ZEN SAND

James W. Heisig & John Maraldo, eds., *Rude Awakenings: Zen, the Kyoto School, & the Question of Nationalism* (1995)

Jamie Hubbard & Paul L. Swanson, eds., *Pruning the Bodhi Tree: The Storm over Critical Buddhism* (1997)

Mark R. Mullins, *Christianity Made in Japan: A Study of Indigenous Movements* (1998)

Jamie Hubbard, *Absolute Delusion, Perfect Buddhahood: The Rise and Fall of a Chinese Heresy* (2001)

James W. Heisig, *Philosophers of Nothingness: An Essay on the Kyoto School* (2001)

Victor Sōgen Hori, *Zen Sand: The Book of Capping Phrases for Kōan Practice* (2003)

Zen Sand

THE BOOK OF CAPPING PHRASES FOR KŌAN PRACTICE

COMPILED, TRANSLATED, AND ANNOTATED BY

Victor Sōgen Hori

University of Hawaiʻi Press
HONOLULU

Printed in the United States of America
Paperback edition 2010

15 14 13 12 11 10 6 5 4 3 2 1

Library of Congress Cataloging-in-Publication Data

Hori, Victor Sōgen.
Zen sand: the book of capping phrases for koan practice / compiled, translated, and annotated by Victor Sōgen Hori.
p. cm.—(Nanzan library of Asian religion and culture)
Includes bibliographical references and index.
ISBN 978-0-8248-3507-1 (pbk : alk. paper)
1. Koan. 2. Spiritual life—Rinzai (Sect) I. Title. II. Series.
BQ9289.5 .H67 2003
294.3'4446—dc21 2002032477

The typesetting for this book was done by the Nanzan Institute for Religion and Culture.

University of Hawai'i Press books are printed on acid-free paper and meet the guidelines for permanence and durability of the Council on Library Resources.

for

Kobori Nanrei,

Former Oshō of Ryōkō-in, Daitoku-ji

&

Nakamura Kan'un-shitsu,

Former Rōshi of the Daitoku-ji Sōdō

Contents

Preface

THE SIZE OF THE present volume rather obscures the purpose of the original Zen phrase books on which it is based. They were hand-written notebooks small enough for monks to carry around in the vest of their kimono or, perhaps more accurately, to *hide* there. Before the use of these books was openly acknowledged, Rinzai Zen monks who were engaged in the kōan practice probably kept their phrase notebooks out of sight just as they kept private their *sanzen* diaries of meetings with the Zen master. There is an old handwritten copy with incense burnmarks on the pages, suggesting that its owner might have had to consult his manual in secret at night, using just the faint glow from a stick of incense to read the characters and dropping burning ash on its pages from time to time. These collections, the product of great and extended spiritual effort, fascinated younger monks, who would make a copy of any notebook a senior monk might let them see. In the course of time, as these notebooks were copied and recopied, more and more phrases were added, so that what started out as secret notebooks ended up becoming an indispensable reference for Zen practice. In time, printers got hold of copies and brought them to a still larger public, until at some point the Zen masters incorporated them into a new practice for ordinary monastic training—the capping phrase.

To this day the books used in Japan are no larger than a paperback and still fit comfortably in the folds of one's kimono. Translating the original text into English and supplying the necessary background material has transformed what weighed less than 100 grams into the cumbersome tome you now hold in your hands.

The title of this book, *Zen Sand*, was inspired by one of its verses:

黄金又是和沙賣　Gold—but to sell it you mix it with sand. (7.55)

An honest broker would not deceive a customer by mixing pure gold with sand, but in Zen things are different. The awakening itself is pure gold, undefiled by language, "not founded on words and letters." To be conveyed to others, it has to be mixed with the sand of language.

In the Rinzai Zen tradition the practitioner is directed not to try to grasp a kōan by fixing on its words or looking for intellectual explanations. One has to embody the kōan so that self and kōan are one. Once a particular kōan has been completed, the rōshi will instruct the practitioner to bring a verse or phrase that captures the insight of that kōan. This phrase is called a *jakugo*, that is, a "capping verse" or "capping phrase." Over the centuries handbooks have been compiled to facilitate the search for these capping phrases—sand to be mixed with the golden experience of enlightened seeing.

In a sense this book may be considered the godchild of the well-known volume *Zen Dust*. In addition to presenting a detailed account of the Rinzai kōan practice, the authors of *Zen Dust,* Miura Isshū Rōshi and Ruth Fuller Sasaki, provided translations for 210 capping phrases that give the reader some hint of their beauty, profundity, and humor. But without a complete translation of one of the traditional *jakugo* handbooks, which usually contain several thousand phrases, the practitioner who lacks familiarity with Chinese and Japanese is unable to carry on the full Rinzai kōan practice. When Ruth Fuller Sasaki died in 1967, she left behind in her temple of Ryōsen-an, located on the premises of Daitoku-ji, a stack of notebooks with the beginnings of a first draft for such a complete translation. *Zen Sand* takes up where *Zen Dust* left off and presents the entire contents of two standard *jakugo* collections.

I began this book in 1976 not with the intention of producing a book for scholarly publication but as an aid for my own personal Zen kōan training. That same year, after completing my requirements for a Ph.D. degree from Stanford University, I had asked Kobori Nanrei, the *oshō* of Ryōkō-in, Daitoku-ji in Kyoto, to ordain me as a Rinzai monk and to sponsor me in monastery training. I then began working on a translation of the *Zengoshū* (*Zen Phrase Collection*), the capping phrase book in use at the Daitoku-ji monastery. As I had had no formal training in classical Chinese (my doctoral studies were in Western philosophy), my ability to read and translate Zen verses from the original texts was quite inadequate. Nevertheless, with the help of dictionaries and grammars, I was able during that year as a Zen novice to struggle my way through to a rudimentary translation of the first half of the *Zengoshū.* On 8 April 1977 (Śākyamuni's birthday), the day when I begged for admission at the gate of the monastery, I had that translation in my monk's bag.

Seven years after I entered the monastery, my first rōshi died. I then wandered from master to master, until at last the winds of karma brought me in 1985 to the Nagaoka Zenjuku, a Zen boarding school, supervised by a traditional Zen rōshi. When I arrived, Asai Gisen Rōshi immediately set up a daily schedule of three *sanzen* (consultations) a day, a schedule that we maintained for five years. Freed of the usual monastic schedule, I was able to focus on kōan work and to return to my translation of *jakugo*. By 1987 I had a complete translation of the 3,040 phrases of the *Zengoshū.*

After twenty years in Japan and thirteen years in full-time Zen practice, I returned to Canada and to academic life, this time in the field of religious studies rather than in Western philosophy. Convinced that I had in my possession a manuscript that would make a useful contribution to scholarship and to Western Buddhist practice,

I set about revising it for publication. Lacking systematic training in classical Chinese Buddhist studies and Chinese literature, I am painfully aware of the inadequacy of my translations. In the Rinzai Zen kōan *jakugo* practice, day by day one follows up one's insight into each kōan by selecting a capping phrase to put on the rōshi's iron anvil. As one of the few people from the English-speaking world ever to have gone through this practice, I feel a special responsibility to introduce this practice to the West. At the same time, I can only hope that someone with better scholarly preparation and a clearer Zen eye will see through the inadequacy of my translations and produce a superior edition.

When I look back at the complex web of people and events that went into making this book a reality, I see at once my greatest debt of gratitude is to my teachers in Zen: Kobori Nanrei Oshō, the priest of Ryōkō-in of Daitoku-ji in Kyoto, who first saw fit to take me in as a disciple, and Nakamura Kan'un-shitsu of Daitoku-ji, my first monastery rōshi, in whose forge I was tempered for my first seven years of Zen monastic life. In addition, I wish to acknowledge my gratitude to all the Zen teachers under whom I subsequently trained: Matsuyama Gaun-an, former rōshi of the Myōshin-ji Sōdō in Kyoto; Hasegawa Daidō, rōshi of the Entsū Sōdō in Imari; Asai Gisen, rōshi of the Nagaoka Zenjuku in Nagaoka; and Sasaki Jōshū, rōshi of Mount Baldy Zen Center in California. In addition, Kobori Geppo, the present *oshō* of Ryōkō-in, has always let me use his temple as my monk's home in Japan.

The quality of one's training depends as much on one's fellow monks as on one's master. At Ryōkō-in, I was fortunate to find myself in a family of dedicated *kyōdai deshi*, brother monks. Besides Kobori Geppo, who completed the kōan training at Rinzai-ji and is the present *oshō* of Ryōkō-in, there was Machida Sōhō, who spent fourteen years at the Daitoku-ji Sōdō and went on to take a Ph.D. and teach at Princeton University; Nishitai Sōkō, who spent twelve years at the Kenchō-ji and Kennin-ji Sōdōs; and Naruse Shōryū, who completed the kōan training at the Eigen-ji Sōdō. In particular I would like to mention the support I received from other Western Zen practitioners who were then engaged in kōan practice: Raymond Sōrei Coffin, Chris Sōju Jay, and John Sōgaku Toler, all of whom trained under Kan'un-shitsu at Daitoku-ji; and Tom Daijō Minick, who trained under Kan'un-shitsu at Daitoku-ji, Morinaga Sōko at Daishu-in, and Harada Shōdō at Sōgen-ji.

From 1990 to 1991 Neil McMullin of Erindale College, University of Toronto, and from 1991 to 1992 Lawrence Sullivan of the Center for the Study of World Religions at Harvard University arranged appointments for me as the Numata Visiting Professor in Buddhist Studies at their respective universities. Masatoshi Nagatomi of Harvard University encouraged me in my work and was instrumental in persuading the Harvard-Yenching Library to acquire further valuable research materials for me not available elsewhere.

My colleagues at McGill University—Professors Arvind Sharma, Katherine Young, and Richard Hayes—graciously rearranged their teaching schedules in order to give me a year of research leave in 1997. The Dean of the Faculty of Religious Studies at the time, Donna Runnalls, gave her support and the Faculty of Graduate Studies and Research at McGill University offered a small but helpful grant enabling me to spend the academic year from 1997 to 1998 at the Nanzan Institute for Religion and Culture in Nagoya, Japan.

The community of scholars and staff at Nanzan contributed immensely to this book. James Heisig, then the Institute Director, sponsored my stay, reconfigured my computers, edited and typeset the entire manuscript, and in every way supported the project with energetic attention. Paul Swanson not only lent me the use of his office and his considerable personal library for an entire year while he was away on sabbatical, but he also read and commented on drafts of large sections of the manuscript and edited the phrase translations. The other senior researchers of the Institute, Watanabe Manabu, Okuyama Michiaki, and Robert Kisala, made me feel at home from the first. The team of junior research fellows—Iwamoto Akemi, Terao Kazuyoshi, and Kondō Mitsuhiro—as well as Peter Knecht, the Director of the Nanzan University Anthropological Institute, generously let me share their daily dinner table and welcomed me into their circle of knowledge, experience, and good judgement. Whenever I could not track down an abstruse reference, I consulted Liang Xiao-hong, a research associate of both the Nanzan Institute and the International Research Institute for Zen Buddhism in Kyoto, and watched as she dissolved my problem into easily comprehensible parts. Okumura Hiroki proofread the Chinese character text of the entire manuscript.

As my translation progressed, I went back to consult with Zen teachers and students engaged in *jakugo* practice. The list of Zen teachers and students who have encouraged and assisted me over the years is a long one. Katō Gessō Rōshi of the Empuku-ji Sōdō in Yawata read through with me the translations of two major sections of the book, the 10-character and 14-character phrases, corrected my interpretations, and helped me track down a number of difficult references. Yasunaga Sōdō, who completed the kōan training under Hirata Seikō Rōshi of Tenryū-ji and is currently the *oshō* of Shōun-ji in the city of Ikeda, also proofread the 10-character and 14-character phrases, correcting mistakes and offering advice on a wide range of subjects, including how to preserve rhythm when translating Chinese poetry into English. He also presented me with a copy of Yamamoto Shungaku's *Wakun Ryakkai Zenrin Kushū,* published in 1920 and now virtually unobtainable.

Harada Shōdō Rōshi of the Sōgen-ji Sōdō in Okayama has been teaching traditional kōan Zen, complete with capping phrases, to Westerners in both Japan and America for many years. I am grateful for the confidence he showed in my book of translations by designating it for use by his students. I want especially to thank those students who, in the course of working with my translations over several years, have raised important questions and suggestions for improvement. I would single out in this regard Stephanie Sōzui Schubert, Mark Dōyū Albin, Larry Dōkyō Zoglin, Sabine Shōe Huskamp, Murlidhare Bodhi Khobragadi, and Jyl Shinjō Brewer. In addition, Frances Mitra Bishop, a teacher in the Philip Kapleau lineage doing further kōan study at Sōgen-ji, took on the enormous task of computerizing my early translations. Priscilla Daichi Storandt, Harada Rōshi's right-hand monk and one of my closest friends for many years, was one of the very first, more than twenty years ago, to press me to prepare my private translations for publication. I wish also to acknowledge the encouragement I received from Gerald Kōzen Sonntag, training under Araki Kokan Rōshi in Ishikawa and Tokyo at the Ningen Zen Kyōdan; Michael Kruse, training as a layman at the Tokugen-ji Sōdō in Nagoya; and those others who have asked to remain anonymous.

Fukushima Keidō, Rōshi of the Tōfuku-ji monastery in Kyoto, generously found time to meet with me to explain certain aspects of Takujū kōan practice and to give me an inside view of how the Shibayama edition of the *Zenrin kushū* was edited. His long time kōan student Jeff Shore, now professor at Hanazono University, read early drafts of some of the introductory chapters with a very critical eye.

For many years now the Institute for Zen Studies at Hanazono University in Kyoto has been publishing extremely useful Zen dictionaries and indexes. Toga Masataka, the director, actively supported my translation project and provided me with several useful research texts. The Institute has been engaged in developing a vast database of computerized Chinese Ch'an and Japanese Zen texts and dictionaries, with a search engine that facilitates character searches over a wide range of primary and secondary texts. I owe immense thanks to Yoshizawa Katsuhiro, director of research at the Institute, for allowing me access to a prototype of this database with search engine and for sharing his detailed research into the colloquial language of classical Ch'an texts. Nishimura Egaku of the Institute installed the database for me and cheerfully offered technical support. Maeda Naomi, the Institute's librarian, on numerous occasions kindly ferreted out books from dark corners of the library and Nishiguchi Yoshio tracked down obscure references for me.

Several persons at the International Research Institute for Zen Buddhism (IRIZ), the second of the two Zen research centers at Hanazono University, also contributed to this book. Michel Mohr read drafts of parts of this book and Sanae Kensei offered guidance about the history of *Kuzōshi* texts. Usami Sachiko and Sakai Etsuko, the librarians for the IRIZ, hunted down texts for me and assisted me in photocopying. I would like also to thank Yanagida Seizan, the founder of the International Research Institute, and Iriya Yoshitaka of Kyoto University, for the enormous body of Zen historical scholarship they have produced.

I would also like to thank Asano Motoshige, leader of the Ashikaga Zendōkai in the city of Ashikaga, and his son, Asano Teruo, for information about Tsuchiya Etsudō, the compiler of the *Zengoshū*, as well as Kurihara Morihito and Tsuchiya Shiomitsu of Utsunomiya, both grandsons of Etsudō, for their helpful conversations.

Shinohara Kōichi of McMaster University helped me in translating Ijūshi's postscript to the 1688 *Zenrin kushū*, and David Pollack of the University of Rochester read and commented on early drafts of the introductory chapters. Feng Liping of Johns Hopkins University checked many of my English translations against the original Chinese, and Nishimura Midori of Sasayama in Japan scrupulously checked every aspect of grammar, nuance, and choice of words. Tsuchida Tomoaki of Nanzan University advised me on *kanbun* readings and Chinese fonts.

Burton Watson, retired professor of Columbia University, has read almost every word that has gone into this book. Dr. Watson has produced many of the translations of the major Chinese classical texts on which my own research relied, and I am deeply gratified at the great personal interest he has taken in my project.

I would like to thank the Asian Scholars Group in Kyoto and the Center for East Asian Studies at Wesleyan University for opportunities to present and receive feedback on some of my views about the origin of the kōan. McGill University provided both research and travel grants. The Japan Foundation gave me one of its Short Term Fellowships to support this research. I thank them both. Thanks also to the Rochester Zen Center, which gave its permission to use its translation of the Four Great Vows (14.320-1), and to the staff of the Nanzan University Library for help in tracking down texts.

Finally, I acknowledge my greatest debt of gratitude to my friend and colleague of many years, Thomas Yūhō Kirchner. A monk who has trained at three different monasteries, Yūhō long ago made his own translations of *jakugo*, all of which he generously turned over to me for my use. In addition, he has introduced me to his wide circle of friends, to whose assistance I turned at every step of the way. Over the years he has never let me forget this translation project and has done everything possible to help me complete it.

In spite of all the expert and learned advice I received from so many people, the translations and the views expressed in this book are my own, and the responsibility for errors that have survived the lengthy process of production lies with me.

Kyūhai (Nine Bows).

Victor Sōgen Hori
McGill University
1 July 2002

INTRODUCTION

Capping-Phrase Practice in Japanese Rinzai Zen

Rinzai kōan practice, as it is presently conducted in the Rinzai monasteries of Japan, involves an element of literary study. Zen monks all have books. They need them to support their kōan practice, and the further they progress, the more their practice involves the study of texts and the writing of words. The Zen school, however, describes itself as "not founded on words and letters, a separate tradition outside scripture." Much of traditional Zen literature heaps ridicule on the idea that one can comprehend or express Zen by means of written explanations. Take, for example, the striking metaphor of Rinzai Gigen, the founder of the Rinzai school:

> There's a bunch of fellows who can't tell good from bad but poke around in the scriptural teachings, hazard a guess here and there, and come up with an idea in words, as though they took a lump of shit, mushed it around in their mouth, and then spat it out and passed it on to somebody else. (Watson 1993b: 61)

Standard images like "do not mistake the finger for the moon" remind the Zen practitioner not to confuse the label with the labeled, the descriptions that point to awakening with the experience of awakening itself. Poetic images like "the mute has had a wonderful dream" express the fact that even the most eloquent person can find no words with which to express the wondrous experience of awakening. Zen teachers also recount stories like that of Tokusan, the scholar of the *Diamond Sutra*, who burned all his previously precious books after he attained awakening (MMK case 28). Why then do Japanese Rinzai monks study books as part of their kōan practice? What books do they study? How can the study of such books be compatible with the struggle to attain the awakening that is beyond language?

Rinzai monasteries in Japan vary in the way they conduct kōan practice, but in the Myōshin-ji–Daitoku-ji branch, when a monk has passed a kōan the Zen teacher will instruct him to bring a "capping phrase," called *jakugo* 着語/著語 or *agyo* 下語. The monk selects a verse or phrase that expresses the insight he has had while meditating on the kōan. He searches for this capping phrase in one of the several Zen phrase books that have been especially compiled for this purpose. If the monk continues into advanced stages of the Rinzai Zen kōan curriculum, he will receive further literary assignments: the writing of explanations in Japanese, called *kakiwake* (書き分け or 書き譯), and the composition of Chinese-style poetry, called *nenrō* 拈弄. Such literary study is not merely an incidental part of kōan training. Monks begin capping-phrase assignments with Jōshū's "Mu," one of the very first kōan, and continue searching for capping phrases throughout their entire training career. The research and writing required to complete *kakiwake* and *nenrō* writing assignments can consume considerable amounts of time during the later stages of a monk's stay in the monastery. If the point of kōan practice is to attain a nonrational, direct insight beyond the boundaries of language and conceptual thought, why is there such literary study in kōan practice? How can *jakugo* practice even be possible in Zen?

My aim in these introductory chapters is not only to describe the *jakugo* practice, but also to explain in general how the practice of meditative insight can be combined with literary study. I will also speculate on how this very interesting Zen practice evolved out of more general practices in Chinese literary culture.

Chapter 1 is more philosophical in tone and discusses the nature of kōan practice. It follows conventional accounts in emphasizing that "passing a kōan" initially involves an experience of insight for which intellectual understanding is neither a substitute nor an aid. At the same time, it argues that there is such a thing as intellectual understanding of the kōan, but it is dependent on the prior experience of insight into the kōan.

Chapter 2 gives an overview of the Rinzai kōan curriculum using the categories of Hakuin's kōan system.

Chapter 3 describes the capping-phrase practice and its importance to both Rinzai kōan practice and to the structure of kōan texts.

Chapter 4 describes the Chinese "literary game" and argues that many of the elements that go into making up the complex image of a kōan—hidden meaning, sudden insight, mind-to-mind transmission, etc.—are features that have been borrowed or adapted from that tradition.

Chapter 5 describes the Zen phrase book, a group of texts that forms its own subgenre among Zen texts. In addition to a short history of the origin of the Zen phrase book, a more detailed, analytical account is presented of the five texts used to support the capping-phrase practice.

Chapter 6 explains the parts of the phrase entries, and also outlines the abbreviations and conventions used in this book.

1

The Nature of the Rinzai Kōan Practice

D. T. SUZUKI'S EARLY works (notably his *Essays in Zen Buddhism Second Series*, 1953) and MIURA and SASAKI's *Zen Dust* (1966) were for a very long time the only major resources available in non-Asian languages for research into the Zen kōan. In recent years, however, a rich bounty of material has appeared. At the level of basic texts, in addition to a steady stream of translations of the traditional "recorded sayings" of the Zen masters from which kōan cases were originally derived,[1] numerous kōan collections, some of them newly created in the West, have also been published in translation.[2] At the scholarly level, major philosophical and historical studies on the nature and development of the kōan have appeared.[3] Despite all these efforts, there is still no philosophical agreement on the nature of the kōan, and indeed little factual information on the actual conduct of kōan practice. Before we attempt to describe the capping-phrase practice, we need a clear picture of the Rinzai kōan practice in general.

A RELIGIOUS PRACTICE

To begin with, like all Buddhist practices, Rinzai kōan practice is religious in nature. This point seems to be forgotten in current accounts. Popular descriptions of the kōan as "riddles" or "paradoxes" make it seem as if the Zen practitioner is interested in little more than the solving of intellectual puzzles. Those interested in enhancing the spontaneity of athletic or artistic performance tend to focus on Zen as a training technique for attaining a state of consciousness in which "the dancer is one with the dance" (GALLWEY 1974, SUDNOW 1978). Scholars who study Zen as a language game give the impression that the practitioner is basically learning a new set of

[1] SASAKI et al. 1971, SASAKI 1975, HOFFMAN 1978, POWELL 1986, PAS 1987, BRAVERMAN 1989, CHIEN 1992, WATSON 1993B, APP 1994, GREEN 1998.

[2] SENZAKI and MCCANDLESS 1964, SHIBAYAMA 1974, HOFFMAN 1977, SEKIDA 1977, CLEARY and CLEARY 1977, AITKEN 1990, CLEARY 1990, SAHN 1993, CLEARY 1993, LOORI 1994, CLEARY 1998.

[3] BUSWELL 1987, HEINE 1994 and 1999, WRIGHT 1998, HEINE and WRIGHT 2000.

rules for language (Sellman 1979, Wright 1992). Others insist that the notion of religious experience (Proudfoot 1985) or Zen experience (Sharf 1995a, 1995b) is a concept manufactured and manipulated for ideological reasons, depicting the practitioner as primarily engaged in some form or other of cultural politics. Critics who suggest that the kōan is a form of "scriptural exegesis" (Sharf 1995a, 108) give the impression that the Zen kōan practice differs little from scholarship in general. These kinds of interpretations of Zen practice are misleading at best. The kōan practice is first and foremost a religious practice, undertaken primarily not in order to solve a riddle, not to perfect the spontaneous performance of some skill, not to learn a new form of linguistic expression, not to play cultural politics, and not to carry on scholarship. Such ingredients may certainly be involved, but they are always subservient to the traditional Buddhist goals of awakened wisdom and selfless compassion.

In saying this, I am making a normative statement, not a description of fact. The fact is, in most Rinzai monasteries today, many of the monks engage in meditation and kōan practice for a mere two or three years in order to qualify for the status of *jūshoku* 住職 (resident priest), which will allow them to assume the role of a temple priest. For many of them, engagement with the kōan may indeed consist in little more than the practice of solving riddles and learning a ritualized language, a fraction of the full practice. In the full practice the Zen practitioner must bring to the engagement the three necessities of the Great Root of Faith, the Great Ball of Doubt, and the Great Overpowering Will (*daishinkon* 大信根, *daigidan* 大疑團, *daifunshi* 大憤志).[4] The kōan is an artificial problem given by a teacher to a student with the aim of precipitating a genuine religious crisis that involves all the human faculties—intellect, emotion, and will.

At first, one's efforts and attention are focused on the kōan. When it cannot be solved (one soon learns that there is no simple "right answer"), doubt sets in. Ordinary doubt is directed at some external object such as the kōan itself or the teacher, but when it has been directed back to oneself, it is transformed into Great Doubt. To carry on relentlessly this act of self-doubt, one needs the Great Root of Faith. Ordinarily, faith and doubt are related to one another in inverse proportion: where faith is strong, doubt is weak; and vice versa. But in Zen practice, the greater the doubt, the greater the faith. Great Faith and Great Doubt are two aspects of the same mind of awakening (*bodaishin* 菩提心). The Great Overpowering Will is needed to surmount all obstacles along the way. Since doubt is focused on oneself, no matter how strong,

[4] These terms are most strongly associated with Hakuin Ekaku Zenji but they appear as a trio in the *Kōhō Oshō zen'yō* 高峯和尚禪要 (Ch. *Kao Feng Ho-shang Ch'an-yao*, ZZ 2; MZZ 122.714) published in 1599, almost a century before Hakuin was born (1686). There is a philosophical discussion in Nishitani 1982, 18–30. The connection of Great Doubt to awakening was emphasized by Ta-hui Tsung-kao (大慧宗杲 J. Daie Sōkō, 1089–163).

wily, and resourceful one is in facing the opponent, that opponent (oneself) is always just as strong, wily, and resourceful in resisting. When self-doubt has grown to the point that one is totally consumed by it, the usual operations of mind cease. The mind of total self-doubt no longer classifies intellectually, no longer arises in anger or sorrow, no longer exerts itself as will and ego. This is the state that Hakuin described as akin to being frozen in a great crystal:

> Suddenly a great doubt manifested itself before me. It was as though I were frozen solid in the midst of an ice sheet extending tens of thousands of miles. A purity filled my breast and I could neither go forward nor retreat. To all intents and purposes I was out of my mind and the *Mu* alone remained. Although I sat in the Lecture Hall and listened to the Master's lecture, it was as though I were hearing from a distance outside the hall. At times, I felt as though I were floating through the air. (*Orategama III*, YAMPOLSKY 1971, 118)

In this state, Hakuin happened one day to hear the temple bell ring. At that moment the ice shattered and he was thrust back into the world. In this experience, called the Great Death (*daishi ichiban* 大死一番), the self in self-doubt is finally extinguished and the Great Doubt is transformed into Great Awakening. As Ta-hui says, "Beneath the Great Doubt, always there is a Great Awakening 大疑之下必有大悟."[5]

Kenshō, the experience of awakening, is more than merely the state of concentrated *samādhi*. When the Great Doubt has totally taken over the self, there is no more distinction between self and other, subject and object. There is no more differentiation, no more attachment. This is merely *samādhi* and not *kenshō*. *Kenshō* is not the self's withdrawal from the conventional world, but rather the selfless self breaking back into the conventional world. It is only when this *samādhi* has been shattered that a new self arises. This self returns and again sees the things of the world as objects, but now as empty objects; it again thinks in differentiated categories and feels attachment, but now with insight into their emptiness.

Again, I am speaking in normative terms. The particular aspects of Zen kōan practice on which scholars have concentrated their attentions—its nondual epistemology, its ritual and performance, its language, its politics—are aspects. They are facets of a practice whose fundamental core is a religious practice.

KŌAN: INSTRUMENT OR REALIZATION?

Most commentators take the approach that the kōan is an *upāya*, an instrument, that deliberately poses a problem unsolvable by the rational mind in order to drive the mind beyond the limits of rationality and intellectual cognition. This approach views the kōan as a psychological technique cunningly designed to

[5] 大慧語録, T 47.886a28.

cause the rational and intellectual functions of mind to self-destruct, thus liberating the mind to the vast realm of the nonrational and the intuitive. Powerful personal accounts of spiritual quest make it seem that the kōan is not a text to be studied for its meaning as one would study an essay or a poem, but rather an existential explosive device with language merely serving as the fuse.

Part of the problem with many such instrumentalist approaches is that it deprives the kōan itself of meaning. The kōan, it is said, cannot be understood intellectually; it gives the appearance of being meaningful only to seduce the meaning-seeking mind to engage with it (Rosemont 1970). This interpretation ignores the mass of evidence contradicting the idea that the kōan is no more than a meaningless, blunt psychological instrument. It is hard to think that the shelves of heavy volumes of kōan commentary produced through the centuries and the lectures in which Zen teachers expound at length on the kōan are all occupied with a technique that is in itself nonsense. It is much more sensible to begin from the assumption that kōan disclose their own meaning (though not necessarily an intellectual one), once they have been properly understood.

A second difficulty is that in trying to demonstrate how the kōan overcomes the dualisms and false dichotomies created by the conventional mind, the instrumental approach introduces dualism and dichotomy back into the picture again. The awakened mind, it is said, has transcended the dualistic dichotomizing of conventional mind and resides in a state of nonduality. The awakened person is thus freer than the average person in being able to choose to act either in the conventional dualistic way or in the awakened nondual way. But the dichotomy between duality and nonduality, conventional thinking and awakened mind, is itself a duality. Rather than being free from dualistic thinking, the awakened mind ends up more tightly locked into dualistic thinking, incessantly forced to choose between being conventional or being awakened.[6]

A much better way of approaching the kōan is by way of the "realizational" model, a term I have borrowed from Hee-jin Kim (1985). The practitioner does not solve the kōan by grasping intellectually the meaning of "the sound of one hand" or "original face before father and mother were born." Rather, in the crisis of self-doubt referred to above, one experiences the kōan not as an object standing before the mind that investigates it, but as the seeking mind itself. As long as consciousness and kōan oppose each other as subject and object, there are still two hands clapping, mother and father have already been born. But when the kōan has overwhelmed the mind so that it is no longer the object but the seeking subject itself, subject and object are no longer two. This is "one hand clapping," the point "before father and mother have been born." This entails a "realization" in the two senses of the term. By making real,

[6] I have borrowed this point from Wright 1992.

i.e., by actually *becoming* an example of, the nonduality of subject and object, the practitioner also realizes, i.e., *cognitively understands,* the kōan. The realization of understanding depends on the realization of making actual.[7]

This realizational account of the kōan solves several problems. On the one hand, it helps explain how the solution to a kōan requires the personal experience of "the sound of one hand" or of "one's original face." On the other, it allows us to see the kōan as not merely a blunt and meaningless instrument, useful only as means to some further end, but as possessed of a meaningful content of its own which can be apprehended intellectually.[8]

"ZEN EXPERIENCE"

If an instrumentalist approach deemphasizes the meaning of the kōan and overemphasizes the experiential aspect, there are scholars on the other end of the spectrum with the opposite approach. Robert Sharf, for example, writes:

> The kōan genre, far from serving as a means to obviate reason, is a highly sophisticated form of scriptural exegesis: the manipulation or "solution" of a particular kōan traditionally demanded an extensive knowledge of canonical Buddhist doctrine and classical Zen verse. (SHARF 1995A, 108)

In claiming that the solving of a kōan is an exercise in scriptural exegesis, Sharf also argues against the traditional claim that one must necessarily have a *kenshō* experience before one can understand Zen. His position is that the idea of a *kenshō* experience has been manufactured and manipulated for ideological purposes by Buddhist modernists (SHARF 1995A, 1995B, 1995C). While it is not possible in this essay to deal with all the details of his position, I feel it necessary to comment on the principal question at stake here.

What does it mean to say that Zen can only be known by experience? The term "experience" needs examination. The ordinary question, "Have you had any experience of living in a foreign country?" usually means nothing more than "Have you ever lived in a foreign country?" "Having experience of" is a loose idiom for describing things one has done or undergone. In a more academic context, however, "experience" has at least two specialized meanings, that are often confused with one another. We may distinguish them as Experience 1: learning or knowing firsthand; and Experience 2: having pure consciousness.

Experience 1 does not entail any epistemological claims about the nature of experience. It simply denies that what is known has been known secondhand, relying on

---

[7] I have borrowed this point about the two senses of "realize" from NISHITANI 1982, 5–6.

[8] I have discussed these questions in greater detail in HORI 2000.

someone else's account. This idea is at work, for instance, in the question, "How do you know it is hot in Indonesia? Have you experienced it for yourself or have you just heard about it from another?" Experience 2, in contrast, does make epistemological claims about the nature of experience. It presupposes a distinction between the rational and the intuitive, the intellectual and nonintellectual, the cognitive and the noncognitive. Its adjective form, "experiential," connotes all these—intuitive, nonintellectual, noncognitive. To experience something in this sense means to have a direct apprehension without any intellectual or conceptual activity. The experience is "pure" precisely to the extent that there is no intellection or conceptualization going on. This idea is at work in the claim, for example, that "mystical experience is not something you attain by thinking. You have to experience it." Although both thinking and experiencing are first-hand, only the latter can be said to be pure.

If "not founded on words and letters" means that Zen must be experienced, we have to ask: Experienced how—as Experience 1 or as Experience 2? If Experience 1, then the claim that Zen must be experienced is true but trivial. If Experience 2, then the claim is important but false.

If the claim that Zen must be experienced amounts to the statement that one must learn or come to know Zen firsthand, then hearing about it or reading a description of it written by someone else does not count as experience. In this sense, the idea that Zen is "not founded on words and letters" really amounts to saying that it is "not founded on the words and letters of another." But there is nothing uniquely Zen about this. Vast areas of human life cannot be experienced vicariously but only be learned or known or accomplished firsthand. In fact, Zen teachers often point out parallel examples from everyday life. I recall a lecture in which the Zen master spoke of five things that people have to do by themselves and for which no one can substitute: eat, sleep, urinate, defecate, and attain *satori.* Although the Zen tradition puts great emphasis on the fact that Zen is "not founded on words and letters" and must be experienced, this claim does not require the concept of a "pure experience."

At the same time, there are many who interpret the dictum that Zen is "not founded on words and letters" to mean that "Zen experience" is Experience 2, pure in the sense of being totally without intellectual or conceptual activity. Elsewhere I have argued that the very notion of a "pure experience" is shot through with conceptual problems, and that the reason for its popularity is that it is used ideologically to promote a kind of individualism: in the same way that there is supposed to be a state of nature in which individuals lived in freedom before society arose to compromise it, so also there is supposed to be a pure consciousness before conceptual thinking and social conditioning arose to defile it (HORI 2000).

But even if the notion of "pure experience" were intelligible, the realization of a Zen kōan would not be experience in this sense. Within the experience of the nonduality of subject and object, there is still intellectual cognition. Ordinary perception presupposes conceptual activity in order to remain clear and intact. One sees the world through concepts like "here," "there," "tree," "table," "red," "loud," bowl," "book," etc. Without these concepts to inform our perception, we would not be able to recognize these flesh-colored things as "hands," to interpret those lines on the wall as a "door," to hear that shrilling sound as a "telephone." All seeing that has meaning is "seeing-as," seeing according to concepts. Without the investment of conceptual activity in perception, the phenomenal world would become a blur of amorphous patches of color, sounds that we would not recognize as speech, sensations without meaning. Zen awakening does not cause perception to lose its crisp, clear form and dissolve into such shapeless forms and cacophonous sounds. The mind of a Zen master is not booming, buzzing confusion. The fact that the world continues to be clearly perceived and that one's surroundings can still be described in ordinary language indicates that the experience associated with Zen awakening cannot be a "pure experience."

The experience of realization in a kōan is indescribable, but only in the very ordinary sense in which *all* immediate experience is basically indescribable. The resistance of the kōan to words is no stronger than the resistance of the aroma of a cup of coffee to verbal expression. The traditional Zen expression of this fact is *reidan jichi* 冷暖自知, "Know for yourself hot and cold." To know the sensation of hot and cold is one thing; to explain it to one who does not know it is another. The experience of the realization in a kōan is not intrinsically indescribable, but only indescribable relative to the repertoire of experiences of the people conversing. When I speak of the aroma of a cup of coffee and the sensation of hot and cold, other people know what I am talking about because they, too, have smelled coffee and felt the sting of hot and cold. But if I should speak of the taste of the durian fruit, the Southeast Asian fruit with the nauseating smell and the wonderful taste, few Western readers will understand what I am talking about.

If one attempts to describe the realization of a kōan to one who has not had the experience, communication naturally fails, and one reverts to saying that it is "not founded on words and letters." But just as any two people who share an experience can talk about it, so there can be discussion about the experience of insight into the Zen kōan. (There is, however, a social prohibition against talking about Zen, which may discourage such discussions from actually taking place.)

So it is quite true that Zen can only be known by experience (in a quite ordinary sense of experience), but this does not imply that Zen is some "pure experience" completely devoid of intellectual activity. A corollary to this conclusion is this: there can be meaningful language about Zen but only between people who have shared its experience. Two aspects of meaning are conjoined in meaningful discourse: *reference*, the object, event, or experience that a word or statement denotes; and *sense*, the significance of a linguistic expression. (The classic example of the distinction is that of "the morning star" and "the evening star," which have different senses but the same reference, namely the planet Venus.) One who is not a connoisseur of wine does not know what "oakiness" *refers* to in wine tasting and therefore does not understand the *sense* of a statement such as, "This wine is too oaky." The same could be said of the entire vocabulary of aesthetic and technical appreciation: words like "highlights," "nose," "fruitiness" in wine tasting; "lushness" and "restraint" in the sound of the strings in music appreciation; "gracefulness" in hockey; "intelligence" in boxing; and so forth. When one does not know the *reference* of these terms in experience, one cannot understand the *sense* of any statement using them.

Many expressions, "splitting migraine," "the pain and pleasure of childbirth," "prolonged melancholia," "the shame of being old," refer to special or particular experiences that many people have never had, and perhaps never will. But few will claim that these experiences are some special class of experience "not founded on words and letters." Because all of us have had some general experiences of "headache," "pleasure," "melancholy," and "shame," we can understand the general sense of these special expressions without having a particular reference for "splitting migraine" or "pain of childbirth" in our repertoire of experiences. The experience of the Zen unity of self and other, however, is so unusual that it does not fall under any more general class. In this case, without one's own experience, one has no point of *reference* for the "sound of one hand" or "original face," and therefore one cannot understand the *sense* of the expressions in which such locutions are used: "Divide the sound of one hand into two"; "How old is the sound of one hand?"; "Make the sound of one hand stand upside down." That does not mean that the language of Zen is meaningless. It is *senseless* only to those who have not had the experience to which it *refers*.

IDEOLOGICAL USE OF EXPERIENCE

Sharf and other scholars have argued that the notion of "religious experience" is an epistemological category created as a useful tool in cultural politics. Sharf writes:

> Nishida, Suzuki, Hisamatsu, and their followers, like Schleiermacher, Otto, and James before them, were reacting to the onslaught of Enlightenment values. They sought to reframe our conceptions of the religious such that a core of spiritual and moral values would survive the headlong clash with secular philosophy, science, and technical progress. They were thus led to posit an "essential core" of religion, conceived of as a private, veridical, ineffable experience inaccessible to empirical scientific analysis. (SHARF 1995A, 135)

That is, those who have described the core of religion as the ineffable experience of the numinous, or of the sacred, or of *satori,* implicitly draw a self-serving line between, on the one hand, those people who have had religious experience (like themselves, practitioners of a religion) and are therefore empowered to be judges of truth and falsehood in matters of religion, and, on the other hand, those people who have not (like the secular and scientific critics of religion) and are therefore incapable of distinguishing truth from falsehood in matters of religion. I do not mean to deny that the notion of "religious experience" has been used in the ideological way described here, to anoint certain persons with the authority to speak on religious matters and disenfranchise others. But "religious experience" is not the only fabled beast lurking in the ideological woods. "Empirical scientific analysis," also known as "academic objectivity," is another such epistemological concept. Proponents not only claim it exists but also use it to draw a self-serving line between those who have it (like themselves, academic scholars) and who are therefore empowered to be the judge of true and false, and those who do not have it (like practitioners of religion) and are therefore incapable of distinguishing the true and the false. In this conflict over who has authority to speak on matter religious, both sides posit epistemological entities, "religious experience" and "scientific objectivity," and both sides claim possession of it to grant themselves authority and to disenfranchise the other. In this conflict, it sounds like two hands clapping, but underneath it is really only one.

It is not necessary to get entangled in this debate to make a more important point: simply because a concept has been used in a political or ideological context does not mean that it has no epistemological value. Sharf's criticism leaves one with the impression that because he has shown that the notion of Zen experience has been used politically, this implies that there is no such thing as genuine Zen experience as traditionally described. What are the grounds for such a stark either/or assumption? There are any number of concepts like gender, color of skin, and religious creed, that have been used as political and ideological tools, but that does not mean that they are empty concepts without real content. Even though the notion of religious experience may be used for ideological purposes, that does not of itself imply that there is no genuine religious experience.

INTELLECTUAL INTERPRETATION OF THE KŌAN

As generation upon generation of Zen teachers have stated, it is a mistake to think that one can solve a kōan merely by analyzing it intellectually. Nevertheless Zen has an intellectually comprehensible vocabulary for discussing the many aspects of Zen awakening. Part of this intellectual vocabulary is technical and philosophical, most of it is symbolic and metaphorical. Some of the technical vocabulary is described in a later chapter: the initial awakening, *honbun* (the Fundamental), dynamic action, verbal expression, Five Ranks, the Ten Precepts, the arousing of compassion for all sentient beings, the straight and the crooked, and so on. The vast majority of the verses and phrases of the capping phrase collections, however, uses symbol and metaphor.

Sometimes the connection between technical vocabulary and symbolic expression is explicitly drawn. For instance, in the headnotes of several verses, the editor of the *ZRKS* uses the technical term *honbun* 本分, "the Fundamental," to explain the graphic symbolism of the verses. In the examples below, the words inside parentheses are translations from the headnotes.

從來心似鐵 *Jūrai kokoro tetsu ni nitari.*

Originally his heart resembles iron.

(ZRKS 5.209n: Originally, the sturdy man; the Fundamental.)

黑風吹不入 *Kokufū fuite mo irazu.*

The black wind blows but cannot enter.

(ZRKS 5.313n: A *watō* 話頭 about the Fundamental.)

明珠絕點翳 *Myōju ten'ei o zessu.*

The bright pearl is beyond all cloudiness.

(ZRKS 5.379: This verse uses the bright pearl to illuminate the Fundamental.)

Other metaphorical expressions for the Fundamental have been repeated so often, they are now Zen clichés: "sound of one hand," "original face," "Mu," "the great matter," "the point of Bodhidharma's coming from the West," etc.

But such examples of technical terminology are uncommon. Most often, the Zen phrase books use metaphorical language without explanation, expecting that the reader will have, or will develop, the eye to see through the metaphor to the underlying meaning. Take, for example, the following three phrases referring to the nonduality of subject and object:

賓主一體	*Hinju ittai.*	Guest and host are one.
理事不二	*Riji funi.*	Principle and fact are not two.
萬物一如	*Banbutsu ichinyo.*	The ten thousand things are one.

This sort of explicit labeling using philosophical terminology is said to "stink of Zen." The Zen tradition rather prefers to use colorful symbolic language.

日落月未上	*Hi ochite tsuki imada noborazu.*	The sun has set but the moon has yet to rise.
一家父子	*Ikke no fushi.*	Father and son in one house.
一刀一段	*Ittō ichidan.*	One sword [cuts into] one piece.

The image in the final line is particularly interesting. The usual expression is *Ittō nidan*, "One sword [cuts into] two pieces," but here the sword of Zen cuts into a single piece, symbolizing a discrimination that is nondual. The metaphorical language is much more striking than the dry technical language.

Although it is true that one can only grasp a kōan by becoming it, that one cannot grasp a kōan merely through intellectual understanding, nevertheless there is an intellectual language, both technical and symbolic, for talking about the many aspects of Zen awakening. Intellectual understanding of the kōan and the experience of the nonduality of subject and object are not opposed to each other, the one excluding the other. Without realization of the point of the kōan, there can be no intellectual understanding of the kōan. With realization comes understanding.

Capping-phrase collections are expressions of Zen awakening in language. The awakening of Zen can only be realized personally; it is "not founded upon words and letters." That is the gold of Zen. But to convey that awakening to others, one must use language. To sell the gold of Zen, one must mix it with sand.

2

The Steps of Kōan Practice

In this chapter, we will consider the stages involved in kōan practice as well as some of the technical terminology that accompanies it. The aim is to present a general picture of the overall training career of full-time practitioners engaged in the kōan curriculum.

KŌAN AND MEDITATION: ENDS OR MEANS?

Although many beginning monks take "passing" the kōan to be the goal of their practice and see meditation as merely the means to that goal, Rinzai teachers caution against this way of thinking. Monks begin and end their daily activities with a period of *zazen* sitting in the *zendō*. From within a period of zazen, monks proceed to the main hall to chant sutras. From within zazen, they go to meals, to *samu* work, and to begging. After returning from the day's activities, they return to the *zendō* for another period of zazen. When they go to bed at night, they are still in a period of zazen that is not ended until the ringing of the bell the next morning. Ritually speaking, therefore, zazen is the one fundamental activity of the monastery, the center from which all else is done.

Zazen is far from being just the means to passing the kōan. The ritual structure of monastery life makes it clear that it is rather the other way around: one works on a kōan in order to do meditation.

Monasteries vary somewhat in their meditation schedules, but most continue to maintain the traditional schedule of two training terms in summer and winter, each containing three or four major *sesshin* 攝心 (a week of intensive meditation practice), and a number of minor *sesshin* filling out the rest of the year. Three *sesshin* a month is common. In addition, regardless of the *sesshin* schedule and unless there is some special reason, the bell for *sanzen* (meeting with the *rōshi* or Zen master) is put out each morning so that monks may confront the rōshi over their kōan at least once a day. In stricter monasteries, monks can expect several hours of meditation and at least two *sanzen* every day throughout most of the year.

SHOKAN 初關, THE FIRST BARRIER

The initial kōan given to monks, known as *shokan* or "the First Barrier," is usually either Hakuin's *Sekishu onjō* (the Sound of One Hand) or Jōshū's *Mu* (MMK 1). Some temples begin with *Honrai no menmoku* (the Original Face, MMK 23). The Chinese glyph *kan* in *shokan* can also mean "gate," so that *shokan* could also be translated "First Entry." I prefer to render it "barrier" to emphasize the difficulty involved in passing through it. Monks are expected to get their first insight, or *kenshō,* into the Fundamental through meditation on one of these kōan. It may take anywhere from half a year to several years to do so. The term *kenshō* needs fuller attention than we will be able to give it here. It contains several layers of meaning in Japanese and, to complicate matters still further, has entered the English language, where Western expectations have given it a new and independent career.[1] Suffice it to remark here that no monk can pass his first kōan without demonstrating *kenshō.* Some academics have surmised that passing a kōan is a form of "scriptural exegesis" presupposing considerable prior study of Buddhist texts. From my own experience as a monk in the Daitoku-ji monastery, I can testify that indeed very few of my fellow monks could be described as intellectuals or as learned in Buddhist teachings. In any case, once past the first barrier, the monk needs further training before he can arrive at and articulate his first insight.

SASSHO 拶所, CHECKING QUESTIONS

A single kōan usually breaks down into parts, the initial "main case" (*honsoku* 本則) and numerous "checking questions" (*sassho* 拶所). *Sassho* perform two functions. First, by means of these questions the rōshi can confirm the monk's original insight into the Fundamental and gauge the depth of that insight. Second, the checking questions push the monk to broaden his insight beyond the Fundamental into particular instances of it. For example, the First Barrier kōan "Sound of One Hand" and "Mu" are typically followed by checking questions such as "What is the Sound of One Hand from in front and from behind?" or "Divide Mu into two." The number of questions ranges anywhere from twenty to a hundred or more, depending on the teaching lineage of the rōshi.[2] Checking questions serve the rōshi as a quick way to uncover deception. The required initial responses to kōan have become fixed over time, and monks sometimes learn the required responses through hearsay.

---

[1] See Hori 2000.

[2] Akizuki 1987 (259–64) has published a list of the 22 *sassho* for the Mu kōan used by the Myōshin-ji rōshi, Kazan Genku; these have been translated in Hori 2000, 290–1. Jeff Shore reports that in the kōan practice at Tōfuku-ji under Fukushima Keidō Rōshi, there are 102 *sassho* for the Mu kōan and 96 for *Sekishu* (personal communication, 10 June 1998).

To confirm that the insight is actually the monk's own and not something he is repeating at second hand, all the rōshi need do is confront him with a few of these checking questions.

Whichever of the two (Sound of One Hand or Mu), the monk receives initially, the novice monk will most likely receive the other of the pair immediately afterwards, so that his entire first year or more is taken up with these two kōan and their *sassho*.

THE INZAN AND TAKUJŪ SCHOOLS

Once past the First Barrier kōan, practice in Rinzai monasteries follows one of two patterns, depending on whether the teaching rōshi belongs to the Inzan school or the Takujū school. Inzan Ien (隱山惟琰, 1751–1814) and Takujū Kosen (卓洲胡僊, 1760–1833) were the direct disciples of Gasan Jitō (峨山慈棹, 1727–1797), who himself was a direct disciple of Hakuin Ekaku (白隠慧鶴, 1686–1769). All monasteries and rōshi presently teaching in Japan associate themselves with one or other of these schools. The two teach basically the same body of kōan and both consider themselves to be transmitting the Zen of Hakuin. But the Inzan school is thought to be sharper and more dynamic in style, while the Takujū school is thought to be more meticulous and low-keyed.

In the Takujū school, Takujū monks work systematically through the *Mumonkan*, beginning with Case 1, advancing to Case 2, Case 3, and so on. On completion of this text, they work on a number of cases from the *Kattō-shū*,[3] and then move on to the *Hekigan-roku*, whose cases they also take up in order, Case 1, Case 2, and so on. In contrast, monks in the Inzan lineage receive kōan from a variety of collections—*Mumonkan*, *Hekigan-roku*, *Kattō-shū*, *Chin'u-shū*—in what appears to be random order. In fact, however, the order is fixed, so much so that a monk transferring from one Inzan school rōshi to another need merely tell the new rōshi his last kōan in order for the new rōshi to know where to continue without leaving any gap or requiring any repetition of work already done.

It is commonly said that, compared to Inzan monks, Takujū monks receive many more *sassho* or checking questions after passing the main case and are asked to provide more *jakugo* (capping phrases). To accommodate the large number of *sassho* and *jakugo* assignments, the *sesshin* schedule in a Takujū monastery often includes more *sanzen* sessions with the rōshi, as many as seven a day. Over the years, the two schools have developed slightly different bodies of Zen verses and phrases from which to draw *jakugo*. The verses and phrases that make up the present volume have been taken from two modern collections, Tsuchiya Etsudō's *Zengoshū* and Shibayama Zenkei's *Zenrin kushū*, in order to encompass the practice of both schools.

---

[3] Shore, personal communication, 10 June 1998.

The two schools are not so divided as to prohibit the occasional crossover of traditions. A monastery's style of kōan practice will depend on the rōshi teaching there at any given time, and although most monasteries have become associated in the course of generations with a particular school, occasionally a *honzan* headquarters of one of the schools will ask a rōshi from the other to take over one of its monasteries. From time to time, a particularly gifted rōshi will make it a point to train under several teachers, learning the style of both schools in order to be able to give instruction in either of them. In addition, many rōshi seem to know that particular kōan are treated differently in the other school, and this knowledge is passed along in their own teaching of those kōan.

KŌAN TAIKEI 公案體系, THE KŌAN SYSTEM

Both the Inzan and Takujū schools teach the kōan system attributed to Hakuin, although it should be noted that there are some grounds for doubting that he was the creator of the present kōan system.[4] Since we are more concerned with the present use of the system, there is no need to go into these historical questions here.

When people speak of Hakuin's kōan system, they usually are referring to a five-fold division of kōan:

Hosshin 法身	*Dharmakāya* or Dharma-body
Kikan 機關	Dynamic Action
Gonsen 言詮	Explication of Words
Hachi nantō 八難透	Eight Difficult-to-Pass
Goi jūjūkin 五位十重禁	Five Ranks and the Ten Grave Precepts

This five-fold division seems to have evolved from earlier classification systems. It is known that the Japanese Zen monk Shōichi Kokushi 聖一國師 (Ben'en Enni 辯圓圓爾 1202–1280) had systematized kōan into categories, but there is some disagreement as to whether he used three or four. The Zen monk and scholar Akizuki Ryōmin describes three categories: *Richi* (理致 Attaining the Principle), *Kikan* (機關 Dynamic Action) and *Kōjō* (向上 Directed Upwards) (Akizuki 1987, 77). Others add a fourth category: *Kōge* (向下 Directed Downwards) (Itō 1970, 36). Nanpō Jōmyō (南浦紹明, 1235–1309), the monk who brought the Yōgi (楊岐) branch of Rinzai Zen to Japan from China, also divided kōan into three categories: *Richi, Kikan,* and *Kōjō* (Akizuki 1987, 77–8; Asahina 1941, 49–50).

Akizuki notes, however, that in Hakuin's system the original fifth category was not *Goi jūjūkin* (Five Ranks and Ten Grave Precepts) but *Kōjō*. He faults the Zen rōshi Asahina Sōgen for first substituting *Goi jūjūkin* as the fifth category, lamenting the fact that both Zen rōshi and lay writers have blindly followed his lead (Akizuki 1987,

[4] Mohr 1999, 315–18.

82). The lack of agreement on precisely what the five categories are has carried over into English-language accounts of Hakuin's system. Miura and Sasaki present Hakuin's system with *Goi jūjūkin* as the fifth category (ZD 62–76), while Shimano gives *Kōjō* (Directed Upwards) as the fifth category and *Goi jūjūkin* as a sixth category (SHIMANO 1988, 79–80). No systematic survey has been conducted to determine what system the majority of Rinzai teaching-rōshi in Japan now follow, but my general impression is that *Goi jūjūkin*, and not *Kōjō*, is usually considered the fifth category.

A complete list of all the categories of kōan in use would have to include not only *Kōjō* but two others as well. At very advanced stages of kōan practice, a monk might receive:

> *Kōjō* (Directed Upwards)
> *Matsugo no rōkan* (末後の牢關 Last Barrier)
> *Saigo no ikketsu* (最後の一訣 Final Confirmation).

I will discuss each of these in greater detail below. Since descriptions of Hakuin's five stages are readily available in English, I will restrict myself to an abbreviated account of his system here.

Hosshin (Dharmakāya) Kōan

The *Hosshin* kōan reveal the *dharmakāya*, the Dharma-body, or the Fundamental. Asahina Sōgen Rōshi explains:

> The simple explanation of Dharma-body, given by the ancients, is that one takes the dharma and makes oneself one with it, but this is just what we mean by true reality (*shinnyo* 眞如), by Dharma-nature, by Buddha-nature, by awakening (*bodai* 菩提), by nirvana, by the original body of the universe. For the Zen practitioner, it means one's own mind nature. In more concrete terms, it is the subject (*shujinkō* 主人公) of our seeing and hearing, of all our consciousness....
>
> The Zen practitioner by illuminating Dharma-body seeks to illuminate himself, to emancipate himself from life-and-death, and to attain unhindered freedom. The *Richi* kōan, the *Kikan* kōan, the *Kōjō* kōan and all other kōan attempt nothing more than to illuminate Dharma-body and radiate freedom through becoming one with the realm of Dharma-body. (ASAHINA 1941, 56)

The Dharma-body kōan are the kōan on which a monk experiences an initial awakening, *kenshō* or *satori*. The First Barrier kōan, the Sound of One Hand, and Jōshū's Mu, fall within this first group. As we see in the formula "If you awaken to *hosshin*, then there is not one single thing" (*Hosshin kakuryō sureba ichi motsu mo nashi* 法身覺了 無一物), the realm of *hosshin* is the realm of the undifferentiated and unconditioned. It is useful, at least provisionally, to think of *Hosshin* kōan as those that introduce the undifferentiated and the unconditional. (Like many other Zen terms, *hosshin* has also a second sense in which the undifferentiated is identical with the differentiated and the unconditioned with the conditioned.)

Kikan (Dynamic Action) Kōan

The *Kikan* or Dynamic Action kōan open up the realm of the differentiated and the dynamic in Zen. The character *ki* 機 in *kikan* is difficult to translate. Originally it denoted a weaver's loom, and in both Chinese and Japanese it is used today in compounds to signify machinery or anything mechanical. In Buddhism it has its own technical meanings, which differ from one branch to the next. Within Zen it has come to be used as a synonym for *hataraki* (working or functioning), and in its wider connotations carries the sense of spirit, dynamism, action, or flair. In general, it implies action rather than stillness and involvement rather than detachment, as, for instance, in the term *zenki* 禪機, which refers to the dynamic activity of the awakened person in the concrete situations of daily life.[5]

Taken together, *Hosshin* kōan and *Kikan* kōan reflect the traditional Chinese contrast between substance (*tai* 體) and function (*yū* 用). The *Hosshin* or "Body of the Buddha" kōan take one to the realm of the ultimate and unconditioned. But it is all too easy to get stuck there, in a condition that Zen calls *deiri no kyūin* 泥裏蚯蚓, "a worm in the mud" (mud being a metaphor for *satori*). *Kikan* kōan pry the monk out of the suffocating *satori* of the undifferentiated and the unconditioned, returning him to the everyday phenomenal world of self and things, of conventionality and discrimination. *Kikan* kōan show that the Fundamental is not merely still and tranquil but also active and dynamic, not only empty and undifferentiated but also full of distinctions and differentiation. To learn this is said to be more difficult than the attainment of the original *satori*, as we see in the following verse.

10.406 涅槃心易明 *Nehan no kokoro wa akirameyasuku,*
差別智難入 *Sabetsu no chi wa irigatashi.*

To clarify the mind of nirvana is easy,
But to enter the wisdom of discrimination is hard.

Gonsen (Explication of Words) Kōan

Gonsen kōan bring to light the fact that while the Fundamental is "not founded on words and letters," it is nevertheless expressed through words and letters. *Gonsen* kōan can be quite long, so that even memorizing them in order to recite them in the presence of the rōshi can be a major task in itself. Despite the fact that a special category exists for verbal expression, in my opinion the *Gonsen* kōan do not present any

[5] For a more detailed discussion of the meaning of this term, see *Ki* in Glossary.

problem with words and language that is not common to all kōan. In every kōan, the Zen practitioner faces the problem of breaking through the surface of words and letters—which may appear to be speaking of something else entirely—to the Fundamental beneath. In this sense the problem of how to express in words and letters what is purportedly not founded on words and letters arises in every kōan and is part of the very nature of kōan practice (see Hori 2000 for a fuller discussion).

Hachi Nantō (Eight Difficult-to-Pass) Kōan

Hakuin selected eight particularly dreadful kōan that he said would give the Zen practitioner chest pains and stomachaches. He urged his monks to risk their lives in order to pass these locked barriers and attain Zen awakening (Akizuki 1987, 89). These *Hachi nantō* kōan, as they are known, are considered a major test for Zen monks, though there seems to be some disagreement about what these kōan are supposed to teach and what their importance is in the overall kōan curriculum. Miura states that one who has completed the *Nantō* kōan understands "*jiji muge hokkai*, the Dharma world where each thing interpenetrates and harmonizes perfectly with every other thing without any hindrance whatsoever, the realm of complete effortlessness" (ZD 61). This description makes it seem as if the point of the *Nantō* kōan is to attain the fourth Hua-yen *dharma-dhātu*. Akizuki, in contrast, argues that the teachers of antiquity created the *Nantō* kōan to show practitioners that after satori there was also the realm of discrimination and differentiation (which is the function of *Kikan* kōan), and then after that, the work of saving sentient beings (Akizuki 1987, 88). I might add that I myself have heard a rōshi remark quite bluntly that the *Nantō* have no significance beyond the fact that Hakuin found them difficult to pass.

Despite this range of opinion about the function of the *Nantō* kōan, most Zen teachers accept a more or less standard explanation, according to which the initial stages of the kōan curriculum are designed to bring the monk to awakening and then to deepen it, while the more advanced stages are meant to cut the monk's attachment to his own awakening and arouse compassion for others. This latter function is attributed to *Nantō* kōan in the version of the curriculum where the fourth and fifth categories are *Nantō* and *Goi Jūjūkin*, and is attributed to *Kōjō* kōan in the version of the curriculum where the fourth and fifth categories are *Nantō* and *Kōjō*. I cite Asahina Sōgen Rōshi's account of the *Nantō* kōan:

> Once a person feels he has attained some degree of satori, he becomes satisfied with the Dharma joy (法悦) of this new world and thus it is hard for him to make any further advance (*kōjō* 向上). In the history of Zen, there are many who at this stage have sat down in self-satisfaction and stopped here. Such people think themselves fine as they are and therefore have no ability to help other people. Indeed on closer reflection, [we see that] they have not even saved themselves. The *Nantō* are a painful stick to the one who undertakes them. They make one

> know what it means to say, "Atop the mountain, another mountain."… That precious satori, which one got by going here, going there, doing this and doing that—[these *Nantō* kōan] take that *satori* and crush it like tree leaves into dust. Zen people call this "the house destroyed and the family scattered." "Holding onto nothing" has been replaced by "absolutely nothing to lose." (Asahina 1941, 61–2)

The *Nantō* kōan, then, are meant to throw the Zen practitioner back into crisis, releasing another Great Doubt, one that is directed not against the conventional self, but against the self that got created with *satori*.

The cycle of attaining awakening and then cutting it off is described in numerous Zen verses, such as the following:

16.57 凡夫若知卽是聖人 *Bompu moshi shiraba, sunawachi kore seijin,*
聖人若會卽是凡夫 *Seijin moshi shiraba, sunawachi kore bompu.*

An ordinary person knows it and becomes a sage;
A sage understands it and becomes an ordinary person.

14.470 握土成金猶可易 *Tsuchi o nigitte kin to nasu koto wa nao yasukarubeshi,*
變金爲土却還難 *Kin o henjite tsuchi to nasu koto wa kaette mata katashi.*

To take earth and turn it into gold may be easy,
But to take gold and turn it into earth, that is difficult indeed.

There is uncertainty now about which eight kōan are included in Hakuin's list. Miura and Sasaki in *Zen Dust* (ZD 57–61) mention the following five kōan:

Nansen's Flower (*Hekigan-roku* Case 40)
A Buffalo Passes the Window (*Mumonkan* Case 38)
Sōzan's Memorial Tower (*Kattō-shū* Case 140)
Suigan's Eyebrows (*Hekigan-roku* Case 8)
Enkan's Rhinoceros Fan (*Hekigan-roku* Case 91)

Shimano (1988: 78–9) gives as an example:

The Old Woman Burns the Hut (*Kattō-shū* Case 162).

Asahina Sōgen (1941: 62–3) gives as additional examples:

Goso Hōen's "Hakuun Said 'Not Yet'" (*Kattō-shū* Case 269)
Shuzan's Main Cable (*Kattō-shū* Case 280).

Akizuki (1987: 90–1) adds:

Nansen Has Died (*Kattō-shū* Case 282)
Kenpō's Three Illnesses (*Kattō-shū* Case 17).

Together these give us ten kōan for Hakuin's list of Eight Difficult-to-Pass Kōan.

Goi (Five Ranks)

The fifth category, *Goi jūjūkin*, contains two subcategories, kōan of the Five Ranks and kōan dealing with the Ten Grave Precepts. The term "Five Ranks" is an abbreviation of "Tōzan's Five Ranks" 洞山五位. Tōzan Ryōkai 洞山良价 (Tung-shan Liang-chieh, 807–869) was the teacher of Sōzan Honjaku 曹山本寂 (Ts'ao-shan Pen-chi, 840–901). The two were cofounders of the Sōtō School of Zen, the name "Sōtō" representing a combination of the first characters of each of their names. For the Japanese Rinzai school, however, Tōzan's Five Ranks are presented in a work authored by Hakuin called *Tōjō goi henshō kuketsu* 洞上五位偏正口訣, "The Five Ranks of the Crooked and the Straight: The Oral Teachings of the [Monk] who Lived on Mount Tō." This work is included in the handbook called *Zudokko* 塗毒鼓 (*The Poison-Painted Drum*), which is one of the standard possessions of practicing monks.

The *Goi* kōan do not introduce the monk to anything new. Rather, they require the monk to systematize all the kōan that he has passed, using the classification system of Tōzan's Five Ranks. The ranks are:

Shōchūhen 正中偏	The Crooked within the Straight
Henchūshō 偏中正	The Straight within the Crooked
Shōchūrai 正中來	The Coming from within the Straight
Kenchūshi 兼中至	The Arrival at Mutual Integration
Kenchūtō 兼中到	Unity Attained.

In Asahina's explanation (1941, 64), *shō* 正 "is emptiness, is truth, is black, is darkness, is principle, is *yin*," while *hen* 偏 "is form, is vulgar, is white, is brightness, is fact, is *yang*." Miura and Sasaki have translated *shō'i* and *hen'i* as "Real" and "Apparent," but I prefer to render them as "Straight" and "Crooked" in order to avoid the implication that "Real" is more real than "Apparent." The practicing monk has met the pair *shō'i* and *hen'i* in kōan practice long before he reaches the Five Ranks. In fact, the distinction between the Fundamental and its particular instantiations, as seen in the First Barrier kōan and its particular *sassho* checking questions, is basically the same distinction as that between *shō'i* and *hen'i*. Kōan almost always divide into two or more parts that invariably see the kōan from the two sides of *shō'i* and *hen'i*. Some commentators claim that the philosophical background of Mahayana Buddhist thought stands behind Zen, and indeed this is one of those places in which that background emerges into clear relief in that the distinction between *shō'i* and *hen'i* can easily be taken as the Zen transformation of the Two Truths.

Although the Five Ranks is associated with Tōzan Ryōkai, the idea of five ranks or positions must have grown out of the Chinese theory of Five Elements or Five Forces. The article on Tōzan's Five Ranks in the *Mochizuki bukkyō daijiten* dictionary of Buddhist terms describes the connections that various commentators have found between the Five Ranks and everything from yin-yang thought to hexagrams of the *I Ching* and Chou Tun-i's diagram of the Supreme Ultimate (MOCHIZUKI 1958, 3864–9). Few useful commentaries on the Five Ranks exist in English. The best starting point is still Chapter Seven of Miura and Sasaki's *Zen Dust,* which contains a slightly abbreviated translation of Hakuin's account of the Five Ranks, *Tōjō goi henshō kuketsu.* One can also consult LUK 1961, POWELL 1986, CHANG 1969, LAI 1983, and TOKIWA 1991.

Of particular interest for many readers will be the relationship between the Five Ranks and the *I Ching.* Since the Five Ranks are constructed from two elements, one positive and one negative (Straight and Crooked, Lord and Vassal, Real and Apparent), it is easy to pair them with hexagrams in the *I Ching,* which themselves are composed of combinations of *yin* and *yang* lines. In fact, Hakuin's own account of the Five Ranks, *Tōjō goi henshō kuketsu,* begins with a diagram of Hexagram 30, Fire upon Fire, but for some reason this diagram has been omitted from the English translation in Miura and Sasaki's *Zen Dust.* Some of the final kōan connected with the Rinzai Five Ranks also treat the hexagrams of the *I Ching.* In working on these kōan, the monk is expected to prepare a set of six woodblocks with *yin* and *yang* faces to be used in the *sanzen* room when he meets the rōshi.

Jūjū kinkai (The Ten Grave Precepts)

Jūjū kinkai, the Ten Grave Precepts, are the precepts against taking life, stealing, misusing sex, lying, intoxication, speaking ill of others, praising oneself, covetousness, anger, and reviling the Three Treasures. The Ten Grave Precepts bring Hakuin's kōan system to completion, since the final end of Rinzai kōan practice is not benefit for oneself but benefit for others. Asahina notes that in these kōan the practicing monk must embody the precepts as *Hosshin,* realize their dynamic activity as *Kikan,* express them in words as *Gonsen,* penetrate them completely as *Nantō,* thoroughly understand their theoretic rationale in the *Goi,* and then practice them faithfully in daily life as *Jūjū kinkai.* At the same time, he regrets that these kōan come at the end of a long system of training, since most monks who begin kōan practice leave their training in mid-course without having come to the Ten Grave Precepts (ASAHINA 1941, 70).

In English there are only a few comments on the Ten Grave Precepts kōan, none of which reflect the way they are taught in Japanese Rinzai training. In their chapter on the Ten Grave Precepts, Miura and Sasaki merely list the precepts and cite a passage from monastery *Admonitions* (ZD 73–6). Shimano observes that the point of these kōan is to get past the habit, especially marked in the West, of always seeing things as either good or bad, and to move to the "ultimate standpoint" beyond the dualistic view of killing or not killing. He places strong emphasis on nonduality, on "no killer and no one to be killed," on "realization of oneness" (SHIMANO 1988, 80–1). Aitken takes the opposite tack, emphasizing the standpoint of the conventional. His lectures on the Ten Grave Precepts rarely use the language of oneness, replacing it with examples of drunken men in hotel rooms, woman chasers in the sangha, and a cranky mother with a demanding daughter (AITKEN 1984, 3–104). In Rinzai kōan training, both the *shō'i* and *hen'i* (straight and crooked, nondual and dual) aspects of the Ten Grave Precepts are given equal emphasis, and the precepts as a whole are presented not merely as rules to guard human behavior against its tendency to wrongdoing, but also as positive expressions of the bodhisattva's practice of "the *samādhi* of freedom in the other," *tajiyū zammai* (他自由三昧). (For normative and nonnormative interpretations of precepts, see also the note at 16.31.)

Kōjō (Directed Upwards)

In the curriculum that seems to be most widely adopted today, the fourth and fifth categories are *Nantō* (Difficult to Pass) and *Goi jūjūkin* (Five Ranks and the Ten Grave Precepts). As we remarked earlier, in what Akizuki claims was the older original kōan system, the fifth category was *Kōjō* (Directed Upwards). Today this category no longer seems to have a well-defined function. In the older curriculum where the fourth and fifth categories were *Nantō* and *Kōjō*, the *Nantō* kōan would simply have been eight kōan considered extremely difficult to pass, and the *Kōjō* kōan would have had the special function of ridding the monk of any "stink of Zen" and of attachment to his awakening.

The variety of different translations of the term *Kōjō* merits comment. I have translated it literally as "Directed Upwards" in view of the fact that Shōichi Kokushi adds the further category *Kōge*, "Directed Downwards." Shimano translates *Kōjō* as "Crowning," but I find this misleading in that it implies a kind of finality or completion. AKIZUKI (1987, 91), writing in Japanese, uses the English term "nonattachment" to explain the function of *Kōjō*. MOHR (1999, 317–8) translates it as "Going beyond," which I find far better in that it implies an open-endedness. *Kōjō* is a reminder that not even the attainment of *satori* or *kenshō* is final, that there is "Atop the mountain, another mountain." After the task of reaching *satori* comes that of ridding oneself of *satori* and working for the salvation of others. This is *Kōjō*. The saying "When you reach the top of the mountain, you must keep going" seems to imply just this sort of further ascent. But the second mountain one has to climb after arriving at the *samādhi* summit of freedom for oneself (*jijiyū zammai* 自自由三昧) begins with a descent downhill, back into the valley as it were, to cultivate for others the *samādhi* of freedom (*tajiyū zammai* 他自由三昧). The final stage of practice is to leave the mountain to work for the benefit of all sentient beings, and of this stage of practice there is no end.

Matsugo no rōkan, The Last Barrier; Saigo no ikketsu, The Final Confirmation

Not much has been written about these last kōan, and needless to say, Zen priests and monks are reluctant to speak of them in public. The Last Barrier kōan is given to the monk as he leaves the monastery. Akizuki gives as examples "Sum up all of the Record of Rinzai in one phrase!" and "Hakuun's 'Not yet'" (1987, 96). But since the monk is leaving the monastery, he is not meant to pass this kōan immediately, but rather to carry it constantly with him and to try again and again to see through it right to the bottom. Finally, some rōshi assign a last kōan called *Saigo no ikketsu*. I have not been able to discover much about this kōan but suspect that it is an alternate name for *Matsugo no rōkan*.

SHŌTAI CHŌYŌ 聖胎長養, LONG NURTURING OF THE SACRED FETUS

The formal kōan training completed in the monastery does nothing more than create a "sacred fetus." A monk who has completed the kōan training is not yet ready to step out into the world and take on a public role. He must first complete another stage called *Shōtai chōyō* (sometimes pronounced *Seitai chōyō*), the "long nurturing of the sacred fetus." This period of withdrawal after the completion of the kōan curriculum is also known as *Gogo no shugyō* 悟後の修行 or "post-*satori* training." (There is some ambiguity in the use of the term, since the same term may also refer to all training after initial *satori*.[6]) As explained in the lectures that rōshi give to their monks, a monk who has completed the kōan curriculum leaves the monastery for several years, hiding his identity as a monk, in order to engage in some activity completely unrelated to monastery practice. The great example is Daitō Kokushi, the "beggar under the bridge." Zen lore has it that after his *satori*, he lived for twenty years with the beggars under the Gojō Bridge in Kyoto, giving his *satori* time to ripen before he went on to found the Daitoku-ji temple.[7] Daitō Kokushi's disciple, Kanzan Egen, it is said, withdrew to the mountains of Ibuka in present-day Gifu Prefecture, where for eight years he tended cattle and tilled the fields (ZD 325). In his *Mujintōron (Discourse on the Inexhaustible Lamp)*, Tōrei Enji cites the long maturation periods of numerous past masters: Hui-neng, the Sixth Patriarch, went south for fifteen years; Nansen Fugan resided for thirty years in a hermitage (where monks eventually gathered and argued about a cat that Nansen had killed); Daibai Hōjō ate pine needles

---

6 See Ruth Fuller SASAKI's rather general comments in ZD 26.

7 Kenneth KRAFT has examined the evidence for the "beggar under the bridge" image of Daitō Kokushi (1992, 41–7). This book also provides an extremely useful account of the importance of the capping phrase in Zen since Daitō is noted as an early Japanese master of the capping-phrase commentary (130–50).

and wore clothes made from lotus stalks for thirty years (14.47–8); Yōgi Hōe spent twenty years in a dilapidated hut where snowflakes bejewelled the floor in the winter (Tōrei 1989, 451–74). During this period of ripening the monk is said to learn to apply the awakening he attained in formal monastery training to the concrete situations of daily life, and he does this by deliberately extinguishing all self-consciousness of *satori*.

The phrase "long nurturing of the sacred fetus" resonates with profound nuances. The term "sacred fetus" itself looks as if it originated in Taoist practices of longevity and immortality, since the point of Taoist inner alchemy practice is to combine breath, vital force, and spirit to create a sacred fetus which is then nurtured through further discipline into immortality.[8] The practice of withdrawing from society also has clear associations with the broader image of the recluse or hermit in Chinese culture. This individual withdrew from public life not because he was incapable of functioning in the world, but because he found the world too disordered for a person of principle to exercise his talents properly. He chose seclusion in order to nourish himself, all the better to reemerge and assume public responsibility at a later time, when a proper leader had appeared and the time was ripe (Vervoorn 1990). A legendary example of this is Chu-ko Liang in the *Romance of the Three Kingdoms*. This master scholar and strategist of war lived in deep seclusion until Liu Pei, the last scion of the Han Empire, visited him three times and was able to persuade him to come forth and join him in the attempt to reestablish an empire (Brewitt-Taylor 1959, 385–407). Reclusion thus symbolizes the fact that, while capable of handling power and rank, the hermit is not attached to these things but puts his self-cultivation and the welfare of people first. Similarly, in *Shōtai chōyō*, the Zen practitioner who has finished his formal training engages in an informal training in which he thoroughly detaches himself from his accomplishments and willingly assumes anonymity for service to others.

---

[8] The term "sacred fetus" was used in both Taoist external alchemy and internal alchemy. According to the *Dōkyō jiten* (*Encyclopedia of Taoism*), in external alchemy the "womb" was the cauldron into which the various ingredients and chemicals were placed for firing and the silver product that was thereby created was called the sacred fetus. In internal alchemy the process for attaining longevity begins on the winter solstice, when *yin* changes to *yang*. On the one-hundreth day thereafter, the ingredients complete their chemical reaction; on the two-hundreth day in the lower cinnabar field the sacred fetus takes firm shape, and on the three-hundreth day it becomes the "womb immortal" that emits true *ch'i* breath-energy (Noguchi et al. 1994, 324).

There are also Buddhist uses. The Buddhist text *Butsu hongyō jikkyō* 佛本行集經 (T 3.655–932) contains the interesting statement, "According to what I have heard, my wife, the Lady Moye Wang, is pregnant with a sacred fetus whose majesty is so great that if she were to give birth, my wife's life would be shortened and before long have to come to an end" (quoted in HYDCD 8.669).

PERSONAL REFLECTIONS

I conclude this short account of the so-called kōan system with a number of supplementary remarks. In day-to-day monastic life, the several categories of kōan make little difference to the practicing monk. Monks themselves do not know to which category the kōan they are presently working on belongs. The categories of kōan are useful to senior monks, who need to reflect on the kōan system as a whole, but monks in the thick of practice seldom speak of *hosshin, kikan, nantō*, or the like.

Moreover, the formal categories of the kōan system give the impression that every kōan can be assigned to a single category, but in fact *hosshin, kikan*, and *gonsen* point to aspects found in all the kōan that every practicing monk easily recognizes even without the formal description. In every kōan the monk must grasp the kōan itself *(hosshin)*, experience its dynamic working *(kikan)*, and use language to express what is "not founded on words and letters" *(gonsen)*. In the same way, the *jakugo* assignments are actually a *gonsen* exercise, even though the word may never be used.

Japanese Rinzai Zen is often criticized, even by its own monks, for allowing the kōan practice to calcify into a rigid formalism. It is not uncommon to hear Rinzai practice faulted for being little more than a ritual recapitulation of kōan responses that the mere passage of time has baptized as orthodoxy. There is some truth to this, but in defense of the practice, I would add that in my own case I never felt anything but admiration for the teachers of the past who had devised a system of training that time and again forced me to plunge deep into *zazen* to find an answer from a place in myself I did not know existed. The fixed response to a kōan resembles the fixed patterns of movements in the martial arts called *kata*. One practices them again and again until they become movements of power, executed precisely and without deliberation. As for whether there are "correct answers" to the kōan, Zen teachers insist that before one engages in the practice a kōan may appear to have a fixed meaning, but that after one has completed the practice, that kōan has no meaning at all, fixed or otherwise.

3

Literary Study in Kōan Practice

KŌAN PRACTICE does not consist merely of meditation and *sanzen*. In the widest sense it also embraces all other aspects of monastery activity, including physical work, ritual and ceremonial practices such as the chanting of sutras, and community life. But even in the more restricted sense of direct engagement with the kōan, it also involves literary study. This study begins in a monk's first year when he is instructed to search for *jakugo* or "capping phrases" for kōan that have been passed, and it continues through to the end of formal training with advanced exercises such as writing lectures, called *kakiwake* (written analysis), and the composition of poetry, called *nenrō* (deft play).

JAKUGO: THE CAPPING PHRASE

When a monk is first instructed to bring a *jakugo*, he will probably not know what a *jakugo* is and will have to ask his fellow monks what he is being asked to do. The ZGDJT (468) gives a useful definition of the *jakugo*:

> *Jakugo* 著語, also *agyo* 下語, *kengo* 揀語. A short commentary appended to a phrase from either the main case or the verse in a Zen text. Though it is clearly a commentary, in it one uses one's eye-for-the-essential either to assess and praise the words or actions of the ancients that support their explanations, or to substitute one's own rendering of their core meaning, freely manipulating the dynamic of life and death. Forms an essential element of certain Zen texts like the *Hekigan-roku* and the *Shōyō-roku*.

As this text makes clear, the *jakugo* assignment reveals both the point or core (*shūshi* 宗旨) of the kōan as well as the eye-for-the-essential (*shūjōgan* 宗乗眼) the monk needs to recognize that core. He is expected to return with a Chinese verse expressing the point of the kōan, or of the *sassho*, as he sees it. Originally, it is said, Zen monks composed their own verses, but with the decline in classical education and facility in composing Chinese verse, modern monks are no longer able to do this. Over time, several thousand such verses have been collected into special Zen collections from which the monk is expected to find an appropriate *jakugo*. The earliest of these books still in use is the *Zenrin kushū* (*The Zen Phrase Collection*), edited by Ijūshi in 1688. This text is in fact a greatly expanded version of an earlier collection known as the *Kuzōshi*, first compiled toward the end of the fifteenth century by Tōyō Eichō Zenji (1426–1504). New collections of Zen *jakugo* phrases have been compiled during the twentieth century, discarding many of the old phrases and adding new ones. These will be described in more detail in Chapter Five.

Several terms are now used for capping phrases with slightly different meanings. The common term *jakugo* (著語, 着語) is written with characters that mean in Japanese "to append a phrase" (*go o tsukeru* 語を着ける, 語を著ける). The variation in the writing of the glyph for *jaku* reflects only the minor nuance between "append" and "attach." A very commonly used term is *agyo* 下語, which also means "appended phrase." The term *kengo* mentioned in the definition from the ZGDJT cited above means simply "selected phrase." Some *jakugo* assignments require a front phrase, a back phrase, and a combined phrase (*zengo* 前語, *gogo* 後語, and *sōgo* 総語). These are meant to express *hen'i,* the Crooked; *shō'i,* the Straight; and the combination of the two. Occasionally *jakugo* and *teigo* 呈語 ("expression") are used as a pair, *jakugo* signifying the *shō'i* verse and *teigo* the *hen'i* verse. Instead of presenting a traditional *jakugo* to a kōan, a monk may also offer a *betsugo* 別語 ("alternate phrase") or *daigo* 代語 ("substitute phrase"). All these terms refer to phrases and verses composed in the Chinese language. In addition, there are capping phrases in Japanese known as *sego* 世語, or "vernacular phrases." Typically these are lines taken from Japanese tanka, haiku, and other traditional forms of Japanese verse. The *Zenrin segoshū (Zen Vernacular Phrase Collection),*[1] a collection of Japanese verses suitable for use as capping phrases, has been compiled for this purpose. *Sego* assignments are relatively rare in comparison with *jakugo* assignments. Finally, there are *heigo* 平語, which are "colloquial phrases" taken from ordinary spoken Japanese.

I recall hearing a Zen rōshi explain the relationship of *agyo* to kōan: an *agyo* complements or highlights a kōan the way *wasabi* mustard complements *sashimi* raw fish, a necktie complements a suit, or a flower complements a scroll. The complement is usually one of contrast: *wasabi* is hot and has a strong taste while *sashimi* is very subtly flavored; a necktie is bright while the suit is dark; a flower is colorful while the scroll is black and white. An *agyo* is usually poetic in the form of an artificially contrived metaphor, while the kōan itself is prosaic in its raw and natural form.

The *jakugo* assignment serves several purposes. First, it is an additional type of checking question through which the Zen master can confirm the monk's insight. But it can also lead to new insight on its own. As the monk pages through the Zen phrase book, he reads each phrase in light of the kōan he has just completed. He may

[1] TSUCHIYA 1957. 773 verses from this collection have been translated in SHIGEMATSU 1988.

happen upon a familiar verse and suddenly see it in a new way. Conversely, a verse in the Zen phrase book may trigger a new insight into the original kōan. When I received the *jakugo* assignment for "Mu," try as I might, I could not find a capping phrase that summed up "Mu." Weeks went by. I lost count of the number of times I read through the *Zen Phrase Book* from cover to cover without success. I was beginning to think there *was* no such verse. Finally, in disgust, the rōshi gave me a hint. All at once an avalanche of suitable verses tumbled off the pages, all of which I had read many times before without making the association. It was as if *every* verse expressed "Mu."

Besides confirming and deepening insight, the *jakugo* assignment functions also as a spur to further practice. As Akizuki explains, when the monk presents a capping-phrase verse he has selected for his kōan and the rōshi accepts it, the rōshi will often discuss some of the other verses that are accepted as *jakugo* for that particular kōan. By seeing the classic *jakugo* for his kōan set side by side with the verse that he has himself selected, the monk realizes the limitations of his own ability to see through the surface of language to the Fundamental beneath, and is impressed with the depth of insight of the ancients (Akizuki 1987, 75–6). Occasionally the rōshi will speak with a bit of pride about the verses he himself selected or composed when he was a monk working on that particular kōan.

Investigation of the kōan through the *jakugo* can become rather complicated. A long kōan may be divided into a number of subsections, each of which may require a *jakugo*. Below is an example of an advanced kōan, Rinzai's Four Discernments *(Rinzai shiryōken)*, with its many divisions and *jakugo* assignments. Not every rōshi uses this structure, but it offers a concrete example of one rōshi's teaching style.

> Rinzai's Four Discernments (*Rinzai shiryōken* 臨濟四料揀 *Rinzai-roku* §10, *Kattō-shū* Case 218):
>
> 1. Remove the person, not the surroundings (Standpoint of principle and fact) 奪人不奪境 (理事の立場)
> 2. Remove the person, not the surroundings (Standpoint of dynamic action) 奪人不奪境 (機關の立場)
> 3. Phrase 語
> 4. Phrase 語
> 5. *Nenrō* verse 拈弄
> 6. Remove the surroundings, not the person (Standpoint of principle and fact) 奪境不奪人 (理事の立場)
> 7. Remove the surroundings, not the person (Standpoint of dynamic action) 奪境不奪人 (機關の立場)
> 8. Phrase 語
> 9. *Nenrō* verse 拈弄
> 10. *Nenrō* verse 拈弄

11. Remove both person and surroundings (Standpoint of principle and fact) 人境兩俱奪 (理事の立場)
12. Remove both person and surroundings (Standpoint of dynamic action) 人境兩俱奪 (機關の立場)
13. Phrase 語
14. Phrase 語
15. *Nenrō* verse 拈弄
16. *Nenrō* verse 拈弄
17. Do not remove either person or surroundings (Standpoint of principle and fact) 人境俱不奪 (理事の立場)
18. Do not remove either person or surroundings (Standpoint of dynamic action) 人境俱不奪 (機關の立場)
19. Phrase 語
20. Phrase 語
21. *Nenrō* verse 拈弄
22. Colloquial phrase for "Remove the person, do not remove surroundings." 奪人不奪境の平語
23. Same as above 同上
24. Colloquial phrase for "Remove the surroundings, do not remove the person" 奪境不奪人の平語
25. Colloquial phrase for "Remove both person and surroundings" 人境兩俱奪の平語
26. Colloquial phrase for "Do not remove either person or surroundings" 人境俱不奪の平語
27. How do you handle the entire Buddhist Canon on the basis of the Four Discernments? 四料揀の立場に一切經典をどうあつかうのか.

Tōzan Goi (洞山五位 Tōzan's Five Ranks) can de divided into 47 parts with numerous *jakugo*. Even an early kōan like "the Cypress Tree in the Garden" divides into 17 parts. In fact, once one has passed the beginning stages, most kōan divide into at least two parts (*shō-i* and *hen'i*—the Straight and the Crooked), often with accompanying *jakugo* for each part.

The verses in the Zen phrase books are drawn from every area of Chinese literature. Although a major portion comes from the writings of Zen masters or from Buddhist sutras, a considerable part is also taken from the massive fund of Chinese poetry up to and including the T'ang Dynasty. Many verses are also taken from the Chinese histories, the Confucian classics, and Taoist works. There are even one or two Taoist chants and children's street songs. By constantly paging through the Zen phrase books, the monk is exposed again and again to the great literary phrases of Chinese history, philosophy, and poetry. In addition to learning the original meaning for each of these verses, he also must learn to read them with a Zen eye. For example, he comes to understand Confucius's statement, "Having heard the Tao in the morning, I can die in the evening" (*Analects* IV, 8) as a kōan. Over time, the experienced monk has memorized so much of the Zen phrase book that it is not necessary for him to spend much time actually reading the text. If assigned a *jakugo*, he may recall an appropriate verse from memory as he sweeps the garden or cuts the carrots.

JAKUGO IN THE KŌAN ITSELF

The practice of appending *jakugo* evolved directly from Chinese Ch'an practices that date back at least to the Sung Dynasty. This practice is so important that it has shaped the structure of basic kōan texts such as the *Hekigan-roku* and *Mumonkan*, two of the main kōan collections used in Rinzai kōan practice.[2] In the *Hekigan-roku,* Setchō Jūken (Ch. Hsüeh-tou Ch'ung-hsien, 980–1052) has compiled one hundred kōan cases and added a verse (called a *ju* 頌) to each. This verse is itself a *jakugo*, a capping verse expressing Setchō's insight into the essence of the kōan. In addition to the *jakugo* that Setchō provided for the kōan as a whole, in fifteen cases he also appended *jakugo* to individual lines of the kōan (Cases 4, 18, 23, 31, 33, 36, 42, 48, 55, 61, 74, 82, 84, 85, 91).

The *Hekigan-roku* is a double-layered *jakugo* text, its second editor, Engo Kokugon (Ch. Yüan-wo K'o-ch'in, 1063–1135), having overlaid an additional layer of commentary on Setchō's original. Engo added an introduction to each case, as well as lengthy

---

[2] The full title of this kōan collection is *Bukka Engo Zenji kekigan-roku* 佛果圜悟禪師碧巖錄 (Ch. *Fo-kuo Yüan-wu Ch'an shih Pi-yen lu*; T no. 2203, 48.139–225). It was first published in 1128 and was soon in wide circulation. Legend says that Engo's disciple Daie Sōkō (大慧宗杲 Ta-hui Tsung-kao, 1089–1163), feeling that the book revealed too much, burned the wooden printing plates for the book. Two centuries later, Chang Ming-yüan 張明遠 reconstituted the text and published a new edition in 1317. Yanagida speculates that Chang was the one who determined the order of the kōan (Iriya et al. 1981, 301). With one exception, modern editions of the *Hekigan-roku* are based on the Chang edition. The one exception is the "One Night Text" (一夜本), so called because Dōgen Zenji, on the night before his departure from China for Japan, copied the entire *Hekigan-roku* in one night. There are significant differences between this text and the Chang edition. Heine 1994 offers a study of this text.

The *Hekigan-roku* evolved from an earlier text entitled *Setchō hyakusoku juko* 雪竇百則頌古 (Setchō's Hundred Kōans with Verse Commentary)—Yanagida calls it "the Ur-Text of the *Hekigan-roku*" (Iriya et al. 1981, 281)—which contains only the Main Case and Setchō's Verse for each kōan. There are no commentaries and no interlinear *jakugo*. Kōan cases 66 to 93 in this text are ordered differently from those in the later *Hekigan-roku.*

The *Zudokko,* which is meant to contain all the basic texts necessary for Rinzai kōan practice, includes the *Setchō hyakusoku juko.* Although the *Zudokko* version is similar in style to the *Hyakusoku juko* (Main Case and Verse but no commentaries or *jakugo*), the order of the cases is the same as that of the *Hekigan-roku.*

prose commentaries to both the Main Case of the kōan and to Setchō's Verse. He then added further line-by-line *jakugo* to both the Main Case and even to Setchō's own *jakugo*. The cases of the *Hekigan-roku* are therefore quite complex in structure, consisting of eight identifiable parts representing three layers of text editing.

Original case	Setchō Jūken Zenji	Engo Kokugon Zenji
		1. *Suiji* 垂示, an Introduction by Engo (called "Pointer" in Cleary and Cleary 1977)
2. *Honsoku* 本則, the Main Case of the kōan	3. *Jakugo* 著語, Setchō's interlinear capping phrases to Main Case in 15 cases	4. *Agyo* 下語, Engo's interlinear capping phrases to both the Main Case and Setchō's capping phrases
		5. *Hyōshō* 評唱, Engo's commentary to the Main Case
	6. *Ju* 頌, Setchō's Verse in response to the Main Case	7. *Jakugo* 著語, Engo's capping phrases to Setchō's Verse
		8. *Hyōshō* 評唱, Engo's Commentary to Setchō's Verse

Kenneth Kraft has aptly described the capping phrase as a "cross between a kōan and a footnote" (1992, 5). Although the capping phrase may appear in a text to be a kind of footnote, its function is not to cite a source, supply a gloss to clarify a difficult passage, or provide further details for those who wish it. The opponents in a kōan dialogue are depicted as being in competition; they are always making strategic moves against each other—probing, defending, feinting, attacking. Setchō's interlinear *jakugo* in the *Hekigan-roku* correspond to the cheering and jeering of the bystander to the match. In Case 4, Setchō responds to Isan's unnecessary praise of Tokusan by countering, "He is putting frost on top of snow." In Case 55, he shows himself aghast at the dialogue in the kōan, exclaiming, "Oh Lord! Oh Lord!" At times the bystanders think they can do better than the competitors themselves. For example, in Case 42, Setchō boasts, "When P'ang first asked, I would have made a snowball and hit him"; and in Case 48, the self-appointed expert claims, "At that time I would have just kicked over the tea stove."

Engo's *jakugo*, like Setchō's, resemble the boos and hurrahs of spectators to a game. Since Engo's *jakugo* are themselves responses to Setcho's *jakugo*, Engo is like someone who responds not only to the players but also to the other spectators. Comments that suggest a better move are not merely criticisms of someone else's move in the game; in the game of Zen one-upmanship, they are themselves moves. In the terminology of modern philosophical analysis, a *jakugo* is not merely a descriptive, it is also a performative. That is, it does not merely describe or characterize an action performed by some other person; it also performs one itself (and that is why they should not be called "Notes" as CLEARY and CLEARY 1977 does).[3]

By way of example, we may look at Case 23 of the *Hekigan-roku*. The text in italics indicates either Setchō's *jakugo* or Engo's *jakugo*.

	Setchō's case	**Engo's *jakugo***
1.	Once when Hofuku and Chōkei were wandering in the mountains,	*These two guys have fallen into the weeds.*
2.	Hofuku pointed with his hand, "This right here is Mystic Peak."	*He's made a pile of bones where there's level ground. Swear off talking about it. Dig up the earth and bury it deep.*
3.	Chōkei said, "That may be so but it's a pity."	*If you lack iron eyes and copper pupils, you will be lost. Two people sick with the same disease are consoling each other. Bury them both in the same hole.*
4.	Setchō's *jakugo*: *When you wander in the mountains with these guys, you can't tell what they will do.*	*Though he [Setchō] has nicely reduced their net worth, still they've got something. On both sides of you, they've got their hands on their swords.*
5.	Another [*jakugo*]: *A hundred thousand years from now, I'm not saying there won't be anyone, just that there will be few.*	*Pompous salesman! Here's another holy man up in the clouds!*
6.	*Later this story was related to Kyōshō,*	*There's good, there's bad.*
7.	*Who said, "If it weren't for Mr. Son [Chōkei], then you would have seen skulls filling the field."*	*Only someone on the same path knows. The great earth is so vast, it makes people so utterly sad. When a slave meets a bondsmaid, they are mutually courteous. If Rinzai and Tokusan had appeared, for sure they would have given them a taste of the stick.*

The original story of this kōan is quite simple. One day while walking with Chōkei, Hofuku pointed with his hand and said, "This right here is Mystic Peak," to which Chōkei said, "That may be so but it's a pity (that you had to say it)." Everything else is *jakugo*. In his *jakugo* at line 4, Setchō, the first editor of the text, expresses his amusement at the clumsy Zen antics of Hofuku and Chōkei each trying to display his enlightenment, but in line 5, he laments that in the future there will be few left with even their level of Zen. Engo Zenji not only reflects Setchō's condescending superior

[3] For more on the performative analysis of the kōan, see HORI 2000. Recent discussions of the structure of the kōan in the *Hekigan-roku* may be found in BUSWELL 1987, 344–5, and FOULK 2000, 28–33.

tone, he even trumps Setchō. In his *jakugo* at line 2, Engo decries the clumsiness of Hofuku, whose unnecessary words destroy the very mysticism they describe. He even finds Chōkei is just as bad as Hofuku ("Bury them both in the same hole"). Then in his *jakugo* to Setchō's *jakugo*, he agrees with Setchō that Hofuku and Chōkei are not completely worthless (line 4), but also lambastes Setchō for his high self-opinion (line 5). Line 7 is open to different interpretations. CLEARY and CLEARY (1977, 154) identify Mr. Son (C. Sun) as Hofuku (C. Pao Fu). But the majority of other commentators identify Son as the informal name for Chōkei (IRIYA et al. 1992, vol. 1, 306; ŌMORI 1994, vol. 1, 187; ASAHINA 1937, vol. 1, 280). Thus taken, the line "If it weren't for Mr. Son [Chōkei], then you would have seen skulls filling the field" means, if it were not for Chōkei, Hofuku would have got away with his atrocious display of Zen. But Engo's *jakugo*, "When a slave meets a bondsmaid, they are mutually courteous," means "It takes one to know one," implying both parties are mutually Zen clowns. The greater part of this kōan consists of *jakugo*. Though they look like footnotes appended to text, none of them supply the information one expects in a footnote; they are all thrusts and parries in the joust of Zen.

The *Mumonkan*, another important kōan collection used in the Rinzai kōan curriculum, is a less complex text, but it, too, would not have its present structure were it not for the practice of *jakugo*. The *Mumonkan* is a collection of forty-eight cases edited by Mumon Ekai (Ch. Wu-men Hui-k'ai 無門慧開). To each of the forty-eight cases Mumon Ekai appends a commentary and a short four-line verse (*ju* 頌) in which he expresses his Zen insight into the matter of the kōan. The four-line verse is his *jakugo*. Each case of the *Mumonkan* contains some moment of Zen insight, but Mumon's *jakugo*, in which he expresses his insight into the kōan, can be just as profound as the insight presented in the main case.

For example, in Case 2, "Hyakujō and the Fox," an old man reveals that long ago he had wrongly claimed that a person of great awakening does not fall into karmic causation, and that his punishment for this mistake was to be reborn for five hundred lives as a fox. The man did not realize it at the time, but his answer, "no falling," was based on a false dichotomy between falling into karma and not falling into karma. Hyakujō releases the fox from punishment by saying that a person of great awakening is not blind to karmic causation, thus avoiding the dichotomy of falling and not falling. Mumon's verse on this kōan begins, "Not falling, not being blind, / Two sides of the same die." Here Mumon goes even further than the main case of the kōan and shows that even Hyakujō's answer, "not blind," sets up another false dichotomy between "not falling" and "not being blind." Mumon's comment even goes so far as to claim that the fox *enjoyed* his five hundred lives.

KAKIWAKE 書き分け, 書き譯 WRITTEN EXPLANATION AND *NENRŌ* 拈弄 DEFT PLAY

Rinzai kōan practice also includes written assignments. This part of the practice is, however, more difficult to research. In the Myōshin-ji/Daitoku-ji monasteries, monks in their seventh or eighth year who have attained some level of maturity will start receiving written assignments, *kakiwake* and *nenrō*. This is not uniform practice in all Rinzai monasteries. In some lineages there may be no written assignments, or written work may be required only once, after the monk has finished the entire kōan curriculum. Since there is no systematic research on this subject, all one can say is that there is a variety of styles; it is impossible to say that there is one predominant pattern to written assignments.

In those monasteries where written assignments form part of the kōan curriculum, after the monk passes a kōan in the usual way, the rōshi assigns the first few lines of the kōan to the monk as a *kakiwake* assignment. *Kakiwake* literally means "written analysis" 書き分け or "written rationale" 書き譯. The monk researches those few lines identifying names of people and places, explaining difficult characters, tracking down the original sources of any quoted passages or set phrases, explaining any technical terms, and so on, and then finally expounds the Zen meaning of the passage. In style and content his essay will resemble the rōshi's regular lectures to the monks. The monk writes his essay with a brush on Japanese *hanshi* paper and in ordinary Japanese. He submits the *kakiwake* essay to the rōshi, who then proceeds to mark the essay in much the same way that a university professor corrects a student's paper. In a few days, the essay is returned to the author with marginal comments in red ink. If the first essay is accepted, the monk is assigned another for the next few lines of the kōan. This procedure continues until the entire kōan has been covered. Even for a short kōan, the entire *kakiwake* essay will comprise several pages, and for a longer kōan, the result will be a small stack of *hanshi*.

On completion of the *kakiwake* essay, which may take several weeks or months, the monk next is directed to write a *nenrō*, a short verse, typically of four lines, in classical Chinese. *Nenrō* literally means "handle playfully," but I have rendered it here "deft play." Whereas the *kakiwake* essay is prosaic, detailed, and discursive, the *nenrō* verse is supposed to be free and imaginative, and written in the form of classical Chinese poetry. The monk's model is the four-line verse that Mumon appends to each kōan in the *Mumonkan*. The *nenrō* verse is much the shorter of the two assignments, but it is also the more difficult.

As is the tradition in Asian scholarship, the *kakiwake* essay is written in an anonymous, impersonal voice. The author does not write in the first person and his personality does not come through in the content. The short *nenrō* verse, in contrast, is meant to be a virtuoso performance in which the monk displays his capacity for seeing more deeply into the kōan than any of the previous masters, turning the kōan on its head to reveal some aspect not noticed before. As Akizuki describes the practice, in contrast to the anonymity of voice in the *kakiwake* essay, the monk ritually adopts an attitude bordering on arrogance: "The old masters said such-and-such, but if it had been me, I would have said so-and-so" (Akizuki 1987, 76). In both *kakiwake* and *nenrō*, the monk will be expected to make free use of *jakugo* and demonstrate his familiarity with the texts and literature of Zen.

Akizuki has published the kōan record for Kazan Genku Rōshi (1837--1917), a rōshi in the Myōshin-ji line (1987, 259–64). He lists two hundred kōan, beginning with Jōshū's Mu and ending with a group that includes the Five Ranks and Ten Grave Precepts. Each main case of a kōan is also followed by *sassho* checking questions, *jakugo* and *sego* capping-phrase assignments, and *kakiwake* and *nenrō* written assignments, for a total of 525 assignments. Here is an example kōan (no. 174): "Tokusan Carries His Bowls" (MMK 13), which displays how the different kōan assignments fit together.

Kōan 174

Main Case: Seppō, disciple of Tokusan, was the rice server. One day, the noon meal was late. Tokusan came down to the eating hall carrying his bowls. Seppō said, "The bell has not yet rung and the drum has not yet sounded. Old Master, where are you going carrying your bowls?" Tokusan without a word bowed and returned to his quarters. Seppō told this to Gantō. Gantō said, "Eminent is Tokusan, but he has still not understood the final word." Tokusan heard about this and sent his attendant to call Gantō to his quarters. He asked Gantō, "Do you not approve of me?" In a whisper, Gantō spoke his mind. The next day, when Tokusan took the lectern, he was very different from usual. In front of the monk's hall, Gantō clapped his hands and laughed, "How joyful it is that the Old Master has understood the final word. From now on, no one in the world can make light of him. But even so, he will live for only three years." Sure enough, in three years he passed away.

Assignment 457: First, in words, what is the point of "Tokusan without a word bowed and returned to his quarters"?

458: What is "The final word"?

459: *Jakugo.*

460: What is "He spoke his mind in a whisper"?

461: *Jakugo.*

462: What do you say to, "But even so, he will live for only three years"?

463: *Jakugo.*

464: Checking question: How about if he did not die in three years?

465: *Kakiwake* for the entire kōan "Tokusan Carries His Bowls."

In this example of an advanced kōan, one has the sense that the story of Tokusan and his two disciples contains a mysterious insight that requires a clear Zen eye to see. As is the standard pattern with every kōan, the monk sits in meditation on the kōan in the usual way until he has had some insight into its matter, and then demonstrates that insight in front of the rōshi. Without such insight into the point of that kōan, there is no point in proceeding to the literary work. After passing the Main Case, the monk receives several *sassho* checking questions (numbers 458, 460, 462, 464 are all checking questions even though the term *sassho* is actually used only once in 464) interspersed with capping-phrase assignments *(jakugo)*. Finally, he writes up the entire kōan as a *kakiwake*.

Completing the entire curriculum of kōan will take about fifteen years, although again there are great individual differences, depending, among other things, on the teaching style of the master and the ability of the monk. Because the monk advanced enough in kōan practice to be working on *kakiwake* and *nenrō* will be a senior monk, it is likely he will not be living in the communal *zendō* but will have a separate room, perhaps by himself, perhaps shared with another monk. Most of the monks in the communal *zendō* are junior monks, the majority of whom plan to leave the monastery after two or three years to become the resident priest of a branch temple somewhere. The younger monks must obey the rule of "No reading and no writing." (Indeed, during my time at Daitoku-ji, a monk was scolded if caught with a pen in his hand.) And in the practice of the kōan, novice monks are often told that the kōan cannot be solved intellectually, that intellectual study will only confuse them in their attempt to penetrate the kōan. For the entire latter half of this 15-year period, the senior monk will continue to work on new kōan each day, maintaining the same *sanzen* schedule as everyone else. While the junior monks are sitting in meditation cultivating the insight not founded on words and letters, the senior monk is constantly studying, writing, and submitting *kakiwake* and *nenrō*.

4

The Kōan and the Chinese Literary Game

AMONG BUDDHIST MEDITATION practices, meditation on the Zen kōan is surely one of the more unusual forms. Why did Buddhist meditation practice in Ch'an/Zen take the form of kōan training? And where did the kōan come from? Are there more primitive forms out of which the kōan evolved? This chapter conducts a short investigation into these questions to establish, first, that kōan training has many features in common with other Chinese practices, which on the one hand help explain why kōan language is so baffling, yet on the other hand show more clearly how an experience said to be "not founded on words and letters" can be so intimately tied to literary practices. Second, this chapter tries to make a contribution to the still unanswered question as to the origin of the kōan. Although there is speculation that the kōan may have evolved from the "pure conversation" tradition of the philosophical Taoists, and although there are strong similarities between the kōan dialogue and the dialogues in *Shih-shuo Hsin-yü: A New Account of Tales of the World* 世說新語 (MATHER 1976), there is to my knowledge no substantial scholarship explaining the origin of the kōan. This chapter advances the hypothesis that one of the parents of the kōan is the Chinese literary game, that the kōan is the child of a mixed marriage between the Chinese literary game and Buddhist teaching and training practices. Judith BERLING (1987) has argued that the emergence of the Ch'an/Zen Recorded Sayings genre must be understood against the previous history of Buddhist sutra literature, which it both continues and undermines. In this essay, I am advancing a parallel argument that the kōan practice also both continues and undermines a prior culture of secular literary and poetic practices. The result is a training practice with many features similar to literary games (competition, on-the-spot spontaneity, turning the tables, and, especially, mind-to-mind transmission) but in the service of a non-literary insight, an awakening "not founded on words and letters."

COMMENTARIAL PRACTICES

Although the Zen kōan is a unique teaching technique, as a literary genre it still has "family resemblances" to several other institutions and practices in early Chinese culture. First of all, it has a family resemblance to the traditional Chinese commentarial practice in which scholars appended commentaries to a classical text, sometimes in the form of verse, sometimes in the form of prose essays, sometimes in the form of line-by-line annotations. As we have already seen, in the *Hekigan-roku* and the *Mumonkan* the compiler has appended a verse to each kōan in the collection. In the Chinese tradition, since structured and rhymed verse was the vehicle of much writing both formal and informal, writers often responded to an original text in verse, especially if the original text was itself composed in verse. A writer was considered skillful to the extent that he could use the rhyming scheme and imagery of the original verse but make these express his own ideas.

Commentaries on philological and philosophical matters took the form of prose essays appended to the text. In China (as in other cultural traditions), these essays tended to get longer and longer, to the point where eventually entire volumes were written to explicate a title or single sentence. With the passage of time, commentaries that originally served merely as an aid to glossing a text ballooned into entire encyclopedias whose categories of knowledge were pegged to the words of the canonical text they were meant to illuminate (HENDERSON 1991, 77–81). In the *Hekigan-roku*, Engo Zenji appends two commentarial essays to each kōan, one for the main case of the kōan and one for Setchō's verse. Although he does not engage in philosophical or text exegesis, his long, discursive prose essays are very much in this style of traditional commentary.

Unlike religious traditions that tried to maintain a distinction between the "sacred text" and the commentary literature written by ordinary humans, in the Chinese commentarial tradition, the stature of the commentary often grew in time to that of the original canonical text, thus blurring the line between canon and commentary. Chu Hsi's commentaries on the Confucian texts, for instance, came to be revered and studied as seriously as the original Confucian texts they were meant to explicate. So, too, in the *Hekigan-roku* the *jakugo* that Setchō Zenji and Engo Zenji append to an original kōan are, in turn, often taken up as kōan themselves, effectively erasing the distinction between kōan and capping phrase, between main text and commentary. Engo Zenji's line-by-line comments on Setchō's line-by-line comments, as we have seen in the previous chapter, form a kind of sub-*jakugo* to the main *jakugo*. In this way, the different features of each case of *Hekigan-roku*—the *ju* verse, the *hyōshō* commentaries (as well as the *suiji* introduction that Engo Zenji has also added), and the *jakugo* appended to *jakugo*—clearly display how deeply the literary genre of the kōan imitates traditional Chinese literary practices.[1]

---

[1] HENDERSON 1991, 51, 56. A further interesting feature of the Chinese commentarial tradition is that the commentator sometimes creates the canon upon which he claims to comment. Before Chu Hsi established the Confucian *Analects*, the *Mencius*, the *Doctrine of the Mean*, and the *Great Learning* as the "Four Books," they had no identity as a unit; in fact, the latter two were not even

It should also be said that at the same time, the use of the *jakugo* in texts like the *Hekigan-roku* represents a departure from traditional commentarial practices. The *jakugo* is a new type of commentary, short and terse, often vulgar, irreverent, and unlearned. It abandons the third-person stance of a detached commentator and assumes the first-person stance of an involved participant in the kōan. The commentator, as we have seen, is a contentious bystander who sometimes actually steps into the game, claiming as much insight as the original players in a game, offering unsolicited instant analysis, and lamenting the obvious clumsiness of the players.

THE KŌAN AND THE CHINESE LITERARY GAME

Authors who discuss the Zen kōan often start by explaining that the Chinese characters for kōan literally mean "public case" and that, just as a magistrate's decision expresses the position of the law on a particular case, so also the kōan expresses the Buddha law on a matter, thus putting an end to all private opinion about it. FOULK (2000), for example, has recently argued that the term *kung-an* (kōan) originally referred to a case on a magistrate's desk and that kōan literature is basically constructed on the metaphor of a magistrate sitting in judgement. I believe, however, that the paradigm of the magistrate sitting in judgement applies more aptly to kōan commentary, but not to original kōan cases themselves. Commentary is a one-sided judgement in which the party being judged does not get a chance to answer back. In the kōan itself (but not in the kōan commentary), the parties to a dialogue are often depicted in mutual thrust and parry with each other. In addition, despite its popularity, the legal metaphor does not explain the more important features that are essential to the kōan—the perplexing language, the sense of fun, the criterion for a good win ("turning the spear around"), insight, and mind-to-mind transmission. I believe another paradigm helps explain all these latter features of the kōan: the Chinese literary game.

In Chinese culture long before the rise of Ch'an/Zen in the T'ang and Sung periods, there was a very old and widespread custom of literary games, chief of which was the game of "capping phrases" or "capping verses," 語次, 連句, 聯句. In a simple version of this game, one person gives the first line of a well-known couplet and challenges the other to recall the second line. The game presupposes that the players have memorized a sizable common stock of Chinese poetry. In other versions of capping-verse games, one person composes an original verse and challenges the other to compose a matching verse with parallel structure, imagery, rhythm, etc. to form a couplet. Alternatively, the two players may compose complete couplets matching each other.

considered independent texts. By identifying them as a unit and writing commentary on them as a unit, he and his fellow scholars effectively canonized them (p. 51).

Or again, four people can compose a quatrain, each person composing one of the lines with an eye to producing an integrated four-line poem. Numerous other variations resulted as players invented rules of their own.

The verses would use the highly allusive language of Chinese poetry, in which one spoke of something without ever mentioning it directly. Part of the fun of capping-phrase games was to speak in such allusive language that the other person missed the connotation. And part of the skill of a good player was the ability to recognize the hidden meaning of the other person's allusions and by "turning the spear around" thrust back using a similar allusion with some other hidden meaning. These general features of the capping-verse game—the use of highly allusive language in which people communicated something without directly saying it (a kind of "mind-to-mind transmission"); two players jousting with each other; the fact that either player could win; the elements of fun, deception, and insight; the fact that the best win "turns the spear around"—are also all features of the Zen kōan dialogue. In fact, the resemblance is so strong that I believe the kōan itself is structured on the paradigm of the capping-verse game. In other words, a Zen kōan is a kind of Chinese capping-verse game, where the two players test and apply, not (merely) their training in poetry, but also the clarity of their awakened eye. The Zen kōan thus derives from two sources. One is the wordless insight of Zen, the insight "not founded on words and letters." The other source for the kōan is the Chinese literary game. To speak about the insight that language could not describe, Chinese Zen monks in the T'ang and Sung periods adapted the capping-phrase game in which for centuries literati had engaged in a highly sophisticated give-and-take of speaking about something without naming it directly. Thus the much later Japanese monastic practice wherein Rinzai Zen monks append a capping phrase to a kōan signifies not a degeneration of the Zen kōan tradition but a return to its origins.

ALLUSION IN CHINESE LITERATURE

The Zen kōan shares with Chinese poetry the rich abundance of literary allusion. As LATTIMORE has pointed out, all allusion has the character of an inside joke, puzzling to those who are not aware of the hidden reference (1973, 405). Moreover, the concealment is done, as the etymology of the word suggests, with a ludic attitude, in a spirit of play. A good allusion masks but also reveals its object of reference in a clever way, such that the dawning revelation brings pleasure to the reader or listener of the verse.

Allusion packs a poem with meaning. In Chinese literature, the mere mention of the name of an ancient virtuous emperor like Yao 堯 or Shun 舜, of a tragic beauty like Yang Kuei-fei 楊貴妃, or of a valiant warrior like General Li Kuang 李廣 將軍 was enough to evoke a wealth of images from the countless stories, legends, and poems that surrounded such figures. Even ordinary words were rich in connotations and could be invested with special meanings. Bamboo, for instance, connoted uprightness and integrity; the pine tree, endurance and fortitude; the plum tree, freshness, youth, and feminine beauty. "Not enough ground even to stick in a pick" 無立錐地 was a standard expression for poverty. The "nomad's flute" 羌笛/胡笳 always conveyed a sense of sadness, and the "cry of the monkey" 猿叫/猿啼 a sense of unbearable loneliness. "Clouds and rain" 雲雨 was a way of referring to amorous intercourse and a "pair of ducks" implied conjugal happiness. "Flowing sands" 流砂 referred to the desolate desert frontier. And so on. Very ordinary words could also carry associations of a more profound sort. The term "three persons," for example, recalled to the mind of the literate reader the famous saying of Confucius, "Where three persons go, for certain there will be a teacher for me" (*Analects* VII, 21). In addition, the range of meanings for a term reached beyond its original context to include its use in allusion by later poets. We might say that the time-honored custom of allusion in Chinese poetry worked like compound interest, meanings multiplying on top of meanings, all becoming part of a large cloud of associations that clung to these terms. The Zen *jakugo*, coming from every branch of Chinese literature as they do, draw upon this immense reservoir of lore and language, of symbol and imagery.

Literary allusion comes naturally to the Zen tradition. The early Ch'an and Zen monks had their own vocabulary of indirect expressions for referring to, without naming, the fundamental experience of the nonduality of subject and object: "sound of one hand," "original face," "Mu," and "the First Patriarch's coming from the West," to mention only the most widely known. To express different aspects of the experience of realization, these masters also took over and adapted the wider stock of allusions, set phrases, and images common among poets in the T'ang and Sung periods. For example:

> 8.59 伐柯伐柯 其則不遠 *Ka o kiri ka o kiru, sono nori tōkarazu.*
>
> To hew an axe handle, to hew an axe handle.
> The model is not far away.

The image of the axe handle used to carve another axe handle in this verse, originally from the early *Book of Songs*, received numerous interpretations throughout its long history and continues to do so today. In its original context, it symbolized a married woman in her role as matchmaker—one married woman creating another. It later came to symbolize ritual, in the sense that the Confucian ruler used ritual to govern by ritual (Saussy 1993, 120–1). It could also symbolize poetic language used to describe the language of poetry (Liu 1988, 41). The image eventually found its way into Zen phrase books. Similar to other Buddhist phrases such as "Ride an ox in search of an ox," it was taken to mean using Buddha-nature to realize Buddha-nature (or alternatively, using attachments to cut off attachments: "A nail pulls out a nail, a stake takes out a stake" (6.186). Even today, the Zen-inspired poetry of Gary SNYDER continues to extend the many uses of the metaphor of the axe handle (1983).

Standard Chinese poetic images such as "pure wind" and "bright moon" take on another meaning in Zen. One could say baldly, "Form is emptiness and emptiness is form" but it is far more elegant to say:

10.279 清風拂明月 *Seifū meigetsu o harai,*
明月拂清風 *Meigetsu seifū o harau.*

The pure wind skims the bright moon,
The bright moon skims the pure wind.

Philosophically, one might say that in emptiness all duality is overcome, and in form all duality is resurrected. But one could also say more poetically:

10.252 春色無高下 *Shunshoku ni kōge naku,*
花枝自短長 *Kashi onozukara tanchō.*

In spring colors, there is neither high nor low,
The flowering branches are, by nature, some long, some short.

A "wooden man" is a puppet and a "stone woman" is a barren woman incapable of bearing children. But in Zen, these negative connotations are set aside and the terms are given a positive connotation. In heavy, more technical language one can say that in the no-self of Zen, the vicissitudes of everyday life are lived through effortlessly. In more literary form, we have:

14.26 木人夜半穿靴去 *Bokujin yahan ni kutsu o ugachisari,*
石女天明戴帽歸 *Sekijo tenmei ni bō o itadaite kaeru.*

Putting on his shoes, the wooden man went away at midnight,
Wearing her bonnet, the stone woman returned at dawn.

One could multiply such examples indefinitely.

Allusion serves political and social functions as well. Because poetry was a medium of official discourse in traditional China, skill in poetic composition and allusion was put to use in a variety of political contexts for a variety of political purposes, some of them honorable, some not. Arthur Waley has pointed out that in the *Tso chuan* 佐傳 chronicles, all officials were expected to know the *Book of Songs* 詩經 in detail, thus providing themselves with a tool of many uses. For example, the Songs were sung as "diplomatic feelers" expressing yet veiling an official's intentions. Similarly, an official might recite one of the Songs as a technique for political persuasion, where a modern politician would offer reason and argument. In one instance mentioned by Waley, an envoy failed to recognize an allusion to the *Songs* and his mission was immediately discredited. Officials also quoted the *Songs* to give their positions moral authority. By skillful allusion to figures mentioned in the *Songs*, an official could admonish his superior without naming him directly and incurring his punishment (Waley 1937a, 335–7).

In addition to such obviously political uses, allusion had social functions. It drew a line between those with inside knowledge and those without. The skillful poet could display his great knowledge of literature and, at the same time, conceal his true intentions to those who knew only the literal, surface meaning of his words. If the allusions in a verse were lost on the listener, he could not know, for example, if he was being subtly ridiculed. If the listener did understand, then he could congratulate himself on his own erudition. What is more, in a social setting where traditional texts were held in reverence, reference to those texts had the force of an appeal to authority. In alluding to a text, the individual in effect implies that he was not simply voicing his own individual opinion but reiterating the wisdom of the ancients. At the same time, the "corporate legitimacy" of the group itself was reinforced by appealing to the great textual authorities of ages past (Lattimore 1973, 411).

These elements are all clearly at work in Zen texts. One scores a point if one can speak of awakening in allusions the other does not catch. And the entire ritual not only recreates an ancient past tradition but also confers legitimacy on those in the present who claim to be its decendants. Kōan after kōan depicts one Zen monk testing the clarity of another's insight through the skillful use of allusion. The monks fiercely compete with one another not in the language of philosophical discourse but in poetic references to "coming from the West," "three pounds of flax," "wash your bowl," and "the cypress tree in the front garden." Mastery of the allusive language of Zen is taken as one of its marks of authority.

ANALOGY IN CHINESE LITERATURE

If the structure of analogy may be taken to be "A1 is to A2 as B1 is to B2," then Chinese thought and literature are full of analogy. The reader of Zen kōan will quickly suspect that analogy is present, but if the principle of resemblance linking the As to the Bs is not revealed, the kōan will remain a mystery. This sense of a hidden truth lurking beneath the surface of the text is not unique to the kōan but runs throughout all of Chinese thought and literature.

The Chinese division of all phenomena into *yin* or *yang*, for example, relies on analogy. As dark is to light, so is night to day, winter to summer, north to south, inside to outside; as female is to male, so is softness to hardness, moisture to dryness, water to earth, moon to sun. Analogical thinking in the Chinese tradition goes beyond resemblances to imply causality as well. For example, why is it that the rivers overflow their banks and flood the earth?—because the emperor dallies too much with his concubines. In both cases, the *yin* element (the waters of the river and the concubines) overpower the *yang* element (the earth and the Emperor). To stop the flooding, the emperor must dismiss some of his concubines. In this case, analogy points to more than surface resemblance; it serves both as metaphor and as causal explanation.[2]

The analogy between flooding and the Emperor's behavior becomes immediately understandable once one sees that *yin-yang* thought classifies them as the same. But without the underlying principle of resemblance, the connection remains shrouded in mystery. One reads much other Chinese literature with a similar feeling of mystery. Consider this passage from the Confucian *Analects*:

> Yen Yu said, "Is the Master on the side of the Lord of Wei?"
> Tzu-kung said, "Well, I shall put the question to him."
> He went in and said, "What sort of men were Po Yi and Shu Ch'i?"
> "They were excellent men of old."
> "Did they have any regrets?"
> "They sought to practice benevolence and could. Why should they regret?"
> On coming out, he said, "The Master is not on his side." (*Analects* VII, 14)

The passage comprises the entire entry for *Analects* VII, 14. It is not a kōan, but as in the kōan, apparently irrelevant items are connected together, leaving the modern reader puzzled. As Nitta Daisaku has pointed out, this passage shares an important feature with the kōan: it "indicates a particular with a particular" (*ji o motte ji o shimesu* 事を以て事を示す), that is, "pointing to the meaning of one particular thing, not by a reason, but by another particular thing" (NITTA 1967, 95). One particular is explained not by means of a general principle of which it is an instance, but by reference to another particular, which is also an example of the same unspoken general principle.[3]

This case is further complicated by the fact that the underlying analogy needs to be explained through an allusion. What lies behind Yen Yu's question to Tzu-kung, "Is the Master on the side of the Lord of Wei?" Yen Yu and Tzu-kung were disciples

---

[2] NEEDHAM AND WANG originally opened discussion on this topic (1956). For later discussions of correlative thinking, see GRAHAM 1986, 1992, and HENDERSON 1984.

[3] Nitta's interesting discussion goes on to claim that answering a particular with a particular reflects Confucius's emphasis on ritual, which gave priority to actual performance of concrete actions and less to philosophical explanations. Confucius was capable of acting much like a Zen master, as we see in the following passage:

> Someone asked for an explanation of the Ancestral Sacrifice. The Master said, I do not know. Anyone who knew the explanation could deal with all things under Heaven as easily as I lay this here; and he laid his finger upon the palm of his hand. (*Analects* III, 11, after WALEY 1938)

The claim to ignorance, the equating of dealing with all under Heaven with moving a finger, and the enigmatic action are all elements to be found in the Zen kōan.

of Confucius and at the time of this particular conversation were staying as guests of the Lord of Wei, Ch'u, son of K'uai-k'uei. The previous Lord of Wei was not Ch'u's father K'uai-k'uei, but his grandfather, Duke Ling. What had happened to the father K'uai-k'uei? Rumor had it that years earlier, Duke Ling's wife, the disreputable Nan-tzu (mentioned at *Analects* VI, 26), carried on an incestuous relationship with her half brother, the handsome Prince Chao (mentioned at VI, 14). K'uai-k'uei, Duke Ling's son (Ch'u's father) was ridiculed because of the Duke's connection with Nan-tzu, and in response K'uai-k'uei plotted to kill her. Before he could accomplish the deed, the plot was discovered and he was forced to flee the state, leaving behind both his own son Ch'u and any chance at succession. When old Duke Ling died, since the son K'uai-k'uei was in exile and no longer heir apparent, K'uai-k'uei's son, Ch'u, succeeded as the next Lord of Wei. This set the stage for a protracted struggle for the state of Wei between father and son, K'uai-k'uei and Ch'u.[4] The three generations are as follows:

Duke Ling, Lord of Wei and the disreputable Nan-tzu
↓
K'uai-k'uei, son of Duke Ling,
plotted to kill Nan-tzu, and when discovered, fled the state.
↓
Ch'u, son of K'uai-k'uei, becomes Lord of Wei;
father and son fight for rulership of Wei.

While Ch'u, then Lord of Wei, was fending off his father's attempts to take control of the state, Confucius came to stay as a guest of the state. When Yen Yu asked, "Is the Master on the side of the Lord of Wei?" he was asking if Confucius sided with Ch'u against his father. In Wei, where generations of the ruling family had engaged in unfilial, disloyal, and incestuous behavior violating the most fundamental precepts of Confucius's teaching, naturally the disciples wanted to know which side the Master supported.

We have further to ask what allusion lies behind Tzu-kung's question, "What sort of men were Po Yi and Shu Ch'i?" Proper etiquette dictated that Tzu-kung not put Yen Yu's question directly to Confucius. Therefore Tzu-kung posed his question indirectly in the form, "What sort of men were Po Yi and Shu Ch'i?" Po Yi and Shu Ch'i were legendary brothers, exemplars of filial piety and loyalty. Two well-known stories illustrate their virtues.

In the first, their father, feeling the younger son, Shu Ch'i, to be the more worthy, designated him as heir and successor rather than his older son, Po Yi. Shu Ch'i, out of respect for his older brother, insisted that Po Yi succeed their father. But older brother

---

[4] The entire story is recounted in the *Tso chuan* (WATSON 1989, 195–200).

Po Yi, like a true filial son, would not disobey the wishes of his father, and refused the throne. In the end, neither took the succession and both fled to another state.

In the second story, King Wu had rebelled against the Yin Dynasty's last evil king. Although King Wu is always depicted in later Chinese history as a virtuous king who deposed a wicked ruler, his rebellion against the throne at the time was an act of disloyalty. Po Yi and Shu Ch'i protested to King Wu but were ignored. As their unbending moral principles prevented them from acquiescing to King Wu, they hid themselves on Mount Shou-yang. Too virtuous to eat the grain of the new dynasty, they fed themselves on a diet of ferns until they eventually died of starvation.[5]

In *Analects* VII, 14, therefore, the family of the Lord of Wei exemplifies those who put personal greed and ambition before filial piety, loyalty, and correct behavior. At the same time, Po Yi and Shu Ch'i are exemplars of those who place filial piety and loyalty before personal gain. Tzu-kung could have asked "What is your moral stance with regard to the family of the Lord of Wei?" but ritual politeness obliged him to ask indirectly, "What sort of men were Po Yi and Shu Ch'i?" Confucius, of course, recognized at once the unstated point of the question. In response to Tzu-kung's inquiry, "Did they have any regrets over their course of action?" he replied, "They sought to practice benevolence and were able to. Why should they have any regrets?" From this reply, Tzu-kung knew at once Confucius's attitude to the Lord of Wei. Since Confucius approved of Po Yi and Shu Ch'i's unbending moral determination, Tzu-kung could report confidently to Yen Yu, "The Master does not support the Lord of Wei."

This form of dialogue, as we say, is shared by the Zen kōan. Where we would expect a statement of general principle (Ch. *li*; J. *ri* 理) such as, "One ought to put filial piety and loyalty before personal advantage" to explain Confucius's attitude, instead *Analects* VII, 14 explains one particular (Ch. *shih*; J. *ji* 事)—Confucius's attitude to the Lord of Wei—by analogy with another particular—his attitude to Po Yi and Shu Ch'i. In so doing, no explicit mention is made of any general principle linking those particulars. Those trained in Chinese literature and history will be able to identify the allusions and fill in on their own the background information needed to construct the analogy, which would then serve the purpose of an explanatory general principle connecting the two particulars. But those without the requisite learning will find mysterious the linking of a particular with a particular without any intermediary.[6]

Allusion refers to a thing without naming it directly. Analogy relates two particu-

---

[5] Ssu-ma Ch'ien, *Shih-chi* 史記伯夷列傳.

[6] The linking of particular to particular again can be seen as part of a larger pattern of correlative thinking. When particular and particular are not only correlated but also causally linked, the relationship was called "resonance" *kan-ying* 感應. *Kan-ying* is a hybrid, midway between a metaphor and a cause. For more on "resonance" and on Chinese correlative thought in general, consult HENDERSON 1984.

lars without revealing the general principle connecting them.[7] These general features of Chinese literature are at work in the Zen kōan, making it an incomprehensible cipher to those not steeped in the literary world of Chinese symbol and metaphor, history and legend. But it would be a mistake to think that the incomprehensibility of a kōan is due merely to an inability to decode the allusions and analogies imbedded in its language. Consider the following three classic Zen dialogues:

> A monk asked Ummon, "What is Buddha?" Ummon replied, "A lump of dried shit." (MMK 21)
>
> A monk asked Tōzan, "What is Buddha?" Tōzan said, "Three pounds of flax." (MMK 18)
>
> A monk asked Jōshū, "What is the point of the First Patriarch's coming from the West?" Jōshū said, "The cypress tree in the courtyard." (MMK 37).

In each case we expect a statement of a general principle, but instead we are given a concrete particular. One senses that there is an analogy at work here, and that if only one knew the basis of the resemblance the logic of the answer would be clear. Or again, one suspects that there must be some obscure allusion behind phrases like "a lump of dried shit" or "three pounds of flax" that would provide the missing information needed to make sense of the kōan.

Here is where allusion and analogy in the kōan differ from allusion and allegory in Chinese literature. One could take "Two hands clap and make a sound. What is the sound of one hand?" as a symbolic analogue for "You know the duality of subject and object. What is the nonduality of subject and object?" The insight one has in seeing that "sound of one hand" means "nonduality of subject and object," I will call horizontal insight. It takes one sideways from one phrase in language to another phrase in language. Such horizontal insight, however, does not solve a kōan. The kōan is solved only when one first realizes (makes real) the nonduality of subject and object in oneself, only when one becomes an instance of that nonduality oneself. It is for this reason that Zen masters instruct their students to become one with the kōan, to *be* the sound of one hand. The insight that arises from realizing the kōan, being the kōan, I will call vertical insight. Vertical insight takes one outside language to experience itself.

To repeat, the fundamental problem in solving a kōan is religious. It is not merely a literary matter of understanding allusion and analogy. It is not merely an epistemological matter of attaining a new kind of awareness, nor a matter of training and drilling oneself to a level of spontaneous improvisation. The kōan is both the means

---

[7] Allegory, says Quintilian, "says one thing in words and another in meaning" (quoted in SAUSSY 1993, 13.

for, and the realization of, a religious experience that finally consumes the self. That experience is the final referent for the symbolic language of "a lump of dried shit," "three pounds of flax," or "the cypress tree in the courtyard."

LITERARY GAMES

As we noted in the previous chapter, kōan have a family resemblance to games in which a pair of opponents are matched against each other in playful competition. The opponents think of themselves as military combatants, along the lines of many of the board games played in China and the West, and view the point of the kōan in terms of winning and losing. They deploy strategy and tactics—feinting, probing, closing in for a sudden strike, and so forth. Later we will consider some examples from the *Hekigan-roku*, where Engo's *agyo* employ the military metaphor.[8]

Chinese, like many languages, employs parallelism in poetic verse: two or more lines with the same structure, rhythm, imagery, and sometimes phonetic rhyme. But the nature of the Chinese language, with its ideographic characters and its lack of inflection, makes the construction of parallel verses relatively easy, with the result that its literature contains an enormous number of paired verses, or couplets.[9] This sets the stage for the Chinese literary game called "capping phrases" or "capping verses" 語次 or 連句 (聯句).[10] This game can be played with two or four or even more persons. In a simple version of this game, one person gives the first line of a well-known couplet and challenges the other to recall the second line.[11] In a more complicated form of the game, one person composes the first line of a couplet and challenges the other to compose a matching verse with parallel structure, imagery, rhythm, etc. to form a couplet. It can also take the form of four people composing a quatrain, each providing a line that integrates into the whole. Or again, several people can work on an extended linked verse, each person composing a line of verse playing upon the rhythm, imagery, and characters of the previous verse. And so on.

Players made up rules over the years, such as restricting images to a given theme or rhyme or Chinese character. There was usually a time limit, often determined by

---

[8] Board games themselves have family resemblances to divination by shamans, since a board game is related to a war game designed to predict the outcome of a proposed military venture. See Needham and Ronan 1978, 46–59, which includes a chart of the "genetic relationships" among games (p. 57), and also Mark 1979.

[9] For studies of parallelism in the Chinese language, see Plaks 1988 and Hightower 1965. For parallelism in other cultures, refer to the Introduction to Fox 1988, 1–28.

[10] For a survey study of Chinese literary games, see Pollack 1976. See also Miner 1979.

[11] Asai Gisen Rōshi, during a *teishō* that discussed capping-phrase games, used the memorable example, "See you later, alligator. / After a while, crocodile."

the burning of a short stick of incense or a fixed length of candle. One person took on the role of host and judge, setting the rules and topic of that particular game and declaring the winner. Tokens, much like poker chips, were used to keep track of wins and losses. Penalities were imposed on the losers, such as having to down a round of drinks, perhaps even as much as "three pints of wine" (OWEN 1977, 275). Such poetry games, with their emphasis on competition, humor, repartee, and erudite invention, were a source of entertainment at all levels of society, from imperial banquets and parties hosted by influential officials to countryside outings and informal gatherings of literati in local drinking establishments. The products of these poetry competitions were not considered serious poetry, partly because the verses were composed just for entertainment and did not contain any morally uplifting message, partly because the quality of verse was much diluted by the wine consumed by the poets (POLLACK 1979, 1–59, 103). Poetry competition also came to be a regular feature of annual festivals such as the Double Ninth Festival and were used as a means of settling disputes, wooing maidens, and so on. In the *Platform Sutra of the Sixth Patriarch*, it is through a poetry competition that the fifth patriarch decides who is to be his successor.

When the culture of literary games was transmitted to Japan, the Japanese extended the game to create "linked verse" (*renku* 連句/ 聯句 or *renga* 連歌). As POLLACK remarks, in China spontaneous verse-linking never lost its character as game and informal amusement, whereas in Japan it was invested with a high degree of seriousness and elevated to formal ceremony (1976, viii; also OWEN 1975, 116). In the case of Japanese *renku* or *renga,* a group of poets compose a 36-, 50-, or 100-verse linked poem, each poet adding a verse that continues the imagery of the previous verse but turns it in a new direction.[12] The game of *Hyakunin isshu* 百人一首, still typically played in Japan at the time of the New Year, is a well-known variation of this custom. It uses a standardized collection of one hundred couplets from one hundred different Japanese poets. The second verse of each couplet is printed on cards and scattered on the tatami mats between two people, usually a young lady and a young man dressed in their traditional New Year's best. As the presiding official intones the first verse of one of the couplets, the young lady and the young man rush to snatch up the card with the matching verse. In an earlier more Confucian age, young men and women had little opportunity for interaction. Such a game, where for a brief instant one's hand might brush against that of a member of the opposite sex, must have had an additional element of excitement.

The Zen kōan and the literary game share too many resemblances not to be considered close relatives. First, as already mentioned, like the players in a literary game, the dialogue partners in a kōan think of themselves as engaged in a competition that

[12] For a historical account of *renku* (or *renga*) see KEENE 1977, MINER 1979. Examples of *renku* can be found in UEDA 1982, 69–111.

they imagine as a kind of military combat. They win; they lose. They engage in strategy, feinting, probing, using surprise, etc. Engo Kokugon's *agyo* to the various kōan in the *Hekigan-roku* clearly adopt the military metaphor. "He carries out his strategy from within his tent" (*Heki* 4, Main Case *agyo*); "He gives up his first position and falls back to his second" (*Heki* 10, Main Case *agyo*); "When you kill someone, make sure you see the blood" (*Heki* 31, Main Case *agyo*); "The sword that kills people, the sword that gives life" (*Heki* 34, Main Case *agyo*); "He captures the flag and steals the drum" (*Heki* 38, Main case *agyo*). In Chinese poetry composition, especially in the context of the imperial examinations, oftentimes characters were judged and careers were determined on the basis of their wit and ability to improvise on the spot (POLLACK 1976, 100). These same qualities are also highly valued in the Zen kōan tradition. An important phrase in the everyday vocabulary of a Zen monastery is *rinki ōhen* 臨機應變 "on-the-spot improvisation."

A second resemblance consists of the fact that in both the literary game and the kōan, players need to be skilled in the art of alluding to a subject without directly naming it. An early predecessor to the capping-verse game was the posing of riddles, a kind of charade in literary form. The practice used a verse form called *yung-wu* 詠物 "writing poetry about an object" or *fu-te* 賦得 "writing a poem on a topic received" (POLLACK 1976, 38, 39). The poet Hui Hung 惠洪 commented that the soul of *yung-wu* poetry was to "bring out the qualities (用) of a thing without bringing up its name" (POLLACK 1976, 44). The host would give each person a slip of paper with a word, perhaps the name of a household object like "broom" or "bucket," perhaps the name of an animal like "dragon" or "tiger." A clever verse referred to the object in such a way as to leave the other dumbfounded as to what it was.

Some of the verses that have found their way into Zen phrase books resemble these riddle-charades. For example:

10.317 扶過斷橋水 *Tasukatte wa dankyō no mizu o sugi,*
伴歸無月村 *Tomonatte wa mugetsu no mura ni kaeru.*

It helps me cross the water where the bridge is broken;
My companion as I return to the village without moon.

The poem is about a traveler's staff, which is unnamed but which anyone versed in Chinese literature would know, and this unnamed object in turn is a symbol for a further unnamed object in Zen. Consider the following examples:

ZRKS 10.65 披毛從此得 *Himō kore yori e,*
作佛亦從他 *Sabutsu mo mata ta ni shitagau.*

Furred creatures are got from this,
Making a Buddha depends on that.

10.19 依稀松屈曲 *Ikitari matsu no kukkyoku,*
彷彿石斕斑 *Hōfutsutari ishi no ranpan.*

It's crooked like the pine,
It's mottled like the stone.

In English translation, "this," "that," and "it," indicate an unmentioned object. In a Zen context one has to ask, what might that unnamed object be?

In the third place, the criteria of a good win in both the literary game and the kōan are the same: surprise, deception, and "reversing the other's spear." Harada Ken'yū comments on the poetry of Han Yü:

> The point in linked-verse poetry is to catch one's opponent unawares. In doing this the writer is himself compelled by unforeseen detours, overhangs, obstacles and abrupt changes in rhythm. There is not time for either omissions or repetitions. Rather, by turning the tables on the handicaps brought by chance or the difficulties one's opponent has thrown at one, a veritable storm of associations is stirred up.[13]

Similarly, in the kōan dialogue monk and master probe each other with disguised allusions, trick questions, and baited traps. Skill in kōan dialogue is to be able to turn the tables against one's opponent.

When a monk asks Baso, "Without getting involved in the 'four propositions and the hundred negations,' show me directly the point of Bodhidharma's coming from the West," Baso smoothly replies, "I'm tired today and can't explain for you" (*Heki* 73 Main Case). The monk took this answer as a refusal to give an answer and did not recognize that this apparent refusal itself was a direct presentation of the point of coming from the West. The monk takes Baso's answer as if it were a descriptive when actually it is a performative.[14] It is much the same as if one were to reply to the question, "What is amnesia?' with the answer "I forgot." The answer, taken descriptively, is a refusal to answer, but taken performatively, is an actual example of what the question asks for. In admiration of the way that Baso has deceived the monk so skillfully, Engo comments in *agyo*, "The monk stumbled past without recognizing it" (*Heki* 73, Main Case *agyo*).

A truly skillful poet recognizes his opponent's strategy, turns it around and uses it to deceive his opponent. When Zen monks do this, the feat is called "turning the other's spear against him" (回槍頭來 or 回転槍頭來, *Heki* 35, Main Case *agyo*; *Heki* 38, Main Case *agyo*; *Heki* 46, Main Case *agyo*) or "mounting the bandit's horse to pursue

[13] Harada Ken'yu 原田憲雄, *Han Yu, Kanshi taikei 11*, 2 韓愈, 漢詩体系十一, quoted in Pollack 1976, xii.

[14] See the discussion on performatives and descriptives in Hori 2000.

him" (騎賊馬趁賊 *Heki* 59, Main Case *agyo*). When, for example, a monk says to Jōshū, "As soon as there are words and speech, this is picking and choosing," Jōshū cleverly lures the monk into words and speech by asking, "Why don't you quote this saying in full?" Engo's *agyo* here is "He mounts the bandit's horse to pursue the bandit" (*Heki* 59, Main Case *agyo*).

The fourth and most significant resemblance between Chinese literary games and the Zen kōan is that they share a similar conception of "mind-to-mind transmission" *ishin denshin* 以心傳心. If Zen is "not founded on words and letters," then it cannot be transmitted from one person to another through verbal explanation or intellectual interpretation. Nevertheless, the Zen tradition attaches great importance to the transmission of the dharma from master to disciple. If the transmission is verbal, then it must be done "mind-to-mind." The story of Śākyamuni holding up a flower (MMK 6) provides the archetype. Surrounded by a group of disciples assembled to hear a discourse on the dharma, Śākyamuni merely held up a flower instead of speaking. No one reacted except his first disciple, Kāśyapa, who broke into a smile. Śākyamuni replied, "I have the all-pervading True Dharma, incomparable Nirvana, exquisite teaching of formless form. It does not rely on letters, and is transmitted outside scriptures. I now hand it to Mahā Kāśyapa" (adapted from Shibayama 1974, 59). Traditionally this story is cited an an example of how transmission in Zen transcends the realm of "words and letters." But the notion of a mind-to-mind transmission outside of language did not originate with Zen. Rather, Zen adopted it from Chinese literary culture.

In Chinese literature the generally dominant place given to allusion and analogy means that language is often used to say one thing and mean another. If everything is said indirectly through allusion and analogy, emotional satisfaction in the game is only achieved if one's opponent is possessed of the same skill and shares the same learned repertoire of literary knowledge. The players are not only opponents, they are also partners in an important sense. Indeed, the game is at its best when the opponent-partners are so well matched that each understands the other's use of images, allusions, or turns of phrase without requiring anything to be explained or deciphered.[15]

In the Confucian literati tradition, such an intimate friend was called a *chiin* (知音; Ch. *chih-yin*), literally, a "connoisseur of sounds." The term refers to the story of Po Ya, who played a lute-like stringed instrument known as the *ch'in*, and his intimate friend, Chung Tzu-ch'i:

> Po Ya was a good lute player and Chung Tzu-ch'i was a good listener. Po Ya strummed his lute, with his mind on climbing high mountains; and Chung Tzu-

[15] Stephen Owen has a good study of the special intimacy between Meng Chiao and Han Yü as expressed in their linked verse (1975, especially 116–36).

> ch'i said: "Good! Lofty like Mount T'ai!" When his mind was on flowing waters, Chung Tzu-ch'i said: "Good! Boundless like the Yellow River and the Yangtze!" Whatever came into Po Ya's thoughts, Chung Tzu-ch'i always grasped it. (GRAHAM 1960, 109–10; see also DEWOSKIN 1982, 105)

The pair were lifelong friends. When Chung Tzu-ch'i died, Po Ya smashed his lute and never played again. Although this episode appears in the *Lieh-tzu*, usually considered a Taoist text, the story of Po Ya and Chung Tzu-ch'i spread throughout Confucian literati culture, where ritual and music were the last two of the six arts of Confucian self-cultivation, and where the ability to play the *ch'in* was seen as a mark of a cultivated individual.[16] Its diffusion is also due to the fact that it symbolized an ideal widely accepted by all schools of thought, whether Taoist, Confucian, or Buddhist: that of *wu wei,* or non-action.

The ideal of *wu wei* does not refer to the simple refusal to take action. This is the crude interpretation ("crude" here being a technical term implying dualistic interpretation). Rather, *wu wei* is a cluster of overlapping concepts that describe the truly accomplished person: one who acts effortlessly without deliberation and conscious intention, without focussing on technique and means, without self-regard and self-consciousness. The true skill of the archer transcends mere technique with a bow and arrow, the true swordsman's ability (the so-called "sword of no-sword") is more than slash and parry with a sword; the true *ch'in* player communicates more than the sound of strings being plucked. Applied to speech, *wu wei* indicates such skill in the use of words that the speaker could communicate without words. This is the prototype for Zen "mind-to-mind transmision." Not only the Zen tradition but the entire educated world of China saw the epitome of learned discourse as one in which the partners were so learned that they communicated more through silence than through words.

Accomplishment in the non-action of *wu wei* always depended on being accomplished in action. First one mastered the bow and arrow or the sword or the *ch'in.* Only then could one push oneself to a state of extreme selflessness in which one could accomplish one's end without reliance on bow and arrow or sword or *ch'in*. The story of Po Ya and Chung Tzu-ch'i exemplified the perfection of those who had thus cultivated themselves in literature, ritual, and music. For the literati, mind-to-mind transmission transcended language not by rejecting it—the "crude" interpretation—but only by being firmly based in language.

Set against this larger context of Chinese literature, the Zen notion of mind-to-mind transmission appears to be a relatively late and particularized adaptation of an

[16] DEWOSKIN 1982 documents the role that music and ideas about music played in Confucian literati culture.

ideal that had circulated in literary circles for centuries. The story of Po Ya and Chung Tzu-ch'i predates by hundreds of years the use of Zen phrases like "mind-to-mind transmission." The *Lieh-tzu*, once thought to date from the Warring States period in China, 403–222 BCE, is now placed around the 3rd or 4th century CE,[17] while the earliest known reference to the story in which "Śākyamuni holds up a flower" is thought to be in the *T'ien-sheng kuang-teng lu* 天聖廣燈錄, published in 1036, nearly seven centuries later (MZZ 135.612a). The story of Śākyamuni and Kāśyapa is now widely thought to imply that Zen experience is quite independent of words and letters, that to attain it one must unlearn language. If the story is read against the background of the tradition from which it comes, however, the lesson it teaches is that the ability to communicate mind-to-mind without language depends on first having mastered words and language.

Given this prior history, it is not surprising to find unidentified allusions to the story of Po Ya and Chung Tzu-ch'i and to the term "connoisseur (or 'hearer') of sounds" (J. *chiin*, Ch. *chih-yin* 知音) frequently in Zen literature, where they are adapted to emphasize the ineffability of the dharma in Zen. I cite four examples:

10.496 若識琴中趣 *Moshi kinchū no omomuki o shiraba,*
何勞絃上聲 *Nanzo genjō no koe ni rō sen.*

When you appreciate the flavor of the lute,
What need to use the sound from the strings?

14.88 掀飜海嶽覓知音 *Kaigaku o kenpon shite chiin o motomu,*
箇箇看來日中斗 *Ko-ko mikitareba nitchū no to.*

I overturn the seas and mountains seeking an intimate,
But it is like a one-by-one search for a star at noon.

ZRKS 10. 440 金風吹玉管 *Kinpū gyokkan o fuku,*
那箇是知音 *Nako ka kore chiin.*

The golden wind blows the jade flute,
Who can appreciate this sound?

10.223 詩向快人吟 *Shi wa kaijin ni mukatte ginji,*
酒逢知己飲 *Sake wa chiki ni aute nomu.*

My songs I sing to those who understand,
Wine I drink with those who know me well.

What is the significance of the story for understanding Rinzai kōan practice? We are used to the idea in Zen writings that language distorts what originally is, that lan-

[17] GRAHAM 1960, xiii.

guage creates false dichotomies imposing artificial categories upon what naturally is, that language cannot transmit the real nature of things as they are.[18] For antecedents of this idea in earlier Chinese literature, one can go directly to the first chapter of the *Tao te ching* ("The Tao that can be spoken of is not the constant Tao") or to the chapter "The Equality of All Things" in the *Chuang-tzu*. But there is another paradigm of language in Chinese literature. In the "expressive-affective conception of poetry" (SAUSSY 1993, 84), the feelings and emotions of the heart were said to naturally express themselves in words, music, and dance. The classic expression of this notion is found in the "Great Preface" to the *Book of Songs*:

> Feeling is moved inwardly and takes form in speech. It is not enough to speak, so one sighs [the words]; it is not enough to sigh, so one draws them out and sings them; it is not enough to draw them out and sing them, so without one's willing it, one's hands dance and one's feet stamp. (after SAUSSY 1993, 77)

Saussy notes that this passage in turn derives from the section on *Records of Music* in the *Record of Ritual* (*Li-chi* 禮記). There, expression in language is depicted as similar to expression in music: just as the melody in the heart spontaneously expresses itself in music, so feelings and emotions spontaneously express themselves in words, sighs, song, and dance. The result is poetry and language.[19]

The assumption is that if the writer's feelings and emotions are expressed in words in spontaneous fashion, it becomes possible for the reader to follow the words back to those feelings and emotions. Stephen Owen speaks here of an underlying paradigm of "linguistic adequacy" according to which language was thought capable of expressing what is in the mind and heart of a writer. The chapter called "The Hearer

[18] For an interesting critical discussion of the notion of the transcendence of language in Zen, see WRIGHT 1992.

[19] The language skeptic, who is wont to claim that language distorts and falsifies the real nature of things, is usually working with the "reference" theory of language, which assumes that a word is just a sound which gets meaning by being conventionally associated with an object. Words are assumed to refer to, denote, or label the object; the sentence is said to describe or report it. Since the relation of word to object, proposition to fact, is merely one of convention, it is always possible to raise doubt about the veracity of linguistic expression. In contrast, the "expressive-affective" theory claims that language is the natural expression of emotion and not just its conventional sign. Note the similarity between the "expressive-affective" theory of language and WITTGENSTEIN's comments on "expression": "The verbal expression of pain replaces crying and does not describe it" (1958, §244); "When someone says, 'I hope he'll come'—is this a report about his state of mind, or a manifestation of his hope?" (§585); "A cry is not a description. But there are transitions. And the words 'I am afraid' may approximate, more or less, to being a cry. They may come quite close to this and also be far removed from it" (§189).

of Sounds (*Chih-yin* 知音)" of the *Wen-hsin tiao-lung* 文心雕龍 by Liu Hsieh 劉勰 puts it this way:

> In the case of composing literature, the emotions are stirred and the words come forth; but in the case of reading, one opens the literary text and enters the emotions [of the writer], goes up against the waves to find the source; and though it be [at first] hidden, it will certainly become manifest. None may see the actual faces of the faraway age, but by viewing their writing, one may immediately see their hearts/minds.[20]

In reading a text, one follows words upstream to their source and enters into the emotions of the writer, reversing the natural and unbroken process by which the written word flows out of the writer's heart. For two people whose cultivation is equally refined, language is not a medium of distortion and falsehood but the very vehicle for immediately seeing into one another's heart and mind.

These two conceptions of language—one in which language is depicted as imposing conceptual categories that falsify experience and prevent us from seeing things as they are, and one in which language is depicted as the means by which people immediately know each other's minds—are both at work in the kōan. For while the rhetoric of Zen constantly emphasizes the fact that it is "not founded on words and letters," implying that language is always inadequate, the kōan practice in which one meditates on a critical phrase promises to transport the practitioner to the enlightened mind of the patriarchs. As Wright remarks, "Given that these sayings epitomize the mental state from which they have come forth, if the practitioner could trace back (*hui-fan*) the saying to its source, he or she would at that moment occupy a mental space identical to that of its original utterer" (2000, 201). Then, in the words of Mumon, one will "see with the same eye and hear with the same ear" as the patriarchs (同一眼見同一耳聞, MMK 1).[21]

---

[20] Quoted in Owen 1985, 59.

[21] One can see this pairing of different attitudes to language dramatized in the *Platform Sutra of the Sixth Patriarch*. In the early part of the *Sutra*, the illiterate Hui-neng wins a poetry competition against the learned and erudite head monk, Shen-hsiu, thus dramatizing the teaching that Zen insight is not founded on words and letters. Yet the same Hui-neng as an aged master declares to his disciples:

> You ten disciples, when later you transmit the Dharma, hand down the teaching of the one roll of the *Platform Sutra;* then you will not lose the basic teaching. Those who do not receive the *Platform Sutra* do not have the essentials of my teaching. . . . If others are able to encounter the *Platform Sutra,* it will be as if they received the teachings personally from me. (Yampolsky 1967, 173)

The first part of the *Sutra* seems to emphasize that language is inadequate, while the latter part seems to subvert this view with the explicit claim that encountering the *Platform Sutra* is the same as encountering Hui-neng himself.

If one begins from the assumption that the Zen tradition has a single, fixed attitude to language—namely, that Zen is not founded on words and letters, and that language cannot express the awakened mind—then Rinzai literary kōan practices can only seem totally misguided. But once one recognizes that Rinzai Zen, like the Chinese literary tradition from which it developed, works with more than one paradigm of language, then the inclusion of literary study as part of kōan practice will be both natural and desirable.

There is one final family resemblance between the Zen kōan curriculum and the traditional Chinese system of imperial examination. In the light of the foregoing, this should come as no surprise. All things being equal, one might suppose that in a religious tradition that stresses sudden enlightenment, the authority of the leaders and teachers of the tradition would be based on a mystical, self-justifying charisma. And indeed, later literature depicts the Ch'an masters of the T'ang Dynasty as iconoclastic, individualistic, and exemplars of the superior authority of experience over literary scholarship. At the same time, the Rinzai kōan system, with its lengthy and detailed fifteen-year curriculum, is much closer to the meritocratic and bureaucratic text-based Chinese examination system for which candidates typically had to study fifteen years or more. In fact, those who successfully complete the Rinzai Zen curriculum need to develop many of the same skills that were required for successful completion of the imperial examinations—a prodigious ability to memorize long passages verbatim, the ability to compose elegant classical Chinese verse, a beautiful calligraphic hand, and so on. The closest present-day counterpart of the classical Chinese Confucian literati scholar is the Japanese Rinzai Zen rōshi. He is one of the last remaining examples of those whose daily lives involve use of the literati scholar's four treasures: writing brush, ink stick, ink stone, and paper.

5

The History of Zen Phrase Books

THE PRESENT VOLUME (*Zen Sand*) is an entirely new compilation that combines two twentieth-century Zen phrase books, the *Shinsan zengoshū* 新纂禪語集 (*A New Compilation of the Zen Phrase Collection*), edited by Tsuchiya Etsudō 土屋悦堂 under the direction of Unkankutsu Shaku Taibi Rōshi 雲關窟釋大眉老師 (Kichūdō 1973), and the *Kunchū zenrin kushū* 訓註禪林句集 (*Annotated Zen Sangha Verse Collection*), edited and revised by Shibayama Zenkei Rōshi 柴山全慶老師 (Kichūdō 1972). These two handbooks, standard possessions of practicing Rinzai monks, are the most recent additions to an ever-evolving line of Zen phrase books.

Zen phrase books (*kushū* 句集), along with kōan collections (*kōan-shū* 公案集), recorded sayings of the patriarchs (*goroku* 語錄), and collected biographies (*dentōroku* 傳燈錄), may be considered a minor subgenre of Japanese Zen literature. This chapter describes the different kinds of Zen phrase books. Broadly speaking, they include books of proverbs or wise sayings, handbooks compiled by early Zen monks as aids to composing Chinese poetry, dictionaries of Chinese dialect or colloquial language, and guidebooks for reading scrolls used in the tea ceremony. It will also attempt an overview of how the Rinzai kōan meditation practice developed and speculate on when the capping-phrase practice came to be incorporated. Finally, we will have a look at the five most important kōan capping-phrase books.

EARLY ZEN PHRASE BOOKS

Golden Phrase Collections: Kinkushū 金句集

From ancient times in China and Japan there have existed collections of proverbs, wise sayings, pithy phrases drawn from Chinese literature, and maxims for everyday actions—"golden phrases." A number of the classics of Chinese literature are in fact basically just such collections, the Confucian *Analects* and the *Tao-te ching* being probably the best-known examples. Such books served two purposes. For the wider public, they provided handy collections of memorable phrases that the educated person might consult in time of self-reflection. More specifically, they were also used as instruction books for school and home. During Japan's Heian period, Minamoto no

Tamenori's *Worldly Phrases* (*Sezoku genbun* 世俗諺文), a selection of golden phrases garnered from classical Chinese texts, was used as such an instruction text. A similar collection, Sugawara Tamenaga's *Annotated "Tube and Calabash"* (*Kanreishō* 管蠡抄), was used during the Kamakura period (IRIYA 1996, 565). Various sorts of Golden Phrase Collections were compiled during the Muromachi period. By this time Zen monks, buoyed up by the literary culture of the Gozan, were beginning to assume the social role of teachers, and their Golden Phrase Collections accordingly came to include more and more phrases from Buddhist sources (IRIYA 1996, 565).

For the Western reader, the *Amakusaban kinkushū* 天草版金句集 is a particularly interesting example of a Golden Phrase Collection. In the late 1500s, the Jesuit Mission of Amakusa in Hizen, western Japan (the area straddling the borders of present-day Saga and Nagasaki Prefectures), published several works to help the Jesuit missionaries learn the language and culture of Japan, the better to propagate Christianity in Japan. One of these was entitled *Qincuxu*, a Portuguese romanization of *Kinkushū*. It was 47 pages long and contained 282 maxims that were probably intended for use by missionaries in their sermons to the Japanese. Each maxim is followed by a short Japanese commentary written not in Japanese *kana* but in Portuguese romanization. Because it is unclear precisely how some of the *kana* were pronounced at the time, the romanized text is invaluable for Japanese philological research, since there is far less ambiguity about the pronunciation of the Portuguese romanization. The maxims were drawn from a variety of Chinese sources such as the Confucian *Analects*, Chinese poetry, etc., as well as from Japanese sources such as the *Seventeen-Article Constitution* of Shōtoku Taishi. Approximately 77, or one-fourth of the sayings, coincide with phrases in the *Kuzōshi*, the Zen phrase book that had been compiled by Tōyō Eichō Zenji around a century earlier (SANAE 1996, 602–3). One of the reasons that Zen verses figure so prominently in the collection is that one of the Jesuits responsible for editing the text was formerly a Zen Buddhist (YOSHIDA 1938, 7).

Zen Poetry Composition Handbooks

Monasteries in medieval Japan were often built to house émigré Chinese masters who ran their monasteries according to Sung Period Chinese monastery rules and who used Chinese language in their teaching (COLLCUTT 1981, 57–90). Under the direction of these monks, and of Japanese monks who had returned to Japan after training in China, early Japanese Zen monks had to become skilled in literary Chinese (POLLACK 1986, 111–57; KRAFT 1992, 51–54), which was used to compose verses for ritual occasions, to record dharma talks, to write monastery documents, and to carve inscriptions on icons and images. The monks at the time did not actually read the Chinese script as Chinese. Instead, the accomplished Japanese monk learned to read classical Chinese text, or *kanbun* 漢文, by giving it a Japanese reading, or *kundoku* 訓讀. This method of transposition attempted to approximate the Chinese pronunciation of the

Chinese characters while rearranging them in the order required by Japanese grammar. Although *kundoku* managed to preserve some of the terseness of the Chinese original and some resemblance to Chinese pronunciation, the elements of tone and rhyme, so important for Chinese poetry, were lost in the process. Unlike Chinese, Japanese does not use tones. As a result, words that can be distinguished tonally in Chinese—high, low, falling, rising, and other variations—ended up as sounding alike in Japanese.

The rules of Chinese poetry divided characters into two basic tone classes, "flat" and "oblique" 平仄 (J. *hyōsoku*, Ch. *p'ing-tse*). Each kind of poetry (5-character 8-line regular verse, 7-character "cut-off" quatrains, and so forth) had its own set of complicated rules to determine the flat/oblique tone for every character in every line. Chinese poetry also used end rhymes, and different kinds of Chinese poetry were accompanied by rules specifying which lines were supposed to rhyme. When the Japanese transposed Chinese into their own grammar and pronunciation, these elements of tone and rhyme were lost. Nonetheless, a Japanese writer accomplished in *kanbun* was expected to compose Chinese prose and poetry according to the Chinese rules of tone and rhyme, and for this had to rely on guidebooks to tell him what character matched with what. (In fact, by the end of the T'ang Dynasty most Chinese themselves needed handbooks of rhyme and tone in order to write poetry correctly, since the Chinese language had itself changed considerably from the time when rhyme and tone were first codified.[1])

Chinese poetry, as we have seen in the previous chapter, is allusive and allegorical. To become proficient in Chinese poetry, one had constantly to study the vast corpus of received literature, tracking down both the source of an allusion for its original meaning and also the many later applications of the allusion that colored the nuances it later came to carry. For this reason, from quite early on handbooks of words and allusions, sanctioned by classical precedent, were compiled in China. An example is the *I-wen lei-chü* 藝分類聚 (*Literary Writings Classified*), compiled by Ou-yang Hsün 歐陽詢 in the T'ang Dynasty (Pollack 1976, 46; see also Owen 1977, 281–93). The early Japanese Zen monks made their own handbooks in which were gathered together verses that would serve as the basis for later examples of allegory and allusion. One such handbook is the *Jōwashū* 貞和集 (*Collection of the Jōwa Era*), in which the Zen poet-monk Gidō Shūshin 義堂周信 (1325–1388) collected some three thousand poems by Chinese monks (Bussho Kankōkai 1983). His diary, *Kūge nichiyō kufū ryakushū* 空華日用工夫略集 (*Summary Collection of Flowers of Emptiness from Daily Practice,* Gidō 1939), also contains numerous examples of verses from Chinese poetry. In his study of extant examples of these poetry composition handbooks,

[1] Pollack, personal correspondence, 18 May 1999.

Sanae reports that their users added numerous marginal notes and attached slips of paper with further examples of compounds, usages, and so forth. These early books were copied by hand, and as the copyist usually incorporated the additional examples from these glosses and inserts into the body of the text, later versions of the same collection quickly became fuller and more detailed (1996, 581).

The handbook most useful for the composition of poetry was the *Shūbun inryaku* 聚分韻略 (*Classified Rhymes*), compiled in 5 fascicles by Kokan Shiren 虎關師錬 in 1306 (Kimura 1995). In it some 8,000 *kanji* were classified according to rhyme and tone class, and within each class the *kanji* were further divided according to meaning under headings such as Heaven and Earth, Season, Plants, Food and Clothing, Artifacts, etc. Each *kanji* was fitted out with a short explanation and examples of compounds in which it appeared. This dictionary proved to be so useful for looking up the flat/oblique tone and rhyme class of *kanji* when composing poetry that it seems to have become something of a best-seller in its time. It was widely circulated in several sizes, including a small portable edition and a larger edition with a wide margin at the top for notes (Sanae 1996, 582).

Poetry composition handbooks were similar in purpose and function. They collected together important and beautiful examples of verse and then categorized them according to rhyme, that is, according to the sound of the final character. First the verses were divided according to the total number of characters they contained (4-character verses, 5-character verses, 7-character verses, etc.). Then they were further grouped according to the rhyme class of the final character. In the first section, for example, the top margin might contain the character 東, pronounced *tung* in Chinese, and below it would be listed all verses ending with characters that rhymed with 東 *tung*, such as 同 *t'ung*, 中 *chung*, and 風 *feng*. Each of the following sections would be headed by a character marking a rhyme class and would contain verses that all have similar end rhyme. In the *Zenrin kushū*, the Rinzai capping-phrase book edited by Ijūshi, several sections contain a supplement in which the verses are ordered according to their final character in exactly this way.

A great many such poetry handbooks were produced in the period from the Kamakura period through the early Edo period. The earliest were handwritten and later versions were set in type; some of them have identifiable authors, others are anonymous; some give only the Chinese characters, while others supply varying degrees of annotative information. Noteworthy among these books is the *Tentetsushū* 點鐵集, a clear predecessor of the *Zenrin kushū*. Compiled by Gyakuō Sōjun 逆翁宗順 (1433–1488) in 1485, its 25 fascicles in 10 volumes contain a massive collection of 4-character, 5-character, and 7-character couplets from both Buddhist and non-Buddhist sources. In this, the largest of the poetry composition books, approximately 43,000 verses were categorized in rhyme classes with headnotes citing original sources (Sanae 1996, 583; Iriya 1996, 572).

Books designed specifically for the composition of Zen poetry have continued to be produced in modern times. One of the most recent is the *Zenrin yōgo jiten* 禪林用語辞典 (*Dictionary of Zen Sangha Language*) compiled by Iida Rigyō and published in 1994. The first half is a dictionary of Zen terms and phrases from 1 character to 7 characters in length (traditional Chinese poetry did not often use lines longer than 7 characters). For each character of each verse, the flat/oblique tone is indicated, allowing nonspeakers of Chinese to follow the rules for ordering tone. The second half consists of a series of indices providing information necessary to the composer of Chinese style verse—characters divided into rhyme class, characters having two pronunciations, a pronunciation index of all characters listed in the first half, etc.

The latest development in Chinese poetry composition aids is the appearance of numerous Internet web sites devoted to Chinese poetry in the Japanese, Chinese, and Korean languages. The sites vary in content but many provide the original Chinese characters, with translation into modern languages, of famous classical poems. Some offer quite specialized collections, such as the site that provides the Chinese poetry written by the Japanese philosopher Nishida Kitarō (http://user2.allnet.ne.jp/nisino/kansi/a003.html). Others are fitted out with audio capability allowing one to hear a reading of the poems in Chinese. Many of these sites provide detailed explanations and step-by-step instructions on how to compose Chinese poetry, with a billboard where newly composed poems can be posted for all to see.

One site in particular (www.vector.co.jp/soft/dl/win95/edu/s0154206.html) is especially useful to the Zen practitioner who has to compose Chinese poetry. Created by the priest of a Zen temple, the site contains a database of Zen poetry based on parts of the *Zenrin kushū* and the *Zenrin geju* 禪林偈頌 (*Zen Sangha Ritual Verses*, composed for ritual occasions such as funerals, founder's day ceremonies, consecration of buildings, etc.) and a *Kanshisen* 漢詩撰 (*Selected Chinese Poetry*) composition tool. The computer poet does not need to know the rules for tone or rhyme since the site provides a template with the flat/oblique tone requirement for every character space of every line as well as the rhyme requirements for the final characters of any line. In the database of poetic phrases, all characters are identified as flat or oblique, making it easy to select out phrases to match the template. It is said that in some golden age in the past, all Zen monks were educated enough in classical Chinese poetry composition to compose their own capping verses. With the invention of this Zen poetry computer composition tool, the golden age may be about to dawn again.

Dialect Books, Hōgo 方語

Among early Zen phrase books were a class of books called *Hōgo*, literally "local speech." The Zen kōan collections and the records of the Zen patriarchs contain numerous examples of vulgar, colloquial, or dialect Chinese that the Japanese did not understand and that required explanation.[2] The headnotes of the *Zenrin kushū*, the classic capping-phrase book, identify many of its phrases as *hōgo* and provide an explanation. For example, verse 4.122 reads *Mimi o ōte suzu o nusumu* 掩耳偷鈴, meaning "He covers his ears to steal the bell." The headnote explains it as *hōgo* for *Donzoku* 鈍賊, "Clumsy thief." Verse 4.192 reads *Reiki o o hiku* 靈龜曳尾, "The spirit turtle sweeps its tail," and the headnote identifies it as *hōgo* for *Ato o haratte ato shōzu* 拂跡跡生, "Erasing traces creates traces." Or again, verse 4.230, *Jisa jiju* 自作自受, "Make it yourself, receive it yourself," is identified as a *hōgo* with the nuance: *Shōnin kase o tsukuru* 匠人作枷, "The master carpenter makes his own fetters" (a Chinese equivalent for "being hoisted on one's own petard"). As is to be expected, dictionary-like collections of such vulgar, dialectic, and colloquial phrases with accompanying explanations were compiled over time. Two kinds of *hōgo* texts were made in Japan: those based on the Chinese learned by the Japanese monks who had gone to China during the Sung (960–1279 CE) and Yüan periods (1260–1368), and those composed during the Ming (1368–1644) and Ch'ing (1644–1911) periods, when monks of the Ōbaku sect from China arrived in Japan (SANAE 1996, 586).

While poetry composition guidebooks helped the Japanese Zen monks learn the classical high culture of T'ang and Sung China, the *hōgo* guidebooks helped familiarize them with low culture. Although the first generation of monks who compiled guidebooks knew they were dealing with colloquial language, most Japanese Zen monks of subsequent generations were probably incapable of distinguishing between literary and colloquial Chinese. Iriya argues that Japanese Zen monks not only mistakenly took Chinese colloquialisms as technical Zen terminology, but also used the strange-sounding Japanized Chinese as a kind of in-house trademark to indulge in elitist attempts to distinguish themselves from other schools of Buddhism (IRIYA 1996, 567).

CAPPING PHRASES AND THE KŌAN CURRICULUM

When did the first capping-phrase collections for monks appear? One would think it but a short single step from golden phrase books, Chinese poetry composition handbooks, and Chinese colloquial phrase and dialect books to these capping-phrase books. Actually, it is a rather long single step.

How did the kōan practice develop? Although much of the history remains obscure, the general outlines are emerging. In the very early period during the seventh and eighth centuries, when Ch'an was developing as a separate school within Chinese Buddhism, the meditation taught in Ch'an temples must have followed

[2] KAWASE argues, however, that *hōgo* means *rakusetsu* ("convenient, advantageous") and is an appropriate title for an introductory handbook (1942, 126).

Indian models closely. It would have focused on *śamatha* and *vipaśyanā*, calmness and insight, and would have instructed the meditator to concentrate on breathing and visualizing parts of the body. The founder of the Chinese T'ien-t'ai school, Chih-i 天台智顗 (538–597), entitled one of his meditation texts *Hsiao chih-kuan* 小止觀, usually translated "The Lesser Calming and Contemplation."[3] The "calming" and "contemplation" in its title are actually translations of *śamatha* and *vipaśyanā*. This text seems to have been the seed text of nearly all later Ch'an meditation manuals for several centuries, right up until the time of Dōgen in the thirteenth century.[4] Early Ch'an monks aimed at calm and contemplation when they meditated; they did not work on the kōan for the simple reason that the kōan had not yet been invented.

The kōan began as stories of "encounter dialogues" between Zen masters and their disciples (J. *kien mondō* 機縁問答). These dialogues were considered a special kind of story. Almost all introductory explanations of the kōan include the quotation of a well-known passage from Chung-feng Ming-pen 中峯明本 (J. Chūhō Myōhon, 1263–1323) explaining that the story is a "public record." In much the same way that a magistrate's decision in a court of law sets a precedent for the correct application of the law to a particular case, so, too, the kōan encapsulates and establishes a correct insight into the dharma of the buddhas and patriarchs.[5] In addition, these stories were used not merely as case studies exemplifying a certain theoretical principle, but also as practical devices to teach and to test Zen practitioners on their own insight. When these stories began to be used explicitly as teaching and testing devices, we may say the kōan was born.

The actual date of birth is, however, uncertain. An early example of the use of the term "kōan" in this sense appears in the *Ching-te ch'uan-teng lu* 景徳傳燈錄 (J. *Keitoku dentō-roku*), where the biography of the Ch'an monk Ch'en Tsun-su (780?–877?) includes the passage: "When the Master saw a monk approaching, he said, 'For an on-the-spot kōan, I give you thirty blows.'"[6] It is an open question, however, whether this use of the term "kōan" represents usage at the time of Ch'en Tsun-su (780?–877?) or at the time of the *Ching-te ch'uan-teng lu* published in the eleventh century (1011). McRae speculates that the characteristic Ch'an encounter dialogue can first be spotted in the records of the teaching of Ma-tsu Tao-i (709–788), but here again the same sort of problem appears: the records of Ma-tsu did not appear until

---

[3] The full name of the version in the Taishō canon is 修習止觀坐禪法要 (T 46.462–75).

[4] See the study by Bielefeldt 1986.

[5] See, for example, Miura and Sasaki 1966, 7–10; Itō 1970, 1–10; Akizuki 1987, 26–7; Foulk 2000, 21–2.

[6] T 51.291b17.

two centuries later in 952, in the *Tsu-t'ang chi* 祖堂集 (J. *Sodō-shū*, *Anthology of the Patriarchal Hall*).[7]

Even as the kōan was being invented outside the monastery walls, monks on the inside were still engaged in Indian-style meditation. In the Sung period (960–1279), Ch'an meditation practice changed. The Chinese Ch'an master Ta-hui Tsung-kao 大慧宗杲 (J. Daie Sōkō, 1089–1163) abandoned meditation based on *śamatha* and *vipaśyanā* practices to create a distinctively Ch'an-style meditation practice called *k'an-hua* 看話, contemplation of the "critical phrase." In addition to using the kōan as a teaching and testing device, Ta-hui saw that the kōan could be used as a focal point in meditation. To use the entire story of an encounter dialogue would encourage discursive thinking. Therefore, Ta-hui isolated the critical phrase (*hua-t'ou* 話頭) in the dialogue, forcing the meditator to penetrate the kōan by a completely different route from that of the intellectual understanding. By boring into the critical phrase, he felt, the meditator would break free of conceptualization and at the same time be overtaken by profound doubt. As this doubt turned away from exterior objects to be directed back to the self, self-doubt grew so large as to absorb the self in its entirety, ultimately destroying all distinction between subject and object, between the doubt and the *hua-t'ou*.[8] The conventional self was destroyed in the Great Death, out of which there would step an awakened self.

The creation of *k'an-hua* meditation planted the seed out of which formal monastic kōan meditation practice grew. It is difficult to determine precisely when monastic kōan meditation training began, but, whenever it got started, in its early years it was very different from the kōan training carried on in Japanese Rinzai monasteries today. Early Chinese Ch'an masters gave kōan instruction to groups of disciples. The texts often depict a master mounting the podium and posing a kōan to the assembled monks standing below, who in turn seem to be competing with each other to display their insight. In present-day Rinzai practice, this kind of group practice has been replaced completely by the meeting of master and disciple in a private room. Chinese monasteries, as well as Japanese monasteries in the twelfth and thirteenth centuries, housed hundreds of monks, so that the practice of *nyusshitsu* 入室 ("entering the room"), in which monks went individually to receive instruction from the master could not have taken place on a daily basis. Chinese Ch'an texts often describe monks struggling with a single kōan for several years, whereas in modern Rinzai practice monks work quickly through a detailed succession of kōan.

It is unlikely that Ch'an monks in the T'ang or Sung periods thought of kōan practice as organized into a system or curriculum, as is the case today. Chinese Ch'an monks roamed freely from monastery to monastery in search of authentic kōan

---

7 See McRae 2000, 51.

8 I am following Buswell's account (1987, 343–56); see also Yü 1979.

teachers, but in modern Japan the Rinzai monk enters one monastery and stays there unless circumstances require a transfer. Despite the formalization and heavy institutional framework, however, modern Japanese Rinzai kōan practice is still easily recognizable as *k'an-hua* meditation.

As mentioned earlier, kōan practice did not initially include the capping-phrase practice. Appending capping phrases to kōan was something that Ch'an masters did, not ordinary Ch'an monks. Already by the mid tenth century collections of "old cases" 古則 were being made. One such early work by Fun'yō Zenshō 汾陽善昭 (Fenyang Shan-chao, 947–1024), called *Fun'yō mutoku zenji goroku* 汾陽無德禪師語錄 (*Fen-yang wu-te ch'an-shih yü-lu*; T 47: 594–629), contains three collections of 100 kōan each, one of which consists of 100 *jakugo* appended to old cases. The other two consist of 100 new kōan that he himself made and 100 old cases for which he provided new answers.

Kenneth Kraft's study of Daitō Kokushi 大燈國師 (1282–1337), the founder of Daitoku-ji and one of the founders of Rinzai Zen in Japan, provides ample evidence that the practice of appending *jakugo* was transmitted from China directly into Rinzai Zen in Japan in the thirteenth and fourteenth centuries (KRAFT 1992). The *Record of Daitō* contains Daitō's commentaries to kōan and kōan texts in which he expresses his responses through capping phrases, of which more than two thousand are spread throughout the *Record*. In his capping phrases Daitō applies traditional Zen verses to new situations and also composes new *jakugo* of his own. In a text entitled simply *Hyakunijussoku* 百二十則 (*One Hundred and Twenty Cases*), Daitō selected 120 kōan to which he has appended interlinear *jakugo*. In another text, *Hekigan agyo* 碧巖下語 (*Hekigan Capping Phrases*), Daitō substituted his own *jakugo* for those appended by Setchō and Engo to the hundred cases of the *Hekigan-roku*. Also significant for a history of the Zen phrase book is an untitled, undated, and unsigned manuscript attributed to Daitō that brings together some 900 capping phrases. If this manuscript was indeed compiled by Daitō Kokushi, it would represent the first capping phrase collection in Japan, predating Tōyō Eichō's *Kuzōshi* by approximately one hundred and fifty years (KRAFT 1992, 210–2).[9]

Ikkyū Sōjun 一休宗純 (1394–1481), in his *Jikaishū* 自戒集 (*Self Precept Collection*), records that as part of the opening ceremonies for a new training hall in 1455—a little more than a century after Daitō—he directed several training activities, including *suiji jakugo* 垂示著語 "Introducing a kōan, appending a verse" (cited in SANAE 1996, 603). In hindsight it seems only natural that the practice of *jakugo* should have taken root within Japanese Zen, not simply because Japanese Zen monks attempted to replicate the practices of their Chinese teachers, but also because much of the literary ambience of Chinese elite culture had also been transplanted to Japan, an ambience

[9] See HIRANO 1988 for a collection of the sayings themselves.

in which poetry was the vehicle of official documents, in which poetic skill was considered the mark of education and intelligence, and in which compendia of verses (類聚) were organized and consulted as encyclopedia.

The practice of creating linked verses or *renga* 連歌 had become a social activity in Japan, supported by members of the imperial family, the warrior class, and the priesthood. In his study of Japanese linked poetry, Miner claims that, during the Momoyama period (1573–1603), the craze for *renga* resembled the tulip mania of Europe during the seventeenth and eighteenth centuries. Lavish banquets and expensive prizes were given to those proficient enough to be declared a Renga Master (MINER 1979, 50). In the Gozan culture of the Kamakura (1185–1333) and Muromachi periods (1338–1573), the writing of poetry was widely considered to be a form of Buddhist practice. It is not surprising, then, that even in the relatively strict and orthodox environment of the Rinzai monastery, training practices should have evolved to include some of the subsidiary activities of a widespread culture of poetry, including that of capping phrases.[10]

TŌYŌ EICHŌ'S *KUZŌSHI* AND IJŪSHI'S *ZENRIN KUSHŪ*

At some point in the evolution of Rinzai monastic practice—we are not sure when—the Zen master's practice of appending capping phrases to kōan became the Zen monk's practice in kōan training.

Every monk in his individual practice was expected to emulate the great T'ang and Sung Chinese masters in appending a capping phrase that expressed his insight into a particular kōan. For this a capping-phrase book is necessary. In Zen monasteries it is often said that in times past Zen monks were well educated and could compose their own Chinese verse capping phrases, whereas modern-day monks lack the training in classical literature to compose such verses on their own. Instead, they turn to a handbook to seek out an appropriate verse.

There were, of course, in every period a handful of monks literate in classical Chinese, but it is doubtful if there was ever a golden age in which all or most Zen monks could manage composition in *kanbun*. In fact, most monks were functionally illiterate and had difficulty reading, let alone composing, Chinese-style verse.[11] Rather than suppose, therefore, that the incorporation of the capping-phrase practice into monastic training explains the emergence of the capping-phrase book, it makes more sense to argue that the cause-effect relation was reversed, that the creation and spread

---

[10] For more detailed discussion of the link between poetry and Buddhist practice, see KRAFT 1992, POLLACK 1986, and EBERSOLE 1983.

[11] In Japan, there was even a tradition of illiterate Zen masters that continued into modern times (KATŌ 1998).

of these manuals are what made possible the incorporation of the *jakugo* practice into monastic training.

Two texts in particular are important for an understanding of the early history of Zen *jakugo* handbooks: the *Kuzōshi* compiled by Tōyō Eichō and the *Zenrin kushū* compiled by Ijūshi.

Kuzōshi 句雙紙 *(Verse Notebook)*

The first two capping-phrase texts, the *Kuzōshi* compiled at the end of the 1400s by Tōyō Eichō Zenji 東陽英朝禪師 (1426–1504) and the *Zenrin kushū* 禪林句集 compiled in 1688 by Ijūshi 已十子 (n. d.), should be discussed together, even though their composition is separated by nearly two centuries. There is a fair amount of looseness in the titling and attribution of authorship for these two texts. Both the terms *Kuzōshi* and *Zenrin kushū* came to be used as generic names for Zen phrase collections. Presently the term *Zenrin kushū* is often used to refer to all monastic capping-phrase books. Moreover, the *Zenrin kushū* is often said to have been edited by Tōyō Eichō even though the work was published nearly two hundred years after his death.[12]

The first collection of Zen capping phrases in Japan seems to have been the untitled text attributed to Daitō Kokushi mentioned above. The document does not appear to be a handbook used by monks engaged in appending verses to kōan as a regular assignment in kōan practice. Most likely it was restricted to the personal use of the master.

The first Zen phrase book used as a capping-phrase handbook for kōan practice was probably the *Kuzōshi,* compiled by Tōyō Eichō Zenji (1426–1504). A priest in the Myōshin-ji lineage, Tōyō Eichō received the *inka,* or certification of enlightenment, from Sekkō Sōshin. He served as temple abbot at both Daitoku-ji and Myōshin-ji, founded the temple Shōtaku-in, and established the Shōtaku sublineage within the Myōshin-ji line.[13] He entitled his compilation of Zen verses *Kuzōshi,* but the exact date is uncertain. Indeed it is difficult to identify anything corresponding to a "publication" of the work, in either the sense of the completion of a printed copy or in that of making it public. Kawase (1942, 120) estimates that the *Kuzōshi* was probably completed after Bunmei, that is, after 1486. Prior to that work Tōyō Eichō had compiled earlier collections known as the *Zensen* 前箭 (*First Arrow*) and the *Gosen* 後箭 (*Later Arrow*),[14] which would indicate that the compiling of Zen phrases was an ongoing project for him, perhaps without a clearly defined date of completion in

[12] For studies of the *Kuzōshi,* its commentary texts, and the *Zenrin kushū,* see Iriya 1996, Kawase 1942, Sanae 1996, Yanagida 1975, Yoshida 1941.

[13] See biographical entry at ZGDJT 84c.

[14] *Zensen wa nao karuku gosen wa fukashi* 前箭猶輕後箭深: "The first arrow still struck lightly, the later arrow went deep."

mind. All of these versions were written by hand and were most likely shown originally only to a small number of disciples.[15]

The *Kuzōshi* was compiled more than five hundred years ago, and in the centuries immediately following served as the model for numerous other versions that copied, expanded, or otherwise imitated it (including the *Amakusaban kinkushū*, mentioned above).[16]

The array of extant *Kuzōshi* texts shows a great many differences. Some versions provide full readings in (usually) *katakana*, along with margin symbols to indicate order of reading of characters. Others provide only margin symbols and the *katakana* for a few verb endings and difficult *kanji*. Of the four texts included in Kimura and Katayama 1984, one provides no explanation of meaning, while three provide *kokoro*, explanations of meaning of varying length and detail. None of the four cites the original sources. These differences need not detain us here. One feature, however, is worth mentioning: the order in which the phrases are classified.

Basically there are two ways of classifying phrases in the *Kuzōshi* texts, by number of characters and by topic. The former is the simpler, taking into account only the number of characters in each verse. The Hōsa Bunko text is an example of this system, containing 1219 phrases ranging from 1 to 14 characters in length and ordered as 1-character, 2-character, 3-character, 4-character, 5-character, 6-character, 7-character,

---

[15] For a discussion of Tōyō Eichō Zenji and the texts that may have served him as models, see Kawase 1942; Yoshida 1941, 1174–5; and Sanae 1996, 60–2.

[16] Despite the existence of several generations of copies and variations of the original text, frequently entitled simply *Kuzōshi* or *Kuzōshishō* 句雙紙抄 (*Annotated Kuzōshi*), this text was not widely available in the twentieth century until quite recently. In 1984, Kimura and Katayama published, in a limited and private edition, photographic facsimiles of four of these early *Kuzōshi* texts:

1. the Muraguchi private collection text reprinted by the Kotenseki Fukusei Sōkan Kankōkai 古典籍覆製叢刊刊行会 (Association for the Reproduction of Classic Texts);
2. the Meireki 2 (1656) woodblock print in the possession of the Komazawa University Library;
3. the unsigned handwritten copy in the possession of the Hōsa Bunko in Nagoya that is estimated to date from mid-Muromachi to early Edo (early 1500s to mid-1600s); and
4. a Genroku 6 (1693) woodblock print text from the Komazawa University Library.

In 1991, Kita published a photo-reproduction of a handwritten copy of the *Kuzōshishō* 句雙紙抄 (*Annotated Kuzōshi*) from the Doi collection that dates from early Edo, and supplied a detailed index of all the words that appear in the annotations. In 1996 Yamada, Iriya, and Sanae reissued a version of the *Kuzōshi* based on the Hōsa Bunko text (number 3 in the list above). This reproduction of the text is accompanied by substantial essays written by Iriya and Sanae on the development of the *Kuzōshi* texts (Yamada et al. 1996). In 2000 the Zen scholar Yanagida Seizan published a photo reproduction of probably a late Edo-period *Kuzōshi* in volume 10B of the *Zengaku tenseki sōkan* series (Yanagida and Shiina 2000).

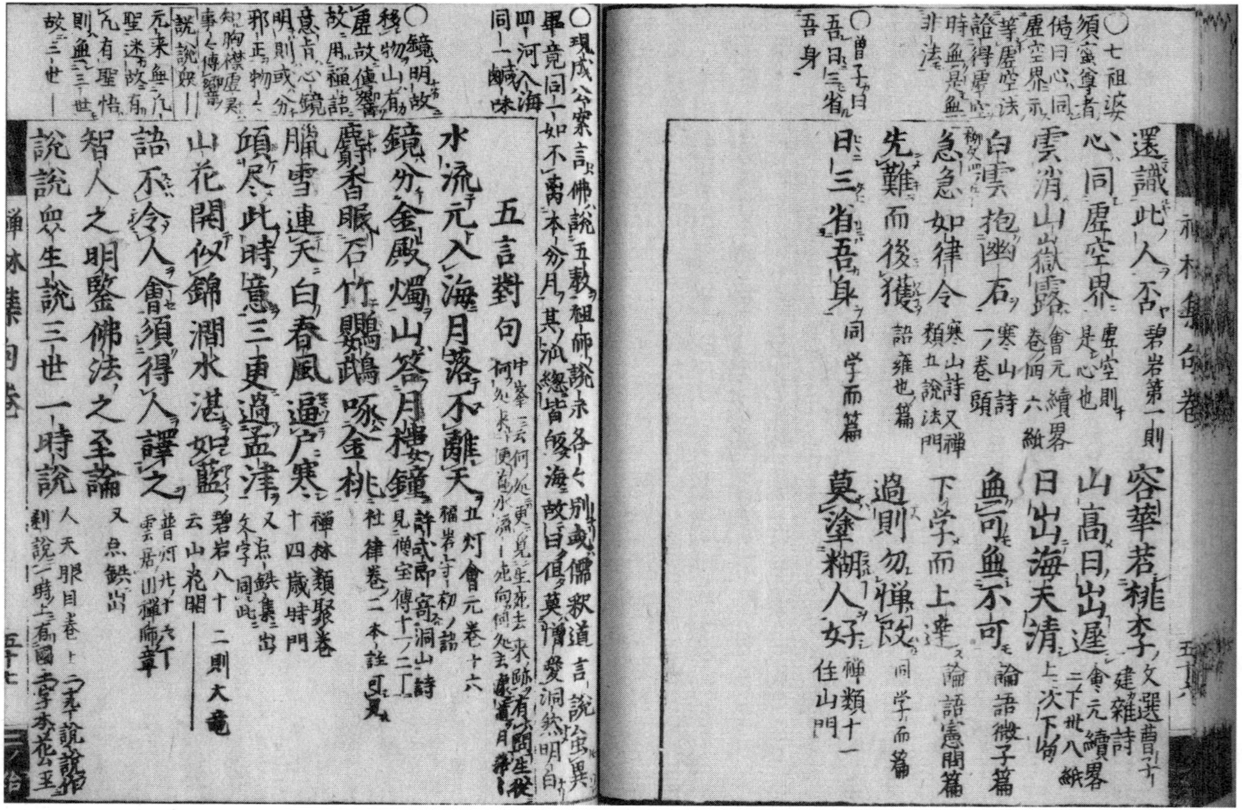

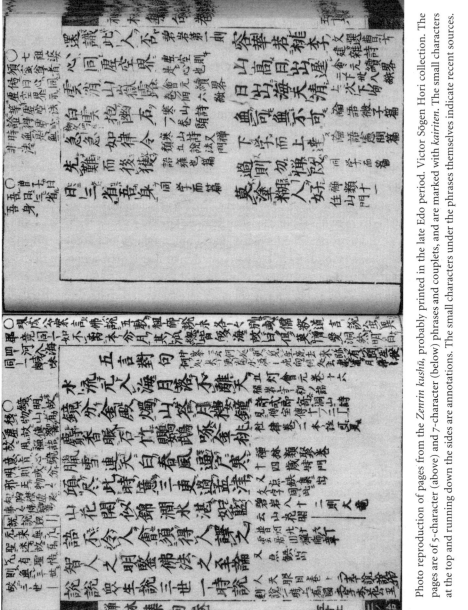

Photo reproduction of pages from the *Zenrin kushū*, probably printed in the late Edo period. Victor Sōgen Hori collection. The pages are of 5-character (above) and 7-character (below) phrases and couplets, and are marked with *kairiten*. The small characters at the top and running down the sides are annotations. The small characters under the phrases themselves indicate recent sources.

蜀志諸葛亮傳

註云是誰 熟是誰

兩句本經 欽文

▲自古

傳灯十四丁 叢林頭偈 宗鏡錄廿九 十四葉云 智者不能知 上賢亦不識

本來成佛非他得 心若眞時道易親 中峯廣錄卷頭偈 同上三首目

直下本來無一物 萬里無雲孤月圓 同上送禪者飯卿 虛堂集四卅四眞讚

六月火雲飛白雪 十方世界鉄渾崙 中峯廣錄九 同上卷末

劫外靈枝不帶春 梅花枝上月三更 空谷集一之十二頌 中峯十二 中八十八葉

百草頭邊風凛凛 千古萬古與人看 中峯十二上七十葉 碧十八則頌

莫謗如來正法輪 自古上賢猶不識 證道歌四十五丁 虛堂集一之九葉

無方便中眞方便 無修證中眞修證 大慧普說 同上對句

文彩縱橫意自殊 未亡見者休尋覓 從容錄五十五葉頌 中峯十三

三人行必有我師 本論語述而篇 永光明藏上六十四葉出

太平天子恩如海 蔭凉軒日錄集 上元日

○同安十玄談 轉位 鑊湯炉炭吹教滅 註 安尽情忘長劫靜 不踏蓮花
不傷 劍樹刀山喝便摧 註 丈夫須立金剛志 劍樹刀山豈自忘

○傳灯廿九 五十一同安察 頌

蓋旧本多誤 乎未見如何 故正之

○同本傳並 無門關 正之 從容錄五廿三葉 求雁清源 同曹山行跡

傳讀也或曰 蓋豈足爲本 白家 白氏家也 蓋不可也 只酒屋猶

七言對

鑊湯爐炭吹教滅 劍樹刀山喝便摧 五灯會元卷十六 人楚石四十七丁

須彌座下烏龜子 莫待重遭點額回 碧巖三則頌評 會元十四 興陽章

只願君王相顧意 臨臺幾度畫蛾眉 閨怨詩也 禪語用

泉州白家酒三盞 喫了猶言未沾脣 傳灯十七曹山章

五鳳樓前問洛陽 金鞭遙指御街長 普灯錄六八十丁

眼中童子目前人 水底金烏天上日 會元卷十六

棊逢敵手難藏行 詩到重吟始見功 禪類五悟道門 集二十六丁

曾騎鉄馬入重城 勅下傳聞六國淸 碧廿四則頌

一曲兩曲無人會 雨過夜塘秋水深 碧卅七則頌 三界無法頌

8-character, 10-character (5-character couplets), 12-character (6-character couplets), and 14-character (7-character couplets) verses.

Classification by topic is more complicated. One standard system of topics was "Eight Realms" (*hakkyōgai* 八境界), which were usually listed as "The Fundamental, Realization, Appearance, Cutting, Direct Pointing, Benefiting Others, Dynamic Connection, and Great Awakening" (本分, 現成, 色相, 裁斷, 直指, 爲人, 機關, 大悟).[17] Within each Realm, the verses were usually listed according to whether the verse was a single line or a couplet, and then according to the number of characters. This produced the following kind of order:

> The Fundamental: 4-character couplets, 4-character singles, 5-character couplets, 5-character singles, 6-character singles, 7-character singles;
>
> Realization: 4-character couplets, 4-character singles, 5-character couplets, 5-character singles, 6-character singles, 7-character singles;
>
> Appearance: 4-character couplets, 4-character singles, 5-character couplets, 5-character singles, 6-character singles, 7-character singles.

And so on for Eight Realms. As can be seen in the Muraguchi Kotenseki text, however, some editions added further topical subclasses to the Eight Realms. In the Muraguchi text these are abbreviated (関, 兩, 落, etc.), and since no explanation accompanies the abbreviations, one can only make educated guesses as to what they mean. Some Zen phrase books abandoned the Eight Realms classification system altogether, substituting their own classification schemes with as many as fifty and sixty different topic classes (YANAGIDA 1975, 2–6; YOSHIDA 1941, 1176–7; SANAE 1996, 594–7).

The Hōsa Bunko text, though ordered according to number of characters, recognizes that the verses can also be categorized into topical classes. At the top of each verse are printed small characters like 本, 學, 機, 用, and so on. These probably indicate some sort of topical classification, but no actual listing of subclasses is given. One has to assume that those who regularly used such handbooks knew what these abbreviations referred to.

By the time of Tōyō Eichō, the Rinzai kōan curriculum had likely evolved to the point where monks were being required to append *jakugo* to kōan, although the practice must still have been in its incipient stages. His *Kuzōshi* contains only a few more than 1,200 verses. If the *Kuzōshi* was being used as a handbook to support a

---

[17] In the photo reproduction from the Doi private collection of the handcopied *Kuzōshishō* published by Kita, the Eight Realms are listed on the second page, making it appear as a sort of subtitle for the entire collection. In that listing, however, the last two realms are not Dynamic Connection and Great Awakening (機關, 大悟) but Dynamism (機) and Barrier Gate (關). The first verses begin immediately on the following page. See KITA 1991.

jakugo practice, the small number of verses alone is evidence that it cannot have been very detailed or developed.

Zenrin kushū 禪林句集 *(Zen Sangha Verse Collection)*

The *Zenrin kushū*, a much larger collection of Zen phrases, may be considered "the revised standard version" of Zen capping-phrase books. In 1688, approximately two hundred years after Tōyō Eichō first compiled the *Kuzōshi*, a scholar-monk who identified himself only as Ijūshi 已十子 created a greatly expanded Zen phrase collection consisting of approximately 4,380 verses (one cannot give a precise number because some verses occur twice, some couplets are simply the same as other couplets but in reverse order, some verses are simply slight 1-character variants of others, etc.). He annotated the text with sources and explanations of the meaning of many of the verses, and changed the title of the collection to *Zenrin kushū*.

The annotations and headnotes cite kōan cases from the *Hekigan-roku* and the *Mumonkan* where that particular verse is used as an *agyo*, a clear indication that the *Zenrin kushū* must have been used at the time in conjunction with kōan practice. Moreover, the large number of verses and the sheer volume of detailed information provided are evidence that the Rinzai kōan practice in the mid-1600s was organized into some sort of curriculum and that the appending of *jakugo* was part of that practice. Although a full three hundred years have elapsed since the time of Ijūshi, even now the *Zenrin kushū* is one of the main capping-phrase collections in use, further proof that it must have been designed from the outset as a handbook for kōan practice. If we are to hazard a guess as to when capping phrases became part of monastic kōan practice, the evidence points to sometime during the two hundred years between the publication of the *Kuzōshi* at the very end of the fifteenth century and the publication of Ijūshi's *Zenrin kushū* in 1688.

Ijūshi himself attached a postscript alluding to the provenance of the work:

> This collection of material from previous sources was compiled by Tōyō Eichō Zenji, seventh-generation descendant of Kanzan Kokushi, the founder of (Myōshin-ji temple in) Hanazono. Eichō made a worthy contribution to the (Zen) school and created an independent line. He may be considered a master of the profound truth, a teacher with the single eye in his forehead with which to illumine the world, raising high the single horn of the *ch'i-lin* and extending the claws and teeth of the lion. The circulation of this collection in the world has thus been received with great appreciation.
>
> This material in its entirety comprises what those who study in the Zen forest learn first. It is like entering the Elementary Learning in Confucian study. Will not a thorough reading give one a ladder for viewing all texts? But if one tries to use it to compose literary works, one will often end up frustrated at not being able to find the original source of the verses contained in it.

I began by studying the Confucian classics, and in mid-life donned the black robes to seek instruction in the court of the Patriarchs. But the years have seen misfortune and the times have been unpropitious, and I have once again returned to Confucian studies. To repay my debt to the many fine Zen teachers from whom I received instruction, I have noted the sources (for the verses), and at the end have appended an additional 500 verses for a total of 6,000. I call it *The Zen Phrase Miscellany*. I have also made a separate collection in five fascicles that I call *Gold Chips from the Dense Forest arranged According to Rhyme*. Selected prose and poetry from numerous authors, outstanding phrases from all works of world-class repute, single verses and couplets used as common Zen sayings—all have been selected and compiled here for the benefit of later generations of students.

The *Zen Phrase Miscellany* mentioned above contains passages from Buddhist sutras, records of the Patriarchs, Taoist texts, Confucian canons, and the prose and poetry of numerous authors. Though I have noted their source, in most cases the verses here are from later texts. Where the original has been abbreviated and a later version cited, I have avoided variant characters. In the *Huai-nan tzu*, it says, "That there was a beginning implies there was also a time without any 'there was a beginning'." I have recklessly persisted in piling up additions the way this phrase does, and have not held my runaway tongue from expressing my own opinions. Even so, the arm does not bend outward. There are still five or six out of each hundred verses whose original source still remains unclear; I await a future scholar of great wisdom to supply them. Those whose pretence exceeds their knowledge will not escape punishment for their sins. But for students of Zen who study its many records, my work may not be lacking in usefulness.

1688 Feast Day of the New Year
At Sengu Sanpu in Rakuhashi
Respectfully,
Ijūshi[18]

[18] Some of Ijūshi's expressions in this postscript merit comment. The single eye in the forehead is the Buddha's eye of awakening that illumines the world, a well-known symbol for those familiar with the *Lotus Sutra*. The *ch'i-lin* is a fantastic animal with a single horn whose rare appearance was considered an omen of good fortune in Chinese mythology (see Glossary). Here the single horn is the symbolic equivalent of the single eye in the Buddha's forehead. Both are metaphors for the great awakening of Zen. The claws and teeth of the lion are a metaphor for the fierce but compassionate techniques of the skillful Zen teacher (see Glossary). When Ijūshi says he first studied Confucianism and then in mid-life donned the "black robes," he means he became a Buddhist monk. "The arm does not bend outward" (6.230) is a well-known Zen saying with many meanings, but here it simply means that there is a limit to how far one can push things. I wish to express my appreciation to Kōichi Shinohara and Burton Watson for help with the translation.

Ijūshi's postscript clearly identifies the two elements that kōan training brings together: the direct insight of awakening (the one eye in the forehead that illumines the world) and the literary study of texts. Although the literary study required of entrants to the Zen sangha is compared to the Elementary Learning in Confucian Studies, if the contents of the *Zenrin kushū* are any indication, there is nothing elementary about it. To read with Zen understanding the thousands of verses culled from hundreds of original sources must have required years, if not decades, of meditation and literary study. The formal, flowery humility of Ijūshi's language aside, one surmises that monastic training in his time must have been a rigorous undertaking.

Internal evidence seems to indicate that Ijūshi's *Zenrin kushū*, with 4,380 verses developed from Tōyō Eichō's 1200-verse *Kuzōshi*. Both texts are ordered according to number of characters as follows: 1-character, 2-character, 3-character, 4-character, 4-character couplets, 5-character, 5-character couplets, 6-character, 6-character couplets, 7-character, 7-character couplets, 8-character, and 8-character couplets. Within each section, however, the phrases are not ordered according to either character or reading. Despite the apparent randomness, there is a rough clustering according to topic. For example, in the ZRKS 4-character phrase section, phrases 70–83 deal with sin, guilt, law, and judgement; phrases 133–44 deal with thieves; phrases 286–9 all contain repeated characters; phrases 290–304 are about doing things twice unnecessarily; phrases 347–51 are about the perfect harmony of matching actions; and so on.

Almost all the verses of Tōyō Eichō's *Kuzōshi* reappear in the *Zenrin kushū*, and in much the same order. It is as if the verses of the *Kuzōshi* have been "spread out" so to speak, with additional verses inserted into the intervals. Compare, for example, the following stretches of verses.

Kuzōshi	***Zenrin kushū***
452 兩肩擔不起 *Ryōken ni ninai okosazu.* Even with both shoulders, you cannot lift it.	5.60 兩肩擔不起 *Ryōken ni ninai okosazu.* Even with both shoulders, you cannot lift it.
	5.61 大地載不起 *Daichi mo nose okosazu.* Not even the great earth can lift it up.
	5.62 芙蕖滴秋露 *Fukyo shūro shitataru.* On lotus leaves autumn dew beads.
453 大地黑漫漫 *Daichi koku manman.* The great earth is utterly black.	5.63 大地黑漫漫 *Daichi koku manman.* The great earth is utterly black.

454 突兀横古路
Tokkotsu to shite koro ni yokotau.
It towers up high blocking the ancient road.

455 虛空無背面
Kokū haimen nashi.
Emptiness has no front or back.

456 通身無影像
Tsūshin yōzō nashi.
The body entire has no shadow.

457 丹靑畫不成
Tanzei egakedomo narazu.
Color it red and blue, still you have not painted it.

5.64 突兀横古路
Tokkotsu to shite koro ni yokotau.
It towers up high blocking the ancient road.

5.65 僧堂入佛殿
Sōdō butsuden ni iru.
The Monks' Hall enters the Buddha Hall.

5.66 横身當宇宙
Mi o yokotawatte uchū ni ataru.
He throws himself into the universe.

5.67 團圞無少剩
Danran shōjō nashi.
Perfect, and not a bit more.

5.68 通身無影像
Tsūshin yōzō nashi.
The body entire has no shadow.

5.69 丹靑畫不成
Tanzei egakedomo narazu.
Color it red and blue, still you have not painted it.

5.70 好手畫不成
Kōshu egakedomo narazu.
Not even an expert can paint it.

All the verses from *Kuzōshi* 452–7 reappear in the *Zenrin kushū* and in the same order with the exception of verse 455. Verse 455 has been dropped, but probably only because a similar phrase appears as 5.96 in a later section in the *Zenrin kushū* (5.96: 光明無背面, *Kōmyō haimen nashi*, "The brilliant light has no back or front").

For want of a better explanation of the relationship of the *Kuzōshi* to the *Zenrin kushū*, one may suppose that the original *Kuzōshi* grew into the *Zenrin kushū* as the original text was hand-copied from one generation to the next. Users may have added marginal notes or paper inserts with further useful Zen phrases. If someone had learned a new phrase on the theme of thieves, for instance, he would have made a note of this in the margin next to another phrase on the topic. When this text and all its notes were transcribed, the copyist would incorporate the phrases noted in the margins of the old text directly into the body of the new copy. In this way the original verses of the *Kuzōshi* would retain their original order but become separated as more and more verses were inserted between them; and at the same time rough clusterings of phrases around specific topics would naturally make their way into the text.

Ijūshi's postscript raises several problems. The *Zenrin kushū* we possess today has approximately 4,380 phrases and verses, but Ijūshi claims that his collection has 6,000. Besides this text, which Ijūshi calls a *Zen Verse Miscellany* (*Zenrin zakku* 禪林雜句), he speaks of having compiled another text called *Gold Chips from the Dense Forest* (*Banrin kinsetsu-shū* 萬林金屑集). It may be that the two texts together contained 6,000 phrases, but Ijūshi's wording does not suggest this. Moreover, it has usually been assumed that Ijūshi increased the number of phrases from the 1,219 in the *Kuzōshi* to 4,380 in the *Zenrin kushū*, but he himself says that he added only another 500.

A further problem is that several sections have an appendix of supplementary phrases 外句增續 that presumably were added by Ijūshi. These supplementary phrases, which total 318 phrases,[19] are arranged according to the rhyme class of their last character, as we saw in the Chinese poetry composition handbooks. It makes more sense to suppose that through two centuries of successive copying along the lines just described, the *Kuzōshi* grew to about 3,700 or 3,800 phrases, and that when Ijūshi edited it, he merely added the supplementary phrases. Even so, the numbers do not quite add up and further investigation is called for.

The present edition of the *Zenrin kushū* lists more than two hundred titles of original sources from which the phrases were taken. These include Confucian writings, texts of philosophical Taoism, the Chinese histories, the *I Ching*, the Chinese poets, Buddhist sūtras, records of the Zen patriarchs, and large quantities of T'ang period poetry. The list of sources extends over all areas of the vast corpus of Chinese literature up through the T'ang period in China (618–960 CE). Although the actual compilation was made in Japan, all the phrases are Chinese and the recurring images in these phrases are all characteristic of Chinese culture at the time of the T'ang: the great vast waterways of China all flowing east, narrow gorges where monkeys shriek like people crying, plaintive barbarian flutes, cruel desert frontiers, luscious lands to the south, women pounding silk at night on fulling blocks, the red dust of the imperial cities, life decided at the point of an official's finger, and so on. This means that the *jakugo* practice required Japanese monks to express their experience of Zen awakening, grounded in the immediacy of the moment, by means of images from a foreign culture and an ever more distant past.

The *Zenrin kushū* that is consulted by present-day monks in training exists in several versions. For the practicing Zen monk, a pocket-size Meiji 27 (1894) reprint is available from Baiyō Shoin. For academic study, the Zen Bunka Kenkyūjo (Research Institute

[19] The numbers are as follows: 40 in the 4-character phrases, 44 in the 5-character phrases, 67 in the 10-character phrases, 30 in the 7-character phrases, 54 in the 14-character phrases, 31 in the 8-character phrases, 10 in the 16-character phrases.

for Zen Culture) at Hanazono University has published a Meiji 19 (1886) reprint with a character index. Numerous other Zen phrase collections were made in the centuries after Ijūshi, but his *Zenrin kushū* has been considered the authoritative edition and continues to be reprinted regularly. From time to time secondhand bookstores still turn up copies of old hand-bound woodblock-print editions whose pages are made of thin mulberry paper folded in half.

Despite its large number of verses, the *Zenrin kushū* has one major failing that makes it impossible for monks to rely on it exclusively. The work was published in 1688. Hakuin Ekaku Zenji was born in 1686 and went on to reform the Rinzai kōan practice, organizing it into the "kōan system" more or less as we know it today. It is unclear just what this reform consisted of and who was responsible for it.[20] But it is now widely accepted that Hakuin revised the kōan system, with the result that Rinzai monasteries everywhere now teach *Hakuin no kenge* (見解), the kōan responses accepted by Hakuin. The *kenge* in turn determine which verses will be accepted as *jakugo* for any given kōan. The *Zenrin kushū*, published before Hakuin's reforms, does not therefore necessarily reflect the kōan answers recognized in Hakuin Zen. This is the reason that new collections of *jakugo* have become necessary.

TWENTIETH-CENTURY CAPPING-PHRASE COLLECTIONS

Three Zen phrase books compiled in the twentieth century are also consulted by Zen monks in the practice of *jakugo*:

> *Zudokko kushū* 塗毒鼓句集 (*Poison-Painted Drum Phrase Collection*), contained in *Zudokko* (*Poison-Painted Drum*), a two-volume Zen monk's handbook compiled by Fujita Genro 藤田玄路 (Kyoto: Kennin-ji Sōdō, 1922);
>
> *Shinsan zengoshū* 新纂禪語集 (*A New Compilation of the Zen Phrase Collection*), compiled by Tsuchiya Etsudō under the direction of Unkankutsu Taibi Rōshi 雲關窟釋大眉老師 (Kyoto: Kichūdō, 1973);
>
> *Kunchū zenrin kushū* 訓註禪林句集 (*Annotated Zen Sangha Verse Collection*), edited and revised by Shibayama Zenkei 柴山全慶 Rōshi (Kyoto: Kichūdō, 1972).

Zudokko kushū 塗毒鼓句集 *(Poison-Painted Drum Phrase Collection)*

The *Zudokko* (*Poison-Painted Drum*) is a two-volume Zen monk's handbook compiled by Fujita Genro (1880–1935), a layman who trained under Takeda Mokurai Rōshi 竹田默雷老師 of the Kennin-ji monastery in Kyoto. Though small in format, the *Zudokko* is an invaluable resource containing nearly all the documents necessary for

[20] See MOHR 1999.

Rinzai practice: all the major kōan collections including the *Hekigan-roku,* the *Mumonkan*, the *Kattō-shū* 葛藤集 (*Tangled Vine Collection*), and the *Chin'u-shū* 鴆羽集 (*Collection of Poison Wings*); the entire *kanji* text of the *Rinzai-roku* and the *Kidō Daibetsugo* 虚堂代別語 (*The Alternate Phrases of Kidō Oshō,* an advanced kōan text); excerpts from the records of the Zen Patriarchs and from Hakuin's writings; and many other Zen documents. The title, *Poison-Painted Drum,* indicates the effects on learners of these Zen teachings. The skin of the drum of Zen is painted with a virulent poison taken from the wing of the poison blackbird; when the drum is beaten, all who hear it die. The *Zudokko* was originally published by the Kennin-ji *sōdō* (monastery). Fujita's Afterword to the second volume of the work is dated Taishō 11 (1922), which we may consider its year of publication.

Fujita Genro was born Fujita Tokujirō 藤田徳次郎 in 1880 in Naniwa, Osaka Prefecture, and at an early age developed a strong interest in Buddhism. After graduating from high school, he made his way to Kyoto, where in 1900 he came into contact with Takeda Mokurai. He left Japan in 1905 to study at New York University as a foreign student and returned to Japan in 1908 (ZGDJT 1073c, Obata 1938, 624–6). He belonged to a prosperous business family, which to this day is active in commerce and the arts. His layman's name, Genro, was conferred by Takeda Mokurai Rōshi. It seems to have been taken from the line in the *Nandō Benken Jūmon* 南堂辨験十門 *(Nandō's Ten Examination Gates):* "You must go by the dark path (*genro*) of the flying bird," *Subekaraku chōdō no genro o yukubeshi* 須行鳥道玄路 (in the second volume of *Zudokko*). The dark path is the path of one who leaves no traces, just as a bird leaves no traces in its path of flight. The "afterwords" he composed for each of the two volumes of the *Zudokko* are written in lines of 4-character verse in the so-called "horse hoof style" (*bateikei* 馬蹄型, because a galloping horse leaves hoofprints in series of four), probably in deliberate imitation of the style of the opening preface of the *Rinzai-roku.* They make frequent allusion to the Chinese classics and display the self-effacing, ironic style of Zen writing. They make it clear that Genro had progressed to a rather advanced stage of kōan practice and that he was a serious amateur scholar of the Chinese classics.

At the end of the second volume of the *Zudokko* is a section simply entitled *Kushū,* "Phrase Collection." It contains 2,397 phrases categorized according to number of characters. Only the characters are printed. No *kundoku* symbols are added between the lines and no readings are given. There is no commentary explaining the meaning and no sources are indicated. As Takeda Mokurai remarks in his foreword to the second volume:

> Companion on the way, layman Genro is the author of the *Poison-Painted Drum.* He has swept up the many poisons of our school and flung them in our faces. He gives no reading for any character; he gives no annotation for any phrase. He does this out of the goodness of his grandmotherly heart.

Some Zen priests argue that this makes the *Zudokko kushū* the best text to use in searching for *jakugo,* since one can read the bare *kanji* without the interference of margin symbols and annotation. For precisely this reason practitioners find it difficult to use. For example, the lay practitioner Tsuchiya Etsudō complained that in the more than 250 years since Tōyō Eichō's *Zenrin kushū* was published (the mistaken attribution of the *Zenrin kushū* to Tōyō Eichō is typical), there had been no new Zen phrase book suitable for looking up *jakugo* except the *Zudokko kushū,* and even this collection was not perfect:

> The *Zudokko kushū* is the only text to address this situation, but it has no margin symbols to indicate the order for reading characters and no *kana* to indicate verb endings. We beginners cannot help but feel hampered in our ability to use it freely. Not only that, one cannot really say that it is a complete collection. It may be considered handy, but that does not mean that it is not inconvenient. For us lay practitioners, it would be desirable to have a single book to serve all our needs. (TSUCHIYA 1973, 2)

Tsuchiya must not have known of the *Wakun ryakkai zenrin kushū* 和訓略解禪林句集 (*The Zenrin kushū with Japanese Readings and Concise Annotation*) compiled by Yamamoto Shungaku that appeared in 1920, two years before the *Zudokko kushū.* This text takes Ijūshi's *Zenrin kushū* as its basic text, appends the full reading in *kana* to each phrase, and adds a short annotation. Since it also claimed to contain 6,000 verses (a claim apparently based on Ijūshi's postscript), this edition should have gone a long way to meet Tsuchiya's complaint that the *Zudokko kushū* lacked sufficient phrases and verses to be complete. Apparently ignorant of Yamamoto's text, Tsuchiya's solution was to produce his own Zen phrase book, the *Zengoshū.*

Zengoshū 禪語集 *(Zen Phrase Collection)*

Tsuchiya Etsudō compiled the *Shinsan zengoshū* 新纂禪語集 (*A New Compilation of the Zen Phrase Collection*) under the direction of Unkankutsu Taibi Rōshi 雲關窟釋大眉老師 (TSUCHIYA 1973). This collection contains 3,040 verses, categorized by number of characters in each verse. Within each category, the verses or phrases are arranged according to the Japanese reading, not according to the Chinese character. That is, they are arranged in a-i-u-e-o order according to the *yomikudashi* reading, not according to the *on-yomi* reading of the first character of each phrase. Although the full *yomikudashi* reading is not given, the usual *kundoku* margin symbols indicate the order for reading the characters. There are no explanatory notes and no citation of sources.

Tsuchiya Etsudō (1899–1978) was born Tsuchiya Kiichi 土屋喜一 in Tochigi Prefecture. He was a mathematics teacher and during his teaching career had been principal of several local schools in the prefecture. He probably first came into contact with

Zen while teaching in the town of Nasu in Tochigi Prefecture, where one of the senior teachers at the same school was a teaching disciple of the well-known Zen monk Nantenbō. About the beginning of Shōwa (late 1920s), Tsuchiya moved to the city of Ashikaga to teach at the Ashikaga Prefectural Middle School (Ashikaga Kenritsu Chūgakkō) and joined the Ashikaga Zendōkai 足利禅堂会, where he became a disciple of its teacher Unkankutsu Shaku Taibi Rōshi (1889–1970), a dharma successor to the well-known Meiji-period rōshi, Shaku Sōen (1859–1919). According to the *Unkan Kōroku nenpyō* (chronology), Tsuchiya received the *kojigō,* or layman's name, of Etsudō during a *sesshin* with Taibi Rōshi in November of 1930 (DAICHŪ-JI 1966, 930).

Although he passed on his teaching responsibilities to other people toward the end of his life, Taibi Rōshi formally led the Suigetsu Dōjō from 1925 until his death in 1970, that is, for the remarkable period of forty-five years. Since Tsuchiya Etsudō formally became a disciple to Taibi Rōshi in 1930, their master-student relationship lasted for more than forty years. During this time Tsuchiya Etsudō was able to compile a Zen phrase book that would correct what he considered the two faults of the *Zudokko kushū*—the lack of margin symbols and *kana* to indicate how the phrases were to be turned into Japanese, and the limitation of 2,397 phrases, a number insufficient for the *jakugo* practice he was engaged in with Taibi Rōshi. According to anecdotal evidence from Asano Genjū 朝野元重, the present leader of the Ashikaga Zendōkai, Tsuchiya Etsudō combed the Chinese classical literature for phrases and verses suitable for use as *jakugo*. These he would take to Taibi Rōshi, who would either approve or disapprove. Over a period of many years, Tsuchiya kept adding to his collection of phrases and verses. The final version of his *Zengoshū* contains 3,040 phrases, or nearly a twenty-five percent increase over the 2,397 phrases of the *Zudokko kushū*.[21] It is the largest of the three *jakugo* phrase books compiled in the twentieth century.

Kunchū zenrin kushū 訓註禪林句集 *(Annotated Zen Sangha Verse Collection)*

The *Kunchū zenrin kushū* of Shibayama Zenkei Rōshi contains 2,646 phrases and verses, arranged according to number of characters and further subdivided according to the *on*-reading of the first Chinese character of the phrase (and not according to the Japanese reading, as is the case in the *Zengoshū*). In addition, each phrase or verse is accompanied by a full reading in *kana* and a short annotation or explanation. In many cases a source is cited. There is also a section following the verses listing all the chief abbots of Daitoku-ji through 490 generations.

This particular text is easily the most usable of the several *jakugo* texts, but it is also

---

[21] I wish to express my appreciation to Tsuchiya Shiomitsu and Kurihara Morito for providing information about their grandfather, Tsuchiya Etsudō; and to Asano Genjū and Asano Teruo for information about the Ashikaga Zendōkai, of which they are the present leaders.

the one that attracts the most criticism. Some complain that the Shibayama collection encourages monks to read the explanations and not the original phrases themselves. Others are annoyed at the way the explanations tend to rely on stereotyped intellectual phrases that are irritating to the practitioner who is seeking words to capture a living experience. Some monasteries even actively discourage their monks from using this text for these reasons.

Shibayama Zenkei Rōshi (1894–1974) began his long career in Buddhism when, under the influence of his devout mother, he entered a Buddhist temple at age fourteen. As he grew older, he grew critical of the Buddhist institution in Japan and for a while left Buddhism for Christianity. He also studied Esperanto and become one of the best Esperanto speakers in Japan at that time. Still on the spiritual search, he heard an inspiring lecture from a Zen rōshi that made him decide to enter a Zen monastery in 1916. After many years of monastery training at Nanzen-ji, he taught as a professor at Hanazono and Ōtani Universities in Kyoto. He was invited back to the Nanzen-ji monastery as its rōshi in 1948 and was elected *kanchō*, or chief abbot, of the entire Nanzen-ji line in 1959. Shibayama Rōshi became known to the West when in 1965 he made the first of several visits to the United States giving special lectures and teaching zazen at selected universities (KUDŌ 1975). His best-known book in English is *Zen Comments on the Mumonkan* (SHIBAYAMA 1974).

Among his many books in Japanese, his revised version of the *Zenrin kushū* is among the standard handbooks that Japanese Rinzai monks consult when assigned *jakugo*. The first edition of his *Zenrin kushū* appeared in 1952, and although probably intended for monks doing kōan practice, it also became popular with people practicing tea ceremony and calligraphy. Consequently Shibayama produced a second, revised, edition in 1972, increasing the number of phrases by 300 and simplifying the ordering system. He mentions in the preface to the second edition that he was greatly assisted by Fukushima Genshō 福島元照, one of his senior monks. Fukushima, now Fukushima Keidō Rōshi, the head of the Tōfuku-ji monastery in Kyoto, states that the number of verses was increased for two reasons: to include phrases and verses often found on tea scrolls, and to include all the *jakugo* used in the Takujū lineage.[22]

The above three Zen phrase books, meant for *jakugo* practice, have all been compiled in the twentieth century. It is inevitable that new *jakugo* collections would appear for at least two reasons. First, there is gradual change. Zen masters in every generation add a new phrase or two and drop an old phrase or two from the corpus of phrases from which they draw *jakugo*. Thus the *Zenrin kushū* by Ijūshi, which may have been appropriate for the Rinzai kōan system at the end of the 1600s, is no longer adequate for the Rinzai kōan system in the twenty-first century. In addition to such gradual

[22] Conversation 8 July 1998, at Tōfuku-ji Sōdō.

change, there is also radical systematic change. Hakuin is said to have revised the entire traditional kōan practice and forged it into the present system. The new systematized kōan responses that Hakuin accepted as correct must surely have caused all teaching rōshi to revise their lists of correct *jakugo*. There is also a third factor, which we are in no position to judge at present. The Hakuin lineage is divided into two sublineages, the Inzan and the Takujū. Though they both teach the Zen of Hakuin, they have developed slightly different sets of responses for their kōan, and consequently slightly different sets of *jakugo*.

ADAPTATIONS AND TRANSLATIONS OF ZEN PHRASE BOOKS

Throughout the Edo period, Zen phrase books continued to appear, but most were reprints of Ijūshi's *Zenrin kushū*, or were modifications of it. Sōtō Sect Zen monks made similar Zen phrase books; the *Zenrin meiku jiten* 禪林名句辞典 compiled by Iida Rigyō is a modern-day Sōtō Sect Zen phrase book (IIDA 1975). There was also, apparently, a Jōdo-shū (Pure Land Buddhist) *Kuzōshi* (SANAE 1996, 593).

Twentieth-century Japan has seen the publication of numerous popular books listing and explaining Buddhist verses and phrases (MATSUBARA 1972, NAKAMURA 1977, KINŌ 1988). Some specialize in particularly Zen language (AKIZUKI 1981, HIRATA 1988). Others single out Buddhist phrases, many from Zen, that have entered into colloquial Japanese (IWAMOTO 1972, HIRO 1988). Introductory books on Zen occasionally include a short section explaining Zen verses and phrases (TAKAHASHI 1988). Moreover, since scrolls with Zen verses are so important for tea ceremony, several books aimed specifically at this reading audience have appeared, often providing detailed information and interesting background to Zen verses. The *Zengokushō* 禅語句抄 (*Annotated Zen Phrases*, Hekian Shūdō 1982) is a useful handbook of Zen verses that indexes both the top and bottom verses of every couplet. NISHIBE Bunjō's *Zengo no ajiwaikata* 禅語の味わい方 (*How to Savor Zen Phrases*, 1985) and the four-volume series *Ichigyōmono* 一行物 (*Scrolls in Single Lines*) by the respected scholar of medieval Japanese Buddhism, HAGA Kōshiro (1973, 1974, 1977, 1984), not only lists Zen phrases but also contains short explanatory lectures.

The Chinese Buddhist publishing industry has likewise produced a number of collections of Zen phrases. Although I have not been able to keep up to date with Chinese publications in this area, I would single out as an interesting example of reverse cultural flow, the *Ch'an-lin hui-yü* 禪林慧語 (*Zen Sangha Words of Wisdom*) edited by Ling Yun, under the supervision of Bai Mu.[23] Compiled by Chinese authors and published in Taiwan, it is partly based on Japanese Zen phrase books and gives among its

[23] See LING Yün, n.d.

sources Gidō Shūshin's *Jōwashū*, Hakuin's *Kaian kokugo*, Dōgen's *Shōbō genzō* and *Eihei kōroku*, and the *Collected Poems of Natsume Sōseki*.

In English, several translations of selected verses from the *Zenrin kushū* have been published over the years. The earliest attempt seems to have been by D. T. Suzuki, whose numerous translations of Zen verses are scattered throughout his voluminous corpus. R. H. Blyth in *Haiku 1: Eastern Culture* gives translations of 73 verses in a section devoted solely to the *Zenrin kushū* and translates several other verses throughout the rest of his book (Blyth 1949, 23–33 and passim). *Cat's Yawn*, the short-lived (July 1940–July 1941) monthly publication of the First Zen Institute of America under the direction of Sasaki Sōkei-an, had a regular feature called "Zenrin Collection," which gave the romanized reading of a Zen verse, its English translation, and the context from which the verse was taken (First Zen Institute of America 1947).

Sōkei-an died in 1945 but his work was continued by his wife, Ruth Fuller Sasaki, who went on to establish the First Zen Institute of America in Japan, a research institute and Zen practice center, at Daitoku-ji in Kyoto. In March 1956 she published a short selection of poems from the *Zenrin kushū* in an article, "Anthology of Zen Poems," which appeared in the Japanese journal *Zen bunka* 4: 22–6. She then collaborated with Isshū Miura Rōshi to produce *Zen Dust*, which includes a translation of 210 Zen verses with original *kanji*, romanized readings, English translations, and occasional notes (Miura and Sasaki 1966, 79–122). Among the many research projects she left behind at the time of her death in 1967, was a plan for a full translation of the *Zenrin kushū* that she and her research associates had been working on. The library of the First Zen Institute of America in Japan, housed at Ryōsen-an in Daitoku-ji, contains a stack of notebooks related to the project. Daitoku-ji kindly allowed me to view these notebooks. I discovered that while there were polished translations for a few of the *Kushū* phrases, the translations of most of the phrases were in various stages of revision, and a large number had not been started at all.

In 1981 Shigematsu Sōiku published *A Zen Forest*, an English translation of 1,234 verses with *kanji*. Although this remains the longest version of the Zen phrase book in English, it is interesting primarily as a sampling of Zen phrases and verses; it does not contain enough phrases and verses to serve as a handbook for *jakugo* practice. Robert E. Lewis, who is associated with the New York Zendō, Shōbō-ji, published in 1996 *The Book of the Zen Grove* (2nd edition), a translation of 631 verses based on the Japanese Shibayama *Zenrin kushū*, with romanized readings, commentary, indices, and a bibliography. In 1991 the Pure Land scholar Hisao Inagaki published *A Glossary of Zen Terms*, a dictionary of 5,500 terms with *kanji* and explanation, focused mainly on 2-character and 4-character *kanji* compounds and set phrases. Although many longer phrases are included and its content overlaps with the 1-character to 4-character phrases of the standard Zen phrase books, the work is not suitable for use as a capping-phrase handbook.

ZEN SAND

This book, *Zen Sand*, combines and translates the contents of the two most widely used twentieth-century Japanese Zen kōan capping-phrase books, Shibayama Zenkei's *Zenrin kushū* and Tsuchiya Etsudō's *Shinsan zengoshū*, providing the original Chinese characters, the classical Japanese reading, and an English translation for 4,022 phrases. It is the largest modern collection of Zen capping phrases in any language, surpassing by far Shibayama's *Zenrin kushū* (2,646 phrases) and Tsuchiya's *Shinsan zengoshū* (3,040 phrases), and second only in size to Ijūshi's *Zenrin kushū* of 1688, which contained approximately 4,380 phrases. In addition to the basic characters, the readings, and the translations, *Zen Sand* also provides a detailed Glossary of supplementary information.

The publication of *Zen Sand* serves two communities: practitioners and scholars. For practitioners, Westerners who have wanted to do the full Rinzai Zen kōan practice have been prevented by the fact that there was no clear account of the overall Zen kōan curriculum with its important literary element, that none of the Western teachers of Zen had ever completed the kōan capping-phrase practice, and that there was no Western-language version of the common capping-phrase books that every Rinzai Zen monk possesses. The publication of *Zen Sand* for the first time makes it possible for Westerners to carry on the traditional capping-phrase practice in either the Inzan or Takujū lineage.

For scholars, *Zen Sand* argues that the rise of the kōan can only be understood against the background of Chinese literary culture, that characteristic features of the kōan dialogue (competition, deceptiveness, on-the-spot spontaneity, turning the tables, and, especially, mind-to-mind transmission) were inherited from its ancestor the Chinese literary game, and then put to work in the service of an awakening "not founded on words and letters." In addition, with its explanation of the kōan system and the capping-phrase practice, *Zen Sand* makes it quite clear that Zen is *free in* language, not *free from* language.

According to the widely accepted stereotypical image, Zen completely rejects language and conceptual thought. Zen enlightenment, it is believed, breaks through the false dichotomies imposed by language and destroys the artificial categories implanted in our minds by social conditioning. Zen enlightenment, it is assumed, directly apprehends things as they are in an ineffable pure consciousness outside the realms of language and intellect. This stereotype, with its crude dichotomy between a realm of intellectual thought and a realm of pure intuition, topples on close inspection from its own internal inconsistencies.[24]

---

[24] For a detailed argument on this point, see HORI 2000.

But as *Zen Sand* makes clear, the kōan practice is not a breaking out of language into a realm of silence but a sophisticated use of language to express and realize awakening. The study of the capping-phrase practice makes explicitly clear that Zen seeks not freedom from language by rejecting it, but freedom in language by mastering it.

6

Guide to Conventions and Abbreviations

The purpose of this final chapter is to provide the reader with the technical apparatus needed to identify the various conventions and abbreviations used in the course of this book.

SOURCES AND ORDERING OF THE VERSES

Zen Sand (ZS) combines the entire contents of Shibayama Zenkei's *Zenrin kushū* (Shiba) and Tsuchiya Etsudō's *Shinsan zengoshū* (ZGS), the two capping-phrase books most frequently used by Rinzai Zen monks.

In general, ZS follows the same order of phrases as ZGS, namely, the Japanese *kana* order (a-i-u-e-o) based on the first syllable of the Japanese reading. This can be seen from the consecutive progression of ZGS numbers in the reference line. Phrases from the Shibayama *Zenrin kushū* were inserted into this order in their appropriate places. This a-i-u-e-o order is broken, however, in the cases of connected verses, as in the example shown below. Where two or more verses are drawn originally from the same longer poem, ZS places them together in order to reconstruct the original verse. The second and third verses in such a series will consequently not be in a-i-u-e-o order.

Other ordering systems would also have been possible. For example, the phrases could have been ordered according to radical and stroke count of the first Chinese character of each verse (the order in the Shibayama text). The ZGS system based on the Japanese reading was followed because it could be used to order the verses either in Japanese or in English romanization.

GUIDE TO THE VERSES

The verses in this book are laid out in a uniform pattern, with standard component parts. The diagram of sample verses below illustrates and explains those component parts.

① ② ③

14.225 五臺山上雲蒸飯 *Godaisanjō kumo han o mushi,*
古佛堂前狗尿天 *Kobutsudōzen inu ten ni nyō su.*

④ ④

On the peak of ⌜Mt. Wu-t'ai⌝, clouds are steaming rice,
⑤ **In front of the ancient Buddha Hall, a dog is pissing at the sky.** ⑧ ➤

⑥ *Heki* 96 Verse 1st Comm.

⑦ KZS #1159, ZGS 14.201, ZGJT 122, ZGJI 618, ZRKS 14.55, Shiba 343

14.226 刹竿頭上煎餶子 *Sekkan tōjō ni taisu o senzu,*
三箇猢猻夜簸錢 *Sanko no koson yoru sen o hiru.*

⑧ ➤ **Toasting dumplings on top of the banner pole,**
Three monkeys are pitching pennies in the night.

Empuku-ji, Shiba 368: *Sekkan tōjō ni tsuisu o senzu.*

ZGS 14 347, ZGJT 250, ZGJI 642, ZRKS 14.220, Shiba 368

① *Numbering of the verses.* The bold numbers in the left margin indicate the number of characters in the verse followed by the number of the verse within that category. Thus 14.225 means verse 225 of the 14-character verses. These numbers are specific to this book.

② *Chinese characters.* In general, traditional, nonsimplified Chinese characters have been used in order to be consistent with the texts, reference works, scrolls, art work, etc. with which this book may be used.

There may be scholarly disagreement over the correct characters with which to write a particular phrase, due in part to the fact that a copyist's mistake can be repeated through later generations of copying, eventually resulting in different versions of the verse or phrase. As a rule, I have followed the corrections to Chinese characters made by the staff of the Zen Bunka Kenkyūjo in their *Teihon Zenrin kushū sakuin* (Zen Bunka Kenkyūjo 1991a). Where there are discrepancies between the two source texts for ZS, I have noted the fact in the annotation line.

The original Chinese text is unpunctuated except to separate lines of poetic verse. In *Zen Sand* the Chinese verse has been laid out in one or two lines according to the available space.

③ *Japanese reading.* The two principal source texts sometimes give different Japanese readings (*yomikudashi*) for the same phrase. When they differ, ZS usually takes the *Zengoshū* reading but also notes the Shibayama reading in the annotation line.

A single Chinese character sometimes has more than one pronunciation. The character 蛇 can be pronounced *da*, as in *ryūda* 龍蛇 "dragon and snake," or *ja* as in *jabara* 蛇腹 "snake belly." 毒蛇, "poison snake," can be pronounced *dokuda* or *dokuja*. The character for "dragon" 龍 is sometimes read *ryō* and sometimes read *ryū*. 走る "to run" is pronounced *hashiru* in some Zen phrases, *washiru* in others. The "Zen" reading of Chinese words and phrases sometimes differs considerably from what is now considered standard reading. 下語 "capping phrase" is read *agyo*, not *gego*; 業風 "wind of karma" is read *goppū*, not *gyōfū*; 江湖 "river and lake" is read *gōko*, no *kōgo*; 法堂 "dharma lecture hall" is read *hattō*, not *hōdō*; 經行 "walking" (between meditation periods) is *kinhin*, not *kyōgyō*; and so on. Different Zen sources will sometimes offer different versions of the correct Zen reading. 少売弄 "petty salesmanship" is read *shōmairō* by ZGDJT 586b and *shanbeirō* by Shibano 41.

The Chinese verses and phrases are often ambiguous, allowing more than one interpretation. ZS follows the Japanese interpretation of the verse or phrase, as indicated by the Japanese reading. This may be somewhat different from an interpretation based directly on the Chinese. Phrase 4.500, for example, reads:

> 詠花吟月　*Hana ni eiji tsuki ni ginzu.*
>
> I sing to the flowers, I chant to the moon.

This could be read, "I sing *of* flowers, I chant *of* the moon," but the traditional Japanese reading is *Hana ni eiji tsuki ni ginzu*, "I sing *to* the flowers, I chant *to* the moon."

Or again, phrase 6.142 reads:

> 巣知風穴知雨　*Sukuu mono wa kaze o shiri, kessuru mono wa ame o shiru.*
>
> Those who live in nests know the wind;
> those who live in holes know the rain.

This can be translated, "Nests know the wind, holes know the rain" but the traditional Japanese reading makes clear 巣 and 穴 are taken not as simply "nests" and "holes" but as persons: *sukuu mono* "those who live in nests" and *kessuru mono* "those who live in holes."

The Zen teachers who were consulted have pointed out that the preferred reading of a particular phrase expresses its *kyōgai*, the spirit, the tone in which the phrase is meant to be uttered. In English, "Am not misbehaving" is too formal and descriptive, but "ain't misbehavin'" actually expresses (a "misbehavin'") attitude. That is its *kyōgai*. Verse 14.533 reads:

> 睡美不知山雨過　*Nemuri bi ni shite shirazu san'u no suguru koto o,*
> 覺來殿閣自生涼　*Samekitatte denkaku onozukara shōryō.*
>
> My nap was wonderful, I wasn't aware mountain rains had passed,
> When I awoke, the pavilion itself was so clean and fresh!

Usually the verb in the second line would be read *shōryō su*. But to insert *su* makes the line descriptive ("It is clean and fresh") when what is wanted is an expressive "So clean and fresh!"

Or again, verse 14.479 reads:

鐵鞋無底飽風霜 *Tetsuai soko nōshite fūsō ni aku,*
歳晩歸來臥石床 *Saiban kaerikitatte sekijō ni fusu.*

My iron sandals are worn right through,
  I've had my fill of wind and frost,
At the end of my years, I've come home to lie
  on my bed of stone.

The usual reading *Tetsuai soko naku shite,* "My iron sandals have no soles," is too formal. Here, for the sake of *kyōgai, naku shite* has been contracted to *nōshite,* a much more colloquial reading. These are the words of a person at the end of a long career. *Naku shite* merely describes his weariness, *nōshite* attempts to express it.

④ *Glossary entry.* Raised corner brackets 「 」 indicate that the enclosed term is listed in the Glossary that follows the verses.

⑤ *English translation.* Some of the phrases are from previously translated works such as the Confucian *Analects,* the *Tao-te ching,* the *Shih-chi,* and Chinese poetry. Where there already existed a good English translation, I have often quoted that translation, but for the vast majority of phrases in ZS, the English translations are my own.

⑥ *Annotation.* Several types of information are provided on the annotation line. The annotation line indicates where a particular phrase appears in one of the two major kōan collections, the *Hekigan-roku (Heki)* and the *Mumonkan* (MMK). It also presents alternate readings, background information, and reference to items in the Glossary. In some cases, where the phrase is well established, for instance, the Confucian *Analects,* it indicates the source. ZS does not attempt, however, to identify an original source for every verse or phrase. To do so would have meant first establishing a correct Chinese character text for each phrase, already a difficult task for many entries, and then tracking that verse or phrase back through many historical layers of documents. ZS leaves the great philological task of establishing the original source for its more than 4,000 phrases to another generation of scholars.

⑦ *Reference.* Limitations of space preclude any detailed explanation of the interpretation. For those wishing further information, the reference line includes the ZGS phrase number and the Shibayama page number, as well as reference to other Zen phrase books, dictionaries, and standard indexes.

⑧ *Linked verses.* The arrow pointing right ➤ at the end of the English translation indicates that the following number is a continuation of the same verse. It is always followed in the succeeding verse by another arrow pointing left ➤. Sometimes there can be several verses linked together in this manner.

ROMANIZATION AND PRONUNCIATION

Romanization of Japanese words follows the standard Hepburn system. The romanization of Chinese follows the Wade-Giles system.

The Rinzai capping-phrase practice is, to the best of my knowledge, carried on only in Japan. The *Zengoshū* and the Shibayama *Zenrin kushū* were compiled in Japan, even though their contents are all written in Chinese. Since this book is for those working in the Japanese tradition, the following conventions have been followed throughout:

1. Names of Zen monks and Zen personalities important to Rinzai kōan practice have been given in their Japanese pronunciation instead of in the Chinese pronunciations, e.g., Rinzai, Mumon, Jōshū, Setchō rather than Lin-chi, Wu-men, Chao-chou, Hsüeh-tou.

   Titles of kōan texts have been given in Japanese, e.g., *Hekigan-roku*, *Mumonkan* rather than *Pi-yen-lu*, *Wu-men-kuan*.
2. Names of Zen monks important primarily to Zen scholarship have been given in their Chinese pronunciation, e.g., Fen-yang Shan-chao.
3. Names of other Chinese persons and places have been given in Chinese pronunciation rather than in Japanese. Thus, for example, Yang Kuei-fei is used rather than Yōkihi, T'ao Yüan-ming rather than Tōenmei, Chuang-tzu rather than Sōshi, Ch'ang-an rather than Chōan.
4. With the exception of Kuan-yin (Ch.), the names of buddhas and bodhisattvas are given in Sanskrit, e.g., Śākyamuni, Mañjuśrī, Samantabhadra. Some other terms, like *yakṣa, asaṃkhyeya,* and *kalpa,* are also given in Sanskrit.

   Diacritical marks have been omitted from Sanskrit words that have entered into standard English (for example, nirvana, sutra, and karma), but are retained in the titles of Sanskrit works.

ABBREVIATIONS

A number of classical sources are cited in *Zen Sand* by title only. For further bibliographical information, consult the list at the end of the Bibliography on page 731.

Agyo — *Agyo* is an interlinear capping phrase, which may be inserted into either the Case or the Verse of the *Hekigan-roku*.

Empuku-ji — A reading given by Katō Gessō Rōshi of the Empuku-ji Sōdō in Yawata-shi, Kyōto-fu.

GKFGS 1.60 — *Shinpen gōko fūgetsu-shū sakkūshō kōgi* 新編江湖風月集鑿空 抄講義 [Pointless Lectures on the *Fūgetsu-shū*, New Edition] by Suzuki

Shijun 鈴木子順 (Tokyo: Reisen-in, 1935), Part 1, page 60. The two parts have separately numbered pages.

Heki 20 Case 20 of the *Hekigan-roku* 碧巖錄 [Blue Cliff Record]. The full title is *Bukka Engo Zenji hekigan-roku* (Ch. *Fo-kuo Yüan-wu Ch'an-shih Pi-yen lu*) 佛果圜悟禪師碧巖錄 [Blue Cliff Record of Zen Master Engo] [T 48: 139–225].

Heki 96 Verse 1st Comm. *Hekigan-roku* Case 96, 1st Commentary to the Verse.

HYDCD 5.124 Vol. v, page 124 of Luo Zhu-feng, ed. 羅竹風主編, *Hanyu dacidian* 漢語大詞典 [Lexicon of Chinese, 12 vols. and Index] (Hanyu Dacidian Chubanshe, 1990).

KSMKJT §374 Entry number 374 of *Kanshi meiku jiten* 漢詩名句辞典 [Dictionary of Well-known Verses from Chinese Poetry], edited by Kamata Tadashi 鎌田正 and Yoneyama Toratarō 米山寅太郎 (Tokyo: Daishūkan, 1980).

KZS #211 Phrase number 211 of the *Kuzōshi* according to the text established in Yamada Toshio 山田俊雄, Iriya Yoshitaka 入矢義高, and Sanae Kensei 早苗憲生, eds., *Teikun Ōrai kuzōshi* 庭訓往来句双紙 (Tokyo: Iwanami Shoten, 1996).

MMK 20 Case 20 of the *Zenshū mumonkan* 禪宗無門關 (Ch. *Ch'an-tsung Wu-men-kuan*) [The Gateless Barrier of the Zen School] compiled by Mumon Ekai 無門慧開 (Ch. Wu-men Hui-k'ai), edited by Shūshō 宗紹 (Ch. Tsung-shao), and published in 1229 [T 48: 292–9].

Morohashi 23345.43 Character number 23345, compound number 43 in *Dai kanwa jiten* 大漢和辭典 [Great Chinese-Japanese Dictionary] compiled by Morohashi Tetsuji 諸橋轍次 (Tokyo: Daishūkan Shoten, 1960).

MZZ 134.331 Vol. 134, page 331 of the *Manji zokuzōkyō*. 卍續藏經 *Wan hsü-ts'ang-ching* [Supplement to the Buddhist Canon]. Taiwan: Hsinwenfeng Pienshenpu, 1983.

na Not Applicable. ZGS na or Shiba na indicates that a particular phrase does not occur in that text.

Ryōkō-in A reading given by Kobori Nanrei, the former *oshō* of Ryōkō-in, Daitoku-ji.

RZR §14 Section 14 of the *Rinzai-roku*, according to the section division in Akizuki Ryōmin 秋月龍珉, *Rinzai-roku* 臨濟錄 [Record of Rinzai]. Tokyo: Chikuma Shobō, 1972. Burton Watson follows the same numbering system in *The Zen Teachings of Master Lin-chi*. (Boston: Shambhala, 1993). The *Rinzai-roku* is *Chinjū Rinzai Eshō Zenji goroku* 鎭州臨濟慧照禪師語錄 (Ch. Chen-chou Lin-chi Hui-chao Ch'an-shih Yü-lu), T 47.495a–506c.

Serenity 從容錄 [Book of Serenity], Takasaki Jikishō 高崎直承, ed. (Tokyo: Kōmeisha, 1934). Citations refer to the English translation of Thomas Cleary, *Book of Serenity* (Hudson, NY: Lindisfarne Press, 1999).

Shiba 14.124 Verse 124 of the 14-character verses in the revised modern version of *Zenrin kushū*, edited by Shibayama Zenkei 柴山全慶, *Kunchū zenrin kushū* 訓註禪林句集 [Annotated Zen Sangha Verse Collection] (Kyoto: Kichūdō, 1972). Do not confuse with ZRKS, which has exactly the same title.

Shinjigen 新字源 [Character Etymologies], Ogawa Tamaki 小川環樹 et al., eds. (Tokyo: Kadokawa Shoten, 1968).

Shōun-ji A reading or information given by Yasunaga Sōdō, the *oshō* of Shōun-ji in the city of Ikeda. Yasunaga Oshō completed the kōan training under Hirata Seikō Rōshi of Tenryū-ji.

SRZGK §1743 Entry number 1743 (not page number 1743) of the *Shoroku zokugokai* 諸錄俗語解 [Explanation of Colloquial Language in Several Texts]. Yoshizawa Katsuhiro 芳澤勝弘, ed. (Kyoto: Zen Bunka Kenkyūjo, 1999).

T *Taishō shinshū daizōkyō* 大正新脩大藏經 [Buddhist Canon Published in the Taishō Era] (Tokyo: Taishō Issaikyō Kankōkai, 1924–1934). T 47.519b refers to volume 47, page 519; a, b, and c refer to top, middle, and bottom thirds of the page.

TSSSTS *Tōshisen santaishi sōgō sakuin* 唐詩選三体詩総合索引 [Joint Index for the *Tōshisen* and *Santaishi*], produced by the Zen Bunka Kenkyūjo (Kyoto: Zen Bunka Kenkyūjo, 1992).

ZD#25 Verse 25 of the "Zen Phrase Anthology," on pages 79–122 of *Zen Dust* by Miura Isshū and Ruth Fuller Sasaki, *Zen Dust: The History of the Koan and Koan Study in Rinzai (Lin-chi) Zen* (Kyoto: The First Zen Institute of America, 1966).

ZD 25 Page 25 of *Zen Dust* above.

ZGDJT *Zengaku daijiten* 禪學大辭典 [Lexicon of Zen Studies], edited by the Komazawa Daigaku Zengaku Daijiten Hensansho (Tokyo: Daishūkan, 1977).

ZGJI *Zengo jii* 禪語字彙 [Zen Glossary] edited by Imai Fukuzan 今井福山 and Nakagawa Shūan 中川渋庵 (Tokyo: Hakurinsha, 1935).

ZGJT *Zengo jiten* 禪語辭典 [Zen Word Dictionary] edited by Iriya

Yoshitaka 入矢義高 and Koga Hidehiko 古賀英彦 (Kyoto: Shibunkaku, 1991).

ZGS 10.188 Phrase number 188 in the 10-character section of *Shinsan zengoshū* 新纂禪語集 [A New Compilation of the Zen Phrase Collection], edited by Tsuchiya Etsudō 土屋悦堂, compiled under the direction of Unkankutsu Shaku Taibi Rōshi 雲關窟釋大眉老師 (Kyoto: Kichūdō, 1973).

ZRKS 10.188 Phrase number 188 in the 10-character phrase section of *Zenrin kushū* (ZRKS). The term *Zenrin kushū* is frequently used as a generic term to refer to all Zen phrase collections, but in this book, ZRKS refers specifically to the *Zenrin kushū* 禪林句集 [Zen Sangha Phrase Collection] compiled in 1688 by Ijūshi 已十子 (Kyoto: Baiyō Shoin reprint). Do not confuse with the book carrying exactly the same title, *Zenrin kushū,* by Shibayama Zenkei (Shibayama 1972). This latter text is designated "Shiba."

PHRASES

Four-Character Phrases

4.1 相去多少 *Aisaru tashō zo.*

How far are they apart?

Heki 25 Verse Comm., 32 Main Case Comm.

ZGS 4.1, Shiba na

4.2 相救相救 *Aisukue, aisukue.*

Help me! Help me!

ZGS 4.2, Shiba na

4.3 屙屎送尿 *Ashi sōnyō.*

Have a shit, take a piss.

Rinzai-roku §13.

ZGS 4.3, Shiba 28, ZGJI 107, ZGDJT 5d, ZGJT 5

4.4 纏脚纏手 *Ashi ni matoi, te ni matou.*

It trips up your feet, it ties your hands.

Heki 83 Main Case Comm.

ZGS 4.4, ZRKS 4.806, Shiba na, ZGJT 329

4.5 啞子喫蜜 *Asu mitsu o kissu.*

A mute is savoring honey.

ZGS 4.5, Shiba 28, ZGJI 107

4.6 拂蹤滅跡 *Ato o harai, ato o messu.*

Erase footprints, wipe out traces.

Heki 26 Main Case Comm., 61 Main Case *agyo*, 88 Intro. Shiba 50: 掃 instead of 拂.

ZGS 4.6, ZRKS 4.90, Shiba 50, ZGJI 107

4.7 作雨作晴 *Ame o nashi hare o nasu.*

To make it rain, to make it shine.

ZGS na, ZRKS 4.367, Shiba 42, ZGJI 108

4.8 雨洗風磨 *Ame ni arai kaze ni migaku.*

Washed by the rain, polished by the wind.

ZGS na, ZRKS 4.583, Shiba 31, ZGJI 108

4.9 知過必改 *Ayamachi o shitte kanarazu aratamu.*

Acknowledge your faults and you must become better.

Heki 4 Main Case *agyo*, 56 Main Case.

ZGS na, Shiba 53, ZGDJT 302

4.10 阿轆轆地 *A roku-roku ji.*

Turning, turning smoothly along.

Heki 39 Main Case Comm., 53 Main Case Comm. ZGS 4.208: 轉 instead of 阿.

ZGS 4.208, ZRKS 4.96, Shiba na, ZGJI 107, ZGJT 4 (阿) and 329 (轉)

4.11 預搔待痒 *Arakajime kaite kayugari o matsu.*

First he scratches, then waits for it to itch.

Heki 18 Main Case *agyo*, 29 Main Case *agyo*.

ZGS na, ZRKS 4.748, Shiba 70, ZGJI 108, ZGDJT 10c, ZGJT 461

4.12 闇室藏燈 *Anshitsu ni tō o kakusu.*

Keep a lamp lit in a dark room.

ZGS 4.7, ZRKS 4.881, Shiba 28, ZGJI 108, ZGDJT 13d

4.13 安心立命 *Anjin ritsumyō.*

Calm your heart and ground your life.

ZGS 4.8: 身 instead of 心, *Anjin ryūmyō.*

ZGS 4.8, ZRKS 4.58, Shiba 28, ZGJI 108, ZGJT 6, KZS #152

4.14 暗夜聞霜 *Anya ni shimo o kiku.*

On a dark night, listening to the frost.

Shiba 28: *Anya ni* instead of *Anya.*

ZGS 4.9, ZRKS 4., Shiba 28

4.15 家貧道富 *Ie mazushiushite michi tomu.*

The house is poor but the Way is wealthy.

ZGS na, ZRKS 4.647, Shiba 33, ZGJI 109, ZGDJT 161d, ZGJT 47

4.16 抱石投河 *Ishi o idaite kawa ni tōzu.*

To hug a rock and throw oneself into the river.

ZGS na, ZRKS 4.232, Shiba 65, ZGJI 109, ZGDJT 24c, ZGJT 421

4.17 一行三昧 *Ichigyō zammai.*

Single practice *samādhi*.

ZGS na, Shiba 29, ZGJI 110, ZGDJT 29c

4.18 一狀領過 *Ichijō ni ryōka su.*

With one verdict, he declares everyone guilty.

Heki 12 Verse *agyo*, 20 Main Case *agyo*, 22 Verse *agyo*, etc., MMK 29.

ZGS na, ZRKS 4.72, Shiba 29, ZGJI 111, ZGDJT 31b, ZGJT 17

4.19 一條白練 *Ichijō no byakuren.*

A single thread of white spun silk.

See also 5.16.

ZGS na, Shiba 29, ZGJI 111, ZGDJT 31c

4.20 一場懡㦬 *Ichijō no mora.*

A shameful scene.

Heki 28 Main Case Comm., 44 Main Case Comm., 55 Main Case *agyo*, etc.

ZGS 4.10, ZRKS 4.751, Shiba 29, ZGJI 111, ZGDJT 31d, ZGJT 17

4.21 一場漏逗 *Ichijō no rōtō.*

An embarrassing scene.

Heki 22 Main Case *agyo*, 63 Main Case *agyo*, 74 Verse *agyo*, MMK 29.

ZGS na, ZRKS 4.750, Shiba 30, ZGJI 111, ZGDJT 31d, ZGJT 17, SRZGK 198 and 1894; Shibayama 1984, 75

4.22 不消一捏 *Ichinetsu o shō sezu.*

It's not worth handling even once.

Heki 16 Verse Comm., 19 Main Case Comm., 25 Main Case Comm., etc. 不消 here is an idiom, "not worth it to…" (ZGJT 397).

ZGS na, ZRKS 4.125, Shiba 62, ZGJI 113, ZGJT 397 and 399

4.23 一網打就 *Ichimō ni tajū su.*

Catch all in one cast of the net.

Heki 52 Main Case *agyo*.

ZGS 4.11, ZRKS 4.801, Shiba 30, ZGJI 114, ZGDJT 36a, ZGJT 18

4.24 一家父子 *Ikka no fūshi.*

Father and son in one house.

ZGS na, ZRKS 4.352, Shiba 29, ZGJI 110

4.25 一水四見 *Issui shiken.*

One water, four ways of seeing.

Shiba 29 has 一見四水. "A god looks at water and sees a jewel, a human sees something to drink, a hungry ghost sees blood, a fish sees a place to dwell."

ZGS na, Shiba 29, ZGDJT 45a, ZGJI 112

4.26 一見便見 *Ikken benken.*

With one glance he sees the difference.

ZGS na, ZRKS 4.536, Shiba 29, ZGJI 110, ZGDJT 40c, KZS #344

4.27 一句道着 *Ikku ni dōjaku su.*

One word says it all.

Heki 76 Main Case *agyo*. Shiba 29: 著 instead of 着.

ZGS 4.12, ZRKS 4.530, Shiba na, ZGJI 110

4.28 一口呑盡 *Ikku ni donjin su.*

Swallow it all in one gulp.

Heki 11 Main Case *agyo*, 49 Verse *agyo*.

ZGS na, ZRKS 4.740, Shiba 29, ZGJI 110, ZGDJT 39c, ZGJT 16, KZS #387

4.29 一坑埋卻 *Ikkyō ni maikyaku su.*

Bury them all in one hole.

Heki 13 Verse *agyo*, 20 Main Case *agyo*, 21 Verse *agyo*, etc.

ZGS na, ZRKS 4.338, Shiba 29

4.30 一箭兩垜 *Issen ryōda.*

One arrow, two hits.

ZGS na, ZRKS 4.725, Shiba 30, ZGJI 112, ZGJT 17

4.31 獲得一箇 *Ikko o kakutoku su.*

Got one!

ZGS 4.13, Shiba na

4.32 一滴一凍 *Itteki ittō.*

One drop of water, one pellet of ice.

ZGS na, ZRKS 4.309, Shiba 30, ZGJI 112

4.33 一刀一斷 *Ittō ichidan.*

One slash [of the sword] cuts into one piece.

ZGS na, Shiba 30, ZGJI 113

4.34 一刀兩斷 *Ittō ryōdan.*

One slash [of the sword] cuts into two pieces.

Variant: 一刀兩段. *Heki* 63 Verse, 76 Main Case *agyo*, 94 Verse *agyo*.

ZGS na, ZRKS 4.262, Shiba 30, ZGJI 113, ZGJT 18, KZS #263

4.35 裂古破今 *Inishie o saki, ima o yaburu.*

It shatters the past and crushes the present.

ZGS na, ZRKS 4.346, Shiba 73, ZGJI 114

4.36 照古鑒今 *Inishie o terashi, ima o kangamu.*

It illuminates the past and reflects the present.

ZGS na, ZRKS 4.343, Shiba 46, ZGJI 114, KZS #288

4.37 亘古亘今 *Inishie ni watari, ima ni wataru.*

It covers the past, it covers the present.

ZGS 4.15, ZRKS 4.344, Shiba na, ZGJI 114, ZGDJT 309a, ZGJT 126, KZS #289

4.38 一拍雙泯 *Ippaku sōmin.*

One clap, two destroyed.

ZGS na, ZRKS 4.256, Shiba 30, ZGJI 113

4.39 一筆勾下 *Ippitsu ni kōge su.*

With one brushstroke he crosses it out.

Heki 44 Main Case *agyo*, 87 Verse *agyo*, 98 Verse *agyo*.

ZGS 4.14, ZRKS 4.767, Shiba na, ZGJI 113, ZGJT 18, KZS #425

4.40 一物也無 *Ichimotsu mo mata nashi.*

There is not even one thing.

Heki 31 Verse *agyo*.

ZGS na, ZRKS 4.649, Shiba 30, ZGJI 114, ZGJT 18

4.41 一理齊平 *Ichiri seihei.*

One principle, complete equality.

ZGS na, ZRKS 4.855, Shiba 30, ZGJI 114, ZGDJT 36d

4.42 坐井觀天 *I ni za shite ten o miru.*

Sitting inside a well, he sees the sky.

ZGS na, ZRKS 4.973, Shiba 42, ZGJI 108, ZGJT 153

4.43 不道不道 *Iwaji, iwaji.*

I won't say! I won't say!

Heki 55 Main Case.

ZGS 4.16, Shiba na, ZGDJT 917d

4.44 魚行水濁 *Uo yukeba mizu nigoru.*

Where the fish goes, the water is murky.

Heki 2 Main Case *agyo*,Verse *agyo*, 9 Verse *agyo*, etc.

ZGS 4.17, ZRKS 4.942, Shiba 37, ZGJI 116, ZGDJT 62d, ZGJT 90

4.45 烏龜鑽壁 *Uki kabe o kiru.*

The blind turtle butts against the wall.

After Shiba 31. ZGS 4.18: 鎖 instead of 鑽; *Uki kabe o tozasu*, "The blind turtle blocks up the wall."

ZGS 4.18, Shiba 31, ZGJI 115, ZGDJT 63a

4.46 烏黑鷺白 *U wa kuroku, ro wa shiroshi.*

Crows are black, herons are white.

KZS #123: *Karasu wa kuroku shi, sagi wa shiroshi.*

ZGS na, ZRKS 4.8, Shiba 31, ZGJI 116, KZS #123

4.47 騎牛求牛 *Ushi ni notte ushi o motomu.*

Riding an ox in search of an ox.

Heki 7 Main Case Comm., *Serenity* 57 Intro.

ZGS 4.19, ZRKS 4.214, Shiba 35, ZGJI 116, ZGJT 80, KZS #246

4.48 雲居羅漢 *Ungo no rakan.*

Cloud-dwelling arhat.

Heki 11 Main Case Comm., 23 Main Case *agyo*, 61 Verse *agyo*, 83 Verse Comm. The phrase "cloud-dwelling arhat" connotes one who is self-satisfied (ZGJI 116).

ZGS na, ZRKS 4.1001, Shiba 31, ZGJI 116, ZGDJT 73b

4.49 雲犀玩月 *Unsai tsuki o moteasobu.*

The cloud-rhinoceros plays with the ⌜moon⌝.

See also 14.245.

ZGS na, Shiba 31, ZGJI 116, ZGDJT 73b

4.50 雲門一曲 *Ummon no ikkyoku.*

⌜Ummon's⌝ tune.

A monk asked Ummon, "What is the Master's tune?" Ummon answered, "The 25th day of the last month of the year" (*Ummon kōroku* §8; T47: 545b).

ZGS na, Shiba 31, ZGDJT 76b

4.51 雲門餬餅 *Ummon kobyō.*

⌜Ummon's⌝ pastry bun.

Heki 77.

ZGS na, Shiba 31, ZGDJT 76c

4.52 雲遊萍寄 *Unyū hyōki.*

Clouds play, waterweeds drift.

ZGS na, Shiba 31, ZGJI 117, ZGDJT 79d

4.53 永字八法 *Eiji happō.*

The ⸢eight model brush strokes of the character *ei*⸣.

ZGS 4.20, Shiba na

4.54 回光返照 *Ekō henshō.*

Turn the light around, reflect back its radiance.

Rinzai-roku §21, *Heki* 93 Verse Comm.

ZGS na, Shiba 33, ZGJI 120

4.55 圓陀陀地 *En da-da ji.*

Serenely perfect.

Heki 43 Verse *agyo.*

ZGS na, ZRKS 4.425, Shiba 32, ZGJI 116, ZGJT 34

4.56 淵默雷轟 *En mokurai todoroku.*

Deep thunderous silence rumbles.

ZGS 4.21, Shiba 32, ZGJI 117

4.57 多添少減 *Ōki ni soe, sukunaki ni genzu.*

Add where there's lots, reduce where there's little.

ZGS na, ZRKS 4.307, Shiba 51, ZGJI 118, ZGDJT 127b, ZGJT 280

4.58 殃門添禍 *Ōmon ni wazawai o sou.*

To misfortune add disaster.

ZGS na, ZRKS 4.52, Shiba 32, ZGJI 118, ZGDJT 125c

4.59 横拈倒用 *Ōnen tōyō.*

Play with it sideways, use it upside down.

Heki 2 Main Case Comm., 76 Verse Comm.

ZGS na, ZRKS 4.965, Shiba 32, ZGJI 118, ZGDJT 122c, ZGJT 38

4.60 可惜呑了 *Oshimubeshi donryō suru koto o.*

What a pity! He swallowed it all!

Ryōkō-in: *Kashaku donryō seri.*

ZGS 4.22, Shiba na

4.61 一任和尚 *Oshō ni ichinin su.*

I leave everything up to the ⸢*oshō*⸣.

ZGS 4.23, ZRKS 4.860, Shiba na

4.62 和尚萬福 *Oshō banpuku.*

All health and happiness to the ⌜*oshō*⌝!

Heki 32 Main Case Comm.

ZGS 4.24, ZRKS 4.203, Shiba na, ZGJI 219, ZGDJT 129c

4.63 可恐可恐 *Osorubeshi, osorubeshi.*

Awful! Awful!

ZGS 4.25, Shiba na

4.64 迷己逐物 *Onore ni mayotte mono o ou.*

To be lost in oneself and chase after things.

Heki 46.

ZGS na, ZRKS 4.1011, Shiba 69, ZGJI 118, ZGDJT 130b, ZGJT 445

4.65 面熱汗下 *Omote nesshite ase kudaru.*

Face burns, sweat drips.

ZGS na, Shiba 69, ZGJI 210, ZGJT 446

4.66 知恩者少 *On o shiru mono sukunashi.*

Few are those who know gratitude.

MMK 34.

ZGS na, ZRKS 4.1008, Shiba 53, ZGJT 302

4.67 以恩報讎 *On o motte ada ni mukuyu.*

He returns gratitude for hate.

ZGS 4.26, Shiba na

4.68 穩密田地 *Onmitsu no denji.*

The field of magnificent ease.

Heki 16 Intro.

ZGS na, Shiba 32, ZGDJT 132b, ZGJT 39

4.69 海晏河清 *Kaian kasei.*

The sea is calm, the rivers are pure.

Heki 18 Main Case, 24 Verse *agyo*, 31 Verse *agyo*.

ZGS 4.27, ZRKS 4.13, Shiba 33, ZGJI 121, ZGDJT 21a, ZGJT 55

4.70 蓋天蓋地 *Gaiten gaichi.*

It covers heaven, it covers earth.

Heki 3 Intro., 5 Main Case Comm., 7 Verse Comm., 22 Main Case Comm., etc.

ZGS 4.28, Shiba na, ZGJI 121, ZGDJT 143c, ZGJT 57

4.71 卻較些子 *Kaette shashi ni atareri.*

He's on the mark.

Heki 1 Main Case *agyo*, Verse *agyo*; 18 Main Case *agyo*, etc.

ZGS 4.29, ZRKS 4.181, Shiba 36, ZGJI 121, ZGDJT 148b, KZS #226

4.72 卻得禮謝 *Kaette raisha o etari.*

Instead, I received a thank you.

ZGS 4.30, Shiba na

4.73 無處回避 *Kaihi suru tokoro nashi.*

No room to twist away.

ZGS na, ZRKS 4.817, Shiba 68, KZS #409

4.74 海蠙含月 *Kaihin tsuki o fukumu.*

The oyster swallows the moonlight.

See *Heki* 90. 海蠙 is actually a sea clam. See 「Moon」.

ZGS na, ZRKS 4.364, Shiba 33

4.75 灰頭土面 *Kaitō domen.*

Ashes on his head, dirt on his face.

Heki 43 Verse Comm.

ZGS 4.31, ZRKS 4.635, Shiba 33, ZGJI 120, ZGDJT 144d, ZGJT 53

4.76 疥癩野干 *Kairai no yakan.*

Scabby leprous animal!

ZGS 4.32, Shiba na

4.77 怪力亂神 *Kai riki ran shin.*

Weird things, feats of strength, disorder, spirits.

Analects VII, 20.

ZGS na, ZRKS 4.830, Shiba 33

4.78 成窠成窟 *Ka o nashi kutsu o nasu.*

Building a nest, making a den.

Heki 3 Intro.

ZGS na, ZRKS 4.857, Shiba 48, ZGJI 120, ZGJT 223

4.79 以蝦爲目 *Ka o motte me to nasu.*

Use shrimps as eyes.

According to the *Laṅkāvatāra sūtra* 7, because the sea urchin has no eyes, it follows shrimps in order to find food (ZGJT 8). Other explanations substitute jellyfish.

ZGS 4.33, ZRKS 4.873, Shiba na, ZGJI 120, ZGDJT 133d, ZGJT 8

4.80 撈蝦摝蜆 *Ka o rō shi, ken o roku su.*

He sifts for shrimp, he scoops for clams.

ZGS na, ZRKS 4.330, Shiba 74, ZGJI 120, ZGJT 492

4.81 瓦解氷消 *Gakai hyōshō.*

The tiles shatter, the ice melts.

Heki 11 Main Case *agyo*, 32 Verse Comm., MMK 19. ZRKS 4.60: *gage* instead of *gakai*.

ZGS na, ZRKS 4.60, Shiba 33, ZGJI 120, ZGJT 51, KZS #153

4.82 崖崩石裂 *Gake kuzure, ishi saku.*

Cliffs crumble, rocks split.

Heki 50 Main Case *agyo*.

ZGS na, ZRKS 4.208, Shiba 34, ZGJI 212

4.83 隱而彌露 *Kakuseba iyo-iyo arawaru.*

The more you hide it, the more it is exposed.

ZGS na, ZRKS 4.131, Shiba 30, KZS #199

4.84 廓然無聖 *Kakunen mushō.*

Vast emptiness, nothing holy.

Heki 1 Main Case, 67 Verse Comm.

ZGS na, Shiba 34, ZGJI 121, ZGDJT 154a, ZGJT 59

4.85 愕然平伏 *Gakuzen to shite heifuku su.*

Astonished, he prostrates himself.

ZGS 4.34, Shiba na

4.86 囫地一聲 *Kaji issei.*

A shout, "HA!"

ZGS na, Shiba 32, ZGJI 119, ZGDJT 133a

4.87 禍事禍事 *Kaji, kaji.*

Disaster! Disaster!

Rinzai-roku §6.

ZGS 4.35, ZRKS 4.81, Shiba 33, ZGJI 120, ZGJT 49, KZS #165

4.88 架上加杻 *Kajō ni chū o kuwau.*

He adds shackles to a ⌜stock⌝.

ZGS 4.36, ZRKS 4.293, Shiba 33, ZGJI 119, ZGJT 46 (variant)

4.89 借風揚帆 *Kaze o karite ho o agu.*

Raise a sail to catch the wind.

ZGS na, ZRKS 4.898, Shiba 44, ZGJI 122, ZGJT 192

4.90 見風使帆 *Kaze o mite ho o tsukau.*

Watch the wind to handle the sail.

Heki 65 Verse Comm.

ZGS 4.37, ZRKS 4.371, Shiba 38, ZGJI 122, ZGJT 65 (variant), KZS #294

4.91 因風吹火 *Kaze ni yotte hi o fuku.*

Use the wind to fan the flames.

Heki 27 Main Case Comm., 27 Intro., 34 Main Case *agyo.*

ZGS na, ZRKS 4.107, Shiba 30, ZGJI 122, ZGJT 28, KZS #186

4.92 無風起浪 *Kaze naki ni nami o okosu.*

No wind, and still he stirs up waves.

MMK Preface, 41. *Heki* 4 Main Case *agyo,* 18 Main Case Comm., 42 Main Case *agyo*, etc.

ZGS 4.38, ZRKS 4.385, Shiba na, ZGJI 122, ZGDJT 161b, ZGJT 441

4.93 風行草偃 *Kaze yukeba kusa fusu.*

Where the wind goes, the grass bends.

Heki 6 Verse Comm., 43 Verse *agyo*, 45 Main Case *agyo*, etc. ZGS 4.39: *noefusu* instead of *fusu.*

ZGS 4.39, ZRKS 4.380, Shiba 64, ZGJI 122, ZGDJT 161b, ZGJT 406

4.94 家賊難防 *Kazoku fusegigatashi.*

It's hard to guard against a ｢thief｣ from within.

ZGS na, ZRKS 4.115, Shiba 33, ZGJI 119, ZGDJT 161d, ZGJT 47, KZS #193

4.95 可知禮也 *Kachi raiya.*

One should know propriety.

ZGS 4.40, ZRKS 4.929, Shiba na, ZGJT 42

4.96 黠兒落節 *Katsuji rakusetsu.*

It's the smart operator who bungles it.

Heki 40 Intro.

ZGS na, ZRKS 4.419, Shiba 34, ZGJI 122, ZGJT 62, KZS #311

4.97 闔國咸知 *Kakkoku mina shiru.*

The entire country knows.

ZGS na, ZRKS 4.547, Shiba 41, KZS #352

4.98 葛藤老漢 *Kattō no rōkan.*

An old fellow full of complications.

Heki 51 Verse *agyo.*

ZGS na, ZRKS 4.408, Shiba 34, ZGJI 122, ZGDJT 166b, ZGJT 62

4.99 活潑潑地 *Kappatsu-patsuji.*

Briskly. Lively.

Variant: *Kappappatchi. Rinzai-roku* §19. *Heki* 49 Verse *agyo*, 60 Main Case Comm., 98 Verse Comm.

ZGS 4.41, ZRKS 4.95, Shiba 34, ZGJI 122, ZGDJT 166d, ZGJT 61, KZS #174, ZD #38

4.100 畫餅充飢 *Gabyō ue ni atsu.*

Satisfy hunger with a picture of pastry.

ZGS na, ZRKS 4.648, Shiba 33, ZGJI 120, ZGDJT 169b, ZGJT 52

4.101 續鳧截鶴 *Kamo o tsugi tsuru o kiru.*

Extending the legs of the duck, cutting the legs of the crane.

ZGS 4.269: *Fu* instead of *kamo. Chuang-tzu,* Outer chapter 3 "Webbed Toes": "Long does not imply excess and short does not imply lack. A duck's legs are short, but to stretch them would be a sorry matter. A crane's legs are long, but to cut them shorter would be sad."

ZGS 4.269, ZRKS 4.167, Shiba 51, ZGJI 123, ZGDJT 171a, ZGJT 276

4.102 刮皮見骨 *Kawa o kezutte hone o miru.*

He cuts away the skin to look at the bones.

ZRKS 4.482: 血 blood instead of 骨 bones.

ZGS na, ZRKS 4.482, Shiba 34, ZGJI 123, ZGDJT 173d, ZGJT 61

4.103 粘皮着骨 *Kawa ni nenji, hone ni tsuku.*

Glued to the skin, stuck to the bones.

Heki 72 Main Case *agyo,* 78 Main Case Comm. ZGJI 123: 著 instead of 着.

ZGS na, ZRKS 4.238, Shiba 59, ZGJI 123, ZGDJT 173d, ZGJT 371

4.104 函蓋相應 *Kangai aiōzu.*

Box and lid fit exactly together.

ZGS na, ZRKS 4.350, Shiba 34, ZGJI 124, ZGJT 64

4.105 函蓋乾坤 *Kangai kenkon.*

⌜Heaven and earth⌝ are box and lid.

Heki 14 Main Case *agyo*, 27 Main Case Comm., 70 Verse *agyo*, etc.

ZGS 4.43, ZRKS 4.919, Shiba 34, ZGJI 124, ZGJT 64

4.106 鑑在機前 *Kan ⌜ki⌝zen ni ari.*

See what is prior to any motion of mind.

Heki 74 Verse Comm. See also 8.304.

ZGS na, ZRKS 4.275, Shiba 35, ZGJI 125, ZGDJT 176a, ZGJT 72, KZS #268

4.107 陥虎之機 *Kanko no ki.*

A trap for a tiger.

Heki 10 Main Case *agyo*, 13 Main Case Comm., 66 Intro and Main Case *agyo*, etc.

ZGS 4.44, ZRKS 4.736, Shiba 35, ZGJI 124, ZGDJT 179a, ZGJT 67, KZS #385

4.108 刺破眼睛 *Ganzei o shiha su.*

Slash the eyeballs.

Heki 5 Verse *agyo*.

ZGS na, ZRKS 4.911, Shiba 43, ZGJI 125, ZGDJT 183c, ZGJT 174 (variant), KZS #434

4.109 突出眼睛 *Ganzei o tosshutsu su.*

He stares goggle-eyed.

Heki 7 Main Case *agyo*. Shiba 35, ZGDJT 183c: 眼睛突出.

ZGS 4.45 ZRKS 4.735, Shiba 35 and 58, ZGJI 125, ZGDJT 183c, ZGJT 73, KZS #384

4.110 眼横鼻直 *Gannō bichoku.*

My eyes lie sideways, my nose stands straight.

ZGS 4.42, ZRKS 4.6, Shiba 35, ZGJI 125, ZGDJT 187b, ZGJT 112, KZS #121

4.111 頑石點頭 *Ganseki tentō su.*

The hard stones nod their heads.

Monk Tao-sheng 道生 (?–434) was ostracized for teaching there were no beings who could not attain Buddhahood. Living in the mountains, he preached to the stones who nodded their heads (ZGDJT 183d).

ZGS 4.46, Shiba 35, ZGDJT 183d

4.112 據款結案 *Kan ni yotte an ni kessu.*

Mete out punishment based on the confession.

Shiba 36, ZGDJT 186d: *an o kessu* instead of *an ni kessu. Heki* 1 Verse Comm, 10 Main Case Comm., 20 Verse Comm., etc. MMK Postscript.

ZGS 4.47, ZRKS 4.32, Shiba 36, ZGJI 124, ZGDJT 186d, ZGJT 89

4.113 官馬相踏 *Kanba aifumu.*

Officers' horses stamp at each other.

Rinzai-roku §30.

ZGS 4.48, ZRKS 4.436, Shiba 34, ZGJI 123, ZGDJT 187d, ZGJT 64, KZS #319

4.114 勘破了也 *Kanpa ryō ya.*

You have seen right to the core.

Heki 4 Verse *agyo,* 6 Verse, 29 Main Case, 84 Verse, 97 Verse.

ZGS 4.49, ZRKS 4.466, Shiba 34, ZGJI 124, ZGDJT 187d

4.115 寒毛卓竪 *Kanmō takuju su.*

Shivering with fear, his hair stood on end.

Heki 2 Verse *agyo,* 77 Main Case Comm., 95 Verse *agyo.*

ZGS 4.50, ZRKS 4.481, Shiba 35, ZGJI 124, ZGDJT 189d, ZGJT 67, KZS #337 (variant)

4.116 絕機絕解 *⌜Ki⌝ o zesshi, ge o zessu.*

Beyond doing, beyond understanding.

Heki 40 Verse Comm.

ZGS na, ZRKS 4.68, Shiba 49, ZGJI 127

4.117 見機而變 *⌜Ki⌝ o mite henzu.*

Watch and change with his moves.

Heki 1 Main Case Comm.

ZGS na, ZRKS 4.390, Shiba 38, ZGJT 106, KZS #299

4.118 飲氣呑聲 *Ki o nomi, koe o nomu.*

He chokes on his anger, he gags when he speaks.

Heki 2 Main Case Comm., 8 Verse *agyo,* 10 Intro., 95 Verse *agyo.*

ZGS na, ZRKS 4.187, Shiba 30, ZGJI 126, ZGJT 28, KZS #230

4.119 弄鬼眼睛 *Ki gansei o rō su.*

He bugs out devil eyes.

Heki 5 Main Case *agyo.*

ZGS na, ZRKS 4.907, Shiba 74, ZGJI 126, ZGDJT 232c, ZGJT 490

4.120 鬼哭神悲 *Ki koku shi, shin kanashimu.*

The devils mourn and the gods grieve.

ZGS na, ZRKS 4.676, Shiba 35

4.121 歸家穩坐 *Kika onza.*

Return home and sit at ease.

Heki 1 Main Case Comm., 14 Main Case Comm.

ZGS na, Shiba 35, ZGDJT 193d

4.122 葵花向日 *Kika hi ni mukau.*

The sunflower faces the sun.

ZGS na, Shiba 35, ZGJI 127, ZGDJT 194c, ZGJT 78

4.123 鬼神潜跡 *Kishin ato o hisomu.*

Devils and gods hide their traces.

ZGS 4.51, Shiba na

4.124 機鋒辛辣 *⌜Ki⌝hō shinratsu.*

His probe is sharp and stinging.

ZGS 4.52, Shiba na

4.125 君暴民亡 *Kimi bō ni shite tami horobu.*

When the lord is violent, the people will perish.

ZGS 4.53, Shiba na,

4.126 照顧脚下 *Kyakka o shōko seyo.*

Turn the light onto your own feet.

ZGS na, Shiba 46, ZGDJT 209b

4.127 脚下泥深 *Kyakka doro fukashi.*

Underfoot the mud is deep.

Heki 36 Verse *agyo.*

ZGS 4.54, Shiba na, ZGJI 290, ZGJT 84

4.128 脚頭脚底 *Kyakutō kyakutei.*

At this step, at that step.

Heki 29 Verse *agyo.*

ZGS 4.55, Shiba na

4.129 逆風張帆 *Gyakufū ni ho o haru.*

Against the wind he spreads his sail.

ZGS na, ZRKS 4.854, Shiba 36, ZGJI 128, ZGJT 85

4.130 久貧乍富 *Kyūhin tachimachi tomu.*

Long poor, suddenly rich.

ZGS na, ZRKS 4.59, Shiba 36, ZGJI 128, ZGJT 85

4.131 久立珍重 *Kyūryū chinchō.*

[I've kept you] standing a long time. Thank you.

Rinzai-roku §1, §6.

ZGS na, Shiba 36, ZGJI 128, ZGDJT 213c, ZGJT 85

4.132 休去歇去 *Kyū shi sari, kesshi sare.*

Stop, cease.

Heki 40 Intro., 97 Verse *agyo*.

ZGS na, Shiba 36, ZGJI 128, ZGDJT 209d

4.133 行住坐臥 *Gyōjū zaga.*

Walking, standing, sitting, lying.

Heki 23 Main Case Comm., 25 Main Case Comm., 47 Intro., etc.

ZGS 4.56, ZRKS 4.623, Shiba 37, ZGJI 129, ZGDJT 223d, KZS #371

4.134 去死十分 *Kyōshi jūbun.*

Ten millimeters away from death.

Heki 28 Main Case *agyo*, 73 Main Case agyo. ZGS 4.57 has 去死充分 but this is a mistake. SRZGK #1392: 十分 ten *fun* is a unit of measurement equal to 一寸, roughly one inch (see「*Fun*」). On a boat, you are one inch away from a watery death.

ZGS 4.57, Shiba na, ZGJI 129, SRZGK #1392

4.135 玉振金聲 *Gyokushin kinsei.*

Jeweled speech, golden voice.

Heki 73 Verse *agyo*: 金聲玉振.

ZGS na, ZRKS 4.656, Shiba 37, ZGJI 130

4.136 承虛接響 *Kyo o ukete hibiki o sessu.*

Listen to silence, follow echoes.

After ZGJT 213.

ZGS na, ZRKS 4.145, Shiba 45, ZGJI 129, ZGJT 213

4.137 當局者迷 *Kyoku ni ataru mono wa mayou.*

His turn and he doesn't know what to do.

Heki 38 Verse *agyo*. Paired with 傍人有眼, "The bystander has the eye." See 4.564 below.

ZGS na, ZRKS 4.236, Shiba 56, ZGJT 336, KZS #258

4.138 虛心坦懷 *Kyoshin tankai.*

Mind empty, heart open.

ZGS na, Shiba 36

4.139 虛靈不昧 *Kyorei fumai.*

Mind empty, no darkness.

ZGS na, Shiba 36

4.140 有擒有縱 *Kin ari jū ari.*

There is taking hold, there is letting go.

Heki 56 Main Case *agyo*, 62 Intro.

ZGS na, ZRKS 4.320, Shiba 70, ZGJI 131, KZS #320

4.141 銀山鐵壁 *Ginzan teppeki.*

Silver mountain, iron wall.

Heki Preface, 42 Intro., 45 Main Case Comm., 57 Intro.

ZGS 4.58, ZRKS 4.16, Shiba 37, ZGJI 131, ZGDJT 236c, ZGJT 95, KZS #1132

4.142 錦上鋪花 *Kinjō ni hana o shiku.*

Spread flowers on brocade.

Heki 21 Intro., 68 Main Case *agyo.*

ZGS 4.59, ZRKS 4.291, Shiba 37, ZGJI 131, ZGJT 95, KZS #272

4.143 推空聽響 *Kū o oshite hibiki o kiku.*

Push open emptiness and listen to the sound.

Variant: 推窓聽響 *Mado o oshite hibiki of kiku,* "Open the window and listen to the sound."

ZGS na, ZRKS 4.717, Shiba 47, ZGJI 132

4.144 空手還鄉 *Kūshu ni shite kyō ni kaeru.*

Empty-handed I return home.

ZGS na, Shiba 38, ZGJI 132, ZGDJT 242d

4.145 當空霹靂 *Kū ni ataru hekireki.*

A thunderclap right out of emptiness.

Heki 37 Intro.

ZGS na, ZRKS 4.761, Shiba 56, ZGJI 132

4.146 句下無私 *Kuge watakushi nashi.*

In his words, there is nothing personal.

ZGS na, Shiba 37, ZGJI 132, ZGDJT 246a

4.147 句句相投 *Ku-ku ai tōzu.*

Every word right on.

Heki 24 Main Case Comm. 50 Intro., 68 Intro.

ZGS na, ZRKS 4.591, Shiba 37, ZGJI 132, ZGDJT 246C

4.148 滯句者迷 *Ku ni todokōru mono wa mayou.*

Bound up in words, a person gets lost.

MMK 37 Verse, *Heki* 13 Verse Comm.

ZGS na, ZRKS 4., Shiba 53, ZGJI 132, ZGDJT 240a, ZGJT 289, KZS #129 (variant)

4.149 藥多病甚 *Kusuri ōku shite yamai hanahadashi.*

The more the medicine, the worse the sickness.

ZGS na, ZRKS 4.672, Shiba 70, ZGJI 133, ZGJT 457

4.150 拏雲攫霧 *Kumo o torae, kiri o tsukamu.*

Seizing clouds, grabbing mist.

Heki 4 Main Case *agyo*, 48 Verse Comm. ZGJI 134: *tsunzaki* instead of *torae.*

ZGS na, ZRKS 4.67, Shiba 52, ZGJI 134, ZGDJT 253b, ZGJT 285

4.151 句裏藏鋒 *Kuri ni hokosaki o kakusu.*

A razor blade hidden in words.

ZGS na, ZRKS 4.123, Shiba 37, ZGJI 132, ZD #42 (variant)

4.152 句裏呈機 *Kuri ni ⌜ki⌝ o tei su.*

His words reveal his sharpness.

Heki 9 Verse, 26 Main Case *agyo*, 50 Verse Comm, 70 Main Case Comm.

ZGS na, ZRKS 4.746, Shiba 37, ZGJI 132, ZGDJT 254a, ZGJT 96, KZS #391

4.153 句裏縛殺 *Kuri ni bakusatsu seraru.*

All tied up in words.

ZGS na, ZRKS 4.707, Shiba 37

4.154 苦屈苦屈 *Kukutsu, kukutsu.*

What suffering! What suffering!

ZGS 4.60, ZRKS 4.721, Shiba na, ZGJI 132, ZGJT 97

4.155 口似磉盤 *Kuchi sōban ni nitari.*

His mouth is like a stone pedestal.

ZGS na, ZRKS 4.421, Shiba 40, ZGJI 133, ZGDJT 249c, ZGJT 124, KZS #312

4.156 口是禍門 *Kuchi wa kore kamon.*

The mouth is the gate of misfortune.

ZGS na, ZRKS 4.77, Shiba 40, ZGJT 124

4.157 口吧吧地 *Kuchi ha-ha ji.*

His mouth goes "Blah, blah!"

ZGS na, ZRKS 4.405, Shiba 40, ZGJI 133

4.158 開口看膽 *Kuchi o hirakeba tan o miru.*

If you open your mouth, we'll see your insides.

Heki 3 Verse *agyo*, MMK 7. ZGJI 133: 見 instead of 看; *tan o arawasu* instead of *tan o miru.*

ZGS 4.61, ZRKS 4.584, Shiba na, ZGJI 133, ZGDJT 249d, ZGJT 56

159 隔靴搔痒 *Kutsu o hedatete kayugari o kaku.*

Wearing shoes, he scratches his itchy foot.

MMK Preface, ZGJI 134: 爬 instead of 搔.

ZGS 4.62, ZRKS 4.833, Shiba 34, ZGJI 134, ZGJT 59

4.160 如愚若魯 *Gu no gotoku, ro no gotoshi.*

Like an idiot, like a fool.

ZGS 4.63, Shiba na

4.161 驚郡動衆 *Gun o odorokashi, shū o ugokasu.*

He shocks the crowds, he moves the masses.

Heki 11 Intro.

ZGS na, ZRKS 4.331, Shiba 37, KZS #284

4.162 君子可八 *Kunshi kahachi.*

The superior person's eight proficiencies.

In Confucianism, the eight qualities of the superior person are humanity, righteousness, ritual, wisdom, filial piety, fraternity, loyalty, and faithfulness (ZGJI 134, ZGDJT 255b).

ZGS 4.64, Shiba 38, ZGJI 134, ZGDJT 255b

4.163 君子一言 *Kunshi no ichigen.*

To the superior person, one word.

This verse can also be interpreted to mean "One word from a superior person." However, 君子一言 is used as part of a couplet 君子一言, 快馬一鞭 "To the superior person, one word; to the superior horse, one flick." There are several variations (快人一言, 好漢一言), all of which describe the keen intuition of a person who understands everything from just a hint (as in 4.174).

ZGS 4.65, ZRKS 4.409, Shiba na.

4.164 傾湫倒嶽 *Keishū tōgaku.*

Upset lakes, overturn mountains.

Heki 63 Intro., 97 Intro.

ZGS 4.66, ZRKS 4.813, Shiba 38, ZGJI 134, ZGDJT 260b, ZGJT 103

4.165 雞頭鳳尾 *Keitō hōbi.*

The head of a chicken and the tail of a phoenix.

ZGS na, ZRKS 4.616, Shiba 38, ZGJI 135

4.166 齩定牙關 *Gekan o kōtei su.*

He locks shut his teeth and jaws.

ZGS na, ZRKS 4.420, Shiba 41, ZGJI 120

4.167 逼塞乾坤 *Kenkon ni hissoku su.*

It's completely dissolved into ⌜heaven and earth⌝.

Heki 76 Intro.

ZGS na, ZRKS 4.20, Shiba 62, ZGJI 171, KZS #128

4.168 玄沙道底 *Gensha iu tei.*

As ⌜Gensha⌝ said.

ZGS 4.67, ZRKS 4.980, Shiba na, ZGJI 136

4.169 拳來趯報 *Kenrai tekihō.*

If he comes with a fist, return with a kick.

Alternative reading: *Kenshi kitareba teki o motte hōzu.* KZS #321: *kenji* instead of *kenshi.*

ZGS 4.68, ZRKS 4.444, Shiba na, ZGJI 136, ZGJT 108, KZS #321

4.170 巻舒齊唱 *Kenjo hitoshiku tonau.*

His speech both grips and liberates.

Heki 5 Intro. See also 8.234.

ZGS na, Shiba 39, ZGJI 135, ZGDJT 287a, ZGJT 107

4.171 現成公案 *Genjō kōan.*

An on-the-spot kōan.

Heki 51 Intro., 63 Verse *agyo.*

ZGS na, Shiba 39, ZGJI 137, ZGDJT 289a, ZGJT 112

4.172 劍刄上事 *Kenninjō no ji.*

A matter decided by ⌜sword blade⌝.

Rinzai-roku §6.

ZGS na, Shiba 39

4.173 有功者賞 *Kō aru mono wa shō su.*

Reward those who have merit.

Heki 97 Verse.

ZGS na, ZRKS 4.39, Shiba 70, ZGJT 29

4.174 舉一明三 *Koichi myōsan.*

For each one raised, understand three.

Analects VII, 8. *Heki* 1 Intro., 13 Intro., 21 Intro., etc.

ZGS na, ZRKS 4.976, Shiba 36, ZGJI 129, ZGDJT 302b, ZGJT 119

4.175 弄巧成拙 *Kō o rō shite setsu to naru.*

Be smart and make a fool of yourself.

ZGS na, ZRKS 4.170, Shiba 74, ZGJI 140, ZGDJT 328d, ZGJT 491

4.176 不知好悪 *Kōo o shirazu.*

He does not know good from bad.

Heki 20 Main Case Comm.: 識 instead of 知.

ZGS na, ZRKS 4.539., Shiba 63, ZGJT 399

4.177 驅耕奪飢 *Kō o kari, ki o ubau.*

He deprives the farmer and steals from the starving.

See 8.147.

ZGS na, ZRKS 4.922, Shiba 38, ZGJI 141

4.178 光陰可惜 *Kōin oshimubeshi.*

Be watchful of your time.

See ⌜light and dark⌝.

ZGS 4.69, Shiba na, ZGJT 126

4.179 光陰如箭 *Kōin ya no gotoshi.*

Time flies like an arrow.

See ⌜light and dark⌝.

ZGS 4.70, ZRKS 4.516, Shiba na

4.180 紅旗閃爍 *Kōki senshaku.*

The red flag waves and flutters.

ZGJI 141: *senreki* instead of *senshaku.*

ZGS 4.71, ZRKS 4.824, Shiba 40, ZGJI 141, KZS #413

4.181 好箇消息 *Kōko no ⌜shōsoku⌝.*

What good news!

Heki 16 Main Case Comm., 25 Verse *agyo*, 46 Main Case *agyo*, etc.

ZGS 4.72, ZRKS 4.461, Shiba 40, ZGJT 131

4.182 向上些子 *⌜Kōjō⌝ no shashi.*

The ultimate point.

ZGS 4.73, Shiba 40

4.183 高祖入關 *Kōso kan ni iru.*

⌜Kao-tsu⌝ enters the land within the passes.

ZGS 4.74, Shiba 41

4.184 勾賊破家 *Kōzoku haka.*

Bring a ⌜thief⌝ into your home and he steals your house.

Heki 42 Main Case *agyo*, 54 Main Case *agyo*, 68 Main Case *agyo*, etc. *Rinzai-roku* §24.

ZGS 4.75, ZRKS 4.117, Shiba 40, ZGJI 139, ZGDJT 318a, ZGJT 125, KZS #194

4.185 入鄉隨俗 *Gō ni itte zoku ni shitagau.*

When you enter a village, follow its customs.

ZGS 4.76, ZRKS 4.365, Shiba na

4.186 公驗分明 *Kōken funmyō.*

Authentic proof of identity.

ZGDJT 246: *kugen* instead of *kōken*; 公驗 is (a) a government certification of a monk's precept ordination, (b) a deed of property. ZGJT 125: travel passport.

ZGS na, ZRKS 4.561, Shiba 40, ZGJI 139, ZGJT 125 (公驗), ZGDJT 246

4.187 恰恰相應 *Kō-kō aiōzu.*

They match each other perfectly.

ZGS na, ZRKS 4.370, Shiba 40, ZGJI 140

4.188 硬剥剥地 *Kō haku-haku ji.*

Claws can't even scratch the surface.

Heki 59 Verse *agyo*.

ZGS na, ZRKS 4.97, Shiba 41, ZGJI 141, ZGDJT 323c, ZGJT 138

4.189 改頭換面 *Kōbe o aratame, omote o kau.*

Replace your head, change your face.

Heki 4 Main Case *agyo*. ZGS 4.191: *zu* instead of *kōbe*.

ZGS 4.191, ZRKS 4.500, Shiba 33, ZGJI 183, ZGJT 54, KZS #342

4.190 擎頭戴角 *Kōbe o sasage, tsuno o itadaku.*

It's rearing its head, it's got horns!

Heki 51 Main Case *agyo*, 81 Verse *agyo*.

ZGS na, ZRKS 4.800, Shiba 38, ZGJI 183, ZGDJT 324c, ZGJT 103, KZS #402

4.191 頭正尾正 *Kōbe tadashiku, o tadashi.*

The head is right, the tail is right.

Heki 56 Main Case *agyo*, *Serenity* 87 Main Case.

ZGS 4.77, ZRKS 4.49, Shiba na, ZGJI 183, ZGDJT 639a, ZGJT 344, KZS #180

4.192 迷頭認影 *Kōbe ni mayoi, kage o tomu.*

He's lost his head, he believes in reflections.

ZGDJT 324c: *mitomu* instead of *tomu*. *Heki* 15 Verse. See ⌜Yajñadatta⌝.

ZGS na, ZRKS 4.228, Shiba 69, ZGDJT 324c, ZGJT 446, KZS #256

4.193 古鑑高懸 *Kokan takaku kaku.*

The ancient mirror is mounted up high.

Heki 74 Intro.

ZGS na, ZRKS 4.904, Shiba 39, ZGJI 137

4.194 五逆聽雷 *Gogyaku rai o kiku.*

The one who committed the ⌜five grave offenses⌝ has heard the thunder.

Shiba 40: It is said that one who commits the five grave offenses will be struck by lightning.

ZGS na, ZRKS 4.680, Shiba 40, ZGJI 139, ZGJT 121, KZS #374

4.195 咬破虛空 *Kokū o kōha su.*

Chew emptiness to pieces.

See Daitō Kokushi's death verse (Kraft 1992, 169–70).

ZGS 4.78, Shiba 40

4.196 虛空打橛 *Kokū ni ketsu o ta su.*

He drives a stake into empty space.

ZGS na, ZRKS 4.863, Shiba 36, ZGJI 138, ZGJT 119

4.197 虛空低頭 *Kokū teitō.*

Emptiness bows its head.

ZGS 4.79, Shiba 36

4.198 黑白二件 *Kokubyaku niken.*

Two cases—black and white.

ZGS 4.80, Shiba na

4.199 擧手動足 *Koshu dōsoku.*

He raises his hands and moves his feet.

ZGS 4.81, ZRKS 4.627, Shiba na, ZGJI 129

4.200 捋虎鬚也 *Koshu o nazuru ya.*

He strokes the tiger's whiskers.

Heki 4 Main Case *agyo*, 26 Verse.

ZGS na, ZRKS 4.102, Shiba 71, ZGJT 469 var, KZS #182

4.201 似鶻捉鳩 *Kotsu no hato o torauru ni nitari.*

Like a falcon striking a pigeon.

Heki 3 Verse Comm., 38 Main Case *agyo*, 77 Intro.

ZGS na, Shiba 43

4.202 鶻眼鷹睛 *Kotsugan yōsei.*

Eagle's eyes, falcon's vision.

ZGS na, ZRKS 4.618, Shiba 41, ZGJI 143, ZGJT 144

4.203 乞兒鬪富 *Kotsuji tomi o tatakawasu.*

Beggars boast about who's richer.

ZGJI 143: *tatakawashimu* instead of *tatakawasu.*

ZGS na, ZRKS 4.641, Shiba 41, ZGJI 143

4.204 事起叮寧 *Koto wa teinei yori okoru.*

Things arise out of politeness.

ZRKS 4.403n: 親甚深卻發恨 "When intimacy deepens, it turns to resentment." Shiba 44, ZRKS 4.403 have 嚀 instead of 寧.

ZGS 4.82, ZRKS 4.403, Shiba 44, ZGJI 143, KZS #304

4.205 言猶在耳 *Koto nao mimi ni ari.*

The words are still in my ears.

Heki 4 Verse *agyo*, 14 Verse *agyo*, 16 Verse *agyo*, etc.

ZGS na, ZRKS 4.510, Shiba 39, ZGJT 111, KZS #347

4.206 詞窮理盡 *Kotoba kiwamari ri tsuku.*

Words depleted, reason spent.

ZGS na, ZRKS 4.715, Shiba 43

4.207 此語最毒 *Kono go mottomo doku nari.*

These words are a deadly poison.

Heki 49 Main Case *agyo.*

ZGS 4.83, ZRKS 4.488, Shiba na, ZGJI 143

4.208 箇自了漢 *Kono jiryō no kan.*

This self-satisfied fellow.

ZGS 4.84, Shiba 40

4.209 這白拈賊 *Kono byakunen zoku.*

This outrageous ⌜thief⌝.

ZGS 4.85, Shiba na

4.210 露箇面目 *Kono menmoku o arawasu.*

It reveals this face.

Heki 16 Main Case Comm.

ZGS na, ZRKS 4.741, Shiba 73, KZS #386

4.211 這野狐精 *Kono yakozei.*

This ⌜wild fox⌝ spirit.

Heki 1 Main Case *agyo*, 8 Verse *agyo*, 22 Main Case *agyo*, 93 Main Case.

ZGS 4.86, ZRKS 4.155, Shiba na, ZGJI 143, ZGDJT 792c, ZGJT 190, KZS #209

4.212 胡人入漢 *Kohito kan ni iru.*

Barbarians have entered the empire of the Han.

Shiba 39: *kojin* instead of *kohito*.

ZGS 4.87, ZRKS 4.843, Shiba 39, ZGJI 137

4.213 枯木寒灰 *Koboku kanpai.*

Dead tree, cold ashes.

ZGS na, ZRKS 4.47, Shiba 39, ZGJI 138, ZGJT 116

4.214 枯木龍吟 *Koboku ryūgin.*

In the ⌜withered⌝ tree, the dragon hums.

ZGS na, Shiba 39

4.215 思之在之 *Kore o omou koto kore ni ari.*

To think of it—is it.

ZGS na, ZRKS 4.520, Shiba 43

4.216 是精知精 *Kore sei, sei o shiru.*

It takes one to know one.

Variant: 識 instead of 知. *Heki* 8 Verse *agyo*, 22 Verse *agyo*, 33 Main Case *agyo*, etc.

ZGS na, ZRKS 4.586, Shiba 48, ZGJI 144, ZGJT 243, KZS #364

4.217 是賊知賊 *Kore zoku zoku o shiru.*

This is a ⌜thief⌝ knowing a thief.

Variant: 識 instead of 知. *Heki* 8 Main Case *agyo*, 22 Verse *agyo*.

ZGS na, ZRKS 4.738, Shiba 48, ZGJI 144, ZGJT 243, KZS #388

4.218 困魚止箔 *Kongyo haku ni tomaru.*

The dazed fish remains in the trap.

Serenity 32 Intro.

ZGS 4.88, ZRKS 4.531, Shiba 41, ZGJI 144, ZGJT 145

4.219 渾身泥水 *Konjin deisui.*

From head to foot, in mud and water.

Heki 71 Verse Comm.

ZGS 4.88, ZRKS 4.771, Shiba na, ZGJI 144, ZGJT 148

4.220 言語道斷 *Gongo dōdan.*

Speech silenced.

ZGS na, ZRKS 4.130, Shiba 39, ZGJI 136, ZGDJT 364b, ZD #41

4.221 言中有響 *Gonchū ni hibiki ari.*

There is a certain resonance in his words.

Heki 26 Main Case *agyo*, 38 Main Case Comm., 42 Main Case *agyo*, etc.

ZGS na, ZRKS 4.112, Shiba 39, ZGJI 137, ZGDJT 368c, ZGJT 111, KZS #189

4.222 渾崙呑棗 *⌜Konron⌝ ni natsume o nomu.*

He gulps down the ⌜jujube⌝ whole.

Heki 39 Main Case *agyo*. *Konron ni* is used adverbially here.

ZGS na, ZRKS 4.607, Shiba 41, ZGJI 144, ZGDJT 370a

4.223 座一走七 *Za ichi sō shichi.*

Sit one, run seven.

ZGS na, ZRKS 4.46, Shiba 42

4.224 不勞再勘 *Saikan suru o rō sezu.*

No need to do it again.

Variant: 不勞重擧 *Heki* 37 Main Case *agyo*, 81 Main Case *agyo*. ZRKS 4.310: *Saikan suru ni rō sezu.*

ZGS na, ZRKS 4.310, Shiba 63, ZGJI 146, ZGJT 400 (variant), KZS #278

4.225 細嚼難飢 *Saishaku wa uegatashi.*

With fine chewing, you are seldom hungry.

MMK 47. See also 8.256.

ZGS na, ZRKS 4.94, Shiba 42, ZGJI 146, ZGDJT 373b, ZGJT 155, KZS #173

4.226 再犯不容 *Saibon yurusazu.*

A second offense is not permitted.

Heki 38 Main Case *agyo*, *Rinzai-roku* §4.

ZGS 4.91, ZRKS 4.35, Shiba 42, ZGJI 146, ZGJT 154, KZS #141, ZD #34

4.227 蹉過了也 *Shaka ryō ya.*

He sailed right past.

Heki 5 Verse *agyo*, 16 Verse *agyo*, 22 Verse *agyo*, etc. ZGS 4.92: *saka* instead of *shaka*. Shiba 42: 嗟 instead of 蹉.

ZGS 4.92, ZRKS 4.178, Shiba 42, ZGJI 145, ZGDJT 465d, ZGJT 152, KZS #221

4.228 坐久成勞 *Zakyū jōrō.*

You've worked hard sitting so long.

Heki 17 Main Case.

ZGS na, ZRKS 4.742, Shiba 42, ZGJI 145, ZGDJT 380b, ZGJT 153

4.229 作家作家 *Sakke, sakke.*

A master teacher, a master teacher.

Heki 49 Verse *agyo*, 79 Main Case *agyo*.

ZGS 4.93, Shiba na

4.230 左之右之 *Sashi ushi.*

On the left, on the right.

Heki 36 Verse *agyo*, 60 Verse *agyo*, 62 Verse *agyo*.

ZGS na, ZRKS 4.317, Shiba 41, ZGJI 145, ZGJT 149

4.231 不妨奇特 *⌜Samatagezu⌝ kitoku naru koto o.*

Yes, quite remarkable!

Heki 1 Main Case Comm., 2 Main Case Comm., 38 Main Case *agyo*, 69 Main Case Comm., etc.

ZGS na, ZRKS 4.434, Shiba 63, ZGJI 147, ZGJT 399

4.232 不妨孤峻 *⌜Samatagezu⌝ koshun naru koto o.*

Ah yes! A lone peak!

Heki 5 Verse Comm., 8 Main Case Comm., 14 Verse *agyo*.

ZGS na, ZRKS 4.45, Shiba 63

4.233 不妨誵訛 *⌜Samatagezu⌝ gōka naru koto o.*

Ah yes! Quite obscure.

Heki 47 Verse Comm., 62 Main Case *agyo*.

ZGS na, Shiba 63, ZGJI 147

4.234 左右逢源 *Sayū minamoto ni au.*

Left and right, you encounter the source.

Serenity 40 Verse *agyo*.

ZGS na, Shiba 42, ZGJI 145, ZGJT 149, KZS #285, 十牛圖

4.235 沙裏淘金 *Sari ni kin o eru.*

Wash the gold from the sand.

ZGS na, ZRKS 4.657, Shiba 42, ZGJI 145, ZGJT 151

4.236 懺悔懺悔 *Zange, zange.*

I repent, I repent.

ZGS 4.94, Shiba na

4.237 斬釘截鐵 *Zantei settetsu.*

Cut nails, shear iron.

Heki 17 Intro.

ZGS 4.95, ZRKS 4.23, Shiba 43, ZGJI 148, ZGJT 166

4.238 三點九橛 *Santen kyūketsu.*

Three points, nine stakes.

ZGS 4.96, Shiba na

4.239 三十二相 *Sanjūni sō.*

The ⌜thirty-two marks⌝ [of the Buddha].

Heki 12 Main Case Comm.

ZGS 4.97, Shiba na, ZGDJT 398b

4.240 三十年後 *Sanjū nen go.*

⌜Thirty years⌝ later.

Heki 77 Verse Comm., 81 Main Case Comm, 96 Verse 3 *agyo.*

ZGS 4.98, Shiba na, ZGJT 160

4.241 取盞便打 *San o totte sunawachi utsu.*

Struck him with the wine cup.

ZGS 4.99, Shiba na

4.242 抛屎撒屙 *Shi o nageuchi, a o sassu.*

Fling shit, spray piss.

ZGS na, ZRKS 4.239, Shiba 65, ZGJI 150

4.243 自作自受 *Jisa jiju.*

He made it himself, he got it himself.

Heki 15 Main Case Comm., 22 Verse *agyo.* ZRKS 4.230: *Hōgo:* "A skilled person makes his own fetters." KZS #257: *Jisaku jiju.*

ZGS 4.105, ZRKS 4.230n, Shiba na, ZGJI 151, ZGDJT 428c, ZGJT 180, KZS #257

4.244 咫尺千里 *Shiseki senri.*

A tiny gap a thousand miles wide.

ZGS na, ZRKS 4.246, Shiba 43, ZGJI 150

4.245 蹈著實地 *Jittchi ni tōjaku su.*

Get your feet on solid ground.

ZGS na, ZRKS 4.88, Shiba 57

4.246 死中得活 *Shichū ni katsu o etari.*

In death come alive.

Heki 4 Verse *agyo*, 54 Main Case *agyo*, 81 Main Case Comm.

ZGS na, Shiba 43, ZGJI 150, ZGDJT 448d, ZGJT 173

4.247 失錢遭罪 *Shissen sōzai.*

To lose the money and suffer punishment as well.

Heki 8 Verse, 91 Verse *agyo*, 95 Main Case Comm., Verse *agyo*.

ZGS 4.106, ZRKS 4.34, Shiba 44, ZGJI 153, ZGDJT 452d, ZGJT 185, KZS #140

4.248 漆桶不會 *Shittsū fue.*

As ignorant as a tub of lacquer.

Heki 5 Main Case.

ZGS 4.107, ZRKS 4.732, Shiba 44, ZGJI 153, ZGDJT 454a, ZGJT 186, KZS #382

4.249 知而故犯 *Shitte kotosara ni okasu.*

To know and yet to transgress.

Heki 47 Verse *agyo*, 55 Main Case *agyo*.

ZGS na, ZRKS 4.71, Shiba 53, ZGJI 158, ZGJT 302, KZS #159, ZD #37

4.250 此錯彼錯 *Shishaku, hishaku.*

This error, that error.

Heki 31 Verse.

ZGS 4.108, ZRKS 4.758, Shiba na, ZGJI 149

4.251 七花八裂 *Shikka hachiretsu.*

Broken to bits.

Literally "Seven flowers, eight bits." *Heki* 2 Verse *agyo*, 13 Main Case *agyo*, 14 Main Case *agyo*, etc.

ZGS na, Shiba 44, ZGJI 152, ZGDJT 445d, ZGJT 184

4.252 七擒八縱 *Shichikin hachijū.*

Seven times take in, eight times let go.

ZGS na, ZRKS 4.42, Shiba 44, ZGJI 152

4.253 七縱八横 *Shichijū hachiō.*

Seven up and down, eight side to side.

Heki 7 Intro., 40 Intro.

ZGS na, ZRKS 4.263, Shiba 44, ZGJI 152, ZGJT 184

4.254 七事隨身 *Shichiji mi ni shitagau.*

He has the ⌜seven articles⌝ on his person.

Heki 17 Verse Comm., 24 Verse *agyo*, 38 Verse Comm., 71 Verse *agyo*.

ZGS 4.109, ZRKS 4.650, Shiba 44, ZGJI 152, ZGDJT 446b, ZGJT 184, KZS #372, BCR 103 and 163

4.255 謝師證明 *Shi no shōmei o sha su.*

To be grateful for the teacher's approval.

ZGS 4.110, Shiba na

4.256 謝師勞疲 *Shi no rōhi o sha su.*

To appreciate the teacher's great labors.

ZGS 4.111, Shiba na

4.257 且請一宿 *Shibaraku kou isshuku.*

I request a night's lodging.

ZGS 4.112, Shiba na

4.258 因邪打正 *Ja ni yotte shō o tasu.*

He uses the crooked to make straight.

ZGS na, ZRKS 4.53, Shiba 30, ZGJI 153, ZGJT 28, KZS #146

4.259 蛇形鼈鼻 *Jagyō beppi.*

The body of a snake, the nose of a turtle.

See *Heki* 22.

ZGS 4.113, ZRKS 4.844, Shiba na

4.260 將錯就錯 *Shaku o motte shaku ni tsuku.*

1. To add one mistake to another. 2. To twist a wrong into a right.

Heki 8 Main Case *agyo*, 16 Main Case *agyo*, 28 Main Case *agyo*, etc. There are several alternate readings and two interpretations. ZGJT 215: *Shaku o motte shaku o nasu.* ZGJI 157: *Shōshaku shūshaku.* ZGDJT 551c: "To skillfully turn a mistake into a solution."

ZGS 4.115, ZRKS 4.116, Shiba 46, ZGJI 157, ZGDJT 551c, ZGJT 215, KZS #192

4.261 捉敗了也 *Shakuhai ryō ya.*

Caught [you]!

Heki 8 Verse *agyo*, 59 Main Case *agyo*.

ZGS 4.116, Shiba na, ZGDJT 765d, ZGJT 274

4.262 尺長寸短 *Shaku wa nagaku sun wa mijikashi.*

A ⌜foot⌝ is long, an ⌜inch⌝ is short.

ZGS 4.117, ZRKS 4.11, Shiba 49

4.263 住持事繁 *Jūji koto shigeshi.*

The temple priest is busy with many things.

Heki 49, 68 Main Case Comm.

ZGS 4.100, Shiba na, ZGDJT 485d, ZGJT 203

4.264 就身打劫 *Shūshin takō.*

Stripped of all personal possessions.

Heki 7 Main Case *agyo*, 55 Main Case *agyo*, 70 Main Case *agyo*. *Takō*, also *tagō*, literally means "to strike *kalpa*" but has come to mean "to steal" (Shiba 45, ZGJT 154).

ZGS na, ZRKS 4.871, Shiba 45, ZGJI 154, ZGJT 201

4.265 待重來答 *Jūrai o matte kotaen.*

He's waiting to come again to answer.

Ryōkō-in: *Kasanete kitatte kotauru o matsu.*

ZGS 4.101, Shiba na

4.266 衆流截斷 *Shūru setsudan.*

Cut off the entire stream.

Var. 截斷衆流 *Setsudan shūru. Heki* 14 Main Case Comm., 21 Main Case Comm., 27 Main Case Comm., etc.

ZGS 4.102, ZRKS 4.918, Shiba 45; variants: ZGJI 154, ZGDJT 664d, ZGJT 252

4.267 熟處難忘 *Jukusho bōjigatashi.*

It is hard to shake old habits.

Jukusho 熟處 is literally "warm spot," the place on a handle which one's hand always grasps.

ZGS 4.103, ZRKS 4.709, Shiba na, ZGDJT 501a, ZGJT 205

4.268 墅著磕著 *Shukujaku katsujaku.*

Direct hit! Smack on!

Heki 27 Verse *agyo*. Shiba 45: *gaijaku* instead of *katsujaku*.

ZGS 4.104, ZRKS 4.913, Shiba 45, ZGJI 154, ZGJT 274

4.269 拗折拄杖 *Shujō o yōsetsu su.*

He breaks the staff.

Heki 17 Verse *agyo*, 28 Verse *agyo*, 65 Verse *agyo*, etc.

ZGS na, ZRKS 4.471, Shiba 71, ZGJT 461

4.270 正按傍提 *Shōan bōtei.*

He confronts straight on, he weasels in sideways.

Heki 66 Intro.

ZGS na, Shiba 48, ZGJI 156, ZGDJT 525b, ZGJT 211

4.271 得少爲足 *Shō o ete tareri to nasu.*

Make do with little.

ZGS na, ZRKS 4.849, Shiba 57, ZGJT 351

4.272 相見了也 *Shōken ryō ya.*

The meeting [with the teacher] is over.

Heki 5 Main Case Comm., ZGDJT 539b: *Shōken shiowareri*, Shiba 76: 已相見了也.

ZGS 4.118, Shiba 76, ZGDJT 539b

4.273 生死根源 *Shōji no kongen.*

The root of ⌜birth-and-death⌝.

ZGS 4.119, Shiba na

4.274 問聖侍去 *Shōji ni toi sare.*

Go ask the ⌜attendant⌝.

ZGS 4.120, Shiba na

4.275 蹤跡難尋 *Shōseki tazunegatashi.*

It is hard to find traces.

ZGS 4.121, Shiba 47

4.276 秤尺在手 *Shōseki te ni ari.*

He has weights and ladles in his hands.

ZGS na, ZRKS 4.660, Shiba 46, ZGJI 156

4.277 秤鎚落井 *Shōtsui i ni otsu.*

The scale weight has fallen into the well.

ZGS 4.262: *hyōtsui* instead of *shōtsui.*

ZGS 4.262, ZRKS 4.665, Shiba 46, ZGJI 156, ZGJT 217

4.278 聖胎長養 *Shōtai chōyō.*

The long nurturing of the ⌜sacred fetus⌝.

Also *seitai* instead of *shōtai.*

ZGS 4.122, Shiba na, ZGJI 162, ZGDJT 566d

4.279 笑中有刀 *Shōchū ni yaiba ari.*

Inside his smile, a dagger.

Heki 35 Verse Comm., 74 Verse *agyo*, 85 Main Case *agyo.*

ZGS 4.123, Shiba 46, ZGJI 156, ZGDJT 568c, ZGJT 217

4.280 正當恁麼 *Shōtō inmo.*

A [person, time] just like this.

Heki 1 Intro.

ZGS na, ZRKS 4.977, Shiba 48, ZGJI 156

4.281 墻壁有耳 *Shōheki ni mimi ari.*

The walls have ears.

ZGS na, ZRKS 4.842, Shiba 46, ZGJT 220

4.282 正法眼藏 *Shōbō genzō.*

Storehouse of the true Dharma eye.

Rinzai-roku §68, *Heki* 6 Main Case Comm., 49 Main Case Comm., 60 Main Case Comm., etc., MMK 6.

ZGS 4.124, Shiba na, ZGDJT 580b

4.283 唱拍相隨 *Shōhaku aishitagau.*

Their singing and clapping go together.

Heki 4 Verse *agyo*, 64 Main Case *agyo.*

ZGS 4.125, ZRKS 4.348, Shiba 46, ZGJI 157, ZGJT 218, KZS #291

4.284 照用齊行 *Shōyū hitoshiku gyōzu.*

Illumination and action are equally realized.

Heki 5 Intro. A passage on illumination and action appears in the Ming edition of the *Rinzai-roku* §8 and is translated as a separate appendix in Watson 1993b, 131–2.

ZGS na, ZRKS 4.319, Shiba 46, ZGJI 157, KZS #281

4.285 有照有用 *Shō ari yū ari.*

There is illumination, there is action.

Heki 25 Main Case Comm., 66 Verse Comm. See note at 4.284 above.

ZGS na, ZRKS 4.937, Shiba 70, ZGJI 157

4.286 笑裏藏鋒 *Shōri ni hokosaki o kakusu.*

A razor blade hidden in a smile.

Heki 35 Verse Comm.

ZGS 4.126, ZRKS 4.146, Shiba 46, ZGJI 156

4.287 且坐喫茶 *Shaza kissa.*

Sit a while and have some tea.

Rinzai-roku §59, *Heki* 38 Main Case Comm. ZGS 4.114: *shoza* instead of *shaza.*

ZGS 4.114, Shiba 44, ZGJT 188

4.288 處處全眞 *Sho-sho zenshin.*

Each and every place is complete truth.

Heki 36 Verse *agyo.*

ZGS 4.127, ZRKS 4.86, Shiba 45, ZGJI 155, ZGDJT 597a, ZGJT 208, KZS #86

4.289 焦尾大蟲 *Shobi no daichū.*

That ⌜big bug⌝ with the burnt tail.

Heki 73 Main Case Comm.

ZGS na, Shiba 46, ZGJI 157, ZGDJT 577b

4.290 不知最親 *Shirazaru mottomo shitashi.*

Not knowing is the most intimate.

ZGS 4.128, ZRKS 4.553, Shiba 63, ZGJI 197, KZS #354

4.291 四楞著地 *Shiryō jakuji.*

Its four legs are planted firmly on the ground.

ZGS na, ZRKS 4.100, Shiba 43, ZGDJT 601a, ZGJT 171

4.292 自領出去 *Jiryō shukko.*

Now pick up your things and go!

Heki 5 Main Case *agyo*, 6 Verse *agyo*, 10 Verse *agyo*, etc. This phrase, originally a judge's final words to a convicted prisoner, meaning "Pick up your own fetters and go to jail!" (Yamada et al. 1996, 121), now has the nuance, "Accept the punishment for your sins" (ZGDJT 601c). ZD #36 *Zuryō shukko.*

ZGS 4.129, ZRKS 4.61, Shiba 43, ZGJI 151, ZGDJT 601c, ZGJT 180, KZS #154n, ZD #36

4.293 振威一喝 *Shin'i ikkatsu.*

He mustered all his strength and gave a "Ka!"

Heki 11 Main Case Comm.

ZGS 4.130, Shiba na

4.294 神出鬼沒 *Shin idete ki bossu.*

Appearing like spirits and vanishing like ghosts.

Heki 83 Main Case Comm.

ZGS 4.131, ZRKS 4.677, Shiba na, ZGJT 228

4.295 心經當體 *Shingyō no tōtai.*

The actual embodiment of the *Heart Sutra.*

ZGS 4.133, Shiba na

4.296 針芥相投 *Shinke aitōzu.*

Needle and mustard seed meet.

From the *Nirvana Sutra* (Southern Text): A needle is set up on the earth. From the Brahma Palace in heaven a tiny mustard seed falls and lands on the tip of the needle (Yamada et al. 1996, 131).

ZGS 4.134, ZRKS 4.349, Shiba 47, ZGJI 159, ZGJT 229, KZS #292

4.297 針剳不入 *Shinsatsu fu'nyū.*

Not even a needle point can get in.

Heki 17 Intro., 42 Verse Comm. Shiba 47: 劄 instead of 剳.

ZGS 4.135, ZRKS 4.478, Shiba 47, ZGJI 159, ZGDJT 611b, ZGJT 159

4.298 心心不異 *Shinjin fui.*

Mind here, mind there are not different.

Rinzai-roku §18, §19.

ZGS 4.136, Shiba na

4.299 眞正成壞 *Shinshō jōe.*

True and correct creation and destruction.

Rinzai-roku §19.

ZGS 4.137, Shiba na

4.300 沒溺深泉 *Shinsen ni motsudeki su.*

He sinks into a deep well.

Variant: 沒溺深坑 *Jinkō ni motsudeki su,* "He sinks into a deep hole." *Rinzai-roku* §6, *Heki* 20 2nd Verse *agyo*, 34 Verse Comm., 55 Verse *agyo*.

ZGS 4.132, ZRKS 4.241, Shiba 66, ZGJI 159, ZGJT 452, KZS #260, 261

4.301 迅雷霹靂 *Jinrai hekireki.*

The rumbling crash of sudden thunder.

Heki 49 Main Case *agyo*.

ZGS na, ZRKS 4.514, Shiba 47

4.302 俊鶻巢雲 *Shunkotsu kumo ni sukuu.*

The fierce falcon makes its nest in the clouds.

ZGS na, ZRKS 4.892, Shiba 45, ZGJI 155, ZGDJT 519b

4.303 蠢動含靈 *Shundō ganrei.*

The squirming of a worm contains a spirit.

Heki 20 Intro.

ZGS 4.138, ZRKS 4.619, Shiba na, ZGJI 155, ZGDJT 521c, ZGJT 138, KZS #370

4.304 巡人犯夜 *Junnin yo o okasu.*

The watchman violates the night curfew.

See 「*Yakō*」.

ZGS 4.139, ZRKS 4.135, Shiba 45, ZGJI 155, ZGDJT 520a, ZGJT 207, KZS #200

4.305 心法倶忘 *Shinpō tomo ni wasuru.*

Mind and things are both forgotten.

Variants: 心法雙忘, 心法兩忘. *Heki* 34 Verse *agyo*, 90 Verse *agyo*.

ZGS 4.140, Shiba na

4.306 隨處作主 *Zuisho ni shu to naru.*

To be master everywhere.

Rinzai-roku §13, §17. ZRKS 4.85: 爲 instead of 作, *Tokoro ni shitagai shu to naru.*

ZGS 4.141, ZRKS 4.85, Shiba 47, ZGJI 160, ZGDJT 631a, ZGJT 240, KZS #169

4.307 水中撈月 *Suichū ni tsuki o torau.*

Reaching for the ⌜moon⌝ in the water.

ZGS 4.142, ZRKS 4.220, Shiba 47, ZGJI 160, ZGJT 235

4.308 隨波逐浪 *Zuiha chikurō.*

Follow the tides and ride the waves.

Heki 8 Intro., 72 Verse *agyo*, 90 Main Case Comm., etc.

ZGS 4.143, ZRKS 4.917, Shiba na, ZGJI 160, ZGJT 240

4.309 水乳相投 *Suinyū aitō zu.*

Water and milk mix with each other.

ZGS na, ZRKS 4.899, Shiba 47, ZGJI 160

4.310 厨庫山門 *Zuku sanmon.*

The kitchen and the temple gate.

Heki 86 三instead of山.

ZGS na, ZRKS 4.811, Shiba 53

4.311 即往不咎 *Sude ni inishi o ba togamezu.*

Don't blame the past.

Analects III, 21. More commonly read *Kiō wa togamezu.*

ZGS 4.144, ZRKS 4.671, Shiba na

4.312 已呑卻了 *Sude ni donkyaku shiowareri.*

Already swallowed it.

ZGS 4.145, Shiba na

4.313 寸鐵入木 *Suntetsu ki ni iru.*

The ⌜inch⌝ of iron pierces the tree.

"Inch of iron" is a dagger (ZGJI 161).

ZGS 4.146, ZRKS 4.17, Shiba na, ZGJI 161, ZGJT 241, KZS #133

4.314 寸鐵在手 *Suntetsu te ni ari.*

He has an ⌜inch⌝ of iron in his hand.

"Inch of iron" is a dagger (ZGJI 161).

ZGS 4.147, ZRKS 4.22, Shiba 48, ZGJI 161

4.315 聖意難測 *Seii hakarigatashi.*

A saint's intentions are hard to fathom.

ZGS na, ZRKS 4.699, Shiba 48

4.316 青山綠水 *Seizan ryokusui.*

Green hills, blue waters.

ZGS 4.148, ZRKS 4.4, Shiba 48, ZGJI 162, ZGJT 244

4.317 成事不説 *Seiji o ba tokazu.*

Don't rehash what's already done.

Analects III, 21. ZRKS 4.669: *Koto o ba nashi tokazu.* ZGS 4.225: *Narishi koto o ba tokazu.*

ZGS 4.225, ZRKS 4.669, Shiba 48, ZGJI 162

4.318 平歩青霄 *Seishō ni heiho su.*

Stroll through the blue heavens.

Heki 27 Main Case *agyo*.

ZGS na, ZRKS 4.19, Shiba 64, ZGJI 162, ZGDJT 646c, ZGJT 413

4.319 獨歩青天 *Seiten ni doppo su.*

Alone I walk the blue heavens.

ZGS na, ZRKS 4.15, Shiba 58, ZGJI 162

4.320 淸風滿地 *Seifū manchi.*

The pure wind fills the earth.

ZGS na, ZRKS 4.927, Shiba 48, ZGJI 162

4.321 淸風明月 *Seifū meigetsu.*

Pure wind, bright ⌜moon⌝.

Heki 31 Verse Comm.

ZGS 4.149, ZRKS 4.3, Shiba 48, ZGJI 162, ZGJT 246, KZS #149

4.322 隻手音聲 *Sekishu onjō.*

The sound of a single hand.

ZGS 4.150, Shiba na, ZGDJT 653a

4.323 隻手遮日 *Sekishu ni hi o saegiru.*

With one hand he blocks out the sun.

ZGS na, ZRKS 4.222, Shiba 49, ZGJI 163, ZGDJT 653a, ZGJT 249

4.324 赤心片片 *Sekishin hen-pen.*

Heart exposed, naked and red.

Heki 1 Verse Comm., 55 Main Case Comm., 57 Main Case Comm.

ZGS na, ZRKS 4.730, Shiba 49, ZGJI 163, ZGDJT 653d, ZGJT 248

4.325 舌上生牙 *Zetsujō ni ge o shōzu.*

He grows fangs on his tongue.

ZGS na, ZRKS 4.304, Shiba 49, ZGJI 164

4.326 雪上加霜 *Setsujō ni shimo o kuwau.*

He puts frost on top of snow.

Heki 4 Main Case and Verse, 28 Main Case *agyo*, 38 Main Case *agyo*, 42 Main Case *agyo*, etc.

ZGS 4.151, ZRKS 4.290, Shiba 49, ZGJI 164, ZGDJT 663c, ZGJT 251, KZS #271

4.327 絕點澄清 *Zetten chōsei.*

Spotless, transparent.

ZGS na, Shiba 49, ZGJI 164, ZGDJT 665c

4.328 切忌道著 *Setsu ni imu dōjaku suru koto o.*

It is forbidden to tell all.

Heki 6 Main Case *agyo*, 23 Main Case *agyo*, 30 Verse *agyo*.

ZGS na, ZRKS 4.423, Shiba 49, ZGJI 163, ZGDJT 660a, ZGJT 250

4.329 說破了也 *Seppa ryō ya.*

Explained it away.

ZGS na, ZRKS 4.404, Shiba 49, ZGJI 164, KZS #305

4.330 如切如磋 *Sessuru ga gotoku, sasuru ga gotoshi.*

So well cut, so finely filed.

See ⌜*Sessa takuma*⌝.

ZGS na, ZRKS 4.598, Shiba 45, ZGJI 163

4.331 縮卻舌頭 *Zettō o shukkyaku su.*

He pulls in his tongue.

Heki 50 Verse *agyo*.

ZGS na, ZRKS 4.282 and 869, Shiba 45, ZGJI 164, ZGJT 205

4.332 舌頭無骨 *Zettō ni hone nashi.*

The tongue has no bones.

ZGS 4.152, ZRKS 4.129, Shiba 49, ZGJI 164, ZGDJT 665d, ZGJT 253

4.333 舌頭落地 *Zettō chi ni otsu.*

The tongue falls onto the ground.

Heki 8 Main Case *agyo*, 100 Main Case Comm.

ZGS 4.153, ZRKS 4.407, Shiba na, ZGJI 16, ZGDJT 665d, KZS #306

4.334 千古榜様 *Senko no bōyō.*

A handbook from an ancient age.

ZGS na, ZRKS 4.337, Shiba 49

4.335 千古無對 *Senko tai nashi.*

For a thousand ages, no answer.

Heki 8 Verse.

ZGS 4.154, ZRKS 4.569, Shiba 50, ZGJI 164

4.336 前三後三 *Zensan gosan.*

Three in front, three behind.

Heki 35 Verse.

ZGS na, ZRKS 4.272, Shiba 50, ZGJT 260

4.337 千錯萬錯 *Sen shaku ban shaku.*

A thousand errors, ten thousand mistakes.

Heki 98 Main Case *agyo*, MMK 2.

ZGS 4.155, ZRKS 4.142, Shiba 50, ZGJI 265, ZGDJT 685a, ZGJT 254

4.338 千聖不傳 *Senshō fuden.*

The thousand saints do not transmit it.

Heki 3 Main Case Comm., 7 Intro., 12 Intro., etc. See also 8.138.

ZGS na, Shiba 50, ZGJI 165, ZGDJT 690b, ZGJT 254

4.339 掀倒禪床 *Zenshō o kentō su.*

He kicks over the zazen seat.

Heki 4 Main Case Comm., 8 Verse Comm., 18 Main Case *agyo*, 38 Main Case *agyo*, etc.

ZGS 4.156, ZRKS 4.101, Shiba na, ZGJT 94, KZS #176

4.340 抛擲前川 *Zensen ni hōteki su.*

He throws it all into the river.

See ⌜Landscape⌝.

ZGS 4.157, Shiba 65

4.341 全提正令 *Zentei shōrei.*

The Truth is manifested in full.

Shibayama 1974, 20.

ZGS na, Shiba 50, ZGJI 166, ZGDJT 593b

4.342 千年滯貨 *Sennen no taika.*

Unsold goods a thousand years old.

ZGS 4.158, Shiba na, ZGJI 356, ZGJT 289 (滯貨)

4.343 千年桃核 *Sennen no tōkaku.*

A thousand-year-old ⌜peach⌝ pit.

Heki 48 Main Case Comm.

ZGS 4.159, Shiba 50, ZGJI 165, ZGDJT 699d, ZGJT 254

4.344 箭鋒相拄 *Senbu aisasou.*

Arrows strike head to head.

Heki 7 Main Case Comm., 42 Verse *agyo*. Shiba 50: *senbō* instead of *senbu*.

ZGS 4.160, ZRKS 4.440, Shiba 50, ZGJI 165, ZGJT 258, KZS #320

4.345 千里同風 *Senri dōfū.*

A thousand miles away and still the same.

ZGS na, ZRKS 4.603, Shiba 50, ZGJI 165, ZGDJT 707c, ZGJT 254

4.346 和贓納欵 *Zō ni washite kan o iru.*

He hands in his confession with the loot.

Shiba 75: 臟 instead of 贓.

ZGS na, ZRKS 4.137, Shiba 75, ZGJI 168, ZGJT 495

4.347 抱贓叫屈 *Zō o idaite kutsu to sakebu.*

Arms full of loot, he yells, "I've been framed."

MMK 30. Shiba 75: 臟 instead of 贓.

ZGS 4.161, ZRKS 4.119, Sh iba 65, ZGJI 168, ZGJT 421

4.348 造次顚沛 *Zōji tenpai.*

A thoughtless moment, a stumble.

ZRKS 4.622n: *Analects* IV, 5: "Even in thoughtless moments, he cleaves to it. Even when he stumbles, he cleaves to it."

ZGS 4.162, ZRKS 4.622, Shiba 51, ZGJT 272

4.349 贓證現在 *Zōshō genzai.*

Here's proof of robbery.

ZGS 4.163, ZRKS 4.138, Shiba na, ZGJI 168, ZGDJT 272 (variant)

4.350 草賊大敗 *Sōzoku taihai.*

The back-country ⌜bandits⌝ have been totally trounced.

Rinzai-roku §4.

ZGS 4.164, ZRKS 4.706, Shiba na, ZGJI 167, ZGDJT 741b, ZGJT 269, KZS #375

4.351 蒼天蒼天 *Sōten sōten.*

"Oh my god! Good heavens!"

Heki 1 Verse *agyo*, 50 Verse *agyo*, 53 Verse *agyo*, etc. The characters literally mean "blue heaven," but the expression is used as a cry of great sadness or grief (ZGJT 167).

ZGS 4.165, ZRKS 4.719, Shiba 51, ZGJI 167, ZGDJT 743d, ZGJT 271, KZS #380

4.352 倒轉鎗頭 *Sōtō o tōten su.*

He has turned the spear around.

Heki 84 Main Case *agyo*. ZRKS 4. 503: 列轉 *retten* instead of 倒轉 *tōten.*

ZGS na, ZRKS 4.503, Shiba 56, ZGJI 168

4.353 觸處淸涼 *Sokusho seiryō.*

Whatever you touch is refreshing.

Heki 70 Verse *agyo.*

ZGS na, ZRKS 4.879, Shiba 47, ZGJI 158, ZGJT 275

4.354 認賊爲子 *Zoku o tomete ko to nasu.*

He mistook a ⌜thief⌝ for his own son.

ZGS 4.166, ZRKS 4.118, Shiba 59, ZGJI 169 (variant), ZGJT 366, KZS #195

4.355 與賊過梯 *Zoku no tame ni kakehashi o sugosu.*

He hands the ⌜thief⌝ a ladder.

Variant: 爲賊過梯. *Heki* 9 Main Case Comm.

ZGS na, ZRKS 4.120, Shiba 71, ZGJI 169, ZGDJT 762b, ZGJT 460, KZS #196

4.356 賊是家親 *Zoku wa kore kashin.*

The ⌜thief⌝ is a member of the family.

ZGS 4.167, ZRKS 4.133, Shiba 51, ZGJI 168, ZGJT 276

4.357 卽心卽佛 *Sokushin sokubutsu.*

Mind itself is Buddha.

MMK 30, *Heki* 44 Main Case.

ZGS na, Shiba 51, ZGDJT 764b, ZGJT 273

4.358 賊身已露 *Zokushin sude ni arawaru.*

The ⌜thief⌝ has made his appearance.

Heki 2 Main Case *agyo.*

ZGS 4.168, ZRKS 4.113, Shiba 51, ZGJI 169, ZGJT 276, KZS #190

4.359 啐啄同時 *Sottaku dōji.*

Pecking out and pecking in together.

Heki 7 Main Case Comm., 16 Main Case Comm. *Sotsu* is the sound of a chick pecking its way out of the shell, and *taku* the sound of the mother hen pecking at the shell from the outside.

ZGS 4.90, ZRKS 4.351, Shiba 51, ZGJI 168, ZGDJT 773c, ZGJT 277

4.360 某呈和尚 *Soregashi ⌜oshō⌝ ni tei su.*

I offer it to the priest.

ZGS 4.169, Shiba na

4.361 某甲罪過 *Soregashi zaika.*

The fault is mine.

Heki 33 Main Case Comm., 34 Main Case Comm.

ZGS 4.170, Shiba na

4.362 某不得便 *Soregashi tayori o ezu.*

1. I have not heard any news. 2. I did not get any advantage.

See 4.517.

ZGS 4.171, Shiba na

4.363 大惠道底 *Daie iu tei.*

As Daie said.

ZGS 4.172, Shiba na

4.364 大機大用 *Dai ⌜ki⌝ daiyū.*

Superb instincts, grand actions.

Haki 11 Main Case Comm., 26 Verse Comm., 32 Verse Comm.

ZGS na, Shiba 52, ZGDJT 789a, ZGJT 292

4.365 太孤危生 *Taiko kisei.*

Solitary and unapproachable.

Heki 3 Intro.

ZGS na, Shiba 52, ZGJI 171, ZGDJT 794a

4.366 大巧若拙 *Taikō wa setsu no gotoshi.*

The great master looks like an idiot.

ZGS na, Shiba 52, ZGDJT 793c, ZGJT 292

4.367 大千捏聚 *Daisen mo netsuju su.*

Gather up even the ⌜great thousand-realm universe⌝.

ZGS na, ZRKS 4.267, Shiba 52, ZGJI 171, KZS #265

4.368 大方無外 *Daihō soto nashi.*

The great earth has no outside.

Heki 22 Intro. See also 8.276. *Daihō* literally means "the great square," since "heaven is round and earth is square."

ZGS 4.173, ZRKS 4.936, Shiba 52, ZGJI 171, ZGDJT 816b, ZGJT 292

4.369 大璞不琢 *Taiboku taku sezu.*

A great jewel in the rough needs no polishing.

ZGS na, Shiba 52, ZGJI 171, ZGDJT 816c

4.370 對面千里 *Taimen senri.*

Face to face a thousand miles away.

ZGS na, ZRKS 4.218, Shiba 52, ZGJI 172, ZGJT 288, KZS #249

4.371 太廉纎生 *Tairen sensei.*

Much too meticulous.

ZGS na, Shiba 52, ZGJI 172

4.372 體露金風 *Tairo kinpū.*

Physically present, the golden wind.

Heki 27.

ZGS 4.174, ZRKS 4.386, Shiba 53, ZGJI 172, ZGDJT 820a, ZGJT 287

4.373 莫謗他好 *Ta o bōzuru nakumba yoshi.*

You should not speak ill of others.

Heki 8 Verse *agyo*.

ZGS 4.175, ZRKS 4.492, Shiba na, ZGJT 435 (variant)

4.374 貴買賤賣 *Takaku katte yasuku uru.*

Buying high, selling low.

ZGS 4.176, ZRKS 4.658, Shiba na, ZGJT 78

4.375 多口阿師 *Taku no ashi.*

Talkative preacher.

Heki 13 Verse *agyo*, 48 Main Case Comm., 50 Verse.

ZGS 4.177, ZRKS 4.406, Shiba na, ZGJI 170, ZGDJT 823a, ZGJT 280

4.376 打成一片 *Dajō ippen.*

Become one.

MMK 1, *Heki* 2 Verse Comm., 6 Verse Comm., 17 Main Case Comm., etc.

ZGS na, Shiba 52, ZGJI 170, ZGDJT 824b, ZGJT 283

4.377 慣戰作家 *Tatakai ni naretaru sakke.*

A master used to battle.

Heki 24 Verse *agyo*, 71 Verse *agyo*.

ZGS na, ZRKS 4.447, Shiba 35, ZGJI 172, ZGDJT 825a, ZGJT 69, KZS #323

4.378 脱體現成 *Dattai genjō.*

As it is right now.

Heki 1 Main Case Comm.

ZGS na, Shiba 53, ZGJI 173, ZGDJT 827d, ZGJT 297

4.379 唾擲便去 *Dajaku shite sunawachi saru.*

He spat and left.

ZGS 4.178, Shiba na

4.380 脱白露淨 *Dappaku rojō.*

Spick-and-span clean.

ZGS 4.179, ZRKS 4.906, Shiba 53, ZGDJT 828b, ZGJT 173

4.381 拖泥帶水 *Dadei taisui.*

Tracking mud, dripping water.

Heki 2 pointer, 37 Verse *agyo*, 64 Main Case *agyo*, etc. KZS #239: *Dei o hiki, mizu o ou.*

ZGS 4.180, ZRKS 4.196, Shiba 51, ZGJI 170, ZGDJT 828c, ZGJT 280, KZS #239

4.382 珠回玉轉 *Tama meguri tama ten zu.*

The pearl spins, the jewel turns.

Heki 36 Main Case Comm.

ZGS na, ZRKS 4.760, Shiba 44, ZGJI 173, ZGJT 196, KZS #395

4.383 誰敢相昧 *Tare ka aete aikuramasan.*

Who would keep you in the dark?

ZGS 4.181, Shiba na

4.384 誰是能擧 *Tare ka kore yoku agen.*

Who will take this up?

ZGS na, ZRKS 4.281, Shiba 47

4.385 擔枷過狀 *Tanka kajō.*

He wears a ⌜stock⌝ with a list of his crimes.

Heki 7 Main Case *agyo*, 30 Verse *agyo*, 37 Main Case Comm., etc.

ZGS 4.182, ZRKS 4.734, Shiba na, ZGJI 173, ZGDJT 834d, ZGJT 298, KZS #383

4.386 擔枷帶鎖 *Tanka taisa.*

He wears a ⌜stock⌝, he's shackled in chains.

ZGS 4.183, ZRKS 4.711, Shiba 53, ZGJI 174, ZGDJT 834d, ZGJT 299

4.387 探竿影草 *Tankan yōzō.*

The scare-pole and the weed lure.

Heki 10 Main Case *agyo*, *Rinzai-roku* §13. The fisherman's scare-pole is a bamboo pole with a clump of bird feathers woven to resemble a bird. He extends it over the water to scare fish in a certain direction. The weed lure is a patch of floating water grass which attracts fish who like to gather under it (ZGJT 300, ZGDJT 835c). Like ⌜teeth and claws⌝, these are metaphors for the master's teaching methods, one ⌜*hajū*⌝ and the other ⌜*hōgyō*⌝.

ZGS 4.184, ZRKS 4.298, Shiba 53, ZGJI 173, ZGDJT 835c, ZGJT 300

4.388 獨步丹霄 *Tanshō ni doppo su.*

Alone I walk the red heavens.

Heki 3 Main Case Comm.

ZGS na, ZRKS 4.15, Shiba 58, ZGDJT 837b, ZGJT 352

4.389 單提獨弄 *Tantei dokurō.*

He presents it himself, he plays with it alone.

Heki 42 Intro.

ZGS 4.185, ZRKS 4.893, Shiba na, ZGJI 173, ZGDJT 838b, ZGJT 299

4.390 拂地而盡 *Chi o haratte tsuku.*

Sweep the ground clean.

Heki 12 Verse Comm., 18 Main Case Comm. (variant).

ZGS na, ZRKS 4.98, Shiba 64

4.391 父嚴子孝 *Chichi gen nareba ko kō nari.*

When the father is strict, the son is devoted.

ZGS 4.186, ZRKS 4.354, Shiba 63, ZGJI 174

4.392 父財子用 *Chichi no zai ko mochiyu.*

The father's wealth, the child spends.

ZGS 4.187, ZRKS 4.356, Shiba na, ZGJI 174

4.393 父羊子證 *Chichi no yō ko arawasu.*

The father's sheep, the son's testimony.

See ⸢Steal a sheep⸣.

ZGS 4.188, ZRKS 4.845, Shiba na

4.394 著衣喫飯 *Jakue kippan.*

Put on your clothes, eat your food.

Rinzai-roku §13, *Heki* 74 Intro.

ZGS 4.189, ZRKS 4.625, Shiba 53, ZGJI 174, ZGDJT 468a, ZGJT 194

4.395 中道實相 *Chūdō jissō.*

The true reality of the Middle Way.

"Middle Way" here refers to Madhyamaka thought in Mahayana Buddhism.

ZGS 4.190, Shiba na

4.396 偸心鬼子 *Chūshin no kisu.*

A little devil with the mind of a thief!

ZGS na, ZRKS 4.592, Shiba 54, ZGJI 182

4.397 張三李四 *Chōzan rishi.*

⸢Chang⸣ number three, ⸢Li⸣ number four.

Chang and Li are very common names in China. Three and four are used only as anonymous designators (ZGDJT 862d, Shiba 54).

ZGS na, ZRKS 4.na, Shiba 54, ZGJI 175, ZGDJT 862d, ZGJT 310

4.398 頂門眼活 *Chōmon ni manako kassu.*

The eye on his forehead is alive.

ZGS na, ZRKS 4.432, Shiba 54, ZGJI 175

4.399 超佛越祖 *Chōbutsu osso.*

Beyond buddhas, surpassing ancestors.

Heki 77 Main Case.

ZGS na, ZRKS 4.103, Shiba 54, ZGJI 175, ZGJT 312, KZS #183

4.400 月白風清 *Tsuki shiroshi, kaze kiyoshi.*

The ⸢moon⸣ is white, the wind is pure.

ZGS 4.192, ZRKS 4.204, Shiba 38, ZGJI 176, ZGDJT 876b

4.401 臥月眠雲 *Tsuki ni fushi, kumo ni nemuru.*

He lies down in moonlight and sleeps on the clouds.

ZGS 4.193, ZRKS 4.708, Shiba 33, ZGJI 176, ZGDJT 876c, ZGJT 52

4.402 月帯重輪 *Tsuki wa jūrin o obu.*

The ⌜moon⌝ wears a double halo.

ZGS 4.194, ZRKS 4.710, Shiba na

4.403 頭上安頭 *Zujō ni zu o anzu.*

Putting another head on top of the head.

Heki 12 Verse *agyo*, 37 Verse *agyo, Rinzai-roku* §19.

ZGS 4.195, ZRKS 4.292, Shiba 57, ZGJI 183, ZGDJT 639a, ZGJT 344, KZS #273

4.404 謹領慈旨 *Tsutsushinde jishi o ryō su.*

We respectfully receive this compassionate teaching.

ZGS 4.196, Shiba na

4.405 低頭便去 *Teitō shite sunawachi saru.*

He bowed and then left.

ZGS 4.197, Shiba na

4.406 換手搥胸 *Te o kaete mune o utsu.*

He beats his breast with alternating hands.

Heki 1 Verse *agyo*, 9 Main Case Comm., 76 Verse *agyo*.

ZGS 4.198, ZRKS 4.501, Shiba na, ZGJI 177, ZGDJT 877d, ZGJT 68, KZS #343

4.407 去溺投火 *Deki o satte hi ni tōzu.*

Escape drowning but fall into the fire.

ZGS na, ZRKS 4.366, Shiba 36, ZGJI 178

4.408 滴水適凍 *Tekisui tekitō.*

A drop of water becomes a bead of ice.

Variant: 滴水滴凍. *Heki* 47 Verse *agyo*.

ZGS na, ZRKS 4.858, Shiba 54, ZGJI 178, ZGJT 322

4.409 覿面相呈 *Tekimen aitei su.*

It's put right into your face.

Heki 2 Verse *agyo*, 3 Verse Comm., 12 Verse Comm., etc. ZGDJT 882b: *sōtei* instead of *aitei*.

ZGS 4.199, ZRKS 4.963, Shiba na, ZGJI 178, ZGDJT 882b

4.410 覿面難藏 *Tekimen zōjigatashi.*

When you're face to face, it's hard to hide.

ZGDJT 882b: *kakushigatashi* instead of *zōjigatashi.*

ZGS na, ZRKS 4.150, Shiba 54, ZGJI 178, ZGDJT 882b, KZS #205

4.411 手蹉脚蹉 *Te tagai ashi tagau.*

Hand missed, foot slipped.

ZGS4.200 has 踋, corrected to 脚 at ZRKS 4.195.

ZGS 4.200, ZRKS 4.195, Shiba na, ZGJI 177, KZS #237

4.412 買鐵得金 *Tetsu o katte kin o etari.*

Buy iron, get gold instead.

MMK 29.

ZGS na, ZRKS 4.655, Shiba 60, ZGJI 178, ZGJT 380

4.413 鐵牛無骨 *Tetsugyū hone nashi.*

An iron bull has no bones.

ZGS 4.201, Shiba 54

4.414 鐵樹開花 *Tetsuju hana o hiraku.*

The iron trees open blossoms.

ZGS na, Shiba 54

4.415 鐵裹摩尼 *Tetsu ni mani o tsutsumu.*

He wraps the *maṇi* jewel in metal.

ZGS na, ZRKS 4.652, Shiba 54, ZGJI 178, ZGJT 324

4.416 鐵輪碎石 *Tetsurin ishi o kudaku.*

The iron wheel crushes rock.

ZGS na, ZRKS 4.468, Shiba 55, ZGJI 178

4.417 掀天搖地 *Ten o ugokashi, chi o yurugasu.*

He moves heaven and shakes earth.

Heki 11 Main Case *agyo.*

ZGS na, ZRKS 4.342, Shiba 37, ZGJI 179, ZGDJT 886b, ZGJT 94 (variant)

4.418 撐天拄地 *Ten o sasae, chi o sasou.*

He props up heaven, he steadies the earth.

Heki 16 Main Case *agyo*, 27 Main Case *agyo*; Shiba 56: 撑 instead of 撐.

ZGS na, ZRKS 4.28, Shiba 56, ZGJI 179, ZGDJT 886b, ZGJT 342, KZS #135

4.419 照天照地 *Ten o terashi, chi o terasu.*

Light up heaven, illuminate earth.

Rinzai-roku §17, *Heki* 8 Main Case Comm.

ZGS na, ZRKS 4.337, Shiba 46, ZGJI 179 (variant), ZGDJT 886c, KZS #286

4.420 模天樣地 *Ten o moshi, chi o yōsu.*

It takes the form of heaven; it takes the shape of earth.

ZGS 4.202, ZRKS 4.243, Shiba na

4.421 天鑑無私 *Tenkan watakushi nashi.*

In the mirror of heaven, there is no private self.

See 8.304.

ZGS na, ZRKS 4.700, Shiba 55, ZGJI 179

4.422 飜了天地 *Tenchi o honryō su.*

Overturn heaven and earth.

ZGS 4.203, Shiba 66

4.423 點滴不施 *Tenteki mo hodokosazu.*

Won't give even a single drop.

Heki 83 Main Case *agyo*, Verse *agyo*.

ZGS 4.204, ZRKS 4.798, Shiba 55, ZGJI 180, ZGDJT 897c, ZGJT 327, KZS #203

4.424 展轉反側 *Tenten hansoku.*

Toss and turn, toss and turn.

ZGS 4.205, Shiba na

4.425 倚天長劍 *Ten ni yoru chōken.*

The long ⌜sword⌝ hanging in the sky.

ZGS na, ZRKS 4.774, Shiba 28, ZGJI 180, ZGJT 12, KZS #397

4.426 天魔膽落 *Temma mo kimo otsu.*

Even a devil will lose his nerve.

ZGS na, ZRKS 4.821, Shiba 55, ZGJI 180, KZS #411

4.427 天高海濶 *Ten wa takaku umi wa hiroshi.*

Heaven is high, the sea is vast.

ZGS 4.206, ZRKS 4.12, Shiba 55, ZGJI 179

4.428 天高地厚 *Ten wa takaku chi wa atsushi.*

Heaven is high, the earth is deep.

ZGS 4.207, ZRKS 4.27, Shiba na, ZGJI 179

4.429 透關破節 *Tōkan hasetsu.*

Penetrate barriers, break through joints.

ZGS na, Shiba 56, ZGJI 182, ZGDJT 912a

4.430 遠問近對 *Tōku toeba chikaku kotau.*

Ask afar and get an answer close by.

ZGS 4.209, ZRKS 4.856, Shiba na, ZGJI 185, ZGDJT 945d, ZGJT 35

4.431 道絕功勳 *Dō kōkun o zessu.*

The Way surpasses merit and distinction.

ZGS na, ZRKS 4.880, Shiba 57

4.432 不遠而來 *Tōshi to sezu shite kitaru.*

Coming from no great distance.

ZGS 4.211, Shiba na

4.433 當軒大坐 *Tōken daiza.*

Under the eaves he's doing a mighty sit.

ZGJT 336, ZGJI 182: *Tōken ni daiza su.*

ZGS na, ZRKS 4.30, Shiba 56, ZGJI 182, ZGDJT 915c, ZGJT 336

4.434 撓鉤搭索 *Dōkō tassaku.*

A steel trap and a rope noose.

ZRKS 4.64: *Nyōkō tassaku.*

ZGS na, ZRKS 4.64, Shiba 57, ZGDJT 919c, ZGJT 349, KZS #155

4.435 東西自在 *Tōzai jizai.*

Free from east and west.

ZGS 4.210, Shiba na

4.436 噇酒糟漢 *Tōshusō no kan.*

Eater of beer dregs.

Heki 11.

ZGS na, ZRKS 4.1000, Shiba 56, ZGJI 184, ZGDJT 927a, ZGJT 342

4.437 倒退三千 *Tōtai sanzen.*

He fell backwards three thousand steps.

Heki 2 Main Case *agyo*, 3 Verse *agyo*, 15 Main Case Comm., etc.

ZGS 4.212, ZRKS 4.247, Shiba 56, ZGJI 182, ZGDJT 934c, ZGJT 339

4.438 刀不斬刀 *Tō tō o kirazu.*

The ⸢sword⸣ does not cut itself.

Shiba 55: *Katana wa katana o kirazu.*

ZGS 4.213, Shiba 55

4.439 銅頭鐵額 *Dōtō tetsugaku.*

Copper head, iron brow.

Heki 70 Verse Comm.

ZGS na, ZRKS 4.633, Shiba 57, ZGJI 184, ZGJT 349

4.440 同道唱和 *Dōdō shōwa su.*

Companions on the Way harmonize together.

Heki 16 Verse Comm.

ZGS na, ZRKS 4.345, Shiba 57, ZGJI 184, ZGDJT 936d, ZGJT 345, KZS #290

4.441 東歩西歩 *Tōho seiho.*

Walk east, walk west.

ZGS 4.214, Shiba 55

4.442 當面蹉過 *Tōmen ni shaka su.*

Face to face, and he sailed right by.

Heki 2 Main Case Comm, 53 Main Case *agyo*, 73 Main Case Comm., 83 Main Case Comm.

ZGS na, ZRKS 4.177, Shiba 56, ZGJI 182, ZGDJT 941d, ZGJT 336, KZS #220

4.443 東涌西沒 *Tōyū seibotsu.*

Rise in the east, sink in the west.

Heki 1 Intro.

ZGS na, ZRKS 4.853, Shiba 56, ZGJI 182, ZGJT 338

4.444 見兎放鷹 *To o mite taka o hanatsu.*

Spotting a rabbit, he releases his hawk.

Heki 27 Intro., 31 Main Case Comm., 77 Main Case Comm., etc.

ZGS na, ZRKS 4.377, Shiba 38, ZGJI 116, ZGJT 106, KZS #295

4.445 撒土撒沙 *Do o sasshi, suna o sassu.*

Spreading dirt, throwing sand.

Heki 9 Verse *agyo*, 36 Verse *agyo*.

ZGS na, ZRKS 4.643, Shiba 42, ZGJI 181, ZGJT 160

4.446 毒悪已露 *Dokuaku sude ni arawaru.*

Poisonous evil has appeared.

ZGS na, ZRKS 4.490, Shiba 57, ZGJI 185

4.447 毒箭中胸 *Dokusen mune ni ataru.*

The poisoned arrow strikes him in the chest.

ZGS na, ZRKS 4.480, Shiba 57, KZS #336

4.448 毒箭攢胷 *Dokusen mune ni atsumaru.*

Poison arrows collect in the heart.

ZGS 4.215, ZRKS 4.480, Shiba na

4.449 髑髏遍野 *Dokuro ya ni amaneshi.*

Skulls fill the field.

Heki 23.

ZGS 4.216, ZRKS 4.457, Shiba 58, ZGJI 185, ZGDJT 954a, ZGJT 353

4.450 遂事不諫 *Togeshi koto o ba togamezu.*

Do not harp on things that are finished.

Analects III, 21. ZGJI 160: *Suiji wa togamezu.*

ZGS 4.217, ZRKS 4.670, Shiba na, ZGJI 160

4.451 兎子望月 *Toshi tsuki o nozomu.*

The rabbit gazes at the ⌜moon⌝.

See *Heki* 90 Comm.

ZGS na, ZRKS 4.359, Shiba 55

4.452 年老心孤 *Toshi oite kokoro ko nari.*

As one gets old, the heart grows lonely.

MMK 17.

ZGS 4.218, ZRKS 4.705, Shiba na, ZGJI 185, ZGJT 369

4.453 土上添泥 *Dojō ni dei o sou.*

Pile mud on top of earth.

ZGS 4.219, Shiba na

4.454 途中善爲 *Tochū yoku osameyo.*

Take care of yourself on the way.

ZGDJT 955a: *Tochū zen'i.*

ZGS 4.220, Shiba na, ZGDJT 955a and 671b, ZGJT 332 and 262

4.455 突出難辨 *Tosshutsu benjigatashi.*

The sudden outbreak was hard to explain.

ZGJT 353: *Tosshutsu shite benzuru koto katashi.*

ZGS na, ZRKS 4.21, Shiba 58, ZGJI 185, ZGJT 353, KZS #129

4.456 怒髪衝冠 *Dohatsu kan o tsuku.*

In anger his hair lifts his hat.

ZGS 4.221, Shiba na

4.457 鳥飛毛落 *Tori tonde ke otsu.*

When birds fly, feathers fall.

Heki 2 Main Case *agyo*, 17 Main Case *agyo*, 29 Intro.

ZGS 4.222, ZRKS 4.378, Shiba 54, ZGJI 186, ZGDJT 957d, ZGJT 311, KZS #296

4.458 入泥入水 *Doro ni iri mizu ni iru.*

Goes into mud, goes into water.

Heki 15 Verse Comm., 16 Main Case Comm., 46 Main Case Comm., etc. Variant: *dei* instead of *doro*.

ZGS na, ZRKS 4.816, Shiba 58, ZGDJT 986b, ZGJT 360, KZS #408

4.459 鈍鳥逆風 *Donchō kaze ni sakarau.*

The stupid bird flies against the wind.

ZGS 4.223, ZRKS 4.242, Shiba 58, ZGJI 186, ZGDJT 961a, KZS #262 (variant)

4.460 鈍鳥栖蘆 *Donchō ro ni sumu.*

The stupid bird nests in the reeds.

ZGS 4.224, ZRKS 4.529, Shiba 58, ZGJI 186, ZGDJT 961a, ZGJT 354

4.461 吞吐不下 *Donto fuge.*

It can't be swallowed, it can't be spit out.

ZD #43: *Dondo fuge.*

ZGS na, ZRKS 4.185, Shiba 58, ZGJI 186, ZD #43

4.462 猶在半途 *Nao hanto ni ari.*

You're only halfway.

Heki 57 Verse *agyo*, 94 Verse Comm.

ZGS na, ZRKS 4.509, Shiba 70

4.463 着何死急 *Nan no shikyū o ka tsuken.*

Why in such an awful hurry?

死, literally "die," is here used as an auxiliary to emphasize 急, hurry (SRZGK #13). Ryōkō-in: *Nan ni jaku shite shi o isogan.*

ZGS 4.226, Shiba na

4.464 何遠之有 *Nan no tōki koto ka kore aran.*

In what sense is it far away?

Analects IX, 30.

ZGS na, ZRKS 4.932, Shiba 32

4.465 那伽大定 *Naga daijō.*

The great Naga *samādhi*.

MMK 42. The Naga, the snake-dragon river god, is always in deep *samādhi*. The Buddha's own *samādhi* is the great Naga *samādhi* (ZGDJT 964c). See also 8.159.

ZGS na, Shiba 58, ZGJI 186, ZGDJT 964c

4.466 入我我入 *Nyūga ganyū.*

It enters me, I enter it.

ZGS 4.227, Shiba na, ZGDJT 985c

4.467 衣錦尚絅 *Nishiki o kite kei o kuwau.*

To dress up in brocade and then add gauze.

ZGS 4.228, Shiba 28

4.468 錦包特石 *Nishiki ni tokuseki o tsutsumu.*

He wraps up his special stone in brocade.

Serenity 14 Intro.

ZGS 4.229, ZRKS 4.654, Shiba na, ZGJI 188, ZGDJT 977d, ZGJT 447

4.469 二祖斷臂 *Niso danpi.*

The Second Patriarch cut off his arm.

See ⌜Eka Daishi cuts off his arm⌝ under ⌜Bodhidharma⌝. MMK 41.

ZGS 4.230, Shiba na, ZGDJT 981c

4.470 落二落三 *Ni ni ochi, san ni otsu.*

He falls into the second and falls into the third.

Heki 98 Main Case Comm.

ZGS na, ZRKS 4.874, Shiba 71, ZGJI 188, ZGJT 469

4.471 日裏看山 *Nichiri ni yama o miru.*

View the mountains under the sun.

ZGS na, ZRKS 4.566, Shiba 58, ZGJI 188, ZGJT 358

4.472 如是我聞 *Nyoze gamon.*

Thus have I heard.

The opening words of a sutra.

ZGS 4.231, Shiba na, ZGDJT 99d

4.473 二龍爭珠 *Niryū tama o arasou.*

Two dragons fight for a jewel.

Heki 65 Main Case Comm. KZS #400: *jiryō* instead of *niryū*.

ZGS 4.232, ZRKS 4.797, Shiba na, ZGJI 188, ZGDJT 996a, ZGJT 357, KZS #400

4.474 任運無作 *Nin'un musa.*

Naturally and without effort.

ZGS na, Shiba 59, ZGJI 189, ZGDJT 996d

4.475 熱喝嗔拳 *Nekkatsu shinken.*

A scorching shout, an angry fist.

ZGS 4.233, ZRKS 4.384, Shiba 59, ZGJI 189

4.476 拈華微笑 *Nenge mishō.*

For lifting a flower, a faint smile.

See「Kāśyapa」and MMK 6.

ZGS na, Shiba 59, ZGDJT 1003a

4.477 腦後一鎚 *Nōgo ni ittsui.*

A hammer blow to the back of the head.

ZGS 4.234, Shiba na

4.478 腦後見腮 *Nōgo ni sai o miru.*

You can see his jawbones from behind his head.

Heki 25 Main Case *agyo*, 30 Main Case *agyo*, 62 Verse *agyo*. In ancient Chinese physiognomy, the size and shape of the bones were read as signs of a person's character. Jawbones so large that they could be seen from behind were said to signify a thieving personality (ZGDJT 1006c).

ZGS na, Shiba 59, ZGJI 454, ZGDJT 1006c, ZGJT 373

4.479 腦後添針 *Nōgo ni hari o sou.*

Stab a needle into the back of his brain.

ZGS na, ZRKS 4.491, Shiba 59, ZGJI 190, KZS #340

4.480 腦後拔箭 *Nōgo ni ya o nuku.*

He removes an arrow from the back of his skull.

Heki 6 Verse *agyo*, 27 Main Case Comm., 81 Main Case *agyo*. During the Five Dynasties period, the warrior Wang Yin was shot from behind by an arrow which came out through his mouth. He removed the arrow and then shot it back, killing his enemy (Shiba 59, ZGJI 190).

ZGS na, ZRKS 4.733, Shiba 59, ZGJI 190, ZGJT 373

4.481 腦門著地 *Nōmon jakuchi.*

Touch forehead to the ground.

ZGS 4.235, ZRKS 4.216, Shiba na, ZGJI 190, ZGDJT 1008a, ZGJT 373, KZS #247

4.482 敗闕不少 *Haiketsu sukunakarazu.*

This is not a minor failure.

Heki 35 Main Case *agyo*.

ZGS na, ZRKS 4.235, Shiba 60, ZGJI 191, ZGJT 379

4.483 背後底聻 *Haigo tei nii.*

It's right behind you!

ZGS 4.236, Shiba na, ZGJI 190, ZGDJT 1010a

4.484 敗將不斬 *Haishō o ba kirazu.*

You do not execute a defeated general.

Heki 38 Verse *agyo*.

ZGS 4.237, ZRKS 4.87, Shiba na, ZGJI 191

4.485 摘葉尋枝 *Ha o tsumami, eda o tazunu.*

Picking through leaves, searching the branches.

Heki 77 Main Case Comm.

ZGS na, ZRKS 4.912, Shiba 54, ZGJI 190, ZGJT 322

4.486 有始有尾 *Hajime ari, owari ari.*

There is a beginning and there is an end.

ZGS na, ZRKS 4.9, Shiba 70, KZS #181

4.487 白雲萬里 *Hakuun banri.*

White clouds for ten thousand miles.

Heki 85 Verse Comm.

ZGS 4.238, ZRKS 4.189, Shiba na, ZGJI 380, ZGDJT 1014b, ZGJT 191, KZS #231

4.488 白圭無玷 *Hakkei kizu nashi.*

The white jade has no flaws.

Heki 8 Verse.

ZGS 4.239, ZRKS 4.718, Shiba 60, ZGJI 191, ZGDJT 1014c, ZGJT 380

4.489 白日青天 *Hakujitsu seiten.*

Bright sun, blue skies.

MMK 25.

ZGS 4.240, ZRKS 4.1, Shiba na, ZGJI 191, KZS #117

4.490 鏌鎁在握 *Bakuya aku ni ari.*

The 「Mo Yeh sword」 is in his grip.

ZGS 4.241, ZRKS 4.820, Shiba 60, ZGJI 192

4.491 破家散宅 *Haka santaku.*

The house is destroyed, the family scattered.

Heki 80 Main Case Comm.

ZGS 4.242, ZRKS 4.465, Shiba 60, ZGJI 190, ZGDJT 1012c, ZGJT 377

4.492 白日迷路 *Hakujitsu michi ni mayou.*

In broad daylight he's lost the way.

ZGS na, ZRKS 4.223, Shiba 60, ZGJI 191, KZS #253

4.493 把住放行 *Hajū hōgyō.*

Grip and hold firm, release and let go.

Heki 76 Intro.

ZGS 4.243, Shiba na, ZGDJT 1019a

4.494 撥草參玄 *Hassō sangen.*

Clear away weeds and seek the profound.

ZGS na, Shiba 60

4.495 撥草瞻風 *Hassō senpū.*

Clear away weeds and gaze into the wind.

ZGS na, Shiba 61

4.496 挽旗奪鼓 *Hata o hiki tsutsumi o ubau.*

Pull down their flags and steal their drums.

Heki 38 Main Case *agyo.*

ZGS na, ZRKS 4.484, Shiba 61, ZGJI 192, ZGJT 165, KZS #338

4.497 八寒八熱 *Hakkan hachinetsu.*

Eight cold, eight hot.

This could be a reference to Chinese seasons; the year had 24 minor seasons, each fifteen days long, of which eight were cold and eight hot. Or it could be a reference to hell, of which there were eight hot and eight cold.

ZGS 4.244, Shiba na

4.498 道得八成 *Hachijō o iietari.*

He spoke eighty percent.

Heki 89 Main Case.

ZGS na, ZRKS 4.865, Shiba 57, ZGJI 192, ZGJT 348

4.499 攢華簇錦 *Hana o atsumete, nishiki o muragarasu.*

Gather flowers, make brocade.

Variant: 花 instead of 華. *Heki* 38 Main Case Comm.

ZGS na, ZRKS 4.934, Shiba 42, ZGJI 192

4.500 詠花吟月 *Hana ni eiji tsuki ni ginzu.*

I sing to the flowers, I chant to the ⌜moon⌝.

ZGS na, Shiba 32

4.501 太深遠生 *Hanahada jin'onsei.*

Awesomely profound.

Heki 59 Verse *agyo.*

ZGS 4.246, Shiba na, ZGJI 171, ZGDJT 801c

4.502 太煞謾人 *Hanahada hito o manzu.*

He really deceives people.

Heki 75 Main Case *agyo.*

ZGS 4.247, ZRKS 4.493, Shiba na, KZS #341

4.503 傾腸倒腹 *Harawata o katamuke, hara o taosu.*

He spills his guts, he turns out his insides.

MMK 20.

ZGS na, ZRKS 4.325, Shiba 38, ZGJI 175, ZGJT 103

4.504 萬箭攢心 *Bansen mune ni atsumaru.*

Ten thousand arrows collect in the heart.

Heki 84 Main Case *agyo.* ZGJI 205: *Mansen kokoro ni atsumaru.*

ZGS 4.248, ZRKS 4.678, Shiba 61, ZGJI 205, ZGDJT 1037a, ZGJT 386, KZS #373

4.505 半合半開 *Hangō hankai.*

Half open, half shut.

The sense here is: "He hems, he haws." Also occurs in reverse order: 半開半合. *Heki* 18 Main Case *agyo*, 30 Verse *agyo*, 34 Verse *agyo*, etc.

ZGS na, ZRKS 4.323, Shiba 61, ZGJI 192, ZGDJT 965a

4.506 萬法一如 *Banpō ichinyo.*

The ⌜ten thousand things⌝ in themselves are one.

Also *Manbō ichinyo. Rinzai-roku* §14.

ZGS na, Shiba 61, ZGJI 420, ZGDJT 1180a

4.507 飯裏有沙 *Hanri ni suna ari.*

A stone in the rice.

MMK 31.

ZGS 4.249, ZRKS 4.151, Shiba 61, ZGJI 193, ZGJT 386, KZS #206

4.508 盤裏明珠 *Banri no meiju.*

Beautiful pearls on the tray.

Heki 65 Main Case *agyo.*

ZGS na, ZRKS 4.50, Shiba 61, ZGJI 193, ZGJT 388

4.509 鼻孔相拄 *Bikū aisasau.*

Nose to nose.

ZGS 4.250, ZRKS 4.783, Shiba na, ZGJI 195

4.510 穿卻鼻孔 *Bikū o senkyaku su.*

He's pierced [the other's] nose.

An oxherd could control a bull if he pierced the bull's nose and passed a roped ring through it. *Heki* 4 Verse *agyo*, 10 Main Case Comm., 26 Verse Comm., etc.

ZGS na, ZRKS 4.459, Shiba 50, ZGJI 195, ZGDJT 677d, ZGJT 257, KZS #332

4.511 失卻鼻孔 *Bikū o shikkyaku su.*

He's lost his nostrils.

Heki 28 Verse Comm., 32 Main Case *agyo*, 51 Main Case Comm. See note to 4.510.

ZGS na, ZRKS 4.217, Shiba 44, ZGJI 195, ZGDJT 1042c, ZGJT 185, KZS #248

4.512 裂轉鼻孔 *Bikū o retten su.*

He twists [the other's] nose.

Heki 53 Main Case *agyo*, 86 Verse *agyo*, 95 Main Case *agyo.*

ZGS 4.252, ZRKS 4.460, Shiba 73, ZGJI 195, ZGDJT 1042d, ZGJT 481

4.513 撞著鼻孔 *Bikū ni tōjaku su.*

He banged his nose against it.

Heki 91 Main Case *agyo.*

ZGS na, ZRKS 4.781, Shiba 56, ZGJT 342

4.514 鼻孔遼天 *Bikū ryōten su.*

He lifts his nose to the sky.

Heki 87 Verse.

ZGS 4.251, ZRKS 4.782, Shiba 62, ZGJI 195, ZGDJT 1042c, ZGJT 392

4.515 指東劃西 *Higashi o yubisashi, nishi o kaku.*

He points to the east, he gestures to the west.

Heki 4 Intro., 18 Main Case *agyo*, *Rinzai-roku* §11.

ZGS na, ZRKS 4.134, Shiba 43, ZGJI 195, ZGJT 175

4.516 皮栲栳禪 *Hikōrō no zen.*

Leather basket Zen.

I.e., heavy duty Zen.

ZGS na, Shiba 61, ZGJI 194, ZGJT 389

4.517 彼此得便 *Hishi tayori o etari.*

1. Here and there, got some news.
2. Here and there, got some benefit.

1. after Shiba 61; 2. after ZRKS 4.315: 彼此落便宜, "Here and there I have fallen into advantage."

ZGS 4.253, ZRKS 4.315, Shiba 61, ZGJI 194 (variant)

4.518 非心非佛 *Hishin hibutsu.*

Neither mind nor Buddha.

MMK 33, *Heki* 44 Main Case.

ZGS na, Shiba 61, ZGJI 194, ZGDJT 1044a, ZGJT 390

4.519 劈口便打 *Hikku sunawachi utsu.*

Slap right on the mouth.

Heki 51 Main Case *agyo.*

ZGS 4.254, Shiba na

4.520 劈腹剜心 *Hippuku wanshin.*

Cut open his chest and tear out his heart.

Heki 98 Main Case *agyo.*

ZGS 4.255, ZRKS 4.24, Shiba 65, ZGJI 200, ZGDJT 1045b, ZGJT 415

4.521 謾人不少 *Hito o manzuru koto sukunakarazu.*

He deceives people not just a little.

ZGS na, ZRKS 4.878, Shiba 67, ZGJI 196, KZS #431

4.522 無瞞人好 *Hito o manzuru nakumba yoshi.*

Better not to deceive people.

ZGS 4.256, Shiba na

4.523 停囚長智 *Hitoya ni todomatte chi o chōzu.*

Kept in prison, he extends his knowledge.

Heki 18 Main Case *agyo*, 51 Main Case *agyo.*

ZGS 4.257, ZRKS 4.280, Shiba 54, ZGJI 154, ZGDJT 1046a, ZGJT 319, KZS #270

4.524 日上月下 *Hi nobori tsuki kudaru.*

The sun rises, the ⌜moon⌝ sets.

Heki 2 Verse.

ZGS 4.258, ZRKS 4.14, Shiba 58

4.525 不惜眉毛 *Bimō o oshimazu.*

He does not care about his ⌜eyebrows⌝.

Heki 27 Intro. and Main Case Comm., 31 Main Case Comm., 51 Main Case Comm.

ZGS na, ZRKS 4.396, Shiba 62, ZGJI 194, ZGJT 399

4.526 惜取眉毛 *Bimō o shakushu seyo.*

Take good care of your ⌜eyebrows⌝.

Heki 31 Verse, 34 Main Case *agyo.*

ZGS 4.259, ZRKS 4.414, Shiba 49, ZGJI 194, ZGDJT 1047d, ZGJT 249

4.527 燎却眉毛 *Bimō o ryōkyaku su.*

He burned off his ⌜eyebrows⌝.

Heki 96 Verse 2 *agyo.*

ZGS na, ZRKS 4.793, Shiba 72, ZGJI 194, ZGDJT 1048a

4.528 披毛戴角 *Himō taikaku.*

[Beings that] wear fur or bear horns.

Rinzai-roku §19.

ZGS 4.260, ZRKS 4.620, Shiba na, ZGJI 194, ZGDJT 1048a, ZGJT 389

4.529 百年妖怪 *Hyakunen no yōkai.*

A hundred-year-old goblin.

ZGS 4.261, Shiba na

4.530 火煖水冷 *Hi wa atataka ni, mizu wa hiyayaka nari.*

Fire is hot, water is cold.

ZGS na, ZRKS 4.7, Shiba 32, ZGJI 194, KZS #122

4.531 賓主共失 *Hinju tomo ni shissu.*

Lose both host and guest.

Heki 92 Main Case *agyo.*

ZGS na, ZRKS 4.567, Shiba 62, ZGJI 196, ZGDJT 1057a

4.532 賓主互換 *Hinju gokan.*

Guest and host interchange.

Heki 20 Main Case Comm., 36 Main Case Comm., 50 Verse *agyo.*

ZGS 4.263, ZRKS 4.499, Shiba 62, ZGJI 196, ZGDJT 1057a, ZGJT 395

4.533 賓主歷然 *Hinju rekinen.*

Guest and host are clearly distinguished.

Rinzai-roku Preface and §4, *Heki* 20 Main Case Comm., 38 Main Case Comm.

ZGS na, ZRKS 4.974, Shiba 62, ZGJI 197, ZGDJT 1057b

4.534 閩蜀同風 *Binshoku dōfū.*

Whether in Min or Szechuan, always the same.

Min, in the southeast, and Szechuan, deep inland to the west, were considered far distant states in early China.

ZGS na, ZRKS 4.587, Shiba 62, ZGJI 208

4.535 和麩糶麵 *Fu ni washite men o uru.*

He sells noodles cut with bran.

ZGS na, ZRKS 4.576, Shiba 75, ZGJI 198, ZGDJT 1096b, ZGJT 495, KZS #576

4.536 傅大士底 *Fudaishi tei.*

As「Fu Daishi」[said, did].

ZGS 4.264, Shiba na

4.537 深辨來風 *Fukaku raifū o ben zu.*

He sees right through your approach.

Heki 4 Main Case Comm., 26 Main Case Comm., 27 Verse *agyo*, etc.

ZGS na, ZRKS 4.799, Shiba 47, ZGJI 198, ZGDJT 1061d, ZGJT 230, KZS #401

4.538 無事生事 *Buji ni ji o shōzu.*

There's no problem, but they make an issue.

Heki 8 Main Case Comm.

ZGS na, ZRKS 4.387, Shiba 68, ZGJI 198, ZGJT 406, KZS #29

4.539 截斷佛祖 *Busso o setsudan su.*

Cut off the buddhas and ancestors.

ZGS na, ZRKS 4.882, Shiba 49, KZS #177

4.540 佛祖不識 *Busso mo shirazu.*

Not even the buddhas and ancestors know.

ZGS na, Shiba 64, ZGJI 199

4.541 佛祖乞命 *Busso mo mei o kou.*

The buddhas and ancestors plead for their lives.

MMK 43.

ZGS 4.265, ZRKS 4.455, Shiba 64, ZGJI 199, ZGDJT 1089d, KZS #331

4.542 罵佛詈祖 *Butsu o nonoshiri, so o nonoshiru.*

He curses the buddhas, he damns the ancestors.

ZGS na, ZRKS 4.486, Shiba 60

4.543 父子唱和 *Fushi shōwa su.*

Father and son harmonize well together.

ZGS 4.266, ZRKS 4.347, Shiba 63, ZGJI 197

4.544 不喞嵧漢 *Fushitsuryū no kan.*

Slovenly fool!

Heki 1 Main Case *agyo*, 6 Verse *agyo*, 27 Verse *agyo*, etc.

ZGS 4.267, ZRKS 4.413, Shiba 62, ZGJI 197, ZGDJT 1073c, ZGJT 398, KZS #308

4.545 不生不死 *Fushō fushi.*

Unborn, undying.

ZGS na, ZRKS 4.928, Shiba 62

4.546 不請勝友 *Fushō no shōyū.*

A best friend needs no invitation.

Heki 62 Intro.

ZGS na, Shiba 62, ZGJI 197, ZGDJT 1075a

4.547 兩不相識 *Futatsunagara aishirazu.*

I do not know the two of them.

ZGS na, ZRKS 4.546, Shiba 72

4.548 刻舟尋劍 *Fune o kizami, ken o tazunu.*

He cuts a mark on the boat rail to search for his ⌜sword⌝.

See ⌜Slash the boat⌝.

ZGS 4.268, ZRKS 4.914, Shiba 41, ZGJI 199, ZGJT 141

4.549 不昧因果 *Fumai inga.*

He does not ignore karma.

MMK 2.

ZGS na, Shiba 63, ZGJI 197, ZGDJT 1098a, ZGJT 399

4.550 不落因果 *Furaku inga.*

He does not fall into karma.

MMK 2.

ZGS na, Shiba 63, ZGJI 197, ZGDJT 1100a

4.551 扶籬摸壁 *Furi moheki.*

Groping along the hedge, feeling along the wall.

Heki 7 Verse *agyo*, 86 Verse *agyo*, 94 Verse *agyo*, etc.

ZGS na, ZRKS 4.334, Shiba 63, ZGJI 197, ZGJT 404

4.552 分疎不下 *Bunso fuge.*

There's no explanation.

Heki 11 Main Case Comm., 58 Main Case Comm., 84 Main Case *agyo*, MMK 19.

ZGS na, ZRKS 4.199, Shiba 64, ZGJI 199, ZGDJT 1103d, ZGJT 411, KZS #241

4.553 米裏有蟲 *Beiri ni mushi ari.*

There are worms in the rice.

ZGS 4.270, ZRKS 4.837, Shiba 64, ZGJI 200

4.554 帶累別人 *Betsunin o tairui su.*

He drags in other people.

Heki 3 Main Case *agyo*, 48 Main Case *agyo*.

ZGS 4.271, ZRKS 4.494, Shiba na, ZGJI 200, ZGDJT 1112c, ZGJT 289

4.555 碧落無碑 *Hekiraku ni hi nashi.*

There is no 「Pi-lo Monument」.

ZGS na, ZRKS 4.958, Shiba 64

4.556 劈頭劈面 *Hekitō hekimen.*

Right to your head, right to your face.

Heki 43 Main Case *agyo*.

ZGS na, ZRKS 4.25, Shiba 64, ZGJI 200, ZGDJT 1111b, ZGJT 415

4.557 買帽相頭 *Bō o kau ni zu o sō su.*

1. To buy a hat, measure your head.
2. After buying a hat, he measures his head.

1. after ZGJI 203, ZGDJT 1012a; 2. after ZGJT 380. *Heki* 16 Main Case *agyo*, 55 Main Case Comm., 82 Verse Comm., etc. ZGDJT 1012a: *Baibō sōtō.*

ZGS 4.275, ZRKS 4.376, Shiba na, ZGJI 203, ZGDJT 1012a, ZGJT 380

4.558 識法者懼 *Hō o shiru mono wa osoru.*

One who knows the law fears it.

Heki 10 Verse Comm., 37 Main Case *agyo*, 50 Verse *agyo*, etc.

ZGS 4.277, ZRKS 4.36, Shiba 44, ZGJI 210, ZGJT 182, KZS #142

4.559 盡法無民 *Hō o tsukuseba tami nashi.*

Apply the law to the limit and the people will perish.

ZGS 4.276, ZRKS 4.74, Shiba na, ZGJI 201, ZGJT 233

4.560 放過一着 *Hōka itchaku.*

He let an opening go by.

ZGS 4.272, Shiba na

4.561 放下便是 *Hōge seba sunwachi ze.*

Let go and at once that's it.

ZGS na, ZRKS 4.608, Shiba 65, ZGJI 201, KZS #369

4.562 放去收來 *Hōko shūrai.*

Let out, take in.

Heki 4 Main Case *agyo*, 14 Main Case Comm., 75 Main Case *agyo*, etc. Shiba 65: *Hokyo shūrai.* ZRKS 4.111 has 収.

ZGS 4.273, ZRKS 4.111, Shiba 65, ZGJI 202, ZGDJT 1125d

4.563 傍人按劍 *Bōjin ken o an zu.*

On your flanks they're gripping their ⌜swords⌝.

Heki 23 Main Case *agyo*. See also 4.137, 4.564.

ZGS na, ZRKS 4.756, Shiba 66, ZGJI 203, ZGJT 428

4.564 傍人有眼 *Bōjin manako ari.*

It is the bystander who has the eye.

Heki 1 Main Case *agyo*, 38 Main Case *agyo*. See also 4.137, 4.563.

ZGS 4.274, ZRKS 4.571, Shiba 66, ZGJI 203, ZGDJT 1140b, ZGJT 428

4.565 忘前失後 *Bōzen shitsugo.*

Forget before, lose track after.

Heki 2 Main Case Comm., 34 Main Case *agyo* and Verse *agyo*.

ZGS na, ZRKS 4.194, Shiba 66, ZGJI 202, ZGJT 427, KZS #236

4.566 棒頭有眼 *Bōtō ni manako ari.*

His stick has an eye.

Heki 20 Main Case Comm., 65 Main Case *agyo*, 75 Main Case, etc.

ZGS na, ZRKS 4.472, Shiba 66, ZGJI 203, ZGDJT 1139c, ZGJT 428, KZS #335

4.567 墨悲糸染 *Boku ito no somu koto o kanashimu.*

⌜Mo-tzu⌝ lamented the dyeing of the thread.

ZGJI 203: 絲 instead of 糸.

ZGS na, Shiba 66, ZGJI 203

4.568 穆如清風 *Boku to shite seifū no gotoshi.*

Mild as a clean breeze.

ZGS na, Shiba 66, 詩經大雅

4.569 烹佛烹祖 *Hotoke o aburi, so o niru.*

Fry the buddhas and boil the ancestors.

ZGJI 198: *Butsu o aburi, so o aburu,* "Grill the buddhas, grill the ancestors."

ZGS na, ZRKS 4.900, Shiba 65, ZGJI 198, ZGJT 425

4.570 法華當體 *Hokke no tōtai.*

The actual embodiment of the *Lotus Sutra.*

ZGS 4.279, Shiba na

4.571 見星悟道 *Hoshi o mite dō o satoru.*

He saw the star and awakened to the Way.

ZGS 4.280, Shiba na

4.572 敲骨打髓 *Hone o tataki, zui o utsu.*

He shatters the bones, he smashes the marrow.

Variant: 取髓 "take the marrow" instead of 打髓. *Rinzai-roku* §8 in Ming edition.

ZGS na, ZRKS 4.476, Shiba 41, ZGJI 204, ZGJT 138

4.573 本地風光 *Honji no fūkō.*

The scenery on the fundamental ground.

Heki 97 Main Case Comm., 99 Verse Comm.

ZGS na, Shiba 66, ZGDJT 1163a, ZGJT 431

4.574 轉凡成聖 *Bon o tenijite shō to nasu.*

Turn ordinary folk into saints.

ZGS na, ZRKS 4.885, Shiba 55, ZGJI 204, ZGJT 329, KZS #178

4.575 梆八囉札 *Bonpa rasatsu.*

Dum! Dum! Drum! Drum!

The sound of the great drum. Shiba 65: *Bonpa rōsa.*

ZGS 4.278, Shiba 65

4.576 本分草料 *Honbun no sōryō.*

Fundamental feed.

Heki 18 Main Case *agyo*, 39 Verse Comm., 48 Main Case *agyo*, etc.

ZGS na, Shiba 66, ZGJI 204, ZGDJT 1168b, ZGJT 431

4.577 本來面目 *Honrai no menmoku.*

Your ⸢original face⸣.

Heki 97 Main Case Comm., 99 Main Case Comm., MMK 23.

ZGS na, Shiba 66, ZGJI 204, ZGDJT 1169c, ZGJT 431

4.578 如麻似粟 *Ma no gotoku, zoku ni nitari.*

Like hemp, like millet.

Heki 17 Verse *agyo*, 23 Verse *agyo*, 25 Main Case *agyo*, etc.

ZGS na, ZRKS 4.597, Shiba 45, ZGDJT 1176b, ZGJT 205

4.579 賣弄不少 *Mairō sukunakarazu.*

Not just a little self-promotion.

ZGS na, ZRKS 4.755, Shiba 60, ZGJI 191

4.580 全依他力 *Mattaku tariki ni yoru.*

Completely depend on another's power.

Heki 32 Main Case *agyo*, 91 Verse *agyo*.

ZGS 4.281, ZRKS 4.43, Shiba na, ZGJI 204

4.581 松直棘曲 *Matsu wa naoku, odoro wa magareri.*

Pines are straight, thorns are bent.

ZGJI 205: *ibara* instead of *odoro*.

ZGS 4.282, ZRKS 4.2, Shiba 45, ZGJI 205, ZGDJT 1173d, ZGJT 213, KZS #118

4.582 間不容髮 *Ma ni hatsu o irezu.*

You can't insert even a hair in between.

ZGDJT 188a: *Kan hatsu o irezu.*

ZGS 4.283, ZRKS 4.714, Shiba na, ZGDJT 188a, ZGJT 68

4.583 眉分八字 *Mayu hachi ji ni wakaru.*

His ⸢eyebrows⸣ divide into the figure eight.

Heki 30. The Chinese character for "eight" consists of two lines sloping down and out 八. This does not, as one might think, express sadness. The eyebrows are raised as when one pays full attention to what is in front of one's eyes (Shiba 61, ZGJT 391).

ZGS na, ZRKS 4.747, Shiba 61, ZGJI 205, ZGDJT 1176c, ZGJT 391, KZS #392

4.584 滿口道著 *Manku ni dōchaku su.*

He gave a full-mouthed explanation.

ZGS na, ZRKS 4.397, Shiba 67, ZGJI 206, ZGJT 436

4.585 滿口氷雪 *Manku no hyōsetsu.*

Mouth full of ice and snow.

ZGS 4.284, ZRKS 4.908, Shiba 67, ZGJI 206

4.586 滿面慚惶 *Manmen no zankō.*

Face completely covered in shame.

Heki 1 Main Case *agyo*, 2 Intro. Shiba 67: 惺 instead of 惶.

ZGS 4.285, ZRKS 4.731, Shiba 67, ZGJI 206, ZGJT 437

4.587 藏身露影 *Mi o kakushite kage o arawasu.*

He hides himself but reveals his shadow.

Heki 28 Main Case *agyo*, 43 Main Case *agyo*, 73 Main Case *agyo*, etc.

ZGS na, ZRKS 4.152, Shiba 51, ZGJI 206, ZGDJT 738c, ZGJT 272, KZS #152

4.588 兼身在内 *Mi o kanete uchi ni ari.*

It is identical with your self, inside.

Heki 13 Verse *agyo*, 33 Verse *agyo*, 91 Main Case *agyo*.

ZGS na, ZRKS 4.148, Shiba 39, ZGJI 206, ZGDJT 1180d, ZGJT 108, KZS #204

4.589 轉身吐氣 *Mi o tenjite ki o haku.*

He spins around, blows out his breath.

Heki 59 Main Case Comm., 72 Verse *agyo*, 79 Main Case Comm., etc.

ZGS na, ZRKS 4.508, Shiba 55, ZGDJT 1180d

4.590 文身斷髮 *Mi o modoroge kami o tatsu.*

He tattoos his body and cuts his hair.

Tattooing the body and cutting the hair were considered barbarian practices in early China. See, for example, *Chuang-tzu*, ch. 1 (Watson 1968, 28).

ZGS na, ZRKS 4.542, Shiba 64, 史記評林四周本記四丁

4.591 和身沒卻 *Mi ni washite bokkyaku su.*

With his body, he submerges himself [in the world].

Heki 23 Verse *agyo*.

ZGS na, ZRKS 4.456, Shiba 75, ZGJI 206

4.592 作縮身勢 *Mi o chijimuru ikioi o nasu.*

To assume a crouching posture.

ZGS 4.286, Shiba na

4.593 未在更道 *Mizai sara ni ie.*

Not yet! Say again!

ZGS na, Shiba 67

4.594 水到渠成 *Mizu itareba mizo naru.*

If water runs there, then there's a channel.

Heki 6 Verse Comm.

ZGS na, ZRKS 4.379, Shiba 47, ZGJI 207, ZGJT 235, KZS #297

4.595 撥水求波 *Mizu o haratte nami o motomu.*

He thrashes the water searching for waves.

ZGS na, Shiba 60

4.596 履水如地 *Mizu o fumu koto chi no gotoshi.*

Stands on water as if on earth.

Rinzai-roku §16.

ZGS na, ZRKS 4.1007, Shiba 72

4.597 塡溝塞壑 *Mizo ni michi, gaku ni fusagaru.*

The channels are full, the waterways are clogged.

Heki 16 Verse *agyo.*

ZGS 4.287, ZRKS 4.18, Shiba 55, ZGJT 329, KZS #130

4.598 道聽途説 *Michi ni kiite to ni toku.*

Hear it on the road and speak it on the Way.

ZGS na, ZRKS 4.410, Shiba 57, ZGJI 206, KZS #307

4.599 密密通風 *Mitsu mitsu ni fū o tsūzu.*

A secret something passes between them.

ZGS 4.288, ZRKS 4.163, Shiba 67, ZGJI 207, KZS #213

4.600 掩耳偸鈴 *Mimi o ōte suzu o nusumu.*

He covers his ears to steal the bell.

Heki 85 Main Case.

ZGS 4.289, ZRKS 4.122, Shiba 32, ZGJI 208, ZGDJT 1185b, ZGJT 34, KZS #198, ZD #40

4.601 明暗雙雙 *Meian sōsō.*

Light and dark, two together.

Heki 51 Verse.

ZGS 4.290, Shiba 68, ZGJI 384

4.602 妙觸宣明 *Myōsoku senmyō.*

Subtle contact releases the radiance.

Heki 78 Main Case.

ZGS na, Shiba 67, ZGJI 208, ZGDJT 1193b, ZGJT 439

4.603 無位眞人 *Mui i no shinnin.*

True person without rank.

Rinzai-roku Preface and §3, *Heki* 32 Main Case Comm., 73 Verse Comm.

ZGS na, Shiba 67, ZGJI 208, ZGDJT 1199c, ZGJT 440

4.604 無依道人 *Mue no dōnin.*

A person of the Way who leans on nothing.

Rinzai-roku §15, §17, §19.

ZGS na, Shiba 67, ZGJI 208, ZGDJT 1200d, ZGJT 441

4.605 無孔鐵鎚 *Muku no tettsui.*

An ⌜iron hammerhead without a socket⌝.

Heki 14 Main Case *agyo*, 29 Main Case *agyo*, 30 Main Case Comm., etc. MMK 17.

ZGS na, ZRKS 4.876, Shiba 67, ZGJI 209, ZGDJT 1202d, ZGJT 441

4.606 無作妙用 *Musa no myōyū.*

The wondrous act of not-doing.

ZGS 4.291, Shiba 68, ZGJI 209, ZGDJT 1204c

4.607 無繩自縛 *Mujō jibaku.*

Without any rope, he ties himslf up.

Heki 73 Main Case *agyo*, *Rinzai-roku* §6, MMK Appendix after Case 48.

ZGS 4.292, ZRKS 4.775, Shiba 68, ZGJI 209, ZGDJT 1208d, ZGJT 441, KZS #398

4.608 目瞪口呿 *Me tō shi, kuchi kyo su.*

Eyes wide open, mouth agape.

ZGS na, ZRKS 4.889, Shiba 70, ZGJI 209, ZGJT 450

4.609 明鏡當臺 *Meikyō tai ni ataru.*

The bright mirror is on the stand.

Heki 9 Intro., 24 Main Case Comm., 28 Verse, etc.

ZGS 4.293, ZRKS 4.563, Shiba 69, ZGJI 209, ZGDJT 1215d, ZGJT 444

4.610 明月藏鷺 *Meigetsu ni ro o kakusu.*

Hide a white heron in the silver moonlight.

ZGS 4.294, ZRKS 4.557, Shiba 68, ZGJI 210, ZGDJT 1216a

4.611 命若懸絲 *Mei kenshi no gotoshi.*

Life hangs by a thread.

ZGS na, ZRKS 4.819, Shiba 68, ZGJI 210

4.612 明皇幸蜀 *Meikō shoku ni miyuki su.*

The Brilliant Emperor has gone to Szechuan.

See ⌜Yang Kuei-fei⌝.

ZGS 4.295, ZRKS 4.847, Shiba 68

4.613 明珠在掌 *Meishu tanagokoro ni ari.*

The bright pearl is in the palm of my hand.

Heki 34 Main Case Comm., 80 Verse *agyo*, 97 Verse, etc.

ZGS na, ZRKS 4.558, Shiba 68, ZGJI 210, ZGDJT 555c, ZGJT 444

4.614 明明歷歷 *Mei-mei reki-reki.*

Bright and clear, detailed and sharp.

ZGS na, ZRKS 4.559, Shiba 68

4.615 抛向面前 *Menzen ni hōkō su.*

Throw it right in your face.

Heki 1 Verse Comm., 5 Main Case.

ZGS 4.296, ZRKS 4.828, Shiba 65, KZS #145

4.616 面壁九年 *Menpeki kyūnen.*

⌜Nine years facing the wall⌝.

Heki 1 Main Case Comm.

ZGS na, Shiba 69, ZGDJT 1221d

4.617 綿綿密密 *Men-men mitsu-mitsu.*

Very detailed, very careful.

ZGS 4.297, Shiba 69, ZGJI 384, ZGDJT 1222a

4.618 綿裏有刀 *Menri ni yaiba ari.*

In the cotton fluff, there is a knife.

ZGS 4.298, ZRKS 4.786, Shiba 69, ZGJI 210

4.619 綿裏包針 *Menri ni hari o tsutsumu.*

Wrap a needle in cotton fluff.

ZGS 4.299, ZRKS 4.393, Shiba 69, ZGJI 210

4.620 作模畫樣 *Mo o nashi yō o kaku.*

He postures, he imitates.

Variant: 作模作樣. *Heki* 18 Main Case *agyo*. *Rinzai-roku* §19.

ZGS 4.300, ZRKS 4.175, Shiba na, ZGJI 210, ZGDJT 1222b, ZGJT 151, KZS #227

4.621 目機銖兩 *Mok⌜ki⌝ shuryō.*

His practiced eye measures precisely.

Heki 1 Intro., 65 Intro.

ZGS na, Shiba 69, ZGJI 211, ZGDJT 1227d, ZGJT 450

4.622 目前分明 *Mokuzen funmyō.*

Before my very eyes, vivid and sharp.

ZGS na, ZRKS 4.556, Shiba 69, ZGJI 211, KZS #356

4.623 摸索不著 *Mosaku fujaku.*

To seek and not find.

Heki 1 Main Case *agyo*, 38 Intro., 56 Intro., etc.

ZGS 4.301, ZRKS 4.174, Shiba 69, ZGJI 210, ZGDJT 1227b, ZGJT 448, KZS #218

4.624 把髻投衙 *Motodori o totte ga ni tō zu.*

He takes his own topknot and presents it to the authorities.

Heki 81 Main Case *agyo*, 84 Main Case *agyo*. When a man was found guilty of a crime punishable by beheading, his topknot would be cut off before his execution (ZGJT 375, ZGJI 211).

ZGS na, ZRKS 4.778, Shiba 60, ZGJI 211, ZGJT 375, KZS #399

4.625 物歸有主 *Mono wa ushu ni ki su.*

Everything returns to its proper place.

ZGS na, ZRKS 4.99, Shiba 64, ZGJI 211, ZGJT 410, KZS #175

4.626 指桃罵李 *Momo o yubisashi sumomo o nonoshiru.*

Pointing to a plum, he damns the ⌜peach⌝.

ZGS na, Shiba 43, ZGJI 211

4.627 文彩已露 *Monsai sude ni arawaru.*

Shapes, colors, have already appeared.

Heki 7 Verse *agyo*. Shiba 64, ZGJI 199: *bunsai* instead of *monsai.*

ZGS 4.302, ZRKS 4.109, Shiba 64, ZGJI 199, ZGDJT 1230d, ZGJT 452

4.628 箭過新羅 *Ya shinra o sugu.*

The arrow has flown off to ⌜Silla⌝.

Heki 1 Main Case *agyo*, 27 Verse *agyo*, 30 Main Case *agyo*, 36 Main Case *agyo*, etc.

ZGS 4.303, ZRKS 4.180, Shiba 50, ZGJI 212, ZGDJT 1234a, ZGJT 258, KZS #225

4.629 藥病相治 *Yakuhei aijisu.*

Drug and disease cure each other.

Rinzai-roku §14, §23. *Heki* 87 Main Case.

ZGS na, ZRKS 4.673, Shiba 70, ZGJI 212, ZGDJT 1236c, ZGJT 457

4.630 柳綠花紅 *Yanagi wa midori, hana wa kurenai.*

The willows are green, the flowers are red.

ZGS 4.304, ZRKS 4.5, Shiba 72, ZGJI 212, ZGJT 473, KZS #120

4.631 也褒也貶 *Yahō, yahen.*

That's great! That's awful!

Heki 39 Main Case *agyo.*

ZGS 4.305, ZRKS 4.326, Shiba na, ZGJI 212

4.632 病在膏肓 *Yamai kōkō ni ari.*

The disease has entered the vital region.

See「Life-and-death illness」.

ZGS na, ZRKS 4.861, Shiba 62

4.633 行吟澤畔 *Yuku-yuku takuhan ni ginzu.*

Strolling, singing on the edge of the pond.

ZGS 4.306, Shiba na

4.634 弓折矢盡 *Yumi ore, ya tsuku.*

Bow broken, arrows all spent.

ZGS 4.307, ZRKS 4.176, Shiba na, ZGJT 86, KZS #219

4.635 鎖斷要關 *Yōkan o sadan su.*

Block off the main arteries.

Heki 31 Main Case Comm.

ZGS na, ZRKS 4.757, Shiba 42, ZGJT 152

4.636 養子之緣 *Yōshi no en.*

The parent's bond with the child.

Heki 3 Main Case *agyo*, 46 Main Case *agyo*. 養子 does not mean an adopted child. The character 養 here means "give birth to" (ZGJT 463, ZGDJT 1250a).

ZGS 4.308, ZRKS 4.389, Shiba na, ZGJI 213, ZGDJT 1250a, ZGJT 463

4.637 揚眉瞬目 *Yōbi shunmoku.*

A lift of the「eyebrows」, a blink of the eyes.

ZGS na, ZRKS 4.626, Shiba 71, ZGJI 213, ZGDJT 1252b, ZGJT 462

4.638 弋不射宿 *Yoku suredomo netori o irazu.*

When hunting, he does not shoot birds at rest.

Analects VII, 26. ZRKS 4.831n: *Hōgo:* A skilled swordsman does not cut a dead man. See also 8.293.

ZGS na, ZRKS 4.831, Shiba 71, ZGJI 213, ZGJT 463

4.639 癩兒牽伴 *Raiji ban o hiku.*

The leper drags along his friends.

Heki 12 Verse *agyo*, 19 Verse *agyo*, 89 Main Case *agyo*, etc.

ZGS 4.309, ZRKS 4.596, Shiba 71, ZGJI 214, ZGDJT 1256d, ZGJT 467, KZS #366, ZD #47

4.640 禮拜了退 *Raihai shiowatte shirizoke.*

Bow and then withdraw.

Heki 2 Main Case, 59 Main Case Comm.

ZGS 4.310, Shiba na

4.641 雷門布鼓 *Raimon no fuko.*

At the Thunder Gate, a ⌜cloth drum⌝.

Above the Thunder Gate entrance to the city of K'uai-chi 會稽 was a huge drum whose boom was heard even in distant Lo-yang. A drum made of cloth, however, makes no sound (ZGJT 466, ZGJI 213).

ZGS 4.311, ZRKS 4.890, Shiba 71, ZGJI 213, ZGDJT 1257d, ZGJT 466

4.642 落草不少 *Rakusō sukunakarazu.*

Not just a few fall into the weeds.

ZGS 4.312, ZRKS 4.968, Shiba 71, ZGJI 214

4.643 理事俱備 *Ri ji tomo ni sonawaru.*

The ⌜real and the apparent⌝ come together.

ZGS na, ZRKS 4.314, Shiba 71, ZGJI 214

4.644 理事不二 *Ri ji funi.*

The ⌜real and the apparent⌝ are not two.

ZGS na, Shiba 72

4.645 狸奴白牯 *Ri'nu byakko.*

The badger and the white bull.

Heki 61 Main Case Comm.

ZGS na, ZRKS 4.612, Shiba 71, ZGJI 214, ZGDJT 1268d, ZGJT 471

4.646 龍天推轂 *Ryūten suikoku.*

The dragon gods put their shoulders to the wheel.

ZGS 4.313, Shiba 72

4.647 龍頭蛇尾 *Ryōtō dabi.*

Head of a dragon, tail of a snake.

Heki 10 Verse *agyo*, 11 Main Case *agyo*, 28 Main Case *agyo*, etc.

ZGS 4.314, ZRKS 4.193, Shiba na, ZGDJT 1277b, ZGJT 474

4.648 牽犂拽耙 *Ri o hiki ha o hiku.*

Leading a water buffalo, pulling a plow.

ZGS 4.315, Shiba na

4.649 壓良爲賤 *Ryō o oshite sen to nasu.*

To force a noble person to be mean.

MMK 6.

ZGS 4.316, ZRKS 4.205, Shiba na, ZGJI 215, ZGDJT 1290c, ZGJT 36

4.650 兩鏡相照 *Ryōkyō aiterasu.*

Two mirrors reflect each other.

Heki 24 Main Case Comm.

ZGS 4.317, ZRKS 4.438, Shiba 72, ZGJI 215, ZGDJT 1282d, ZGJT 476

4.651 兩口一舌 *Ryōku ichizetsu.*

Two mouths, one tongue.

ZGS na, ZRKS 4.600, Shiba 72, ZGJI 215, ZGDJT 1282d, KZS #367

4.652 兩彩一賽 *Ryōsai issai.*

Both odd and even on one throw of the dice.

Heki 39 Main Case *agyo*, MMK 2. Shiba 29, ZGJI 111: 一彩両賽. Shiba 72: 采 instead of 彩.

ZGS na, ZRKS 4.266, Shiba 72, ZGJI 111, ZGJT 17, KZS #264

4.653 龍聚鳳翔 *Ryōshū hōshō.*

Dragons gather, phoenixes wheel in the air.

ZGS na, Shiba 72, ZGJI 215

4.654 兩刄相傷 *Ryōjin aisokonau.*

Two blades slash each other.

Heki 4 Verse *agyo*.

ZGS na, ZRKS 4.439, Shiba 72, ZGDJT 1286c, ZGJT 476

4.655 驪龍玩珠 *Riryū tama o moteasobu.*

The black dragon plays with its pearl.

Heki 62 Verse *agyo*. See「Black dragon pearl」.

ZGS na, ZRKS 4.773, Shiba 72, ZGJI 214, ZGJT 472

4.656 有禮有樂 *Rei ari, gaku ari.*

There are rites, there is music.

ZGS 4.318, ZRKS 4.335, Shiba na

4.657 靈龜曳尾 *Reiki o o hiko.*

The spirit turtle sweeps its tail.

Heki 4 Main Case *agyo*, 12 Intro., 27 Verse Comm., etc.

ZGS 4.319, ZRKS 4.192, Shiba 73, ZGJI 217, ZGJT 481, KZS #234, ZD #45

4.658 冷笑一番 *Reishō ichiban.*

A sneer.

ZGS 4.320, Shiba na

4.659 冷暖自知 *Reidan jichi su.*

Know for yourself hot and cold.

MMK 23, KZS #355: *Reinan onozukara shiru.*

ZGS 4.321, ZRKS 4.555, Shiba 73, ZGJI 216, ZGDJT 1305d, ZGJT 353, KZS #355

4.660 據令而行 *Rei ni yotte gyō zu.*

He acted according to law.

Heki 19 Verse *agyo*, 31 Verse *agyo*, 34 Main Case Comm., etc.

ZGS na, ZRKS 4.770, Shiba 36, ZGJI 216, ZGDJT 1300d, ZGJT 89

4.661 令不虚行 *Rei midari ni gyōzu.*

He does not rule arbitrarily.

Heki 26 Main Case *agyo*. MMK 14.

ZGS na, Shiba 73, ZGJI 216, ZGJT 479

4.662 羚羊挂角 *Reiyō tsuno o kaku.*

The antelope hooks its horns [into the trees].

See「Horn-hooking antelope」.

ZGS na, Shiba 73

4.663 看樓打樓 *Rō o mite rō o ta su.*

See tit, give tat.

Heki 41 Main Case *agyo*.

ZGS na, ZRKS 4.763, Shiba 34, ZGJI 218, ZGDJT 1315c, ZGJT 65

4.664 認驢作馬 *Ro o mitomete uma to nasu.*

He mistook a donkey for a horse.

ZGS 4.323, Shiba na, ZGJI 218, ZGJT 336

4.665 渡驢渡馬 *Ro o watashi, uma o watasu.*

He lets donkeys pass, he lets horses pass.

Heki 52 Main Case.

ZGS na, ZRKS 4.329, Shiba 55, ZGJI 218

4.666 螻蟻蚊虻 *Rōgi bunmo.*

Crickets, ants, mosquitoes, horseflies.

ZGS 4.322, ZRKS 4.617, Shiba na, ZGJI 219

4.667 臘月扇子 *Rōgetsu no sensu.*

A fan in December.

ZGS 4.324, ZRKS 4.638, Shiba 74, ZGJI 219, ZGJT 493

4.668 労而無功 *Rō shite kō nashi.*

Work hard and accomplish nothing.

Heki 84 Verse *agyo*, 91 Main Case.

ZGS 4.325, ZRKS 4.805, Shiba 74, ZGJT 490, KZS #406, ZD #48

4.669 老鼠做大 *Rōso dai o nasu.*

The old rat has gotten big.

ZGS 4.326, Shiba na

4.670 魯祖面壁 *Roso menpeki.*

Roso faces the wall.

A student asked Roso Hōun 魯祖寶雲 (Ch. Lu-tsu), a disciple of Baso Dōitsu 馬祖道一 (Ch. Ma-tsu Tao-i), "Why are you sitting facing the wall?" Roso just continued to sit facing the wall (ZGDJT 1322c, 1119b).

ZGS 4.327, Shiba na, ZGDJT 1322c

4.671 魯般縄墨 *Roban ga jōboku.*

⌜Lu Pan⌝ draws a line.

Lu Pan is the god of carpenters. *Jōboku* 縄墨 literally means "cord black." A carpenter draws a line by stretching taut a string dyed with black ink and snapping it against his board (ZGDJT 1323c).

ZGS na, Shiba 73, ZGDJT 1323c, Giles 1939 #1424.

4.672 驢駝馬載 *Ro ni da shi, ba ni sai su.*

Load onto donkeys, pack onto horses.

Heki 33 Verse, 97 Main Case *agyo*. ZGS 4.328: 馱 instead of 駝. ZGDJT 1322c: *ba ni no su* instead of *ba ni sai su*.

ZGS 4.328, ZRKS 4.796, Shiba na, ZGJI 218, ZGDJT 1322c, ZGJT 486

4.673 露地白牛 *Roji no byakko.*

The white ox on the bare ground.

Rinzai-roku §36, *Heki* 94 Intro.

ZGS na, Shiba 73, ZGJI 217, ZGDJT 1321c, ZGJT 485

4.674 露柱懐胎 *Rochū kaitai.*

The post nurtures something in its womb.

ZGS na, ZRKS 4.964, Shiba 74, ZGJI 217, ZGJT 485

4.675 露柱燈籠 *Rochū tōrō.*

The post, the lantern.

Heki 15 Main Case Comm., 21 Main Case Comm.

ZGS na, Shiba 74, ZGJI 217, ZGJT 485

4.676 撞著露柱 *Rochū ni dōchaku su.*

He's crashed into the post.

Heki 78 Main Case *agyo.*

ZGS na, ZRKS 4.727, Shiba 57, ZGJI 217, ZGDJT 1322d, ZGJT 342, KZS #381

4.677 漏逗不少 *Rōtō sukunakarazu.*

Not just a little old and decrepit.

Heki 2 Verse Comm., 3 Main Case *agyo*, 28 Main Case *agyo*, etc.

ZGS na, ZRKS 4.753, Shiba 74, ZGJI 218, ZGJT 492, KZS #394

4.678 我甚勞倦 *Ware hanahada rōken su.*

I am very tired and weary.

ZGS 4.329, Shiba na

4.679 我到無功 *Ware mukō ni itaru.*

I ended up with no merit.

ZGS 4.330, Shiba na

4.680 和敬清寂 *Wa kei sei jaku.*

Harmony, respect, purity, tranquillity.

The four fundamentals of the tea ceremony.

ZGS na, Shiba 74

4.681 和光同塵 *Wakō dōjin.*

Soften one's light and mingle in the dust.

ZGS na, Shiba 75

4.682 和尚年尊 *⌜Oshō⌝ nenson.*

The priest is very old in years.

Heki 91 Main Case.

ZGS na, ZRKS 4.432, Shiba 75, ZGJI 219, KZS #318

Five-Character Phrases

5
字

5.1 相牽入火坑 *Aihiite kakyō ni iru.*

They drag each other into the fire pit.

Heki 36 Main Case *agyo.*

ZGS 5.1, ZRKS 5.261, Shiba 100, ZGJI 221, ZGDJT 2d, KZS #515

5.2 惡水驀頭澆 *Akusui makutō ni sosogu.*

Pour filthy water right on his head.

Heki 1 Main Case Comm., 55 Main Case *agyo*, 78 Main Case *agyo.*

ZGS na, ZRKS 5.273, Shiba 76, ZGJI 221, ZGJT 5, KZS #527

5.3 啞子喫苦瓜 *Asu kuka o kissu.*

The mute eats a bitter melon.

Heki 3 Verse *agyo*, 75 Main Case *agyo.*

ZGS 5.2, Shiba 76, ZGJI 221, ZGDJT 5c

5.4 如啞子得夢 *Asu no yume o uru ga gotoshi.*

Like a mute who has had a dream.

MMK 1.

ZGS na, Shiba 94, ZGJI 221

5.5 亞夫擊摧玉 *Afu utte tama o kudaku.*

The servant smashes the jewel to pieces.

ZGS 5.3, Shiba na, HYDCD (亞夫) 1.542

5.6 阿房曳衣底 *Abō koromo o hiku tei.*

The way they trail their robes in the ⌜O-pang Palace⌝.

ZGS 5.4, Shiba na

5.7 欲雨山色近 *Ame furan to hosshite sanshoku chikashi.*

Just before it rains, the mountains look closer.

ZGS 5.5, Shiba 119

5.8 雨降地上濕 *Ame futte chijō uruou.*

Rain falls and wets the ground.

MMK 34 Verse.

ZGS na, ZRKS 5.5, Shiba 79, KZS #437

5.9 臨危不悚人 *Ayauki ni nozonde hito o osorezu.*

Facing danger, he fears no one.

ZGS na, ZRKS 5.295, Shiba 120, ZGJI 221, KZS #545

5.10 過則勿憚改 *Ayamatte wa sunawachi aratamuru ni habakaru koto nakare.*

If you have faults, do not hesitate to correct them.

Analects I, 8.

ZGS na, ZRKS 5.468, Shiba 80

5.11 莫謂得便宜 *Iu nakare bengi o etari to.*

Speak not of gaining advantage.

ZGS 5.197, Shiba na

5.12 何處不稱尊 *Izure no tokoro ka son to shō sezaru.*

What place cannot be called a place of honor?

MMK 46.

ZGS na, ZRKS 5.75, Shiba 79, ZGJI 225, KZS #461

5.13 聞一以知十 *Ichi o kiite motte jū o shiru.*

He hears one part and understands all ten.

Analects V, 8.

ZGS na, ZRKS 5.428, Shiba 113

5.14 一鏃破三關 *Ichizoku hasankan.*

One arrow smashes three barriers.

Heki 56 Main Case.

ZGS na, ZRKS 5.211, Shiba 78, ZGJI 224, ZGJT 19, ZGDJT 32c

5.15 一擊忘所知 *Ichigeki shochi o bōzu.*

One "tock!" and he forgot all he knew.

"Tock" here is the sound of stone striking bamboo. From the story of how Kyōgen Chikan attained awakening (Shibayama 1974, 55–6).

ZGS na, Shiba 77, ZGJI 223, ZGDJT 217d

5.16 一條白練去 *Ichijō no byakuren ni shi sare.*

Become a single thread of white spun silk.

ZGS na, Shiba 77, ZGJI 223

5.17 一大事因緣 *Ichidaiji innen.*

The one great matter, cause and condition.

ZGS na, Shiba 78, ZGJI 224, ZGDJT 32c

5.18 一念萬年去 *Ichinen bannen ni shi sare.*

Make one moment of thought into an eternity.

ZGS na, Shiba 78, ZGJI 224

5.19 一馬生三寅 *Ichima san'in o shōzu.*

One horse gives birth to three tigers.

ZGS na, ZRKS 5.344, Shiba 78, ZGJT 19

5.20 一無位眞人 *Ichi mui no shinnin.*

The true person without rank.

Rinzai-roku §3, *Heki* 32 Main Case Comm., 73 Verse Comm.

ZGS na, Shiba 78, ZGJI 522

5.21 一盲引衆盲 *Ichimō shūmō o hiku.*

One blind person leads a group of the blind.

MMK 46 Verse, *Heki* 5 Main Case *agyo*, 9 Main Case Comm.

ZGS 5.6, ZRKS 5.420, Shiba 78, ZGJI 224, ZGJT 20, KZS #484

5.22 一句定綱宗 *Ikku kōshū o sadamu.*

One word wraps up the entire net of teachings.

ZGS na, ZRKS 5.404, Shiba 77, ZGJT 18

5.23 一箇鐵橛子 *Ikko no tekkessu.*

An iron stake.

Heki 44 Main Case *agyo*.

ZGS na, ZRKS 5.221, Shiba 77, ZGJI 223, ZGJT 19

5.24 一切在和尚 *Issai* ⌜*oshō*⌝ *ni ari.*

It's all up to the priest.

ZGS 5.7, Shiba na

5.25 一箭中紅心 *Issen kōshin ni ataru.*

One arrow hits the red heart.

The Chinese archery target had a red center (ZGJT 19, ZGJI 223).

ZGS na, ZRKS 5.308, Shiba 77, ZGJI 223, ZGJT 19, KZS #520

5.26 一髮繋千鈞 *Ippatsu senkin o tsunagu.*

Hang a ton on a single strand of hair.

"Ton" here translates *senkin* (1,000 *chün*). See ⌜Catty⌝.

ZGS 5.8, Shiba na

5.27 一髮引千鈞 *Ippatsu senkin o hiku.*

A single strand of hair pulls a ton.

"Ton" here translates *senkin* (1,000 *chün*). See ⌜Catty⌝.

ZGS 5.9, Shiba na

5.28 一箭過西天 *Issen saiten o sugu.*

The arrow has shot past India.

Rinzai-roku §62.

ZGS 5.10, Shiba 77, ZGJI 223, ZGJT 19

5.29 一箭落雙鵰 *Issen sōchō o otosu.*

With one arrow he shoots down two hawks.

Heki 87 Verse *agyo*. See ⌜General Li⌝.

ZGS na, ZRKS 5.155, Shiba 77, ZGJI 223, ZGJT 19, KZS #481

5.30 賺殺一船人 *Issen no hito o rensatsu su.*

He duped people by the boatload.

ZGJI 223: *Issen no hito o kensatsu su. Heki* 31 Main Case *agyo*, 43 Main Case *agyo*, 47 Verse *agyo*, et al.

ZGS 5.11, ZRKS 5.252, Shiba na, ZGJI 223, ZGJT 482, KZS #508

5.31 一隊野狐精 *Ittai no yakosei.*

A pack of ⌜wild foxes⌝.

ZGS 5.12, ZRKS 5.105, Shiba na, ZGJI 224, ZGJT 19

5.32 何處是妄語 *Izure no tokoro kore mōgo.*

In what way are these words false?

ZGS 5.13, Shiba na

5.33 今請與一盞 *Ima kou issan o ataeyo.*

Please now, give me a cupful.

ZGS 5.14, Shiba na

5.34 恐喪盡兒孫 *Osoraku wa jison o sōjin su.*

There's a chance he may kill off all his descendants.

ZGS 5.15, Shiba na

5.35 無可無不可 *Ka mo naku fuka mo nashi.*

I have no "thou shalt" or "thou shalt not."

Analects XVIII, 8; WALEY 1938, 222.

ZGS na, ZRKS 5.464, Shiba 116

5.36 海月澄無影 *Kaigetsu sunde kage nashi.*

Moonlight luminous on the sea—no shadows.

Rinzai-roku §66.

ZGS na, ZRKS 5.381, Shiba 80, ZGJI 227, Watson 1993: 123

5.37 蝦跳不出斗 *Ka odoru mo to o idezu.*

The shrimp can't jump out of the scoop.

Heki 6 Main Case *agyo*, 13 Verse *agyo*, 31 Main Case *agyo*, 89 Main Case *agyo*. Shiba 80: 鰕 instead of 蝦.

ZGS 5.16, ZRKS 5.231, Shiba 80, ZGJI 227, ZGJT 50, ZGDJT 103d and 133c, KZS #502

5.38 家家觀世音 *Ka-ka kanzeon.*

⌜Kuan-yin⌝ in every house.

ZGS 5.17, Shiba na, ZGJT 47

5.39 餓狗喫繂綍 *Gaku kenri o kissu.*

A starving dog will eat rags.

ZGS 5.18, Shiba na

5.40 餓狗嚙枯髏 *Gaku koro o kamu.*

The starving dog chews an old skull.

ZGS 5.19, Shiba na, ZGJI 227, ZGDJT 151b

5.41 鑊湯無冷處 *Kakutō ni reisho nashi.*

There's no cool spot in a cauldron of boiling water.

ZGS 5.20, ZRKS 5.219, Shiba 81, ZGJI 228, ZGJT 60

5.42 臨崖看虎兕 *Gake ni nozonde koji o miru.*

At the brink of the cliff, he sees the tiger.

Heki 43 Main Case *agyo*.

ZGS na, ZRKS 5.373, Shiba 120, ZGJI 228, ZGJT 478, ZGDJT 134b

5.43 果然上鈎來 *Kanen to shite tsuribari ni noborikitaru.*

As expected, he took the hook and he's coming up.

Heki 42 Main Case *agyo*. ZRKS 5.256: 鉤 instead of 鈎.

ZGS na, ZRKS 5.256, Shiba 80, KZS #511

5.44 果然把不着 *Kanen to shite hafujaku.*

As expected, you can't grasp it.

ZGS 5.21, Shiba 80

5.45 畫梅香芬芬 *Gabai kō fun-fun.*

The painting of the plum, how rich its fragrance!

ZGS 5.22, Shiba 80

5.46 畫瓶盛糞汁 *Gabei ni funjū o moru.*

An ornate jar filled with shit soup.

ZGS 5.23, Shiba na

5.47 寒光射斗牛 *Kankō togyū o iru.*

The cold light illuminates the ⌜Dipper and the Ox⌝.

See also 5.190.

ZGS 5.24, ZRKS 5., Shiba 81, ZGJI 229

5.48 韓信臨朝底 *Kanshin chō ni nozomu tei.*

Like ⌜Han Hsin⌝ appearing at the imperial court.

ZGS 5.25, ZRKS 5.424, Shiba 82, ZGJI 230, ZGJT 72

5.49 眼前是什麼 *Ganzen kore nan zo.*

What is this before your very eyes?

Heki 2 Main Case *agyo*, 25 Verse Comm.

ZGS 5.26, Shiba 82

5.50 欵出囚人口 *Kan wa shūjin no kuchi yori izu.*

The confession comes from the prisoner's mouth.

Heki 15 Main Case *agyo*.

ZGS 5.27, ZRKS 5.268, Shiba 81, ZGJI 229, ZGJT 66, ZGDJT 1881, KZS #525

5.51 寒時終不熱 *Kan no toki wa tsui ni nessezu.*

Right through the cold season, not a bit of warmth.

ZGS na, ZRKS 5.32, Shiba 81

5.52 肝膽向人傾 *Kantan hito ni mukatte katamuku.*

He spills his guts to other people.

ZGS na, ZRKS 5.456, Shiba 81, ZGJI 229

5.53 邯鄲學唐歩 *Kantan tōho o manabu.*

In Han-tan, he studies the T'ang way of walking.

A country youth came to the capital city of Han-tan and tried to learn the refined Han-tan way of walking. Not only did he fail to learn the new way of walking, but he also forgot his old way of walking (*Chuang-tzu*, ch. 17). ZRKS 5.328: *tōbu* instead of *tōho*.

ZGS na, ZRKS 5.328, Shiba 81, ZGJI 229, ZGJT 64

5.54 拔卻眼中橛 *Ganchū no ketsu o bakkyaku su.*

Remove the stake from your eye.

ZGS na, ZRKS 5.25, Shiba 111, ZGJI 230, ZGJT 384

5.55 棺木裏瞠眼 *Kanbokuri ni dōgan su.*

Even in his coffin he's still blinking his eyes.

Heki 2 Verse *agyo*, 42 Main Case *agyo*, 81 Main Case *agyo*.

ZGS na, ZRKS 5.257, Shiba 82, ZGJI 230, ZGJT 68, ZGDJT 189b

5.56 官路販私鹽 *Kanro ni shiko o han su.*

He sells private salt on the public roads.

In the Han Dynasty, the production, sale, and taxation of salt was supervised by the salt official 鹽官.

ZGS 5.28, Shiba na

5.57 墮在鬼窟裏 *Kikutsuri ni dazai su.*

He's fallen into the cave of ghosts.

Heki 36 Verse *agyo*. KZS #543: 落 instead of 墮.

ZGS na, ZRKS 5.353, Shiba 101, ZGJI 230, ZGJT 285, KZS #543

5.58 龜毛長三尺 *Kimō nagaki koto sanjaku.*

The ⌜turtle hairs⌝ are three feet long.

ZGS na, ZRKS 5.275, Shiba 82, ZGJI 231, ZGJT 77

5.59 脚下太泥深 *Kyakka hanahada doro fukashi.*

Beneath your feet the mud is very deep.

Heki 21 Main Case Comm.

ZGS 5.29, ZRKS 5.265, Shiba na, ZGJI 231, ZGJT 84 (variant), KZS #517

5.60 脚跟隨他轉 *Kyakkon ta ni shitagatte tenzu.*

His feet follow someone else's around.

Heki 53 Main Case *agyo*.

ZGS na, ZRKS 5.153, Shiba 82, ZGJI 231, KZS #479

5.61 脚跟未點地 *Kyakkon imada chi ni tensezu.*

He hasn't got his feet on the ground yet.

Rinzai-roku §52.

ZGS na, ZRKS 5.264, Shiba 83, ZGJI 231, ZGJT 84, KZS #516, Watson 1993, 110

5.62 依舊是侍者 *Kyū ni yotte kore jisha.*

This is the ⌜attendant⌝ from many years back.

ZGS 5.30, Shiba na

5.63 急急如律令 *Kyū-kyū nyo ritsu ryō.*

Quickly! quickly! As prescribed by law!

In the later Han period, public legal documents often ended with these words enjoining subjects to implement the law immediately. The phrase was then taken up by practicers of magic. A charm inscription would be written on paper and then burned or swallowed by the person needing the charm. Meanwhile, the magician recited the charm ending with "Quickly, quickly, etc." (ZGJT 87, PALMER 1986).

ZGS 5.31, ZRKS 5.465, Shiba 83, ZGJI 231, ZGJT 87

5.64 九日是重陽 *Kyūjitsu kore chōyō.*

The day of nines is "repeated *yang*."

See ⌜Double ninth⌝.

ZGS na, ZRKS 5.394, Shiba 83

5.65 鄉原德之賊 *Kyōgen wa toku no zoku nari.*

The village worthies are the thieves of virtue.

Mencius VII, B, 37.

ZGS 5.32, ZRKS 5.14, Shiba 84

5.66 虛懷養天眞 *Kyokai tenshin o yashinau.*

With an empty breast nurture the heavenly truth.

ZGS na, Shiba 83

5.67 金鳳宿龍巢 *Kinpō ryūsō ni shuku su.*

The golden phoenix makes its home in a dragon's lair.

ZGS na, ZRKS 5.367, Shiba 84, ZGJI 232

5.68 銀椀裏盛雪 *Ginwanri ni yuki o moru.*

Heap up snow in a silver bowl.

Heki 13 Main Case.

ZGS 5.33, ZRKS 5.224, Shiba 84, ZGJI 232, ZGJT 95

5.69 打鼓普請看 *Ku o utte fushin shite miyo.*

Beat the signal drum, get everyone to help.

Heki 5 Main Case.

ZGS na, ZRKS 5.144, Shiba 101, ZGJI 237, ZGJT 284, ZGDJT 240b

5.70 空手牽鐵牛 *Kūshu ni shite tetsugyū o hiku.*

With empty hands he pulls the iron ox.

ZGS na, ZRKS 5.86, Shiba 84, ZGJI 233

5.71 斬草蛇頭落 *Kusa o kireba datō otsu.*

Cutting grass, he lops off the head of a snake.

ZGS na, ZRKS 5.329, Shiba 92, ZGJI 234, ZGJT 166

5.72 以草打一揮 *Kusa o motte da suru koto ikki.*

He strikes a blow with a blade of grass.

ZGS 5.34, Shiba na

5.73 閉口道一句 *Kuchi o tojite ikku o ie.*

Close your mouth and say one word.

ZGS 5.35, Shiba na

5.74 開口重千斤 *Kuchi o hirakeba, omoki koto senkin.*

Open your mouth [and your words] weigh 1,000 ⌜catties⌝.

ZGS 5.36, ZRKS 5.335, Shiba na, ZGJI 234

5.75 雲消山嶽露 *Kumo kiete sangaku arawaru.*

The clouds disperse and mountain peaks appear.➛

ZGJI 556: 雪 snow instead of 雲 clouds.

ZGS na, ZRKS 5.461, Shiba 79

5.76 日出海天清 *Hi idete kaiten kiyoshi.*

➛The sun comes out, sea and sky are clear.

ZGS na, ZRKS 5.462, Shiba 109

5.77 雲靜日月正 *Kumo shizuka ni shite jitsugetsu tadashi.*

With the clouds serene, sun and ⌜moon⌝ are precisely seen.

ZGS na, Shiba 79, ZGJI 234, ZGJT 32

5.78 溪梅一朶香 *Keibai ichida kanbashi.*

Fragrant, the lone plum tree by the valley stream.

ZGS na, ZRKS 5.20, Shiba 85, ZGJI 235, KZS #439

5.79 屐齒印青苔 *Gekishi seitai ni in su.*

Wooden clogs leave marks in the green moss.

ZGS na, Shiba 85

5.80 月下彈琵琶 *Gekka ni biwa o danzu.*

Under the ⌜moon⌝, he strums his lute.

ZGS 5.39, Shiba 85

5.81 絹糸結富嶽 *Kenshi fugaku o musubu.*

A silk thread ties up Mount Fu.

ZGS 5.38, Shiba 85,

5.82 子能繼父業 *Ko wa yoku chichi no gyō o tsugu.*

The son continues his father's work well.

ZGS 5.60, ZRKS 5.143, Shiba na, ZGJI 236

5.83 論劫不論禪 *Kō o ronjite, zen o ronzezu.*

He talks forever, but there's not a word of Zen.

ZGS na, ZRKS 5.8, Shiba 122, ZGJI 239, ZGJT 495, ZGDJT 303a

5.84 後園驢喫草 *Kōen no ro kusa o kissu.*

The backyard donkey is eating grass.

ZGS 5.40, ZRKS 5.276, Shiba na, ZGJI 239, ZGJT 134

5.85 黄河向北流 *Kōga wa kita ni mukatte nagaru.*

The Yellow River flows north.

Tradition says, "All rivers in China flow east."

ZGS na, ZRKS 5.316, Shiba 88, ZGJI 239, ZGJT 137, KZS #544

5.86 向後須參取 *Kōgō subekaraku sanshu subeshi.*

Hereafter you must strive to attain it.

ZGS 5.41, Shiba na

5.87 好事不如無 *Kōji mo naki ni wa shikazu.*

Even a good thing isn't as good as nothing at all.

Heki 69 Verse *agyo*, 86 Main Case.

ZGS 5.42, Shiba 87, ZGJI 238, ZGJT 131, ZGDJT 312a, KZS #463

5.88 巧匠不留跡 *Kōshō ato o todomezu.*

A skilled craftsman leaves no traces.

Heki 88 Verse *agyo*.

ZGS 5.43, ZRKS 5.300, Shiba 86, ZGJI 238, ZGJT 126

5.89 向上關捩子 *⌜Kōjō⌝ no kanreisu.*

The key to the ultimate barrier.

Shiba 86: 棙 instead of 捩.

ZGS na, Shiba 86, ZGJT 129, ZGDJT 314b

5.90 紅塵飛碧海 *Kōjin hekkai ni tobu.*

⌜Red dust⌝ blows in the blue sea.➛

ZGS na, ZRKS 5.447, Shiba 87,

5.91 白浪起青岑 *Hakurō seishin ni okoru.*

➛White waves rise on the blue peaks.

ZGS na, ZRKS 5.448, Shiba 111

5.92 荒草鋤不盡 *Kōsō sukedomo tsukizu.*

Cut away weeds, but you can't be rid of them.

Shiba 88: *Kōsō sukitsukusazu.*

ZGS 5.44, Shiba 88

5.93 荒草曾不鋤 *Kōsō katsute sukazu.*

The wild grasses have never been cut.

Rinzai-roku §1.

ZGS na, ZRKS 5.405, Shiba 88, ZGJI 239, ZGJT 136, Watson 1993:10

5.94 荒草裏横身 *Kōsōri ni mi o yokotau.*

He throws himself into the wild grass.

Heki 15 Main Case *agyo.*

ZGS na, ZRKS 5.272, Shiba 88, KZS #526

5.95 江南一枝春 *Kōnan isshi no haru.*

A branch of spring from south of the Yangtze.

From the state of Wu in the south, Lu K'ai 陸凱 sent a single branch of a ⌜plum⌝ blossom to Fan Yeh 范曄 in ⌜Ch'ang-an⌝, where it was still winter (Shiba 87).

ZGS na, Shiba 87

5.96 剜好肉作瘡 *Kōniku o egutte kasa to nasu.*

He cuts a wound into healthy flesh.

ZGJI 238: *Kōnikujo kizu o eru.*

ZGS na, ZRKS 5.114, Shiba 122, ZGJI 238, ZGJT 497

5.97 好肉上剜瘡 *Kōnikujō ni kasa o eguru.*

He cuts a wound into healthy flesh.

Heki 3 Intro. Shiba 87: *Kōnikujō ni kizu o eguru.*

ZGS 5.45, ZRKS 5.286, Shiba 87, ZGJI 238, ZGJT 131

5.98 光明無背面 *Kōmyō haimen nashi.*

Light has no back or front.

KZS #455: 虛空 "emptiness" instead of 光明 "brilliant light."

ZGS na, ZRKS 5.50, Shiba 86, ZGJI 239, KZS #455

5.99 蛟龍得雲雨 *Kōryū un'u o etari.*

The rain dragon has got its rain cloud.

A Chinese saying to mean that a great person has acquired the means to accomplish a great task (*Shinjigen* 886).

ZGS na, Shiba 88

5.100 紅輪當宇宙 *Kōrin uchū ni ataru.*

The red disc fills the universe.

"Red disc" here refers to the ⌜sun⌝.

ZGS na, ZRKS 5.445, Shiba 87

5.101 紅爐一點雪 *Kōro itten no yuki.*

In the red furnace, one snowflake.

ZGS 5.46, ZRKS 5.163, Shiba 87, ZGJT 135, KZS #485

5.102 古鏡裏含銘 *Kokyōri ni mei o fukumu.*

The back of the old mirror has an inscription.

ZGS 5.47, Shiba na

5.103 虛空打筋斗 *Kokū kinto o ta su.*

Emptiness turns a somersault.

ZGS 5.48, Shiba 83

5.104 虛空駕鐵船 *Kokū tessen ni ga sa.*

Emptiness rides an iron ship.

ZGS 5.49, ZRKS 5.47, Shiba 83, ZGJI 237, KZS #445

5.105 虛空咲點頭 *Kokū waratte tentō su.*

Emptiness laughs and nods it head.

ZGS 5.50, ZRKS 5.357, Shiba 83, ZGJI 237

5.106 黑烏吹漆桶 *Kokuu shittsū o fuku.*

A ⌜black crow⌝ is spouting black lacquer.

ZGS na, ZRKS 5.374, Shiba 88, ZGJI 239

5.107 黑風吹不入 *Kokufū fukedomo irazu.*

The black wind blows but cannot enter.

ZGS na, ZRKS 5.313, Shiba 88, ZGJI 240

5.108 虎口裏横身 *Kokōri ni mi o yokotau.*

He throws himself into the tiger's mouth.

Heki 5 Intro., 15 Verse Comm., 56 Main Case Comm., 75 Main Case *agyo.*

ZGS na, ZRKS 5.122, Shiba 86, ZGJI 236, ZGJT 38, KZS #471

5.109 虎口裏奪飡 *Kokōri ni san o ubau.*

Steal food from the tiger's mouth.

ZGS na, ZRKS 5.120, Shiba 86, ZGJI 236

5.110 試露爪牙看 *Kokoromi ni sōge o araweseyo min.*

Try showing your ⌜claws and teeth⌝ for once.

ZGS na, ZRKS 5.364, Shiba 92, ZGJI 240, ZGJT 178

5.111 按牛頭喫草 *Gozu o anjite kusa o kisseshimu.*

Pushing the ox's head down, he feeds it grass.

Heki 76 Verse, 94 Main Case *agyo*, MMK 17.

ZGS 5.52, ZRKS 5.296, Shiba 76, ZGJI 232, ZGJT 7, KZS #536

5.112 壺中日月長 *Kochū jitsugetsu nagashi.*

In the pot, sun and ⌜moon⌝ shine eternally.

ZD #58.

ZGS 5.51, ZRKS 5.161, Shiba 86, ZGJI 237, ZGJT 119

5.113 乞兒弄飯椀 *Kotsuji hanwan o rō su.*

The beggar plays with the rice bowl.

ZGS 5.53, ZRKS 5.193, Shiba 89, ZGJI 143, ZGJT 240, KZS #491

5.114 這不喞噌漢 *Kono fushitsuryū no kan.*

This stupid fool!

Heki 1 Main Case *agyo.*

ZGS 5.56, Shiba na

5.115 是外無別事 *Kono hoka ni betsuji nashi.*

Outside of this there is nothing.

ZGS 5.57, Shiba na

5.116 這掠虚頭漢 *Kono ryakkyotō no kan.*

This phony thief!

Heki 10 Main Case.

ZGS na, ZRKS 5.19, Shiba 93, ZGJI 240

5.117 拶殺這老漢 *Kono rōkan o sassetsu su.*

I pushed this old man to his limit.

Heki 2 Main Case *agyo*, 45 Main Case *agyo*. KZS #528: 賊 instead of 漢.

ZGS 5.58, ZRKS 5.274, Shiba na, ZGJI 240, ZGJT 159, KZS #528

5.118 激發箇老漢 *Kono rōkan ni gekihatsu seraru.*

I was strongly moved by this old man.

ZGS 5.54, Shiba na

5.119 枯木不逢春 *Koboku haru ni awazu.*

A dead tree greets no spring.

ZGS 5.59, ZRKS 5.18, Shiba 86, ZGJI 237

5.120 枕之作臥勢 *Kore o makura to shite fu su ikioi o nasu.*

Using this as a pillow, he lay down in a sleeping position.

ZGS 5.55, Shiba na

5.121 此箇破草鞋 *Kore kono hasōai.*

This worn-out straw sandal.

ZGS 5.61, Shiba na

5.122 是什麼心行 *Kore nan no shingyō zo.*

What's going on in his mind?

Heki 39 Main Case *agyo*, 66 Main Case *agyo*, 69 Main Case, 79 Main Case *agyo*.

ZGS 5.62, Shiba na

5.123 金剛王寶劍 *Kongō ō hōken.*

The treasure ⌜sword⌝ of the ⌜*Vajra*⌝ King.

Rinzai-roku §43, *Heki* 8 Intro. and Main Case Comm., 63 Verse *agyo*, 84 Verse *agyo*.

ZGS na, Shiba 84, ZGJI 422, ZGJT 145, ZGDJT 364c

5.124 金剛嚼生鐵 *Kongō santetsu o kamu.*

The ⌜*Vajra*⌝ King chews up raw iron.

ZGS 5.63, ZRKS 5.207, Shiba 84, ZGJI 241, KZS #497

5.125 跳出金剛圈 *Kongōken o chōshutsu su.*

He leaps right out of the ⌜*vajra*⌝ trap.

Heki 78 Verse *agyo*.

ZGS na, ZRKS 5.251, Shiba 103, ZGJI 241, ZGJT 312

5.126 渾身寒如氷 *Konshin samū shite kōri no gotoshi.*

My whole body is as cold as ice.

ZGS na, ZRKS 5.58, Shiba 89

5.127 今年二十五 *Konnen nijūgo.*

This year, twenty-five.

ZGS 5.64, Shiba na

5.128 言鋒冷似水 *Gonbō mizu yori mo suzushi.*

His words cut more than cold water.

Shiba 85: *Genbō mizu yori mo hiyayaka nari.*

ZGS 5.65, ZRKS 5.13, Shiba 85, ZGJI 235

5.129 崑崙嚼生鐵 *Konron santetsu o kamu.*

⌜Chaos⌝ chews up raw iron.

ZGS na, Shiba 89, ZGJI 241, ZGJT 147, ZGDJT 370a, KZS #449

5.130 崑崙擘不開 *Konron tsunzakedomo hirakezu.*

Though you hack away at ⌜chaos⌝, it will not open.

Rinzai-roku §38. Shiba 89: 渾 instead of 崑. ZRKS 5.55: 破 instead of 開.

ZGS na, ZRKS 5.55, Shiba 89, ZGJI 509, ZGDJT 370a, KZS #450

5.131 崑崙著鐵袴 *Konron tekko o tsuku.*

⌜Chaos⌝ dons an armor-plated apron.

ZGS na, ZRKS 5.310, Shiba 89, ZGJI 241, ZGJT 147, KZS #521

5.132 崑崙無縫罅 *Konron hōka nashi.*

⌜Chaos⌝ has no seams.

ZGS 5.66, ZRKS 5.165, Shiba 89, ZGJI 241

5.133 柴頭掛胡蘆 *Saitō ni koro o kaku.*

There's a gourd hanging on the hedge.

ZGS 5.67, Shiba 90

5.134 彩鳳舞丹霄 *Saihō tanshō ni mau.*

The flashing phoenix dances in the red sunset.

ZGS 5.68, ZRKS 5.384, Shiba 90, ZGJI 242

5.135 幸是老和尚 *Saiwai ni kore rō ⌜oshō⌝.*

Fortunately it's the old priest.

ZGS 5.69, ZRKS 5.ns, Shiba na,

5.136 賴値師指示 *Saiwai ni shi no shiji ni au.*

We are fortunate to receive the master's instruction.

ZGS 5.70, Shiba na

5.137 茶烟永日香 *Saen eijitsu kanbashi.*

The fragrance of parched tea lingers all day long.

ZGS na, Shiba 90

5.138 作者知機變 *Sakusha ⌜ki⌝ hen o shiru.*

A master knows how to change on the move.

Heki 10 Verse, 46 Verse Comm.

ZGS na, ZRKS 5.290, Shiba 90, ZGJI 157, ZGJT 242, KZS #533

5.139 殺活在手裡 *Sakkatsu shuri ni ari.*

Life and death are in one's hands.

ZGS 5.71, Shiba 90

5.140 更參三十年 *Sara ni sanzeyo sanjūnen.*

Train more, another ⌜thirty years⌝.

Heki 4 Verse Comm., 20 Verse 2 *agyo*, 57 Main Case Comm., MMK 19.

ZGS 5.72, Shiba 87, ZGJI 242, ZGJT 133

5.141 投簪泣井傍 *San o tōjite seibō ni naku.*

Having dropped her hairpin in, she cries by the well.

See ⌜Houbai⌝.

ZGS 5.73, Shiba 106

5.142 横身三界外 *Sangai no soto ni mi o yokotau.*

He throws himself outside the ⌜three worlds⌝.

ZGS na, ZRKS 5.342, Shiba 79, ZGJT 38

5.143 山形拄杖子 *Sangyō no shujōsu.*

My staff rough-cut from the mountains.

Heki 18 Main Case. *Sangyō no shujōsu*: a rough unfinished staff directly from the mountains, apparently in fashion among monks during the T'ang and Sung (Shiba 91, ZGJI 243).

ZGS na, ZRKS 5.124, Shiba 91, ZGJI 243, ZGJT 163, KZS #474

5.144 三才並泰昌 *Sansai narabi ni taishō.*

The three are aligned and sing songs of peace.

The three are heaven, earth, and humans 天地人 (Shiba 91).

ZGS na, Shiba 91

5.145 山色清淨身 *Sanshoku shōjōshin.*

The mountains in color are the pure [Buddha] body.

See 14.190.

ZGS na, Shiba 92

5.146 三歩退拜謝 *Sanpo shirizoite haisha su.*

He takes three steps backwards and bows in gratitude.

ZGS 5.74, Shiba na

5.147 憐兒不覺醜 *Ji o awarende minikuki o oboezu.*

1. Love a child and forget your own ugliness.
2. A beloved child is not ugly.

1. after Shiba 121, ZGJI 244.2. after ZD #55, ZGJT 482. *Heki* 38 Main Case Comm., MMK 28.

ZGS 5.75, ZRKS 5.150, Shiba 121, ZGJI 244, ZGJT 482, ZD #55, KZS #478

5.148 直心是道場 *Jikishin kore dōjō.*

Straightforward mind—this is the place of practice.

ZGS na, Shiba 104, ZGJI 256, ZGJT 183, ZGDJT 421b

5.149 慈眼視衆生 *Jigen shujō o miru.*

See all sentient beings with the eye of compassion.

Kannon-gyō: Jigen shi shujō.

ZGS na, Shiba 93, ZGDJT 426a

5.150 時時勤拂拭 *Ji-ji ni tsutomete fusshiki seyo.*

Always strive to clean and polish it.

Platform Sutra §6, Shen-hsiu's verse. *Heki* 28 Verse Comm.

ZGS na, Shiba 93

5.151 屎臭氣薫人 *Shishū ki hito ni kunzu.*

The smell of his shit carries to others.

Heki 98 Main Case Comm.

ZGS 5.76, ZRKS 5.299, Shiba na, ZGJI 243, ZGJT 174, KZS #538

5.152 自屎不覺臭 *Jishi kusaki o oboezu.*

He doesn't know the smell of his own shit.

Heki 77 Verse *agyo*, 79 Main Case *agyo*.

ZGS 5.77, ZRKS 5.95, Shiba 92, ZGJI 244, ZGJT 180, ZGDJT 431b, KZS #464

5.153 侍者點火來 *Jisha hi o tenjite kitare.*

⌜Attendant⌝, light a lamp and bring it.

ZGS 5.78, Shiba na

5.154 死水不藏龍 *Shisui ryū o kakusazu.*

Stagnant water does not harbor dragons.

Heki 20 Verse Comm., 95 Verse Comm.

ZGS 5.79, ZRKS 5.115, Shiba 92, ZGJI 243, ZGJT 173, KZS #507

5.155 日午點金燈 *Jitsugo kintō o tenzu.*

At noon, light the golden lantern.

ZGS na, ZRKS 5.223, Shiba 109, ZGJI 263

5.156 日午打三更 *Jitsugo sankō o da su.*

At noon, beat the drum signal for midnight.

Heki 86 Verse *agyo*. See ⌜Watch⌝.

ZGS na, ZRKS 5.238, Shiba 109, ZGJI 263, ZGJT 358

5.157 知而問禮也 *Shitte tou wa rei nari.*

To know and yet to enquire is politeness.

ZGS na, ZRKS 5.425, Shiba 103

5.158 室內一盞燈 *Shitsunai issan no tō.*

Within the room, a single saucer lamp.

Heki 17 Main Case Comm.

ZGS 5.80, ZRKS 5.271, Shiba 93, ZGJI 244, ZGJT 185, GKFGS 1.150.

5.159 照破四天下 *Shitenka o shōha su.*

It illuminates the four corners of the earth.

Heki 3 Verse Comm., 26 Main Case Comm., 85 Intro.

ZGS 5.81, Shiba 95

5.160 兒不嫌母醜 *Ji wa haha no minikuki o kirawazu.*

The child does not hate its mother's ugliness.

MMK 28.

ZGS 5.82, ZRKS 5.152, Shiba 92, ZGJI 244

5.161 有麝自然香 *Ja areba jinen ni kanbashi.*

Where there is ⌜deer musk⌝, there it is naturally fragrant.

ZGS na, ZRKS 5.97, Shiba 119, ZGJI 245

5.162 晝蛇强添足 *Ja o egaite shiite ashi o sou.*

He insists on ⌜adding feet when drawing a snake⌝.

ZGS 5.85, Shiba 80

5.163 釋迦彌勒聻 *Shaka miroku nii.*

Śākyamuni and ⌜Maitreya⌝!

ZGS 5.86, Shiba na

5.164 蹉過也不識 *Shaka suredomo mata shirazu.*

He stumbled right past it without knowing.

Heki 1 Main Case Comm., 29 Verse *agyo.*

ZGS na, ZRKS 5.43, Shiba 90, ZGJT 152

5.165 斫額望天衢 *Shakugaku shite tenku o nozomu.*

Shade the eyes and gaze at heaven's streets.

ZGS 5.87, ZRKS 5.408, Shiba na, ZGJI 245

5.166 杓卜聽虚聲 *Shakuboku ni kyosei o kiku.*

He listens to the empty voice of the divination dipper.

Heki 38 Main Case Comm. To make a prediction, a diviner would spin a dipper in a pot of water and when it came to rest, would go out in the direction indicated by the dipper handle, where a voice would tell the future outcome (ZGJI 245, ZGJT 191).

ZGS 5.88, ZRKS 5.361, Shiba 93, ZGJI 245, ZGJT 191, ZGDJT 471a

5.167 愁人知夜長 *Shūjin yoru no nagaki o shiru.*

A person in sorrow knows the night is long.

ZGS na, ZRKS 5.349, Shiba 94, ZGJI 245, ZGJT 202, 東坡詩愁人怨夜長

5.168 脩竹不受暑 *Shūchiku sho o ukezu.*

Deep in the bamboo, one does not get the heat.

ZGS na, ZRKS 5.39, Shiba 94, ZGJI 245

5.169 秋露滴芙蕖 *Shūro fukyo ni shitataru.*

Autumn dew beads on the lotus leaves.

Heki 36 Main Case.

ZGS na, ZRKS 5.62, Shiba 94,

5.170 熟睡饒儋語 *Jukusui ni sengo ōshi.*

Sound asleep, he's mumbling fast and furious.

Heki 38 Main Case Comm.

ZGS 5.89, ZRKS 5.422, Shiba na, ZGJI 246, ZGJT 205

5.171 拄杖常在手 *Shujō tsune ni te ni ari.*

He always has his staff in hand.

ZGS na, ZRKS 5.236, Shiba 93, ZGJI 245

5.172 拄杖撥乾坤 *Shujō kenkon o harau.*

My staff sweeps ⌜heaven and earth⌝.

ZGS na, ZRKS 5.407, Shiba 93, ZGJI 245

5.173 出現十方佛 *Shutsugen jippō butsu.*

The buddhas of the ⌜ten directions⌝ appear.

ZGS 5.90, Shiba na

5.174 須彌安鼻孔 *Shumi ni bikū o yasunzu.*

He puts nostrils on Mount ⌜Sumeru⌝.

Similar to putting holes on ⌜Hun-tun⌝ (ZGJI 245).

ZGS na, ZRKS 5., Shiba 93, ZGJI 245

5.175 春來草自生 *Shunrai kusa onozukara shōzu.*

Spring comes, grass grows by itself.

Shiba 94: *Haru kitatte kusa onozukara shōzu.*

ZGS 5.95, ZRKS 5.26, Shiba 94, ZGJI 508, ZGJT 206

5.176 馳書不到家 *Sho o hasete ie ni itarazu.*

The letter's been sent, but it hasn't reached the house.

ZGS na, Shiba 103, ZGJI 246, ZGDJT 600b

5.177 靜處蘇婆訶 *Jōsho sowaka.*

This place of serenity, *svāhā*.

Sowaka is the Japanese for *svāhā*, the Sanskrit term appended to the end of a chant to indicate completion and to invoke good fortune (ZGJI 249, Shiba 98).

ZGS 5.83, ZRKS 5.76, ZGJI 249, ZGJT 225, ZGDJT 560b; Shiba 98, 娑 instead of 蘇

5.178 小女可以備 *Shōjo motte sonaubeshi.*

A young girl must make the offering.

ZGS 5.84, Shiba na

5.179 小魚呑大魚 *Shōgyo taigyo o nomu.*

The little fish swallows the big fish.

ZGS na, ZRKS 5.188, Shiba 95, ZGJI 246, ZGDJT 535d, ZGJT 210, KZS #489

5.180 焦穀不生芽 *Shōkoku ge o shōzezu.*

Scorched grain will not sprout.

Heki 95 Main Case *agyo.*

ZGS na, ZRKS 5.244, Shiba 95, ZGJI 246, ZGJT 218, ZGDJT 542c

5.181 小慈妨大慈 *Shōji daiji o samatagu.*

Little compassion obstructs great compassion.

ZGS na, ZRKS 5.431, Shiba 95, ZGJI 246, ZGJT 210, ZGDJT 551b

5.182 松樹千年翠 *Shōju sennen no midori.*

The pine tree, a thousand years of green.

ZGS na, Shiba 95, ZGJI 516

5.183 淨地上撒屙 *Jōchijō ni a o sassu.*

He pisses where it is clean.

ZGS 5.91, ZRKS 5.385, Shiba na, ZGJI 247

5.184 諸佛居何處 *Shobutsu izure no tokoro ni ka iru.*

Where are all the buddhas?

ZGS 5.92, Shiba na

5.185 調高賞音稀 *Shirabe takōshite shōin mare nari.*

Few can appreciate music so refined.

ZGS 5.93, ZRKS 5.213, Shiba 104, ZGJI 256

5.186 塵外年光滿 *Jingai nenkō mitsu.*

Away from this world of ⌜dust⌝, time is complete.

ZGS na, Shiba 96

5.187 針眼裏藏身 *Shinganri ni mi o zōsu.*

He conceals himself in the eye of the needle.

ZGS na, ZRKS 5.189, Shiba 96, ZGJI 247, ZGJT 229, KZS #490

5.188 眞玉泥中異 *Shingyoku deichū ni i nari.*

True jade stands out in mud.

ZGS na, ZRKS 5.396, Shiba 95, ZGJI 247

5.189 親言出親口 *Shingen wa shinku yori izu.*

Kind words come from a kind mouth.

Heki 10 Verse *agyo*, 63 Verse *agyo.*

ZGS 5.94, ZRKS 5.292, Shiba 96, ZGJI 247, ZGJT 231, KZS #534

5.190 神光射斗牛 *Shinkō togyū o iru.*

The divine light illuminates the ⌜Dipper and the Ox⌝.

See also 5.47.

ZGS na, ZRKS 5.131, Shiba 96, ZGJI 247, ZGDJT 610a

5.191 神光照天地 *Shinkō tenchi o terasu.*

The divine light illuminates heaven and earth.

Heki 96 Verse.

ZGS na, ZRKS 5.145, Shiba 96, ZGJI 247

5.192 隨後婁藪也 *Zuigo rōsō ya.*

A fool just following others around!

Heki 55 Main Case *agyo*.

ZGS 5.96, ZRKS 5.291, Shiba na, ZGJI 248, ZGJT 239

5.193 水上掛燈籠 *Suijō ni tōrō o kaku.*

Hang a lantern over the water.

ZGS na, ZRKS 5.181, Shiba 96, ZGJI 248

5.194 水底走金烏 *Suitei ni kin'u hashirashimu.*

In the depths of the water, make the ⌜golden crow⌝ fly.

ZGS na, ZRKS 5.182, Shiba 97, ZGJI 248

5.195 水底石牛吼 *Suitei ni sekigyū hoyu.*

In the depths of the water, the stone ox lows.

ZGS na, ZRKS 5.203, Shiba 97, ZGJI 248

5.196 芻狗趁鐵牛 *Sūku tetsugyū o ou.*

A ⌜straw dog⌝ herds the iron ox.

ZGS na, ZRKS 5.208, Shiba 97, ZGJI 248

5.197 已相見了也 *Sude ni shōken shiowareri.*

The meeting [with the master] is already over.

ZGS na, ZRKS 5.184, Shiba 76, KZS #488

5.198 靑黄赤白黑 *Sei ō shaku byaku koku.*

Blue, yellow, red, white, black.

ZGS 5.97, Shiba na

5.199 逼生蠶作繭 *Seisan o semete mayu o tsukurashimu.*

He forces baby silkworms to produce thread.

ZGS na, ZRKS 5.319, Shiba 112, ZGJI 248, ZGJT 393, KZS #522

5.200 聖朝無棄物 *Seichō ni kibutsu nashi.*

Nothing is wasted in the court of saints.

ZGS 5.98, ZRKS 5.53, Shiba 97, ZGJI 249

5.201 井底種林檎 *Seitei ni ringo o uyu.*

He plants apples at the bottom of the well.

ZRKS 5.37: *rinkin* instead of *ringo*.

ZGS na, ZRKS 5.37, Shiba 97, ZGJI 248

5.202 清波無透路 *Seiha tōro nashi.*

Through the pure waves, there is no path.

Heki 39 Main Case Comm.

ZGS na, Shiba 97, ZGJI 249, ZGJT 246, ZGDJT 648d

5.203 清風來故人 *Seifū kojin kitaru.*

The pure wind arrives like an old friend.

ZGS na, Shiba 97

5.204 赤脚上刀山 *Sekkyaku ni shite tōzan ni noboru.*

In bare feet he climbs the ⌜mountain of blades⌝.

MMK 17.

ZGS na, ZRKS 5.197, Shiba 98, ZGJI 250, ZGJT 248, KZS #492

5.205 石虎叫連宵 *Sekko renshō ni sakebu.*

The stone tiger roars all night long.

ZGS na, ZRKS 5.455, Shiba 98, ZGJI 249

5.206 石人相耳語 *Sekijin aijigo su.*

Stone statues whisper to each other.

Shiba 98: *ainigo* instead of *aijigo*.

ZGS 5.99, Shiba 98, ZGJI 250

5.207 石女夜生兒 *Sekijo yoru ji o shōzu.*

The ⌜stone woman⌝ gives birth to a child at night.

ZGS na, Shiba 98, ZGJI 250, ZGDJT 656a, KZS #483

5.208 切忌渾崙呑 *Setsu ni imu ⌜konron⌝ ni nomu koto o.*

Don't just blindly swallow it whole.

渾崙 *konron* here is used as an adverb.

ZGS na, ZRKS 5.340, Shiba 98, ZGJI 250, ZGDJT 660a

5.209 舌根裏藏身 *Zekkonri ni mi o zōsu.*

His self disappears into his tongue.

ZGS na, ZRKS 5.130, Shiba 98, ZGJI 250

5.210 說是說不是 *Ze to toki, fuze to toku.*

He says, "It's this." He says, "It isn't this."

ZGS 5.100, Shiba na

5.211 錢出急家門 *Sen wa kyūka no mon yori izu.*

Money flees the gate of a house in trouble.

ZGS na, ZRKS 5.309, Shiba 99, ZGJI 251, ZGJT 258, ZGDJT 670c

5.212 千眼看不見 *Sengan miru mo mamiezu.*

Though even a thousand eyes look, they cannot see.

ZGS na, ZRKS 5.227, Shiba 98, ZGJI 250, KZS #499

5.213 全機不覆藏 *Zen⌜ki⌝ fukuzō sezu.*

Totally in action, nothing hidden.

ZGS na, ZRKS 5.418, Shiba 99, ZGJI 251

5.214 千古動悲風 *Senko hifū o ugokasu.*

From a thousand ages past, a sad wind has been stirring.

Heki 68 Verse.

ZGS na, ZRKS 5.450, Shiba 99, ZGJI 250, ZGJT 254

5.215 先師無此語 *Senshi kono go nashi.*

The old master never said that.

Katto-shū 9.

ZGS 5.101, ZRKS 5.216, Shiba 99

5.216 千聖跳不出 *Senshō mo chō fu shutsu.*

Not even the thousand sages can leap out.

Heki 47 Main Case *agyo*. ZGS na, Shiba 99, ZGJI 250

5.217 草鞋裏踍跳 *Sōairi ni botchō su.*

In straw sandals he leaps and bounds.

ZGS na, ZRKS 5.27, Shiba 100, ZGJI 251

5.218 草鞋和露重 *Sōai tsuyu ni washite omoshi.*

The straw sandals are heavy with dew.

ZGS na, Shiba 100, ZGJI 251

5.219 曹源一滴水 *Sōgen no ittekisui.*

One drop of water from Ts'ao-yüan.

Heki 7 Main Case Comm., 35 Verse Comm. See ⌜Pao-lin ssu⌝ under ⌜Sixth Patriarch⌝.

ZGS na, Shiba 100, ZGJT 269, ZGDJT 724b

5.220 相續也大難 *Sōzoku mata tainan.*

To maintain focus moment to moment is very difficult.

Heki 4 Verse Comm., 20 Main Case Comm., 46 Main Case Comm., 59 Main Case Comm.

ZGS 5.102, Shiba na, ZGDJT 741b

5.221 回轉鎗頭來 *Sōtō o kaiten shite kitareri.*

He's turned the spear around and come back.

Heki Main Case 35 *agyo*.

ZGS na, ZRKS 5.393, Shiba 80, ZGJI 252, ZGJT 53

5.222 僧堂入佛殿 *Sōdō butsuden ni iru.*

The Monks' Hall enters the Buddha Hall.

See ⌜Seven-hall complex⌝.

ZGS na, Shiba 100, ZGJT 271

5.223 賊過後張弓 *Zoku sugite nochi yumi o haru.*

He draws his bow after the ⌜thief⌝ has fled.

Heki 4 Main Case *agyo*, 88 Main Case *agyo*, et al.

ZGS 5.103, ZRKS 5.102, Shiba 100, ZGJI 252, ZGJT 276, KZS #468

5.224 奪賊鎗煞賊 *Zokusō o ubatte zoku o korosu.*

Steal the ⌜bandit's⌝ own spear to kill him.

ZGS 5.104, ZRKS 5.139, Shiba 102, ZGJI 252, ZGJT 297, ZGDJT 762b

5.225 作賊人心虛 *Zoku to naru hito kokoro kyo nari.*

One who is a ⌜thief⌝ has an empty mind.

Variants: *kokoro ko nari* (Asahina 1937, vol. 1, 123), *kokoro itsuwaru* (Shiba 90). *Heki* 8 Main Case.

ZGS na, ZRKS 5.101, Shiba 90, ZGJI 252, KZS #467

5.226 騎賊馬趁賊 *Zokuba ni notte zoku o ou.*

Mount the ⌜bandit's⌝ horse and chase him.

Heki 15 Main Case Comm., 27 Main Case Comm., 59 Main Case *agyo.*

ZGS 5.105, ZRKS 5.104, Shiba na, ZGJI 252, ZGJT 80

5.227 楚山入漢水 *Sozan kansui ni iru.*

The mountains of Ch'u run into the rivers of Han.

ZGS 5.106, Shiba na, ZGJI 251

5.228 祖師西來意 *Soshi seirai i.*

The point of ⌜Bodhidharma's coming from the west⌝.

ZGS na, Shiba 100, ZGJI 251, ZGJT 264, ZGDJT 769b

5.229 某甲不着便 *Soregashi bin o tsukezu.*

It is inconvenient for me.

There are several interpretations of 不着便. See ⌜*Bin, ben*⌝.

ZGS 5.107, Shiba na

5.230 大功不立賞 *Taikō wa shō o rissezu.*

Great merit does not receive praise.

Heki 88 Verse *agyo.*

ZGS 5.108, ZRKS 5.248, Shiba 101, ZGJI 253, ZGJT 292

5.231 大士講經竟 *Daishi kōkyō owannu.*

The great master has finished preaching the sutra.

Heki 67 Main Case *agyo.*

ZGS 5.109, Shiba na

5.232 大小大宗師 *Daishōdai no shūshi.*

A great master and teacher indeed!

ZGS 5.110, Shiba na

5.233 大地黑漫漫 *Daichi koku manman.*

The great earth is utterly black.

Heki 68 Verse *agyo.*

ZGS 5.111, ZRKS 5.63, Shiba 101, ZGJI 253, ZGDJT 805d, KZS #453

5.234 大地絕消息 *Daichi ⌜shōsoku⌝ o zessu.*

The great earth is beyond talking about.

ZGS na, ZRKS 5.79, Shiba 101, ZGJI 253

5.235 大地絕纖埃 *Daichi sen'ai o zessu.*

The great earth is beyond any ⌜dust⌝.

Heki 36 Verse.

ZGS na, ZRKS 5.397, Shiba 101, ZGJI 254, ZGJT 292, ZGDJT 805d

5.236 大道透長安 *Daidō chōan ni tōru.*

The great road passes through ⌜Ch'ang-an⌝.

ZGS 5.112, ZRKS 5.98, Shiba 101, ZGJI 254, ZGJT 293, KZS #465

5.237 大德不踰閑 *Daitoku wa nori o koezu.*

A person of great virtue does not exceed the law.

Analects XIX, 11.

ZGS na, ZRKS 5.449, Shiba 102

5.238 對面隔千里 *Taimen senri o hedatsu.*

Face to face a thousand miles apart.

ZGS na, ZRKS 5.141, Shiba 102, ZGJI 254, ZGJT 288, KZS #477

5.239 只箇一念子 *Tada kono ichinensu.*

Just this one thought.

ZGS 5.113, Shiba na

5.240 達者暗裏驚 *Tassha anri ni odoroku.*

In the dark, the expert is startled.

ZGS 5.114, ZRKS 5.46, Shiba na, ZGJI 255

5.241 溪深杓柄長 *Tani fukōshite shakuhei nagashi.*

For a deep stream, the dipper handle is long.

ZGS na, ZRKS 5.191, Shiba 85, ZGJI 235, ZGDJT 829c

5.242 求珠不離泥 *Tama o motomuru ni doro o hanarezu.*

Searching for the pearl, he's stuck in the mud.

ZGS na, ZRKS 5.318, Shiba 83, ZGJI 255, ZGJT 86

5.243 誰是最上人 *Tare ka kore saijō no hito.*

Who is this superior person?

ZGS 5.115, Shiba na

5.244 擔折知柴重 *Tan orete shiba no omoki o shiru.*

When the carrying pole breaks you know the firewood is heavy.

ZGS na, ZRKS 5.345, Shiba 102, ZGJI 255, ZGJT 299

5.245 丹青畫不成 *Tanzei egakedomo narazu.*

Color it red or blue, still you can't paint.

ZGS na, ZRKS 5.69, Shiba 102, KZS #457

5.246 斷碑横古路 *Danpi koro ni yokotau.*

A broken monument lies across the old road.

ZGS 5.116, ZRKS 5.427, Shiba 103, ZGJI 255

5.247 地肥茄子大 *Chi koete nasu dai nari.*

When the ground is fertile, the eggplants are large.

ZGS na, ZRKS 5.119, Shiba 103, ZGJI 255

5.248 池塘春草生 *Chitō shunsō shōzu.*

On the banks of the pond, spring grass grows.

Shiba 103: 生春草.

ZGS 5.117, ZRKS 5.33, Shiba 103

5.249 坐地開眼睡 *Chi ni za shite manako o hiraite nemuru.*

He sits on the ground and sleeps with eyes open.

ZGS 5.118, Shiba na

5.250 着床作臥勢 *Chakushō shite fusu ikioi o nasu.*

He spread out the bedding and assumed a sleeping position.

ZGS 5.119, Shiba na

5.251 重疊關山路 *Chōjōtari kanzan no michi.*

Row on row of mountains block my path.

Heki 39 Main Case Comm.

ZGS na, ZRKS 5.263, Shiba 94, ZGJT 203

5.252 鳥道絕東西 *Chōdō tōzai o zessu.*

The path of the bird transcends east and west.

ZGS 5.120, Shiba 103

5.253 張良躡足底 *Chōryō ashi o fumu tei.*

It is like ⌜Chang Liang⌝ stepping on [the commander's] foot.

See also 14.460.

ZGS 5.121, Shiba na

5.254 通身是手眼 *Tsūshin kore shugen.*

The body entire is hands and eyes.

Heki 89.

ZGS 5.122, ZRKS 5.391, Shiba 104, ZGJI 256, ZGDJT 874c, ZGJT 315

5.255 通身無影像 *Tsūshin yōzō nashi.*

The body entire is without shadow.

Heki 90 Main Case *agyo.*

ZGS 5.123, ZRKS 5.68, Shiba 104, ZGJI 256, ZGJT 315, ZGDJT 874d, KZS #456

5.256 痛處下針錐 *Tsūsho shinsui o kudasu.*

He inserts needles just where it hurts.

ZGS na, ZRKS 5.134, Shiba 104, ZGJI 257

5.257 和月賣珊瑚 *Tsuki ni washite sango o uru.*

They sell ⌜coral⌝ in the light of the ⌜moon⌝.

See also 14.291.

ZGS 5.124, ZRKS 5.388, Shiba 122, ZGJI 257

5.258 露濕草鞋重 *Tsuyu uruōte sōai omoshi.*

Wet with dew, the straw sandals are heavy.

ZGS 5.125, ZRKS 5.315, Shiba na, ZGJI 257, ZGJT 485

5.259 撒手臥長空 *Te o sasshite chōkū ni fu su.*

Stretch out your arms and lie down in the vast sky.

ZGS na, ZRKS 5.387, Shiba 91, ZGJI 257

5.260 把手拽不入 *Te o totte hikedomo irazu.*

Take him by the hand, still he won't come in.

ZGS na, ZRKS 5.57, Shiba 111, ZGJI 257, ZGJT 375, ZGDJT 878

5.261 泥水洗玉石 *Deisui ni gyokuseki o arau.*

He washes jade in muddy water.

ZGS 5.126, Shiba na

5.262 庭前柏樹子 *Teizen no hakujushi.*

The cypress tree in the front garden.

MMK 37.

ZGS na, Shiba 104, ZGJI 534, ZGDJT 879d

5.263 泥裏洗土塊 *Deiri ni dokai o arau.*

He's washing a clod of earth in mud.

Heki 14 Verse *agyo*, 15 Verse *agyo*, 20 Verse *agyo*, *et al.*

ZGS 5.127, ZRKS 5.260, Shiba 105, ZGJI 257, ZGJT 321, KZS #514

5.264 覿面無消息 *Tekimen* ⌜*shōsoku*⌝ *nashi.*

Face to face and nothing to say.

ZGS na, ZRKS 5.142, Shiba 105, ZGJI 257, ZGJT 322

5.265 鐵丸無縫罅 *Tetsugan hōka nashi.*

The iron ball has no seams.

ZGS 5.128, ZRKS 5.42, Shiba 105, ZGJI 258, ZGDJT 882d, KZS #442

5.266 鐵牛生石卵 *Tetsugyū sekiran o shōzu.*

The iron ox lays a stone egg.

ZGS na, ZRKS 5.412, Shiba 105, ZGJI 258

5.267 鐵鈷舞三臺 *Tekko santai o mau.*

The iron thunderbolt dances the ⌜three steps⌝.

See ⌜*Vajra*⌝.

ZGS 5.129, ZRKS 5.312, Shiba 105, ZGJI 258, ZGJT 324

5.268 豎起鐵脊梁 *Tessekiryō o juki su.*

Straighten up that iron backbone.

ZGS na, ZRKS 5.204, Shiba 94, ZGJI 258

5.269 鐵船水上浮 *Tessen suijō ni ukabu.*

An iron boat floats upon the water.

ZGS 5.130: 浮水上 instead of 水上浮.

ZGS 5.130, ZRKS 5.51, ZGJI 258, ZGJT 324, ZGDJT 884c, KZS #447

5.270 鐵鎚舞春風 *Tettsui shunpū ni mau.*

The iron hammer dances in the spring wind.

ZGS 5.132, ZRKS 5.366, Shiba 105, ZGJI 258

5.271 鐵蛇横古路 *Tetsuda koro ni yokotau.*

An iron snake lies across the ancient road.

ZGS 5.131, ZRKS 5.45, Shiba 105, ZGJI 258, ZGDJT 884a, KZS #443

5.272 踏破鐵圍山 *Tetchisen o tōha su.*

He stomps to pieces the ⌜ring of iron mountains⌝.

ZGS na, Shiba 107, ZGJI 258

5.273 天曉失卻火 *Ten akete hi o shikkyaku su.*

Dawn breaks and they put out the torches.

ZGS na, ZRKS 5.89, Shiba 106, ZGJI 258

5.274 疑殺天下人 *Tenka no hito o gisatsu su.*

He totally confounds everyone under heaven.

Heki 21 Main Case *agyo.*

ZGS na, ZRKS 5.253, Shiba 82, ZGJI 258, ZGJT 81, KZS #510

5.275 天高群星近 *Ten takōshite gunsei chikashi.*

The heavens are so high yet the stars are so close.

ZGS na, Shiba 106, ZGJI 259

5.276 電光裡走馬 *Denkōri ni uma o hashirasu.*

He runs horses in lightning.

ZGS 5.133, Shiba na

5.277 燈下不剪爪 *Tōka ni tsume o kirazu.*

Don't cut your nails under a lamp.

ZGS 5.134, Shiba 107

5.278 同坑無異土 *Dōkō ni ido nashi.*

There's no different dirt in the same hole.

Heki 12 Verse *agyo*, 67 Main Case *agyo*, 89 Main Case *agyo.*

ZGS na, ZRKS 5.230, Shiba 107, ZGJI 260, ZGJT 345, KZS #501

5.279 東山水上行 *Tōzan suijōkō.*

The east mountain walks upon the water.

ZGS na, Shiba 107, ZGJI 260, ZGJT 338, ZGDJT 921a

5.280 道無南北祖 *Dō ni namboku no so nashi.*

On the Way, there are no Northern and Southern patriarchs.

ZGS na, Shiba 107, ZGDJT 905d

5.281 道士請便坐 *Dōshi kou sunawachi za seyo.*

Practitioners of the Way, just sit!

ZGS 5.135, Shiba na

5.282 道中西來意 *Dōchū seirai i.*

To be on the Way—the point of ⌜Bodhidharma's coming from the west⌝.

ZGS 5.136, Shiba na

5.283 如稻麻竹葦 *Tōma chikui no gotoshi.*

Like rice stalks, flax, bamboo, and reeds.

ZGS 5.137, Shiba 94

5.284 冬嶺秀孤松 *Tōrei koshō hiizu.*

On a winter peak a single pine stands lone and tall.

Shiba 106: *Tōrei shūko no matsu.*

ZGS 5.138, Shiba 106

5.285 同途不同轍 *To o onajiushite wadachi o onajiusezu.*

Our road is the same but we travel in different wheel tracks.

Heki 2 Main Case Comm., 26 Verse Comm.

ZGS 5.139, ZRKS 5.228, Shiba 107, ZGJI 259, ZGJT 345, ZGDJT 904b, KZS #500

5.286 獨坐大雄峯 *Dokuza daiyūhō.*

The Great Hero Peak sits in majestic solitude.

Heki 26.

ZGS 5.140, ZRKS 5.88, Shiba 108, ZGJI 261, ZGDJT 948c, KZS #462

5.287 獨坐鎮寰宇 *Dokuza kan'u o chin su.*

Alone he sits commanding his fortress-universe.

ZGS na, ZRKS 5.74, Shiba 108, ZGJI 261, ZGJT 352

5.288 獨掌不浪鳴 *Dokushō midari ni narazu.*

The sound of a single hand is rarely heard.

Heki 18 Main Case.

ZGS 5.141, ZRKS 5.100, Shiba 108, ZGJI 261, ZGJT 353, KZS #466

5.289 禿箒舞天風 *Tokusō tenpū ni mau.*

The bald broom dances in the heavenly wind.

ZGS 5.142, Shiba 107

5.290 特來見和尚 *Toku ni kitatte ⌜oshō⌝ ni mamiyu.*

He came especially to meet the priest.

ZGS 5.143, Shiba na

5.291 特地一場愁 *Tokuchi ichijō no urei.*

That's a very sad situation.

Heki 43 Main Case *agyo.*

ZGS na, ZRKS 5.311, Shiba 108, ZGJI 261, ZGJT 350

5.292 都盧一團鐵 *Toro ichidan no tetsu.*

All is one lump of iron.

ZGS 5.144, ZRKS 5.52, Shiba 106, ZGJT 315, KZS #448

5.293 鈍鳥不離巢 *Donchō su o hanarezu.*

The dull-witted bird does not leave its nest.

ZGS 5.145, ZRKS 5.288, Shiba 108, ZGJI 262, ZGDJT 961a, KZS #532

5.294 鈍刀不截骨 *Dontō hone o kirazu.*

A dull knife does not cut bone.

ZGS na, ZRKS 5.183, Shiba 108, ZGJI 262, KZS #487

5.295 那吒擎鐵鎚 *Nata tettsui o sasagu.*

⌜Nata⌝ raises his iron hammer.

ZGS 5.146, ZRKS 5.128, Shiba 109, ZGJI 262, ZGJT 356, KZS #475

5.296 尚是第二機 *Nao kore daini ⌜ki⌝.*

This is still secondary mind.

ZGS 5.147, Shiba na, ZGJI 90, ZGDJT 811b

5.297 汝親見皷山 *Nanji shitashiku kusan o miyo.*

You, take a close look at Drum Mountain.

Drum Mountain is located in present-day Fujian Province.

ZGS 5.148, Shiba na

5.298 放汝三十棒 *Nanji ni yurusu sanjū bō.*

I will pardon you from thirty blows.

ZGS 5.149, Shiba na

5.299 汝不離門外 *Nanji monge o hanarezu.*

You cannot go beyond the gate.

ZGS 5.150, Shiba na

5.300 如衣錦夜行 *Nishiki o kite yoru yuku ga gotoshi.*

Like dressing up in brocade and then going out at night.

See ⌜*Yakō*⌝.

ZGS 5.151, Shiba 94

5.301 日日是好日 *Nichi-nichi kore kōnichi.*

Every day is a good day.

Heki 6.

ZGS na, Shiba 109, ZGJI 264, ZGJT 358, ZGDJT 982b, KZS #459

5.302 日輪正當午 *Nichirin masa ni go ni ataru.*

The sun wheel reaches high noon.

ZGS na, ZRKS 5.333, Shiba 110, ZGJT 358

5.303 日下挑孤燈 *Nikka ni kotō o kakagu.*

In sunlight he hangs out a lantern.

ZGS na, Shiba 109, ZGJI 263, ZGDJT 982d

5.304 如實知自心 *Nyojitsu ni jishin o shiru.*

Actually know your own mind.

ZGS 5.152, Shiba na, ZGDJT 991c

5.305 奴見婢慇懃 *Nu wa hi o mite ingin.*

When manservant meets maidservant, they are polite to each other.

Heki 22 Main Case *agyo*, 23 Main Case Comm. 89 Main Case Comm.

ZGS 5.153, ZRKS 5.3, Shiba 106, ZGJI 259, ZGJT 332, ZGDJT 1000b

5.306 涅槃像妙處 *Nehanzō no myōjo.*

The wondrous picture of the Buddha's *parinirvāṇa*.

ZGS 5.154, Shiba na

5.307 念念不停流 *Nennen fuchōryū.*

Thought after thought, the flow never stops.

Heki 80 Main Case.

ZGS na, ZRKS 5, Shiba 110, ZGJI 264, ZGJT 370

5.308 腦後添一錐 *Nōgo ni issui o sou.*

Into the back of his brain stick a ⌜pick⌝.

ZGJI 264: 腦後少一錐 *Nōgo ni issui o kaku*, "He was pardoned from a stab in the back of the brain."

ZGS 5.155, ZRKS 5.135, Shiba 110

5.309 白雲抱幽石 *Hakuun yūseki o idaku.*

The white clouds embrace mysterious rocks.

ZGS 5.156, ZRKS 5.463, Shiba 111, ZGJT 380, 寒山詩 §1

5.310 白狀底一句 *Hakujōtei no ikku.*

A word of confession.

ZGS 5.157, Shiba na

5.311 白馬入蘆花 *Hakuba roka ni iru.*

A white horse enters the white reed flowers.

Heki 13 Main Case *agyo.*

ZGS 5.158, ZRKS 5.267, Shiba 111, ZGJI 265, ZGJT 380

5.312 鉢盂裏走馬 *Hatsuuri ni uma o hashirasu.*

Race a horse inside a bowl.

ZGS na, ZRKS 5.84, Shiba 111

5.313 八風吹不動 *Happū fukedomo dōzezu.*

Though the ⌜eight winds⌝ blow, it does not move.

ZGS na, ZRKS 5.451, Shiba 111, ZGJI 265, ZGDJT 1029b, 寒山詩 §295.

5.314 花散鳥不來 *Hana chirite tori kitarazu.*

The flowers are scattered and no birds come.

ZGS 5.159, Shiba na

5.315 把針失卻線 *Hari o totte sen o shikkyaku su.*

He took up the needle but lost the thread.

ZGS na, ZRKS 5.337, Shiba 111

5.316 嚼飯餵嬰兒 *Han o kande eiji o yashinau.*

She chews the rice to feed to the baby.

ZGS 5.160, ZRKS 5.314, Shiba na, ZGJI 266, ZGJT 193, KZS #546

5.317 樊噲踏鴻門 *Hankai kōmon o fumu.*

⌜Fan K'uai⌝ stands at the Hung-men Gate.

ZGS 5.161, ZRKS 5.436, Shiba na

5.318 萬里一條鐵 *Banri ichijō no tetsu.*

For ten thousand miles, one bar of iron.

ZGS 5.162, ZRKS 5.44, Shiba 112, ZGJI 266, ZGJT 387, ZGDJT 1039d, KZS #444

5.319 萬里無片雲 *Banri hen'un nashi.*

For ten thousand miles, not a wisp of cloud.

ZGS 5.163, ZRKS 5.452, Shiba 112, ZGJI 267

5.320 日出乾坤輝 *Hi idete kenkon kagayaku.*

The sun appears lighting up ⌜heaven and earth⌝.

ZGS na, ZRKS 5.1, Shiba 109, ZGJI 267, KZS #435

5.321 鼻孔長三尺 *Bikū nagaki koto sanjaku*

His nose is three feet long.

He holds his nose high, a sign of arrogance (ZGJI 267).

ZGS na, ZRKS 5.454, Shiba 112, ZGJI 267, ZGDJT 1042c

5.322 彼此不著便 *Hishi tayori o tsukezu.*

Here, there—completely beyond communication.

There are several interpretations of 不著便. See ⌜*Bin, ben*⌝.

ZGS na, ZRKS 5.305, Shiba 112, ZGJI 267, ZGDJT 1043b, KZS #519

5.323 砒礵藏石密 *Hisō sekimitsu o zō su.*

Arsenic possesses a sweet taste.

Shiba 112: 蜜 instead of 密.

ZGS 5.164, Shiba 112

5.324 殺人須見血 *Hito o koroshite wa subekaraku chi o miru beshi.*

When you kill someone, make sure you see the blood.

Heki 31 Main Case *agyo*. Shiba 90, ZRKS 5.125: 煞 instead of 殺.

ZGS 5.165, ZRKS 5.125, Shiba 90, ZGJI 268, ZGJT 159, ZGDJT 1045c, KZS #473

5.325 煞人不用刀 *Hito o korosu ni tō o mochiizu.*

He kills people without using a ⌜sword⌝.

Heki 13 Verse Comm.

ZGS na, ZRKS 5.239, Shiba 91, ZGJI 268, ZGJT 159, KZS #505

5.326 煞人不眨眼 *Hito o korosu ni manako o sassezu.*

When you kill someone, no blinking.

Heki 4 Verse Comm.

ZGS na, ZRKS 5.108, Shiba 91, ZGJT 160 (眨)

5.327 披毛戴角去 *Himō taikaku shi saru.*

He leaves wearing fur and bearing horns.

ZGS 5.166, Shiba na

5.328 眉毛横眼上 *Bimō ganjō ni yokotau.*

⌜Eyebrows⌝ lie sideways above the eyes.

ZGS na, ZRKS 5.202, Shiba 112, ZGJI 267, ZGJT 392, KZS #495

5.329 猫兒屋頭尿 *Byōji okutō ni nyō su.*

The cat pisses on the roof.

ZGS 5.167, Shiba na, ZGJI 268, ZGDJT 1191a

5.330 平常心是道 *Byōjōshin kore dō.*

Everyday mind is the Way.

MMK 19.

ZGS na, Shiba 114, ZGJI 269, ZGDJT 1107d

5.331 氷凌上走馬 *Hyōryōjō ni uma o hashirasu.*

He races his horse across ice.

ZGS na, Shiba 113

5.332 貧兒思舊債 *Hinji kyūsai o omou.*

The beggar is thinking of his old debts.

Heki 1 Main Case *agyo*, 98 Main Case *agyo*.

ZGS 5.168, ZRKS 5.232, Shiba na, ZGJI 268, ZGJT 395, KZS #503

5.333 父子相投和 *Fushi aitōwa su.*

Father and son match perfectly.

Heki 81 Main Case Comm.

ZGS 5.169, ZRKS 5.4, Shiba 113, ZGJI 269, ZGDJT 1073a

5.334 無事是貴人 *Buji kore ki'nin.*

No cares! That's nobility.

Rinzai-roku §12.

ZGS na, Shiba 116, ZGJI 269, ZGJT 406, ZGDJT 1073a

5.335 普州人送賊 *Fushū no hito zoku o okuru.*

The man from P'u-chou is seeing off a ⌜thief⌝.

Heki 22 Main Case *agyo*, 39 Verse *agyo*. ZRKS 5.205n: "All of P'u-chou is a place of thieves."

ZGS 5.170, ZRKS 5.205, Shiba 113, ZGJI 269, ZGDJT 1074b, KZS #496

5.336 佛眼覰不見 *Butsugen miredomo mizu.*

Though the Buddha eye looks, it does not see.

Heki 24 Intro.

ZGS na, ZRKS 5.411, Shiba 113, ZGJI 269, ZGJT 408

5.337 佛祖開口難 *Busso kuchi o hiraku koto katashi.*

The buddhas and patriarchs can't open their mouths.

ZGS 5.171, Shiba na

5.338 蚊子咬鐵牛 *Bunsu tetsugyū o kamu.*

The mosquito bites the iron bull.

Heki 58 Main Case *agyo.*

ZGS 5.172, ZRKS 5.48, Shiba 113, ZGJI 269, ZGDJT 1103c, ZGJT 411, KZS #446

5.339 平地起波瀾 *Heichi ni haran o okosu.*

On a flat plain he raises waves.

Heki 55 Verse *agyo.*

ZGS 5.173, ZRKS 5.113, Shiba 114, ZGDJT 1108b, KZS #498

5.340 別是一家風 *Betsu ni kore ikkafū.*

Ah! This is the house's own style.

Heki 64 Verse *agyo.*

ZGS na, ZRKS 5.16, Shiba 114, ZGJI 270, ZGDJT 1112c, ZGJT 416

5.341 別是一壺天 *Betsu ni kore ikko no ten.*

Ah! So this is heaven in a pot!

ZGS na, ZRKS 5.453, Shiba 114, ZGJI 270

5.342 遍界不曾藏 *Henkai katsute kakusazu.*

The world in all its totality has never been hidden.

ZGS na, ZRKS 5.111, Shiba 114, ZGJI 279

5.343 徧地是刀鎗 *Henchi kore tōsō.*

Throughout the land, ⌜swords⌝ and spears.

ZGS 5.174, ZRKS na; Shiba 114 has 瘡 instead of 鎗.

5.344 寶劍在手裡 *Hōken shuri ni ari.*

The jeweled ⌜sword⌝ is in his hand.

ZGS 5.175, ZRKS 5.198, ZGJI 271, KZS #493; Shiba 115 has 裏 instead of 裡.

5.345 方木逗圓孔 *Hōboku enkō ni tōru.*

A square peg passes through a round hole.

Heki 25 Main Case Comm., 48 Verse *agyo.*

ZGS na, ZRKS 5.222, Shiba 115, ZGJI 271, ZGJT 420, ZGDJT 1143b

5.346 北斗裏藏身 *Hokutori ni mi o zō su.*

He hides himself in the ⌜North Star⌝.

ZGS na, ZRKS 5.132, Shiba 115, ZGJI 272, ZGJT 429, KZS #476

5.347 撲落不他物 *Bokuraku tamotsu ni arazu.*

What's fallen down is not anyone else's matter.

Heki 78 Main Case *agyo.*

ZGS na, ZRKS 5.249, Shiba 115, ZGJI 272, ZGJT 429

5.348 歩歩是道場 *Ho-ho kore dōjo.*

Every single step is a place of practice.

KZS #458: *Bu-bu kore dōjō.*

ZGS na, ZRKS 5.72, Shiba 114, ZGJI 271, KZS #458

5.349 歩歩清風起 *Ho-ho seifū okoru.*

At every step the pure wind rises.

KZS #460: *Bu-bu seifū okoru.*

ZGS 5.176, ZRKS 5.73, Shiba 115, ZGJI 271, KZS #460

5.350 煩惱卽菩提 *Bonnō soku bodai.*

Delusive passions are themselves ⌜*bodhi*⌝.

ZGS 5.177, Shiba na, ZGDJT 1167c

5.351 本來無一物 *Honrai mu ichimotsu.*

Fundamentally there is not one thing.

Heki 94 Verse Comm. See ⌜Sixth Patriarch⌝.

ZGS na, Shiba 115, ZGJI 272, ZGJT 431, ZGDJT 1169c

5.352 眨眼便蹉過 *Manako o sō sureba sunawachi shaka.*

If you blink, you will sail right past.

Shiba 100 reads 蹉過 as *saka,* but as *shaka* for 5.164.

ZGS na, Shiba 100, ZGJI 100, ZGJT 100

5.353 孟八郎秤金 *Manparō kin o hakaru.*

The no-account spendthrift is counting his money.

Man 孟 (Ch. *Meng*) is an abbreviation of *manran* 孟浪 (Ch. *Meng-lang*), meaning "wild, irresponsible." 八郎, often used as proper name for an eighth son, here just names everyman (ZGJT 436).

ZGS na, ZRKS 5.443, Shiba 118, ZGJT 436

5.354 轉身一轉出 *Mi o tenjite itten shite izu.*

He spins around once and then leaves.

ZGS 5.178, Shiba na

5.355 横身當宇宙 *Mi o yokotaete uchū ni ataru.*

He flings himself directly into the universe.

ZGS na, ZRKS 5.66, Shiba 79, ZGJI 273, ZGJT 38, KZS #454

5.356 打水魚頭痛 *Mizu o uteba, gyotō itamu.*

If you slap the water, you hurt the heads of the fish.

ZGS 5.179, ZRKS 5.28, Shiba na, ZGJI 274

5.357 擔水河頭賣 *Mizu o ninatte katō ni uru.*

He hauls water and to sell by the river.

Heki 57 Verse *agyo.*

ZGS 5.180, ZRKS 5.294, Shiba 102, ZGJI 274, ZGJT 299, ZGDJT 1182b

5.358 水急不流月 *Mizu kyū ni shite tsuki o nagasazu.*

The streams flow swiftly but do not carry away the ⌜moon⌝.

ZGS na, ZRKS 5.359, Shiba 96, ZGJI 274

5.359 入水見長人 *Mizu ni itte chōjin o miru.*

Get into the water and see who is taller.

ZGS 5.181, ZRKS 5.117, Shiba 110, ZGJI 274, ZGJT 360

5.360 密卻在汝邊 *Mitsu wa kaette nanji ga hen ni ari.*

The secret is in yourself.

MMK 23.

ZGS na, ZRKS 5.430, Shiba 116, ZGJI 273

5.361 密裏有砒礵 *Mitsuri ni hisō ari.*

In the honey there's arsenic.

KZS #506: 蜜 instead of 密.

ZGS na, ZRKS 5.241, Shiba 116, ZGJI 274, KZS #506

5.362 密室不通風 *Misshitsu ni kaze o tsūzezu.*

Not even the wind can penetrate into his secret room.

ZGS 5.182, ZRKS 5.200, Shiba 116, ZGJI 273, ZGDJT 1184b, KZS #494

5.363 面南見北斗 *Minami ni mukatte hokuto o miru.*

Facing south, he sees the ⌜North Star⌝.

Heki 28 Verse.

ZGS 5.183, ZRKS 5.106, Shiba 117, ZGJI 274, ZGJT 447

5.364 看看臘月盡 *Miyo miyo rōgetsu tsuku.*

Pay attention! The twelfth month is ending.

ZGS na, ZRKS 5.334, Shiba 81, ZGJI 274, ZGJT 65

5.365 無義老凍膿 *Mugi no rōtōnō.*

Worthless old clot of pus.

ZGS 5.184, Shiba na

5.366 無言誠有功 *Mugon makoto ni kō ari.*

Silence is truly effective.

ZGS 5.185, Shiba 116

5.367 無手者好打 *Mushu no mono yoku utsu.*

The person without hands gives a good punch.

ZGS na, ZRKS 5.12, Shiba 117

5.368 無底破漆桶 *Mutei no hashittsū.*

The bottomless broken lacquer tub.

ZGS na, ZRKS 5.398, Shiba 117, ZGJI 275

5.369 無佛處作佛 *Mubutsu no tokoro sabutsu.*

Where there are no buddhas, make buddhas.

Heki 7 Intro. ZGJI 275: *Mubutsu no tokoro butsu o saku su.*

ZGS na, ZRKS 5.348, Shiba 117, ZGJI 275, ZGDJT 1080d

5.370 明鏡裏藏身 *Meikyōri ni mi o zō su.*

He hides himself in the bright mirror.

ZGS 5.186, Shiba 117

5.371 明珠絕點翳 *Meishu ten'ei o zessu.*

The bright pearl has no trace of cloudiness.

ZGS na, ZRKS 5.379, Shiba 117, ZGJI 275

5.372 揑目强生花 *Me o hinette shiite hana o shōzu.*

By rubbing his eyes hard, he makes flowers appear.

ZGS 5.187, ZRKS 5.327, Shiba na, ZGJI 275, ZGJT 368

5.373 孟軻鄒人也 *Mōka wa sū no hito nari.*

Mencius was a man from Tsou.

ZGS 5.188, Shiba na

5.374 猛虎畫娥眉 *Mōko gabi o egaku.*

The fierce tiger paints its ⌜eyebrows⌝.

ZGS 5.189, ZRKS 5.77, 386, Shiba 118, ZGJI 276

5.375 猛虎當路坐 *Mōko michi ni attate za su.*

A fierce tiger sits across your path.

ZGS na, ZRKS 5.110, Shiba 118, ZGJI 276, ZGDJT 1223b, ZGJT 449

5.376 木馬上金梯 *Mokuba kintei ni noboru.*

The wooden horse climbs a golden ladder.

ZGS na, ZRKS 5.160, Shiba 118, ZGJI 276

5.377 目前無異草 *Mokuzen ni isō nashi.*

There are no unusual weeds before my eyes.

ZGS 5.190, Shiba na

5.378 本立而道生 *Moto tachite dō naru.*

Establish the foundation and the Way opens.

Analects 1, 2. Shiba 115: *Moto tatte michi shōzu.*

ZGS 5.191, ZRKS 5.164, Shiba 115

5.379 出門便是草 *Mon o izureba sunawachi kore kusa.*

Go out the gate and immediately there are weeds.

ZGS 5.192, Shiba na, ZGJI 276

5.380 門外雨滴聲 *Monge no utekisei.*

Outside the gate, the sound of raindrops.

ZGS 5.193, Shiba na

5.381 門前下馬臺 *Monzen no gebadai.*

The hitching post by the gate.

ZGS 5.194, Shiba na

5.382 夜深明月孤 *Yoru fukōshite meigetsu ko nari.*

In the deep of the night, the luminous ⌜moon⌝ alone.

Shōun-ji: *yo* instead of *yoru.*

ZGS na, ZRKS 5.169, Shiba 118

5.383 夜雨過瀟湘 *Yau shōshō o sugu.*

Night rain passes through ⌜Hsiao-hsiang⌝.

ZGS na, ZRKS 5.325, Shiba 118

5.384 夜叉空裏走 *Yasha kūri ni hashiru.*

The ⸢*yakṣa*⸣ runs through the sky.

ZGS na, ZRKS 5.129, Shiba 118, ZGJI 277

5.385 山呼萬歳聲 *Yama wa yobu banzai no koe.*

The mountains ring with shouts of "⸢Ten thousand years!⸣"

ZGS 5.195, ZRKS 5.148, Shiba 91, ZGJI 277

5.386 山寒花發遲 *Yama samūshite hana hiraku koto ososhi.*

In cold mountains flowers bloom late.

ZGS na, ZRKS 5.24, Shiba 91, ZGJI 277

5.387 山高月上遲 *Yama takōshite tsuki no noboru koto ososhi.*

In high mountains the ⸢moon⸣ is late to rise.

ZGS na, ZRKS 5.190, Shiba 91, ZGJI 277

5.388 山深雪未消 *Yama fukōshite yuki imada kiezu.*

Deep in the mountains the snow has yet to melt.

ZGS na, ZRKS 5.21, Shiba 92, ZGJI 277, ZGJT 164, KZS #440

5.389 野鹿叫林底 *Yaroku rintei ni sakebu.*

Wild deer cry in the deep forest.

ZGS 5.196, Shiba na

5.390 擔雪塡古井 *Yuki o ninatte kosei o uzumu.*

They haul snow to fill the old well.

ZGS 5.198, Shiba 102, ZGJI 212, ZGJT 299, ZGDJT 1246b

5.391 依樣畫猫兒 *Yō ni yotte byōji o egaku.*

He uses a model to paint a cat.

Heki 93 Main Case, Verse *agyo*. Shiba 77: 胡盧 calabash instead of 猫兒 cat.

ZGS 5.199, ZRKS 5.9, Shiba 77, ZGJI 278, ZGJT 9

5.392 鷂子過新羅 *Yōsu shinra o sugu.*

The hawk has flown off to ⸢Silla⸣.

Heki 1 Verse Comm.

ZGS na, ZRKS 5.287, Shiba 119, ZGJI 278, ZGJT 463, KZS #531

5.393 能聚兮聚兮 *Yoku atsumeyo atsumeyo.*

Gather it in well, gather it in.

ZGS 5.200, Shiba na

5.394 善射不中的 *Yoku iru mono wa mato ni atarazu.*

One who takes careful aim does not hit the target.

ZGS 5.201, ZRKS 5.322, Shiba 99, ZGJI 278

5.395 能使得爺錢 *Yoku yasen o tsukaietari.*

He made good use of his father's money.

ZGS 5.202, ZRKS 5.151, Shiba 110, ZGJI 278

5.396 好和聲便打 *Yoshi koe ni washite sunawachi utan.*

Better hit him whenever he speaks.

Heki 37 Main Case *agyo.*

ZGS na, ZRKS 5.172, Shiba 87, ZGJI 279

5.397 雷罷不停聲 *Rai yande koe o todomezu.*

The thunder has stopped, but the rumbling has not ended.

ZGS na, ZRKS 5.323, Shiba 119, ZGJI 279

5.398 夜更飢鼠驕 *Yo fukete kiso ogoru.*

When night falls, the starving rat grows bold.

ZGS 5.203, Shiba na

5.399 禮拜甚分明 *Raihai hanahada funmyō.*

His ritual bows are extremely impressive.

ZGS na, ZRKS 5.80, Shiba 121, ZGJI 281

5.400 爛泥裏有棘 *Randeiri ni ubara ari.*

There are thorns in the slime and mud.

Heki 9 Main Case *agyo*, 28 Main Case *agyo*. ZGJI 279: *Randeiri ni toge ari.*

ZGS 5.204, ZRKS 5.102, Shiba 119, ZGJI 279, ZGJT 470

5.401 利劍不如錐 *Riken sui ni shikazu.*

A sharp ⌜sword⌝ is no match for an ⌜awl⌝.

ZGS na, ZRKS 5.121, Shiba 120, ZGJI 279

5.402 梨花一枝春 *Rika isshi no haru.*

The pear blossoms—a spray of spring!

ZGS na, ZRKS 5.23, Shiba 120, ZGJI 279

5.403 驪龍吐明珠 *Riryō meishu o haku.*

The ⌜black dragon⌝ coughs up its bright pearl.

ZGS na, ZRKS 5.194, Shiba 120, ZGJI 280

5.404 龍生金鳳子 *Ryū kin hōsu o umu,*

The dragon gave birth to a golden phoenix,➛

Rinzai-roku §59.

ZGS na, ZRKS 5.376, Shiba 120, ZGJI 280

5.405 衝破碧瑠璃 *Heki ruri o shōha su.*

➛That shattered the turquoise-blue sky.

Rinzai-roku §59. ZKRS 5.377 has 琉 for 瑠.

ZGS na, ZRKS 5.377, Shiba 95, ZGJI 270

5.406 臘月火燒山 *Rōgetsu no hi yama o yaku.*

December fires burn the mountain.

Heki 17 Main Case Comm. Mountain villagers cleared off the mountain at the end of the year by burning it (ZGJI 282, ZGJT 493).

ZGS na, ZRKS 5.270, Shiba 121, ZGJI 282, ZGJT 493

5.407 螻蟻搖鐵柱 *Rōgi tetchū o yurugasu.*

Crickets and ants shake the iron pillar.

ZGS 5.205, Shiba na

5.408 老拳不妄發 *Rōken midari ni hassezu.*

A veteran does not often use his fist.

ZGS 5.206, ZRKS 5.173, Shiba na, ZGJI 282, ZGJT 489, KZS #486

5.409 聾人爭得聞 *Rōjin ikade ka kiku koto o en.*

How can a deaf person hear?

Heki 95 Main Case.

ZGS na, ZRKS 5.297, Shiba 121, KZS #537

5.410 老鼠入牛角 *Rōso gokaku ni iru.*

The old rat crawled into the ox horn.

ZGS 5.207, Shiba 121, ZGJI 282, ZGJT 489

5.411 六耳不同謀 *Rikuji hakarigoto o onajiusezu.*

Six ears—their comprehension is not the same.

Heki 26 Verse Comm. Six ears are three people (ZRKS 5.229n).

ZGS na, ZRKS 5.229, Shiba 121, ZGJI 280, ZGJT 494

5.412 驢屎比麝香 *Roshi jakō ni hi su.*

Donkey shit compares with ⌜deer musk⌝.

Heki 77 Main Case Comm.

ZGS 5.208, ZRKS 5.250, Shiba na, ZGJI 281, ZGJT 486

5.413 驢屎似馬糞 *Roshi bafun ni nitari.*

Donkey shit is like horse manure.

ZGS 5.209, ZRKS 5.250, Shiba na

5.414 驢揀濕處尿 *Ro wa shissho o erande nyō su.*

Donkeys choose wet places to piss.

ZGS 5.211, ZRKS 5.392, Shiba na, ZGJI 282, ZGJT 486

5.415 露柱掛燈籠 *Rochū ni tōrō o kaku.*

Hang a lantern on the outdoor pillar.

Heki 83 Verse *agyo*.

ZGS 5.210, ZRKS 5.279, Shiba 121, ZGJI 281, ZGJT 485

5.416 纔行三五歩 *Wazuka ni aruku koto sangoho.*

He goes only a short three or five steps.

MMK 31.

ZGS 5.212, Shiba na

5.417 和氣兆豊年 *Waki wa hōnen o chō su.*

Calm weather is a sign of a prosperous year.

ZGS na, ZRKS 5.9, Shiba 122

5.418 合咲不合哭 *Warau beshi koku su bekarazu.*

Laugh, don't cry.

Heki 12 Verse.

ZGS na, ZRKS 5.368, Shiba 88

5.419 吾無隱乎爾 *Ware nanji ni kakusu koto nashi.*

I am not keeping anything from you.

Analects VII, 23.

ZGS 5.213, Shiba 86

5.420 話頭也不識 *Watō mo mata shirazu.*

They don't know the point of his talk.

Heki 49 Main Case, 67 Main Case Comm.

ZGS na, ZRKS 5.414, Shiba 122, ZGJI 282

Six-Character Phrases

6.1 阿哆哆阿波波 *A ta ta, a ha ha.*

Ahhh! Yahhh!

Variant: 阿吒吒阿波波. The wailing of those in hell. However, in T'ang colloquial language, 阿波波 represented laughter (ZGJI 283).

ZGS 6.1, Shiba na, ZGJI 282

6 字

6.2 阿呵呵露風骨 *A ka ka fūkotsu o arawasu.*

His laugh "Ha ha!" reveals the bones of his style.

ZGS na, ZRKS 6.129, Shiba 123, ZGJI 283

6.3 蛙面水鹿角蜂 *Amensui rokkakuhō.*

Water on the frog's face, a bee on the deer's horn.

ZGS 6.2, ZRKS 6.236, Shiba 123, ZGJI 283

6.4 莫錯認定盤星 *Ayamatte jōbanjō o mitomuru koto nakare.*

Don't fix your attention on the graduation marks.

Heki 18 Verse Comm., 21 Main Case, 84 Verse Comm. See ⌜Steelyard⌝. See also 10.156.

ZGS 6.3, ZRKS 6.278, Shiba 144, ZGJI 283

6.5 行燈暗行燈暗 *Antō kurashi, antō kurashi.*

The lantern's gone out! The lantern's gone out!

ZGS 6.4, Shiba na

6.6 咦淨地上撒屙 *Ii jōchijō ni a o sassu.*

Oh! He's pissing in a sacred space.

ZGS 6.5, Shiba na

6.7 具威儀謝答話 *Igi o gu shite tōwa o sha su.*

Donning formal clothes, he gives thanks for the response.

ZGS 6.6, Shiba na

6.8 池印月鏡含像 *Ike wa tsuki o in shi, kagami wa zō o fukumu.*

The pond reflects the ⌜moon⌝, the mirror holds an image.

ZGS na, ZRKS 6.69, Shiba 140, ZGJI 284, ZGDJT 22d

6.9 去卻一拈得七 *Ichi o kokyaku shi shichi o nentoku su.*

He threw out one but picked up seven.

Heki 6 Verse.

ZGS na, ZRKS 6.183, Shiba 128, ZGJI 284, ZGDJT 28a, ZGJT 88, KZS #638

6.10 一合相不可得 *Ichi gōsō fukatoku.*

The merging of all into one—this cannot be grasped.

Heki 83 Main Case *agyo*, 87 Main Case *agyo*. From the *Diamond Sutra.*

ZGS na, ZRKS 6.150, Shiba 124, ZGJI 284, ZGJT 20

6.11 因一事長一智 *Ichiji ni yotte itchi o chōzu.*

With each single thing add a single wisdom.

ZGJI 285: 經 instead of 因.

ZGS na, ZRKS 6.146, Shiba 125, ZGJI 285, KZS #614

6.12 一二三三二一 *Ichi ni san, san ni ichi.*

One two three, three two one.

ZGS 6.8, ZRKS 6.209, Shiba 124

6.13 一二三四五六 *Ichi ni san shi go roku.*

One two three four five six.

Heki 21 Main Case *agyo*, 47 Verse.

ZGS 6.9, ZRKS 6.210, Shiba 124, ZGJI 323, ZGDJT 33b, ZGJT 21

6.14 一棒打不回頭 *Ichibō ni ta suredomo kōbe o megurasazu.*

Though you hit him with a stick, he doesn't turn his head.

MMK 28, *Heki* 4 Main Case Comm., 7 Main Case Comm.

ZGS 6.10, ZRKS 6.279, Shiba 124, ZGJI 285

6.15 一火弄泥團漢 *Ikka deidan o rō suru no kan.*

A bunch of fellows playing with balls of mud.

Heki 36 Main Case *agyo*, 48 Main Case *agyo*. 一火 or 一伙 is a T'ang military term meaning a single group (ZGDJT 37d).

ZGS na, ZRKS 6.214, Shiba 124, ZGJI 284, ZGDJT 37d

6.16 一花開天下春 *Ikka hiraite tenka haru nari.*

A single blossom opens and the world is in spring.

ZGS 6.11, ZRKS 6.172, Shiba 124, ZGJI 284, ZGJT 20

6.17 一手擡一手搦 *Isshu tai, isshu jaku.*

Lift with one hand, lower with the other.

Heki 16 Intro., 36 Main Case *agyo*, 48 Main Case *agyo*, etc.

ZGS 6.12, ZRKS 6.28, Shiba 124, ZGJI 285 (variant), ZGDJT 43c, ZGJT 20

6.18 一簞食一瓢飲 *Ittan no shi, ippyō no in.*

A single dish of food, a single gourd of drink.

See *Analects* VI, 9.

ZGS na, Shiba 124

6.19 未知生焉知死 *Imada shō o shirazunba izukunzo shi o shiran.*

If you've never understood life, how will you understand death?

Analects XI, 11. Shiba 147: *sei* instead of *shō*.

ZGS na, ZRKS 6.76, Shiba 147

6.20 井覰驢驢覰井 *I ro o mi, ro i o miru.*

The well gazes at the ass, the ass gazes at the well.

ZGS 6.13, ZRKS 6.107, Shiba 137, ZGJI 283, ZD #94; variant: *sei* instead of *i*

6.21 描不成畫不就 *Utsusedomo narazu, egakedomo narazu.*

It can't be copied, it can't be painted.

MMK 23 Verse, *Serenity* 49 Intro.

ZGS 6.15, ZRKS 6.47, Shiba 145, ZGJI 286, ZGDJT 1054b, ZGJT 395

6.22 烏自黑鷺自白 *U wa onozukara kuroku, ro wa onozukara shiroshi.*

Crows are naturally black, herons are naturally white.

ZGS 6.16, Shiba na

6.23 益州布揚州絹 *Ekijū no nuno, yōjū no kinu.*

The cloth of I-chou, the silk of Yang-chou.

ZGS 6.7, ZRKS 6.71, Shiba na, ZGJI 286

6.24 烟霞不遮梅香 *Enka baikō o saegirazu.*

Smoke and mist cannot cover up the fragrance of the plum.

Shiba 125: 煙 instead of 烟.

ZGS 6.14, ZRKS 6.98, Shiba 125, ZGJI 286

6.25 黃金鎚白玉鑿 *Ōgon no tsuchi, hakugyoku no nomi.*

A hammer of gold and a drill of white jade.

ZRKS 6.93: *saku* instead of *nomi.*

ZGS na, ZRKS 6.93, Shiba 132, ZGJI 286

6.26 可惜勞而無功 *Oshimubeshi, rō shite kō naki koto o.*

What a pity, all that work for nothing!

Heki 91 Main Case.

ZGS 6.17, ZRKS 6.42, Shiba 126

6.27 推不去挽不來 *Osedomo sarazu, hikedomo kitarazu.*

Push, it will not go; pull, it will not come.

ZGS 6.18, ZRKS 6.48, Shiba 136, ZGJI 287

6.28 無友不如己者 *Onore ni shikazaru mono o tomo to suru koto nakare.*

Have no friends not equal to yourself.

Trans. from Legge 1985, *Analects* 1, 8.

ZGS 6.19, ZRKS 6.274, Shiba na

6.29 面赤者心不直 *Omote akaki mono kokoro naokarazu.*

One with a red face has a crooked mind.

ZGS 6.20, ZRKS 6.na, Shiba 148, KZS #620

6.30 面赤不如語直 *Omote no akakaran yori wa go no naokaran ni wa shikazu.*

Better to speak straight than to be red-faced [with shame].

Heki 34 Main Case *agyo*, 58 Main Case *agyo*. Shiba 148: *naoki ni shikazu* instead of *naokaran ni wa shikazu*.

ZGS 6.21, ZRKS 6.153, Shiba 148, ZGJT 447

6.31 知恩方解報恩 *On o shitte wa masa ni on o hōzen koto o ge su.*

One who truly understands gratitude knows to repay it.

Rinzai-roku §56.

ZGS 6.22, ZRKS 6.145, Shiba 140, ZGJI 287, ZGDJT 132d, ZGJT 303

6.32 薤園裡賣葱草 *Kaienri ni sōsō o uru.*

He sells leeks near the onion fields.

ZGS 6.23, ZRKS 6., Shiba 127

6.33 指槐樹罵柳樹 *Kaiju o yubisashite ryūju o nonoshiru.*

He points to a locust tree but scolds the willow.

Heki 12 Main Case *agyo*.

ZGS na, ZRKS 6.104, Shiba 134, ZGJI 288, ZGDJT 140b, ZGJT 174

6.34 卻是老僧罪過 *Kaette kore rōsō no zaika.*

It's this ⌜old monk⌝ who is at fault.

Heki 34 Main Case Comm.

ZGS 6.24, Shiba na

6.35 歸去來歸去來 *Kaeri nan iza, kaeri nan iza.*

Homeward bound! Homeward bound!

ZGS 6.25, ZRKS 6., Shiba na, 陶淵明歸去來兮辭

6.36 鰐魚死民心安 *Gakugyo shi shite minshin yasushi.*

When the crocodile is dead, the people's minds are at ease.

ZGS na, Shiba 127

6.37 家醜莫向外揚 *Kashū wa soto ni mukatte aguru koto nakare.*

Don't show others the shameful secrets of our house.

ZGS na, ZRKS 6.203, Shiba 126, ZGJI 288, ZGJT 47, KZS #581

6.38 迦葉貧阿難富 *Kashō no hin, anan no tomi.*

The poverty of ⌜Kāśyapa⌝, the wealth of ⌜Ānanda⌝.

ZGS 6.26, ZRKS 6.252, Shiba na, ZGJI 287

6.39 頭不缺尾不剩 *Kashira kakezu, o amarazu.*

Head not too short, tail not too long.

ZGS 6.27, ZRKS 6.50, Shiba na, KZS #568

6.40 被風吹別調中 *Kaze ni betchō no naka ni fukaru.*

Blown by the wind into a completely different tune.

Heki 7 Verse *agyo*, 65 Main Case Comm. For other interpretations, see 14.18.

ZGS na, Shiba 145, ZGJI 597, ZGJT 9

6.41 風從虎雲從龍 *Kaze wa tora ni shitagai, kumo wa ryū ni shitagau.*

Wind comes with the tiger, clouds come with the dragon.

ZGS 6.28, ZRKS 6.63, Shiba 146, ZGJI 288, KZS #575

6.42 渇不飲盗泉水 *Kassuredomo tōsen no mizu o nomazu.*

Though thirsty he refuses to drink the water of Stolen Spring.

Confucius refused to drink the water of Stolen Spring because the spring had a bad name (淮南子, 說山訓, cited in Morohashi 23006.43). This story has become a metaphor for virtue and uprightness.

ZGS 6.30, Shiba na

6.43 活卓卓孤逈逈 *Kattaku-taku, ko kei-kei.*

Full of vim and vigor, off in a world apart.

ZGS na, Shiba 127, ZGJI 288, ZGDJT 165d

6.44 跨瞎驢追猛虎 *Katsuro ni matagatte, mōko o ou.*

Astride a blind donkey, pursuing a fierce tiger.

ZGS 6.31, ZRKS 6.250, Shiba 131, ZGJI 288

6.45 果然現大人相 *Kanen to shite daijin no sō o genzu.*

As expected, showing the signs of being a great person.

Shiba 126: *Kazen to shite taijin no sō o genzu.*

ZGS 6.29, Shiba 126

6.46 彼蒼天喪父母 *Ka no sōten fubo o ushinau.*

That desperate cry when father and mother have perished.

ZGS 6.32, Shiba na

6.47 蝦蟆窟裸出來 *Gama kutsuri yori idekitaru.*

The toad emerges from its hole.

Heki 72 Main Case *agyo*.

ZGS na, ZRKS 6.142, Shiba 126, ZGJI 288, ZGDJT 170b, ZGJT 50, KZS #644

6.48 上是天下是地 *Kami wa kore ten shimo wa kore chi.*

Above are the heavens, below is the earth.

Heki 6 Verse *agyo*, 18 Main Case *agyo*.

ZGS na, ZRKS 6.246, Shiba 135, ZGJT 221

6.49 臥龍不鑑死水 *Garyū shisui o kangamizu.*

You won't see a dragon sleeping in dead water.

Heki 95 Verse.

ZGS 6.34, ZRKS 6.161, Shiba 126, ZGJI 288, ZGJT 52, KZS #626

6.50 火爐頭無賓主 *Karotō ni hinjū nashi.*

In the fireplace there is no host or guest.

ZGS na, ZRKS 6.43, Shiba 126, ZGJI 287

6.51 荷葉團松葉細 *Kayō wa maruku shōyō wa hososhi.*

Lotus leaves are round, pine needles are slender.

ZGS 6.33, Shiba na, ZGJI 288

6.52 甘草甘黄蓮苦 *Kansō wa amaku ōren wa nigashi.*

Sweet grass is sweet, yellow lotus is bitter.

In Chinese medicine, sweet grass and yellow lotus are medicinal plants (ZGJI 289).

ZGS na, ZRKS 6.34, Shiba 127, ZGJI 289, ZGJT 63, KZS #564

6.53 眼裏沙耳裏土 *Ganri no suna, niri no do.*

Sand in the eyes, dirt in the ears.

Heki 25 Verse: 塵「dust」 instead of 沙 sand.

ZGS na, ZRKS 6.115, Shiba 127, KZS #591

6.54 擬議白雲萬里 *Gigiseba hakuun banri.*

Hesitate and you are off in white clouds for ten thousand miles.

ZGS 6.35, ZRKS 6.92, Shiba na, ZGJI 289, ZGJT 81, KZS #602

6.55 龜毛長兎角短 *Kimō wa nagaku, tokaku wa mijikashi.*

⌜Turtle hairs⌝ are long, ⌜rabbit horns⌝ are short.

ZGS 6.37, ZRKS 6.72, Shiba 128, ZGJI 289

6.56 脚下泥深三尺 *Kyakka doro fukaki koto sanjaku.*

Beneath your feet, the mud is three feet deep.

Heki 36 Verse *agyo.*

ZGS 6.38, ZRKS 6.266, Shiba na, ZGJI 290, ZGJT 84

6.57 不喜舊路逢人 *Kyūro hito ni au o yorokobazu.*

I don't enjoy meeting people on the ancient road.

ZGS 6.39, Shiba na, ZGJI 290

6.58 下喬木入幽谷 *Kyōboku yori kudarite yūkoku ni iru.*

Come down from the tall trees and enter the dark valley.

ZGS 6.40, ZRKS 6.232, Shiba na, ZGJI 290, ZGDJT 229c, ZGJT 40

6.59 起來大作舞出 *Kirai ōi ni mai o nashite izu.*

He comes, does a great dance, and leaves.

ZGS 6.41, Shiba na

6.60 急水上打毬子 *Kyūsuijō ni kyūsu o tasu.*

Playing ball on running water.

Heki 80 Main Case.

ZGS na, ZRKS 6.254, Shiba 128, ZGJI 290, KZS #600

6.61 强將下無弱兵 *Kyōshōka ni jakuhei nashi.*

Under a strong general, there are no weak soldiers.

ZGS na, ZRKS 6.116, Shiba 128, ZGJT 91, KZS #592

6.62 行亦禪坐亦禪 *Gyō mo mata zen, za mo mata zen.*

Action is also Zen, sitting is also Zen.

ZGS na, Shiba 129, ZGDJT 214b

6.63 金烏急玉兎速 *Kin'u kyū ni, gyokuto sumiyaka nari.*

The ⌜golden crow⌝ is swift, the ⌜jade rabbit⌝ is fast.

Heki 12 Verse.

ZGS na, Shiba 129, ZGJT 291, KZS #565

6.64 賣金須買金人 *Kin o uru wa subekaraku kin o kau hito narubeshi.*

To sell gold, you must first become a buyer of gold.

ZGS na, ZRKS 6.197, Shiba 144, ZGJI 291, ZGJT 379

6.65 空手來空手去 *Kūshu ni shite kitari kūshu ni shite saru.*

Empty-handed I come, empty-handed I go.

ZGJT 98: 空手去空手歸 *Kūshu ni shite yuki, kūshu ni shite kaeru,* "Empty-handed he went, empty-handed he returned."

ZGS 6.42, ZRKS 6.147, Shiba 129, ZGJI 291, ZGJT 98, KZS #618

6.66 草茸茸煙羃羃 *Kusa jō-jō kemuri beki-beki.*

Choked with weeds, shrouded in smoke.

Heki 6 Verse, 34 Verse Comm.

ZGS na, ZRKS 6.7, Shiba 138, ZGJI 291, ZGJT 169

6.67 雲冉冉水漫漫 *Kumo zen-zen, mizu man-man.*

Clouds scud along, water brims boundless.

Heki 62 Verse.

ZGS 6.43, ZRKS 6.215, Shiba 125, ZGJI 291, ZGJT 32

6.68 雲在天水在缾 *Kumo ten ni ari, mizu hei ni ari.*

Clouds in the sky, water in the bottle.

ZGS na, ZRKS 6.85, Shiba 125, ZGJI 291

6.69 君子周而不比 *Kunshi wa shū shite hi sezu.*

The superior person embraces all and does not compare.

Analects II, 14.

ZGS 6.44, Shiba 129

6.70 君子千里同風 *Kunshi senri dōfū.*

The superior person is the same in manner even a thousand miles away.

ZGS 6.45, ZRKS 6.140, Shiba 129, ZGDJT 255b, KZS #611

6.71 乾三連坤六斷 *Ken sanren, kon rokudan.*

Heaven is three solids; earth is six brokens.

See ⌜Eight trigrams⌝. KZS #555: *rikudan* instead of *rokudan.*

ZGS 6.46, ZRKS 6.20, Shiba na, ZGJI 292, KZS #555

6.72 嚴師出好弟子 *Genshi kō deshi o idasu.*

A strict teacher produces good disciples.

ZGS 6.47, ZRKS 6.198, Shiba na

6.73 竪起拳頭出去 *Kentō o juki shite idesaru.*

Raising a fist, he leaves.

ZGS 6.48, Shiba na

6.74 見不見聞不聞 *Ken fuken, mon fumon.*

Seeing without seeing, hearing without hearing.

Heki 56 Intro.

ZGS 6.49, ZRKS 6.282, Shiba na

6.75 向去底卻來底 *Kōkyotei kyaraitei.*

The way [one] came, the way [one] left.

The particle 底 makes the phrase which precedes it adjectival or adverbial. The reading *kyaraitei* follows ZGS 6.50.

ZGS 6.50, Shiba na

6.76 江月照松風吹 *Kōgetsu terashi shōfū fuku.*

The ⌜moon⌝ gleams on the water, wind blows through the pines.

ZGS 6.51, ZRKS 6.288, Shiba 132, ZGJI 293, ZGDJT 308b

6.77 好語不可説盡 *Kōgo wa tokitsukusu bekarazu.*

A good talk should not explain everything.

ZGS na, ZRKS 6.109, Shiba 132, ZGJI 293, ZGJT 131

6.78 好兒不使爺錢 *Kōji yasen o tsukawazu.*

A good son does not use his father's money.

ZGS 6.52, ZRKS 6.133, Shiba 132, ZGJI 294, KZS #605

6.79 黃尚書李僕射 *Kō shōsho, ri bokuya.*

Huang the premier, Li the first minister.

ZGS 6.53, Shiba na

6.80 高天跼厚地蹐 *Kōten ni segukumari, kōchi ni nukiashi su.*

Crouch under the high heavens, tiptoe over the deep earth.

ZGS 6.54, ZRKS 6.73, Shiba 132, ZGJI 294

6.81 頭鬔鬆耳卓朔 *Kōbe hōsō, mimi takusaku.*

Hair out of place, but ears alert.

Heki 90 Intro.

ZGS na, ZRKS 6.171, Shiba 142, ZGJI 306, ZGJT 344

6.82 紅爐上一點雪 *Kōrojō itten no yuki.*

In the red hot furnace, a flake of snow.

Heki 69 Intro.

ZGS 6.55, Shiba 132, ZGJI 294, ZGDJT 328c, ZGJT 135

6.83 入香爐入線香 *Kōro ni iri, senkō ni iru.*

Enter into the burner, enter into the incense.

ZGS 6.56, Shiba na

6.84 呼虛空名什麼 *Kokū o yonde nan to ka nazuku.*

When you address emptiness, what name do you use?

ZGS 6.57, Shiba na

6.85 入虎穴捋虎鬚 *Koketsu ni itte koshu o nazu.*

Enter the tiger's den and stroke the tiger's whiskers.

ZGS na, ZRKS 6.144, Shiba 144, ZGJI 293, KZS #612

6.86 此去漢陽不遠 *Koko o satte kanyō tōkarazu.*

Leave here and Han-yang is not far away.

ZGS 6.58, ZRKS 6.189, Shiba na, ZGJI 294

6.87 箇箇立在轉處 *Ko-ko tenjo ni ryūzai su.*

Each and every one stands in a place of transformation.

Heki 10 Intro., 26 Verse Comm., 39 Main Case Comm., etc.

ZGS na, ZRKS 6.255, Shiba 131

6.88 踞地金毛獅子 *Koji kinmō no shishi.*

A golden lion crouching on the ground.

Rinzai-roku §43.

ZGS na, Shiba 128

6.89 胡長三黑李四 *Kochō san kokuri shi.*

Red-bearded ⌜Chang⌝ number three, black-haired ⌜Li⌝ number four.

ZRKS 6.187: *uchō* instead of *kochō*.

ZGS na, ZRKS 6.187, Shiba 131, ZGJI 293, ZGJT 118

6.90 牛頭沒馬頭回 *Gozu bosshite mezu kaeru.*

When Oxhead withdraws, Horsehead turns around.

Heki 5 Verse, 49 Intro.

ZGS 6.59, ZRKS 6.218, Shiba 128, ZGJI 290

6.91 踞虎頭收虎尾 *Kotō ni kyo shite, kobi o osamu.*

Ride the tiger's head and control the tiger's tail.

Heki 49 Main Case, 54 Verse.

ZGS 6.60, ZRKS 6.135, Shiba 128, ZGJI 293, KZS #606

6.92 此地無金二兩 *Kono chi kin ni ryō nashi.*

Here there are not two ounces of gold.

This is part of a longer couplet: 此地無金二兩俗人沽酒三升 *Kono chi kin ni ryō nashi, zokujin shu sanshō o kau,* "Here, there are not two ounces of gold, the layman buys three jugs of wine." A man once hid his money in the ground but then erected a sign, "Here, there are not two ounces of gold." A priest disguised himself to buy wine but then blurted out, "I am a layman buying three jugs of wine" (Shiba 133).

ZGS na, ZRKS 6.238, Shiba 133, ZGJI 573

6.93 此語永劫不忘 *Kono go eigo ni wasurezu.*

This word will not be forgotten for endless ages.

ZGS 6.61, Shiba na

6.94 五百年一間生 *Gohyakunen ni hitotabi kanshō su.*

One such person is born only every five hundred years.

Heki 26 Verse *agyo.*

ZGS na, Shiba 131, ZGJI 293, ZGJT 121

6.95 古廟裡香爐去 *Kobyōri no kōro ni shi sare.*

Go and become the incense burner in the old shrine.

ZGS na, Shiba 130

6.96 古佛過去久矣 *Kobutsu kako suru koto hisashi.*

The old Buddha left long ago.

ZRKS 6.97: *sugisatte* instead of *kako suru koto.*

ZGS na, ZRKS 6.97, Shiba 130, ZGJI 292 and 236, ZGDJT 358a, ZGJT 115

6.97 古佛與露柱交 *Kobutsu to rochū to aimajiwaru.*

The old Buddha merges with the post.

ZGS 6.62, Shiba 130

6.98 護法爲心切也 *Gohō wa kokoro no setsu naru ga tame nari.*

The Dharma is maintained through zeal in the heart.

ZGS 6.63, Shiba 131

6.99 米不咬破一粒 *Kome ichiryū o kōha sezu.*

Not a single grain of rice is chewed.

ZGS 6.64, Shiba na

6.100 是甚麼繫驢橛 *Kore nan no keroketsu zo.*

What kind of donkey hitching post is this?

Heki 1 Main Case *agyo*, 31 Main Case *agyo* (variant).

ZGS 6.65, Shiba 137

6.101 是放開是捏聚 *Kore hōkai ka, kore netsujū ka.*

Now letting go, now taking in.

ZGS na, ZRKS 6.68, Shiba 137, ZGJI 295, KZS #577

6.102 金剛圈栗棘蓬 *Kongōken, rikkyokubō.*

A pitfall with sharp thorns.

See ⌜*Vajra*⌝.

ZGS 6.66, ZRKS 6.55, Shiba na, ZGJI 295, ZGJT 146, KZS #572

6.103 今日有明日無 *Konnichi wa u, myōnichi wa mu.*

Today there is, tomorrow there isn't.

ZGS 6.67, Shiba na, ZGJI 295

6.104 今日打着一箇 *Konnichi ikko o tajaku su.*

Today I struck one.

ZGS 6.68, Shiba na

6.105 今日始知數量 *Konnichi hajimete sūryō o shiru.*

Today for the first time I understand number and weight.

ZGS 6.69, Shiba na

6.106 爲混沌畫眉去 *Konton no tame ni mayu o egakisaru.*

They've drawn ⌜eyebrows⌝ for ⌜Hun-tun⌝.

ZGS na, ZRKS 6.226, Shiba 123, ZGJI 295

6.107 賴遇和尚印可 *Saiwai ni ⌜oshō⌝ no inka ni au.*

How fortunate to receive the priest's ⌜*inka*⌝.

ZGS 6.70, Shiba na

6.108 倒騎牛入佛殿 *Sakashima ni ushi ni notte butsuden ni iru.*

Mounted backwards on an ox, he rides into the Buddha Hall.

Heki 86 Verse.

ZGS na, ZRKS 6.130, Shiba 142, ZGJI 295, ZGJT 339, KZS #601

6.109 昨日雨今日晴 *Sakujitsu wa ame, konnichi wa hare.*

Yesterday rain, clear skies today.

ZGS 6.36: *Kinō* instead of *sakujitsu*.

ZGS 6.36, ZRKS 6.64, Shiba 132, ZGJI 295

6.110 回顧左右茫然 *Sayū o kaiko shite bōzentari.*

Looking left and right, he stands there in a daze.

ZGS 6.71, Shiba na

6.111 山花咲野鳥語 *Sanka warai yachō kataru.*

Mountain flowers bloom, wild birds sing.

ZGS 6.72, ZRKS 6.4, Shiba 133, ZGJI 296

6.112 賛不欣罵不嗔 *San suredomo yorokobazu, nonoshiredomo ikarazu.*

Though praised, he does not rejoice; though reviled, he does not anger.

Shiba 133: *homuredomo* instead of *san suredomo*.

ZGS 6.73, ZRKS 6.49, Shiba 133, ZGJI 313

6.113 三人證龜作鼈 *Sannin kame o shō shite betsu to nasu.*

Three men testified on the terrapin, and declared it a softshell.

Heki 17 Main Case Comm.

ZGS 6.74, ZRKS 6.178, Shiba 133, ZGJI 296, ZGJT 161, KZS #633

6.114 養兒始知父慈 *Ji o yashinōte hajimete chichi no ji o shiru.*

Raise a child and at once you understand your own parents' love.

Rinzai-roku §24. Shiba 150: 養子方 *Ko o yashinatte masa ni* instead of 養兒始.

ZGS 6.80, ZRKS 6.132, Shiba 150, ZGJI 292, ZGJT 463, KZS #604

6.115 獅子吼無畏説 *Shishiku mui no setsu.*

The lion's roar—a fearless sermon.

ZGS 6.81, ZRKS 6.77, Shiba 134, ZGJI 297, ZGDJT 430a, 証道歌

6.116 死蛇弄得令活 *Shida o rō shiete kasseshimu.*

He can play with dead snakes and bring them to life.

ZGS 6.82, ZRKS 6.269, Shiba na, ZGJI 297

6.117 叱叱叱者畜生 *Shitsu shitsu shitsu kono shukusan.*

Get! Get! Get! You animal!

ZGJI 297: *chikusan* instead of *shukusan*.
ZGS 6.83, ZRKS 6.231, Shiba na, ZGJI 297, ZGJT 185

6.118 領承師老婆心 *Shi no rōbashin o ryōshō su.*

We receive the master's grandmotherly kindness.
ZGS 6.84, Shiba na

6.119 十字街頭掛牌 *Jūji gaitō ni hai o kaku.*

Put up a sign at the town intersection.
ZGS 6.75, ZRKS 6.275, Shiba na, ZGJI 298

6.120 十字街頭吹笛 *Jūji gaitō ni fue o fuku.*

Play a flute at the town intersection.
ZGS 6.76, ZRKS 6.276, Shiba na, ZGJI 298

6.121 宗師家有三毒 *Shū shike sandoku ari.*

The Zen master has ⌜three poisons⌝.
ZGS 6.77, Shiba na

6.122 十日風五日雨 *Jūjitsu no kaze, gojitsu no ame.*

Wind on the tenth, rain on the fifth.
ZGJI 298: 十日雨五日風, "Rain on the tenth, wind on the fifth." *Heki* 9 Main Case Comm.
ZGS 6.78, ZRKS 6.37, Shiba na, ZGJI 298

6.123 繡房事不可言 *Shūbō no koto wa iu bekarazu.*

Do not talk of what goes on in the women's quarters.
ZGS 6.79, Shiba na

6.124 十目視十手指 *Jūmoku no miru tokoro, jisshu no yubisasu tokoro.*

What ten eyes behold, what ten hands point to.
Trans. from LEGGE 1985, *Great Learning*, c.VI.3. KZS #556: *sasu* instead of *yubisasu*.
ZGS na, ZRKS 6.21, Shiba 134, KZS #556

6.125 主山高安山低 *Shuzan wa takaku, anzan wa hikushi.*

The main mountain is high, the surrounding mountains are low.
Variation: 按 instead of 安. Heki 57 Main Case *agyo*. See ⌜Landscape⌝.
ZGS 6.85, ZRKS 6.192, Shiba na, ZGJI 297 (variant), KZS #563

6.126 拄杖子呑乾坤 *Shujōsu kenkon o nomu.*

The staff swallows up ⌜heaven and earth⌝.
Heki 60 Verse.
ZGS na, ZRKS 6.159, Shiba 134, ZGJI 297, KZS #624

6.127 春山青春水碧 *Shunzan wa aoku shunsui wa midori nari.*

Spring mountains are green, spring waters are blue.

KZS #549: 綠 instead of 碧.

ZGS 6.91, ZRKS 6.3, Shiba 134, ZGJI 298, ZGJT 206, KZS #549

6.128 唱彌高和彌寡 *Shō iyo-iyo takakereba, wa iyo-iyo sukunashi.*

The higher you sing, the fewer those who can sing with you.

ZGS na, ZRKS 6.58, Shiba 135, ZGJI 298, ZGJT 218

6.129 峭巍巍孤迥迥 *Shō gi-gi ko kei-kei.*

Majestic and aloof, off in a world apart.

See also 6.40.

ZGS na, ZRKS 6.13, Shiba 135, ZGJI 298

6.130 生薑終不改辣 *Shōkyō tsui ni karaki koto o aratamezu.*

In the end you cannot change the fact that ginger is hot.

Shiba 137: *shōga* instead of *shōkyō.*

ZGS 6.87, ZRKS 6.151, Shiba 137, ZGJI 300, ZGDJT 535c, ZGJT 244, KZS #619

6.131 湘之南潭之北 *Shō no minami tan no kita.*

South of Hsiang and north of T'an.

Heki 18. Hsiang-t'an is the name of an area in Hunan Province (ZGJT 218). "South of Hsiang and north of T'an" is like saying, "North of San Fran- and south of -cisco."

ZGS na, ZRKS 6.16, Shiba 135, ZGJI 298, ZGDJT 576a, ZGJT 218, KZS #627

6.132 上大人丘乙己 *Jō tai jin, kyū itsu ki.*

Jō tai jin kyū itsu ki.

The first line of a copy book used for teaching children Chinese characters. The characters do not make a sentence. Corresponds to "ABC…" in English.

ZGS na, ZRKS 6.143, Shiba 135, ZGJI 298, ZGJT 221

6.133 淨躶躶赤洒洒 *Jō ra-ra shaku sha-sha.*

Clean and naked, totally fresh.

Heki 6 Verse Comm., 27 Main Case *agyo*. Shiba 135: 赤灑灑 instead of 赤洒洒.

ZGS 6.88, ZRKS 6.15, Shiba 135, ZGJI 298, ZGDJT 591a, ZGJT 225, KZS #553

6.134 如入芝蘭之室 *Shiran no shitsu ni iru ga gotoshi.*

Like entering a room full of irises and orchids.

逢善友則如入芝蘭之室逢惡友則如入鮑魚之廛 "Meeting a good friend is like entering a room of irises and orchids, meeting an evil friend is like entering the fish market" (ZGJI 710).

ZGS na, Shiba 134, ZGJI 710

6.135 突出心肝五臟 *Shinkan gozō o tosshutsu su.*

He's thrust out his heart, liver, and all five organs.

The five organs of the body are heart, lungs, liver, kidneys, and stomach. See ⌜Five phases⌝. *Heki* 12 Verse Comm.

ZGS na, ZRKS 6.126, Shiba 143, ZGJI 298, KZS #598

6.136 心眼爛然如月 *Shingan ranzen to shite tsuki no gotoshi.*

The mind's eye is as bright as the ⌜moon⌝.

ZGS 6.89, ZRKS 6.294, Shiba na, ZGJI 298

6.137 嗔拳不打笑面 *Shinken shōmen o ta sezu.*

An angry fist does not strike a laughing face.

ZGS 6.90: 瞋 instead of 嗔.

ZGS 6.90, ZRKS 6.154, Shiba 136, ZGJI 299, ZGJT 230, KZS #621

6.138 仁者天下無敵 *Jinsha wa tenka ni teki nashi.*

A person of virtue has no enemies in the world.

ZGS 6.92, Shiba 136

6.139 森羅影裏藏身 *Shinra eiri ni mi o kakusu.*

Hide oneself in the forest of many shadows.

ZGS 6.93, ZRKS 6.131, Shiba 136, ZGJI 299

6.140 迅雷不及掩耳 *Jinrai mimi o ōu ni oyobazu.*

Sudden thunder, no chance to cover the ears.

Heki 37 Verse *agyo*.

ZGS na, ZRKS 6.186, Shiba 136, ZGJI 277, ZGJT 233

6.141 水上推胡蘆子 *Suijō ni korosu o osu.*

Pushing a gourd on water.

ZGS 6.94, Shiba 136, ZGJI 299

6.142 巣知風穴知雨 *Sukuu mono wa kaze o shiri, kessuru mono wa ame o shiru.*

Those who live in nests know the wind; those who live in holes know the rain.

ZRKS 6.65: *Su ni sumu mono wa kaze o shiri, ana ni sumu mono wa ame o shiru.*

ZGS 6.95, ZRKS 6.65, Shiba 138, ZGJI 299, ZGJT 279, KZS #576

6.143 淸寥寥白的的 *Sei ryō ryō haku teki teki.*

Serene and pure, sharp and clear.

Heki 34 Verse Comm.

ZGS na, ZRKS 6.12, Shiba 137, ZGJI 300, ZGDJT 650d, ZGJT 246

6.144 青天也須喫棒 *Seiten mo mata subekaraku bō o kissu beshi.*

The blue sky, too, must get a taste of the stick.

ZGS na, ZRKS 6.194, Shiba 137, ZGJI 300, KZS #630

6.145 雪團打雪團打 *Setsudan ta, setsudan ta.*

The snowball hit! The snowball hit!

Heki 42 Verse.

ZGS 6.96, ZRKS 6.273, Shiba 137, ZGJI 300

6.146 切忌開眼作夢 *Setsu ni imu manako o hiraite yume o nasu koto o.*

Detestable, to dream with the eyes open.

ZGS 6.97, Shiba na

6.147 殺人刀活人劍 *Setsunintō katsuninken.*

The blade that kills, the「sword」that brings to life.

MMK 11 Verse. Shiba 133: *Satsujintō katsujinken.*

ZGS 6.98, ZRKS 6.57, Shiba 133, ZGJI 295, ZGDJT 666b, ZGJT 159, KZS #571

6.148 說不說知不知 *Setsu fusetsu, chi fuchi.*

Speaking without speaking, knowing without knowing.

Heki 56 Intro.

ZGS 6.99, ZRKS 6.283, Shiba na

6.149 有錢使得鬼走 *Sen areba ki o tsukaiete hashirashimu.*

With money you can make devils run around.

ZGS na, ZRKS 6.207, Shiba 149, ZGJI 301, ZGJT 29

6.150 是亦剗非亦剗 *Ze mo mata kezuri, hi mo mata kezuru.*

Shave away right, shave away wrong.

ZGS 6.100, ZRKS 6.270, Shiba na, ZGJI 300

6.151 禪名關敎名網 *Zen o kan to nazuke kyō o mō to nazuku.*

Zen is called a barrier and the teachings a snare.

ZGS 6.101, ZRKS 6.253, Shiba na, ZGJI 301

6.152 呑卻山河大地 *Senga daichi o donkyaku su.*

He swallowed up the mountains, the rivers, and the great earth.

ZGS 6.102, ZRKS 6.268, Shiba 143, ZGJI 296

6.153 照破山河萬朶 *Senga banda o shōha su.*

Illuminate completely the mountains, the rivers, and myriad blossoms.

ZGS na, ZRKS 6.166, Shiba 135, ZGJI 296, KZS #628

6.154 千虛不如一實 *Senkyo ichijitsu ni shikazu.*

A thousand lies cannot match one truth.

ZGS 6.103, ZRKS 6.267, Shiba 138, ZGJI 300, ZGJT 254

6.155 千邪不如一直 *Senja ichijiki ni shikazu.*

A thousand twists cannot match one straight.

ZGS 6.104, ZRKS 6.230, Shiba 138, ZGJI 300

6.156 千年田八百主 *Sennen no den, happyaku no shu.*

In a thousand years a field has eight hundred masters.

ZGS 6.105, ZRKS 6.18, Shiba na, ZGJI 301, ZGJT 255

6.157 千聞不如一見 *Senbun ikken ni shikazu.*

To hear a thousand times is not as good as seeing once.

Heki 30 Main Case *agyo*. KZS #607: *senmon* instead of *senbun*.

ZGS 6.106, ZRKS 6.136, Shiba 138, ZGJT 255, KZS #607

6.158 前三三後三三 *Zen san san go san san.*

Before three and three, behind three and three.

Heki 35 Main Case.

ZGS na, ZRKS 6.16, Shiba 138, ZGJI 301, ZGDJT 683d, ZGJT 260, KZS #554

6.159 喪車後懸藥袋 *Sōshago ni yakutai o kaku.*

Hang a medicine pouch on the back of the hearse.

Heki 55 Main Case *agyo*, 64 Verse *agyo*.

ZGS na, ZRKS 6.158, Shiba 138, ZGJT 270, KZS #617

6.160 滄海濶白雲閑 *Sōkai hiroku hakuun kan nari.*

The blue sea vast, the white clouds serene.

ZGJI 302: 蒼 instead of 滄.

ZGS na, Shiba 139, ZGJI 302

6.161 藏頭白海頭黑 *Zōtō haku, kaitō koku.*

Tsang's head is white; Hai's head is black.

Heki 50 Verse Comm., 73 Main Case.

ZGS 6.107, ZRKS 6.280, Shiba 139, ZGJI 302, ZGDJT 750b, ZGJT 272

6.162 賊不打貧兒家 *Zoku wa hinji no ie o ta sezu.*

A ⌜thief⌝ does not strike the house of a poor man.

Heki 33 Main Case *agyo*, 41 Main Case *agyo*.

ZGS na, ZRKS 6.102, Shiba 139, ZGJI 302, ZGJT 277, KZS #588

6.163 某甲遇不慮難 *Soregashi furyo no nan ni au.*

I met an unexpected disaster.

ZGS 6.108, Shiba na

6.164 大覺果滿境界 *Daikaku kaman no kyōgai.*

The bearing of a greatly awakened one at full maturity.

ZGS 6.109, Shiba na

6.165 大衆一同饡飯 *Daishū ichido sanpan.*

Everyone in the assembly eats together.

ZGS 6.110, Shiba na

6.166 大道廢仁義始 *Daidō sutarete jingi hajimaru.*

Virtue begins when the Great Way is abandoned.

ZGS 6.111, Shiba na

6.167 一匝大千世界 *Daisen sekai o issō su.*

Take in the ⌜great thousand-fold universe⌝ in one embrace.

ZGS 6.112, Shiba na

6.168 他殺不如自殺 *Tasatsu wa jisatsu ni shikazu.*

Killing another does not compare to killing oneself.

Heki 6 Main Case Comm. ZGJI 302: *Ta o korosan yori mizukara korosu ni shikazu.*

ZGS 6.113, Shiba na, ZGJI 302

6.169 只恐有人不肯 *Tada osoraku wa hito no ukegawazaru aran koto o.*

I fear only there will be someone who does not agree.

ZGS 6.114, Shiba na

6.170 唯爲人甚近也 *Tada hito no tame ni suru koto no hanahada chikashi.*

To live for others means you are very close indeed.

ZGS 6.115, Shiba na

6.171 只露目前些子 *Tada mokuzen no shashi o arawasu.*

To reveal the little something right in front of your eyes.

Heki 40 Main Case Comm.

ZGS 6.116, Shiba na

6.172 打成一片田地 *Tajō ippen no denchi.*

Become the ground of one.

Heki 27 Verse Comm.: 若向這裏盡古今凡聖乾坤大地打成一片, "If you direct yourself here, then all past and present, foolish and wise, the universe and the great earth become one."

ZGS na, ZRKS 6.233, Shiba 139, ZGJI 285

6.173 痴兀兀兀兀痴 *Chi kotsu-kotsu, kotsu-kotsu chi.*

Stupidly stubborn, stubbornly stupid.

ZRKS 6.87: 癡 instead of 痴.

ZGS na, ZRKS 6.87, Shiba 140

6.174 父不嚴子不孝 *Chichi gen narazareba ko kō narazu.*

If the father is not strict, the son is not filial.

ZGJI 303: 父不慈子不孝, "If the father is not compassionate, the son is not filial."

ZGS 6.117, ZRKS 6.134, Shiba 146, ZGJI 303 (variant)

6.175 父不傳子不記 *Chichi tsutaezu, ko wa ki sezu.*

The father does not transmit it, the son does not record it.

Shiba 146: *shirusazu* instead of *ki sezu.*

ZGS 6.118, ZRKS 6.19, Shiba 146, ZGJI 303

6.176 父攘羊子證之 *Chichi hitsuji o nusumeba, ko kore o arawasu.*

If the father ⌜steals a sheep⌝, the child reveals it.

Shiba 146: *shō su* instead of *arawasu.*

ZGS 6.119, ZRKS 6.101, Shiba 146, ZGJI 303, KZS #586

6.177 長安東洛陽西 *Chōan no higashi, rakuyō no nishi.*

East of ⌜Ch'ang-an⌝, west of ⌜Lo-yang⌝.

ZGS 6.120, ZRKS 6.79, Shiba na

6.178 朝三千暮八百 *Chō sanzen bo happyaku.*

In the morning 3,000; in the evening 800.

Heki 66 Verse *agyo.*

ZGS 6.121, ZRKS 6.17, Shiba 140, ZGJI 304, ZGDJT 862d, ZGJT 311

6.179 作張三作李四 *Chōsan to nari, rishi to naru.*

Become Smith, become Jones.

Chōsan (⌜Chang⌝ number three) and *Rishi* (Li number four) are translated Smith and Jones.

ZGS 6.122, Shiba na

6.180 長者長短者短 *Chōja wa chō, tanja wa tan.*

A long thing is long, a short thing is short.

ZGS na, ZRKS 6.82, Shiba 140, ZGJI 304

6.181 長鞭不搆馬腹 *Chōben bafuku ni itarazu.*

Not even a long whip reaches a horse's belly.

ZGS 6.123, Shiba 140

6.182 頂門眼通天竅 *Chōmon no manako tenkyō ni tsūzu.*

The eye in the forehead penetrates the farthest corners of heaven.

ZGS na, ZRKS 6.75, Shiba 140, ZGJI 304

6.183 鎮州出大蘿蔔 *Chinjū ni dairafu o idasu.*

They produce giant radishes in Chen Province.

Heki 30 Main Case. Chen Province is where Jōshū lived (Shiba 140).

ZGS na, ZRKS 6.44, Shiba 140, ZGJI 363, ZGJT 314

6.184 月印水水印月 *Tsuki mizu ni in shi, mizu tsuki ni in su.*

The ⌜moon⌝ reflects in the water, the water reflects in the moon.

ZGS 6.124., ZRKS 6.264, Shiba 130, ZGJI 304

6.185 庭前花生耶死 *Teizen no hana, sei ka shi ka.*

The flower in the garden, is it alive or dead?

ZGS 6.125, Shiba na

6.186 釘出釘橛出橛 *Tei tei o idashi ketsu ketsu o idasu.*

A nail pulls out a nail, a stake takes out a stake.

ZGS na, ZRKS 6.8, Shiba 141, ZGJI 304

6.187 鄭州梨青州棗 *Teishū no nashi seishū no natsume.*

The pears of Cheng Province, the jujubes of Ch'ing Province.

ZGS na, ZRKS 6.211, Shiba 141, ZGJI 305, ZGDJT 879a, ZGJT 320

6.188 鐵牛通身無骨 *Tetsugyū tsūshin hone nashi.*

Not a bone in the body of the iron ox.

ZGS na, ZRKS 6.125, Shiba 141, ZGJI 305, KZS #597

6.189 天不文地不理 *Ten ayanarazu, chi ayanarazu.*

Heaven has no rhyme; earth has no reason.

Shiba 141: *Ten bun narazu, chi ri narazu,* "Heaven has no astronomy, earth has no geography."

ZGS 6.126, ZRKS 6.39, Shiba 141, ZGJI 305

6.190 藏天下於天下 *Tenka o tenka ni kakusu.*

Hide the world within the world.

ZGS 6.127, ZRKS 6.120, Shiba na, ZGJI 305, KZS #595

6.191 天下人不知價 *Tenka no hito atai o shirazu.*

No one in the world knows its worth.

Heki 8 Verse *agyo.*

ZGS 6.128, ZRKS 6.138, Shiba 141, ZGJI 305, KZS #609

6.192 天下人無實頭 *Tenka no hito no jittō naru nashi.*

People in this world lack a real head.

ZGS na, ZRKS 6.122, Shiba 141, ZGJI 305

6.193 回天關轉地軸 *Tenkan o megurashi, chijiku o tenzu.*

Swing the barrier of heaven, turn the axle of earth.

ZGS 6.129, ZRKS 6.61, Shiba 127, ZGJI 305, KZS #574

6.194 天無門地無戸 *Ten ni mon naku, chi ni to nashi.*

Heaven has no gate, earth has no door.

ZGS 6.130, ZRKS 6.53, Shiba 142, ZGJI 305, KZS #569

6.195 天星數地砂數 *Ten no seisū, chi no shasū.*

The number of stars in the heavens, the number of grains of sand on earth.

ZGS 6.131, Shiba na

6.196 天蒦外地地外 *Ten no tengai, chi no chigai.*

Heaven beyond heaven, earth beyond earth.

ZGS 6.132, ZRKS 6.235, Shiba na

6.197 天是天地是地 *Ten wa kore ten chi wa kore chi.*

Heaven is heaven, the earth is the earth.

Heki 2 Verse Comm., 9 Main Case Comm., 62 Main Case Comm.

ZGS 6.133, ZRKS 6.2, Shiba 141, ZGJI 305, ZGJT 325, KZS # 548

6.198 轉轆轆阿轆轆 *Ten roku-roku, a roku-roku.*

Rolling, rolling along; turning, turning along.

ZGS 6.134, Shiba 142

6.199 同行必有一智 *Dōkō kanarazushimo itchi ari.*

Among fellow travelers, there will always be one who is wise.

ZGS na, ZRKS 6.139, Shiba 142, ZGJI 306, KZS #610

6.200 東山下左邊底 *Tōzanka no sahentei.*

Somewhere around East Mountain.

Tung-shan (East Mountain) is where the famous Zen master Goso Hōen (五祖法演 Wu-tsu Fa-yen 1024?– 1104) resided for thirty years (ZGDJT 920d).

ZGS 6.135, Shiba 142, ZGJI 306

6.201 刀上蜜酒中鴆 *Tōjō no mitsu, shuchū no chin.*

Honey on the ⌜sword⌝, poison in the wine.

See ⌜Poison blackbird⌝.

ZGS 6.136, ZRKS 6.242, Shiba 142, ZGJI 306

6.202 咄咄咄力口希 *Totsu totsu totsu riki i ki.*

Hah! Hah! Hah! …Kaa!

Totsu, a word without meaning, is a shout of great effort. The fourth and fifth characters, 力 and 口, combine to form the character 囗, pronounced *ka*, another great shout. The last character, also without meaning, is used here to intensify the previous characters. The verse originated with Ummon Zenji but has become well known in Japan because Sen no Rikyū, founder of the tea ceremony, used it in his death poem just before he committed suicide, as ordered by Hideyoshi. ZGS 6.137 and ZRKS 240 both have 囗 instead of 口.

ZGS 6.137, ZRKS 6.240, Shiba 143, ZGJI 307, ZGDJT 955b, ZGJT 353

6.203 土肉痩山骨現 *Doniku yase sankotsu arawaru.*

The earth flesh shrinks back, the mountain bones appear.

ZGS 6.138, Shiba na

6.204 射虎不勞沒羽 *Tora o ite rō sezu shite tsubasa o bossu.*

Effortlessly he buried the feathers of his arrow in the tiger.

ZGS 6.139, ZRKS 6.262, Shiba na, ZGJI 307

6.205 捉則逸放則隨 *Toraureba sunawachi isshi, hanateba sunawachi shitagau.*

Grasp it and at once it escapes, release it and it immediately follows.

ZGS 6.140, Shiba 139

6.206 聞名不如見面 *Na o kiku yori omote o min ni wa shikazu.*

Hearing the name is no match for seeing the face.

MMK 28 Verse.

ZGS 6.141, ZRKS 6.99, Shiba 146

6.207 猶是弄精魂漢 *Nao kore seikon o rō suru kan.*

This is just a fellow who toys with spirits.

Heki 81 Main Case *agyo*.

ZGS na, ZRKS 6.195, Shiba 149, ZGJI 307, KZS #639

6.208 尚是老僧有孫 *Nao kore rōsō son ari.*

Now this ⌜old monk⌝ has a descendant.

ZGS 6.142, Shiba na

6.209 半河南半河北 *Nakaba wa kahan nakaba wa kahoku.*

Half south of the river, half north.

Heki 6 Main Case *agyo*, 15 Verse *agyo*, 76 Verse *agyo*, etc.

ZGS 6.143, ZRKS 6.163, Shiba 145, ZGJI 307, ZGDJT 965a, ZGJT 385

6.210 皷南山舞北山 *Nanzan ni ko seba hokuzan ni mau.*

When they drum on South Mountain, they dance on North Mountain.

ZGS 6.144, Shiba na

6.211 南山雲北山雨 *Nanzan wa kumo hokuzan wa ame.*

Clouds on South Mountain, rain on North Mountain.

Heki 83 Verse.

ZGS na, ZRKS 6.31, Shiba 143, ZGJI 308, KZS #560

6.212 何望和尚慈悲 *Nanzo ⌜oshō⌝ no jihi o nozoman.*

Why expect sympathy from the priest?

ZGS 6.145, Shiba na

6.213 南地竹北地木 *Nanchi no take hokuchi no ki.*

Bamboo in the southern regions, trees in the north.

Heki 12 Verse.

ZGS 6.146, ZRKS 6.32, Shiba 143

6.214 日面佛月面佛 *Nichimen butsu gachimen butsu.*

Sun-faced Buddha, Moon-faced Buddha.

Heki 3. In the present *kalpa*, a thousand Buddhas will appear to save sentient beings. Number 202 is the Sun-faced Buddha who lives 1,800 years. Number 858 is the Moon-faced Buddha who lives only a day and a night (ZGDJT 982c; Nakamura 1981, 1053). ZGJI 308 reverses this explanation.

ZGS 6.147, ZRKS 6.165, Shiba 143, ZGJI 308, ZGDJT 982c, KZS #634

6.215 二八女出畫堂 *Nihachi no onna gadō o izu.*

A girl of sixteen comes forth from the decorated hall.

ZGS 6.148, Shiba na

6.216 膿滴滴血洒洒 *Nō teki-teki, ketsu sha-sha.*

Pus drip-drip, blood drop-drop.

ZGS 6.149, Shiba na

6.217 囊裏豈可藏錐 *Nōri ani sui o kakusu bekenya.*

How can you hide a sharp pick in a bag?

Heki 67 Verse *agyo.*

ZGS na, ZRKS 6.224, Shiba 144, ZGJI 308, ZGJT 373

6.218 鉢裏飯桶裏水 *Hatsuri no han tsūri no mizu.*

Rice in the bowl, water in the keg.

Heki 50 Main Case, Verse.

ZGS na, ZRKS 6.167, Shiba 144, ZGJI 309, ZGJT 144, KZS #635

6.219 把得抛向坑裏 *Hatoku shite kyori ni hōkō su.*

Grab him and throw him into the pit.

Rinzai-roku §19.

ZGS 6.150, Shiba na

6.220 花簇簇錦簇簇 *Hana zoku-zoku, nishiki zoku-zoku.*

Masses of flowers, swaths of brocade.

Heki 12 Verse, 61 Main Case *agyo.*

ZGS 6.151, ZRKS 6.6, Shiba 126, ZGJI 309, ZGDJT 1029d, ZGJT 45, KZS #551

6.221 太煞減人威光 *Hanahada hito no ikō o genzu.*

He really cuts away a person's authority.

Heki 1 Verse Comm., 15 Verse *agyo.* ZRKS 6.234 (variant): 太煞減人斤両 *Hanahada hito no kinryō o genzu,* "He certainly takes away a person's money."

ZGS 6.152, ZRKS 6.234, Shiba na

6.222 春不種秋不實 *Haru uezareba aki minorazu.*

No planting in spring, no crop in autumn.

ZGS 6.153, ZRKS 6.52, Shiba na

6.223 會萬物爲自己 *Banbutsu o e shite jiko to nasu.*

Comprehend the ⌜ten thousand things⌝ and make them oneself.

Heki 40 Main Case Comm.

ZGS 6.154, Shiba 127

6.224 萬物皆備於我 *Banbutsu mina ware ni sonawaru.*

The ⌜ten thousand things⌝ are all within me.

Mencius VII, A, 4.

ZGS 6.155, Shiba na

6.225 火不燥水不濕 *Hi mo kawakasazu, mizu mo uruosazu.*

Fire does not dry, water does not wet.

ZGS na, ZRKS 6.85, Shiba 125, ZGJI 309

6.226 火就乾水流濕 *Hi wa kawakeru ni tsuki, mizu wa uruoeru ni nagaru.*

Fire burns in dry places, water flows in wet places.

ZGS 6.156, ZRKS 6.54, Shiba na, ZGJI 309, ZGJT 40

6.227 問東便乃答西 *Higashi o towaba sunawachi nishi o kotau.*

Asked about east, straightway he answers about west.

ZGS na, ZRKS 6.118, Shiba 149, ZGJI 453 (variant), KZS #593

6.228 砒礵不干鐵鎚 *Hisō tettsui o okasazu.*

Not even arsenic will take on the iron hammer.

ZGS na, ZRKS 6.113, Shiba 145, ZGJI 309

6.229 臂膊不向外曲 *Hihaku soto ni mukatte magarazu.*

The arm does not bend outward.

ZGS 6. 86, KZS #629: 手臂 *shuhi* instead of 臂膊 *hihaku*. *Heki* 1 Main Case *agyo*.

ZGS 6.86, ZRKS 6.180, Shiba 145, ZGJI 310, ZGJT 391, KZS #629

6.230 百不知百不會 *Hyaku fuchi hyaku fue.*

One hundred he does not know, one hundred he does not understand.

ZGJT 393: "one hundred" here intensifies the negative. "He totally does not know, he totally does not understand."

ZGS 6.157, ZRKS 6.221, Shiba 145, ZGJI 310, ZGJT 393

6.231 不可説不可取 *Fukasetsu fukashu.*

Indescribable, ungraspable.

ZGS 6.158, ZRKS 6.284, Shiba na, ZGJI 310

6.232 不思善不思惡 *Fushizen fushiaku.*

Think not good, think not evil.

MMK 23.

ZGS na, Shiba 146, ZGJI 311, ZGDJT 1072c

6.233 不是心不是佛 *Fuzeshin fuzebutsu.*

Not mind, not Buddha.

MMK 27, *Heki* 28 Main Case.

ZGS 6.159, ZRKS 6.285, Shiba na, ZGJI 482, ZGDJT 1077b

6.234 不是不是不是 *Fuze fuze fuze.*

Not this, not this, not this.

ZGS 6.160, Shiba na

6.235 佛法王法一般 *Buppō to ōhō to ippan.*

The Buddha's law and the king's law are one.

Heki 38 Main Case.

ZGS 6.161, ZRKS 6.265, Shiba na, ZGJI 312, KZS #615

6.236 文王沒文在斯 *Bunnō bosshite bun koko ni ari.*

After ⸢King Wen⸣ died, his culture came to me.

Analects IX, 5: 文王既沒文在茲乎 *Bunnō sude ni bossu, bun koko ni arazaran ya,* "King Wen has died, but am I not the repository of his culture?" (after YOSHIKAWA 1996, vol. II, 287).

ZGS 6.162, Shiba na

6.237 僻地裏罵官人 *Hekichiri ni kanjin o nonoshiru.*

In the provinces, they insult officials.

Heki 91 Main Case *agyo.*

ZGS na, ZRKS 6.185, Shiba 146, ZGJI 312, ZGJT 415

6.238 碧落碑無贗本 *Hekiraku no hi ni ganpon nashi.*

There is no replica of the ⸢Pi-lo Monument⸣.

ZGS 6.163, ZRKS 6.78, Shiba na, ZGJI 312, ZGJT 415

6.239 建法幢立宗旨 *Hōtō o tatete shūshi o rissu.*

Erect the banner of the Dharma, set forth the teaching of our school.

Heki 21 Intro., 60 Intro.

ZGS 6.164, ZRKS 6.271, Shiba na, ZGJI 313

6.240 鳳豈喰烏鵲食 *Hō ani ujaku no shoku o kuwan ya.*

How can a phoenix eat the food of crows and magpies?

ZGS na, ZRKS 6.137, Shiba 147, ZGJI 313, KZS #608

6.241 握母指咬中指 *Boshi o nigitte chūshi o kamu.*

Clench your thumb in your fist and bite your middle finger.

Kaian Kokugo (variant): 握左手咬中指, "Grasp the left hand and bite the middle finger" (IIDA Tōin 1955, 139, 149, 215).

ZGS 6.165, Shiba 123, ZGJI 295 (variant)

6.242 法身般若解脱 *Hosshin hannya gedatsu.*

Dharma-body, wisdom, emancipation.

ZGS 6.166, Shiba na

6.243 法身報身應身 *Hosshin, hōjin, ōjin.*

The Dharma-body, the reward-body, the transformation-body.

See ⌜Three bodies of the Buddha⌝.

ZGS 6.167, Shiba na

6.244 獻佛不假香多 *Butsu ni kenzuru ni kō no ōki o karazu.*

Paying homage to the Buddha is not a matter of lots of incense.

Heki 58 Main Case Comm. ZRKS 6.148: 不在香多 *kō no ōki ni arazu.*

ZGS na, ZRKS 6.148, Shiba 130, ZGJI 311, ZGJT 110

6.245 麻矢直蓬矢曲 *Mashi wa naoku, hōshi wa magareri.*

A hemp arrow is straight, a wormwood arrow is bent.

ZGS na, ZRKS 6.86, Shiba 147, ZGJI 313, KZS #583

6.246 松不直棘不曲 *Matsu naokarazu, ibara magarazu.*

Pine needles are not straight, thorns are not curved.

KZS #562: *odoro* instead of *ibara.*

ZGS 6.168, ZRKS 6.33n, Shiba na, KZS #562

6.247 松自直 棘自曲 *Matsu wa onozukara naoku ibara wa onozukara magareri.*

Pine needles are naturally straight, thorns are naturally curved.

ZGS na, ZRKS 6.33, Shiba 135, ZGJI 314

6.248 眼卓朔耳卓朔 *Manako takusaku, mimi takusaku.*

Eyes peeled, ears cocked.

Heki 94 Intro.

ZGS 6.169, ZRKS 6.281, Shiba na, ZGJI 314

6.249 旋身一轉更去 *Mi o megurashi itten shite sunawachi saru.*

Turn around once and leave.

ZGS 6.170, Shiba na

6.250 水淺不泊船處 *Mizu asōshite fune o todomuru tokoro ni arazu.*

Shallow water has no place for boats to harbor.

MMK 11.

ZGS na, ZRKS 6.173, Shiba 136

6.251 南天台北五台 *Minami wa tendai kita wa godai.*

In the south is T'ien-t'ai, to the north is ⌜Wu-t'ai⌝.

T'ien-t'ai and Wu-t'ai are mountains famed as Buddhist holy places in China.

ZGS 6.171, ZRKS 6.30, Shiba na, ZGJI 314

6.252 無孔笛最難吹 *Mukuteki mottomo fukigatashi.*

A flute without holes is impossible to blow.

ZGS na, ZRKS 6.169, Shiba 147, ZGJI 315

6.253 賣弄無孔鐵鎚 *Muku no tettsui o mairō su.*

He's peddling an ⌜iron hammerhead without a socket⌝.

ZGS na, ZRKS 6.196, Shiba 144, ZGJI 315 (variant), KZS #579

6.254 無舌人能解語 *Muzetsu no hito yoku go o gesu.*

The one with no tongue understands words well.

ZGS 6.172, ZRKS 6.286, Shiba na, ZGJI 315, ZGDJT 1202c

6.255 明皎皎白的的 *Mei kō-kō haku teki-teki.*

Brilliant illumination, sharp and clear.

ZGS 6.173, ZRKS 6.11, Shiba 148, ZGJI 315, KZS #552

6.256 捨明珠弄魚目 *Meishu o sutete gyomoku o rōsu.*

He throws away a luminous pearl to play with a fish eye.

ZGS na, ZRKS 6.127, Shiba 134, ZGJI 315, KZS #599

6.257 明歷歷露堂堂 *Mei reki-reki, ro dō-dō.*

Brilliant and fully present.

ZGS 6.174, ZRKS 6.263, Shiba 148, ZGJI 315

6.258 用盲人作什麼 *Mōjin o mochiite nani o ka nasan.*

What can you do with a blind man?

ZGS 6.175, ZRKS 6 na, Shiba na

6.259 盲人端的有眼 *Mōjin tanteki manako ari.*

The blindest of the blind has an eye.

ZGS na, ZRKS 6.124, Shiba 148, ZGJI 315

6.260 作模作樣什麼 *Mo o nashi yō o nashite nani o ka sen.*

With your posing and putting on airs, what do you think you are doing?

ZGS 6.176, Shiba na

6.261 文殊三處度夏 *Monju sanjo ni ge o wataru.*

⌜Mañjuśrī⌝ passed the training term in three places.

See ⌜Three periods⌝.

ZGS 6.177, Shiba na

6.262 猛虎不食其子 *Mōko sono ko o kurawazu.*

Not even the fiercest tiger eats its own child.

ZGS na, ZRKS 6.10, Shiba 148, ZGJI 316, ZGJT 449

6.263 野干鳴獅子吼 *Yakanmei, shishiku.*

The fox's yelp, the lion's roar.

ZGS 6.178, Shiba 149, ZGJI 316, KZS #586

6.264 也太奇也太奇 *Yataiki yataiki.*

Ah, marvelous! Ah, marvelous!

ZGS 6.179, ZRKS 6.277, Shiba 149, ZGJI 316, Nishibe 181

6.265 入柳綠入花紅 *Yanagi ni itte wa midori, hana ni itte wa kurenai.*

Go into the willows—that's green; go into the flowers—that's red.

ZGS 6.180, Shiba na

6.266 柳不綠花不紅 *Yanagi midori narazu hana kurenai narazu.*

The willows are not green, the flowers are not red.

ZGS 6.181, ZRKS 6.258, Shiba 151, ZGJI 316

6.267 山有榛隰有苓 *Yama ni shin ari, sawa ni rei ari.*

The mountains have alder trees, the marshes have tubers.

ZGS 6.182, Shiba na

6.268 山是山水是水 *Yama wa kore yama, mizu wa kore mizu.*

Mountains are mountains, rivers are rivers.

Heki 2 verse Comm., 40 Verse *agyo*, 62 Main Case Comm., etc.

ZGS 6.183, ZRKS 6.1, Shiba 133, ZGJI 316, ZGDJT 1238d, ZGJT 164, KZS #547

6.269 懸羊頭賣狗肉 *Yōtō o kakete kuniku o uru.*

He displays a sheep's head but sells dog flesh.

MMK 6.

ZGS 6.184, ZRKS 6.103, Shiba 130, ZGJI 360, ZGJT 110, KZS #587

6.270 能知者須能用 *Yoku shiru mono wa subekaraku yoku mochiiru beshi.*

One who knows well must act well.

ZGS 6.185, ZRKS 6.243, Shiba na

6.271 豫讓藏身呑炭 *Yojō mi o zōshite sumi o nomu.*

⌜Yü Jang⌝ disguised his body and swallowed charcoal.

ZGS 6.186, ZRKS 6.245, Shiba 150

6.272 呼則易遣則難 *Yobu koto wa sunawachi yasuku, yaru koto wa sunawachi katashi.*

Easy to call, hard to send away.

Heki 56 Main Case *agyo*, 75 Verse.

ZGS na, ZRKS 6.182, Shiba 131, ZGJI 317, ZGJT 115

6.273 用禮拜作什麼 *Raihai o mochiite nani o ka nasan.*

What are you doing by prostrating?

ZGS 6.187, Shiba na

6.274 樂樂樂白自目 *Raku gaku gyō wa haku ji moku.*

The characters *raku, gaku, gyō* are distinguished by *haku, ji, moku.*

The three characters *raku, gaku, gyō* 樂, 樂, 樂, differ only in the top center graphs, 白, 自, 目 which themselves are the characters *haku, ji, moku.*

ZGS 6.188, Shiba na

6.275 鸞鳳不栖荆棘 *Ranpō keikyoku ni sumazu.*

The phoenix does not nest in a tree of thorns.

ZGS na, ZRKS 6.193, Shiba 150, ZGJI 317, ZGJT 470, KZS #578

6.276 李花白桃花紅 *Rika wa shiroku, tōka wa kurenai nari.*

Plum blossoms are white, ⌜peach⌝ blossoms are pink.

ZGS 6.189, ZRKS 6.5, Shiba 151, ZGJI 318, KZS #550

6.277 利劍不斬死漢 *Riken shikan o kirazu.*

A skilled swordsman does not cut a dead man.

Heki 98 Main Case Comm.

ZGS 6.190, ZRKS 6.157, Shiba 150, ZGJI 318, ZGJT 471, KZS #623

6.278 龍得水虎靠山 *Ryū wa mizu o e, tora wa yama ni yoru.*

Dragons take to their waters, tigers return to their hills.

Heki 8 Intro., 9 Main Case Comm., 25 Verse Comm., etc.

ZGS 6.191, Shiba na

6.279 良賈深藏如虛 *Ryōko wa fukaku kakushite munashiki ga gotoku su.*

A good merchant hides his goods and appears to have nothing.

ZGS 6.192, ZRKS 6.261, Shiba 151, ZGJI 318, KZS #589

6.280 兩箇無孔鐵鎚 *Ryōko muku no tettsui.*

Two ⌜iron hammerheads without sockets⌝.

Heki 30 Main Case Comm., 31 Verse *agyo.*

ZGS na, ZRKS 6.248, Shiba 151, ZGJI 318, ZGDJT 1283c

6.281 臨濟下座端的 *Rinzai geza no tanteki.*

Rinzai came straight down from his seat.

ZGS 6.193, Shiba na

6.282 臨濟最後難關 *Rinzai saigo no nankan.*

Rinzai's last difficult barrier.

ZGS 6.194, Shiba na

6.283 瑠璃瓶裏添花 *Ruri binri hana o sou.*

Stand a flower in a lapis lazuli vase.

ZGS na, ZRKS 6.24, Shiba 151, ZGJI 318

6.284 冷地裡學客舂 *Reichiri ni kyakushō o manabu.*

Imitate the "visitor who husked" in a cold place.

ZGS na, Shiba 152, ZGDJT 1306a

6.285 螻蟻撼於鐵柱 *Rōgi tetchū o ugokasu.*

The ants are shaking the iron post.

Heki 57 Verse. ZGJI 319, ZGJT 493: *yurugasu* instead of *ugokasu;* KZS #646: *rugi* instead of *rōgi.*

ZGS 6.195, ZRKS 6.217, Shiba 152, ZGJI 319, ZGJT 493, KZS #646

6.286 脱籠頭卸角駄 *Rōtō o dasshi, kakuda o orosu.*

He unloads his baskets and takes off his pack.

Heki 21 Intro.

ZGS 6.196, ZRKS 6.179, Shiba na, ZGJI 319, ZGJT 297, KZS #643

6.287 當爐不避熱鐵 *Ro ni atatte nettetsu o sakezu.*

In the furnace, there is no escaping the hot steel.

ZGS 6.197, ZRKS 6.244, Shiba na, ZGJI 319

6.288 吾道一以貫之 *Waga michi itsu motte kore o kan su.*

My Way has a unity which runs right through it.

Analects IV, 15. Variant: *tsuranuku* instead of *kan su.*

ZGS 6.198, ZRKS 6.45, Shiba na, ZGJI 319

6.289 禍不入愼家門 *Wazawai wa shinka no mon ni irazu.*

Misfortune does not enter the gate of the cautious.

ZGS 6.199, ZRKS 6.249, Shiba 126, ZGJI 50, ZGJT 50, KZS #603

6.290 軟似綿硬似鐵 *Wata yori mo yawaraka ni, tetsu yori mo katashi.*

Softer than cotton fluff, harder than iron.

ZGS 6.200, ZRKS 6.259, Shiba na, ZGJI 319

6.291 我不要那賤器 *Ware wa nan no senki o yō sezu.*

I need no money box.

ZGS 6.201, Shiba na

6.292 我還道得道得 *Ware mata iietari iietari.*

I could speak, I could speak.

ZGS 6.202, Shiba na

Seven-Character Phrases

7.1 朝聞道夕死可也 *Ashita ni michi o kiite yūbe ni shi sutomo ka nari.*

Having heard the Way in the morning, I can die in the evening.

Analects IV, 8. Shiba 181: *Ashita ni michi o kikeba.*

ZGS 7.1, Shiba 181, ZRKS 7.42

7.2 惡語傷人恨不消 *Akugo hito o yabutte urami shōsezu.*

For evil words that wound a person, resentment never fades.

ZGS na, ZRKS 7.323, Shiba 153, ZGJI 320

7.3 透網金鱗猶滯水 *Ami o tōru kinrin nao mizu ni todokōru.*

The golden fish that escaped the net still lingers in the water.

ZGS 7.2, ZRKS 7.23, Shiba 185, KZS #660

7.4 遺恨十年磨一劍 *Ikon jūnen ikken o migaku.*

Nursing resentment for ten years, he's sharpened his ⌜sword⌝.

ZGS 7.3, Shiba na

7.5 一雨普潤周沙界 *Ichiu amaneku uruoshite shakai ni amaneshi.*

One rain wets everything, covering the entire world.

ZGS 7.4, Shiba 153

7.6 一段風光畫不成 *Ichidan no fūkō egakedomo narazu.*

This unique scenery cannot be painted.

ZGS 7.5, ZRKS 7.94, Shiba 155, KZS #820, *Ten Oxherding Pictures* 3

7.7 一條紅線手中牽 *Ichijō no kōsen shuchū ni hiku.*

The one red thread runs through your hand.

ZRKS 7.286n: 竹庵三玄三要頌: 臨濟命根元不斷一條紅線手中牽, "Rinzai's life runs unbroken from its root. / The one red thread runs through your hand" (Chiku-an's Verse on the Three Mysteries and Three Necessities).

ZGS 7.6, ZRKS 7.286, Shiba na, ZGJI 322, KZS #679

7.8 一條絛三十文買 *Ichijō no tō sanjūmon ni kau.*

Buy a braid for thirty cents.

ZGS 7.7, Shiba na

7.9 一念瞋恚頭戴角 *Ichinen no shin'i kashira ni tsuno o itadaku.*

In a moment of anger he grows horns on his head.

ZGS 7.8, Shiba 155

7.10 一毛頭上定乾坤 *Ichimōtōjō ni kenkon o sadamu.*

Arrange ⌜heaven and earth⌝ on the tip of a single hair.

ZGS na, ZRKS 7.45, Shiba 155, ZGJI 324, KZS #662

7.11 一葉落知天下秋 *Ichiyō ochite tenka no aki o shiru.*

In the fall of a single leaf, one knows that now autumn is here.

ZGS 7.9, ZRKS 7.90, Shiba 156

7.12 一葉翻空天下秋 *Ichiyō kū ni hirugaeru tenka no aki.*

A single leaf flutters in the air and it's autumn throughout the land.

ZGS 7.10, ZRKS 7.56, Shiba 156

7.13 一葉舟中載大唐 *Ichiyō shūchū ni daitō o nosu.*

He places the Great T'ang Empire on a leaf boat.

Heki 58 Verse *agyo.*

ZGS 7.11, ZRKS 7.183, Shiba 156, KZS #737

7.14 一爐沈水一甌茶 *Ichiro no jinsui ichiō no cha.*

A burner fragrant with incense and a potful of tea.

ZGS na, ZRKS 7.385, Shiba 156 沈水 means 沈香

7.15 一回擧著一回新 *Ikkai kojaku sureba ikkai arata nari.*

Each time you bring it up it is new.

Heki 30 Verse *agyo.*

ZGS 7.12, ZRKS 7.497, Shiba na

7.16 一家有事百家忙 *Ikka koto areba hyakka isogawashi.*

Something happens at one house and a hundred houses are abuzz.

ZGS 7.13, ZRKS 7.149, Shiba na, ZGJT 21

7.17 一喝如雷聞者喪 *Ikkatsu rai no gotoku kiku mono sō su.*

A shout like thunder, all who hear it die.

ZGS 7.14, ZRKS 7.575 , Shiba 153, ZGJI 321

7.18 一曲琵琶奏月明 *Ikkyoku no biwa getsumei ni sō su.*

A song from the lute rises in the moonlight.

ZGS 7.15, ZRKS 7.195, Shiba 153, GKFGS 1.164

7.19 一句講了一切經 *Ikku ni issaikyō o kōryō su.*

With one word expound the entire Buddhist canon.

Shiba 154: *Ikku ni kōryō su issaigyō.*

ZGS 7.16, Shiba 154

7.20 一句講了臨濟錄 *Ikku ni kōryō su rinzairoku.*

With one word expound the *Record of Rinzai.*

ZGS 7.17, Shiba na

7.21 一箇半箇千萬箇 *Ikko hanko senmanko.*

One, or a half, or ten million.

ZGS 7.18, Shiba na

7.22 一枝梅花和雪香 *Isshi no baika yuki ni washite kanbashi.*

How fragrant the spray of plum blossoms dusted by the snow.

ZGS 7.19, ZRKS 7.48, Shiba 154

7.23 一心只在梅花上 *Isshin tada baika no ue ni ari.*

Oneness of mind—there in the ⌜plum⌝ blossoms.

ZGS 7.20, ZRKS 7.572, Shiba 154, ZGJI 323

7.24 一塵不立話方行 *Ichijin rissezu wa masa ni gyōzu.*

Without raising a speck of dust, he does just as he says.

ZGS na, ZRKS 7.184, Shiba 154, KZS #738, GKFGS 1.89-90

7.25 一寸常懷一丈恩 *Issun tsune ni omou ichijō no on.*

For each inch, I am aware of ten feet of debt.

ZGS 7.21, ZRKS 7.334, Shiba na, ZGJI 323

7.26 一寸龜毛重七斤 *Issun no kimō omoki koto shichi kin.*

A one-inch ⌜turtle hair⌝ weighs seven pounds.

ZGS 7.22, ZRKS 7.574, Shiba 154, ZGJI 323

7.27 一聲雞唱乾坤曉 *Issei tori wa tonau kenkon no akatsuki.*

The single crow of the cock brings dawn over ⌜heaven and earth⌝.

ZGS 7.23, ZRKS 7.569, Shiba 154

7.28 一聲霹靂驚天地 *Issei no hekireki tenchi o odorokasu.*

One crack of thunder startles heaven and earth.

ZGS 7.24, ZRKS 7.332, Shiba 154, KZS #694

7.29 一聲幽鳥到窓前 *Issei no yūchō sōzen ni itaru.*

The song of an unseen bird comes to my window.

ZGS 7.25, ZRKS 7.570, Shiba 154, ZGJI 323

7.30 一聲雷震淸飇起 *Issei rai furuute seihyō okoru.*

With a crash of rolling thunder a pure whirlwind rises.

Heki 49 Main Case *agyo*. Shiba 155: 風 instead of 飇.

ZGS 7.26, ZRKS 7.571, Shiba 155

7.31 一超直入如來地 *Itchō jiki nyū nyoraiji.*

With one leap enter the stage of the Tathāgata straightway.

ZGS 7.27, ZRKS 7.573, Shiba 155, ZGJI 323, ZGJT 23; Yung Chia, "Song of Enlightenment"

7.32 一鳥不鳴山更幽 *Itchō nakazu yama sara ni yū nari.*

With no bird singing the mountain is still more mysterious.

ZGS 7.28, ZRKS 7.135, Shiba 154, ZGJI 323, ZD #135

7.33 一對眼睛烏律律 *Ittsui no ganzei u ritsu-ritsu.*

My two eyes are as 「black as crows」.

See 14.479–480.

ZGS na, ZRKS 7.189, Shiba 155

7.34 一夫作難七廟墮 *Ippu nan o nashi shichi byō dasu.*

One man started the trouble and destroyed seven ancestral shrines.

See 「Han Kao-tsu」.

ZGS 7.29, Shiba na, Morohashi 1.1967

7.35 不動一歩行千里 *Ippo o dōzezu shite senri o yuku.*

Without moving one step, he goes a thousand miles.

ZGS 7.30, Shiba 192

7.36 一畝地三蛇九鼠 *Ippo no chi sanda kyūso.*

One square yard of land has three snakes and nine rats.

ZGS 7.31, Shiba 155

7.37 自古上賢猶不識 *Inishie yori jōken mo nao shirazu.*

From olden times it is the brilliant intellectuals who do not know.

ZGS 7.32, ZRKS 7.593, Shiba na

7.38 衣弊履穿頭半白 *I yabure, ri ugatte, kōbe nakaba shiroshi.*

Tattered clothing, torn shoes, head half white.

ZGJI 321: *kutsu* instead of *ri*. Empuku-ji: *e yabure.*

ZGS 7.33, ZRKS 7.26, Shiba na, ZGJI 321

7.39 飢來喫飯困來眠 *Uekitareba han o kisshi konjikitareba nemuru.*

When hungry, I eat; when tired, I sleep.

Heki 78 Verse Comm.

ZGS 7.34, ZRKS 7.512, Shiba 160

7.40 烏龜帶劍上燈臺 *Uki ken o obite tōdai ni noboru.*

The ⌜black⌝ turtle straps on a ⌜sword⌝ and mounts the lantern.

ZGS 7.35, Shiba na

7.41 烏雞夜半咬生鐵 *Ukei yahan ni santetsu o kamu.*

The ⌜black⌝ rooster at midnight chews raw iron.

ZGS 7.36, Shiba 157

7.42 雨後青山青轉青 *Ugo no seizan sei utata sei.*

Green mountains after rain, the green is even greener.

ZGS 7.37, ZRKS 7.557, Shiba 156, ZGJI 325

7.43 雨竹風松皆説禪 *Uchiku fūshō mina zen o toku.*

Rain in the bamboo, wind in the pines are all talking Zen.

ZGS na, Shiba 156, ZGJI 325

7.44 雨中春樹萬人家 *Uchū no shunju banjin no ie.*

In every household, spring trees in the rain.

ZGS na, Shiba 156

7.45 優鉢羅華火裏開 *Upparage kari ni hiraku.*

The blue lotus blooms in the flames.

The blue lotus is the same as the ⌜*uḍumbara*⌝ flower (Shiba 196).

ZGS na, ZRKS 7.361, Shiba 196

7.46 有佛處請指出看 *Ubutsu no tokoro kou shishutsu shite miyo.*

Please point out to me the place where the buddhas are.

ZGS 7.38, Shiba na

7.47 遠山無限碧層層 *Enzan kagiri naki heki sō-sō.*

Mountains endless into the distance, layer upon layer of blue.

Heki 20 Verse 2. See also 14.629.

ZGS 7.39, ZRKS 7.288, Shiba 157, ZGJI 326, ZD 39

7.48 燕雀何知鴻鵠志 *Enjaku nanzo kōkō no kokorozashi o shiran ya?*

How can a sparrow know the aspiration of a wild swan?

ZGS 7.40, ZRKS 7.3, Shiba na, KZS #648, 史記陳勝傳.

7.49 出圓通又入圓通 *Entsū o idete mata entsū ni iru.*

Leaving complete perfection, enter complete perfection.

ZGS na, ZRKS 7.504, Shiba 172, ZGJI 326, KZS #799, GKFGS 1.104-5

7.50 閻浮樹下笑呵呵 *Embujuge warai ka-ka.*

"Ha, Ha!" laughing beneath the ⌜*jambū* tree⌝.

Heki 14 Verse.

ZGS 7.41, ZRKS 7.217, Shiba na

7.51 大破關中收圖書 *Ōi ni kanchū o yabutte tosho o osamu.*

He destroys the stronghold within the passes, and takes the maps and documents.

See ⌜Hsiao Ho⌝.

ZGS 7.42, Shiba na

7.52 大似胡猻咬生鐵 *Ōi ni koson ni nite santetsu o kamu.*

Like a barbarian ape he bites raw iron.

ZGS na, ZRKS 7.481, Shiba 179

7.53 黄金色上更添黄 *Ōgon shikijō ni sara ni kō o sou.*

To gleaming gold he adds more gleam.

See also 14.702.

ZGS 7.44, ZRKS 7.197, Shiba na, ZGJI 326, KZS #749, GKFGS 1.148.

7.54 黄金擔子千鈞重 *Ōgon no tansu senkin omoshi.*

The gold carrying pole weighs 1,000 pounds.

ZGS 7.46, ZRKS 7.278, Shiba na

7.55 黄金又是和沙賣 *Ōgon mata kore suna ni washite uru.*

It's gold, but to sell it you mix it with sand.

ZRKS 7.307, ZGJI 327

7.56 黄金鑄出鐵崑崙 *Ōgon o chūshutsu su tek⌜konron⌝.*

Smelt gold from black iron.

ZGS 7.45, ZRKS 7.503, Shiba 165, ZGJI 326

7.57 抛御黄金拾瓦礫 *Ōgon o hōkyaku shite gareki o hirou.*

He throws away gold and picks up rubble.

ZGS 7.43, ZRKS 7.515, Shiba 192

7.58 抛御黄金捧碌甎 *Ōgon o hōkyaku shite rokusen o sasagu.*

He throws away gold but carries around rubble.

ZGS na, ZRKS 7.325, Shiba 193, ZGJI 327, ZGJT 422

7.59 王孫去後絕消息 *Ōson satte nochi shōsoku nashi.*

Since the prince left, there's been no news.

ZGS 7.47, Shiba na

7.60 和尚有如是機鋒 *⌜Oshō⌝ kaku no gotoki no ⌜ki⌝hō ari.*

The priest has just such a Zen blade.

ZGS 7.48, Shiba na

7.61 和尚莫以良爲賤 *⌜Oshō⌝ ryō o motte sen to nasu nakare.*

The priest should not make what is refined into what is mean.

ZGS 7.49, Shiba na

7.62 摽有梅其實七兮 *Ochite ume ari sono mi nanatsu.*

Plums fell, there were seven.

ZGS 7.50, Shiba 190, *Book of Songs* 20

7.63 各各眉毛横眼上 *Ono-ono bimō ganjō ni yokotau.*

All ⌜eyebrows⌝ lie sideways over the eyes.

ZGJI 329: *kaku-kaku* instead of *ono-ono.*

ZGS 7.51, ZRKS 7.19, Shiba 157, ZGJI 329, KZS #657

7.64 自有金剛王寶劍 *Onozukara kongō ōhōken ari.*

You yourself possess the jeweled ⌜sword⌝ of the ⌜*Vajra*⌝ King.

ZGS 7.52, ZRKS 7.145, Shiba na, KZS #796

7.65 不覺老從頭上來 *Oboezu rō no zujō yori kitaru koto o.*

Before I knew it, old age had descended upon my head.

ZGS 7.53, ZRKS 7.402, Shiba na, ZGJI 327

7.66 飲光眉向花前展 *Onkō no bi wa kazen ni mukatte nobu.*

The "drinker of light" raised his ⌜eyebrows⌝ at the flower.

See ⌜Kāśyapa⌝.

ZGS 7.54, ZRKS 7.107, Shiba na

7.67 鵞王擇乳非鴨類 *Gaō chichi o erabu kamo no rui ni arazu.*

The king goose that extracts the milk is no ordinary duck.

Rinzai-roku §13. From water mixed with milk, the king goose separates out just the milk and drinks it (ZGJI 328, ZGJT 53).

ZGS na, ZRKS 7.122, Shiba 158, ZGJI 328

7.68 海神知貴不知價 *Kaijin tattoki o shitte atai o shirazu.*

The sea god knows it is precious but has no knowledge of its worth.

Heki 6 Main Case *agyo.*

ZGS 7.55, ZRKS 7.125, Shiba 158, ZGJI 328

7.69 卻來虎穴奪全威 *Kaette koketsu ni kitatte zen'i o ubau.*

Then he went to the tiger's cave and took away all its power.

ZGS 7.56, ZRKS 7.280, Shiba na, ZGJI 328, KZS #673

7.70 無限輪鎚擊不開 *Kagiri naki rintsui utedomo hirakezu.*

Though you swing forever with a hammer, still it will not open.

Heki 9 Verse.

ZGS na, ZRKS 7.496, Shiba 195, ZGJI 329, ZGJT 442

7.71 鑊湯爐炭三萬尺 *Kakutō rotan sanmanjaku.*

Boiling cauldron and burning coals for thirty thousand feet.

ZGS 7.57, Shiba na

7.72 客盃弓影元非蛇 *Kyakuhai no kyūei moto ja ni arazu.*

The bow reflected in the guest's cup is not really a snake.

See ⌜Snake in the wine cup⌝.

ZGS 7.58, ZRKS 7.84, Shiba na, ZGJI 408

7.73 客盃弓影生蛇疑 *Kyakuhai no kyūei jagi o shōzu.*

The bow reflected in the guest's cup makes him wonder, "Is it a snake?"

See ⌜Snake in the wine cup⌝.

ZGS na, ZRKS 7.80, Shiba 161, ZGJI 332

7.74 學海波瀾一夜乾 *Gakkai no haran ichiya ni kawaku.*

The waves of the seas of learning have dried up in a single night.

Heki 87 Main Case Comm.

ZGS 7.59, ZRKS 7.508, Shiba 158

7.75 迦葉門前風凜凜 *Kashō monzen kaze rin-rin.*

In front of ⌜Kāśyapa's⌝ gate the wind is piercing cold.

ZGS 7.60, ZRKS 7.110, Shiba na

7.76 話盡山雲海月情 *Katari tsukusu san'un kaigetsu no jō.*

We talk on and on of our impressions of mountains and clouds, sea and ⌜moon⌝.

Heki 53 Verse. After years apart, two close friends meet and can talk only of the scenery. See also 14.24.

ZGS 7.61, ZRKS 7.114, Shiba 198, KZS #787

7.77 活中有眼還同死 *Katchū manako ari kaette shi ni onaji.*

If you have an eye that's alive, then you are the same as dead.

Heki 41 Verse, 80 Verse Comm.

ZGS na, ZRKS 7.513, Shiba 158, ZGJI 329

7.78 蝦蟆窟裏出頭來 *Gama kutsuri yori shuttō shi kitaru.*

The frog sticks its head out of its hole.

ZGS na, ZRKS 7.209, Shiba 157

7.79 火裏蓮華朶朶開 *Kari no renge da-da hiraku.*

The lotus blossoms bloom profusely in the fire.

ZRKS 39 (variant): 旱地蓮華朶朶開 *Kanchi no renge dada hiraku*, "The lotus blossoms bloom profusely in the parched earth." ZGS 7.62, Shiba 157: 花 instead of 華.

ZGS 7.62, ZRKS 7.39, Shiba 157

7.80 可憐飛燕倚新粧 *Karen nari hien no shinshō ni yoru o.*

How lovely! Flying Swallow freshly powdered and perfumed.

Flying Swallow is the beautiful Chao Fei-yen (I C. BCE), a lady in the court of Han Emperor Ch'eng. It was said she was so light she could dance on the palm of a man's hand (Maeno 1962, vol. III, 133; Pauline Yu 1980, 154).

ZGS 7.63, Shiba na

7.81 巖下風生虎弄兒 *Ganka kaze shōjite tora ji o rō su.*

At the foot of the cliff, a breeze blows, a tiger plays with its cub.

ZGS 7.64, ZRKS 7.295, Shiba 160, ZGJI 331

7.82 寒鴈聲聲度翠微 *Kangan sei-sei suibi o wataru.*

The winter geese honk across the blue mountains.

ZRGS #65, Shiba na

7.83 含元殿裏問長安 *Gangen denri ni chōan o tou.*

In the Han-yüan Palace he asks where ⌜Ch'ang-an⌝ is.

ZRKS 7.383n: To ask where the capital city is while you are in the capital city.

ZGS na, ZRKS 7.383, Shiba 159, ZGJI 331

7.84 喚取機關木人問 *Kikan bokujin o kanshu shite toe.*

Call a clockwork ⌜wooden man⌝ and ask.

ZGS na, ZRKS 7.436, Shiba 159, Yung Chia, *Song of Enlightenment*

7.85 澗水松風悉説法 *Kansui shōfū kotogotoku seppō.*

The valley streams, the wind in the pines—all expound the Dharma.

See ⌜Pine wind⌝.

ZGS 7.66, ZRKS 7.430, Shiba 158, ZGJI 330

7.86 肝膽心腸都吐盡 *Kan tan shin chō subete hakitsukusu.*

Vomits up everything—liver, gall, heart, intestines.

ZGS 7.67: 膓 instead of 腸.

ZGS 7.67, ZRKS 7.339, Shiba 158, ZGJI 330, KZS #698

7.87 觀音三十二應身 *Kannon sanjūni ōjin.*

The thirty-two bodily appearances of ⌜Kuan-yin⌝.

ZGS 7.68, Shiba na

7.88 眼裏耳裏絶瀟灑 *Ganri niri zetsu shōsha.*

The eyes, the ears—perfectly clean!

Heki 42 Verse.

ZGS na, Shiba 160, ZGJI 331, KZS #659

7.89 寒流石上一株松 *Kanryū sekijō isshu no matsu.*

On a rock in a cold stream, a single pine.

ZGS 7.69, Shiba na. 盧仝逢鄭三遊山

7.90 見義不爲無勇也 *Gi o mite sezaru wa yū naki nari.*

To see what is right and not do it is lack of courage.

Analects II, 24. *Heki* 56 Main Case *agyo*, 75 Main Case Comm.

ZGS 7.70, ZRKS 7.424, Shiba na, KZS #763

7.91 向鬼窟裏作活計 *Kikutsuri ni mukatte kakkei o nasu.*

In a ghost haunt he carries on his daily life.

Heki 1 Verse *agyo*, 21 Main Case *agyo*, 54 Main Case *agyo*, 62 Main Case *agyo*, etc.

ZGS 7.71, ZRKS 7.207, Shiba 165, KZS #769

7.92 昨日有雨今日晴 *Sakujitsu wa ame ari konnichi wa hare.*

Yesterday it rained, today it's clear.

ZGS 7.72, Shiba na

7.93 爲君幾下蒼龍窟 *Kimi ga tame ni ikutabi ka sōryūkutsu ni kudaru.*

For your sake, how many times have I gone down into the blue dragon's cave!

Heki 3 Verse. Shiba 153: *Kimi ga tame ni ikutabi ka kudaru sōryū no kutsu.*

ZGS 7.73, ZRKS 7.218, Shiba 153, KZS #703

7.94 君向瀟湘我向秦 *Kimi wa shōshō ni mukai ware wa shin ni mukau.*

You are headed for ⌜Hsiao-hsiang⌝ and I am headed for Ch'in.

Heki 24 Verse *agyo,* 51 Verse *agyo.* See also 14.41.

ZGS 7.74, ZRKS 7.225, Shiba na, ZGJI 331

7.95 脚跟下放大光明 *Kyakkonka ni daikōmyō o hanatsu.*

From under your heels a great light shines.

Heki 1 Main Case *agyo.*

ZGS 7.75, ZRKS 7.140, Shiba 161, ZGJI 331

7.96 脱下舊鞋著新鞋 *Kyūai o datsuge shite shin'ai o tsuku.*

He throws away his old sandals and puts on new ones.

ZGS 7.76, ZRKS 7.150, Shiba na, ZGJI 333

7.97 蚯蚓段段孰是眞 *Kyūin dan-dan izure ka kore shin.*

A worm cut into two—which half is the true worm?

ZGS 7.77, Shiba na

7.98 九重城裏五節會 *Kyūjūjōri gosetsu no e.*

In the ⌜nine-tiered imperial palace⌝, the ⌜five festive occasions⌝.

ZGS 7.78, Shiba na.

7.99 玉不玉矣玉玲瓏 *Gyoku gyoku narazu shite gyoku reirō.*

The jade that is not jade is the jade that gleams and sparkles.

ZGS 7.79, Shiba na

7.100 金香爐下鐵崑崙 *Kinkōroka no tetsu konron.*

Under the golden incense burner, iron ⌜chaos⌝.

The pedestal of a large incense burner was sometimes sculpted to look like fierce beings, part animal and part god.

ZGS 7.80, ZRKS 7.405, Shiba 160, KZS #806

7.101 銀山鐵壁千萬重 *Ginzan, teppeki, senbanjü.*

Silver mountains, iron walls—range upon range without end.

ZGS 7.81, ZRKS 7.93, Shiba 163, ZGJI 334, KZS #813

7.102 金翅鳥王當宇宙 *Konjichōō uchū ni ataru.*

⸢*Garuda*⸣, king of birds, perches on the universe.

Heki 3 Verse Comm.

ZGS na, ZRKS 7.20,413, Shiba 162, ZGJI 334

7.103 錦上鋪花又一重 *Kinjō ni hana o shiku mata ichijū.*

Upon brocade, spread another layer of flowers.

ZGS 7.82, ZRKS 7.432, Shiba na, KZS #676

7.104 錦上添花別是春 *Kinjō ni hana o sou betsu ni kore haru.*

Flowers heaped upon brocade, truly this is spring.

ZGS 7.83, ZRKS 7.284 Shiba 162, ZGJI 334

7.105 錦心繡口向人開 *Kinshin shūku hito ni mukatte hiraku.*

He unfolds for others brilliant thoughts and eloquent words.

ZGS na, ZRKS 7.282, Shiba 163, ZGJI 334, KZS #720

7.106 金毛跳入野狐窟 *Kinmō odotte yakokutsu ni iru.*

The golden lion leaps into the ⸢wild fox's⸣ cave.

ZGS 7.84, ZRKS 7.173, Shiba na, ZGJI 334, KZS #741

7.107 金毛獅子輥繡毬 *Kinmō no shishi shūkyū o korogasu.*

The golden lion rolls the embroidered ball around.

ZGS 7.85, ZRKS 7.435, Shiba 162, ZGJI 334

7.108 金毛獅子無處討 *Kinmō no shishi tazunuru ni tokoro nashi.*

The golden lion has no place to turn to.

Heki 84 Verse.

ZGS 7.86, ZRKS 7.446, Shiba na, ZGJI 334, KZS #758

7.109 金毛獅子變成狗 *Kinmō no shishi henjite inu to naru.*

The golden lion transformed into a dog.

See also 14.562.

ZGS 7.87, ZRKS 7.396, Shiba 162, ZGJI 334

7.110 求心歇處卽無事 *Gushin yamu tokoro sunawachi buji.*

Where the seeking mind comes to rest, there is nothing in particular.

Rinzai-roku §11.

ZGS na, Shiba 161, ZGJI 333

7.111 句裏呈機劈面來 *Kuri ni ⌜ki⌝ o teishi hekimen ni kitaru.*

Within his words he thrusts a blade right at your face.

See also 7.110, 7.382. *Heki* 9 Verse. ZRKS 7.117, ZGJI 335: *hitsumen* instead of *hekimen.*

ZGS na, ZRKS 7.117, Shiba 163, ZGJI 335, KZS #792

7.112 開口不在舌頭上 *Kuchi o hiraku koto wa zettōjō ni arazu.*

Speaking is not a matter of using your tongue.

MMK 20.

ZGS 7.88, ZRKS 7.347, Shiba 158, ZGJI 335

7.113 口吐紅蓮養病身 *Kuchi ni guren o haite byōshin o yashinau.*

He vomits up red flowers caring for his sick body.

Heki 11 Main Case Comm.

ZGS 7.89, Shiba na

7.114 屈原既放游江潭 *Kutsugen sude ni hanatarete kōtan ni asobu.*

After he was banished, ⌜Ch'ü Yüan⌝ wandered the river banks.

ZGS 7.90, Shiba na

7.115 九曲黄河混底流 *Kyūkyoku no kōga soko ni konjite nagaru.*

The Yellow River with its nine bends flows murky right to its bottom.

ZGS 7.91, Shiba 161

7.116 岣嶁峯頭神禹碑 *Kuro hōtō shin'u no hi.*

The monument to the divine ⌜Yü⌝ atop Mount Kou-lou.

ZGS 7.92, ZRKS 7.483, Shiba 165

7.117 摶空金翅取猛龍 *Kū o utsu konji mōryū o toru.*

The golden ⌜*Garuda*⌝ bird sweeps the skies, snapping up fierce dragons.

ZRKS 7. 412: *hautsu* instead of *utsu.*

ZGS na, ZRKS 7.412, Shiba 189, ZGJI 335, GKFGS 1.179.

7.118 養雞意在五更天 *Kei o yashinau i goko no ten ni ari.*

The point of raising chickens is in the early morning sky.

See ⌜Watch⌝.

ZGS 7.93, ZRKS 7.22, Shiba na

7.119 慶喜阿閦見佛國 ***Keiki ashuku ni bukkoku o miru.***

See the Buddha-land in the delightful Akṣobhya.

The Buddha once used his divine powers to show ⌜Ānanda⌝ a vision of Akṣobhya Buddha in his Buddha-land in the south. Then he made the vision disappear. All things are as unsubstantial as this, said the Buddha (ZGDJT 257c).

ZGS 7.94, Shiba na, ZGDJT 257c

7.120 荊棘林中一條路 *Keikyokurinchū ichijō no michi.*

Through the forest of thorns, a single path.

ZGS 7.95, ZRKS 7.2, Shiba 163, ZGJI 336, KZS #647

7.121 溪邊掃葉夕陽僧 *Keihen sōyō su sekiyō no sō.*

A monk at twilight is gathering leaves by the banks of the stream.

ZGS na, Shiba 163

7.122 桂輪孤朗碧天濶 *Keirin hitori hogaraka ni shite hekiten hiroshi.*

The cassia circle serene in the vast blue sky.

See ⌜Moon⌝.

ZGS 7.96, ZRKS 7.400, Shiba 163, ZGJI 336

7.123 外空内空内外空 *Gekū naikū naigekū.*

Outside—empty, inside—empty, inside and outside—empty.

ZGS 7.97, ZRKS 7.11, Shiba na, ZGJI 328

7.124 月明豈在珊瑚枝 *Getsumei ani sangoshi ni aran ya.*

Moonlight—does it always fall on the branches of the ⌜coral⌝?

ZGS 7.98, ZRKS 7.306, Shiba na, ZGJI 336

7.125 逼塞乾坤鎖宇宙 *⌜Kenkon⌝ ni hissoku shite uchū o tozasu.*

Withdrawing into the universe, he commands the universe.

KZS #655: 逼塞面前鎖宇宙, Withdrawing into right-before-your-eyes, he commands the universe.

ZGS 7.99, ZRKS 7.491, Shiba na, ZGJI 336, KZS #655

7.126 請爲一堂設饡飯 *Kou ichidō no tame ni sanpan o mōkeyo.*

Please prepare food for the whole assembly.

ZGS 7.100, Shiba na

7.127 紅焔叢中駿馬嘶 *Kōen sōchū shunme inanaku.*

In the midst of red flames, the fleet-footed horse neighs.

ZGS 7.101, Shiba na

7.128 引得黄鶯下柳條 *Kōō o hikiete ryūjō o kudarashimu.*

He lured the golden warbler down from the willow branch.

Heki 40 Main Case *agyo.*

ZGS 7.102, ZRKS 7.182, Shiba na, KZS #735

7.129 好手還同火裏蓮 *Kōshu kaette kari no ren ni onaji.*

A master craftsman is like a lotus in fire.

Heki 43 Main Case Comm. See ⌜Five Ranks⌝.

ZGS 7.103, ZRKS 7.274, Shiba 165, ZGJI 339, ZD 315-23.

7.130 巧匠揮斧不露刃 *Kōshō ono o furutte yaiba o arawasazu.*

A master craftsman swings his axe without showing the blade.

ZGJI 339: *ha* instead of *yaiba.* Empuku-ji: *saeba* instead of *yaiba.*

ZGS 7.104, ZRKS 7.309, Shiba na, ZGJI 339

7.131 黃鶴樓前鸚鵡洲 *Kōkakurōzen ōmushū.*

In front of the ⌜Yellow Crane Pavilion⌝ is the ⌜Isle of Parrots⌝.

ZGS na, ZRKS 7.322, Shiba 166

7.132 曠劫無明當下灰 *Kōgō no mumyō tōka ni kai su.*

Vast ⌜*kalpa*⌝ of ignorance immediately turn into ash.

ZRKS 7.151: *tōka ni hai su.*

ZGS na, ZRKS 7.151, Shiba 166

7.133 高祖殿前樊噲怒 *Kōsō denzen hankai ikaru.*

⌜Kao-tsu⌝ got angry at ⌜Fan K'uai⌝ in front of the hall.

ZGS 7.105, Shiba na

7.134 功至無功汗馬高 *Kō wa mukō ni itatte kanba takashi.*

When merit attains no-merit, there has been great effort indeed.

Kanba, here translated "great effort," literally means "sweat horse."

ZGS 7.106, ZRKS 7.260, Shiba 165, ZGJI 339, KZS #713

7.135 虛空消殞鐵山摧 *Kokū shōin shite tessen kudaku.*

Emptiness disintegrates, the iron mountain shatters.

ZGS 7.107, ZRKS 7.75, Shiba 161, ZGJI 338, KZS #818

7.136 虛空說法何須口 *Kokū seppō nanzo kuchi o mochiin?*

When emptiness preaches the Dharma, what mouth does it use?

ZGS 7.108, ZRKS 7.148, Shiba na, ZGJI 338

7.137 黑漆桶裏黃金色 *Kokushittsūri ōgon no iro.*

In the ⌜black lacquer⌝ tub, the glitter of gold.

ZGS 7.109, ZRKS 7.394, Shiba 166, ZGJI 341

7.138 黑漆桶裏盛黑汁 *Kokushittsūri ni kokujū o moru.*

Pour black ink into the ⌜black lacquer⌝ tub.

Heki 86 Verse *agyo.*

ZGS 7.110, ZRKS 7.448, Shiba 167, KZS #860

7.139 黑漆崑崙雲外走 *Kokushitsu no konron ungai ni hashiru.*

⌜Black⌝ ⌜chaos⌝ runs beyond the clouds.

ZGS 7.111, ZRKS 7.352, Shiba 341

7.140 黑漆崑崙夜裏走 *Kokushitsu konron yari ni hashiru.*

⌜Black⌝ ⌜chaos⌝ runs in the night.

ZGS 7.112, ZRKS 7.428, Shiba 166, ZGJI 341

7.141 黑漆崑崙踏雪行 *Kokushitsu konron yuki o funde yuku.*

⌜Black⌝ ⌜chaos⌝ walks across the snow.

ZGS 7.113, Shiba 166, ZGJI 341

7.142 心若眞時道易親 *Kokoro moshi shin naru toki wa dō shitashimi yasushi.*

When the mind is true, it is easily intimate with the Way.

ZGS na, ZRKS 7.583, Shiba 173, ZGJI 341

7.143 孤舟載月洞庭湖 *Koshū tsuki o nosu dōteiko.*

A lone boat laden with the ⌜moon⌝ on ⌜Lake Tung-t'ing⌝.

ZGS 7.114, ZRKS 7.404, Shiba 164

7.144 五臺拍手峨嵋笑 *Godai te o haku sureba gabi warau.*

When ⌜Mount Wu-t'ai⌝ claps its hands, Mount O-mei laughs.

Mount Wu-t'ai and Mount O-mei are two well-known mountains in China. ZGJI 339: *Godai te o uteba gabi warau.*

ZGS 7.115, ZRKS 7.166, Shiba 165

7.145 骨頭節節是黄金 *Kottō setsu-setsu kore ōgon.*

All your bones and joints are made of gold.

ZGS na, ZRKS 7.191, Shiba 167, ZGJI 341, GKFGS 1.183

7.146 虎頭虎尾一時收 *Kotō kobi ichiji ni osamu.*

In a single moment he takes both the tiger's head and the tiger's tail.

Heki 54 Verse.

ZGS 7.116, ZRKS 7.181, Shiba 164, ZGJI 337, KZS #733

7.147 虎頭戴角出禪扃 *Kotō tsuno o itadaite zenkei o izu.*

Out of the Zen gate comes a tiger with horns.

ZGS 7.117, ZRKS 7.540, Shiba na, ZGJI 337, KZS #752

7.148 虎頭生角出荒草 *Kotō ni tsuno o shōjite kōsō o izu.*

Out of the wild grass comes a tiger with horns.

Heki 70 Verse.

ZGS 7.118, ZRKS 7.416, Shiba 164

7.149 騎虎頭兮收虎尾 *Kotō ni notte kobi o osamu.*

Ride the tiger's head, tame the tiger's tail.

ZGS 7.119, ZRKS 7.343, Shiba na, ZGJI 337

7.150 持箇渾身入地獄 *Kono konshin o motte jigoku ni iru.*

With this very body I enter hell.

ZGS na, Shiba 171, ZGJI 342

7.151 收虎尾兮捋虎鬚 *Kobi o osamete koshu o nazu.*

He takes the tiger's tail, he strokes the tiger's whiskers.

Heki 85 Verse.

ZGS 7.120, ZRKS 7.447, Shiba na, ZGJI 337, KZS #759

7.152 孤峯頂上坐草裡 *Kohō chōjō sōri ni zasu.*

On the lone mountain peak he sits in the weeds.

ZGS 7.121, Shiba na

7.153 孤峯雲散千谿月 *Kohō kumo wa sanzu senkei no tsuki.*

Clouds scattered round the lone peak—the ⌜moon⌝ in a thousand valleys.

ZGS na, Shiba 164, ZGJI 337

7.154 枯木花開劫外春 *Koboku hana hiraku gōgai no haru.*

The withered tree flowers in a spring beyond time.

ZGS 7.122, ZRKS 7.152, Shiba 165, ZGJI 338, KZS #724, ZD #134

7.155 葫蘆棚上掛冬瓜 *Koro hōjō ni tōgan o kaku.*

On a trellis for squash he hangs a winter melon.

ZRKS 7.227: 猪頭 "boar's head" instead of "squash."

ZGS na, ZRKS 7.227, Shiba 165, ZGJI 338

7.156 孤輪獨照江山靜 *Korin hitori terashite kōzan shizuka nari.*

The solitary ⌜moon⌝ shines alone, the rivers and mountains are still.➛

A couplet from *Rinzai-roku* §66.

ZGS 7.123, ZRKS 7.437, Shiba 164, ZGJI 617

7.157 自笑一聲天地驚 *Mizukara warau issei tenchi odoroku.*

➛A burst of laughter startles all heaven and earth.

ZGS 7.351, ZRKS 7.438, Shiba 171, ZGJI 617

7.158 是什麼熱椀鳴聲 *Kore nan no netsuwan myōshō zo.*

What's this squeaking noise from a hot bowl?

Heki 25 Verse Comm.

ZGS 7.124, Shiba na

7.159 閫外安危策已成 *Kongai no anki saku sude ni naru.*

On the borders security measures are now in effect.➛

ZGS 7.125, ZRKS 7.321, Shiba na, GKFGS 1.165

7.160 全鋒不戰屈人兵 *Zenbu tatakawazu hito no hei o kussu.*

➛Without using a single spear they lay low the opposing soldiers.

ZGS 7.211, ZRKS 7.281, Shiba na, KZS #674

7.161 今古永超圓智體 *Konko nagaku koyu enchi no tai.*

Now as always, eternally transcending the state of perfect wisdom.

Rinzai-roku §60.

ZGS na, ZRKS 7.440, Shiba 167, ZGJI 342

7.162 金剛脚下鐵崑崙 *Kongō kyakka no tetsu konron.*

Beneath the feet of the ⌜*Vajra*⌝ gods, iron ⌜chaos⌝.

ZGS 7.126, ZRKS 7.78, Shiba 162, ZGJI 342, KZS #802

7.163 金剛杵打鐵山摧 *Kongō no sho tessen o utte kudaku.*

The ⌜*vajra*⌝ club strikes, splitting the iron mountain.

ZGS na, ZRKS 7.388, Shiba 162, ZGJI 342

7.164 金剛正眼輝乾坤 *Kongō shōgen kenkon ni kagayaku.*

The true eye of the ⌜*Vajra*⌝ God illumines ⌜heaven and earth⌝.

ZGS na, ZRKS 7.34, Shiba 162, ZGJI 342, KZS #190

7.165 金剛腦後添生鐵 *Kongō nōgo ni santetsu o sou.*

The ⌜*vajra*⌝ guardian fits an iron helmet to his head.

ZGS 7.127, ZRKS 7.506, Shiba 162, ZGJI 342

7.166 崑崙著靴空中走 *Konron kutsu o tsukete kūchū ni hashiru.*

⌜Chaos⌝ puts on shoes and runs through the air.

ZGS 7.128, ZRKS 7.168, Shiba 167, ZGJI 342

7.167 崑崙騎象舞三臺 *Konron zō ni notte santai o mau.*

⌜Chaos⌝ mounts an elephant and dances the ⌜three steps⌝.

ZGS 7.129, ZRKS 7.382, Shiba na, ZGJI 342

7.168 左轉右轉隨後來 *Saten uten shirie ni shitagai kitaru.*

Turn left, turn right, it follows right behind.

Heki 17 Verse, 18 Verse *agyo.*

ZGS na, ZRKS 7.58, Shiba 167, KZS #798

7.169 再來不直半文錢 *Sairai hanmonsen ni atarazu.*

A second try is not worth half a cent.

Heki 1 Main Case *agyo,* Verse *agyo*; 45 Verse *agyo.*

ZGS 7.130, ZRKS 7.155, Shiba na, ZGJI 343, KZS #728

7.170 倒騎象王追麒麟 *Sakashima ni zōō ni notte kirin o ou.*

Riding backwards on an elephant, he pursues a ⌜*ch'i-lin*⌝.

ZGS 7.131, ZRKS 7.200, Shiba 185, ZGJI 343

7.171 倒騎鐵馬上須彌 *Sakashima ni tetsuma ni notte shumi ni noboru.*

Riding backwards on an iron horse, he climbs Mount ⌜Sumeru⌝.

KZS #668: *tetsuba* instead of *tetsuma.*

ZGS na, ZRKS 7.33, Shiba 185, ZGJI 343, KZS #668

7.172 昨夜三更月到窓 *Sakuya sanko tsuki mado ni itaru.*

Last night at the third ⌜watch⌝ the ⌜moon⌝ came to my window.

ZGS 7.132, ZRKS 7.57, Shiba 168

7.173 殺人活人不眨眼 *Setsunin katsunin manako o sassezu.*

Whether killing a person or bringing to life—no blinking.

Shiba 168: *Satsujin katsujin manako o sō sezu.*

ZGS 7.203, ZRKS 7.355, Shiba 168, ZGJI 377

7.174 塞雁聲聲度翠微 *Saigan sei-sei suibi o wataru.*

The frontier geese honk-honk across the shimmering blue mountains.

ZGS na, ZRKS 7.40, Shiba 167

7.175 猿繞霜枝一夜啼 *Saru wa sōshi o megutte ichiya naku.*

Monkeys clinging to the frosted branches shriek all night.

ZGS 7.133, Shiba 156

7.176 三脚蝦蟆呑巨鼇 *Sankyaku no kama kyogō o nomu.*

The ⌜three-legged frog⌝ swallows the ⌜giant turtle⌝.

ZGS na, ZRKS 7.527, Shiba 168, ZGJI 424

7.177 珊瑚枝枝撐著月 *Sango shishi tsuki o tōjaku su.*

The ⌜coral's⌝ many branches are suffused with the ⌜moon⌝.

Heki 13 Main Case Comm., 100 Main Case.

ZGS 7.134, ZRKS 7.104, Shiba 169, ZGJI 345

7.178 三更杲日黑漫漫 *Sankō kōjitsu koku man-man.*

At the third ⌜watch⌝ in a brilliant sun—endless blackness.

ZGS na, ZRKS 7.486, Shiba 168, ZGJI 344

7.179 三箇柴頭品字煨 *Sanko no saitō honji ni wai su.*

Stacked like the character 品, three pieces of firewood burn.

ZGS 7.135, ZRKS 7.530, Shiba 168, ZGJI 344

7.180 三脚驢兒跳上天 *Sankyaku no roji odotte ten ni noboru.*

The three-legged donkey leaps into heaven.

ZGS 7.136, ZRKS 7.378, Shiba 168, ZGJI 344

7.181 三尺杖子攪黄河 *Sanjaku no jōsu kōga o kakimidasu.*

With his three-foot stick he stirs up the Yellow River.

Heki 33 Verse *agyo.*

ZGS 7.137, Shiba na, ZGJI 345

7.182 三尺杖頭挑日月 *Sanjaku no jōtō jitsugetsu o kakagu.*

He raises sun and ⌜moon⌝ on the top of his three-foot staff.

ZGS 7.138, ZRKS 7.398, Shiba 168, ZGJI 345

7.183 三尺鏌鎁横在手 *Sanjaku no bakuya yokoshima ni te ni ari.*

The three-foot sword ⌜Mo Yeh⌝ is level in his hand.

ZGS 7.139, ZRKS 7.579, Shiba na

7.184 三尺鏌鋣清四海 *Sanjaku no bakuya ⌜shikai⌝ o kiyomu.*

The three-foot sword ⌜Mo Yeh⌝ purifies the whole world.

ZGS 7.140, ZRKS 7.175, Shiba na, KZS #744

7.185 三十年後有人知 *Sanjūnengo hito no shiru aran.*

⌜Thirty years⌝ from now someone will know.

ZGS 7.141, Shiba na

7.186 三千里外有知音 *Sanzenrigai chiin ari.*

I have an ⌜intimate friend⌝ more than three thousand miles away.

ZGS 7.142, ZRKS 7.299, Shiba na, KZS #683

7.187 三千里外沒交涉 *Sanzenrigai mokkyōshō.*

We're more than three thousand miles away. All connections are cut!

Heki 83 Main Case *agyo.*

ZGS na, Shiba 179, ZGJI 345

7.188 生鐵秤鎚被蟲蝕 *Santetsu no shōtsui mushi ni mushibamaru.*

The iron scale weights have been eaten by worms.

ZGS na, ZRKS 7.539, Shiba 176, ZGJI 354

7.189 三人行必有我師 *Sannin ayumeba kanarazu waga shi ari.*

Where three persons go, for certain one will be a teacher for me.

Analects VII, 21.

ZGS na, ZRKS 7.598, Shiba 169

7.190 十字街頭破草鞋 *Jūji gaitō hasōai.*

At the busy intersection, a worn-out sandal.

ZGS 7.143, Shiba 171

7.191 十分春色滿人間 *Jūbun no shunshoku, jinkan ni mitsu.*

Spring in all its colors fills the human world.

ZGS 7.144, ZRKS 7.46, Shiba na, ZGJI 349, KZS #664

7.192 四海而今清似鏡 *⌜Shikai⌝ ima kagami yori kiyoshi.*

The entire world is now clearer than a mirror.

ZGS 7.145, ZRKS 7.54, Shiba 179

7.193 四海香風從此起 *⌜Shikai⌝ no kōfū kore yori okoru.*

A fragrant breeze in every quarter arises from here.

ZGS 7.146, ZRKS 7.381, Shiba 179

7.194 獅子教兒迷子訣 *Shishi ji o oshiu meishi no ketsu.*

The lion teaches the cub by making it lose its way.

MMK 15 Verse. Shiba 170: *oshiyu* instead of *oshiu.*

ZGS 7.148, ZRKS 7.273, Shiba 170, ZGJI 347

7.195 侍者將衣來安寢 *Jisha koromo o mochikitatte anshin.*

The ⌜attendant⌝ brings the robes and sleeps in late.

ZGS 7.149, Shiba na

7.196 死諸葛走生仲達 *Shiseru shokatsu ikeru chūdatsu o hashirasu.*

Even in death, ⌜Chu-ko⌝ makes the still-living Chung-ta run.

ZGS 7.150, Shiba 170

7.197 弄得死蛇成活龍 *Shida o rō shiete katsuryū to nasu.*

He played with a dead snake and turned it into a live dragon.

ZGS 7.151, ZRKS 7.231, Shiba 198, ZGJI 346

7.198 叱咤神威孰敢當 *Shitta no jin'i tare ka aete ataran.*

Who can confront the awesome anger of the gods?

ZRKS 7.550: *shittataru* instead of *shitta no.*

ZGS 7.152, ZRKS 7.550, Shiba na

7.199 十箇指頭八箇丫 *Jikko no shitō hakko no a.*

Ten fingers, eight crotches.

ZGS na, ZRKS 7.297, Shiba 171, ZGJI 349

7.200 十方世界一團鐵 *Jippō sekai ichidan no tetsu.*

The world in all ⌜ten directions⌝—one lump of iron.

ZGS 7.153, ZRKS 7.261, Shiba 171, ZGJI 632, 662

7.201 十方世界鐵崑崙 *Jippō sekai tetsu konron.*

The world in all ⌜ten directions⌝—iron ⌜chaos⌝.

ZGS 7.154, ZRKS 7.587, Shiba 200, ZGJI 350

7.202 獻師不堪用有餘 *Shi ni kenzuru ni yūyo o mochiuru ni taezu.*

When serving the master, you cannot use leftovers.

ZGS 7.155, Shiba na

7.203 詩學李杜文師韓 *Shi wa rito o manabi bun wa kan o shi to su.*

For poetry, study ⌜Li Po⌝ and ⌜Tu Fu⌝; for prose, take Han Yü as a teacher.

ZGS 7.156, Shiba na

7.204 詩至重吟初見功 *Shi wa jūgin ni itatte hajimete kō o miru.*

In poetry, only after many readings is your merit visible.

See also 14.237.

ZGS na, Shiba 170

7.205 四百四病一時發 *Shihyakushibyō ichiji ni hassu.*

Four hundred and four illnesses break out all at once.

Heki 3 Main Case *agyo*. There are a hundred diseases each for the four great elements of earth, water, fire, and wind. Add the four elements themselves to make 404 diseases (ZGJI 149).

ZGS 7.157, ZRKS 7.10, Shiba 170, ZGJI 346, KZS #651

7.206 釋迦彌勒樂堯年 *Shaka miroku gyōnen o tanoshimu.*

Śākyamuni and ⌜Maitreya⌝ enjoy the years of ⌜Yao⌝.➛

ZGS 7.158, ZRKS 7.464, Shiba na, ZGJI 678

7.207 文殊普賢歌舜日 *Monju fugen shunjitsu o utau.*

➛⌜Mañjuśrī⌝ and ⌜Samantabhadra⌝ sing of the days of ⌜Shun⌝.

ZGS 7.368, ZRKS 7.465, Shiba na, ZGJI 678 reverses order of couplet

7.208 射工含沙待影過 *Shakō suna o fukunde kage no suguru o matsu.*

The ⌜sand-spitter⌝ fills its mouth with sand and waits for shadows to pass.

ZGS 7.159, Shiba na, ZGJI 348

7.209 謝三郎不知四字 *Shasanrō shiji o shirazu.*

⌜Hsieh San-lang⌝ does not know even the four characters.

MMK 41.

ZGS 7.160, Shiba 171

7.210 娑婆往來八千度 *Shaba ōrai hassendo.*

Going back and forth to this ⌜*sahā*⌝ world eight thousand times.

ZGS 7.161, Shiba na

7.211 宗通説通大自在 *Shūtsū settsū daijizai.*

A master of the practice, a master of the teaching—completely free.

ZGS 7.162, Shiba na

7.212 秋風過去春風至 *Shūfū sugisatte shunpū itaru.*

The autumn breeze has passed, the spring wind arrives.

ZGS 7.163, ZRKS 7.44, Shiba na, ZGJI 349

7.213 袖裏金鎚劈面來 *Shūri no kintsui hitsumen ni kitaru.*

The golden hammer up his sleeve lands square in your face.

ZGS 7.164, ZRKS 7.179, Shiba na, ZGJI 349, KZS #734

7.214 樹上鯉魚開口笑 *Jujō no rigyo kuchi o hiraite warau.*

Up in the trees, the carp opens wide its mouth and laughs.

ZGS 7.165, ZRKS 7.487, Shiba 171, ZGJI 349

7.215 莫把商音作羽音 *Shōin o totte hain o nasu koto nakare.*

Do not take the note *shang* for the note *yü*.

The ancient Chinese musical scale had five notes: 宮 *kung*, 商 *shang*, 角 *chüeh*, 徵 *chih*, and 羽 *yü*.

ZGS 7.166, Shiba na

7.216 蕭何賣卻假銀城 *Shōka maikyaku su kaginjō.*

⸢Hsaio Ho⸣ sells a phony city of silver.

Heki 43 Main Case *agyo*.

ZGS 7.167, ZRKS 7.417, Shiba 172; ZGJI 351, KZS #754

7.217 燒甎打著連底冰 *Shōsen tajaku su rentei no kōri.*

The flaming tile broke through the solid layers of ice.

ZGS 7.168, ZRKS 7.147, Shiba 172

7.218 秤鎚搦出黃金汁 *Shōtsui shiboridasu ōgon no shiru.*

He wrings gold juice from the scale weights.

ZGS na, ZRKS 7.293, Shiba 172, ZGJI 351, KZS #675

7.219 焦尾大蟲元是虎 *Shobi no daichū moto kore tora.*

That ⸢big bug⸣ with the scorched tail was once a tiger.

ZGS 7.169, ZRKS 7.536, Shiba 172, ZGJI 351

7.220 丈夫面上傅紅粉 *Jōbu menjō ni kōfun o tsuku.*

He applies rouge to his healthy face.

ZGS 7.170, Shiba 173

7.221 蟭螟眼裏五須彌 *Shōmei ganri no goshumi.*

Five Mount ⸢Sumerus⸣ in the eye of the ⸢mite⸣.

ZGS 7.171, ZRKS 7.180, Shiba 173, ZGJI 351, KZS #732

7.222 燒葉爐中無宿火 *Shōyō rochū shukka nashi.*

In the pit of burning leaves there is no residual heat.

ZGS 7.172, Shiba na

7.223 燒葉爐頭火筯忙 *Shōyō rotō kacho isogashi.*

In the pit of burning leaves the fire tongs are busy.

ZGS 7.173, Shiba na

7.224 上下四維無等匹 *Jōge shiyui tōhitsu nashi.*

Above, below, and in the four directions, no rivals.

Heki 6 Verse. *Shi yui* 四維 are actually the four in-between directions, NW, NE, SW, and SE.

ZGS na, Shiba 173, ZGJI 351

7.225 杖林山下竹筋鞭 *Jōrinzanka chikkinben.*

The bamboo-root whip from Chang-lin Mountain.

Heki 12 Main Case Comm. Shiba 173: *Jōrinzanka chikkonben.*

ZGS 7.174, Shiba 173

7.226 不知明月落誰家 *Shirazu meigetsu ta ga ie ni ka otsu.*

I do not know into whose house the bright moonlight will fall.

See also 14.52.

ZGS 7.175, ZRKS 7.477, Shiba 192, ZGJI 352

7.227 紫羅帳裏撒眞珠 *Shirachōri ni shinju o sassu.*

Sprinkle pearls on the purple silk curtain.

Heki 10 Verse Comm.

ZGS 7.176, ZRKS 7.555, Shiba 170, ZGJI 346

7.228 調古神清風自高 *Shirabe furi shin kiyōshite fū onozukara takashi.*

His elegant style was pure in spirit, his manner naturally refined.

ZGS na, Shiba 181

7.229 要識眞金火裏看 *Shinkin o shiran to yōseba kari ni miyo.*

If you want to know true gold, test it in the fire.

MMK 20 Verse, *Heki* 20 Main Case Comm, 65 Main Case *agyo.*

ZGS 7.177, ZRKS 7.276, Shiba 196, ZGJI 352

7.230 深閨燈影語寃讎 *Shinkei no tōei ni enshū o kataru.*

By lamplight in the inner chamber they speak of deception and revenge.

ZGS 7.178, Shiba na

7.231 神箭三匝白猿號 *Shinsen sansō shite hakuen sakebu.*

The divine arrow circled three times and the white monkey screamed its last.

ZGS 7.179, Shiba 174

7.232 盡大地藏身無處 *Jindaichi mi o kakusu ni tokoro nashi.*

On this whole wide earth, there is no place to hide.

ZGS 7.180, Shiba 174

7.233 針頭不用重添鐵 *Shintō mochiizu kasanete tetsu o souru koto o.*

It is useless to add extra metal to the head of a needle.

ZGS 7.181, ZRKS 7.142, Shiba 174, ZGJI 352

7.234 新婦騎驢阿家牽 *Shinpu ro ni noreba ako hiku.*

The bride rides the donkey led by the mother of the groom.

ZGS na, Shiba 174, ZGJI 353

7.235 針鋒頭上翻筋斗 *Shinpō tōjō ni kinto o hirugaesu.*

On the point of a needle, turn a somersault.

ZGS 7.182; Shiba 174: 飜 instead of 翻.

7.236 俊狗咬人不露牙 *Shunku hito o kamu ni kiba o arawasazu.*

A crack dog doesn't show its fangs when it bites a man.

Heki 48 Main Case Comm.

ZGS 7.183, ZRKS 7.203, Shiba 172, ZGJI 350

7.237 春光爛漫花爭發 *Shunkō ranman to shite hana arasoi hiraku.*

In the wild spring sun, flowers riot in bloom.➛

ZGS 7.184, ZRKS 7.160, Shiba na, 普燈錄十六

7.238 子規啼落西山月 *Shiki nakiotosu seizan no tsuki.*

➛The cuckoo calls the ⌜moon⌝ down over the western mountains.

ZGS 7.147, ZRKS 7.161, Shiba 169, ZGJI 346

7.239 迅雷吼破澄潭月 *Jinrai kuha su chōtan no tsuki.*

Crashing thunder shatters the ⌜moon⌝ in the still pool.

ZGS 7.185, ZRKS 7.98, Shiba 174, ZGJI 353

7.240 睡虎眼有百步威 *Suiko no manako ni hyappo no i ari.*

The eye of the sleeping tiger sends fear a hundred paces.

ZGS 7.186, Shiba 174, ZGJI 354

7.241 醉後郎當愁殺人 *Suigo rōtō to shite hito o shūsatsu.*

Drunk and disheveled, he causes everyone grief.

Heki 99 Main Case *agyo.*

ZGS 7.187, ZRKS 7.12, Shiba 175, ZGJI 354, KZS #653

7.242 垂手還同萬仞崖 *Suishu kaette banjin no gai ni onaji.*

His helping hand is more like a towering stone wall.

Heki 43 Verse. Shiba 175: 刄 instead of 仞. See ⌜*Suishu*⌝.

ZGS na, ZRKS 7.302

7.243 水面無塵波洗濤 *Suimen chiri naku nami nami o arau.*

On the water's dustless surface, waves wash over waves.

ZGS 7.188, Shiba na

7.244 吹毛用了急須磨 *Suimō mochiowatte kyū ni subekaraku masubeshi.*

When you finish using the ⌜hair-cutter sword⌝, quickly sharpen it.

ZGS na, ZRKS 7.500, Shiba 175, KZS #791

7.245 洗硯端池生玉蓮 *Suzuri o aratte tanchi ni gyokuren o shōzu.*

Wash the inkstone at the side of the pond and jade lotuses are born.

ZGS 7.189, Shiba na

7.246 已知聖澤深無限 *Sude ni shiru seitaku no fukōshite kagiri naki koto o.*

We already know the limitless depth of imperial virtue.

聖澤 literally means "holy pond" but is used here in the sense of imperial virtue (Morohashi 29074.208).

ZGS 7.190, Shiba na, TSSSTS 48

7.247 精金入火色轉鮮 *Seikin hi ni itte iro utata azayaka nari.*

Refined gold put in fire shines brighter still.

ZGS 7.191, Shiba na

7.248 精金百錬出紅爐 *Seikin hyakuren kōro o izu.*

Pure gold refined one hundred times comes out of the red furnace.

ZGS 7.192, ZRKS 7.442, Shiba 177, KZS #753, GKFGS 1.97

7.249 靑山涌出黃金宅 *Seizan yūshutsu su ōgon no taku.*

The blue mountains radiate forth a golden house.

ZGS na, ZRKS 7.368, Shiba 176

7.250 井梧翻葉動秋聲 *Seigo ha o hirugaeshite shūsei o ugokasu.*

Leaves tumble from the empress tree by the well, making the rustling sounds of autumn.

ZGS 7.193, ZRKS 7.49, Shiba na

7.251 齊女擊碎連環玉 *Seijo gekisai su renkan no tama.*

The girl from Ch'i smashes to pieces the jeweled necklace.

ZGS 7.194, Shiba na

7.252 靑天白日怒雷奔 *Seiten hakujitsu dorai washiru.*

On a bright clear day, angry thunder rumbles.

Shiba 176: 晴 instead of 靑.

ZGS 7.195, ZRKS 7.342, Shiba 176, ZGJI 354, GKFGS 2.34.

7.253 淸風匝地有何極 *Seifū sōchi nan no kiwamari ka aran.*

The pure wind encircling the earth, what limits does it have?

Heki 1 Verse.

ZGS 7.196, ZRKS 7.422, Shiba 176, ZGJI 354

7.254 駕與靑龍不解騎 *Seiryū ni gayo suredomo noru koto o ge sezu.*

Even if you put him on Green Dragon, he wouldn't know how to ride it.

Heki 20 Main Case *agyo*, 54 Main Case *agyo*. Green Dragon is the name of a legendary swift-footed horse.

ZGS 7.197, ZRKS 7.220, Shiba 158, ZGJI 354, KZS #707

7.255 石火光中急轉身 *Sekka kōchū kyū ni mi o tenzu.*

In a flash of light he spins his body around.

ZGS 7.198, ZRKS 7.260, Shiba na, ZGJI 354

7.256 赤脚波斯過孟津 *Sekkyaku no hashi moshin o sugu.*

The ⌜barefoot Persian⌝ crossed [the Yangtze River] at the Meng Ford.

ZGS 7.199, Shiba na

7.257 赤洪崖打白洪崖 *Sekkōgai hakkōgai o utsu.*

The great red cliff strikes the great white cliff.

ZGS 7.200, Shiba na

7.258 絕學無爲閑道人 *Zetsugaku mui no kandōnin.*

A relaxed person of the Way—beyond learning, without effort.

Heki 44 Main Case Comm.

ZGS na, Shiba 177

7.259 説似一物即不中 *Setsuji ichimotsu soku fuchū.*

Try to explain even one thing and already you've missed the mark.

ZGS na, ZRKS 7.15, Shiba 177, ZGJI 355, ZGJT 253

7.260 雪上加霜又一重 *Setsujō ni shimo o kuwau mata ichijū.*

On top of snow he adds a layer of frost.

Heki 85 Main Case *agyo*, 90 Main Case *agyo*, 97 Main Case *agyo*.

ZGS 7.201, ZRKS 7.451, Shiba 177, ZGJI 355, KZS #765

7.261 舌頭三寸鑄生鐵 *Zettō sanzun santetsu o iru.*

With his three-⸢inch⸣ tongue, he forges raw iron.

ZGS 7.202, ZRKS 7.576, Shiba na, ZGJI 355

7.262 千機萬機一時轉 *Sen⸢ki⸣ banki ichiji ni tenzu.*

One thousand acts, ten thousand impulses moving all at once.

ZGS 7.204, ZRKS 7.65, Shiba na, ZGJI 355

7.263 千手大悲遮不得 *Senju daihi mo saegiru koto o ezu.*

Not even the thousand-handed Great Compassionate One can turn it off.

See ⸢Kuan-yin⸣.

ZGS na, Shiba 177, ZGJI 355

7.264 千手大悲提不起 *Senju daihi mo tei fuki.*

Not even the thousand-handed Great Compassionate One can offer it.

See ⸢Kuan-yin⸣.

ZGS 7.205, Shiba na

7.265 千重關鎖擊難開 *Senjū no kansa utedomo hirakigatashi.*

Strike the barrier of a thousand chains, still it won't open.

ZGS 7.206, ZRKS 7.198, Shiba na, ZGJI 355

7.266 千聖從來不識伊 *Senshō mo jūrai kare o shirazu.*

Even the thousand holy ones have never known him.

ZGS na, ZRKS 7.53, Shiba 177, ZGJI 355

7.267 拳倒禪床便出去 *Zenshō o kentō shite sunawachi idesaru.*

He knocked over the zazen seat and straightway left.

ZGS 7.207, Shiba na

7.268 扇子踍跳舞三臺 *Sensu botchō shite sandai o mau.*

The fan leaps up and dances the ⸢three steps⸣.

ZGS 7.208, Shiba 178, ZGJI 356

7.269 前箭猶輕後箭深 *Zensen wa nao karuku kōsen wa fukashi.*

The first arrow still struck lightly, the later arrow went deep.

Heki 29 Main Case *agyo,* 36 Main Case *agyo,* 46 Main Case *agyo* etc., MMK 15 Verse.

ZGS 7.209, ZRKS 7.105, Shiba 178, ZGJI 357, KZS #782

7.270 栴檀葉葉香風起 *Sendan yō-yō kōfū okoru.*

From the leaves of the sandalwood tree a fragrant wind rises.

ZGS 7.210, ZRKS 7.63, Shiba 178, KZS #801

7.271 千峯盤屈色如藍 *Senpō bankutsu iro ai no gotoshi.*

A thousand peaks twist and turn, their color like indigo.

Heki 35 Verse.

ZGS 7.212, ZRKS 7.305, Shiba 177, ZGJI 356

7.272 千里萬里一條鐵 *Senri banri ichijō no tetsu.*

A thousand miles, ten thousand miles—one solid bar of iron.

ZGS 7.213, ZRKS 7.18, Shiba 177, ZGJI 356, KZS #656

7.273 曹溪鏡裏絕塵埃 *Sōkei kyōri jin'ai o zessu.*

The mirror of ⸢Ts'ao-ch'i⸣ has no dust.

Heki 5 Verse.

ZGS 7.214, ZRKS 7.370, Shiba 178

7.274 相識猶如不相識 *Sōshiki wa nao fusōshiki no gotoshi.*

Being close to him is the same as not being close to him.

See 14.614.

ZGS 7.215, Shiba 178, ZGJI 357

7.275 曹操賜關羽錦囊 *Sōsō kan'u no kinnō o tamau.*

Ts'ao Ts'ao bestows a brocade bag on Kuan Yü.

In the Chinese novel *San kuo chih yen-i* 三國志演義 (*Romance of the Three Kingdoms*), Kuan Yü is one of the three heroes who pledges to support the Han. In ch. 25, their enemy Ts'ao Ts'ao tries to win over Kuan Yü's loyalty. Among other tactics, he gives Kuan Yü a brocade bag for his luxurious beard (Brewitt-Taylor 1959, 259–69).

ZGS 7.216, Shiba na

7.276 擾擾怱怱水裏月 *Jō-jō sō-sō suiri no tsuki.*

Shattered and shimmering, the ⸢moon⸣ in the water.

Heki 15 Verse. ZGS 7.217: 怱怱擾擾.

ZGS 7.217, Shiba 173, ZGJI 352

7.277 象峯八十眞境界 *Zōhō hachijū shin no kyōgai.*

The true spirit of the eighty of Elephant Peak.

ZGS 7.218, Shiba na

7.278 蒼龍依水起雲雷 *Sōryū mizu ni yotte unrai o okosu.*

The blue dragon takes to the water, raising clouds and thunder.

ZGS 7.219, ZRKS 7.96, Shiba na, ZGJI 358, KZS #793

7.279 入觸界不被觸惑 *Sokkai ni itte sokuwaku o kōmurazu.*

He enters the realm of touch without succumbing to touch.

Rinzai-roku §19.

ZGS 7.220, ZRKS 7.532, Shiba na

7.280 賊不入愼家之門 *Zoku wa shinka no mon ni irazu.*

A ⌜thief⌝ will not enter the gate of a watchful household.

ZGS 7.221, ZRKS 7.66, Shiba 179, ZGJI 358, KZS #804

7.281 多少人喪身失命 *Tashō no hito sōshin shitsumyō su.*

Many people are destroying themselves, losing their lives.

Heki 13 Verse *agyo.*

ZGS na, ZRKS 7.7, Shiba 179, ZGJI 359

7.282 太阿寶劍本是鐵 *Taia no hōken moto kore tetsu.*

⌜*T'ai-a*⌝, the treasure sword, was originally iron.

ZGS 7.223, Shiba na

7.283 大圓鏡光黑如漆 *Daien kyōkō kuroki koto urushi no gotoshi.*

The brilliance of the great mirror wisdom is as ⌜black as lacquer⌝.

ZGS 7.224, Shiba na

7.284 醍醐毒藥一時行 *Daigo dokuyaku ichiji ni gyōzu.*

He gives the milk of wisdom and the poisonous drug at the same time.

Heki 74 Main case *agyo.* See ⌜Five flavors⌝.

ZGS 7.225, ZRKS 7.221, Shiba 180, ZGJI 360, KZS #709

7.285 大地撮來無寸土 *Daichi sasshi kitaru ni sundo nashi.*

Try to grasp the great earth and there is not even a clod of dirt.

ZGS 7.226, ZRKS 7.494, Shiba 179, ZGJI 359, KZS #777

7.286 大地山河絕纖埃 *Daichi senga sen'ai o zessu.*

On the mountains, rivers, and the great earth, not a speck of dust.

ZGS 7.227, ZRKS 7.86, Shiba 179, ZGJI 359, KZS #807

7.287 大地茫茫愁殺人 *Daichi bō-bō to shite hito o shūsatsu su.*

The great earth is so vast it saddens people terribly.

Heki 23 Main Case *agyo*, 77 Verse *agyo*.

ZGS na, ZRKS 7.6, Shiba 179, ZGJI 359, KZS #652

7.288 大聲不入於里耳 *Taisei ri'ni ni irazu.*

Great music is lost on the ears of the villagers.

After Watson 1968, 140.

ZGS na, Shiba 180. 莊子天地篇

7.289 大唐打鼓新羅舞 *Daitō ni tsutsumi o uteba shinra ni mau.*

When they beat the drum in T'ang [China], they dance in ⌜Silla⌝ [Korea].

Heki 24 Main Case *agyo*.

ZGS 7.228, ZRKS 7.127, Shiba 180, ZGJI 360

7.290 太平天子恩如海 *Taihei no tenshi on umi no gotoshi.*

Our debt to the Emperor of Great Peace is as vast as the ocean.

ZGS 7.229, ZRKS 7.599, Shiba na, ZGJI 360

7.291 大鵬一擧九萬里 *Taihō ikkyo su kyūmanri.*

The great ⌜roc⌝ flies 90,000 miles in one flap of its wings.

ZGS 7.230, ZRKS 7.164, Shiba 180, ZGJI 360, KZS #736

7.292 大鵬展翅取龍呑 *Taihō tsubasa o nobete ryū o totte nomu.*

The great ⌜roc⌝ spreads its wings, pecks up dragons, and gulps them down.

ZGS na, ZRKS 7.535, Shiba 180, ZGJI 360,

7.293 大冶精金無變色 *Taiya no seikin henshoku nashi.*

Gold refined by a great smith never changes color.

ZGS 7.231, ZRKS 7.380, Shiba 180

7.294 誰家無明月淸風 *Ta ga ie ni ka meigetsu seifū nakaran.*

At whose house is there no bright ⌜moon⌝ and pure wind?

Heki 6 Main Case *agyo*.

ZGS 7.232, ZRKS 7.495, Shiba 175, ZGJI 361, ZGJT 238, KZS #778

7.295 誰家竈裡火無烟 *Ta ga ie no sōri ni ka hi ni kemuri nakaran.*

In the hearth of whose house does smoke not come from fire?

ZGS 7.233, ZRKS 7.265, Shiba 175, KZS #717

7.296 貴懸羊頭賣狗肉 *Tattoku yōtō o kakete kuniku o uru.*

He hangs out a lamb's head but sells dog meat.

ZRKS 7.562: *takaku* instead of *tattoku*.

ZGS na, ZRKS 7.562, Shiba 160, ZGJI 360

7
字

7.297 玉作精神雪作膚 *Tama o seishin to nashi yuki o hada to nasu.*

Jewels are its spirit, snow is its skin.

Shōun-ji: *gyoku* instead of *tama.* Shiba 161: A poem about the beauty of ⌜plum⌝ blossoms.

ZGS na, ZRKS 7.375, Shiba 161, ZGJI 361

7.298 斷弦須是鸞膠續 *Dangen wa subekaraku kore rankō ni te tsugubeshi.*

A broken bowstring must be mended with phoenix glue.

ZGS 7.234, Shiba na

7.299 團團珠遶玉珊珊 *Dan-dan tama meguri gyoku san-san.*

The pearls roll round, the jewels chime.

Heki 33 Verse.

ZGS 7.235, ZRKS 7.204, Shiba 180

7.300 知音自有松風和 *Chiin onozukara shōfū no wa suru ari.*

⌜Intimates⌝ naturally have the same rapport as wind and pines.

See also ⌜Pine wind⌝.

ZGS 7.236, ZRKS 7.159, Shiba na, ZGJI 362

7.301 知音知後更誰知 *Chiin shitte nochi sara ni tare ka shiran.*

More my ⌜intimate⌝ companion, who else knows more?

ZGS 7.237, ZRKS 7.252, Shiba 181

7.302 直下本來無一事 *Jikige honrai ichiji nashi.*

Right now, fundamentally there is not one thing.

From Hui-neng's poem. See ⌜Sixth Patriarch⌝.

ZGS 7.238, ZRKS 7.584, Shiba na.

7.303 地獄門前鬼脱卯 *Jigoku monzen ki datsubō su.*

At the gates of hell, the demons are not signing in.

Chinese administrators reported for work at the hour of the hare (卯刻 6 AM) and signed a registry (卯簿). Failing to sign in was 脱卯 *datsubō* (ZGJI 77).

ZGS 7.239, ZRKS 7.524, Shiba na, ZGJI 362, ZGJT 181

7.304 痴人積雪作銀山 *Chijin wa yuki o tsunde ginzan to nasu.*

The fool piles up snow to make a silver mountain.

ZGS 7.240, Shiba na

7.305 長安城裏任閑遊 *Chōanjōri ni kanyū ni makasu.*

He gives himself over to leisure in ⌜Ch'ang-an⌝.

Heki 64 Verse.

ZGS 7.241, ZRKS 7.425, Shiba 181, ZGJI 362

7.306 醉殺長安輕薄兒 *Chōan no keihakuji o suisatsu su.*

They get the ⌜Ch'ang-an⌝ playboys dead drunk.

ZGS 7.242 , Shiba na, Maeno 1962, vol. III, 181-3.

7.307 張公喫酒李公醉 *Chōkō sake o kissureba rikō you.*

When Duke ⌜Chang⌝ drinks wine, Duke ⌜Li⌝ gets drunk.

Book of Serenity Case 17 "Added Sayings Case"

ZGS 7.243, ZRKS 7.242, Shiba 181, ZGJT 310, KZS #710

7.308 澄潭不許蒼龍蟠 *Chōtan yurusazu sōryū no wadakamaru koto o.*

A clear still pool does not allow the blue dragon to coil up and hide.

Heki 18 Verse, 20 Verse Comm., 95 Verse Comm.

ZGS 7.244, ZRKS 7.444, Shiba 181, ZGJI 363, ZGJT 312, KZS #756

7.309 朝來同見千家雨 *Chōrai onajiku miru senke no ame.*

Morning comes, everywhere's the same, rain on a thousand houses.

ZGS 7.245, Shiba na,

7.310 鴆酒一盃當面傾 *⌜Chinshu⌝ ippai tōmen ni katamuku.*

A cup of poison wine, you drank in front of me.

ZGS 7.246, ZRKS 7.233, Shiba 182, KZS #774, GKFGS 2.94-5.

7.311 鴆鳥入水魚皆死 *Chinchō mizu ni itte uo mina shi su.*

When the ⌜poison blackbird⌝ enters the water, all the fish die.

ZGS 7.247, ZRKS 7.468, Shiba 181, ZGJI 651, ZGJT 314

7.312 通身是病通身藥 *Tsūshin kore yamai tsūshin kore kusuri.*

The whole body is sickness, the whole body is medicine.

ZGS 7.248, ZRKS 7.301, Shiba 182, ZGJI 364

7.313 通身紅爛火裏看 *Tsūshin kuran kari ni miyo.*

When your whole body is aflame, look into the fire.

ZGS na, ZRKS 7.51, Shiba 182, ZGJI 613

7.314 月在靑天水在瓶 *Tsuki wa seiten ni ari, mizu wa byō ni ari.*

The ⌜moon⌝ is in the blue sky, the water is in the bottle.

ZGS 7.249, ZRKS 7.259, Shiba 164, ZGJI 364, KZS #666

7.315 頭頭全露法王身 *Zu-zu mattaku hōōshin o arawasu.*

This thing, that thing, everything reveals the Dharma King's body.

ZGS 7.250, ZRKS 7.399, Shiba 185, ZGJI 363

7.316 常呑一箇鐵崑崙 *Tsune ni nomu ikko no tetsu ⌜konron⌝.*

The black iron ball is stuck in my throat.

ZGS na, Shiba 173

7.317 泥牛觸碎蒼龍窟 *Deigyū shokusai su sōryūkutsu.*

The mud ox crushes the blue dragon's cave.

ZGS 7.251, ZRKS 7.366, Shiba na, ZGJI 365

7.318 泥牛蹴浪鼓瞋牙 *Deigyū nami o kette shinga o ko su.*

The mud ox kicks the waves and racks its angry horns.

ZGS 7.252, Shiba na

7.319 難提掇處轉有則 *Teitetsu shigataki tokoro utata nori ari.*

For times when give and take are difficult, just then there are rules.

ZGS 7.253, Shiba na

7.320 翻手作雲覆手雨 *Te o hirugaeseba kumo to nari te o kutsugaeseba ame.*

Palm up it's cloudy, palm down it rains.

ZGS 7.254, Shiba 194. 杜甫貧交行

7.321 的的分明箭後路 *Teki-teki funmyō nari sengo no michi.*

Clearly apparent, the flight of the arrow.

Heki 56 Verse.

ZGS na, ZRKS 7.211, Shiba 182, ZGJI 596

7.322 信手拈來着着親 *Te ni makasete nenji kitareba jaku-jaku shitashi.*

Let your hand fall where it may, and whatever it grasps feels just right.

Shiba 187: 任 instead of 信.

ZGS na, ZRKS 7.208, Shiba 174, 187

7.323 鐵牛擎出黄金角 *Tetsugyū sasageidasu ōgon no tsuno.*

The iron ox offers up a golden horn.

ZGS na, ZRKS 7.77, Shiba 182, ZGJI 365: 骨 bone instead of 角 horn.

7.324 鐵作心肝也皺眉 *Tessa no shinkan mo mata mayu o shibamu.*

Even someone with cast-iron guts would frown.

ZGS na, ZRKS 7.367, Shiba 182, ZGJI 365

7.325 鐵山突兀拄天地 *Tessan tokkotsu to shite tenchi o sasou.*

The iron mountain thrusts up, supporting heaven and earth.

ZGS 7.255, ZRKS 7.68, Shiba 183, ZGJI 365

7.326 鐵樹花開別是春 *Tetsuju hana hiraku betsu ni kore haru.*

The iron tree sends out flowers, this is truly spring.

ZGS 7.256, ZRKS 7.577, Shiba 183, ZGJI 365, ZGJT 321

7.327 鐵樹花開二月春 *Tetsuju hana hiraku nigatsu no haru.*

The iron tree blossomed in the second month.

See also 14.699.

ZGS na, ZRKS 7.310, Shiba 183, ZGJI 385

7.328 鐵鎚擊碎黃金骨 *Tettsui gekisai su ōgon no kotsu.*

The iron hammer shatters the golden bone.

Heki 99 Verse.

ZGS na, ZRKS 7.457, Shiba 183, ZGJI 365

7.329 鐵壁銀山絕來往 *Teppeki ginzan raiō o zessu.*

Iron walls and silver mountains cut off all coming and going.

ZGS 7.257, ZRKS 7.95, Shiba 183, ZGJI 366, KZS #816

7.330 鐵鞭擊碎驪龍珠 *Tetsuben gekisai su riryū no tama.*

The iron whip shatters the ⌜black dragon's pearl⌝.

ZGS 7.258, ZRKS 7.397, Shiba 183, ZGJI 366

7.331 手把玉鞭敲金門 *Te ni gyokuben o totte kinmon o tataku.*

He takes the jade whip in hand and raps on the golden gate.

ZGS 7.259, ZRKS 7.115, Shiba na, ZGJI 365, KZS #788

7.332 信手拗折珊瑚枝 *Te ni makasete ōsetsu su sangoshi.*

He lets his hands break every ⌜coral⌝ branch they touch.

ZGS 7.260, ZRKS 7.169, Shiba na, ZGJI 365

7.333 出頭天外笑呵呵 *Tengai ni shuttō shite warai ka-ka.*

Step outside heaven and laugh, "Ha! Ha!"

ZGS 7.261, ZRKS 7.460, Shiba na, ZGJI 366

7.334 天明賊人投古井 *Ten akete zokujin kosei ni tō su.*

When dawn comes, the ⌜thieves⌝ throw themselves into the old well.

ZGS na, ZRKS 7.498, Shiba 183, ZGJI 366

7.335 天下衲僧跳不出 *Tenka no nōsō chōfushutsu.*

No monk under heaven can jump out.

Heki 1 Main Case Comm., 4 Main Case *agyo*, 8 Main Case *agyo*, etc.

ZGS 7.262, ZRKS 7.112, Shiba na, ZGJI 366, ZGJT 325, KZS #823

7.336 換卻天下人眼睛 *Tenka no hito no ganzei o kankyaku su.*

He replaces the eyeballs of everyone under heaven.

ZGS 7.263, ZRKS 7.581, Shiba 159

7.337 坐斷天下人舌頭 *Tenka no hito no zettō o zadan su.*

He cuts off the tongues of everyone in the world.

Heki 4 Main Case *agyo*, 5 Main Case Comm., 8 Intro., 10 Verse Comm., etc.

ZGS 7.264, ZRKS 7.223, Shiba 167, ZGJI 355, ZGJT 153

7.338 電光石火存機變 *Denkō sekka* ⌜*ki*⌝*hen o sonsu.*

In the flash of a spark he adapts to change.

Heki 26 Verse.

ZGS na, ZRKS 7.338, Shiba 184

7.339 天上人間唯我知 *Tenjō jinkan tada ware shiru.*

Among gods and humans, only I know.

Heki 73 Verse.

ZGS 7.265, ZRKS 7.505, Shiba na, ZGJI 366, ZGJT 325

7.340 轉身蹈破鐵崑崙 *Tenshin tōha su tetsu* ⌜*konron*⌝.

Wheeling his body around, he stamps to pieces the iron ball.

ZGS 7.266, ZRKS 7.79, Shiba na

7.341 倚天長劍逼人寒 *Ten ni yoru chōken hito ni sematte susamaji.*

The long ⌜**sword**⌝ **standing against the sky chills all it approaches.**

ZGS 7.267, ZRKS 7.146, Shiba 160, ZGJI 367, ZGJT 12, KZS #797

7.342 兎子懷胎産大蟲 *Toshi kaitai daichū o sanzu.*

The rabbit conceives and gives birth to a tiger.

See *Heki* 90.

ZGS na, ZRKS 7.341, Shiba 184

7.343 桃花似錦柳如烟 *Tōka wa nishiki ni nitari yanagi wa kemuri no gotoshi.*

The ⌜**peach**⌝ **blossoms are like brocade, the willows like mist.**

ZGS na, ZRKS 7.349, Shiba 185, ZGJI 368

7.344 凍合玉樓寒起粟 *Tōgo gyokurō kan zoku o okosu.*

The jeweled pavilion is frozen shut, the cold makes goosebumps rise.

ZGS 7.268, Shiba na

7.345 同死同生爲君訣 *Dōshi dōshō kimi ga tame ni kessu.*

To die together, to live together—for you I've decided.

Heki 15 Verse.

ZGS na, ZRKS 7.544, Shiba 185, ZGJI 369, ZGJT 346

7.346 不離當處常湛然 *Tōsho o hanarezu tsune ni tannen.*

Not apart from right-here, always clear.

ZGS 7.269, ZRKS 7.16, Shiba 192, KZS #658, Yung Chia, "Song of Enlightenment".

7.347 同中還有不同意 *Dōchū kaette fudōi ari.*

It's precisely those who are alike who do not get along.

ZGS na, ZRKS 7.371, Shiba 185

7.348 洞中春色人難見 *Tōchū no shunshoku hito migatashi.*

Spring colors inside a cave are hard for people to see.

ZGS 7.270, Shiba 184

7.349 洞房深處説私情 *Tōbō fukaki tokoro shijō o toku.*

Deep within a vaulted cavern I speak my private feeling.

ZGS 7.271, Shiba 184

7.350 蟷螂張斧當隆車 *Tōrō wa ono o hatte ryūsha ni ataru.*

The praying mantis, waving its claws, attacks the carriage.

ZGS 7.272, Shiba na

7.351 燈籠露柱打筋斗 *Tōrō rochū kinto o utsu.*

The lamps and posts turn somersaults.

ZGS 7.273, Shiba na

7.352 兎角龜毛過別山 *Tokaku kimō betsuzan o sugu.*

⌜Rabbit horns and turtle hairs⌝ lie across another mountain.

ZGS 7.274, Shiba na

7.353 德行顏淵閔子騫 *Tokugyō gan'en binshiken.*

For virtuous action—⌜Yen Yüan⌝ and ⌜Min Tzu-ch'ien⌝.

Analects XI, 2.

ZGS 7.275, Shiba na

7.354 德不孤兮必有隣 *Toku wa ko narazu kanarazu tonari ari.*

The virtuous are never alone—they always have neighbors.

Analects IV, 25.

ZGS 7.276, ZRKS 7.156, Shiba na

7.355 毒龍行處草不生 *Dokuryū yuku tokoro kusa shō sezu.*

Where the poison dragon goes, weeds do not grow.

ZGS 7.277, ZRKS 7.565, Shiba 1886, ZGJI 369, KZS #785

7.356 髑髏識盡喜何立 *Dokuro shiki tsukite yorokobi nanzo rissen.*

The skull is exhausted consciousness, how can joy arise?

Heki 2 Verse.

ZGS 7.278, Shiba na

7.357 杜鵑啼在百花枝 *Token naite hyakka no eda ni ari.*

Cuckoos cry in a hundred flowering branches.

ZGS 7.279, ZRKS 7.29, Shiba 184, ZGJI 635

7.358 杜鵑啼處花狼藉 *Token naku tokoro hana rōzeki.*

Where the cuckoo calls, flowers [fall] in wild disarray.

ZGS na, ZRKS 7.279, Shiba 184, ZGJI 367, ZGJT 331

7.359 兜率與泥犁同境 *Tosotsu to nairi to dōkyō.*

Heaven and hell, the same realm.

ZGS 7.280, ZRKS 7.479, Shiba na

7.360 曇華再發一枝春 *Donge futatabi hiraku isshi no haru.*

The ⌜*uḍumbara*⌝ tree blooms again—spring in a single branch.

ZGS 7.281, ZRKS 7.108, Shiba na, ZGJI 370

7.361 那吒十面千眸動 *Nata jūmen senbō ugoku.*

⌜Nata's⌝ ten faces and thousand eyes are moving.

ZGS 7.282, ZRKS 7.100, Shiba na, ZGJI 370

7.362 七生人間滅此賊 *Nana tabi ningen ni umarete kono zoku o messen.*

Be born a human seven times and eradicate these ⌜thieves⌝.

ZGS 7.283, Shiba na

7.363 南山打鼓北山舞 *Nanzan ni tsutsumi o uteba hokuzan ni mau.*

When they beat the drum on South Mountain, they dance on North Mountain.

ZGS 7.284, ZRKS 7.30, Shiba 186, ZGJI 370, ZGJT 356, KZS #665

7.364 南山北山轉滂霈 *Nanzan hokuzan utata hōhai.*

On South Mountain and North Mountain, never-ending rain.

ZGS 7.285: 雱 instead of 滂.

ZGS 7.285, Shiba 186

7.365 南山鼈鼻要驚人 *Nanzan no beppi hito o odorokasan koto o yōsu.*

Use the turtle-nose monster of South Mountain to scare people.

See *Heki* 22.

ZGS na, ZRKS 7.331, Shiba 186

7.366 乳虎墜地氣食牛 *Nyūko chi ni ochite ki ushi o kurau.*

The moment a newborn tiger touches the ground, it wants to eat an ox.

ZGS 7.286, Shiba 187

7.367 似則似是則不是 *Nitaru koto wa sunawachi nitari ze naru koto wa sunawachi ze narazu.*

As for resemblance, it certainly resembles; but as for being it, it certainly is not.

Heki 1 Main Case Comm., 8 Main Case Comm.

ZGS 7.287, ZRKS 7.543, Shiba na, ZGJI 371

7.368 日裏麒麟看北斗 *Nichiri no kirin hokuto o miyo.*

For the ⌜*ch'i-lin*⌝ in the sun, look to the North Star.

ZGS na, ZRKS 7.526, Shiba 187, ZGJI 371

7.369 人間天上一般春 *Ningen tenjō ippan no haru.*

Throughout heaven and earth, spring everywhere.

Variant: *jinkan* instead of *ningen.*

ZGS 7.288, ZRKS 7.376, Shiba na, ZGJI 371

7.370 鼠入錢筒伎已窮 *Nezumi sentō ni itte gi sude ni kiwamaru.*

The rat that crawled into the money tube is at its wit's end.

ZGS 7.222: read *so* instead of *nezumi*; 技 instead of 伎. A bamboo tube, whose inside diameter matched the size of coins, was used as a money container.

ZGS 7.222, ZRKS 7.545, Shiba 178, ZD #49

7.371 拈來瓦礫是黃金 *Nenji kitareba gareki mo kore ōgon.*

Play with it and even broken tile is gold.

ZGS 7.289, ZRKS 7.226, Shiba 187, ZGJI 371, KZS #772. GKFGS 1.189.

7.372 野有伏兵雁行亂 *No ni fukuhei areba gangyō midareru.*

If soldiers are hiding in the field, the flight of the geese is disturbed.

ZGS 7.290, Shiba na

7.373 白雲鎖斷萬重關 *Hakuun sadan su banjū no kan.*

The white clouds cut off the ten-thousand-tiered barrier.

ZGS 7.291, ZRKS 7.62, Shiba 188, ZGJI 373

7.374 白雲重疊鎖青山 *Hakuun jūjō seizan o tozasu.*

Piles of white clouds block the blue mountains.

ZGS 7.292, ZRKS 7.61, Shiba na

7.375 白雲斷處家山妙 *Hakuun tayuru tokoro kasan myō nari.*

Where the white clouds part, my mountain home is wonderful.

ZGS 7.293, ZRKS 7.52, Shiba 188, ZGJI 373

7.376 白雲片片嶺上飛 *Hakuun hen-pen reijō ni tobu.*

Tufts of white cloud float over the mountain peak.

ZGS 7.294, ZRKS 7.165, Shiba 188

7.377 馬駒蹈殺天下人 *Baku tōsatsu su tenka no hito.*

The colt will trample to death everybody in the world.

Heki 73 Verse.

ZGS 7.295, ZRKS 7.230, Shiba 188, ZGJI 372, ZGJT 378

7.378 白雲流水共悠悠 *Hakuun ryūsui tomo ni yū-yū.*

White clouds and flowing streams—together serene into the distance.

ZGS na, Shiba 189, ZGJI 373

7.379 柏樹子話有賊機 *Hakujushi no wa ni zok⌜ki⌝ ari.*

The story of the Cypress Tree has the power to rob you.

Verse by Kanzan Kokushi 關山國師: 庭前の柏樹, "The Cypress Tree in the Garden."

ZGS na, Shiba 189

7.380 取鏌鎁劍爭殺活 *Bakuya no ken o totte sakkatsu o arasou.*

Fighting with the ⌜Mo Yeh sword⌝ in hand, he kills and brings to life.

Heki 9 Intro.

ZGS 7.296, ZRKS 7.174, Shiba na, ZGJI 373, KZS #743

7.381 白浪滔天平地起 *Hakurō tōten heichi ni okoru.*

From a flat plain rise white waves that leap to the skies.

Heki 50 Verse.

ZGS 7.297, ZRKS 7.243, Shiba 189, ZGJI 373

7.382 始覺全身在帝鄉 *Hajimete oboyu zenshin no teikyō ni aru koto o.*

I suddenly realized I was totally inside the imperial capital.

ZGS 7.298, ZRKS 7.554, Shiba 170, GKFGS 2.97-8

7.383 始知師有此機鋒 *Hajimete shiru shi ni kono ⌜ki⌝hō aru koto o.*

Suddenly I saw that the master had this Zen blade.

ZGS 7.299, Shiba na

7.384 波斯説夢入市中 *Hashi yume o toite shichū ni iru.*

The ⌜Persian⌝ explains the dream and enters the marketplace.

ZGS 7.300, Shiba na, ZGJI 372

7.385 如馬前相撲相似 *Bazen no sōbaku no gotoku ni ainitari.*

It's like ⌜wrestling in front of horses⌝.

Heki 26 Main Case Comm., 95 Main Case Comm.

ZGS 7.301, Shiba na

7.386 八兩元來是半斤 *Hachiryō ganrai kore hankin.*

Eight ounces are basically half a pound.

See ⌜Catty⌝.

ZGS 7.302, ZRKS 7.170, Shiba na, ZGJI 374

7.387 八角磨盤空裏走 *Hakkaku no maban kūri ni washiru.*

The ⌜eight-cornered mortar stone⌝ wheels across the sky.

Heki 47 Main Case *agyo.*

ZGS 7.303, ZRKS 7.102, Shiba 189, ZGJI 373, ZGJT 383, ZD #133, KZS 776

7.388 八臂那吒行正令 *Happi no nata shōrei o gyōzu.*

Eight-armed ⌜Nata⌝ carries out his orders.

ZGS 7.304, ZRKS 7.101, Shiba 189 and ZGJI 374: 行正令 "wields his sticks." KZS #819

7.389 跛鼈拂眉立晩風 *Habetsu mayu o haratte banpū ni tatsu.*

The lame tortoise touches up its ⌜eyebrows⌝ and sits in the evening breeze.

ZGS 7.305, Shiba na

7.390 跛鼈盲龜入空谷 *Habetsu mōki kūkoku ni iru.*

The lame tortoise and the blind turtle enter the empty valley.

Heki 12 Verse.

ZGS 7.306, Shiba na, ZGJI 372

7.391 破襴衫裏包清風 *Haransanri ni seifū o tsutsumu.*

He wraps up the pure wind in a torn robe.

ZGS 7.307, Shiba 188

7.392 出林猛虎鼓唇牙 *Hayashi o izuru mōko shinga o ko su.*

Coming out of the forest, the fierce tiger smacks its lips and fangs.

ZGS 7.308, ZRKS 7.269, Shiba na, ZGJI 374, KZS #722

7.393 幡竿尖上鐵龍頭 *Hankansenjō no tetsu ryūtō.*

On the point of the banner pole, the iron dragon's head.

ZGS 7.309, ZRKS 7.377, Shiba na

7.394 萬象之中獨露身 *Banzō shichū dokuroshin.*

Among the ⌜ten thousand things⌝, one body alone appears.

Heki 6 Verse Comm.

ZGS 7.310, ZRKS 7.476, Shiba 190, ZGJI374, ZGJT 387, KZS #742

7.395 萬重關鎖一時開 *Banjū no kansa ichiji ni hiraku.*

Ten thousand chain barriers break open all at once.

ZGS 7.311, ZRKS 7.71, Shiba na, ZGJI 374

7.396 和盤托出夜明珠 *Ban ni wa shite takushutsu su yameiju.*

On a matching plate, he arranges mounds of ⌜night-shining jewels⌝.

Shiba 198: *yamei* instead of *no tama yameju.*

ZGS 7.312, ZRKS 7.113, Shiba 198, ZGJI 375, KZS #786

7.397 以半斤放向和尚 *Hankin o motte ⌜oshō⌝ ni hōkō su.*

He throws half a pound at the abbot.

See ⌜Catty⌝.

ZGS 7.313, Shiba na

7.398 萬里區區獨往還 *Banri ku-ku to shite hitori ōkan su.*

Ten thousand miles to faraway places, alone he goes back and forth.

Heki 29 Verse.

ZGS 7.314, ZRKS 7.257, Shiba 190, KZS #716

7.399 萬里無雲孤月圓 *Banri kumo naku kogetsu madoka nari.*

No clouds for ten thousand miles, the lone ⌜moon⌝ is a perfect sphere.

ZGS 7.315, ZRKS 7.585, Shiba 190, ZGJI 375

7.400 飯裏忽逢沙一粒 *Hanri tachimachi suna ichiryū ni au.*

In the middle of the cooked rice he suddenly comes upon a grain of sand.

Shiba 189: 砂 instead of 沙.

ZGS 7.316, ZRKS 7.551, Shiba 189, ZGJI 374

7.401 封微子啓爲殷後 *Bishikei o fū shite in no ato to nasu.*

He enfeoffed Wei Tzu-ch'i to carry on the lineage of Yin.

When ⌜Wu Wang⌝ established a new dynasty by overthrowing Chou, the last evil king of the Yin Dynasty, he also enfeoffed Wei Tzu-ch'i, a relative to Chou, to carry on ancestral sacrifices to the Yin. See also ⌜Chieh⌝ and ⌜Chou⌝.

ZGS 7.317, Shiba na

7.402 美玉精金無定價 *Bigyoku seikin teika nashi.*

Beautiful jewelry and refined gold have no fixed price.

KZS #723: *Migyoku seikin jōka nashi.*

ZGS na, ZRKS 7.132, Shiba 190, ZGJI 376

7.403 美食不中飽人喫 *Bishoku hōjin no kitsu ni atarazu.*

Delicious food does not appeal to a person with a full stomach.

MMK 17.

ZGS 7.318, ZRKS 7.126, Shiba 190, ZGJI 376, ZGJT 392

7.404 逼折貶向火爐頭 *Hissetsu shite karotō ni henkō su.*

He broke it and threw it into the ⌜fire pit⌝.

ZGS 7.319, Shiba na

7.405 陷人坑子年年滿 *Hito o otoshiiru kōsu nen-nen mitsu.*

The man-trap fills up year by year.

ZGS 7.320, ZRKS 7.196, Shiba na, ZGJI 376, KZS #748, GKFGS 1.155

7.406 咬人獅子爪牙張 *Hito o kamu shishi sōge haru.*

The man-eating lion flexes its ⌜claws and fangs⌝.

ZGS 7.321, ZRKS 7.316, Shiba na, ZGJI 377, KZS #691

7.407 令人長憶李將軍 *Hito o shite nagaku ri shōgun o omowashimu.*

It will make people remember ⌜General Li⌝ for a long time.

Heki 71 Verse.

ZGS 7.322, ZRKS 7.234, Shiba na, ZGJI 666, ZGJT 479

7.408 揚人是非作什麼 *Hito no zehi o agete nan to ka nasan.*

Judging people right and wrong, what do you think you are doing?

ZGS 7.323, Shiba na

7.409 入火眞金色轉鮮 *Hi ni itte shinkin iro utata azayaka nari.*

When true gold is put into fire, its color becomes even brighter.

ZGJI 375: *akiraka* instead of *azayaka.*

ZGS 7.324, ZRKS 7.262, Shiba 187, ZGJI 375, ZGJT 361, ZD #141

7.410 捏不成團劈不開 *Hineredomo dan to narazu tsunzakedomo hirakezu.*

Though kneaded, it won't make a ball; though chopped, it won't split.

ZGS na, ZRKS 7.268, Shiba 187, ZGJI 371, KZS #715

7.411 日到西峯影漸長 *Hi wa seihō ni itatte kage yōyaku nagashi.*

As the sun nears the western mountains, the shadows grow gradually longer.

ZGS 7.325, ZRKS 7.27, Shiba na, ZGJI 375

7.412 日出東方夜落西 *Hi wa tōhō yori ide, yoru nishi ni otsu.*

The sun rises in the east and at night sets in the west.

ZGS 7.326, ZRKS 7.13, Shiba 186, ZGJI 376, ZGJT 359

7.413 剔起眉毛還不見 *Bimō o tekki sureba kaette miezu.*

Plucking out the ⌜eyebrows⌝ makes it even more difficult to see.

Heki 22 Verse.

ZGS 7.327, ZRKS 7.137, Shiba na, ZGJI 376

7.414 百戰金吾出鳳城 *Hyaku sen no kingo hōjō o izu.*

Chin-wu, victor of one hundred battles, leaves the Phoenix City.

Chih Chin-wu 執金吾, a military officer under Han Emperor Wu, was famous for fighting a hundred battles and winning a hundred times (ZGJI 377; GKFGS 1.100).

ZGS na, ZRKS 7.187, Shiba 191, KZS #740, GKFGS 1.100

7.415 百草頭邊風凛凛 *Hyakusō tōhen kaze rin-rin.*

Over the heads of the hundred grasses, the wind is biting cold.

ZGS na, ZRKS 7.590, Shiba 191, ZGJI 377

7.416 百花春至爲誰開 *Hyakka haru itatte ta ga tame ni ka hiraku.*

The hundred flowers that come with the spring, for whom do they bloom?

Heki 5 Verse.

ZGS na, ZRKS 7.516, Shiba 191

7.417 百雜碎兮鐵團欒 *Hyaku zassai tetsu danran.*

Smashed to smithereens, the iron ball.

ZGS 7.328, Shiba na, ZGJI 310

7.418 百尺竿頭坐底人 *Hyakushaku kantō ni za suru tei no hito.*

The one who sits atop a hundred-foot pole.

MMK 46.

ZGS 7.329, ZRKS 7.32, Shiba 191, ZGJI 377, KZS #667

7.419 百姓日用不相知 *Hyakusei wa hibi ni mochiite aishirazu.*

Ordinary people do not know that they use it every day.

ZGS 7.330, ZRKS 7.133, Shiba 191, KZS #725

7.420 百錬黃金再入爐 *Hyakuren no ōgon futatabi ro ni iru.*

Gold refined one hundred times goes back into the furnace.

ZGS 7.331, ZRKS 7.237, Shiba na

7.421 百錬精金無變色 *Hyakuren no seikin henshoku nashi.*

Gold refined one hundred times does not discolor.

ZGS 7.332, Shiba na

7.422 病身最覺風霜早 *Byōshin mottomo obou fūsō no hayaki koto o.*

The sick first feel the onset of wind and frost.

ZGS 7.333, ZRKS 7.9, Shiba na, ZGJI 378

7.423 風露新香隱逸花 *Fūro arata ni kōbashi in'ikka.*

Wind and dew and the fresh scent of chrysanthemums.

ZGS na, Shiba 192

7.424 不斷煩惱入涅槃 *Fudan bonnō nyū nehan.*

Without cutting off delusive passion, enter nirvana.

Shiba 191: *Bonnō o danzezu shite nehan ni iru.*

ZGS 7.334, Shiba 191

7.425 佛心之子毒蛇心 *Busshin no shi dokuda no shin.*

The child of the Buddha-mind is the mind of the poisonous snake.

ZGS 7.335, ZRKS 7.568, Shiba na, ZGJI 378

7.426 騎佛殿出山門去 *Butsuden ni notte sanmon o idesaru.*

Riding the Buddha Hall, he passes out the Mountain Gate.

Heki 28 Verse *agyo*. See「Seven-hall complex」.

ZGS 7.336, ZRKS 7.103, Shiba

7.427 隨分著衣喫飯去 *Bun ni shitagatte jakue kippan ni shi saru.*

Each in your place, just get dressed and eat your food.

ZGS na, Shiba 176

7.428 糞火堆上話長短 *Funkataijō wa chōtan.*

On a smoking shit pile, he discourses on this and that.

ZGS na, Shiba 192

7.429 忿怒那吒失卻威 *Fundo no nata i o shikkyaku su.*

Angry ⌜Nata⌝ has lost his authority.

ZGS 7.337, Shiba na

7.430 忿怒那吒撞帝鐘 *Fundo no nata teishō o tsuku.*

Angry ⌜Nata⌝ strikes the imperial bell.

ZGS 7.338, Shiba na

7.431 丙丁童子來求火 *Heitei dōji kitarite hi o motomu.*

The lamp-lighter novice comes seeking fire.

Story in *Heki* 7 Main Case Comm.

ZGS na, ZRKS 7.285, Shiba 194, ZGJI 379, ZGJT 412

7.432 霹靂過頭猶瞌睡 *Hekireki kōbe o suguredomo nao kassui su.*

Though thunder booms overhead, still he sleeps like a log.

ZGS 7.339, Shiba 193, ZGJI 379

7.433 得便宜是落便宜 *Bengi o uru kore bengi ni otsu.*

To gain an advantage is to be trapped by advantage.

Heki 66 Verse.

ZGS 7.340, ZRKS 7.225, Shiba na, ZGJT 352, KZS #770

7.434 鳳離金網鶴抛籠 *Hō kinmō o hanare tsuru kago o nageutsu.*

The phoenix escaped the golden net, the crane threw over its cage.

ZGS 7.341, Shiba 193, GKFGS 2.6.

7.435 木人不恐獅子吼 *Bokujin shishiku o osorezu.*

The ⌜wooden man⌝ does not fear the lion's roar.

ZGS na, ZRKS 7.345, Shiba 195, ZGJI 380

7.436 星在秤兮不在盤 *Hoshi wa shō ni atte ban ni arazu.*

The graduations are on the balance arm, not in the balance pan.

Heki 39 Verse.

ZGS na, ZRKS 7.420, Shiba 176, ZGJI 380

7.437 奪得寶珠村裏賣 *Hōju o ubaiete sonri ni uru.*

He managed to steal jewels and then sell them in the village.

ZGS 7.342, ZRKS 7.158, Shiba na, KZS #731

7.438 棒頭有眼明如日 *Bōtō ni manako ari akiraka naru koto hi no gotoshi.*

On the staff there is an eye bright as the sun.

Heki 20 Main Case Comm., 65 Main Case *agyo.*

ZGS na, ZRKS 7.312, Shiba 193, ZGJI 380, ZGJT 428

7.439 茫茫四海少知音 *Bō-bōtaru shikai chiin mare nari.*

The four seas are vast, a true「intimate」is rare indeed.

Heki 99 Verse *agyo.*

ZGS 7.343, ZRKS 7.247, Shiba na, ZGJI 380, ZGJT 427

7.440 牡丹花下睡猫兒 *Botankaka no suimyōji.*

Under the peony blossom, a sleeping cat.

ZGS 7.344, ZRKS 7.406, Shiba 193, ZGJI 380

7.441 不離魔界入佛界 *Makai o hanarezu shite bukkai ni iru.*

Without leaving the demon world, enter the Buddha world.

ZGS 7.345, Shiba 192

7.442 卷盡五千四十八 *Makitsukusu gosen yonjū hachi.*

Roll up the 5,048.

Heki 15 Verse *agyo.* In this lifetime, the Buddha's teaching amounted to 5,048 sutra rolls (ZGJI 381).

ZGS 7.346, ZRKS 7.120, Shiba na, ZGJI 381, ZGJT 107

7.443 又是千年茄子根 *Mata kore sennen nasu no ne.*

Again this thousand-year-old eggplant root.

ZGS 7.347, Shiba na

7.444 也勝秋露滴芙渠 *Mata shūro no fukyo ni shitataru ni masareri.*

It surpasses even lotus leaves glistening with autumn dew.

Heki 36 Main Case.

ZGS na, ZRKS 7.514, Shiba 195

7.445 開眼堂堂入鑊湯 *Manako o hiraite dō-dō to shite kakutō ni iru.*

With open eyes he fearlessly enters the boiling cauldron.

ZGS 7.348, ZRKS 7.300, Shiba na, ZGJI 331, ZGJT 56

7.446 萬壑松風供一啜 *Mangaku no shōfū ittotsu ni kyōsu.*

In ten thousand valleys, the ⌜pine winds⌝ all together take a sip.

Shōun-ji: *bangaku* instead of *mangaku.*

ZGS na, Shiba 190, GKFGS 1.17

7.447 滿架薔薇一院香 *Manka no shōbi ichiin kambashi.*

The tables are laden with roses, the entire temple is fragrant.

ZGS na, ZRKS 7.364, Shiba 194, ZGJI 381

7.448 滿船明月載得歸 *Mansen no meigetsu noseete kaeru.*

I loaded my boat full of moonlight and came home.

ZGS 7.349, ZRKS 7.172, Shiba 194

7.449 滿天風雨毛骨寒 *Manten no fūu mōkotsu samushi.*

Sky full of wind-driven rain, I'm cold to my hair and bones.

ZGS 7.350, ZRKS 7.111, Shiba na, ZGJI 382

7.450 萬兩黄金也合消 *Manryō no ōgon mo mata shōsubeshi.*

Even a ton of gold will dwindle away.

ZGS na, ZRKS 7.138, Shiba 190, ZGJI 381

7.451 汲水僧歸林下寺 *Mizu o kumu sō wa rinka no tera ni kaeru.*

The monk who drew the water returns to his forest temple.

See also 14.648.

ZGS 7.352, ZRKS 7.25, Shiba 335, ZGJT 86

7.452 水自茫茫花自紅 *Mizu wa onozukara bō-bō hana onozukara kurenai nari.*

The waters are naturally vast, the flowers are naturally red.

Ten Oxherding Pictures, 9.

ZGS 7.353, ZRKS 7.384, Shiba 175, ZGJI 382

7.453 水欺龍臥出前山 *Mizu garyū o azamuite zensan o izu.*

The waters steal by the sleeping dragon and leave by the mountains in front.

Garyū o azamuite 欺臥龍 is literally "to deceive the sleeping dragon." This describes the way a stream quietly flows around dragon-shaped hills. For "mountains in front," see ⌜Landscape⌝.

ZGS 7.354, ZRKS 7.403, Shiba na, ZGJI 382, ZGJT 407

7.454 塡溝塞壑無人會 *Mizo ni michi tani ni fusagaru hito no e suru nashi.*

It floods the channels and overflows the valleys, and yet no one understands.

Heki 16 Verse *agyo.*

ZGS na, Shiba 184, KZS #712

7.455 看盡湘南淸絕地 *Mitsukusu shōnan seizetsu no chi.*

I have seen all of Hsiang-nan, a land of surpassing purity.

ZGS 7.355, ZRKS 7.72, Shiba 159, KZS #809

7.456 密密工夫不漏風 *Mitsu-mitsu taru kufū kaze o morasazu.*

Meticulous effort, not even the wind can leak through.

ZGS 7.356, ZRKS 7.549, Shiba 194, ZGJI 382

7.457 看時不見暗昏昏 *Miru toki miezu an kon-kon.*

When you look, you cannot see—utter darkness.

Heki 86 Main Case.

ZGS 7.357, ZRKS 7.136, Shiba na, KZS #729

7.458 明眼衲僧會不得 *Myōgen no nōsō e futoku.*

The clear-eyed ⌜patch-robed monk⌝ cannot understand.

Heki 73 Verse.

ZGS 7.358, ZRKS 7.395, Shiba 195

7.459 無角鐵牛眠少室 *Mukaku no tetsugyū shōshitsu ni nemuru.*

The hornless iron ox sleeps in the little room.

ZGS 7.359, ZRKS 7.485, Shiba 194, ZGJI 383, ZGJT 44

7.460 無孔鐵鎚生節目 *Muku no tettsui setsumoku o shōzu.*

On the ⌜iron hammerhead without a socket⌝, seams and knots appear.

ZGS 7.360, ZRKS 7.373, Shiba na, ZGJI 383

7.461 無孔鐵鎚當面擲 *Muku no tettsui tōmen ni nageutsu.*

Throw the ⌜iron hammerhead without a socket⌝ right in his face.

Heki 29 Main Case *agyo.*

ZGS 7.361, ZRKS 7.92, Shiba 195, ZGJI 383, ZGJT 441, KZS #811

7.462 無相光中常自在 *Musō kōchū tsune ni jizai.*

Within formless light, always free.

ZGS 7.362, Shiba na

7.463 明月蘆花君自看 *Meigetsu roka kimi mizukara miyo.*

You must see for yourself the reed flowers in moonlight.

Heki 62 Verse.

ZGS 7.363, ZRKS 7.415, Shiba 195, ZGJI 384, ZD #143

7.464 明月蘆花不似他 *Meigetsu roka ta ni shikazu.*

Bright ⌜moon⌝ and [white] reed flowers do not resemble each other.

See 14.736.

ZGS 7.364, ZRKS 7.154, Shiba na, ZGJT 445

7.465 吐出明珠照膽寒 *Meiju o hakidashi tan o terashite susamaji.*

It spews forth so brilliant a jewel, its light chills me to the core.

ZGS na, ZRKS 7.295, Shiba 184, ZGJI 384, KZS #677, GKFGS 1.2

7.466 明窓下古鏡照心 *Meisō no moto kokyō shōshin.*

By the light of the window, illuminating one's mind in the ancient mirror.

An ancient text was likened to a mirror, in whose wisdom one could see one's own mind illuminated.

ZGS 7.365, Shiba na

7.467 吹面不寒楊柳風 *Men o fukedomo samukarazu yōryū no kaze.*

Though it blows on my face, it is not cold—the willow wind.

ZGS 7.366, ZRKS 7.119, Shiba 176

7.468 出門不踏來時路 *Mon o idete wa fumazu raiji no michi.*

Leaving from the gate, I do not walk the road by which I came.

ZRKS 7.118: 出門不蹈來時路.

7.469 問處分明答處親 *Monjo funmyō nareba tōsho shitashi.*

Get the question clear and you are already close to the answer.

ZGS 7.369, ZRKS 7.157, Shiba na, ZGJI 386, ZGJT 453, KZS #730

7.470 夜半金雞生鐵卵 *Yahan no kinkei tetsuran o shōzu.*

The golden cock at midnight lays iron eggs.

ZGS 7.370, Shiba na, KZS #812

7.471 夜半金雞帶雪飛 *Yahan no kinkei yuki o obite tobu.*

Wreathed in snow, the golden cock flies at midnight.

ZGS na, ZRKS 7.523, Shiba 196

7.472 山帶夕陽半邊紅 *Yama wa sekiyō o obite hanpen kurenai nari.*

Mountains tinged by the setting sun, half around us is red.

ZGS 7.371, Shiba 169, ZGJI 386

7.473 把斷要關絕往來 *Yōkan o hadan shite ōrai o zessu.*

Shut down the main checkpoints, cut off all coming and going.

ZGS na, ZRKS 7.109, Shiba 188

7.474 善用者不露鋒鋩 *Yoku mochiuru mono wa hōbō o arawasazu.*

A seasoned user does not show the tip of his spear.

ZGS 7.372, ZRKS 7.37, Shiba 178, ZGJI 387

7.475 能使爺錢何故聻 *Yoku yasen o tsukau nani ga yue zo nii.*

Why is he using so much of his father's money?

ZGS 7.373, Shiba na

7.476 呼來山頭一片雲 *Yobikitasu santō ippen no kumo.*

I call over the lone cloud on the mountain top.

ZGS 7.374, Shiba 164

7.477 來者須教喪膽魂 *Raisha wa subekaraku tankon o sōseshimubeshi.*

All comers will certainly lose their lives.

ZGS na, ZRKS 7.330, Shiba 196, ZGJI 332

7.478 來來去去作什麼 *Rai-rai kyo-kyo shite nani o ka nasu.*

Coming and going, coming and going, what do you think you are doing?

Rinzai-roku §48, §64.

ZGS 7.375, ZRKS 7.541, Shiba na, ZGJI 387

7.479 落花流水甚茫茫 *Rakka ryūsui hanahada bō-bō.*

Falling flowers, flowing waters, limitless, vast.

Heki 25 Verse.

ZGS 7.376, ZRKS 7.434, Shiba 196

7.480 狸奴白牯放毫光 *Ri'nu byakko gōkō o hanatsu.*

The badger and the white bull emit a glorious light.

Gōkō 毫光 "glorious radiance" is the brilliant light which shines from between the ⸢eyebrows⸣ of Buddha (BKGDJT 405).

ZGS 7.377, ZRKS 7.130, Shiba 197, ZGJI 388, ZD #134

7.481 龍袖拂開全體現 *Ryūshū hokkai shite zentai arawasu.*

The dragon shakes his sleeves showing his whole body.

Shiba 197: *ryōshū* instead of *ryūshū.*

ZGS 7.378, Shiba 197, KZS #745

7.482 龍在潛淵鶴在巣 *Ryū wa sen'en ni arite, tsuru wa su ni ari.*

Dragons live in deep secret pools, cranes live in nests.

ZGS 7.379, ZRKS 7.443, Shiba 197, ZGJI 388, GKFGS 1.140

7.483 不透龍門待幾時 *Ryūmon o tōrazumba ikutoki ka matan.*

If you won't pass through the dragon gate, what are you waiting for?

ZGS 7.380, ZRKS 7.24, Shiba na, ZGJI 388, KZS #661

7.484 兩箇猢猻探水月 *Ryōko no koson suigetsu o saguru.*

A pair of monkeys are reaching for the 「moon」 in the water.

ZGS 7.381, ZRKS 7.205, Shiba na, ZGJI 389

7.485 兩刃交鋒不須避 *Ryōjin hokosaki o majiete sakuru koto o mochiizu.*

Two blades have crossed points, there's no pulling back.

The fourth verse from Tung Shan's 「Five Ranks」. *Heki* 43 Main Case Comm.

ZGS 7.382, ZRKS 7.426, Shiba 197, ZGJI 389, ZGJT 476, KZS #766

7.486 兩箇泥牛戰入海 *Ryōko no deigyū tatakatte umi ni iru.*

Two mud oxen fought each other into the sea.

ZGS na, ZRKS 7.521, Shiba 197

7.487 兩頭毒蛇見者死 *Ryōtō no dokuda miru mono wa shi su.*

The two-headed poisonous snake, all who look upon it die.

ZGS 7.383, ZRKS 7.553, Shiba na, ZGJI 389

7.488 良馬何曾勞鞭影 *Ryōme nanzo katsute ben'ei o rōsen.*

With a good horse, should one have to use even the hint of a whip?

Refer to *Heki* 65.

ZGS 7.384, ZRKS 7.433, Shiba na, ZGJI 389

7.489 凛凛威風四百州 *Rin-rin taru ifū shihyaku shū.*

His commanding presence extends over 400 provinces.

Heki 26 Main Case *agyo,* 54 Verse. The T'ang Empire in China was said to have 400 provinces (ZGJI 385).

ZGS 7.385, ZRKS 7.81, Shiba na, ZGJI 389, ZGJT 478, KZS #789

7.490 凜凜威風逼人寒 *Rin-rin taru ifū hito ni sematte susamaji.*

His commanding presence sends shivers through people.

ZGS 7.386, ZRKS 7.85, Shiba 197, ZGJI 389, KZS #790

7.491 玲瓏八面起淸風 *Reirō hachimen seifū o okosu.*

Crystal clear on every face, it makes the pure wind rise.

ZGS 7.387, ZRKS 7.232, Shiba 197

7.492 臘月蓮華拂拂香 *Rōgetsu renge futsu-futsu kambashi.*

The lotus flower in December, the air is heavy with its fragrance.

ZGS na, ZRKS 7.248, Shiba 198, ZGJI 391

7.493 六月火雲飛白雪 *Rokugatsu no kaun haku setsu o tobasu.*

The fiery clouds of summer drive the white snow.

ZGS na, ZRKS 7.586, Shiba 198, ZGJI 391

7.494 鷺鷥股裏多割肉 *Roji no kori ni ōku wa niku o saku.*

Scrape a mound of flesh from the heron's leg.

ZGS 7.388, Shiba na, ZGJI 390

7.495 鷺鷥立雪非同色 *Roji yuki ni tatsu, dōshoku ni arazu.*

When a heron stands in the snow, its colors are not the same.

ZGS 7.389, ZRKS 7.153, Shiba 198, ZGJI 390, ZGJT 485

7.496 莫沾老僧袈裟角 *Rōsō no kesa kado o uruosu koto nakare.*

Don't let the corner of the ⸢old monk's⸣ robe get wet.

ZGS 7.390, Shiba na

7.497 脱卻籠頭卸角駄 *Rōtō o dakkyaku shi kakuda o orosu.*

He removes the baskets and takes off the saddle packs.

Heki 17 Verse, 21 Intro.

ZGS 7.391, Shiba na, ZGJI 599

7.498 老倒無端入荒草 *Rōtō hashi naku kōsō ni iru.*

Old, uncaring, he wanders into the wild weeds.

ZGS 7.392, ZRKS 7.308, Shiba na, ZGJI 391, KZS #685

7.499 我今日小出大遇 *Ware konnichi shōshutsu taigū.*

Today, though we made small progress, we have had a great encounter.

A ritual phrase on parting with a teacher. See 8.55.

ZGS 7.393, Shiba na

7.500 我非無神通菩薩 *Ware ni jintsū bosatsu naki ni arazu.*

It is not true there is no divine power or bodhisattva in me.

ZGS 7.394, Shiba na

7.501 還我無孔鐵鎚來 *Ware ni muku no tettsui o kaeshi kitare.*

Give me back the ⌜iron hammerhead without a socket⌝.

Heki 46 Verse *agyo.*

ZGS 7.395, ZRKS 7.67, Shiba na, ZGJI 508, KZS #805

7.502 笑一場時哭一場 *Warai ichijō no toki koku ichijō.*

When you laugh, you cry.

ZGS na, ZRKS 7.314, Shiba 172, ZGJI 391, KZS #688

7.503 堪咲人來捋虎鬚 *Warau ni taetari hito no kitatte koshu o nazuru koto o.*

I can't stop laughing—he came to stroke the tiger's whiskers.

Heki 26 Verse. ZGS 7.396: 笑 instead of 咲.

ZGS 7.396, ZRKS 7.421, Shiba na, ZGJI 332

Eight-Character Phrases

8.1 非敢後也 馬不進也 *Aete okuretaru ni arazu uma susumazaru nari.*

It was not courage that kept me behind. My horses were slow.

Analects XI, 13 (Waley 1938, 118–19).

ZGS 8.1, Shiba na

8.2 朝遊檀特 暮到羅浮 *Ashita ni dantoku ni asobi, kure ni rafu ni itaru.*

In the morning I travel to T'an-t'e, in the evening I go to Lo-fu. 8 字

T'an-t'e (J. Dantoku) is Daṇḍaka, or Daṇḍaloka (Skt.), a mountain in north India where the Buddha is said to have performed his bodhisattva practice (Mochizuki, 3520). Lo-fu (J. Rafu) is the name of the mountain in China where ⌜Ko Hung⌝ trained in Taoist immortality practices.

ZGS 8.2, ZRKS 8.258, Shiba na, ZGJI 393, ZGJT 312

8.3 朝隮于西 崇朝其雨 *Ashita ni wa nishi ni noboru, sōchō sore ame furu.*

In the morning I climb to the west; in the early dawn, it rains.

ZGS 8.3, Shiba na

8.4 朝到西天 暮歸東土 *Ashita ni wa saiten ni itari, kure ni wa tōdo ni kaeru.*

In the morning I reach India, in the evening I return to China.

Heki 44 Main Case *agyo*. The characters for India are 西天, literally "West Heaven," and for China 東土, literally "East Earth."

ZGS 8.4, ZRKS 8.207, Shiba 277, ZGJI 393, ZGJT 312, KZS #919

8.5 豈不夙夜 謂行多露 *Ani shuku ya ni sezaranya, omowaku michi ni tsuyu ōkaran.*

Why did I not go in the early morn? I thought the way too wet with dew.

ZGS 8.5, Shiba na, *Book of Songs* 17

8.6 鞍上無人 鞍下無馬 *Anjō hito naku anka uma nashi.*

Above the saddle no person, below the saddle no horse.

ZGS 8.6, Shiba 199

8.7 收得安南 又憂塞北 *Annan o osameete mata saihoku o ureu.*

Having put down An-nan in the south, he worries about Sai-pei in the north.

ZGS 8.7, ZRKS 8.85, Shiba na, ZGJI 393, ZGJT 199

8.8 暗穿玉線 密度金針 *An ni gyokusen o ugachi, hisoka ni kinshin o do su.*

In darkness they sew with jewel thread, in secret they stitch with the golden needle.

ZGS 8.8, ZRKS 8.247, Shiba 199, ZGJI 393, KZS #870

8.9 伊字三點 那箇是正 *Iji santen nako ka kore shō.*

Of the three dots of the character ∴, which is correct?

The character 伊 here is not used for meaning. It represents the pronunciation *i* of the Sanskrit character written with three dots ∴.

ZGS 8.9, Shiba na, ZGDJT 24

8.10 發憤忘食 樂以忘憂 *Ikidōri o hasshite shoku o wasure,*
Tanoshinde motte urei o wasuru.

So intent he forgot to eat, so pleased he forgot his bitterness.

Analects VII 18.

ZGS 8.10, Shiba na

8.11 意中削句 句中削機 *Ichū ni ku o kezuri kuchū ni ⌜ki⌝ o kezuru.*

Carve words out of meaning, carve action out of words.

ZGS 8.11, Shiba na

8.12 一翳在眼 空華亂墜 *Ichiei manako ni araba, kūge rantsui su.*

Let one mote get in your eye and ⌜flowers of emptiness⌝ fall in disarray.

ZGS na, ZRKS 8.395, Shiba 200, ZGJI 394, ZGJT 22 (variant)

8.13 一言既出 駟馬難追 *Ichigen sude ni izureba shime mo oigatashi.*

A team of horses can't catch a word once uttered.

Serenity Case 89 Added Sayings.

ZGS na, ZRKS 8.136, Shiba 200, ZGJI 395 (variant), ZGJT 22 (variant)

8.14 不經一事 不長一智 *Ichiji o hezareba, itchi o chō zezu.*

One thing not experienced is one wisdom not gained.

ZGS 8.12, ZRKS 8.94, Shiba 232, ZGJI 395 (variant), ZGJT 400 (variant), KZS #878

8.15 放下一著 落在第二 *Itchaku o hōge sureba, daini ni rakuzai su.*

If you let him take the first move, then you fall into his second.

Shiba 234: 放過一着 *Ichi jaku o hōka sureba* instead of 放下一著. *Heki* 10 Main Case *agyo*, 24 Main Case Comm.

ZGS 8.13, ZRKS 8.222, Shiba 234, ZGJI 396, ZGJT 424

8.16 一日不作 一日不食 *Ichijitsu nasazareba ichijitsu kurawazu.*

A day without working is a day without eating.

ZGS na, Shiba 201, ZGJI 397, ZGDJT 33b

8.17 一人傳虛 萬人傳實 *Ichinin kyo o tsutaureba, bannin jitsu to tsutau.*

If one person tells a lie, ten thousand pass it on as truth.

Heki 47 Verse *agyo*, 96 Verse 1 *agyo*.

ZGS 8.14, ZRKS 8.231, Shiba na

8.18 一念忘機 太虚無玷 *Ichinen* ⌜*ki*⌝ *o bōzureba, taikyo kizu nashi.*

Once forget all impulses, then great emptiness is flawless.

ZGS na, ZRKS 8.314, Shiba 201, ZGJI 397, ZGDJT 34a

8.19 一棒打殺 狗也不喫 *Ichibō ni tasatsu shite, ku mo mata kurawazu.*

Struck dead by a single blow from the stick, not even the dogs will eat him.

ZGS 8.15, ZRKS 8.303, Shiba na, ZGJI 397

8.20 一輪皎潔 萬里騰光 *Ichirin kōketsu to shite banri hikari o agu.*

The pure white ⌜moon⌝ sends its light ten thousand miles.

ZGS 8.16, Shiba na

8.21 一靈皮袋 皮袋一靈 *Ichirei hitai hitai ichirei.*

One spirit, one bag of skin; one bag of skin, one spirit.

ZGS 8.17, Shiba na, ZGJI 398

8.22 一回見面 千載知名 *Ikkai men o mite senzai na o shiru.*

If you see its face once, you know its name for a thousand years.

ZGS na, ZRKS 8.29, Shiba 200

8.23 一句截流 萬機寢削 *Ikku setsuru ban*⌜*ki*⌝ *shinsaku.*

One word cuts the flow, myriad impulses cease.

Heki 38 Main Case Comm. ZGJI 395: *Ikku setsuru shite banki shinsaku su.*

ZGS na, ZRKS 8.263, Shiba 200, ZGJI 395, ZGJT 22

8.24 一家父子 和氣如春 *Ikke no fushi waki haru no gotoshi.*

Parents and children in one family, as harmonious as the spring.

ZGS 8.18, Shiba na, ZGJI 110

8.25 一犬吠虛 萬犬傳實 *Ikken kyo ni hoe, manken jitsu to tsutau.*

When one dog howls false, ten thousand dogs pass it on as true.

Shiba 200: 一犬吼虛 千猱啀實 *Ikken kyo o hoereba, sendō jitsu to igamu,* "When one dog howls false, a thousand monkeys shriek it as true."

ZGS 8.19, Shiba na; variants: ZGJI 395, ZGJT 22, KZS #880

8.26 拈出一箇 膠盆子了 *Ikko no kōbonsu o nenshutsu shi owannu.*

He has put out a pot of glue.

Rinzai-roku §19.

ZGS 8.20, Shiba na

8.27 一切善惡 都莫思量 *Issai no zen'aku subete shiryō suru nakare.*

Do not think at all about good and bad.

ZGS 8.21, Shiba na, ZGJI 395

8.28 一手指天 一手指地 *Isshu wa ten o yubisashi, isshu wa chi o yubisasu.*

One hand points to heaven, one hand points to earth.

Heki 16 Verse Comm.

ZGS 8.22, ZRKS 8.223, Shiba na, ZGJI 22, ZGJT 395

8.29 一生與人 抽釘拔楔 *Isshō hito no tame ni tei to nuki ketsu to nuku.*

A life devoted to helping people pull out nails and remove their blocks.

Heki 6 Main Case Comm., 62 Main Case Comm., 100 Main Case Comm.

ZGS na, Shiba 200

8.30 一心不生 萬法無咎 *Isshin shōzezareba banpō toga nashi.*

Think no thought and all is flawless.

ZGS na, Shiba 200, ZGJI 396, ZGJT 44

8.31 一長三短 四句百非 *Itchō santan shiku hyappi.*

One long, three shorts, the ⌜four propositions and the hundred negations⌝.

Refer to *Heki* 73. See ⌜Four propositions and hundred negations⌝.

ZGS 8.23, Shiba na, ZGJI 148, ZGJT 170

8.32 一朝無憂 終身有樂 *Itchō yū nakereba shūshin raku ari.*

Have one morning without worry and forever after be at ease.

ZGS na, Shiba 201, ZGJI 396

8.33 一燈萬燈 燈燈無盡 *Ittō bantō tōtō mujin.*

One lamp, ten thousand lamps, lamp after lamp without end.

See ⌜Inexhaustible lamp⌝.

ZGS 8.24, Shiba na

8.34 一東二冬 叉手當胸 *Ittō nitō shashu tōkyō*

Dum! Da-dum! Hands in ⌜*shashu*⌝, against the chest!

ZGJT 23: The characters 東 and 冬 are used not for meaning but to represent drum beats.

ZGS na, ZRKS 8.115, Shiba na, ZGJT 23

8.35 一夫當關 萬夫莫開 *Ippu kan ni atareba banpu mo hiraku nashi.*

If one stalwart guards the gate, then ten thousand men cannot enter.

ZGS 8.25, Shiba na

8.36 潛泉魚鼓 波而自躍 *Izumi ni hisomu uo nami o ko shite mizukara odoru.*

Fish lurking in the pond thrash the waves and leap into the air.

Rinzai-roku §19

ZGS 8.26, Shiba na

8.37 何官無私 何水無魚 *Izure no kan ni ka watakushi nakaran,*
Izure no mizu ni wa uo nakaran.

In what public official is there no private feeling? In what stream are there no fish?

ZGS 8.27, Shiba 203, ZGJI 398, ZGDJT 26b

8.38 賤如泥沙 貴如金璧 *Iyashiki koto wa deisha no gotoku,*
Tattoki koto wa kinpeki no gotoshi.

As worthless as a lump of mud, as precious as a gold jewel.

ZGS 8.28, ZRKS 8.378, Shiba na, ZGJI 398, ZGJT 259

8.39 曰作家眼目僧禮拜 *Iwaku sakke no ganmoku sō raihai su.*

It is said that the monk prostrates himself before the eye of the master.

ZGS 8.29, Shiba na

8.40 不信因果 正法自壞 *Inga o shinzezumba shōbō onozukara e su.*

Without belief in karma, the true Dharma by itself declines.

ZGS 8.30, Shiba na

8.41 內無所得 外無所求 *Uchi ni shotoku naku, hoka ni shogu nashi.*

Inside nothing to attain, outside nothing to seek.

Sutra of Forty-Two Articles.

ZGS na, ZRKS 8.204, Shiba 230, ZGJI 399

8.42 有佛處請試指出看 *Ubutsu no tokoro kou kokoromi ni shishutsu seyo min.*

I ask of you, please point out where the Buddha is.

ZGS 8.31, Shiba na

8.43 戲海獰龍 摩天俊鶻 *Umi ni tawamureru dōryū, ten o masuru shunkotsu.*

A fierce dragon playing in the seas, a great hawk careening through the skies.

ZGS na, ZRKS 8.284, Shiba 206, ZGJI 399

8.44 漆不厭黑 粉不厭白 *Urushi wa koku o itowazaru, fun wa haku o itowazu.*

Lacquer does not mind being ⌜black⌝, powder does not mind being white.

ZGS 8.32, Shiba na

8.45 雲月是同 溪山各異 *Ungetsu kore onaji, keizan ono-ono kotonaru.*

Ever the same, the ⌜moon⌝ among the clouds; different from each other, the mountain and the valley.

Shibayama 1974, 251; MMK 35.

ZGS na, Shiba 201

8.46 提奬嬰兒 撫憐赤子 *Eiji o teishō shi, sekishi o buren su.*

He comforts new-born babies, he takes compassion on little infants.

ZGS 8.33, Shiba na

8.47 應無所住 而生其心 *Ō mu sho jū ni shō go shin.*

Arouse the mind that abides in no place.

Shiba 203: *Masa ni jū suru tokoro nōshite, sono kokoro o shōzubeshi.* See ⌜Sixth Patriarch⌝.

ZGS na, Shiba 203, ZGJI 401, ZGDJT 125b

8.48 辨王庫刀 振塗毒鼓 *Ōkō no katana o benji, zudokko o furuu.*

He knows the ⌜sword in the king's storehouse⌝ and wields the ⌜poison-painted drum⌝.

ZGS na, ZRKS 8.269, Shiba 234, ZGJI 400, KZS #938

8.49 王登寶殿 野老謳歌 *Ō hōden ni nobori yarō ōka su.*

When the king ascends the jeweled palace, the old people in the country sing.

Rinzai-roku §10.

ZGS 8.34, ZRKS 8.272, Shiba 202, ZGJI 401

8.50 王勅已行 諸侯避道 *Ōchoku sude ni yuite shokō michi o saku.*

The king's decree has already gone forth and all the lords avoid the roads.

Heki 43 Verse *agyo*. ZGS 8.66 (variant): 狗銜赦書 *Inu shasho o fukumeba,* "The dog has taken the imperial script in its mouth," instead of 王勅已行, "The king's decree has already gone forth."

ZGS na, ZRKS 8.81, Shiba na, ZGJI 401, ZGJT 36

8.51 可惜此器 不遇知音 *Oshimubeshi kono ki chiin ni awazu.*

I regret that in this person I did not meet a true ⌜intimate⌝.

ZGS 8.35, Shiba na

8.52 不知恩人 不放舊債 *Onjin o shirazu kyūsai o hanatazu.*

He ignores those who helped him and shrugs off his old debts.

ZGS 8.36, Shiba na

8.53 見怪不怪 其怪自壞 *Kai o mite kai to sezareba, sono kai onozukara e su.*

Don't see the strange as strange, and its strangeness will just disappear.

Heki 22 Main Case *agyo*. ZRKS 8.184, KZS #911: *sono ke onozukara yaburu.*

ZGS na, ZRKS 8.184, Shiba 210, ZGJI 403, ZGJT 107, KZS #911

8.54 爲學日益 爲道日損 *Gaku o osamuru mono wa hi ni mashi,*
Michi o osamuru mono wa hi ni sonsu.

One devoted to study increases day by day,
One devoted to the Way decreases day by day.

Tao-te ching, ch. 48.

ZGS na, Shiba 199, ZGJI 403

8.55 學人今日 小出大遇 *Gakunin konnichi shōshutsu taigū.*

Today we students have made small progress, but we have had a great encounter.

ZGJI 403: A ritual compliment from students to their teacher.

ZGS na, ZRKS 8.429, Shiba 204, ZGJI 403

8.56 戒器不全 定水不貯 *Kaiki mattakarazareba jōsui takuwaerarezu.*

If the precept vessel is not whole, it will not collect the water of *samādhi.*

See「Three learnings」.

ZGS na, Shiba 204, ZGJI 402

8.57 快人一言 快馬一鞭 *Kaijin no ichigen, kaiba no ichiben.*

For an alert person, one word; for a sharp horse, one flick of the whip.

Heki 38 Intro., 70 Intro.

ZGS 8.37, ZRKS 8.128, Shiba 204, ZGJI 402, ZGJT 54

8.58 卻是撞着 祖師面目 *Kaette kore soshi no menmoku ni dōchaku su.*

This is a slap right in the patriarch's face.

ZGS 8.38, Shiba na

8.59 伐柯伐柯 其則不遠 *Ka o kiri, ka o kiru, sono nori tōkarazu.*

To hew an axe handle, to hew an axe handle, the model is not far away.

Book of Songs 158; *Doctrine of Mean* XIII, 2.

ZGS 8.39, ZRKS 8.358, Shiba na

8.60 學者參禪 師家面壁 *Gakusha sanzen shike menpeki.*

The student comes seeking Zen, but the master faces the wall.

ZGS 8.40, Shiba na

8.61 迦葉作舞 顏淵顰眉 *Kashō mai o nashi Gan'en mayu o hisomu.*

⸢Kāśyapa⸣ dances and Yen Yüan knits his brow in a frown.

Kāśyapa is the first disciple of the Buddha and Yen Yüan of Confucius.

ZGS 8.41, Shiba na

8.62 牙上生牙 爪上生爪 *Gajō ni ga o shōji, sōjō ni sō o shōzu.*

Grow teeth on top of teeth, claws on top of claws.

Heki 95 Main Case Comm. See ⸢Teeth and claws⸣.

ZGS na, ZRKS 8.78, Shiba na, ZGJI 402

8.63 風吹樹動 悉辨來機 *Kaze fuite ki ugoki, kotogotoku rai⸢ki⸣ o benzu.*

The blowing wind and swaying trees have all seen right through the student.

ZGS 8.42, Shiba na

8.64 風吹不入 水洒不着 *Kaze fukedomo irazu mizu sosogedomo tsukazu.*

The wind blows but cannot enter it, the water falls but cannot wet it.

ZRKS 8.22: 著 instead of 着.

ZGS 8.43, ZRKS 8.22, Shiba 234, ZGJI 403, ZGJT 407, KZS #835

8.65 活捉生擒 不勞餘力 *Kassoku seikin yoryoku o rō sezu.*

Took him alive and kicking, without working up a sweat.

Heki 79 Intro.

ZGS na, ZRKS 8.190, Shiba 204

8.66 不在河南 正在河北 *Kanan ni arazumba masa ni kahoku ni ari.*

I will not be in Ho-nan, I will be in Ho-pei.

Ho-nan and Ho-pei are south and north of the Yellow River respectively. This verse, whose source is *Heki* 9 Main Case *agyo*, is similar to verse 8.171, whose source is *Rinzai-roku* Preface and §56. A common interpretation of these verses is that they express freedom from dualisms like that between north and south (e.g., Shiba 233). However, Shōun-ji says it is better to translate this verse, "I will not be in Ho-nan, I will be in Ho-pei," to retain the implication that there is a difference between north and south.

ZGS 8.44, ZRKS 8.185, Shiba na, KZS #914, Watson 1993, 114

8.67 如鐘在簴 似鏡當臺 *Kane no kyo ni aru ga gotoku, kagami no tai ni ataru ni nitari.*

Like a bell in a tower, like a mirror on a stand.

ZGS na, ZRKS 8.234, Shiba 219, ZGJI 404

8.68 蝦蟇蚯蚓 泥猪疥狗 *Gama, kyūin, deicho, kaiku.*

Toads, worms, mud hogs, scabby dogs.

ZGS 8.45, ZRKS 8.89, Shiba na

8.69 上透霄漢 下徹黄泉 *Kami shōkan ni tōri, shimo kōsen ni tessu.*

Above it extends beyond the Milky Way, below it reaches the「Yellow Springs」.

Heki 97 Verse *agyo*.

ZGS 8.46, ZRKS 8.61, Shiba 220, ZGJI 404, ZGJT 222, KZS #856

8.70 上無諸佛 下無衆生 *Kami shobutsu naku, shimo shujō nashi.*

Above no buddhas, below no sentient beings.

ZGS 8.47 , ZRKS 8.362, Shiba 220

8.71 上無攀仰 下絕己躬 *Kami hangyō naku, shimo kokyū o zessu.*

Above nothing to revere, below ego exhausted.

Heki 17 Verse Comm., 25 Verse Comm.

ZGS 8.48, ZRKS 8.20, Shiba 220, ZGJI 404, ZGJT 222, ZGS #833

8.72 遇家裏人 說家裏事 *Kari no hito ni ōte, kari no koto o toku.*

When you meet family folks, you talk family matters.

ZGS na, ZRKS 8.88, Shiba 209, ZGJI 402, KZS #876

8.73 瓦礫生光 眞金失色 *Gareki hikari o shōji, shinkin iro o shissu.*

Rubble emits light, pure gold loses its luster.

Heki 31 Intro.

ZGS 8.49, ZRKS 8.352, Shiba 203, ZGJI 402, KZS #900

8.74 彼死我死 向何處會 *Kare shi shi ware shi su, izure no tokoro ni mukatte ka awan.*

He dies, I die, where shall we meet?

ZGS 8.50, Shiba na

8.75 干戈叢裡 七縱八横 *Kanka sōri shichiju hachiō.*

Bristling with shields and spears, from back to front and side to side.

ZGS 8.51, Shiba na

8.76 官不容針 私通車馬 *Kan ni wa hari o mo irezu, watakushi ni wa shaba o tsūzu.*

Officially, not even a needle may enter; privately, horses and carriages go through.

Rinzai-roku §66.

ZGS 8.52, ZRKS 8.169, Shiba 204, ZGJI 405, ZGJT 64, ZD #183

8.77 還丹一粒 點鐵成金 *Kantan ichiryū tetsu o tenjite kin to nasu.*

One gram of ⌜restored cinnabar⌝ touches iron and makes gold.

ZGDJT 293a: *gentan* instead of *kantan*.

ZGS na, ZRKS 8.192, Shiba 205, ZGJI 406, ZGDJT 293a

8.78 有陷虎機 無斬蛟劍 *Kanko no ki ari, zankō no ken nashi.*

He has the desire to trap a tiger but he hasn't even a ⌜sword⌝ to cut a lizard.

ZGS na, ZRKS 8.270, Shiba 237, ZGJI 405

8.79 換骨靈方 頤神妙術 *Kankotsu no reihō, ishin no myōjitsu.*

A spiritual prescription to transform your bones,
A miracle method to cultivate your mind.

Heki Intro.

ZGS na, Shiba 205, ZGJT 406

8.80 剜卻眼睛 掀卻腦蓋 *Ganzei o wankyaku shi, nōgai o kinkyaku shu.*

Gouge out his eyes, pry off his skullbone.

ZGS na, ZRKS 8.130, Shiba 240, ZGJT 406

8.81 寒來重衣 熱來弄扇 *Kan kitaraba e o kasane, netsu kitaraba sen o rō su.*

When the cold comes, wear more clothes; when the heat comes, use a fan.

ZGS na, Shiba 204, ZGJI 405

8.82 寒爐無人 獨臥虚空 *Kanro hito naku, hitori kokū ni ga su.*

Hearth gone cold, no one around, alone he dozes in emptiness.

ZGS na, Shiba 205, ZGJI 406

8.83 眼中無翳 空裏無花 *Ganchū ni ei naku, kūri ni hana nashi.*

No spots in my eyes, no ⌜flowers in the sky⌝.

ZGS na, ZRKS 8.38, Shiba 205, ZGJI 406, 699

8.84 眼裏泉聲 耳裏山色 *Ganri wa sensei, niri wa sanshoku.*

In my eyes, the sound of springwater; in my ears, the colors of the hills.

ZGS na, Shiba 206

8.85 岸眉横雪 河目含秋 *Ganbi yuki o yokotau, kamoku aki o fukumu.*

His brows are cliffs mantled with snows, his eyes are streams filled with autumns.

Serenity 47 Verse.

ZGS na, Shiba 205, ZGJI 406

8.86 氣呑佛祖 眼蓋乾坤 *Ki busso o nomi, manako kenkon o ōu.*

His spirit swallows buddhas and patriarchs, his eye covers ⌜heaven and earth⌝.

ZGS na, ZRKS 8.122, Shiba 206, ZGJI 407

8.87 聞時富貴 見後貧窮 *Kiku toki wa fūki, mite nochi wa hinkyū.*

What I heard was fabulous wealth, what I saw was desperate poverty.

ZGS na, ZRKS 8.394, Shiba 234, ZGJI 407

8.88 以機奪機 以毒攻毒 *⌜Ki⌝ o motte ki o ubai, doku o motte doku o semu.*

With dynamism steal dynamism, with poison attack poison.

ZGS 8.53, ZRKS 8.329, Shiba 199, ZGJI 407, KZS #933

8.89 機不離位 墮在毒海 *⌜Ki⌝ kurai o hanarezareba dokkai ni dazai su.*

If you don't get your mind off rank, you will fall into the poison sea.

Heki 15 Verse Comm., 25 Intro.

ZGS 8.54, ZRKS 8.360, Shiba 206, ZGJI 407, ZGJT 79, ZD #68, p.318

8.90 機前語活 棒頭眼開 *⌜Ki⌝zen ni go kasshite, bōtō ni manako hiraku.*

His Zen energy gives life to words, his stick awakens your eye.

ZGS na, ZRKS 8.384, Shiba 206, ZGJI 407, ZGJT 79

8.91 龜上覓毛 兎邊求角 *Kijō ni ke o motome, tohen ni tsuno o motomu.*

Looking for hair on a tortoise, searching for horns on a rabbit.

See ⌜Rabbit horns and turtle hairs⌝.

ZGS 8.55, ZRKS 8.49, Shiba 206, ZGJI 407, ZD #174

8.92 鏡水圖山 鳥飛不渡 *Kyōsui tozan tori tobi watarazu.*

Water like a mirror, peaks as in pictures—birds fly but do not cross.

Heki 38 Main Case Comm.

ZGS 8.56, Shiba 207

8.93 牙如劍樹 口似血盆 *Kiba kenju no gotoku, kuchi ketsubon ni nitari.*

His teeth are like a tree of ⌜swords⌝, his mouth is like a bowl of blood.

Heki 4 Main Case Comm., MMK 28.

ZGS 8.57, ZRKS 8.15, Shiba 203, KZS #830

8.94 君君臣臣 父父子子 *Kimi wa kimi tari, shin wa shin tari,*
Fu wa fu tari, shi wa shi tari.

Let the ruler be a ruler and the official an official.
Let the father be a father and the son a son.

Analects XII, 11.

ZGS 8.58, Shiba na

8.95 君向西秦 我之東魯 *Kimi wa seishin ni mukai, ware wa tōro ni iku.*

You head west to Ch'in, I go east to Lu.

Heki 70 Main Case *agyo*, 82 Main Case Comm.

ZGS na, ZRKS 8.80, Shiba 210, ZGJI 408, ZGJT 99

8.96 狂狗逐塊 瞎驢趁隊 *Kyōku tsuchikure o oi, katsuro wa tai o ou.*

A mad dog chases the dirt clod, the blind donkey follows the pack.

ZGJT 90: The dog attacks the dirt clod rather than the person who threw it.

ZGS na, ZRKS 8.40, Shiba 207, ZGJI 409, ZGJT 90

8.97 教外別傳 不立文字 *Kyōge betsuden furu moji.*

A separate transmission outside doctrine, not founded on words and letters. ➛

See ⌜Bodhidharma's verse⌝. MMK 6, couplet reversed. Shiba 207: *furyū monji.*

ZGS na, Shiba 207

8.98 直指人心 見性成佛 *Jikishi jinshin kenshō jōbutsu.*

➛Pointing directly at human mind, seeing nature, become Buddha.

Heki 1 Main Case Comm., 9 Main Case Comm., 14 Main Case Comm.

ZGS 8.175, ZRKS 8.308, Shiba 227, ZGJI 445, ZGJT 183

8.99 玉兎東昇 金烏西墜 *Gyokuto higashi ni nobori, kin'u nishi ni otsu.*

The ⌜jade rabbit⌝ rises in the east, the ⌜golden crow⌝ sets in the west.

ZGS na, ZRKS 8.107, Shiba 207

8.100 金不換金 水不濺水 *Kin wa kin ni kaezu, mizu wa mizu ni sosogazu.*

You can't turn gold into gold, you can't wet water with water.

ZGS 8.61, Shiba 208

8.101 金以火試 人以言試 *Kin wa hi o motte kokoromi, hito wa gen o motte kokoromu.*

Test gold with fire, test people with their words.

ZGS 8.62, ZRKS 8.124, Shiba 208, ZGJI 410 var, ZGJT 94 (variant), KZS #889

8.102 金雞唱曉 玉鳳啣花 *Kinkei akatsuki o tonae, gyokuhō hana o tsuibamu.*

The ⌜golden crow⌝ serenades the dawn, the jade phoenix plucks a flower.

ZGS na, ZRKS 8.56, Shiba 208, ZGJI 410

8.103 金塵入眼 毒刺投心 *Kinjin manako ni iri, dokushi kokoro ni tōzu.*

He throws gold dust into your eyes and stabs poison thorns into your heart.

ZGS na, ZRKS 8.367, Shiba 208

8.104 金屑雖貴 落眼成翳 *Kinsetsu tattoshi to iedomo, manako ni ochite ei to naru.*

Though gold dust is precious, in the eyes it obscures the vision.

Heki 25 Main Case Comm., 60 Main Case Comm., *Rinzai-roku* §35.

ZGS 8.59, ZRKS 8.28, Shiba 208, ZGJI 410, ZGJT 94, KZS #838, ZD #171

8.105 金鎚影動 寶劍光寒 *Kintsui kage ugoite, hōken hikari susamaji.*

The shadow of the golden hammer moves, the light of the treasure ⸢sword⸣ chills.

ZGS 8.60, ZRKS 8.151, Shiba 208, ZGJI 410, KZS #899

8.106 金毛獅子 奮威出窟 *Kinmō no shishi i o furutte kutsu o izu.*

The golden lion in all its majesty strides from its cave.

ZGS na, ZRKS 8.142, Shiba 209, ZGJI 410, KZS #898

8.107 銀碗盛雪 明月藏鷺 *Ginwan ni yuki o mori, meigetsu ni ro o kakusu.*

Put snow in a silver bowl, hide a heron in the light of the ⸢moon⸣.

Shiba 209: 盌 instead of 碗.

ZGS 8.63, Shiba 209

8.108 敲空有響 打木無聲 *Kū o tataku ni hibiki ari, ki o utsu ni koe nashi.*

Strike the sky and there is an echo, strike wood and there is no sound.

ZGS 8.64, ZRKS 8.387, Shiba 214, ZGJI 411

8.109 空手而來 空手而去 *Kūshu ni shite kitari, kūshu ni shite saru.*

Empty-handed he came, empty-handed he left.

ZGS 8.65, Shiba na, ZGDJT

8.110 狗子還有 佛性也無 *Kusu ni kaette busshō ari ya mata nashi ya.*

Does a dog have Buddha-nature or does it not?

MMK 1. This is the traditional reading (e.g., Hirata 1969, 14–15). However, according to Shōunji, the correct reading should be simply *Kusu ni kaette busshō ari ya,* for which the translation would be, "Does a dog have a Buddha-nature?"

ZGS na, Shiba 209, ZGJI 410

8.111 開口卽錯 動舌卽乖 *Kuchi o hirakeba sunawachi ayamari,*
Shita o ugokaseba sunawachi somuku.

Open your mouth and at once you're wrong,
Move your tongue and at once you transgress.

ZGS 8.67, ZRKS 8.69, Shiba na, ZGJI 411

8.112 口齩霜刄 足撥飛鋒 *Kuchi ni sōjin o kami, ashi ni hihō o harau.*

His mouth chews with blades of ice, his feet flash like flying spears.

ZGS 8.68, Shiba na

8.113 國有憲章 三千條罪 *Kuni ni kenshō ari sanzenjō no tsumi.*

The country has constitutional law—and 3,000 criminal offenses.

Heki 82 Verse.

ZGS 8.69, ZRKS 8.53, Shiba na, ZGJI 411, ZGJT 141

8.114 雲收萬嶽 月上中峯 *Kumo wa bangaku ni osamari, tsuki wa chūhō ni noboru.*

Clouds gather on the many mountains, the ⌜moon⌝ rises over the central peak.

See ⌜Landscape⌝.

ZGS na, ZRKS 8.155, Shiba 201, ZGJI 412

8.115 雲歸碧洞 露滴蘭叢 *Kumo wa hekidō ni ki shi, tsuyu wa ransō ni shitataru.*

The clouds gather round the blue caves, dew trickles on the orchid clusters.

ZGS na, Shiba 201, ZGJI 412

8.116 車不横推 理不曲斷 *Kuruma yoko ni osazu, ri magete danzezu.*

You do not push a cart from the side, nor cut crookedly across the grain.

ZGS 8.70, ZRKS 8.265, Shiba 217, ZGJI 412, ZGJT 188

8.117 君子愛財 取之以道 *Kunshi wa zai o aisuru mo kore o toru ni michi o motte su.*

Though the prince loves wealth, he obtains it through the Way.

ZGJI 412 (variant): 君子愛財取之有道 *Kunshi wa zai o aisu, kore o toru ni michi ari,* "The prince loves wealth, to obtain it there is a Way."

ZGS 8.71, Shiba 210, ZGJI 412

8.118 君子盛德 容皃若愚 *Kunshi wa seitoku atte yōbō orokanaru ga gotoshi.*

The prince possesses unsurpassed virtue and the face of a fool.

ZGS 8.72, Shiba na

8.119 薫天富貴 徹骨貧窮 *Kunten no fūki, tekkotsu no hinkyū.*

Wealth and honor fragrant to the sky, poverty that cuts to the bone.

ZGS 8.73, Shiba na

8.120 荊棘參天 蒺藜滿地 *Keikyoku santen, shitsuri manchi.*

Thorns fill the sky, brambles cover the earth.

ZGS 8.74, ZRKS 8.262, Shiba na, ZGJI 412, KZS #939

8.121 逈然獨脱 不與物拘 *Keinen dokudatsu ni shite mono to kakawarazu.*

Remote and free, not caught up on things.

Rinzai-roku §19.

ZGS na, Shiba 210

8.122 如擊石火 似閃電光 *Geki sekka no gotoku, sen denkō ni nitari.*

Like a shooting spark, like a flash of lightning.

Heki 1 Verse Comm., 5 Verse Comm., 7 Main Case Comm., 8 Verse Comm., et al.

ZGS 8.75, ZRKS 8.34, Shiba 218, ZGJI 413, ZGJT 362, KZS #842

8.123 桀無由助 顏弗足希 *Ketsu tasukuru ni yu naku, gan no nozomu ni tarazu.*

Couldn't do anything with Chieh, couldn't do anything for Yen.

See ⌜Chieh⌝ and ⌜Yen Hui⌝.

ZGS 8.76, Shiba na

8.124 下坡不走 快鞭難逢 *Geba hashirazareba kaiben aigatashi.*

If you don't race even on the downhill, you won't get that welcome spur.

"Spur" translates 鞭, literally "whip." *Heki* 81 Main Case *agyo*. Similar to *Hashiru uma ni muchi*, "The whip is for the running horse." A master teaches only an eager student, one who does not coast on the downhill. However, this verse appears in many texts with 便 instead of 鞭. "If you do not run even on the downhill, you will miss the convenient ferry" (ZGJT 40).

ZGS 8.77, ZRKS 8.198, Shiba na, ZGJT 40

8.125 求賢以德 致聖以道 *Ken o motomuru ni toku o motte su,*
Sei o itasu ni michi o motte su.

Seek wisdom through virtue,
Seek the holy through the Way.

ZGS na, Shiba 206

8.126 乾坤震裂 山嶽搖動 *Kenkon o shinretsu shi sangaku o yōdō su.*

He makes heaven and earth shake, he causes mountain peaks to shudder.

ZGS na, ZRKS 8.312, Shiba 210, ZGJI 413

8.127 打破乾坤 獨歩靑天 *Kenkon o taha shite seiten o doppo su.*

He shatters ⌜heaven and earth⌝ and alone walks the blue sky.

ZGS 8.78, Shiba na

8.128 乾坤大地 一時露出 *Kenkon daichi ichiji ni roshutsu su.*

The universe and the great earth are at once revealed.

Heki 32 Verse *agyo.*

ZGS 8.79, ZRKS 8.37, Shiba na, ZGJI 413, KZS #845

8.129 劍去刻舟 守株待兎 *Ken satte funabata o kizami, kuize o mamotte to o matsu.*

Losing his ⌜sword⌝, he notches the boat rail; watching the stump, he waits for rabbits.

See ⌜Slash the boat⌝, ⌜Wait by the stump for a rabbit⌝.

ZGS 8.80, ZRKS 8.254, Shiba 211, ZGJI 414, KZS #864

8.130 元首明哉 股肱良哉 *Genshu akiraka naru kana, kokō yoi kana.*

How brilliant the emperor, how excellent his ministers.

ZGS 8.81, ZRKS 8.98, Shiba na, ZGJI 414 cites 書經

8.131 元正啓祚 萬物咸新 *Genshō keiso banbutsu mina arata nari.*

In this New Year, may good fortune increase. All things everywhere are renewed.

Heki 44 Main Case Comm.

ZGS na, ZRKS 8.315, Shiba 211, ZGJI 414, ZGJT 111

8.132 欲得現前 莫存順逆 *Genzen o en to hosseba, jungyaku o son suru koto nakare.*

If you want to obtain what's right before your eyes, don't take the opposite as real.

ZGS na, Shiba 238

8.133 權柄在手 殺活臨時 *Kenpei te ni ari, sakkatsu toki ni nozomu.*

Scepter in hand, he waits for the time to kill or awaken.

Heki 9 Intro (variant). ZGS 8.82: 自在 instead of 臨時.

ZGS 8.82, ZRKS 8.32, Shiba na, ZGJI 414, KZS #841

8.134 黄絹幼婦 外孫齏臼 *Kōken yōbu gaison saikyū.*

"Yellow silk," "infant lady," "outside grandchild," "pickling mortar."

This phrase is a Chinese character cipher that, when deciphered, yields 絕妙好辭, *zetsumyō kōji,* "absolute mystery, fine discourse." 黄絹 means "yellow silk" or more generally "colored thread" 色糸. Combined into one character, they form 絕 *zetsu,* "absolute." 幼婦 means "infant woman" or more generally "small woman" 小女, which when combined into one character form 妙 *myō,* "mystery." 外孫 denotes one's grandchild who has married out; such an event is considered "good" or "fine" 好. The character 齏 (ZGS has 齑) means "pickled vegetables," whose flavor is "salty" 辛. And the last character is 臼 "mortar," a utensil which "receives" 受. These last two characters combine to form 辤, which is a variant way of writing 辭, "discourse." See also 12.102.

ZGS 8.83, Shiba 213, ZGJI 419

8.135 好個師僧 也恁麼去 *Kōko no shisō mata inmo ni shisaru.*

A fine-looking monk, but he, too, goes off like this.

MMK 31.

ZGS 8.84, Shiba na

8.136 高山流水 只貴知音 *Kōzan ryūsui tada chiin o tattobu.*

In all the high peaks and the flowing waters, I value only my ⌜intimate friend⌝.

ZGS na, ZRKS 8.160, Shiba 213, ZGJI 418, ZGJT 136

8.137 杲日麗天 清風匝地 *Kōjitsu ten ni kagayaki, seifū chi o meguru.*

The bright sun touches the heavens, the pure wind circles the earth.

Heki 42 Intro.

ZGS na, ZRKS 8.5, Shiba 213, ZGJI 418

8.138 向上一路 千聖不傳 *Kōjō no ichi ro senshō fuden.*

The one path directed upward the thousand sages do not transmit.

Heki 3 Main Case Comm., 12 Intro., 40 Main Case Comm.

ZGS na, Shiba 213, ZGJI 418, ZGDJT 314b

8.139 劫石易消 村話難改 *Kōseki wa keshiyasuku, sonwa wa aratamegatashi.*

The ⌜*kalpa* stone⌝ is easy to wear away, but village talk is hard to amend.

ZGS 8.85, Shiba na, ZGJI 420

8.140 好雪片片 不落別處 *Kōsetsu hen-pen bessho ni ochizu.*

Beautiful snow! Flake after flake, they fall in no other place.

Heki 42. KZS #846: *kōsetsu* is an exclamatory.

ZGS na, ZRKS 8.42, Shiba 213, ZGJI 418, ZGJT 132, KZS #846

8.141 浩然之氣 塞天地間 *Kōzen no ki tenchi no kan ni fusagaru.*

His vast spirit fills the space between heaven and earth.

ZGS 8.86, Shiba na

8.142 皇天無私 惟德是仰 *Kōten watakushi naku, kore toku kore aogu.*

The great heaven is impersonal, it honors only the virtuous.

書經蔡仲之命: 皇天無親惟德是輔.

ZGS 8.87, Shiba na

8.143 黄頭結舌 碧眼呑聲 *Kōtō shita o musubi, hekigan koe o nomu.*

⌜Yellow Head⌝ is tongue-tied, ⌜Blue Eyes⌝ is speechless.

ZGS na, ZRKS 8.322, Shiba 214, ZGJI 419

8
字

8.144 剛刀雖利 不斬無罪 *Kōtō ri nari to iedomo muzai o kirazu.*

Though the ⌜*vajra*⌝ sword is sharp, it does not cut the innocent.

ZGS 8.88, ZRKS 8.230, Shiba 214, ZGJI 420

8.145 功成不處 電光難追 *Kō natte sho sezu, denkō mo oigatashi.*

Having attained merit he does not stay, a lightning flash is also hard to follow.

ZGS 8.89, ZRKS 8.135, Shiba na, ZGJI 417

8.146 洪波浩渺 白浪滔天 *Kōha kōbyō hakurō tōten.*

Giant waves on endless water, white waves wash the sky.

ZGS 8.90, Shiba 213: 洪 instead of 浩

8.147 驅耕夫牛 奪飢人食 *Kōfu no ushi o kari, kijin no jiki o ubau.*

He drives away the farmer's ox and steals the starveling's food.

Heki 3 Main Case Comm.

ZGS 8.91, ZRKS 8.134, Shiba 209, ZGJI 419, KZS #891

8.148 頭枕天台 脚踏南嶽 *Kōbe tendai o makura shi, ashi nangaku o fumu.*

He pillows his head on Mount T'ien-t'ai and rests his feet on South Peak.

ZRKS 8.317: 頭枕衡山脚蹈北嶽 *Kōbe kōzan o makura shi, ashi hokugaku o fumu,* "He pillows his head on Mount Heng-shan and rests his feet on North Peak."

ZGS 8.92, ZRKS 8.317, Shiba na, ZGJI 452

8.149 非高明智 爭得此人 *Kōmei no chi ni arazumba ikade ka kono hito o en.*

If you yourself lack refined wisdom, how can you expect to find such a person?

ZGS na, Shiba 232

8.150 毫釐有差 天地懸隔 *Gōri mo sa areba, tenchi haruka ni hedataru.*

If you allow even a hair's difference, then heaven and earth are split far apart.

信心銘 *Faith in Mind.*

ZGS 8.93, ZRKS 8.428, Shiba na, ZGDJT 327b

8.151 不入紅爐 爭辨眞僞 *Kōro ni irazareba ikade ka shingi o benzen.*

Without entering the burning furnace, how can you distinguish true from false?

ZGS 8.94, ZRKS 8.300, Shiba 233, ZGJI 418

8.152 五逆聞雷 曾參顏回 *Gogyaku rai o kiki, sōshin gankai.*

One who commits the ⌜five sins⌝ hears thunder—Tseng Ts'an and ⌜Yen Hui⌝.

ZRKS 8.345: Tseng Ts'an (J. Sōshin) and Yen Hui (J. Gankai) are both disciples of Confucius, known for their earnest attitude toward self-cultivation. See also 4.194.

ZGS na, ZRKS 8.345, Shiba 212

8.153 鵠不浴白 鴉不染黑 *Koku wa yoku sezu shite shiroku, a wa somezu shite kuroshi.*

The swan is white without bathing, the crow is black without dyeing.

Chuang-tzu, ch. 14.

ZGS 8.95, ZRKS 8.73, Shiba na, ZGJI 419

8.154 不入虎穴 爭得虎兒 *Koketsu ni irazunba ikadeka koji o en.*

Without entering the tiger's lair, how will you take the tiger's cub?

Heki 26 Main Case Comm.

ZGS na, ZRKS 8.183, Shiba 233, KZS #184

8.155 心如波旬 面似夜叉 *Kokoro hajun no gotoku, omote yasha ni nitari.*

A heart like a ⌜*pāpīyas*⌝, a face like a ⌜*yakṣa*⌝.

ZGS 8.96, Shiba na

8.156 心不負人 面無慚色 *Kokoro hito ni somukazareba, omote ni hazuru iro nashi.*

If the heart does not betray others, the face will not color with shame.

ZGS 8.97, ZRKS 8.171, Shiba 220, ZGJI 420, ZGJT 226, KZS #901

8.157 坐斷古今 鐵輪碎石 *Kokon o zadan shite, tetsurin ishi o kudaku.*

It cuts off past and present, as an iron wheel crushes stone.

ZGS na, ZRKS 8.168, Shiba 214, ZGJI 416, ZGJT 165, ZGJT 153

8.158 五十歩咲 他先百歩 *Gojuppo ni shite ta no hyappo ni sakidatsu koto o warau.*

One who retreats fifty paces mocks one who retreats a hundred.

Mencius II, A, 3.

ZGS na, ZRKS 8.9, Shiba 212, ZGJI 417

8.159 業識忙忙 那伽大定 *Gosshiki bō-bō mo naga daijō naran.*

The turmoil of consciousness is the great Naga *samādhi.*

MMK 42. For "great Naga *samādhi,*" see 4.465.

ZGS na, ZRKS na, Shiba 207

8.160 呉天嘯月 楚路遊花 *Goten tsuki ni usobuki, soro hana ni asobu.*

Sing to the ⌜moon⌝ in Wu's skies, wander on the flowered byways of Ch'u.

Shiba 212: *soji* instead of *soro.*

ZGS 8.98, Shiba 212

8.161 古洞風清 寒潭月皎 *Kodō kaze kiyoku, kantan tsuki shiroshi.*

A clean wind in the old cave, a silver ⌜moon⌝ over the deep pool.

ZGS na, Shiba 211, ZGJI 416

8.162 不植梧桐 爭得鳳來 *Godō o uezu, ikadeka hō no kitaru koto o en.*

If you do not plant a parasol tree, how will you get a phoenix to roost?

ZRKS 8.103: *Godō o uezunba ikadeka hō o rai suru o en.* ZGJT 417: "The phoenix is said to nest in the Chinese parasol tree."

ZGS na, ZRKS 8.103, Shiba 233, ZGJI 417

8.163 虎班易見 人班難見 *Koban wa miyasuku, jinban wa migatashi.*

A tiger's stripes are easy to see, a person's stripes are hard to see.

ZGS na, ZRKS 8.13, Shiba 212, ZGJI 416, KZS #828

8.164 孤峯遙秀 不掛烟蘿 *Kohō haruka ni hiide enra o kakezu.*

The lone peak soars so high no shred of mist clings to it.

ZGS na, Shiba 212

8.165 枯木生花 鐵樹抽枝 *Koboku hana o shōji, tetsuju eda o nukinzu.*

The dead tree flowers, the iron tree extends branches.

This verse often appears with the couplet reversed. Some variants have 石樹 *sekiju* "stone tree" instead of "dead tree," and 蚰 instead of 抽.

ZGS na, ZRKS 8.141 and 8.145, ZGJI 416, Shiba na, KZS #892

8.166 仰之彌高 鑽之彌堅 *Kore o aogeba iyo-iyo takaku, kore o kireba iyo-iyo katashi.*

Gaze up and it rises even higher, drill into it and it becomes even harder.➛

Analects IX, 10.

ZGS na, Shiba 207, ZGJI 421

8.167 瞻之在前 忽焉在後 *Kore o miru ni mae ni aru ka to sureba, kotsuen to shite shirie ni ari.*

➛When I looked, it seemed to be in front, and then suddenly it was behind.

Analects IX, 10.

ZGS na, ZRKS 8.4, Shiba 224, KZS #827

8.168 視之不見 聽之無聲 *Kore o miredomo miezu, kore o kikedomo koe nashi.*

When I look I do not see, when I listen there is no sound.

Tao-te ching, ch. 14.

ZGS na, ZRKS 8.417, Shiba 216, ZGJI 421, ZGJT 177

8.169 喚之無聲 看之無形 *Kore o yobu ni koe naku, kore o miru ni katachi nashi.*

There is no voice by which to call it, there is no shape by which to see it.

ZGS na, ZRKS 8.224, Shiba 204, ZGJI 421

8.170 維鵲有巣 維鳩居之 *Kore kasasagi su areba, kore hato kore ni oreri.*

If the magpie has a nest, then a pigeon will be in it.

ZGS 8.99, Shiba na

8.171 不是河南 便歸河北 *Kore kanan ni arazumba, sunawachi kahoku ni ki sen.*

When I'm not in Ho-nan, I return to Ho-pei.

Rinzai-roku Preface and §56. Ho-nan and Ho-pei are south and north of the Yellow River respectively. See note at 8.66.

ZGS na, Shiba 233

8.172 金剛王寶 劍當頭截 *Kongō ō hōken tōtō ni kiru.*

The treasure sword of the ⌜*Vajra*⌝ King cuts everything it strikes.

ZGS 8.100, ZRKS 8.51, Shiba na, ZGJI 422, KZS #851

8.173 透金剛圈 呑栗棘蓬 *Kongōken o tōri rikkyokubō o nomu.*

He escapes the diamond pitfall and eats up the prickly thorns.

See ⌜*Vajra*⌝.

ZGS na, ZRKS 8.121, Shiba 229, ZGJI 422, ZGJT145

8.174 言語道斷 心行處滅 *Gongo dōdan shingyō shometsu.*

Speech silenced, thoughts destroyed.

ZGS 8.101, Shiba 211

8.175 金翅擘海 怒雷破山 *Konji umi o tsunzaki, dorai yama o yaburu.*

⌜*Garuda*⌝ churns the ocean, angry thunder smashes the mountains.

Same as 8.322 but couplet is reversed. This is the more common form. Shiba 208: *kinji* for *konji.*

ZGS 8.102, ZRKS 8.264, Shiba 208

8.176 言詮不及 意路不到 *Gonsen fukyū iro futō.*

Words cannot touch it, thought cannot reach it.

ZGS na, Shiba 211

8.177 左眼半斤 右眼八兩 *Sagan hankin, ugan hachiryō.*

The left eye—half a pound; the right eye—eight ounces.

Heki 56 Verse *agyo*, 12 Verse *agyo*, 65 Verse *agyo*. See ⌜Catty⌝.

ZGS 8.103, ZRKS 8.235, Shiba 214, ZGJI 149, ZGJT 422

8.178 左轉右轉 自由自在 *Saten uten jiyu jizai.*

Turn left, turn right, utterly free!

ZGS 8.104, Shiba na

8.179 左撥右轉 右轉左撥 *Sahatsu uten, uten sahatsu.*

Wave left and turn right, turn right and wave left.

Heki 31 Main Case Comm.

ZGS na, ZRKS 8.396, Shiba 214, ZGJI 422, ZGJT 150

8.180 三界無安 猶如火宅 *Sangai wa yasuki koto naku, nao kataku no gotoshi.*

In the ⌜three worlds⌝, there is no rest; it is like being in a burning house.

Parable of the burning house, *Lotus Sutra*, ch. 3.

ZGS 8.105, ZRKS 8.294, Shiba na, ZGJI 424

8.181 三界無法 何處求心 *Sangai muhō izure no tokoro ni ka shin o motomen.*

In the ⌜three worlds⌝, there are no dharmas. Where is one to seek for mind?

Heki 37 Main Case Comm. and Verse.

ZGS na, Shiba 215, ZGJI 424

8.182 三徑就荒 松菊猶存 *Sankei are ni tsuite shōgiku nao son seri.*

The three garden paths were overrun with weeds, but the pines and chrysanthemums were still there.

See ⌜Yüan-ming⌝. Shōun-ji: *Sankei wa kō ni tsuki, shōgiku wa nao son seri.*

ZGS 8.106, Shiba na

8.183 殘羹餿飯 狗亦不顧 *Zankō sōhan inu mo mata kaerimizu.*

Leftover soup, spoiled rice, not even dogs will look at them.

ZGS 8.107, Shiba na

8.184 三代禮樂 在緇衣中 *Sandai no reigaku wa shie no uchi ni ari.*

The ritual composure of the ⌜Three Dynasties⌝ lives in these black robes.

ZGS 8.108, ZRKS 8.1, Shiba 215, ZGJI 425, ZGJT 161

8.185 三段不同 收歸上科 *Sandan onajikarazu, osamete jōka ni ki su.*

The three steps do not agree, leave them and return to the top level.

There are several interpretations of this verse. ZGJI 425: The three steps are the three Buddha-bodies; *jōka* refers to *dharmakaya.* ZGJT 160: The three steps are parts of a sutra: introduction, text, and commentary. No explanation of *jōka.* Daitoku-ji Sōdō Rōshi *teishō,* 15 October 1979: A commentary to a sutra text is dropped one character space, a commentary to the commentary is dropped two character spaces, a third commentary is dropped three character spaces—thus forming three steps. *Jōka* is the original text which starts at the top of the page.

ZGS 8.109, ZRKS 8.278, Shiba na, ZGJI 425, ZGJT 160

8.186 三郎郎當 三郎郎當 *Sanrō rōtō, sanrō rōtō.*

Slovenly San-lang! Slovenly San-lang!

See ⌜Hsieh San-lang⌝.

ZGS 8.110, Shiba na

8.187 三世諸佛 口掛壁上 *Sanze no shobutsu kuchi hekijō ni kaku.*

The buddhas of the ⌜three worlds⌝ have hung up their mouths on the wall.

ZGS na, ZRKS 8.288, Shiba 215, ZGJI 425 (variant), ZGJT 161

8.188 參須實參 悟須實悟 *San wa subekaraku jitsusan naru beku,*
Go wa subekaraku jitsugo narubeshi.

Practice must be true practice,
Awakening must be true awakening.

ZGS na, Shiba 215, ZGJI 426

8.189 聽事不眞 喚鐘作甕 *Ji o kiite shin narazareba, kane o yonde motai to nasu.*

Hearing the facts wrong is like calling a crock a bell.

MMK 7.

ZGS 8.111, Shiba 227, ZGJI 421, ZGJT 313

8.190 紫燕黄鸝 深談實相 *Shien kōri fukaku jissō o danzu.*

The purple swallows and yellow nightingales are in deep discussion about true nature.

ZGS na, ZRKS 8.426, Shiba 216, ZGJI 427

8.191 自覺覺他 覺行圓滿 *Jikaku kakuta kakugyō enman.*

Self-awakening, awakening others, the discipline for awakening, complete fulfilment.

ZGS 8.112, Shiba na

8.192 色卽是空 空卽是色 *Shiki soku ze kū, kū soku ze shiki.*

Form itself is emptiness, emptiness itself is form.

Heart Sutra.

ZGS na, Shiba 217

8.193 四十九年 一字不説 *Shijūku nen ichiji fusetsu.*

For forty-nine years, not one word spoken.

Refer *Heki* 14, 15.

ZGS 8.113, ZRKS 8.225, Shiba 216, ZGJI 436

8.194 親者不問 問者不親 *Shitashiki mono wa towazu, tou mono wa shitashikarazu.*

An ⌜intimate friend⌝ does not ask; one who asks is not an intimate.

ZGS na, ZRKS 8.390, Shiba 221, ZGJI 428

8.195 至道無難 唯嫌揀擇 *Shidō bunan yuiken kenjaku.*

The Great Way is without difficulty, just avoid picking and choosing.

信心銘 *Faith in Mind. Heki* 2 Main Case, 9 Main Case Comm., 57 Main Case, 58 Main Case, 59 Main Case.

ZGS na, Shiba 216

8.196 獅子一吼 野干脳裂 *Shishi ikku sureba yakan nōretsu su.*

The lion gives one roar and scrambles the brains of the ⌜wild fox⌝.

ZGS na, Shiba 216

8.197 獅子哮吼 百獣脳裂 *Shishi kōku sureba hyakujū nōretsu su.*

When the lion roars, the brains of the hundred beasts are rent.

ZGS 8.114, ZRKS 8.30, Shiba 216, ZGJI 427, ZGJT 176, KZS #839

8.198 獅子咬人 韓獹逐塊 *Shishi hito o kami, kanro kai o ou.*

A lion bites the man, but the Han-lu hound chases after the clod of earth.

ZGJI 125: The Han-lu hound is a stupid dog that chases the clod, not the man.

ZGS 8.115, ZRKS 8.149, Shiba na, ZGJI 427 and 125 (*kanro*), ZGJT 176

8.199 獅子嚬呻 象王回顧 *Shishi hinshin sureba zōō kaiko su.*

When the lion growls, the king elephant turns its head.

ZGS na, ZRKS 8.156, Shiba 217, ZGJI 168, KZS #894

8.200 事事物物 天眞獨朗 *Ji-ji butsu-butsu tenshin hitori hogaraka.*

In every fact and every thing, the fundamental reality alone shines.

天眞 translates *bhūta-tathatā* (Skt.), "the fundamental reality."

ZGS 8.116, Shiba na

8.201 舌捲春雷 眼懸秋月 *Shita shunrai o maki, manako shūgetsu o kaku.*

From his tongue rolls spring thunder, in his eye hangs the autumn ⌜moon⌝.

ZGS 8.117, Shiba na, ZGJI 428

8.202 自他不二 錯生人我 *Jita funi ayamatte ninga o shōzu.*

Self and other are not two; in error, we create "they" and "I."

ZGS 8.118, Shiba na

8.203 七尺拄杖 三尺竹篦 *Shichishaku no shujō sanjaku no shippei.*

A seven-foot staff, a three-foot ⌜*shippei*⌝.

ZGS 8.119, ZRKS 8.19, Shiba na, ZGJI 428, KZS #832

8.204 七顛八倒 目瞪口呿 *Shitten battō mokutō shi kuko su.*

He tosses and turns; gazing vacantly, his mouth hangs open.

ZGS 8.120, Shiba na

8.205 實際理地 不染一塵 *Jissai richi ichijin ni somazu.*

The ground of actuality is not defiled by even a mote of ⌜dust⌝.

ZGS na, ZRKS 8.406, Shiba 217, ZGJI 428

8.206 實際理地 醉見身界 *Jissai richi yōtte shinkai o miru.*

We drunkenly see the ground of actuality as "my world."

實際 translates *bhūta-koṭi*, "actuality."

ZGS 8.121, Shiba na

8.207 十方虛空 悉皆消殞 *Jippō kokū kotogotoku mina shōin su.*

The ⌜ten directions⌝ are empty, everything has vanished.

ZGS 8.122, ZRKS 8.241, Shiba 218

8.208 四佛智見 四智如來 *Shibutsu chiken shichi nyorai.*

The four Buddhist insights, the four wisdoms, the Tathāgata.

ZGS 8.123, Shiba na

8.209 四邊誵訛 八面玲瓏 *Shihon gōka hachimen reirō.*

Its four sides are incomprehensible but its eight faces are crystal clear.

Heki 97 Verse *agyo.*

ZGS 8.124, ZRKS 8.79, Shiba na, ZGJI 426, ZGJT 141 (*gōka*)

8.210 寂然不動 如春在花 *Jakunen fudō haru no hana ni aru ga gotoshi.*

Serene and still, like springtime in the flowers.

ZGS na, ZRKS 8.281, Shiba 218

8.211 蛇呑鼈鼻 虎咬大蟲 *Ja beppi o nomi, tora daichū o kamu.*

The snake swallows a turtle-nose monster, the tiger bites a ⌜big bug⌝.

For turtle-nose monster, see *Heki* 22.

ZGS na, ZRKS 8.86, Shiba 217, KZS #875

8.212 秋月離離 秋色依依 *Shūgetsu ri-ri shūshoku i-i.*

Autumn ⌜moon⌝—so far far away; autumn colors—how near, how near.

ZGS 8.125, Shiba na, ZGJI 429

8.213 須彌不高 大海不深 *Shumi takakarazu, daikai fukakarazu.*

Mount ⌜Sumeru⌝ is not high, the great ocean is not deep.

ZGS 8.126, Shiba na

8.214 諸葛殘謀 殺魏將軍 *Shokatsu hakarigoto o nokoshite gi shōgun o korosu.*

⌜Chu-ko⌝ left behind a strategy that killed the Wei general.

ZGS 8.127, Shiba na

8.215 上求菩提 下化衆生 *Jōgu bodai geke shujō.*

Above to seek awakening, below to save sentient beings.

ZGS 8.128, Shiba na

8.216 牀窄先臥 粥薄後坐 *Sho semaku shite mazu fu shi, kayu usuku shite okurete za su.*

First he lay down on his narrow bed, later he sat down to a thin gruel.

ZGS 8.129, Shiba na

8.217 上天之載 無聲無臭 *Jōten no koto wa oto mo naku ka mo nashi.*

The acts of high heaven have neither sound nor smell.

ZGS 8.130, Shiba 220, *Book of Songs* 235.

8.218 生佛一如 妄爲凡聖 *Shōbutsu ichinyo midari ni bonshō to nasu.*

Buddhas and sentient beings are one, but willy-nilly we divide them into sacred and profane.

ZGS 8.131, Shiba na

8.219 正法眼藏 涅槃妙心 *Shōbō genzō nehan myōshin.*

The treasury of the Dharma eye, the marvelous mind of nirvana.

MMK 6.

ZGS na, Shiba 223, ZGDJT 583b

8.220 諸法實相 何厭何憎 *Shohō jissō nanzo itowan nanzo nikuman.*

All things in their real aspect—what is there to regret, what is there to hate?

ZGS 8.132, Shiba na

8.221 不慕諸聖 不重己靈 *Shosei o shitawazu, korei o mo omonzezu.*

He does not revere the saints, he does not care about the soul.

ZGS na, ZRKS 8.335, Shiba 233, ZGJI 431, ZGJT 401

8.222 眞不掩僞 曲不藏直 *Shin itsuwari o ōwazu, kyoku jiki o kakusazu.*

The true does not conceal the false, the bent does not contain the straight.

Heki 42 Main Case *agyo*.

ZGS na, ZRKS 8.119, Shiba 221, ZGJI 433, ZGJT 229, KZS #119 (order reversed)

8.223 心境一如 物我不二 *Shinkyō ichinyo motsuga funi.*

Mind and its surroundings are one, things and self are not two.

ZGS 8.133, Shiba na

8.224 眞空無相 亂存執取 *Shinkū musō midari ni shisshu o son su.*

True emptiness is without form, mistakenly we create something to grasp.

ZGS 8.134, Shiba na

8.225 心外無法 滿目青山 *Shinge muhō manmoku seizan.*

Outside of mind there are no things, but the eyes are filled with blue mountains.

Heki 7 Main Case Comm.

ZGS 8.135, ZRKS 8.399, Shiba 220, ZGJI 432, ZGJT 226

8.226 身心脱落 脱落身心 *Shinjin datsuraku, datsuraku shinjin.*

Body-mind cast off, cast off body-mind.

ZGS na, Shiba 221, ZGJI 433, ZGDJT 616a

8.227 神仙秘訣 父子不傳 *Shinsen hiketsu fushi fuden.*

The secret techniques of gods and immortals are not passed on from father to son.

Heki 73 Verse Comm.

ZGS na, ZRKS 8.131, Shiba 221, ZGJT 228

8.228 針頭削鐵 鷺股割肉 *Shintō ni tetsu o kezuri, rokō ni niku o saku.*

Shave iron from the tip of a needle, scrape flesh from a heron's leg.

ZGS 8.136, ZRKS 8.84, Shiba 221, ZGJI 433, KZS #874

8.229 眞獅子兒 能獅子吼 *Shin no shishiji yoku shishi ku su.*

A true lion's cub gives a good lion's roar.

Shiba 221: 善 instead of 能. *Heki* 4 Main Case *agyo*.

ZGS 8.137, ZRKS 8.177, Shiba 221, ZGJI 433, ZGJT 229, KZS #910

8.230 盡大地撮 來無寸土 *Jindaichi sasshikitaru ni sundo nashi.*

In this vast world there is not even a clod of earth to grasp.

ZGS 8.138, Shiba na

8.231 心安如海 膽量如斗 *Shin yasuki koto umi no gotoku, tanryō to no gotoshi.*

A mind as still as the sea, a heart as deep as the Big Dipper.

ZGS na, Shiba 220, ZGJI 420

8.232 春風如刀 春雨似膏 *Shunpū wa katana no gotoku, shun'u wa abura ni nitari.*

The spring wind [stings] like a ⌜sword⌝, the spring rain is [slick] as oil.

Shiba 218: *Shunpū wa yaiba no gotoku.*

ZGS 8.139, ZRKS 8.23, Shiba 218, ZGJI 430, ZGJT 206

8.233 春風入門 千花生觜 *Shunpū mon ni ireba senka kuchibashi o shōzu.*

When the winds of spring enter the gate, the thousand flowers send forth shoots.

ZGS 8.140, ZRKS 8.146, Shiba na, ZGJI 430

8.234 照用同時 卷舒齊唱 *Shōyū dōji kenjo hitoshiku tonau.*

His insight is simultaneous with act, his speech equally grips and liberates.

Heki 5 Intro.

ZGS na, Shiba 219, ZGJI 432

8.235 垂絲千尺 意在深潭 *Suishi senjaku kokoro shintan ni ari.*

He dropped a line a thousand feet, aiming for something deep in the pool.

ZGS na, ZRKS 8.90, Shiba 222, ZGJI 434, ZGJT 237, KZS #877

8.236 隨處作主 遇緣卽宗 *Zuisho ni shu to nari, en ni ōte shū ni soku su.*

Be master wherever you go, become one in every condition.

MMK 47.

ZGS na, Shiba 222

8.237 隨處作主 立處皆眞 *Zuisho ni shu to nareba, rissho ni mina shin nari.*

Be master wherever you go, then wherever you are, things are as they truly are.

ZGS 8.141, Shiba 222, ZGJI 431

8.238 水中鹽味 色裏膠青 *Suichū no enmi, shikiri no kōsei.*

Salt in water, sizing in dye.

ZGS na, ZRKS 8.97, Shiba 222, ZGJI 434, ZGJT 236

8.239 背倚寒巖 面如滿月 *Se kangan ni yori, omote mangetsu no gotoshi.*

He takes a winter cliff for his backrest, he has a face like the full ⌜moon⌝.

ZGS na, Shiba 231

8.240 齊女維打 姜女維嗔 *Seijo kore uchi, kyōjo kore ikaru.*

When the girl from Ch'i slaps, the girl from Chiang gets angry.

ZGS 8.142, Shiba na

8.241 聲前一句 千聖不傳 *Seizen no ikku senshō fuden.*

The one word prior to speech the thousand sages have never passed on.

ZGS na, Shiba 223

8.242 股肱淸朝 槖籥黎庶 *Seichō kokō to shite reisho ni takuyaku su.*

When the "arms and legs" of the court are pure, then the black-haired people are like a bellows.

股肱 "arms and legs" is a conventional expression for officials who serve a ruler (Morohashi 29284.11). The "black-haired people" is a Ch'in expression for common people. 槖籥 is a blacksmith's bellows (Morohashi 15533.28).

ZGS 8.143, Shiba na

8.243 把定世界 不漏纖毫 *Sekai o hajō shite sengō o morasazu.*

He takes the world in hand and not a strand of hair slips through.

Heki 85 Intro.

ZGS na, ZRKS 8.297, Shiba 231, ZGJI 435, ZGJT 375

8.244 石火莫及 電光罔通 *Sekka mo oyobu koto naku, denkō mo tsūzuru koto nashi.*

A spark cannot catch him, lightning cannot touch him.

Rinzai-roku §66.

ZGS 8.144, ZRKS 8.217, Shiba 223, ZGJI 436, ZGJT 247, KZS #922, Watson 1993, 124

8.245 石人點頭 露柱拍手 *Sekijin tentō sureba, rochū te o haku su.*

When the stone man nods his head, the wooden pillar claps its hands.

ZGS 8.145, ZRKS 8.65, Shiba 223, ZGJI 437, ZGJT 247, KZS #858

8.246 蟬噪高樹 蛩吟古砌 *Semi wa kōju ni sawagi, kirigirisu wa kozei ni ginzu.*

Cicadas shrill in the tall trees, crickets chirp under old stone steps.

ZGS 8.146, ZRKS 8.111, Shiba na, ZGJI 437

8.247 潛行密用 如愚如魯 *Sengyō mitsuyū, gu no gotoku ro no gotoshi.*

His training is hidden, his practice secret; he seems a fool or an idiot.

ZGS na, Shiba 224

8.248 栴檀林中 必無雜樹 *Sendanrinchū kanarazu zōju nashi.*

In the sandalwood forest there are no ordinary trees.

ZGS 8.147, ZRKS 8.173, Shiba na, KZS #902

8.249 前頭綠水 後面青山 *Zentō wa ryokusui, kōmen wa seizan.*

In front, blue waters; behind, green hills.

ZGS 8.148, ZRKS 8.400, Shiba 224, ZGJI 438

8.250 千兵易得 一將難求 *Senpyō wa eyasuku, isshō wa motomegatashi.*

A thousand soldiers are easy to raise, but one general is hard to find.

Heki 13 Verse *agyo*, 49 Verse *agyo*, 54 Verse *agyo*.

ZGS 8.149, ZRKS 8.175, Shiba 223, ZGJI 438, ZGJT 255, KZS #903

8.251 千峯向岳 百川趣海 *Senpō gaku ni mukai, hyakusen umi ni omomuku.*

The thousand peaks face the mountain, the hundred rivers head toward the sea.

ZGS 8.150, ZRKS 8.46, Shiba 223, ZGJI 438

8.252 巢父飲牛 許由洗耳 *Sōho ushi ni mizukai, kyoyū mimi o arau.*

⌜Ch'ao-fu⌝ waters his ox, ⌜Hsü Yu⌝ washes his ears.

ZD #188n. Hsü Yu and Ch'ao-fu were two men of ancient China, famous for their spotless integrity. When Emperor ⌜Yao⌝ offered his throne to him, Hsü Yu hurried to wash his ears in the stream to cleanse them of defilement. When Ch'ao-fu heard of this, he led his ox upstream to avoid drinking the dirty water in which Hsü Yu had washed his ears.

ZGS 8.151, ZRKS 8.290, Shiba na, ZGJI 439, ZGJT 270, ZD #188

8.253 雙放雙收 箭過新羅 *Sōhō sōshū ya shinra o sugu.*

Let both go, take both in; the arrow has flown off to ⌜Silla⌝.

ZGS 8.152, Shiba na

8.254 蒼龍得水 老虎靠山 *Sōryū mizu o ete, rōko yama ni yoru.*

The blue dragon takes to the water, the old tiger lives in the mountains.

Variant: 毒龍得水, "The poison dragon takes to the water."

ZGS 8.153, ZRKS 8.299, Shiba225, ZGJI 439

8.255 賊是小人 智過君子 *Zoku wa kore shōjin, chi kunshi ni sugitari.*

The ⌜thief⌝ is a minor fellow but in cunning he surpasses an eminent man.

Rinzai-roku §54, *Heki* 59 Main Case *agyo.*

ZGS 8.154, ZRKS 8.277, Shiba 225, ZGJI 439, KZS #887 , Watson 1993, 112

8.256 麁飡易飽 細嚼難飢 *Sosan wa akiyasuku, saishaku wa uegatashi.*

With coarse chewing you are quickly satisfied,
With fine chewing you are seldom hungry.

MMK 47.

ZGS 8.155, ZRKS 8.193, Shiba 225, ZGJI 439, ZGJT 265

8.257 祖師心印 七花八裂 *Soshi no shin'in shikka hachiretsu.*

The true mind-seal of the patriarchs smashed to pieces.

ZGS na, ZRKS 8.309, Shiba 225, ZGJI 152 Shikka hachi retsu, ZGJT 264

8.258 楚人一炬 可憐焦土 *Sojin no ikko ni awaremubeshi shōdo to narinu.*

How sad —the man of Ch'u's single torch has scorched the earth.

From Tu Mu 杜牧, "O-pang-kung fu" 阿房宮賦. See ⌜O-pang Palace⌝ and ⌜Hsiang Yü⌝.

ZGS 8.156, Shiba na

8.259 夫善竊者 鬼神莫知 *Sore yoku nusumu mono wa kijin mo shiru koto nashi.*

He is so good at stealing, not even the gods and demons are aware.

Shiba 233: 殺 "killing" instead of 竊 "stealing."

ZGS 8.157, ZRKS 8.27, Shiba 233, ZGJI 440

8.260 太阿寶劍 本是生鐵 *Taia no hōken moto kore santetsu.*

The jeweled sword ⌜T'ai-a⌝ was originally raw iron.

ZGS 8.158, ZRKS 8.59, Shiba 226, ZGJI 442, KZS #853

8.261 掀飜大海 趯倒須彌 *Daikai o kenpon shi, shumi o tekitō su.*

He tips over the great sea, he kicks over Mount ⌜Sumeru⌝.

Heki 20 Intro.

ZGS 8.159, ZRKS 8.33, Shiba na, ZGJI 440, ZGJT 95, KZS #842

8.262 太虛無雲 淸鏡無痕 *Taikyo kumo naku, seikyō ato nashi.*

There are no clouds in the vast emptiness, no traces left in the bright mirror.

ZGS 8.160, ZRKS 8.106, Shiba 226, ZGJI 442, KZS #884

8.263 大湖浸月 長橋伏浪 *Daiko tsuki o hitashi, chōkyō nami ni fu su.*

The ⌜moon⌝ is steeped in the great lake, the long bridge lies down across its waves.

ZGS 8.161, Shiba na

8.264 太公招手 子夏揚眉 *Taikō te o manekeba, shika mayu o agu.*

⌜T'ai-kung⌝ waved his hand, Tzu-hsia raised his ⌜eyebrows⌝.

Tzu-hsia is a disciple to Confucius. Several of his sayings are included in *Analects* XIX.

ZGS na, ZRKS 8.77, Shiba 226, ZRMKJT na

8.265 大道無門 千差有路 *Daidō mumon sensa michi ari.*

The Great Way has no gate, the thousand byways are its path.

8
字

MMK Mumon's Preface. Shibayama (1974, 9) translates, "Gateless is the Great Way. / There are thousands of ways to it," as if the great Way and the thousands of byways were different.

ZGS na, Shiba 225

8.266 透得此關 乾坤獨歩 *Kono kan o tōtoku seba, kenkon o doppo sen.*

Pass through this barrier and alone you walk ⌜heaven and earth⌝.

MMK Mumon's Preface.

ZGS na, Shiba na

8.267 大機圓應 大道無方 *Dai ⌜ki⌝ ennō, daidō muhō.*

Great action adapts totally; in the Great Way there are no skillful means.

ZGS na, Shiba 225, ZGJI 441

8.268 大用現前 不存軌則 *Daiyū genzen kisoku o son sezu.*

Great activity manifests itself unbound by convention.

Heki 3 Intro., 8 Intro., 79 Intro.

ZGS 8.162, ZRKS 8.424, Shiba 226, ZGJI 442, ZGJT 293

8.269 鷹拏燕雀 鶻打寒鳩 *Taka wa enjaku o uchi, hayabusa wa kankyū o utsu.*

The hawk attacks the small birds, the falcon strikes the winter pigeon.

ZGS 8.163, Shiba na

8.270 澤廣藏山 狸能伏豹 *Taku hirōshite yama o zō shi, ri yoku hyō o fu su.*

The broad marsh flats engulf the hills, a badger makes the panther lie down.

Heki 4 Main Case Comm., 38 Main Case Comm.,

ZGS 8.164, ZRKS 8.186, Shiba na, ZGJI 442, ZGJT 295, KZS #906

8.271 相維辟公 天子穆穆 *Tasukuru kore heki kō ari, tenshi boku-boku tari.*

The lords assist, the emperor is congenial and mild.

ZGS 8.165, Shiba na

8.272 唯解見前 不解見後 *Tada mae o miru koto o ge shite, shirie o miru koto o ge sezu.*

He knows only to look ahead, he doesn't know to look behind.

ZGS 8.166, ZRKS 8.208, Shiba na

8.273 竪窮三際 横亘十方 *Tate ni sansai o kiwame, yoko ni jippō ni wataru.*

Vertically it contains the ⌜three moments⌝, horizontally it embraces the ⌜ten directions⌝.

Shiba 218: 亙 instead of 亘.

ZGS 8.167, ZRKS 8.8, Shiba 218, ZGJI 443, ZGJT 198

8.274 他馬莫騎 他弓莫牽 *Ta no uma o noru koto nakare, ta no yumi o hiku koto nakare.*

Do not ride another's horse, do not draw another's bow.

MMK 45 Verse.

ZGS 8.168, Shiba na, ZGJI 440, ZGJT 278

8.275 爲他語脈 裏被轉卻 *Ta no tame ni gomyakuri ni tenkyaku seraren.*

For the sake of others, he lets himself get sent round the maze of words.

ZGS 8.169, Shiba na

8.276 大方無外 大圓無内 *Taihō hoka naku, taien uchi nashi.*

The great square has no outside, the great circle has no inside.

Earth is square and heaven is round. *Heki* 22 Intro.

ZGS na, ZRKS 8.349, Shiba 226, ZGJI 441, ZGJT 295

8.277 珠回玉轉 八面玲瓏 *Tama mawari tama tenzu, hachimen reirō.*

Pearls roll, gems tumble, every facet gleaming and sparkling.

ZGS 8.170, Shiba na, ZGJI 429

8.278 玉本無瑕 彫文喪德 *Tama moto kizu nashi, bun o ette toku o sōsu.*

The original jewel is flawless but engraving a design destroys its quality.

Shiba 207: 雕 instead of 彫, *bun o hotte* instead of *bun o ette.*

ZGS 8.171, ZRKS 8.164, Shiba 207

8.279 依稀端午 彷彿重陽 *Tango ni iki to shite, chōyō ni hōfutsu tari.*

It resembles the fifth day of the fifth month, it is like the ninth day of the ninth month.

See「Five festive occasions」.

ZGS 8.172, Shiba na

8.280 含血吐人 先汚其口 *Chi o fukunde hito ni hakeba, mazu sono kuchi o kega su.*

If you suck up blood to spit it on others, first you dirty your own mouth.

ZGJI 443: 噴 instead of 吐.

ZGS 8.173, ZRKS 8.14, Shiba na, ZGJI 443, ZGJT 73, KZS #829

8.281 智鑑高明 識量寛大 *Chikan kōmei shikiryō kandai.*

Wise and high-minded, liberal and large-hearted.

ZGS 8.174, Shiba na

8.282 住着智見 破正梵行 *Chiken ni jūchaku sureba shōbongyō o ha su.*

If you get stuck at wisdom, then you destroy correct Buddhist practice.

ZGS 8.176, Shiba na

8.283 父爲子隱 子爲父隱 *Chichi wa ko no tame ni kakushi, ko wa chichi no tame ni kakusu.*

The father conceals it for his son, the son conceals it for his father.

See ⌜Steal a sheep⌝.

ZGS 8.177, ZRKS 8.26, Shiba 233, ZGJI 444, ZGJT 403, KZS #837

8.284 重賞之下 必有勇夫 *Jūshō no shita ni kanarazu yūfu ari.*

Under a person of great merit, there will always be courageous men.

Heki 26 Verse *agyo*.

ZGS 8.178, ZRKS 8.178, Shiba 218, ZGJT 203

8.285 有條攀條 無條攀例 *Jō areba jō o yoji, jō nakereba rei o yozu.*

If there is a rule, follow the rule; if there is no rule, follow precedent.

Heki 10 Intro, 77 Intro.

ZGS 8.179, ZRKS 8.199, Shiba 237, ZGJI 432, ZGJT 30

8.286 朝打三千 暮打八百 *Chōda sanzen, boda happyaku.*

In the morning, three thousand blows; in the evening, eight hundred.

Heki 60 Verse *agyo*, 61 Main Case *agyo*, 66 Main Case *agyo*, 78 Verse *agyo*, 82 Verse *agyo*, 84 Verse *agyo*.

ZGS 8.180, Shiba 227, ZGJI 445, ZGJT 312, KZS #840

8.287 頂門眼照 破四天下 *Chōmon no manako shitenka o shōha su.*

The eye in the forehead illuminates everything under the four heavens.

Heki 26 Main Case Comm. ZGJI 445: "Everything under the four heavens" refers to the four continents surrounding Mount ⌜Sumeru⌝.

ZGS na, ZRKS 8.327, Shiba 227, ZGJI 445

8.288 頭角崢嶸 狀似鐵牛 *Zukaku sōkō katachi tetsugyū ni nitari.*

He looks like an iron ox with sharp flaring horns.

Related to *Heki* 38.

ZGS na, Shiba 229, ZGJI 445

8.289 頭上是天 脚下是地 *Zujō wa kore ten, kyakka wa kore chi.*

Above the head is heaven, beneath the feet is earth.

ZGS na, ZRKS 8.109, Shiba 229, ZGJI 446

8.290 頭上漫漫 脚下漫漫 *Zujō manman, kyakka manman.*

Above the head—vast and boundless; beneath the feet—vast and boundless.

Heki 2 Verse *agyo*, 34 Verse *agyo*, 96 Verse 2nd *agyo*.

ZGS 8.181, ZRKS 8.279, 420, Shiba 229, ZGJI 446, ZGJT 344

8.291 頭頭顯露 物物全眞 *Zuzu genro motsumotsu zenshin.*

Each thing—clear and revealed; every object—entirely true.

Shiba 230: *kenro* instead of *genro*.

ZGS 8.182, ZRKS 8.305, Shiba 230, ZGJI 446

8.292 插翼猛虎 戴角大蟲 *Tsubasa o sashihasamu mōko, tsuno o itadaku daichū.*

A fierce tiger that has sprouted wings, a wild beast that has grown horns.

Heki 81 Verse Comm.

ZGS 8.183, ZRKS 8.197, Shiba na, ZGJI 446, KZS #918

8.293 釣而不網 弋不射宿 *Tsuri suredomo ami sezu, yoku suredomo nedori o izu.*

When fishing, he does not use nets; when hunting, he does not shoot birds at rest.

Analects VII, 26.

ZGS 8.184, Shiba 226

8.294 泥多佛大 水長船高 *Dei ōkereba butsu dai nari, mizu nagakereba fune takashi.*

In deep mud, the Buddha is bigger; on broad waters, the ships are taller.

Heki 29 Main Case *agyo*.

ZGS 8.256 order reversed, ZRKS 8.102, Shiba 228, ZGJI 447, ZGJT 321

8.295 弄泥團漢 有什麼限 *Deidan o rō suru no kan, nan no kagiri ka aran?*

The fellow making balls in the mud, when will he ever have done!

Heki 48 Verse *agyo*, 81 Main Case, 93 Verse *agyo*.

ZGS 8.185, ZRKS 8.132, Shiba 239, ZGJI 447, ZGJT 491

8.296 帝網重重 主伴無盡 *Teimō jūjū shuban mujin.*

⌜Indra's net⌝, reflections of reflections, selves and others, without end.

ZGS 8.186, Shiba 227, ZGJI 447

8.297 以手摩頂 且坐喫茶 *Te o motte itadaki o ma shi, shibaraku za shite cha o kissu.*

He rubs his head with his hand, he sits awhile then drinks his tea.

ZGS 8.187, ZRKS 8.ns, Shiba na

8.298 點鐵成金 點金成鐵 *Tetsu o ten shite kin to nasu, kin o ten shite tetsu to naru.*

He touches iron and it turns to gold, he touches gold and it turns to iron.

8
字

Heki 85 Intro.

ZGS na, ZRKS 8.252, Shiba 228, ZGJI 448, ZGJT 327, KZS #872

8.299 呼天爲地 呼地爲天 *Ten o yonde chi to nashi, chi o yonde ten to nasu.*

He calls heaven earth, he calls earth heaven.

ZGS 8.188, Shiba na

8.300 天高東南 地傾西北 *Ten wa tōnan ni takaku, chi wa seihoku ni katamuku.*

Heaven is high in the southeast, earth slopes in the northwest.

In Han cosmology, dome-shaped heaven did not fit neatly over the flat earth. The northwest support pillar had been knocked aslant so that heaven leaned down there and earth sloped downwards from the horizontal in the southeast. That is why the stars do not revolve around a point directly overhead and why there are four seasons every year (Major 1993, 26, 72).

ZGS na, ZRKS 8.2, Shiba 228, ZGJI 449, KZS #825

8.301 天不能蓋 地不能載 *Ten mo ōu koto atawazu, chi mo nosuru koto atawazu.*

Heaven cannot cover it, earth cannot support it.

Heki 7 Intro.

ZGS na, ZRKS 8.105, Shiba 228, ZGJI 448, ZGJT 326

8.302 在天同天 在人同人 *Ten ni arite wa ten ni onaji, hito ni arite wa hito ni onaji.*

In heaven, be one with heaven; among people, be one with people.

ZGS na, Shiba 215

8.303 天下重器 王者大統 *Tenka no jūki ōja no daitō.*

A precious vessel in the world, the great lineage of the kings.

ZGS 8.189, Shiba na

8.304 天鑑無私 鑑在機先 *Tenkan watakushi naku, kan wa ⌜ki⌝sen ni ari.*

The mirror of heaven has no self, it sees what is prior to any motion of mind.

ZGS na, Shiba 228

8.305 天上天下 唯我獨尊 *Tenjō tenge yuiga dokuson.*

Above heaven and below heaven, only I am the Honored One.

Heki 6 Verse Comm., 16 Verse Comm., 31 Verse *agyo*, 45 Main Case Comm., 55 Verse *agyo*, 55 Main Case, 96 Verse 2 *agyo*. ZRKS 8.330n: "The World-Honored One upon his birth walked seven paces, with his eye surveyed the four directions, pointed one finger to heaven and one finger to earth and uttered, 'Above heaven and below heaven, only I am the Honored One.'"

ZGS na, ZRKS 8.330, Shiba 228, ZGJI 448, ZGJT 326

8.306 不在天台 定在南岳 *Tendai ni arazumba sadamete nangaku ni aran.*

If he is not on T'ien-t'ai, then for sure he is on Nan-yüeh.

ZGS 8.190, Shiba na

8.307 天地一指 萬物一馬 *Tenchi isshi banbutsu itsuba.*

Heaven and earth—one finger; the ⸢ten thousand things⸣—one horse.

Chuang-tzu, ch. 2

ZGS 8.191, Shiba 228, ZGJI 449

8.308 天堂未就 地獄先成 *Tendō imada narazaru ni jigoku mazu naru.*

The halls of heaven are not yet built, but hell has already been constructed.

ZGS 8.192, ZRKS 8.83, Shiba na, ZGJI 449, ZGJT 326, KZS #867

8.309 電飛雷走 山崩石裂 *Den tobi rai hashiri yama kuzure ishi saku.*

Lightning flies, thunder rolls, mountains crumble, rocks split.

ZGS 8.193, Shiba na

8.310 天無四壁 地絕八維 *Ten ni shiheki naku, chi ni hachii o zessu.*

Heaven does not have four walls, earth does not have eight cardinal directions.

ZGS 8.194, ZRKS 8.62, Shiba 228, ZGJI 448

8.311 如天普蓋 似地普擎 *Ten no amaneku ōu ga gotoku, chi no amaneku sasaguru ga gotoshi.*

Like heaven covering everything, like earth supporting everything.

Heki 64 Main Case Comm., 80 Main Case Comm.

ZGS 8.195, Shiba 219

8.312 東夷南蠻 北狄西戎 *Tōi nanban hokuteki seijū.*

Eastern savages, southern barbarians, northern aborigines, western wild men.

ZGS 8.196, Shiba na

8.313 東家作驢 西家作馬 *Tōka ni ro to nari, saika ni uma to naru.*

In the east house, it's a donkey; in the west house, it's a horse.

ZGS 8.197, Shiba na, ZGJI 450

8.314 東西不辨 南北不分 *Tōzai ben zezu, nanboku wakatazu.*

East and west are not distinguished, north and south are not divided.

Heki 33 Intro.

ZGS 8.198, Shiba na

8.315 東西南北 一等家風 *Tōzai namboku ittō no kafū.*

East, west, south, north—all one house style.

Heki 31 Verse *agyo.*

ZGS na, ZRKS 8.3, Shiba 229, ZGJI 450, ZGJT 338, KZS #826

8.316 東南得友 西北失友 *Tōnan ni tomo o e, seihoku ni tomo o ushinau.*

In the southeast, I made a friend; in the northwest, I lost a friend.

ZGS 8.199, Shiba na

8.317 桃季不言 下自成蹊 *Tōri mono iwazaredomo, shita onozukara kei o nasu.*

Peach and ⌜plum⌝ blossoms say not a word, but below them footpaths naturally appear.

ZGS na, Shiba 229

8.318 開戸見之 不視其所 *To o hiraite kore o miredomo sono tokoro o mizu.*

Though he's opened the door and sees it, he does not see where it is.

ZGS 8.200, Shiba na

8.319 德安四海 威肅三邊 *Toku shikai o yasunji, i sanben o shuku su.*

His virtue calms the ⌜four seas⌝, his authority rules the ⌜three borders⌝.

ZGS 8.201, Shiba na

8.320 鳶飛戾天 魚躍于淵 *Tobi tonde ten ni itari, uo fuchi ni odoru.*

The bird flies up to heaven, fish leap in the deep pools.

ZGS 8.202, Shiba 202, *Book of Songs* 239.

8.321 兎馬有角 牛羊無角 *Tome ni tsuno ari, gyūyō ni tsuno nashi.*

The rabbit and horse have horns, the ox and goat do not.

See ⌜Rabbit horns⌝. *Heki* 55 Verse.

ZGS 8.203, ZRKS 8.95, Shiba 228, ZGJI 450, ZGJT 331

8.322 怒雷破山 金翅擘海 *Dorai yama o yaburi, konji umi o tsunzaku.*

Angry thunder smashes the mountains, ⌜*Garuda*⌝ churns the ocean.

Same as 8.175, but with couplet reversed. 8.175 is the more common form.

ZGS 8.204, Shiba na

8.323 鳥飛毛落 魚行水濁 *Tori tobeba ke ochi, uo yukeba mizu nigoru.*

Where the bird flies, feathers fall; where the fish swims, the water is murky.

This couplet also appears with verses in reverse order.

ZGS 8.205, Shiba na, ZGJI 399, KZS #

8.324 呑舟魚不 遊數仭谷 *Fune o nomu uo wa sūjin no tani ni asobazu.*

A fish that can swallow a boat does not swim in shallow valley streams.

Shiba 230: *Donshū no uo wa sūjin no tani ni asobazu.*

ZGS 8.206, Shiba 230, ZD#187

8.325 爭名者朝 爭利者市 *Na o arasou mono wa chō shi, ri o arasou mono wa shi su.*

They fight over name in the court, they fight over profit in the market.

ZGS 8.207, Shiba na

8.326 立名認相 皆爲欺誑 *Na o tatete sō o mitomu, mina gikyō to naru.*

Make a name, establish a position—all is deception.

ZGS 8.208, Shiba na

8.327 南山起雲 北山下雨 *Nanzan ni kumo o okoshi, hokuzan ni ame o kudasu.*

On South Mountain clouds rise, on North Mountain rain falls.

Heki 83 Main Case.

ZGS 8.209, ZRKS 8.21, Shiba 230, ZGJI 453, ZGJT 356, KZS #834

8.328 南北東西 烏飛兎走 *Nanboku tōzai u tobi to hashiru.*

North south east west, the crow flies, the rabbit runs.

Heki 58 Verse.

ZGS 8.210, ZRKS 8.206, Shiba na, ZGJI 453

8.329 裳錦褧裳 衣錦褧衣 *Nishiki o mo ni shite kei mo shi, nishiki o kite keii su.*

Over a brocade skirt, she wears net; over a brocade jacket, she wears gauze.

ZGS 8.211, Shiba na

8.330 耳底泉聲 眼前山色 *Nitei wa sensei, genzen wa sanshoku.*

In my ears, the sound of springs; before my eyes, the colors of the mountains.

ZGS na, ZRKS 8.154, Shiba 217, ZGJI 427

8.331 入鄽垂手 爲人度生 *Nitten ⌜suishu⌝ i'nin doshō.*

Entering the market with extended hands for the salvation of all people.

Ten Oxherding Pictures, 10.

ZGS 8.212, Shiba na

8.332 雞寒上樹 鴨寒下水 *Niwatori samū shite ki ni nobori, kamo samū shite mizu ni kudaru.*

When chickens are cold, they go up into trees; when ducks are cold, they go down to water.

ZGS 8.213, ZRKS 8.114, Shiba 210, ZGJI 454 , ZGJT 103, ZD #178

8.333 人人本具 箇箇圓成 *Nin-nin hongu ko-ko enjō.*

Each and every person is originally endowed, each and every one complete.

ZGS 8.214, ZRKS 8.414, Shiba 222, ZGJI 454

8.334 腦後見腮 莫與往來 *Nōgo ni sai o mireba, tomo ni ōrai suru koto nakare.*

If you can see his jaws from behind his head, have nothing to do with him.

Heki 25 Main Case *agyo*, 30 Main Case *agyo*, 62 Verse *agyo*.

ZGS 8.215, ZRKS 8.120, Shiba na, ZGJI 454, ZGJT 373 (variant)

8.335 農夫歌野 商人舞市 *Nōfu ya ni utai, shōnin ichi ni mau.*

Farmers sing in the field, merchants dance in the market.

ZGS 8.216, Shiba na

8.336 野有死麕 白茅包之 *No ni shikin ari, hakubō kore o tsutsumu.*

In the fields there is a dead fawn; with white rushes it is covered.

ZGS 8.217, Shiba na, *Book of Songs* 23

8.337 運籌帷幄 決勝千里 *Hakarigoto o iaku ni megurashi katsu koto o senri ni kessu.*

Plotting strategy inside a battle tent, he decides a victory a thousand miles away.

Heki 4 Main Case Comm. See ⌜Chang Liang⌝.

ZGS 8.218, ZRKS 8.248, Shiba 202, KZS #781, Watson 1993, 107

8.338 破鏡鳥機 動欲食母 *Hakyōchō no ki yayamosureba haha o kurawan to suru.*

The ⌜broken-mirror bird⌝ feels a desire to eat its mother.

ZGS 8.219, Shiba na, ZGJI 455

8.339 白日青天 莫寐語好 *Hakujitsu seiten migo suru koto nakumba yoshi.*

On a bright day under blue skies, one shouldn't be talking in one's sleep.

ZGS 8.220, ZRKS 8.341, Shiba na, ZGJI 455

8.340 八面玲瓏 白圭無瑕 *Hachimen reirō hakkei kizu nashi.*

Every surface gleams, a flawless crystal jewel.

ZGS 8.221, Shiba na

8.341 蚌含明月 兎子懷胎 *Hamaguri meigetsu o fukumi, toshi kaitai su.*

The oyster swallows moonbeams, the rabbit conceives a child in its womb.

Heki 90 Main Case. See ⌜Moon⌝.

ZGS 8.222, Shiba 235

8.342 掩鼻偸香 空遭罪責 *Hana o ōte kō o nusumu mo munashiku zaiseki ni au.*

You held your nose to avoid the smell, but in vain, now face your punishment.

ZGJT 34: 掩鼻偸香 "you held your nose to avoid the smell" means the same as 掩耳偸鈴 "he covers his ears to steal the bell" (4.600).

ZGS na, ZRKS 8.370, Shiba 202, ZGJI 458. ZGJT 34

8.343 飯裡有砂 泥中有棘 *Hanri ni isago ari, deichū ni ubara ari.*

Sand in the rice, thorns in the mud.

ZGS 8.223, Shiba na

8.344 偏守眞空 斷諸智種 *Hitoe ni shinkū o mamori, kono chishu o tatsu.*

Earnestly guard true emptiness and cut off any seeds of wisdom.

ZGS 8.224, Shiba na

8.345 咬人獅子 不露爪牙 *Hito o kamu shishi sōge o arawasazu.*

The man-eating lion does not show its 「teeth and claws」.

ZGS 8.225, ZRKS 8.182, Shiba 213, ZGJI 458, KZS #913

8.346 人無遠慮 必有近憂 *Hito to shite tōki omonpakari nakumba kanarazu chikaki urei ari.*

If one pays no heed to what is distant, then sorrow will arise close by.

Analects xv, 11.

ZGS 8.226, ZRKS 8.376, Shiba na

8.347 穿人鼻孔 換人眼睛 *Hito no bikū o ugachi, hito no ganzei o kau.*

He pierces people's nostrils, he replaces the pupils of their eyes.

KZS #850: An oxherd pierces an ox's nostrils in order to pass a rope through it.

ZGS na, ZRKS 8.50, Shiba 224, ZGJI 459, KZS #850

8.348 如人飲水 冷暖自知 *Hito no mizu o nonde reidan jichi suru ga gotoshi.*

Like drinking water and knowing for yourself hot and cold.

MMK 23.

ZGS 8.227, ZRKS 8.246, Shiba na, ZGJI 459, ZGJT 363, KZS #863

8.349 入火不燒 入水不溺 *Hi ni itte mo yakezu, mizu ni itte mo oborezu.*

Entering fire he is not burned, entering water he is not drowned.

Rinzai-roku §19.

ZGS 8.228, ZRKS 8.194, Shiba 229, ZGJI 457, ZGJT 361, ZD #185, Watson 1993, 50

8.350 亹亹文王 令聞不已 *Bi-bi taru bunnō reibun yamazu.*

Earnest and energetic was 「Wen Wang」, endlessly he is praised.

ZGS 8.229, Shiba na

8.351 冰窟開花 炎天落雪 *Hyōkutsu no kaika, enten no rakusetsu.*

Flowers blooming in a frozen cave, snow falling from a blazing sky.

ZGS na, ZRKS 8.320, Shiba 232, ZGJI 459

8.352 冰凌上行 劍刄上走 *Hyōryōjō ni yuki, kenninjō ni washiru.*

He walks on ice, he runs on the edge of a ⌜sword⌝.

Heki 41 Intro., 46 Intro.

ZGS 8.230, ZRKS 8.249, Shiba 232, ZGJT 394, KZS #866

8.353 鼻雷齁齁 梁塵振飛 *Birai kōkō ryōjin furuitobu.*

Thunderous snoring, dust flies from the beams.

ZGS 8.231, Shiba na

8.354 蘋葉風涼 桂花露香 *Hin'yō kaze suzushiku, keika tsuyu kōbashi.*

Fresh wind in the floating grass, fragrant dew on the laurels.

ZGS na, ZRKS 8.113, Shiba 232, ZGJI 459

8.355 武王一怒 安天下民 *Buō hitotabi ikatte tenka no tami o yasunzu.*

⌜Wu Wang⌝ once arose in anger and brought peace to the people of the world.

Mencius I, B, 3.

ZGS 8.232, Shiba 234

8.356 伏屍百萬 流血漂楯 *Fukushi hyakuman, ryūketsu tate o tadayowasu.*

A million fallen corpses, flowing blood washes away their shields.

ZGS 8.233, Shiba na, ZGJI 460

8.357 逢佛殺佛 逢祖殺祖 *Butsu ni ōte wa butsu o koroshi, so ni ōte wa so o korosu.*

Meet the Buddha, kill the Buddha; meet the patriarchs, kill the patriarchs.

Rinzai-roku §19, MMK 1.

ZGS 8.234, ZRKS 8.292, Shiba 235, ZGJI 460, ZGJT 425

8.358 文王在上 萬國則之 *Bunnō kami ni ari, bankoku kore ni nottoru.*

⌜Wen Wang⌝ is in command, all states follow him.

First verse is from *Book of Songs* 235.

ZGS 8.235, Shiba na

8.359 文質彬彬 然後君子 *Bunshitsu hin-pin to shite shikashite nochi ni kunshi nari.*

Talent and training refined create the superior person.

Analects VI, 16.

ZGS 8.236, Shiba na

8.360 不憤不啓 不悱不發 *Funsezareba kei sezu, hi sezareba hassezu.*

If he makes no effort, I do not respond; if he does not strive, I will not begin.

Analects VII, 8.

ZGS 8.237, Shiba na

8.361 坌掃堆頭 更添壒𡎺 *Funsō taitō ni sara ni kassatsu o sou.*

On a pile of manure, heaping more shit.

ZGS 8.238, Shiba na, ZGJI 461, ZGJT 410

8.362 寶應老漢 看取眉毛 *Hōō rōkan bimō o kanshu seyo.*

Old man Pao-ying, watch out for your ⌜eyebrows⌝.

ZGS 8.239, Shiba na

8.363 采葑采菲 無以下體 *Hō o tori hi o toru, katai o motte suru nashi.*

Whether it's green or root vegetables, you don't select them by their lower parts.

Book of Songs 35.

ZGS 8.240, Shiba na

8.364 法尚應捨 何況非法 *Hō sura nao masa ni sutsu beshi, nanzo iwanya hihō o ya.*

Even the Dharma must be cast aside, how much more so the non-Dharma?

ZGS 8.241, Shiba na, ZGDJT 1118b

8.365 寶所在近 更進一歩 *Hōjo chikaki ni ari, sara ni ippo susumeyo.*

The treasure is very close, take one more step.

ZGS na, Shiba 235

8.366 方地爲輿 高天作蓋 *Hōchi o yo to nashi, kōten o gai to nasu.*

He makes the square earth his carriage, he makes the round heavens his canopy.

A chariot and its canopy were sometimes likened to square earth and round heaven (Major 1993, 35–6).

ZGS 8.242, ZRKS 8.159, Shiba na, ZGJI 462

8.367 墨悲絲染 詩讃羔羊 *Boku wa ito no somu o kanashimi, shi wa kōyō o san su.*

⌜Mo-tzu⌝ lamented the dyeing of thread, the *Songs* praise those wearing skins of lamb.

Book of Songs 18 praises dignified court officials: "In the skins of the young lamb sewn / With white silk of four hundred strands" (Waley 1937a, 23).

ZGS 8.243, Shiba na, ZGJI 203

8.368 法窟爪牙 奪命神符 *Hokkutsu no sōge, datsumyō no shinpu.*

The ⌜teeth and claws⌝ of the Dharma cave, the ⌜life-stealing magic charm⌝.

ZGS 8.244, Shiba na, ZGJI 585

8.369 歩歩蹈著 綠水青山 *Ho-ho tōjaku su, ryokusui seizan.*

With every step, walk the green waters and blue hills.

ZGS 8.245, ZRKS 8.228, Shiba 234, ZGJI 462, KZS #930

8.370 凡聖同居 龍蛇混雜 *Bonshō dōgo, ryūda konzatsu.*

Saints and commoners dwell together, dragons and snakes intermingle.

Heki 35.

ZGS 8.246, ZRKS 8.157, Shiba 235, ZGJI 463, ZGJT 432, ZD #182

8.371 前不搆村 後不迭店 *Mae son ni itarazu, shirie ten ni itarazu.*

Won't reach the village ahead, can't return to the lodge behind.

Heki 63 Verse Comm., 65 Verse *agyo*, 72 Main Case Comm., 76 Main Case *agyo*, 91 Verse *agyo*, 98 Main Case Comm.

ZGS na, ZRKS 8.218, Shiba 224, ZGJI 463, ZGJT 261, KZS #927

8.372 前無釋迦 後無彌勒 *Mae ni shaka naku, shirie ni miroku nashi.*

In front, no Śākyamuni; behind, no ⌜Maitreya⌝.

ZGS na, Shiba 224

8.373 將謂猴白 更有猴黑 *Masa ni omoeri kōhaku to, sara ni kōkoku aru koto o.*

Certainly you know about ⌜Houbai⌝—but there was also ⌜Houhei⌝.

Serenity 40.

ZGS 8.247, ZRKS 8.302, Shiba 219, ZGJI 463, ZGJT 215

8.374 松老雲閒 曠然自適 *Matsu oi kumo shizuka ni shite, kōnen to shite jiteki su.*

He was an aging pine, a still cloud, empty and content with himself.

Rinzai-roku Intro. Shiba 219: 閒 instead of 閑.

ZGS na, Shiba 219

8.375 末後牢關 最後一橛 *Matsugo no rōkan, saigo no ikketsu.*

The last hard barrier, the one final stake.

These two phrases often refer to the last kōan of training.

ZGS 8.248, Shiba na

8.376 先行其言 而後從之 *Mazu sono gon o okonaite nochi kore ni shitagau.*

First put those words into practice and then continue to follow them.

ZGS 8.249, Shiba na

8.377 圓如太虛 無缺無餘 *Madoka naru koto taikyo ni onaji, kakuru koto naku amaru koto nashi.*

Perfection is like the great emptiness, nothing lacking and nothing in excess.

信心銘 *Faith in Mind*. Shiba 202: 同 instead of 如.

ZGS 8.250, Shiba 202, ZGJI 400

8.378 眼如銅鈴 口似扁擔 *Manako wa dōrei no gotoku, kuchi wa hentan ni nitari.*

His eyes are like copper bells, his mouth is like a carrying pole.

The two ends of a shoulder carrying pole bend grimly down.

ZGS 8.251, Shiba na

8.379 眼似流星 機如掣電 *Manako wa ryūsei no gotoku, ⌜ki⌝ wa seiden no gotoshi.*

His eyes are like shooting stars, his moves like lightning.

MMK 8, *Heki* 24 Intro.

ZGS na, Shiba 205, ZGJI 464

8.380 眼見東南 心在西北 *Manako tōnan o mite kokoro saihoku ni ari.*

His eye looks southeast, but his heart is in the northwest.

Heki 4 Main Case *agyo.*

ZGS na, ZRKS 8.16, Shiba 205, ZGJI 464, KZS #879

8.381 慢藏誨盜 冶容誨淫 *Manzō tō o michibiki, yayō in o michibiku.*

Lax security invites theft, make-up leads to lewdness.

ZGJI 412: *Kura o man zuru wa tō o oshiyuru nari, yō o iru wa in o oshiyuru nari.*

ZGS 8.252, Shiba na, ZGJI 412

8.382 萬法歸一 一亦不守 *Manbō itsu ni ki su, itsu mo mata mamorazu.*

The ⌜ten thousand things⌝ return to One, and the One itself we do not retain.

信心銘 *Faith in Mind.*

ZGS na, ZRKS 8.45, Shiba 231, ZGJI 465

8.383 滿面慚惶 强而惺惺 *Manmen no zankō shiite sei-sei.*

Face full of shame, completely at a loss.

ZGS 8.253, Shiba na

8.384 眉藏寶劍 袖掛金鎚 *Mayu ni hōken o kakushi, sode ni kintsui o kaku.*

He hides a treasure ⌜sword⌝ in his ⌜eyebrows⌝, he has a golden hammer in his sleeve.

Heki Case 100 Verse Comm.

ZGS na, ZRKS 8.125, Shiba 232, ZGJI 465, ZGJT 392

8.385 慢鳴塗毒 鼓喪兒孫 *Midari ni zudokko o narashite jison o sō su.*

Wildly he beat the ⌜poison-painted drum⌝ and killed off his descendants.

ZGS 8.254, Shiba na

8.386 水到渠成 風行草偃 *Mizu itatte kyo nari, kaze yuite kusa fu su.*

Where water flows, channels form; when the wind blows, the grasses bend.

This couplet also appears in reversed order. *Heki* 6 Verse Comm., 43 Verse *agyo*, 45 Main Case *agyo*.

ZGS 8.255, Shiba na, ZGJI 404, ZGJT 235

8.387 水不洗水 金不博金 *Mizu mizu o arawazu, kin kin ni kaezu.*

Water does not wash water, gold is not changed into gold.

ZGS 8.257, Shiba na

8.388 水不借路 路不借水 *Mizu michi o karazu, michi mizu o karazu.*

Water doesn't ask for a channel, a channel doesn't ask for water.

ZGS na, ZRKS 8.12, Shiba 222, ZGJI 466

8.389 密糸密糸 糸糸密糸 *Misshi misshi shishi misshi.*

Fine thread, fine thread, thread after thread, fine thread.

ZGS 8.258, Shiba na

8.390 水結成冰 冰釋成水 *Mizu musunde kōri to nari, kōri tokete mizu to naru.*

Water freezes and turns to ice, ice melts and turns to water.

ZGS 8.259, Shiba na

8.391 密用金針 縫頭已露 *Mitsu ni kinshin o mochiyu, hōtō sude ni arawaru.*

Secretly he uses the golden needle, already the stitches have appeared.

ZGS na, Shiba 235, ZGJI 465

8.392 稇載而往 垂橐而歸 *Mite nosete yuki, taku o tarete kaeru.*

He went fully laden and returned with sacks hanging empty.

ZGJI 446: *tsumi nosete* instead of *mite nosete.*

ZGS 8.260, ZRKS 8.92, Shiba na, ZGJI 446

8.393 耳聽如聾 口説如啞 *Mimi kiite rō no gotoku, kuchi toite a no gotoshi.*

He hears with the ears of the deaf, he speaks with the mouth of a mute.

Heki 42 Main Case.

ZGS na, ZRKS 8.357, Shiba 217, ZGJI 466

8.394 明修棧道 暗度陳倉 *Myō ni sandō o shū shi, an ni chinsō o watasu.*

By daylight, he repaired the hanging road; at night, he crossed over from Ch'en-ts'ang.

See ⌜Han Kao-tsu⌝.

ZGS 8.261, ZRKS 8.219, Shiba 236, ZGJI 468, ZGJT 445, KZS #923

8.395 無病著艾 不是好心 *Mubyō ni gai o tsuku, kore kōshin ni arazu.*

To apply ⸢moxa⸣ when not sick is not being sound in mind.

ZGS na, ZRKS 8.350, Shiba 236, ZGJI 467, ZGJT 442, KZS #859

8.396 無說無聞 是眞般若 *Musetsu mumon kore shin no hannya.*

No speaking, no hearing—this is true wisdom.

Heki 6 Verse Comm., 90 Verse Comm.

ZGS na, ZRKS 8.316, Shiba 236, ZGJI 466, ZGJT 442

8.397 明足以察 秋毫之末 *Mei wa shūgō no matsu o motte sassuru ni taru.*

Clarity is being able to see the tips of ⸢autumn down⸣.

ZGS 8.262, Shiba na

8.398 鳴鶴在陰 其子和之 *Meikaku in ni ari, sono ko kore ni wa su.*

The calling crane is hidden in shadow, but its young respond to its cry.

ZGS na, Shiba 23

8.399 不識明珠 返成瓦礫 *Meishu o shirazu kaette gareki to nasu.*

Unaware it was a jewel, he thought it just rubble.

ZGS na, ZRKS 8.166, Shiba 233, ZGJI 468

8.400 面前一絲 長時無間 *Menzen no isshi chōji muken.*

Never a break in the single thread right in front of you.

Heki 90 Intro.

ZGS na, ZRKS 8.200, Shiba 236, ZGJI 468

8.401 前面瑪瑙 後面眞珠 *Menzen wa menō, kōmen wa shinju.*

In front, agate; behind, pearls.

ZGS na, Shiba 224

8.402 毛吞巨海 芥納須彌 *Mō kokai o nomi, ke ni shumi o iru.*

A hair swallows the great ocean, a mustard seed contains Mount ⸢Sumeru⸣.

ZGS 8.263, ZRKS 8.293, Shiba 237, ZGJI 412

8.403 拔猛虎鬚 截蒼龍角 *Mōko no hige o nuki, sōryū no tsuno o kiru.*

He plucks the whiskers of the fierce tiger, he cuts off the horns of the blue dragon.

ZGS 8.264, ZRKS 8.342, Shiba 232, ZGJI 469

8.404 木馬嘶風 泥牛吼月 *Mokuba kaze ni inanaki, deigyū tsuki ni hoyu.*

The wooden horse neighs at the wind, the mud ox bellows at the ⌜moon⌝.

ZGS 8.265, ZRKS 8.236, Shiba 237, ZGJI 469

8.405 沒意智漢 何境界在 *Motsuichi no kan nan no kyōgai ka aran.*

That numskull, what kind of world does he live in?

ZGS 8.266, Shiba na

8.406 本自天然 不假雕琢 *Moto onozukara tennen chōtaku o karazu.*

From the start it is naturally so, it does not need any sculpting.

ZGS na, ZRKS 8.275, Shiba 235, ZGJI 469

8.407 應物現形 如水中月 *Mono ni ōjite katachi o gen zuru koto, suichū no tsuki no gotoshi.*

It matches its form to things, as does the ⌜moon⌝ to water.

Rinzai-roku §17, *Heki* 47 Main Case Comm., 89 Main Case Comm.

ZGS 8.267, Shiba na, ZGJI 469, ZGJT 37

8.408 閉門造車 出戸合轍 *Mon o tojite kuruma o tsukuri, to o idete wadachi ni gassu.*

Behind closed gates, he makes a cart; out the door, he fits it to the wheel ruts.

ZGS 8.268, Shiba na

8.409 從門入者 不是家珍 *Mon yori iru mono wa kore kachin ni arazu.*

What comes in through the gate is not the treasure of the house.

Heki 5 Main Case Comm., 22 Main Case Comm., MMK Mumon's Preface.

ZGS na, Shiba 218, ZGJI 470, ZGJT 204

8.410 箭既離弦 無返回勢 *Ya sude ni yumi o hanarete, henkai no ikioi nashi.*

The arrow has already left the bow, it cannot come back.

Heki 37 Main Case *agyo*.

ZGS na, ZRKS 8.359, Shiba 224, ZGJI 470, ZGJT 258

8.411 不許夜行 投明須到 *Yakō o yurusazu, mei ni tōjite subekaraku itarubeshi.*

You may not go out at night, you must come when day breaks.

Heki 41. See ⌜*Yakō*⌝.

ZGS 8.269, ZRKS 8.36, Shiba 232, ZGJI 470, ZGJT 401, KZS #844, ZGDJT 1237a

8.412 夜半正明 天曉不露 *Yahan shōmei, tengyō furo.*

Midnight is truly bright, at dawn nothing appears.

ZGS 8.270, ZRKS 8.351, Shiba 236, ZGJI 470, ZGDJT 1237d, ZGJT 455

8.413 山高水深 雲閑風靜 *Yama takaku shite mizu fukaku, kumo kan ni shite kaze shizuka nari.*

High mountains and deep streams, quiet clouds and gentle winds.

ZGS na, Shiba 215, ZGJI 470

8.414 要行便行 要坐便坐 *Yukan to yōsureba sunawachi yuki, zasen to yōsureba sunawachi zasu.*

When he wants to go, he just goes; when he wants to sit, he just sits.

ZGS 8.271, ZRKS 8.295, Shiba 238, ZGJI 471, ZGJT 462, KZS #934

8.415 雪北嶺冷 梅南枝香 *Yuki wa hokurei ni susamaji, ume wa nanshi ni kōbashi.*

The snow on the northern peaks is cold, the ⌜plum⌝ blossoms on the southern branches are fragrant.

ZGS 8.272, ZRKS 8.153, Shiba na, ZGJI 471

8.416 坐斷要津 不通凡聖 *Yōshin o zadan shite, bonshō o tsūzezu.*

He cuts off the only crossing, and allows neither saints nor commoners through.

Variant: 把斷 *hadan* instead of 坐斷 *zadan*. Both versions appear in *Hekigan-roku* (for 坐斷, *Heki* 52 Verse *agyo*, 57 Intro; for 把斷, *Heki* 27 Main Case Comm., 73 Main Case Comm.).

坐斷: ZGS na, Shiba 215, ZGJI 471, ZGDJT 1250c
把斷: ZGS na, ZRKS 8.355, Shiba 231, ZGJT 375, KZS #931

8.417 把定要津 壁立萬仭 *Yōshin o hajō shite, hekiryū banjin.*

He controls the only crossing, like a cliff ten thousand feet high.

Rinzai-roku Intro.

ZGS na, ZRKS 8.313, Shiba 231, ZGJI 471, KZS #931, WATSON 1993, 3

8.418 善游者溺 善騎者落 *Yoku oyogu mono wa obore, yoku noru mono wa ochiru.*

One who swims well drowns, one who rides well falls.

ZGS 8.273, Shiba na

8.419 能學下惠 不師其跡 *Yoku kakei o manande, sono ato shi to sezu.*

They learned much from ⌜Hsia-hui⌝, but they did not imitate his acts.

ZGS 8.274, ZRKS 8.239, Shiba na, ZGJI 471, 472;

8.420 雷聲浩大 雨點全無 *Raisei kōdai ni shite, uten mattaku nashi.*

Vast rumbling thunder and not a drop of rain.

Heki 10 Verse *agyo.*

ZGS 8.275, ZRKS 8.158, Shiba na, ZGJI 471, ZGJT 466, KZS #895

8.421 李花不白 桃花不紅 *Rika shirokarazu, tōka wa kurenai narazu.*

Plum blossoms are not white, ⌜peach⌝ blossoms are not pink.

ZGS na, ZRKS 8.398, Shiba 238, ZGJI 472

8.422 龍吟雲起 虎嘯風生 *Ryū ginzureba kumo okori, tora usobukeba kaze shōzu.*

The dragon roars and clouds arise, the tiger growls and winds blow.

Heki Case 99 Intro.

ZGS 8.276, ZRKS 8.26 , Shiba 238, ZGJI 472, ZGJT 474, KZS #890

8.423 作龍上天 作蛇入草 *Ryū to natte ten ni nobori, ja to natte kusa ni iru.*

Becoming a dragon, he rises to the sky; turning into a snake, he enters the grass.

ZGS 8.277, ZRKS 8.338, Shiba 214, ZGJI 473

8.424 如龍無足 似蛇有角 *Ryū no ashi naki ga gotoku, hebi no tsuno aru ni nitari.*

Like a dragon without feet, like a snake with horns.

Heki 51 Main Case *agyo.*

ZGS 8.278, ZRKS 8.188, Shiba 219, ZGJI 472, ZGJT 472

8.425 如龍得水 似虎靠山 *Ryū no mizu o uru ga gotoku, tora no yama ni yoru ni nitari.*

He is like a dragon settling into water, or a tiger at home in the mountains.

Heki 31 Intro.

ZGS 8.279, ZRKS 8.127, Shiba 219, ZGJI 473, ZGJT 474, KZS #882

8.426 六爻未動 一氣潛回 *Rikkō imada dō sezaru ni ikki hisoka ni mawaru.*

The six lines are unmoving, but therein a single element secretly turns.

Rikkō: the six lines of *I ching* hexagrams. See ⌜Eight trigrams⌝.

ZGS 8.280, ZRKS 8.242, Shiba 239, ZGJI 472

8.427 陸地行舟 虛空馳馬 *Rikuchi ni fune o yari, kokū ni uma o ha su.*

He sails his boat on dry land, he rides his horse in the empty sky.

ZGS 8.281, ZRKS 8.54, Shiba 238, ZGJI 472

8.428 良醫之門 病者愈多 *Ryōi no mon byōsha hanahada ōshi.*

At a good doctor's gate, the sick are great in number.

ZGS 8.282, Shiba na, ZD #192

8.429 兩手托開 問取趙州 *Ryōte takkai shite jōshū o monshu su.*

With both hands open, he receives Jōshū's question.

ZGS 8.283, Shiba na

8.430 兩段不同 鷺鷥立雪 *Ryōdan onajikarazu roji yuki ni tatsu.*

The two are not the same—a heron standing in the snow.

ZGS 8.284, ZRKS 8.57, Shiba 239, ZGJI 473

8.431 良馬窺鞭 已遲八刻 *Ryōme muchi o ukagau mo sude ni chi hakkoku.*

A good horse anticipates the whip but already that's way too late.

ZGS 8.285, ZRKS 8.150, Shiba 238, ZGJI 473

8.432 綠竹含煙 靑山鎖翠 *Ryokuchiku kemuri o fukumi, seizan sui o tozasu.*

The green bamboo hold in the mist, the blue mountains encircle the azure sky.

ZGS na, ZRKS 8.66, Shiba 239

8.433 禮儀三百 威儀三千 *Reigi sambyaku, igi sanzen.*

Formality and manners, three hundred; dignity and decorum, three thousand.

ZGS 8.286, Shiba na

8.434 狼毒肝膓 生鐵面目 *Rōdoku no kanchō, santetsu no menmoku.*

Guts of wolf poison, face of raw iron.

ZGS 8.287, ZRKS 8.43, Shiba 239, ZGJI 475, KZS #847

8.435 六道四生 遊戲三昧 *Rokudō shishō yuge zammai.*

The ⌜six realms⌝ and ⌜four births⌝ are the playground of *samādhi*.

ZGS 8.288, Shiba na

8.436 驢事未去 馬事到來 *Roji imada sarazaru ni baji tōrai su.*

The donkey business isn't finished yet, but the horse business has arrived.

ZGS na, ZRKS 8.104, Shiba 239, ZGJI 474, ZGJT 486, KZS #853

8.437 吾王庫内 無如是刀 *Waga ō konai kaku no gotoki no katana nashi.*

In our king's storehouse, there is no such sword.

Heki 95 Verse *agyo*. Shiba 203: 我王庫中無如是事 *Waga ō ko no uchi ni kaku no gotoki no ji nashi,* "In our king's storehouse, there is no such thing." See ⌜Sword in the king's storehouse⌝.

ZGS 8.289, ZRKS 8.216, Shiba 203, ZGJI 476, ZGJT 51, KZS #928

8.438 我這裏無 這箇消息 *Waga shari shako no shōsoku nashi.*

I have no comment.

Heki 49 Verse *agyo*.

ZGS 8.290, ZRKS 8.321, Shiba 202, ZGJT 216 (*shōsoku*)

8.439 纔失正念 卽犯他物 *Wazuka ni shōnen o shissureba sunawachi tabutsu o okasu.*

If you lose right thought even a moment, you violate someone else.

ZGS 8.291, Shiba na

8.440 我有嘉賓 鼓瑟吹笙 *Ware ni kahin ari, koto o hiki fue o fuku.*

I have an important guest. We will play the harps and blow the flutes.

ZGS 8.292, Shiba na, *Book of Songs* 161

8.441 和和婆婆 有句無句 *Wa-wa ba-ba uku muku.*

Blah, blah, blah, blah, yes and no.

See 「Four propositions and hundred negations」.

ZGS 8.293, Shiba na, ZGJI 115 (*uku muku*)

8.442 椀子落地 成七八片 *Wansu chi ni ochite shichi happen to naru.*

The bowl fell to the ground and broke into pieces, seven or eight.

ZGS 8.294, Shiba na

Nine-Character Phrases

9.1 一箇打着一箇打不着 *Ikko wa tajaku, ikko wa tafujaku.*

One hit, one missed.

ZGS 9.1

9.2 奪卻衣鉢曰物歸有主 *Ehatsu o dakkyaku shite iwaku motsu wa ushu ni ki su.*

Stealing the robe and bowl, he says, "These things are going back to their owner."

ZGS 9.2

9.3 溺者入水拯者亦入水 *Oboruru mono mizu ni iri, sukuu mono mata mizu ni iru.*

The drowning person is in the water, the rescuer is also in the water.

ZGS 9.3, ZGJI 709

9.4 玉璽未彰文萬邦稽首 *Gyokuji imada mon o arawazaru ni banpō keishu su.*

The imprint of the imperial seal has yet to appear, and yet all states bow in homage.

ZGJI 477: 玉璽釆彰文.

ZGS 9.4, ZGJI 477

9.5 兄弟鬩于墻外禦其侮 *Keitei kaki ni semegedomo, soto sono anadori o fusegu.*

Brothers quarrel within their own fence, but outside they ward off any insult [together].

ZGS 9.5, *Book of Songs* 164

9.6 項王叱咤喑啞千人廢 *Kōō shitta in'a sennin hai su.*

King Hsiang roared in thunderous anger and a thousand people perished.

See 「Hsiang Yü」.

ZGS 9.6

9.7 孔子適周問禮於老子 *Kōshi shū ni yuki rei o rōshi ni tou.*

Confucius went to Chou and requested instruction in ritual from Lao-tzu.

ZGS 9.7, 史記孔子世家

9.8 時日害喪予及女偕亡 *Kono hi itsu ka horobin, ware nanji to tomo ni horobin.*

O Sun, when wilt thou perish? We care not if we have to die with thee.

Trans. from Lau 1970, 50. *Mencius* I, A, 2.

ZGS 9.8

9.9 金剛正眼照破四天下 *Kongō no shōgen shitenka o shōha su.*

The true eye of the ⌜*Vajra*⌝ King illuminates the four quarters of the world.

ZGS 9.9, ZGJI 478

9.10 獅子身中蟲喰獅子肉 *Shishi shinchū no mushi shishi no niku o kurau.*

The worms within the lion's body eat the flesh of the lion.

Heki 53 Main Case Comm.

ZGS 9.10, ZGJI 478, ZGDJT 430a, ZGJT 177

9.11 護得常住物恰如眼目 *Jōjū no mono o mamoriete, atakamo ganmoku no gotoshi.*

He cared for the ⌜permanent things⌝ as he would his eyes.

ZGS 9.11, ZGJI 478, ZGDJT 555d, ZGJT 223

9.12 吹毛斬不入風吹不動 *Suimō kiredomo irazu, kaze fukedomo ugokazu.*

The ⌜hair-cutter sword⌝ cannot cut into it, the blowing wind cannot move it.

ZGS 9.12, ZGJI 479

9.13 呑炭橋下伏三刺緋衣 *Sumi o nonde kyōka ni fu shite mitabi hie o sasu.*

He swallowed charcoal, hid beneath the bridge, and stabbed the crimson robe three times.

See ⌜Yü Jang⌝.

ZGS 9.13

9.14 齊宣王見孟子於雪宮 *Sei no sennō mōshi o sekkyū ni miru.*

King Hsüan of Ch'i met with Mencius in the Snow Palace.

ZGS 9.14, *Mencius* I, B, 4

9.15 曰勿向外揚家醜便打 *Soto ni mukatte kashū o aguru koto nakare to itte sunawachi utsu.*

Saying, "You must not reveal the family's shame to others," he gave a slap.

ZGS 9.15

9.16 多年重擔一時脱卻了 *Ta'nen no jūtan ichiji ni dakkyaku shi owannu.*

Years of built-up burdens dropped in a single moment.

ZGS 9.16, ZGJI 480

9.17 東家人死西家人助哀 *Tōka no hito shi sureba, seika no hito ai o tasuku.*

When someone in the east house dies, those in the west house assist in mourning.

Heki 1 Main Case *agyo*, 32 Main Case *agyo*, 38 Main case *agyo*, etc.

ZGS 9.17, ZGJI 481, ZGDJT 909b, ZGJT 338

9.18 衲僧家那一句作麼生 *Nōsōge na no ikku somosan.*

You ⸢patched-robe monk⸣, what's your one word?

ZGS 9.18, ZGJI 481

9.19 衲僧家冷暖自知一句 *Nōsōge reidan onozukara ikku o shiru.*

The ⸢patched-robe monk's⸣ one word when he knows for himself hot and cold.

ZGS 9.19, ZGJI 481

9.20 破鏡鳥子常有食母機 *Hakyōchō no ko tsune ni haha o kurau no ki ari.*

The ⸢broken-mirror bird⸣ constantly feels the impulse to eat its mother.

ZGS 9.20, ZGJI 481

9.21 如人夜間背手摸枕子 *Hito no yahan ni haishu shite chinsu o saguru ga gotoshi.*

Like a person's hand in the middle of the night searching behind for the pillow.

Heki 89 Main Case.

ZGS 9.21

9.22 蝮蛇吞象三年而出骨 *Fukuda zō o nomi sannen ni shite hone o idasu.*

The cobra swallowed an elephant and three years later ejected the bones.

ZGS 9.22, ZGJI 482

9.23 穆穆文王於緝熙敬止 *Boku-boku taru bunnō aa, shūki ni shite kei shite todomaru.*

August is Wen, the King. Oh, to be reverenced in his glittering light!

Trans. after Waley 1937, 250. Alternate reading: *Boku-boku taru bunnō aa, tsugi akiraka ni shite tsutsushimeri.*

ZGS 9.23, *Book of Songs* 235

9.24 逝者如斯夫不舍晝夜 *Yuku mono wa kaku no gotoki ka, chūya o okazu.*

It passes on and on like this, never ceasing day or night.

ZGS 9.24, *Analects* IX, 16

9.25 囉囉招囉囉遙囉囉送 *Ra-ra shō, ra-ra yō, ra-ra sō.*

La-dee-dum, la-dee-dee, la-dee-da.

ZGJI 104, ZGJT 465, SRZGK #575: 囉囉哩 *ra-ra-ri* is the rhythm of singing and clapping of hands.

ZGS 9.25, ZGJI 104, ZGJT 465

9.26 兩鏡相照中心無影像 *Ryōkyō aiterashite chūshin yōzō nashi.*

Two mirrors reflect each other; in between, there is no image.

ZGS 9.26, ZGJI 483

9.27 云領領以拄杖送一送 *Ryō-ryō to itte shujō o motte sō issō su.*

Nodding "Yes, yes," he takes the stick and gives a jab.

ZGDJT 1290c: 領領 means "nod in agreement." ZGJT 269: 送一送 is "give a jab."

ZGS 9.27, ZGDJT (領領) 1290c, ZGJT (送一送) 269

9.28 我亦知汝向第二頭道 *Ware mo mata shiru, nanji ga daini tō ni mukatte iu koto o.*

I also know that you are talking on a secondary level.

ZGS 9.28

Ten-Character Phrases

10.1 相逢相不識　*Aiōte aishirazu,*
共語不知名　*Tomo ni katatte na o shirazu.*

We meet but do not know each other,
We speak without knowing names.

ZGS 10.1: 不相 instead of 相不.

ZGS 10.1, Shiba 273, ZD #88, ZGJT 268, ZGJI 484, ZRKS 10.430

10.2 相逢不下馬　*Aiōte uma yori kudarazu,*
各自走前程　*Kakuji ni zentei ni hashiru.*

Meeting we do not dismount from our horses,
But each of us rushes on ahead.

ZGS 10.2, Shiba na, ZGJT 267, ZGJI 484, ZRKS 10.330

10.3 相見元無事　*Aimite moto buji,*
不來卻思君　*Kitarazareba satte kimi o omou.*

When we meet, it is nothing really.
But if you do not come, I think of you all the more.

ZGS 10.3, Shiba na

10.4 曉送千峯日　*Akatsuki ni okuru, senpō no hi,*
春回大地華　*Haru wa meguru, daichi no hana.*

Dawn brings sun to a thousand peaks,
Spring returns with flowers across the broad earth.

ZGS 10.4, Shiba na

10.5 削足而適履　*Ashi o kezutte ri ni kanai,*
殺頭而便冠　*Atama o soide kanmuri ni ben ni su.*

He trims his feet to match his shoes,
He carves his head to fit his hat.

ZGS 10.5, Shiba na, ZGJI 484

10.6 朝進東門營　*Ashita ni tōmon no kan ni susumi,*
暮上河陽橋　*Kure ni kayō no hashi ni noboru.*

In the morning he advances to the East Gate camp,
In the evening he climbs to the River Sun Bridge.

ZGS 10.6, Shiba 276, TSSSTS 4

10.7 朝見雲片片 *Ashita ni wa kumo no hen-pentaru o mi,*
暮聽水潺潺 *Kure ni wa mizu no sen-sentaru o kiku.*

Mornings watching wisps of clouds,
Evenings listening to the splashing stream.

ZGJI 484: 看 instead of 見. Shiba 275: 朝見雲泛泛夕聞水潺潺 *Ashita ni wa kumo no han-pantaru o mi, Yūbe ni wa mizu no sen-sentaru o kiku.*

ZGS 10.7, Shiba 275, ZGJI 484, ZRKS 10.561

10.8 豈不憚艱險 *Ani kanken o habakarazan ya,*
深懷國士恩 *Fukaku kokushi no on o omou.*

Is he one to flee from trouble and conflict?
Deeply he ponders the obligations of a statesman.

ZGS 10.8, Shiba na, TSSSTS 3

10.9 聽雨寒更盡 *Ame o kiite kankō tsuki.*
開門落葉多 *Mon o hirakeba rakuyō ōshi.*

Listening to the rain, I passed the cold night hours.
When I opened the doors, there were many fallen leaves.

ZGS 10.9, Shiba 276, ZGJI 484, ZRKS 10.415

10.10 不雨花猶落 *Ame furazaru ni hana nao ochi,*
無風絮自飛 *Kaze naki ni jo onozukara tobu.*

Though no rain falls, blossoms still fall;
Though no breeze stirs, willow down floats by.

Shiba 284: *narazaru* instead of *furazaru.*

ZGS 10.10, Shiba 284, ZGJI 484, ZRKS 10.150

10.11 臨危而不變 *Ayauki ni nozonde henzezaru wa,*
方是丈夫兒 *Masa ni kore jōbu no ji.*

Faced with danger, he does not flinch;
This is truly a man of strength.

Heki 75 Main Case *agyo*. Empuku-ji: *jōhu* instead of *jōbu.*

ZGS na, Shiba 295, KZS #1067

10.12 錯認驢鞍橋 *Ayamatte roankyō o mitomete,*
作阿爺下頷 *Aya no kagan to nasu.*

He saw the bridge of a donkey's saddle
And thought it was his papa's chin.

Heki 98 *agyo.*

ZGS 10.11, Shiba 259, ZGJT 159, ZGJI 485, ZRKS 10.199, KZS #1027

10.13 可憐傅大士 *Awaremubeshi fudaishi,*
處處失樓閣 *Shosho rōkaku o shissu.*

Pity「Fu Daishi」,
He lost his mansions in so many places.

ZGS 10.12, Shiba na

10.14 庵中閑打坐 *Anchū shizuka ni taza sureba,*
白雲起峯頂 *Hakuun hōchō ni okoru.*

As I sit quietly in my hut,
White clouds arise on the mountain peaks.

ZGS na, Shiba 241, ZGJI 485, ZGJT 7, ZRKS 10.404

10.15 暗裏施文彩 *Anri ni monsai o hodokoshi,*
明中不見蹤 *Meichū ni ato o mizu.*

In the darkness he applies patterns and colors,
In the light no trace of them is seen.

Shiba 241: *Anri ni bunsai o hodokoshi.*

ZGS 10.13, Shiba 241, ZGJI 485, KZS #982, ZRKS 10.124

10.16 環家萬里夢 *Ie ni kaeru, banri no yume,*
爲客五更愁 *Kyaku to naru, goko no urei.*

To return home—my dream for ten thousand miles.
To be the traveler—my worries at four in the morning.

ZGS 10.14, Shiba na

10.17 家無白澤圖 *Ie ni hakutaku no zu nakereba,*
如此有妖怪 *Kaku no gotoki no yōkai ari.*

If the house has no「White Glade talisman」,
Then it will have goblins like these.

ZGS na, Shiba 247, ZGJI 486, ZGJT 47, ZRKS 10.14

10.18 家貧未是貧 *Ie hin ni shite imada kore hin narazu,*
道貧愁殺人 *Dō hin ni shite hito o shūsatsu su.*

Poverty at home is not yet poverty;
Poverty on the Way is the extreme of misery.

ZGS na, Shiba 246, ZGJI 486, ZGJT 48, ZRKS 10.69

10.19 依稀松屈曲 *Ikitari matsu no kukkyoku,*
彷彿石爛斑 *Hōfutsutari ishi no ranpan.*

It's crooked like the pine,
It's mottled like the stone.

ZGS 10.15, Shiba 242, ZGJT 9, ZRKS 10.132, ZGJI 485

10.20 石壓笋斜出 *Ishi oshite takanna naname ni ide,*
岸懸花倒生 *Kishi ni kakatte hana sakashima ni shōzu.*

Pressed by a rock, the bamboo grows at a slant;
Hanging from a cliff, the flower grows upside down.

Shiba 271: *Ishi asshite jun naname ni ide.*

ZGS 10.16, Shiba 271, ZGJI 486, ZGJT 247, ZRKS 10.13, ZGJT 247

10.21 石從空裏立 *Ishi wa kūri yori tachi,*
火向水中焚 *Hi wa suichū ni mukatte taku.*

Stones stand in midair,
Fire burns under water.

ZGS 10.17, Shiba 271, ZGJI 486, ZGJT 247, ZRKS 10.38

10.22 石長無根樹 *Ishi wa mukon no ju o chōji,*
山含不動雲 *Yama wa fudō no kumo o fukumu.*

The rock grows a rootless tree,
The mountains embrace motionless clouds.

ZGS na, Shiba 271, ZGJI 486, ZRKS 10.107

10.23 坐石雲生衲 *Ishi ni za sureba kumo nō ni shōji,*
添泉月入瓶 *Izumi o sōreba tsuki kame ni iru.*

When I sit on a rock, clouds are born in my robe;
When I ladle up springwater, the ⌜moon⌝ enters my water jar.

ZGS 10.18, Shiba 258, ZRKS 10.324, KZS #990

10.24 一雁過連營 *Ichigan ren'ei o sugi,*
繁霜覆古城 *Hansō kojō o ōu.*

A goose flies over the rows of camps,
Heavy frost covers the old city.

ZGS 10.19, Shiba na, TSSSTS 63

10.25 一言盡十方 *Ichigen jin jippō,*
一句該萬象 *Ikku banzō o kanu.*

One word exhausts the ⌜ten directions⌝,
One phrase covers the ⌜ten thousand things⌝.

Empuku-ji: *banshō* instead of *banzō*.

ZGS 10.20, Shiba na

10.26 一言盡十方 *Ichigen jin jippō,*
一句超萬象 *Ikku banzō o koyu.*

One word exhausts the ⌜ten directions⌝,
One phrase transcends the ⌜ten thousand things⌝.

Empuku-ji: *banshō* instead of *banzō*.

ZGS 10.21, Shiba na

10.27 一言纔出口 *Ichigen wazuka ni kuchi o izureba,*
地上繡絪開 *Chijō shūin hiraku.*

If even one word issues forth from his mouth,
Then across the earth spreads a living brocade.

ZGS 10.22, Shiba na

10.28 一字不著劃 *Ichiji kaku o tsukezu,*
八字無兩丿 *Hachiji ryōketsu nashi.*

The character 一 has no further strokes,
The character 八 does not have two 丿 strokes.

ZGS 10.23, Shiba na, ZGJI 487, ZRKS 10.39

10.29 一二三四五 *Ichi ni san shi go,*
直道三二一 *Jiki ni iu san ni ichi.*

One, two, three, four, five.
Speaking directly: three, two, one.

ZGS 10.24, Shiba na

10.30 一二三四五 *Ichi ni san shi go,*
六七八九十 *roku shichi hachi ku jū.*

One, two, three, four, five,
Six, seven, eight, nine, ten.

ZGS 10.25, Shiba na

10.31 一夜落花雨 *Ichiya rakka no ame,*
滿城流水香 *Manjō ruisui kanbashi.*

One night the flowers fell in the rain,
And throughout the city the waters flowed fragrant.

ZGS 10.26, Shiba 244, ZGJI 489, ZGJT 24, ZRKS 10.171, KZS #1060

10.32 如斬一綟絲 *Ichireishi o kiru ga gotoshi,*
一斬一切斬 *Ichizan issai zan.*

It's like cutting a bundle of threads—
One cut cuts all.

Heki 19 Intro.

ZGS 10.27, Shiba 266, ZGJI 490

10.33 如染一綟絲 *Ichireishi o somuru ga gotoshi,*
一染一切染 *Issen issai sen.*

It's like dyeing a bundle of threads—
One dying dyes all.

Heki 19 Intro.

ZGS 10.28, Shiba na

10.34 一氣走五百里 *Ikki ni hashiru koto gohyakuri,*
更不回頭 *Sara ni kōbe o megurasazu.*

He runs five hundred miles in one dash,
Without once turning his head.

ZGS 10.29, Shiba na

10.35 拈起一莖草 *Ikkyōsō o nenki shite,*
作丈六金身 *Jōroku no konjin to nasu.*

Picking up a single blade of grass,
He turns it into a ⌜sixteen-foot⌝ golden Buddha.

ZGS 10.30, Shiba 280, ZGJI 487, ZGJT 222 (*konjin*), ZRKS 10.360

10.36 一金成萬器 *Ikkin banki to nari,*
萬器成一金 *Banki ikkin to naru.*

One chunk of metal becomes ten thousand vessels,
Ten thousand vessels become one chunk of metal.

ZGS 10.31, Shiba 242, ZRKS 10.297

10.37 一句合頭語 *Ikku gattō no go,*
萬劫繫驢橛 *Mangō no keroketsu.*

A phrase whose words are exactly right,
Will be your ⌜donkey hitching post⌝ for ten thousand ⌜*kalpa*⌝.

Heki 42 Verse Comm.

ZGS 10.32, Shiba na, ZGJI 487, ZGJT 23, ZGDJT 39c, ZRKS 10.182, KZS #1063

10.38 一句定乾坤 *Ikku kenkon o sadame,*
一劍平天下 *Ikken tenka o tairagu.*

One word determines the universe,
One ⌜sword⌝ brings peace to the world.

ZGS 10.33, Shiba 243, ZGJI 487, ZGJT 23, ZRKS 10.182, KZS #1034

10.39 一九與二九 *Ikku to niku to,*
相逢不出手 *Aiōte te o idasazu.*

One nine and two nines
Meet but do not extend their hands.

ZGS 10.34, Shiba 243, ZRKS 10.86

10.40 一莖兩莖曲 *Ikkyō ryōkyō wa magareri,*
三莖四莖斜 *Sankyō shikyō wa naname nari.*

One stem, two stems are bent;
Three stems, four stems are slanted.

ZGS 10.35, Shiba na, ZGJI 487, ZRKS 10.87

10.41 一呼百諾來 *Ikko sureba hyakudaku shite kitari,*
一笑萬人賀 *Isshō sureba bannin ga su.*

Call once and a hundred people respond,
Laugh once and ten thousand people rejoice.

ZGS 10.36, Shiba 243

10.42 道取一尺 *Isshaku o dōshu sen yori wa*
不如行取一寸 *Issun o gyōshu suru ni shikazu.*

Speaking one ⌜foot⌝
Is not as good as doing one ⌜inch⌝.

ZGS 10.37, Shiba 279

10.43 一尺絹擣練 *Isshaku no kinu ni mo ren o uchi,*
一盃酒上樓 *Ippai no sake ni mo rō ni noboru.*

Each foot of silk is kneaded and pounded,
Even one cup of wine is taken up to the roof.

See ⌜Fulling block and club⌝. It was considered a great pleasure to drink wine high up under the ⌜moon⌝.

ZGS na, Shiba 243, ZGJI 488, ZRKS 10.216

10.44 一聲鳴歷歷 *Issei natte reki-reki,*
十指起淸風 *Jisshi seifū o okosu.*

A single voice sings out limpid and clear,
Ten fingers raise the pure wind.

ZGS 10.38, Shiba na, ZGJI 488, ZRKS 10.527

10.45 一聲雷發動 *Issei rai hatsudō sureba,*
蟄戸一時開 *Chikko ichiji ni hiraku.*

At one crash of thunder,
The sleeping insects open their doors all at once.

ZGS 10.39, Shiba na, ZGJI 488, ZRKS 10.173, KZS #1035

10.46 一點梅花蘂 *Itten baika no zui,*
三千世界香 *Sanzen sekai kanbashi.*

With one pistil of the plum flower,
The ⌜three thousand worlds⌝ are fragrant.

ZGS 10.40, Shiba 243, ZGJI 466, ZRKS 10.472

10.47 一生二 *Ichi ni o shōji,*
二生三 *Ni san o shōji,*
三生萬物 *San banbutsu o shōzu.*

One gives birth to two,
Two gives birth to three,
Three gives birth to the ⌜ten thousand things⌝.

ZGS 10.41, Shiba na; *Tao-te ching*, ch. 42

10.48 一片月生海 *Ippen no tsuki umi ni shōji,*
幾家人上樓 *Ikuka no hito rō ni noboru.*

A crescent ⌜moon⌝ rises from the sea,
In how many houses will people go up to the roof?

ZGS 10.42, Shiba 243, ZGJI 489, ZGJT 24, ZRKS 10.21

10.49 一峯雲片片 *Ippō kumo hen-pen,*
雙澗水潺潺 *Sōkan mizu sen-sen.*

One peak with wisps of clouds,
Two mountain streams of splashing water.

ZGS 10.43, Shiba 243, ZGJI 489

10.50 一葉一釋迦 *Ichiyō mo isshaka,*
一鬚一彌勒 *Isshu mo ichi miroku.*

One leaf is one Śākyamuni,
One hair is one ⌜Maitreya⌝.

ZGS na, Shiba 244, ZRKS 10.227

10.51 鷸蚌争不休 *Itsu bō no arasoi yamazu,*
終入漁人手 *Tsui ni gyojin no te ni iru.*

The snipe and the mussel cannot cease their struggle.
In the end, the fisherman takes them in hand.

When the snipe tries to eat the mussel, the mussel clamps onto the bird's beak.

ZGS 10.44, Shiba na

10.52 渭北春天樹 *Ihoku shunten no ju,*
江東日暮雲 *Kōtō nichibo no kumo.*

North of Wei River, trees in the spring sky;
East of the Yangtze, clouds in the setting sun.

ZGS 10.45, Shiba 242

10.53 威雄震十方 *Iyū jippō ni furui,*
聲價動寰宇 *Seika kan'u o ugokasu.*

His majesty reaches the ⌜ten directions⌝,
His fame moves the world.

ZGS 10.46, Shiba na, ZGJI 485, ZRKS 10.36, KZS #957

10.54 陰陽不到處 *In'yō futō no tokoro,*
一片好風光 *Ippen no kōfūkō.*

Where the sun and shade do not reach,
There is marvelous scenery indeed.

ZGS 10.47, Shiba 244, ZD #80, ZGJI 490, ZRKS 10.139, KZS #984

10.55 烹魚煩則碎 *Uo o niru koto wazurawashikereba kudake,*
治民煩則散 *Tami o osamuru koto wazurawashikereba sanzu.*

In cooking fish, too much handling breaks them to pieces;
In governing people, too much meddling makes them flee.

ZGS 10.48, Shiba na, ZGJI 491

10.56 有梅添月色 *Ume ari gesshoku o soe,*
無竹缺秋聲 *Take nōshite shūsei o kaku.*

With a plum tree we get also the light of the ⌜moon⌝,
But without bamboo we lack the sounds of autumn.

ZGS na, Shiba 292, ZGJI 491, ZRKS 10.133

10.57 赦有罪寵女 *Yūzai no chōjo o yurushi,*
斬無罪卑女 *Muzai no hijo o kiru.*

He pardons the beautiful guilty girl,
And beheads the ugly innocent one.

ZGS 10.49, Shiba na

10.58 牛飲水成乳 *Ushi no nomu mizu wa chichi to nari,*
蛇飲水成毒 *Ja no nomu mizu wa doku to naru.*

The water a cow drinks turns to milk,
The water a snake drinks turns to poison.

ZGS 10.50, Shiba 250, ZGJI 491

10.59 宇宙無雙日 *Uchū sōjitsu naku,*
乾坤只一人 *Kenkon tada ichinin.*

In the universe there are not two suns,
In ⌜heaven and earth⌝ there is only one person.

ZGS 10.51, Shiba 244, ZGJI 490, ZRKS 10.321

10.60 雨中看杲日 *Uchū ni kōjitsu o mi,*
火裏酌清泉 *Kari ni seisen o kumu.*

**In the middle of the rain, see the bright sun shining;
In the midst of fire, dip from the clear spring.**

ZGS 10.52, Shiba 244, ZGJI 490, ZRKS 10.233, KZS #1030

10.61 下馬飲君酒 *Uma yori orite kimi ni sake o nomashimu,*
問君何所之 *Tou kimi izure no yuku tokoro zo.*

**Getting off his horse, he gives you a drink of wine
And asks, "Where are you going?"**

ZGS 10.53, Shiba na, TSSSTS 4

10.62 海枯終見底 *Umi karete tsui ni soko o miru mo,*
人死不知心 *Hito shi shite shin o shirazu.*

**When the sea dries up, we see its bottom,
But when a person dies, we do not know their mind.**

ZGS 10.54, Shiba 247, ZGJT 55, ZGJI 491, ZRKS 10.35, KZS #963

10.63 海暗三山雨 *Umi wa kurashi sanzan no ame,*
花明五嶺春 *Hana wa akiraka nari gorei no shun.*

**Dark ocean—rain on the three mountains;
Bright flowers—spring on the five peaks.**

ZGS 10.55, Shiba 247

10.64 梅瘦占春少 *Ume yasete haru o shimeru koto sukunaku,*
庭寛得月多 *Niwa hirō shite tsuki o uru koto ōshi.*

**Withered plum trees barely retain the spring,
But the garden opens up to receive the ⌜moon⌝.**

ZGS na, Shiba 282, ZGJI 491, ZRKS 10.181

10.65 梅只雪霜先 *Ume wa tada sessō no saki,*
花猶風雨後 *Hana wa nao fūu no nochi.*

**Plums only before the snow and frost,
Flowers even after the wind and rain.**

ZGS na, Shiba 281, ZRKS 10.346, ZGJI 491

10.66 雲門棒頭短 *Ummon bōtō mijikaku,*
藥山杓柄長 *Yakusan shakuhei nagashi.*

**Ummon's stick is short,
Yakusan's ⌜*shippei*⌝ is long.**

ZGJI 492: Ummon was famous for his one-word answers, not for his use of the stick; Yakusan used neither the stick nor the shout in teaching. He used a ⌜*shippei*⌝, a short bamboo rod.

ZGS na, Shiba 245, ZGJI 492, ZRKS 10.485

10.67 越鳥巣南枝 *Etchō nanshi ni sukui,*
胡馬嘶北風 *Koma hokufū ni inanaku.*

The birds of Yüeh nest in the southern branches,
The Mongol horses neigh into the northern wind.

ZGS 10.56, Shiba na, ZGJI 492

10.68 遠鷗浮水靜 *En'ō mizu ni ukande shizuka ni,*
輕燕受風斜 *Keien kaze o ukete naname nari.*

Faraway gulls float quietly on the water,
Flying swallows take the wind on the slant.

ZGS 10.57, Shiba 245

10.69 遠山見有色 *Enzan miru ni iro ari,*
近水聞無聲 *Kinsui kiku ni koe nashi.*

When I see the far off mountains, they have colors;
When I hear the nearby waters, they have no sound.

Shiba 245: 遠観山有色, 近聽水無聲 *Tōku mite yama ni iro ari, chikaku kiite mizu ni koe nashi.*

ZGS 10.58, Shiba 245, ZGJI 492, ZRKS 10.576 (variant)

10.70 烟村三月裏 *Enson sangatsu no uchi,*
別是一家春 *Betsu ni kore ikka no haru.*

In the third month when the village is [shrouded] in mist,
Ah! the entire household is in spring.

ZGS na, Shiba 245, ZGJI 492, ZRKS 10.551

10.71 不貪王母桃 *Ōbo ga momo o musaborazu,*
自在仙家棗 *Onozukara senka no natsume ari.*

I do not covet the ⌜peach⌝ of the ⌜Queen Mother [of the West]⌝,
I have my own ⌜jujube⌝ of immortality.

ZGS 10.59: 有 instead of 在, Shiba na, ZRKS 10.403

10.72 鸚鵡叫煎茶 *Ōmu sencha to sakebu,*
與茶元不識 *Cha o ataunedomo moto shirazu.*

The parrot calls for green tea,
But offer tea and it won't understand.

ZGS na, Shiba 246, ZGJI 492, ZRKS 10.400

10.73 黄蓮未是苦 *Ōren wa imada kore nigakarazu,*
甘草未是甘 *Kansō wa imada kore amakarazu.*

Yellow lotus isn't really bitter,
Sweet grass isn't really sweet.

Herbs in Chinese medicine. Empuku-ji: *kanzō* instead of *kansō*.

ZGS na, Shiba 257, ZGJI 507, ZRKS 10.303, KZS #1075

10.74 屋衰人不見 *Oku sutarete hito miezu,*
蘆折雁何之 *Ro orete gan izuku ni ka yuku.*

In the abandoned house, not a person to be seen.
The reeds are broken and where have the geese gone?

ZGS 10.60, Shiba na

10.75 爲己鎖者多 *Onore ga tame ni tozasu mono wa ōku,*
爲他鎖者少 *Ta no tame ni tozasu mono wa sukunashi.*

Many are those who bind themselves,
Few are those bound by others.

ZGS 10.61, Shiba na, ZGJI 493

10.76 懷州牛喫禾 *Kaijū no ushi ka o kissureba,*
益州馬腹張 *Ekijū no uma hara haru.*

When the cows of Huai-chou eat grain,
The stomachs of horses in I-chou swell.

Heki 96 Verse 1 Comm.

ZGS 10.62, Shiba 247, ZGJI 494, ZGJT 56, ZRKS 10.237, KZS #1032

10.77 華岳連天碧 *Kagaku renten no midori,*
黄河混底流 *Kōga kontei no nagare.*

The green of ⌜Hua-shan⌝ reaches right to the sky,
The ⌜Yellow River⌝ flows turbulent right to the bottom.

ZGS 10.63, Shiba 247, ZGJI 493, ZGJT 48, ZRKS 10.284

10.78 鏡藉重磨瑩 *Kagami wa jūma o karite kagayaki,*
金須再煉精 *Kin wa sairen o mochiite sei nari.*

The mirror shines from many polishings,
Gold becomes pure from repeated refining.

ZGS na, Shiba 251, ZGJI 499, ZGJI 374, KZS #1005

10.79 鏡分金殿燭 *Kagami wa kinden no shoku o wakachi,*
山答月樓鐘 *Yama wa getsurō no kane ni kotau.*

The mirror reflects the candles in the golden hall,
The mountain echoes the bell of the ⌜moon⌝ tower.

ZGS 10.64, Shiba 251, ZGJI 494, ZRKS 10.2, KZS #944

10.80 隔牆弄胡蝶 *Kaki o hedatete kochō o rō shi,*
臨水擲蝦蟆 *Mizu ni nozonde gama o nageutsu.*

Outside the house wall, they play with butterflies;
At the river, they throw at frogs.

ZGS 10.65, Shiba 248, ZGJT 59, 寒山詩 §39

10.81 格外辨龍蛇 *Kakuge ni ryūda o benji,*
機前擒虎兒 *⌜Ki⌝zen ni koji o torau.*

Cool and detached, he separates snakes from dragons;
In one fell swoop, he catches the tiger's cub.

ZGS 10.66, Shiba 248, ZGJI 494, ZRKS 10.289, KZS #975

10.82 角婢紅羅縝 *Kakuhi wa kōra no shin,*
閹奴紫錦裳 *Endo wa shikin no shō.*

For the women attendants, red gauze head scarves;
For the male servants, purple brocade robes.

ZGS 10.67, Shiba na, ZGJI 494, 寒山詩 §65

10.83 笠重吳山雪 *Kasa wa omoshi gosan no yuki,*
履香楚地花 *Kutsu wa kanbashi sochi no hana.*

My bamboo hat is weighed down with Wu mountain snow,
My shoes are scented with flowers from fields in Ch'u.

Shiba 294: 天 "skies" instead of 山 "mountains"; 鞋 *ai* "sandals" instead of 履 *kutsu* "shoes."

ZGS 10.68, Shiba 294, ZGJI 494, ZRKS 10.166

10.84 入花山求花 *Kazan ni itte hana o motome,*
向明月求月 *Meigetsu ni mukatte tsuki o motomu.*

In hills full of flowers, he looks for flowers;
In moonlight, he looks for the ⌜moon⌝.

ZGS 10.69, Shiba na, ZGJI 493

10.85 風暖鳥聲碎 *Kaze atataka ni shite chōsei kudake,*
日高花影重 *Hi takaushite kaei omoshi.*

The winds are warm, bird songs shatter the stillness;
With the sun up high, flowers pile their shadows on each other.

ZGS 10.70, Shiba 286, ZGJI 494, TSSSTS 180

10.86 風狂螢墮草 *Kaze kurutte hotaru kusa ni ochi,*
雨驟鵲驚枝 *Ame niwaka ni shite kasasagi eda ni odoroku.*

In the swirling wind, fireflies drop to the grass;
Caught by sudden showers, crows on the branches are startled.

ZGJI 494: 落 instead of 墮; ZRKS 10.536: 墜 instead of 墮.

ZGS na, Shiba 286, ZGJI 494, ZRKS 10.536

10.87 風定花猶落 *Kaze shizumatte hana nao ochi,*
鳥鳴山更幽 *Tori naite yama sara ni yū nari.*

The wind stops, but the flowers still fall;
A bird sings and the mountain is quieter still.

ZGS 10.71, Shiba 286, ZGJT 407, ZGJI 494, ZRKS 10.156

10.88 無風荷葉動 *Kaze naki ni kayō ugoku.*
決定有魚行 *Ketsujō uo no yuku koto aran.*

Without a breeze the lotus petals stir.
It's obvious a fish swims there.

Shiba 289: *ketsujō shite.*

ZGS 10.72, Shiba 289, ZGJI 494, ZGJT 443, ZRKS 10.499

10.89 風爲什麼色 *Kaze nan no iro o ka nashi.*
雨從何處來 *Ame izure no tokoro yori ka kitaru.*

What is the color of the wind?
Where does the rain come from?

Shiba 285: *Kaze nan no iro o ka nasu, Ame izuko yori kitaru.*

ZGS 10.73, Shiba 285

10.90 風吹南岸柳 *Kaze wa nangan no yanagi o fuki,*
雨打北池蓮 *Ame wa hokuchi no hasu o utsu.*

The wind blows the willows on the southern bank,
The rain strikes the lotus in the north pond.

ZGS 10.74, Shiba 286, ZGJI 495, ZRKS 10.274

10.91 側見雙翠鳥 *Katawara ni miru sōsuichō,*
巢在三珠樹 *Sukūte sanjuju ni aru o.*

Off to the side, I see two kingfishers
Nesting in the tree of three pearls.

ZGS 10.75, Shiba na, TSSSTS 3

10.92 喝下絕機思 *Kakka ⌜ki⌝shi o zesshi,*
棒頭開正眼 *Bōtō shōgen o hiraku.*

With the shout, stop motion of mind;
With the stick, open the true eye.

ZGS na, Shiba 248, ZGJI 495, ZRKS 10.482

10.93 曾慣雪霜苦 *Katsute sessō no ku ni narete,*
楊花落也驚 *Yōka no ochiru ni mo mata odoroku.*

Having once experienced the pain of snow and frost,
He shudders at the falling of white willow down.

ZGS na, Shiba 273, ZGJI 495, ZRKS 10.223

10.94 瓜田不納履 *Kaden ni ri o osamezu,*
梨下不整冠 *Rika ni kanmuri o tadasazu.*

Don't wear your shoes in the melon patch,
Don't adjust your hat under the pear tree.

A proverb warning against behavior which may arouse suspicion. Bending over to tie your shoes in a melon patch may look like you are stealing a melon. Raising your arms under a pear tree may look like you are stealing a pear (古楽府, 君子行 cited in *Shinjigen* 662).

ZGS 10.76, Shiba 246

10.95 臥龍纔奮迅 *Garyū wazuka ni funjin,*
丹鳳便翺翔 *Tanpō sunawachi kōshō su.*

If the sleeping dragon stirs ever so slightly,
The red phoenix soars aloft.

ZGS 10.77, Shiba 247, ZGJI 493, ZRKS 416

10.96 寒雲抱幽石 *Kan'un yūseki o idaki,*
霜月照清池 *Sōgetsu seichi o terasu.*

Cold clouds embrace lonely rocks,
The frosty ⌜moon⌝ shines upon the clear pond.

ZGS 10.78, Shiba 248, ZGJI 495

10.97 寒蟬抱枯木 *Kansen koboku o idaki,*
泣盡不回頭 *Nakitsukushite kōbe o megurasazu.*

The autumn cicada clings to the dead tree.
Crying singlemindedly, it never turns its head.

ZGS 10.79, Shiba 248, ZGJI 495

10.98 岩前瑞草多 *Ganzen zuisō ōku,*
磵下靈苗足 *Kanka reibyō taru.*

The foot of the cliff is thick with ⌜auspicious grass⌝,
The valley floor is covered with ⌜spiritual shoots⌝.

ZGS 10.80, Shiba na

10.99 寰中天子勅 *Kanchū wa tenshi no choku,*
塞外將軍令 *Saigai wa shōgun no rei.*

Within the imperial domains, the decree of the emperor;
Beyond the frontiers, the command of the general.

Heki 44 Verse, 73 Main Case *agyo* (敕 instead of 勅).

ZGS 10.81, Shiba 249, ZGJT 71, ZGJI 496, ZRKS 10.265, KZS #1021

10.100 聞説愁難遣 *Kikunaraku urei yarigatashi to,*
斯言謂不眞 *Kono gen shin narazu to iu.*

I've heard it said sorrow is hard to banish,
But these words are not true.

ZGS 10.82, Shiba na

10.101 來説是非者 *Kitatte zehi o toku mono wa,*
便是是非人 *Sunawachi kore zehi no hito.*

One who approaches with "right and wrong" talk
Is a "right and wrong" person.

MMK 18, *Heki* 74 Main Case *agyo*. To talk "right and wrong" is to spread gossip.

ZGS na, Shiba 293, ZGJI 497, ZGJT 466, ZRKS 10.141, KZS #985

10.102 携君石上琴 *Kimi ga sekijō no koto o tazusaete,*
彈我窓前月 *Wa ga sōzen no tsuki o danzu.*

You take up the lute atop the rock,
I strum in the moonlight by the window.

ZGS na, Shiba 253, ZGJI 497, ZRKS 10.251

10.103 勸君金屈巵 *Kimi ni susumu kinkusshi,*
滿酌不須辭 *Manshaku ji suru koto o mochiizu.*

I offer you this gold wine jug.
Please don't refuse a brimming cup.➛

ZGS 10.83, Shiba 249, TSSSTS 69

10.104 花發多風雨 *Hana hiraite fūu ōshi,*
人生足別離 *Jinsei betsuri taru.*

➛Flowers bloom to many winds and rains,
A person's life is filled with partings.

ZGS 10.84, Shiba na

10.105 君家住何處 *Kimi no ie wa izure no tokoro ni ka jū su,*
妾住在横塘 *Shō wa jū shite ōtō ni ari.*

"Where is the house in which you live?"
"My humble dwelling is over on yonder bank."➛

Shiba 253: in line 1, 在 instead of 住, *Kimi ga ie izuko ni ka aru.*

ZGS 10.85, Shiba 253, TSSSTS 64

10.106 停船暫借問 *Fune o todomete shibaraku shamon su,*
或恐是同郷 *Aruiwa osoru kore dōkyō naran.*

➛"Stop your boat and let's talk a little.
Perhaps we are from the same place."

ZGS 10.86, Shiba na

10.107 君看此花枝 *Kimi miyo kono kashi,*
中有風露香 *Naka ni fūro no kanbashiki ari.*

Just look at this flower branch—
Within is the fragrance of the wind and dew.

ZGS 10.87, Shiba 253, ZGJI 497, ZRKS 10.70

10.108 君看雙眼色　*Kimi miyo sōgan no iro,*
不語似無愁　*Katarazareba urei naki ni nitari.*

Look at the expression in her eyes—
She doesn't speak and looks as if she has no cares.

ZGS 10.88, Shiba na, ZGJI 497, ZRKS 10.165

10.109 久旱逢初雨　*Kyūkan shou ni ai,*
他郷遇舊知　*Takyō kyūchi ni au.*

After a long drought, we greet the first rain.
In another village, I run into an old friend.

ZGS 10.89, Shiba na, ZGJT 85, ZGJI 498, ZRKS 10.80

10.110 九夏寒岩雪　*Kyūge kangan no yuki,*
三冬枯木花　*Santō koboku no hana.*

Through the ninety days of summer, snow on the cold cliffs;
During the three months of winter, flowers on the ⌜withered⌝ tree.

Shiba 249: *kyūka* instead of *kyūge.*

ZGS 10.90, Shiba 249, ZGJI 498, ZRKS 10.397

10.111 舊竹生新筍　*Kyūchiku shinjun o shōji,*
新花長舊枝　*Shinka kyūshi ni chōzu.*

Old bamboo produces new shoots,
New blossoms grow out on old branches.

ZGS 10.91, Shiba 250, ZGJI 498

10.112 舊令尹政　*Kyūreiin no matsurigoto*
必以告新令尹　*Kanarazu motte shinreiin ni tsugu.*

The older councillor's conduct of government,
Without fail, is passed on to the new councillor.

ZGS 10.92, Shiba na; *Analects* v, 18

10.113 窮鼠反咬猫　*Kyūso kaette neko o kami,*
闘雀不畏人　*Tōjaku hito o osorezu.*

A cornered rat will turn and bite the cat,
Fighting sparrows do not fear people.

ZGS 10.93, Shiba 250, ZGJI 498

10.114 窮鳥入懐則　*Kyūchō futokoro ni ireba,*
弋者亦救之　*Yokusha mo mata kore sukuu.*

If the desperate bird flees into the bosom of his vest,
Then even the hunter will save it.

ZGS 10.94, Shiba 250

10.115 曉月尋花去 *Gyōgetsu hana o tazunete sari,*
春風帶酒歸 *Shunpū sake o obite kaeru.*

Under a dawn ⌜moon⌝, he went off to seek flowers;
In the spring breeze, he returned rather tipsy.

ZGS 10.95, Shiba 251

10.116 經來白馬寺 *Kyō wa kitaru hakubaji,*
僧到赤烏年 *Sō wa itaru sekiu'nen.*

The sutras came to the Temple of the White Horse,
The monks arrived in the Year of the Red Crow.

It is said that Buddhist sutras first arrived in China at the Temple of the White Horse during the time of Emperor Ming of the Later Han Dynasty, and that according to the zodiac, monks arrived during the Year of the Red Crow (Shiba 253).

ZGS na, Shiba 253, ZGJI 499, ZRKS 10.212

10.117 斬得匈奴首 *Kyōdo no kōbe o kiriete,*
還歸細柳營 *Kaette sairyūei ni ki su.*

Having cut off the head of the barbarian,
He returns to the ⌜Hsi-liu Garrison⌝.

ZGS 10.96, Shiba na, ZGJT 167, ZGJI 499, ZRKS 10.267, KZS #1022

10.118 曲終人不見 *Kyoku oete hito miezu,*
江上數峯青 *Kōjō sūhō aoshi.*

The song ends, no one in sight;
Over the river, several peaks are blue.

ZGS 10.97, Shiba 251, ZGJT 92, ZGJI 499, ZRKS 10.252, KZS #1013

10.119 玉樓巣翡翠 *Gyokurō ni hisui o sukuwashime,*
金殿鎖鴛鴦 *Kinden ni ennō o tozasu.*

He has kingfishers nest in the jade tower,
He keeps mandarin ducks in the golden palace.

ZGS 10.98, Shiba 252, ZRKS 10.213

10.120 歸來坐虛室 *Kaerikitatte kyoshitsu ni za sureba,*
夕陽在吾西 *Sekiyō waga nishi ni ari.*

I have come back to sit in my empty room,
The evening sun to the west of me.

ZGS 10.99, Shiba 249, ZGJT 494, ZGJI 499, ZRKS 10.520

10.121 金屑眼中翳 *Kinsetsu wa ganchū no ei,*
衣珠法上塵 *Eju wa hōjō no chiri.*

Gold dust in the eyes obstructs vision,
⌜A jewel in the clothing⌝, to the Dharma, is dirt.

ZGS 10.100, Shiba 252, ZGJT 94, ZGJI 499, ZRKS 10.439

10.122 空山不見人 *Kūzan hito o mizu*
但聞人語響 *Tada jingo no hibiki o kiku.*

Empty mountains, no one in sight,
Only an echo of someone's voice.

ZGS 10.101, Shiba na, TSSSTS 61

10.123 空手把鋤頭 *Kūshu ni shite jotō o tori,*
歩行騎水牛 *Hokō ni shite suigyū ni noru.*

Empty-handed, grasp the spade;
Walking on foot, ride the water buffalo.➛

⌜Fu Daishi's⌝ verse. See also 20.5.

ZGS 10.102, Shiba 252, ZGJT 98, ZGJI 500, ZRKS 10.49

10.124 人從橋上過 *Hito kyōjō yori sugureba,*
橋流水不流 *Hashi wa nagarete, mizu wa nagarezu.*

➛When a person walks over the bridge,
The bridge flows, the water doesn't.

ZGS 10.103, Shiba 268, ZGJT 365, ZGJI 544, ZRKS 10.508

10.125 打鼓弄琵琶 *Ku o uchi, biwa o rō su,*
相逢兩會家 *Aiō ryōeka.*

Beating the drum and strumming the lute,
Two old masters are meeting each other.

Heki 22 Main Case Comm., 92 Main Case *agyo.*

ZGS 10.104, Shiba na, ZGJT 284, ZGJI 504, ZRKS 10.247

10.126 九月十三晴 *Kugatsu jūsan harereba,*
釘靴掛斷繩 *Kutsu ni tei shite danjō ni kaku.*

If the weather is good on 13 September,
He will hang his sandals on a nail with a piece of rope.

"Good weather on 13 September means that continued rains are expected, so hang up your walking shoes and forget about traveling" (ZGJI 498).

ZGS 10.105, Shiba na, ZGJI 498

10.127 苦瓠連根苦 *Kuko wa ne ni tsuranatte nigaku,*
甜瓜徹蔕甜 *Kanka wa hozo ni tesshite amashi.*

The bitter gourd is bitter to the root,
The sweet melon is sweet through the stem.

Heki 87 Main Case *agyo*, 90 Main Case *agyo*. Shiba 252: *kuka* instead of *kuko*.

ZGS 10.106, Shiba 252, ZGJT 97, ZGJI 500, ZRKS 10.238, KZS #1014

10.128 草作青青色 *Kusa wa sei-seitaru iro o nashi,*
春風任短長 *Shunpū tanchō ni makasu.*

The grasses are green, green in color;
Long or short, the spring wind lets them be.

ZGS na, Shiba 273, ZGJI 500, ZRKS 10.388

10.129 鯨呑海水盡 *Kujira kaisui o nomitsukushite,*
露出珊瑚枝 *Sangoshi o roshutsu su.*

The whale has drunk up all the water in the sea
And exposed the branches of the coral.

ZGS 10.107, Shiba na, ZGJT 103, ZGJI 501, ZRKS 10.323, KZS #997

10.130 鯨呑洗鉢水 *Kujira senpatsu no mizu o nomi,*
犀觸點燈船 *Sai tentō no fune ni fureru.*

The whale drinks the wash water from the bowl,
The rhinoceros adjusts the boat of the oil lamp.

ZGS 10.108, Shiba na, TSSSTS 161

10.131 國清才子貴 *Kuni kiyō shite saishi tattoku,*
家富小兒驕 *Ie tonde shōni ogoru.*

When the country is uncorrupted, the talented person is highly valued;
When the house is rich, the younger son is arrogant.

MMK 17 Verse.

ZGS 10.109, Shiba 258, ZGJT 141, ZGJI 501, ZRKS 10.62, KZS #1045

10.132 國破山河在 *Kuni yaburete senga ari,*
城春草木深 *Shiro haru ni shite sōmoku fukashi.*

Though the nation is torn apart, the mountains and rivers remain;
The city in spring is deep in grass and trees.➛

ZGS 10.110, Shiba na, 杜甫春望

10.133 感時花濺涙 *Toki ni kanjite wa hana ni mo namida o sosogi,*
恨別鳥驚心 *Wakare o urande wa tori ni mo kokoro o odorokasu.*

➛Moved by the moment, I weep even at flowers;
Sad at parting, even birds suddenly disturb my heart.

ZGS 10.111: 惜 instead of 恨, Shiba 248

10.134 狗吠乞兒後 *Ku wa kotsuji no ato ni hoe,*
牛耕農夫前 *Ushi wa nōfu no mae ni kō su.*

The dog barks behind the beggar,
The ox plows in front of the farmer.

Empuku-ji: *shirie* instead of *ato.*

ZGS 10.112, Shiba 252, ZGJI 490

10.135 雲掩仲秋月 *Kumo wa chūshū no tsuki o ōi,*
雨打上元燈 *Ame wa jōgen no tomoshibi o utsu.*

Clouds veil the mid-autumn ⌜moon⌝,
Rain beats on the New Year's lantern.

ZGS 10.113: 中 instead of 仲.

ZGS 10.113, Shiba 244

10.136 無雲生嶺上 *Kumo no reijō ni shōzuru naku,*
有月落波心 *Tsuki no hashin ni otsuru ari.*

No clouds arise on the peak,
The ⌜moon⌝ falls into the midst of the waves.

ZGS 10.114, Shiba 289, ZGJI 501, ZRKS 10.511

10.137 薫風自南來 *Kunpū minami yori kitari,*
殿閣生微涼 *Denkaku biryō o shōzu.*

A fragrant breeze comes from the south,
The palace pavilion is now fresh and cool.

Empuku-ji: *Kunpū jinanrai.*

ZGS 10.115, Shiba 253, ZGJT 99, ZGJI 501, ZRKS 10.16, KZS #947

10.138 雞聲茅店月 *Keisei bōten no tsuki,*
人跡板橋霜 *Jinseki bankyō no shimo.*

At cock crow, the ⌜moon⌝ over the traveler's inn,
Footprints on the frosted boards of the bridge.

ZGS 10.116, ZGJI 502, Shiba na, TSSSTS 167

10.139 溪聲洗耳清 *Keisei mimi o aratte kiyoku,*
松蓋觸眼緑 *Shōgai me ni furete midori nari.*

The sound of the stream washes my ears clean,
The canopy of pines touches green to my eyes.

ZGS 10.117, Shiba 253

10.140 擊碎擊碎 *Gekisai seyo, gekisai seyo,*
不擊碎增瑕纇 *Gekisai sezareba karai o masan.*

Smash it, smash it!!
If you don't smash it, the faults will just increase.

ZGS 10.118, Shiba na

10.141 煙歸碧海夕 *Kemuri hekkai ni kaeru yūbe,*
雁度青天時 *Gan seiten o wataru toki.*

In the evening, as haze returned to the emerald sea,
At the moment when geese crossed the blue sky.

ZGS 10.119, Shiba na

10.142 擧起軒轅鑑 *Ken'en no kan o koki sureba,*
蚩尤頓失威 *Shiyū ton ni i o shissu.*

If you lift up the mirror of Hsien-yüan,
Ch'ih Yu at once loses his ferocity.

Hsien-yüan is the personal name of ⌜Huang-ti⌝.

ZGS 10.120, Shiba na

10.143 劍刄上走馬 *Kenninjō ni uma o hashirashime,*
火焰裏藏身 *Kaenri ni mi o zō su.*

He drives his horses on the blade of a ⌜sword⌝,
And hides himself in the burning fire.

ZGS 10.121, Shiba 254, ZGJT 108, ZGJI 502, ZRKS 10.48, KZS #967

10.144 劍刄上求人 *Kenninjō ni hito o motome,*
電光中垂手 *Denkōchū ni te o taru.*

He seeks a man on the blade of a ⌜sword⌝,
He drops his hands in a flash of lightning.

Te o taru can also be read ⌜*suishu*⌝.

ZGS 10.122, Shiba 254, ZGJI 502, ZRKS 10.278, KZS #970

10.145 劍握甑人手 *Ken wa sōjin no te ni nigiri,*
魚在謝郎船 *Uo wa sharō ga fune ni ari.*

The ⌜sword⌝ is in the grip of the ⌜man from Tseng⌝,
The fish are in ⌜Hsieh-lang's⌝ boat.

ZGS 10.123, Shiba na, ZGJI 502, ZRKS 10.37, KZS #964

10.146 言鋒冷似氷 *Genpō kōri yori mo hiyayaka ni,*
利舌硬如鐵 *Rizetsu tetsu yori mo katashi.*

His knife-like words are colder than ice,
His sharp tongue is harder than steel.

ZGS 10.124, Shiba na

10.147 沅湘流不盡 *Genshō nagarete tsukizu,*
屈子恨何深 *Kusshi urami nanzo fukaki.*

The Yüan and Hsiang Rivers flow without cease.
How deep is ⌜Ch'ü-tzu's⌝ bitterness?

ZGS 10.125, Shiba na

10.148 紅霞穿碧落 *Kōka hekiraku o ugachi,*
白日繞須彌 *Hakujitsu wa shumi o meguru.*

A red haze cuts the blue heavens,
The white sun enwraps Mount ⌜Sumeru⌝.

ZGS na, Shiba 257, ZGJI 506, ZGJT 135, ZRKS 10.365, KZS #1007

10.149 高高峯頂立 *Kō-kōtaru hōchō ni tachi,*
深深海底行 *Shin-shintaru kaitei ni yuku.*

Stand on the crest of a high, high peak;
Walk the bottom of the deep, deep sea.

ZGS 10.126, Shiba 257, ZGJI 506, ZRKS 10.343

10.150 黄昏雞報曉 *Kōkon tori akatsuki o hōji,*
半夜日頭明 *Han'ya nittō akiraka nari.*

At sunset, the rooster announces the dawn;
At midnight, the sun is shining brightly.

ZGS na, Shiba 257, ZGJI 507, ZGJT 137, ZRKS 10.106

10.151 高山白浪起 *Kōzan hakurō okori,*
海底紅塵颺 *Kaitei kōjin agaru.*

White waves roll on the high mountains,
Red dust rises on the bottom of the sea.

ZGS 10.127, Shiba na, ZGJI 506

10.152 好事不出門 *Kōji mon o idezu,*
惡事行千里 *Akuji senri o yuku.*

Good works do not go further than the gate,
But bad deeds go a thousand miles.

ZGS 10.128, Shiba 257, ZGJT 132, ZGJI 506, ZRKS 10.471

10.153 巧匠運斤斧 *Kōshō kinpu o megurashi,*
斫木不抨繩 *Ki o kiru ni nawa o tsuruutazu.*

The master craftsman swings his axe,
Cuts the wood without using a line.

ZGS 10.129, Shiba na, ZGJT 126, ZGJI 505, ZRKS 10.53

10.154 江上思鱸客 *Kōjō suzuki o omou kyaku,*
人間失馬翁 *Ningen uma o shissuru no ō.*

On the river, the traveler who dreamed about perch;
In the world, ⌜the old man who lost his horse.⌝

See ⌜Chang Han⌝.

ZGS 10.130, Shiba 256, ZGJI 505, ZRKS 10.206

10.155 江上萬餘里 *Kōjō banyori,*
何謁聖明君 *Nanzo seimei no kimi ni essen.*

Upriver more than ten thousand miles,
How will we ever meet a lord of superior virtue?

ZGS 10.131, Shiba na

10.156 識取鉤頭意 *Kōtō no i o shikishu seyo,*
莫認定盤星 *Jōbanjō o mitomuru koto nakare.*

Know the meaning of the ⌜steelyard's⌝ hook,
Don't fix your attention on the graduation marks.

Heki 2 Main Case Comm., 86 Main Case Comm., 87 Main Case Comm.

ZGS 10.132, Shiba na, ZGJT 183, ZGJI 507, ZRKS 10.193, KZS #1026

10.157 在江南爲橘 *Kōnan ni atte wa tachibana to nashi,*
在江北爲枳 *Kōhoku ni atte wa karatachi to nasu.*

South of the river, it's a tangerine;
North of the river, it's an orange.

ZGS 10.133, Shiba 259, ZGJI 505, ZRKS 10.383, KZS #1010

10.158 到江呉地盡 *Kō ni itatte gochi tsuki,*
隔岸越山多 *Kishi o hedatete essan ōshi.*

At the river, the land of ⌜Wu⌝ comes to an end;
Across the banks are the many mountains of ⌜Yüeh⌝.

ZGS 10.134, Shiba 278, ZGJT 339, ZGJI 505, ZRKS 10.313

10.159 江碧鳥逾白 *Kō midori ni shite tori iyo-iyo shiroku,*
山青花欲然 *Yama aō shite hana moen to hossu.*

Against the green river, the birds are even whiter;
On the blue mountains, the flowers look ready to burst into flame.

ZGS 10.135, Shiba 256, ZGJI 505, TSSSTS 64

10.160 不入洪浪裏 *Kōrō no uchi ni irazumba,*
爭見弄潮人 *Ikade ka ushio o rōsuru hito o min.*

If you do not throw yourself into the breakers,
How will you ever meet the one who frolics in the waves?

ZGS na, Shiba 284, ZGJI 506, ZGJT 403, ZRKS 10.115

10.161 養子莫教大 *Ko o yashinōte dai narashimuru koto nakare,*
大了作家賊 *Dai ni shiowareba kazoku to naru.*

When you raise a son, do not let him get big;
If he gets big, he will steal the house.

ZGS 10.136, Shiba na, ZGJT 463, ZGJI 503, ZRKS 10.382

10.162 古澗寒泉湧 *Kokan kansen waki,*
青松雪後凋 *Seishō setsugo shibomu.*

An icy spring gushes up in the ancient valley
And the green pine withers after the snows.

ZGS na, Shiba 255, ZGJI 503, ZRKS 10.461

10.163 虛空無背面 *Kokū haimen naku,*
鳥道絕東西 *Chōdō tōzai o zessu.*

The empty sky has no front or back,
The path of the bird transcends east and west.

ZGS 10.137, Shiba 251, ZGJI 504, ZRKS 10.197

10.164 湖光迷翡翠 *Kokō hisui o mayowashi,*
草色醉蜻蜓 *Sōshiki seitei o yowashimu.*

The light of the lake confuses the kingfishers,
The color of the grass makes the dragonflies drunk.

ZGS 10.138, Shiba 255, ZGJI 504, ZRKS 10.130, TSSSTS 160

10.165 五更一盂粥 *Gokō ichiu no shuku,*
辰時一頓飯 *Shinji itton no han.*

At the fifth ⌜watch⌝, one bowl of gruel;
At the hour of the dragon, one round of rice.

The fifth watch of the night is 3–5 AM. The hour of the dragon is 7–9 AM.

ZGS na, Shiba 256, ZGJI 504, ZRKS 10.118

10.166 志密行亦密 *Kokorozashi mitsu nareba gyō mo mata mitsu nari,*
功深悟亦深 *Kō fukakereba go mo mata fukashi.*

If your resolution is solid, your practice will also be solid;
If your training is deep, your awakening will also be deep.

ZGS 10.139, Shiba 262, ZGJI 507, ZRKS 10.523

10.167 試搖枝頭雪 *Kokoromi ni shitō no yuki o ugokase,*
定有夜來花 *Sadamete yarai no hana aran.*

Try shaking the snow off the branches,
For sure, flowers have opened during the night.

Empuku-ji: *sadande* instead of *sadamete.*

ZGS 10.140, Shiba 262, ZGJI 507, ZRKS 10.433

10.168 江山千里舊 *Kōzan senri no kyū,*
賓主一時新 *Hinju ichiji ni arata nari.*

Mountains and rivers for thousands of miles are ageless,
But host and guest at every instant are new.

ZGS na, Shiba 256, ZGJI 505, ZRKS 10.555

10.169 腰纏十萬貫 *Koshi ni jūmangan o matōte,*
乘鶴下揚州 *Tsuru ni norite yōjū ni kudaru.*

He straps one hundred thousand strings of cash onto his hips,
Takes off on a crane and alights in Yang-chou.

Shiba 292. Empuku-ji: *Koshi ni matou jūmangan.*

ZGS 10.141, Shiba 292

10.170 古松談般若 *Koshō hannya o danji,*
幽鳥弄眞如 *Yūchō shinnyo o rō su.*

The old pine is talking *prajñā*-wisdom,
The hidden bird is playing with true suchness.

ZGS 10.142, Shiba 255, ZGJI 503, ZRKS 10.448

10.171 護生須是殺 *Goshō wa subekaraku kore korosubeshi,*
殺盡始安居 *Koroshitsukushite hajimete ango.*

Saving your life is what you must kill;
Kill it completely and you will rest in peace.

ZGJT 123: *Shō o mamoru ni wa subekaraku korosubeshi.*

ZGS na, Shiba 256, ZGJI 504, ZGJT 123, ZRKS 10.229, KZS #1029

10.172 瓠子曲彎彎 *Kosu wa magatte wan-wan,*
冬瓜直儱侗 *Tōga wa naoku shite rōtō.*

The gourd is bent and twisted,
The winter melon flops straight down.

Shiba 255: *naōshite* instead of *naoku shite.*

ZGS 10.143, Shiba 255, ZGJI 504, ZRKS 10.123

10.173 呉楚東南坼 *Goso tōnan ni sake,*
乾坤日夜浮 *Kenkon nichiya ni ukabu.*

It separates ⌜Wu⌝ and Ch'u into east and south,
⌜Heaven and earth⌝ float on it day and night.

ZGS 10.144, Shiba 256, TSSSTS 28

10.174 鶻欲搏者潛 *Kotsu no utan to hossuru mono wa hisomi,*
蠖欲伸者屈 *Kaku no nobin to hossuru mono wa kussu.*

He who would strike like a falcon hides himself;
He who would stretch like the inchworm draws himself back.

ZGS 10.145, Shiba na, ZGJI 508

10.175 劫石有消日 *Gosseki wa shō suru hi ari tomo,*
此恨幾時休 *Kono urami iku toki ka yaman.*

Though even the ⌜*kalpa* stone⌝ will one day wear away,
When will this resentment cease?

Empuku-ji: *gosshaku* instead of *gosseki.*

ZGS 10.146, Shiba na

10.176 劫石有消日 *Gosseki wa shō suru hi ari tomo,*
洪音無盡時 *Kōin wa tsukuru toki nashi.*

Though even the ⌜*kalpa* stone⌝ will one day wear away,
This vast sound will never come to an end.

Empuku-ji: *gosshaku* instead of *gosseki*

ZGS 10.147, Shiba 257, ZGJI 507

10.177 兀然無事坐 *Gotsunen to shite buji ni shite za sureba,*
春來草自生 *Shunrai kusa onozukara shōzu.*

Sitting quietly doing nothing, spring comes,
Grass grows by itself.

ZGS 10.148, Shiba 258

10.178 此地別燕丹 *Kono chi entan ni wakaru,*
壯士髮衝冠 *Sōshi hatsu kan o tsuku.*

At this spot, he took leave of Prince Tan of Yen;
The hair of this brave man bristled beneath his cap.➛

See ⌜Ching K'o⌝.

ZGS 10.149, Shiba na, TSSSTS 58

10.179 昔時人已沒 *Sekiji no hito sude ni bosshite,*
今日水猶寒 *Konnichi mizu nao samushi.*

➛The men of ancient times have passed away,
Today the river waters still run cold.

ZGS 10.150, Shiba na

10.180 此夜一輪滿 *Kono yō ichi rin miteri,*
淸光何處無 *Seikō izure no tokoro ni ka nakaran.*

Tonight the ⌜moon⌝ has reached its full,
What place is not suffused with its pure radiance?

ZGS 10.151, Shiba 262, ZGJT 172, ZGJI 508, ZRKS 10.20

10.181 語不令人會 *Go hito o shite eseshimezareba,*
須得人譯之 *Subekaraku hito o ete kore o yaku subeshi.*

If your words do not make people understand,
You must get the right person to explain them.

ZGS 10.152, Shiba na, ZRKS 10.7

10.182 枯木倚寒巖 *Koboku kangan ni yoru,*
三冬無暖氣 *Santō danki nashi.*

The old pine stands on the frozen rock,
For the three months of winter, not a breath of warm air.

ZGS 10.153: 嵓 instead of 巖, Shiba 255, ZGJT 117

10.183 古木鳴寒鳥 *Koboku kanchō naki,*
空山啼夜猿 *Kūzan yaen naku.*

On the dead branch a winter bird cries,
In the empty mountains the night monkeys howl.

ZGS 10.154, Shiba 255: 野 "wild" for 夜 "night", TSSSTS 3

10.184 枯木裏龍吟 *Kobokuri no ryūgin,*
髑髏裏眼睛 *Dokurori no ganzei.*

The dragon-hum in the dead tree,
The eyeball in the dry skull.

Heki 2 Verse Comm.

ZGS 10.155, Shiba 255, ZGJI 503, ZD #82, ZRKS 10.240

10.185 愛之欲其生 *Kore o ai shite wa sono sei o hosshi,*
惡之欲其死 *Kore o nikunde wa sono shi o hossu.*

When you love it, you want it to live;
When you hate it, you want it to die.

ZGS 10.156, Shiba na; *Analects* xii, 10.

10.186 視之而弗見 *Kore o miredomo miezu,*
聽之而弗聞 *Kore o kikedomo kikoezu*

Though you look, it cannot be seen;
Though you listen, it cannot be heard.

ZGS 10.157, Shiba 262

10.187 打破蔡州城 *Saishūjō o taha shite,*
殺卻吳元濟 *Gogensai o sekkyaku su.*

He demolished the city of Ts'ai-chou,
And killed Wu Yüan-chi.

In 817, during the T'ang Dynasty, Wu Yüan-chi (J. Gogensai) led a rebellion against the emperor and took the city of Ts'ai-chou. The emperor called in his army, which broke into the city, captured Wu Yüan-chi and took him to ⌜Ch'ang-an⌝ to be executed (ZGJT 283, Morohashi 3365.544).

ZGS 10.158, Shiba 273, ZGJT 284, ZGJI 509, ZRKS 10.505

10.188 棹穿輕靄去 *Sao wa keiai o ugatte sari,*
帆逐暮烟歸 *Ho wa boen o ōte kaeru.*

The pole leaves piercing the mist,
The sail returns chasing the evening haze.

ZGS 10.159, Shiba na

10.189 仗策謁天子 *Saku o tsuetsuite tenshi ni esshi,*
驅馬出關門 *Uma o katte kanmon o izu.*

Whip in hand, he goes to an audience with the emperor;
Racing his horse, he rides out the barrier gate.

ZGS 10.160, Shiba na, TSSSTS 3

10.190 昨夜一聲鴈 *Sakuya issei no kari,*
淸風萬里秋 *Seifū banri no aki.*

Last night the wild goose gave a cry;
The pure wind spread autumn for ten thousand miles.

ZGS 10.161: 雁 instead of 鴈, Shiba 259, ZGJI 510, ZRKS 10.152

10.191 昨夜寒風起 *Sakuya kanpū okoru,*
今朝括地霜 *Konchō katchi no shimo.*

Last night a cold wind rose,
This morning an earth-gripping frost.

ZGS 10.162, Shiba na, ZGJI 510, ZRKS 10.352

10 字

10.192 托來藏日月 *Sasage kitareba jitsugetsu o kakushi,*
放下貯乾坤 *Hōge sureba kenkon o takuwau.*

When you offer them up, sun and ⌜moon⌝ are concealed;
When you set them down, ⌜heaven and earth⌝ are retained.

ZGS na, Shiba 274, ZGJI 510, ZRKS 10.459

10.193 座上無老僧 *Zajō ni rōsō naku,*
目前無闍梨 *Mokuzen ni jari nashi.*

On my seat there is no ⌜old monk⌝,
Before my eyes there is no teacher.

"Old monk" is used to refer to the first person (ZGJT 487); *jari* is often used as a second person pronoun (ZGDJT 478). Thus this verse can be translated, "On my seat there is no me, / Before my eyes there is no you" (ZGJT 154).

ZGS 10.163, Shiba na, ZGJT 154, ZGJI 509, ZRKS 10.222, KZS #1025

10.194 坐底見立底 *Zatei ni ryūtei o mi,*
立底見坐底 *Ryūtei ni zatei o miru.*

Those sitting see those standing,
Those standing see those sitting.

ZGS na, Shiba 258, ZGJI 509, ZRKS 10.478, *Jōshū-roku* §334.

10.195 更無尋覓處 *Sara ni jinmyaku suru tokoro nashi,*
鳥跡印空中 *Chōseki kūchū ni in su.*

There is nowhere to search for them—
The traces that a bird leave in the sky.

ZGS 10.164, Shiba 257, ZGJI 510, ZRKS 10.545

10.196 山櫻火燄輝 *San'ō kaen kagayaki,*
山鳥歌聲滑 *Sanchō kasei nameraka nari.*

The mountain cherries glow like burning fire,
The mountain birds sing with a liquid sound.

Shiba 260: 炎 instead of 燄; ZGJI 511: 焔 instead of 燄.

ZGS 10.165, Shiba 260, ZGJI 511, ZRKS 10.575

10.197 山果携兒摘 *Sanka ji o tazusaete tsumi,*
荒田共婦鋤 *Kōden fu to tomo ni suku.*

Taking my child in hand, I pick mountain fruit;
And together with my wife dig the hillside fields.

ZGS 10.166: 皐 instead of 荒, Shiba 260, 寒山詩 §31

10.198 山果青猿摘 *Sanka seien tsumi,*
池魚白鷺銜 *Chigyo hakuro fukumu.*

The mountain fruit picked by the blue monkeys,
The fish in the pond eaten by the white herons.

ZGS 10.167, Shiba 260, ZGJI 512

10.199 山河並大地 *Senga narabi ni daichi,*
全露法王身 *Mattaku hōōshin o arawasu.*

Mountains and rivers and the great earth
Completely reveal the Dharma King's body.

ZGS 10.168, Shiba 260, ZGJT 164, ZGJI 512, ZRKS 10.146, KZS #1058

10.200 山花開似錦 *Sanka hiraite nishiki ni nitari,*
澗水湛如藍 *Kansui tataete ai no gotoshi.*

Mountain flowers bloom like brocade,
The valley streams brim indigo blue.

Heki 82 Main Case.

ZGS 10.169, Shiba 260, ZGJI 512, ZRKS 10.6, KZS #952

10.201 三月初三雨 *Sangatsu shozan ame fureba,*
桑葉無人取 *Sōyō hito no toru nashi.*

If it rains on the third of March,
There will be no one to pick the mulberry leaves.

ZGS 10.170, Shiba na

10.202 不遊三級浪 *Sankyū no nami ni asobazumba,*
爭識禹門高 *Ikadeka umon no takaki koto o shiran.*

If you do not press through the ⌜three-stage⌝ waves,
How will you know the height of ⌜Yü's⌝ gate?

ZGS 10.171, Shiba 284, ZGJI 510, ZRKS 10.333, KZS #999

10.203 三間得幽寂 *Sangen yūjaku o u,*
數歩藏清深 *Sūho seishin o kakusu.*

Just three nooks but it is serene and quiet;
The few steps contain a deep purity.

"Three nooks" translates 三間, where 間 is the distance between house posts. "Nooks" tries to capture the nuance that the scholar's study is tiny. Its small garden has a path only a "few steps" long.

ZGS na, Shiba 259, ZGJI 511, ZRKS 10.524

10.204 三日不相見 *Sanjitsu shōken sezumba,*
莫作舊時看 *Kyūji no kan o nasu nakare.*

If we haven't met in three days,
You can't take the same view as last time.

ZGS 10.172, Shiba na, ZGJT 162, ZGJI 511, ZRKS 10.82, KZS #954

10.205 三尺一丈六 *Sanjaku to ichijōroku to,*
且同攜手歸 *Shibaraku onajiku te o tazusaete kaeru.*

The three-foot and the「sixteen-foot」,
Return hand-in-hand together.

ZGS 10.173: 與 instead of 一, Shiba 259, ZGJT 162, ZGJI 511, ZRKS 10.307

10.206 山勢臨江盡 *Sansei kō ni nozonde tsuki,*
鐘聲出塢微 *Shōsei iu o idete bi nari.*

The mountains lose height as they approach the river,
The boom of the bell fades as it leaves the slopes.

ZGS na, Shiba 260, ZGJI 512, ZRKS 10.170

10.207 要知山上路 *Sanjō no michi o shiran to yōseba,*
須是去來人 *Subekaraku kore kyorai no hito narubeshi.*

If you want to know the path on the mountain,
You must be one who comes and goes on it.

Heki 34 Main Case Verse. ZGJT 462: *hosseba* instead of *yōseba.*

ZGS na, ZGJI 512, ZGJT 462, ZRKS 10.127, Shiba 292, KZS #1072

10.208 三冬枯木秀 *Santō koboku hiide,*
九夏雪花飛 *Kyūka sekka tobu.*

Through the three months of winter the old tree stands tall,
During the ninety days of summer snowflakes fly.

ZGS na, Shiba 260, ZGJI 511, ZGJT 162, ZRKS 10.100

10.209 不明三八九 *Sanpakku o akiramezumba,*
對境所思多 *Kyō ni tai shite shoshi ōshi.*

If you are unclear about 3, 8, and 9,
Then about the world you will have many thoughts.

3+8+9=20. Twenty was sometimes written with the character 念, pronounced *nien* in Ch. 念 usually means "thought," "thinking" (ZGJI 511; Mathews §4716b).

ZGS 10.174, Shiba 284, ZGJI 511

10.210 强欲登高去 *Shiite takaki ni nobori saran to hossu,*
無人送酒來 *Hito no sake o okurikitaru nashi.*

If you insist on climbing high places,
No one will bring you any wine.

ZGS 10.175, Shiba na, TSSSTS 64

10.211 十年歸不得 *Jūnen kaeru koto o ezumba,*
忘卻來時道 *Raiji no michi o bōkyaku su.*

Ten years unable to return,
I've forgotten the road by which I came.

Shiba 265: *ezareba* instead of *ezumba. Heki* 34 Verse.

ZGS 10.176, Shiba 265, ZGJT 202, ZGJI 515, ZD# 77, ZRKS 10.129, KZS #1073, 寒山詩 §4

10.212 秋風吹渭水 *Shūfū isui o fukeba,*
落葉滿長安 *Rakuyō chōan ni mitsu.*

When autumn winds blow on the river Wei,
Falling leaves fill ⌜Ch'ang-an⌝.

ZGS 10.177, Shiba 264, ZGJT 200, ZGJI 514, ZD# 84, ZRKS 10.325

10.213 欲得周郎顧 *Shūrō ga ko o en to hosshite,*
時時誤拂絃 *Ji-ji ni ayamatte gen o harau.*

Wanting to get Chou-lang to turn his head again,
From time to time she plucks the wrong string.

ZGS 10.178, Shiba na, ZGJI 514, ZRKS 10.61, KZS #961

10.214 死脱夏天衫 *Shishite wa dassu katen no san,*
生著冬月襖 *Ikite wa tsuku tōgetsu no ō.*

Die in taking off your summer gown,
Live in putting on your winter coat.

ZGS 10.179, Shiba na, ZGJI 512, ZRKS 10.72

10.215 竹篦生鐵鑄 *Shippei santetsu o iri,*
石火迸青天 *Sekka seiten ni hotobashiru.*

With his bamboo rod he forges raw iron;
Sparks fly through the blue sky.

ZGS na, Shiba 274, ZGJI 531, ZRKS 10.563

10.216 十方無虛空 *Jippō kokū naku,*
大地無寸土 *Daichi sundo nashi.*

Throughout the ⌜ten directions⌝ there is no emptiness,
On the great earth there is not a clod of dirt.

ZGS 10.180, Shiba 264, ZGJI 515, ZRKS 10.28

10.217 十方同聚會 *Jippō dōjue,*
箇箇學無爲 *Ko-ko gaku mui.*

From the ⌜ten directions⌝, they gather into one assembly,
And one by one, each learns non-action.➛

Poem by ⌜Layman P'ang⌝.

ZGS 10.181, Shiba na

10.218 此是選佛場 *Kore wa kore senbutsujō,*
心空及第皈 *Shinkū kyūdai shite kaeru.*

➛Here at the Buddha selection ground,
With emptiness of mind, they pass the trials and go home.

Shiba 262: 歸 instead of 皈.

ZGS 10.182, Shiba 262, ZGJT 172, ZGJI 508, ZRKS 10.540

10.219 十方薄伽梵 *Jippō bogyaban,*
一路涅槃門 *Ichiro nehanmon.*

The bhagavat of the ⌜ten directions⌝
Have one way to nirvana.

MMK 48. Bhagavat here mean buddhas (Shibayama 1974, 326).

ZGS na, Shiba 264, ZGJI 515, ZGJT 202, ZRKS 10.443

10.220 十方無影像 *Jippō yōzō naku,*
三界絕行蹤 *Sangai gyōshō o zessu.*

In the ⌜ten directions⌝ there are no images;
In the ⌜three worlds⌝ all traces have gone.

ZGS na, Shiba 264, ZGJI 515, ZRKS 10.547

10.221 十方無壁落 *Jippō hekiraku naku,*
四面又無門 *Shimen mata mon nashi.*

The ⌜ten directions⌝ are without walls,
The four quarters are without gates.

Heki 36 Verse Comm., 60 Main Case *agyo.*

ZGS 10.183, Shiba 264, ZGJT 202, ZGJI 515, ZD# 75, ZRKS 10.92, KZS #1066

10.222 不知何處寺 *Shirazu izure no tokoro no tera zo,*
風送鐘聲來 *Kaze shōsei o okuri kitaru.*

I do not know where the temple is,
But the wind carries the sound of its bell.

ZGS na, Shiba 284, ZGJI 517, ZRKS 10.432

10.223 詩向會人吟 *Shi wa kaijin ni mukatte ginji,*
酒逢知己飲 *Sake wa chiki ni ōte nomu.*

My songs I sing to those who understand,
Wine I drink with those who know me well.

Shiba 262: 快 instead of 會.

ZGS 10.184, Shiba 262, ZGJT 196, ZGJI 510, ZRKS 10.78, KZS #1064

10.224 任經霜與雪 *Shimo to yuki o furu ni makasete,*
不改舊時容 *Kyūji no katachi o aratamezu.*

Indifferent to the passing of frost and snow,
It never changes its age-old shape.

ZGS 10.185, Shiba na

10.225 錫帶吳天雪 *Shaku ni wa obu goten no yuki,*
瓶添漢地泉 *Hei ni wa sou kanchi no sen.*

The staff is covered with snow from ⌜Wu⌝,
The jug holds water from the springs of Han.

ZGS 10.186, Shiba na, ZGJI 513

10.226 麝香眠石竹 *Jakō sekichiku ni nemuri,*
鸚鵡啄金桃 *Ōmu kintō o tsuibamu.*

The ⌜musk deer⌝ sleeps among the rushes,
The parrot pecks at a golden ⌜peach⌝.

ZGS 10.187, Shiba 263, ZRKS 10.3

10.227 不因射鵰手 *Shachū no te ni yorazumba,*
誰識李將軍 *Tare ka rishōgun o shiran.*

If not by the hand that shot the eagle,
How can one know ⌜General Li⌝?

Shiba 283: *shashū* instead of *shachū*.

ZGS 10.188, Shiba 283, ZGJT 402, ZGJI 513, ZRKS 10.334

10.228 得衆則得國 *Shu o ereba kuni o eru,*
失衆則失國 *Shu o ushinaeba kuni o ushinau.*

By gaining the people, the kingdom is gained,
By losing the people, the kingdom is lost.

ZGS 10.189, Shiba na; *Great Learning* x, 5

10.229 終日走紅塵 *Shūjitsu kōjin ni hashitte,*
失卻自家珍 *Jika no chin o shikkyaku su.*

Running about in the red ⌜dust⌝ all day long,
You have lost your precious family treasure.

Shiba 264: *Shūjitsu kōjin ni washiri.*

ZGS 10.190, Shiba 264, ZRKS 10.261, KZS #1019

10.230 袖中藏日月 *Shūchū ni jitsugetsu o zōshi,*
掌内握乾坤 *Shōnai ni kenkon o nigiru.*

He hides the sun and ⌜moon⌝ in his sleeves,
And holds ⌜heaven and earth⌝ in his hands.

ZGS na, Shiba 264, ZGJI 514, ZRKS 10.256

10.231 宿昔青雲志 *Shukushaku seiun no kokorozashi,*
蹉跎白髮年 *Satatari hakuhatsu no toshi.*

In the old days I had ambitions as high as the blue sky,
Now I am a worn out old man with white hair.

ZGS 10.191, Shiba 265, TSSSTS 59

10.232 出身猶可易 *Shusshin wa nao yasukarubeshi,*
脱體道應難 *Dattai ni iu koto wa masa ni katakarubeshi.*

To attain release from self is easy,
But to speak after liberation is difficult.

Heki 46 Main Case.

ZGS na, Shiba 265, ZGJT 206, ZGJI 515, ZRKS 10.516

10.233 出沒太虛中 *Shutsubotsu taikō no uchi,*
吹毛曾不動 *Suimō katsute dōzezu.*

Appearing and disappearing in vast emptiness,
The ⌜hair-cutter sword⌝ never moves.

ZGS 10.192, Shiba na, ZGJI 515, ZRKS 10.41

10.234 主賓分兎馬 *Shuhin tome o wakachi,*
棒喝辨龍蛇 *Bōkatsu ryūda o benzu.*

Host and guest separate the rabbits from the horses,
The ⌜stick and shout⌝ distinguish the dragons from the snakes.

ZGS 10.193, Shiba 263, KZS #1006, ZGJI 514, ZRKS 10.384

10.235 餓死首陽山 *Shuyōzan ni gashi suru mo,*
誓不食周栗 *Chikatte shū no zoku o hamazu.*

Even if they starved to death on ⌜Mount Shou-yang⌝,
They vowed not to eat the grain of Chou.

See ⌜Po Yi and Shu Ch'i⌝.

ZGS 10.194, Shiba na, ZD #199

10.236 正狗不偸油 *Shōku abura o nusumazu,*
雞銜燈盞走 *Kei tōsan o fukunde hashiru.*

A good dog doesn't steal oil,
But the cock runs away with the lamp bowl in its beak.

ZGS 10.195, Shiba na, ZGJI 516

10.237 昭君則住胡 *Shōkun wa sunawachi ko ni yuki,*
西施則歸越 *Seishi wa sunawachi etsu ni kaeru.*

⌜Chao Chün⌝ went away to the Hu barbarians,
⌜Hsi-shih⌝ returned to Yüeh.

ZGS 10.196, Shiba na

10.238 跳出生死關 *Shōji no kan o chōshutsu shite,*
驀過荊棘林 *Keikyokurin o bakka su.*

Leap right over the barrier of life and death,
Gallop straight through the forest of thorns.

ZGS na, Shiba 276, ZGJI 520, ZRKS 10.467

10.239 松樹千年翠 *Shōju sennen no midori,*
不入時人意 *Toki no hito no kokoro ni irazu.*

The thousand-year green of this pine
Does not enter the minds of people today.

ZGS 10.197, ZGJI 516, ZRKS 10.427, Shiba 266

10.240 樵夫入深山 *Shōfu shinzan ni iri,*
碧潭漁史釣 *Hekitan gyoshi tsuru.*

The woodsman goes deep into the hills,
The fisherman angles the blue pools.

ZGS na, Shiba 267

10.241 鐘聲來舊寺 *Shōsei kyūji ni kitari,*
月色下新池 *Gesshoku shinchi ni kudaru.*

The tolling of the bell comes to the old temple,
Moonlight falls on a new pond.

ZGS na, Shiba 267, ZGJI 517, ZRKS 10.164

10.242 聖僧堂裡坐 *Shōsō wa dōri ni za shi,*
金剛門外立 *Kongō wa monge ni tatsu.*

The ⌜holy monk⌝ is sitting in the *zendō*,
The ⌜*vajra*⌝ kings stand outside the gate.

ZGS 10.198, Shiba na, ZGJI 521

10.243 牀頭三尺劍 *Jōtō sanjaku no ken,*
瓶裏一枝梅 *Heiri isshi no ume.*

On the rack, a three-foot ⌜sword⌝;
In the vase, a single plum bough.

ZGS 10.199, Shiba 266

10.244 蜀先主三顧 *Shoku no senshu*
孔明於草蘆 *Kōmei o sōro ni sanko su.*

Three times the ruler of Shu
Visited K'ung-ming in his thatch-roofed hut.

See ⌜Chu-ko⌝.

ZGS 10.200, Shiba na

10.245 深山古廟裡 *Shinzan kobyōri,*
無轉智大王 *Mutenchi no daiō.*

Deep in the mountains, in his old shrine,
A great king of unchanging wisdom.

ZGS 10.201, Shiba na, ZGDJT 1211

10.246 人生不滿百 *Jinsei hyaku ni mitazu,*
常懷千載憂 *Tsune ni senzai no urei o idaku.*

The span of human life does not reach a hundred years,
Yet we constantly bear the sorrows of a thousand.

ZGS 10.202, Shiba 268, ZGJT 232, ZGJI 516, ZRKS 10.570, 寒山詩 §138

10.247 神通並妙用 *Jintsū narabi ni myōyū,*
荷水也搬柴 *Mizu o ninai mata shiba o hakobu.*

Divine powers, works of wonder,
Hauling water, carrying wood.

Heki 42 Main Case Comm.

ZGS 10.203, Shiba 267, ZGJT 234, ZGJI 518, ZRKS 10.32, KZS #951

10.248 心隨萬境轉 *Shin wa bankyō ni shitagatte tenzu*
轉處實能幽 *Tenjō jitsu ni yoku yū nari.*

Mind changes with its myriad surroundings.
The way it changes is truly mysterious.➛

Heki 22 Verse Comm., *Rinzai-roku* §19

ZGS 10.204, Shiba 267, ZGJT 226, ZGJI 507, ZRKS 10.445

10.249 隨流認得性 *Nagare ni shitagatte shō o nintoku sureba,*
無喜亦無憂 *Ki mo naku mata yū mo nashi.*

➛If you follow its flow and perceive its nature,
Then there is neither joy nor sorrow.

ZGS 10.205, Shiba 269, ZGJT 240, ZGJI 539, ZRKS 10.479, ZD #89.

10.250 樹密猿聲響 *Ju mitsu ni shite ensei hibiki,*
波澄鴈影深 *Nami sunde gan'ei fukashi.*

The cries of monkeys ring though the dense forest,
Images of geese lie deep in the still waters.

ZGS na, Shiba 264, ZGJI 514, ZRKS 10.137, TSSSTS 160

10.251 春山疊亂青 *Shunzan ranjō o tatami,*
春水漾虛碧 *Shunsui kyoheki o tadayowasu.*

The spring mountains make mad piles of green,
The spring waters splash transparently blue.

Shiba 265: 漂 instead of 漾.

ZGS 10.206, Shiba 265, ZGJI 515, ZRKS 10.221

10.252 春色無高下 *Shunshoku ni kōge naku,*
花枝自短長 *Kashi onozukara tanchō.*

In spring colors, there is neither high nor low;
Flowering branches are by nature some long, some short.

Shiba 265: *Shunshoku kōge naku.*

ZGS 10.207, Shiba 265, ZGJT 207, ZGJI 516, ZRKS 10.12, KZS #953

10.253 春鳥啼春風 *Shunchō shunpū ni naki,*
春魚弄春水 *Shungyo shunsui o rō su.*

The spring birds sing in the spring wind,
The spring fish play in the spring waters.

ZGS 10.208, Shiba na

10.254 俊鳥不栖林 *Shunchō hayashi ni sumazu,*
活龍不滯水 *Katsuryū mizu ni todokōrazu.*

A fierce eagle does not nest in the forest,
A live dragon does not remain in the water.

ZGS 10.209, Shiba 265, ZGJI 515, ZRKS 10.356

10.255 舜無卓錐地 *Shun ni takusui no chi naku,*
禹無十戸聚 *U ni jikko no shū nashi.*

⌜Shun⌝ did not have enough ground even to stick in a ⌜pick⌝,
⌜Yü's⌝ village was a cluster of not even ten houses.

ZGS 10.210, Shiba 266

10.256 春來遊寺客 *Shunrai yūji no kyaku,*
花落閉門僧 *Hana ochite mon o tozuru no sō.*

When spring comes people visit at the temple;
As the petals fall the monk closes the gate.

ZGS na, Shiba 266, ZGJI 542

10.257 春眠不覺曉 *Shunmin akatsuki o oboezu,*
處處聞啼鳥 *Sho-sho teichō o kiku.*

Springtime sleeping late, unaware of the dawn;
Here and there, hear the song of the bird.➛

ZGS 10.211, Shiba 266, TSSSTS 62

10 字

10.258 夜來風雨聲 *Yarai fūu no koe,*
花落知多少 *Hana otsuru koto shinnu tashō zo.*

➛Last night there was the sound of wind and rain.
Who knows how many flowers fell?

ZGS 10.212, Shiba 291; Maeno 1963. vol. III, 51-2

10.259 不因樵子路 *Shōshi no michi ni yorazumba,*
爭到葛洪家 *Ikade ka kakkō ga ie ni itaran.*

If you do not go by the woodcutter's path,
How will you ever reach the House of ⌜Ko Hung⌝?

ZGJI 517: 徑 instead of 路.

ZGS na, Shiba 283, ZGJT 402, ZGJI 517, ZRKS 10.315, KZS #996

10.260 少林無師句 *Shōrin mushi no ku,*
曹溪絕學禪 *Sōkei zetsugaku no zen.*

⌜Shao-lin⌝—the verse of one who would not teach.
⌜Ts'ao-chi⌝—the Zen that cannot be learned.

ZGS na, Shiba 266, ZGJI 516, ZRKS 10.494

10.261 晉楚失其富 *Shinso mo sono tomi o shisshi,*
賁育失其勇 *Fun'iku mo sono yū o shissu.*

[The states of] Chin and Ch'u have lost their wealth,
[The warriors] Pen and Yü have lost their courage.

Chin and Ch'u were states during the Warring States Period. Meng Pen 孟賁 and Hsia Yü 夏育 were warriors famed in early China for their courage (ZGJI 517). See also 15.5.

ZGS na, Shiba 267; ZGJI 492, 517, 687

10.262 盡大地是藥 *Jindaichi kore kusuri,*
那箇是自己 *Nako ka kore jiko.*

The great earth is itself medicine,
What is the self?

Heki 87.

ZGS na, Shiba 268, ZRKS 10.518

10.263 秦樓歌夜月 *Shinrō yagetsu ni utai,*
魏闕醉春風 *Giketsu shunpū ni you.*

On the palaces of Ch'in, they sing to the night ⌜moon⌝;
At the gates of Wei, they are drunk in the spring breeze.

ZGS 10.213, Shiba 268, ZGJI 518, ZRKS 10.355

10.264 瑞氣靄然樓 *Zuiki ai'nentaru rō,*
紫烟凝鳳闕 *Shien hōketsu ni koru.*

An air of good fortune surrounds the tower,
A purple haze gathers round the Phoenix Perch.

ZGJT 240 has 龍楼 "Dragon Tower" instead of 然楼, and says that "Dragon Tower" and 鳳闕 "Phoenix Perch" are both names of imperial palaces.

ZGS na, Shiba 269, ZGJI 519, ZGJT 240, ZRKS 10.406

10.265 翠羽立高枝 *Suiu kōshi ni tachi,*
危巣帶落暉 *Kisō rakki ō obu.*

The kingfisher perches on a lofty branch,
Its teetering nest wears the glow of the setting sun.

ZGS 10.214, Shiba na

10.266 坐水月道場 *Suigetsu no dōjō ni za shite,*
修空華萬行 *Kūge no mangyō o shū su.*

Sitting in the Moon Water *dōjō*,
Tracing ⌜flowers in the sky⌝.

ZGS 10.215, Shiba 258

10.267 水上青青翠 *Suijō sei-seitaru midori,*
元來是浮萍 *Ganrai kore fuhyō.*

The brilliant blue on the water's surface
Once was floating duckweed.

ZGS 10.216, Shiba 268, ZGJI 519, ZRKS 10.236

10.268 吹毛截不入　*Suimō kiredomo irazu,*
輸鎚擊不開　*Rintsui utedomo hirakazu.*

**Not even the ⌜hair-cutter sword⌝ can cut into it,
Not even the hammer wheel can break it open.**

ZGS 10.217, Shiba 269, ZGJI 519

10.269 已見寒梅發　*Sude ni kanbai no hiraku o mi,*
復聞啼鳥聲　*Mata teichō no koe o kiku.*

**I have already seen the blooming of the winter plum
And heard the songs of the singing birds.**

ZGS 10.218, Shiba 241, TSSSTS 61

10.270 靑郊鳴錦雉　*Seikō kinchi naki,*
綠水漾金鱗　*Ryokusui kinrin tadayou.*

**In the green fields the colored pheasant sings,
In the blue waters the golden fish swims.**

ZGS 10.219, Shiba na

10.271 靑山自靑山　*Seizan wa onozukara seizan,*
白雲自白雲　*Hakuun wa onozukara hakuun.*

**The blue mountains are just blue mountains,
The white clouds are just white clouds.**

Empuku-ji: *Seizan onozukara seizan, Hakuun onozukara hakuun.*

ZGS 10.220, Shiba 270, ZGJI 521, ZRKS 10.366, KZS #1003

10.272 靑山元不動　*Seizan moto fudō,*
白雲自去來　*Hakuun onozukara kyorai su.*

**The blue mountains by nature are immoveable,
The white clouds of themselves come and go.**

ZGS 10.221, Shiba 270, ZGJT 244, ZGJI 521, ZRKS 10.312, KZS #1084

10.273 生蛇入竹筒　*Seija chikutō ni iri,*
盲龜入空谷　*Mōki kūkoku ni iru.*

**The live snake enters the bamboo tube,
The blind tortoise enters the empty valley.**

ZGS 10.222, Shiba na, ZGJI 520

10.274 聖人無恒心　*Seijin kōshin nashi,*
以民心爲心　*Minshin o motte shin to nasu.*

**The sage has no fixed mind,
He makes the people's mind his mind.**

ZGS 10.223, Shiba na; *Tao-te ching,* ch. 49.

10.275 西川十樣錦 *Seisen jūyō no nishiki,*
添花色轉鮮 *Hana o soete iro utata azayaka nari.*

Ten varieties of West River brocade—
Add flowers and their colors are even more vivid.

ZGS 10.224, Shiba 270, ZGJI 521, ZRKS 10.338, KZS #994

10.276 西川斬畫像 *Seisen ni gazō o kireba,*
陝府人頭落 *Senpu no hito kōbe otsu.*

When posters of their faces were slashed in Hsi-ch'uan,
The heads of people in Shen-fu fell.

During the T'ang Dynasty, it was said that when posters of wanted An Lu-shan rebels were slashed in Hsi-ch'uan, the heads of those people in distant Shen-fu fell off one by one (ZGJI 520).

ZGS 10.225, Shiba 270, ZGJI 520, ZRKS 10.298

10.277 靑天轟霹靂 *Seiten ni hekireki o todorokashi,*
陸地起波濤 *Rikuchi ni hatō o okosu.*

The blue heavens boom with rumbling thunder,
On dry land tidal waves arise.

ZGS 10.226, Shiba 271, ZGJT 244 top verse, ZGJI 521, ZRKS 10.276, KZS #973

10.278 西風一陣來 *Seifū ichijinrai,*
落葉兩三片 *Rakuyō ryōsanpen.*

A surprise attack of west wind
Tears away leaves in twos and threes.

ZGS 10.227, Shiba 270, ZGJI 521, ZRKS 10.18

10.279 淸風拂明月 *Seifū meigetsu o harai,*
明月拂淸風 *Meigetsu seifu o harau.*

The pure breeze skims the bright ⌜moon⌝,
The bright moon skims the pure breeze.

ZGS 10.228, Shiba 271, ZGJI 521, ZRKS 10.266, KZS #972

10.280 淸流無間斷 *Seiryū kandan naku,*
碧樹不曾凋 *Hekiju katsute shibomazu.*

Clear streams flow without cease,
Evergreen trees never wither.

ZGS 10.229, Shiba na, ZGJI 521, ZRKS 10.109

10.281 石火迸靑天 *Sekka seiten ni hotobashiri,*
旱雷轟宇宙 *Kanrai uchū ni todoroku.*

A spark leaps across the blue sky,
A bolt from the blue rumbles through the universe.

ZGS 10.230: *hodobashiri* instead of *hotobashiri.*

ZGS 10.230, Shiba 271, ZGJI 522, ZRKS 10.228

10.282 石上栽花後 *Sekijō hana o uete nochi,*
生涯共是春 *Shōgai tomo ni kore haru.*

After you have planted the flower on the rock,
Your life, too, will always be spring.

ZGS na, Shiba 271, ZGJI 522, ZRKS 10.419

10.283 石人機似汝 *Sekijin no ⌜ki⌝ nanji ni nitaraba,*
也解唱巴歌 *Mata haka o utauru koto o gesu.*

If the stone man's spirit were like yours,
He would know how to sing rough country songs.

Heki 96 Verse Comm.

ZGS na, Shiba 271, ZGJI 522, ZGJT 247, ZRKS 10.195

10.284 世尊不説説 *Seson fusetsu no setsu,*
迦葉不聞聞 *Kashō fumon no mon.*

The World-Honored One spoke without speaking,
⌜Kāśyapa⌝ heard without hearing.

ZGS na, Shiba 270, ZGJT 242, ZGJI 520, ZRKS 10.447

10.285 世尊有密語 *Seson mitsugo ari,*
迦葉不覆藏 *Kashō fukuzō sezu.*

The World-Honored One had a secret word,
But ⌜Kāśyapa⌝ did not keep it hidden.

ZGS 10.231, Shiba 270, ZGJT 241, ZGJI 520, ZRKS 10.121

10.286 折脚鐺内 *Sekkyaku shōnai ni*
煎猫頭煮鴆羽 *Myōtō o iri chin'u o niru.*

In a broken-legged cauldron
He stews cats' heads and boils ⌜poison bird wings⌝.

See also 20.10.

ZGS 10.232, Shiba na, ZGJT 250

10.287 説説衆生説 *Setsu setsu shujō setsu,*
三世一時説 *Sanze ichiji no setsu.*

Speaking, speaking, all sentient beings are speaking;
The ⌜three worlds⌝ all speak at once.

ZGS 10.233, Shiba na, ZGJT 250, ZRKS 10.9

10.288 雪庭一滴血 *Settei itteki no chi,*
染出少林春 *Some idasu shōrin no haru.*

With a drop of blood the snow garden
Is stained and brings forth the spring of ⌜Shao-lin⌝.

ZGS 10.234, Shiba 272, ZGJI 522

10.289 透過是非關 *Zehi no kan o tōka shite,*
不住羅籠裏 *Rarōri ni todomarazu.*

Having passed through the barrier of right and wrong,
He does not linger by his cage.

ZGS na, Shiba 278, ZGJI 520, ZGJT 340, ZRKS 10.158, KZS #1059

10.290 有錢千里通 *Zeni areba senri mo tsūji,*
無錢隔壁聾 *Zeni nakereba kabe o hedatete rō su.*

When you have money, you can communicate with the world;
When you have no money, your next door neighbor is deaf.

ZGS 10.235, Shiba na, ZGJT 30, ZGJI 523, ZRKS 10.185

10.291 善惡如浮雲 *Zen'aku fūun no gotoku,*
起滅倶無處 *Kimetsu tomo ni tokoro nashi.*

Good and bad are like floating clouds,
Nowhere do they arise or dissolve.

ZGS 10.236, Shiba na

10.292 千江同一月 *Senkō dōitsugetsu,*
萬戸盡逢春 *Banko kotogotoku haru ni au.*

On a thousand rivers, one and the same ⌜moon⌝—
Ten thousand houses all greet the spring.

ZGS 10.237, Shiba 272, ZGJI 523, ZGJT 255, ZRKS 10.160

10.293 千牛拽不回 *Sengyū hikedomo kaerazu,*
快鷂趁不及 *Kaiyō oedomo oyobazu.*

A thousand bulls pull, but cannot turn it;
A swift falcon flies, but cannot cross it.

ZGS na, Shiba 272, ZGJI 522, ZRKS 10.58

10.294 前山烟霧外 *Zenzan enmu no soto,*
不知世上遊 *Sejō no yū o shirazu.*

Beyond the mist of yonder mountains,
I do not know the pleasures of the world.

ZGS 10.238, Shiba na

10.295 千山添翠色 *Senzan suishoku o soe,*
萬樹鎖銀花 *Banju ginka o tozasu.*

The thousand mountains array their emerald color,
The ten thousand trees are filled with silver flowers.

ZGS na, Shiba 272, ZGJI 523, ZRKS 10.558

10.296 千山鳥飛絕 *Senzan tori tobi tae,*
萬徑人跡滅 *Bankei jinseki messu.*

In the thousand hills, birds fly no more;
On the myriad paths, all human trace has gone.➛

Shiba 272: 千山飛鳥絕 *Senzan hichō tae.*

ZGS 10.239, Shiba 272, 唐詩三百首柳宗元江雪

10.297 孤舟簑笠翁 *Koshū saryū no ō,*
獨釣寒江雪 *Hitori kankō no yuki ni tsuri su.*

➛On a lone boat, in straw rain cape, an old man
Fishes alone in the cold river snow.

Shiba 255: *Hitori tsuru kankō no yuki.*

ZGS 10.240, Shiba 255

10 字

10.298 泉聲中夜後 *Senzei chūya no nochi,*
山色夕陽時 *Sanshoku sekiyō no toki.*

The bubbling of the spring after midnight,
The coloring of the hills in the setting sun.

ZGS 10.241, Shiba 272, ZD #79, ZGJI 523, ZGJT 257

10.299 前釋迦不前 *Zen shaka susumazu,*
後彌勒不後 *Ato miroku okurezu.*

In front Śākyamuni does not go ahead,
Behind ⌜Maitreya⌝ does not follow.

ZGS 10.242, Shiba na, ZGJI 523

10.300 前頭說一體 *Zentō ni wa ittai to toki,*
這裏說不同 *Shari ni wa fudō to toku.*

Outwardly he says, "All are one,"
Privately he says, "They're not the same."

Heki 40 Verse Comm.

ZGS 10.243, Shiba na, ZGJI 523, ZRKS 10.151, KZS #986

10.301 前頭驚殺人 *Zentō ni wa hito o kyōsetsu shi,*
後頭笑殺人 *Kōtō ni wa hito o shōsetsu su.*

In front, he shocks them to death;
Behind, he kills them with laughter.

ZGS 10.244, Shiba na, ZGJI 523, ZRKS 10.556

10.302 罕逢穿耳客 *Senni no kyaku ni au koto mare nari,*
多遇刻舟人 *Ōku wa fune o kizamu hito ni au.*

We seldom meet a ⌜pierced-eared traveler⌝.
We often meet men who ⌜slash their boats⌝.

Heki 55 Main Case *agyo.*

ZGS 10.245, Shiba na, ZGJT 63, ZGJI 523, ZGJI 523, ZRKS 10.244

10.303 欲窮千里目 *Senri no me o kiwamen to hosshite,*
更上一層樓 *Sara ni issō ro ni noboru.*

If you want to attain thousand-mile eyes,
Climb up one more storey on the tower.

ZGS na, Shiba 293, ZGJI 523, ZGJT 464, ZRKS 10.88, KZS #1065

10.304 其知可及 *Sono chi ni wa oyobubeshi,*
其愚不可及也 *Sono gu ni wa oyobubekarazu.*

It is possible to attain his wisdom,
But it is not possible to attain his stupidity.

ZGS na, Shiba 249; *Analects* v, 20.

10.305 相識滿天下 *Sōshiki tenka ni mitsu,*
知心能幾人 *Chishin yoku ikunin zo.*

My acquaintances fill the world,
But how many of them really know my mind?

ZGS 10.246, Shiba na, ZGJI 524, ZGJT 267, ZRKS 10.79, KZS #1050

10.306 桑樹猪揩背 *Sōju ni wa cho senaka o suri,*
長江鴨洗頭 *Chōkō ni wa ahiru kashira o arau.*

Against the mulberry tree, the wild boar scratches its back;
In the long river, the ducks dip their heads.

ZGS 10.247, Shiba na, ZGJI 524, ZRKS 10.268

10.307 僧投寺裡宿 *Sō wa jiri ni tōjite shuku shi,*
賊打不防家 *Zoku wa fubō no ie o ta su.*

The monk heads for a temple to lodge overnight,
The thief strikes the house that is not guarded.

ZGS 10.248, Shiba na

10.308 疎簾見雪巻 *Soren yuki o mite maki,*
深戸映花關 *Shinko hana ni eijite tozasu.*

**Roll up the door curtain to view the snow,
Shut the inner door against the brilliance of the flowers.**

ZGS 10.249: 踈 instead of 疎.

ZGS 10.249, Shiba 273, ZGJI 524, ZRKS 10.496, TSSSTS 165

10.309 大隱隱朝市 *Daiin wa chōshi ni kakure,*
小隱隱山林 *Shōin wa sanrin ni kakuru.*

**A great recluse hides himself in court and market,
A small recluse hides himself in hills and woods.**

ZGS 10.250, Shiba 274, ZGJI 525, ZRKS 10.525

10.310 大海任魚躍 *Daikai wa uo no odoru ni makase,*
長空任鳥飛 *Chōkū wa tori no tobu ni makasu.*

**The great ocean lets the fish jump,
The vast sky lets the birds fly.**

ZGS 10.251, Shiba na, ZGJI 525

10.311 大海波濤涌 *Daikai hatō waki,*
千江水逆流 *Senkō mizu sakashima ni nagaru.*

**The great seas surge with tidal waves,
In a thousand rivers, the waters flow backwards.**

ZGS na, Shiba 274, ZGJI 525, ZRKS 10.207

10.312 諦觀法王法 *Taikan hōōhō,*
法王法如是 *Hōōhō nyoze.*

**Clearly behold the Dharma of Dharma King;
The Dharma of Dharma King is thus.**

Heki 92 Main Case and Verse.

ZGS na, Shiba 277, ZGJI 527, ZGJT 289, ZRKS 10.450

10.313 大行山下賊 *Taikō sanka no zoku,*
南嶽嶺頭雲 *Nangaku reitō no kumo.*

**⌜Bandits⌝ beneath Mount T'ai-hang,
Clouds over the Southern Peak.**

ZGS 10.252, Shiba na, ZGJI 526, ZGJT 286, ZRKS 10.

10.314 大千沙界内 *Daisen shakai no uchi,*
一箇自由身 *Ikko jiyūshin.*

**Within all the ⌜great thousand-realm universe⌝
There is one person completely free.**

ZGS 10.253, Shiba na, ZGJI 526, ZRKS 10.157

10.315 大明無私照 *Taimei shishō naku,*
至公無私親 *Shikō shishin nashi.*

There is no private shining of the great light,
A civic stateman has no personal favorites.

Shiba 274: *Taimei ni shishō naku, Shikō ni shishin nashi.*

ZGS 10.254, Shiba 274

10.316 高捲吟中箔 *Takaku ginchū no sudare o maite,*
濃煎睡後茶 *Komayaka ni suigo no cha o senzu.*

Singing a song, he rolls up the bamboo blind;
After a nap he brews some dark tea.

ZGS 10.255, Shiba 257, ZD #81, ZGJI 527, ZRKS 10.179

10.317 扶過斷橋水 *Tasukatte wa dankyō no mizu o sugi,*
伴歸無月村 *Tomonatte wa mugetsu no mura ni kaeru.*

It helps me cross the water where the bridge is broken,
My companion as I return to the village without moon.➛

MMK 44. Shiba 285: *tasukete* instead of *tasukatte.*

ZGS 10.256, Shiba 285, ZGJI 527, ZGJT 404, ZRKS 10.282, 靈隱寺慈覺禪師語

10.318 只知途路遠 *Tada toro no tōki koto o shitte,*
不覺又黄昏 *Oboezu mata kōkon.*

➛Thinking only that the road was long,
I was not aware that dusk had come again.

Shiba 262 omits *koto.*

ZGS 10.257, Shiba 262, ZGJI 528, ZRKS 10.486

10.319 只改舊時相 *Tada kyūji no sō o aratamete,*
不改舊時人 *Kyūji no hito o aratamezu.*

He's changed only his former appearance,
He hasn't changed his former self.

ZGS na, Shiba 261, ZGJT 169, ZGJI 528, ZRKS 10.218, KZS #1023

10.320 不唯騎虎頭 *Tada kotō no noru nomi narazu,*
亦解收虎尾 *Mata kobi o osamuru koto o ge su.*

Not only did he ride the tiger's head,
He also knew how to handle the tiger's tail.

Heki 85 Verse Comm.

ZGS 10.258, Shiba na, ZRKS 10.239, KZS #1033

10.321 只在此山中 *Tada kono sanchū ni ari,*
雲深不知處 *Kumo fukō shite tokoro o shirazu.*

We know only that he is in these mountains,
But not where—the clouds are so deep.

ZGS 10.259, Shiba 261, ZGJI 528, TSSSTS 69

10.322 只見錐頭利 *Tada suitō no ri o mite,*
不知鑿頭方 *Sakutō no hō o shirazu.*

He sees only the sharpness of the ⌜gimlet⌝,
He does not know the squareness of the chisel.

Heki 66 Main Case *agyo.*

ZGS 10.260, Shiba 261, ZGJI 526, ZGJT 170, ZRKS 10.198, KZS #1038

10.323 只可自怡悦 *Tada mizukara ietsu subeshi,*
不堪持贈君 *Ji shite kimi ni okuru ni taezu.*

Only I myself can enjoy it,
It is not something I can send you.

ZGS 10.261, Shiba 261, ZD #78, ZGJI 528, ZGJT 169, ZRKS 10.13, 陶弘景詔問山中何所有賦詩以答 (Mair 1994, 187)

10.324 只得雪消去 *Tada yuki no shōshi saru koto o ete,*
自然春到來 *Jinen ni haru tōrai.*

Only when the snow has melted away
Does spring naturally come.

ZGS 10.262, Shiba na, 477, ZGJI 528, ZRKS 10.477

10.325 只許老胡知 *Tada rōko no chi o yurushite,*
不許老胡會 *Rōko no e o yurusazu.*

I admit I know of the ⌜old barbarian⌝,
But I don't admit I've met him.

Heki 1 Verse Comm., 41 Verse Comm., 47 Verse Comm., 51 Verse *agyo*, MMK 9.

ZGS 10.263, Shiba 261, ZGJI 528, ZGJT 170, ZRKS 10.111, KZS #1067

10.326 譬如翻錦機 *Tatoeba kinki o hirugaesu ga gotoshi,*
背面共是花 *Haimen tomo ni kore hana.*

For example, it is like turning over brocade weaving:
Both front and back are flowers.

ZGS 10.264, Shiba 283, ZGJI 529, ZRKS 10.421

10.327 逶溪今歳柳 *Tani o meguru konsai no yanagi,*
傍竹去年梅 *Take ni sou kyonen no ume.*

By the stream are this year's willows,
With the bamboo are last year's plums.

ZGS 10.265, Shiba 267, ZGJI 501 ZRKS 10.396

10.328 谷暗千旗出 *Tani kurōshite senki ide,*
山鳴萬乘來 *Yama natte banjō kitaru.*

Darkening the valley, thousands of flags appear;
Making the mountains thunder, ten thousand chariots arrive.

ZGS 10.266, Shiba 258, TSSSTS 19

10.329 多年籠中鳥 *Ta'nen rōchū no tori,*
今日負雲蜚 *Konnichi kumo o ōte tobu.*

The bird, caged these many years,
Today soars, trailing clouds upon its wings.

ZGS 10.267, Shiba na, ZGJI 525, ZRKS 10.74, KZS #1056

10.330 被他獅子皮 *Ta no shishi hi o kite,*
還作野干鳴 *Kaette yakan mei o nasu.*

He wears the skin of a lion
But has the bark of a fox.

ZGS 10.268, Shiba na, ZGJI 525, ZRKS 10.332, KZS #992.

10.331 傭他癡聖人 *Ta no chiseijin o yatōte,*
擔雪共塡井 *Yuki o ninōte tomo ni sei o uzumu.*

He hires another fool
And together they haul snow to fill in the well.

Shiba 292: 痴 instead of 癡.

ZGS 10.269, Shiba 292

10.332 珠藏澤自媚 *Tama kakusarete taku onozukara kobi,*
玉韞山含輝 *Tama tsutsumarete yama kagayaki o fukumu.*

A stream that hides a jewel is naturally clearer,
A mountain that contains jade gives off a glow.

ZGS 10.270, Shiba na

10.333 偶來松樹下 *Tamatama shōju no moto ni kitarite,*
高枕石頭眠 *Makura o takōshite sekitō ni nemuru.*

I came by chance to the base of the pine
And slept without a care, a stone for my pillow.➤

ZGS 10.271, Shiba na, TSSSTS 70

10.334 山中無暦日 *Sanchū rekijitsu nashi,*
寒盡不知年 *Kan o tsukuredomo toshi o shirazu.*

➤In the mountains there is no counting of days,
At winter's end I do not know the year.

ZGS 10.272, Shiba 261

10.335 玉潤窓前竹 *Tama wa uruou sōzen no take,*
花繁院裏梅 *Hana wa shigeshi inri no ume.*

Jade-like dew dampens the bamboo by my window,
Flowers bloom thick on the courtyard plum.

ZGS 10.273, Shiba 252

10.336 玉向泥中潔 *Tama wa deichū ni mukatte isagiyoku,*
松經雪後貞 *Matsu wa setsugo o hete tei nari.*

The jewel is purer in the midst of the mud,
The pine is more upright after enduring the snow.

ZGS 10.274, Shiba 251, ZRKS 10.214, KZS #1042

10.337 達磨不會禪 *Daruma zen o e sezu,*
夫子不知字 *Fūshi ji o shirazu.*

⌜Bodhidharma⌝ does not understand Zen,
Confucius does not know letters.

ZGS na, Shiba 274, ZGJI 529, ZRKS 10.381

10.338 誰知蓆帽下 *Tare ka shiran sekimō no moto,*
元是昔愁人 *Moto kore sekishū no hito naran to wa.*

Who knew that under the straw hat
Was someone so steeped in suffering?

Shiba 269: 有此 instead of 元是: *Kono sekishū no hito aru koto o.* ZGJI 530: *Moto kore sono kami no shūjin naran to wa.*

ZGS na, Shiba 269, ZGJT 238, ZGJI 530, ZRKS 10.308, KZS #1076, 寒山詩 §37

10.339 誰知砧杵裏 *Tare ka shiru chinsho no uchi,*
有此斷腸人 *Kono danchō no hito aru koto o.*

Who knows that within this ⌜fulling block⌝
Is this heartbroken woman?

ZGS 10.275, Shiba 269, ZGJI 530, ZRKS 10.295, KZS #1074

10.340 誰知遠烟浪 *Tare ka shiru tōki enrō ni,*
別有好思量 *Betsu ni kōshiryō aru koto o.*

Who can know that far off in the misty waves
Another, yet more excellent realm of thought exists?

Trans. from ZD #76. *Heki* 24 Main Case.

ZGS 10.276, Shiba na, ZD #76, ZGJI 530, ZGJT 238, ZRKS 10.126, KZS #983

10.341 直透萬重關 *Jiki ni banjū no kan o tōri,*
不住青霄裡 *Seishōri ni mo todomarazu.*

Having passed right through a myriad barriers,
He does not stop even in the blue sky.

Shiba 276: 宵 instead of 霄.

ZGS 10.277, Shiba 276, ZGJT 184, ZGJI 529, ZRKS 10.68, KZS #1055

10.342 父頑母嚚象傲 *Chichi gan ni, haha gin ni, shō ogoru,*
克諧以孝 *Yoku yawaraguru ni ko o motte su.*

Though his father was mulish, his mother insincere,
And his half-brother Hsiang arrogant, he was mild and filial.

See ⌜Shun⌝.

ZGS 10.278, Shiba na

10.343 長安一片月 *Chōan ippen no tsuki,*
萬戸擣衣聲 *Banko koromo o utsu koe.*

A sliver of ⌜moon⌝ over ⌜Ch'ang-an⌝;
From thousands of houses, the tap-tap of pounding cloth.

See ⌜Fulling block⌝.

ZGS 10.279, Shiba 275, TSSSTS 3

10.344 長者長法身 *Chōja wa chōhosshin,*
短者短法身 *Tanja wa tanhosshin.*

A long thing is a long Buddha-body,
A short thing is a short Buddha-body.

Heki 50 Verse *agyo.*

ZGS 10.280, Shiba 275, ZGJT 310, ZGJI 531, ZRKS 10.474

10.345 趙王因好劍 *Chōō ken o konomu ni yotte,*
闔國人帶刀 *Kakkoku no hito tō o obu.*

Because the King of Chao took delight in the ⌜sword⌝,
Throughout his state men wore swords.

ZGS 10.281, Shiba 276, ZGJI 531, ZRKS 10.327

10.346 踏破澄潭月 *Chōtan no tsuki o tappa shi,*
穿開碧落天 *Hekiraku no ten o senkai su.*

He stamps to pieces the ⌜moon⌝ in the still pool,
He tears open the blue sky.

Shiba 279: 蹈 instead of 踏, *tōha* instead of *tappa.*

ZGS 10.282, Shiba 279, ZGJT 343, ZGJI 531, ZRKS 10.254, KZS #1018

10.347 塵埋床下履 *Chiri wa shōka no ri o ume,*
風動架頭巾 *Kaze wa katō no kin o ugokasu.*

Dust buries the shoes beneath the bed,
Wind stirs the kerchief on the rack.

ZGS 10.283, Shiba na

10.348 張三喫鐵棒 *Chōsan tetsubō o kissureba,*
李四忍疼痛 *Rishi tōtsū o shinobu.*

When Third Son ⌜Chang⌝ gets a taste of the metal rod,
Fourth Son ⌜Li⌝ suffers the pain.

ZGS na, Shiba 275, ZGJI 531, ZRKS 10.257

10.349 陣雲横海上 *Jin'un kaijō ni yokotawari,*
拔劍攪龍門 *Ken o nuite ryūmon o kaku.*

Clouds of battle lie across the sea,
Drawn ⌜swords⌝ threaten the Dragon Gate.

ZGS 10.284, Shiba na, ZGJI 518, ZRKS 10.262, KZS #971

10.350 頭角混泥塵 *Zukaku deijin ni konji,*
分明露此身 *Funmyō ni kono shin o arawasu.*

Head smeared with mud and dirt,
Thus does he clearly reveal himself.

ZGS 10.285, Shiba 279, ZGJI 532, ZRKS 10.371

10.351 頭上太高生 *Zujō wa taikōsei,*
末後太低生 *Matsugo wa taiteisei.*

In the beginning, very high;
At the end, very low.

Heki 4 Main Case *agyo.*

ZGS na, Shiba 279, ZGJI 532, ZRKS 10.387

10.352 頭頭無取捨 *Zu-zu shusha naku,*
處處絶疎親 *Sho-sho soshin o zessu.*

With things, neither grasp nor let go;
With places, transcend far and near.

Heki 42 Main Case Comm.: 頭頭非取捨處處沒張乖.

ZGS na, Shiba 279, ZRKS 10.452

10.353 月落潭無影 *Tsuki ochite tan ni kage naku,*
雲生山有衣 *Kumo shōjite yama ni koromo ari.*

When the ⌜moon⌝ sets, the deep pool has no reflections;
Clouds rise and the mountains are decked in robes.

ZGS 10.286, Shiba 254, ZGJI 533, ZRKS 10.458

10.354 月高城影盡 *Tsuki takōshite jōei tsuki,*
霜重柳條疎 *Shimo omōshite ryūjō so nari.*

With the ⌜moon⌝ on high, the city loses its shadows;
Heavy with frost, the willow branches are sparse.

ZGS 10.287, Shiba 253, ZGJI 533, ZRKS 10.154, TSSSTS 176

10.355 月到天心處 *Tsuki no tenshin ni itaru tokoro,*
風來水面時 *Kaze no suimen ni kitaru toki.*

Where the ⌜moon⌝ rises to the center of the sky,
When the wind comes to the face of the water.

ZGS 10.288, Shiba na

10.356 月到中秋滿 *Tsuki no chūshū ni itatte michi,*
風從八月涼 *Kaze no hachigatsu yori suzushi.*

The ⌜moon⌝ grows full as it reaches mid-autumn;
The breeze from the eighth month onward is cool.

ZGS 10.289, ZGJT 105, ZGJI 533, ZRKS 10.342, Shiba 254

10.357 月隨碧山轉 *Tsuki wa hekizan ni shitagatte tenji,*
水合青天流 *Mizu wa seiten ni gasshite nagaru.*

The ⌜moon⌝ sails along the blue mountains,
The streams flow in harmony with the blue sky.

ZGS na, Shiba 254, ZGJI 533, ZRKS 10.530

10.358 月知明月秋 *Tsuki wa meigetsu no aki o shiri,*
花知一樣春 *Hana wa ichiyō no haru o shiru.*

The ⌜moon⌝ knows autumn with its bright moon,
The flowers know the same kind of spring.

ZGS na, Shiba 254, ZGJI 533, ZRKS 10.194

10.359 抱妻罵釋迦 *Tsuma o idaite shaka o nonoshiri,*
醉酒打彌勒 *Sake ni yōte miroku o ta su*

Hugging his wife, he curses Śākyamuni;
Drunk with wine, he strikes ⌜Maitreya⌝.

ZGS 10.290, Shiba na

10.360 泣露千般草 *Tsuyu ni naku sempan no kusa,*
吟風一樣松 *Kaze ni ginzu ichiyō no matsu.*

A thousand grasses weep tears of dew,
A lone pine tree sighs in the breeze.

See ⌜Pine wind⌝.

ZGS 10.291, Shiba 250, ZD #72, ZGJI 534, ZGJT 86, ZRKS 10.19, í[¡ §3

10.361 鶴飛千尺雪 *Tsuru wa tobu senjaku no yuki,*
龍起一潭冰 *Ryū wa okoru ittan no kōri.*

The crane flies the thousand-foot snows,
The dragon rises from a pool of ice.

ZGS 10.292, Shiba 248, ZGJI 534, ZGJT 59, ZRKS 10.328

10.362 手把黄金鎚 *Te ni ōgon no tsuchi o totte,*
敲落天邊月 *Tenpen no tsuki o kōraku su.*

He takes the golden hammer in hand,
And strikes down the ⌜moon⌝ from the heavens.

ZGS na, Shiba 263, ZGJI 534, ZRKS 10.269, KZS #968

10.363 泥牛光影亂 *Deigyū kōei midare,*
石女素衣完 *Sekijo soi mattashi.*

The mud cow's shadow is broken up,
The ⌜stone woman's⌝ plain clothes are perfectly neat.

ZGS 10.293, Shiba na

10.364 庭臺深夜月 *Teidai shinya no tsuki,*
樓閣靜時鐘 *Rōkaku seiji no kane.*

On the garden deck, the ⌜moon⌝ in the deep of night;
From the high tower, a bell in a moment of stillness.

ZGS na, Shiba 276, ZGJI 534, ZRKS 10.497

10.365 撒手長空外 *Te o chōkū no hoka ni sassu,*
時人總不知 *Toki no hito sō ni shirazu.*

He thrust his hands outside the vast sky,
But no one at the time was aware of it.

ZGS 10.294, Shiba 259, ZRKS 10.249, KZS #1016

10.366 手把白玉鞭 *Te ni hakugyoku no muchi o totte,*
驪珠悉擊碎 *Riju kotogotoku gekisai su.*

He takes the white jeweled whip in hand,
And completely smashes the ⌜black dragon pearl⌝.

Heki 82 Verse.

ZGS 10.295, Shiba 263, ZGJI 534, ZRKS 10.152, KZS #987

10.367 泥佛不渡水 *Deibutsu mizu o watarazu,*
神光照天地 *Shinkō daichi o terasu.*

The mud Buddha does not cross the water,
But the divine light illuminates heaven and earth.

Heki 96 Verse 1.

ZGS na, Shiba 277, ZGJT 321 (first line), ZRKS 10.519

10.368 鐵蛇鑽不入 *Tetsuda kiredomo irazu,*
鐵鎚打不碎 *Tettsui utedomo kudakezu.*

An iron snake cannot cut into it,
An iron hammer cannot smash it.

ZGS 10.296, Shiba 277, ZGJI 535, ZRKS 10.178, KZS #1062

10.369 掇轉鐵圍山 *Tetchisen o tetten shi,*
現出金剛山 *Kongōsen o genshutsu su.*

He whirls the ⌜ring of iron mountains⌝ around,
And makes the Diamond Mountain appear.

ZGS 10.297, Shiba na, ZGJT 323, ZGJI 535, ZRKS 10.258

10.370 望天不見天 *Ten o nozonde ten o mizu,*
覷地不見地 *Chi o mite chi o mizu.*

He gazes at the sky, but does not see the sky;
He stares at the ground, but does not see the ground.

ZGS na, Shiba 288, ZGJI 536, ZRKS 10.574

10.371 天下有道則見 *Tenka michi areba sunawachi araware,*
無道則隱 *Michi nakereba sunawachi kakuru.*

When the Way exists in this world, then appear;
When the Way does not exist, then keep concealed.

ZGS 10.298, Shiba na; *Analects* VIII, 13

10.372 貪看天上月 *Tenjō no tsuki o musabori mite,*
失卻掌中珠 *Shōchū no tama o shikkyaku su.*

He covets the ⌜moon⌝ he sees in the sky above
And loses the pearl in the palm of his hand.

ZGS 10.299, Shiba 280, ZGJI 536, ZRKS 10.204, KZS #1040

10.373 天台華頂秀 *Tendai kachō hiide,*
南嶽石橋高 *Nangaku shakkyō takashi.*

The Hua peak of T'ien-t'ai juts straight up,
The stone bridge atop Nan-yüeh is high.

Shiba 277: 岳 instead of 嶽.

ZGS 10.300, Shiba 277, ZGJI 536, ZRKS 10.27

10.374 出頭天外看 *Tengai ni shuttō shite miyo,*
誰是我般人 *Tare ka kore wa ga tsura no hito.*

Stick your head outside the sky,
Who is there to face you?

ZGS na, Shiba 265, ZGJI 535, ZGJT 206, ZRKS 10.155, KZS #988

10.375 天高群象正 *Ten takōshite gunshō tadashiku,*
海濶百川朝 *Umi hirōshite hyakusen chō su.*

Heaven is high and all things are in proper order,
The sea is vast and the hundred rivers flow toward it.

ZGS na, Shiba 277, ZGJI 536, ZGJT 326, ZRKS 10.169

10.376 天晴一雁遠 *Ten harete ichigan tōku,*
海濶孤帆遲 *Umi hirōshite kohan ososhi.*

Clear skies, a lone goose in the distance;
On the broad ocean, a single slow sail.

ZGS 10.301, Shiba na

10.377 天共白雲曉 *Ten wa hakuun to tomo ni ake,*
水和明月流 *Mizu wa meigetsu ni washite nagaru.*

Sky and white clouds together brighten into dawn,
Water flows in harmony with the bright ⌈moon⌉.

ZGS 10.302, Shiba 277, ZGJT 326, ZGJI 536, ZRKS 10.172, KZS #1061

10.378 東家杓柄長 *Tōka no shakuhei wa nagaku,*
西家杓柄短 *Seika no shakuhei wa mijikashi.*

In the East House the dipper handle is long,
In the West House the dipper handle is short.

Heki 53 Verse *agyo.*

ZGS 10.303, Shiba 278, ZGJI 537, ZGJT 339, ZRKS 10.504, KZS #1015

10.379 桃花零落盡 *Tōka reiraku shitsukushite,*
何處見靈雲 *Izure no tokoro ni ka reiun o min.*

The ⌈peach⌉ blossoms have all fallen away,
Where now shall I meet ⌈Reiun⌉?

ZGS 10.304, Shiba na, ZGJI 537, ZRKS 10.521

10.380 遠觀山有色 *Tōku mite yama ni iro ari,*
近聽水無聲 *Chikaku kiite mizu ni koe nashi.*

Seen from afar, the mountains have color;
Heard from close by, the water has no sound.

ZGS 10.305, Shiba 245, ZGJI 538, ZRKS 10.576

10.381 入道不通理 *Dō ni itte ri ni tsūsezumba,*
復身還信施 *Mi o kaeshite shinse o kaesu.*

One who enters the Way but does not penetrate to its principle
Should renounce his status and return all the believers' donations.

Rinzai-roku §21.

ZGS na, Shiba 280, ZGJI 538, ZRKS 10.572

10.382 動容揚古路 *Dōyō koro ni agu,*
不墮悄然機 *Shōzen no ⌜ki⌝ ni dasezu.*

In his everyday actions he expresses the ancient way,
He does not fall back into self-satisfaction.

ZGS 10.306, Shiba 279, ZGJI 537, ZGJT 346, ZRKS 10.273, KZS #969

10.383 燈籠上作舞 *Tōrōjō ni mai o nashi,*
露柱裏藏身 *Rochūri ni mi o kakusu.*

He dances on top of the lantern,
He hides himself in the lamppost.

ZGS 10.307, Shiba 278, ZGJI 537, ZRKS 10.470

10.384 洞深雲出晩 *Tō fukōshite kumo no izuru koto osoku,*
澗曲水來遲 *Tani magatte mizu no kitaru koto ososhi.*

From the deep clefts the mists take a long time leaving,
In the winding valleys the waters come along slowly.

ZGS na, Shiba 278, ZGJI 537, ZRKS 10.176

10.385 等閑垂一釣 *Tōkan ni itchō o tarete,*
驚起碧潭龍 *Hekitan no ryū o kyōki su.*

Nonchalantly I dropped a line
And startled awake the dragon in the deep pool.

ZRKS 10.242: *Naozari ni itchō o tarete.*

ZGS na, Shiba 278, ZGJI 537, ZRKS 10.242, KZS #1077

10.386 桃李火中開 *Tōri kachū ni hiraki,*
黄昏後日出 *Kōkongō ni hi izu.*

⌜Peach⌝ and plum trees bloom in the midst of fire;
After evening falls, the sun rises.

ZGS na, Shiba 278, ZGJI 537, ZGJT 340, ZRKS 10.60

10.387 時與道人偶 *Toki ni dōjin to gū shi,*
或隨樵者行 *Aruiwa shōsha ni shitagatte yuku.*

At times one goes with a person of the Way,
At times one follows a woodcutter.

ZGS 10.308, Shiba na, TSSSTS 5

10.388 獨坐人不知 *Dokuza hito shirazu,*
孤月照寒泉 *Kogetsu kansen o terasu.*

I sit alone in my secret place,
The lone ⌜moon⌝ shines on the cold spring.

ZGS 10.309, Shiba 279

10.389 獨坐幽篁裡 *Dokuza yūkō no uchi,*
彈琴復長嘯 *Dankin mata chōshō.*

I sit secluded, alone within the bamboo,
Strumming the lute, drawing the notes out long.➛

ZGS 10.310, Shiba 279, TSSSTS 61

10.390 深林人不知 *Shinrin hito shirazu,*
明月來相照 *Meigetsu kitarite aiterasu.*

➛In my secret place deep in the grove,
The bright ⌜moon⌝ comes to shine on me.

ZGS 10.311, Shiba 268

10.391 鳥啼人不見 *Tori naite hito miezu,*
花落木猶香 *Hana ochite ki nao kanbashi.*

A bird cries, no one in sight;
The flowers fall, but the woods are still fragrant.

ZGS 10.312, Shiba 275, ZGJI 538, ZRKS 10.220, KZS #1024

10.392 鳥栖無影樹 *Tori wa sumu muyōju,*
花發不萌枝 *Hana wa hiraku fubōshi.*

Birds perch on shadowless trees,
Flowers open on budless branches.

ZGJT 538, Shiba 275: *Tori wa sumu muyō no ju, Hana wa hiraku fubō no eda.*

ZGS 10.313, Shiba 275, ZGJI 538, ZRKS 10.271

10.393 鳥宿池中樹 *Tori wa shuku su chichū no ju,*
僧敲月下門 *Sō wa tataku gekka no mon.*

A bird nests in the tree by the pond,
A monk knocks on the moonlit gate.

Shiba 275: 邊 instead of 中.

ZGS 10.314, Shiba 275, TSSSTS 167

10.394 似虎多雙角 *Tora ni nite sōkaku ōku,*
如牛缺尾巴 *Ushi no gotoku ni shite biha o kaku.*

It looks like a tiger, but it has these two horns;
It looks like a cow, but it lacks a swishy tail.

ZGS 10.315, Shiba na, ZRKS 10.24

10.395 嫩竹抽新笋 *Donchiku shinjun o nuki,*
枯松長老枝 *Koshō rōshi o chōzu.*

Young bamboo produces new shoots,
The ⌜withered⌝ pine holds out its ancient branches.

ZGS 10.316: 筝 instead of 笋, Shiba 280

10.396 富嫌千口少 *Tonde wa senkō mo sukunashi to kirai,*
貧厭一身多 *Mazushiushite wa isshin mo ōshi to itou.*

If you are wealthy, you dislike a thousand mouths as too few;
If you are poor, you resent even one person as too many.

Shiba 285: *Hin ni shite wa isshin mo ōshi to itou.*

ZGS 10.317, Shiba 285, ZGJI 538, ZGJT 404, ZD p. 285, ZRKS 10.217

10.397 泣把李陵袂 *Naite riryō no tamoto o tori,*
歸思欲沾襟 *Kishi eri o uruosan to hossu.*

Weeping, ⌜Su Wu⌝ grasped ⌜Li Ling's⌝ sleeve;
Sad at his departure, Li's tears soaked his vest.

ZGS 10.318, Shiba 250

10.398 長伸兩脚睡 *Nagaku ryōkyaku o nobete nemureba,*
無僞亦無眞 *Gi mo naku mata shin mo nashi.*

When you stretch out both legs and sleep,
There is neither false nor true.

僞 "false" and 眞 "true" can also be translated as "conventional and ultimate," the categories of the Two Truths.

ZGS 10.319, Shiba 275, ZRKS 10.120, KZS #981

10.399 隨流常出沒 *Nagare ni shitagatte tsune ni shutsubotsu shi,*
不滯往來蹤 *Ōrai no ato ni todokōrazu.*

He goes with the flow, ever rising and sinking,
Without tangling in the traces of coming and going.

ZGS 10.320, Shiba na, ZGJI 539, ZRKS 10.548

10.400 啼時驚妾夢 *Naku toki shō ga yume o odorokashite,*
不得到遼西 *Ryōsei ni itaru koto o ezarashimu.*

When [the bird] sings, it disturb my dreams
And keeps me from going to Liao-hsi.

ZGS 10.321, Shiba na, TSSSTS 70

10.401 衲被蒙頭坐 *Nappi mōtō ni shite za sureba,*
冷暖了無知 *Reidan tsui ni shiru koto nashi.*

If you do zazen covered in a shroud,
You'll know nothing at all about hot and cold.

⌜Bodhidharma⌝ is often depicted sitting with a long shroud covering his head.

ZGS 10.322, Shiba na, ZGJI 540, ZRKS 10.320, KZS #1069

10.402 揮涙斬丁公　*Namida o furutte chōkō o kiri,*
咬牙封雍齒　*Kiba o kande yōshi o hōzu.*

Shedding tears, he beheads Duke Ting;
Clenching his teeth, he gives Yung Ch'ih a fief.

Two historical allusions. (1) In the rivalry between ⌜Liu Pang⌝ and ⌜Hsiang Yü⌝, the general Duke Ting betrayed Hsiang Yü and went to the side of Liu Pang. Liu Pang had him beheaded as a warning to traitors (Giles 1939, 735). (2) General Yung Ch'ih helped place Liu Pang on the throne and then, with several others became discontent, feeling unjustly treated by the new emperor. Liu Pang then enfeofed Yung Ch'ih, giving him the high title of Marquis just because he was least friendly with the emperor (ibid., 979).

ZGS 10.323, Shiba na

10.403 日日是好日　*Nichi nichi kore kōnichi,*
風來樹點頭　*Kaze kitatte ju tentō su.*

Every day is a good day.
When the wind blows, the tree nods.

Heki 6.

ZGS 10.324, Shiba na, ZGJI 539, ZRKS 10.320

10.404 鬧市裏天子　*Nyōshiri no tenshi,*
百草頭老僧　*Hyakusōtō no rōsō.*

The Son of Heaven in the noisy city,
The ⌜old monk⌝ in the hundred weeds.

ZGS 10.325, Shiba na, ZGJT 349, ZGJI 538, ZRKS 10.335, KZS #1000

10.405 人人脚跟下　*Ninnin kyakkonka,*
有一坐具地　*Ichi zagu no chi ari.*

Beneath the feet of every person
Is space for one sitting mat.

Variant: 痕 instead of 跟.

ZGS na, Shiba 268, ZGJT 365, ZGDJT 1092a, ZGJI 540, ZRKS 10.488

10.406 涅槃心易明　*Nehan no shin wa akirameyasuku,*
差別智難入　*Shabetsu no chi wa irigatashi.*

To clarify the mind of nirvana is easy,
But to enter the wisdom of discrimination is hard.

ZGJI 540: 涅槃心易曉, 差別智難明.

ZGS 10.326, Shiba na, ZGJI 540

10.407 拂葉動秋色　*Ha o haratte shūshoku o ugokashi,*
捲簾分月花　*Sudare o maite gekka o wakatsu.*

Shake the leaves and stir the colors of autumn,
Roll up the screen and appreciate the ⌜moon⌝ and flowers.

ZGS na, Shiba 286, ZGJI 541, ZRKS 10.293

10 字

10.408 作馬去東家 *Ba to natte tōka ni sari,*
成驢入西家 *Ro to natte seika ni iru.*

It left the east house as a horse,
But entered the west house as a donkey.

ZGS na, Shiba 259, ZGJI 491, ZRKS 10.507

10.409 白玉按劍立 *Hakugyoku ken o anjite tachi,*
朱絃流水聲 *Shugen ryūsui no koe.*

At the glint of a jewel, he stands with hand to ⌜sword⌝;
At the red string, the sound of running water.

At a flash of light from a sparkling jewel, an ignorant person is suspicious and stands with hand on his sword; when the red lute string is plucked, a clever person recalls a song of running water and at once hears its sound (ZGJI 541, Shiba 282).

ZGS na, Shiba 282, ZGJI 541, ZRKS 10.348

10.410 破鏡不重照 *Hakyō kasanete terasazu,*
落花難上枝 *Rakka eda ni noborigatashi.*

Broken mirrors never again reflect,
Fallen flowers cannot return to the branch.

ZGS 10.327, Shiba 281, ZGJT 377, ZGDJT 1013a, ZGJI 540, ZRKS 10.45, KZS #959

10.411 陌頭楊柳枝 *Hakutō yōryū no eda,*
已被春風吹 *Sude ni shunpū ni fukaru.*

On the roadside, the willow branches
Already are blown by the spring winds.

ZGS 10.328, Shiba na, TSSSTS 59

10.412 白髮三千丈 *Hakuhatsu sanzenjō,*
緣愁似個長 *Urei ni yorite kaku no gotoku nagashi.*

White hair thirty thousand feet long—
From worry and sorrow it has become this long.

ZGS 10.329, Shiba 282, TSSSTS 60

10.413 白鷺沙汀立 *Hakuro shatei ni tachi,*
蘆花相對開 *Roka aitai shite hiraku.*

White herons stand on the sandy beach,
White reed flowers open against each other.

ZGS 10.330, Shiba 282, ZGJI 541, ZGJT 380, ZRKS 10.190

10.414 過橋村酒美 *Hashi o sugite sonshu bi nari,*
隔岸野花香 *Kishi o hedatete yaka kanbashi.*

The village across the bridge has good wine;
On the other bank, the wild flowers are fragrant.

ZGS 10.331, Shiba 247, ZGJI 541

10.415 始隨芳草去 *Hajime wa hōsō ni shitagatte sari,*
又逐落花回 *Mata rakka o ōte kaeru.*

First, I went following the sweet grasses;
Now I return chasing falling leaves home.

Heki 36.

ZGS 10.332, Shiba 262, ZGJI 542, ZRKS 10.85, KZS #1052

10.416 辱莫辱多欲 *Hazukashime wa tayoku yori hazukashiki wa naku,*
樂莫樂無求 *Tanoshimi wa motome naki yori tanoshiki wa nashi.*

There is no shame more shameful than having many desires,
There is no joy more joyous than non-seeking.

ZGS 10.333, Shiba na, ZGJI 541

10.417 欲問花來處 *Hana no raisho o towan to hossureba,*
東君亦不知 *Tōkun mo mata shirazu.*

Do you want to ask where flowers come from?
Not even the Master of the East knows.

The Master of the East is the Green Emperor who presides over the coming of spring (ZGJI 541).

ZGS na, Shiba 293, ZGJI 542, ZRKS 10.506

10.418 移花兼蝶到 *Hana o utsushite wa chō no itaru o kane,*
買石得雲饒 *Ishi o katte wa kumo o eru koto ōshi.*

By transplanting flowers, I also get the butterflies to come;
When I buy rocks, I get also masses of clouds.

Shiba 242: *Ishi o kōte wa kumo o ete ōshi.*

ZGS 10.334, Shiba 242, ZGJI 542, ZGJT 13, ZRKS 10.434

10.419 花開無根樹 *Hana wa mukon no ju ni hiraki,*
魚跳萬仭峯 *Uo wa banjin no mine ni odoru.*

Flowers blossom on rootless trees,
Fish leap on the lofty peaks.

Shiba 246: *Hana wa hiraku mukon no ju, Uo wa odoru banjin no mine.*

ZGS 10.335, Shiba 246

10.420 破衲逐雲飛 *Hanō kumo o ōte tobi,*
草鞋隨路轉 *Sōai michi ni shitagatte tenzu.*

A torn robe chases after clouds;
Straw sandals tumble along the road.

ZGS 10.336, Shiba 281, ZGJI 540

10.421 萬機休罷處 *Ban⌜ki⌝ kyūhi no tokoro,*
一曲韻無私 *Ikkyoku in watashi nashi.*

Where the ten thousand impulses have come to rest,
There is a melody without private tune.

This verse contains an untranslatable pun. The character 曲 *kyoku* is used (1) as a counter for songs, e.g., "one tune," "two tunes"; and (2) to mean bent or crooked, e.g., 私曲 *shikyoku* "unfairness, corruption" (literally "private twistedness"). The second line says there is an *ikkyoku*, "one tune," which is not *shikyoku*, "privately twisted." No word in English means both "tune" and "twisted."

ZGS na, Shiba 282, ZGJI 543, ZRKS 10.481

10.422 萬里無雲時 *Banri kumo naki toki,*
青天須喫棒 *Seiten subekaraku bō o kissubeshi.*

When there are no clouds for ten thousand miles,
Even the blue sky must get a taste of the stick.

ZGS na, Shiba 282, ZGJI 543, ZGJT 387, ZRKS 10.489

10.423 母在一子寒 *Haha areba isshi samuku,*
母去三子寒 *Haha saraba sanshi samukaran.*

If mother is here, then one child is cold;
If mother is gone, won't three children be cold?

See ⌜Min Tzu-ch'ien⌝.

ZGS 10.337, Shiba 288, ZGJI 542

10.424 破鼈上天台 *Habetsu tendai ni nobori,*
盲龜入空谷 *Mōki kūkoku ni iru.*

A crippled turtle climbs Mount T'ien-t'ai,
A blind tortoise enters the empty valley.

ZGS 10.338, Shiba 281, ZGJT 377

10.425 入林不動草 *Hayashi ni itte kusa o ogokasazu,*
入水不立波 *Mizu ni itte nami o tatezu.*

He enters the forest, but does not disturb the grass;
He enters the water, but does not cause waves.

ZGS na, Shiba 280, ZGJI 542, ZGDJT 1031a, ZRKS 10.163

10.426 出林虎方怒 *Hayashi o idete tora masa ni ikari,*
横岡蟒正嗔 *Oka ni yokotawatte mō masa ni ikaru.*

Coming from the trees—a fierce tiger.
Lying across the hill—an angry python.

ZGS 10.339, Shiba na, ZGJI 542, ZRKS 10.25

10.427 萬口同一舌 *Bankō dōichizetsu,*
四海同一家 *Shikai dōikka.*

Ten thousand mouths have one and the same tongue,
The ⌜four seas⌝ are one and the same house.

ZGS 10.340, Shiba na, ZGJI 543, ZRKS 10.89, KZS #1053

10.428 爲萬物根源 *Banbutsu no kongen to nari,*
作天地太祖 *Tenchi no taiso to naru.*

Become the root source of the ⌜ten thousand things⌝,
Be the progenitor of heaven and earth.

ZGS na, Shiba 242, ZGJI 543, ZRKS 10.509

10.429 日出乾坤耀 *Hi idete kenkon kagayaki,*
雲收山岳青 *Kumo osamatte sangaku aoshi.*

When the sun appears, ⌜heaven and earth⌝ shine;
When the clouds disperse, the mountain peaks are blue.

Shiba 280: 雨收 *ame osamatte,* "when the rains end," instead of 雲收 *kumo osamatte,* "when the clouds disperse."

ZGS 10.341, Shiba 280

10.430 覓火和烟得 *Hi o motomete wa kemuri ni washite e,*
擔泉帶月歸 *Izumi o ninatte wa tsuki o obite kaeru.*

Seeking fire, I found it mingled with smoke;
Bearing spring water, I return home clad in the ⌜moon⌝.

ZGS 10.342 has 覔 for 覓, Shiba 287, ZD #73, ZGJT 416, ZGJI 543, ZRKS 10.52, KZS #1043

10.431 砒礵能活人 *Hisō yoku hito o kassu,*
甘露亦殺人 *Kanro mo mata hito o korosu.*

Arsenic is good for giving people life,
And sweet nectar for killing people.

ZGS na, Shiba 283, ZRKS 10.399

10.432 謂火不燒口 *Hi to iu mo kuchi o yakazu,*
謂水不溺身 *Mizu to iu mo mi o oborasazu.*

Though you say "fire," you don't burn your mouth;
Though you say "water," you don't drown your body.

ZGS 10.343, Shiba na, ZGJI 543

10.433 火不待日熱 *Hi wa hi o mattazu shite atsuku,*
風不待月涼 *Kaze wa tsuki o mattazu shite suzushi.*

Fire is hot without needing the sun,
Wind is cool without needing the ⌜moon⌝.

ZGS na, Shiba 246, ZGJI 543, ZGJT 40, ZRKS 10.436

10.434 臂長衫袖短 *Hiji nagaku shite sanshu mijikaku,*
脚痩草鞋寬 *Ashi yasete sōai hiroshi.*

If you have long arms, your shirt sleeves are short;
If you have small feet, your straw sandals are big.

ZGS 10.344, Shiba na, ZGJT 391, ZGJI 544, ZRKS 10.311

10.435 人皆苦炎熱 *Hito wa mina ennetsu o kurushimu,*
我愛夏日長 *Ware wa kajitsu no nagaki o ai su.*

People suffer from the sizzling heat,
But I love the length of summer days.

ZGS 10.345, Shiba na

10.436 微風吹幽松 *Bifū yūshō o fuki,*
近听聲愈好 *Chikaku kikeba koe iyo-iyo yoshi.*

A light breeze blows in the lonely pine;
If you listen closely, the sound is even better.

Heki 34 Verse Comm. Shiba 283: 聽 instead of 听. See「Pine wind」.

ZGS 10.346, Shiba 283, ZGJI 544, ZD #85, ZRKS 10.409, 寒山詩 §4

10.437 皮膚脱落盡 *Hifu datsuraku shitsukushite,*
唯有一眞實 *Tada ichi shinjitsu nomi ari.*

Shed your skin completely
And there is one true reality alone.

ZGS 10.347, Shiba 282, ZD #86, ZGJI 543, ZGJT 389, ZRKS 10.414, 寒山詩 §158

10.438 眉毛碎須彌 *Bimō shumi o kudaki,*
鼻孔呑大海 *Bikō taikai o nomu.*

His eyebrows crush Mount「Sumeru」to pieces,
His nostrils suck up the great seas.

ZGS na, Shiba 283

10.439 百萬一時盡 *Hyakuman ichiji ni tsuku,*
含情無片言 *Jō o fukunde hengen nashi.*

A million of their money, all gone in a moment;
They swallow their feelings, uttering not a word.

ZGS 10.348, Shiba na, TSSSTS 62

10.440 打破毘耶城 *Biyajō o taha shite,*
靠倒維摩詰 *Yuimakitsu o kōtō su.*

Crush to pieces Vaiśālī City,
Knock down「Vimalakīrti」.

ZGS na, Shiba 273, ZGJI 544, ZRKS 10.412

10.441 豹隱南山霧 *Hyō wa nanzan no kiri ni kakure,*
鵬搏北海風 *Hō wa hokkai no kaze ni utsu.*

The leopard hides in the mists of the southern mountains,
The ⌜roc⌝ beats the winds of the north seas.

ZGS na, Shiba 283, ZGJI 545, ZRKS 10.43, KZS #958

10.442 氷蠶不知寒 *Hyōsan kan o shirazu,*
火鼠不知暑 *Kaso sho o shirazu.*

The winter silkworm does not know cold,
The summer mouse does not know heat.

ZGS 10.349, Shiba na, ZGJI 545

10.443 風花亂紫翠 *Fūka shisui o midashi,*
雲外有煙林 *Ungai enrin ari.*

The wind in the flowers ruffles the purples and blues,
Beyond the clouds there is a misty forest.

ZGS na, Shiba 286, ZGJI 546, ZRKS 10.526

10.444 富貴中富貴 *Fūki chū no fūki,*
作家中作家 *Sakke chū no sakke.*

A noble among nobles,
A master among masters.

Heki 58 Verse *agyo.*

ZGS na, Shiba 285, ZGJI 546, ZRKS 10.243

10.445 布皷當軒撃 *Fuko noki ni attate utsu,*
誰是知音者 *Tare ka kore ⌜chiin⌝ no mono.*

I have struck the ⌜cloth drum⌝ hanging under the eaves.
Who is it that really knows this sound?

Heki 57 Verse.

ZGS na, Shiba 285, ZGJI 545, ZRKS 10.81

10.446 夫子温良恭 *Fūshi wa on, ryō, ken,*
謙讓以得之 *kyō, jō motte kore o u.*

Confucius gained it by being warm, straightforward,
Courteous, moderate, and respectful.

ZGS 10.350, Shiba 284; *Analects* 1, 10

10.447 碎佛祖玄關 *Busso no genkan o kudaki,*
瞎人天眼目 *Ninden no ganmoku o kassu.*

Smash the entranceway of the Buddha and ancestors,
Split the eyeball of gods and humans.

ZGS na, Shiba 259, ZGJI 546, ZRKS 10.46, KZS #966

10.448 佛殿裏燒香 *Butsudenri ni shōkō shi,*
山門頭合掌 *Sanmontō ni gasshō su.*

In the Buddha Hall, offer incense;
At the Mountain Gate, put hands in *gasshō*.

ZRKS 10.319: *Butsudenri ni kō o yaki.*

ZGS na, Shiba 286, ZGJI 547, ZGJT 409

10.449 婦搖機軋軋 *Fu wa ⌜ki⌝ o yurugashite atsu-atsu,*
兒弄口喎喎 *Ji wa kuchi o rōshite ka-ka.*

My wife rocks her loom clack-clack,
My baby plays with its mouth ga-ga.

ZGS 10.351, Shiba 285, ZGJI 546, 寒山詩 §21

10.450 父母所生身 *Fubo shoshō no mi,*
速證大覺位 *Sumiyaka ni daikaku kurai o shō su.*

The body you received at birth from your parents
Immediately testifies to the status of your great enlightenment.

ZGS 10.352, Shiba na

10.451 武陵春已老 *Buryō haru sude ni oite,*
臺榭綠陰多 *Taisha ryokuin ōshi.*

In Wu-ling spring is already past its peak,
The pavilion's green shadows are many.

ZGS 10.353, Shiba 285, ZGJT 405, ZGJI 546, ZRKS 10.50

10.452 文章千古事 *Bunshō senko no koto,*
得失寸心知 *Tokushitsu sunshin shiru.*

In texts are matters from a thousand past ages;
The mind can learn a little of gain and loss.

ZGS na, Shiba 287, ZGJI 547, ZRKS 10.542

10.453 文王爲世子日 *Bunnō seishi naru no hi*
見王季三 *ōki o mamiyuru koto mitabi.*

On the day that ⌜King Wen⌝ became emperor,
He paid respect to King Chi three times.

ZGS 10.354, Shiba na, *Book of Rites*, sect. 8.

10.454 文王一怒而 *Bunnō hitotabi ikari,*
安天下之民 *Tenka no tami o yasunzu.*

⌜King Wen⌝ once got angry
And brought peace to all the world's people.

Mencius I, B, 3. Shiba 287: *ikatte* instead of *ikari.*

ZGS 10.355, Shiba 287, Mencius I, B3.

10.455 弊衣纏痩骨 *Hei sōkotsu ni matoi,*
衰髪覆蒼顔 *Suihatsu sōgan o oou.*

His protruding bones are wrapped in ragged robes,
Sickly hair covers his aging face.

ZGS 10.356, Shiba na

10.456 平原秋樹色 *Heigen shūju no iro,*
沙麓暮鐘聲 *Sharoku boshō no koe.*

The color of P'ing-yüan's autumn trees,
The sound of Sha-lu's evening bell.

P'ing-yüan and Sha-lu are names of places in China.

ZGS 10.357, Shiba 287, ZGJI 547

10.457 碧玉盤中珠 *Hekigyoku banchū no tama,*
瑠璃殿上月 *Ruridenjō no tsuki.*

The pearl in the blue jade bowl,
The ⌜moon⌝ above the lapis lazuli palace.

ZGS 10.358, Shiba 287, ZGJI 547, ZRKS 10.339, KZS #1002

10.458 法法本來法 *Hō hō honrai hō,*
心心無別心 *Shin shin mubesshin.*

This thing, that thing, are all originally dharmas;
This thought, that thought, are nothing other than mind.

ZGS na, Shiba 288, ZGJI 548, ZGDJT 1141d, ZRKS 10.393

10.459 卸帽穿雲去 *Bō o oroshite kumo o egachisari,*
披蓑帶雨歸 *Sa o hiraite ame o obite kaeru.*

Pulling down his hat, he left piercing the clouds;
Unfurling his cape, he returns wrapped in the rain.

ZGS 10.359, Shiba na, ZGJI 549, ZRKS 10.367

10.460 棒下無生忍 *Bōka no mushōnin,*
臨機不讓師 *⌜Ki⌝ ni nozonde shi ni yuzurazu.*

With the stick, he shows no restraint;
In practice, he will not spare even his master.

Heki 38 Main Case Comm., 47 Verse Comm. The translation of this verse is patterned after *Analects* xv, 35: 當仁不讓於師, "When it comes to goodness, one need not avoid competing with one's teacher" (Waley 1938, 200).

ZGS 10.360, Shiba 288, ZGJT 428, ZRKS 10.64, KZS #1046

10.461 牡丹一日紅 *Botan ichijitsu no kurenai,*
滿城公子醉 *Manjō kōshi you.*

The peonies all bloomed red one day,
And throughout the town the noble sons got drunk.

ZGS na, Shiba 288, ZGJI 547, ZRKS 10.301

10.462 削圓方竹杖 *Hōchikujō o sakuen shi,*
輓卻紫茸氈 *Shijōsen o bankyaku su.*

He whittles a square staff round,
He pulls the fuzz out of a purple felt rug.

ZGS 10.361, Shiba na, ZGJI 547, ZGJT 157, ZRKS 10.290

10.463 房房虛索索 *Bō-bō kyo saku-saku,*
東壁打西壁 *Tōheki saiheki o utsu.*

Room after room is empty and stark,
The east wall runs into the west wall.

ZGS 10.362, Shiba na, 寒山詩 §167

10.464 打破鳳林關 *Hōrinkan o taha shite,*
著靴水上立 *Kutsu o haite suijō ni tatsu.*

He smashes down the Phoenix Forest Barrier,
And in his boots stands upon the water.

Shiba 274: 鳳凰 instead of 鳳林, *tsukete* instead of *haite.*

ZGS 10.363, Shiba 274, ZGJI 548, ZRKS 10.71

10.465 牧人驅犢返 *Bokujin toku o katte kaeri,*
獵馬帶禽歸 *Ryōma tori o obite kaeru.*

The oxherd returns driving his calves,
The hunter's horse comes back laden with birds.

Shiba 288: *Bokujin koushi o katte kaeri, Ryōma tori o onde kaeru.*

ZGS 10.364, Shiba 288, TSSSTS 17

10.466 步步行舌頭 *Ho-ho zettō ni yuki,*
步步歸話頭 *Ho-ho watō ni kaeru.*

With every step out—your kōan.
With every step back—your kōan.

ZGS 10.365, Shiba na

10.467 薪盡火滅後 *Maki tsuki hi messhitaru nochi,*
密室爛如泥 *Misshitsu tadarete dei no gotoshi.*

The wood has been used up and the fire is dead,
The shut-up room swelters like hot mud.

ZGS 10.366, Shiba na

10.468 枕有思郷涙 *Makura ni kyō o omou no namida ari,*
門無問病人 *Mon ni yamai o tou no hito nashi.*

On the pillow are my tears from thinking of home;
At the gate no one asks about my illness.

ZGS 10.367, Shiba na

10.469 將謂胡鬚赤 *Masa ni omoeri ko shushaku to,*
更有赤鬚胡 *Sara ni shakushu ko aran to wa.*

I thought the barbarian had a red beard,
And sure enough, isn't this a red-bearded barbarian?

MMK 2.

ZGS 10.368, Shiba 267, ZGDJT 1173a, ZGJI 549, ZRKS 10.26, KZS #948

10.470 將謂吾負汝 *Masa ni omoeri ware nanji ni somuku to,*
元來汝負我 *Ganrai nanji ware ni somuku.*

All the time I thought I was opposing you,
But really it was you who were opposing me.

MMK 17.

ZGS na, Shiba 267, ZGJI 549, ZRKS 10.54

10.471 松無古今色 *Matsu ni kokon no iro naku,*
竹有上下節 *Take ni jōge no fushi ari.*

The pine has no old or new color,
The bamboo has upper and lower joints.

ZGS 10.369, Shiba 266, ZGJI 549, ZGDJT 1173d, ZRKS 10.30, KZS #950

10.472 有眼不曾見 *Manako atte katsute mizu,*
有耳不曾聞 *Mimi atte katsute kikazu.*

He has eyes, but has never seen;
He has ears, but has never heard.

Heki 26 Main Case *agyo* (verse 1 only), 82 Verse *agyo.*

ZGS na, Shiba 291, ZGJT 30, ZRKS 10.455

10.473 横身當宇宙 *Mi o yokotaete uchū ni ataru,*
誰是出頭人 *Tare ka kore shuttō no hito.*

Jump right in against the universe,
What kind of person will come out of this?

ZGS na, Shiba 245, ZGJI 550, ZGJT 38 (Verse 1 only), ZRKS 10.557

10.474 三描仙不就 *Mitabi sen o egaite narazu,*
終不與君傳 *Tsui ni kimi ga tame ni tsutaezu.*

I've tried to draw immortality three times without success.
In the end I've not gotten through to you.

ZGS 10.370, Shiba na

10.475 路遠驚日曛 *Michi tōku shite hi no kuraki ni odoroki,*
擔折知柴重 *Tan orete shiba no omoki o shiru.*

The road still long, he is surprised that it is sunset,
Aware only of the firewood bending down his shoulder pole.

ZGS 10.371, Shiba na, ZGJI 255 (Verse 2), ZGJT 299 (Verse 2)

10.476 路逢達道人 *Michi ni tatsudō no hito ni awaba,*
不將語默對 *Gomoku o motte taisezare.*

On the road, if you meet an expert in the Way,
Do not greet him with either words or silence.

MMK 36.

ZGS na, ZGJI 550, ZGJT 484, ZRKS 10.513, Shiba 296

10.477 有水皆含月 *Mizu ari mina tsuki o fukumu,*
無山不帶雲 *Yama to shite kumo o obirazaru nashi.*

Every stream contains the ⌜moon⌝,
No mountains are unwreathed in clouds.

ZGS 10.372, Shiba 291, ZGJI 551, ZGJT 30, ZRKS 10.168

10.478 掬水月在手 *Mizu o kiku sureba, tsuki te ni ari,*
弄花香滿衣 *Hana o rō sureba, kō e ni mitsu.*

I scoop up water and the ⌜moon⌝ is in my hands,
I play with flowers and their fragrance clings to my clothes.

ZGS 10.373, Shiba 249, ZD 71, ZGJT 82, ZRKS 10.11, KZS #946

10.479 汲水疑山動 *Mizu o kunde wa yama no ugoku ka to utagai,*
揚帆覺岸行 *Ho o agete wa kishi no yuku ka to oboyu.*

When you draw water, you wonder if the mountains are moving;
When you hoist the sail, you think the cliffs are gliding by.

ZGS 10.374, Shiba 250, ZGJI 551, ZRKS 10.191, TSSSTS 168

10.480 看盡瀟湘景 *Mitsukusu shōshō no kei,*
和舟入畫圖 *Fune ni washite gato ni iru.*

I have seen it all, the scenery of ⌜Hsiao-hsiang⌝,
And in my boat I ⌜enter the painting⌝.

ZGS 10.375, Shiba 248, ZGJI 517, ZRKS 10.34

10.481 水流元入海 *Mizu nagarete moto umi ni iri,*
月落不離天 *Tsuki ochite ten o hanarezu.*

Water flows but always enters the sea,
The ⌜moon⌝ goes down but never leaves the heavens.

ZGS 10.376, Shiba 269, ZGJT 236, ZGJI 551, ZRKS 10.1, KZS #943

10.482 水帶荷花白 *Mizu wa kaka o obite shiroku,*
烟和楊柳青 *Kemuri wa yōryū ni wa shite aoshi.*

The water around the lotus flowers is clear,
The mist in the willow branches is blue.

Shiba 269: *onde* instead of *obite.*

ZGS 10.377, Shiba 269, ZRKS 10.350

10.483 水廣則魚大 *Mizu hirokereba uo dai nari,*
君明則臣惠 *Kimi mei nareba shin kei ari.*

When the waters are broad, the fish are large;
When the lord's virtue shines, his ministers are clever.

ZGS 10.378, Shiba na, ZGJI 551

10.484 妙在一漚前 *Myō wa ichiō no mae ni ari,*
豈容千聖眼 *Ani senshō no manako o iren ya.*

The subtle point is in the moment before the first foam appears.
How can the eyes of even a thousand sages take it in?

ZGS na, Shiba 289, ZGJI 552, ZRKS 10.202n

10.485 霧海之南針 *Mukai no nanshin,*
夜途之北斗 *Yato no hokuto.*

A compass on a foggy sea,
The ⌜North Star⌝ in the middle of the night.

"Compass" is *nanshin*, literally "south needle," a poetic contrast to "north star." The early Chinese compass was developed from magnetic spoons and needles which pointed south. See Needham et al. 1962, 245–93.

ZGS 10.379, Shiba na

10.486 無手人行拳 *Mushu no hito ken o gyōji,*
無口人叫喚 *Muku no hito kyōkan su.*

The person without a hand swings a fist,
The person without a mouth gives a shout.

ZGS na, Shiba 289, ZGJI 552, ZGJT 442, ZGDJT 1201c, ZRKS 10.99

10.487 空留一片石 *Munashiku ippen no ishi o todomete,*
萬古在燕山 *Banko enzan ni ari.*

Alone it remains, one bit of rock,
From the far distant past, here on Mount Yen.

On Mount Yen there was an inscribed stone memorial to a general of the Later Han who long ago had won a victory there over the Hsiung-nu tribes.

ZGS 10.380, Shiba 252, TSSSTS 66

10.488 擧目望江山 *Me o agete kōzan o nozomeba,*
遍界無相識 *Henkai sōshiki nashi.*

I raise my eyes to gaze at the mountains and rivers;
In the whole world, I have no acquaintance.

ZGS 10.381, Shiba na, ZGJI 552, ZRKS 10.460

10.489 明鏡忽臨臺 *Meikyō tachimachi dai ni nozonde,*
當下分妍醜 *Tōge ni kenshū o wakatsu.*

As soon as the bright mirror is put on its stand,
At once it distinguishes the beautiful from the ugly.

Heki 65 Verse.

ZGS 10.382, Shiba 290, ZGJI 552, ZRKS 10.286

10.490 明明百草頭 *Mei-meitari hyakusōtō,*
明明祖師意 *Mei-meitari soshii.*

Radiant the hundred grasses,
Radiant the mind of the patriarchs.

ZGS na, Shiba 290, ZGJI 552, ZGDJT 1218d

10.491 仰面不見天 *Men o aoide ten o mizu,*
低頭不見地 *Kōbe o tarete chi o mizu.*

He turns his face upwards, but does not see the sky;
He hangs his head down, but does not see the ground.

ZGS 10.383, Shiba na, ZGJI 506

10.492 猛將立雄基 *Mōshō yūki o tatsu,*
誰窺其藩籬 *Tare ka sono hanri o ukagawan.*

The fierce general has constructed a strong base.
Who approaches such a fort?

ZGS 10.384, Shiba na

10.493 木雞鳴子夜 *Mokkei shiya ni naki,*
芻狗吠天明 *Sūku tenmei ni hoyu.*

The wooden cock crows at midnight,
The ⌜straw dog⌝ barks at dawn.

ZGS 10.385, Shiba 290, ZGJI 553, ZGJT 429, ZRKS 10.138, KZS #1057

10.494 木馬飛上天 *Mokuba tonde ten ni nobori,*
泥牛走入海 *Deigyū washite umi ni iru.*

The wooden horse soars up to the sky,
The mud ox gallops into the sea.

ZGS 10.386, Shiba na, ZGJI 553

10.495 若識琴中趣 *Moshi kinchū no omomuki o shiraba,*
何勞絃上聲 *Nanzo genjō no koe ni rō sen.*

When you appreciate the flavor of the lute,
What need is there for sound from the strings?

ZGS 10.387, Shiba 263, ZGJI 553, ZRKS 10.235, KZS #1031

10.496 若是鳳凰兒 *Moshi kore hōōji naraba,*
不向那邊討 *Nahen ni mukatte tazunezu.*

If this were the offspring of a phoenix,
It would not be hanging around in those places.

ZGS na, Shiba 263, ZGJI 553, ZGJT 193, ZRKS 10.200, KZS #1039

10.497 若逢親切問 *Moshi shinsetsu no mon ni awaba,*
端的不饒君 *Tanteki kimi ni yurusazu.*

If he gets a question right to the point,
Surely he won't show you any mercy.

ZGS 10.388, Shiba na, ZGJI 553, ZRKS 10.103

10.498 若不同床臥 *Moshi dōshō ni fusazumba,*
爭知被底穿 *Ikade ka hitei no ugataru koto o shiran.*

If you do not lie down in the same bed,
How will you know that the bottom is torn?

Heki 40 Verse *agyo*, 41 Main Case *agyo*. Shiba 263: *fusezumba* instead of *fusazumba*.

ZGS 10.389, Shiba 263, ZGJI 553, ZGJT 193, ZRKS 10.77, KZS #1049

10.499 若人求佛慧 *Moshi hito butsue o motomen to seba,*
通達菩提心 *Bodaishin ni tsūtachi seyo.*

If people would seek Buddha-wisdom,
Let them attain ⌜*bodhi*-mind⌝.

ZGS 10.390, Shiba na

10.500 元是一精明 *Moto kore ichi seimei,*
分爲六和合 *Wakarete riku wagō to naru.*

Originally it is a single pure radiance,
It divides into a sixfold seamless harmony.

Rinzai-roku §11: 本 instead of 元. ZRKS 10.174n: "Originally it is one thing but it is endowed with the six sense-bases—eye, ear, nose, tongue, body, mind."

ZGS 10.391, Shiba 254, ZGJI 554, ZRKS 10.174

10.501 出門何所見 *Mon o idete nan no miru tokoro zo,*
春色滿平蕪 *Shunshoku heibu ni mitsu.*

When you go out of the gate, what do you see?
Fields of hay full of the colors of spring.

ZGS 10.392, Shiba na

10.502 出門逢釋迦 *Mon o idete wa shaka ni ai,*
入門逢彌勒 *Mon ni itte wa miroku ni au.*

Go out the gate and you meet Śākyamuni,
Enter the gate and you meet ⌜Maitreya⌝.

ZGS 10.393, Shiba 265, ZGJI 554, ZRKS 10.187, KZS #1036

10.503 閉門推出月 *Mon o tōjite tsuki o suishutsu shi,*
穿井鑿開天 *I o hotte ten o sakkai su.*

Close the door and you draw out the ⌜moon⌝,
Dig a well and you cut a way into heaven.

Shiba 287: *tozashite* instead of *tojite*. Empuku-ji: *ugatte* instead of *hotte.*

ZGS 10.394, Shiba 287, ZGJI 554, ZRKS 10.484

10.504 野火燒不盡 *Yaka yakedomo tsukizu,*
春風吹又生 *Shunpū fuite mata shōzu.*

Field-fire cannot burn them all completely away.
When the spring wind blows, they grow again.

ZGS 10.395, Shiba 291, ZGJT 456, ZGJI 555, ZRKS 10.231

10.505 夜行莫踏白 *Yakō shiroki o fumu koto nakare,*
不水定是石 *Mizu ni arazareba sadamete kore ishi naran.*

When you walk at night never step on anything white.
If it is not water, most likely it is a rock.

Shiba 290: *Yakō ni shiroki o fumu koto nakare, Mizu ni arazumba sadamete kore ishi naran.*

ZGS 10.396, Shiba 290, ZGJI 554

10.506 野水浮輕楫 *Yasui keishū o ukabe,*
暖煙生紫蓴 *Dan'en shizen o shōzu.*

On the meadow pond floats a punt;
In the warm mists purple water shields are born.➛

Variant: 野水浮輕舟淡淵生紫蓴 *Yasui keishū o ukabe, Tan'en shizen o shōzu,* "On the meadow pond floats a boat; / In the limpid pools purple water shields are born." Water shield is an aquatic plant with floating oval leaves and purple flowers.

ZGS 10.397, Shiba na

10.507 晩來望湖上 *Banrai kojō o nozomeba,*
多是罟魚人 *Ōku wa kore uo o ami suru no hito.*

➛As evening comes, I look out over the lake.
Many men there are catching fish in nets.

Variant: 晩來望樓上多是網魚人 *Banrai rōjō yori nozomeba, Ōku wa kore uo o ami suru no hito,* "As evening comes, I look out from the pavilion. / Many men there are catching fish in nets."

ZGS 10.398, Shiba na

10.508 愛山登萬仭 *Yama o ai shite banjin ni nobori,*
樂水浮千舟 *Mizu o tanoshinde senshū o ukabu.*

In love with mountains, I climbed ten thousand feet high;
Delighting in water, I sailed a thousand boats.

ZGS 10.399, Shiba 241, 寒山詩 §176

10.509 山晩雲和雪 *Yama kurete kumo yuki ni washi,*
天寒月照霜 *Ten samū shite tsuki shimo o terasu.*

On the darkening mountains clouds mix with snow,
Under a shivering sky the ⌜moon⌝ shines upon the frost.

ZGS 10.400, Shiba na, TSSSTS 178

10.510 山向岳邊止 *Yama wa gakuhen ni mukatte todomari,*
水流海上消 *Mizu wa kaijō ni nagarete shō su.*

The mountain stops at the face of the cliff,
Flowing waters vanish into the sea.

ZGS 10.401, Shiba 260, ZGJI 555, ZRKS 10.462

10.511 山帶新晴雨 *Yama wa shinsei no ame o obi,*
谷留閏月花 *Tani wa jungetsu no hana o todomu.*

The mountains deck themselves anew in sun and rain,
The valleys retain the flowers of the ⌜repeated month⌝.

ZGS na, Shiba 261, ZGJI 555, ZRKS 10.413

10.512 山虚風落石 *Yama munashiku shite kaze ishi ni ochi,*
樓靜月侵門 *Rō shizuka ni shite tsuki mon o okasu.*

In the empty mountains wind falls against the rocks,
In the silent pavilion the ⌜moon⌝ strikes against the gate.

ZGS 10.403, Shiba na

10.513 不因夜來鴈 *Yarai no kari ni yorazumba,*
爭知海門秋 *Ikade ka kaimon no aki o shiran.*

If you do not go by the geese that come during the night,
How will you know when it is autumn at Sea Gate?

Shiba 284: 雁 instead of 鴈.

ZGS 10.403, Shiba 284, ZGJI 555, ZGJT 402, ZRKS 10.113

10.514 夜來風雪惡 *Yarai fūsetsu arashi,*
木折古巖前 *Ki wa oru kogan no mae.*

During the night the wind and snow were bad,
Trees broke in front of the old cliff.

ZGS 10.404, Shiba 291: 岩 instead of 巖, ZGJI 555, ZRKS 10.42 and 560

10.515 行到水窮處 *Yuite wa itaru mizu no kiwamuru tokoro,*
坐看雲起時 *Za shite wa miru kumo no okoru toki.*

Walking, I reach the place where streams run out;
Sitting, I see the moment when the clouds arise.

ZGS 10.405, Shiba 251, ZGJI 556, ZGJT 133, ZRKS 10.31, KZS #955, TSSSTS 198

10.516 維摩懶開口 *Yuima kuchi o hiraku ni monoushi,*
枝上一蟬吟 *Shijō issen ginzu.*

⌜Vimalakīrti⌝ refuses to open his mouth,
But on a bough a cicada is singing.

Heki 84.

ZGS 10.406, Shiba na, ZGJI 555, ZRKS 10.94

10.517 幽州猶自可 *Yūjū wa nao onozukara ka nari,*
最苦是江南 *Mottomo kurushiki wa kore kōnan.*

⌜Yu-chou⌝ is still bearable,
But there is nothing worse than ⌜Chiang-nan⌝.

Heki 21 Main Case *agyo.*

ZGS 10.407, Shiba 292, ZGJI 556, ZGJT 459, ZRKS 10.250

10.518 幽鳥語喃喃 *Yūchō go nannan,*
辭雲入亂峯 *Kumo o ji shite rampō ni iru.*

A hidden bird twitters, "Nam, nam";
Leaving the clouds, it drops into the ragged hills.

ZGS 10.408, Shiba 292, ZGJI 556, ZGJT 459, ZRKS 10.291

10.519 雪消山骨露 *Yuki shō shite sankotsu araware,*
雲出洞中明 *Kumo idete tochū akiraka nari.*

When the snow melts, the bones of the mountains are revealed;
When the clouds disperse, the inside of the cave brightens.

ZGJI 556: *kiete* instead of *shō shite.*

ZGS 10.409, Shiba 272, ZGJI 556, ZRKS 10.10

10.520 雪續溪橋斷 *Yuki wa keikyō no taetaru o tsugi,*
煙彰山舍藏 *Kemuri wa sansha no kakururu o arawasu.*

Snow covers the gap in the broken bridge,
Smoke reveals where the mountain hut is hidden.

ZGS na, Shiba 272, ZGJI 557

10.521 夜靜溪聲近 *Yoru shizuka ni shite keisei chikaku,*
庭寒月色深 *Niwa samū shite gesshoku fukashi.*

In the still of the night the valley stream sounds close by,
In the winter garden the moonlight is deeper still.

ZGS 10.410, Shiba 291, ZGJI 557, ZRKS 10.568, TSSSTS 178

10.522 能爲萬象主 *Yoku banzō no shu to nari,*
逐四時不凋 *Shiji o ōte shibomazu.*

Truly become master of the ⌜ten thousand things⌝,
And you will not waste away chasing the four seasons.

Empuku-ji: *banshō* instead of *banzō.*

ZGS na, Shiba 281, ZGJI 557, ZGJT 372, ZRKS 10.429

10.523 横鋪四世界 *Yokoshima ni shi sekai o shiki,*
堅蓋一乾坤 *Tate ni ichi kenkon o ōu.*

Horizontally, it lays out the four worlds;
Vertically, it covers ⌜heaven and earth⌝.

Four Worlds: four *dharma-dhātu.*

ZGS na, Shiba 245, ZGJI 557, ZRKS 10.402

10.524 夜坐連雲石 *Yoru wa ren'un no ishi ni zashi,*
春栽帶雨松 *Haru wa taiu no matsu o uyu.*

Evenings we sit on stones that merge into clouds,
In the spring we plant pines wreathed in rain.

ZGS na, Shiba 291, ZGJI 557, ZRKS 10.279

10.525 癩馬繫枯樁 *Raima kotō ni tsunagi,*
黑牛臥死水 *Kokugyū shisui ni ga su.*

A leprous horse is tied to an old post,
A black ox lies down in dead water.

ZGS na, Shiba 293, ZGJI 558, ZGJT 467, ZRKS 10.490

10.526 羅籠不肯住 *Rarō suredomo aete todomarazu,*
呼喚不回頭 *Kokan suredomo kōbe o megurasazu.*

Cage him and he will not stay put,
Call and he will not turn his head.

Heki 62 Main Case Comm.

ZGS 10.411, Shiba 293, ZGJI 557, ZGJT 465, ZRKS 10.465

10.527 欄干雖共倚 *Rankan tomo ni yoru to iedomo,*
山色看不同 *Sanshoku miru koto onajikarazu.*

Though we lean upon the same balustrade together,
We do not see the colors of the mountains the same.

ZGS 10.412, Shiba na, ZGJI 558, ZRKS 10.344

10.528 亂聲千葉下 *Ransei sen'yō no moto,*
寒影一巣孤 *Kan'ei issō ko nari.*

Beneath the rustling of a thousand leaves,
In the cold shadow, one nest alone.

ZGS 10.413, Shiba na, TSSSTS 202

10.529 理極忘情謂 *Ri kiwamatte jōi o wasuru,*
如何得喩齊 *Ikan zo yusei suru koto o en.*

Reason is at its limits, feeling and intellect forgotten—
What can be likened to this?➛

Heki 34 Verse Comm., 90 Verse Comm. The four verses 529-532 form one poem, "Fa-yen's Verse on Perfect True Nature" 法眼圓成實相.

ZGS 10.414, Shiba na

10.530 到頭霜夜月 *Tōtō sōya no tsuki,*
任運落前溪 *Nin'un zenkei ni otsu.*

➛From its zenith, the frosty night ⌜moon⌝
Sets softly into yonder valley.➛

ZGS 10.415, Shiba 278, ZGJT 339, ZGJI 537, ZRKS 10.22

10.531 果熟兼猿重 *Kajuku shite saru o kasanete omoku,*
山深路似迷 *Yama fukō shite michi mayou ni nitari.*

➛The ripened fruits are heavy with monkeys,
The hills stretch on so far—surely we'll lose our way.➛

ZGS 10.416: 遙似路 instead of 深路似.

ZGS 10.416, Shiba 246, ZGJI 493

10.532 擧頭殘照在 *Kōbe o agureba zanshō ari,*
元是住居西 *Moto kore jūkyo no nishi.*

➛When I look up, light still lingers;
It comes from west of where I live.

ZGS 10.417, Shiba 251, ZGJI 537, KZS #1012

10.533 理上絕疎親 *Rijō soshin o zesshi,*
法中無彼比 *Hōchū ni hishi nashi.*

Principle goes beyond the near-and-far,
Facts have no this-and-that.

ZGS na, Shiba 293, ZGJI 558, ZRKS 10.449

10.534 驪珠光燦爛 *Riju hikari sanran,*
蟾桂影婆娑 *Senkei kage basha.*

The ⌜black pearl's⌝ gleam is a brilliant radiance;
The ⌜moon's⌝ light is a shimmering glow.

蟾桂 are literally "toad and cassia tree." See ⌜Black dragon pearl⌝.

ZGS na, Shiba 294, ZGJT 472, ZGJI 559, ZRKS 10.253, KZS #1017

10.535 柳色黄金懶 *Ryūshoku ogon monouku,*
梨花白雪香 *Rika hakusetsu kanbashi.*

The willows reluctantly color into gold,
Snow white pear blossoms are fragrant.

ZGS 10.418, Shiba 294, ZGJI 559, ZGJT 473, ZRKS 10.280, 李白宮中行樂詞

10.536 流水寒山路 *Ryūsui kanzan no michi,*
深雲古寺鐘 *Shin'un koji no kane.*

A running stream, the cold mountain path,
Deep in the clouds, the old temple bell.

ZGS 10.419, Shiba 294, ZGJI 559

10.537 定龍蛇眼正 *Ryūda o sadamuru manako tadashiku,*
擒虎兒機全 *Koji o torauru ⌜ki⌝ mattashi.*

His eye correctly distinguishes snake from dragon;
He is full ready to pounce on any tiger's cub.

Empuku-ji: *Ryūda o sadamuru ni manako tadashiku, Koji o torauru ni ki mattashi.* ZGJI 559: 搭 instead of 定.

ZGS 10.420, Shiba 276, ZGJI 559, ZRKS 10.500, KZS #1078

10.538 龍吟初夜後 *Ryū wa ginzu shoya no nochi,*
虎嘯五更前 *Tora wa usobuku gokō no mae.*

The dragon shrieks after the fall of night,
The tiger roars before the break of day.

ZGS na, Shiba 294, ZGJI 559, ZRKS 10.125, KZS #1071

10.539 良匠無棄材 *Ryōshō ni wa sutsuru zai naku,*
明君無棄士 *Meikun ni wa sutsuru samurai nashi.*

A good craftsman has no lumber to throw away,
An enlightened sovereign has no men to squander.

Empuku-ji: *Ryōshō ni wa kizai naku, Meikun ni wa kishi nashi.*

ZGS 10.421, Shiba na

10.540 兩頭共坐斷 *Ryōtō tomo ni zadan shite,*
八面起清風 *Hachimen seifū o okosu.*

When you have cut off both heads,
From all eight directions the pure wind rises.

ZGS 10.422, Shiba 294, ZGJI 559, ZRKS 10.510

10.541 兩頭倶截斷 *Ryōtō tomo ni setsudan shite,*
一劍倚天寒 *Ikken ten ni yotte susamaji.*

It cuts off your two heads,
One cold ⌜sword⌝ poised against the sky.

ZGS 10.423, Shiba 294, ZGJI 559, ZRKS 10.370, KZS #1004

10.542 寥寥天地間 *Ryō-ryōtaru tenchi no kan,*
獨立有何極 *Dokuritsu shite nan no kiwamari ka aran.*

In the awesome quiet between heaven and earth,
Standing free—where is there an end?

ZGS 10.424, Shiba 294, ZGJI 560, ZRKS 10.380

10.543 林下十年夢 *Rinka jūnen no yume,*
湖邊一咲新 *Kohen isshō arata nari.*

Ten years in the forest dreaming,
Then by the lake laughing a new laugh.

Shiba 295: 笑 instead of 咲.

ZGS 10.425, Shiba 295, ZD #74, ZGJI 560, ZRKS 10.75

10.544 林中不賣薪 *Rinchū ni takigi o urazu,*
湖上不鬻魚 *Kojō ni uo o hisagazu.*

You don't sell firewood in a forest,
You don't sell fish on a lake.

ZGS 10.426, Shiba 295, ZGJI 560

10.545 脱卻娘生袴 *Rōshō no hakama o dakkyaku shite,*
還著破襴衫 *Kaette haransan o tsuku.*

Taking off the trousers made by his mother,
He puts on the ragged gown of the student.

ZGS 10.427, Shiba na, ZGJI 561, ZRKS 10.363

10.546 臘雪連天白 *Rōsetsu ten ni tsuranatte shiroku,*
春風逼戸寒 *Shunpū to ni sematte samushi.*

The year end snows fill the skies with white,
The spring winds press cold against the doors.

ZGS 10.428, Shiba 296, ZGJI 652, ZRKS 10.4

10.547 嶺梅先破玉 *Reibai mazu tama o yaburi,*
江柳未遙金 *Kōryū imada kin o ugokasazu.*

The mountain plums are first to break their buds,
The riverside willows have not yet hung out their golden catkins.

Shiba 295: 搖 instead of 遙.

ZGS na, Shiba 295, ZGJI 560, ZGJT 481, ZRKS 10.364

10.548 裂開也在我 *Rekkai mo mata ware ni ari,*
揑聚也在我 *Netsuju mo mata ware ni ari.*

To destroy—is within me.
To put together—is also within me.

ZGS na, Shiba 295, ZGJI 561

10.549 結廬古城下 *Ro o kojō no moto ni musunde,*
時登古城上 *Toki ni kojō no ue ni noboru.*

He built his hut by an ancient city,
Sometimes he climbs atop the old city wall.

ZGS 10.429, Shiba na

10.550 結廬在人境 *Ro o musunde jinkyō ni ari,*
而無車馬喧 *Shikamo shaba no kamabisushiki nashi.*

I built a little hut where people live,
But there is no noise of wagons and horses.➤

The five verses from 550-554 form one poem, T'ao Yüan-ming's 陶淵明 "Drinking Wine" 飲酒.

ZGS 10.430, Shiba na

10.551 問君何能爾 *Kimi ni tou nanzo yoku shikaru,*
心遠地自偏 *Kokoro tōku shite chi onozukara hen nari.*

➤I ask you, how can this be?
For a heart that's detached, anywhere becomes a place remote.➤

ZGS 10.431, Shiba na

10.552 採菊東籬下 *Kiku o tōri no moto ni totte,*
悠然見南山 *Yūzen to shite nanzan o miru.*

➤Gathering chrysanthemums at the eastern hedge,
Quietly I gaze upon the southern hills.➤

ZGS 10.432, Shiba 258, ZGJI 497, ZGJT 155, ZRKS 10.119, KZS #1070

10.553 山氣日夕佳 *Sanki nisseki ka nari,*
飛鳥相共還 *Hichō aitomo ni kaeru.*

➤In the clean mountain air at sunset,
Two birds wing home together.➤

ZGS 10.433, Shiba na

10.554 此間有眞意 *Kono kan shin'i ari,*
欲辨已忘言 *Benzen to hosshite sude ni gen o wasuru.*

➤Here there is true meaning,
But when I go to express it, I find I have forgotten the words.

ZGS 10.434, Shiba na

10.555 蘆花映明月 *Roka meigetsu ni eiji,*
明月映蘆花 *Meigetsu roka ni eizu.*

White reed flowers shine on the bright ⌜moon⌝,
The bright moon shines on the white reed flowers.

Heki 62 Verse Comm.

ZGS 10.435, Shiba na, ZGJI 561

10.556 六月買松風 *Rokugatsu shōfū o kawaba,*
人間恐無價 *Ningen osoraku atai nakaran.*

If one would buy the ⌜pine wind⌝ in June,
Would there be anyone who could match its price?

ZGS 10.436, Shiba na, ZGJI 562, ZGJT 494, ZRKS 10.17

10.557 六月滿天雪 *Rokugatsu manten no yuki,*
渾身冷如鐵 *Konshin tetsu yori mo tsumetashi.*

In the sixth month, the sky is full of snow.
My entire body is colder even than iron.

ZGS na, Shiba 296, ZGJI 562, ZRKS 10.97, ZGJI 562

10.558 露地藏白牛 *Roji byakugo o zō shi,*
長空呑日月 *Shōkū jitsugetsu o nomu.*

The lane hides a white ox,
The vast sky swallows the sun and ⌜moon⌝.

ZGS 10.437, Shiba 296

10.559 吾心似秋月 *Wa ga kokoro shūgetsu ni nitari,*
碧潭淸皎潔 *Hekitan kiyō shite kōketsu.*

My heart is like the autumn ⌜moon⌝,
Shining so clearly in the pool of limpid blue.➤

ZGS 10.438, Shiba 256, ZGJT 122, ZGJI 562, 寒山詩 §5

10.560 無物堪比倫 *Mono no hirin ni taetaru wa nashi,*
教我如何説 *Ware o shite ikanga tokashimen.*

**➤Nothing compares with this.
Tell me, how am I to explain?**

ZGS 10.439, Shiba 289, ZGJI 554, ZRKS 10.29

10.561 易分霜裏粉 *Wakachiyasuki wa sōri no fun,*
難辨雪中梅 *Benjigataki wa setchū no ume.*

**It is easy to distinguish flour in the frost,
It is hard to distinguish the plum flowers in the snow.**

ZGS 10.440, Shiba 242, ZGJI 562, ZGJT 10, ZRKS 10.309

10.562 欲別牽郎衣 *Wakaren to hosshite rō ga koromo o hiku,*
郎今到何處 *Rō ima izure no tokoro ni ka itaru.*

**At parting, I clung to my husband's robe.
Husband, where are you by now?**

ZGS 10.441, Shiba na, TSSSTS 69

10.563 使我爲良臣 *Ware o shite ryōshin o tarashimeyo,*
勿使爲忠臣 *Chūshin narashimuru nakare.*

**Let me be a conscientious servant,
Do not make me be a loyal servant.**

ZGS 10.442, Shiba na

10.564 投我以木瓜 *Ware ni okuru ni bokka o motte sudomo,*
報之以瓊琚 *Kore ni mukuyuru ni keikyo o motte sen.*

**Though he threw me a quince,
I returned a jade.**

ZGS 10.443, Shiba na, ZGJI 563

10.565 我行荒草裏 *Ware wa kōsōri ni yuki,*
汝又入深村 *Nanji wa mata shinson ni iru.*

**I walk in the midst of wild grasses,
You enter the deep villages again.**

ZRKS 10.76 (variant): 汝又入深林, "You enter the deep forests again."

ZGS 10.444, Shiba na, ZGJI 562, ZGJT 52, ZRKS 10.76

10.566 吾本來茲土 *Ware moto kono do ni kitaru koto wa,*
傳法救迷情 *Hō o tsutaete meijō o sukuwan to nari.*

**When I first came to this land,
It was to save people from delusion and passion by spreading the Dharma.➤**

566-567 are the "Verse of the First Patriarch, the Priest Bodhidharma" (Yampolsky 1967, 176).

ZGS 10.445, Shiba na

10.567 一華開五葉 *Ichige goyō o hiraki,*
結果自然成 *Kekka jinen ni naru.*

➤A lotus opens five leaves,
And of itself bears fruit.

Empuku-ji: *Ikke goyō o hiraki, Kekka jinen jō.*

ZGS 10.446, Shiba 242, ZGJI 486, ZGJT 23, ZRKS 10.579

10.568 椀子落地 *Wansu chi ni ochite*
楪子成七八片 *Chansu shichi-happen to naru.*

The bowl fell to the ground
And the plate broke into seven or eight pieces.

Heki Verse *agyo.*

ZGS 10.447, Shiba 296, ZGJT 497, ZGJI 563

Eleven-Character Phrases

11.1 可憐渾沌氏 *Awaremubeshi kontonshi,*
七日而其死乎 *Shichinichi ni shite sore shi sen ka.*

Pity Mr. ⌜Hun-tun⌝.
He died after seven days!

ZGS 11.1

11.2 道得三十棒 *Iiurumo sanjūbō,*
道不得三十棒 *Iiezarumo sanjūbō.*

If you can speak, you get thirty blows;
If you cannot speak, you get thirty blows.

ZGS 11.2, ZGJI 566

11.3 君子之言幽而 *Kunshi no gen wa yū ni shite,*
必有驗平明 *Kanarazu heimei ni shirushi ari.*

The superior person's words are mysterious,
But always prove clear.

See also 21+.10.

ZGS 11.3

11.4 好一釜羹 *Kōippu no atsumono,*
被兩顆鼠糞汚卻 *Ryōka no sofun ni okyaku seraru.*

A potful of my best stew,
Dirtied by two lumps of rat shit!

This is Hakuin's *jakugo* to "Form itself is emptiness, emptiness itself is form" in *Dokugo shingyō* (Waddell 1996, 31).

ZGS 11.4, ZGJI 564

11.5 五羖入而秦喜 *Goko itte shin yorokobi,*
毅出而燕懼 *Ki idete en osoru.*

When ⌜Lord Five Ram-Skins⌝ entered, Ch'in rejoiced;
When General Yi left, Yen trembled in fear.

For General Yi, see ⌜Yüeh Yi⌝.

ZGS 11.5

11.6 見秋毫之末者 *Shūgō no matsu o miru mono mo,*
不自見其睫 *Mizukara sono shō o mizu.*

Though one may be able to see the tips of ⌜autumn down⌝,
One cannot see one's own eyelashes.

ZGS 11.6, ZGJI 564

11.7 子在齊聞韶 *Shi wa sei ni imashite shō o kiku koto,*
三月不知肉味 *Sangatsu niku no aji o shirazu.*

When the Master was in Ch'i, he heard the Shao
And for three months, he did not know the taste of meat.

The Shao is music originally composed for an imperial dance performance, which Confucius considered both beautiful and good. *Analects* VII, 13.

ZGS 11.7

11.8 盡十方法界 *Jin jippō hokkai,*
盡是自己光明 *Kotogotoku kore jiko no kōmyō.*

All dharma worlds in the ⌜ten directions⌝
Are the luminous brilliance of the self.

ZGS 11.8

11.9 秦時轆轢鑽 *Shinji no takurakusan,*
貶向大食國裏 *Dai shokkokuri ni henkō su.*

That useless tool from the Ch'in era,
Dump it in the land of the Saracens.

Takurakusan 轆轢鑽, a now useless tool used long ago in the time of the First Emperor of Ch'in when he built the ⌜O-pang Palace⌝ (ZGJI 247).

ZGS 11.9, ZGJI 564

11.10 擧千鈞之重者 *Senkin no omoki o aguru mono mo,*
不自擧其身 *Mizukara sono mi o agezu.*

One who can lift a thousand-pound weight
Still cannot lift his own body.

ZGS 11.10, ZGJI 565

11.11 鐸以聲自毀 *Taku wa sei o motte mizukara kobotare,*
膏燭以明自鑠 *Kōshoku mei o motte mizukara torakasu.*

To produce sound, the bell cracks itself;
To produce light, the candle consumes itself.

The ZGS 11.11 reading for 鑠 is *torakasu*. The usual reading is *tokeru*.

ZGS 11.11

11.12 衲僧門下一毫不偸常住物 *Nōsōmonka ichigō mo jōjū no mono o nusumazu.*

A ⌜patch-robed monk⌝ does not steal even a hair from the ⌜permanent things⌝.

ZGS 11.12

11.13 欲知佛性義 *Busshō no gi o shiran to hosseba*
當觀時節因緣 *Masa ni jisetsu innen o kan zubeshi.*

To understand the principle of Buddha-nature
Contemplate [the nature of] time and causality.

Heki 14 Main Case Comm., 39 Intro., 48 Main Case Comm. See also 12.114.

ZGS 11.13

11.14 萬劫難遇有密義 *Mangō aigataki mitsugi ari,*
不説不説 *Fusetsu, fusetsu.*

This secret—so rarely met even in ten thousand ages—
I will not tell, I will not tell.

ZGS 11.14, ZGJI 566

11.15 蘭生幽宮 *Ran no yūkyū ni shōzu,*
不爲莫服而不芳 *Oburu nashi to nashite hō arazumba aran.*

Orchids grow in the hidden quarters of the palace.
Though never displayed, they never cease emitting their fragrance.

ZGS 11.15, ZGJI 566

Twelve-Character Verses

12.1 相罵饒儞接觜 *Ainonoshiru koto wa nanji ni yurusu, kuchibashi o tsuge,*
相唾饒儞潑水 *Aidasuru koto wa nanji ni yurusu, mizu o sosoge.*

When we're reviling one another, you may give me tit for tat;
When we're spitting at one another, you may spew me with slobber.

Trans. from ZD #117. *Heki* 2 Main Case Comm., 9 Main Case Comm., 58 Main Case Comm.

ZGS 12.1, ZRKS 12.25, Shiba 309, ZGJI 567, ZGDJT 2d, ZGJT 268, ZD #117

12.2 家貧難辨素食 *Ie hin ne shite soshoku o benjigataku,*
事忙不及草書 *Koto isogashiku shite sōsho suru ni oyobazu.*

Their house is so poor, they don't know what a simple meal is;
They're so busy with work, they can't even scribble off a few notes.

MMK 21.

ZGS 12.2, ZRKS 12.60, Shiba 299, ZGJI 567, ZGJT 48, KZS #1120

12.3 争如著衣喫飯 *Ikadeka jakue kippan ni shikan,*
此外更無佛祖 *Kono hoka sara ni busso nashi.*

What compares with just getting dressed or eating your food?
Aside from this, there are no buddhas and ancestors.

ZGS 12.3, ZRKS 12.130, Shiba 309, ZGJI 567

12.4 一塵飛而翳天 *Ichijin tonde ten o kakushi,*
一芥墮而覆地 *Ikke ochite chi o ōu.*

A single mote of ⸢dust⸣ flies up and hides all the heavens,
A single ⸢mustard seed⸣ falls and covers the whole earth.

ZGJT 25: *Ichijin tonde ten o ōi.*

ZGS 12.4, ZRKS 12.126, Shiba 298, ZGJI 568, ZGJT 25

12.5 一人跨三脚驢 *Ichinin wa sankyaku no ro ni matagari,*
一人騎三角虎 *Ichinin wa sankaku no tora ni noru.*

One sits astride a three-legged donkey,
The other rides a three-horned tiger.

ZGS 12.5, Shiba 298

12.6 一人順水張帆 *Ichinin wa junsui ni ho o hari,*
一人逆風把梶 *Ichinin wa gyakufū ni kaji o toru.*

One sets his sail with the current,
The other holds his rudder against the wind.

ZGS 12.6, ZRKS 12.110, Shiba 298, ZGJI 568

12.7 一人辯如懸河 *Ichinin wa ben kenga no gotoku,*
一人口似木訥 *Ichinin wa kuchi bokutotsu ni nitari.*

One person's eloquence is like a rushing stream,
Another person's speech is a rigid stutter.

ZGS 12.7, Shiba na

12.8 一毛頭上獅子 *Ichimōtōjō no shishi,*
示現百億毛頭 *Hyakuoku mōtō ni jigen su.*

The lion on one hair
Displays itself on one billion hairs.

ZGS na, ZRKS 12.141, Shiba 299, ZGJI 568

12.9 一喝大地震動 *Ikkatsu daichi shindō shi,*
一棒須彌粉碎 *Ichibō shumi funsai su.*

At one shout, the great earth trembles;
At one blow of the stick, Mount ⌜Sumeru⌝ shatters to pieces.

See ⌜Stick and shout⌝.

ZGS 12.8, Shiba 297, ZGJI 567, KZS #1097

12.10 一切聲是佛聲 *Issai no shō wa kore busshō,*
一切色是佛色 *Issai no shiki wa kore busshiki.*

Every sound is the Buddha's voice,
Every form is the Buddha-form.

Heki 79 Main Case. Shiba 298: *issai no koe* instead of *issai no shō*; *issai no iro* instead of *issai no shiki*. The character 色 when read *shiki* implies shape or form (as opposed to emptiness), when read *iro* implies color.

ZGS 12.9, ZRKS 12.124, Shiba 298, ZGJI 568, ZGJT 25

12.11 一指指狗子 *Isshi wa kusu o yubisashi,*
一指指主事出去 *Isshi wa shuji o yubisashite idesaru.*

With one finger pointing to the dog
And one finger pointing to the head monk, he leaves.

ZGS 12.10, Shiba na

12.12 一炷烟中得意 *Isshū enchū ni i o ete,*
九衢塵裏偸閑 *Kyūku jinri kan o nusumu.*

Once one attains the mind in one burning stick of incense,
Then one can steal a rest even in the ⌜dust⌝ clouds of the nine avenues.

ZGS na, ZRKS 12.155, Shiba 298, ZGJI 568

12.13 奪卻衣鉢曰 *Ihatsu o dakkyaku shite iwaku,*
爲什麼在某手裡 *Nan to shite ka soregashi shuri ni aru to.*

Having stolen the robe and bowl, he says,
"How did these come to be in my hands?"

ZGS 12.11, Shiba na

12.14 意蹈毘盧頂顆 *I wa biru chōnei o fumi,*
行拜童子足下 *Gyō wa dōji no sokka o hai su.*

His ideal is to stand on ⌜Vairocana's⌝ crown,
His practice is to prostrate at the feet of a child.

ZGS 12.12, Shiba na

12.15 不可以有心得 *Ushin o motte u bekarazu,*
不可以無心求 *Mushin o motte motomu bekarazu.*

It is not to be attained with mind,
It is not to be sought with no-mind.

ZGS na, ZRKS 12.152, Shiba 315, ZGJI 569

12.16 内無玲瓏機智 *Uchi ni ruri no kichi naku,*
外無花藻文章 *Soto ni kasō no bunshō nashi.*

Within there is no azure gem of living wisdom,
Without there is no air of literary refinement.

ZGS na, ZRKS 12.17, Shiba 312, ZGJI 569

12.17 碎衣珠於醉客 *Eju o suikaku ni kudaki,*
劈金鎖於病猿 *Kinsa o byōen ni tsunzaku.*

Smash the ⌜jewel in the robe⌝ of the drunken visitor,
Shatter the ⌜golden chain on the sick monkey⌝.

ZGS na, ZRKS 12.6, Shiba 305, ZGJI 567

12.18 不住圓覺伽藍 *Engaku garan ni jū sezu,*
不守三期禁制 *Sango no kinsei o mamorazu.*

No staying in the temple of awakening,
No keeping the regulations of the ⌜three periods⌝.

ZGS 12.13, ZRKS 12.3, Shiba 315, ZGJI 569, KZS #1091

12.19 王孫遊兮不歸 *Ōson asonde kaerazu,*
春草生兮萋萋 *Shunsō shōjite seisei.*

The young lord plays about and does not come home,
Spring grass grows in lush profusion.

ZGS 12.14, ZRKS 12.10 (cites 楚詞), Shiba na, ZGJI 569

12.20 戒潔滄海之珠 *Kai wa sōkai no tama yori mo isagiyoku,*
性朗碧天之月 *Shō wa hekiten no tsuki yori mo hogaraka nari.*

The precepts are purer than the pearl in the azure seas,
Buddha-nature is brighter than the ⌜moon⌝ in the blue heavens.

ZGS na, ZRKS 12.75, Shiba 300, ZGJI 570

12.21 迦葉聆箏起舞 *Kashō sō o hiite mai okoshite,*
淵明聞鐘皺眉 *Enmei kane o kiite mayu o shibamu.*

⌜Kāśyapa⌝ listens to the harp and dances,
⌜Yüan-ming⌝ hears the bell and wrinkles his eyebrows.

ZGS 12.15, Shiba na

12.22 聽鐘知有古寺 *Kane o kiite wa koji aru koto o shiri,*
見烟覺有野村 *Kemuri o mite wa yason aru koto o oboyu.*

On hearing the bell, he knows there is an old temple;
On seeing the smoke, he knows there is a country village.

Shiba 310: *Kane o kiite koji aru o shiri, Kemuri o mite yason aru o obou.*

ZGS 12.16, Shiba 310, ZGJI 570

12.23 上無片瓦蓋頭 *Kami henga no kōbe o ōu naku,*
下無寸土立足 *Shimo sundo no ashi o rissuru nashi.*

Above, he hasn't a scrap of tile over his head;
Below, he hasn't an inch of earth on which to stand.

ZGS 12.17, Shiba na, ZGJI 570, ZGJT 222

12.24 鴈無遺蹤之意 *Kari ni ishō no i naku,*
水無沈影之心 *Mizu ni chin'ei no kokoro nashi.*

The wild geese do not intend to leave traces,
The water has no mind to absorb their image.

ZGS na, ZRKS 12.154, Shiba 301, ZGJI 570, ZD #130

12.25 彼采艾兮 *Kare mogusa o toran,*
一日不見 *Ichijitsu mo awazareba,*
如三歳兮 *Sansai no gotoshi.*

Oh, he is plucking mugwort.
For a single day I have not seen him,
But it seems like three years.

Trans. from Waley 1937a, 48.

ZGS 12.18, Shiba na; *Book of Songs* §72

12 字

12.26 寒時寒殺闍梨 *Kan no toki wa jari o kansatsu shi,*
熱時熱殺闍梨 *Netsu no toki wa jari o nessatsu su.*

When it's cold, it kills you with cold;
When it's hot, it kills you with heat.

Heki 43.

ZGS 12.19, ZRKS 12.4, Shiba 300, ZGJI 570, ZGJT 67, KZS #1092

12.27 欲爲君盡君道 *Kimi ga tame ni kimi no michi o tsukusan koto o hosshi,*
欲爲臣盡臣道 *Shin no tame ni shin no michi o tsukusan koto o hossu.*

If one wishes to be a ruler, one must be devoted to the way of the ruler;
If one wishes to be a minister, one must be devoted to the way of the minister.

ZGS 12.20, Shiba na, *Mencius* IV, A, 2.

12.28 豁開胸襟法藏 *Kyōkin no hōzō o kakkai shi,*
運出自己家珍 *Jiko no kachin o unshutsu su.*

Reveal the Dharma treasury within your breast
And deliver forth your own house treasures.

ZGS na, ZRKS 12.63, Shiba 300, ZGJI 571

12.29 去年梅今歳柳 *Kyonen no ume konsai no yanagi,*
顔色馨香依舊 *Ganshoku keikō kyū ni yoru.*

Last year's plum and this year's willow—
Their color and fragrance are as of old.

Trans. from ZD #124.

ZGS 12.21, ZRKS 12.98, Shiba 301, ZGJI 570, ZD #124

12.30 去年貧未是貧 *Kyonen no hin wa imada kore hin narazu,*
今年貧始是貧 *Konnen no hin wa hajimete kore hin.*

Last year's poverty wasn't quite poverty,
But this year's poverty is really poverty.

ZGS 12.22, ZRKS 12.51, Shiba 301, ZGJT 88, ZD #121

12.31 許由臨岸洗耳 *Kyoyū kishi ni nozonde mimi o arai,*
巢父不飲牛水 *Sōfu mizu o ushi ni nomasazu.*

⌜Hsü Yu⌝ washed his ears at the river bank,
⌜Ch'ao-fu⌝ refused to let his ox drink the water.

Hsü Yu was so virtuous that when Emperor ⌜Yao⌝ offered him the throne, he washed his ears in the stream to clean them of defilement. Ch'ao-fu, just as virtuous, refused to let his ox drink the dirty water (ZGJI 571).

ZGS na, ZRKS 12.156, Shiba 302, ZGJI 571, ZD #188

12.32 君召不俟駕行 *Kimi messeba ga o matazu shite yuki,*
父召唯而不諾 *Chichi messeba i shite daku sezu.*

When your lord summons, you go without waiting for a carriage.
When your father calls, you do not [just] reply,"Yes."

Books of Rites, ch. 1, quoted in *Analects* x, 13. See also 13.8.

ZGS na, Shiba 303

12.33 口欲談而辭喪 *Kuchi danzen to hosshite ji sōshi,*
心欲緣而慮亡 *Kokoro enzen to hosshite ryo bōzu.*

When the mouth tries to speak about it, words fail;
When the mind wants to relate to it, thoughts die.

Heki 33 Main Case Comm.

ZGS 12.23, ZRKS 12.16, Shiba 304, ZGJI 571, ZGJT 124, ZD #114

12.34 雲無心而出岫 *Kumo mushin ni shite kuki o ide,*
水盈科而或流 *Mizu ana ni michite aruiwa nagaru.*

Without a thought, clouds float off the mountain peaks.
Water fills the hollows and flows away.

ZGS 12.24, ZRKS 12.79, Shiba 299

12.35 雲無心以出岫 *Kumo mushin ni shite kuki o ide,*
鳥倦飛而知還 *Tori tobu ni unde kaeru koto o shiru.*

Without a thought, clouds float off the mountain peaks.
Tired from flying, the birds know when to return.

ZGS 12.25, Shiba 299

12.36 勁松彰於歲寒 *Keishō wa saikan ni araware,*
貞臣見於國危 *Teishin wa kokki ni arawaru.*

The sturdiness of the pine is seen in the winter cold,
The upright minister is recognized in a nation's crisis.

ZGS 12.26, ZRKS 12.69, Shiba 303, ZGJI 571

12.37 劍刄上論殺活 *Kenninjō sekkatsu o ronji,*
棒頭上別機宜 *Bōtōjō* ⌜*ki*⌝*gi o wakatsu.*

He expounds life and death with his ⌜sword⌝,
He makes his decisions with his stick.

Heki 61 Intro.

ZGS 12.27, ZRKS 12.146, Shiba 303, ZGJI 571

12.38 護鵝之戒如雪 *Goga no kai wa yuki no gotoku,*
守臘之行若冰 *Shurō no gyō wa kōri no gotoshi.*

The virtuous deed of saving the duck is like [pure] snow,
The midwinter discipline is [as hard to endure] as ice.

A monk came to beg food at the gate of a jeweler who was polishing a jewel. When the jeweler went inside for something to give, a duck saw the jewel and, mistaking it for food, swallowed it. When the jeweler returned and discovered his jewel missing, he accused the monk. He tied up the monk and beat him with a stick until blood ran from his ears, mouth, and nose. Just then, the duck approached and lapped up the blood. Enraged, the jeweler struck the duck and killed it. Seeing the duck die, the monk shed tears and then explained how the duck had swallowed the jewel. The jeweler cut open the duck's stomach and found his jewel. He raised his voice in great sorrow, but by this time the monk had already disappeared (ZRKS 12.59n).

ZGS na, ZRKS 12.59, Shiba 304, ZGJI 572

12.39 要明向上鉗鎚 *Kōjō no kantsui o akiramen to yōseba,*
須是作家爐鞴 *Subekaraku kore sakke no rohai narubeshi.*

If you want to know what superior ⌜tongs and hammer⌝ are,
Then you must experience a great master's ⌜fire pit and bellows⌝.

Heki 43 Intro. Shiba 319: *kentsui* instead of *kantsui*. See ⌜Directed upwards⌝.

ZGS 12.28, ZRKS 12.39, Shiba 319, KZS #1113

12.40 拈起向上鉗鎚 *Kōjō no kantsui o nenki shite,*
扶竪正法眼藏 *Shōbō genzō o fuju su.*

Pick up the ultimate ⌜tongs and hammer⌝
And establish the treasury of the true Dharma eye.

Heki 45 Intro. See ⌜Directed upwards⌝.

ZGS 12.29, ZRKS 12.48, Shiba na, ZGJI 573, KZS #1114

12.41 認箇照照靈靈 *Kono shō-shō rei-rei to mitomete,*
落在驢前馬後 *Rozen bago ni rakuzai su.*

Thinking it radiance and spirituality,
He's fallen into leading asses and following horses.

Heki 99 Main Case Comm. Shiba 313: *tomete* instead of *mitomete.*

ZGS 12.30, ZRKS 12.1, Shiba 313, ZGJI 573, ZD #111

12.42 不是只口門窄 *Kore tada kumon no semaki ni arazu,*
滿口說未盡耳 *Manku ni tokite imada tsukusazaru nomi.*

It is not that the mouth is small;
Not even a full mouth can completely explain.

ZGS 12.31, ZRKS 12.31, Shiba na, ZGJI 573

12.43 坐中有江南客 *Zachū kōnan no kyaku ari,*
樽前莫唱鷓鴣 *Sonzen shako o tonauru koto nakare.*

If you are sitting with a traveler from ⌜Chiang-nan⌝
And having a few drinks, don't sing "Quails in the Sky."

See also 14.258. "Quails in the Sky" is the name of a lyric tune (Feng Liping, personal communication, 4 February 2000).

ZGS 12.32, Shiba na

12.44 三家村裏交眉 *Sanka sonri ni mayu o majie,*
萬仞崖頭移歩 *Banjin gaitō ni ho o utsusu.*

See eye to eye with the folks in the three-house village,
Stretch a leg out to the 10,000-fathom cliff.

See ⌜eyebrows⌝.

ZGS 12.33, Shiba na

12.45 驚起三聖瞎驢 *Sanshō no katsuro o kyōki shi,*
趯倒趙州畧彴 *Jōshū no ryakushaku o tekitō su.*

He startles Sanshō's blind donkey,
And topples Jōshū's log bridge.

For Sanshō, see *Rinzai-roku* §68; for Jōshū's bridge, see *Heki* 52.

ZGS 12.34, ZRKS 12.81, Shiba 302, ZGJI 574

12.46 逐鹿者不見山 *Shika o ou mono wa yama o mizu,*
攫金者不見人 *Kin o tsukamu mono wa hito o mizu.*

One who hunts for deer doesn't see the mountains,
One who steals money doesn't see people.

ZGS 12.35, ZRKS 12.35, Shiba 310, ZGJT 60, KZS #1110, ZD #118

12.47 詩三百一言以蔽之 *Shi sanbyaku ichigen motte kore o ōu,*
曰思無邪 *Iwaku omoi yokoshima nashi.*

The three hundred verses of the *Book of Songs*—one phrase embraces them all:
"In thoughts, nothing crooked."

ZGS 12.36, Shiba 306; *Analects* II, 2.

12.48 獅子不咬麒麟 *Shishi kirin o kamazu,*
猛虎不飡伏肉 *Mōko funiku o kurawazu.*

The lion does not bite a ⌜*ch'i-lin*⌝,
A fierce tiger does not eat the flesh of a corpse.

KZS #1119: *Mōko funiku o san sezu.*

ZGS 12.37, ZRKS 12.55, Shiba 306, ZGJI 575, ZGJT 177, KZS #1119

12.49 獅子不飡鵰殘 *Shishi chōzan o kurawazu,*
快鷹不打死兎 *Kaiyō shito o tasezu.*

The lion does not devour what the vulture leaves,
The swift hawk does not strike the dead rabbit.

ZGS 12.38, ZRKS 12.56, Shiba na, ZGJI 575, KZS #1123

12.50 士爲知己者死 *Shi wa onore o shiru mono no tame ni shishi,*
女爲愛己者容 *Nyo wa onore o ai suru mono no tame ni katachizukuru.*

A warrior dies for one who knows him,
A woman dresses for one who loves her.

See ⌜Yü Jang⌝.

ZGS 12.39, Shiba na

12.51 突出釋迦鼻孔 *Shaka no bikū o tosshutsu shi,*
豁開達磨眼睛 *Daruma no ganzei o kakkai su.*

Make Śākyamuni flare his nostrils,
And make ⌜Bodhidharma⌝ bug out his eyes.

ZGS 12.40, ZRKS 12.151, Shiba na, ZGJI 575

12.52 從來把本修行 *Jūrai hahon no shugyō,*
不敢棄捐因果 *Aete inga o kien sezu.*

From the beginning the discipline of grasping the fundamental
Has never presumed to neglect cause and effect.

ZGS 12.41, ZRKS 12.50, Shiba na, ZGJI 576

12.53 商鞅立法車轢 *Shōō no rippō wa shareki shi,*
吳起刻剝肢解 *Goki no kokuhaku wa shikai su.*

⌜Shang Yang⌝ put into law "dragging by chariots,"
⌜Wu Ch'i's⌝ tyranny was "dismembering the body."

ZGS 12.42: *kuruma reki* instead of *shareki.*

ZGS 12.42, Shiba na

12.54 性自了了常知 *Sei onozukara ryō-ryō to shite tsune ni shiru,*
何須諸佛開示 *Nanzo shobutsu no kaishi o mochiin.*

Your nature of itself has always been clearly known to you.
Why do you need the instruction of the buddhas?

ZGS 12.43, ZRKS 12.159, Shiba na, ZGJI 577

12.55 小麥化成蝴蝶 *Shōbaku wa keshite kochō to nari,*
蚯蚓化成百合 *Kyūin keshite yuri to naru.*

Wheat changes and turns into butterflies,
Worms change and become lilies.

ZGS 12.44, Shiba na, ZGJI 576

12.56 淨躶躶絕承當 *Jō ra-ra jōtō o zesshi,*
赤洒洒沒窠臼 *Shaku sha-sha kakyū o bossu.*

Totally clean—all connections cut;
Completely bare—old habits cast away.

ZGS 12.45: *kakyū nashi* instead of *kakyū o bossu.*

ZGS 12.45, ZRKS 12.54, Shiba 307, ZGJI 576, KZS #1117, SRZGK §1273 (承當), SRZGK §1486 (窠臼).

12.57 處處眞處處眞 *Sho-sho shin, sho-sho shin,*
塵塵盡本來人 *Jin-jin kotogotoku honraijin.*

Everywhere real, everywhere real;
This ⌜dust⌝, that dust, are all original self.

ZGS na, ZRKS 12.122, Shiba 306, ZGJI 576, KZS #1118

12.58 諸天捧花無路 *Shoten hana o sasaguru ni michi naku,*
外道潛覷不見 *Gedō mo hisoka ni miru ni miezu.*

The devas find no path on which to strew flowers;
The heretics, secretly spying, find nothing to see.

Heki 16 Intro, 97 Verse Comm. ZGJI 576 (variant): 外道潛窺無門, "The heretics have no gate through which to spy."

ZGS 12.46, ZRKS 12.52, Shiba na, ZGJI 576, ZD #122

12.59 心空無相而 *Shinkū musō ni shite,*
其妙用通貫十方 *Sono myōyū jippō ni tsūkan su.*

Mind empty and without signs,
Its wondrous workings penetrate the ⌜ten directions⌝.

ZGS 12.47, Shiba na

12.60 震之東兌之西 *Shin no higashi, da no nishi,*
離之南坎之北 *Ri no minami, kan no kita.*

Chen is east, Tui is west,
Li is south, K'an is north.

See ⌜Eight trigrams⌝.

ZGS 12.48, ZRKS 12.111, Shiba na, ZGJI 577

12.61 進則墮坑落壍 *Susumu toki wa kyō ni ochi zen ni otsu,*
退則猛虎啣脚 *Shirizoku toki wa mōko ashi o fukumu.*

Going forward, he tripped and fell into a hole;
Going backwards, a fierce tiger bit his leg.

Heki 56 Verse *agyo.*

ZGS 12.49, ZRKS 12.33, Shiba na, ZGJT 230, KZS #1107

12.62 雖有截流之機 *Setsuru no ⌜ki⌝ ari to iedomo,*
且無隨波之意 *Shibaraku zuiha no i nashi.*

Though he has the mind that cuts off the stream,
He has no will to ride the waves.

ZGS na, ZRKS 12.117, Shiba 308, ZGJI 577

12 字

12.63 坐斷千聖路頭 *Senshō no rotō o zadan shi,*
打破群魔境界 *Gumma no kyōgai o taha su.*

He shuts down the path of the thousand wise men
And smashes the realm of the demon swarm.

ZGS 12.50, ZRKS 12.108, Shiba 304, ZGJI 577, KZS #1098

12.64 戰戰兢兢 *Sen-sen kyō-kyō to shite,*
如臨深淵 *Shin'en ni nozomu ga gotoku,*
如履薄氷 *Hakuhyō o fumu ga gotoshi.*

Be fearful and alert,
As if peering into an abyss,
As if treading on thin ice.

Book of Songs, §196; *Analects* VIII, 3. See also 12.142 and 21⁺.27.

ZGS 12.51, Shiba 308

12.65 驚走陜府鐵牛 *Senbu no tetsugyū o kyōsō shi,*
嚇殺嘉州大象 *Kashū no daizō o kakusetsu su.*

He scares away the ⌜Iron Ox of Shen-fu⌝,
He frightens to death the ⌜giant statue of Chia-chou⌝.

Heki 38 Verse *agyo.*

ZGS 12.52, ZRKS 12.86, Shiba 302, ZGJI 523, KZS #1130

12.66 大象不遊兎徑 *Daizō wa tokei ni asobazu,*
大悟不拘小節 *Daigo wa shōsetsu ni kakawarazu.*

An elephant does not play around on rabbit runways,
Great awakening does not concern itself with trivia.

ZGS 12.53, ZRKS 12.136, Shiba 309, ZGJI 578, ZGJT 294; Yung Chia, *Song of Enlightenment*

12.67 變大地爲黄金 *Daichi o henjite ōgon to nashi,*
攪長河爲酥酪 *Chōga o kaite soraku to nasu.*

He changes the great earth into gold,
He churns the long river into refined butter.

Shiba 316: *daiji* instead of *daichi.* See ⌜Five flavors⌝.

ZGS 12.54, ZRKS 12.132, Shiba 316, ZGJI 578, ZGJT 417

12.68 唯堯則之 *Tada Gyō nomi kore ni nottoru,*
蕩蕩乎民無能名焉 *Tō-tō ko to shite tami yoku nazukuru koto nashi.*

Only ⌜Yao⌝ could match it.
It was so vast the people could find no name for it.

ZGS 12.55, Shiba na; *Analects* VIII, 19

12.69 只爲入草求人　*Tada kusa ni itte hito o motomuru ga tame ni,*
不覺通身泥水　*Tsūshin no deisui o oboezu.*

In the weeds I was so intent upon finding that person,
I did not realize my whole body was covered in mud.

ZGS 12.56, Shiba na

12.70 只此一圈攣　*Tada kono ikkenren,*
天下衲僧跳不出　*Tenka no nōsō chofushutsu.*

Just this one circle,
No monk in the world can jump out.

ZGS 12.57, Shiba na

12.71 只有受璧之心　*Tada juheki no shin atte,*
全無割城之意　*Mattaku katsujō no i nashi.*

He has only the desire to seize the jewel;
He has no intention at all of ceding the cities.

See ⌜Hsiang-ju⌝.

ZGS 12.58, ZRKS 12.57, Shiba na, ZGJI 579

12.72 只見溪回路轉　*Tada tani meguri michi tenzuru o mite,*
不知身在桃源　*Shirazu mi no tōgen ni aru koto o.*

Seeing only winding streams and twisting paths,
He is unaware he is in the ⌜peach⌝ blossom spring.

ZGS 12.59, ZRKS 12.113, Shiba 305, ZGJI 579, ZD #127

12.73 只有湛水之波　*Tada tansui no nami atte,*
且無滔天之浪　*Katsu tōten no nami nashi.*

There are only swells of deep clear water;
No breakers leap to the sky.

ZGS 12.60, ZRKS 12.123, Shiba na, ZGJI 579, ZGJT 170

12.74 縱令驊騮捉鼠　*Tatoi karyū mo nezumi o torauru toki wa,*
則不及跛猫兒　*Sunawachi hamyōji ni oyobazu.*

If the fleet horse ⌜Hua-liu⌝ were to try to catch a mouse,
It would still be no match for even a lame-legged cat.

ZGS 12.61, Shiba na

12.75 譬如北辰居其所而　*Tatoeba hokushin no sono tokoro ni ite,*
衆星拱之　*Shūsei kore ni mukau ga gotoshi.*

He is like the North Star, which remains in its place
While all other stars encircle it.

ZGS 12.62, Shiba na; *Analects* II, 1

12
字

12.76 達磨不居少室 *Daruma shōshitsu ni kyo sezu,*
六祖不住曹溪 *Rokuso sōkei ni jū sezu.*

⌜Bodhidharma⌝ did not live in ⌜Shao-shih⌝,
The ⌜Sixth Patriarch⌝ did not dwell at ⌜Ts'ao-ch'i⌝.

ZGS 12.63, ZRKS 12.88, Shiba 309, ZGJI 579

12.77 達磨不來東土 *Daruma tōdo ni kitarazu,*
二祖不往西天 *Niso seiten ni yukazu.*

⌜Bodhidharma⌝ did not come to China,
The ⌜Second Patriarch⌝ did not go to India.

ZGS 12.64, ZRKS 12.36, Shiba 310, ZGJI 579, ZGDJT 833c, ZGJT 296, KZS #1111

12.78 誰有取親喪沐浴着珠而行者 *Tare ka oya no sō o tori mokuyoku tama o tsukete yuku mono aranya.*

Who would, while in mourning for his parents, bathe, put on jewelry, and go out?

ZGS 12.65, Shiba na

12.79 丹之所藏者赤 *Tan no zō suru tokoro no mono wa akaku,*
漆之所藏者黑 *Urushi no zō suru tokoro no mono wa kuroshi.*

That in which cinnabar is stored is red,
That in which lacquer is stored is black.

ZGS 12.66, ZRKS 12.64, Shiba na

12.80 近則不離方寸 *Chikaki toki wa hōsun o hanarezu,*
遠則十萬八千 *Tōki toki wa jūman hassen.*

When near, it is not an inch away;
When far, it is 108,000 [miles] away.

ZGS 12.67, ZRKS 12.102, Shiba 302, ZGJI 580

12.81 父有迷子之訣 *Chichi ni meishi no ketsu ari,*
子有打爺之拳 *Ko ni taya no ken ari.*

The father's method is to make the child lose its way;
The child has a fist to strike its father.

ZGS 12.68, ZRKS 12.92, Shiba 316, ZGJI 580, KZS #1135

12.82 定盤之星難明 *Jōban no hoshi wa akiramegatashi,*
野狐之趣易墮 *Yako no omomuki ni wa ochiyasushi.*

It is hard to make out the graduation marks of the balance pan,
But it is easy to fall into the schemings of the ⌜wild fox⌝.

Heki 三教老人 Preface.

ZGS 12.69, ZRKS 12.8, Shiba 311, ZGJI 581, KZS #1094

12.83 趙壁本無瑕纇 *Chōheki moto karai nashi,*
相如謾誑秦王 *Shōjo midari ni shinnō o taburakasu.*

The ⌜Chao jewel⌝ was really without flaw,
Hsiang-ru audaciously fooled the King of Ch'in.

ZGS 12.70, ZRKS 12.89, Shiba 310, ZGJI 580, KZS #1131

12.84 豆種不生麻麥 *Zushu mabaku o shōsezu,*
草根不産松椿 *Sōkon shōchin o sansezu.*

Bean seeds do not grow into flax or wheat,
Roots of grass do not produce pines or camellias.

ZGS 12.71, ZRKS 12.114, Shiba na, ZGJI 581

12.85 天際日上月下 *Tensai hi nobori tsuki kudaru,*
檻前山深水寒 *Kanzen yama fukaku mizu samushi.*

At the edge of heaven, the sun rises and the ⌜moon⌝ sets;
Beyond the balustrade, the mountains are deep and the waters cold.

Heki 2 Verse.

ZGS 12.72, ZRKS 12.105, Shiba 311, ZGJI 581, ZGJT 362

12.86 遇唐虞則禮樂 *Tōgu ni au tokinba sunawachi reigaku,*
逢桀紂則干戈 *Ketchū ni au tokinba sunawachi kanka.*

When you meet ⌜Yao or Shun⌝, there is ritual and music.
When you meet ⌜Chieh or Chou⌝, there are shields and spears.

ZGS 12.73, ZRKS 12.20, Shiba na, ZGJI 582, KZS #1100

12.87 燈籠跳入露柱 *Tōro odotte rochū ni iri,*
佛殿走出山門 *Butsuden hashite sammon o izu.*

The lanterns leap into the pillars,
The Buddha Hall runs out the mountain gate.

ZGS 12.74, ZRKS 12.101, Shiba 312, ZGJI 582 (variant), KZS #1137

12.88 説盡江湖風波 *Tokitsukusu gōko no fūha,*
論量柴米貴賤 *Ronryō su saimai no kisen.*

All their talk about the scenery of the ⌜river and the lake⌝
Was about comparing the cost of food and rice.

ZGS 12.75, Shiba na, ZGJI 572

12.89 以德勝人者昌 *Toku o motte hito ni masaru mono wa sakae,*
以力勝人者亡 *Chikara o motte hito ni masaru mono wa horobu.*

One who excels others in virtue will prosper,
One who excels others in strength will die away.

ZGS 12.76, ZRKS 12.104, Shiba 297, ZGJI 582

12.90 毒蛇鼻頭揩痒 *Dokuja bitō ni kayugari o kaki,*
饑鷹爪下奪肉 *Kiyō sōka ni niku o ubau.*

Scratch the itch on the nose of the poisonous snake,
Pry meat from the talons of the hungry hawk.

See also 12.132, 12.133.

ZGS 12.77, ZRKS 12.91, Shiba na, ZGJI 582

12.91 南瞻部洲展鉢 *Nan'enbushū ni hatsu o nobe,*
西瞿耶尼喫飯 *Saikuyani ni han o kissu.*

In the south continent lay out your bowls,
And in the west continent eat your meal.

See「Sumeru」.

ZGS 12.78, ZRKS 12.71, Shiba 312, ZGJI 582

12.92 拈御膩脂帽子 *Nishi mōsu o nenkyaku shi,*
脱御鶻臭布衫 *Kosshū fusan o dakkyaku su.*

He has taken off his greasy hat
And discarded his sweat-smelling underwear.

Heki 12 Verse Comm. This verse sometimes appears with 郤 instead of 御, but this is a mistake.

ZGS 12.79, ZRKS 12.23, Shiba na, ZGJI 582, ZGJT 371, KZS #1103

12.93 日月雖有盛明 *Nichigetsu jōmyō ari to iedomo,*
不照覆盆之下 *Fukubon no shita o terasazu.*

Though sun and「moon」are radiant and bright
They cannot reach under an inverted tray.

Variant: *jitsugetsu* instead of *nichigetsu.*

ZGS 12.80, ZRKS 12.67, Shiba na, ZGJI 575, KZS #1121

12.94 日月照臨不到 *Nichigetsu mo shōrin shi itarazu,*
天地蓋覆不盡 *Tenchi mo gaifuku shi tsukusazu.*

Sun and「moon」cannot illuminate it completely,
Heaven and earth cannot cover it entirely.

Variant: *jitsugetsu* instead of *nichigetsu.*

ZGS 12.81, ZRKS 12.22, Shiba 312, ZGJI 575, KZS #1102, ZD #115

12.95 入息不居陰界 *Nissoku onkai ni kyo sezu,*
出息不渉萬緣 *Shussoku ban'en ni watarazu.*

Breathing in, he does not linger in the world of the「*skandha*」;
Breathing out, he is not entangled in the ten thousand conditions.

Shiba 313: *Nissoku onkai ni orazu. Serenity* 3 Main Case.

ZGS 12.82, ZRKS 12.49, Shiba 313, ZGJI 583, ZGJT 361, ZD #120

12.96 截斷人天路頭　*Ninden no rotō o setsudan shite,*
打開五無間獄　*Gomugengoku o takai su.*

He cuts off the pathways to heaven and humans,
And smashes open the ⌜five hells⌝.

ZGS 12.83, ZRKS 12.115, Shiba 308, ZGJI 583

12.97 人人領略釋迦　*Nin-nin shaka o ryōryaku shi,*
箇箇平欺達磨　*Ko-ko daruma o heiki su.*

Each person awakens Śākyamuni,
Each thing deceives ⌜Bodhidharma⌝.

ZRKS 12.77: *heigo su* instead of *heiki su.*

ZGS na, ZRKS 12.77, Shiba 307, ZGJI 583, KZS #1127

12.98 拈華曉稱迦葉　*Nenge no akatsuki kashō to shōshi,*
傳衣夜喚盧能　*Den'e no yoru ronō to yobu.*

The dawn when the flower was raised, he was called ⌜Kāśyapa⌝;
The night when the robe was transmitted, he was called ⌜Lu-neng⌝.

ZGS 12.84, ZRKS 12.74, Shiba 313, ZGJI 583, KZS #1125

12.99 拈起衲僧鼻孔　*Nōsō no bikū o nenki shite,*
穿開佛祖心肝　*Busso no shinkan o senkai su.*

He twists the nose of the ⌜patch-robed monk⌝
And rips out the guts of the buddhas and ancestors.

ZGS na, ZRKS 12.131, Shiba 314, ZGJI 583

12.100 展則彌綸法界　*Noburu toki wa hokkai ni mirin shi,*
收則絲髮不立　*Osamuru toki wa shihatsu mo rissezu.*

Expanded, it fills the entire Dharma universe;
Contracted, there's no room for even a single hair to stand.

Rinzai-roku §23. Variant: 收則毫髮不存, *Osamuru toki wa gōhatsu mo sonsezu.*

ZGS 12.85, ZRKS 12.34, Shiba 311, ZGJI 583, ZGJT 328, KZS #1108

12.101 腦門上播紅旗　*Nōmonjō ni kōki o age,*
耳背後輪雙劍　*Ni haigo ni sōken o mawasu.*

Above his head, he raises the red flag;
And behind his ears, he whirls two ⌜swords⌝.

Heki 37 Intro. ZGJI 583: *kōki o kakage.*

ZGS na, ZRKS 12.85, Shiba 314, ZGJI 583, ZGJT 373

12.102 把住黄絹幼婦　*Hajū suru toki wa kōken yōfu,*
放行外孫韲臼　*Hōgyō suru toki wa gaison saikyū.*

Take in and you have "Yellow silk, infant lady";
Release and you have "Outside grandchild, pickling mortar."

12
字

This verse is a cryptogram which, when deciphered, means, "Take in and you have absolute mystery 絕妙, Release and you have fine discourse 好辭." See explanation at 8.134.

ZGS na, ZRKS 12.40, Shiba 314, ZGJI 583

12.103 破布囊裡眞珠 *Hafu nōri no shinju,*
識者方知是寶 *Shiru mono wa masa ni shiru kore takara naru koto o.*

The pearl in the torn rag—
Only one who knows sees a treasure.

ZGS 12.86, ZRKS 12.83, Shiba 315, ZGJI 584, KZS #1126

12.104 列萬象於目前 *Banshō o mokuzen ni tsurane,*
裁群機於量外 *Gun⌜ki⌝ o ryōgai ni saisu.*

Everything is arrayed before one's very eyes,
All thought is cut off in the realm beyond measure.

ZGS na, ZRKS 12.5, Shiba 320, ZGJI 584, KZS #1129

12.105 爲萬物之根源 *Banbutsu no kongen to nari,*
作天地之太祖 *Tenchi no taiso to naru.*

It is the source of the ⌜ten thousand things⌝,
It is the great ancestor of heaven and earth.

ZGS 12.87, ZRKS 12.53, Shiba 297, KZS #1115

12.106 乞火不若取燧 *Hi o kou wa sui o toru ni shikazu,*
寄水不若鑿井 *Mizu ni yoru wa sei o ugatsu ni shikazu.*

If you want fire, better use a flint drill,
If you need water, best dig a well.

ZGS 12.88, Shiba na, ZGJI 584

12.107 求美則不得美 *Bi o motomureba sunawachi bi o ezu,*
不求美則美矣 *Bi o motomezareba sunawachi bi nari.*

If you seek beauty, you will not get it;
If you do not seek beauty, you will get it.

Shiba 301: *Bi o motomuru toki wa sunawachi bi o ezu, Bi o motomezaru toki wa sunawachi bi nari.*

ZGS 12.89, Shiba 301, ZGJI 584

12.108 有斐君子 *Hitaru kunshi ari,*
如切如磋 *Sessuru ga gotoku sasuru ga gotoku,*
如琢如磨 *Takusuru ga gotoku masuru ga gotoshi.*

For a person of superior refinement
It is like cutting and grinding,
Like filing and polishing.

Book of Songs, §55; *Analects* 1, 15. See ⌜*Sessa takuma*⌝.

ZGS 12.90, Shiba na

12.109 等是普同供養 *Hitoshiku kore fudō kuyō,*
誰知飯裏有沙 *Tare ka shiran hanri ni isago aru koto o.*

This is a donated meal for everyone alike.
But who knows, there may be stones in the rice.

ZGS 12.91, ZRKS 12.129, Shiba na, ZGJI 585

12.110 一願皇帝萬歳 *Hitotsu ni wa kōtei banzai to negai,*
二願群臣千秋 *Futatsu ni wa gunshin senshū to negau.*

First, we pray for 10,000 years for the emperor;
Second, we pray for 1,000 autumns for his many officials.

ZGS 12.92, ZRKS 12.65, Shiba na

12.111 逢人且説三分 *Hito ni aute wa katsu sanbu o toke,*
未可全施一片 *Imada mattaku ippen o hodokosu bekarazu.*

Explain only thirty percent to another person;
Do not give away everything at once.

MMK 33. Variant: *Hito ni aute wa shibaraku sanbun o toke* (Hirata 1969, 124).

ZGS 12.93, ZRKS 12.147, Shiba 317, ZGJI 585, ZGDJT 1045c, ZGJT 425 (variant)

12.112 眉毛觸碎須彌 *Bimō shumi o sokusai shi,*
鼻孔飲乾大海 *Bikū daikai o onken su.*

His eyebrows smash to pieces Mount ⌜Sumeru⌝,
His nostrils suck dry the great ocean.

ZGS 12.94, ZRKS 12.94, Shiba na, ZGJI 584

12.113 坐斷毘盧頂顛 *Biru chōnei o zadan shite,*
曾不見有佛祖 *Katsute busso aru koto o mizu.*

Having cut off completely ⌜Vairocana's⌝ head,
I do not see any buddhas or ancestors.

ZGS 12.95, ZRKS 12.27, Shiba na, ZGJI 584, ZGJT 153, KZS #1,099, ZD #125

12.114 欲識佛性義理 *Busshō no giri o shiran to hosseba,*
當觀時節因緣 *Masa ni jisetsu innen o kan zubeshi.*

To understand the principle of Buddha-nature,
Contemplate [the nature of] time and causality.

Heki 21 Main Case Comm., 48 Main Case Comm. See also 11.13.

ZGS 12.96, ZRKS 12.116, Shiba 319, ZGJI 586, ZGJT 464, KZS #1090, ZD #128

12.115 不萠枝上花開 *Fubō shijō ni hana hiraki,*
無影樹頭鳳舞 *Muyō jutō ni hō mau.*

On the branches without buds, flowers bloom;
On the tree without shadow, the phoenix dances.

ZGS 12.97, ZRKS 12.12, Shiba 315, ZGJI 585

12.116 父母所生鼻孔 *Fubo shosei no bikū,*
卻在別人手裏 *Kaette betsujin no shuri ni ari.*

Your own nostrils received at birth from your parents
Are in someone else's hands.

Heki 47 Main Case Comm., 53 Main Case *agyo.*

ZGS na, ZRKS 12.42, Shiba 316, ZGJI 586, ZGJT 403

12.117 糞箕掃帚拈起 *Funki sōsō nenki shite,*
便行誰分先後 *Sunawachi yukeba tare ka sengo o wakatan.*

Pick up the shit-basket and broom and then leave at once.
Who can tell who was first and who later?

ZGS 12.98, Shiba na

12.118 蔽芾甘棠 *Heihitaru kantō,*
勿剪勿伐 *Kiru koto nakare utsu koto nakare,*
召伯所茇 *Shōhaku no yadorishi nari.*

Young and tender is this sweet pear tree.
Do not lop it or knock it,
For the Lord of Shao took shelter under it.

Book of Songs §16. Trans. from WALEY 1937A, 135.

ZGS 12.99, Shiba na

12.119 放行光蔽五天 *Hōgyō sureba hikari goten o ōi,*
把住風馳萬里 *Hajū sureba kaze banri o hasu.*

Release, and light floods the Five Heavens;
Grasp, and the breeze crosses 10,000 miles.

ZGS 12.100 has 鳳 "phoenix" instead of 風 "breeze."

ZGS 12.100, ZRKS 12.138, Shiba 317, ZGJI 586

12.120 換北斗作南辰 *Hokutō o kaete nanshin to nashi,*
轉金烏爲玉兎 *Kin'u o tenjite gyokuto to nasu.*

He changes the ⌜North Star⌝ into the ⌜southern dragon⌝,
He turns the ⌜golden crow⌝ into the ⌜jade rabbit⌝.

ZGS 12.101 has 喚 "call" instead of 換 "change."

ZGS 12.101, ZRKS 12.78, Shiba 300, ZGJI 587

12.121 非法無以談空 *Hō ni arazu shite motte kū o danzuru koto naku,*
非會無以説法 *E ni arazu shite motte hō o toku koto nashi.*

Without the Dharma one cannot talk about emptiness,
Without understanding one cannot expound the Dharma.

ZGS 12.102, ZRKS 12.13, Shiba na, ZGJI 586

12.122 法法本自圓成 *Hō-hō moto onozukara enjō,*
念念悉皆具足 *Nen-nen kotogotoku mina gusoku su.*

Each and every thing, originally, is perfectly realized;
Each and every moment of thought is thus endowed.

ZGS na, ZRKS 12.150, Shiba 317, ZGJI 586

12.123 將謂龍頭蛇尾 *Masa ni ieri ryūtō dabinaru koto o,*
誰知蛇尾龍頭 *Tare ka shiran dabi ryōtō.*

Yes, you can say that this is a dragon's head with a snake's tail;
But who realizes that it is a snake's tail with a dragon's head?

ZGS 12.103, Shiba na

12.124 眼不見玄黃色 *Manako genkō no iro o mizu,*
耳不聞絲竹聲 *Mimi shichiku no koe o kikazu.*

Eyes do not see the colors of dark and gold,
Ears do not hear the sounds of strings and flutes.

ZGS 12.104, ZRKS 12.28, Shiba 300

12.125 吟哦滿目青山 *Manmoku no seizan o ginga shi,*
指點門前湖水 *Monzen no kosui o shiten su.*

I sing of the blue mountains that fill my eyes
And point to the lake waters before my gates.

ZGS na, ZRKS 12.46, Shiba 303, ZGJI 587

12.126 水至清則無魚 *Mizu itatte kiyoki toki wa uo naku,*
人至察則無徒 *Hito itatte akiraka naru toki wa to nashi.*

Water that is completely pure has no fish;
A person who is totally open has no companions.

Shiba 307: *Mizu itatte sumu toki wa uo naku, Hito itatte sassuru toki wa to nashi.* ZGS 12.105: 到 instead of 至.

ZGS 12.105, Shiba 307, ZGJI 588

12.127 妙高峯頂行船 *Myōkōhōchō ni fune o yari,*
揚子江上走馬 *Yōsukōjō ni uma o washirasu.*

Send a boat up the High Wondrous Peak,
Run a horse on the Yangtze River.

For "High Wondrous Peak," see ⸢Sumeru⸣.

ZGS 12.106, Shiba 318

12.128 彌勒不入樓閣 *Miroku rōkaku ni irazu,*
善財不須彈指 *Zenzai danshi o mochiizu.*

⌜Maitreya⌝ has not entered the many-storeyed tower,
So ⌜Sudhana⌝ is not awaiting the snap of his fingers.

ZGS 12.107, ZRKS 12.18, Shiba 317, ZGJI 587, ZGJT 439, KZS #1093

12.129 寧可熱鐵纏身 *Mushiro nettetsu o mi ni matou beku mo,*
不受信心人衣 *Shinjin no hito no koromo o ukezu.*

I would rather have hot metal wrapped around my body
Than put on the robe of one of those believers.

ZGS na, ZRKS 12.26, Shiba 313, ZGJI 588, ZGJT 367

12.130 面上夾竹桃花 *Menjō wa kyōchiku tōka,*
肚裏參天荊棘 *Zuri wa santen no keikyoku.*

On the surface he is like an oleander blossom;
But inside, his guts are like a sky-scraping tree of thorns.

ZGS 12.108, ZRKS 12.93, Shiba 318, ZGJI 589, ZGJT 447, KZS #1136

12.131 猛虎頷下金鈴 *Mōko ganka no kinrei,*
蒼龍窟裏明珠 *Sōryū kutsuri no meishu.*

The golden bell under the jaw of the fierce tiger,
The bright jewel in the cave of the blue dragon.

ZGS 12.109, ZRKS 12.87, Shiba 318, ZGJI 589

12.132 猛虎口中奪鹿 *Mōko kuchū ni shika o ubai,*
饑鷹爪下分兎 *Kiyō sōka ni to o wakatsu.*

Seize the deer from the mouth of the fierce tiger,
Pry the rabbit from the talons of the hungry hawk.

Shiba 318: *mōko kōchū* instead of *mōko kuchū*; *roku* instead of *shika*. See also 12.90.

ZGS 12.110, ZRKS 12.90, Shiba 318, ZGJI 589, KZS #1133

12.133 猛虎口裏横身 *Mōko kuri ni mi o yokotae,*
毒蛇頭上揩痒 *Dokuja zujō ni kayugari o kaku.*

Lie down between the jaws of the tiger,
Scratch the itch on the poison snake's head.

Shiba 319: *mōko kōri* instead of *mōko kuri*. See also 12.90.

ZGS 12.111, ZRKS 12.100, Shiba 319, ZGJI 589, KZS #1128

12.134 木札羹鐵釘飯 *Mokusakkō tetteihan,*
使人吞吐不下 *Hito o shite donto fuge narashimu.*

Wood-chip stew, iron-nail rice—
People can't swallow them or spit them out.

See also 4.461.

ZGS 12.112, Shiba 319, ZGJI 316

12.135 若是本分衲僧　*Moshi kore honbun no nōsō naraba,*
不喫這般茶飯　*Shahan no sahan o kissezu.*

If this were a ⌜patch-robed monk⌝ of the ⌜fundamental⌝,
He would not eat such food as this.

Heki 74 Verse *agyo.*

ZGS 12.113, ZRKS 12.120, Shiba 306, ZGJI 589

12.136 若非獅子之兒　*Moshi shishi no ji ni arazumba,*
野干漫爲開口　*Yakan midari ni kuchi o hiraku koto o nasan.*

If he were not a lion's child,
The wild ones would be yapping away freely.

ZGS 12.114, ZRKS 12.37, Shiba na, ZGJI 589

12.137 文殊不識寒山　*Monju kanzan o shirazu,*
普賢不識拾得　*Fugen jittoku o shirazu.*

⌜Mañjuśrī⌝ does not know ⌜Han-shan⌝,
⌜Samantabhadra⌝ does not know ⌜Shih-te⌝.

ZGS 12.115, ZRKS 12.125, Shiba 316, ZGJI 589

12.138 不假文殊神通　*Monju no jintsū o karazu,*
休要罔明彈指　*Mōmyō no danshi o yōsuru koto o yameyo.*

Do not borrow ⌜Mañjuśrī's⌝ supernatural powers,
And stop using Wang-ming's snap of the fingers.

See MMK 42.

ZGS 12.116, ZRKS 12.44, Shiba na, ZGJI 590

12.139 登山則戮虎豹　*Yama ni nobotte sunawachi kohyō o kiri,*
入水則斬蛟龍　*Mizu ni itte wa sunawachi kōryō o kiru.*

To climb mountains means killing tigers and leopards,
To enter the river means slaying snakes and dragons.

Heki, 三教老人 Preface.

ZGS 12.117, ZRKS 12.9, Shiba 311, ZGJI 590, KZS #1096

12.140 游宴中有鴆毒　*Yūen no naka ni chindoku ari,*
談笑中有戈矛　*Danshō no naka ni kabō ari.*

In the feast there is ⌜poisoned wine⌝,
In the laughing conversation there are spears.

ZGS 12.118, Shiba na, ZGJI 590

12.141 厭浥行露 *Yōyūtaru michi no tsuyu,*
豈不夙夜 *Ani shukuya ni sezaranya,*
謂行多露 *Omowaku michi ni tsuyu ōkaran.*

The paths are drenched in dew.
True, I said, "Early in the night,"
But I fear to walk in so much dew.

Book of Songs §17. Trans. from WALEY 1937A, 65.

ZGS 12.119, Shiba na

12.142 啓予手啓予足 *Yo ga te o hirake yo ga ashi o hirake,*
今而後吾知免 *Ima ni shite nochi ware manukaruru koto o shiru.*

Uncover my hands, uncover my feet.
Now and hereafter, I know I am saved.

Analects VIII, 3.

ZGS 12.120, Shiba na

12.143 喜則濫賞無功 *Yorokobu toki wa midari ni kō naki o shōshi,*
怒則濫殺無罪 *Ikaru toki wa midari ni zai naki o korosu.*

When feeling good, one brashly rewards even the unworthy;
When angry, one blindly sentences the innocent to death.

ZGS 12.121, Shiba na, ZGJI 590

12.144 六王畢四海一 *Rikuō owatte shikai hitotsu nari,*
蜀山兀阿房出 *Shokuzan kotsu to shite abō o izu.*

When the six kings were destroyed, the world was one.
The Szechwan mountains were laid bare and the ⌜O-pang Palace⌝ emerged.

From Tu Mu 杜牧, "O-pang kung-fu" 阿房宮賦. ZGJI 685 (variant): 六王畢後四海一蜀山兀而阿房秀.

ZGS 12.122, Shiba na, ZGJI 685

12.145 利劍斬處無痕 *Riken kiru tokoro ato naku,*
殺活咸歸劍下 *Sekkatsu kotogotoku kenka ni kisu.*

The sharp ⌜sword⌝ cuts without leaving a scar.
Life and death depend entirely on this sword.

ZGS 12.123, ZRKS 12.2, Shiba na, ZGJI 590

12.146 靈山河沙聖衆 *Ryōzen gasha no shōju,*
黄梅七百高僧 *Ōbai nanahyaku no kōsō.*

On ⌜Vulture Peak⌝, holy ones numerous as the sands of the Ganges;
On ⌜Yellow Plum Mountain⌝, seven hundred high priests.

ZGS 12.124, ZRKS 12.66, Shiba na, ZGJI 591, KZS #1124

12.147 兩刄倚天長劍 *Ryōjin ten ni yoru chōken,*
一團印鐵鑄就 *Ichidan intetsu inasu.*

Two ⌜swords⌝, like one long sword against the sky,
Are fused into a single mass of wrought iron.

ZGS na, ZRKS 12.143, Shiba 320, ZGJI 591

12.148 離婁不辨正色 *Rirō shōshiki o benzezu,*
師曠豈識玄絲 *Shikō ani genshi o shiran ya.*

If ⌜Li Lou⌝ cannot discern the true shape,
How then can ⌜Shih K'uang⌝ distinguish the subtle tune?

Heki 88 Verse. Shiba 320: *riru* instead of *rirō*.

ZGS 12.125, ZRKS 12.84, Shiba 320, KZS #1138, ZD #123

12.149 臨濟喝得口破 *Rinzai kasshiete kuchi yabure,*
德山棒得手穿 *Tokusan bōshiete te ugatsu.*

Rinzai could give a shout that would tear his mouth,
Tokusan could give a whack with his stick that would break his hand.

See ⌜Stick and shout⌝.

ZGS 12.126, ZRKS 12.47, Shiba na, ZGJI 591

12.150 出爐鞴而放光 *Rohai o idete hikari o hanachi,*
入鉗鎚而成器 *Kantsui ni itte ki to naru.*

Coming out of the ⌜forge⌝, it glows bright;
And going under the ⌜tongs and hammer⌝, it turns into a vessel.

ZGS 12.127, ZRKS 12.103, Shiba na, ZGJI 591

12.151 我心憂傷念昔 *Waga kokoro yūshō mukashi o omou,*
先人明發不寐 *Sennin no mei hasshite inerarezu.*

With a sad and still hurting heart, I thought about those days.
Because of that person from long ago, all night long I did not sleep.

ZGS 12.128, Shiba na

12.152 雖與我同條生 *Ware to dōjō ni shōzu to iedomo,*
不與我同條死 *Ware to dōjō ni shisezu.*

Though we were born of the same lineage,
We do not die of the same lineage.

Heki 15 Verse Comm., 51 Main Case.

ZGS na, ZRKS 12.24, Shiba 308, ZGJI 591, ZGJT 239, ZD #116.

Thirteen-Character Phrases

13.1 發憤忘食 *Ikidori o hasshite shoku o wasure,*
樂以忘憂 *Tanoshimi o motte urei o wasure,*
不知老將至 *Oi no masa ni itaran to suru o shirazu.*

A person so intent that he forgets to eat,
So happy that he forgets his worries,
Unaware that he is getting old.

ZGS 13.1; *Analects* VII, 18

13.2 有佛處住不得 *Ubutsu no tokoro jū suru koto o ezare,*
無佛處急須走過 *Mubutsu no tokoro kyū ni subekaraku sōka subeshi.*

Don't remain where the Buddha is,
And run quickly past where the Buddha isn't.

Heki 95 Intro. (variant): 有佛處不得住無佛處急走過.

ZGS 13.2, ZGJI 569

13.3 行雲流水墜葉飛花 *Kōun ryūsui tsuiyō hika,*
爲君擧揚久 *Kimi ga tame ni koyō suru koto hisashi.*

Drifting clouds and flowing water, falling leaves and flying petals,
Have been doing it just for you for a long long time.

ZGS 13.3, ZGJI 592

13.4 胡王好音而 *Koō on o konomi,*
秦穆公以女樂誘之 *Shin no bokkō nyogaku o motte kore o sasou.*

The barbarian king had a taste for music,
Duke Mu of the Ch'in lured him with women and song.

ZGS 13.4

13.5 不動聲色而 *Shōshiki ni dōzezu shite,*
措天下於泰山之安 *Tenka o taisan no yasuki ni oku.*

Set the world into the stillness of Mount T'ai,
Unmoved by sight or sound.

ZGS 13.5

13.6 水碓三千餘口 *Suitai sanzen'yo ku,*
他珍寶貨賄稱之 *Ta no chinpō kawai kore ni kanau.*

A watermill grindstone with more than 3,000 scratches
Is a match for your rare jewels and valuable possessions.

ZGS 13.6

13.7 聖人不凝滯於物而 *Seijin wa mono ni gyōtai sezu shite,*
能與世推移 *Yoku yo to tomo ni suii su.*

The sage is not stuck on things,
But moves skillfully with the world.

ZGS 13.7

13.8 父召不用諾 *Chichi shō seba daku o mochiizu,*
君命召不俟駕行矣 *Kimi meijite shō seba ga o matazu shite yuku.*

When your father calls, you do not [just] reply, "Yes."
When your lord summons, you go without waiting for a carriage.

See also 12.32.

ZGS 13.8, ZGJI 593

13.9 鄭州梨青州棗 *Teishū no nashi, seishū no sō,*
萬物無過出處好 *Banbutsu wa shussho no yoki ni sugitaru wa nashi.*

Like the pears of Cheng and the ⌜jujubes⌝ of Ch'ing,
All things are unsurpassed in their place of origin.

ZGS 13.9

13.10 人性上不可添一物 *Hito no shō no ue ni wa ichimotsu o sou bekarazu,*
若有須吹滅 *Moshi araba subekaraku suimetsu subeshi.*

Do not add even one thing to a person's nature;
If there is something, then you must blow it off.

ZGS 13.10

13.11 亂者治之本 *Ran wa chi no moto.*
亂極則治 *Ran kiwamareba sunawachi osamaru.*
治極則亂 *Chi kiwamareba sunawachi midaru.*

Chaos is the basis of order.
Chaos at its limit is order.
Order at its limit is chaos.

ZGS 13.11

13.12 我這裡一種亦不要 *Waga shari isshu mo mata yō sezu,*
況二種三種 *Iwanya nishu, sanshu o ya.*

I do not need even one thing,
Much less two or three.

ZGS 13.12

Fourteen-Character Verses

14.1 相逢相見呵呵笑　*Aiōte aimite ka-ka to shite warai,*
屈指擡頭月半天　*Yubi o kusshi kōbe o motagureba tsuki hanten.*

We meet and recognize each other laughing, "Ha ha!"
A rare moment to raise our faces to the ⌜moon⌝ above!

屈指 *yubi o kusshi* literally means "bend the fingers," as is done in counting. It implies a very small number, and by extension, something rare or unusual (HYDCD 4.30).

ZGS 14.1, ZGJI 595, ZRKS 14.388, HYDCD 4.30

14.2 相送當門有脩竹　*Aiokutte mon ni atareba shūchiku ari,*
爲君葉葉起淸風　*Kimi ga tame ni yō-yō seifū o okosu.*

As I escort you to the gate, there are tall bamboo.
Just for you, their leaves are raising a pure wind.

ZGS 14.2, ZGJI 595, ZRKS 14.394, Shiba 370

14.3 靑出於藍靑於藍　*Ao wa ai yori idete ai yori mo aoshi,*
冰生於水寒於水　*Kōri wa mizu yori shōjite mizu yori mo samushi.*

The blue which comes from indigo is bluer than indigo,
The ice made from water is colder than the water.

Shiba 367: *Kōri wa mizu yori shōjite mizu yori mo suzushi.*

KZS #1212, ZGS 14.3, ZGJT 245, ZGJI 640, ZRKS 14.299, Shiba 367

14.4 丫鬟子女畫蛾眉　*Akan no shijo gabi o egaki,*
鸞鏡臺上話似癡　*Rankyōdaijō hanashi chi ni nitari.*

Young maiden, hair done up, paints her arched ⌜eyebrows⌝,
And to the phoenix mirror on its stand, prattles away like a fool.➛

ZGS 14.4, ZGJT 3(丫), Shiba na.

14.5 自說玉顏難比並　*Onozukara toku gyokugan hihei shigatashi to,*
卻來架上著羅衣　*Kaette kajō ni kitatte rae o tsuku.*

➛She says to herself, "My beautiful face is hard to match."
Then coming to the clothes rack, she puts on a robe of sheer silk.

ZGS 14.5, Shiba na

14.6 晨搖玉佩趨金殿　*Ashita ni gyokuhai o yurugashite kinden ni hashiri,*
夕奉天書拜瑣闈　*Yūbe ni tensho o hōjite sai o hai su.*

In the mornings, his jade tassels swinging, he hurries to the Golden Palace.
In the evenings, having received imperial edicts, he bows out by the blue gate.

ZGS 14.6, Shiba na, TSSSTS 48

14.7 朝辭白帝彩雲間 *Ashita ni ji su hakutei saiun no kan,*
千里江陵一日還 *Senri no kōryō ichi nichi ni kaeru.*

In the morning I left White King City in many-colored clouds
And returned a thousand miles to Chiang-ling in a day.➛

White King City is in Szechuan, and Chiang Ling several hundred miles away in Hubei Province.

ZGS 14.7, Shiba na, TSSSTS 74

14.8 兩岸猿聲啼不住 *Ryōgan no ensei naite todomarazu,*
輕舟已過萬重山 *Keishū sude ni sugu banjū no yama.*

➛On both banks monkeys shrieked without cease,
But my leaf boat's already shot past those endless ranks of mountains.

ZGS 14.8, Shiba 399

14.9 雨散雲收山嶽露 *Ame sanshi kumo osamatte sangaku arawaru,*
珊瑚枝上掛金鉤 *Sango shijō kinku o kaku.*

Rains pass, the clouds recede, and mountains appear.
In the branches, glistening like coral, hangs a golden crescent.

ZGS 14.9, Shiba na

14.10 雨過雲凝曉半開 *Ame sugi kumo kotte akatsuki nakaba hiraku,*
數峯如畫碧崔嵬 *Sūhō egaku ga gotoku heki saikai.*

Rains pass, clouds recede, half breaks the dawn.
So many mountains—as in a painting—with blue peaked crags.

ZGS 14.10, ZGJI 596, Shiba 327

14.11 可憐無限弄潮人 *Awaremubeshi kagiri naki ushio o rō suru no hito,*
畢竟還落潮中死 *Hikkyō kaette chōchū ni ochite shi su.*

Pity him endlessly playing with the tide,
In the end he will fall into it and die.

Heki 79 Verse.

ZGS 14.11, ZGJT 42, ZGJI 596, ZRKS 14.39, Shiba 330

14.12 透網金鱗要衝天 *Ami o tōru kinrin ten o tsukan to yōsu,*
拏雲攫霧飜然去 *Kumo o hikotsurae kiri o tsukande honnen to shite saru.*

The golden fish jumps out of the net and leaps at the sky;
Trailing a wake of mist and spray, suddenly it's gone.

ZGS 14.12, Shiba na

14.13 怪得香魂長入夢 *Ayashimietari kōkon no nagaku yume ni iru koto o,*
三生骨肉是梅花 *Sanshō no kotsuniku kore baika.*

How mysterious that fragrant spirits have long entered my dreams.
My flesh and bones from three past lives are now these plum blossoms.

ZGS 14.13, ZGJI 596, ZRKS 14.373, Shiba na

14.14 莫怪坐來頻勸酒 *Ayashimu nakare zarai shikiri ni sake o susumuru koto o,*
自從別後見君稀 *Wakarete yori nochi kimi o miru koto mare nari.*

Don't wonder that I'm sitting here serving you more wine.
After you leave, seldom will I get to see you.

ZGS 14.14, Shiba na

14.15 安禪不必須山水 *Anzen wa kanarazushimo sansui o mochiizu,*
滅卻心頭火自涼 *Shintō o mekkyaku sureba hi mo onozukara suzushi.*

Quiet meditation does not always need hills and streams.
Once mind is extinguished, even fire itself is refreshing.

Heki 43 Main Case Comm.

KZS #1172, ZGS 14.15, ZGJT 6, ZGJI 597, ZD #158, ZRKS 14.105, Shiba 321

14.16 莫言深遠無人到 *Iu koto nakare shin'on ni shite hito no itaru nashi to,*
滿目青山是故人 *Manmoku no seizan kore kojin.*

Don't say that we're so far removed that no one visits us;
The blue mountains that fill our eyes are our old friends.

ZGS na, ZGJI 679, ZRKS 14.412, Shiba 383

14.17 有意氣時添意氣 *Iki aru toki iki o sou,*
不風流處也風流 *Fūryū narazaru tokoro mata fūryū.*

You add more spirit when you have spirit,
But that's style when you have no style.

KZS #1187, ZGS na, ZGJT 31, ZGJI 597, ZD#164, ZRKS 14.201, Shiba 397

14.18 依稀似曲纔堪聽 *Iki to shite kyoku ni nite wazuka ni kiku ni taetari,*
又被風吹別調中 *Mata kaze ni betchō no uchi ni fukaru.*

It sounded so like a melody, I had to give a listen,
But then it was blown by the wind into another tune entirely.

ZGS na, ZGJT 9, ZGJI 597, ZRKS 14.190, Shiba 321, *Jōshū-roku* §478

14.19 歸家擔子兩頭脱 *Ie ni kaette tansu ryōtō dassu,*
柴自青兮火自紅 *Shiba wa onozukara aoku hi wa onozukara kurenai nari.*

Returning home, he rests both ends of his carrying pole.
Brushwood of itself is green, fire of itself is scarlet.

ZGS 14.16, ZGJI 598, ZRKS 14.375, Shiba 334, GKFGS 1.187

14.20 幾片落花隨水去 *Iku hen no rakka mizu ni shitagatte sari,*
一聲長笛出雲來 *Issei no chōteki kumo o idete kitaru.*

Petals from fallen flowers drift away on the water,
A note from the long flute floats forth from the clouds.

ZGS 14.17, ZGJI 598, ZRKS 14.243, Shiba na

14.21 聊與東風論箇事 *Isasaka tōfū to kono ji o ronzu,*
十分春色屬誰家 *Jūbun no shunshoku ta ga ie ni ka zoku su.*

I have discussed this somewhat with the east wind:
What house owns these full spring colors?

ZGS 14.18, ZGJI 598, ZRKS 14.328, Shiba na

14.22 依然百丈山頭月 *Izentari hyakujō santō no tsuki,*
五百生前汝是誰 *Gohyaku shōzen nanji wa kore ta so.*

The ⌜moon⌝ on the peak of Mount Hyakujō is the same as always.
Five hundred lifetimes ago, who were you?

ZGS 14.19, Shiba na

14.23 一毫端現寶王刹 *Ichigōtan ni hōōsetsu o genji,*
微塵裏轉大法輪 *Mijinri ni daihōrin o tenzu.*

On the tip of a hair manifest the land of the Jewel King,
In a mote of ⌜dust⌝ turn the great wheel of the Dharma.

ZGS na, ZGJI 599, ZRKS 14.308, Shiba 323

14.24 一重山盡又一重 *Ichi jū yama tsukite mata ichi jū,*
話盡山雲海月情 *Kataritsukusu san'un kaigetsu no jō.*

Beyond one range of mountains—yet another range.
We talk on and on of our impressions of mountains and clouds, sea and ⌜moon⌝.

Two close friends, after years of separation, meet unexpectedly. Their feelings for each are so strong, they cannot express them in words. Instead they talk endlessly about the scenery.

ZGS 14.153, ZGJI 600, Shiba 324

14.25 一樹春風有兩般 *Ichi jū no shunpū ryō han ari,*
南枝向暖北枝寒 *Nanshi wa dan ni mukai hokushi wa kan.*

The spring wind in a single tree has two sides.
The southern branches face its warmth, the northern branches its cold.

ZGS 14.22, ZGJI 600, ZRKS 14.376, Shiba na

14.26 一段風流玉琢成 *Ichi dan no fūryū tama migaki nasu,*
一枝留得舊風流 *Isshi todomeetari kyūfūryū.*

A degree of elegance, this polished jade;
One branch retains the ancient elegance.

ZGJI 601: The first verse is originally about a chrysanthemum, the second about a plum flower.

ZGS 14.23, ZGJI 601, ZRKS 14.150, Shiba 325

14.27 一人佛殿裏誦經 *Ichi nin wa butsudenri ni jukyō shi,*
一人明窓下把針 *Ichi nin wa meisō no shita ni hashin su.*

One chants sutras in the Buddha Hall,
The other takes needle in hand by the open window.

ZGS 14.24, Shiba na

14.28 一毛頭上重拈出 *Ichi mōtōjō kasanete nenshutsu sureba,*
憤怒那吒失卻威 *Fundo no nada i o shikkyaku su.*

If you can put one hair on top of another,
Fierce ⌜Nata⌝ will lose his power.

ZGS 14.25, ZGJI 602, ZRKS 14.404, Shiba na

14.29 一粒粟中藏世界 *Ichi ryūzokuchū ni sekai o zō shi,*
半升鐺内煮山川 *Hanshotōnai ni sansen o niru.*

Put the universe inside a grain of millet,
And inside a half-pint pot, boil up some mountains and rivers.

ZGS 14.26, ZGJT 26, ZGJI 602, ZRKS 14.344, Shiba 326

14.30 進一瓜而斬三妾 *Ikka o susumete sanshō o kiri,*
放二桃而殺三子 *Nitō o hanatte sanshi o korosu.*

He proffers one melon and slays three concubines,
He gives ⌜two peaches⌝ and kills three retainers.

ZGS 14.27, Shiba na

14.31 一火鑄成金彈子 *Ikka ni inasu kindansu,*
團圝都不費鉗鎚 *Danran subete kentsui o tsuiyasazu.*

With his single flame he forges golden pellets,
All perfectly round, without using ⌜tongs and hammer⌝.

ZGS na, ZGJI 598, ZRKS 14.217, Shiba 322

14.32 一曲兩曲無人會 *Ikkyoku ryōkyoku hito no e suru nashi,*
雨過夜塘秋水深 *Ame sugite yatō shūsui fukashi.*

One song, two songs, no one understands.
Rain passes, and in the night pools autumn waters are deep.

Heki 37 Verse.

KZS #1144, ZGS 14.20, ZGJT 25, ZGJI 599, ZRKS 14.9, Shiba 322

14.33 一口吸盡西江水 *Ikku ni kyūjin su seikō no mizu,*
洛陽牡丹新吐蘂 *Rakuyō no botan arata ni zui o haku.*

In one gulp I have swallowed all the waters of the West River.
The peonies of ⌜Lo-yang⌝ spew out their stamens anew.

Heki 42 Main Case Comm., 73 Main Case Comm.

ZGS 14.28, ZGJT 25, ZGJI 599, ZRKS 14.149, Shiba 323

14.34 一句當陽本現成 *Ikku tōyō moto genjō,*
平平仄仄仄平平 *Hyō-hyō-soku-soku, soku-hyō-hyō.*

One verse perfectly applies, it expresses the fundamental:
One-two-three-four, one-two-three.

Each Chinese character is pronounced in one of four tones. One tone, called *hyō* 平 in Japanese, is flat or level in pitch. The other three, all classed together as *soku* 平仄, are inflected, either rising or falling in pitch. The rules of Chinese poetry specify the *hyō/soku* of every character in any given line of verse. The second line should read, "flat-flat-inflected-inflected, inflected-flat-flat," but has been changed here to an English equivalent of chanted rhythm or rhyme.

ZGS na, ZGJI 599, ZRKS 14.425, Shiba 323

14.35 一句明明該萬象 *Ikku mei-mei to shite banzō o kanu,*
重陽九日菊花新 *Chōyō kyūjitsu kikka arata nari.*

This brilliant verse expresses all the ⌜ten thousand things⌝,
On the ⌜double ninth⌝ holiday the chrysanthemeum flowers are new.

KZS #1165, ZGS na, ZGJI 599, ZRKS 14.74, Shiba 323

14.36 一拳拳倒黃鶴樓 *Ikken ni kentō su kōkakurō,*
一趯趯飜鸚鵡洲 *Itteki ni tekihon su ōmushū.*

With one fist strike down the ⌜Yellow Crane Pavilion⌝,
With one kick overturn the ⌜Isle of Parrots⌝.

Heki 16 Verse Comm. Empuku-ji: *Ikken kentō su kōkakurō, Itteki tekihon su ōmushū.* ZGS 14.29: 翻 instead of 飜.

KZS #1155, ZGS 14.29, ZGJT 25, ZGJI 599, ZRKS 14.45, Shiba 323

14.37 一拶當機怒雷吼 *Issatsu ki ni atatte dorai hou,*
驚起須彌藏北斗 *Shumi o kyōki shite hokuto o kakusu.*

In one fell swoop, roaring with angry thunder,
He startles ⌜Sumeru⌝ and obliterates the ⌜North Star⌝.

Shiba 324: *Shumi o kyōki shite hokuto ni kakuru,* "He startles awake Mount Sumeru and withdraws into the North Star."

ZGS na, ZGJI 600, ZRKS 14.416, Shiba 324

14.38 一種是聲無限意 *Isshu kono koe kagiri naki no i,*
有堪聽與不堪聽 *Kiku ni taetaru to kiku ni taezaru to ari.*

The same sound has infinite meanings,
Both worthy of being heard and unbearable to hear.

ZGS 14.30, ZGJI 600, ZRKS 14.306, Shiba 324

14.39 一心只在梅花上 *Isshin tada baika no ue ni ari,*
凍損吟身也不知 *Ginshin o tōson suru mo mata shirazu.*

My mind completely absorbed in the plum blossoms.
My self enraptured and unaware of being frozen.

ZGS 14.31, Shiba na

14.40 一聲一聲又一聲 *Issei issei mata issei,*
不管人間銀髮生 *Kan sezu ningen ginpatsu no shōzuru koto o.*

My! My! Oh my!
But it's not my job to watch people's hair go white.

ZGS 14.32, ZGJI 600, ZRKS 14.356, Shiba na

14.41 一聲羌笛離亭晩 *Issei no kyōteki ritei no kure,*
君向瀟湘我向秦 *Kimi wa shoshō ni mukai ware wa shin ni mukau.*

The sound of the nomad's flute on the eve of our parting,
You are headed for ⌜Hsiao-hsiang⌝ and I am headed for Ch'in.

ZGS 14.33, ZGJI 600, Shiba na

14.42 一聲玉笛起高樓 *Issei no gyokuteki kōrō yori okoru,*
狼藉梅花滿地休 *Rōzekitaru baika manchi ni kyū su.*

A single note from the jade flute rises from the high tower.
Scattered plum blossoms carpet the ground.

ZGS 14.34, ZGJI 600, ZRKS 14.196, GKFGS 1.151, Shiba na

14.43 一聲霹靂頂門開 *Issei no hekireki chōmon hiraku,*
喚起從前自家底 *Kanki su jūzen jika no tei.*

One peal of thunder opens the crown of the head,
Calling awake one's own former self.

ZGS 14.35, ZGJI 601, ZRKS 14.140, Shiba na

14.44 一戰功成早掣身 *Issenkō nari hayaku mo mi o sei su,*
釣竿輕動五湖雲 *Chōkan keidō su goko no kumo.*

He fought a war with distinction and then quickly retired.
His fishing pole makes the clouds [reflected] in ⌜Five Lakes⌝ tremble.

ZGS 14.36, Shiba na

14.45 一箭尋常落一鵰 *Issen yonotsune itchō o otosu,*
更加一箭已相饒 *Sara ni issen o kuwaete sude ni aiyurusu.*

With one arrow you are to shoot down an eagle.
If you add another arrow, that's a free shot.

Heki 1 Main Case Comm.

ZGS 14.37, ZGJT 26, ZGJI 601, Shiba na

14.46 一陣西風吹雨過 *Ichijin no seifū ame o fuki sugu,*
夕陽總在海棠花 *Yūyō wa subete kaidō no hana ni ari.*

A gust of west wind blows the rain away,
The evening sun is all in the roses.

ZGS na, ZGJI 601, ZRKS 14.197, Shiba 325, GKFGS 1.153

14.47 一池荷葉衣無盡 *Itchi no kayō e tsukuru nashi,*
數樹松花食有餘 *Sūju no shōka shoku suru ni amari ari.*

With a pond of lotus leaves I am never out of clothes,
Pine nuts from a few trees provide more than enough to eat.➛

Verse by Daibai Hōjō (752–839) on *shōtai chōyō*. See ⌜Sacred fetus⌝.

ZGS 14.38, Shiba na

14.48 剛被世人知住處 *Shiite sejin ni jūsho o shirarete,*
又移茅舍入深居 *Mata bōsha o utsushite shinkyō ni iru.*

➛Unfortunately, my dwelling has become known by the world.
I will move my hut again deeper into seclusion.

ZGS 14.39, Shiba na

14.49 一擲千金渾是膽 *Itteki senkin subete kore tan,*
家無四壁不知貧 *Ie ni shiheki naki mo hin o shirazu.*

What guts to throw away a thousand gold cash all at once!
Not even four walls to his house, yet he knows no poverty.

ZGS 14.40, Shiba 325

14.50 一趯趯飜四大海 *Itteki ni tekihon su shidaikai,*
一拳拳倒須彌山 *Ikken ni kentō su shumisen.*

With one kick, I overturn the four great oceans,
With one blow, I knock down Mount ⌜Sumeru⌝.

ZGS 14.41, ZGJI 601, ZRKS 14.472, Shiba 325

14.51 一等共行山下路 *Ittō tomo ni yuku sanka no michi,*
眼頭各自見風烟 *Gantō kakuji ni fūen o miru.*

Together we walk the mountain path,
Each one's eyes see different wind and mist.

ZGS 14.42, ZGJI 601, ZRKS 14.142, Shiba na

14.52 一把骨頭捧去後 *Ippa no kottō kakagesatte nochi,*
不知明月落誰家 *Shirazu meigetsu ta ga ie ni ka otsu.*

After this collection of bones has been borne away,
I do not know into whose house the bright moonlight will fall.

ZGS na, ZGJT 26, ZGJI 601, ZRKS 14.102, Shiba 326

14.53 一把柳絲收不得 *Ippa no ryūshi shūfutoku,*
和風搭在玉欄干 *Kaze ni washite tōzai su gyokurankan.*

Can't catch even a handful of those willow strands
Streaming in the wind over the jade balustrade.

KZS #1171 (variant): *kashite* instead of *washite.*

KZS #1171, ZGS 14.43, ZGJI 601, ZRKS 14.95, Shiba 326

14.54 一片白雲横谷口 *Ippen no hakuun kokku ni yokotawari,*
幾多歸鳥夜迷巣 *Ikuta no kichō ka yoru su ni mayou.*

White clouds block the inlet to the valley.
Many birds seeking their nests at night will go astray.

ZGS 14.44, ZGJT 26, ZGJI 602, ZRKS 14.280, Shiba 326

14.55 一二三四五六七 *Ichi ni san shi go roku,*
碧眼胡僧不知數 *Hekigan kosō mo sū o shirazu.*

One, two, three, four, five, six.
The blue-eyed ⌜barbarian monk⌝ does not know numbers.

ZGS na, Shiba 325

14.56 如今抛擲西湖裏 *Ima hōteki su seiko no uchi,*
下載淸風付與誰 *Asai no seifū tare ni ka fuyo sen.*

Just now I threw away everything into West Lake.
With whom can I share this clean feeling of release?

Heki 45 Verse. ZGJT 363, Shiba 360: *Nyokon hōteki su seiko no uchi, Seifū o asai shite tare ni ka fuyo sen.*

ZGS 14.45, ZGJT 363, ZGJI 659, ZRKS 14.184, Shiba 360

14.57 慇懃爲説西來意 *Ingin tame ni toku seirai i,*
暮樓鐘皷月黄昏 *Borō no shōko tsuki kōkon.*

So kind of them to explain the point of the coming from the West.
The bell and drum towers at evening, the golden ⌜moon⌝ at twilight.

See ⌜Patriarch came from the West⌝ under ⌜Bodhidharma⌝.

ZGS 14.46, ZGJI 602, ZRKS 14.385, Shiba 327

14.58 幾處吹笳明月夜 *Iku sho ka ka o fuku meigetsu no yoru,*
何人倚劍白雲天 *Nanbito ka ken ni yoru hakuun no ten.*

Where does the flute music come on from this moonlit night?
Who is that man leaning on his ⌜sword⌝ under this white-clouded sky?

ZGS 14.47, Shiba na, TSSSTS 57

14.59 鶯逢春暖歌聲滑 *Uguisu wa shundan ni ōte kasei nameraka ni,*
人遇時平笑臉開 *Hito wa jihei ni ōte shoken hiraku.*

Nightingales greet the warmth of spring with melodious song,
Men greet times of peace by breaking into smiles.

ZGS 14.48: 瞼 instead of 臉, ZGJI 603, ZRKS 14.248, Shiba 330

14.60 雨後有人耕綠野 *Ugo hito no ryokuya ni tagayasu ari,*
月明無犬吠花村 *Getsumei inu no kason ni hoyuru nashi.*

After the rains men cultivate the green fields,
In the moonlight no dogs bark in the flowering villages.

ZGS 14.49, ZGJI 603, ZRKS 14.246, Shiba na

14.61 雨前初見花間葉 *Uzen ni wa hajimete miru kakan no yō,*
雨後兼無葉底花 *Ugo ni wa kanete nashi yōtei no hana.*

Before the rain there were a few leaves among the flowers,
But after the rain there was not a flower among the leaves.➛

ZGS 14.50, ZGJI 603, Shiba na, TSSSTS 112

14.62 蛺蝶飛來過墻去 *Kyōchō tobikitatte kaki o sugisaru,*
卻疑春色在隣家 *Kaette utagau shunshoku no rinka ni aru ka to.*

➛A butterfly flutters in and passes over the hedge.
I wonder if its spring colors are now in my neighbor's house.

ZGS 14.51, ZGJI 611, Shiba 336

14.63 歸馬于華山之陽 *Uma o kazan no minami ni kaeshi,*
放牛于桃林之野 *Ushi o tōrin no ya ni hanatsu.*

He sends the horses back to south of the ⌜Flower Peak⌝,
He releases the oxen in the pastures of ⌜Peach⌝ Forest.

ZGS 14.52, ZGJI 603, Shiba na, 史記留侯世家

14.64 梅須遜雪三分白 *Ume wa subekaraku yuki ni sanbu no shiroki o yuzuru beshi,*
雪亦輸梅一段香 *Yuki mo mata ume ni ichidan no ka o maku.*

The plum must concede that the snow is whiter by a third;
But the snow, on the other hand, loses a point on fragrance to the plum.

ZGS 14.53, ZGJI 603, ZRKS 14.245, Shiba 381

14.65 雲門胡餠趙州茶 *Ummon no kobyō, Jōshū no cha,*
惠崇蘆雁趙昌花 *Ejō ga rogan, Chōchō ga hana.*

Yun-men's pastry bun, Jōshū's tea,
Hui-ch'ung's reed goose, Chao-ch'ang's flower.

Masters and their masterpieces. For Ummon's pastry bun, see *Heki* 77; Jōshū's tea, see *Heki* 22 Main Case Comm. Hui-ch'ung and Chao-ch'ang were Sung period painters, famous for paintings of birds and flowers respectively (ZGJI 531; Nishibe 1985, 78).

ZGS 14.54, ZGJI 603, ZRKS 14.378, Shiba 328

14.66 叡嶽三千房雪月 *Eigaku sanzen bō no setsugetsu,*
長安十萬戸風烟 *Chōan jūman ko no fūen.*

On Mount Jui, three thousand cabins under the snowy ⌜moon⌝,
In ⌜Ch'ang-an⌝, one hundred thousand houses in the misty wind.

ZGS 14.55, Shiba na

14.67 越王勾踐破呉歸 *Etsuō kōsen go o yabutte kaeru,*
義士還家盡錦衣 *Gishi ie ni kaette kotogotoku kin'i su.*

Kou Chien, King of Yüeh, conquered ⌜Wu⌝ and then returned.
His loyal followers returned home all in robes of brocade.➛

ZGS 14.56 , Shiba 329, Obata 77, TSSSTS 74–5

14.68 宮女如花滿春殿 *Kyūjo hana no gotoku shunden ni mitsu,*
只今惟有鷓鴣飛 *Tada ima tada shako no tobu ari.*

➤Court women, like flowers, thronged the palace in spring,
But now only a partridge flies.

ZGS 14.57, Shiba 335

14.69 鴛鴦繡出從君看 *En'ō o shūshutsu shite kimi ga miru ni makasu,*
莫把金針度與人 *Kinshin o totte hito ni doyo suru koto nakare.*

The ⌜mandarin ducks⌝ that I've embroidered I will let you see,
But the golden needle that made them, do not give to another.

Heki 40 Main Case *agyo.*

ZGS 14.58, ZGJI 604, ZD#154, ZRKS 14.42, Shiba 329

14.70 燕子不來春又老 *Enshi kitarazu haru mata oiyu,*
滿襟離思落花風 *Mankin ni rishi rakka no kaze.*

No swallows come as spring begins to wane.
Thoughts of parting fill my breast, flowers fall in the wind.

ZGS 14.59, Shiba na

14.71 隨緣赴感靡不周 *En ni shitagai kan ni omomuite amanekarazu to iū koto nashi,*
而常處此菩提座 *Shikamo tsune ni kono bodaiza ni sho su.*

Led by impulse on the spur of each moment, he is always everywhere,
Yet always he is on this ⌜*bodhi*⌝ seat.

ZGS 14.60, Shiba na

14.72 隨緣來矣隨緣去 *En ni shitagatte kitari, en ni shitagatte saru,*
掛角羚羊不見蹤 *Tsuno o kakuru reiyō ato o mizu.*

It wandered in and wandered out,
No trace seen of the ⌜horn-hooking antelope⌝.

ZGS 14.61, Shiba na

14.73 王好惡逆 *Ō akugyaku o konomeba,*
則民苦塗炭而其世亡矣 *Tami totan ni kurushinde sono yo horobu.*

If the king has a taste for vice and wrong-doing,
Then the people will suffer extreme misery and his reign will come to ruin.

ZGS 14.62, Shiba na

14.74 黃金打就玉鸚鵡 *Ōgon dashū su gyoku ōmu,*
一聲聲作鷓鴣啼 *Isseisei wa shako no naki o nasu.*

The jeweled parrot made of gold,
Sound for sound gives the call of the partridge.

KZS #1206, ZGS 14.63, ZRKS 14.283, Shiba na

14.75 漚生漚滅水還在 *Ō shō ō metsu mizu mata ari,*
風急浪平月印潭 *Kaze kyū ni nami tairaka ni shite tsuki tan ni insu.*

Bubbles form and break, but there's always water;
In strong winds or smooth waves, the ⌜moon⌝ reflects in the deep.

ZGS 14.64, Shiba na

14.76 横按鏌鎁全正令 *Ō ni bakuya o anjite shōrei o mattō shi,*
太平寰宇斬癡頑 *Taihei no kan'u ni chigan o kiru.*

Strap on the ⌜Mo-yeh sword⌝ and the law rules supreme;
In the empire of the great peace, the foolish and greedy are slain.

Alternate translation line 1: "When the Mo-yeh sword is leveled sideways." ZGJI 681: *Yoko ni bakuya o anjite….*

KZS #1183, ZGS 14.65, ZGJT 38, ZGJI 681, ZRKS 14.259, Shiba na

14.77 横拈鏌鎁居閫外 *Ō ni bakuya o nenjite kongai ni iru,*
當鋒誰最夜重圍 *Hō ni ataru tare ka mottomo yoru i o omōsu.*

Swinging the ⌜Mo-yeh sword⌝, he stands outside the gates,
His spear at the ready. Who would lay siege in the deepest night?

ZGS 14.66, Shiba na

14.78 王令已行徧天下 *Ōrei sude ni okonawarete tenka ni amaneshi,*
將軍塞外絕烟塵 *Shōgun saigai ni enjin o zessu.*

The king's command now governs all under heaven;
Beyond the frontiers, his generals have settled the ⌜dust⌝ of battle.

KZS #1179, ZGS 14.67, ZGJI 604, ZRKS 14.253, Shiba 329, *Rinzai-roku* §10

14 字

14.79 屋漏兒啼薪亦盡 *Oku mori ji naki shin mo mata tsuku,*
呼嗟縮首未會休 *Kosa shite kubi o chijimete imada katsute kyūsezu.*

The roof leaks, the baby is crying, the firewood's all been used.
He lets out a moan and hangs his head down—still no rest.

ZGS 14.68, Shiba na

14.80 可惜年年明月夜 *Oshimubeshi nen-nen meigetsu no yoru,*
漁家只作舊時看 *Gyoka tada kyūji no kan o nasu koto o.*

What a shame! Year after year, nights of bright ⌜moon⌝,
And the fisherman just sees things in the same old way.

ZGS na, ZGJI 604, ZRKS 14.446, Shiba 330

14.81 同來翫月人何處 *Onajiku kitatte tsuki o moteasobi shi hito izure no tokoro zo,*
風景依稀似去年 *Fūkei iki to shite kyonen ni nitari.*

Where is my companion who gazed with me at the ⌜moon⌝?
This scenery only resembles that of last year.

ZGS 14.69, Shiba na, TSSSTS 94.

14.82 自是鳳凰臺上客 *Onozukara kore hōō daijō no kyaku,*
眼高看不到黄金 *Manako takōshite mite ōgon ni itarazu.*

For after all he was the visitor at the Phoenix Terrace,
Whose lofty vision did not stop at the sight of gold.

Ref. to *Heki* 1.

ZGS 14.70, ZGJI 604, GKFGS 2.52, ZRKS 14.421, Shiba 355

14.83 不覺觸佗蚯蚓怒 *Oboezu ta no kyūin no ikari ni furete,*
迅機顚蹶欲飜天 *Jinki tenketsu ten o hirugaesan to hossu.*

Unawares, I touched that worm and triggered its fury.
Now writhing and twisting, it wants to leap into the sky.

ZGS 14.71, Shiba na; Iida Tōin 1955, 43

14.84 徐行踏斷流水聲 *Omomuro ni yuite tōdan su ryūsui no koe,*
縱觀寫出飛禽跡 *Hoshiimama ni mite utsushiidasu hikin no ato.*

As I step slowly along to the sounds of running water,
My wandering gaze catches the traces of flying birds.

Heki 6 Verse.

ZGS 14.72, ZGJI 604, Shiba 360

14.85 寃親平等秋天月 *Onshin byōdō shūten no tsuki,*
影入恒河不止痕 *Kage wa kōga ni itte ato o todomezu.*

Love and hate are all the same to the ⌜moon⌝ in the autumn sky.
Shadows sink into the River Ganges and leave no trace.

ZGS 14.73, Shiba na

14.86 遠公遁跡廬山嶺 *Onkō ato o nogaru rozan no mine,*
開士幽居祇樹林 *Kaishi yūkyo su gijurin.*

Mount Lu—where Master Yüan withdrew leaving not a trace,
The Jeta Forest—where the Bodhisattvas lived in seclusion.

ZGS 14.74, Shiba na

14.87 有械事者有械心 *Kaiji aru mono wa kaishin ari,*
有機心者有機事 *Kishin aru mono wa kiji ari.*

He who is fettered has a fettered mind,
He who has a dynamic mind does dynamic things.

ZGS 14.75, Shiba na

14.88 掀翻海嶽覓知音 *Kaigaku o kenpon shite chiin o motomu,*
箇箇看來日中斗 *Ko-ko mikitareba nitchū no to.*

I overturn the seas and mountains seeking an ⌜intimate friend⌝,
But it is like a one-by-one search for a star at noon.

ZGS 14.76, ZGJI 606, ZRKS 14.202, Shiba na

14.89 掀翻海岳求知己 *Kaigaku o kenpon shite chiki o motome,*
擬亂乾坤致太平 *Kenkon o hatsuran shite taihei o itasu.*

I overturn sea and mountain seeking an ⌜intimate friend⌝,
Setting ⌜heaven and earth⌝ in order, I deliver the great peace.

ZGS 14.77, Shiba na

14.90 海底泥牛銜月走 *Kaitei no deigyū tsuki o fukunde hashiri,*
巖頭石虎抱兒眠 *Gantō no sekko ji o idaite nemuru.*

The mud ox on the sea floor runs with the ⌜moon⌝ in its mouth,
The stone tiger on the cliff sleeps with its cub in its embrace.

Shiba 332: 啣 instead of 銜 and 岩 instead of 巖.

ZGS na, ZGJI 606, ZRKS 14.464, Shiba 332

14.91 回風度雨渭城西 *Kaifū dou ijō no nishi,*
細草新花踏作泥 *Saisō shinka funde dei to nasu.*

Swirling winds, sweeping rains, west of the city of Wei,
Slender shoots, new blossoms, tramped into the mud.

ZGS 14.78, Shiba na

14.92 卻恨含情掩秋扇 *Kaette uramu jō o fukunde shūsen o ōu koto o,*
空懸明月待君王 *Munashiku meigetsu o kakete kunnō o matsu.*

How bitter, to swallow her feelings and be discarded like a fan in autumn,
Sitting alone in the moonlight, she waits for the Emperor.

ZGS 14.79, Shiba na

14.93 卻嫌脂粉汚顏色 *Kaette kirau shifun no ganshoku o kegasu koto o,*
淡掃蛾眉朝至尊 *Awaku gabi o haratte shison ni chō su.*

Not wanting to discolor her face with rouge and powder,
She lightly brushes her ⌜moth eyebrows⌝ and goes to an audience with the emperor.

ZGS 14.80, Shiba 335

14 字

14.94 卻將錦樣鶯花地 *Kaette kinyō ōka no ji o motte,*
變作元暉水墨圖 *Henjite genki ga suiboku no zu to nasu.*

Even the golden brocade-like land of nightingales and flowers,
Can be changed into a water and ink painting by Yüan-hui.

Hsieh Yüan-hui 謝元暉 was a Chin master painter (Iida Tōin 1955, 423).

ZGS 14.81, ZRKS 14.57, Shiba na

14.95 擘開華嶽連天色 *Kagaku renten no iro o hekkai shi,*
放出黄河徹底淸 *Kōga tettei no sei o hōshutsu su.*

Split open ⌜Flower Peak⌝, whose colors touch the skies;
Release the Yellow River, transparent down to the bottom.

ZGS 14.82, ZGJT 416, ZGJI 605, ZRKS 14.46, Shiba 389

14.96 無限心中不平事 *Kagiri naki shinchū fuhei no ji,*
一宵淸話又成空 *Isshō no seiwa ni mata kū to naru.*

The endless problems that upset my mind,
With one night's talk have dispersed to nothing.

ZGS 14.83, Shiba na, TSSSTS 123

14.97 欲知無限傷春意 *Kagiri naki haru o itamashimuru i o shiran to hosseba,*
盡在停針不語時 *Kotogotoku hari o todomete katarazaru toki ni ari.*

If you want to see her endless discontent at spring,
It's all there when her needle stops in silence.

Variant: 可憐無限傷春意 *Awaremubeshi kagiri naki haru o itamashimuru i.*

ZGS 14.84, ZGJT 42, ZGJI 597, 606, ZRKS 14.319, Shiba na

14.98 閣中帝子今何在 *Kakuchū no teishi ima izure ni ka aru,*
檻外長江空自流 *Rangai no chōkō munashiku onozukara nagaru.*

The princes of this palace, where are they now?
Beyond the balustrades, the Long River just flows on past.

ZGS 14.85, Shiba na, TSSSTS 6

14.99 學道之人不知眞 *Gakudō no hito shin o shirazu,*
只爲從前認識神 *Tada jūzen shikishin o mitomuru ga tame nari.*

Practitioners of the Way do not know the truth,
They only recognise discriminating mind.➛

Empuku-ji: *Gakudō no hito shin o shirazaru wa.*

ZGS 14.86, Shiba na, Shibayama 1974, 93

14.100 無始劫來生死本 *Mushi gōrai shōji no moto,*
癡人喚作本來人 *Chijin yonde honrai shin to nasu.*

➛From beginningless time, this has been the cause of birth-and-death,
Yet fools take it for the original self.

ZGS na, ZGJT 443 and ZGJI 675 (variants), ZRKS 14.453, Shiba 393, Shibayama 1974, 93

14.101 鑊湯爐炭淸涼界 *Kakutō rotan wa seiryōkai,*
劍樹刀山遊戲場 *Kenju tōzan wa yugejō.*

The boiling cauldrons and burning coals [of Hell] are a cool, refreshing world,
The ⌜tree of swords and mountain of blades⌝ are a playground.

Empuku-ji: *Kakutō rotan seiryōkai, Kenju tōzan yugejō.*

ZGS 14.88, ZGJI 606, Shiba 332

14.102 鑊湯爐炭吹敎滅 *Kakutō rotan fuite messeshime,*
劍樹刀山喝便摧 *Kenjutōzan kasshite sunawachi kudaku.*

Blow out the boiling cauldron and the burning coals [of Hell],
With a shout, shatter the ⌜tree of swords and mountain of blades⌝.

Heki 6 Verse Comm.

ZGS 14.89, ZGJT 60, ZGJI 606, ZRKS 14.1, Shiba 332

14.103 岳陽城上聞吹笛 *Gakuyōjōjō suiteki o kiku,*
能使春心滿洞庭 *Yoku shunshin o shite dotei ni mitashimu.*

From above Yüeh-yang City, I hear the blowing of a flute.
Truly it fills ⌜Lake Tung-t'ing⌝ with the feeling of spring.

ZGS 14.90, Shiba na, TSSSTS 79

14.104 佳人一笑嬋姸刄 *Kajin no isshō senkentaru yaiba,*
斷盡人間寸寸膓 *Tachitsukusu ningen sun-sun no chō.*

The smile of a beautiful woman is a charmed blade
For cutting out men's guts bit by little bit.

ZGS 14.91, ZGJI 605, Shiba na

14.105 知數摩醯難辨色 *Kazu o shiru makei iro o benjigatashi,*
入楊綠矣入花紅 *Yanagi ni itte wa midori, hana ni itte wa kurenai.*

⌜Maheśvara⌝ knows numbers but cannot distinguish colors.
But when you enter willows, that's green, and when you enter flowers, that's red.

ZGS 14.92, ZRKS 14.58, Shiba na

14.106 風蕭蕭兮易水寒 *Kaze shō-shō to shite ekisui samushi,*
壯士一去不復還 *Sōshi hitotabi satte mata kaerazu.*

The wind is sighing over the cold waters of the River I,
Once this brave man leaves, he will not be returning.

See ⌜Ching K'o⌝.

ZGS 14.93, Shiba na, 史記刺客列傳

14.107 風送泉聲來枕上 *Kaze sensei o okutte chinjō ni kitari,*
月移花影到窓前 *Tsuki kaei o utsushite sōzen ni itaru.*

The wind carries the sound of spring waters to my pillow,
The ⌜moon⌝ brings the shadows of flowers to my window.

ZGS 14.94, Shiba 387

14.108 風送斷雲歸嶺去 *Kaze dan'un o okutte mine ni kaerisari,*
月和流水過橋來 *Tsuki ryūsui ni washite hashi o sugikitaru.*

The wind brings wisps of clouds back to the peaks,
The ⌜moon⌝ flows with the water past the bridge.

ZGS 14.95, ZGJI 606, ZRKS 14.154, Shiba 388

14.109 不因風捲浮雲淨 *Kaze no fu'un o maite kiyou suru ni yorazumba,*
爭見長空萬里天 *Ikade ka min chōkū banri no ten.*

Without the clearing wind to roll away the drifting clouds,
How could we see this vast sky and mile after mile of heaven?

ZGS 14.96, Shiba na

14.110 風攪飛泉送冷聲 *Kaze hisen o kakimidashite reisei o okuru,*
前峯月上竹窓明 *Zenpō tsuki nobotte chikusō akiraka nari.*

Wind, stirring the suspended mist, sends a cooling sound.
The ⌜moon⌝ over the nearby hills lights my bamboo window.➛

ZGS 14.97, Shiba 387, 寂室

14.111 老來殊覺山中好 *Rōrai koto ni oboyu sanchū no yoki o,*
死在巖根骨也清 *Shi shite gankon ni areba hone mata kiyoshi.*

➛As I get old, I especially recall how wonderful were the mountains.
When I die, my bones will lie clean beneath their cliffs.

ZGS 14.98, Shiba 401

14.112 風吹不動天邊月 *Kaze fukedomo dōzezu tenpen no tsuki,*
雪壓難摧碉底松 *Yuki osedomo kudakegatashi kantei no matsu.*

Though the wind may blow, the ⌜moon⌝ in the sky does not move;
Though the snow may cover them, the pines in the ravine do not break.

ZGS 14.99, ZGJI 606, ZRKS 14.31, Shiba 387

14.113 風吹碧落浮雲盡 *Kaze hekiraku o fuite fuun tsuki,*
月上青山玉一團 *Tsuki seizan ni noboru tama ichidan.*

Wind sweeps the blue sky, whipping the floating clouds away,
And over the green hills, up floats the ⌜moon⌝ like a globe of jade.

ZGS 14.100, ZGJI 606, ZRKS 14.87, Shiba 387

14.114 荷盡已無擎雨蓋 *Ka tsukite sude ni ame ni sasaguru gai naku,*
菊殘猶有傲霜枝 *Kiku nokoshite nao shimo ni hokoru eda ari.*

The lotus are gone, no longer lifting parasols to the rain,
But chrysanthemums remain, their branches still resisting the frost.

Empuku-ji: *Ka tsukite sude ni ame ni sasaguru no gai naku, Kiku nokotte nao shimo ni ogoru no eda ari.*

ZGS 14.101, ZGJI 605, Ogawa 1962, II, 38, Watson 1994, 119, ZRKS 14.341, Shiba 331, 蘇東坡贈劉景文

14.115 曾騎鐵馬入重城 *Katsute tetsuma ni notte chōjō ni iru,*
勅下傳聞六國清 *Choku kudatte tsutaekiku rikkoku no kiyoki koto o.*

Driving armored horses, he has occupied numerous cities.
The imperial edict has come down proclaiming peace in the six states.

Heki 24 Verse. Six states: the states which the first emperor of Ch'in conquered to form the first empire (Iriya et al. 1992, vol. 1, 318).

KZS #1143, ZGS na, ZGJI 607, ZRKS 14.8, Shiba 371

14.116 曾經巴峡猿啼處 *Katsute hakyō saru no naku tokoro o hereba,*
鐵作心肝也斷腸 *Tessa no shinkan mo mata danchō.*

In the Pa Gorge, if you pass the place where the monkeys cry,
Even a heart made of iron will be cut to the quick.

KZS #1211, ZGS na, ZGJT 270, ZGJI 607, ZRKS 14.296, Shiba 371

14.117 濶步文翁房裏月 *Kappō su bunnō bōri no tsuki,*
閑尋杜甫宅邊松 *Shizuka ni tazunu toho takuhen no matsu.*

Striding along—the ⌜moon⌝ in ⌜Wen Weng's⌝ rooms.
Quietly visiting—the pine by Tu Fu's house.

Wen Weng, not to be confused with ⌜Wen Wang⌝ 文王, was an official during the Han period, known for his love of learning. During the reign of Emperor Wu, he set up a system of schools in remote barbarian areas. Mentioned in ⌜Tu Fu's⌝ poetry (Morohashi 13450.70; HYDCD 6.1530).

ZGS 14.102, Shiba na

14.118 我儂更勝渠些子 *Gadō sara ni kare ni masaru shashi,*
說到驢年不點頭 *Toite ronen ni itaru mo tentō seji.*

"I'm still a little better than he,"
He says, and not till the Year of the Donkey will he bow his head.

In the twelve-year cycle of the Chinese zodiac, there are years for Tiger, Hare, Dragon, etc., but no year of the Donkey.

ZGS 14.103, Shiba na

14.119 家童爲問深深意 *Kadō tame ni tou shinshin no i,*
笑指紗窓月正秋 *Waratte shasō o yubisaseba tsuki masa ni aki nari.*

The houseboy asked about the ultimate point,
So smiling, I pointed out the silk-paned window to the autumn ⌜moon⌝.

ZGS 14.104, ZGJI 605, Shiba na

14.120 科頭箕踞長松下 *Katō ni shite kikyo su chōshō no moto,*
白眼看他世上人 *Hakugan ni shite ta no sejō no hito o miru.*

Bare-headed, legs splayed apart, he sits under the tall pines,
And bug-eyed stares at the worldly people.

Empuku-ji: *Katō ni kikyō su chōshō no moto, Hakugan ni kanta su sejō no hito.*

ZGS 14.105, Shiba na, TSSSTS 78

14.121 聞鐘則宿雲外寺 *Kane o kiite wa sunawachi shuku su ungai no tera,*
見月則上湖邊樓 *Tsuki o mite wa sunawachi noboru kohen no rō.*

I hear the bell and at once I am staying in the temple beyond clouds,
I see the ⌜moon⌝ and at once I am climbing the platform by the lake.

ZGJI 607: *Kane o kiku toki wa ungai no tera ni shuku su, Tsuki o miru toki wa kohen no rō o noboru.*

ZGS 14.106, ZGJI 607, Shiba na

14.122 蛾眉螓首一群女 *Gabi shinshu ichigun no jo,*
各戴花枝錦繡肩 *Ono-ono kashi o itadaku kinshū no kata.*

A flock of pretty girls, with ⌜moth eyebrows⌝ in broad clear faces,
Each carries a flower spray and is clad in embossed brocade.

Shiba 607: *Gabi shinshu ichigun no onna, Ono-ono kashi o hasamu sanshū no kata.*

ZGS 14.107, Shiba 331

14.123 上好財則臣害林 *Kami zai o konomeba sunawachi shin rin o gai shi,*
上好魚則臣害澗 *Kami uo o konomeba sunawachi shin tani o gai su.*

If the emperor wants his precious possession, at once his ministers destroy a forest;
If the emperor wants fish, immediately they destroy a pond.

Line 1 refers to a folk story: One day the king's precious monkey escaped and fled back to the forest. The king ordered the forest burned to recover the monkey. Line 2 probably is a deliberate play on the saying "Disaster extends to the fish in the pond." See ⌜Inferno at the gate⌝.

ZGS 14.108, Shiba na

14.124 荷葉團團團似鏡 *Kayō dan-dan to shite kagami yori mo madoka nari,*
菱角尖尖尖似錐 *Ryōkaku sen-sen to shite kiri yori mo surudoshi.*

Lotus leaves are round, rounder than a mirror;
Water-chestnut thorns are sharp, sharper even than a ⌜gimlet⌝.➛

Empuku-ji: *Kayō wa dan-dan to shite kagami yori mo maruku, Ryōkaku wa sen-sen to shite kiri yori mo surudoshi.*

ZGS 14.109, ZGJT 48, ZGJI 605, ZRKS 14.284, Shiba 331

14.125 風吹柳絮毛毬走 *Kaze ryūjo o fuite mōkyū washiri,*
雨打梨花蛺蝶飛 *Ame rika o utte kyōchō tobu.*

⤚Wind blows the willow catkins and wooly puffs sail away,
Rain strikes the pear blossoms and butterflies take flight.

KZS #1168, ZGS 14.110, ZGJT 407, ZGJI 607, ZRKS 14.84, Shiba 387

14.126 寒雲籠雪夕陽重 *Kan'un yuki o komete sekiyō omoku,*
山月照梅夜色清 *Sangetsu ume o terashite yashoku kiyoshi.*

Cold clouds are laden with snow in the deepening twilight,
The mountain ⌜moon⌝ lights a plum tree with clean night colors.

ZGS 14.111, ZGJI 608, Shiba 333

14.127 閒蟻爭曳蜻蜓翼 *Kangi arasoihiku seitei no tsubasa,*
新燕雙憩楊柳枝 *Shin'en narabiikou yōryū no eda.*

Ants fight each other and pull apart the dragonfly's wings,
But swallows rest side by side on the willow twig.

ZGS 14.112: 間 for 閒, 並 for 雙, and 憩 for 憇.

ZGS 14.112, Shiba 334

14.128 蠶婦携籃多菜色 *Sanpu ran o tazusaete saishoku ōku,*
村童偸筍過疎籬 *Sondo takanna o nusunde sori o sugu.*

The silkworm nursery girls lug baskets full of vegetable greens,
The village boys steal bamboo shoots and run off through the hedge.

ZGS 14.113, Shiba 351 *Hakuin funyū nehan no ju*

14.129 寒山不語拾得笑 *Kanzan wa katarazu jittoku wa warau,*
跳出龍門萬仞來 *Ryūmon banjin o chōshutsu shi kitaru.*

⌜Kanzan⌝ does not speak but Jittoku laughs,
They come leaping ten thousand fathoms off the ⌜Dragon Gate⌝.

ZGS 14.114, ZGJI 608, ZRKS 14.301, Shiba na

14.130 寒松一色千年別 *Kanshō isshiki sennen betsu nari,*
野老拈花萬國春 *Yarō hana o nenzu bankoku no haru.*

The winter pine is different, evergreen for a thousand years.
An old peasant plucks a flower—spring in a myriad lands.

ZGS 14.115, ZGJI 608, ZRKS 14.139, Shiba 333

14.131 寒水欲春冰彩薄 *Kansui haru naran to hosshite hyōsai usuku,*
曉山初霽雪峯高 *Gyōzan hajimete harete seppō takashi.*

Winter waters long for spring, their icy features fade;
Dawn breaks in the mountains over high snow peaks.

ZGS 14.116, ZGJI 608, ZRKS 14.166, Shiba 333

14
字

14.132 失卻眼睛無所覓 *Gansei o shikkyaku shite motomuru tokoro nashi,*
梅花新發去年枝 *Baika arata ni hiraku kyonen no eda.*

I have lost my eyes, they are nowhere to be found;
But plum blossoms open again on last year's branches.

ZGS 14.117, ZGJI 609, ZRKS 14.387, Shiba 355

14.133 紈素不畫意高哉 *Gansō kakazu i takai kana,*
若著丹青墮二來 *Moshi tansei o tsukureba ni ni dashikitaru.*

How high was his mind before his sheet of unpainted silk,
But when he applied colors, he fell into dualism.➤

ZGS 14.118, Shiba na

14.134 無一物中無盡藏 *Mu ichi motsu chū mujinzō,*
有花有月有樓臺 *Hana ari tsuki ari rōtai ari.*

➤"There is not one thing" is an infinite storehouse,
With flowers, the ⌜moon⌝, and tall towers.

ZGS 14.119, ZGJI 674, Shiba 393

14.135 眼中童子目前人 *Ganchū no dōji mokuzen no hito,*
水底金烏天上日 *Suitei no kin'u tenjō no hi.*

That boy in my mind's eye is the person right before my eyes,
The ⌜golden crow⌝ at the bottom of the water is the sun in the sky.

KZS #1141, ZGS 14.120, ZGJT 73, ZGJI 609, ZRKS 14.6, Shiba na

14.136 寒時普天普地寒 *Kan no toki wa futen fuchi kan,*
熱時普天普地熱 *Netsu no toki wa futen fuchi netsu.*

When it's cold, all heaven and earth are cold;
When it's hot, all heaven and earth are hot.

Empuku-ji: *Kanji wa futen fuchi kan, Netsuji wa futen fuchi netsu.*

ZGS 14.121, Shiba na

14.137 觀音妙智慈悲力 *Kannon myōchi jihi no riki,*
荆棘林生優鉢花 *Keikyokurin ni uhatsuge o shōzu.*

The power of ⌜Kuan-yin's⌝ marvelous wisdom and compassion
Makes the ⌜*uḍumbara*⌝ flower bloom in the thorn forest.

ZGS 14.122, ZGJI 609, ZRKS 14.438, Shiba na

14.138 寒梅的的西來意 *Kanbai teki-teki seirai i,*
一片西飛一片東 *Ippen wa nishi ni tobi ippen wa higashi.*

The winter plum is clearly the meaning of the ⌜coming from the West⌝.
One petal flies west, one flies east.

Variation: instead of 寒梅 *kanbai,* "winter plum," 現成 *genjō,* "this right here."

ZGS 14.123, ZGJI 616 *(genjō),* ZRKS 14.366, Shiba 341

14.139 久雨不晴看丙丁 *Kyūu harezumba heitei o miyo,*
久晴不雨看戊己 *Kyūsei furazumba boki o miyo.*

In the long rainy season without sun, see the element of fire;
In the long sunny weather without rain, see the element of earth.

In Chinese astrology, the ten celestial stems are associated in pairs with the five elements. The stems *hei* 丙 and *tei* 丁 are the pair associated with the element of fire; the stems *bo* 戊 and *ki* 己 are the pair associated with the element of earth.

ZGS 14.124, Shiba na

14.140 九秋皓月當空照 *Kyūshū no kōgetsu kū ni atatte terashi,*
一片白雲山上來 *Ippen no hakuun sanjō yori kitaru.*

The bright autumn ⌜moon⌝ hangs shining in the sky,
A wisp of white cloud comes rising over the mountain.

ZGS 14.125, ZGJI 610, ZRKS 14.162, Shiba 335

14.141 九尾野狐多變體 *Kyūbi no yako hentai ōshi,*
金毛獅子解轉身 *Kinmo no shishi tenshin o gesu.*

The nine-tailed ⌜wild fox⌝ often changes its shape,
The golden-haired lion knows how to transform its body.

ZGS 14.126, ZGJI 610, ZRKS 14.331, Shiba na

14.142 巍巍乎舜禹之有天下也而不與焉 *Gi-gi kotari shun'u no tenka o tamotte shikōshite azukarazu.*

Majestic were ⌜Shun and Yü⌝ who held possession of the empire, yet remained unattached.➛

Analects VIII, 18–19.

ZGS 14.127, Shiba na

14.143 大哉堯之爲君也 *Dai naru ka na gyō no kuntaru koto ya,*
巍巍乎唯天爲大 *Gi-gi ko to shite tada ten nomi dai nari to nasu.*

➛Great indeed was ⌜Yao⌝ as sovereign! Only heaven was as great!

ZGS 14.128, Shiba na; Yoshikawa 1978 I, 270–2.

14.144 機中織錦秦川女 *Kichū nishiki o oru shinsen no onna,*
碧紗如煙隔窓語 *Hekisa kemuri no gotoku mado o hedatete kataru.*

At her loom a maid of Ch'in-ch'uan is weaving brocade,
Murmuring behind a window screen of mist blue gauze.➛

ZGS 14.129, Shiba na, TSSSTS 8

14.145 停梭悵然憶遠人 *Osa o todomete chōzen to shite enjin o omou,*
獨宿空房淚如雨 *Hitori kūbō ni shuku shite namida ame no gotoshi.*

➛She stops her shuttle in sadness, thinking of someone far away,
Sleeping alone in her empty room, her tears fall like rain.

Empuku-ji: *Hi o todomete chōzen to shite enjin o omou, Hitori kūbō ni shuku shite nanda ame no gotoshi.*

ZGS 14.130, Shiba na, TSSSTS 8

14.146 君向江邊取釣竿 *Kimi wa kōhen ni mukatte chōkan o tori,*
我隨巨海看波瀾 *Ware wa kyokai ni shitagatte haran o miru.*

You sit by the stream holding your fishing pole,
I travel the vast oceans watching the waves.

ZGS 14.137, ZRKS 14.300, Shiba 339

14.147 勸君盡此一杯酒 *Kimi ni susumu kono ippai no sake o tsukuseyo,*
西出陽關無故人 *Nishi no kata yōkan o izureba kojin nakaran.*

I'm urging you to have another cup of wine,
Out west of Yang Pass, you won't have old friends.

ZGS 14.131, Shiba 334, TSSSTS 116

14 字

14.148 君看陌上二三月
那樹枝頭不帶春

Kimi miyo hakujō no ni san getsu,
Naju no shitō ni ka haru o obizaru.

Look in the avenues during the second or third month.
What tree's branches are not wreathed in spring?

ZGS 14.132, ZGJI 610, ZRKS 14.323, Shiba na

14.149 鄉國不知何處是
雲山漫漫使人愁

Kyōkoku wa shirazu izure no tokoro ka kore naru,
Unzan manman to shite hito o shite ureeshimu.

My native country, I do not know where it would be.
Mountains buried in clouds, they make a person sad.

ZGS 14.133, Shiba na, TSSSTS 92

14.150 漁翁睡重春潭闊
白鳥不飛舟自橫

Gyoō nemuri omoushite shuntan hiroshi,
Hakuchō tobazu fune onozukara yokotawaru.

Old fisherman fast asleep on a broad spring pond,
No swans fly, the boat drifts by itself.

ZGS 14.134: 濶 instead of 闊, ZGJI 611, ZRKS 14.63, Shiba 336

14.151 玉戸簾中卷不去
擣衣砧上拂還來

Gyokko renchū makedomo sarazu,
Tōi chinjō haraedomo mata kitaru.

She rolls down the jade door curtain, but it will not go away;
She brushes off her silk-pounding block, but still it comes.

ZGS 14.135, Shiba na, TSSSTS 14–5

14.152 玉殿深沈夜將半
斷猿空叫月明中

Gyokuden shinchin to shite yoru masa ni nakaba naran to su,
Dan'en munashiku sakebu getsumei no uchi.

The Jade Palace steeped in silence, nearly midnight—
A lone monkey cries forlornly in the light of the ⌜moon⌝.

ZGS 14.136, Shiba 337

14.153 玉堂金馬非吾事
土甕新蒭晚粒香

Gyokudō kimba goji ni arazu,
Doyō shinsū banryū kōbashi.

The Jade Academy and the Golden Horse [Gate] are not our concern;
Ours is earthen jugs, new hay, and the aroma of the late harvest grain.

The Jade Academy is the Hanlin Academy, the Imperial College of Literature. The Golden Horse Gate refers to the military academy established in the Han Dynasty by Emperor Wu (GKFGS 1.125).

ZGS 14.137, Shiba na, GKFGS 1.124–6

14.154 巨鰲莫戴三山去
吾欲蓬萊頂上行

Kyogō sanzan o itadaite saru koto nakare,
Ware wa hōrai chōjō ni yukan to hossu.

⌜Giant turtle⌝, bearing the ⌜three mountains⌝, do not go away,
I wish to go to the top of Mount P'eng-lai.

ZGS 14.138, Shiba na

14.155 去國一身輕似葉 *Kyokoku isshin ha yori mo karuku,*
高名千古重於山 *Kōmei senko yama yori mo omoshi.*

Setting out from home, what he had was as light as leaves,
But his fame for a thousand ages is heavier than the mountains.

KZS #1189, ZGS 14.139, ZGJT 88, ZRKS 14.205, Shiba 335

14.156 去年貧有錐無地 *Kyonen no hin wa sui atte chi naku,*
今年貧無錐無地 *Konnen no hin wa sui mo naku chi mo nashi.*

In last year's poverty, we had an ⌜awl⌝ but no ground to stick it in.
In this year's poverty, we have neither awl nor ground.

ZGS 14.140, ZGJI 611, ZRKS 14.108, Shiba 336

14.157 虛名萬事雪填井 *Kyomei banji yuki i o uzumu,*
幻影百年風繫繩 *Genyō hyakunen kaze nawa o tsunagu.*

The empty names of the ⌜ten thousand things⌝—fill a well with snow.
Illusory shadows for a hundred years—tie a rope to the wind.

ZGS 14.141, Shiba na

14.158 巨靈擡手無多子 *Kyorei te o motaguru ni tashi nashi,*
分破華山千萬重 *Bunpa su kazan no senbanjū.*

It was no great effort for the ⌜Giant Spirit⌝ to raise his hand,
But he split the million strata of ⌜Flower Peak⌝.

Heki 32 verse, MMK 3.

KZS #1152, ZGS 14.142, ZGJT 89, ZGJI 611, ZRKS 14.41, Shiba 336

14.159 許由本不受堯天 *Kyoyu moto gyōten o ukezu,*
只臥箕山山頂月 *Tada kizan sanchō no tsuki ni ga su.*

⌜Hsü Yu⌝ simply refused Emperor Yao's empire,
He just lies out under the ⌜moon⌝ on top of Mount Chi-shan.

ZGJI 611: Hsü Yu refused Emperor Yao's offer to make him his successor.

ZGS na, ZGJI 611, ZRKS 14.334, Shiba 336

14.160 莫嫌襟上斑斑色 *Kirau koto nakare kinjō hanpan no iro,*
是妾燈前滴淚縫 *Kore shō ga tōzen namida o shitatatte nuu.*

Don't disdain the discolored spots on this coat—
By lamplight I sewed it with my tears.

Shiba 382, Empuku-ji: *Kore shō ga tōzen nanda o tarete nuu.*

ZGS 14.143, ZGJI 612, Shiba 382

14.161 莫嫌冷淡無滋味 *Kirau koto nakare reitan ni shite jimi naki koto o,*
一飽能消萬劫飢 *Ippō yoku mango no ue o shōsu.*

Don't complain that it's cold and tasteless.
Once you have eaten your fill, the hunger of a million ⌜*kalpa*⌝ disappears.

ZGS 14.144, ZGJT 435, ZGJI 61, ZRKS 14.50, Shiba 383

14.162 自從金革銷聲後 *Kinkaku koe o shōshite yori nochi,*
惟聽堯民擊壤歌 *Tada kiku gyōmin gekijō no uta.*

Since the clanging of arms has come to an end,
We hear only ⌜Yao's⌝ people singing and stomping their feet.

ZGS 14.145, ZGJT 180, ZGJI 612, ZRKS 14.349, Shiba 354

14.163 金果早朝猿摘去 *Kinka sōchō saru tsumisari,*
玉花晚後鳳啣來 *Gyokka kurete nochi hō fukumikitaru.*

In the early morning monkeys pluck away the golden fruit,
In the evening the phoenix brings jade flowers in its beak.

ZGS 14.146, Shiba 337

14.164 錦鏡亭前風凜凜 *Kinkyōteizen kaze rin-rin,*
妙高峯頂雪漫漫 *Myōkōhōchō yuki man-man.*

Before the pavilion of brocade and mirrors the wind howls and whines,
On the top of ⌜Wonder Peak⌝, snow spreads far and wide.

ZGS 14.147, ZRKS 14.169, Shiba na

14.165 金雞啄破瑠璃卵 *Kinkei takuha su ruri no ran,*
玉兎挨開碧落門 *Gyokuto aikai su hekkai no mon.*

The golden pheasant breaks open the lapis lazuli egg,
The ⌜jade rabbit⌝ pushes open the blue sky gate.

ZGS 14.148, ZGJT 94, ZGJI 612, ZRKS 14.317, Shiba 337

14.166 金沙灘上觀音面 *Kinsa nanjō kannon no omote,*
劫火光中幻化身 *Gokka kōchū genka no shin.*

On the banks of the Golden Sands River the face of ⌜Kuan-yin⌝,
In the light of the ⌜doomsday fire⌝ her transformed appearance.

ZGS na, ZGJI 612, ZRKS 14.455, Shiba 337

14.167 金針曾不露鋒鋩 *Kinshin katsute hōbō o arawasazu,*
惹得無絲玉線長 *Mushi shite gyokusen o hikiete nagashi.*

The golden needle has never revealed its point,
But it draws the threadless jade thread out long.

ZGS na, ZGJI 612, GKFGS 1.102, ZRKS 14.12, Shiba 338

14.168 近來傳得安心法 *Kinrai tsutaetari anjin no hō,*
萬壑松風枕上聞 *Bangaku no shōfū chinjō ni kiku.*

I have recently learned a method for peace of mind:
From my pillow, I listen to the ⌜pine wind⌝ in the myriad valleys.

ZGS 14.149, ZGJI 613, ZRKS 14.362, Shiba 337

14.169 金龍不守於寒潭 *Kinryū kantan o mamorazu,*
玉兎豈栖於蟾影 *Gyokuto ani sen'ei ni sumanya.*

The ⌜golden dragon⌝ does not remain in the winter pool,
How can the ⌜jade rabbit⌝ remain in the moonlight?

"Moonlight" is literally "light of the toad." See ⌜Sun⌝, ⌜Moon⌝.

KZS #1177, ZGS 14.150, ZGJI 613, ZRKS 14.158, Shiba 338

14.170 金爐香盡漏聲殘 *Kinro kō tsukite rōsei nokoru,*
剪剪輕風陣陣寒 *Sen-sentaru kyōfū jinjin to shite samushi.*

Incense gone from the gold censer, water continues to drip;
Stab after stab of swirling wind, shiver after shiver of cold.➛

ZGS 14.151, Shiba na

14.171 春色惱人眠不得 *Shunshoku hito o nayamashite nemuru koto ezu,*
月移花影上欄干 *Tsuki kaei utsushite rankan ni jō su.*

➛Spring colors disturb people so they cannot sleep,
Moonlight makes flower shadows creep up the balustrade.

Shiba 359: *Shunshoku hito o nayamashimete nemuri o ezu, Tsuki kaei o utsushite rankan ni noborashimu.* Empuku-ji: *Tsuki kaei utsushite rankan ni noboru.*

ZGS 14.152, Shiba 359

14.172 銀盌盛來千世界 *Ginwan morikitaru sen sekai,*
冰壺映徹十虛空 *Hyōko eitetsu su jūkokū.*

In this silver bowl are heaped a thousand worlds,
In this jar of ice are reflected ten empty voids.

ZGS 14.153, ZGJT 95, Shiba na

14.173 空山無我來往跡 *Kūzan waga raiō no ato nashi,*
異日相逢又何邊 *Ijitsu aiau mata izure no hen zo.*

Empty mountains, no trace of my coming or going.
Some other day we shall meet—but where?

ZGS 14.154, Shiba na

14.174 藕絲孔裏騎大鵬 *Gūshikuri daihō ni nori,*
等閑挨落天邊月 *Tōkan ni oshiotosu tenpen no tsuki.*

Inside the hollow lotus stem I ride the great ⌜roc⌝,
With ease I knock down the ⌜moon⌝ in the heavens.

Variation: instead of 藕絲孔裏 *gūshikuri*, "inside the hollow lotus stem," 針鋒影裏 *shinpōyōri*, "in the glint of a needle's point." See also 14.345.

ZGS 14.155, 14.306; ZGJT 229, ZGJI 614, 635; ZRKS 14.322, Shiba 338, 362

14.175 傾國傾城漢武帝 *Kuni o katamuke shiro o katamuku kan no butei,*
爲雲爲雨楚襄王 *Kumo to nari ame to naru so no jōō.*

For Emperor Wu of Han, she destroyed a state and toppled a city,
For King Hsiang of Ch'u, she turned into clouds and turned into rain.

See ⌜Hsi-shih⌝ and ⌜Clouds and rain⌝. Empuku-ji: *Keikoku keisei kan no butei.*

ZGS 14.156, Shiba na, TSSSTS 7–8

14.176 朽木不可雕也糞 *Kuchitaru ki oba haerubekarazu,*
土之牆不可杇也 *Fundo no kaki oba nurubekarazu.*

Rotten wood cannot be carved,
Nor can a wall of dried dung be worked with a trowel.

ZGS 14.157, Shiba na; *Analects* v1, 9

14.177 雲逐風來得自由 *Kumo kaze o oikitatte jiyu o e,*
風隨雲去無拘束 *Kaze kumo ni shitagaisatte kōsoku nashi.*

Clouds come chasing the wind, free as can be;
The wind leaves with the clouds without any ties.

ZGS 14.158, Shiba na

14.178 雲耶山耶吳耶越 *Kumo ka yama ka, go ka etsu ka,*
水天髣髴青一髮 *Suiten hōfutsu sei ippatsu.*

Are those clouds or mountains, the state of ⌜Wu⌝ or ⌜Yüeh⌝?
Sea would blur into sky but for a blue hairline.

ZGS 14.159, Shiba na

14.179 雲遮劍閣三千里 *Kumo kenkaku o saegiru sanzenri,*
水隔瞿塘十二峯 *Mizu kutō o hedatsu jūnihō.*

Clouds block in Chien Ko for three thousand miles,
The river splits Ch'ü T'ang into its twelve peaks.

Chien Ko, literally Sword Parapet, was a mountain stronghold on the way to Szechuan whose sharp vertical peaks resembled swords. Ch'ü T'ang is famous steep gorge in Szechuan (Shiba 328).

ZGS 14.160, Shiba 328

14.180 雲横秦嶺家何在 *Kumo shinrei ni yokotawatte ie izuku ni ka aru,*
雪擁藍關馬不前 *Yuki rankan o yōshite uma susumazu.*

Clouds hang over the Ch'in Ling Peak—where would my house be?
Snow blocks in the Lan Station and my horse cannot go on.

Ch'in Ling Peak is in Shenhsi Province. Lan Station was a checkpoint in the mountains south of Ch'ang-an.

ZGS 14.161, Shiba 327

14.181 雲想衣裳花想容　*Kumo ni wa ishō ka to omoi, hana ni wa katachi ka to omou,*
春風拂檻露華濃　*Shunpū kan o haratte roka komayaka nari.*

Clouds remind me of her dress, flowers remind me of her face;
Spring breezes sweep the floral hedge, flowers are damp with dew.

See ⌜Yang Kuei-fei⌝.

ZGS 14.162, Shiba 328, TSSSTS 72

14.182 雲在嶺頭閑不徹　*Kumo wa reitō ni atte kanputetsu,*
水流磵下太忙生　*Mizu wa kanka ni nagarete taibōsei.*

Clouds dwell on the mountain peaks completely still;
Water flows down through the valleys, bubbling busily.

KZS #1158, ZGS 14.163: 澗 instead of 磵, ZGJT 32, ZGJI 614, ZRKS 14.53, Shiba 328

14.183 雲開月色家家白　*Kumo hirakete gesshoku ya-ya shiroku,*
春過山花處處紅　*Haru sugite sanka sho-sho kurenai nari.*

Clouds have parted, and, lit by the ⌜moon⌝, every house is white;
Spring has left and mountain flowers everywhere are red.

ZGS 14.164, ZGJI 614, ZRKS 14.127, Shiba 327

14.184 雲掃長空巢月鶴　*Kumo chōkū o haratte tsuki ni sukuu no tsuru,*
寒清入骨不成眠　*Kansei hone ni itte nemuri narazu.*

Clouds sweep the vast sky, a crane nests in the ⌜moon⌝;
This piercing cold has gotten into my bones—I cannot sleep.

ZGS na, ZGJI 614, Shiba 328

14.185 停車坐愛楓林晚　*Kuruma o todomete sozoro ni aisu fūrin no kure.*
霜葉紅於二月花　*Sōyō wa nigatsu no hana yori mo kurenai nari.*

He stops his carriage just to enjoy the sunset in the maples,
Whose frost-bitten leaves are redder than spring flowers.

Alternate reading: *oshimu* instead of *aisu, jigatsu* instead of *nogatsu.*

ZGS 14.165, Shiba 375, TSSSTS 110

14.186 群陰剥盡一陽生　*Gun'in hakujin shite ichiyō shōzu,*
草木園林盡發萌　*Sōmoku enrin kotogotoku hō o hassu.*

Peeling the many shadows away, the one sun appears,
And all the grass, trees, and forests send forth new shoots.

ZGS na, ZGJI 614, ZRKS 14.163, Shiba 339

14.187 誦經群羊來跪聽　*Kyō o jū sureba gunyō kitari hizamazuite kiki,*
習定鳥巢衣襵中　*Jō o naraeba tori eshō no uchi ni sukuu.*

When he chanted sutras, flocks of sheep came to kneel and listen;
When he practiced *samādhi,* birds nested in the folds of his robe.

ZGS na, ZRKS 14.460, Shiba 361

14.188 渓磵豈能留得住 *Keikan ani yoku todomuredomo todomuru koto o en ya,*
直歸大海作波濤 *Jiki ni taikai ni ki shite hatō to naru.*

Though you may try, can you really stop the valley stream?
Straightway it runs to the sea and turns into waves.

Heki 11 Verse Comm.

ZGS na, ZGJI 615, ZRKS 14.124, Shiba 339

14.189 輕輕觸著便無明 *Kei-kei ni sokujaku sureba sunawachi mumyō,*
只這無明元是道 *Tada kono mumyō moto kore dō.*

The slightest contact is at once ignorance,
But this ignorance is fundamentally the Way.

Shiba 340: 着 instead of 著.

ZGS na, ZGJI 615, ZRKS 14.395, Shiba 340

14.190 溪聲便是廣長舌 *Keisei sunawachi kore kōchōzetsu,*
山色豈非淸淨身 *Sanshoku ani shōjōshin ni arazaran ya.*

The splashing of the brook is the eloquence of the Buddha.
Are not mountains in color the pure [Buddha] body?

Heki 37 Verse Comm. See 「Inch and foot」.

ZGS 14.167, ZGJT 103, ZGJI 615, ZRKS 14.454, Shiba 339, 蘇東坡七贈東林總長老

14.191 閨中少婦不知愁 *Keichū no shōfu urei o shirazu,*
春日凝粧上翠樓 *Shunjitsu yosooi o korashite suirō ni noboru.*

In her chambers the young wife knew no cares.
On a spring day, she powdered her face and climbed the blue tower.➤

ZGS 14.168, Shiba 340, TSSSTS 76

14.192 忽見陌頭楊柳色 *Tachimachi hakutō yōryū no iro o mite,*
悔教夫婿覓封侯 *Kuyuraku wa fusei o shite hōkō o motomeshimeshi koto o.*

➤Then suddenly seeing the avenues glowing green with willows,
She regretted letting her husband go off in search of noble rank.

ZGS 14.169, Shiba na

14.193 蕙帳空兮夜鶴怨 *Keichō munashiushite yakaku urami,*
山人去兮曉猿驚 *Sanjin satte gyōen odoroku.*

Orchids were his curtains—now empty, the night cranes grieve,
The mountain dweller is gone, and the dawn monkeys are dismayed.

Orchid curtains connote a mountain hermitage where long tendrils of orchids form a curtain-door (ZGJI 615, Iida Tōin 1955, 199).

ZGS 14.170, ZGJI 615, Shiba 340

14.194 擊碎驪龍頷下珠 *Gekisai su riryū ganka no tama,*
敲出鳳凰五色髓 *Kōshutsu su hōō goshiki no zui.*

Smash to pieces the jewel under the jaw of the black dragon,
Crush out the five-colored marrow of the phoenix.

ZRKS 43: *Riryū ganka no tama o gekisai su, Hōō goshiki no zui o kōshutsu su.* Empuku-ji, Shiba 340: *Tatakiidasu hōō gosshiki no zui.*

KZS #1153, ZGS 14.171, ZGJT 104, ZGJI 682, ZRKS 14.43, Shiba 340

14.195 乾坤無地卓孤笻 *Kenkon kokyō o taku suru ni chi nashi,*
且喜人空法亦空 *Shaki suraku wa nin kū hō mo mata kū.*

In ⌜heaven and earth⌝, no place to plant my staff,
Rejoice! Persons are empty! Things are empty, too!➛

This and the next verse form one poem. About to be cut down by Mongol (Yüan) warriors with swords, Mugaku Sogen (無學祖元 1226–1286), a Chinese monk, composed this four-line poem. He survived and later went to Japan where he founded the temple of Engaku-ji in Kamakura and was given the title Bukkō Kokushi 佛光國師. "No place to plant my staff" here means "no place to hide," "no room to maneuver."

ZGS 14.172, Shiba na

14.196 珍重大元三尺劍 *Chinchō su daigen sanjaku no tsurugi,*
電光影裡斬春風 *Denkōyōri ni shunpū o kiru.*

➛How splendid this three-foot ⌜sword⌝ of the great Yüan Dynasty!
In a lightning flash, it slices the spring breeze.

Empuku-ji: *Chinchō su taigen no ken, Denkōyōri shunpū o kiru.*

ZGS 14.173, ZGJI 650, Shiba na

14.197 無可嫌著眼界平 *Kenjaku su beki nakereba gankai tairaka ni,*
不藏秋毫心地直 *Shūgō o kakuseba shinchi naoshi.*

If there were no rejecting things, you would see the world with equality;
If there were no concealing tiny details, your heart would be direct.

ZGS na, ZGJI 616, ZRKS 14.415, Shiba 393

14.198 玄都觀裏桃千樹 *Gentōkanri no momo senju,*
盡是劉郎去後栽 *Kotogotoku kore ryūrō satte nochi uu.*

The thousand ⌜peach⌝ trees of the Temple of the Land of Immortals,
Were all planted after Liu Lang had left.

Liu Lang (J. Ryūrō) was exiled from the capital. Years later when he was allowed to return, thousands of trees had been planted in the Taoist temple and he was greeted by masses of flowers.

ZGS 14.174, Shiba na, TSSSTS 90

14.199 劍爲不平離寶匣 *Ken wa fuhei no tame ni hōkō o hanare,*
藥因療病出金瓶 *Kusuri wa ryōbyō ni yotte kinpei o izu.*

Remove the ⌜sword⌝ from its jeweled scabbard when there is injustice,
Bring out the medicine from its golden flask when there is illness.

KZS #221, ZGS 14.175, ZGJT 108 var, ZGJI 616, ZRKS 14.221, Shiba 341

14.200 見惑頓斷如金剛 *Kenwaku tondan kongo no gotoku,*
思惑漸斷如藕絲 *Shiwaku zendan gūshi no gotoshi.*

Intellectual delusions break off suddenly like the ⌜*vajra*⌝ diamond,
Emotional delusions are gradually severed like threads of lotus root.

Shiba 341: 修惑 *shūwaku* instead of 思惑 *shiwaku.*

ZGS 14.176, Shiba 341

14.201 孤猿叫落中岩月 *Koen sakebiotosu chūgan no tsuki,*
野客吟餘半夜燈 *Yakaku ginjiamasu hanya no tomoshibi.*

A lone monkey cries the ⌜moon⌝ down over the cliffs,
A country traveler still sings long past the midnight lamp.

ZGS 14.177, Shiba 342

14.202 釣鼇時下一圈攣 *Gō o tsutte toki ni ikkenren o kudasu,*
天下衲僧跳不出 *Tenka no nōsō chōfushutsu.*

He lowers the trap with which he caught the great turtle,
No ⌜patch-robed monk⌝ in the world will be able to jump out.

ZGS 14.178, Shiba na

14.203 黄河界上空來往 *Kōga kaijō munashiku raiō,*
直至而今未樹功 *Jiki ni ima ni itaru made imada kō o tatezu.*

The Yellow River, wandering pointlessly across the earth,
To this day has not accomplished a thing.

ZGS 14.179, Shiba na, GKFGS 1.41

14.204 紅霞碧靄籠高低 *Kōka hekiai kōtei o komu,*
芳草野花一様春 *Hōsō yaka ichiyō no haru.*

Rosy mists and blue haze cover high and low,
Sweet grass and wild flowers are everywhere in spring.

ZGS 14.180: 艸 instead of 草, ZGJI 619, Shiba 345

14.205 紅旗曜日催征騎 *Kōki hi ni kagayaite seiki o moyōshi,*
駿馬嘶風捲陣雲 *Shunme kaze ni inanaite jin'un o maku.*

Red flags flashing in the sun urge the horsemen on,
Their big chargers neigh into the wind and churn up the dustclouds of battle.

ZGS 14.181, Shiba na

14.206 江國春風吹不起 *Kōkoku no shunpū fukitatazu,*
鷓鴣啼在深花裏 *Shako naite shinkari ni ari.*

Over the river country, spring winds have not yet stirred.
Partridges are crying, deep within the flowers.➛

Heki 7 Verse. Empuku-ji: *Kōkoku no shunpū fukedomo tatazu.*

ZGS 14.182, ZGJT 132, ZGJI 619, ZRKS 14.194, Shiba 344

14.207 三級浪高魚化龍 *Sankyū nami takōshite uo ryū to ke su,*
癡人猶戽野塘水 *Chijin nao kumu yatō no mizu.*

**➤The waters surge at ⌜Three Stages⌝ where fish transform into dragons,
But fools still trawl the night water by the banks.**

Heki 7 Verse, 100 Verse Comm.

KZS #1157, ZGS 14.183, ZGJT 162, ZGJI 624, ZD #155, ZRKS 14.52, Shiba 348

14.208 黃沙百戰穿金甲 *Kōsa hyakusen kinkō o ugatsu,*
不破楼蘭終不還 *Rōran o yaburazumba tsui ni kaerazu.*

**A hundred battles on the desert sands have worn my armor through,
But I'll not go home until I've destroyed ⌜Lou-lan⌝.**

ZGS 14.184, Shiba 345, TSSSTS 76

14.209 江上晩來堪畫處 *Kōjō banrai egaku ni taetaru tokoro,*
漁人披得一蓑歸 *Gyonin issa o hishiete kaeru.*

**Evening falls on the river, a scene almost unpaintable.
Throwing on his straw raincoat, the fisherman returns home.**

Variant: 簑 instead of 蓑.

KZS #1162, ZGS 14.185, ZGJT 132, ZGJI 619, ZD #156, ZRKS 14.67, Shiba 344

14.210 行人尋路遙招手 *Kōjin michi o tazunete haruka ni te o maneku mo,*
恐畏魚驚不告津 *Osoraku wa uo no odorokan koto o osorete shin o tsugezaran.*

**The traveler seeking the road waved his hand from afar,
But fearing to disturb the fish, I did not tell him of the crossing.**

ZGS 14.186, Shiba na; Iida Tōin 1955, 606

14 字

14.211 絳幘雞人報曉籌 *Kōsaku no keijin gyōchū o hōzu,*
尚衣方進翠雲裘 *Shōe masa ni susumu suiun no kyū.*

**The red-capped wake-up warden has announced daybreak,
The imperial robe-keeper brings the blue-cloud-pattern robes.**

ZGS 14.187, Shiba na, TSSSTS 45, 134

14.212 江天一色無纖塵 *Kōten isshiki senjin nashi,*
皎皎空中孤月輪 *Kōkōtari kūchū no kogetsurin.*

**River and sky are one color—not a speck of ⌜dust⌝,
Pure white, the full ⌜moon⌝ alone in the sky.**

ZGS 14.188, Shiba na

14.213 紅粉青蛾映楚雲 *Kōfun seiga soun ni eizu,*
桃花馬上石榴裙 *Tōka bajō sekiryū kun.*

**She's beautiful, powdered and rouged, radiant against Ch'u's clouds,
Riding in pomegranate skirts on a ⌜peach⌝-colored pony.**

ZGS 14.189, Shiba 345, TSSSTS 71

14.214 紅粉易粧端正女 *Kōfun yosōiyasushi tanshō no onna,*
無錢難作好兒郎 *Zeni nakushite gōjirō to narigatashi.*

With rouge and powder it is easy to make oneself into an attractive woman,
Without money it is difficult to make oneself a desirable man.

ZGS 14.190, ZGJT 135 ZGJI 619, ZRKS 14.98, Shiba na

14.215 孔門弟子無人識 *Kōmon no deshi hito no shiru nashi,*
碧眼胡僧笑點頭 *Hekigan no kōsō waratte tentō.*

Among the disciples of Confucius no one understands,
But the blue-eyed ⌜barbarian monk⌝ laughs and nods his head.

Shiba 344: *teishi* instead of *deshi.*

ZGS 14.191, ZGJT 125, ZGJI 619, ZRKS 14.297, Shiba 344

14.216 拈將紅葉書秋思 *Kōyō o nenji motte shūshi o sho shi,*
摘得黄花當晩飡 *Kōka o tsumiete bansan ni atsu.*

I pick colored leaves on which to write autumn thoughts,
I pluck yellow flowers to serve at evening meal.

ZGS 14.192 and ZRKS 159: 拈將; ZGJI 619 and Shiba 380: 拈持; 飡 variant for 餐.

ZGS 14.192, ZGJI 619, ZRKS 14.159, Shiba 380

14.217 香爐峯雪捲簾見 *Kōrohō no yuki wa sudare o maite miru,*
遺愛寺鐘欹枕聞 *Iaiji no kane wa makura o sobadatete kiku.*

I roll up the blind to see the snow on Incense Bowl Peak,
From my pillow I raise an ear to hear the bell of I-ai Temple.

Shiba 345: *Kōrohō no yuki wa sudare o kakagete miru.*

ZGS 14.193, Shiba 345

14.218 胡笳一曲斷人腸 *Koka ikkyoku hito no harawata o tatsu,*
坐客相看涙如雨 *Zakyaku aimite namida ame no gotoshi.*

Oh, the plaint of the nomad's flute is heartbreaking.
Seated guests gaze at each other, tears run like rain.

ZGS 14.193, Shiba na, TSSSTS 81

14.219 呉宮花艸埋幽徑 *Gokyū no kasō yūkei o uzume,*
晉代衣冠成古丘 *Shindai no ikan kokyū to naru.*

Flowers and grass in the ⌜Wu⌝ palace have buried its lonely pathways.
The robed [officials] of the Chin Dynasty have gone to old gravemounds.➛

ZGS 14.195, Shiba na, TSSSTS 45

14.220 三山半落青天外 *Sanzan nakaba wa otsu seiten no soto,*
二水中分白鷺洲 *Nisui chūbun su hakuroshū.*

**➤The ⌈three mountains⌉ are half suspended beyond the blue sky,
The stream divides into two at White Heron Islet.**

ZGS 14.196, ZRKS 14.54, Shiba na

14.221 黑風袞袞六花輕 *Kokufū konkon rikka karushi,*
天列陰崖勢欲傾 *Tenretsu no ingai ikioi katamukan to hossu.*

**Relentless black wind whips the white snow;
The dark cliffs, looming against the sky, look about to fall.**

ZGS 14.197, Shiba na

14.222 腰不繫兮鞋不穿 *Koshi tsunagazu, ai ugatazu,*
面未洗兮頭未裹 *Omote imada arawazu, kashira imada tsutsumazu.*

**He hasn't tied his waistband or put on his shoes,
He hasn't washed his face yet or put on his hat.**

ZGS 14.198, Shiba na

14.223 故人西辭黃鶴樓 *Kojin nishi no kata kōkakurō o ji shite,*
煙花三月下楊州 *Enka sangatsu yōshū ni kudaru.*

**My old friend set off from the ⌈Yellow Crane Pavilion⌉ in the west,
And mid flowers and mists in the third month, went down to Yang-chou.**

ZGS 14.199, Shiba na, TSSSTS 74

14.224 孤蟾獨輝千山靜 *Kosen hitori kagayaki senzan shizuka ni,*
長嘯一聲天地驚 *Chōshō issei tenchi odoroku.*

**The lone ⌈toad⌉ shines brilliant, the thousand mountains are still.
At the long drawn-out roar, heaven and earth are startled.**

ZGJI 617: The first verse alludes to the ⌈moon⌉, the second verse to a tiger.

ZGS 14.200, ZGJI 617, ZRKS 14.157, Shiba na

14.225 五臺山上雲蒸飯 *Godaisanjō kumo han o mushi,*
古佛堂前狗尿天 *Kobutsudōzen inu ten ni nyō su.*

**On the peak of Mount ⌈Wu-t'ai⌉ clouds are steaming rice,
In front of the ancient Buddha Hall a dog is pissing at the sky.➤**

Heki 96 Verse First Comm.

KZS #1159, ZGS 14.201, ZGJT 122, ZGJI 618, ZRKS 14.55, Shiba 343

14.226 刹竿頭上煎餢子 *Sekkan tōjō ni taisu o senzu,*
三箇猢猻夜簸錢 *Sanko no koson yoru sen o hiru.*

**➤Toasting dumplings on top of the banner pole.
Three monkeys are pitching pennies in the night.**

14
字

Empuku-ji, Shiba 368: *Sekkan tōjō ni tsuisu o senzu:* 鎚 instead of 槌.

ZGS 14.347, ZGJT 250, ZGJI 642, ZRKS 14.220, Shiba 368

14.227 壺中自有佳山水 *Kochū onozukara kasansui ari,*
終不重尋五老峯 *Tsui ni kasanete gorōhō o tazunezu.*

The waterpot already contains beautiful mountain scenery,
No need to go all the way out to ⌜Mount of Five Elders⌝.

ZGS 14.202, Shiba 342

14.228 蝴蝶夢中家萬里 *Kochō muchū ie banri,*
杜鵑枝上月三更 *Token no shijō tsuki sankō.*

In my ⌜butterfly's dream⌝, home is ten thousand miles away;
On the branch there's a cuckoo, above is the ⌜moon⌝ at midnight.

ZGS 14.203, Shiba na, TSSSTS 153

14.229 劫火洞然毫末盡 *Gokka tōnen to shite gōmatsu tsuku,*
青山依舊白雲中 *Seizan kyū ni yotte hakuun no uchi.*

The ⌜doomsday fire⌝ has scorched every last little thing away,
But, as of old, the blue mountains rise among the white clouds.

Empuku-ji: *gōka* instead of *gokka.*

ZGS 14.204, ZGJT 140, ZGJI 620, ZRKS 14.106, Shiba 345

14.230 古殿深沈曉未開 *Koden shinchin to shite akatsuki imada hirakezu,*
玉簫吹徹鳳凰臺 *Gyokushō suitessu hōōdai.*

The deep stillness of the ancient palace before the break of day
Is pierced by the sound of a jade flute from the Phoenix Tower.

ZGS 14.205, ZGJI 616, Shiba 342

14.231 古殿深沈人不見 *Koden shinchin hito miezu,*
滿庭桂花風露香 *Mantei no keika fūro kanbashi*

In the deep stillness of the ancient palace, not a person in sight.
The garden is filled with cassia flowers, fragrant in the dewy air.

ZGS na, Shiba 342

14.232 此翁白頭眞可憐 *Kono ō hakutō makoto ni awaremubeshi,*
伊昔紅顏美少年 *Kore mukashi kōgan no bishōnen.*

Truly a pity, this white-haired old man—
Once long ago he was a handsome, rosy-cheeked youth.➛

ZGS 14.206, Shiba na, TSSSTS 8

14.233 公子王孫芳樹下 *Kōshi ōson hōju no moto,*
清歌妙舞落花前 *Seika myōbu rakka no mae.*

➤The son of a nobleman beneath the fragrant trees—
He sang so clearly, danced so lightly, amid the falling petals.

ZGS 14.207, Shiba 343

14.234 此曲祇應天上有 *Kono kyoku tada masa ni tenjō ni arubeshi,*
人間能得幾回聞 *Ningen yoku iku tabi ka kiku koto o en.*

This melody can only exist in heaven.
In the world of men, how often can one hear it?

ZGS 14.208, Shiba na

14.235 將此深心奉塵刹 *Kono jinshin o motte jinsetsu ni hōzu,*
是則名爲報佛恩 *Kore o sunawachi nazukete button ni hōzu to nasu.*

With deep feeling he serves in the realm of ⌜dusts⌝,
And calls it paying back his debts to Buddha.

ZGS 14.209, Shiba na

14.236 取箇眼兮耳必聾 *Kono manako o totte mimi kanarazu rōshi,*
捨箇耳兮目雙瞽 *Kono mimi o sutete me narabikosu.*

Take away the eyes and the ears go deaf,
Throw away the ears and the eyes go blind.

Heki 56 Verse.

ZGS na, ZGJT 196, ZGJI 621, ZRKS 14.209, Shiba na

14
字

14.237 碁逢敵手難藏行 *Go wa tekishu ni aute yukute o kakushigataku,*
詩到重吟始見功 *Shi wa jūgin ni itatte hajimete kō o miru.*

In chess, it's hard to hide your strategy from a skillful opponent;
In poetry, only after many readings is your merit visible.

ZGS 14.211, ZGJT 122, ZGJI 618, ZRKS 14.7, Shiba 343

14.238 五鳳樓前問洛陽 *Gohō rozen ni rakuyō o toeba,*
金鞭遙指御街長 *Kinben haruka ni yubisasu gyogai no nagaki koto o.*

In front of the ⌜Tower of Five Phoenixes⌝, if you should ask where ⌜Lo-yang⌝ is,
The golden whip will grandly point out the length of the ⌜imperial avenue⌝.

ZGS 14.212, ZGJI 618, ZRKS 14.5, Shiba 343

14.239 不是一番寒徹骨 *Kore ichibankan hone ni tessezumba,*
爭得梅花撲鼻香 *Ikade ka baika no hana o utte kōbashiki koto o en.*

If not for this bone-chilling cold,
How else could the fragrance of the plum flower strike my nose?

ZGS 14.213, ZGJT 403, ZRKS 14.25, Shiba 386

14.240 不是殃門累及吾 *Kore ōmon no wazawai ware ni oyobu ni arazu,*
彌天過犯不容誅 *Miten no kabon chū o yurusazu.*

The ⌜inferno at the gate⌝ will not spread to me.
My many crimes will fill the sky but punishment will not be exacted.

ZGS 14.214, Shiba na

14.241 今日親聞獅子吼 *Konnichi shitashiku shishiku o kiku,*
他時定作鳳凰兒 *Taji sadamete hōōji to naran.*

Today, listen closely to the growl of this lion cub.
Some other time, it will surely become the offspring of a phoenix.

KZS #1182, ZGS na, ZGJI 622, ZRKS 14.210, Shiba 346

14.242 今夜不知何處宿 *Konya shirazu izure no tokoro ni ka shuku sen,*
平沙萬里絕人煙 *Heisa banri jin'en o tatsu.*

I do not know where I will sleep tonight.
Flat sand for a thousand miles and no sign of people or fire.

ZGS 14.215, Shiba 346, TSSSTS 80

14.243 細雨濕衣看不見 *Saiu e o uruoshite miru ni mizu,*
閑花落地聽無聲 *Kanka chi ni ochite kiku ni koe nashi.*

Misty rain dampens my robe—look, but it cannot be seen.
Faded flowers fall to the earth—listen, but they have no sound.

ZGS 14.216, ZGJI 623, ZRKS 14.386, Shiba 346, TSSSTS 134

14.244 細雨洒花千點涙 *Saiu hana ni sosogu senten no namida,*
淡烟籠竹一堆愁 *Tan'en take o komu ittai no urei.*

Fine rain sprays the flowers with a thousand tears,
Thin mist clutches the bamboo in a wistful embrace.

ZGS 14.217, ZGJI 623, ZRKS 14.330, Shiba 346

14.245 犀因翫月紋生角 *Sai wa tsuki o moteasobu ni yotte mon tsuno ni shōji,*
象被驚雷花入牙 *Zō wa rai ni odorokasarete hana kiba ni iru.*

Playing with the ⌜moon⌝, the rhinoceros acquired the grain in its horn;
Being frightened by thunder put the pattern into the ivory of the elephant's tusks.

Both rhinoceros horn and elephant ivory display a distinct pattern or grain when polished.

ZGS 14.218, ZGJT 155, ZGJI 623, ZRKS 14.298, Shiba na

14.246 倒跨金毛獅子兒 *Sakashima kinmō ni shishiji o matagatte,*
無位眞人上五臺 *Mui no shinjin gotai ni noboru.*

Backwards he rides the golden lion cub,
The true person without rank climbs Mount ⌜Wu-t'ai⌝.

ZGS na, ZGJT 623, ZGJI 623, ZRKS 14.347, Shiba 377

14.247 倒把少林無孔笛 *Sakashima ni shōrin no mukuteki o totte,*
逆風吹了順風吹 *Gyakufū ni fukiowatte junpū ni fuku.*

He holds the holeless flute of ⌈Shao-lin⌉ upside down,
And after blowing it backwards, he blows it straight.

ZGS na, ZGJI 623, ZRKS 14.88, Shiba 378

14.248 向道莫行山下路 *Saki ni iu sanka no michi o yuku koto nakare to,*
果然猿叫斷腸聲 *Kazen to shite saru sakebu danchō no koe.*

They told me before not to go on the path by the mountains.
Sure enough, the monkeys shrieked with heartbreaking cries.

ZGS 14.219, ZGJT 128, ZGJI 619, ZRKS 14.101, Shiba 344

14.249 昨日今日事不同 *Sakujitsu konnichi ji onajikarazu,*
一般寒雨一般風 *Ippan wa kan'u ippan wa kaze.*

Yesterday and today things are not the same.
Before was winter rain, now it is windy.

ZGJI 623: *Ippan* 一般 here means 一方 *ippō*, "on the one hand."

ZGS 14.220, ZGJI 623, ZRKS 14.310, Shiba na

14.250 昨日友今日寃讎 *Sakujitsu no tomo konnichi no enshū,*
昨日花今日塵埃 *Sakujitsu no hana konnichi no jin'ai.*

Yesterday's friend is today's enemy,
Yesterday's flower is today's ⌈dust⌉.

ZGS 14.221, Shiba na

14.251 昨夜風敲門外竹 *Sakuya kaze tataku mongai no take,*
也知賊不打貧家 *Mata shiru zoku no hinka o tasezaru koto o.*

Last night it was the wind knocking the bamboos outside the gate.
I knew that no robber would strike the house of a poor man.

ZGS 14.222, ZGJI 623, ZRKS 14.379, Shiba na, GKFGS 1.73

14.252 昨夜金烏飛入海 *Sakuya kin'u tonde umi ni iri,*
曉天依舊一輪紅 *Gyōten kyū ni yotte ichirin kurenai nari.*

Last night the ⌈golden crow⌉ glided into the sea.
In the dawn sky, as of old, there is a single circle of red.

KZS #1151, ZGS 14.223, ZGJI 623, ZRKS 14.40, Shiba 347

14.253 昨夜虛空開口笑 *Sakuya kokū kuchi o hiraite warau,*
祝融呑卻洞庭湖 *Shukuyū donkyaku su dōteiko.*

Last night emptiness opened its mouth to laugh,
And ⌈Chu Jung⌉ swallowed ⌈Lake Tung-t'ing⌉ in one gulp.

ZGS na, ZGJT 158, ZGJI 623, ZRKS 14.359, Shiba 347

14 字

14.254 昨夜三更失卻牛
今朝天明失卻火
Sakuya sankō ushi o shikkyaku shi,
Konchō tenmei hi o shikkyaku su.

Last night, at the third watch, I lost the ox.
This morning, as the sky brightened, I lost the fire.

Variation: instead of 今朝天明, "this morning as the sky brightened," 天曉起來 *tengyō okikitatte,* "as dawn arrived."

ZGS 14.224, ZGJI 623, Shiba 347

14.255 昨夜秋風生八極
今朝流水漲前溪
Sakuya shūfū hakkyoku ni shōji,
Konchō ryūsui zenkei ni minagiru.

Last night the autumn wind rose in the ⌜eight extremities⌝,
This morning flowing water fills the nearby valleys.

ZGS 14.225, Shiba na

14.256 昨夜七峯牽老興
千思萬想到天明
Sakuya shichihō rōkyō o hiku,
Senshi bansō tenmei ni itaru.

Last night Seven Peaks stirred old desires
And he had a thousand thoughts, a million musings, to the break of day.

ZGS 14.226, Shiba na

14.257 昨夜泥牛鬪入海
直到而今無消息
Sakuya deigyū tatakatte umi ni iri,
Jiki ni ima ni itaru made shōsoku nashi.

Last night mud oxen fought each other into the sea.
Since then, we've had no news of them.

ZGS 14.227, Shiba 348

14.258 坐中若有江南客
聽取鷓鴣聲外聲
Zachū moshi kōnan no kyaku araba,
Chōshū seyo shako shōgai no shō.

If you are sitting with a traveler from ⌜Chiang-nan⌝,
Hear from him the song beyond song of the quail.

Variant: *seigai* instead of *shōgai.* See also 12.43.

ZGS 14.228, ZGJI 622, Shiba na

14.259 更把一枝無孔笛
等閑吹出萬年歡
Sara ni isshi no mukuteki o totte,
Tōkan ni fukiidasu mannen no kan.

And picking up the flute without holes,
He casually blew forth eternal joy.

ZGS na, ZRKS 14.401, Shiba 344

14.260 猿抱子歸青嶂後
鳥啣花落碧巖前
Saru ko o idaite seishō no shirie ni kaeri,
Tori hana o fukunde hekigan no mae ni otsu.

Monkeys, clasping their young, withdraw behind the green peaks;
Birds, holding flowers, alight before the blue cliffs.

ZGS 14.229: 銜 instead of 啣. Shiba 329: 岩 instead of 巖. ZRKS 122n2: A monk asked Kassan E Zenji, "What sort of place is Kassan's place?" Kassan replied, "Monkeys, clasping their young, withdraw behind the green peaks. Birds, holding flowers, alight before the blue cliffs." ZGJI 624: It is said that the *Blue Cliff Record* got its title from this phrase.

KZS #1199, ZGS 14.229, ZGJT 34, ZGJI 624, ZD #159, ZRKS 14.122, Shiba 329

14.261 珊瑚枕上兩行涙 *Sangochinjō ryōkō no namida,*
半是思君半恨君 *Nakaba wa kore kimi o omoi nakaba wa kimi o uramu.*

On the coral pillow, two streams of tears.
Half longing for you, half resenting you.

ZGS 14.230, ZGJI 627, Shiba 351

14.262 殘星數點雁横塞 *Zansei sūten kari sai ni yokotawari,*
長笛一聲人倚樓 *Chōteki issei hito rō ni yoru.*

A few stars remain as geese cross the frontier;
At the sound of the long-flute, he leans against the tower.

ZGS 14.231, ZGJI 627, ZRKS 14.153, Shiba 351, TSSSTS 146

14.263 山影入門推不出 *San'ei mon ni itte osedomo idezu,*
月光鋪地掃不盡 *Gekkō chi ni shiite haraedomo tsukizu.*

The mountain's shadow has crept into the gate—though pushed, it will not leave.
Moonlight covers the ground—though swept, it still remains.

ZGS 14.232, ZGJI 626, Shiba 350

14.264 山岳連天常吐碧 *Sangaku ten ni tsuranatte tsune ni midori o haki,*
深溪和月轉流光 *Shinkei tsuki ni washite utata hikari o nagasu.*

Mountain peaks stretch to heaven, emitting green without cease;
Deep valleys reflect the ⌜moon⌝ in flowing streams of endless light.

ZGS 14.233, Shiba na

14.265 山家富貴銀千樹 *Sanka no fūki ginsenju,*
漁夫風流玉一簑 *Gyofu no fūryū tama issa.*

The treasures of a mountain man, thousands of silvered trees;
The elegance of a fisherman, his rain-jeweled cape.

ZGS 14.234, ZGJI 626, Shiba 350

14.266 拗折山形拄杖子 *Sangyō no shujōsu o ōsetsu shite,*
從來大地黑漫漫 *Jūrai daichi koku manman.*

I have broken my plain mountain staff.
The great earth has always been deep, deep black.

Empuku-ji: *Sangyō no shujōsu o yōsetsu shite.* See also 5.143.

ZGS 14.235, ZGJI 626, Shiba na

14.267 山禽引子哺紅果 *Sankin shi o hiite kōka o hoshi,*
溪女得錢留白魚 *Keijo sen o ete hakugyo o todomu.*

The mountain bird leads its young with red berries in its mouth,
The girl by the stream lures white fish with coins.

ZGS 14.236, Shiba na

14.268 三世諸佛不知有 *Sanze no shobutsu aru koto o shirazu,*
狸奴白牯卻知有 *Ri'nu byakko kaette aru koto o shiru.*

The buddhas of the ⌜three worlds⌝ do not know what is,
But it is the badger and the white bull who know what is.

Heki 61 Main Case Comm., *Serenity* 69.

ZGS na, ZGJT 163, ZGJI 625, ZRKS 14.36, Shiba 349

14.269 山東老將尚童顏 *Santō no rōshō nao dōgan,*
曾臂紅旗到賀蘭 *Katsute kōki o hiji ni shite garan ni itaru.*

The old general from east of the mountains, when still a youth,
Once carried a red banner in his arm and went as far as Ho-lan.

Ho-lan was a mountain on the border between the early Chinese empire and central Asia.

ZGS 14.237, Shiba na

14.270 山僧活計茶三畝 *Sansō ga kakkei cha sanpo,*
漁父生涯竹一竿 *Gyofu no shōgai take ikkan.*

This mountain monk's livelihood is three square yards of tea bush,
A fisherman's life is his single bamboo pole.

ZGS 14.238, ZGJI 626, ZRKS 14.410, Shiba 350

14.271 山頭月掛雲門餅 *Santō tsuki wa kaku ummon no mochi,*
屋後松煎趙州茶 *Okugo matsu wa niru jōshū no cha.*

Over the mountains hangs the ⌜moon⌝—Ummon's dumpling;
Behind the house, steeping in the pines—Jōshū's tea.

ZGS 14.239, ZGJI 627, Shiba 351

14.272 三喚砒霜藏石蜜 *Sankan no hisō sekimitsu o zōshi,*
三應笑面露愁腸 *Sannō no shōmen shūchō o arawasu.*

[The Master's] three calls—his harsh cruelty concealed a stony sweetness,
[The attendant's] three replies—his smiling face revealed a mind in distress.

See MMK 17. Shiba 348: 礵 instead of 霜.

ZGS 14.240, Shiba 348, GKFGS 1, 180

14.273 三玄三要是何物 *Sangen sanyō kore nani mono zo,*
處處笙歌醉似泥 *Sho-sho no shōka yōte dei ni nitari.*

The ⌜three dark gates⌝ and the ⌜three necessities⌝—what can they be?
Everywhere we're playing flutes and singing and getting drunk as mud.

See *Rinzai-roku* §9.

ZGS 14.241, ZGJI 625, ZRKS 14.350, Shiba 348

14.274 三皇五帝是何物 *Sankō gotei kore nani mono zo,*
辛苦曾經二十年 *Shinku shite katsute furu nijūnen.*

The ⌜three sovereigns and five emperors⌝—what are they?
We've had twenty years of hard labor.

ZGS 14.242, Shiba na, GKFGS 1.60

14.275 三更月照幽窓外 *Sankō tsuki terasu yūsō no hoka,*
松竹青青碧欲流 *Shōchiku sei-sei to shite midori nagaren to hossu.*

At midnight, the ⌜moon⌝ is shining outside my silent window.
The pines and bamboo are so green their verdant color seems about to overflow.

ZGS 14.243, ZGJI 625, ZRKS 14.233, Shiba 348

14.276 三千世界海中漚 *Sanzen sekai kaichū no ō,*
一切賢聖如電拂 *Issai no kenjō denpotsu no gotoshi.*

The ⌜three thousand worlds⌝ are just froth on the ocean,
And wise men and saints are like a flicker of lightning.

See also 14.409.

ZGS na, Shiba 349

14.277 三千刹界眼中盡 *Sanzen sekkai ganchū ni tsuki,*
十二因緣心裏空 *Jūni innen shinri ni kūzu.*

The ⌜three thousand worlds⌝ exhausted in the eye,
The ⌜twelve causal conditions⌝ void in the heart.

ZGS 14.244, Shiba na

14.278 三千劍客今何在 *Sanzen no kenkyaku ima izuku ni ka aru,*
獨許莊周致太平 *Hitori yurusu sōshū ga taihei o itasu o.*

Where are the three thousand swordsmen now?
I recognize that Chuang Chou by himself brought about the great peace.

ZGJI 625, ZGJT 163: Chuang Chou is Chuang-tzu. *Chuang-tzu*, ch. 30, "Discoursing on Swords," describes King Wen of Chao, who was so fascinated by swords he let his state decline. He supported 3,000 swordsmen to watch them fight. Chuang-tzu, through his discourse on swords, made the king give up the sword.

ZGS 14.245, ZGJT 163, ZGJI 625, ZRKS 14.252, Shiba 349

14.279 三冬鐵樹滿林花 *Santō no tetsuju manrin no hana,*
六月黃河連底冰 *Rokugatsu no kōga rentei no kōri.*

Iron trees in the dead of winter—yet the forest is full of flowers.
The Yellow River in the peak of summer—yet it's frozen solid to the bottom.

ZGS 14.246, ZGJI 626, ZRKS 14.289, Shiba 349

14.280 三年辛苦已栽竹 *Sannen shinku shite sude ni take o uu,*
一夜工夫又作梅 *Ichiya no kufū mata ume to naru.*

After three years of bitter pain I planted bamboo,
And with one night's effort they blossomed into plums.

ZGS 14.247, ZGJI 626, ZRKS 14.357, Shiba 349

14.281 三邊一箭收功後 *Sanben no issen kō o osamete nochi,*
四海何愁不太平 *Shikai nanzo uroen taihei narazaru o.*

On the ⸢three borders⸣, now that the one arrow has achieved its effect,
There's no need to worry that the ⸢four seas⸣ are not at peace.

ZGS 14.249, ZGJT 163, ZGJI 626, ZRKS 14.257, Shiba na

14.282 三要印開朱點側 *Sanyō inkai shite shuten sobadatsu,*
未容擬議主賓分 *Imada gigi o irezaru ni shuhin wakaru.*

Lift the seal of ⸢three necessities⸣, the red imprint is sharp.
Before any hesitation can enter, host and guest have separated.

Rinzai-roku §9. *Heki* 98 Main Case *agyo.*

ZGS na, ZGJT 163, ZGJI 626. ZRKS 14.76, Shiba 350

14.283 子曰 *Shi notamawaku,*
參乎吾道一以貫之 *Shin ya, waga michi wa itsu wo motte kore wo tsuranukeri,*
曾子曰唯 *Sōshi no iwaku i.*

The Master said,
"Shen! My way has one [thread] that runs right through it."
Master Tseng said, "Yes."

Trans. from Waley 1938, *Analects* iv, 15.

ZGS 14.249, Shiba na

14.284 十字街頭窮乞兒 *Jūjigaitō no kyūkotsuji,*
腰間掛箇風流袋 *Yōkan ni kono fūryūtai o kaku.*

At the corner of the avenue, a beggar in gravest poverty
Hangs about his waist an elegant bag.

ZGS 14.250, ZGJI 631, ZRKS 14.397, Shiba 358

14.285 十年枕上塵中夢 *Jūnen chinjō jinchū no yume,*
半夜燈前物外心 *Hanya tōzen motsuge no shin.*

Ten years on my pillow, dreams in the midst of ⸢dust⸣.
Then at midnight, by lamplight, the mind beyond things.

ZGS 14.251, ZGJI 632, ZRKS 14.470, Shiba 358

14.286 四海盡歸皇化裏 *Shikai kotogotoku kōkari ni kisu,*
三邊誰敢犯封疆 *Sanpen tare ka aete hōkyō o okasan.*

The ⌜four seas⌝ have all returned to the realm of the emperor.
On the ⌜three borders⌝, who dares to violate the boundaries?

KZS #1171, ZGS 14.252, ZGJT 171, ZGJI 627, ZRKS 14.251, Shiba 353

14.287 四海只知天子貴 *Shikai tada tenshi no tōtoki koto o shitte,*
不知天子作何顏 *Tenshi nan no kanbase o nasu ka o shirazu.*

The ⌜four seas⌝ know only of the emperor's loftiness.
They do not know what face he has.

ZGS 14.253, Shiba na

14.288 四海浪平龍睡穩 *Shikai nami tairaka ni shite ryū no nemuru koto odayaka ni,*
九天雲靜鶴飛高 *Kyūten kumo shizuka ni shite tsuru no tobu koto takashi.*

The waves of the ⌜four seas⌝ are still and the dragon sleeps peacefully,
The clouds of the ⌜nine heavens⌝ are at rest and the stork flies high.

Shiba 353: *Kyūten kumo shizuka ni shite kakuhi takashi.*

ZGS 14.254, ZGJT 171, ZGJI 628, Shiba 353

14.289 四五百條花柳巷 *Shigohyakujō karyū no chimata,*
二三千處管絃樓 *Nisanzensho kangen no rō.*

Four or five hundred streets in the flower and willow quarter,
Two or three thousand halls for flutes and strings.

ZGS 14.255, Shiba na

14 字

14.290 四方八面絕遮欄 *Shihō hachimen sharan o zessu,*
萬象森羅齊漏泄 *Banzō shinra hitoshiku rōsetsu su.*

In the four quarters and eight directions, there are no barriers.
The ⌜ten thousand things⌝ all spill forth in teeming array.

Empuku-ji: *Banzō shinra hitoshiku rōsetsu shi.*

KZS #1150, ZGS 14.256, ZGJI 628, ZRKS 14.35, Shiba 353

14.291 支遁鶴矣右軍鵝 *Shiton ga tsuru, yugun ga ga,*
夜來和月賣珊瑚 *Yarai tsuki ni washite sango o uru.*

Chih Tun's cranes and Yuchün's geese:
As night falls, they sell coral bathed in the ⌜moon⌝.

Chih Tun (J. Shiton, 314–366), also known as Tao-lin 道林, was born into a Buddhist family and became an army general. He was said to be fond of cranes, a fitting image, since in later life he followed Taoist thought (ZGDJT 458b), where cranes are a symbol of longevity. After retiring he became good friends with the Taoist poet-calligrapher Wang I-chih, also called Yuchün (J. Yugun), "Army of the Right," because he commanded this army. Yuchün was fond of geese (Morohashi 3250.39). Moonlight was thought to encourage the growth of coral. The literary image here is of two masters who bring out each other's beauty as do coral and moonlight.

ZGS na, ZGDJT 458b, ZRKS 14.311, Shiba 352

14.292 頻呼小玉元無事 *Shikiri ni shōgyoku to yobu mo moto buji,*
只要檀郎認得聲 *Tada yōsu danrō ga koe o nintoku sen koto o.*

Again and again she calls Little Jade, but for no real purpose,
Just so that her lover can hear her voice.

MMK 17. ZGJI 629: Till married a man and woman were not to speak to each other. A woman summons her servant Little Jade only so that the man, who may be passing by downstairs, will hear her voice.

ZGS 14.257, ZGJT 395, ZGJI 629, ZRKS 14.65, Shiba 385

14.293 紫金光聚照山河 *Shikon kōjū senga o terasu,*
天上人間意氣多 *Tenjō ningen iki ōshi.*

Purple-gold light illumines the mountains and rivers;
In heaven above and in the world below, spirit abounds.➤

ZGS 14.258, ZGJI 628, ZRKS 14.352, Shiba 353

14.294 曾敕文殊領徒衆 *Katsute monju ni choku shite toshū o ryō su,*
毘耶城裏問維摩 *Biyajōri ni yuima o towashimu.*

➤He sends ⌜Mañjuśrī⌝ as his messenger to lead the disciples
And visit with ⌜Vimalakīrti⌝ at the Vaiśālī Palace.

ZGS 14.259, Shiba na

14.295 獅子窟中無異獸 *Shishikutchū ni ijū nashi,*
象王行處絕狐蹤 *Zōō yuku tokoro koshō o zessu.*

In the lion's cave there is no other beast;
Where the king elephant goes, no ⌜fox⌝ leaves its trace.

ZGS 14.260, ZGJT 177, ZGJI 628, ZRKS 14.422, Shiba 354

14.296 死鼠周人之玉璞 *Shiso wa shūnin no gyokuhaku,*
山雞楚國之鳳凰 *Sankei wa sokoku no hōō.*

A dead rat is the unpolished gem of the people of Chou,
A mountain pheasant is the phoenix of the land of Ch'u.

ZGS 14.261, Shiba na

14.297 七月七日長生殿 *Shichigetsu shichijitsu chōshōden,*
夜半無人私語時 *Yahan hito naku shigo no toki.*

On the seventh day of the seventh month, in the Hall of Long Life,
At midnight and alone by himself, he spoke intimate words.➤

The next two verses are connected lines from "Everlasting Sorrow" by Po Chü-i 白居易長恨歌. See ⌜Yang Kuei-fei⌝.

ZGS 14.262, Shiba na

14.298 在天願作比翼鳥 *Ten ni atte wa negawaku wa hiyoku no tori to naran,*
在地願爲連理枝 *Chi ni atte wa negawaku wa renri no eda to naran.*

**➛"In the sky I vow we shall be birds with shared wings,
On the earth I vow we shall be branches with a common grain.➛**

See ⌜Matrimonial harmony⌝.

ZGS 14.253, Shiba na

14.299 天長地久有時盡 *Ten nagaku chi hisashiki mo toki atte tsuku,*
此恨綿綿無絶期 *Kono urami wa men-men tayuru toki nashi.*

**➛Even the vast sky and the broad earth must someday come to an end,
But this bitterness lingers on and on, and does not cease."**

ZGS 14.264, Shiba na

14.300 十洲三島鶴乾坤 *Jisshū santō tsuru no kenkon,*
四海五湖龍世界 *Shikai goko ryū no sekai.*

**The ⌜ten isles⌝ and the ⌜three islands⌝ are the universe of the crane,
The ⌜four seas⌝ and the ⌜five lakes⌝ are the realm of the dragon.**

KZS #1216, ZGS 14.265, ZGJI 632, ZRKS 14.281, Shiba 358

14.301 十洲春盡花凋殘 *Jisshū haru tsukite hana chōzan,*
珊瑚樹林日杲杲 *Sango jurin hi kō-kō.*

**On the ⌜ten isles⌝ spring has gone and the flowers withered,
But in the coral tree forest the dazzling sun shines bright.**

Heki 70 Verse.

ZGS 14.266, ZGJI 632, ZRKS 14.182, Shiba 358

14.302 榔栗横擔不顧人 *Shitsuritsu ō ni ninatte hito o kaerimizu,*
直入千峯萬峯去 *Jiki ni senpō banpō ni irisaru.*

**His staff sideways across his shoulders and without a backward glance,
Straightaway he strides into the thousand hills and myriad peaks.**

Heki 25 Main Case. ZRKS 14.126: *Sokuritsu ō ni ninatte hito o kaerimizu.* ZGJI 630: *Shitsuritsu yokozama ni ninatte hito o kaerimizu.* Also: *Shitsuritsu ōtan hito o kaerimizu.*

ZGS 14.267, ZGJT 186, ZD #160, ZRKS 14.126, Shiba 355

14.303 事到極處則難説 *Ji no kyokusho ni itaru tokinba sunawachi tokigataku,*
理到極處則難明 *Ri no kyokusho ni itaru tokinba sunawachi akiramegatashi.*

**Facts at their ultimate are hard to explain,
Reason at its ultimate is hard to illuminate.**

Shiba 355: *itatte* instead of *itaru tokinba.*

ZGS 14.268, ZGJI 629, ZRKS 14.239, Shiba 355

14 字

14.304 不因紫陌花開早 *Shihaku hana hiraku hayaki ni yorazumba,*
爭得黄鶯下柳條 *Ikadeka kōō no ryūjō o kudaru koto o en.*

If not for flowers blooming early in the avenues of the capital,
Why else would yellow warblers alight on the willow boughs?

ZGS 14.269, ZGJT 403, ZGJI 628, ZRKS 14.345, Shiba na

14.305 釋迦彌勒舞堯風 *Shaka miroku gyōfū ni mai,*
文殊普賢歌舜日 *Monju fugen shunjitsu ni utau.*

Śākyamuni and ⌜Maitreya⌝ dance in ⌜Yao's⌝ breeze,
⌜Mañjuśrī and ⌜Samantabhadra⌝ sing in ⌜Shun's⌝ sun.

ZGS 14.270, Shiba na

14.306 芍藥花開菩薩面 *Shakuyaku hana hiraku bosatsu no men,*
椶櫚葉散夜叉頭 *Shuroha sanzu yasha no kashira.*

The peony flower blossoms into the face of a bodhisattva,
The palm shoots out its leaves into the head of a ⌜*yakṣa*⌝.

Empuku-ji: *Shakuyaku hana wa hiraku bosatsu no omote, Shuroha wa sanzu yasha no kashira.*

KZS #1167, ZGS 14.271, ZGJT 191, ZGJI 630, ZRKS 14.83, Shiba na

14.307 借問故園隱君子 *Shamon su koen no inkunshi,*
時時來往住人間 *Ji-ji raiō shite ningen ni jūsuru ka to.*

I asked him, the old recluse of my home village,
"Always going back and forth, ever think of staying in the world of people?"

ZGS 14.272, Shiba na, TSSSTS 81–2

14.308 借問梅花何處落 *Shamon su baika izure no tokoro ni ka otsuru,*
風吹一夜滿關山 *Kaze fuite ichiya kanzan ni mitsu.*

I wonder where these plum blossoms will fall.
The wind blows, and in one night they fill the mountain passes.

"Plum Blossoms" is the name of a flute melody.

ZGS 14.273, Shiba na, TSSSTS 220–1

14.309 衆花盡處松千尺 *Shūka tsukuru tokoro matsu senjaku,*
群鳥喧時鶴一聲 *Gunchō kamabisushiki toki tsuru issei.*

Where masses of flowers finally end, a thousand-foot pine;
When flocks of birds twitter, the single cry of a crane.

ZGS 14.274, ZGJI 631, ZRKS 14.277, Shiba 357

14.310 終日行而未曾行 *Shūjitsu gyōjite imada katsute gyōzezu,*
終日說而未曾說 *Shūjitsu toite imada katsute tokazu.*

All day long practicing, but still haven't practiced a thing;
All day long preaching, but still haven't preached a thing.

Heki 16 Intro.

ZGS 14.275, ZGJT 201, ZGJI 631

14.311 終年無客長閉關 *Shūnen kyaku nakushite nagaku kan o tozu,*
終日無心長自閑 *Shūjitsu kokoro nakushite nagaku onozukara kan nari.*

All year long no guests, my gate is always closed,
All day long nothing in mind, I'm always at ease.

Empuku-ji: *nōshite* instead of *nakushite.*

ZGS 14.276, Shiba na

14.312 重賞功前見勇夫 *Jūshō kōzen ni yūfu o mi,*
鐵鞭高擧碎珊瑚 *Tetsuben takaku agete sango o kudaku.*

By his great achievement, one recognizes the courageous hero,
Raising the iron whip high, he smashes the coral.

ZGS 14.277, Shiba na

14.313 從前汗馬無人識 *Jūzen no kamba hito no shiru nashi,*
只要重論蓋代功 *Tada yōsu kasanete gaidai no kō o ronzen koto o.*

We are not aware of the great efforts made in the past,
But we should again and again discuss the achievements of the first founders.

Kanba, here translated as "great effort," literally means "sweat horse." *Heki* 7 Intro.

KZS #1186, ZGS 14.278, ZGJT 204, ZGJI 632

14.314 愁人莫向愁人説 *Shūjin shūjin ni mukatte toku koto nakare,*
説向愁人愁殺人 *Shūjin ni sekkō sureba hito o shūsatsu su.*

A sad man should not speak to a sad man,
If he speaks to a sad man, he will deepen his sadness.

Heki 3 Verse *agyo*, 40 Verse *agyo.*

ZGS 14.279, ZGJT 202, ZGJI 631, ZRKS 14.304, Shiba 357

14.315 秋天曠野行人絕 *Shūten kōya kōjin tayu,*
馬首東來知是誰 *Bashu tō rai suru wa shiru kore ta zo.*

Under an autumn sky on an empty plain, not a traveler in sight,
A horseman comes from the east [west]. Who could that be?

Variant: 西 *sei,* "west," instead of 東 *tō,* "east." Shiba 356: *Bashu tō [sei] rai su shinnu kore ta zo.*

ZGS 14.280, ZGJI 631, Shiba 356, TSSSTS 76

14.316 秋葉風吹黄颯颯 *Shūyō kaze fuite kō sassatsu,*
晴雲日照白磷磷 *Seiun hi terashite haku rinrin.*

Wind blows in the autumn leaves, their yellows rustle.
The sun shines through bright clouds, a brilliant white.

ZGS 14.281, Shiba na

14.317 秋容萬里江楓盡 *Shūyō banri kōfū tsuku,*
人在澗溪橋上南 *Hito wa kankei kyōjō no minami ni ari.*

Autumn scenery for miles and miles, all lakes and maples.
There's someone south of the bridge over the valley stream.

ZGS 14.282, Shiba na

14.318 宿鷺亭前風擺柳 *Shukuroteizen kaze yanagi o uchiharai,*
錦官城裡雨催花 *Kinkanjōri ame hana o moyousu.*

By the Roosting Crane Pavilion, wind shakes the willows;
In the City of Brocade, rain sets off the flowers.

ZGS 14.283, Shiba na

14.319 樹色到京三百里 *Jushoku kyō ni itaru sambyakuri,*
河流歸漢幾千年 *Karyū kan ni kisu iku sennen.*

The green of the trees stretches to the capital three hundred miles.
The Yellow River has flowed into the land of Han for how many thousand years?

ZGS 14.284, Shiba na, TSSSTS 131

14.320 衆生無邊誓願度 *Shujō muhen seigan dō,*
煩惱無盡誓願斷 *Bonnō mujin seigan dan.*

All beings without number, I vow to liberate.
Endless blind passions, I vow to uproot.➤

This and the next verse are *shigu seigan,* 四弘誓願, the Four Great Vows, recited daily in the Zen monastery. This translation courtesy of the Rochester Zen Center.

ZGS 14.285, Shiba na

14.321 法門無量誓願學 *Hōmon muryō seigan gaku,*
佛道無上誓願成 *Butsudō mujō seigan jō.*

➤Dharma gates beyond measure, I vow to penetrate.
The Great Way of Buddha, I vow to attain.

ZGS 14.286, Shiba na

14.322 拄杖子踍跳上天 *Shujōsu botchō shite ten ni nobori,*
盞子裡諸佛說法 *Sanshiri no shobutsu hō o toku.*

My staff leaps up to the sky,
In my cup, many buddhas speak the Dharma.

ZGS 14.287, ZGJI 630, Shiba na.

14.323 須彌頂上無根草 *Shumi chōjō mukonsō,*
不受春風花自開 *Shunpū o ukezu shite hana onozukara hiraku.*

Atop Mount ⌜Sumeru⌝, on rootless grasses,
Untouched by the spring wind, flowers bloom by themselves.

KZS #1160, ZGS 14.288, ZGJI 631, ZRKS 14.59, Shiba na

14.324 修羅惡發把須彌 *Shura aku hasshite shumi o tori,*
一擲跨跳上梵天 *Ikkaku botchō shite bonten ni noboru.*

The ⌜*asura*⌝, enraged, seize Mount ⌜Sumeru⌝,
And in one vault leap up into Brahma's heaven.

ZGS 14.289, ZGJI 631, ZRKS 14.268, Shiba na

14.325 盡情收拾歸家去 *Jō o tsukushite shūshū shite ie ni kaerisaru,*
半掩柴扉春晝長 *Nakaba wa saihi o ōte shunchū nagashi.*

Emotions all spent, he's packed up and left for home.
The door of his hut stands open, on these long spring days.

ZGS 14.290, Shiba na

14.326 情閑巖樹看愈好 *Jō kan ni shite ganju mireba iyoiyo yoshi,*
室靜磵泉聞轉幽 *Shitsu shizuka ni shite kansen kikeba utata yū nari.*

With mind serene, one sees the cliffs and trees so much better;
With the room silent, the flowing spring sounds even more quiet.

ZGS 14.291, ZGJI 634, Shiba na

14.327 松檜蒼蒼歷幾歲 *Shōkai sō-sō to shite iku toshi o ka hetaru,*
莫敎駁畔鳥聲稀 *Samo araba are ganpan chōsei no mare naru koto o.*

Pines and cedars, thick and green, have been here how many years?
Never mind. The call of the cliff birds is rare indeed.

ZGS na, ZGJI 633, Shiba na

14.328 松根石上與誰説 *Shōkon sekijō tare to tomo ni ka tokan,*
月到中峯猶未歸 *Tsuki chūhō ni itatte nao imada kaerazaru ga gotoshi.*

With whom am I talking on the Pine Root Rock?
The ⌜moon⌝ has reached the central peak and I won't be returning just yet.

See ⌜Landscape⌝.

ZGS 14.292, Shiba na

14.329 繩床靜坐無餘事 *Jōshō ni seiza shite yoji nashi,*
深院遲遲春晝長 *Shin'in chi-chi to shite shunchū nagashi.*

I sit quietly on a woven cushion with nothing left to do.
Secluded in a distant temple faraway, I relax during long spring days.

ZGS 14.293, Shiba na

14.330 生死路頭君自看 *Shōji rotō kimi mizukara miyo,*
活人全在死人中 *Katsujin wa mattaku shinjin no uchi ni ari.*

See for yourself that on the path of life and death,
The live person is completely inside the dead person.

ZGS na, ZGJI 639, ZRKS 14.460, Shiba 366

14
字

14.331 生前富貴草頭露 *Shōzen no fūki wa sōtō no tsuyu,*
身後風流陌上花 *Shingo fūryū hakujō no hana.*

When alive, your wealth is the dew on the grass;
After death, your fame is the flowers by the roadside.

ZGS na, ZGJI 639, ZRKS 14.437, Shiba 366

14.332 燒甎打著連底冰 *Shōsen tajaku su rentei no kōri,*
赤眼撞著火柴頭 *Sekigan dōjaku su kasaitō.*

The flaming tile broke through the solid layers of ice,
⌜Red eyes⌝ collides with the burning brush.

Shiba 361: 着 instead of 著.

ZGS 14.294, ZGJI 634 (variant), Shiba 361

14.333 湘潭雲荏暮山出 *Shōtan kumo tsukite bosan ide,*
巴蜀雪消春水來 *Hashoku yuki shōshite shunsui kitaru.*

When Hsiang-t'an's clouds disperse, the evening mountains appear;
When Pa-shu's snows vanish, the spring waters flow.

Shiba 361: 盡 instead of 荏; TSSSTS 131.

ZGS 14.295, ZGJI 634, ZRKS 14.19, Shiba 361

14.334 焦遂五斗方卓然 *Shōsuigoto masa ni takuzen,*
高談雄辯驚四筵 *Kōdan yūben shien o odorokasu.*

Chiao Sui was even more impressive after drinking five flagons.
His lofty speeches and eloquent discourse would amaze all around.

ZGS 14.296, Shiba na, TSSSTS 10

14.335 少帝長安開紫極 *Shōtei chōan ni shikyoku o hiraki,*
雙懸日月照乾坤 *Jitsugetsu o narabekakete kenkon o terasu.*

The young emperor has taken the throne in ⌜Ch'ang-an⌝,
Now sun and moon together will shine over ⌜heaven and earth⌝.

"Sun and moon": the old and new emperors (TSSSTS 73).

ZGS 14.297, Shiba na, TSSSTS 73

14.336 丈夫自有衝天氣 *Jōfu onozukara shōten no ki ari,*
不向如來行處行 *Nyorai no gyōsho ni mukatte yukazu.*

A realized person naturally has energy that extends to heaven
And does not try to go where the Tathāgata has gone.

ZGS 14.298, ZGJT 222, ZGJI 634, ZRKS 14.383, Shiba na

14.337 蟭螟眼裏放夜市 *Shōmei ganri ni yashi o hanachi,*
大蟲舌上打鞦韆 *Daichū zetsujō ni shūsen o tasu.*

Hold a night festival in a ⌜mite's⌝ eye,
Ride a swing on the tiger's tongue.

ZGS 14.299, Shiba na

14.338 昭陽殿裏恩愛絕 *Shōyōdenri onnai o zessu,*
蓬萊宮中日月長 *Hōraikyūchū jitsugetsu nagashi.*

The devoted love of the Chao Yang Hall has ended,
The days and months in the ⌜P'eng-lai⌝ Palace are so long.

Originally built as the concubines' residence for Emperor Wu of the Han Dynasty, the Chao Yang Hall is more famous for later being the residence of ⌜Yang Kuei-fei⌝, the great love of Emperor Hsuan Tsung of the T'ang Dynasty.

ZGS 14.300, Shiba na

14.339 自小出家今已老 *Shō yori shukke shite ima sude ni ou,*
見人無力下禪床 *Hito o mite zensho o kudaru ni chikara nashi.*

Ordained when small, now I'm old.
I can't get down even to say hello.

ZGS na, ZGJI 633, ZRKS 14.193, Shiba 354

14.340 自小爲僧今六十 *Shō yori sō to narite ima rokujū,*
不曾擡手揖公卿 *Katsute te o motagete kōkei o iusezu*

Ordained as a monk when small, now I'm sixty.
I've yet to raise my hands and bow to their lordships.

ZGS 14.301, Shiba na

14.341 處處綠楊堪繫馬 *Sho-sho no ryokuyō uma o tsunagu ni taetari,*
家家門底透長安 *Ka-ka no montei chōan ni tooru.*

Everywhere the green willows are suitable for tying the horses,
The gate of every house leads to ⌜Ch'ang-an⌝.

ZGS 14.302, ZGJT 208, ZGJI 633, Shiba na

14.342 不識盧公何處去 *Shirazu rokō izure no tokoro ni ka saru,*
白雲流水共悠悠 *Hakuun ryūsui tomo ni yū-yū.*

We do not know where Master Lu has gone,
But the white clouds and flowing water are vast, immense.

ZGS 14.303, Shiba na

14.343 新秋簾幕千家雨 *Shinshū renbaku senke no ame,*
落日樓臺一笛風 *Rakujitsu rōtai itteki no kaze.*

It's just turned autumn, and on the screens of a thousand houses, rain;
Sunset, and from the mansion rooftops, the sound of a flute on the breeze.

Empuku-ji: *shinshū renmaku.*

ZGS 14.304, ZGJT 230, ZGJI 636, ZRKS 14.29, Shiba 363, TSSSTS 146

14.344 新婦面上添笑靨 *Shinpu menjō ni shōyō o soe,*
卻向錦繡幕裡行 *Kaette kinshūmakuri ni mukatte iku.*

The new bride, her face set in a dimpled smile,
Proceeds toward the curtains of embroidered brocade.

ZGS 14.305, Shiba 363

14.345 針鋒影裏騎大鵬 *Shinpōyōri taihō ni nori,*
等閑推落天邊月 *Tōkan ni oshiotosu tenpen no tsuki.*

Riding the great ⌜roc⌝ in the shadow of a needle's point,
With ease I knock down the ⌜moon⌝ from the heavens.

See also 14.174.

ZGS 14.306, ZGJT 229, ZGJI 635, ZRKS 14.322, Shiba 362

14.346 仁者見之謂之仁 *Jinsha wa kore o mite kore o jin to ii,*
智者見之謂之智 *Chisha wa kore o mite kore o chi to iu.*

A man of benevolence sees it and calls it benevolence,
A man of wisdom sees it and calls it wisdom.

ZGS 14.307, ZGJT 233, ZGJI 637, ZRKS 14.79, Shiba 364, 易經繫辞

14.347 眞金須是紅爐煅 *Shinkin wa subekaraku kore kōrō ni kitaubeshi,*
白玉還他妙手磨 *Hakugyoku wa ta no myōshu no masuru ni kaesu.*

True gold must be refined in the red-hot furnace,
Give white jade to a skilled hand for polishing.

ZGS 14.308, ZGJI 636, ZRKS 14.291, Shiba 362

14.348 參差松竹烟凝薄 *Shinshitaru shōchiku kemuri kotte usuku,*
重疊峯巒月上遲 *Jūjōtaru hōran tsuki noboru koto ososhi.*

In pines and bamboo tall and short, the thin mist is freezing;
Mountain peaks pile one upon another, the ⌜moon⌝ slowly rising.

ZGS 14.310, ZGJI 627, ZRKS 14.155, Shiba na

14.349 森森翠翰雪長拂 *Shin-shintaru suikan yuki nagaku harau,*
密密寒枝鳥不栖 *Mitsu-mitsutaru kanshi tori sumazu.*

The deep forests of green pines have long shrugged off the snow;
In the tangles of winter branches, birds do not roost.

ZGS 14.311, ZGJI 636, ZRKS 14.167, Shiba na

14.350 秦不耕兮漢不耘 *Shin tagayasazu kan kusagirazu,*
钁頭邊事杳無聞 *Kakutōhen no ji yō to shite kiku koto nashi.*

During the Ch'in no one tilled, and during the Han no one weeded.
There's no mention of anyone farming in those days.➛

ZGS 14.312, ZGJI 635, Shiba na, GKFGS 1.25

14.351 年來又有秋成望 *Nenrai mata shūsei no nozomi ari,*
三合清風半合雲 *Sango no seifū hango no kumo.*

➛Now with the passing years, we're looking to an autumn harvest
Of three parts pure wind and one-half measure of clouds.

ZGS 14.313, Shiba na

14.352 深溪絶無樵子語 *Shinkei taete shōshi no go naku,*
陰崖卻有獵人來 *Ingai kaette ryōjin no kitaru ari.*

Deep in the valley, no voices of lumberjacks.
By the shadowed cliff, a hunter appears.

ZGS 14.314, ZGJI 636, Shiba 362

14.353 深林漏月寒猿叫 *Shinrin tsuki o morashite kan'en sakebi,*
舊巣受風宿鶴鳴 *Kyūsō kaze o ukete shukkaku naku.*

In the deep forest filtered with moonlight, monkeys screech in the cold.
Its nest catches the wind and a roosting stork cries.

ZGS 14.315, ZGJI 636, Shiba 363

14.354 春江潮水連海平 *Shunkō no chōsui umi ni tsuranatte tairaka ni,*
海上明月共潮生 *Kaijō no meigetsu ushio to tomo ni shōzu.*

Spring rivers and tide waters join flat in the sea,
The bright ⌜moon⌝ over the ocean is born on the rising tide.

ZGS 14.316, ZGJI 632, Shiba 359, TSSSTS 13–4

14.355 春山無伴獨相求 *Shunzan tomonaku shite hitori aimotomu,*
伐木丁丁山更幽 *Batsuboku chō-chō to shite yama sara ni yū nari.*

Spring on the mountain, alone I've come to look for you.
The chop, chop of felling timber, the mountain is still more quiet.

Shiba 359: *Shunzan tomonaku hitori aimotomu, Batsuboku teitei yama sara ni kasuka nari.*

ZGS 14.317, Shiba 359, TSSSTS 53

14.356 春宵一刻價千金 *Shunshō ikkoku atai senkin,*
花有清香月有陰 *Hana ni seikō ari tsuki ni kage ari.*

Twilight in spring—a moment worth a thousand gold coins,
When flowers have that clean fragrance and the ⌜moon⌝ a haze.

ZGS 14.318, Shiba 359

14.357 春風强自分南北 *Shunpū shiite onozukara nanboku o wakatsu,*
畢竟枝梢共一根 *Hikkyō shishō tomo ni ikkon.*

The spring wind naturally divides north and south,
But branches and twigs originally have one root.

ZGS 14.319, Shiba na

14.358 春風春雨又開花 *Shunpū shun'u mata kaika,*
春雨春風又落花 *Shun'u shunpū mata rakka.*

Spring wind, spring rain, and again the flowers have bloomed;
Spring rain, spring wind, and again the flowers have fallen.

ZGS 14.320, Shiba na

14.359 春風得意馬蹄疾 *Shunpū i o ete batei hayashi,*
一日看盡長安花 *Ichijitsu ni mitsukusu chōan no hana.*

Inspired by the spring wind the horse's hooves are fleet.
In one day I have seen all the flowers of ⌜Ch'ang-an⌝.

KZS #1209, ZGS 14.321, ZGJT 207, ZGJI 633, ZRKS 14.290, Shiba 359

14.360 駿駒一躍三千界 *Shunku ichiyaku su sanzenkai,*
空解門前下馬臺 *Kūge monzen gebadai.*

The fleet horse in one bound leaps the ⌜three thousand worlds⌝.
Alone and unused is the hitching post by the gate.

ZGS 14.322, ZGJI 633, Shiba na

14.361 俊鶻遼天呈羽翮 *Shunkotsu ten ni itatte ukaku o teishi,*
金毛出窟振全威 *Kinmō kutsu o idete zen'i o furuu.*

The bold falcon soaring high in the skies displays its feathered wings,
The golden lion coming from its cave displays its total majesty.

ZGS 14.323, ZGJI 633, ZRKS 14.271, Shiba 360

14.362 俊鷹豈肯籬邊立 *Shunyō ani aete rihen ni tatan ya,*
直透青霄萬萬尋 *Jiki ni seishō ban-ban jin ni tōru.*

How can the peerless falcon just sit perched on a hedge?
In a flash, it soars ten thousand feet into the blue heaven.

ZGS 14.324, ZGJI 633, ZRKS 14.342, Shiba na

14.363 醉歸扶路人爭笑 *Suiki michi ni tasukerarete hito arasoiwarai,*
十里珠簾半上鉤 *Jūri no shuren nakaba kō ni noboru.*

When he came home drunk, clinging by the road, people roared with laughter.
For ten miles the elegant house screens were rolled up to the halfway hook.

ZGS 14.325, Shiba na

14.364 水光瀲灩晴偏好 *Suikō ren'en harete hitoe ni yoshi,*
山色空濛雨亦奇 *Sanshoku kūmō ame mata ki nari.*

The light on its waters, its endless waves on a clear day are especially fine.
But the coloring of the mountains under a drizzling rain is also unique.➤

ZGS 14.326, Shiba na, 蘇東坡題杭州西湖詩

14.365 若把西湖比西施 *Moshi seiko o totte seishi ni hiseba,*
淡粧濃抹兩相宜 *Tanshō nōmatsu futatsu nagara aiyoshi.*

➛If you compare West Lake to the lady ⌜Hsi-shih⌝,
Both look beautiful either in plain dress or rich attire.

ZGS 14.327, ZGJI 677, ZRKS 14.377, Shiba 356

14.366 垂死病中驚坐起 *Suishi no byōchū odoroite zaki su,*
暗風吹雨入寒窓 *Anpū ame o fuite kansō ni iru.*

Though deathly ill, I sat bolt upright in shock.
A dark wind was driving in rain through the cold window.

ZGS 14.328, Shiba na, TSSSTS 92

14.367 吹毛匣裏冷光寒 *Suimō kōri reikō susamaji,*
外道天魔皆拱手 *Gedō tenma mina te o tandaku su.*

The cold glint of the ⌜hair-cutter sword⌝ in its case sets them shivering.
All the heretics and devas clasp their hands together in fear.

Heki 65 Main Case Comm., ZGJI 638: *Gedō tenma mina te o komanuku.*

KZS #1198, ZGS 14.329, ZGJI 638, ZRKS 14.181, Shiba na

14.368 數聲淸磬是非外 *Sūsei no seikei zehi no hoka,*
一箇閑人天地間 *Ikko no kanjin tenchi no kan.*

Clear-sounding chimes beyond right and wrong,
One person at ease between heaven and earth.

ZGS 14.330, Shiba na

14.369 數片白雲籠古寺 *Sūhen no hakuun koji o kome,*
一條綠水繞青山 *Ichijō no ryokusui seizan o meguru.*

Tattered white clouds veil the old temple,
A single green stream winds around the blue mountains.

ZGS 14.331, ZGJT 240, ZGJI 638, ZRKS 14.381, Shiba 365

14.370 已收滴博雲間戍 *Sude ni tekihaku unkan no jū o osame,*
欲奪蓬婆雪外城 *Hōba setsugai no shiro o ubawan to hossu.*

I already control Ti Po, that stronghold within the clouds,
Now I want to seize P'eng P'o, the castle beyond the snows.

ZGS 14.332, Shiba na, TSSSTS 82

14.371 淸風欲發鴉飜樹 *Seifū hassen to hosshite a ju ni hirugaeru,*
闕月初昇犬吠雲 *Ketsugetsu hajimete nobotte inu kumo ni hoyu.*

A clean wind about to rise, crows fly to the trees;
On the first rise of the crescent ⌜moon⌝, dogs howl at the clouds.

Shiba 367: 翻 instead of 飜.

ZGS 14.333, ZGJI 641, ZRKS 14.143, Shiba 367

14.372 靑山綠水元依舊 *Seizan ryokusui moto kyū ni yoru,*
明月淸風共一家 *Meigetsu seifū tomo ni ikka.*

The green mountains and blue streams are as they have always been,
The bright ⌜moon⌝ and pure wind are both of one house.

ZGS 14.334, ZGJT 245, ZGJI 640, ZRKS 14.20, Shiba 366

14.373 靑山綠水草鞋底 *Seizan ryokusui sōaitei,*
明月淸風柱丈頭 *Meigetsu seifū shujōtō.*

The green mountains and their blue waters beneath my straw sandals,
The bright ⌜moon⌝ and the pure wind above my monk's staff.

ZGS 14.335, ZGJI 640, Shiba 366

14.374 靑山只解磨古今 *Seizan tada kokon o masuru koto o gesu,*
流水何曾洗是非 *Ryūsui nanzo katsute zehi o arawan.*

The blue mountains have ground to dust past and present.
Do the flowing streams run according to right and wrong?

ZGS 14.336, ZGJT 245, ZGJI 640, ZRKS 14.384, Shiba 366

14.375 靑松不礙人來往 *Seishō hito no raiō o saegirazu,*
野水無心自去留 *Yasui mushin ni shite onozukara kyoryū su.*

The green pines do not hinder people from coming and going,
The field streams stop and go without a care.

ZGS 14.337, ZGJT 245 (variant), ZGJI 641, ZRKS 14.70, Shiba na

14.376 晴川歷歷漢陽樹 *Seisen reki-rekitari kanyō no ju,*
芳草萋萋鸚鵡洲 *Hōsō sei-seitari ōmuchū.*

Across the bright shining river—the trees of Han-yang.
Fragrant grasses, lush and profuse—on the ⌜Isle of Parrots⌝.➛

ZGS 14.338, Shiba na, TSSSTS 45, 140

14.377 日暮鄉關何處是 *Nichibo kyōkan izure no tokoro ka kore naru,*
烟波江上使人愁 *Enpa kōjō hito o shite ureeshimu.*

➛At the day's end, my home village, where would it be?
Mist and waves on the river make a person sad.

ZGS 14.339, Shiba na

14.378 靑蛇上竹一種色 *Seija take ni noboru isshu no iro,*
黃蝶隔牆無限情 *Kōchō kaki o hedatsu mugen no jō.*

The oneness of colors when the green snake climbs the bamboo,
The infinite feeling when a yellow butterfly flies over the hedge.

ZGS 14.340, Shiba na

14.379 青燈夜雨湘江上 *Seitō yau shōkō no hotori,*
添得平沙落雁圖 *Soeetari heisha rakugan no zu.*

Blue lamplight, night rain on the River Hsiang.
Add to this geese landing on the flat sands, as in a painting.

ZGS 14.341, ZGJI 641, ZRKS 14.199, Shiba na , ZRKS 14.199n2: GKFGS 1.32

14.380 昔人既乘白雲去 *Sekijin sude ni hakuun ni jōjite saru,*
此地空餘黃鶴樓 *Kono chi munashiku amasu kōkakurō.*

Once long ago a man mounted a white cloud and left.
Now in this place nothing remains but the ⸢Yellow Crane Pavilion⸣.

ZGS 14.342, Shiba na, TSSSTS 45, 140

14.381 石女舞成長壽曲 *Sekijo mai nasu chōjū no kyoku,*
木人唱起太平歌 *Bokujin tonaeokosu taihei no uta.*

The ⸢stone woman⸣ dances the dance of long life,
The ⸢wooden man⸣ sings songs of great peace.

KZS #1180, ZGS 14.343, ZGJI 641, ZRKS 14.255, Shiba 367

14.382 石火光中分緇素 *Sekka kōchū ni shiso o wakachi,*
閃電機裏辨端倪 *Sendenkiri ni tangei o benzu.*

In the twinkling of a spark, he separates black from white;
In a flash of lightning, he distinguishes beginning and end.

Heki 16 Verse Comm.

ZGS 14.344, ZGJI 641, ZRKS 14.27, Shiba 367

14.383 石虎哮吼上九天 *Sekko kōkō shite kyūten ni nobori,*
泥牛入海無尋處 *Deigyū umi ni itte tazuneru ni tokoro nashi.*

With a roar the stone tiger rises into the ⸢nine heavens⸣,
Slipping into the sea, the mud ox is nowhere to be found.

ZGS 14.345, Shiba 367

14.384 世尊隻眼通三界 *Seson no sekigen sangai ni tsūji,*
外道雙眸貫五天 *Gedō no sōbō goten o tsuranuku.*

The World-Honored One's single eye penetrates the ⸢three worlds⸣,
The heretic's two eyes pierce the ⸢five heavens⸣.

ZGS 14.346, ZGJI 639, ZRKS 14.272, Shiba 365

14.385 雪後始知松柏操 *Setsugo hajimete shiru shōhaku no misao,*
事難方見丈夫心 *Koto katōshite masa ni arawaru jōbu no shin.*

Only after snow do we appreciate the steadfast pine and oak.
It is in times of difficulty that strength of character truly appears.

ZGS 14.348, ZGJT 251, ZGJI 642, Shiba 368, ZRKS 14.368

14.386 千溪萬壑歸滄海 *Senkei bangaku sōkai ni kishi,*
四海八蠻朝帝都 *Shikai hachiban teito ni chōsu.*

The thousand streams, the ten thousand channels return to the open sea;
The four seas, the eight barbarian tribes pay tribute at the imperial capital.

KZS #1219, ZGS 14.349, ZGJI 642, ZRKS 14.254, Shiba na

14.387 千溪日晩樵歌路 *Senkei hi kuru shoka no michi,*
歸去來兮歸去來 *Kaeri nan iza kaeri nan iza.*

As the sun sets over a thousand valleys, woodsmen sing on the road,
"Going home, we are going home."

ZGS 14.350, Shiba na

14.388 千江有水千江月 *Senkō mizu ari senkō no tsuki,*
萬里無雲萬里天 *Banri kumo nashi banri no ten.*

A thousand rivers have water, a thousand rivers of ⌜moon⌝,
A million miles without a cloud, a million miles of sky.

ZGS 14.351, ZGJT 255, ZGJI 642, ZRKS 14.24, Shiba 369

14.389 千古萬古黑漫漫 *Senko banko koku man-man,*
塡溝塞壑無人會 *Mizo ni michi tani ni fusagaru hito no e suru nashi.*

From a thousand, ten thousand ages past, a complete and utter darkness
Floods the channels, overflows the valleys and yet no one understands.

Heki 16 Verse *agyo.*

ZGS 14.352, ZGJT 255, ZGJI 642, ZRKS 14.315, Shiba na

14.390 泉州白家酒三盞 *Senshū hakke no sake sansan,*
喫了猶言未沾唇 *Kisshi owatte nao iu imada kuchibiru uruosazu to.*

At the House of Pai in Ch'üan-chou, you've had three cups of wine.
Though you've drunk, still you say, "I have yet to wet my lips."

MMK 10 (variant): *kisshi tsukushite* instead of *kisshi owatte.* ZRKS 14.4n: The House of Pai in Ch'üan-chou is a winemaker. There are many variations of this verse with different names for winemaker and place.

KZS #1140, ZGS na, ZGJT 244 (variant), ZGJI 640 (variant), ZD #151, ZRKS 14.4, Shiba 369

14.391 千峯雨霽露光冷 *Senpō ame harete rokō hiyayaka ni,*
月落松根蘿屋前 *Tsuki wa otsu shōkon raoku no mae.*

The rain has lifted from a thousand peaks, dew drops are shimmering cold,
Moonlight falls on the pine roots before the ivied cottage.➛

ZGS 14.353, Shiba 369

14.392 擬寫等閑此時意 *Tōkan ni kono toki no i o utsusan to gi sureba,*
一溪雲鎖水潺潺 *Ikkei kumo tozashite mizu sen-sen.*

➛Long I wonder how to catch the feel of this moment
With the stream shrouded in mist and the water trickling.

ZGS 14.354, Shiba 334

14.393 千峯勢到嶽邊止 *Senpō no ikioi wa gakuhen ni itatte tomi,*
萬派聲歸海上消 *Manpa no koe wa kaijō ni ki shite shō su.*

The thousand hills lose their stature at the foot of the mountains,
The sounds of the ten thousand streams cease on their return to the sea.

ZGS na, ZGJT 256, ZGJI 643 ZRKS 14.51, Shiba 369

14.394 千峯萬峯不敢住 *Senpō banpō aete todomarazu,*
落花流水太芒芒 *Rakka ryūsui hanahada bō-bō.*

A thousand peaks, ten thousand peaks—without end.
Fallen flowers, flowing water—on and on without cease.

ZGS 14.356, Shiba 369

14.395 泉石膏肓不可醫 *Senseki no kōkō iyasubekarazu,*
曉鐘吟到夕陽時 *Gyōshō ginji itaru sekiyō no toki.*

Can't cure this ⸢life-and-death disease⸣ of wandering the mountains and springs,
From the ring of the morning bell to the time of the evening sun.

ZGS 14.357, Shiba na

14.396 疎影横斜水清淺 *Soei ōsha mizu seisen,*
暗香浮動月黄昏 *Ankō fudō tsuki kōkon.*

Shadows of plums straight and crooked on clear shallow water,
Their lingering fragrance floats about the twilight ⸢moon⸣.

ZRKS 14.16n: 疎影 is a literary term for plums.

ZGS 14.359, ZGJI 643, ZRKS 14.16, Shiba 370, 林和靖梅花詩

14.397 桑柘樹頭聞布穀 *Sōsha jutō ni fukoku o kiki,*
春風影裏牧耕牛 *Shunpū eiri ni kōgyū o boku su.*

In the mulberry bushes I hear the pigeons calling,
In the lee of the spring wind I tend the oxen plowing.

ZGS 14.360, ZGJI 643, ZRKS 14.224, Shiba na

14.398 桑柘影斜秋社散 *Sōsha kage naname ni shite shūsha sanzu,*
家家扶得醉人歸 *Ka-ka suijin o tasukeete kaeru.*

The mulberries are casting long shadows, the autumn festival has dispersed,
The drunks are all being helped home.

ZGS 14.361, ZGJI 643, Shiba na, TSSSTS 112

14.399 草色青青柳色黄 *Sōshoku sei-sei ryūshoku ki nari,*
桃花歷亂李花香 *Tōka rekiran rika kanbashi.*

Grass colors green, willows color gold,
⸢Peach⸣ blooms in profusion, plum blossoms fragrant.

ZGS 14.362, Shiba 370, TSSSTS 78–9

14.400 霜天月落夜將半 *Sōten tsuki ochite ya masa ni nakaba naran to su,*
誰共澄潭照影寒 *Dare to tomo ni ka chōtan kage o shōshite samuki.*

The ⌜moon⌝ is setting in the frosty sky, it's almost midnight.
With whom can I share these winter images caught in the still pond?

Heki 40 Verse.

ZGS 14.363, ZGJI 644, Shiba na

14.401 象罔到時光燦爛 *Zōmō itaru toki hikari sanran,*
離婁行處浪滔天 *Rirō iku tokoro nami tōten.*

When ⌜Hsiang-wang⌝ came, its light was dazzlingly bright,
Where ⌜Li Lou⌝ went, the waves dashed to the sky.

Heki 88 Verse Comm.

ZGS 14.364, Shiba 371

14.402 鼠入錢筒技已窮 *So sentō ni itte gi sude ni kiwamaru,*
十年蹤跡眼頭空 *Jūnen no shōseki gantō ni kūzu.*

Like a mouse caught in a money tube, he was at wits' end—
Ten years of traces disappeared from sight.➛

A bamboo tube whose mouth was exactly the diameter of a coin was used as a money container.

ZGS 14.365, Shiba na, GKFGS 47

14.403 而今又問平田路 *Ima mata tou heiden no michi,*
山舍半吹黄葉風 *Sansha nakaba fuku kōyō no kaze.*

➛Now again he's on the path across the open fields.
The wind's blowing yellow leaves into the mountain hut.

Shiba 354: *Jikon mata tou heiden no michi.*

ZGS 14.366, Shiba 354

14.404 其安也潛鱗在淵 *Sono an ya senrin fuchi ni ari,*
其逸也翔鳥脱絆 *Sono itsu ya shōchō han o dassu.*

Peace—a deepwater fish rests in the depths.
Freedom—a flying bird loosened from its fetters.

ZGS 14.367, Shiba na

14.405 昔年覓火和烟得 *Sekinen hi o motomete kemuri ni washite u,*
今日擔泉帶月歸 *Konnichi izumi o ninaeba tsuki o obite kaeru.*

Years ago, seeking fire, I found it mingled with smoke.
Today, carrying spring water, I return wrapped in the ⌜moon⌝.

Shiba 368: *Sono kami hi o motomuru ni kemuri ni washite e, Konnichi izumi o ninatte wa tsuki o onde kaeru.*

ZGS na, ZGJI 642, ZRKS 14.72, Shiba 368

14.406 村落夜深猶未眠 *Sonraku yo fukōshite nao imada nemurazu,*
寒砧應是小嬋娟 *Kanchin masa ni kore shōsenken narubeshi.*

Midnight in the village, someone is still awake.
Still at the cold ⌜fulling blocks⌝, "Ah, these are going to be slightly elegant indeed!"

ZGS 14.368, Shiba na, *Shinjigen* 1750

14.407 太液芙蓉未央柳 *Taieki no fuyō biau no yanagi,*
芙蓉如面柳如眉 *Fuyō wa men no gotoku yanagi wa mayu no gotoshi.*

The lotus flowers of the pond, the willows of the palace:
The lotus flowers are like her face, the willows like her ⌜eyebrows⌝.

ZGS 14.369, ZGJI 644, Shiba na

14.408 大湖三萬六千頃 *Taiko sanman rokusen kei,*
月在波心説向誰 *Tsuki wa hashin ni ari tare ni ka sekkō sen.*

T'ai-hu, the great lake, stretches over thirty-six thousand acres;
The ⌜moon⌝ floats deep under the waves. To whom can I tell this?

ZGS 14.370, ZGJT 286, ZGJI 645, ZRKS 14.6, Shiba na

14.409 大千沙界海中漚 *Daisen shakai kaichu no ou,*
一切賢聖如電拂 *Issai no kenshō denpotsu no gotoshi.*

The ⌜thousand-fold universe⌝ is just froth on the ocean,
And wise men and saints are like a flicker of lightning.

See also 14.276.

ZGS 14.371, Shiba na

14.410 大地撮來粟米粒 *Daichi sasshikitaru zokubeiryū,*
一毫頭上現乾坤 *Ichimōtōjō ni kenkon o genzu.*

Pick up the great earth in a pellet of grain;
And on the tip of a hair, manifest ⌜heaven and earth⌝.

ZGS na, ZGJI 645, ZRKS 14.477, Shiba 372

14.411 大底有大底生涯 *Taitei wa taitei no shōgai ari,*
小底有小底活計 *Shōtei wa shōtei no kakkei ari.*

A big person has a big person's career,
A small person leads a small person's life.

ZGS na, ZGJI 645, ZRKS 14.406, Shiba 372

14.412 大抵還他肌骨好 *Taitei wa ta no kikotsu no yoki ni kaesu,*
不塗紅粉自風流 *Kōfun o nurazaredomo onozukara fūryū.*

On the whole she relies on the original beauty of her skin and features.
Without painting herself with rouge and powder, she has a charm of her own.

ZGS 14.372, ZGJT 286, ZGJI 645, ZRKS 14.69, Shiba 371

14.413 太平元是將軍致 *Taihei moto kore shōgun itasu,*
不許將軍見太平 *Yurusazu shōgun taihei o miru koto o.*

The great peace was actually the general's achievement
But the general was not allowed to see it.

ZGJI 646, KZS #1149: *Taihei moto kore shōgun no chi, Shōgun no taihei o miru koto o yurusazu.*

KZS #1149, ZGS 14.373, ZGJT 286, ZGJI 646, ZRKS 14.32, Shiba na

14.414 大鵬展翅蓋十洲 *Taihō tsubasa o nobete jisshū o ou,*
籬邊燕雀空啾啾 *Rihen no enjaku munashiku shūshū.*

When the giant ⌜roc⌝ spreads its wings, it looms over the ten isles;
In the bushes, sparrows and swallows shriek pitifully.

ZGS 14.374, ZGJT 294, ZRKS 14.358, Shiba na

14.415 大野兮涼飈颯颯 *Taiya ryōhyō satsusatsu,*
長天兮疎雨濛濛 *Chōten sou mōmō.*

Harsh winds gust across the great plains,
Misty rains darken the enormous sky.

Heki 27 Verse.

ZGS 14.375, ZGJI 645, Shiba 372

14.416 大洋海底紅塵起 *Taiyō kaitei ni kōjin okori,*
須彌頂上水橫流 *Shumi chōjō ni mizu ōryū su.*

On the bottom of the great ocean red ⌜dust⌝ rises,
On the top of Mount ⌜Sumeru⌝ water flows.

ZGS 14.376, Shiba na

14.417 大陽門下無星月 *Taiyō monka seigetsu naku,*
天子殿前無貧兒 *Tenshi denzen hinji nashi.*

At the gate of the sun there are neither stars nor ⌜moon⌝,
In front of the emperor's palace there are no poor.

ZGS 14.377, ZRKS 14.90, Shiba na

14.418 誰家別舘池塘裏 *Ta ga ie no bekkan zo chitō no uchi,*
一對鴛鴦畫不成 *Ittai no en'ō egakedomo narazu.*

In the pond of whose estate
Is there a pair of ⌜mandarin ducks⌝ too beautiful to paint?

ZGS 14.378, ZGJT 238, ZGJI 648, ZRKS 14.286, Shiba 365

14.419 竹密不妨流水過 *Take mitsu ni shite ryūsui suguru o samatagezu,*
山高豈礙白雲飛 *Yama takōshite ani hakuun no tobu koto o saen ya.*

Dense bamboo does not interrupt the flow of water,
Nor does a high mountain block the drift of the clouds.

ZGS 14.379, ZGJT 304, ZGJI 646, ZRKS 14.37, Shiba 373

14.420 惟愛清臺新曆日 *Tada ai su seidai shin rekijitsu,*
懶觀韓子送窮文 *Miru ni monoushite kanshi no sōkyū no bun.*

We love the star-viewing deck and the New Year calendar,
But we are tired of reading Han-tzu's "Text for Sending Off the God of Poverty."

ZGJT 12: The traditional celebrations of the New Year included one that was not so much fun, the year-end recitation of Han-tzu's "Text for Sending Off the God of Poverty."

ZGS na, ZGJT 12, ZGJI 647, ZRKS 14.223, Shiba 322

14.421 只今惟有西江月 *Tada ima tada seikō no tsuki nomi ari,*
曾照吳王宮裏人 *Katsute terasu goō kyūri no hito.*

Now there is only the ⌜moon⌝ on the West River,
But once it shone on someone in the palace of the King of ⌜Wu⌝.

ZGS 14.380, Shiba na, TSSSTS 74

14.422 戰矣哉暴骨沙礫 *Tatakawan kana hone o sareki ni sarashi,*
降矣哉終身夷狄 *Kudaran kana mi o iteki ni oen.*

Fight, and bleach your bones in the desert sands;
Surrender, and end your life in a barbarian land.

ZGS 14.381, ZGJI 647, Shiba na

14.423 只願君王相顧意 *Tada kunnō no aikaerimiru i o negatte,*
臨臺幾度畫蛾眉 *Tai ni nozonde ikutabi ka gabi o egaku.*

My only wish is to receive the favor of my lord.
Before my mirror, how many times have I painted ⌜moth eyebrows⌝?

ZRKS 14.3: *Tada negau kunnō no aikaerimiru i o.*

KZS #1139, ZGS 14.382, ZGJI 646, ZRKS 14.3, Shiba 352

14.424 但得心閑隨處樂 *Tada shin kan naru koto o eba tokoro ni shitagatte tanoshiman,*
不論朝市與雲山 *Chōshi to unzan to o ronzezu.*

If you once attain a heart at peace, you enjoy wherever you are,
Whether at the morning market or atop a clouded mount.

ZGS 14.383, Shiba na

14.425 只箇一點無明焰 *Tada kono itten no mumyō no honō,*
鍊出人間大丈夫 *Neriidasu ningen no daijōbū.*

Just this single ignorant ember
Was worked up into a supreme example of humanity.

ZGS 14.384, ZRKS 14.91, Shiba 352

14.426 只此更無回避處 *Tada kore sara ni kaihi no tokoro nashi,*
森森頭角畫不成 *Shinshin taru zukaku egakedomo narazu.*

There is simply nowhere for it to turn and hide;
Its majestic horns, no artist could draw.

ZGS na, ZRKS 14.336, Shiba 352, *Oxherding Picture* 3

14.427 只知牛瘦角不瘦 *Tada shiru ushi yasete tsuno yasezaru koto o,*
不覺心高句亦高 *Oboezu kokoro takōshite ku mo mata takaki koto o.*

I knew only that even if a cow gets thin, its horns will not.
But I did not know that when one's heart is elevated, so also are one's words.

ZGS 14.385, Shiba na, GKFGS 1.163

14.428 祇因雕巧失其體 *Tada chōkō ni yotte sono tai o ushinau,*
不見全文在世門 *Zenmon no seken ni aru koto o mizu.*

He loses the essence by skillful sculpting;
The complete figure is not to be seen in worldly learning.

Kidō-roku has a slightly different version with a clearer meaning: 祇因彫巧失眞體, 不見全文在世間 *Tada eru koto takumi ni shite shintai o ushinau, Zenbun no seken ni aru koto o mizu,* "He loses the true essence by his skill in sculpting; / The complete figure is not to be seen in the world" (Kokuyaku Zenshū Sōsho Kankōkai 1974, Second Collection, vol. vii, 256–7).

ZGS 14.386, Shiba na

14.429 朶朶湖山千古佛 *Da-da no kozan sen kobutsu,*
重重烟樹一樓臺 *Jū-jū enju ichi rōtai.*

The mountains and lakes in vast array are thousands of old buddhas;
The misted trees, layer upon layer, are a many-storeyed tower.

ZGS 14.387: 煙 instead of 烟.

ZGS 14.387, ZGJI 644, GKFGS 1.9; ZRKS 14.354, Shiba 371

14.430 只看棚頭弄傀儡 *Tada hōtō ni kairai o rō suru o miyo,*
抽牽全籍裏頭人 *Chūken mattaku ritō no hito ni yoru.*

Just look at puppets performing on the box stage,
Every movement controlled by the person behind.

Rinzai-roku §9.

ZGS na, ZGJI 646, ZRKS 14.78, Shiba 352

14.431 只有文殊知此數 *Tada monju nomi atte kono kazu o shiru,*
前三三與後三三 *Zen san-san to go san-san.*

Only ⌜Mañjuśrī⌝ knows such a number:
In front three by three, in back three by three.

Heki 35.

ZGS na, ZGJI 646, ZRKS 14.324, Shiba 353

14.432 唯有夜猿知客恨 *Tada yaen no kakukon o shiru ari,*
嶧陽溪路第三聲 *Ekiyō keiro daisansei.*

Only the night monkeys know this traveler's loneliness;
On the Mount I-yang river trail comes their third and saddest cry.

ZGS 14.388, Shiba 322, TSSSTS 88

14.433 只見落紅風拂盡 *Tada rakkō kaze no haraitsukusu o miru,*
豈知庭樹綠陰多 *Ani shiran ya teiju ryokuin no ōki koto o.*

I saw only the wind blowing all the red flowers away.
How could I know that the garden trees were lush with green shade?

ZGS 14.389, ZGJI 647, ZRKS 14.145, Shiba na

14.434 縱然一夜風吹去 *Tatoi ichiya kaze fukisaru mo,*
只在蘆花淺水邊 *Tada roka sensui no hen ni aran.*

Even if in the night the wind blows it adrift,
It will still be by the reeds in the shallows.

ZGS 14.390, Shiba na, TSSSTS 119

14.435 譬如見西施何必 *Tatoeba seishi o miru ga gotoshi, nanzo kanarazushimo,*
識姓名然後知美 *seimei o shitte, shikashite nochi ni bi o shiran.*

For example, it is like looking at「Hsi-shih」.
Must we first learn her name to know she is beautiful?

ZGS 14.391, Shiba na

14.436 多年曆日如能用 *Ta'nen no rekijitsu moshi yoku mochiiba,*
免被巡官指上推 *Junkan no shijō ni osaruru koto o manukaren.*

One has many years and days, if one uses them well.
One can avoid being led away at the point of an official's finger.

ZGS 14.392, Shiba na

14.437 達磨眼睛總不會 *Daruma no ganzei masa ni fue,*
尋常呼作一聯詩 *Yonotsune yonde ichiren no shi to nasu.*

「Bodhidharma's」 eye is not well understood.
Usually, at the mention of his name, one thinks of his poem.

ZGS 14.393, ZRKS 14.409, Shiba na

14.438 誰把金梭橫玉線 *Ta ka kinsa o totte gyokusen o yokotau,*
織成十丈錦通紅 *Orinasu jūjō no kintsūkō.*

Who, with a golden shuttle, laid down these golden threads
And wove them into this ten-foot brocade entirely red?

ZGS 14.394, ZGJI 648, ZRKS 14.198, Shiba 365, GKFGS 1.12

14.439 孰知不向邊庭苦 *Tare ka shiran hentei ni mukatte kurushimazaru koto o,*
縱死猶聞俠骨香 *Tatoi shi su to mo nao kyōkotsu no kanbashiki o kikan.*

Who would have guessed? Though on the frontier, I am not suffering.
And if I die, they will still smell "the fragrance of a valorous man's bones."

ZGS 14.395, Shiba na, TSSSTS 78

14.440 誰料此山諸草木 *Tare ka hakaran kono yama no shosōmoku,*
盡能排難化爲人 *Kotogotoku yoku nan o haishite keshite hito to naran to wa.*

Who could have imagined that the grasses and trees on this mountain
Would remove the danger completely by taking the appearance of people?

When Fu Chien (苻堅, 357–384), ruler of the Former Ch'in Dynasty, attacked the Chin Dynasty, he mistook the grasses and trees on Mount Pa-kung for Chin soldiers and fled (Morohashi 1450.181; Rogers 1968, 169). The Chin was thus saved from danger.

ZGS 14.396, Morohashi 1450.181, ZRKS 14.456, Shiba na

14.441 短袴長衫白苧巾 *Tanko chōsan hakuchokin,*
咿咿月下急推輪 *I i to shite gekka ni kyū ni rin o osu.*

In shortened pants, long shirts, and white hemp kerchiefs,
Heaving and panting, they roll their wagons on swiftly in the moonlight.➤

ZGS 14.397, ZGJI 648, Shiba 372

14.442 洛陽路上相逢著 *Rakuyō no rojō aibujaku su,*
悉是經商買賣人 *Kotogotoku kore keishō baibai no hito.*

➤Then, coming together on the streets of ⌜Lo-yang⌝—
Lo! All are roadside merchants, buyers and sellers.

ZGS 14.398, ZGJI 681, Shiba 397

14.443 彈指圓成八萬門 *Danshi ni enjō su hachiman mon,*
刹那滅卻三祇劫 *Setsuna ni mekkyaku su san gikō.*

A snap of the fingers accomplishes the eighty thousand teachings
And in a split second destroys three *asaṃkhyeya* ⌜*kalpa*⌝.

See ⌜*Asogikō*⌝. ZGS 14.399.

ZGS 14.399, ZGJI 648, ZRKS 14.325, Shiba 373

14.444 丹鳳朱城白日暮 *Tanpō shujō hakujitsu kure,*
青牛紺幰紅塵度 *Seigyū kanken kōjin wataru.*

The crimson phoenix over the scarlet city in the setting sun;
Black bulls, blue-hooded carriages pass through the red ⌜dust⌝.

The crimson phoenix here is a decorative icon over the gate of the imperial residence in the capital city (Maeno 1962, vol. 1, 180).

ZGS 14.400, Shiba na, TSSSTS 15–16

14.445 竹影掃堦塵不動 *Chikuei kai o haratte chiri dōzezu,*
月穿潭底水無痕 *Tsuki tantei o ugatte mizu ni ato nashi.*

Bamboo shadows sweep the stairs, yet not a mote of ⌜dust⌝ is stirred.
Moonbeams pierce the bottom of the pool, yet leave no trace in the water.

ZGS 14.401: 拂階 instead of 掃堦.

ZGS 14.401, ZD #170, ZRKS 14.339, Shiba 373

14.446 竹中一滴曹溪水 *Chikuchū no itteki sōkei no mizu,*
漲起江西十八灘 *Minagiriokoru kōsei no jūhachi dan.*

A drop of water among the bamboo at ⌜Ts'ao-ch'i⌝,
Overflowed and gave rise to the eighteen rapids of ⌜Chiang-hsi⌝.

ZGS 14.402, ZGJI 649, Shiba na

14.447 知章騎馬似乘船 *Chishō ga uma ni noru wa fune ni noru ni nitari,*
眼花落井水底眠 *Ganka i ni ochite suitei ni nemuru.*

Chih-chang rides on horseback as on a reeling boatdeck,
Bleary-eyed, he plunges into a well to sleep at the bottom of the water.

From Tu Fu, "Song of Eight Immortals Drinking" 飲定八仙歌. Taoists advanced in immortality practices were said to love drinking and to be able to sleep under water.

ZGS 14.403, KSMKJT #474. ZRKS 14.466, Shiba na, TSSSTS 10

14.448 知轉錦江成渭水 *Chi wa kinkō ni tenjite isui to nashi,*
天廻玉壘作長安 *Ten wa gyokurui o megurashite Chōan to nasu.*

The earth moves and the Chin-chiang River runs into the Wei;
The sky reels and Mount Yü-lei rises in ⌜Ch'ang-an⌝.

Both the Chin-chiang and Mount Yü-lei are located in Szechuan in the far west, while the Wei River and Ch'ang-an are located in north-central China.

ZGS 14.404, Shiba na, TSSSTS 73

14.449 忠臣付仕於二君 *Chūshin nikun ni tsukaezu,*
貞婦不見於兩夫 *Teifu ryōfu ni mamiezu.*

A loyal minister does not serve two lords,
A faithful wife does not cleave to two husbands.

ZGS 14.405, Shiba na, 史記田單傳

14.450 仲尼厄而作春秋 *Chūji yaku ni shite shunjū o tsukuri,*
屈原放乃賦離騷 *Kutsugen hanatarete sunawachi risō o fu su.*

Out of his suffering, Confucius wrote the *Spring and Autumn Annals.*
On being exiled, Ch'ü Yüan composed his long poem, "Encountering Sorrow."

Chūji 仲尼 (Ch. Chung-ni) is another name for Confucius.

ZGS 14.406, Shiba na

14.451 長安風月明於晝 *Chōan no fūgetsu hiru yori mo akiraka nari,*
那箇男兒摸壁行 *Nako no danji ga kabe o moshite yuku.*

⌜Ch'ang-an⌝ bathed in moonlight is brighter than the day.
Who are those fellows groping their way along the wall?

Shiba 373: 子 instead of 兒.

ZGS 14.407, ZGJI 649, Shiba 373

14.452 朝三暮四一何少 *Chōsan boshi hitoe ni nanzo sukunakaran,*
朝四暮三何大多 *Chōshi bosan nanzo hanahada ōki.*

⌜Three in the morning and four in the evening⌝, how is that any less?
Four in the evening and three in the morning, how is that any more?

ZGS na, ZGJI 650, ZRKS 14.468, Shiba 374

14.453 趙州狗子無佛性 *Jōshū no kusu mubusshō,*
萬疊青山藏古鏡 *Banjō no seizan kokyō ni kakuru.*

Jōshū's dog has no Buddha-nature,
But the ancient mirror contains range upon range of blue mountains.➛

ZGS 14.408, Shiba na

14.454 赤脚波斯入大唐 *Sekkyaku no hashi daitō ni iri,*
八臂那吒行正令 *Happi no nada shōrei o gyōzu.*

➛The ⌜barefoot Persian⌝ enters the empire of the T'ang
And eight-armed ⌜Nata⌝ imposes the true law.

ZGS 14.409, Shiba 368

14.455 趙女乘春上畫樓 *Chōjo haru ni jōjite garō ni noboru,*
一聲歌發滿城秋 *Issei uta wa hassu manjō no aki.*

Pretty lady of Chao, stirred by the spring, climbs the painted pavilion.
With just one song, her voice fills the city with autumn.

ZGS 14.410, Shiba na, TSSSTS 93

14.456 苕箒用來隨日禿 *Chōshō mochiikitatte hi ni shitagatte tsubu,*
塵埃難上簸箕唇 *Jinnai nobosegatashi hakishin.*

With use the broom gets balder by the day,
Making it harder to sweep up ⌜dust⌝ into the basket.

ZGS 14.411, Shiba na, GKFGS 2.69

14.457 長春殿上金鐘動 *Chōshundenjō kinshō ugoki,*
萬歲山前玉漏遲 *Banzaisanzen gyokuro ososhi.*

In the Palace of Eternal Spring, golden bells are swaying;
Before the Mountain of Ten Thousand Years, a jade water clock is slowly dripping.

ZGS 14.412, ZGJI 650, ZRKS 14.411, Shiba 374, 宋詩選

14.458 長天粘水水粘天 *Chōten mizu ni nenji mizu ten ni nenzu,*
一片氷輪上下圓 *Ippen no hyōrin jōge madoka nari.*

A vast sky stretches to the water, water reaches for the sky.
A single icy sphere is round, utterly round.

ZGS 14.413, Shiba na, GKFGS 2.67

14.459 長天夜夜淸如鏡 *Chōten ya-ya kiyoki koto kagami no gotoshi,*
萬里無雲孤月圓 *Banri kumo naku kogetsu madoka nari.*

Every night the vast sky is as clear as a mirror;
Ten thousand miles, no clouds, the lone ⌜moon⌝ round.

ZGS 14.414, ZGJI 650, Shiba na

14.460 張良躡足封韓信 *Chōryō ashi o funde kanshin o hōzu,*
呂后依目留漢王 *Ryokō me ni yotte kan'ō o tomu.*

⌜Chang Liang⌝ stepped on the [commander's] foot and had ⌜Han Hsin⌝ enfeofed,
⌜Empress Lü⌝ with her eyes detained the King of Han.

In the campaign which led to the founding of the Han Dynasty, general Han Hsin defeated the state of Ch'i and sent word to his commander Liu Pang that he wished to be made its king. Liu Pang was angered, but advisor Chang Liang stepped on Liu Pang's foot and whispered into his ear to make Han Hsin king in order to retain his loyalty (Watson 1993a, vol. ii, 175). The incident behind the second verse has not been identified.

ZGS 14.415, Shiba na

14.461 直木不可以爲輪 *Chokuboku wa motte wa to nasu bekarazu,*
曲木不可以爲桷 *Kyokuboku wa motte kaku to nasu bekarazu.*

You cannot make a ring from straight wood,
You cannot make a rafter from crooked wood.

ZGS 14.416, Shiba na

14.462 喚回枕上三更夢 *Chinjō sankō no yume o yobikaeshite,*
惹動江南萬斛愁 *Kōnan bankoku no urei o hikiugokasu.*

Recalling midnight dreams on my pillow,
I stir up the countless heavy sorrows of ⌜Chiang-nan⌝.

ZGS 14.417, ZRKS 14.133, Shiba na

14.463 墜葉雖憐踈雨感 *Tsuiyō wa sou no kan o awaremu to iedomo,*
黄粱爭似暮雲親 *Kōryō ikade ka boun no shitashiki ni shikan.*

Though fallen leaves evoke sadness in a gentle shower,
Does it match the intimacy of yellow millet with the evening clouds?

Shiba 374: 疎 instead of 踈.

ZGS 14.418, ZGJI 651, Shiba 374; Iida Tōin 1954, 82

14.464 通玄不是人間世 *Tsūgen wa kore ningense ni arazu to,*
滿目靑山何處尋 *Manmoku no seizan izure no tokoro ni ka tazunan.*

The [Mountain of] Mystery is not in the human world.
Blue mountains fill the eyes—where should one search for it?

ZGS na, ZGJI 651, ZRKS 14.240, Shiba 374

14.465 通身罪犯是黃金 *Tsūshin zaibon kore ōgon,*
對面橀贓而拷賊 *Taimen azō zoku o utsu.*

Their unmitigated guilt is solid gold.
Confront them with their stolen goods and flog the thieves.➛

ZGS 14.419, Shiba na, 佛光語錄

14.466 人間天上可憐生 *Ningen tenjō karensei,*
淸平世界添荊棘 *Seihei sekai keikyoku o sou.*

➛The human world and heaven above are charming,
The world of pure serenity is strewn with thorns and nettles.

ZGS 14.472, Shiba na

14.467 月落烏啼霜滿天 *Tsuki ochi karasu naite shimo ten ni mitsu,*
江楓漁火對愁眠 *Kōfū gyoka shūmin ni taisu.*

Crows caw after the setting of the ⌜moon⌝, frost fills the sky.
Fishermen's lamps and the river maples disturb my fitful sleep.

ZGS 14.420, Shiba 341, TSSSTS 88, 102

14.468 月從雪後皆奇夜 *Tsuki wa setsugo yori mina kiya,*
天到梅邊有別春 *Ten wa baihen ni itatte besshun ari.*

Moonrise after snow, everywhere a wondrous night;
Heaven touches the plum blossoms, a special spring.

ZGS 14.421, ZGJI 651, ZRKS 14.141, Shiba 340

14.469 月沈野水光明藏 *Tsuki yasui ni shizumu kōmyōzō,*
蘭吐春山古佛心 *Ran shunzan ni haku kobusshin.*

Moonlight sinks in the meadow water—the storehouse of light,
Orchids breathe their scent on the spring hills—the mind of the ancient buddhas.

ZGS 14.422, Shiba 341, GKFGS 2.2

14.470 握土成金猶可易 *Tsuchi o nigitte kin to nasu koto wa nao yasukarubeshi,*
變金爲土卻還難 *Kin o henjite tsuchi to nasu koto wa kaette mata katashi.*

To take earth and turn it into gold may be easy;
But to take gold and turn it into earth, that is difficult indeed.

ZGS 14.423, ZGJT 6, ZGJI 652, ZRKS 14.33, Shiba na

14.471 等閑識得東風面 *Tōkan ni tōfū no omote o shikitoku su,*
萬紫千紅總是春 *Banshi senkō masa ni kore haru.*

Caressed by the touch of the east wind,
A myriad purples, a thousand reds, the height of spring.

ZGS na, ZGJI 656, ZRKS 14.452, Shiba 378

14.472 道冠儒履佛袈裟 *Dōkan juri bukkesa,*
和合三家成一家 *Sanka o wagō shite ikke to nasu.*

A Taoist hat, Confucian shoes, and a Buddhist robe
Combine the three houses into one.

ZGS na, Shiba 379

14.473 常憶江南三月裏 *Tokoshie ni omou kōnan sangatsu no uchi,*
鷓鴣啼處百花香 *Shako naku tokoro hyakka kanbashi.*

In my thoughts always, ⌜Chiang-nan⌝ in the third month,
The singing of quails, the fragrance of hundreds of blossoms.

MMK 24.

ZGS 14.424, ZGJI 652, ZRKS 14.15, Shiba 362

14.474 弟昆各自逞功能 *Teikon kakuji ni konō o takumashiusu,*
獨有家兄徹骨貧 *Hitori kakei nomi ari tekkotsu no hin.*

The other disciples all displayed their talents and abilities.
Only my elder brother was impoverished right down to his bones.

ZRKS 14.97: *Teikon kakuji ni konō o tei su.*

ZGS 14.425, ZGJI 652, ZRKS 14.97, Shiba na

14.475 鄭子將行罷使臣 *Teishi masa ni yukan to shite shishin o yamu,*
囊無一物獻尊親 *Nō ni ichimotsu no sonshin ni kenzuru nashi.*

Cheng-tzu has stepped down as envoy and is about to leave office.
In his traveling bags he hasn't a single thing for his parents.

The implication is that Cheng-tzu was honest and did not use his position to enrich himself. (Maeno 1962, vol. iii, 207)

ZGS 14.426, Shiba na, TSSSTS 82

14.476 庭樹不知人去盡 *Teiju wa shirazu hito saritsukuru o,*
春來還發舊時花 *Shunrai mata hiraku kyūji no hana.*

The garden trees are unaware the people have gone away.
When spring comes, they send forth flowers as always.

ZGS 14.427, Shiba na, TSSSTS 81

14.477 庭前有月松無影 *Teizen ni tsuki ari matsu ni kage nashi,*
欄外無風竹有聲 *Rangai kaze nōshite take ni koe ari.*

The front garden has moonlight, yet the pine has no shadow;
The balustrade has no wind, yet the bamboo rustles.

ZGS 14.428, ZGJI 653, ZRKS 14.114, Shiba 375

14.478 的的朱簾白日映 *Teki-tekitaru shuren hakujitsu eiji,*
娥娥玉顔紅粉粧 *Ga-gataru gyokugan kōfun yosōu.*

Glittering, glittering, a curtain of jewels catches the bright sun.
Dazzling, dazzling, a face like jade, she applies her red cosmetics.

ZGS 14.429, Shiba na, TSSSTS 7

14.479 鐵鞋無底飽風霜 *Tetsuai soko nōshite fūsō ni aku,*
歳晩歸來臥石床 *Saiban kaerikitatte sekijō ni fusu.*

My iron sandals are worn through, I've had enough of wind and frost.
At the end of my years, I've come home to lie on my bed of stone.➛

ZGS 14.430, Shiba 375, GKFGS 1.43

14.480 一對眼睛烏律律 *Ittsui no ganzei u ritsu-ritsu,*
半隨雲影掛寒堂 *Nakaba wa un'ei ni shitagatte kandō ni kaku.*

➛My two eyes as ⌜black as crows⌝
Now follow the play of clouds, now come to rest in the cold hall.

ZGS 14.431, Shiba na

14.481 鐵牛昨夜眠空室 *Tetsugyū sakuya kūshitsu ni nemuri,*
吼破三更無月天 *Kōha su sankō mugetsu no ten.*

The iron bull last night slept in the empty room.
At midnight his bellow pierced the moonless sky.

ZGS 14.432, Shiba na

14.482 鐵狗吠開巖上月 *Tekku baikai su ganjō no tsuki,*
泥牛觸破嶺頭雲 *Deigyū shokuha su reitō no kumo.*

The iron dog's howling arouses the ⌜moon⌝ above the cliffs,
The mud ox's horns gore away the clouds on the peak.

Shiba 375: 嶺 instead of 巖.

ZGS na, ZGJI 653, ZRKS 14.121, Shiba 375

14.483 鐵壁迸開雲片片 *Teppeki heikai su kumo hen-pen,*
黑山輥出月團團 *Kokuzan konshutsu su tsuki dan-dan.*

Iron cliffs set swirling wisps of clouds;
Out of the dark mountains rolls a round, round ⌜moon⌝.

ZGS 14.433, ZGJT 324, ZGJI 653, ZRKS 14.267, Shiba 375

14.484 天際雪埋千尺石 *Tensai yuki wa uzumu senjaku no ishi,*
洞門凍折數株松 *Dōmon tōsetsu su sūshu no matsu.*

Sky-high snows bury the thousand foot crags;
At the mouth of the cave pines are frozen, broken.

ZGS 14.434, ZGJI 654, ZRKS 14.173, Shiba 376

14.485 天上有星皆拱北 *Tenjō ni hoshi ari mina kita ni tandaku su,*
人間無水不朝東 *Ningen mizu to shite higashi ni chō sezaru nashi.*

In heaven above, all stars are oriented to the ⌜North Star⌝,
On earth, there are no rivers that do not pay tribute to the east.

"Pay tribute to the east" here means to flow to the east.

ZGS 14.435, ZGJT 326, ZGJI 654, ZRKS 14.137, Shiba na

14.486 天上碧桃和露種 *Tenjō no hekitō tsuyu ni washite ue,*
日邊紅杏倚雲栽 *Nippen no kōkyō kumo ni yotte uu.*

In heaven, the blue ⌜peaches⌝ are planted with the dew;
Round the sun, the red apricots are sown near the clouds.

ZGS na, ZGJI 654, ZRKS 14.227, Shiba 376

14.487 天地猶空秦日月 *Tenchi nao kūzu shin no jitsugetsu,*
山河不見漢君臣 *Senga ni mo mizu kan no kunshin.*

The world is empty of the sun and ⌜moon⌝ of Ch'in,
On the mountains and rivers the lords of Han are not seen.

ZGS 14.436, ZGJI 654, ZRKS 14.60, Shiba 376

14.488 天無四壁地無門 *Ten ni shiheki naku chi ni mon nashi,*
何處堪埋阿母身 *Izure no tokoro ni ka amo no shin o uzumuru ni taen.*

Heaven has not four walls, earth has no gate.
Where can I bury my mother's body?

ZGS 14.437, Shiba na, GKFGS 1.59

14 字

14.489 滕王高閣臨江渚 *Tōō no kōkaku kōsho ni nozomeri,*
佩玉鳴鑾罷歌舞 *Haigyoku meiran kabu o yamu.*

King T'eng's High Palace still overlooks the waters of the Yangtze,
But gone are the jeweled sashes, the ringing carriages, the song and dance.➤

ZGS 14.438, Shiba na, TSSSTS 6

14.490 畫棟朝飛南浦雲 *Gatō ashita ni tobu nanpo no kumo,*
朱簾暮捲西山雨 *Shuren kure ni maku seizan no ame.*

➤In the mornings the clouds of Nanbu would rise above the muraled roof beams,
In the evenings the jeweled blinds were rolled for the showers on the western hills.

ZGS 14.439, Shiba 331

14.491 凍雞未報家林曉 *Tōkei imada hōzezu karin no akatsuki,*
隱隱行人過雪山 *In-intaru kōjin sessen o sugu.*

In the cold the cock has not yet announced dawn to the houses in the woods,
In the haze, a traveler crosses the snow-covered mountains.

ZGS 14.440, ZGJI 656, ZRKS 14.172, Shiba 378

14.492 東行西行天地寛 *Tōkō seikō tenchi hiroshi,*
左轉右轉珠走盤 *Saten uten tama ban ni washiru.*

Go east, go west—in the wide world,
Roll left, roll right—like pearls round a tray.

Empuku-ji: *Tōgyō seigyō tenchi hiroshi, Saten uten tama ban ni hashiru.*

ZGS 14.441, ZGJI 655, Shiba na

14.493 桃紅李白薔薇紫 *Tōkō rihaku shōbishi,*
問著春風總不知 *Shunpū ni monjaku suredomo masa ni shirazu.*

「Peach blossoms」 are pink, plum flowers white, roses dark red.
You may ask the spring breeze why, but it won't know a thing.

ZGS 14.442, ZGJT 340, ZGJI 655, ZRKS 14.418, Shiba 378

14.494 東西南北無門戸 *Tōzai namboku monko nashi,*
大地山河不覆藏 *Daichi senga fuzō sezu.*

North, south, east, west have no door;
The great earth, mountains, and rivers conceal nothing.

ZGS 14.443, ZGJI 655, ZRKS 14.75, Shiba na

14.495 童子不知霜雪苦 *Dōji wa shirazu sōsetsu no ku,*
只取瓦礫打寒水 *Tada gareki o totte kanpyō o utsu.*

A child, not knowing the pain of frost and snow,
Takes a broken tile and beats the cold ice.

ZGS 14.444, ZGJI 656, Shiba na

14.496 刀不斬刀 *Tō tō o kirazu,*
水不斬水 *mizu mizu o kirazu,*
虚空不斬虚空 *kokū kokū o kirazu.*

A 「sword」 does not cut a sword,
Water does not cut water,
***Śūnyatā* does not cut *śūnyatā*.**

ZGS 14.445, Shiba na

14.497 堂堂意氣走雷霆 *Dō-dōtaru iki raitei o hashirashime,*
凛凛威風掬霜雪 *Rin-rintaru ifū sōsetsu o kiku su.*

His majestic spirit is like driving thunder,
His austere severity chills like frost and snow.

KZS #1193, ZGS 14.446, ZGJI 656, ZRKS 14.269, Shiba 379

14.498 東風吹落杏花枝 *Tōfū fukiotosu kyōka no eda,*
千里紅香在何處 *Senri no kōkō izure no tokoro ni ka aru.*

The east wind has blown the apricot flowers from their branches.
Their red fragrance that stretched for endless miles—where has it gone?

ZGS 14.447, ZGJI 655, ZRKS 14.89, Shiba na

14.499 東風吹散梅梢雪 *Tōfū fukisanzu baishō no yuki,*
一夜挽回天下春 *Ichiya ni bankai su tenka no haru.*

The east wind scatters the snow from the tips of the plum,
And in one night spring returns to the world.

ZGS 14.448, ZGJI 655, ZRKS 14.232, Shiba 377

14.500 東邊是觀音勢至 *Tōhen wa kore kannon seishi,*
西邊是文殊普賢 *Saihen wa kore monju fugen.*

On the east side, ⌜Kuan-yin⌝ and ⌜Mahāsthāmaprāpta⌝,
On the west side, ⌜Mañjuśrī⌝ and ⌜Samantabhadra⌝.

ZGS 14.449, Shiba na

14. 501 東弗于逮日下東 *Tōhotsuutai wa jikka no higashi,*
西瞿耶尼月氏西 *Saikuyani wa gesshi no nishi.*

Tōhotsuutai lies east of Jih-hsia,
Saikuyani lies west of Yüeh-chih.

See ⌜Sumeru⌝.

ZGS 14.450, Shiba na

14.502 如刀能割不自割 *Tō yoku sakedomo mizukara sakazaru ga gotoku,*
如眼能看不自看 *Manako yoku miredomo mizukara mizaru ga gotoshi.*

Like the ⌜sword⌝ that cuts well but still does not cut itself,
Like the eye that sees well but still does not see itself.

ZGJI 655: *Tō no yoku kitte mizukara kirazaru ga gotoku, Manako no yoku mite mizukara mizaru ga gotoshi.*

ZGS 14.451, ZGJI 655, ZRKS 14.449, Shiba 360

14.503 兎角龜毛眼裏栽 *Tokaku kimō ganri ni uu,*
鐵山當面勢崔嵬 *Tessan tōmen ikioi ni saikai.*

When ⌜rabbit horns and turtle hairs⌝ are planted in your eye,
Then ⌜iron mountains⌝ rise to confront you with their awesome crags.

ZGS 14.452, ZGJT 331, ZGJI 655, ZRKS 14.302, Shiba 376, ZGJT 331

14.504 圖畫當年愛洞庭 *Toga sono kami dōtei o ai su,*
波心七十二峯青 *Hashin shichijū ni hō aoshi.*

While sketching that year, I came to love ⌜Lake Tung-t'ing⌝.
In the bosom of its waves were seventy-two peaks of blue.➤

Heki 20, First Verse Comm.

ZGS 14.453, Shiba 377

14.505 而今高臥思前事 *Ima kōga shite zenji o omoeba,*
添得盧公倚石屏 *Soeetari rokō no sekihei ni yoru o.*

⤙Now in a moment of leisure I recall those past events.
To that sketch I've added Master Lu leaning against a stone wall.

Empuku-ji: *Jikon kōga shite zenji o omoeba.* Master Lu usually refers to the Sixth Patriarch, but here Setchō Zenji may be referring to himself (Iriya et al., 1992, vol. 1, 274; Ōmori 1994, vol. 1, 163).

ZGS 14.454, Shiba na

14.506 桃花端的悟靈雲 *Tōka no tanteki reiun satoru,*
添得玄沙劫外春 *Soeetari gensha gōgai no haru.*

⌜Peach⌝ blossoms at their ultimate awakened ⌜Reiun⌝.
And to this, ⌜Gensha⌝ added a spring beyond time.

Shiba 378: *Tōka no tanteki reiun o satorashime.*

ZGS na, ZGJI 655, ZRKS 14.451, Shiba 378

14.507 髑髏盡是長城卒 *Dokuro kotogotoku kore chōjō no sotsu,*
日暮沙場飛作灰 *Nichibo sajō tonde hai to naru.*

These skulls all once were soldiers on the Great Wall.
As the sun fades on the desert sand, they fly to ash.

ZGS 14.455, Shiba na, TSSSTS 83

14.508 抖擻多年穿破衲 *Tosō su ta'nen no senpa'nō,*
襤衫一半逐雲飛 *Ransan ippan kumo o ōte tobu.*

Having cast off that tattered robe of so many years,
In just his undercloak he flies off on the clouds.

ZGS 14.456, Shiba na

14.509 十謁朱門九不開 *Totabi shumon ni esshite kutabi hirakazu,*
滿身風雪又歸來 *Manshin no fūsetsu mata kaerikitaru.*

Ten visits at the red mansion gate, nine times it does not open.
Though completely exhausted by wind and snow, still he returns.

ZGS 14.457, Shiba 357, HYDCD 1.829

14.510 在途中不離家舍 *Tochū ni atte kasha o hanarezu,*
離家舍不在途中 *Kasha o hanarete tochū ni arazu.*

One, though on the way, has not left home.
Another, though he has left home, is not on the way.

Rinzai-roku §8

ZGS 14.458, Shiba na

14.511 都府樓纔見瓦色　*Tofurō wa wazuka ni kawara no iro nomi o mi,*
觀音寺只聽鐘聲　*Kannonji wa tada shōsei o kiku.*

Government office tower—I can just see the tint of its tiles,
⌜Kuan-yin⌝ Temple—I can only hear the sound of its bell.

ZGS 14.459, Shiba 377

14.512 富與貴是人所欲　*Tomi to tattoki to wa kore hito no hossuru tokoro nari,*
貧與賤是人所惡　*Mazushiki to iyashiki to wa kore hito o nikuminzuru tokoro nari.*

Wealth and respect are what people desire,
Poverty and meanness are what they dislike.

Analects IV, 5; trans. from LEGGE 1985.

ZGS 14.460, Shiba na

14.513 嫩色柔香遠更濃　*Tonshoku jūkō tō shite sara ni komayaka nari,*
春來無處不茸茸　*Shunrai tokoro to shite jō-jōtarazaru nashi.*

The new colors, soft and fragrant, are even stronger seen from afar.
When spring comes, there is no place not in luxuriant growth.

ZGS 14.461, Shiba na

14.514 就中明暗相凌處　*Nakanzuku meian aishinogu tokoro,*
天外出頭誰解看　*Tengai ni shuttō shite tare ka miru koto o gesen.*

First, from where ⌜light and dark⌝ contest each other,
Step out beyond the sky. Who knows what you can see?

ZGS na, ZRKS #267n, Shiba 357

14.515 衲被蒙頭萬事休　*Nappi mōtō banji kyūsu,*
此時山僧都不會　*Kono toki sanzō subete fue.*

Head covered in a shroud, all things come to rest.
At this moment, this ⌜mountain monk⌝ understands nothing at all.

"Head covered in a shroud" is the traditional way of depicting ⌜Bodhidharma⌝.

Heki 61 Main Case Comm., 80 Main Case Comm. ZGS 14.462, Shiba na

14.516 猶把琵琶半遮面　*Nao biwa o totte nakaba omote o saegiru,*
不令人見轉風流　*Hito o shite miseshimezaru utata fūryū.*

She holds her lute half-hiding her face.
Not allowing anyone to see, she is even more alluring.

Shiba 356: 手把琵琶半遮面 *Te ni biwa o totte nakaba omote o saegiru.*

ZGS 14.463, ZGJI 658, ZRKS #305n, Shiba 356

14.517 收下南岳嶺頭雲 *Nangaku reitō no kumo o shūka shi,*
捉得太行山下賊 *Taikōsanka no zoku o shakutoku su.*

Release clouds on the Southern Peak,
Capture the thieves on Mount T'ai-hang.

ZGS 14.464, Shiba na

14.518 射殺南山老大蟲 *Nanzan no rōdaichū o shasatsu shite,*
行人從此路頭通 *Kōjin kore yori rōtō tsūzu.*

With his arrow he killed the old tiger of South Mountain.
Travelers from now on can travel on the roads.

For *rōdaichū*, see ⌜Big bug⌝.

KZS #1194, ZGS 14.465, ZRKS 14.275, Shiba na

14.519 南村北村雨一犁 *Nanson hokuson ame ichiri,*
新婦餉姑翁哺兒 *Shinpu wa ko ni karei shi, ō wa ji ni ho su.*

In South Village, in North Village, they're plowing after the rain.
The bride's brought lunch for her new mom and papa feeds the baby.

ZGS 14.466, ZGJI 658, Shiba 379

14.520 南北東西歸去來 *Nanboku tōzai kaeri nan iza,*
夜深同看千巖雪 *Yoru fukōshite onajiku miru sengan no yuki.*

North, south, east, west—let us return
And in the deep night together view the snow on a thousand peaks.

Heki 51 Verse. Shiba 379: 岩 instead of 巖.

ZGS 14.467, ZGJI 658, ZRKS 14.183, Shiba 379

14.521 南北東西無路入 *Nanboku tōzai michi no iru nashi,*
鐵山當面勢崔嵬 *Tessan tōmen ikioi saikai.*

North, south, east, west—no road penetrates.
Iron mountains rise sheer before you with their awesome crags.

ZGS 14.468, Shiba na

14.522 西望鄉關腸欲斷 *Nishi ni kyōkan o nozomeba harawata taen to hossu,*
對君衫袖淚痕斑 *Kimi ni taisureba sanshū ruikon han nari.*

Gazing west toward my native land, I feel as though my heart will rend;
Meeting you, the sleeve of my coat is stained with tears.

ZGS 14.469, Shiba na, TSSSTS 52

14.523 二十四聖皆點額 *Nijūshi sei mina tengaku su,*
觀音一人登龍門 *Kannon ichinin ryūmon ni noboru.*

The twenty-four holy ones all bowed their heads,
⌜Kuan-yin⌝ alone ascended the ⌜Dragon Gate⌝.

ZGS na, ZGJI 659, ZRKS 14.365, Shiba 380

14.524 日月星辰一時暗 *Nichigetsu seishin ichi ji ni kurashi,*
全機透出上頭關 *Zenki tōshutsu su jōtō no kan.*

Sun, moon, and stars all at once darken.
With all your energy, burst through the supreme barrier.

Heki 2 Intro. (first verse only).

ZGS 14.470, ZGJI 630, ZRKS 14.333, Shiba na

14.525 耳裡藏得須彌山 *Jiri kakushietari shumisen,*
眼裡著得四大海 *Ganri tsukeetari shidaikai.*

The ear encloses Mount ⌜Sumeru⌝,
The eye contains the ⌜Four Seas⌝.

ZGS 14.471, Shiba na

14.526 截斷人間是與非 *Ningen no ze to hi o setsudan shite,*
白雲深處掩柴扉 *Hakuun fukaki tokoro saihi o ōu.*

He's cut off worldly quibbling over right and wrong,
And deep in the white clouds, closes his brushwood door.

ZGS 14.473, ZGJI 659, ZRKS 14.368, Shiba 368

14.527 人間富貴一時樂 *Ningen no fūki ichiji no raku,*
地獄辛酸萬劫長 *Jigoku no shinsan mangō nagashi.*

Wealth and honor in the world are momentary pleasures,
But the pain and grief of hell are ten thousand ⌜*kalpa*⌝ long.

ZGS 14.474, ZGJI 659, ZRKS 14.473. Shiba na

14.528 人間路到三峯盡 *Ningen no michi wa sanpō ni itatte tsuki,*
天下秋隨一葉來 *Tenka no aki wa ichiyō ni shitagaikitaru.*

The path of humans ends at the Three Peaks,
Autumn comes to the world beginning with one leaf.

See ⌜Mount of Five Elders⌝.

KZS #1145, ZGS 14.475, ZGJI 659, ZRKS 14.13, Shiba 363

14.529 人面不知何處去 *Ninmen wa shirazu izure no tokoro ni ka saru,*
桃花依舊笑春風 *Tōka kyū ni yotte shunpū ni emu.*

I don't know where that person's face has gone,
But the ⌜peach⌝ blossoms laugh in the spring wind as she used to do.

The same character 笑 can mean both to bloom and to laugh.

ZGS 14.476, ZGJT 232, ZGJI 637, ZRKS 14.103, Shiba 363

14
字

14.530 願作輕羅著細腰 *Negawaku wa keira to natte saiyō ni tsukan,*
願爲明鏡分嬌面 *Negawaku wa meikyō to natte kyōmen o wakatan.*

My wish—to become a fine silk robe and cover your slender waist.
My wish—to be a bright mirror and reflect your charming face.

ZGS 14.477, Shiba na, TSSSTS 7

14.531 與君相向轉相親 *Kimi to aimukatte utata aishitashimi,*
與君雙棲共一身 *Kimi to narabisunde isshin o tomo ni sen.*

The more I see you, the fonder I grow.
Let us live together and become one.

ZGS 14.478, Shiba na

14.532 願待來年蠶麥熟 *Negawaku wa rainen sanbaku no juku suru o matte,*
羅睺羅兒與一錢 *Ragora no ji ni issen o ataen.*

Please wait till next year when the silkworms and barley are ready
To give beggar Rāhula a coin.

ZGS 14.479, Shiba na, ZGJI 647

14.533 睡美不知山雨過 *Nemuri bi ni shite shirazu san'u no suguru koto o,*
覺來殿閣自生涼 *Samekitatte denkaku onozukara shōryō.*

My nap was wonderful, I wasn't aware mountain rains had passed.
When I awoke, the pavilion itself was so clean and fresh!

KZS #1205, ZGS 14.480, ZGJI 660, ZRKS 14.214, Shiba 364

14.534 年年歳歳花相似 *Nen-nen sai-sai hana ainitari,*
歳歳年年人不同 *Sai-sai nen-nen hito onajikarazu.*

From year to year flowers resemble each other,
From year to year people are never the same.

ZGS 14.481, Shiba 380, TSSSTS 8

14.535 年來老大渾無力 *Nenrai rōdai ni shite subete chikara nashi,*
偸得忙中些子閑 *Nusumietari bōchū shashi no kan.*

Now old in years, all my strength has gone.
In the midst of busyness, I steal moments of leisure.

KZS na#, ZGS 14.482, ZGJI 660, ZRKS 14.99, Shiba na

14.536 梅花嘲笑槐安事 *Baika chōshō su kaian no ji,*
燕舞鶯歌半熟中 *Enbu ōka hanjuku no uchi.*

The plum blossoms are laughing at my adventures in the land of ⌜Huai-an⌝,
The swallows are dancing, the nightingales singing, and the millet is only half cooked.

ZGS 14.483, Shiba na

14.537 梅邊殘月無疎影 *Baihen no zangetsu soei nashi,*
竹裏淸風有落花 *Chikuri no seifū rakka ari.*

The morning ⸢moon⸣ in the plums casts no shadows,
The clean breeze through the bamboo leaves fallen flowers.

ZGS 14.484, ZGJI 661, Shiba 381

14.538 白雲鎖斷巖前石 *Hakuun sadan su ganzen no ishi,*
掛角羚羊不見蹤 *Tsuno o kakuru reiyō ato o mizu.*

White clouds enclose the rocks on the cliff face,
No trace seen of the ⸢horn-hooking antelope⸣.

ZGS 14.485, ZGJI 661, ZRKS 14.128, Shiba na

14.539 白雲盡處是靑山 *Hakuun tsukuru tokoro kore seizan,*
行人更在靑山外 *Kōjin wa sara ni seizan no soto ni ari.*

Where the white clouds end, there are blue mountains.
The traveler is even further beyond those blue mountains.

ZGS 14.555, ZRKS 14.200, ZGJT 414: 平蕪 *heibu,* "grass plains," instead of白雲 *hakuun,* "white clouds."

ZGS na, ZRKS 14.200; ZGJT 381, 414; ZGJI 661, Shiba 382

14.540 白雲深處金龍躍 *Hakuun fukaki tokoro kinryū odori,*
碧波心裏玉兎驚 *Hekiha shinri gyokuto odoroku.*

Deep in the white clouds the ⸢golden dragon⸣ dances;
Within the blue waves, the ⸢jade rabbit⸣ is startled.

Heki 24 Verse Comm.

KZS #1147, ZGS 14.486, ZGJI 661, ZRKS 14.23, Shiba 381

14.541 白雲深處僧炊飯 *Hakuun fukaki tokoro sō han o kashigi,*
綠樹蔭中人呼舟 *Ryokuju inchū hito fune o yobu.*

Deep in the white clouds a monk boils rice,
In the shade of the green trees someone calls for a boat.

ZGS 14.487, Shiba na

14.542 伯牙絕絃於子期 *Hakuga gen o shiki ni tachi,*
仲尼覆醢於子路 *Chūji kai o shiro ni kutsugaesu.*

⸢Po Ya⸣ cut the strings for Tzu-ch'i,
Confucius overturned the salt-preserves for Tzu-lu.

Hearing of the death of his disciple Tzu-lu, Confucius overturned a crock of salted vegetables.

ZGS 14.488, Shiba na

14.543 白玉琢成西子骨 *Hakugyoku migakinasu seishi ga kotsu,*
黃金鑄就伍員心 *Ōgon chūshū su goin ga kokoro.*

⸢Hsi-shih's⸣ bones are white polished jade,
⸢Wu Yuan's⸣ heart is refined gold.

ZGS na, ZGJI 661, ZRKS 14.318, Shiba 382

14.544 陌上堯樽傾北斗 *Hakujō no gyōson hokuto o katamuke,*
樓前舜樂動南薫 *Rōzen no shungaku nankun o ugokasu.*

Above the paths the Big Dipper pours into goblets of ⌜Yao⌝,
In front of the tower ⌜Shun's⌝ music stirs the south wind's warmth.

Trans. from Pauline Yu 1980, 96.

ZGS 14.489, Shiba na

14.545 白水滿時雙鶴下 *Hakusui mitsuru toki sōkaku kudari,*
綠槐高處一蟬吟 *Ryokkai takaki tokoro ichizen ginzu.*

On the clear brimming waters a pair of cranes alight,
High in the green locust trees a cicada is shrilling.

ZGS 14.490, Shiba na

14.546 驀然鐵棒如風至 *Bakuzentaru tetsubō kaze no gotoku ni itari,*
失卻從前眼裏花 *Shikkyaku su jūzen ganri no hana.*

Sudden as the wind, the iron rod strikes,
Clearing away all those old stars in the eye.

Shiba 383.

ZGS na, ZGJI 662, ZRKS 14.266, Shiba 383

14.547 白馬金鞍從武皇 *Hakuba kin'an bukō ni shitagai,*
旌旗十萬宿長楊 *Seiki jūman chōyō ni shuku su.*

On white horses with golden saddles they followed Emperor Wu,
With one hundred thousand banners they stopped at Ch'ang-yang.

ZGS 14.491, Shiba na, TSSSTS 76

14.548 白髮田家一老翁 *Hakuhatsu denke no ichirōō,*
欲行翻更伏兒童 *Yukan to hosshite hirugaette sara ni jidō ni fusu.*

An old white-haired peasant about to depart
Turns again and bows to the little boy.

ZGS 14.492, Shiba na

14.549 白蘋風細秋江暮 *Hakuhin kaze wa komayaka nari shūkō no kure,*
古岸舡歸一帶煙 *Kogan fune wa keru ittai no kemuri.*

White sea grasses in a light breeze, autumn river dusk,
By the old banks, a boat returns swathed in mist.

ZGS 14.493, ZGJI 661, Shiba na

14.550 薄暮層巒雲擁腰 *Hakubo sōran kumo koshi o yōsu,*
傾盆一雨定明朝 *Bon o katamukuru ichiu sadande myōchō.*

As twilight tinges the mountains, clouds mass on the slopes,
Tomorrow morning surely rain will pour as from an upturned tub.

ZGS 14.494, Shiba na

14.551 白狼河北音書斷　*Hakuro kahoku insho tae,*
丹鳳城南秋夜長　*Tanpōjōnan shūya nagashi.*

From north of the White Wolf River the letters have stopped;
Here, south of Red Phoenix City, the autumn nights are long.

Shiba 382: 絕 instead of 斷.

ZGS 14.495, Shiba 382, TSSSTS 42

14.552 白鷺下田千點雪　*Hakuro den ni kudaru senten no yuki,*
黃鶯上樹一枝花　*Kōō ju ni noboru isshi no hana.*

White herons alighting in a field—thousands of snowflakes!
A yellow nightingale perched in a tree—a flowering branch!

ZGS 14.496, ZGJT 381, ZGJI 661, ZD #165, ZRKS 14.206, Shiba 382

14.553 無端更渡桑乾水　*Hashi naku sara ni sōkan no mizu o watarite,*
卻望幷州是故鄉　*Kaette heishū o nozomeba kore kokyō.*

Here I find myself crossing back over the waters of the Sang-kan,
And looking back over my shoulder, Ping-chou feels to me now like my native home.

ZGS 14.497, Shiba na, TSSSTS 93

14.554 馬上相逢無紙筆　*Bajō aiōtte shihitsu nashi,*
憑君傳語報平安　*Kimi ni yotte dengo shite heian o hōzeshimu.*

Meeting you on horseback, I have neither paper nor brush.
Carry my words for me, tell them I'm safe and sound.

ZGS 14.498, Shiba na; TSSSTS 80, 109

14 字

14.555 波上碧雲飜雨露　*Hajō no hekiun uro o hirugaeshi,*
日中青蓋蔭龜魚　*Nitchū no seigai kigyo o ou.*

Above the waves in azure clouds, rain and mist tumble;
In the midday sun a canopy of blue covers the turtles and fish.

ZGS 14.499, Shiba na

14.556 芭蕉葉上無愁雨　*Bashō yōjō ni shūu nashi,*
只是時人聽斷腸　*Tada kore toki no hito kiite danchō su.*

On the banana leaves it is not the rain that is melancholy,
But just that those who hear it feel heartbroken.

ZGS 14.500, ZGJI 661, ZRKS 14.120, Shiba 381

14.557 芭蕉無耳聞雷開　*Bashō mimi nakushite rai o kiite hiraki,*
葵花無眼隨日轉　*Kika manako nakushite hi ni shitagatte tenzu.*

Banana leaves have no ears, yet open on hearing the thunder;
Hollyhocks have no eyes, yet turn to face the sun.

ZGS 14.501, ZGJI 661, ZRKS 14.71, Shiba na

14.558 八萬四千非鳳毛 *Hachiman shisen hōmō ni arazu,*
三十三人入虎穴 *Sanjūsannin koketsu ni iru.*

The eighty-four thousand were not phoenix feathers.
Thirty-three men entered the tiger's cave.

Heki 15 Verse. "84,000" refers to the disciples of the Buddha who gathered on Vulture Peak. Only ⌜Kāśyapa⌝ smiled when the Buddha held up the flower. The others were not "phoenix feathers." "Thirty-three men" refers to the twenty-eight patriarchs of India and the six patriarchs in China. ⌜Bodhidharma⌝ is counted twice, as the twenty-eighth Indian patriarch and the first Chinese patriarch (ZGJI 662).

ZGS 14.502, ZGJT 382, ZGJI 662, ZRKS 14.61, Shiba 383

14.559 八葉白蓮一肘間 *Hachiyō no byakuren itchū no aida,*
炳現阿字素光色 *Hei to shite arawaru aji sokō no iro.*

The eight-petaled white lotus within a cubit span—
The ⌜character "A"⌝ clearly appears in brilliant hues.➤

ZGS 14.503, Shiba na, 塗毒鼓續編鳩羽集附則 13

14.560 禪智倶入金剛縛 *Zen chi tomo ni iru kongō no baku,*
召入如來寂靜智 *Messhite iru nyorai jakujō no chi.*

➤Zen and wisdom together enter into the diamond *mudrā*
And invite in the Tathāgata's nirvana wisdom.

ZGS 14.358, Shiba na

14.561 八角樹上魚生子 *Hakkaku jujō uo ko o shōji,*
急水灘頭鳥掛巣 *Kyūsui dantō tori su o kaku.*

Up in the eight-branched tree the fish lay their young,
On the rapids of the rushing river, birds build their nests.

ZGS 14.504, ZGJI 662, Shiba na

14.562 八角磨盤空裡走 *Hakkaku no maban kūri ni washiru,*
金毛獅子變成狗 *Kinmo no shishi henjite ku to naru.*

The ⌜eight-cornered mortar stone⌝ flies through the air,
The golden lion was transformed into a dog.

ZGDJT 1026, ZGS 14.505, ZGJT 383 First verse, ZGJI 662, Shiba 383

14.563 把定則雲横谷口 *⌜Hajō⌝ suru tokinba kumo kokkō ni yokotawari,*
放下也月落寒潭 *⌜Hōge⌝ sureba mata tsuki kantan ni otsu.*

Take hold, clouds lie across the valley's mouth.
Release, the ⌜moon⌝ drops into the limpid winter pond.

ZGS 14.506, ZGJI 661, ZRKS #118, Shiba 381

14.564 穿花蛺蝶深深見
點水蜻蜓欵欵飛

Hana o ugatsu kyōchō shin-shin to shite mie,
Mizu ni tenzuru seitei kan-kan to shite tobu.

Butterflies pierce the flowers long and deep;
Dragonflies dip into the water, hovering slowly.

ZGS 14.507, ZGJI 663, Shiba 370

14.565 花開不假栽培力
自有春風管對伊

Hana hiraku koto saibai no chikara o karazu,
Onozukara shunpū no kare o kantai suru ari.

Flowers bloom without need for cultivation,
The spring wind naturally watches over them.

ZGS na, ZGJI 663, ZRKS 14.117, Shiba 331

14.566 花簇簇處鷓鴣啼
草薫薫時鴛鴦飛

Hana zoku-zokutaru tokoro shako naki,
Kusa kun-kuntaru toki en'ō tobu.

Where flowers crowd upon flowers, a quail cries;
When the grasses are heavy with scent, ⌜mandarin ducks⌝ fly.

ZGS 14.508, ZGJI 663, ZRKS 14.14, Shiba na

14.567 逢花欲問簾中主
一笑紅唇不敢言

Hana ni aute towan to hossu renchū no shu,
Isshō no kōshin aete iwazu.

Seeing this flower, I want to ask who is behind the screen—
A smile and red lips that dare not speak.

The verse puns on the character 笑 which can mean (a flower's) bloom and (a woman's) smile.

ZGS 14.509, ZGJI 663, Shiba na

14.568 花發鷄冠媚早秋
誰人能染紫絲頭

Hana hiraite keikan sōshū ni kobu,
Ta ga hito ka yoku somu shishitō.

Flowers bloom flaunting red crests in the early fall.
Who has dyed these purple threads so well?➛

ZGS 14.510, Shiba na

14.569 有時風動頻相倚
似向堦前鬬不休

Aru toki kaze ugoki shikiri ni aiyoru,
Kaizen ni mukatte tatakatte kyūsezaru ni nitari.

➛At those times when the wind stirs, they sway against each other
Before the steps, as if in ceaseless debate.

Empuku-ji: *Toki atte kaze ugoki shikiri ni aiyoru.*

ZGS 14.511, Shiba na

14.570 花開花落狂風吹
自有馨香滿天地

Hana hiraki hana ochite kyōfū fuku,
Onozukara keikō no tenchi ni mitsuru ari.

Flowers bloom, then fall, blown by whirling gusts.
Quietly their fragrance permeates earth and sky.

ZGS 14.512 , Shiba na

14.571 展翅鵬騰六合雲 *Hane o nobete hōtō su rikugō no kumo,*
搏風鼓蕩四溟水 *Kaze ni hōtte kutō su shimei no mizu.*

Spreading its wings, the ⌜roc⌝ soars over the clouds of the ⌜six directions⌝;
Beating the wind, it churns up the waters of the ⌜four seas⌝.

Heki 89 Verse. 六合雲 *rikugō no kumo,* literally "six compound clouds," refers to the six senses. 四溟水 *shimei no mizu* is literally "four murky seas."

ZGS 14.513, Shiba na

14.572 隔林彷彿聽機杼 *Hayashi o hedatete hōfutsu to shite kijō o kiku,*
知有人家翠微中 *Ninka no aru o shiru suibi no uchi.*

Beyond the trees I hear the faint click of a weaver's shuttle,
And know that someone is at home within that delicate green.

ZGS 14.514, Shiba na

14.573 春入千林處處花 *Haru wa senrin ni iru sho-sho no hana,*
秋沈萬水家家月 *Aki wa bansui ni shizumu ka-ka no tsuki.*

Spring fills a thousand forests—flowers are everywhere;
Autumn falls on ten thousand streams—moonlight in every house.

ZGS 14.515, ZGJI 663, Shiba 360

14.574 破了當年重用去 *Haryō sono kami kasanete mochiisaru,*
和煙搭在玉欄干 *Kemuri ni washite tōzai su gyokurankan.*

Gone! Those years have all been used up.
Wrapped in the mist, I lean on the jade balustrade.

ZGS na, ZRKS , Shiba na

14.575 遙憐停手頻渾淚 *Haruka ni awaremu te o todomete shikiri ni namida o furuu koto o,*
搗月聲聲斷又連 *Tsuki o tsuku sei-sei taete mata tsuranaru.*

How sad—her hand stops, tears tremble and fall.
She thumps at the moonlight, stops, then starts again.

See ⌜Fulling block⌝. The moonlight falls across her fulling block.

ZGS 14.517, Shiba na

14.576 萬古業風吹不盡 *Banko goppū fukitsukizu,*
又隨月色過羅浮 *Mata gesshoku ni shitagatte rafu o sugu.*

The wind of karma from endless past ages blows without cease.
Again, by the light of the ⌜moon⌝, I cross over Mount Lo-fu.

For Mount Lo-fu, see ⌜Ko Hung⌝.

ZGS 14.518, ZGJI 664, Shiba na

14.577 萬古碧潭空界月 *Banko no hekitan kūkai no tsuki,*
再三撈摝始應知 *Saisan rōroku shite hajimete masa ni shirubeshi.*

In the blue pool from a thousand ages past, the ⌜moon⌝ of emptiness.
Reach for it again and again and again, at last you will know it.

KZS #1170, ZGS 14.519, ZGJT 387, ZGJI 664, Shiba 384

14.578 萬山不隔今夜月 *Banzan hedatezu konya no tsuki,*
一片淸光分外明 *Ippen no seikō bungai ni akiraka nari.*

The ten thousand mountains cannot keep away the ⌜moon⌝ tonight,
A crescent of pure light, bright beyond measure.

ZGS 14.520, ZGJI 664, Shiba na

14.579 萬事無心一釣竿 *Banji mushin nari itchōkan,*
三公不換此江山 *Sankō ni mo kaezu kono kōzan.*

I care not about the ⌜ten thousand things⌝, only about my fishing pole.
I would not exchange for three dukedoms these mountains and streams.

Empuku-ji: *Banji mushin itchōkan.*

ZGS 14.521, ZGJI 664, ZRKS 14.471, Shiba na

14.580 萬乘旌旗何處在 *Banjō no seiki izure no tokoro ni ka aru,*
平臺賓客有誰憐 *Heidai no hinkaku tare atte ka awareman.*

Where now are the ten thousand chariots and banner flags?
Does anyone grieve for the guests at the P'ing Pavilion?

Rulers of states in early China sometimes maintained guest quarters to receive itinerant visitors to their courts who claimed to be experts on warfare, civil government, and ethics. King Hsiao of the state of Liang named his the P'ing Pavilion.

ZGS 14.522, Shiba na, TSSSTS 77

14.581 萬象森羅開活眼 *Banzō shinra katsugen o hiraku,*
更於何處覓醫王 *Sara ni izure no tokoro ni oite iō o motomen.*

All the ⌜ten thousand things⌝ of the universe have opened their living eye.
Beyond this, where else should one seek the Medicine King?

The Buddha is sometimes called the Medicine King and the Great Physician.

ZGS na, ZGJI 664, ZRKS 14.423, Shiba 384

14.582 半陂飛雨半陂晴 *Hanpa wa hiu hanpa wa hare,*
漁曲翻秋野調淸 *Gyokyoku aki ni hirugaette yachō kiyoshi.*

One bank is in flying rain, the other bank is in sun.
A fisherman's song lilts through the crisp autumn meadows.

This reading follows ZGS 14.523. Alternative reading: *Gyokyoku shūya ni hirugaette shirabe kiyoshi,* "A fishing song lilts through fall meadows, its melody clear."

ZGS 14.523, ZGJI 664, Shiba na

14.583 萬里煙塵一點無 *Banri enjin itten mo nashi,*
太平時節合歡娯 *Taihei no jisetsu kango subeshi.*

For ten thousand miles, no hint of smoke and ⌜dust⌝;
In this time of great peace, all rejoice.

ZGS 14.524, Shiba na, GKFGS 1.55

14.584 微雨績天烟織雪 *Biu ten ni tsumuide kemuri yuki o ori,*
寒風簸水月篩梅 *Kanpū mizu o hite tsuki ume o furuu.*

Fine rain like sky-spun thread, mist like woven snow;
Winter wind ruffles the water, moon filters through the plums.

ZGS 14.525, ZGJI 666, ZRKS 14.229, Shiba na

14.585 日落長沙秋色遠 *Hi ochite chōsa shūshoku tōshi,*
不知何處弔湘君 *Shirazu izure no tokoro ni ka shōkun o tomurawan.*

Sunset over Ch'ang-sha, fall colors stretch into the distance.
I know not where to mourn for the ⌜Princesses of the Hsiang⌝.

ZGS 14.526, Shiba na, TSSSTS 74

14.586 日晩江南望江北 *Hi kurete kōnan yori kōhoku o nozomeba,*
寒鴉飛盡水悠悠 *Kan'a tobitsukite mizu yū-yū.*

At sunset from the south bank, I gaze north across the river.
Winter crows fly out of sight, waters wide and serene.

ZGS 14.527, Shiba na, TSSSTS 106

14.587 彼此征途雖有異 *Hi shi seito i ari to iedomo,*
須知同日到天庭 *Subekaraku shirubeshi dōjitsu tentei ni itaru.*

Though he and I travel by different roads,
Know this: we shall both reach T'ien-t'ing on the same day.

ZGS 14.528, Shiba na

14.588 微子去之箕子爲 *Bishi wa kore o sari kishi wa*
之奴比干諫而死 *kore ga do to naru hikan isamete shi su.*

The lord of Wei fled from him, the lord of Chi was enslaved by him,
Pi Kan admonished him and was killed.

Analects XVIII, 1. See ⌜Chieh and Chou⌝.

ZGS 14.529, Shiba na

14.589 翡翠踏翻荷葉雨 *Hisui tōhan su, kayō no ame,*
鷺鷥衝破竹林烟 *Roji shōha su, chikurin no kemuri.*

Kingfishers scatter raindrops from the lotus leaves,
White herons drive the mist from the bamboo grove.

ZGS 14.530, ZGJI 665, Shiba 384

14.590 約臂黃金寬一寸 *Hiji ni yaku suru ōgon yuruki koto issun,*
逢人猶道不相思 *Hito ni aute nao iu aiomowazu to.*

The golden bracelet on her arm is too loose by an inch,
Yet on meeting people she says, "No, I'm not thinking of him."

ZGS 14.531, ZGJI 666, ZD #166, ZRKS 14.208, Shiba 396

14.591 微塵眼底三千界 *Bijin gantei sanzenkai,*
拄杖頭邊四百州 *Shujō tōhen shihyakushū.*

In a dust mote in the eye, three thousand worlds;
On the head of a staff, four hundred states.

ZGS na, ZRKS 14.364, Shiba 385

14.592 令人轉憶謝三郎 *Hito o shite utata shasanrō o omowashimu,*
一絲獨釣寒江雪[雨] *Isshi hito ri tsuru kankō no yuki [ame].*

It reminds people of「Hsieh San-lang」,
Who with a single line would fish on the snowy [rainy] winter river.

ZGS 14.532, ZGJI 666, ZRKS 14.170, Shiba na

14.593 一自赤心來報國 *Hitotabi sekishin ni shite kitatte kuni o hōzeshi yori,*
邊頭刁斗不曾聞 *Hentō tōto katsute kikazu.*

Once you become straight in spirit and repay your debt to your country,
You will no longer hear pots being beaten on the frontier.

To rally troops for battle, army commanders would beat drums and bang pots.

ZGS na, ZGJT 26, ZGJI 666, ZRKS 14.250, Shiba 324

14.594 一與山門作境致 *Hitotsu ni wa sanmon no tame ni kyōchi to nashi.*
二與後人作標榜 *Futatsu ni wa kōjin no tame ni hyōbō to nasu.*

First, I want to make a setting for the temple gate.
Second, I want to make a marker for later generations.

Rinzai-roku §49.

ZGS 14.533, Shiba 326

14.595 美如西施離金闕 *Bi naru koto wa seishi ga kinketsu o hanaruru ga gotoku,*
嬌似楊妃倚玉樓 *Kyō naru koto wa yōki ga gyokurō ni yoru ni nitari.*

Beauty is「Hsi-shih」leaving the gold court palace,
Charm is「Yang Kuei-fei」leaning against the jade tower.

Shiba 385: 矯 instead of 嬌.

ZGS 14.534, ZGJT 392, ZGJI 665, ZRks 314, Shiba 385

14.596 毘婆尸佛早留心 *Bibashibutsu hayaku shin o todomuru mo,*
直到如今不得妙 *Jiki ni ima ni itaru made myō o ezu.*

Though「Vipaśyin」Buddha long ago set his mind to it,
Through all this time, he has yet to attain the mystery.

ZGS 14.535, ZGJT 391, ZGJI 665, ZRKS 14.382, Shiba 384

14.597 得成比目何辭死 *Himoku to naru koto o eba nanzo shi o ji sen,*
願作鴛鴦不羨仙 *En'ō to naran koto o negatte sen o urayamazu.*

If I could be paired fish with you, I would not begrudge even death.
Let us become mandarin ducks and we will not envy even the immortals.

See ⌜Matrimonial harmony⌝.

ZGS 14.536, Shiba na, TSSSTS 6

14.598 百尺竿頭進一歩 *Hyakushaku kantō ni ippo o susume,*
十方刹土現全身 *Jippō setsudo ni zenshin o genzu.*

Advance one step from the top of a hundred-foot pole,
Reveal yourself completely in all the lands in the ⌜ten directions⌝.

MMK 46.

KZS #1191, ZGS 14.537, ZGJI 666, ZRKS 14.262, Shiba 385

14.599 百千毒鼓同時響 *Hyakusen no dokku dōji ni hibiku,*
吼破虛空無點痕 *Kokū o kōha shite tenkon nashi.*

One hundred thousand ⌜poison-painted drums⌝ thunder all at once.
Shattering the void, not a trace remains.

ZGS 14.538, ZGJI 667, Shiba na

14.600 百年三萬六千日 *Hyakunen sanman rokusen nichi,*
得忻忻處且忻忻 *Kin-kin o uru tokoro katsu kin-kin.*

In a hundred years there are thirty-six thousand days,
So if there is a moment to be happy, be happy.

ZGS 14.539, ZGJT 394, ZGJI 667 , ZRKS 14.408, Shiba na

14.601 百鍊黃金鑄鐵牛 *Hyakuren no ōgon tetsugyū o iru,*
十分高價與人酬 *Jūbun no kōka hito ni ataete mukuishimu.*

From gold refined a hundred times, I have cast an iron ox
And will make it repay my debts to others at full value.

ZGS 14.540, ZRKS 14.214, Shiba na

14.602 毘盧愛飲彌勒酒 *Biru aishinomu Miroku no sake,*
文殊醉倒普賢扶 *Monju suitō sureba Fugen tasuku.*

⌜Vairocana⌝ loves to drink ⌜Maitreya's⌝ wine.
When ⌜Mañjuśrī⌝ falls down drunk, ⌜Samantabhadra⌝ cares for him.

ZGS 14.541, ZGJI 665, ZRKS 14.399, Shiba 385

14.603 風花雪月任流轉 *Fūka setsugetsu ruten ni makasu,*
金剛腦後添生鐵 *Kongō nōgo santetsu o sou.*

Letting wind and flowers, snow and ⌜moon⌝, drift and tumble,
The ⌜*Vajra*⌝ guardian fits an iron helmet to his head.

ZGS 14.542, ZRKS 14.506, ZGJT 146, Shiba na

14.604 風前腸斷趙如意 *Fūzen harawata tatsu chō nyoi,*
錦繡帳中有呂后 *Kinshū chōchū ryokō ari.*

Helpless little Chao Ju-i—it was so heartbreaking,
For behind the drapes of embroidered brocade lurked the ⸢Empress Lü⸣.

ZGS 14.545, ZRKS #na, Shiba na

14.605 巫峽山頭窈窕女 *Fukyō no santō yōchōtaru onna,*
朝爲行雲暮爲雨 *Asa ni wa kōun to nari kure ni wa ame to naru.*

On the crags of the shaman's mountain lives a mysterious woman.
She is the morning clouds, the evening rain.

See ⸢Clouds and rain⸣.

ZGS 14.544, ZGJI 668, Shiba na

14.606 浮世如夢事全非 *Fusei yume no gotoku ji mattaku hi nari,*
坐見庭前紅葉飛 *Sozoro ni miru teizen kōyō no tobu o.*

This floating world is just a dream, all things unreal,
Blankly I gaze at red leaves tumbling in the garden.➛

ZGS 14.545, Shiba na

14.607 春去秋來不知老 *Haru sari aki kitatte oyuru o shirazu,*
垢塵猶著舊裳衣 *Kōjin nao tsuku kyūjōe.*

➛Spring and fall come and go, but I'm not aware of getting old.
Hmm, more ⸢dust⸣ has collected on my old clothes.

ZGS 14.546, Shiba na

14.608 佛祖未生空劫前 *Busso imada shōsezu kūgō no mae,*
正偏不落有無機 *Shōhen umu no ki ni ochizu.*

Before the ⸢*kalpa*⸣ of annihilation, when Buddhas and patriarchs had yet to appear,
The ⸢real⸣ and the ⸢apparent⸣ hadn't got entangled in the workings of having and not-having.

ZGS 14.547, Shiba na

14.609 佛祖大機歸掌握 *Busso no daiki shōaku ni ki shi ,*
人天命脈受指呼 *Ninden no myōmyaku shiko o uku.*

The great energy of the buddhas and patriarchs is in his grip,
The lifelines of the men and gods are at his fingertips.

Heki 11 Intro.

ZGS 14.548, ZRKS 14.335, Shiba na

14.610 就船買得魚偏美 *Fune ni tsuite kaiete uo hitoe ni bi nari,*
蹈雪沽來酒倍香 *Yuki o funde kaikitatte sake masumasu kanbashi.*

Fish bought right from the boat has more flavor,
Wine got by tramping through snow tastes a lot better.

ZGJT 201: *Fune ni tsuite kaietaru uo hitoe ni umashi,* 舩 instead of 船. Shiba 357: 踏 instead of 蹈.

ZGS 14.549, ZGJT 201, ZGJI 668, ZRKS 14.171, Shiba 357

14.611 粉骨碎身未足酬 *Funkotsu saishin imada mukuyuru ni tarazu,*
一句了然超百億 *Ikku ryōnen to shite hyaku oku o koyu.*

Break your bones, destroy your body—that still won't repay your debts.
But one clear word would be worth more than ten million atonements.

Heki 1 Main Case Comm.

ZGS 14.550, ZGJT 410 (variant), ZGJI 669, Shiba 388, ZGDJT 39, 証道歌

14.612 文章已變南山霧 *Bunshō sude ni henzu nanzan no kiri,*
羽翼應搏北海風 *Uyoku masa ni utsubeshi hokkai no kaze.*

Its spots have already changed into South Mountain mist,
Its wings will beat against the North Sea wind.

ZGJI 669: The first verse refers to a leopard, the second verse alludes to the great ⌜roc⌝.

ZGS 14.551, ZGJI 669, ZRKS 14.156, Shiba na

14.613 分明紙上張公子 *Funmyō nari shijō no chōkōshi,*
盡力高聲喚不譍 *Chikara o tsukushite kōsei ni yobedomo kotaezu.*

It is clearly the Duke Chang on the paper,
But though you call him with all your might, he will not answer.

Shiba 388: 應 instead of 譍.

KZS #1164, ZGS 14.552, ZGJI 669, ZRKS 14.73, Shiba 388

14.614 平生肝膽向人傾 *Heisei no kantan hito ni mukatte katamuku,*
相識猶如不相識 *Sōshiki wa nao fusōshiki no gotoshi.*

He is always spilling his guts to others,
So being close to him is the same as not being close to him.

ZGJT 413: *Heisei kantan hito nu mukatte katamuke, Aishiru mo nao aishirazari ga gotoshi.*

ZGS 14.553, ZGJT 413, ZGJI 669, ZRKS 14.135, Shiba 389

14.615 平生報國心如火 *Heisei hōkoku no kokoro hi no gotoshi,*
一夜春風吹作灰 *Ichiya shunpū fuite hai to naru.*

Always his spirit of patriotism burned like a flame.
Then one night the spring wind blew and it turned to ash.

ZGS 14.554, Shiba na

14.616 平蕪盡處是青山 *Heibu tsukuru tokoro kore seizan,*
行人更在青山外 *Kōjin sara ni seizan no hoka ni ari.*

The grass plain ends at the blue mountains,
But the traveler is even further beyond the blue mountains.

ZGS 14.555, ZGJT 414, ZRKS 14.200, Shiba na

14.617 平陽歌舞新承寵 *Heiyō no kabu arata ni chō o sazuku,*
簾外春寒賜錦袍 *Rengai no haru samuku shite kinpō o tamau.*

One of the dancing girls from P'ing-yang has just received his praise.
Outside the screens in the spring chill, he offers her his brocade jacket.

ZGS 14.556, Shiba na, TSSSTS 75

14.618 衝開碧落松千尺 *Hekiraku o shōkai su matsu senjaku,*
截斷紅塵水一溪 *Kōjin o setsudan su mizu ikkei.*

Piercing the blue sky—a thousand-foot pine;
Cutting the red ⌜dust⌝—the water of a single stream.

ZGS 14.557, ZGJT 220, ZGJI 669, ZRKS 14.130, Shiba 361

14.619 遍界乾坤皆失色 *Henkai kenkon mina iro o shissu,*
須彌倒卓半空中 *Shumi tōtaku su hankū no uchi.*

The entire world, all heaven and earth, lose their color;
Mount ⌜Sumeru⌝ looms high in the sky.

KZS #1196, ZGS na, ZGJI 670, ZRKS 14.276, Shiba 389

14.620 偏正未曾離本位 *Henshō imada katsute hon'i o hanarezu,*
無生豈涉語因緣 *Mushō ani go innen ni wataran ya.*

While ⌜apparent and real⌝ have yet to emerge from the fundamental state,
Does the unborn presume to chatter about karma?

ZGS 14.558, ZGJT 418, ZGJI 670, ZRKS 14.371, Shiba na

14.621 茅簷相對坐終日 *Bōen aitai shite za suru koto shūjitsu,*
一鳥不鳴山更幽 *Itchō nakazu yama sara ni yū nari.*

Under the thatched eaves, all day I've sat facing it.
With no bird singing, the mountain is yet more still.

ZGS 14.559, ZRKS 7 135n, Shiba na

14.622 脱帽露頂王公前 *Bō o dasshi chō o arawasu ōkō no mae,*
揮毫落紙如雲烟 *Go o furutte kami ni otoseba un'en no gotoshi.*

He doffs his hat and exposes his head before the lords.
He wields his brush, lowers it to paper and lo—clouds and mist arise.

The calligrapher Chang Hsü 張旭, when drunk, would throw all decorum to the wind (remove his formal headgear), stick his head into a pot of ink, and, using his own hair as a brush tip, would write free-flowing (clouds and mist) calligraphy (Maeno 1962, vol. 1, 112).

ZGS 14.560, Shiba na, TSSSTS 10

14.623 謀臣猛將今何在 *Bōshin moshō ima izuku ni ka aru,*
萬里清風只自知 *Banri no seifū tada jichi su.*

Those able ministers and fierce generals, where are they now?
Only the pure wind for ten thousand miles knows.

Heki 61 Verse.

ZGS 14.561, ZGJI 671, ZRKS 14.178, Shiba na

14.624 蓬頭稚子學垂綸 *Hōtō no chishi suirin o manabu,*
側坐莓苔艸映身 *Maitai ni sokuza shite kusa mi ni eizu.*

Tousle-haired infant is learning how to dangle a line,
Lolling in the moss with the shadows of grass across his body.

ZGS 14.562, Shiba na

14.625 暴富乞兒休説夢 *Bōfu kotsuji yume o toku koto o yameyo,*
誰家竈裡火無烟 *Ta ga ie no sōri ni ka hi ni kemuri nakaran.*

Beggar-boy suddenly rich, stop telling us your fantasies!
In whose house is there not smoke from the hearth fire?

ZGS 14.563, ZGJT 238, Shiba 390

14.626 茫茫宇宙人無數 *Bō-bō taru uchū hito musū,*
幾箇男兒是丈夫 *Ikko no danji kore jōbu.*

In this vast universe there are people without number.
How many of them are people of stature?

ZGS na, ZGJI 671, ZRKS 14.441, Shiba 390

14.627 眸裏山川皆白盡 *Bōri no sansen mina hakujin su,*
埋殘草屋一絲煙 *Umenokosu sōoku isshi no kemuri.*

The hills and streams before my eyes have all faded into white,
But left unburied is a thatched hut with a single thread of smoke.

ZGS 14.564, Shiba na

14.628 鳳輦不來春欲盡 *Hōren kitarazu haru tsukinan to hossu,*
空留鶯語到黄昏 *Munashiku ōgo o todomete kōkon ni itaru.*

The Phoenix Carriage does not come, spring has almost gone.
The lonely call of the nightingale lingers as dusk arrives.

ZGS 14.565, Shiba na, TSSSTS 94

14.629 堪對暮雲歸未合 *Taisuru ni taetari boun no kaette imada gassezaru ni,*
遠山無限碧層層 *Enzan kagiri naki heki sō-sō.*

I never tire of the evening clouds before the dark descends—
Mountains endless into the distance, layer upon layer of blue.

Heki 20, Verse 2. Shiba 333: *Boun no kaette imada gassezaru ni taisuru ni taetari.*

ZGS 14.566, Shiba 333

14.630 木人夜半穿靴去　*Bokujin yahan ni kutsu o ugachisari,*
石女天明戴帽歸　*Sekijo tenmei ni bō o itadaite kaeru.*

Putting on his shoes, the ⌜wooden man⌝ went away at midnight;
Wearing her bonnet, the ⌜stone woman⌝ returned at dawn.

Shiba 395: *Mokujin* instead of *bokujin.*

ZGS 14.567, ZGJT 429, ZGJI 671, ZRKS 14.26, Shiba 395

14.631 法界徧周元妙圓　*Hokkai henshū moto myōen,*
一氣頭上得完全　*Ikki˙zujō kanzen o u.*

The entire Dharma world is wondrously complete.
In one breath, you can get it all.

Variant: *Ikkitōjō kanzen o etari.*

ZGS 14.568, Shiba na

14.632 法界何曾問自他　*Hokkai nanzo katsute jita o tou,*
見聞知覺眼中華　*Kenmon chikaku ganchū no hana.*

In the Dharma world, do you ask about self and other?
Seeing, hearing, knowing, and feeling are ⌜flowers in the eye⌝.

ZGS na, ZGJI 670, ZRKS 14.436, Shiba 390

14.633 拂子跨跳過流沙　*Hossu botchō shite ryūsha o sugu,*
奪轉胡僧一隻履　*Datten su kosō no isseki ri.*

The ⌜whisk⌝ leaps across the flowing sands
And snatches back the ⌜barbarian monk's⌝ single shoe.

ZGS 14.569, ZRKS 414, Shiba na

14.634 品字柴頭煨正煖　*Honji no saitō wai shite masa ni atataka nari,*
不知風雪到梅花　*Shirazu fūsetsu no baika ni itaru koto o.*

The cozy flames of the three-log fire have warmed us up.
We're not thinking of the wind and snow on the plum blossoms.

In a three-log fire, the logs are piled up like the character *hon* 品.

ZGS 14.570, ZRKS 14.369, Shiba na

14.635 奔車之上無仲尼　*Honsha no ue ni chūji naku,*
覆舟之下無伯夷　*Fukushū no moto ni hakui nashi.*

You will not find Confucius on a fleeing carriage,
Nor ⌜Po Yi⌝ under an overturned boat.

ZGS 14.571, Shiba na

14.636 將謂黃連甜似蜜 *Masa ni omoeri ōren wa mitsu yori mo amashi to,*
誰知蜜苦似黃蓮 *Tare ka shiru mitsu no ōren yori mo nigaki koto o.*

Everyone thinks that wormwood is sweeter than honey,
But who knows that honey is more bitter than wormwood?

ZGS 14.572, ZGJT 214, ZGJI 672, ZRKS 14.288, Shiba 361

14.637 爲政心閑物自閑 *Matsurigoto o nasu ni, kokoro shizuka nareba mono onozukara shizuka nari,*
朝看飛鳥暮飛還 *Ashita ni miru hichō kure ni wa tonde kaeru.*

In government, if the mind is at peace, things of themselves are at peace.
I watch the birds fly off at dawn and return home at dusk.

ZGS 14.573, Shiba na, TSSSTS 84

14.638 滿街楊柳綠絲煙 *Mangai no yōryū ryokushi no kemuri,*
畫出長安二月天 *Egakiidasu chōan nigatsu no ten.*

Streets filled with willows, green streamers in mist—
Picture the skies of ⌜Ch'ang-an⌝ in spring.

二月, the second month in the Chinese lunar calendar, would be mid-spring.

ZGS 14.574, Shiba 391

14.639 滿口氷霜徹骨寒 *Manku no hyōsō hone ni tesshite samushi,*
就中消息共誰論 *Kono uchi shōsoku tare to tomo ni ka ronzen.*

Mouth full of ice and frost, I'm chilled to the bone.
With whom can I talk about this condition?

ZGS 14.575, ZGJI 672, ZRKS 14.403, Shiba 391

14.640 滿船明月一竿竹 *Mansen no meigetsu ikkan no take,*
家在五湖歸去來 *Ie wa goko ni ari kaeri nan iza.*

With my boat loaded with moonlight and a bamboo pole,
My home is the ⌜Five Lakes⌝ and I'm going home.

ZGS 14.576, ZGJI 672, Shiba na

14.641 滿地落花春已過 *Manchi no rakka haru sude ni sugu,*
綠陰空鎖舊苺苔 *Ryokuin munashiku tozasu kyūmaitai.*

Fallen flowers cover the ground, already spring has gone.
Green shadows silently cover the old moss.

ZGS 14.577, ZGJI 672, Shiba 391

14.642 滿把驪珠撒向人 *Manpa no riju hito ni sankō su,*
醉倒玉樓扶不起 *Gyokurō o suitō shite tasukete okosazu.*

After throwing handfuls of black pearls at people,
He fell drunk by the jade tower and couldn't be helped up.

See「Black dragon pearl」.

ZGS na, ZGJI 672, ZRKS 14.417, Shiba 391

14.643 満面塵灰煙火色 *Manmen no jinkai enka no iro,*
兩鬢蒼蒼十指黑 *Ryōbin wa sō-sō jisshi wa kuroshi.*

Face covered in「dust」and ash, darkened by smoke and fire,
Hair white at the temples, and all ten fingers black.

ZGS 14.578, Shiba na

14.644 不見西湖林處士 *Mizu ya seiko no rin shoshi,*
一生受用只梅花 *Isshō no juyū tada baika.*

I've never seen the「Hermit Lin」of West Lake.
He devoted his life to tending plum blossoms.

ZGS 14.579, ZRKS 14.179, Shiba 386

14.645 路不賚粮笑復歌 *Michi kate o tsutsumazu warai mata utau,*
三更月下入無何 *Sankō gekka buka ni iru.*

On the road without any food, laughing and singing;
Midnight under the「moon」, I enter nothingness.

ZGS 14.580, Shiba na, GKFGS 1.38

14.646 路逢劍客須呈劍 *Michi ni kenkyaku ni awaba subekaraku ken o tei subeshi,*
不是詩人莫獻詩 *Kore shijin ni arazumba shi o kenzuru koto nakare.*

If you meet a swordsman on the road, you present your「sword」;
If you meet someone not a poet, you do not present your poems.

Heki 38 Main Case Comm., *Rinzai-roku* §66, MMK 33.

KZS #1184, ZGS 14.581, ZGJI 673, ZRKS 14.185, Shiba 400

14.647 道泰不傳天子令 *Michi yasūshite tsutaezu tenshi no rei,*
時清盡唱太平歌 *Toki kiyōshite kotogotoku utau taihei no uta.*

When the way is tranquil, imperial edicts are not issued;
In an age of purity, everyone sings the songs of great peace.

ZGS 14.582, ZGJT 349, ZGJI 673, ZRKS 14.34, Shiba na

14.648 汲水僧歸林下寺 *Mizu o kumu sō wa rinka no tera ni kaeri,*
待船人立渡頭沙 *Fune o matsu hito wa totō no sha ni tatsu.*

The monk who drew the water returns to his forest temple,
The man who waits for a boat stands on the ferry sandbank.

ZGS 14.583, ZGJT 86, Shiba 335

14.649 水自竹邊流出冷 *Mizu wa chikuhen yori nagareidete hiyayaku,*
風從花裏過來香 *Kaze wa kari yori sugikitatte kanbashi.*

Water flows cold from the bamboo's edge,
The breeze blows fragrant through the flowers.

KZS #1146, ZGS 14.584, ZGJT 236, ZGJI 673, ZD #152, ZRKS 14.18, Shiba 364

14.650 自携瓶去沽村酒 *Mizukara hei o tazusaesatte sonshu o kai,*
卻著衫來作主人 *Kaette san o tsukekitatte shujin to naru.*

He himself carried the jar to buy some village wine.
Now he changes clothing and becomes head of the house.

ZGS 14.585, ZGJT 180, ZGJI 673, ZD #169, ZRKS 14.337, Shiba 354

14.651 自笑一生無定力 *Mizukara warau isshō jōriki naki koto o,*
行藏多被業風吹 *Gyōzō ōku wa goppū ni fukaru.*

Even I laugh: my whole life I've had no powers of concentration,
Bobbing in and out of the waves, blown by the wind of karma.

ZGS na, ZGJI 673, ZRKS 14.393, Shiba 355

14.652 身在南蕃無所預 *Mi wa nanban ni arite azuku tokoro nashi,*
心懷百憂復千慮 *Kokoro ni idaku hyakuyū mata senryo.*

Here in this southern outback, a place where I don't belong,
My heart holds a hundred sorrows, a thousand memories.

ZGS 14.586, Shiba na, TSSSTS 12

14.653 妙解豈容無著問 *Myōge ani mujaku no toi o iren ya,*
漚和爭負截流機 *Ōwa ikadeka setsuru no ki ni somukan.*

How can ⌜Mañjuśrī⌝ handle Wu-chu's questions?
How can skillful means conflict with the cutting off of delusions?

Rinzai-roku §9; ZRKS 77n: *Ōwa* is skillful means. Shiba 392: 着 instead of 著.

ZGS na, ZGJI 674, ZRKS 14.77, Shiba 392

14.654 妙明一句威音外 *Myōmei no ikku ion no hoka,*
折角泥牛雪裏眠 *Sekkaku no deigyū setsuri ni nemuru.*

This phrase of wonderful clarity is beyond Imposing Sound,
The broken-horned mud ox sleeps in the snow.

Lotus Sutra, ch. 20 describes a buddha named King of Imposing Sound who lived many million ⌜*kalpa*⌝ ago.

ZGS na, ZGJI 674, ZRKS 14.465, Shiba 392

14.655 妙峯孤頂難人到 *Myōbukochō hito no itaru koto katashi,*
只看白雲飛又歸 *Tada miru hakuun tonde mata kaeru koto o.*

The summit of ⌜Wondrous Peak⌝ is hard for people to climb.
I just sit here watching the white clouds come and go.

ZGS 14.587, Shiba 391

14.656 妙用全施該世界 *Myōyū zense sekai o kane,*
木人閑歩火中來 *Bokujin shizuka ni kachū o ayumikitaru.*

The wondrous activity is totally enacted in the world,
The ⌜wooden man⌝ walks calmly through the fire.

ZGS na, ZGJI 674, ZRKS 14.434, Shiba 392

14.657 欲得不招無間業 *Muken no gō o manekazaru o en to hosseba,*
莫謗如來正法輪 *Nyorai no shōbōrin o bōsuru koto nakare.*

If you want to avoid the *karma* of hell,
Don't slander the Tathāgata's wheel of the true Dharma.

Heki 46 Main Case Comm. Empuku-ji: *Mugengō o manekazaru o en to hosseba.* See ⌜Five hells without interval⌝.

ZGS 14.589, Shiba na

14.658 無業一生莫妄想 *Mugō isshō maku mōzō,*
瑞巌只喚主人公 *Zuigan tada yobu shujinkō.*

Mugō's whole life was "Don't fantasize!"
Zuigan just kept calling, "Oh Master!"➛

This and the next verse form one poem. Funshū Mugō Zenji (汾州無業 Ch. Fen-chou Wu-yeh, 760–821) was a disciple of Baso Dōitsu. When practitioners would pose questions to him, he would answer, "Don't fantasize" (ZGDJT 1172, 1203). For Zuigan, see MMK 12.

ZGS 14.590, ZGJI 675, Shiba na

14.659 空山白日蘿窓下 *Kūzan hakujitsu rasō no moto,*
聽罷松風午睡濃 *Shōfū o kikiyande gosui komayaka nari.*

➛Empty mountains, bright sun—beneath the ivied window;
No longer hearing the wind in the pines—a luxurious afternoon nap.

ZGS 14.591, ZGJI 614, Shiba 338

14.660 夢中射落蟭螟窠 *Muchū ni iotosu shōmei no ka,*
開眼看來無縫罅 *Manako o hiraite mikitareba hōka nashi.*

In my dream I shot down a nest of midges,
But when I opened my eyes and looked, there were no traces.

KZS #1196, ZGS 14.592, ZGJI 675, ZRKS 14.279, Shiba 394

14.661 無邊刹界浪痕平 *Muhen no sekkai rōkon tairaka nari,*
獨駕泥牛耕月色 *Hitori deigyū ni ga shite gesshoku ni tagayasu.*

In this world infinitely vast, all waves have been smoothed away.
Alone, mounted on a mud ox, he plows in the moonlight.

ZGS 14.593, Shiba na

14.662 無影樹下合同船 *Muyōjuge no gōdōsen,*
瑠璃殿上無知識 *Ruridenjō ni chishiki nashi.*

Under the tree without shadow, a ferryboat;
In the Jewel Palace, no knowledge.

Heki 18.

ZGS 14.594, ZGJI 675, Shiba na

14.663 名花傾國兩相歡 *Meika keikoku futatsu nagara aiyorokobu,*
常得君王帶笑看 *Tsune ni kunnō no emi o obite miru koto o etari.*

That fair flower and that beautiful woman both rejoice,
For always they receive the emperor's smiling gaze.➛

"Beautiful woman" is literally "overturn a state" 傾國. See ⌜Hsi-shih⌝.

ZGS 14.595, Shiba na, TSSSTS 73

14.664 解釋春風無限恨 *Shunpū kagiri naki no urami o kaishaku shite,*
沈香亭北倚欄干 *Chinkōtei hokurankan ni yoru.*

➛The endless longing that comes on the spring wind melts away
As she leans on the north balustrade of the Ch'en-hsiang Pavilion.

Shiba 332: *Shunpū mugen no urami o kaishaku shite.*

ZGS 14.596, Shiba 332, TSSSTS 73

14.665 明月自來還自去 *Meigetsu onozukara kitari mata onozukara saru,*
更無人倚玉欄干 *Sara ni gyokurankan ni hito no yoru nashi.*

The bright ⌜moon⌝ just comes and goes.
Once again, there is no one leaning on the jade balustrade.

ZGS 14.597, Shiba 394, TSSSTS 95

14.666 猛虎不顧几上肉 *Mōko kijō no niku o kaerimizu,*
洪爐豈鑄囊中錐 *Kōro ani nōchū no sui o in ya.*

The fierce tiger does not look at meat on a board.
In a giant furnace, do you forge needles?

"Needles" translates 囊中錐, "drill bit in a bag." See ⌜Awl⌝.

ZGS 14.598, ZGJT 449, ZGJI 676, ZRKS 14.93, Shiba 394

14.667 猛將豈在家中死 *Mōshō ani kachū ni shinu koto aran ya,*
胡蜂不戀舊時窠 *Kohō kyūji no ana o ren sezu.*

Does a fierce general meet his death residing at home?
Stinging hornets do not long for their old nest.

ZGS 14.599: *Mōshō ani kachū ni atte shisen ya, Kohō kyūji no ana o koishitawazu.*

ZGS 14.599, ZGJI 676, ZRKS 14.370, Shiba 394

14.668 木雞含卵立棺木 *Mokkei tamago o fukunde kanboku ni tachi,*
瓦馬逐風歸本貫 *Gaba kaze o aute honkan ni kaeru.*

The wooden hen brooding on its eggs stands on the coffin,
The tile horse chasing the wind returns to its home ground.

ZGS 14.600, Shiba na

14.669 若無舉鼎拔山力 *Moshi kyotei batsuzan no chikara nakumba,*
千里烏騅不易騎 *Senri no usui mo noriyasukarazu.*

Without the power to lift cauldrons and uproot mountains,
He could not so easily have ridden the fleet-footed Dapple.

See ⌜Hsiang Yü⌝. Empuku-ji: *Moshi kanae o age yama o nuku chikara nakumba.*

ZGS 14.601, ZGJT 194, ZGJI 676, ZRKS 14.64, Shiba 356

14.670 若教轉眄一回首 *Moshi tenpen ikkai shuseshimeba,*
三十六宮無粉光 *Sanjūrokkyū funkō naken.*

If you could get her to cast a glance, once to turn her head,
Then in the thirty-six palaces there would be no beauty to match hers.

See ⌜Chao Chün⌝.

ZGS 14.602, Shiba na, 韓子蒼背面美人圖詩

14.671 如人暗中書字 *Moshi hito anchū ji o sho sureba,*
字雖不成文彩已露 *ji narazu to iedomo monsai sude ni arawaru.*

It is like a person writing characters in the dark.
They may not be characters, but something has already taken shape.

ZGS 14.603, Shiba na

14.672 沒底籃兒盛白月 *Mottei no ranji ni byakugetsu o mori,*
無心椀子貯清風 *Mushin no wansu ni seifū o takuwau.*

I put the white ⌜moon⌝ into a bottomless basket
And keep the pure breeze in the bowl of mindlessness.

Shiba 390: *Bottei no ranji ni byakugetsu o mori.*

KZS #1181, ZGS 14.604, ZGJI 671, ZRKS 14.309, Shiba 390

14.673 最愛江南三月後 *Mottomo aisu kōnan sangatsu no nochi,*
靑山綠樹囀黃鸝 *Seizan ryokuju kōri tenzu.*

What I love best is ⌜Chiang-nan⌝ in mid-spring,
Blue mountains and green trees, yellow orioles singing.

ZGS 14.605, ZGJI 677, ZRKS 14.231, Shiba 347

14.674 本爲修行利濟人 *Moto shugyō wa hito o risai sen ga tame nari,*
誰知翻成不喞噌 *Tare ka shiran kaette fushitsuryū to naran to wa.*

Originally I carried on the practice in order to help others.
Who would have guessed I'd become a useless fool?

ZGS na, Shiba 390

14.675 文殊提起殺人刀 *Monju teiki su setsunintō,*
淨名抽出活人劍 *Jōmyō chūshutsu su katsuninken.*

⌜Mañjuśrī⌝ holds aloft the ⌜sword⌝ that slays people.
⌜Vimalakīrti⌝ draws the sword that gives people life.

KZS #1173, ZGS 14.606, ZGJI 678, ZRKS 14.107, Shiba 388

14.676 門前綠樹無啼鳥 *Monzen no ryokuju teichō naku,*
庭下蒼苔有落花 *Teika no sōtai rakka ari.*

In the green trees by the gate, no birds sing;
On the green garden moss, flowers have fallen.

ZGS 14.607, ZGJI 678, ZRKS 14.238, Shiba 395

14.677 不出門庭三五步 *Montei sangoho o idezu,*
看盡江山千萬重 *Mitsukusu kōzan no senbanjū.*

Not going but three or five steps from my house gate,
My gaze takes in mountains and rivers in endless array.

KZS #1214, ZGS 14.608, ZGJI 678, ZRKS 14.343, Shiba na

14.678 入門懶見妻兒面 *Mon ni itte miru ni monoushi saiji no omote,*
撥盡寒爐一夜灰 *Abakitsukusu kanro ichiya no hai.*

On returning, he ignores his wife and children,
And rakes up the night's ashes in the fireplace gone cold.

ZGS 14.609, Shiba na

14.679 藥忌是誰除未得 *Yakki kore tare ka nozoku koto o imada ezaran,*
夜深飢鼠觸燈臺 *Yoru fukaushite kiso tōdai ni furu.*

Take this, avoid that—who has yet managed to get around this?
But in the deep of the night, a starving rat jiggles the oil lamp.

Yakki 藥忌 are the active and passive sides of treating an illness: taking medicine and avoiding anything harmful. Hungry rats targeted the vegetable or animal oil in lamps. Eventually they would cause the flame to go out (GKFGS 1.132–3).

ZGS 14.610, ZGJT 457, Shiba na, GKFGS 1.132

14.680 夜半和風到窓紙 *Yahan kaze ni washite sōshi ni itaru,*
不知是雪是梅花 *Shirazu kore yuki ka kore baika ka.*

At midnight, blown by wind against my paper windows,
I cannot tell: Is it snow or the petals of plum flowers?

ZGS 14.611, ZGJI 679, ZRKS 14.228, Shiba 396

14.681 山高海深人不測
古往今來轉青碧

Yama takaku umi fukaushite hito hakarazu,
Koō konrai utata seiheki.

Mountains are high, seas are deep, beyond the measure of humans;
From past into present, ever more green, still more blue.

Heki 83 Verse Comm.

ZGS 14.612, Shiba 350

14.682 山如洛下層層出
江自巴中渺渺來

Yama wa rakka no gotoku sō-sō to shite ide,
Kō wa hachū yori byō-byō to shite kitaru.

Mountains piled upon mountains rise round ⌜Lo-yang⌝;
From the land of Pa the rivers comes forth in a wide slow flow.

ZGS 14.615, Shiba na

14.683 夜明簾外排班立
萬里歌謡道太平

Yamyōrengai han o hai shite tatsu,
Banri kayō taihei o iu.

Beyond the screen of ⌜night-shining jewels⌝ they stand in two rows,
In the ten thousand villages they talk of great peace.

ZGS 14.614, Shiba na

14.684 夜來一陣狂風起
吹落桃華知幾多

Yarai ichijin no kyōfū okoru,
Tōka o fukiotoshite shirannu ikuta zo.

Last night gusts of wild wind
Blew down the ⌜peach⌝ blossoms—who knows how many!

ZGS na, ZGJI 679, ZRKS 14.467, Shiba 396

14.685 野老不嫌公子醉
相將携手御街遊

Yarō kirawazu kōshi no yoi,
Aihikiite te o tazusaete gyogai ni asobu.

The old peasant is not offended by the prince's drunkenness;
Pulling each other along by the hand, they play in the ⌜imperial avenue⌝.

ZGS 14.615, Shiba na

14.686 野老從教不展眉
且圖家國立雄基

Yarō samo araba are mayu o nobezaru koto o,
Shibaraku hakaru kakaku no yūki o rissuru koto.

Let the old peasants be who won't relax their frowns.
I will ponder how to establish a solid basis for home and country.

Heki 61 Verse.

ZGS 14.616, Shiba na

14.687 由基矯矢而猿號 *Yūki ya o tamete saru sakebi,*
蒲且虚絃而鳧落 *Hosho gen o munashiushite fu otsu.*

Yu Chi drew forth an arrow and the monkey screamed,
P'u Chü emptied his bow and a duck fell.

For Yu Chi, see *Heki* 69 Verse Comm.

ZGS 14.617, Shiba na

14.688 雪深深處愁猿移 *Yuki no shin-shintaru tokoro shūen utsuri,*
雲遠遠峯訪客歸 *Kumo no en-entaru mine kyaku o tōte kaeru.*

Where the snow lies deep, monkeys are silently stirring.
From clouded peaks far away, a traveler returns from a visit.

ZGS 14.618, ZGJI 680, Shiba na

14.689 雪封雪封雪卻迷 *Yuki fūji yuki fūjite yuki kaette mayoi,*
月滿月滿月不照 *Tsuki michi tsuki michite tsuki terasazu.*

The snow blocks all, the snow blocks all, but it is the snow that is lost.
The ⌜moon⌝ is full, the moon is full, but the moon does not shine.

ZGS 14.619, Shiba na

14.690 夢回一曲漁家傲 *Yume wa kaeru ikkyoku no gyoka ogori,*
月淡江空見白鷗 *Tsuki awaku kō munashiushite hakuō o miru.*

Last night's dream brings back a song, "The Fisherman's Treat."
As the ⌜moon⌝ begins to fade on the empty river, he gazes at the white gulls.

Shiba 393: *Yume wa kaeru ikkyoku gyoka no ogori.*

ZGS 14.620, ZGJI 680, Shiba 393, GKFGS 1.2

14.691 醉來黑漆屏風上 *Yoikitaru kokushitsu byōbu no ue,*
草寫盧仝月蝕詩 *Sōsha su rodō ga gesshoku no shi.*

He got totally drunk, and on a black screen
He scribbled Lu T'ung's ⌜moon⌝-eclipse poem.

Lu T'ung 盧仝 (d. 835?) was a mid-T'ang Dynasty poet whose poem on the eclipse of the moon attracted considerable attention (Morohashi 23050, 137, 138: 14330.187).

ZGS 14.621, ZGJI 680, ZRKS 14.263, Shiba na

14.692 陽氣未回吹律琯 *Yōki imada kaerazu rikkan o fuku,*
野梅先發向南枝 *Yabai mazu hasshite nanshi ni mukau.*

While *yang* has not yet returned to blow the pipe,
The wild plums already begin to blossom on southern branches.

"While *yang* has not yet returned" is the period before the winter solstice when *yin* dominates and nights are increasingly longer; after the solstice, *yang* dominates and days are increasingly longer. "To blow the pipe" refers to the Chinese method for signalling the arrival of *yang*. Chinese music has 12 tones, 6 *yin* and 6 *yang*. The reed or bamboo pipe which played the *yang* tones was filled with ash and let stand. When the wind had blown the pipe empty and caused a note to sound, it was said that *yin* had changed to *yang* (ZGJT 462; ZGJI 680, 402).

ZGS 14.622, ZGJT 462, ZGJI 680, 402, ZRKS 14.164, Shiba na

14.693 醉臥沙場君莫笑 *Yōte sajō ni fusu kimi warau koto nakare,*
古來征戰幾人歸 *Korai seisen ikubaku hito ka kaeru.*

Don't laugh at me lying drunk on the battlefield.
How many have ever come back from war?

ZGS 14.623, Shiba na, TSSSTS 72

14.694 夜靜水寒魚不食 *Yoru shizuka ni mizu samushite uo hamazu,*
滿船空載月明歸 *Mansen munashiku getsumei o nosete kaeru.*

Still night, cold waters, no fish are biting.
Alone, I fill my boat with moonlight and go home.

ZGS 14.624, ZGJT 455, ZGJI 681, ZRKS 14.165, Shiba 395

14.695 好住白雲紅樹裏 *Yoshi hakuun kōju no uchi ni jū shite,*
與君同唱太平歌 *Kimi to onajiku tonau taihei no uta.*

I love to live amid the white clouds and crimson trees,
And sing with you the songs of great peace.

ZGS 14.625, ZGJI 681, ZRKS 14.11, Shiba na

14.696 夜發淸溪向三峽 *Yoru seikei o hasshite sankō ni mukau,*
思君不見下渝州 *Kimi o omoedomo mamiezu yushū ni kudaru.*

Tonight I leave Ch'ing-hsi for the Three Gorges,
Going down to Yü-chou and thinking of you whom I cannot see.

Shiba 396: *Yoru seikei o hasshite sankyō ni mukau.*

ZGS 14.626, Shiba 396, TSSSTS 73

14.697 尋常一樣窓前月 *Yonotsune ichiyō sōzen no tsuki,*
纔有梅花便不同 *Wazuka ni baika areba sunawachi onajikarazu.*

The ⌜moon⌝ by the window has its usual appearance,
But with plum flowers there, suddenly it's different.

ZGJI 637: *Jinjō ichiyō sōzen no tsuki.*

ZGS 14.627, ZGJI 637, ZD #157, ZRKS 14.82, Shiba 364

14.698 尋常多是論三五 *Yonotsune ōku wa kore sango o ronzu,*
惟有今宵分外明 *Tada konshō nomi atte bungai akiraka nari.*

Usually there is much talk about ⌜moon⌝ on the fifteenth,
But tonight it is exceptionally bright.

In the old calendar, the moon was full on the fifteenth day of the month.

ZGS 14.628, ZGJI 637, ZRKS 22, Shiba na

14.699 夜傳衣鉢曹溪去 *Yoru ihatsu o tsutaete sōkei ni saru,*
鐵樹花開二月春 *Tetsuju hana hiraku nigatsu no haru.*

At night the ⌜robe and bowl⌝ were transmitted, and he left for ⌜Ts'ao-ch'i⌝.
The iron tree blossomed in the second month.

ZGS na, ZGJI 681, ZRKS 14.450, Shiba 396

14.700 夜冷井邊聞落葉 *Yoru hiyayaka ni shite seihen ni rakuyō o kikeba,*
已驚秋色到梧桐 *Sude ni odoroku shūshoku no gōtō ni itaru koto o.*

In the cold night, when I hear leaves falling by the well,
I fear that autumn colors have reached the *wutung* tree.

ZGS 14.629, ZRKS 14.211, Shiba na

14.701 夜深各自知寒冷 *Yoru fukōshite kakuji kanrei o shiru,*
莫待齊腰三尺深 *Matsu koto nakare saiyō sanjaku no fukaki o.*

Late at night, you know for yourself what it's like to be freezing cold.
You don't need to wait until it's up to your waist three feet deep.

ZGS 14.630, Shiba na

14.702 讀到三行多一句 *Yonde sankō ni itatte ikku ōshi,*
黃金色上更添黃 *Ōgon shikijō ni sara ni kō o sou.*

I've read to the third line, there's no need to add another verse.
To gleaming gold, that would add more gleam.

ZGS 14.631, Shiba na, GKFGS 1.148

14.703 來年更有新條在 *Rainen sara ni shinjō no aru ari,*
惱亂春風卒未休 *Shunpū ni nōran shite tsui ni imada kyū sezu.*

Next year it will again have new branches
And whipped by the spring wind will not know a moment's rest.

The branches are the long tendrils of a willow. ZGJI 674, KZS #1207: 明年 instead of 來年.

KZS #1207, ZGS 14.632, ZGJT 466, ZGJI 674, ZRKS 14.285, Shiba na

14.704 落花有意隨流水 *Rakka i atte ryūsui ni shitagai,*
流水無情送落花 *Ryūsui jō nakushite rakka o okuru.*

The fallen flowers drift away with longing on the flowing water,
The flowing water carries the fallen flowers away without a care.

Shiba 398: *Ryūsui jō nōshite rakka o okuru. Serenity* 52, Added Sayings.

ZGS 14.633, ZGJT 469, ZGJI 681, ZRKS 14.17, Shiba 398

14.705 落花三月睡初醒 *Rakka sangatsu nemuri hajimete samu,*
碧眼黃頭皆作夢 *Hekigan kōzu mina yume o nasu.*

When flowers fell in the third month, I'd just awakened from sleep.
The ⌜Blue-eyed⌝ One and the ⌜Yellow-headed One⌝ were making dreams.

Shiba 398: *Hekigan kōtō mina yume o nasu.*

ZGS 14.634, ZGJT 469, ZGJI 681, ZRKS 14.313, Shiba 398

14.706 落霞與孤鶩齊飛 *Rakka to koboku to hitoshiku tobi,*
秋水共長天一色 *Shūsui chōten to tomo ni isshiki.*

The sunset mist hangs in the air with a lone goose,
The autumn waters are one color with the endless sky.

ZGS 14.635, ZGJT 469, ZGJI 681, ZRKS 14.131, Shiba 398

14.707 落木千山天遠大 *Rakuboku senzan ten ondai,*
澄江一道月分明 *Chōkō ichidō tsuki funmyō.*

Bare trees on a thousand hills, a vast and endless sky;
The single thread of a shining river, ⌜moon⌝ gleaming bright.

ZGS 14.636, ZGJI 682, ZRKS 14.144, Shiba 398

14.708 洛陽三月春如錦 *Rakuyō sangatsu haru nishiki no gotoshi*
多少工夫織得成 *Tashō no kufū ka oriete nasu.*

The third month in ⌜Lo-yang⌝, springtime like a tapestry brocade—
A bit of effort was required to weave it.

ZGS 14.637, Shiba na

14.709 羅睺羅擊平中險 *Ragora heichū no ken o utte,*
阿難陀聞險處平 *Ananda kensho no hyō o kiku.*

Rāhula struck the steep within the level,
⌜Ānanda⌝ heard the level within the steep.

Shiba 397: 阿彌陀 "Amida" instead of 阿難陀 "Ānanda."

ZGS na, ZGJI 681, ZRKS 14.426, Shiba 397

14.710 羅襦寶帶爲君解 *Raju hōtai kimi ga tame ni toki,*
燕歌蝶舞爲君開 *Enka chōbu kimi ga tame ni hiraku.*

Their fine silk robes and jeweled belts they will remove for you,
The songs of Yen and the dances of Tieh they will perform for you.

The women of Yen were reputed to be extremely fine at singing; the women of Chao were reputed to be especially good dancers (Maeno 1962, vol. 1, 76). Shiba 397: 趙 instead of 蝶.

ZGS 14.638, Shiba 397, TSSSTS 7

14.711 利劍拂開天地靜 *Riken hokkai shite tenchi shizuka ni,*
霜刀擧處斗牛寒 *Sōtō kosuru tokoro togyū susamaji.*

The keen-edged ⌜sword⌝ sweeps all away, heaven and earth are still.
Raise that chilling blade and even the constellations shiver.

KZS #1154, ZGS 14.639, ZGJT 471, ZGJI 682, ZRKS 14.44, Shiba na

14.712 理盡詞窮路亦窮 *Ri tsuki kotoba kiwamatte michi mo mata kiwamaru,*
鳳離金網鶴拋籠 *Hō kinmo o hanare kaku rō o nageutsu.*

Where reason is spent, words give out and the path has come to an end.
The phoenix escapes the golden net and the crane kicks over the cage.

ZGS 14.640, Shiba na, GKFGS 2.6

14.713 定龍蛇兮眼何正 *Ryūda o sadamuru manako nanzo tadashikaran,*
擒虎兕兮機不全 *Koji o torauru ni ki mattakarazu.*

How good is his eye for telling snakes from dragons?
His will to capture the tiger is not yet total.

Heki 11 Comm.

ZGS 14.641, ZGJI 683, ZRKS 14.188, Shiba na

14.714 龍得水時添意氣 *Ryū mizu o eru toki iki o soe,*
虎靠山處長威獰 *Tora yama ni yoru tokoro inyō o chōzu.*

When the dragon reaches water, it fills with spirit;
When the tiger is in the mountains, it increases its ferocity.

ZGS 14.642, ZGJT 474, ZGJI 683, Shiba na

14.715 要使良駒行遠道 *Ryōku o shite endō o yukashimen to yōseba,*
臨歧只得痛加鞭 *Ki ni nozomi tada etari itaku muchi o kuwauru koto o.*

If you want to make a good horse travel a long trail,
At any turnoff, just lay on the whip until it hurts.

ZGS 14.643, Shiba na

14.716 兩箇黃鸝鳴翠柳 *Ryōko no kōri suiryū ni naki,*
一行白鷺上青天 *Ikkō no hakuro seiten ni noboru.*

A pair of yellow warblers sing in the green willows,
A line of snowy herons ascends the blue heaven.

ZGS 14.644, Shiba na

14.717 牕含西嶺千秋雪 *Mado ni wa seirei senshū no yuki o fukumi,*
門泊東吳萬里船 *Mon ni wa tōgo banri no fune o hakusu.*

My window frames the Western Mountains, snow-capped for a thousand autumns.
Through my gate, lo! A ten-thousand-league boat from Eastern Wu now at rest.

ZGS 14.645, Shiba na

14.718 了事衲僧消一箇 *Ryōji no nōsō ikko o shōsu,*
長連床上展足臥 *Chōren shōjō ashi o nobete fusu.*

All we need is a single monk devoted to the one matter,
To stretch out his legs and lie down on the meditation bench.

Heki 78 Verse. 了事 does not mean "awakened" here. 消 here is colloquial for "need" (KZS 1197n).

KZS #1197, ZGS 14.646, ZGJI 683, Shiba na

14.719 遼東白鶴去無跡 *Ryōtō no hakkaku satte ato nashi,*
三山半落青天外 *Sanzan nakaba wa otsu seiten no hoka.*

The white crane from the distant east leaves without a trace,
The ⌜three mountains⌝ hang suspended beyond the blue sky.

ZGS na, ZGJI 683, Shiba 399

14.720 良藥苦口利於病 *Ryōyaku kuchi ni nigōshite yamai ni ri ari,*
忠言逆耳利於行 *Chūgen mimi ni sakarau mo okonai ni ri ari.*

Good medicine is bitter to the taste, but works against illness;
Frank advice grates your ear, but is good for your behavior.

ZGS 14.647, ZRKS 14.100, Shiba 399

14.721 莫把綠雲爲彩鳳 *Ryokuun o totte saihō to nasu koto nakare,*
休將飛雪作楊花 *Hisetsu o motte yōka to nasu koto o yameyo.*

Don't mistake a green cloud for a colored phoenix,
And stop taking willow down for flying snow.

ZGS 14.648, ZRKS 14.295, Shiba na

14.722 輪劍直衝龍虎陣 *Rinken jiki ni tsuku ryūko no jin,*
馬喪人亡血滿田 *Uma sōshi hito bōjite chi den ni mitsu.*

With swinging ⌜swords⌝, they charged the ⌜dragon-tiger formation⌝,
Horses fell, men died, and the fields were steeped in blood.

ZGS 14.649, ZGJI 683, ZRKS 14.242, Shiba na

14.723 抛出輪王三寸鐵 *Rinnō sanzun no tetsu o hōshutsu shite,*
方知遍界是刀鎗 *Masa ni shiru henkai kore tōsō naru koto o.*

The King of the Dharma Wheel released his three-⌜inch⌝ iron tongue
And then we really understood that ours is a world of ⌜swords⌝ and spears.

ZGS 14.650, ZGJI 683, ZRKS 14.215, Shiba 389

14.724 凛凛孤風不自誇 *Rin-rintaru kofū mizukara hokorazu,*
端居寰海定龍蛇 *Kankai ni tankyo shite ryōda o sadamu.*

Fearsome and solitary in demeanor, he does not boast of himself,
But, seated squarely in the universe, decides who is snake, who is dragon.

Heki 11 Verse.

KZS #1185, ZGS 14.651, ZGJT 478, ZGJI 683, ZD #162, ZRKS 14.186, Shiba 399

14.725 瑠璃階上布赤沙 *Ruri kaijō shakusha o shiki,*
碼碯盤中撒眞珠 *Me'nō banchū ni shinjū o sassu.*

Over the lapis lazuli steps, spread red sand;
On the agate tray, sprinkle pearls.

KZS #1210, ZGS 14.652, ZGJI 683, ZRKS 14.294, Shiba 400

14.726 靈琴不引人間韻 *Reikin wa ningen no in o hikazu,*
知音肯度伯牙門 *Chiin aete hakuga no mon ni wataran ya.*

His soul harp no longer strums people's songs,
For his ⌜intimate companion⌝ no longer crosses ⌜Po Ya's⌝ gate.

ZGS 14.653, Shiba na

14.727 禮非玉帛而不表 *Rei wa gyokuhaku ni arazareba arawarezu,*
樂非鐘鼓而不傳 *Gaku wa shōko ni arazareba tsutawarazu.*

Ritual decorum is not expressed without jewels and silks,
Music cannot be conveyed without bells and drums.

ZGS 14.654, ZGJT 479, ZRKS 14.112, Shiba 400

14.728 蓮社當年結未齊 *Rensha sono kami musunde imada hitoshikarazaru ni,*
遠公頭若暮雲低 *Onkō no kōbe wa boun no taruru ga gotoshi.*

The Lotus Society formed that year is still not all-inclusive,
Master Hui's head is [as white] as if enclosed in evening clouds.

The White Lotus Society was formed by Hui-yüan (J. Eon, 334–417) at the Tung-lin ssu temple on Mount Lu for studying the *Nirvana Sutra* and reciting the Buddha's name. This verse can be taken two ways. (1) Hui-yüan's head has turned white from his efforts to save people by including them into the Lotus Society. (2) Hui-yüan excluded Hsieh Ling-yün (J. Sha Rei-un), claiming he lacked a pure heart. The verse can then imply, as Hui-yüan is already white-haired with age, that we must hurry if we are to do something for Hsieh Ling-yün's salvation.

ZGS 14.655, Shiba na, GKFGS 1.22

14.729 老樹臥波寒影動 *Rōju nami ni fushite kan'ei ugoki,*
野烟浮草夕陽昏 *Yaen kusa ni ukande yūyō kurashi.*

The cold reflection of an ancient tree shimmers across the ripples,
Mist in the fields floats over the grass in the twilight dark.

ZGS na, ZGJI 685, ZRKS 14.132, Shiba 400

14.730 樓臺上下火照火 *Rōtai jōge hi hi o terashi,*
車馬往來人見人 *Shaba ōrai hito hito o miru.*

Up and down the terraces and pavilions, lights shine on lights;
Back and forth on horse or carriage, people look at people.

ZGS 14.656, ZGJI 685, ZRKS 14.360, Shiba 401

14.731 老倒疎慵無事日 *Rōtō sorai buji no hi,*
安眠高臥對青山 *Anmin kōga seizan ni taisu.*

Lazy in my old age, days with nothing to do,
Peacefully sleeping without care, facing the blue mountains.

KZS #1161, ZGS 14.657, ZGJI 685, ZRKS 14.62, Shiba 401

14.732 廬山烟雨浙江潮 *Rozan no en'u sekko no ushio,*
不到千般恨未消 *Itarazareba senpan urami imada shōsezu.*

Misty rain on Mount Lu, tide in the River Che;
If I do not go there, a thousand regrets will never let me be.➛

ZGS 14.658, Shiba na, ZRMKJT 382, ZGDJT 1321

14.733 到得歸來無別事 *Itariekaerikitatte betsuji nashi,*
廬山烟雨浙江潮 *Rozan wa en'u sekko wa ushio.*

➛I went and returned, it was nothing special:
Misty rain on Mount Lu, tide in the River Che.

ZGS 14.659, ZRKS 14.219, Shiba 377

14.734 不識廬山眞面目 *Rozan no shin menmoku o shirazaru wa,*
只緣身在此山中 *Tada mi no kono sanchū ni aru ni yoru.*

I do not know the true face of Mount Lu,
For I myself am in the mountain.

ZGS 14.660, ZGJI 635, ZRKS 14.405, Shiba 386

14.735 魯酒薄而邯鄲圍 *Roshū wa usuku shite kantan kakomare,*
宋羹疏而鄭軍誇 *Sōkō wa sakan ni shite teigun hokoru.*

Because the wine of Lu was watery, Han-tan was beseiged;
Because the stew of Sung was plentiful, the troops of Cheng boasted.

The ruler of Chao presented rich wine to the lord of Ch'u while the ruler of Lu presented watery wine. Chao, however, failed to bribe the lord's wine steward, who, out of spite, switched the wines. The lord of Ch'u, angered at Chao for its thin wine, attacked its capital city, Han-tan (Watson 1968, 109). On the eve of battle with Cheng, Hua Yüan of Sung slaughtered a sheep and fed stew to his troops. There was not enough for his carriage driver. The next day in battle, the driver ran his carriage straight into the Cheng troops, who then took Hua Yüan prisoner (Iida Tōin 1955, 429; Watson 1989, 74).

ZGS 14.661, Shiba na

14 字

14.736 鷺鷥立雪非同色 *Roji yuki ni tatsu dōshoku ni arazu,*
明月蘆花不似他 *Meigetsu roka ta ni shikazu.*

The heron standing in the snow is not similar to it in color,
Bright moon and [white] reed flowers do not resemble each other.

ZGJT 445: *Meigetsu roka kare ni shikazu.*

ZGS 14.662; ZGJT 485, 445; Shiba na

14.737 爐中有火無心撥 *Rochū ni hi ari mushin ni shite abaku,*
處處縱橫任意遊 *Sho-sho jūō i ni makasete asobu.*

Thoughtlessly I stir up flames in the fire pit,
Up and down, side to side, everywhere.

ZGS 14.665, Shiba na

14.738 吾宗無語又無傳 *Wa ga shū ni go naku mata den nashi,*
此去西天道八千 *Koko satte saiten michi hassen.*

Our sect has neither word nor transmission;
From here, the road to India is eight thousand miles.

"Eight thousand miles" here connotes an impossibly long distance.

ZGS 14.664, ZGJI 686, ZRKS 14.363, Shiba na

14.739 吾奴不識錦囊重 *Wa ga nu wa shirazu kinnō no omoki koto o,*
裹得青山暮色歸 *Seizan no boshoku o tsutsumiete kaeru.*

My servant does not know why the brocade bag is so heavy,
But we're coming home with the sunset colors of the blue mountains wrapped in it.

ZGS 14.665, ZGJI 686, ZRKS 14.355, Shiba na

14.740 堪笑日月不到處 *Warau ni taetari jitsugetsu futō no tokoro,*
箇中別是一乾坤 *Kono naka betsu ni kore ichi kenkon.*

Wonderful is the place where sun and ⌜moon⌝ do not reach,
Within there is another ⌜heaven and earth⌝.

ZGJI 686, ZRKS 478, Shiba 332

14.741 我憶南泉好言語 *Ware wa omou nansen no kōgongo,*
如是痴鈍亦復稀 *Nyoze no chidon mo mata mare nari.*

I recall Nansen's wonderful words,
A fool like that is rare indeed.

ZGS 14 666, Shiba na

14.742 盱水盡頭居士宅 *Usui no tsukuru hotori koji no taku,*
白雲深處法王家 *Hakuun fukaki tokoro hōōke.*

At the source of the River Hsü there's a layman's cabin,
Deep in the white clouds is the Dharma King's home.

ZRKS 14.372n: (verses 3 and 4) "Who knows how long the tree without roots has stood? And now there is someone seeking a flower in December."

ZGS na, Shiba na, ZRKS 14.372

Fifteen-Character Phrases

15.1 透出一字福壽延長 *Ichiji o tōshutsu shite fukuju enchō,*
透不得藏身無路 *Tō futoku ni shite mi o kakusu michi nashi.*

If you can penetrate the one character, you increase your fortune and long life;
If you cannot penetrate it, there is no place you can hide.

See also 15.9 below.

ZGS 15.1

15.2 蓋天蓋地只一箇 *Gaiten gaichi tada ikko,*
釋迦達磨一棒打殺 *Shaka daruma ichibō ni tasetsu su.*

Covering earth, covering heaven, just one thing;
Śākyamuni and⸢Bodhidharma⸣ I kill with one blow of the stick.

ZGJI 687: 只一琴 instead of 只一箇.

ZGS 15.2, ZGJI 687

15.3 頭長三尺 *Kōbe nagaki koto sanjaku,*
脚短一寸 *Ashi mijikaki koto issun,*
相對無言獨足立 *Aitai shite mugon dokusoku ni shite tatsu.*

Its head is long—three feet;
Its legs are short—one inch;
It faces me in silence standing on one leg.

ZGS 15.3

15.4 見齊師則減師半德 *Ken shi ni hitoshiki toki wa sunawachi shi ni hantoku o genzu,*
見過師方堪傳授 *Ken shi ni sugite masa ni denju suru ni taetari.*

If your *kenshō* is equal to your teacher's, then you have diminished his merit by half;
If your *kenshō* surpasses your teacher's, only then are you competent to receive transmission.

Heki 11 Main Case Comm., 46 Verse Comm., *Rinzai-roku* §56. This verse more commonly appears as a quatrain: 見與齊師, 減師半德, 見過於師, 方堪傳授. For other interpretations of this verse, see ⸢*Genshi hantoku*⸣.

ZGS 15.4, ZGJI 615, ZGJT 107, ZGDJT 284a

15.5 晉楚失其富 *Shin so mo sono tomi o shisshi*
賁育失其勇 *Hon iku mo sono yū o shisshi*
王侯失其貴 *Ō kō mo sono tattoki o shissu.*

[The states of] Chin and Ch'u have lost their wealth,
[The warriors] Pen and Yü have lost their courage,
The king and his vassals have lost their authority.

See explanation at 10.261.

ZGS 15.5, ZGJI 492 and 687

15字

15.6 觀大海者難言水 *Daikai o miru mono wa mizu o iigataku,*
遊聖人門者難成言 *Seijin no mon ni asobu mono wa gen nashigatashi.*

One who has seen the great ocean finds it difficult to speak of water,
One who has studied with a wise man finds it hard to put him into words.

ZGS 15.6

15.7 泰山其頽乎 *Taisan sore kuzuren ka.*
梁木其壞乎 *Ryōboku sore yaburen ka.*
哲人其萎乎 *Tetsujin sore yaman ka.*

Won't Mount T'ai crumble?
Won't the strong roofbeam break?
Won't the wise man pass away?

Confucius intoned these words and told of having a dream in which he foresaw his own death. He then took to bed, and seven days later died (禮記檀弓上 44).

ZGS 15.7

15.8 二桃殺三士 *Nitō sanshi o korosu,*
誰能爲此謀 *Tare ka yoku kono hakarigoto o nasu,*
相國齊晏子 *Shōkoku sei no anshi.*

With two「peaches」he kills three warriors.
Who devised this clever scheme?
Yen-tzu, first minister of the state of Ch'i.

ZGS 15.8

15.9 若人見得福壽延長 *Moshi hito kentoku seba fukujū enchō,*
見不得藏身無路 *Ken futoku naraba mi o kakusu ni michi nashi.*

If one can see, one increases fortune and long life;
If one cannot see, there is no place to hide.

See also 15.1.

ZGS 15.9

15.10 吾盾之堅莫能陥 *Waga tate no kataki yoku tōru naku,*
吾矛之於物無不陥 *Waga hoko no mono ni okeru tōrazaru nashi.*

My shield, so hard nothing penetrates it;
My spear, so sharp there is nothing it cannot pierce.

ZGS 15.10, *Han Fei Tzu* §40.

Sixteen-Character Phrases

16.1 或吹火而然　*Aruiwa hi o fuite moe,*
或吹火而滅　*Aruiwa hi o fuite, messu.*
所以吹者異也　*Yuen wa fuku mono kotonareba nari.*

One blows on the fire and it burns,
One blows on the fire and it goes out.
The purpose for blowing is different.

ZGS 16.1, Shiba na, ZGJI 690

16.2 穀則異室　*Ikite wa neya o koto ni suru mo,*
死則同穴　*Shi shite wa ana onajiusen.*
謂予不信　*Ware o makoto araji to omowaba,*
有如皦日　*Akirakeki hi no gotoku nari.*

Alive, they never shared a house,
But in death they had the same grave.
You thought I had broken faith,
But I was as true as the bright sun above.

Trans. from Waley 1937a, #58.

ZGS 16.2, Shiba na

16.3 一佛成道觀見法界　*Ichibutsu jōdō kanken hokkai,*
草木國土悉皆成佛　*Sōmoku kokudo shikkai jōbutsu.*

When one Buddha attains the way and sees the Dharma world,
The grasses and trees, the land and the earth, one and all become Buddha.

ZGS 16.3, Shiba na, ZGDJT 34d

16.4 一箇如武侯布八陣　*Ikko wa bukō ga hachijin o shiku ga gotoku,*
一箇似子房燒棧道　*Ikko wa shibō ga sandō o yaku ni nitari.*

One is like Marquis Wu deploying the ⌜eight formations⌝,
One is like Tzu-fang burning the trestle pathway.

Marquis Wu is the famed military strategist ⌜Chu-ko Liang⌝. Tzu-fang refers to ⌜Chang Liang⌝, advisor to ⌜Liu Pang⌝.

ZGS 16.4, Shiba na

16.5 一雙孤雁撲地高飛　*Issō no kogan chi o utte takaku tobu,*
一對鴛鴦池邊獨立　*Ittsui no en'ō chihen ni hitori tatsu su.*

A pair of lone geese thump the ground and sail into the sky,
Mated ducks are standing alone out by the pond.

ZGS 16.na, ZRKS 16.22, Shiba 402

16.6 禹以夏王桀以夏亡 *U wa ka o motte ōtari, ketsu wa ka o motte horobu.*
湯以殷王紂以殷亡 *Tō wa in o motte ōtari, chū wa in o motte horobu.*

⌜Yü⌝ was ruler of the Hsia Dynasty, ⌜Chieh⌝ brought the Hsia to ruin.
T'ang was the ruler of the Yin Dynasty, ⌜Chou⌝ brought the Yin to ruin.

ZGS 16.5, Shiba na

16.7 嗜異味者必得異病 *Imi o tashinamu mono wa kanarazu ibyō o e,*
作奇態者必得奇窮 *Kitai o nasu mono wa kanarazu kikyū o u.*

One who seeks strange flavors always gets a strange disease,
One who affects a different manner invariably goes to extremes.

ZGS 16.6, Shiba na, ZGJI 690

16.8 狼跋其胡載疐其尾 *Ōkami sono shitakuchibi o funde sunawachi sono o ni tauri,*
狼疐其尾載跋其胡 *Ōkami sono o ni taure sunawachi sono shitakuchibi o fumu.*

The wolf steps on its beard and then falls on its tail,
The wolf falls on its tail and then steps on its beard.

Book of Songs #160.

ZGS 16.7, Shiba na

16.9 不曰堅乎磨而不磷 *Kataki o iwazu ya migakedomo usurogazu,*
不曰白乎涅而不緇 *Shiroki o iwazu ya kuri ni suredomo kuromazu.*

Is it not said, "So hard, no grinding can wear it thin"?
Is it not said, "So white, no dying can make it black"?

Analects XVII, 7. YOSHIKAWA: *Katashi to iwazu ya, mashite usuragazu; Shiroshi to iwazu ya, desshite kuromazu* (1978, vol. II, 261).

ZGS 16.8, Shiba na

16.10 夏蟲不可以語於氷 *Kachū ni wa motte hyō o kataru bekarazu,*
井蛙不可以語於海 *Seia ni wa motte umi o kataru bekarazu.*

The summer insects cannot speak of ice,
The frog in the well cannot talk of the sea.

ZGS 16.9, Shiba na, ZGJI 691

16.11 關關雎鳩在河之洲 *Kan-kantaru shokyū wa kawa no su ni ari,*
窈窕淑女君子好逑 *Yōchōtaru shukujo wa kunshi no kōkyū.*

"Fair, fair," cry the ospreys on the island in the river.
Lovely is the noble lady, fit bride for our lord.

Trans. from WALEY 1937A, #87. *Book of Songs* #1. ZGS 16.10: 述 corrected to 逑.

ZGS 16.10, Shiba na

16.12 義之筆劃入石三分 *Gishi ga hikkaku ishi ni iru koto sanbu,*
李杜文章光燄萬丈 *Rito ga bunshō kōen banjō.*

I-chih's brushstrokes scored the stone 3 mm. deep,
⌜Li Po⌝ and ⌜Tu Fu's⌝ verses shone with a light 10,000 meters high.

Variant: 義之筆法有入石三分. See ⌜*Fun*⌝. I-chih is Wang I-chih (J. Ōgishi 王義之, 303–379), famous for his brush writing.

ZGS 16.11, Shiba na

16.13 刮龜毛於鐵牛背上 *Kimō o tetsugyū haijō ni kezuri,*
截兎角於石女腰邊 *Tokaku o sekijo yōhen ni kiru.*

He shaves the ⌜tortoise hairs⌝ off the iron bull's back,
He cuts the ⌜rabbit horns⌝ from the ⌜stone woman's⌝ back.

Shiba 406: 削 instead of 刮.

ZGS 16.12, ZRKS 16.10, ZGJI 692; Shiba 406

16.14 堯風蕩蕩野老謳歌 *Gyōfū tō-tō to shite yarō ōka shi,*
舜日熙熙漁人皷棹 *Shunjitsu ki-ki to shite gyojin sao o ko su.*

When ⌜Yao's⌝ influence spread throughout the land, peasants raised their voices in song;
When ⌜Shun's⌝ radiance shone over his domain, fishermen drummed their oars.

ZGS 16.13, ZRKS 16.24, Shiba na, ZD #203

16.15 玉人獻寶楚王誅之 *Gyokujin takara o kenzureba soō kore o korosu,*
李斯竭忠胡亥極刑 *Rishi chū o tsukuseba kogai kei o kiwamu.*

The jewel smith presented a treasure, but the king of Ch'u punished him;
Li Ssu was a paragon of loyalty, but Hu-hai exacted the extreme penalty.

Variant: *kenjite* instead of *kenzureba, tsukushite* instead of *tsukuseba.* See ⌜*Ho* jewel⌝ and ⌜Li Ssu⌝.

ZGS 16.14, Shiba 404

16 字

16.16 漁歌烟浦咸稱富貴 *Gyo wa empo ni utatte mina fūki to shō shi,*
樵唱雲村共樂昇平 *Shō wa unson ni tonaete tomo ni shōhei o tanoshimu.*

Fishermen sing on the misted bays, all praising their good fortune;
Lumbermen chorus by their cabins in the clouds, together rejoicing in the era of peace.

ZGJI 692: 唱雲樹共平樂太. Shiba 403: 雲樹 instead of 雲村.

ZGS 16.15, ZRKS 16.16, Shiba 403, ZGJI 692, ZD #198

16.17 金以火試玉以石試 *Kin wa hi o motte kokoromi, tama wa ishi o motte kokoromi,*
水以杖試人以言試 *Mizu wa jō o motte kokoromi, hito wa gen o motte kokoromu.*

Gold is tested by fire, a jewel is tested by a stone;
Water is tested with a pole, a person is tested by his word.

ZGS 16.404, Shiba 404, ZGJI 692

16.18 雲凝大野徧界不藏 *Kumo daiya ni kotte henkai kakusazu,*
雪覆蘆花難分朕迹 *Yuki roka o ōte chinseki o wakachigatashi.*

Clouds mass over the great plain, not hiding the vast world beyond;
Snow covers the [white] reed flowers blurring their outline.

Heki 13 Intro.

ZGS 16.17, Shiba 402, ZGJI 693

16.19 劍輪飛處日月沈輝 *Kenrin tobu tokoro jitsugetsu kagayaki o shizume,*
寶杖敵時乾坤失色 *Hōjō teki suru toki kenkon iro o shissu.*

Where the ⌜sword⌝ wheel flies, sun and ⌜moon⌝ lose their light;
When the treasure staff strikes, ⌜heaven and earth⌝ pale in color.

ZGS na, ZRKS 16.1, Shiba 405

16.20 建廣厦必先擇工匠 *Kōka o taten ni wa kanarazu mazu kōshō o erabu,*
發三軍必先拜良將 *Sangun o hassen ni wa kanarazu mazu ryōshō o haisu.*

To build a great mansion, you must first select a master carpenter;
To command three armies, you must first commission a great general.

ZGS 16.18, Shiba na, ZGJI 695

16.21 高高峯頂立不露頂 *Kō-kōtaru hōchō ni tatte chō o arawasazu,*
深深海底行不濕脚 *Shin-shintaru kaitei ni yuite ashi o uruosazu.*

He stands on the high peak without showing his head,
He walks the ocean depths without wetting his feet.

ZGS 16.19, ZRKS 16.18, Shiba 406, ZGJI 694, ZGJT 137

16.22 姑蘇台畔不語春秋 *Koso taihan shunjū o katarazu,*
衲僧面前豈論玄妙 *Nōsō menzen ani genmyō o ronzen ya.*

On the ⌜Ku-su Terrace⌝ we do not discuss the *Spring and Autumn Annals,*
In front of a ⌜patch-robed monk⌝ would you theorize about the dark mystery?

ZGS 16.na, ZRKS 16.9, Shiba 405, ZGJI 694, ZD #196.

16.23 孤峯頂上嘯月眠雲 *Kohōchōjō tsuki ni usobuki kumo ni nemuru,*
大洋海中翻波走浪 *Taiyō kaichū nami o hirugaeshi nami ni hashiru.*

On lonely peaks he whistles at the ⌜moon⌝ and sleeps in the clouds,
In the vast ocean he splashes in the surf and rides the waves.

ZGS 16.20, ZRKS 16.17, Shiba 405, ZGJI 694, ZD #200

16.24 孤峯頂上目視雲霄 *Kohōchōjō manako ni unshō o mi,*
古渡頭邊和泥合水 *Kototōhen wadei gassui.*

Atop the solitary peak your eyes gaze at the clouds,
At the old ferry dock you're covered with muck and water.

ZGS 16.21, ZRKS 16.3, Shiba 405, ZGJI 694, ZD #193

16.25 處孤峯者救入荒草 *Kohō ni oru mono wa sukutte kōsō ni irashime,*
墮荒草者救處孤峯 *Kōsō ni dasuru mono wa sukutte koho ni orashimu.*

The one atop the lone peak, when saved, is put out into the wild grass;
The one in the wild grass, when saved, is put atop the lone peak.

ZGS 16.22, Shiba na

16.26 仰之彌高鑽之彌堅 *Kore o aogeba iyo-iyo takaku, kore o kireba iyo-iyo katashi,*
瞻之在前忽焉在後 *Kore o mite mae ni aru ka to sureba kotsuen to shite shirie ni ari.*

The more I look up at it, the higher it becomes; the more I bore into it, the harder it becomes.
When I look and think it is ahead, suddenly it is behind.

Analects IX, 10.

ZGS 16.23, Shiba 404, ZGJI 421

16.27 求之不得寤寐思服 *Kore o motomete ezareba gobi ni mo omoiomou,*
悠哉悠哉輾轉反側 *Yū naru ka na yū naru kana tenten shi hansoku su.*

I search but cannot find her—awake, asleep, thinking of her,
Endlessly, endlessly, turning, tossing from side to side.➛

Trans. from Watson 1984, 18. Shiba 403: 寤寐 instead of 寤寐.

ZGS 16.24, Shiba 403

16.28 參差荇菜左右采之 *Shinshitaru kōsai wa sau ni kore o toru,*
窈窕淑女琴瑟友之 *Yōchōtaru shukujo wa kinshitsu shite kore o itsukushimu.*

➛A ragged fringe is the floating heart; left and right we pick it.
The mild-mannered good girl—harp and lute make friends with her.

ZGS 16.25, Shiba na

16 字

16.29 寒則向火熱則乘涼 *Samukereba hi ni mukai, atsukereba ryō ni jōzu,*
飢則喫飯困則打眠 *Uereba han o kisshi, konzureba nemuri o tasu.*

When cold, face the fire; when hot, go up where it's cool;
When hungry, eat something; when tired, take a nap.

Heki 74 Main Case Comm. ZGJI 695: *damin su* instead of *nemuri o tasu.*

ZGS 16.26, Shiba na, ZGJI 695, ZGJT 65

16.30 實際理地不立一塵 *Jissai richi ichijin o rissezu,*
佛事門中不捨一法 *Butsuji monchū ippō o sutezu.*

In the realm of ultimate reality, not one speck of dust is raised;
Within the gates of the Buddha works, not one dharma is thrown away.

Shiba 406: 致 instead of 地; ZGJI 695.

ZGS 16.27, Shiba 406

16.31 諸惡莫作衆善奉行 *Shoaku makusa shuzen bugyō,*
自淨其意是諸佛教 *Jijō goi kore shobutsu no kyō.*

Commit no evil, do every good;
Purify your own mind—this is the teaching of the many buddhas.

This well-known verse has traditionally been translated in the imperative. However, ZGDJT 523 says that in the original Sanskrit and Pali versions this verse is not in the imperative and does not state prohibitions. In that case, the translation should be:

No evil is committed, all good is done;
The purity of one's own mind is the teaching of the many Buddhas.

ZGS 16.28, Shiba na, ZGJI 696, ZGDJT 523b

16.32 女無美惡入宮見妬 *Jo wa biaku to naku kyū ni itte wa netamareru,*
士無賢愚入朝見嫉 *Shi wa kengu to naku chō ni itte wa nikumareru.*

Any woman, beautiful or ugly, on entering the palace is regarded with jealousy;
Any man, clever or stupid, on entering the court is regarded with hostility.

ZGS 16.29, Shiba na, ZGJI 691

16.33 身體髮膚受之父母 *Shintai happu kore o fubo ni uku,*
不敢毀傷孝之始也 *Aete kishō sezaru wa kō no hajime nari.*

Body and bones, hair and skin—these we receive from our father and mother;
Keeping them from damage or injury—this is the beginning of filial piety.

ZGS 16.30, Shiba na, 孝經 1

16.34 乃積乃倉乃裹餱糧 *Sunawachi tsumi sunawachi kura ni shi sunawachi kōryō o tsutsumu,*
于橐于囊思戢用光 *Taku ni nō ni osamete motte ōi ni sen koto o omoeri.*

He stocked and stored; he placed provisions in bags and sacks.
He brought harmony and so glory to his state.

Trans. from Lau 1970, 66. *Mencius* i, b, 5.

ZGS 16.31, Shiba na

16.35 成王削桐葉爲圭而封小弱弟周公入賀 *Seiō tōyō o kezuri kei to nashite, shōjaku no tei o hōzu, shūko irite ga su.*

King Ch'eng clipped a paulownia leaf and, making it into a sceptre, enfeofed his little boy brother. ⌜Duke Chou⌝ celebrated the occasion.

ZGS 16.32, Shiba na

16.36 齊婢含冤三年不雨 *Seihi en o shinonde sannen ame furazu,*
鄒衍下獄六月飛霜 *Sūen goku ni kudatte rikugetsu shimo o tobasu.*

The maid of Ch'i endured false accusation and for three years it did not rain,
Tsou Yen was thrown into jail and frost formed in the sixth month.

Shiba 407: *fukunde* instead of *shinonde.* As a result of court intrigues in the state of Ch'i 齊, a false accusation was made against Lady Hsiao 孝婦 and heaven sent no rain for three years (漢書于定國傳, cited at Morohashi 12.1422). Both ZGS 16.33 and Shiba 407 have 齊婢, but this must be a misprint for 齊婦 "the lady of Ch'i." Tsou Yen was a just official who, falsely slandered, was thrown into jail; as a consequence frost formed, although it was mid-summer. 鄒衍 is also written 騶衍 (Morohashi 39562.7).

ZGS 16.33, Shiba 407

16.37 背倚寒岩面如滿月 *Se wa kangan ni yori omote wa mangetsu no gotoshi,*
盡大地人只觀半截 *Jindaichi no hito tada hansetsu o miru.*

He leans his back against the cold cliffs, his face like the full ⌜moon⌝;
The people throughout this vast land see only a half.

ZGS 16.34, Shiba na, ZGJI 699

16.38 善財七日尋覓不得 *Zenzai shichijitsu junmyaku shite futoku,*
趙州五年分疎不下 *Jōshū gonen bunso fuge.*

⌜Sudhana⌝ searched seven days without result,
For five years Jōshū had nothing to say.

For the incident regarding Sudhana, see *Heki* 23 Main Case Comm. For the incident regarding Jōshū, see *Heki* 58.

ZGS 16.35, Shiba na

16.39 陝府鐵牛不覺膽顫 *Senpu no tetsugyū mo oboezu kimo furui,*
嘉州大象通身汗流 *Kashū no daizō mo tsūshin ase nagaru.*

The ⌜Iron Ox of Shen-fu⌝ can't help the churning in its guts,
The ⌜giant statue of Chia-chou's⌝ whole body runs with sweat.

ZGS 16.36, Shiba na, ZGJI 696

16.40 出其東門有女如雲 *Sono tōmon o izureba jo ari kumo no gotoshi,*
雖則如雲匪我思存 *Sunawachi kumo no gotoshi to iedomo wa ga omoi no aru ni arazu.*

Outside the Eastern Gate are girls as many as clouds;
But though they are as many as clouds, there is none on whom my heart dwells .

Trans. from Waley 1937, #36.

ZGS 16.37, Shiba na

16 字

16.41 攪酥酪醍醐爲一味 *Soraku daigo o kaite ichimi to nashi,*
鎔缾盤釵釧爲一金 *Byōban saisen o tokashite ikkin to nasu.*

Stir curds and whey with butter and cream to make one flavor,
Melt pails and tubs with hairpins and bracelets to make one ingot.

ZGS 16.38, Shiba 403

16.42 追大鵬於藕絲竅中 *Taihō o gūshi kyōchū ni oi,*
納須彌於蟭螟眼裏 *Shumi o shōmei ganri ni iru.*

Chase the great ⌜roc⌝ into the vein of a lotus stalk,
Drop Mount ⌜Sumeru⌝ into the eye of a flea.

ZGS 16.na, ZRKS 16.7, Shiba 407, ZGJI 697, ZD #195

16.43 太隧之中其樂融融 *Taisui no naka sono tanoshimi yū-yū,*
太隧之外其樂洩洩 *Taisui no soto sono tanoshimi ei-ei.*

Within the great tunnel, genial, genial is my joy!
Outside the great tunnel, far-flung, far-flung is my joy!

From *Tso chuan,* Duke Yin First Year 春秋左傳隱元. Because she hated him and actively schemed against him, Duke Chuang put his own mother into an underground prison and swore an oath, "Not until we reach the Yellow Springs [below the earth] shall we meet again." Later he repented but could not break a sworn oath. Instead, he dug into the earth, i.e., towards the Yellow Springs, and then made a tunnel to his mother's prison. This allowed him to meet his mother without breaking his oath. The first verse is spoken by Duke Chuang, the second verse by his mother (WATSON 1989, 1–4).

ZGS 16.39, Shiba na

16.44 鵊羽狼膽猫頭狐涎 *Chin'u rōtan myōtō kozen,*
一釜煉來抛向面前 *Ippu ni nerikitatte menzen ni hōkō su.*

⌜Blackbird wings⌝, wolf gall, cat's heads, ⌜fox slobber⌝:
He stirs them all up in a pot, then throws them in your face.

Shiba 407: *koen* instead of *kozen.*

ZGS 16.40, Shiba 407, ZGJI 698

16.45 同天下利者得天下 *Tenka to onajiku ri suru mono wa tenka o e,*
擅天下利者失天下 *Tenka o hoshiimama ni shite ri suru mono wa tenka o ushinau.*

One who shares the fortunes of the world gains the world,
One who exploits the fortunes of the world loses the world.

ZGJI 698: *Tenka no ri ni dō suru mono wa tenka o e, Tenka no ri o sen ni shite ri suru mono wa tenka o ushinau.*

ZGS 16.41, Shiba na, ZGJI 698

16.46 天寒人寒針頭削鐵 *Tenkan jinkan shintō ni tetsu o kezuri,*
滴水滴凍畫餅充飢 *Tekisui tekitō gabei ue ni atsu.*

Till heaven and humans freeze over, shave metal from a needle;
Till each drop of water turns to ice, feed pictures of food to the starving.

ZGS 16.42: *atsu* instead of *mitsu.* ZGJI 698: *ten samuku, hito samuku* instead of *tenkan jinkan.*

ZGS 16.42, ZRKS 16.6, Shiba 408, ZGJI 698

16.47 天何言哉四時行焉 *Ten nani o ka iū ya shiiji okonaware,*
地何言哉百物生焉 *Chi nani o ka iū ya hakumotsu sei su.*

What does heaven say? Yet the four seasons roll on.
What does earth say? Yet the hundred creatures are born.

Analects XVII, 19; *Heki* 47 Intro. Both ZGS 16.43 and Shiba 408 read 四時 as *shiiji.* Shiba 408: *naru* instead of *sei su.*

ZGS 16.43, Shiba 408, ZGJI 698

16.48 天馬駒日行數千里 *Tenma no ku nichi ni sūsenri o yuku,*
橫行竪走奔馳如飛 *Ōkō jusō honchi tobu ga gotoshi.*

The sky colt races thousands of miles in a day;
Back and forth, far and wide, it gallops as fast as flying.

Heki 26 Verse Comm.

ZGS 16.44, Shiba na

16.49 唐棣之華偏其反而 *Tōtei no hana hirugaette sore hirugaereri,*
豈不爾思室是遠而 *Ani nanji o omowazaran ya shitsu kore tōkereba nari.*

The flowers of the cherry tree, how they wave about!
It's not that I do not think of you, but your home is far away.

Trans. from Lau 1979, 100. *Analects* ix, 30.

ZGS 16.45, Shiba na, ZGJI 699

16.50 東涌西沒南涌北沒 *Tōyu saimotsu nanyu hokumotsu,*
中涌邊沒邊涌中沒 *Chūyu henmotsu henyu chūmotsu.*

You can pop up in the east and vanish in the west, pop up in the south and vanish in the north,
Pop up in the middle and vanish in the borderland, pop up in the borderland and vanish in the middle.

Trans. from Watson 1993b, 38. *Rinzai-roku* §16. Here 涌 is traditionally read *yu*, not *yū* (Akizuki 1972, 71–2).

ZGS 16.46, Shiba na, ZGJI 698

16.51 鳥之將死其鳴也哀 *Tori no masa ni shinan to suru toki sono naku ya kanashi,*
人之將死其言也善 *Hito no masa ni shinan to suru toki sono iū ya yoshi.*

Sad is the cry of a dying bird,
Good are the words of a dying man.

Trans. from Lau 1979, 92. *Analects* viii, 4.

ZGS 16.47, Shiba na

16.52 伯夷死名於首陽下 *Hakui shi shite shuyō no moto ni na ari,*
盜跖死利於東陵上 *Tōseki shi shite tōryō no hotori ni ri ari.*

⌜Po Yi⌝ died at the foot of Mount Shou-yang for the sake of honor;
⌜Robber Chih⌝ died atop Mount Tung-ling because of greed.

Chuang-tzu, ch 8.

ZGS 16.48, Shiba na

16.53 白雲堆裏不見白雲 *Hakuun tairi hakuun o mizu,*
流水聲中不聞流水 *Ryūsui seichū ryūsui o kikazu.*

Inside a mass of white clouds one sees no white clouds,
Inside the sound of flowing water one hears no flowing water.

ZGS 16.49, ZRKS 16.21, Shiba 408, ZGJI 699

16.54 萬仭嶮崕人跡不到 *Banjin no kengai jinseki futō no tokoro,*
處亂葛藤抽枝垂蔓 *Kattō midare chūshi suiman.*

Sheer cliffs 10,000 fathoms high, where footsteps have never reached;
A place rife with tangled vines, where branches jut and creepers dangle.

ZGS 16.50, Shiba na

16.55 不萠枝上金鳳翺翔 *Fuhōshijō kinhō kōshō shi,*
無影樹邊玉象圍繞 *Muyōjuhen gyokuzō igyō su.*

Round the tree without buds the golden phoenix wheels,
Round the tree with no shadow the jade elephant circles.

ZGS 16., Shiba 409, ZGJI 700

16.56 弊帷不棄爲埋馬也 *Heii uma o uzumuru tame ni sutezu,*
弊蓋不棄爲埋狗也 *Heigai inu o uzumuru tame ni sutezu.*

You do not throw away a ragged tent, as it is useful when burying a horse;
You do not throw away a broken lid, as it is useful when burying a dog.

ZGS 16.51, Shiba na

16.57 凡夫若知卽是聖人 *Bonpu moshi shiraba sunawachi kore seijin,*
聖人若會卽是凡夫 *Seijin moshi eseba sunawachi kore bonpu.*

An ordinary person knows it and becomes a sage,
A sage understands it and becomes an ordinary person.

MMK 9.

ZGS 16.52, ZRKS 16.34, Shiba 409, ZGJI 700, ZD #207

16.58 説妙談玄太平姦賊 *Myō to toki gen to danzu taihei no kanzoku,*
行棒下喝亂世英雄 *Bō o gyōji katsu o kudasu ransei no eiyu.*

He preaches the ineffable, he expounds the mystery—a debauched thief in the time of great peace.
He swings the stick, he roars "Kaa!"—the hero of this age of confusion.

ZGS 16.53, ZRKS 16.5, Shiba na, ZGJI 701

16.59 若作酒醴爾惟麴蘖 *Moshi shurei o tsukuru (tsukaraba), nanji kore kikugetsu,*
若作和羹爾惟鹽梅 *Moshi wakō o tsukuru (tsukaraba), nanji kore anbai.*

Be to me the yeast and malt for making wine and spirits,
Be to me the salt and plum for making broth.

ZGS 16.54, Shiba na, 書經, 説命下

16.60 桃之夭夭其葉蓁蓁 *Momo no yō-yōtaru sono ha shin-shin tari,*
之子于歸宜其家人 *Kono ko koko ni totsuide sono kajin ni yo karan.*

Buxom is the ⌜peach⌝ tree—how thick its leaves!
Our lady going home brings good to the people of her house.

Trans. from Waley 1938, 106.

ZGS 16.55, Shiba 408

16.61 隔山見烟早知是火 *Yama o hedatete kemuri o mite wa hayaku kore hi naru o shiri,*
隔墻見角便知是牛 *Kaki o hedatete tsuno o mite wa sunawachi kore ushi naru o shiru.*

Beyond the mountains see smoke, and know at once there's a fire;
Beyond the fence see horns, and know right away there's an ox.

Heki 1 Intro., 24 Main Case Comm. Shiba 403: 煙 instead of 烟.

ZGS 16.56, ZRKS 16.30, Shiba 403, ZGJI 702, ZGJT59, ZD #205

16.62 爐鞴之所鈍鐵猶多 *Rohai no tokoro dontetsu nao ōku,*
良醫之門病者愈甚 *Ryōi no mon ni byōsha iyo-iyo hanahadashi.*

At the blacksmith's forge, even more scrap iron;
At the gate of the good doctor, ever more sick.

ZGS 16.na, ZRKS 16.2, Shiba 409, ZGJI 703, ZGJT 483, ZD #192

16.63 我有嘉賓中心喜之 *Ware ni kahin ari chūshin kore o yorokobu,*
鍾皷既設一朝右之 *Shōko sude ni mōke itchō kore o susumu.*

I have a fine guest and wholeheartedly rejoice in him;
Bells and drums are ready, all morning I host him.

ZGS 16.57, Shiba na, *Book of Songs* #175

Seventeen-Character Phrases

17.1 織者日以進 / 耕者日以退 / 事相反成功一也

Oru mono wa hibi ni motte susumi,
Tagayasu mono wa hibi ni motte shirizoku.
Koto aihan suru mo kō o nasu wa itsu nari.

One who weaves moves forward day after day; one who tills moves backward day after day.
But though opposite to each other, their result is the same.

ZGS 17.1, ZGJI 704

17.2 咸池承雲九韶六英 / 人之所樂 / 鳥獸聞之驚

Kanchi shōun kyūshō rikuei,
Hito no tanoshimu tokoro.
Chōjū kore o kiite odoroku.

These melodies—"Heaven's Pond," "Receiving Clouds," "The Nine Tunes," "The Six Heroes"—
Are what men find pleasant,
But the birds and beasts hear them and are frightened.

Chuang-tzu, ch. 18.

ZGS 17.2, ZGJI 704

17.3 狂者東走 / 逐者亦東走 / 走同而所以走則異

Kyōja higashi ni hashireba,
Ou mono mo mata higashi ni hashiru.
Hashiru koto onajiushite hashiru yuen wa sunawachi kotonaru.

The madman runs east and his pursuer also runs east.
Their running is the same but their reasons for running are different.

ZGS 17.3, ZGJI 704

17.4 芻蕘野人築壇祈 / 雛子到死不得男子一人

Sūzō yajin dan o kizukite inoru.
Sūshi shi ni itaru mo danshi ichinin o ezu.

The grass-cutters, woodsmen, and fieldmen built platforms and prayed.
But right until they died, the little ones did not get even one son.

ZGS 17.4

17.5 先照後用 / 先用後照 / 照用同時 / 照用不同時

Senshō goyū,
Senyū goshō,
Shōyū dōji,
Shōyū fudōji.

Insight first, action later;
Action first, insight later.
Insight and action together,
Insight and action apart.

ZGS 17.5, ZGJI 704, ZGDJT 691d

17.6 孰謂微生高直
或乞醯焉
乞諸其隣而與之

Tare ka biseikō o choku nari to iu,
Aru hito su o kou,
Kore o sono tonari ni koute kore ni atau.

How can we call even Wei-sheng Kao upright?
When someone asked him for vinegar,
He went and begged it from the people next door, and then gave it as though it were his own gift.

Trans. from Waley 1938, 113. *Analects* v, 23.

ZGS 17.6

17.7 鶴鳴于九皐
聲聞于野
魚潛在淵或在于渚

Tsuru wa kyūkō ni naki,
Koe ya ni kikou,
Uo wa hisonde fuchi ni ari aruiwa nagisa ni ari.

The cranes cry in the Nine Pools,
Their voices are heard in the wild.
Fish sink into the pools or rest in the shoals.

Book of Songs #184.

ZGS 17.7, ZGJI 704

17.8 翡翠以羽自殘
龜以智自害
丹以含色磨肌

Hisui hane o motte jizan shi,
Ki wa chi o motte jigai shi,
Tan wa iro o fukumu o motte ki o masu.

The kingfisher is killed for its wings,
The turtle is destroyed for knowledge,
The *tan* crystal's sheen is ground for the color it contains.

The kingfisher's beautifully colored feathers were highly prized. The turtle's shell was used in divination. The *tan* crystal was used to make the pigment for "Chinese red."

ZGS 17.8, ZGJI 705

17.9 晝爾于茅
宵爾索綯
亟其乘屋
其始播百穀

Hiru wa nanji yuite chi kari,
Yoru wa nanji nawa nae,
Sumiyaka ni sore ya ni nobore,
Sore hajimete hyakkoku o shikan.

By day, you cut the long grass,
In the evening you braid it into rope;
Quickly climb the thatch roof,
Then begin the sowing of the many grains.

Book of Songs #154.

ZGS 17.9

17.10 文王左右天下 *Bunnō wa tenka o sayu shite,*
不以絲毫私 *motte shigō o watakushi sezu,*
以民心爲心已 *tami no kokoro o motte kokoro to nasu nomi.*

⌜King Wen⌝ governed all under heaven.
Without the least self-interest
He made people's feelings his own.

ZGS 17.10

Eighteen-Character Phrases

18.1 一味不能合異鼎之甘 *Ichimi itei no amaki koto o gassuru koto atawazu,*
獨木不能致鄧林之茂 *Dokuboku tōrin no shigeki o itasu koto atawazu.*

A single flavor cannot match the seasoning of a good kettle of stew;
A lone tree cannot attain the luxurious growth of the Teng-lin Forest.

ZGS 18.1, Shiba 410, ZGJI 706

18.2 擊碎我法二空見泥獄 *Gahō nikū no ken deigoku o gekisai shi,*
踏斷今時那邊瞎兎徑 *Konji nahen no kattokei o tōdan su.*

Destroy that mud hell they call "self and object, both empty."
Stamp out that dead-end rabbit alley called "the here-and-now."

ZGS 18.2, Shiba 411

18.3 火雲蒸太虛太虛不熱 *Kaun taikyo o musedomo taikyo atsukarazu,*
清風掃太虛太虛不涼 *Seifū taikyo o haraedomo taikyo suzushikarazu.*

Though fiery clouds heat the great sky, the great sky does not become hot,
Though pure winds blow upon the great sky, the great sky does not become cool.

ZGS na, Shiba 410

18.4 雁過長空影沈寒水 *Kari chōkū o sugi kage kansui ni shizumu mo,*
雁無遺蹤意水無沉影心 *Kari ni ishō no i naku mizu ni chin'ei no kokoro nashi.*

Geese cross the vast sky, their image sinking into the cold waters.
The geese do not intend to leave traces, the water has no mind to reflect their image.

Shiba 411: 沈 instead of 沉.

ZGS 18.3, Shiba 411, ZGJI 706

18.5 羯諦羯諦波羅羯諦波羅僧羯諦菩提蘇婆訶 *Gyatei gyatei hara gyatei hara sō gyatei bōji sowaka.*

Gone! Gone! Gone beyond! Gone completely beyond! ⌜*Bodhi*⌝! *Svāhā!*

This mantra comprises the last lines of the *Heart Sutra* and is often translated as above into English. But Genjō Hosshi 玄奘法師, who translated the Sanskrit into Chinese, deliberately avoided translating the meaning of this mantra. Instead, he used Chinese characters to indicate how the syllables of the phrase were to be pronounced. If mantras are to be chanted for their sound and not for their meaning, then the mantra should be rendered in its original Sanskrit form: *Gate gate pāragate pārasaṃgate bodhi svāhā.*

ZGS 18.4, Shiba na

18.6 狡兎死走狗烹　*Kōto shi shite sōku nirare,*
飛鳥盡良弓藏　*Hichō tsukite ryōkyū kakure,*
敵國破謀臣亡　*Tekkoku yaburete bōshin horobu.*

When the wily rabbits have been killed, the hunting dogs get boiled;
When the soaring birds have gone, the good bows get put away;
When the enemy states have been destroyed, the policy advisors are eliminated.

A saying common to several old texts. See, for example, *Shih-chi* 92 (WATSON 1993, *Han* I, 181).

ZGS 18.5, Shiba 412

18.7 是曰性十重禁須臾離　*Kore ni iwaku shō jūjūkin shuyu mo hanarureba,*
則即落二見惡無不造　*Sunawachi niken ni ochite aku tsukurazaru wa nashi.*

It is said, one whose nature strays even one moment from the ten grave precepts
At once falls into the duality of views and will not avoid doing wrong.

ZGS 18.6, Shiba na

18.8 乞兒亦不顧底破漆桶　*Kotsuji mo mata kaerimizaru tei no hashittsū,*
瘦馬亦不食底蔓葛藤　*Sōba mo mata kurawazaru tei no mankattō.*

A broken tub that a beggar would not look at twice,
A tangle of rotting vines that a scrawny horse would not eat.

ZGS 18.7, Shiba 412, ZGJI 706

18.9 十分爽氣兮淸磨暑秋　*Jūbun no sōki kiyoku shoshū o mashi,*
一片閑雲兮遠分天水　*Ippen no kan'un tōku tensui o wakatsu.*

A complete change of air cleans the heat of autumn,
Far off a single lazy cloud divides the sea from sky.

ZGS na, Shiba 414, ZGJI 706

18.10 唐虞日孳孳以致於王　*Tōgu wa hi ni shi-shi to shite motte ō o itashi,*
桀紂日怏怏以致於死　*Ketchū wa hi ni ō-ō to shite motte shi o itasu.*

⌜T'ang and Yü⌝ achieved kingship through their daily diligence,
⌜Chieh and Chou⌝ brought about death through their daily resentments.

ZGS 18.8, Shiba na

18.11 伯牙善鼓琴鍾子期善聽　*Hakuga yoku kin o ko shi shōshiki yoku kiku,*
鍾子期死伯牙斷絃　*Shōshiki no shisuru ya hakuga gen o tatsu.*

⌜Po Ya⌝ played his lute so beautifully and Chung Tzu-ch'i listened so intently.
When Chung Tzu-ch'i died, Po Ya cut the strings.

ZGS 18.9, Shiba na

18.12 居廟堂之高則憂其民　*Byōdō no takaki ni oreba sono tami o ureu,*
居江湖之遠則憂其君　*Gōko no tōki ni oreba sono kimi o ureu.*

On the heights of the imperial shrine he worries for his people;
On the distant lakes and rivers they worry for their lord.

ZGS 18.10, Shiba na

18.13 蛇出一寸知其大與小
人出一言知其長與短

Hebi wa issun o izureba sono dai to shō to o shiri,
Hito wa ichigen o idaseba sono chō to tan to o shiru.

If a snake emerges even one inch, one knows if it is big or small;
If a man says even one word, one knows if he is great or small.

ZGS 18.11, Shiba 413

18.14 山生金反自刻
木生蠹反自食
人生事反自賊

Yama kin o shōjite kaette mizukara kizamare,
Ki kikuimushi o shōjite kaette mizukara kuraware,
Hito koto o shōjite kaette mizukara sokonau.

Mountains produce gold and get themselves gouged,
Trees produce borers and themselves are eaten away,
Men produce problems and cause their own ruin.

ZGS 18.12, Shiba na, ZGJI 707

18.15 以指喩指之非指不若
以非指譬指之非指也

Yubi o motte yubi no yubi ni arazaru ni tatoen yori shikazu,
Yubi ni arazaru o motte yubi no yubi ni arazaru ni tatoen ni wa.

Using a finger to indicate that a finger is not a finger is not as good as
Using a non-finger to indicate that a finger is not a finger.

Chuang-tzu, ch. 2

ZGS 18.13, Shiba na

18.16 李陵振臂一呼創病皆起
擧刃指虜胡馬奔走

Riryō hiji o furutte ikko sureba sōbyō mina tachi,
Katana o agete ryo o yubisaseba koba mo honsō su.

When ⌜Li Ling⌝ waved his arm and gave a shout, the sick and wounded would all rise;
When he raised his ⌜sword⌝ and pointed at the enemy, the barbarian horsemen would run away.

ZGS 18.14: *kizuki yameru mono* instead of *sōbyō*.

ZGS 18.14, Shiba 417

18.17 令尹子文三仕爲令尹無喜色
三已之無慍色

Reiin shibun mitabi tsukaete reiin taredomo yorokoberu iro mo naku,
Mitabi kore o yameraruredom ikaru iro mo nashi.

The Grand Minister Tzu-wen was three times appointed to the office of minister and he showed no sign of pleasure;
Three times he was deposed from the office and he showed no displeasure.

Analects v, 18.

ZGS 18.15, Shiba na

Nineteen-Character Phrases

19.1 忘足履之適也 *Ashi o wasururu wa kutsu no kanaeru,*
忘腰帶之適也 *Koshi o wasururu wa obi no kanaeru,*
忘是非心之適也 *Zehi o wasururu wa kokoro no kanaeru.*

You forget your feet when your shoes are comfortable.
You forget your waist when your belt is comfortable.
You forget right and wrong when your mind is comfortable.

Trans. from Watson 1968, 206. *Chuang-tzu* , ch. 19. Variant: *Ashi o wasururu wa kutsu no teki nari, Koshi o wasururu wa obi no teki nari, Zehi o wasururu wa kokoro no teki nari.*

ZGS 19.1, Shiba na, ZGJI 708

19.2 意到句不到 *I itarite ku itarazu,*
句到意不到 *Ku itarite i itarazu.*
意句倶不到 *I ku tomo ni itarazu,*
意句倶到 *I ku tomo ni itaru.*

Got the meaning but not the words,
Got the words but not the meaning.
Got neither the meaning nor the words,
Got both the meaning and the words.

ZGS 19.2, Shiba na, ZGJI 708

19.3 君子無終食之間違仁 *Kunshi wa shoku o owasuru no aida mo jin ni tagau koto nashi.*
造次必於是 *Zōji ni mo kanarazu koko ni oite shi,*
顚沛必於是 *tenpai ni mo kanarazu koko ni oite su.*

The superior person does not, even for the space of a single meal, act contrary to virtue.
In moments of haste, he cleaves to it.
In seasons of danger, he cleaves to it.

Trans. from Legge 1985. *Analects* iv, 5.

ZGS 19.3, Shiba na

19.4 孤標方外兮爲照世之燈 *Kohyō hōgai shōse no tō nari,*
象駕崢嶸人天之軌躅 *Zōga sōkō ninden no kitaku.*

In solitary splendor beyond the mundane, a lamp to illumine the world;
Astride an elephant resplendent on high, in the tracks of mortals and gods.

ZGS 19.4, Shiba na

19.5 伸左手搔佛首卽非無 *Sashu o nobashite busshu o kaku koto wa sunawachi naki ni arazu,*
屈右手觸狗頭何日免得 *Ushu o magete kutō ni fururu koto wa izure no hi ni ka manukareen.*

Extend your left hand, you may be scratching a Buddha's head;
Crook your right arm, no way you'll miss feeling a dog's head.

This verse has been corrected according to the original in the *Dokugo shingyō* 毒語心經, Hakuin's commentary on the *Heart Sutra*. In ZGS 19.5, ZGJI 708, the first character of the first line is 握 "grasp," instead of 伸 "extend," and the first character of the second line is 展 "extend," instead of 屈 "crook." See Waddell 1996, 16; Shibayama 1980.

ZGS 19.5, Shiba na, ZGJI 708

19.6 石門有盜泉 / *Sekimon ni tōsen ari,*
軟重千斤試使夷齊飲 / *nanjū senkin kokoromi ni isei o shite nomashimuru mo,*
終當不易心 / *tsui ni masa ni kokoro o kaezaru beshi.*

At Stonegate there is Stolen Spring.
If you try to coax or pressure ⌜Po Yi⌝ or ⌜Shu Ch'i⌝ to drink from it,
To the end they will not waver in their determination.

A well at Ssu-shui 泗水 in Shantung Province is called Stolen Spring. Legend says that Confucius, though thirsty, refused to drink from this well because of its name. Since then, refusal to drink the water of Stolen Spring implies that the person is strict and upright in behavior.

ZGS 19.6, Shiba na

19.7 朝與下大夫言侃侃如也 / *Chō ni shite ataifu to iu toki wa kan-kanjotari,*
與上大夫言誾誾如也 / *Jōdaifu to iu toki wa gin-ginjotari.*

At court, when conversing with the Under Ministers, his attitude is friendly and affable;
When conversing with the Upper Ministers, it is restrained and formal.

Trans. from Waley 1936, 146. *Analects* x, 2.

ZGS 19.7, Shiba na

19.8 毛嬙麗姬人之所美也 / *Mōshō riki wa hito no bi to suru tokoro nari.*
魚見之深入鳥見之高飛 / *Uo wa kore o mite fukaku iri, tori wa kore o mite takaku tobu.*

Mao-ch'iang and Lady Li—people consider them beautiful,
But when fish see them, they dive to the bottom, and when birds see them, they fly away.

Chuang-tzu, ch. 2.

ZGS 19.8, Shiba na, ZGJI 708

19.9 龍可狎擾者也 / *Ryū wa kōzō subeki mono nari,*
然喉下有逆鱗徑尺 / *Shikaredomo kōka ni gyakurin no keishaku naru mono ari,*
人嬰之則殺 / *Hito kore ni kakareba korosaru.*

The dragon can be tamed,
But on the underside of its throat it has scales a foot in diameter that curl back from the body,
And anyone who chances to brush against them is sure to die.

Watson 1964, *Han Fei Tzu*, 79.

ZGS 19.9, Shiba na

Twenty-Character Phrases

20.1 朝出芙蓉基　*Ashita ni fuyō no moto o idete,*
夕歸芙蓉基　*Yūbe ni fuyō no moto ni kaeru.*
宿宿二三宿　*Shuku shuku ni san shuku,*
未離芙蓉基　*Imada fuyō no moto o hanarezu.*

In the morning I leave the foot of the mountain,
In the evening I return to the foot of the mountain.
Two, three lodgings away,
And still I have not left the foot of the mountain.

In classical Chinese, 芙蓉 referred to the lotus flower. The term was also used of mountain peaks, and in Japan 芙蓉峯 referred to Mount Fuji, since the eight high points surrounding Fuji's volcanic mouth were said to resemble the eight petals of a lotus (Mochizuki 30694.10).

ZGS 20.1, Shiba 415

20.2 似石含玉不知玉之無瑕　*Ishi no tama o fukunde tama no kizu naki koto o shirazaru ni nitari,*
如地擎山不知山之孤峻　*Chi no yama o sasagete yama no shun naru koto o shirazaru ga gotoshi.*

It is like the stone—unaware of the flawless perfection of the jewel that it possesses within itself.
It resembles the earth—unaware of the solitary grandeur of the mountain that it supports.

ZGS 20.2, Shiba 413, ZGJI 709

20.3 溺者入水　*Oboruru mono mizu ni ireba,*
拯者亦入水　*Sukuu mono mo mata mizu ni iru.*
入水同而　*Mizu ni iru koto wa onajiushite,*
所以入水者則異　*Mizu ni iru yuen [no] wa sunawachi kotonaru.*

The drowning person is in the water,
The rescuer is also in the water.
Their being in the water is the same,
But their reason for being in the water is different.

ZGS 20.3, Shiba na, ZGJI 709

20.4 漢兵既得地　*Kanpei sude ni chi o u,*
四面楚歌聲　*Shimen soka no koe.*
大王意氣盡　*Taiō iki tsuki,*
賤妾何聊生　*Sensho nanzo sei o rōzen.*

The soldiers of Han already hold the land,
From all four sides come voices singing the songs of Ch'u.
The great king has exhausted all his strength.
But how can I, a lowly concubine, go on living?

See「Hsiang Yü」.

ZGS 20.4, Shiba na

20.5 空手把鋤頭　*Kūshu ni shite jotō o tori,*
步行騎水牛　*Hokō ni shite suigyū ni noru,*
人從橋上過　*Hito kyōjō yori sugureba,*
橋流水不流　*Hashi wa nagarete mizu wa nagarezu.*

Empty-handed, grasp the spade;
While walking on foot, ride the water buffalo;
When a person walks over the bridge,
The bridge flows, the water doesn't.

「Fu Daishi's」 verse 傅大士頌. *Heki* 96 Verse 1 Comm. See also 10.123-4.

ZGS 20.4, Shiba na, ZGJI 709

20.6 吳王好劍客　*Goō kenkaku o kononde,*
百姓多瘢瘡　*hyakusei hansō ōku.*
楚王好細腰　*Soō saiyō o kononde,*
宮中多餓死　*kyūchū gashi ōshi.*

Because the King of Wu liked swordsmen,
many common people were cut and slashed.
Because the King of Ch'u liked narrow waists,
many in the palace died of starvation.

ZGS 20.6, Shiba 412

20.7 三日下厨下　*Sanjitsu chūka ni kudari,*
洗手作羹湯　*Te o aratte kōtō o tsukuru,*
未諳姑食性　*Imada ko no shokusei o soranzezu,*
先使小姑嘗　*Mazu shōko o shite nameshimu.*

On the third day, she goes down to the kitchen
And washes her hands to make the stew.
She hasn't yet learned her mother-in-law's taste in food
And asks her sister-in-law to check the flavor.

ZGS 20.7 (variant): 入厨下 instead of 下厨下, 遣 instead of 使.

ZGS 20.7, Shiba 413, ZGJI 709

20.8 仕官千日失在一朝　*Shikan senjitsu shitsu itchō ni ari,*
殊不知趙州風流亦勞而無功　*Koto ni shirazu Jōshū no fūryū mata rō shite kō naki o.*

Ah! To serve as an official for thousands of days and then to lose it all in one morning.
Not known at all is Jōshū's way—to labor away, all to no avail.

The first line occurs in *Heki* 48 Main Case.

ZGS 20.8, Shiba na, ZGJI 710

20.9 賊仁者謂之賊 *Jin o sokonau mono kore o zoku to iu,*
賊義者謂之殘 *Gi o sokonau mono kore o zan to iu,*
殘賊之人謂之一夫 *Zanzoku no hito kore o ippu to iu.*

A man who mutilates benevolence is a mutilator,
While one who cripples rightness is a crippler.
He who is both a mutilator and a crippler is an "outcast."

Trans. from Lau 1970, 66. *Mencius* I, B, 8.

ZGS 20.9,Shiba na, ZGJI 710

20.10 折脚鐺内煎猫頭煮鴆羽 *Sekkyaku shōnai ni myōtō o senji chin'u o ni*
曲木牀上吐狐涎鳴狼牙 *Kyokumoku jōjō ni kozen o haki rōge o narasu.*

In a broken-legged cauldron, he stews cats' heads and boils ⌜poison bird wings⌝;
On the lecture seat, he spews ⌜fox slobber⌝ and clicks his wolf fangs.

See also 10.286.

ZGS 20.10, Shiba 414, ZGJI 710

20.11 樂民之樂者 *Tami no tanoshimi o tanoshimu mono wa,*
民亦樂其樂 *Tami mo mata sono tanoshimi o tanoshimu.*
憂民之憂者 *Tami no urei o ureu mono wa,*
民亦憂其憂 *Tami mo mata sono urei o ureu.*

The people will delight in the joy
Of him who delights in their joy,
And will worry over the troubles
Of him who worries over their troubles.

Trans. from Lau 1970, 63. *Mencius* I, B, 4.

ZGS 20.11, Shiba 417

20.12 趙州露刄劍寒霜光焰焰 *Jōshū no rojinken kansō hikari en-en,*
更擬問如何分身作兩段 *Sara ni ikan to towan to gi sureba mi o wakatte ryōdan to naru.*

Jōshū's naked ⌜sword⌝ gleams with a shivering light;
If you go to ask anything, it will slash you in two.

ZGS 20.12, Shiba 414, ZGJI 710

20.13 德雲閑古錐 *Tokuun no kankosui,*
幾下妙峯頂 *ku tabi ka kudaru myōhōchō.*
傭他痴聖人 *Ta no chiseijin o yatōte yuki o ninōte,*
擔雪共塡井 *tomo ni sei o uzumu.*

Tokuun, that old blunt drillhead,
How many times has he come down from Wonder Peak?
He hires another fool
And together they haul snow to fill in the well.

See ⌜Sudhana⌝.

ZGS 20.na, Shiba 415

20.14 走不以手縛手走不能疾 *Hashiru ni te o motte sezare domo te o baku shite hashireba hayaki koto atawazu,*
飛不以尾屈尾飛不能遠 *Tobu ni ō o motte sezaredomo ō o kusshite tobeba tōki koto atawazu.*

Though the hands are not used in running, if you bind your hands you cannot run fast.
Though the tail is not used in flying, if one bends the tail one cannot fly far.

ZGS 20.13, Shiba na, ZGJI 710

20.15 菩提元無樹 *Bodai moto ju nashi,*
明鏡亦非臺 *Meikyō mata dai ni arazu,*
本來無一物 *Honrai mu ichi motsu,*
何處惹塵埃 *Izure no tokoro ni ka jin'ai o hikan.*

⌜*Bodhi*⌝ is originally not a tree,
There is no bright mirror on a stand.
Fundamentally there is not one thing.
Where then can ⌜dust⌝ collect?

See ⌜Sixth Patriarch⌝.

ZGS 20.14, Shiba 416

20.16 若人欲了知三世一切佛 *Moshi hito sanze issai no hotoke o ryōchi sen to hosseba,*
應觀法界性一切唯心造 *Masa ni hokkaishō wa issai yuishinzō naru koto o kanzubeshi.*

One who would awaken to all the buddhas of the ⌜three worlds⌝
Must see the nature of the *dharma-dhātu,* that all is created by mind alone.

Heki 97 Main Case Comm.

ZGS 20.15, Shiba 413, ZGJI 711

20.17 有物先天地 *Mono ari tenchi ni sakidatsu,*
無形本寂寥 *Katachi naku shite moto sekiryō,*
能為萬象主 *Yoku banzō no shu to natte,*
不逐四時凋 *Shiji o ōte shibomazu.*

There is something prior to heaven and earth,
Formless, originally silent and solitary.
Master of the ⌜ten thousand things⌝,
It follows the four seasons and never wanes.

A modification of verses from *Tao-te ching,* chs. 1 and 25.

ZGS 20.16, Shiba na, ZGJI 711

Twenty-One-and-More Character Phrases

21⁺.1 阿字一刀下於八識田中
生死又斬涅槃又斬
生死涅槃猶如昨夢矣

Aji no ittō hasshiki denchū ni kudasu.
Shōji mata kiri nehan mata kiru.
Shōji nehan nao sakumu no gotoshi.

Drop the ⌜sword⌝ of the ⌜character "A"⌝ into the field of the ⌜eight consciousnesses⌝.
It cuts away *saṃsāra*, cuts away nirvana,
And *saṃsāra* and nirvana become like last night's dreams.

ZGS 21⁺.1, Shiba na

21⁺.2 豈可絕人逃世以爲潔哉
天下若已平則無用變易之
正天下無道故欲以道易之耳

Ani hito o tachi yo o nogarete motte ketsu to nasu bekenya.
Tenka moshi sude ni tairaka nareba kore o hen'eki suru ni yū nashi.
Tenka no mudō o tadasu yue ni dō o motte kore o kaen to hossuru nomi.

Why must one become pure by shunning people and fleeing the world?
If the world is already at peace, why change it?
The world is without the Way, I want only to use the way to change and correct this.

ZGS 21⁺.2, Shiba na

21⁺.3 有時拈一莖草作丈六金身
有時拈丈六金身作一莖草

Aru toki wa ikkyōsō o nenjite jōroku no konjin to nashi,
Aru toki wa jōroku no konjin o nenjite ikkyōsō to nasu

At times one turns a single blade of grass into a ⌜sixteen-foot⌝ golden Buddha.
At times one turns a sixteen-foot golden Buddha into a single blade of grass.

Heki 8 Intro.

ZGS 21⁺.3, Shiba 416

21⁺.4 有時坐於孤峯頂上垂手十字街頭
有時居於十字街頭作睡孤峯頂上

Aru toki wa kohōchōjō ni zashite jūjigaitō ni te o tare,
Aru toki wa jūjigaitō ni kyo shite kohōchōjō ni sui o nasu

At times you sit atop the lone mountain peak and let your hands dangle into the busy intersection;
At times, while in the busy intersection, you drowse off on the lone mountain peak.

ZGS 21⁺.4, Shiba na

21⁺.5 一簞食一瓢飲
在陋巷人不堪其憂
回也不改其樂賢哉回也

Ittan no shi ippyō no in,
Rōkō ni ari hito sono urei ni taezu,
Kai ya sono tanoshimi o aratamezu ken naru kana kai ya.

With a single bamboo-dish of rice, a single gourd-dish of drink,
And living in his mean narrow lane, while others could not have endured the distress,
He did not allow his joy to be affected by it. Admirable indeed was the virtue of Hui.

Trans. from LEGGE 1985, *Analects* VI, 9. Hui is Yen Hui 顏回 (J. Gankai), a favorite disciple of Confucius.

ZGS 21+.5, Shiba 410

21+.6 出弔於東郭氏公孫丑曰昔者辭以病今日弔或者不可乎 *Idete tōkakushi ni chō su. Kōsonchū iwaku kinō wa jisuru ni yamai o motte shi konnichi wa chō su aruiwa fuka naran ka.*
孟子曰昔者疾今日愈如之何不弔 *Mōshi iwaku kinō wa yamai konnichi wa iyu kore o ikanzo chō sezu.*

[He] went on a visit of condolence to the Tung-kuo family. Kung-sun Ch'ou said, "Yesterday you excused yourself on the ground of illness, yet today you go on a visit of condolence. This is perhaps ill-advised."
Mencius said, "I was ill yesterday, but I am recovered today. Why should I not go on a visit of condolence?"

Trans. from LAU 1970, 86. *Mencius*, II, B, 2.

ZGS 21+.6, Shiba na

21+.7 苟有正念工夫則 *Iyashikumo shōnen kufū araba,*
不泥行相不拘威儀 *Gyōsō ni nazumazu igi ni kodawarazu,*
卽理卽事卽坐卽行 *Ri ni soku shi ji ni soku shi, za ni soku shi gyō ni soku shi,*
卽是卽非卽動卽靜 *Ze ni soku shi hi ni soku shi, dō ni soku shi jō ni soku shi,*
卽法卽非法卽世間卽出世間 *Hō ni soku shi hihō ni soku shi, seken ni soku shi shusseken ni soku su.*
只要不失正念 *Tada shōnen o ushinawazaran koto o yō su.*

Have right mindfulness and constant application
And you will not get mired in appearances nor get taken in by dress and robes.
You will be one with reason and one with fact, one with sitting and one with going,
One with yes and one with no, one with movement and one with stillness,
One with the Dharma and one with the non-Dharma, one with the world and one with renouncing the world.
This is the only necessity: do not lose right mindfulness.

ZGS 21+.7, Shiba na

21+.8 堯舜率天下以仁民從之 *Gyō shun tenka o hikiiru ni jin o motte shi tami kore ni shitagau,*
桀紂率天下以暴民從之 *Ketchū tenka o hikiiru ni bō o motte shi tami kore ni shitagau,*
衲僧率天下以何民從之 *Nōsō tenka o hikiiru ni nani o motte shite ka tami kore ni shitagawan.*

⌜Yao and Shun⌝ ruled the world with benevolence and the people followed them.
⌜Chieh and Chou⌝ ruled the world with violence and the people followed them.
With what will the ⌜patch-robed monk⌝ rule the world and will the people follow him?

ZGS 21+.8, Shiba na

21+.9 邦有道卽知邦無道卽愚 / *Kuni ni dō areba sunawachi chi kuni ni dō nakereba sunawachi gu,*
其知可及也其愚不可及也 / *Sono chi oyobu beki nari, sono gu oyobu bekarazaru nari.*

So long as the Way prevailed in his country, he showed wisdom; but when the Way no longer prevailed, he showed his folly.
To such wisdom as his we may all attain, but not to such folly.

Trans. from Waley 1938, *Analects* v, 20.

ZGS 21+.9, Shiba na

21+.10 君子之言幽而必有驗乎明 / *Kunshi no gon wa yū ni shite kanarazu mei ni shirushi ari,*
遠而必有驗乎近 / *En shite kanarazu kin ni shirushi ari,*
大而有驗乎小 / *Dai ni shite shō ni shirushi ari,*
微而必有驗乎著 / *Bi ni shite kanarazu chaku ni shirushi ari.*

The superior person's words are mysterious, but always prove clear;
distant, but always prove intimate;
large, but always prove detailed;
minute, but always stand forth.

必 has been inserted into the third line. ZGS 20+.10 omits it.

ZGS 21+.10, Shiba na

21+.11 鷄鳴丑 / *Keimei ushi,*
愁見起來還漏逗 / *Ureimiru okikitatte mata rōtō,*
裙子褊衫箇亦無 / *Kunsu hensan ko mo mata nashi,*
袈裟形相些些有 / *Kesa no gyōsō isasaka ari,*
裩無襠袴無口 / *Kon ni tō naku, ko ni kuchi nashi,*
頭上靑灰三五斗 / *Zujō no seikai san go to,*
本爲修行利濟人 / *Moto shugyō suru wa hito o risai sen ga tame nari,*
誰知翻成不喞嚁 / *Tare ka shiran kaette fushitsuryū to naran to wa.*

The cock crows—2 AM!
I look up drearily, get up with listless unconcern.
I haven't a single robe or undershirt,
Only the *kesa* has a little of its form.
My underwear has no seat, my pants have no legs.
My head's got three scoops of dan, five of druff.
I first entered practice to help save others.
Who knew I'd end up a fool like this?

From Jōshū's "Song of the Twelve Hours of the Day" (趙州十二時歌).

ZGS 21+.11, Shiba na

21+.12 孔子名丘字仲尼其先宋人 / *Kōshi na wa kyū, azana wa chūji, sono saki wa sō no hito nari.*
父叔梁紇母顏氏 / *Chichi wa shukuryōkotsu, haha wa ganshi.*
以魯襄公二十二年庚戌之歳十一月庚子 / *Ro no jōkō nijūni nen kōjutsu no toshi jūichi gatsu kōshi,*
生孔子於魯昌平鄉陬邑 / *Kōshi o motte kōshi o ro no shōheikyō no sūyū ni umu.*

Confucius: his name was Ch'iu, his courtesy name was Chung-ni.
His ancestors were people of Sung. His father was Shu Liang-he, his mother was from the Yen family.
In the year Keng-hsü, the twenty-second year of the reign of Duke Hsiang of Lu, in the month Keng-tzu,
Confucius was born in Tsou in the district of Ch'ang-p'ing in Lu.

ZGS 21+.12, Shiba na

21+.13 有美玉於斯 / *Koko ni bigyoku ari.*
韞匵而藏諸 / *Untoku shite kore o zō sen ka.*
求善賈而沽諸 / *Zenko o motomete kore o uran ka.*
子曰沽之哉沽之哉 / *Shi notamawaku, kore o uran kana kore o uran kana.*
我待賈者也 / *Ware wa ko o matsu mono nari.*

I have a beautiful gem here.
Should I put it into a case and hide it away?
Or should I try to get a good price and sell it?
The Master said, "Sell it! Sell it! But I would wait for the right merchant."

Analects IX, 12.

ZGS 21+.13, Shiba na

21+.14 吳中有臣室 / *Gochū ni shinshitsu ari.*
其子婦臨蓐欲產 / *Sono shi no tsuma shitone ni nozonde uman to su.*
以其時不吉勸令忍勿生 / *Sono toki no fukitsu naru o motte susumete shinonde shōzuru koto o nakarashimu.*
逾時子母俱斃 / *Toki o koete shibo tomo ni taoru.*

In the capitol of Wu, there was a minister's lady.
This noble's wife stared at the mattress waiting to give birth.
But the time was not propitious and she forced herself not to give birth.
When the time had passed, both mother and child had died.

ZGS 21+.14, Shiba na

21+.15 兀兀坐定思量箇不思量底 / *Gotsu gotsu to shite zajō shite kono fushiryō-tei o shiryō seyo.*
不思量底如何思量非思量 / *Fushiryō-tei ikan ga shiryō sen. Hi shiryō.*

Sit dead-still in *sāmadhi* and ponder the imponderable.
How to ponder the imponderable? By not-pondering.

ZGS 21+.15, Shiba na, 普勸坐禪儀

21⁺.16	無差別平等不準佛法惡平等故	*Sabetsu naki no byōdō wa buppō ni junzezu, aku byōdō naru ga yue ni,*
	無平等差別不準佛法惡差別故	*Byōdō naki no sabetsu wa buppō ni junzezu, aku sabetsu naru ga yue ni.*

Equality without discrimination is not the Buddha-dharma—it is bad equality.
Discrimination without equality is not the Buddha-dharma—it is bad discrimination.

ZGS 21⁺.16, Shiba na

21⁺.17	山河大地萬象森羅	*Senga daichi banzō shinra,*
	醯雞蟞蝨草芥人畜	*Keikei beppō sōkai jinchiku,*
	一一放大光明	*Ichi ichi daikōmyō o hanatsu,*
	一一壁立萬仞	*Ichi ichi hekiryū banjin.*

Mountains and rivers, the great earth and the ⌜ten thousand things⌝ in total array:
Insects and plants, people and animals—
Each one radiates the great illumination,
Each one stands 10,000 fathoms high.

醯雞 are tiny insects that feed on the scum of fermenting alcohol (Morohashi 40036.2).

ZGS 21⁺.17, Shiba na

21⁺.18	脩脛者使之跖钁	*Shūkei naru mono wa kore o shite kaku o fumashime,*
	强脊者使之負土	*Kyōseki naru mono wa kore o shite tsuchi o owashime,*
	眇者使之準	*Byō naru mono wa kore o shite junzeshime,*
	傴者使之塗	*Segukumaru mono wa kore o shite nurashimu.*

Let one who has long legs uses them to step on a spade.
Let one who has a strong back use it to carry earth.
Let one who has a squint eye use it to line things up.
Let one who has a bent back use it to paint.

Huai-nan-tzu 淮南子齋俗訓, cited in Morohashi 29535.30.

ZGS 21⁺.18, Shiba na

21⁺.19	有女同車	*Jo ari kuruma o onajiushite,*
	顏如蕣華	*Kanbase shunka no gotoshi,*
	將翺將翔	*Masa ni kakeri masa ni furumau,*
	佩玉瓊琚	*Haigyoku keikyo,*
	彼美孟姜	*Ka no kaoyoki mōkyō,*
	洵美且都	*Makoto ni kaoyoku shite mata miyabiyaka nari.*

In the same carriage there is a girl
Whose face is the bloom of a morning glory,
She set dancing
Waistband gems and jewel pendants.
The Chiang's lovely first daughter,
Beautiful and refined.

Book of Songs #83.

ZGS 21⁺.19, Shiba na

21+.20 上大人、丘乙己、化三千 *Jōdaijin, kyū itsuki, ke sanzen,*
七十士、爾少生、八九子 *Shichijū shi, ji shōsei, hakku shi,*
可作仁、可知禮也 *Ka sajin, ka chirei ya.*

The great sage Confucius alone taught three thousand,
And seventy became disciples. You young ones, eight or nine,
Cultivate kindness and know propriety.

Alternate reading: *Taijin ni nobosu, kyū itsu sude ni sanzen shichijū shi o kaseri, shōsei hachi kyū shi ka nari, jin o nashi rei o shirubeki nari.* This phrase is an old Chinese rhyme for teaching 25 Chinese characters and Confucian precepts to young children. Quoted in Hakuin's *Kaian-kokugo* 槐安國語 (Iida Tōin 1955, 109); also translated in Miyazaki 1981, 114.

ZGS 21+.20

21+.21 爲人君止於仁 *Hito no kun to narite wa jin ni todomari,*
爲人臣止於敬 *Hito no shin to narite wa kei ni todomari,*
爲人子止於孝 *Hito no shi to narite wa kō ni todomari,*
爲人父止於慈 *Hito no fu to narite wa ji ni todomari,*
與國人交止於信 *Kuni no tami to majiwarite wa shin ni todomaru.*

As a sovereign, he rested in benevolence.
As a minister, he rested in reverence.
As a son, he rested in filial piety.
As a father, he rested in kindness.
In communication with his subjects, he rested in good faith.

Trans. from Legge 1985, *Great Learning* III.

ZGS 21+.21, Shiba na

21+.22 水中鹽味、色裡膠青 *Suichū no enmi, shikiri no kōsei,*
决定是有、不見其形 *Ketsujō shite kore yu naredomo, sono katachi o mizu,*
心王亦爾、身内居停 *Shinnō mo mata shikari, shinnai ni kyōjō shite,*
面門出入、應物隨情 *Menmon ni shutsunyū su, mono ni ōji jō ni shitagatte,*
自在無礙 *Jizai muge.*

Salt in the water, glue within the dye—
For sure they are there but you cannot see their form.
Thus the soul-king resides in the body going in and out the portals of the face,
Adjusting to things, following feeling,
Free and unhindered.

ZGS 21+.22, Shiba na, 心王銘

21+.23 齊景公有馬千駟 *Sei no keikō uma senshi ari,*
死之日民無德而稱焉 *Shi suru no hi tami toku to shite shosuru nashi.*
伯夷叔齊餓于首陽之下 *Hakui shukusei shuyō no moto ni ga su,*
民到于今稱之 *Tami ima ni itaru made kore o sho su.*

Duke Ching of Ch'i had a thousand teams of horses,
But on the day of his death the people could think of no good deed for which to praise him.
「Po Yi and Shu Ch'i」 starved at the foot of Mount Shou-yang,
Yet the people sing their praises down to this very day.

Trans. from Waley 1938, *Analects* xvi, 12.

ZGS 21+.23, Shiba na

21+.24 節彼南山維石巖巖 *Setsutaru kano nanzan, kore ishi gan-gantari.*
赫赫師尹民具爾瞻 *Kaku-kakutaru shi in, tami to tomo ni nanji o miru.*
有國者不可以不愼 *Kuni o motsu mono motte tsutsushimazumba aru bekarazu.*

"Lofty is that southern hill, with its rugged masses of rocks!
Greatly distinguished are you, O [Grand] Teacher Yin, the people all look up to you."
Rulers of states may not neglect to be too careful.

Trans. from Legge 1985, *The Great Learning, Commentary* x, 4.

ZGS 21+.24, Shiba na

21+.25 前面是眞珠瑪瑙 *Zenmen wa kore shinjū menō,*
後面是瑪瑙眞珠 *Gomen wa kore menō shinjū,*
東邊是觀音勢至 *Tōhen wa kore kannon seishi,*
西邊是文殊普賢 *Saihen wa kore monju fugen,*
中間有一首幡 *Chūkan ni isshu no hata ari,*
被風吹着 *Kaze ni suijaku serarete,*
道胡盧胡盧 *Koro-koro to iu.*

The front face—pearls and agate;
The back face—agate and pearls.
To the east—⌈Kuan-yin⌉ and ⌈Mahāsthāmaprāpta⌉;
To the west—⌈Mañjuśrī⌉ and ⌈Samantabhadra⌉.
In the middle there is a banner
Blown by the wind—
"Flap, flap."

Variant: 有箇旛子 *Chūkan ko no hansu ari* instead of *Chūkan isshu no hata ari.*

ZGS 21+.25, Shiba na

21+.26 善來四君子 *Zenrai shikunshi,*
茲謝遠來 *Koko ni onrai o sha su.*
來坐吾明窻下 *Wa ga meisō no moto ni raiza seyo.*
吾廬空疎而 *Wa ga ro kūsō ni shite,*
無可充供養 *Kuyō ni atsu beki nashi.*
壁間幸 *Hekikan saiwai ni,*
有鱗鱗皴皴底物 *Rin-rin shun-shun tei no mono ari.*
掛在年于茲 *Kazai suru koto koko ni toshi ari.*
以待諸君來 *Motte shokun no kitaru o matte*
各與七八頓 *Kaku shichi hachi ton o ataete.*
貶向無佛世界 *Mubutsu sekai ni henkō sen.*

Four gentlemen have kindly come from afar—
My deepest appreciations!
May you be seated by our bright windows.
My thatched roof is merely a shelter
With nothing to offer.
But fortunately on the wall there is
Something reptile-skinned, chipped and cracked all over,
That's been hanging up there for years.
I've been waiting for you gentlemen to arrive
To give you each seven or eight whacks with it.
And then I'll drop into the world without buddhas.

槐安國語卷二 (IIDA Tōin 1955, 255).

ZGS 21+.26, Shiba na

21+.27 曾子有疾召門弟子曰啓予足啓予手 *Sōshi yamai ari monteishi o yonde iwaku, wa ga ashi o hirake wa ga te o hirake.*
詩云戰戰兢兢如臨深淵如履薄冰 *Shi ni iwaku, sen-sen kyō-kyō shin'en ni nozomu ga gotoku hakuhyō o fumu ga gotoshi to.*

When master Tseng was ill, he called the disciples of his school and said,
"Uncover my feet, uncover my hands.
It is said in the *Book of Songs,* 'Be fearful and alert, As if peering into an abyss,
As if treading on thin ice.'"

Analects VIII, 3. See also 12.64 and 12.142.

ZGS 21+.27, Shiba na

21+.28 滄浪之水清兮可以濯吾纓 *Sōrō no mizu sumaba motte wa ga ei o araubeshi,*
滄浪之水濁兮可以濯吾足 *Sōrō no mizu nigoraba motte wa ga ashi o araubeshi.*

If the blue water is clear,
It is fit to wash my chin-strap.
If the blue water is muddy,
It is only fit to wash my feet.

Trans. from LAU, *Mencius* IV, A, 8.

ZGS 21+.28, Shiba na

21+.29 楚王亡其猿而林木爲之殘 *Soō sono saru o ushinaite rinboku kore ga tame ni sokonaware,*
宋王亡其珠池中魚爲之殫 *Sōō sono tama o ushinaite chichū no uo kore ga tame ni tsuku.*

Because the King of Ch'u lost his monkey, he destroyed the forest;
Because the King of Sung lost his jewel, all the fish in the pond died.

Variant: 君 instead of 王, 玉 instead of 珠.

ZGS 21+.29, Shiba 415

21+.30 力拔山兮氣蓋世
時不利兮騅不逝
騅不逝兮可奈何
虞兮虞兮奈若何

Chikara yama o nuki yo o ōu,
Toki ni ri arazu sui yukazu,
Sui yukazaru no ikan to mo ga subeshi,
Gu ya gu ya nanji o ikan sen.

My strength plucked up the hills, my might shadowed the world;
But the times were against me, and Dapple runs no more.
When Dapple runs no more, what then can I do?
Ah Yü, my Yü, what will your fate be?

Trans. from WATSON 1993, *Han* 1, 45; *Shi-chi* 7.

ZGS 21+.30, Shiba na

21+.31 趙州曰金剛般若波羅密經
如是我聞一時佛在舍衛國
此中透出一字千里同風

Jōshū iwaku kongo hanyahara mikkyō,
Nyoze gamon ichiji butsu zai shaeikoku,
Kono naka ichiji o tōshutsu sureba senri dōfū.

Jōshū said, "The *Diamond Sutra* says: 'Thus have I heard.
At one time the Buddha was in the kingdom of Śrāvastī….'
If you pierce even one word of this, then you will be 'for a thousand miles, always the same.'"

The first part is from *Jōshū-roku* §442. For *Senri dōfū*, see 4.345.

ZGS 21+.31, Shiba na

21+.32 東家母死其子哭之不哀
西家子見之返謂其母曰
社何愛速死吾必悲哭社
夫欲其母之死者雖死亦不能悲哭矣

Tōke no haha shi su. Sono ko kore o koku shite kanashimazu.
Saike no ko kore o mite kaette sono haha ni itte iwaku,
Sha nanzo sumiyaka ni shi suru koto o oshiman, ware kanarazu sha o hikoku sen.
Sore sono haha no shi o hossureba, shi to iedomo mata hikoku suru koto atawazu.

When a mother of a house on the east side died, her son mourned for her but was not sad.
The son in a house on the west side saw this, and on returning home said to his mother,
"Mother, why should you mind if you die an early death? I would certainly mourn for you."
But one who wishes for the death of his mother could not possibly grieve and mourn her death.

淮南子, 説山訓.

ZGS 21+.32, Shiba na

21+.33 滔滔武溪、一何深
鳥飛不度、獸不能臨
嗟哉武溪兮多毒淫

Tō-tōtaru bukei, itsu ni nanzo fukaki,
Tori tobi watarazu, jū nozomu koto atawazu.
Aa bukei dokuin ōshi.

The vast, flowing River Wu-ch'i. My, how deep!
Birds cannot fly across, animals cannot be seen.
Alas! the Wu-ch'i overflows with poison.

The Wu-ch'i River is located in Henan Province.

ZGS 21+.33, Shiba na

21+.34 與人共其樂者 *Hito to sono raku o tomo ni suru mono wa,*
人必憂其憂 *Hito kanarazu sono urei o ureu.*
與人同其安者 *Hito to sono yasuki o onajiku suru mono wa,*
人必拯其危 *Hito kanarazu sono ki o sukuu.*

If you share your pleasures with others,
Others will bear your sorrows;
If you make common peace with others,
Others will support you in trouble.

ZGS 21+.34, Shiba na

21+.35 暮春春服既成 *Boshun ni wa shunpuku sude ni nari,*
冠者五六人童子六七人 *Kanja gorikunin dōji rikushitsunin,*
浴乎沂風乎舞雩詠而歸 *Ki ni yoku shite buu ni fū jite ei jite kaeran.*

At the end of spring, when the making of spring clothing is complete,
With five or six youths who have been capped and with six or seven boys,
I would wash in the River I, enjoy the breeze among the rain altars, and return home singing.

Analects XI, 25. At the time of Confucius, new clothing was made in the spring and men took the cap at age twenty as a sign of maturity.

ZGS 21+.35, Shiba na

21+.36 厲之人夜半生其子 *Minikuki no hito yahan sono ko o umeri,*
遽取火而視之 *Niwaka ni hi o totte kore o miru,*
汲汲然而 *Kyū-kyūzen to shite,*
唯恐其似己也 *Tada sono onore ni nin koto o osoru.*

When the leper woman gives birth to a child in the dead of the night,
She rushes to fetch a torch and examine it,
Trembling with terror
Lest it look like herself.

Chuang-tzu, ch., 12. Trans. from WATSON 1968, 140.

ZGS 21+.36, Shiba 417

21+.37 明月之光可以遠望而可以細書 *Meigetsu no hikari wa motte tōku nozomubeku shite motte komaka ni sho subekarazu,*
深霧之朝可以細書而不可以遠望 *Shinmu no asa wa motte komaka ni sho subeku shite motte tōku nozomubekarazu.*

The light of the bright ⌜moon⌝ is for gazing into the distance and not for doing fine calligraphy,
A morning of deep mist is for doing fine calligraphy and not for gazing into the distance.

ZGS 21+.37, Shiba na

21+.38 毛嬙西施善毀者不能蔽其娟 *Mōshō seishi wa yoku soshiru mono mo sono ken o ōu koto atawazu,*
嫫姆倭傀善譽者不能掩其醜 *Bobo wakai wa yoku homuru mono mo sono shū o ōu koto atawazu.*

Not even one who maligns Mao-ch'iang and ⌜Hsi-shih⌝ can conceal their beauty,
Not even one who glorifies Mo-mu or Wei-k'uei can conceal their ugliness.

Mao-ch'iang and Hsi-shih were famed in Chinese legend and history for their great beauty; Mo-mu and Wei-k'uei were equally renowned for their ugliness (Morohashi 796.5).

ZGS 21+.38, Shiba na

21+.39 幼而不孫弟 *Yō ni shite sontei narazu,*
長而無述焉 *Chōjite noburu koto naku,*
老而不死 *Oite shi sezu,*
是爲賊 *Kore zoku to nasu to,*
以杖叩其脛 *Tsue o motte sono hagi o tataku.*

"Those who, when young, show no respect to their elders
Achieve nothing worth mentioning when they grow up.
Merely to live on, getting older and older,
Is to be a useless pest."
And he struck him across the shins with a stick.

Trans. from Waley 1938, *Analects* xiv, 46.

ZGS 21+.39, Shiba na

21+.40 龍泉與刀斧同鐵利鈍懸殊 *Ryūsen to tōfu to tetsu o onajiusuredomo ridon haruka ni koto nari,*
駑駘與驥馬同途遲速有異 *Dotai to kiba to michi o onajiusuredomo chisoku kotonaru koto ari.*

The Dragon Spring Sword and an axe are both made of iron, but there is a vast difference in their sharpness,
A plodding nag and a fleet stallion are both on the track but there is a difference in their speed.

ZGS 21+.40, Shiba na

21+.41 與歷代祖師 *Rekidai no soshi to,*
把手共行眉毛厮結 *Te o totte tomo ni yuki, bimō aimusunde,*
同一眼見同一耳聞 *Dōichigen ni mi, dōichiji ni kiku.*
豈不慶快 *Ani keikai narazu ya.*

To walk hand in hand with the patriarchs of the ages,
To join eyebrow to eyebrow,
To see with the exact same eye, to hear with the exact same ear—
How can one not be overjoyed?

MMK 1.

ZGS 21+.41, Shiba na

21+.42 吾黨之直者異於是 *Wa ga tō no choku naru wa kore ni kotonari.*
父爲子隱 *Chichi wa ko no tame ni kakushi,*
子爲父隱 *Ko wa chichi no tame ni kakusu.*
直在其中矣 *Naoki wa sono uchi ni ari.*

Among us, in our part of the country, those who are upright are different from this.
The father conceals the misconduct of the son
And the son conceals the misconduct of the father.
Uprightness is to be found in this.

Trans. from Legge 1985, *Analects* xiii, 18.

ZGS 21+.42, Shiba na

21+.43 吾十有五而志于學 *Ware jūyūgo ni shite gaku ni kokorozashi,*
三十而立 *Sanjū ni shite tachi,*
四十而不惑 *Shijū ni shite madowazu,*
五十而知天命 *Gojū ni shite tenmei o shiri,*
六十而耳順 *Rokujū ni shite mimi shitagau.*
七十而從心所欲不踰矩 *Shichijū ni shite kokoro no hossuru tokoro ni shitagatte nori o yuezu.*

At fifteen, I had my mind bent on learning.
At thirty, I stood firm.
At forty, I had no doubts.
At fifty, I knew the decrees of heaven.
At sixty, my ear was an obedient organ.
At seventy, I could follow what my heart desired, without transgressing what was right.

Trans. from Legge 1985, *Analects* ii, 4.

ZGS 21+.43, Shiba na

GLOSSARY
BIBLIOGRAPHY
INDEX

Glossary

THE VERSES AND phrases used as Rinzai kōan capping phrases are taken from classical Chinese literature. They employ a large number of allusions, poetic images, and symbols that assume a considerable background knowledge of the history, myths, culture, and literature of China. Rather than supply the necessary background information as annotations to the verses themselves, a format that would require numerous repetitions of the same information, the explanations have been gathered together here in the form of a general Glossary.

The Glossary has been composed primarily with readers in mind who have little or no background in Japanese or Chinese culture and language, and who are doing kōan training in the Japanese Rinzai tradition. At the same time, a certain amount of more technical information, including Chinese characters of terms and names cited, is given for the sake of completeness.

Where a more or less standard English translation of a term exists, the entry will be listed under that translation. A small number of commonly used Sanskrit terms are listed under the original Sanskrit. Otherwise, where a standard English translation does not exist, entries have been arranged according to their Japanese pronunciation.

Because this book is designed for people working in the Japanese Zen tradition, the names of persons directly connected with Ch'an have been rendered in their Japanese pronunciation rather than in their Chinese, e.g., Rinzai, Mumon, Jōshū, and Setchō rather than Lin-chi, Wu-men, Chao-chou, and Hsüeh-tou. The Chinese pronunciation has always been provided. There are, however, a number of exceptions to this rule. For example, the entry for Bodhidharma is given under the Sanskrit, "Bodhidharma," not under "Daruma" (J.) or "Tamo" (Ch.). Also, in discussing the Sixth Patriarch, it is now more common to use the Chinese name, Hui-neng, rather than the Japanese name, Enō, a custom we will follow here. In any event, alternative pronunciations and translations have been cross-referenced.

Glossary entries occasionally refer to examples from the phrases themselves to illustrate the explanation. For further examples, consult the cumulative Index at the end of this volume.

Terms marked in **bold print** have their own entry in the Glossary.

"A" (the character) *Aji* (J.) 阿字

In Esoteric Buddhism, *aji* represents अ, the first letter of the Sanskrit alphabet. The first letter is said to contain all the other letters. It is also the first letter of the Sanskrit word *anutpāda,* "unborn," and thus symbolizes the original nature of the universe, neither arising nor passing away.

In the Esoteric practice known as "seeing the letter A," *ajikan* 阿字觀, the practitioner meditates upon a diagram of the letter अ drawn upon the full moon or a lotus flower and through it becomes one with Dainichi Nyorai (Vairocana) Buddha.

Adding feet when drawing a snake *Ja o egaite ashi o sou* (J.) 畫蛇添足

This saying is a Chinese proverb to illustrate the foolishness of doing too much. Several attendants of a lord had received a flask of wine, enough for one but not enough for them all. They decided to have a competition, the winner to take all the wine. The task was to draw a snake. One man finished first and grabbed the wine. Congratulating himself on his speed and skill, he said to himself, "I even have enough time to add feet." So he added feet. When another man finished his drawing, he declared that a snake does not have feet and took the wine. Thus the man who finished first lost the wine.

Anan ➛ Ānanda

Ānanda (Skt.) Ananda (J.) 阿難陀

Ānanda is one of the Buddha's "ten great disciples" (十大弟子). It is said that he served the Buddha as attendant for 25 years, during which time he attended most of the Buddha's lectures. Because of his great memory, at the First Council he was able to recite exactly the Buddha's words, which were then recorded to form the *sūtra-piṭaka.* In Zen phrases, Ānanda, most advanced in learning, is sometimes contrasted with the other great disciple of the Buddha, **Kāśyapa**, who was most advanced in meditation and ascetic practice.

Apparent and real ➛ Five Ranks

Attendant *Jisha, inji, sannō* (J.) 侍者, 隱侍, 三應

There are several terms for the attendant monk who serves the master of a Zen monastery. The most common term is *jisha* 侍者 (5.62, 5.153, 7.195). In the Northern Sung period, a master of a large monastery had two attendants, but by the Yüan period the number of attendants had increased to five: an incense attendant, a secretary attendant, a guest attendant, a robe attendant, and a "hot water and medicine" attendant who cooked for him (燒香侍者, 書状侍者, 請客侍者, 衣鉢侍者, 湯藥侍者; ZGDJT 432a, 343a). In the modern Rinzai monastery, however, the usual terms for attendant are *inji* 隱侍 (short for *inryō* 隱寮 *no jisha,* "attendant of the rōshi's quarters") and *sannō.* The term *sannō* literally means "three responses" 三應 and is taken from the well-known kōan "The Master Calls Three Times" MMK 17 (14.272). See also ***Shōji.***

Asōgikō (J.) 阿僧祇劫

Asōgi is the Japanese pronunciation for the Sanskrit term *asaṃkhya* or *asaṃkhyeya*, which means "countless," "limitless." The *kō* in *Asōgikō* means **kalpa.** *Asōgikō* is therefore an incalculably long aeon of time. Conze describes "incalculable" as "a number so high that neither human nor heavenly mathematicians can calculate it. It is, in any case, more than 10 followed by 27 noughts" (Conze 1959, 31).

The fifty stages of the bodhisattva's practice are divided into three periods. There are differing accounts of this division but one popular account says that the first 40 stages (十信, 十住, 十行, 十迴向) are accomplished in the first *asaṃkhyeya kalpa*; the last ten practices (十地) are divided into two groups, 1 to 7 and 8 to 10, each of which requires an *asaṃkhyeya kalpa* (Oda 1954, 603–4; ZGDJT 387).

Asura (Skt.) *Ashura, shura* (J.) 阿修羅, 修羅

Asura are fighting gods. Their realm is one of the **six realms** of rebirth. Asura are said to be gods who have fallen out of heaven because of their penchant for fighting. They are associated with war, battlefields, and violence in general. They are included in the **eight beings**.

Auspicious grass and spiritual shoots *Zuisō reimyō* 瑞草靈苗

Auspicious grass, *zuisō*, is a mysterious plant without roots and without buds. They can be taken as symbolic of plants that exist outside the usual realm of life-and-death, *saṃsāra*. Spiritual shoots, *reimyō*, connote awakened mind in general, and outstanding disciples or descendants in particular (10.98; ZGDJT 1306d, ZGJI 561).

Autumn down *Shūgō* (J.) 秋毫

In ancient China, it was said that some animals and birds shed their old coats at the end of the summer and grew new coats in the autumn. The new hairs had very fine tips. The tips of this autumn down became a symbol for anything fine, tiny, difficult to distinguish. Also written 秋豪 (Morohashi 24940.46; 24940.49).

Awl, pick, gimlet, drill *Sui* (J.) 錐

An awl or a pick is a sharp needle-shaped hand tool used for puncturing holes into leather, picking apart knotted rope, breaking ice, etc. If the sides of the round shaft head are beveled so that it has a point with three or four flat sides, it becomes a drill, the handle of which is twirled between the two flat surfaces of the hand. The Chinese expression "not enough ground in which to stick a pick" 無立錐地 connotes extreme poverty. In phrases like "He sees only the sharpness of the gimlet, he does not know the squareness of the chisel" 只見錐頭利, 不知鑿頭方 (10.322), the gimlet's sharpness and the chisel's squareness represent the two aspects of Zen practice, ***hajū*** and ***hōgyō***. The phrase "drill bit in a bag" 囊中錐 has two connotations. On the one hand, it connotes something quite small (as in 14.666); on the other hand, it connotes something quite prominent, since the point will pierce through the bag cloth (6.217).

In a completely different context, "withered old drill" *rōkosui* 老古錐 is a set term that refers to the mature Zen practitioner. See ***Kareta.***

Bandit ➛ **Thief**

Barbarian monk ➛ under **Bodhidharma**

Big bug *Daichū* (J.) 大蟲

Daichū literally means "big bug," but it is a colloquial expression for a tiger that has lost its fierce appearance. Its tail has been singed, as shown by the expression "the big bug with the burnt tail" (*shōbi no daichū* 焦尾大蟲), and it is also said to be toothless (*mushi no daichū* 無齒大蟲). It is possible to translate *daichū* as "tiger," but *Zen Sand* verses often pair and contrast the feeble "big bug" and the "fierce tiger," as in "This big bug with the burnt tail was originally a tiger" (7.219). The contrast is important, since *daichū* is one of several phrases, like "withered old drill" (*rōkosui* 老古錐), which describe the ***kareta*** aspect of a mature Zen practitioner. For lack of a better translation, we translate the characters literally: "big bug" (ZGDJT 578).

Bin, ben (J.) 便

This character occurs in several important idioms. For some usages, there is disagreement on its meaning. The character 便 may indicate "convenience," or it may indicate "news" or "communication." The phrase 某甲不着便 (5.229) has been translated "It is inconvenient for me," but it is possible to translate it also as "No news has reached me." The core phrase 不着便 and its variant 不著便 occur in other longer phrases. Shiba 112 reads 5.322 彼此不著便 as *Hishi tayori o tsukezu*, taking 便 as some kind of communication. Based on the gloss "not in any place reached by differentiation or language," *Zen Sand* translates this phrase as "Chit-chat does not get through." "Chit-chat" translates the term 彼此 *hishi* "there and here," which implies dualism or differentiation. The same phrase also occurs in *Heki* 33 Main Case in 早是不著便, which Ōmori glosses as "You haven't greeted me" (1994, vol. 1, 267). In these two cases 便 is used to mean some sort of communication, in one case in a logical context and in the other in a practical context.

The phrase also occurs in *Heki* 42 Main Case *agyo* in 從頭到尾不著便. Iriya, Mizoguchi, and Sueki interpret both occurrences in *Heki* 33 and *Heki* 42 to mean "at a total loss" (1992, II, 33, 115, 116). The ZGJT, which Iriya edited with his students, gives the same explanation (ZGJT 339).

Birds with shared wings ➛ under **Matrimonial harmony**

Birth-and-death *Shōji* (J.) 生死

Shōji literally means "birth-death" and translates the Sanskrit Buddhist term *saṃsāra*.

Black crow | Black lacquer 黑烏 | 黑漆

The characters 烏 "crow" and 漆 "lacquer" connote the color black. Although in English "pitch" literally means "tar," the expression "pitch black" just means "deep black." Similarly, although the characters in compounds such as 烏龜 (7.40) and 烏雞 (7.41) literally mean "crow turtle" and "crow rooster," the terms just mean "black turtle" and "black rooster." "Black lacquer" *kokushitsu* 黑漆 is another compound that often just means deep black, as in "black chaos" (7.139–7.141), not "black lacquer chaos." The set phrase "black lacquer tub" *kokushittsū* 黑漆桶 is a metaphor for a state in which nothing can be discriminated (7.137–7.138). The phrase "my two eyes black as crows" (*ittsui no ganzei u ritsu-ritsu* 一對眼睛烏律律, 7.33, 14.480) could imply both that the eyes are colored black or that the eyes do not discriminate things.

Blackbird, Blackbird wings ➛ **Poison blackbird**

Black dragon pearl *Riju, riryūju, riryōju* (J.) 驪珠 | 驪龍珠

A fabulous gem kept underneath the chin of the sleeping black dragon. To attempt to steal the pearl is a metaphor for risking one's life. See, for example, the story in *Chuang-tzu*, ch. 32, "Lieh Yü-k'ou" (Watson 1968, 360).

Blind donkey *Katsuro* (J.) 瞎驢

When Rinzai was about to pass away, he sat up in bed and said, "After I am gone, you must not destroy my True Dharma Eye." His first disciple, Sanshō, said, "Who would dare to destroy the Master's True Dharma Eye?" The Master asked, "If someone asked you, what would you say?" Sanshō gave a shout, "Kaa!" The Master said, "Who knows? My True Dharma Eye may well be destroyed by this blind donkey here!" Then, remaining in upright sitting position, he entered nirvana (*Rinzai-roku* §68, translation adapted from Watson 1993b, 126).

Blue-eyed barbarian ➛ BARBARIAN under **Bodhidharma**

Bodai (J.) *Bodhi* (Skt.) 菩提

Bodai is the Japanese pronunciation for the Sanskrit term *bodhi*, the wisdom of awakening. The characters 菩提, pronounced *p'u-t'i* in Chinese, attempted to recreate the pronunciation of bodhi and not to translate the meaning of the term. Other terms, "way" 道, "awakening" 覺, "wisdom" 智, etc. tried to translate the meaning.

Bodhi ➛ *Bodai*

Bodhidharma, Great Teacher Daruma Daishi (J.) 達磨大師

According to Zen tradition, Bodhidharma (also written 達摩) is the Indian monk who first brought Ch'an/Zen from India to China. He is revered as the twenty-eighth Indian patriarch after Śākyamuni and the first patriarch of the Ch'an/Zen sect in China. Biographies of Bodhidharma in texts like the *Keitoku dentō-roku* 景徳傳燈錄—published much later, in 1004—say he arrived in China in 527, but recent research has suggested other dates (for example, ZGDJT 831c notes birth and death dates of 346–495). Dumoulin (1990, vol. 1, 85–94) has tried to separate the historical Bodhidharma from the image of Bodhidharma in Zen history. The Japanese scholar Sekiguchi Shindai, in a book-length study of seventeen early documents, has concluded that the legend of Bodhidharma combines the biographies of three figures—the historical Bodhidharma, an intermediate figure Dharmatrāta, and Daruma, the founder of the Zen sect—together with elements taken from the biographies of other Zen monks (Sekiguchi 1967).

Because Rinzai kōan training uses elements of the Bodhidharma legend to express points in its teaching, the historical factuality of the Bodhidharma legend is not a great concern. The following points of the Bodhidharma legend are important for the understanding of capping phrases.

ANCESTRY AND LINEAGE

Legend says Bodhidharma was born the third son of a Brahman king and received the Dharma from the twenty-seventh patriarch Prajñātāra, thus becoming the twenty-eighth patriarch of Buddhism. He is the central figure linking the Ch'an / Zen patriarchs in China, and later Japan, to Śākyamuni Buddha, as if all the Buddhist patriarchs formed a Chinese-style ancestral lineage (the Chinese character for "patriarch" 祖 is the same as for "ancestor").

APPEARANCE AND ICONOGRAPHY

In iconography, Bodhidharma is usually shown with a red robe pulled up to cover his head and large grotesque eyes (because he has no eyelids). He has blue eyes, a red beard (see MMK 4), a hairy chest, and earrings. He has long earlobes, a trait that seems to be borrowed from the iconography of the Buddha (see **Thirty-two marks**). He is also referred to as the "**pierced-eared traveler**" (see below) although this has nothing to do with earrings. He is usually shown in one of two postures, one in seated meditation and one standing, often on a single reed, and often carrying a single shoe over his shoulder.

BARBARIAN

Bodhidharma is called the "barbarian monk" 胡僧 *kosō* (J.), the "blue-eyed barbarian" 碧眼胡僧 *hekigan no kosō* (J.) (since blue eyes in China are a sign of foreign origin), and "the old barbarian" 老胡 *rōko*, although this last term can sometimes be used of Śākyamuni himself. His beard, hairy chest, and earrings also mark him as a barbarian. See also **BAREFOOT PERSIAN.**

BAREFOOT PERSIAN *Sekkyaku (shakkyaku) no hashi* (J.) 赤脚波斯

Another literary term referring to Bodhidharma. *Hashi* 波斯, 波嘶, pronounced *po-ssu*, is an old Chinese term for Parsa or Persia (ODA 1954, 1395). *Sekkyaku, shakkyaku* 赤脚, "barefoot," implies that he is a barbarian. ZGDJT also interprets bare feet to symbolize the freedom of someone well grounded (474–4).

BODHIDHARMA RETURNS TO INDIA CARRYING A SINGLE SHOE 隻履歸天

When he died, Bodhidharma was buried on Hsiung Erh (熊耳 Bear Ear) Mountain. Later a monk traveling in the mountains between India and China reported meeting Bodhidharma carrying one shoe and traveling towards India. Bodhidharma's grave was opened but there was nothing inside except one shoe (OGATA 1990, 73–4).

BODHIDHARMA TRANSMITS THE DHARMA TO FOUR DISCIPLES

Some biographies of Bodhidharma contain a story in which he asks four of his disciples to show their understanding. With each successive answer he says, "You have gained my skin," "You have gained my flesh," "You have gained my bone," and finally "You have gained my marrow." This story is sometimes held up as an example of "mind-to-mind transmission" (*ishin denshin* 以心傳心). If so, it uses body-to-body transmission as a metaphor for mind-to-mind transmission. Some versions of the story have Bodhidharma declaring he is 150 years old and implying that it is time for him to return to India to die. Some versions have three disciples instead of four, blood for skin, or a different order to the answers (SEKIGUCHI 1967, 159–63).

BODHIDHARMA'S VERSE

Bodhidharma is said to be the author of the four-line poem:

敎外別傳 *Kyōge betsuden*
不立文字 *Furyū monji* (*Furu moji*)
直指人心 *Jikishi jinshin*
見性成佛 *Kenshō jōbutsu.*

A separate transmission outside doctrine,
Not founded on words or letters,
Pointing directly at human mind,
Seeing nature, become Buddha.

EKA DAISHI CUTS OFF HIS ARM *Eka danpi* (J.) 慧可斷臂

Eka 慧可 (Ch. Hui-k'o) visited Bodhidharma, waited long in the snow, asking to be instructed in the Dharma. Bodhidharma refused until Eka cut off his arm as a sign of his determination. In MMK 41, when Eka says, "Your disciple's mind is not yet at rest. I beg the master to give my mind rest," Bodhidharma answers, "Bring your mind and I will give you rest." Eka replies, "I have searched for my mind and cannot find it." Bodhidharma replies, "I have set your mind totally at rest." Shibayama has a *teishō* on this kōan (1974, 292–9). Eka went on to become Bodhidharma's successor and the second patriarch in Chinese Ch'an/Zen.

ENCOUNTER WITH EMPEROR WU OF THE LIANG

Emperor Wu was known as a Buddhist emperor. He not only promoted the construction of monasteries and the spread of Buddhism in general, but also personally entered monasteries for short intervals.

In reply to Emperor Wu's question, "What is the supreme first truth (無上第一義), Bodhidharma gave the answer, "Vast emptiness, nothing holy" (廓然無聖). To the question, "Who stands before me?" he answered "Do not know" (不識). See *Heki* 1.

These phrases, expressing the difference between Emperor Wu's Buddhism and Bodhidharma's Zen, have become parts of the standard vocabulary of all Zen monks. Disappointed with Emperor Wu, Bodhidharma crossed the Yangtze River on a single reed and traveled north.

NINE YEARS FACING THE WALL *Kyūnen menpeki* (J.) 九年面壁

In a cave on Shao-shih Peak, Bodhidharma sat in meditation for "nine years facing the wall." To prevent himself from falling asleep, it is said that he cut off his eyelids, and where the eyelids fell, tea bushes grew. For this reason Zen monks drink tea to keep themselves awake during meditation. Because he did not move, his arms and legs atrophied and fell off. The Japanese *daruma* doll has no arms or legs; shaped like a squat rounded bowling pin, whenever it is pushed over it rights itself.

It was during this period that Eka came to seek instruction in the Dharma from Bodhidharma.

"THE PATRIARCH CAME FROM THE WEST"

Bodhidharma's country of origin is said to have been either Persia (*Hashi* 波斯) or India (*Nantenjuku* 南天竺 or *Saiten* 西天). He is said to have come from the West (the term for India 西天 means "Western Heaven"), and the set phrase "the point of the patriarch's coming from the west" 祖師西來意 (*soshi seirai i*) is a conventional way of referring to the fundamental point of Zen.

The kōan index 禪門公案大成 *(Zen School Kōan Compilation)* lists 118 kōan whose main question is "What is the point of the patriarch's coming from the west?" (Otobe 1918, 50–90).

D. T. Suzuki discusses a variety of possible answers to this kōan (1953, 227–53). The character 意 is sometimes translated as "meaning" (as in "What is the meaning of Bodhidharma's coming from the west?"), and sometimes as "intention" (as in "What was Bodhidharma's intention in coming from the west?"). The translation used in *Zen Sand,* "point," attempts to straddle these two interpretations.

PIERCED-EARED TRAVELER *Senni no kyaku* (J.) 穿耳客
PIERCED-EARED BARBARIAN MONK *Senni no kosō* (J.) 穿耳胡僧

The term *senni no kyaku* (10.302) can refer to any awakened monk, but *senni no kosō* is usually a reference to **Bodhidharma**. The term "pierced-eared" has no connection to the fact that Bodhidharma wore earrings. ZGJT 63 cites 止觀輔行:

> Of those who have heard the Buddha-Dharma during their lifetimes and become wise, copper can be passed right through their skulls; but of those who are still ignorant, copper cannot be passed through their skulls.

The following story, though taken from a thirteenth-century Japanese text called the *Shasekishū*, describes the same measuring of Dharma understanding:

> In India lived a Brahman who bought skulls. He would place a copper chopstick into the ear sockets and pay most for those skulls which the chopstick penetrated deeply, less for those which it penetrated slightly, and nothing for those which it would not penetrate at all. His reasoning was that the earholes of those who heard the Law in ancient times were deep, the earholes of those who heard little were shallow, and the earholes of those who heard nothing were impenetrable. The man bought the skulls of those who heard the Law, erected stupa, and performed services for them. For this he was born into the heavens (Morrell 1985, 120).

ROBE AND BOWL

Because he foresaw that people would doubt, Bodhidharma gave his robe and bowl to Hui-k'o as proof that he was the true successor. Bodhidharma's robe and bowl, as symbols of true transmission, also appear in the story of how Hui-neng, who later went on to become the Sixth Patriarch, received transmission from Hung-jen, the Fifth Patriarch.

SHAO-LIN, SHAO-SHIH, SUNG-SHAN

After leaving Emperor Wu, Bodhidharma settled into a temple called Shao-lin ssu 少林寺 (J. Shōrin-ji) on Shao-shih Peak 少室 (J. *Shōshitsu*) on a mountain called Sung-shan 嵩山 (J. *Sūzan*). All of these names—Shao-lin, Shao-shih, Sung-shan—occur in Zen phrases and imply that the phrase is about Bodhidharma, although he may not be mentioned by name.

VERSE UPON TRANSMISSION *Denbō no ge* (J.) 傳法の偈

Bodhidharma uttered a verse on transmitting the Dharma to his disciple.

吾本來茲土	*Ware moto kono do ni kitaru koto wa*
傳法救迷情	*Hō o tsutaete meijō o sukuwan to nari.*
一華開五葉	*Ichige goyō o hiraki,*
結果自然成	*Kekka jinen ni naru.*

I first came to this land,
To spread the Dharma and save people from delusive passion.
A lotus opens five leaves,
And of itself bears fruit.

The *Platform Sutra of the Sixth Patriarch* contains a collection of the verses uttered by the first five Zen patriarchs upon transmission of the Dharma to a successor (YAMPOLSKY 1967, 176–7).

Brahma Bonten (J.) 梵天

Originally an Indian god, Bonten (Brahma) was absorbed into Buddhism, along with Nata, Vaiśravaṇa and others. He is the lord of heaven and functions as a protector of Buddhism.

Branches with a common grain ➛ under **Matrimonial harmony**

Broken mirror *Hakyō* (J.) 破鏡

"Broken mirror" will sometimes connote unfaithfulness between lovers (e.g., 10.410). In an old Chinese legend, a couple who had to part broke a mirror in two as a sign of their promise to be faithful to each other. Each kept half of the mirror, awaiting the time when they could put the two halves together again. But while the man was away, the woman took a new lover. Her half of the broken mirror turned into a magpie and flew off to the former lover to inform him of what had happened. The bird in this story, however, does not seem to have any connection with the **Broken-mirror bird.**

Broken-mirror bird *Hakyōchō* (J.) 破鏡鳥

The broken-mirror bird is said to want to eat its parent (8.338). The *Shih-chi* describes an imperial ceremony in which are sacrificed an owl, which wants to eat its mother, and a "broken-mirror" 破鏡 bird, which wants to eat its father (史記封禪書). Morohashi also lists a reference to the *Laṅkāvatāra sūtra* that mentions an evil bird called "broken mirror" 破鏡, which wants to eat its parent (Morohashi 24124.27).

Butterfly's dream *Kochō no yume* (J.) 蝴蝶夢

In *Chuang-tzu,* chapter 2, Chuang-tzu recounts that he dreamed he was a butterfly. When he awoke, he did not know if he were a person dreaming he was a butterfly, or a butterfly dreaming he was a person.

Cangue ➛ **Stock**

Catty *Kin* (J.) *Chin* (Ch.) 斤

A catty is an ancient Chinese unit of weight. From the Chou through the Warring States periods it was equivalent to 256 grams, or a little more than half a pound; 30 *kin* (斤) was equal to 1 *kin* (鈞, Ch. *chün*). See *Shinjigen*, 1223–4.

Chang (Ch.) Chō (J.) 張

Chang is an extremely common name in China. "Third Son Chang, Fourth Son Li" 張三李四 is a set phrase, equivalent to "Tom and Dick" or "Smith and Jones," names for the common person.

Chang Han (Ch.) Chōkan (J.) 張翰

Chang Han (258?–319?) was a government official, originally of the state of Wu, sent to a distant outpost. One day while traveling on a river, the autumn breeze brought back memories of the delicious rice, soup, and fish of his home in Wu. Immediately he resigned his post, ordered a carriage, and returned many thousands of miles home (Morohashi 9812.148).

Chang Liang (Ch.) Chōryō (J.) 張良

In founding the Han Dynasty, Liu Pang (see **Han Kao-tsu**) was assisted by the "Three Heroes" 三傑. Among them was Chang Liang. Physically weak and often ill, he did not participate much in actual fighting. He practiced austerities, followed special diets (such as going without grain), and sometimes secluded himself in his house for a year at a time (WATSON 1993A, *Han I*, 109). But he was the brilliant military strategist about whom it was said, "Plotting strategy inside a battle tent, he decides a victory a thousand miles away" (8.337). When Liu Pang entered the capital of Ch'in, on the advice of Chang Liang, he refrained from the usual plundering of the city and the slaughter of its civilians (referred to in 7.51) and thereby gained a reputation for supporting the common people. (Sometimes Hsiao Ho is credited with this policy. See under **Han Kao-tsu**.)

In another example of clever strategy, on retreat from the capital, Chang Liang advised Liu Pang to burn the wooden trestle pathway over which they had just crossed (the only passable route through a steep gorge) in order to show that Liu Pang had no intention of returning east to contend for supremacy of the Ch'in capital. This is the event referred to in 16.4: "One is like Tzu-fang burning the trestle pathway." Deceiving his rival into complacency, Liu Pang later did return east, defeated Hsiang Yü, and established the empire of the Han (WATSON 1993A, *Han I*, 103). (See **Han Kao-tsu** below for other interpretations of this incident.)

Verse 14.460 contains the line "Chang Liang stepped on the [commander's] foot and had Han Hsin enfeofed." One of Liu Pang's generals, the brilliant Han Hsin, had defeated the state of Ch'i and sent word by envoy to his commander Liu Pang that he wished to be made its local king. Liu Pang was angered when he received the envoy's message and started to curse, but advisor Chang Liang stepped on Liu Pang's foot and whispered into his ear (so that Han Hsin's envoy would not hear) that he should make Han Hsin the local king in order to retain his loyalty (WATSON 1993A, *Han I*, 175).

Chao Chün (Ch.) Shōkun (J.) 昭君

Chao Chün, the "Brilliant Lady," is one of Chinese history's famous beauties (10.237, 14.670). She was born Wang Ch'iang in 53 BCE, the daughter of a Han official, and died in 18 CE, the widow of a barbarian chieftain. Schooled in Confucian virtue, she grew into a young lady of delicate beauty, great cultural refinement, and strong moral sense. When she was seventeen, an imperial minister seeking beautiful girls for the imperial harem took her to the capital. Because there were so many women, the emperor did not actually see the women but inspected paintings made by the court painter. The court painter expected bribes from the women and their families. Because of her strong moral upbringing, Wang Ch'iang refused to bribe the painter, who, in retaliation, disfigured her portrait by adding a mole under her right eye.

The Han emperors entered into treaties with the barbarian Hsiung-nu, in which the Han gave gifts, supplies, and an imperial princess to keep them pacified. Emperor Yüan Ti 元帝 (r. 48–33 BCE) selected Wang Ch'iang to send to the Hsiung-nu. At the formal handover to the Hsiung-nu envoys, he saw her for the first time. Realizing that his ministers and the court painter had kept the most beautiful of his women away from him, he had them executed and tried to substitute another woman. However, Wang Ch'iang herself, now titled Chao Chün, the Brilliant Lady, insisted that if the emperor failed to present her to the Hsiung-nu, in revenge they would cause much damage to the Han empire. Sadly he realized that she was right and sent her to the barbarians.

As queen of the Hsiung-nu, Chao Chün learned to ride, hunt, and drink goat's milk tea. She gave birth to a son, who became one of many princes under the Great Khan, who had already had sons by two previous queens and several other women. In 32 BCE the Great Khan died, leaving Chao Chün a young widow and mother at age twenty-two. Ordered by the Han emperor to conform to Hsiung-nu custom, she acquiesced when the new Great Khan took over all of his father's women, including Chao Chün. She became his queen, and by the young Khan, Chao Chün gave birth to two daughters. The young Khan, however, was struck by a virulent disease and Chao Chün was again a widow at age thirty-three. One of her daughters was sent to the Han imperial court as a lady in waiting, and the second daughter was married to a minister then in office. Her son, who was a contender for the position of Khan, was murdered by a rival. She spent the rest of her days mourning his loss (SHU 1981C).

Chaos ➤ ***K'un-lun***

Chao jewel ➤ **Hsiang-ju**

Ch'ang-an Chōan (J.) 長安

Now the present-day city of Sian in Shensi Province, the ancient city of Ch'ang-an was the capital during the Han and T'ang dynasties. In Chinese literature and history, the name of Ch'ang-an had a romantic ring. OBATA describes the city as follows: "Beside the main castle with its ninefold gates, there were thirty-six imperial palaces that reared over the city their resplendent towers and pillars of gold, while innumerable mansions and villas of noblemen vied with one another in magnificence. By day the broad avenues were thronged with motley crowds of townsfolk, gallants on horseback, and mandarin cars drawn by yokes of black oxen. And there were countless houses of pleasure, which opened their doors at night, and which abounded in song, dance, wine, and pretty women with faces like the moon" (1935, 4). By the seventh century Ch'ang-an was the largest city in the world, with a population of one million (STEINHARDT 1990, 93).

The city was laid out as a symmetrical grid of straight north-south and east-west streets dividing the city into wards. A great outer wall, reaching thicknesses of 9–12 metres, defined the square perimeter, making the city a virtual fortress. The imperial palace complex rose at the north end of Vermilion Bird Avenue, the wide north-south thoroughfare that bisected the city. Several other palaces were scattered throughout the city, and imperial tombs dotted the northwestern suburbs. The emperor maintained a large park where he hunted animals. From time to time the emperor and his entourage made procession to the various altars, where he conducted rituals. Magnificently equipped soldiers with golden whips (14.238) stood guard around imperial buildings and accompanied the emperor on his processions along **imperial avenues** reserved exclusively for the emperor and his family (14.238).

Ch'ang-an was the terminus of the Silk Road, the great travel route that stretched across central Asia to reach India, the Middle East, Africa, and the Mediterranean. An eastward extension reached Nara in Japan. Even during the Han, Ch'ang-an was already a cosmopolitan city with a significant international population of foreign merchants, envoys of foreign states, and Buddhist monks (SCHAFER 1963, 7–39).

During the T'ang, the city contained 130 Buddhist monasteries and 40 Taoist monasteries. These numbers are small in comparison to the 1,367 religious buildings in the Northern Wei capital of Lo-yang, but the monasteries were often vast complexes occupying entire city blocks (STEINHARDT 1990, 102). Envoy ships from Japan brought students and monks eager to learn the culture of the T'ang and the teachings of Buddhism. The Japanese so admired Chinese culture that they imported the Chinese imperial city plan and constructed the Japanese capitals of Heijō (now Nara), Nagaoka, and Heian (now Kyoto) in imitation of Ch'ang-an (STEINHARDT 1990, 108–21).

Ch'ao-fu ➛ **Shun**

Chiang-hu ➛ **River and Lake**

Chiang-hsi ➛ **River and Lake**

Chiang-nan (Ch.) Kōnan (J.) 江南

Chiang-nan was a southern region reputed to be a paradise, famed for its beautiful landscape, women, food, etc. It was often contrasted with **Yu-chou**, which was a northwestern boundary state in ancient China with a reputation for being cold, barren, and desolate.

Chieh and Chou (Ch.) Ketchū (J.) 桀紂

Just as **Yao** and **Shun** are held up as the epitome of the virtuous ruler in Chinese legend, the pair King Chieh and King Chou are remembered as the classic examples of evil tyrants (12.86). Chieh was the last king of the Hsia Dynasty (2205–1766 BCE). GILES says that after coming to power, he "for many years indulged in cruel brutality and lust almost unparalleled in history" (1939, 139). Chou was the last king of the Yin Dynasty (1766–1122 BCE). "To please his consort, the infamous Ta Chi, he [Chou] made a lake of wine, hung up quarters of meat on a forest of trees, and held a great banquet during which naked youths and women were made to pursue each other among the meat-laden trees." In the story behind *Analects* XVIII, 1, Chou is also said to have torn the heart out of the body of an uncle who reproached him for bad government.

Ching K'o (Ch.) Keika (J.) 荊軻

Ching K'o does not appear by name in *Zen Sand*, but his story is assumed in several of the verses. During the Warring States period (403–221 BCE), Ching K'o was sent by Prince Tan of the state of Yen to assassinate the king of Ch'in, the man who later went on to become Ch'in Shih Huang Ti, the ruthless founder of the first unified empire of China. Ching K'o knew that he would not return alive from his mission. He became the topic of poetry by later poets, and lines from these poems are used as kōan capping phrases (e.g., 10.178–10.179).

Ching K'o's biography is included in Chapter 86 of the *Shih-chi*, "Assassin-Retainers" (WATSON 1993A, 167–78, where his name is rendered Jing ke); see also YANG and YANG 1979, 392–402; and Mair 1994, 671–83). Chen Kaige has made a full-length film, *The Emperor and the Assassin*, about Ching K'o and the king of Ch'in. In this movie, when Ching K'o sets out on his attempt to assassinate the king of Ch'in, the couplet at 10. 178–10.179 is recited.

Chinshu ➛ **Poison blackbird**

Chou ➛ **Duke of Chou**

Chu Jung (Ch.) Shukuyū (J.) 祝融

In early Chinese mythology, Chu Jung is the name of the fire god who, among other acts, executed Kun, the father of **Yü**, the hero who saved China from the great flood. By association, the characters in the name Chu Jung can also mean fire in general. There is also a Chu Jung Peak in Hunan Province (the same province that contains **Lake Tung-t'ing** [14.253]). BIRRELL 1993 (79, 81) has a brief mention of Chu Jung (where it is spelled Chu Yung).

Chu-ko (Ch.) Shokatsu (J.) 諸葛

In the *Romance of the Three Kingdoms* 三國誌, Chu-ko Liang 諸葛亮 (also called Chu-ko K'ung-ming 諸葛孔明, Shokatsu Kōmei in J.) was the celebrated military strategist in the army of Shu 蜀. The ruler of Shu was Liu Pei 劉備 (J. Ryūbi, 161–223), last ruler of the Later Han Dynasty. Before Liu Pei became emperor, Chu-ko was living in seclusion in the countryside. Liu Pei visited Chu-ko, asking him three times to come out of seclusion from his grass-roofed hut and help the new emperor (10.244). This is the origin of 三顧 (J. *sanko*), the custom of showing respect by making a request three times.

Chapters 53 and 54 of the *Romance of the Three Kingdoms* describe the final confrontation between Chu-ko Liang and the leader of the opposing Wei army, Ssu-ma I 司馬懿, whose style name was Chung-ta 仲達 (J. Chūdatsu). He was a fierce general, said to be the only man whom Chu-ko feared. In the skirmishes between them, Ssu-ma I, always afraid of getting caught in one of Chu-ko's ingenious traps, never met Chu-ko head-on. Chu-ko, however, was failing in health and knew that he would soon die. After his death, as his coffin was being transported back to Shu, Ssu-ma I attacked, thinking his opportunity had finally come to defeat the Shu army. He walked right into a trap in which the Shu army, carrying the Prime Minister's banners of Chu-ko Liang, surrounded and counter-attacked. Ssu-ma I's army panicked, and he himself fled for his life. This is the background for 7.196, 8.214. See BREWITT-TAYLOR 1959, 450–69.

Chü Ling ➛ Flower Peak

Ch'i-lin (Ch.), *Kirin* (J.) 麒麟

In Chinese legend, the *ch'i-lin* is a fabulous animal with the body of a deer, the tail of an ox, a hide of many colors, a belly colored yellow, and one fleshy horn. It does not tread on grass nor eat anything living. The male is *ch'i* and the female is *lin*. Sighting a *ch'i-lin* was rarely reported, but when it did occur the sighting was always considered a great good omen.

Chung Tzu-ch'i ➛ Intimate, intimate friend

Ch'ü-tzu ➛ Ch'ü Yüan

Ch'ü Yüan (Ch.) Kutsugen (J.) 屈原

Also known as Ch'ü-tzu 屈子 (J. Kusshi) and Ch'ü P'ing 屈平 (J. Kuppei), Ch'ü Yüan (340?–278 BCE) was a government official during the period of the Warring States. He is remembered in Chinese literature as the model selfless and loyal minister who suffered slander and banishment. The *Shih-chi*, ch. 84, contains a short biography. Ch'ü Yüan was minister to King Huai of the state of Ch'u at a time when the state of Ch'in in the west had already started on the road to the military conquest of all China. A jealous court rival of Ch'ü Yüan slandered him to the king and had him removed from office. Although he no longer had official position at court, Ch'ü Yüan continued to give advice to King Huai, advice that the reckless King Huai, intent on military adventure, ignored to his disadvantage. Eventually King Huai was taken prisoner and died a hostage in a foreign state. Banished from the country by his enemies at court, Ch'ü Yüan wandered through southern China and finally drowned himself in Mi-lo 汨羅 River in Chiang-t'an 江潭 (J. Kōtan) (WATSON 1993A, *Han I*, 435–43). This took place on the fifth day of the fifth month, and still today, this day is an annual festival in which people fill small bamboo tubes with offerings of rice and throw them into the river to the spirit of Ch'ü Yüan.

An early collection of poetry inspired by Ch'ü Yüan's martyrdom is the *Ch'u tz'u* 楚辭 (J. *Soji*), *The Songs of Ch'u*, translated as *Songs of the South* by David HAWKES (1985). The only poem in the collection that can be attributed with confidence to Ch'ü Yüan himself is the *Li Sao* 離騷 (J. *Risō*), translated as "Encountering Sorrow," a lament on the petty evil of court intrigue and the weakness of an unprincipled ruler (14.450). Hawkes has a complete translation as well as a detailed account of the Ch'ü Yüan legend (HAWKES 1985; NIENHAUSER et al. 1986, 347–9, 352–3).

Ch'un ch'iu ➛ **Spring and autumn**

Claws and teeth ➛ **Talons and tusks**

Cloth drum *Fuko* (J.) 布鼓

A cloth drum, no matter how hard it is struck, makes no sound. (ZGDJT 1069)

Clouds and rain *Un'u* (J.) 雲雨

"Clouds and rain" is a literary phrase that, at its crudest, connotes sexual intercourse and, at more elevated levels, implies intimate encounter with a goddess (14.175, 14.605). It is an abbreviation of "morning clouds, evening rain" 朝雲暮雨 (J. *Chōun bou*). The source of these uses is "Rhapsody on the Kaotang Shrine" by the poet Sung Yü, in the early poetry collection *Wen Hsüan (Literary Selections)*. The poem tells how the ancient king, Hsiang, hunting on Mount Wushan ("Shaman Mountain"), lay down for a daytime nap. In his dream he was visited by a beautiful goddess who shared his bed. When she left, she said:

> I live on the sunny side of Shaman Mount,
> Among the defiles of a lofty hill.
> Mornings, I am Dawn Cloud,
> Evenings, I am Pouring Rain.
> (translation from XIAO 1996, 325–39)

SCHAFER 1980 has an extended discussion of the figure of the divine women in Chinese legend and literature.

Cold Mountain ➛ **Han-shan**

Coming from the west ➛ PATRIARCH CAME FROM THE WEST under **Bodhidharma**

Coral *Sango* (J.) 珊瑚

Coral is one of the traditional eight jewels: gold, silver, lapis lazuli, mother of pearl, agate, coral, amber, pearl (金銀瑠璃硨磲瑪瑙珊瑚琥珀眞珠 *Kon gon ruri shako menō sango kohaku shinju*). Folk legend said that coral branches grew under the influence of moonlight and that their tips had a halo of light (ZGJI 345; 7.177). In order to understand the meaning of coral in Zen verses, it is worthwhile remembering that the moon is a traditional symbol for awakened mind. It is otherwise difficult to understand verses like 7. 124 or 7.332.

Crooked ➛ **Five Ranks**

Datsumyō no shinpu (J.) 奪命神符

Literally "a divine tally for stealing your life away," this is a "metaphor for the spiritual power attained after the experience of the Great Death" (ZD 279).

Deer musk *Jakkō* (J.) 麝香

Oil from the musk deer, taken from the musk gland around the navel, was considered both a particularly exotic aromatic and a medicinal drug (5.412, 10.226). Barbarian rulers of kingdoms in Manchuria and Yunnan sent gifts of this perfume as tribute to the Chinese emperor during the T'ang (SCHAFER 1963, 158; Morohashi 47682.3).

Diamond Mountain ➛ **Sumeru, Mount**

Dipper and Ox *Togyū* (J.) 斗牛

"The Dipper and the Ox" imply the entire heavens. In traditional Chinese astrology/astronomy, the sky was divided into the four directions, which were in turn subdivided into seven lodges. The Dipper and the Ox were two of the lodges, but the compound Dipper-Ox was used as an abbreviation for all twenty-eight lodges (*Shinjigen* 448).

Directed upwards *Kōjō* (J.) 向上

The characters for *kōjō* literally mean "directed upwards," but in Zen they imply the path of awakening. "The *kōjō* path is not transmitted by even a thousand sages. Seekers struggle with its form but they are like monkeys trying to grasp reflections in water" (傳燈錄七, 盤山寶積章, quoted in ZGDJT 314b). Here *kōjō* may be translated "ultimate" (5.89).

In some accounts of the Rinzai kōan system, *kōjō* is an advanced category of kōan given to students near the end of the entire curriculum (see Introduction). For these kōan, the literal translation "directed upwards" has been retained, since *kōjō* kōan are sometimes contrasted with another category of kōan, *kōge* 向下 "directed downwards." Shōichi Kokushi (1202–1280) said, "The Buddhas and ancestors have produced [kōan] of principle, of dynamic action, those directed upwards, those directed downwards" (AKIZUKI 1987, 77).

In other contexts *kōjō* has been translated "superior" (compare 12.39 and 12.40).

Donkey hitching post *Keroketsu* (J.) 繫驢橛

A donkey hitching post is a post hammered into the ground, to which a donkey is tied. It is used in Zen verses as a symbol of unfreedom, that which prevents one from free movement, a hobble.

Doomsday fire ➛ under ***Kalpa***

Double ninth *Chōyō* (J.) 重陽

The ninth day of the ninth month, a festive holiday (5.64, 8.279, 14.35). See also **Five festive occasions**. The characters literally mean "Double Yang," since nine was the greatest *yang* number. During the T'ang period it was customary on the Double Ninth day to climb to a high place such as a hill or tower, to cut a twig of dogwood to wear in the hair as a protection from evil spirits, and to drink chrysanthemum wine together with friends. For a discussion of the theme of double ninth in Chinese poetry, see DAVIS 1968.

Dragon Gate *Ryūmon* (J.) *Lung Men* (Ch.) 龍門

When **Yü** the Great drained the waters that flooded the world at that time, he cut a three-step 三級 (J. *sankyū*) waterfall (10.202, 14.207) through mountains to open up a passage for the Yellow River. This waterfall became known as the Dragon Gate. Legend says that, on the third day of the third month, when the peach trees are in flower, vigorous carp that can scale this three-tiered waterfall will transform into dragons. Climbing the Dragon Gate is a general metaphor for success and transformation after long effort (7.483, 10.349, 14.129, 14.523; ZGDJT 1278b).

Dragon Spring sword *Ryōsenken, ryūsenken* (J.) 龍泉劍

Ryōsen is the name of a famous sword in Chinese legend. In one version of the story, it is part of a pair, the other sword being the famous **T'ai-a Sword**. In another version, a swordsmith tempered his swords by alternately firing them and thrusting them into water. One of his swords, when thrust into spring water, turned into a dragon. He called the sword thereafter Dragon Spring (Morohashi 48818.377).

Dragon-tiger formations *Ryūko no jin* (J.) 龍虎陣

The dragon and tiger formations are formations of troops in Chinese military science. See **Eight formations.**

Drillhead ➛ ***Kareta***

Duke of Chou 周公

The Duke of Chou was the brother of King Wu, who with his father, **King Wen**, founded the Chou Dynasty. When King Wu died, the throne went to his son Ch'eng 成, still a young boy. The Duke, as uncle to Ch'eng, became regent to the young king. The Duke is revered as an model upright statesman who never succumbed to the temptation to take the throne for himself.

One day when Ch'eng was playing with his younger brother, he clipped the leaf of a tree into the shape of a sceptre and said to his brother, "With this sceptre I grant you a fief." Duke Chou, the regent, overheard this, and declaring a day of ceremony, started to make preparations for a real enfeofment. When Ch'eng said, "I said it only in play," the Duke replied, "The Son of Heaven says nothing in jest. As he has spoken, the ministers will duly record it, carry it out with proper ceremony, and celebrate the occasion with music and song." And the younger brother was duly made a feudal lord over a state (史記晉世家).

Dust *Jin, jin'ai* (J.) 塵 | 塵埃

The term "dust" is a Buddhist metaphor to denote the sources of sensation, which in Buddhist thought are said to defile the original purity of mind. The "six dusts" are sight, sound, taste, smell, touch, and thought. The world of the six dusts is the phenomenal world known through sense perception. Many Chinese expressions are influenced by the metaphor of dust: "red dust," "mote in the eye," "flowers in the eye," etc.

Eight beings *Hachibushū* (J.) 八部衆

The eight kinds of supernatural beings, often repeated in such texts as the *Kannon Sutra*, are: gods, *naga* (or water gods), ***yakṣa***, *gandharva* (musician spirits who feed on incense and emit fragrance), ***asura***, ***garuda***, *kinnara* (music spirits with a human body and a horse's head), and *mahoraga* (music spirits with human body and head of a snake) (天龍夜叉乾闥婆阿修羅迦樓羅緊那羅摩睺羅迦 *ten ryū yasha kendatsuba ashura karura kinnara magoraga*).

Eight consciousnesses *Hasshiki* (J.) 八識

In the Consciousness-only school of Buddhism, the eight consciousnesses include the basic six consciousnesses (seeing, hearing, smelling, tasting, feeling, and consciousness) plus *manas* or mind, and *ālaya* or the so-called storehouse consciousness.

Eight-cornered mortar stone *Hakkaku no maban* (J.) 八角磨盤

The eight-cornered mortar stone, a weapon mentioned in Indian mythology, is a grindstone with eight sharpened points. It symbolizes huge destructive power capable of destroying everything at once (ZGJT 383).

Eight formations *Hachijin* (J.) 八陣

"Eight formations" was a technical term in early Chinese military science to describe eight ways of deploying an army for battle. There is, however, no single explanation of them, although the eight types of battle formation were thought to correspond to the **eight trigrams** and thus to embody different combinations of the powers of *yin* and *yang* and the Tao. Needham gives a chart of eight formations: Heaven, Earth, Wind, Clouds, Flying Dragon, Winged Tiger, Soaring Bird, Curling Snake (NEEDHAM and YATES 1994, 58–66).

Eight model brush strokes of the character *ei* *Eiji happō* (J.) 永字八法

In Chinese calligraphy there are no more than eight basic brush strokes, all of which appear in the model character 永. The character's meaning, "long" or "eternal," is not relevant to its use here.

Eight poles, eight extremities *Hakkyoku* (J.) 八極

Ancient Chinese geography depicted the earth as laid out in a flat three-by-three grid of nine states or countries. Seen from the point of view of people living in the central state, in each of the eight directions there was a state or country that one could reach if one went to extreme distances. These are the eight extremities. For an overview of Chinese geographical ideas at the time of the Han, see MAJOR 1993, esp. ch. 4, and ALLAN 1991.

Eight trigrams *Hakka* (J.) *Pa kua* (Ch.) 八卦

In the Chinese divination text, *I ching*, a trigram 卦 is a diagram composed of three lines. Lines can be either solid (*yang* lines) or broken (*yin* lines). There are eight possible combinations and each such trigram is named and given a philosophical significance.

☰	☱	☲	☴	☳	☵	☶	☷
乾	兌	離	巽	震	坎	艮	坤
Ch'ien	*Tui*	*Li*	*Sun*	*Chen*	*K'an*	*Ken*	*K'un*
Heaven	Marsh	Fire	Wood	Thunder	Water	Mountain	Earth

Trigrams taken in pairs produce a hexagram (also 卦), a stack of six lines (六爻). There are 64 possible combinations of hexagrams. Some *Zen Sand* verses explicitly refer to the *I ching* (8.426, 12.60). In addition, the *I ching* character combination 乾坤 (Ch. *ch'ien/k'un*, J. *ken/kun*), which means "heaven and earth" or "the universe," has entered Chinese language in general and occurs in numerous verses in *Zen Sand*. It implies that the universe consists of dualities. Thus, in addition to "heaven and earth," the term might also be translated "**light and dark**," "male and female," etc., depending on the context.

In the Rinzai kōan curriculum, there is a final set of kōan based on hexagrams of the *I ching*. A standard translation of the *I ching* is WILHELM 1967. Several new translations have recently appeared, among them LYNN 1994.

Eight winds *Happū* (J.) 八風

The eight winds that move human feeling are the winds of gain and loss, defamation and eulogy, praise and blame, suffering and pleasure 利衰毀譽稱譏苦樂 (ZGJI 265).

Empress Lü Ryokō (J.) 呂后

Empress Lü was the wife of **Han Kao-tsu**, the first emperor of the Han Dynasty. Verses in *Zen Sand* (e.g., 14.604) point to one incident in particular from her colorful life. Though the emperor had a son by Empress Lü who was designated the heir apparent, the emperor himself favored his son by Lady Ch'i, one of his consorts, because of all his eight sons, her son, Chao Ju-i 趙如意, most resembled him. In fact, Kao-tsu intended to displace the son of Empress Lü and install Chao Jui as the heir apparent when the little boy came of age. In her jealousy, the Empress Lü had the child Ju-i poisoned and then tortured Lady Ch'i by cutting off her hands and feet, gouging out her eyes, forcing her to drink a chemical that destroyed her voice, and forcing smoke into her ears to make her deaf. Finally, she was cast into a toilet pit where she was exhibited as a "human pig." Empress Lü's story forms chapter 9 of the *Shih-chi* (Watson 1993a, *Han I*, 267–84).

Enter the painting *Gato ni iru* (J.) 入畫圖

A good painting was said to be so realistic that the viewer entered the painting, stepping into the world it represented.

Eyebrows *Bimō* (J.) 眉毛

Eyebrows are mentioned in several Chinese idioms. It was said that if one defamed the dharma, one's eyebrows would fall out. Since the dharma is said to be beyond words and letters, to speak even a little is to defame the dharma (ZGJT 399). This association is behind the kōan "Ts'ui Yen's Eyebrows" (*Heki* 9). "To shave the eyebrows" 剔起眉 means to get better vision. It implies that one cannot see clearly because the eyebrows are so long and shaggy. "To cross eyebrows" 交眉 is an idiom meaning "to be friendly, to exchange cordial greetings," like "rubbing elbows" in English. "Ritual raising to the level of the eyebrows" 齊眉禮 is the lifting of any food or drink to the level of the eyebrows before serving to guests as a show of respect (*Shinjigen* 1172). This is still the common practice in Japanese Zen monasteries.

Shapely eyebrows were also considered a sign of feminine beauty. See **Moth eyebrows.**

Fan K'uai (Ch.) Hankai (J.) 樊噲

Fan K'uai was originally a dog butcher who early attached himself to Liu Pang, the rebel who went on to found the Han Dynasty (see also **Han Kao-tsu**). The verse 5.317 "Fan K'uai stands at the Hung-men Gate" refers to the critical meeting of Liu Pang with his military rival Hsiang Yü at the Hungmen Gate. Though supposedly a friendly meeting, Fan K'uai sensed the danger to Liu Pang and stayed close beside him, preventing his assassination. The incident is described in the *Shih-chi*, ch. 7 (WATSON 1993A, *Han I*, 30–2).

Fireplace ➛ ***Karōtō***

Fire pit and bellows, forge *Rohai* (J.) 爐鞴

The characters individually mean "fire pit" and "bellows," the equipment in a blacksmith's workplace. The Zen master's *dōjō* is likened to a blacksmith's forge. In *Zen Sand*, the term "forge" has also been used to translate *kantsui* or *kentsui* 鉗鎚, which means "**Tongs and hammer**," a similar image for the Zen master's teaching methods.

Fish with paired eyes ➛ **Matrimonial harmony**

Five Emperors ➛ **Three Sovereigns and the Five Emperors**

Five festive occasions *Go setsu no e* | *gosetchie, gosekku* (J.) 五節會, 五節句

The five festivals were observed on the first day of the first month, third day of the third month, fifth day of the fifth month, seventh day of the seventh month, and ninth day of the ninth month. These are all the days on which a *yang* number is duplicated in the day and month position. See also **Double ninth.**

Five flavors *Gomi* (J.) 五味

The term "five flavors" is used in two contexts, one Chinese and one Buddhist. In accordance with the Chinese typology of **Five phases**, it classifies flavors into five: sour, bitter, sweet, spicy, and salty. In Buddhism, however, it refers to five kinds of products that can be made from milk: fresh milk, yogurt, coagulated cream, butter, and a highly refined buttery product called in Sanskrit *maṇḍa*, or *sarpirmaṇḍa* (J. *daigo* 醍醐, sometimes translated in *Zen Sand* as "milk of wisdom"). The last of these was said to possess both the finest flavor and the power to cure illness. The five flavors were used as a metaphor in Tendai Buddhism for the Five Periods of the Buddha's teaching, with *daigo* as a metaphor for the Nirvana teaching and for Buddha nature itself (Mochizuki 1958, 1299).

A related term is *soraku* 酥酪 (Skt. *ghṛta*). On the one hand it was considered a refined product (see 12.67 where it is translated "refined butter"). But on the other hand, it was considered unrefined in contrast with *daigo,* the most refined milk product, as in *soraku daigo* 酥酪醍醐 (16.41), which has been translated "curds and whey" in order to capture that contrast.

Five grave offenses ➛ **Five sins**

Five heavens *Goten* (J.) 五天

The ancient term for India was Western Heaven (J. *Tenjiku* 天竺). The five heavens are the five areas of India: north, south, east, west, and center (ZGDJT 353). More generally, the term is used to mean the universe in general (14.384).

Five hells without interval *Gomugengoku* (J.) 五無間獄

For the sake of smoother reading, this term has been abbreviated to "five hells" (e.g., 12.96). *Gomugengoku* is actually a single hell but with five kinds of punishment. Although accounts differ according to text, the realm of hell (Skt. *naraka*, J. *jigoku* 地獄) is subdivided into eight hot hells, eight cold hells, and three other hells. The worst of the eight hot hells, located deepest underground, is for those beings who commit the **Five sins.** This is *avīci* (Skt.), known as the hell of five kinds of punishment "without interval." "Without interval" has more than one meaning. *Mugen* 無間 translates *anantara* (Skt.), which can mean (1) immediate, direct and (2) continuous, without a break. This hell is so called for any of five reasons: (1) beings who commit the worst sins are reborn there immediately without passing through an intermediate birth; (2) their suffering is continuous and without break; (3) the time of their suffering is also continuous and without break; (4) the beings live endlessly there; or (5) the beings have bodies of 80,000 *yojana* in size completely filling hell, which is also 80,000 *yojana* in size, thus allowing them to be tortured without cease (ZGDJT 1203c, Oda 1954, 574; Daitō 1991, 94).

The *avīci* hell has a "tree of swords and the mountain of blades" 劍樹刀山, (J. *kenju tōzan*). The tree has branches consisting of swords protruding outwards (8.93). The mountain is a mass of swords all arranged with blades pointing upwards (14.101, 14.102). Sinners have to climb both the tree and the mountain with bare hands and feet. There is also a sword wheel 劍輪 (J. *kenrin*) in *avīci* hell, another means of inflicting endless suffering (HYDCD 752; 14.102).

Five lakes *Goko* (J.) 五湖

There are several areas in China that have bodies of water called "five lakes" (Morohashi 257.385). For capping phrases, it is not particularly important to identify the five lakes geographically; the term connotes scenic beauty and a sense of leisure.

Five phases *Gogyō* (J.) *Wu hsing* (Ch.) 五行

The Chinese classification of all things into two great classes, yin and yang, was extended into a system of five classes, or five phases. The five basic classes are metal, wood, fire, water, earth. Almost anything imaginable is divisible into five classes: time (years, seasons, hours of the day, imperial reigns, etc.), place (directions, city space, household space, etc.), colors, food, numbers, clothing, animals, kinds of ritual, organs of the body, planets and stars, offices in the bureaucracy, tones of music, etc.

As with yin and yang, the five phases are not thought of as fixed and unchanging essences but as phases of cyclical change. According to one explanation (the "mutual overcoming order"), earth overcomes water, water overcomes fire, fire overcomes metal, metal overcomes wood, and wood overcomes earth. In another system (the "mutual production order"), wood produces fire, fire produces earth, earth produces metal, metal produces water, and water produces wood. There were, however, other competing systems (MAJOR 1993, 186–9).

The five phases provide a comprehensive system for determining what set of things are consistent with each other and in what order events should proceed. The system of five phases thus provides the philosophical basis for theories of music, culinary taste, art, good government, ritual, divination, etc. For longer discussions, see HENDERSON 1984, MAJOR 1993, SMITH 1991.

Five Ranks *Goi* (J.) 五位

See the extended discussion in chapter 1 of the Introduction (pages 23–6).

Five sins *Gogyakuzai* (J.) 五逆罪

The five grave sins in Buddhism are usually listed as killing one's father, killing one's mother, killing an arhat, shedding the blood of a buddha's body, and causing dissension in the sangha. There is some variation in the items of this list, depending on the text one consults.

Five *skandha* (Skt.) *Goun* (J.) 五蘊

Since Buddhism denies that there is an essential self, it offers an alternative analysis of the human personality—the theory of the five *skandha,* translated variously as "aggregates" or "elements." The original term connotes a "heap," or random collection whose whole is no greater than the sum of its parts. That is, no "self" is created when the elements of the heap are piled together. The human personality consists of the five *skandha,* which are form, feeling, thought, volition, and consciousness. The *Heart Sutra* explicitly denies that any of the *skandha* has an essential core. In the words of the well-known formula, it says "Form itself is emptiness and emptiness itself is form," and then goes on to say that the same is true for all the other *skandha.*

Flower Peak Hua-shan, Hua-yüeh (Ch.) Kazan, Kagaku (J.) 華山, 華嶽

Hua-shan or Hua-yüeh (Ch.), literally "Flower Peak," is the western member of the so-called Five Peaks of China and stands in the province of Shensi. Hua-shan has several peaks and steep cliffs between which flows the Yellow River. Legend says that long ago the mountain was a single peak and the Yellow River flowed around it. Then the Giant Spirit of the Yellow River, Chü Ling 巨靈 (J. Kyorei), split the mountain open with his hand, allowing the Yellow River to flow through. Today one may still see the imprint of the god's fingers and palm atop Hua-shan, while his footprint is visible atop Shou-yang Mountain (BIRRELL 1993, 42; KZS #1152n).

Flowers in the eye *Ganchū no hana* (J.) 眼中華 | *Ganri no hana* (J.) 眼裏華
Flowers in the sky *Kūge* (J.) 空花 | 空華

Pressing a finger against the eyeballs causes spots to appear before the eyes (5.372). These are the "flowers in the eye" or "flowers in the sky." They are not existent in themselves but created in the eye of the observer. In the verses of *Zen Sand*, not only are the objects of the sensible world said to be flowers in the eye, but so also is awakening itself. Since the character for "sky" can also be read as "emptiness" (*śūnyatā*), the term can also be read "flowers of emptiness."

Flowers of emptiness ➛ **Flowers in the eye**

Foot ➛ **Inch and foot**

Forge ➛ **Fire pit and bellows, Tongs and hammer**

Forked hands *Shashu* (J.) 叉手

Monks carry the hands in one of two positions: *gasshō* 合掌 —palms flat together in "prayer position"—or *shashu* (literally, "forked hands")—the fork between thumb and first finger of one hand inserted into the fork of the opposite hand, both hands held flat against the chest (8.34). According to Mujaku Dōchū, *gasshō* is derived from an Indian ritual form, while *shashu* is a Chinese ritual form (quoted in ZGJT 187). The two positions have a bit of a *yin-yang* relation: when one enters the zendō, the hands are in *gasshō,* but when one exits, they are in *shashu*; when one approaches the altar for offering incense, they are in *shashu,* but when one returns from the altar to do three bows, they are in *gasshō.*

When standing or walking in their long robes, monks always have their hands either in *gasshō* or *shashu.* Almost any individual act—picking up a teacup or bowl, getting up from sitting in meditation, receiving something offered, etc.—is preceded and followed by a *gasshō*. *Shashu* is the default position: when not in *gasshō,* the hands are in *shashu.*

In contrast to either *gasshō* and *shashu* is **suishu.**

Four births *Shishō* (J.) 四生

In early Buddhist thought, living things were said to be born in four possible ways: from the womb (humans, mammals), from eggs (fish, birds, reptiles), from moisture (mosquitoes), and from transformation (butterflies, moths). This phrase is often paired together with *rokudō*, **six realms**, as a literary expression for *saṃsāra*, the cycle of birth and death.

Four *dharma-dhātu*, four dharma realms *Shihokkai* (J.) *Ssu-fa-chieh* (Ch.) 四法界

The four *dharma-dhātu* or dharma realms of Hua-yen Buddhism are generated through combination of the two basic elements: 事 (J. *ji,* Ch. *shih*), and 理 (J. *ri,* Ch. *li*), variously translated as "phenomenon" and "noumenon," or "fact" and "principle." The four realms are:

1. 事法界 (J. *jihokkai*, Ch. *shih-fa-chieh*), the realm of phenomena;
2. 理法界 (J. *rihokkai*, Ch. *li-fa-chieh*), the realm of noumena;
3. 理事無礙法界 (J. *riji muge hokkai*, Ch. *li-shih wu-ai fa-chieh*), the realm of unhindered mutual interpenetration of noumena and phenomena;
4. 事事無礙法界 (J. *jiji muge hokkai*, Ch. *shih-shih wu-ai fa-chieh*), the realm of unhindered mutual interpenetration of phenomena and phenomena.

Four propositions and the hundred negations *Shiku hyappi* (J.) 四句百非

The four propositions refer to Nagarjuna's tetralemma: 一異無有, or "identity, difference, negation, and affirmation." Logically, if P is any statement, then the four propositions are P, not-P, neither P nor not-P, both P and not-P. These basic four propositions are then manipulated to get the hundred negations. Each proposition contains the entire set of four, thus the four contain a total of sixteen. Since these all exist in each of the **three worlds** of matter, form, and formlessness, their total number is forty-eight. Each of these exists in an already arisen state and in an about-to-arise state, which makes ninety-six. Add to these the original four propositions to get one hundred propositions. Since these one hundred propositions are non-actual, they are called negations. Thus one hundred negations (ZGJI 148–9). This terminology arises in several kōan (e.g., *Heki* 73).

The phrase *uku muku* 有句無句 (*Kattō-shū* 35) refers to two of the four propositions. An affirmative proposition is *uku* 有句 and a negative proposition is *muku* 無句.

Four seas *Shikai* (J.) 四海

The term literally means "four seas," and in particular cases it can mean the seas in the four directions surrounding Mount Sumeru. But in most Zen verses, it usually connotes "everyone," "the world," "everywhere," and it would be inappropriate to translate it literally as if there were some strong connection with seas and oceans.

Four worlds *Shi sekai* (J.) 四世界

A reference to the **four *dharma-dhātu*** of Hua-yen Buddhism.

Fox, fox slobber ➛ Wild fox

Fu Daishi (J.) Fu Ta-shih (Ch.) 傅大師

Layman Fu Daishi (497–569) spent his life in extreme ascetic discipline. After being exposed to Buddhism, he lived with his family under a pair of sala trees at the foot of Pine Mountain. He did manual labor by day and talked about Buddhism to all and sundry in the evening. During the famine of 527–529 he sold his house and fields to buy food for the starving villagers. Eventually the emperor installed him in a temple near the capital, but he left it to build a Buddha Hall again under the sala trees. In 548 he once more gave away all his fields and property to the people and proposed to immolate himself after a month of fasting; by this act he hoped to alleviate the suffering caused by the recent military disasters. However, nineteen of his disciples volunteered to take his place and hundreds of others engaged in extreme ascetic practices in order to persuade him not to immolate himself. Some years later, when famine again struck the land, Fu Daishi once again gave everything away and worked in the fields to help the poor (ZD, 262–4).

Fulling block and club *Chinsho* (J.) 砧杵

This character compound consists of 砧 (J. *chin*), a stone block upon which silk cloth was pounded, and 杵 (J. *sho*), the wooden pestle or club for pounding. Women's work in ancient China included weaving silk and making clothes (a man's work was tilling in the fields and fighting in the army). After weaving, the finished silk cloth was extremely stiff and had to be beaten on a fulling block to make it soft enough to wear (10.43, 10.343, 14.406). In poetry, the fulling block and club became a metaphor for a solitary wife whose husband had been sent to the frontier (e.g., 10.339). See Birrell for other literary uses of this metaphor (1986, 307).

Fun (J.) 分

A small unit for measuring length in ancient China. In the first to third centuries CE, it was 0.2304 cm; in the third century, 0.2412 cm; in the sixth and seventh centuries, 0.2951 cm; and during the seventh to tenth centuries, 0.311 cm (*Shinjigen*, 1224–5).

Fundamental ➛ *Honbun*

Gai* ➛ *Moxa

Garuda (Skt.) *Konji* (J.) 金翅

The characters 金翅, which literally mean "golden winged," are sometimes read *kinji*, but following Nakamura (1981, 422), we read them as *konji*. The *garuda* bird is one of the **Eight beings** in Buddhism.

In Indian legend it is the fierce, beautiful, and magnificent king of the birds. In Chinese Buddhist literature the *garuda* of Indian legend starts to resemble the great **roc** of Chinese legend, described in texts like *Chuang-tzu*, ch. 1. Gold in color, its wing span is said to be 3,360,000 miles wide. It lives around the base of Mount Sumeru, the gigantic central mountain of the universe.

General Li Ri Shōgun (J.) 李將軍

General Li Kuang 李廣, a Han general, early established a reputation as a fierce fighter, a clever strategist, and a leader admired by the common soldier. He rendered eminent service in fighting the Hsiung-nu nomads, who came to know and respect him. He was a great archer. Among the many stories told about him, it is said that one day he mistook a rock for a tiger in the grass and shot an arrow with such force that it imbedded itself in the rock. In another story, he shot down two eagles with one arrow. His biography is ch. 109 of the *Shih-chi* (see WATSON 1993A, *Han* II, 117–28; also WATSON 1974, 12–23).

Gensha ➛ ***Shasanrō***

Genshi hantoku (J.) 減師半徳

Phrase 15.4 reads "If your *kenshō* is equal to your teacher's, then you have diminished his merit by half; if your *kenshō* surpasses your teacher's, then you are competent to receive transmission." The phrase *genshi hantoku*, however, can also be translated to mean that the disciple's merit, not the teacher's merit, is diminished, e.g., "If your view equals your teacher's, you have less than half your teacher's virtue" (CLEARY and CLEARY 1977, 74, 326; see also ASAHINA 1935, 171; SASAKI 1975, 57). Some reference texts are ambiguous on this point (IRIYA 1991, 199). *Zen Sand* follows those commentators who say that it is the teacher's merit that is diminished (AKIZUKI 1972, 212; ZGJT 107; WATSON 1993B, 115).

Giant Spirit ➛ **Flower Peak**

Giant statue of Chia-chou *Kashū no daizō* (J.) 嘉州大象

Chia-chou was a district in present-day Szechuan. The giant statue was a Buddhist image, 360 feet in height, carved into the sheer face of a cliff at Wu Hsia, one of the gorges on the upper Yangtze River (KZS #1130n).

Giant turtle *Kyogō* (J.) 巨鼇

The Chinese, like the Indians, had a myth that the earth rested ultimately on the back of a great turtle. The turtle thus came to symbolize solidity, such that pillars, posts, stone tablets, etc. were often placed on stone footings designed in the shape of a turtle (WILLIAMS 1976, 403–6).

In addition, for the ancient Chinese, "heaven is round, earth is square" and "heaven is round, earth is flat." Sarah Allan has argued that, because of these associations, the early Chinese associated the turtle with the shape of the cosmos, since its shell has a round dome over a flat base that roughly resembles five squares (ALLAN 1991). Perhaps for this reason the turtle shell was used for divination (plastromancy) along with the scapula bones of oxen (scapulimancy). The remains of these turtle shells and scapula bones are the famous "oracle bones."

Gibbon, orangutan *Shōjō* (J.) *Hsing-hsing* (Ch.) 猩猩

This term is translated into English as "gibbon," "orangutan," and sometimes "ape." Several kinds of legend about the gibbon circulated in early China (SCHAFER 1963, 208–10; 1967, 231–3) but in *Zen Sand*, important is the fact that a gibbon, like a parrot, was thought to be able to talk.

Gimlet ➛ **Awl**

Goi ➛ **Five Ranks**

Going out at night *Yakō* (J.) 夜行

In the Chinese city, citizens were not allowed to walk the streets at night. Curfew was imposed at the end of the day when the city gates were closed and the drums in the towers were beat to mark the time. Anyone found on the streets thereafter was taken into custody and brought before court. Curfew remained in place until the next morning when the city gates were opened again to the sound of drum beats. Phrase 4.304 reads "The watchman violates the night curfew." To catch violators, watchmen patrolled the streets at night. That is, to enforce the rule, they themselves broke the rule (ZGDJT 520a, ZGJT 207).

Gōko ➛ **River and lake**

Golden crow ➛ **Sun**

Golden chain on the sick monkey *Kinsa byōen* (J.) 金鎖病猿

The golden chain on the sick monkey is the awakening of the practitioner. To shatter the golden chain on the sick monkey (劈金鎖於病猿, 12.17) is to cut the practitioner's attachment to his own awakening (ZGJI 567).

Golden dragon ➛ **Sun**

Goose *Kari, gan* (J.) 雁 | 鴈

The goose is a migratory bird that travels long distances. It is often depicted in Chinese poetry as crossing high across a serene sunset sky. It has a special nuance, however, frequently appearing in stories of people separated by long distances but bound together by loyalty or love. See, for example, the story of **Su Wu**, who was kept in captivity by the Hsiung-nu for nineteen years until he tied a letter to a goose that flew all the way back to the capital and was shot down by the emperor. In poetry, the goose is sometimes associated with the lone wife thinking of her far-off husband who has been conscripted as a soldier to man a frontier garrison or to work on the Great Wall. The People's Republic of China postal service still uses as its logo the image of a goose carrying a letter (BIRRELL 1993, 308; WILLIAMS 1976, 216–7).

Great thousand-realm universe ➛ **Three thousand worlds**

Hair-cutter sword *Suimōken* (J.) 吹毛劍

Among the many famous swords in Chinese legend is the hair-cutter sword, *Suimōken*, so called because it was so sharp that it would cut a hair that was blown by the wind against it (*Heki* 100).

Han Hsin (Ch.) Kanshin (J.) 韓信

Along with **Chiang Liang** and **Hsiao Ho**, Han Hsin was one of the "Three Heroes" who assisted Liu Pang in establishing the Han Dynasty (see **Han Kao-tsu**).

Although Han Hsin was of lowly birth, he was recognized as a man of courage and ability. Through his loyalty and military accomplishments, he rose through the ranks, finally becoming commander-in-chief, and was rewarded with a fiefdom of his own within the empire. During his time, however, other people tried on several occasions to involve Han Hsin in plots to seize power from the emperor. On one occasion, Han Hsin knew that the emperor suspected him of disloyalty and that he would most likely be taken prisoner and executed if he appeared at court, but nevertheless he decided to make a court appearance (5.48). He uttered the famous words, "When the cunning hares are dead, the good dog is boiled." Eventually he was killed in a court intrigue. See the biography of the Marquis of Huai-yin in WATSON 1993A, *Han 1*, 163–84.

Han Kao-tsu (Ch.) Kan no Kōso (J.) 漢高祖

The founder of the Han Dynasty is usually known by his posthumous title, "Han Kao-tsu," which literally means "High ancestor of the Han (Dynasty)." His polite name was Liu Chi (劉季), his familiar name Liu Pang (劉邦). The story of the fall of the Ch'in Dynasty (221–215 BCE) and the establishment of the Han Dynasty is one of the great historical dramas of China. Ch'in Shih Huang Ti, the First Emperor of Ch'in, had succeeded in conquering the many warring states of early China and forging a single Chinese empire in 221 BCE. Though he proclaimed that his Ch'in Dynasty would last for 10,000 generations, the new empire was riven by internal revolt a few years after its founding when the emperor died in 209 BCE. While the Ch'in empire under the Second Ch'in emperor tried to maintain its hold on power, many rebel groups, angry at the cruel and authoritarian First Emperor, openly revolted and eventually coalesced around two figures, the fierce general **Hsiang Yü** and the more temperate Liu Pang, who went on to become Han Kao-tsu, the first ancestor of the Han Dynasty.

Liu Pang was leading a group of men who had been ordered to work on the First Emperor's great mausoleum (where many centuries later the terra cotta warriors would be discovered). Fearful of the extremely harsh working conditions, his men started to run away. Since the punishment would be the same for failing to prevent his men from running away or for actively revolting, Liu Pang released all his men. Thus began the career of the commoner who rose to found an empire. Phrase 7.34 reads, "One man started the trouble and destroyed the seven ancestral shrines" (quoted from the "Faults of Ch'in" by Chia I in *Shih-chi*, ch. 6; WATSON 1993A, *Qin*, 80). This is a way of saying that the rebellion started by Liu Pang eventually led to the overthrow of the Ch'in Dynasty and the establishment of the Han Dynasty. Noble families had ancestor temples whose size reflected their social rank. Lesser-ranking nobility had ancestor temples with one, three, or five shrines, depending on rank. Only the emperor had a temple with seven ancestral shrines: a central shrine to the first ancestor and then three shrines each on the left and right sides of the corridor leading to the central shrine (Morohashi 6.433).

In the beginning, Hsiang Yü and Liu Pang cooperated in their struggle to overthrow the Ch'in. Through a combination of tactical skill and good fortune, Liu Pang managed to enter and capture the Ch'in capital city of Hsien-yang 咸陽 in Kuan-chung, "the land within the passes" (the event referred to in 4.183). The two had earlier agreed that whoever entered the capital first would take possession of it for himself. Later historians say that Liu Pang treated the deposed Ch'in ruler with courtesy, forbade his generals from looting the capital, and instituted a compassionate legal code to replace the former harsh Ch'in code. That is the point of 7.51, "He destroys the stronghold within the passes and takes the maps and documents"—the maps and documents being the only things needed for proper government. Four months later, however, Hsiang Yü arrived, forcing Liu Pang out. Hsiang Yü immediately put the former Ch'in ruler to death, allowed his men to sack and burn the city, and carved up the country, parceling out fiefs to his generals and allies. Liu Pang was given a remote piece of land far to the south, an area called Han.

Phrase 8.394 reads "By daylight, he repaired the hanging road; at night, he crossed over from Ch'en-ts'ang." This verse is about the military tactic used by Liu Pang when he withdrew from Hsien-yang. There are differing accounts of this tactic. Shibayama (Shiba 236) says it was devised by Chōryō (Ch. Chang Liang), but ZGJT 445 and KZS #923 say it was devised by Kanshin (Ch. Han Hsin). In 206 BCE, when Hsiang Yü arrived and forced him out, Liu Pang left by a hanging road through a narrow gorge, a trestle structure made of poles inserted sideways into the cliff face. Shiba 236n and KZS 923n say he repaired this hanging road, giving the impression he would return again to attack from this direction, but he actually advanced using the old road from Ch'en-ts'ang and successfully surprise-attacked his enemy. This is the story as transmitted in footnotes to Zen texts. The *Shih-chi*, ch. 8, however, says that Liu Pang burned the hanging road behind him to give the impression he would never return. Four months later he returned to begin the long campaign that ended in victory over Hsiang Yü in 202 BCE. See also the explanation in WADDELL 1996, 78.

Hsiang Yü was militarily more powerful and on more than one occasion Liu Pang faced certain defeat but managed to escape final destruction with just a handful of men. Throughout his struggles with Hsiang Yü, Liu Pang was assisted by the so-called "Three Heroes" 三傑, the military strategist **Chiang Liang**, the general **Han Hsin**, and the judicious administrator **Hsiao Ho**. With their aid, Liu Pang forged military alliances with local rulers, rallied his soldiers to fight for him out of loyalty, won the trust of the common people, and finally defeated Hsiang Yü to become the founding ancestor of the Han.

Han-shan (Ch.) Kanzan (J.) Cold Mountain 寒山

Han-shan (J. Kanzan), whose name means "Cold Mountain," is a legendary figure who may have been an actual person, a poet during the mid-T'ang period (around 750). He is always paired together with his friend Shih-te 拾得, (J. Jittoku, "the foundling"). According to legend, Han-shan and Shih-te were two recluses who lived near a Buddhist monastery but who were much too eccentric and irreverent to actually join the monkhood. Han-shan wrote poetry and lived on the mountain behind the monastery; Shih-te worked in the monastery kitchen and fed leftovers to Han-shan. They are always depicted as saying and doing nonsensical things, gleefully laughing at some private joke. In iconography, Han-shan is often shown with paper and a writing brush in hand; Shih-te is often shown with a broom. Han-shan and Shih-te were said to be reincarnations of **Mañjuśrī** and **Samantabhadra**, respectively. Han-shan's poetry has been translated many times.

Heaven and earth ➛ under **Eight trigrams**

Hermit Lin Rin shoshi (J.) 林處士

Hermit Lin is Lin Ho-ching 林和靖 of the Sung Dynasty, who built a small hut for himself on West Lake, did not enter town for twenty years, and was buried in the grave he dug for himself beside his hut. He never married and had no children. He grew plum trees and raised cranes, thus was nicknamed "Plum-wife, crane-child" (Morohashi 14551.222).

Hexagram ➛ under **Eight trigrams**

Ho jewel Wa (J.) 和

Phrase 16.15 reads "The jewel smith presented a treasure, but the king of Ch'u punished him." A man named Pien Ho 卞和 found a large piece of jade and presented it to his king, but the king thought it was a mere stone and punished Ho by cutting off his left leg. When the king died and his successor took the throne, Ho again presented the jade and this time had his right foot cut off. He wept for three days and nights after which the king enquired again. This time the jade was recognized to be truly a jewel (Shiba 404; WATSON 1964, Han Fei Tzu, 80). *Shih-chi,* ch. 81, says this jade was the jewel at the center of the conflict between Lin Hsiang-ju and the king of Ch'in, where it is called "the disc of Chao" 趙璧 (J. *chōheki*). See **Hsiang-ju**.

Hōgyō ➛ **Taking in and letting go**

Holy monk ➛ ***Shosō***

Holy attendant ➛ ***Shōji***

Honbun (J.) The fundamental 本分

This term is used in two senses. In ordinary usage, it means one's duty or social responsibility. But in Zen, it indicates the fundamental nature of a realized person, unconcerned with either awakening or ignorance. It also indicates actuality itself, as-it-is-ness itself (ZGJI 60, ZGDJT 1168a, ZGJT 430).

The "fundamental" was also the first of the "eight realms," a standard system for organizing phrases in early Zen phrase books. See the explanation on page 14 above.

Horn-hooking antelope *Tsuno o kakeru (kakuru) reiyō* (J.) 掛角羚羊

Shinjigen §6279 has this entry: "(1) An antelope that, at night when it sleeps, hooks its horns into the branches of a tree to avoid harm; (2) A Zen expression used in poetry for skill so subtle nothing about it can be said to be skillful" (see also ZGDJT 877).

Houbai (Ch.) Kōhaku (J.) 猴白

A thief named Houbai one day met a woman named Houhei 猴黒 (J. *Kōkoku*) standing next to a well. She said, "I dropped a bag with 100 gold coins down this well. Get it for me and I will give you half as reward." Houbai went down the well but could find nothing. When he climbed out, he found his clothes had all been stolen. In other versions of this story, Houhei says she has dropped her hairpin into the well (ZGJT 463).

Houhei ➛ Houbai

Hsi-liu Garrison Sairyūei (J.) 細柳營

The Hsi-liu ("Slender Willow") Garrison was a military base in Hsi-liu, an area southwest of Hsien-yyang in Shensi during the Former Han period. Because of the severity of its military discipline, the term "Hsi-liu Garrison" came to imply a crack military unit or a military base of superior officers (*Shinjigen*, 773).

Hsi-shih, Hsi-tzu (Ch.) Seishi (J.) 西施, 西子

See also **Wu**. Hsi-shih is one of Chinese history's most beautiful women. At age sixteen, Hsi-shih was already the perfection of beauty. Her complexion was said to rival the moon, her eyebrows were long and arched, her hair was long and glossy, and her swaying walk had the alluring grace of the languorous willow. Frowning made her even more beautiful. Homely girls tried to imitate her beautiful frown but merely succeeded in making themselves ugly (*Chuang-tzu*, ch. 14). Her "bones were white polished jade," a phrase that in classical Chinese indicated great beauty. She was the woman of whom it was originally said that her beauty could "overturn a state, topple a city" (傾國傾城). Her beauty is measured in such political terms because her story is inextricably woven into the history of the long struggle between the powerful kingdoms of **Wu** and Yüeh during the Spring and Autumn period (770–403 BCE) in Chinese history. Hsi-shih's beauty led to the final destruction of the kingdom of Wu in 473 BCE. See SHU (1981B) for an account of the legend of Hsi-shih.

Hsi Wang Mu ➛ Queen Mother of the West

Hsia-hui (Ch.) Kakei (J.) 下惠

Liu Hsia-hui 柳下惠 (J. Ryū Kakei) was a sage teacher in the Chou Dynasty. Instead of emulating his sageliness, his disciples copied only his rough casualness and his irreverence for ritual (8.419; ZGJI 471, 472). He is mentioned in *Mencius* II, A, 9: "Liu Hsia-hui… was not ashamed of a prince with a tarnished reputation, neither did he disdain a modest pose. When in office, he did not conceal his own talent, and always acted in accordance with the Way. When he was passed over he harboured no grudge, nor was he distressed even in straitened circumstances" (LAU 1970, 84).

Hsiang-ju (Ch.) Shōjo (J.) 相如

In the Warring States period, the minor state of Chao had for generations possessed an unusual jade disc (趙璧 *chōheki*, "the disc of Chao"), made from the **Ho jewel**. The king of the powerful state of Ch'in heard of the disc and offered to trade fifteen cities for it. Chao, a militarily weak state, could not refuse and sent Lin Hsiang-ju 藺相如 with the disc to the Ch'in king. Hsiang-ju, however, perceived that the king had no real intention of ceding fifteen cities and said to the king, "The jewel has a flaw. If you will give it to me, I will show you where it is." Once he had the jewel back in his hands, he backed himself up against a pillar and threatened to smash the disc against the pillar if the king did not follow proper ritual, fast and purify himself for five days, and honestly offer the fifteen cities. The king promised to do so. While waiting for the king to complete five days of preparation, Hsiang-ju sent one of his attendants dressed in disguise back to Chao via a secret route with the disc. On discovering this, the king of Ch'in reluctantly agreed with Hsiang-ju that killing him would not bring back the disc and so released him (*Shih-chi,* ch. 81, YANG and YANG 1979, 139–51).

Hsiang-wang (Ch.) Zōmō (J.) 象罔

Hsiang-wang is a person who appears in the *Chuang-tzu,* ch. 12. Hsiang-wang means "shape indistinct." WATSON translates the name "Shapeless" (1968, 128–9). One day the emperor was traveling on the river and lost his pearl in the water. He sent three people to find it. They were "Knowledge" 知, Li Chu 離朱 (also known as **Li Lou**), famous for his keen eyesight, and Ch'ih-kou 喫詬, whose name means "Wrangling Debate." When none of them was able to find it, he sent Hsiang-wang, "Shapeless," who succeeded in recovering it. This is the story behind phrase 14.401. The story personifies the claim that the pearl of wisdom cannot be obtained by knowledge, discrimination, or language; it can only be obtained by something without precise shape or form.

Hsiang Yü (Ch.) Kōu (J.) 項羽

The Ch'in Emperor was the first to unify the many states of China into a single empire under one ruler in 221 BCE. Though he predicted that his empire would last ten thousand generations, in fact, internal rebellion brought the dynasty to an end in 207 BCE after a mere fifteen years. The spontaneous rebellions and uprisings that erupted in different parts of the Ch'in empire in 210 BCE were at first uncoordinated and easily suppressed by the Ch'in army. Then Hsiang Yü, who was from a military family in Ch'u, arose to unite the different rebellions into an organized resistance. He swiftly established a reputation as a forceful leader (9.6) and a cunning tactician superior to the generals that the Ch'in deployed against him. He was famous for his great strength. It was said he could lift great three-legged metal cauldrons weighing 4000–5000 *kin* and could uproot mountains. His warhorse, Dapple, could run 1000 *ri* in a day (14.669).

He was, however, not the only able military leader in the field. Liu Pang, who later became the first Han emperor (**Han Kao-tsu**), had started his own rebellion and gathered forces loyal to him. Liu Pang was supported by **Chang Liang**, **Han Hsin**, and **Hsiao Ho**, who managed to secure important territories for Liu Pang, keep his army properly supplied, and provide him with good political advice. In the final confrontation, which is one of the great dramatic moments in Chinese history, Hsiang Yü found himself surrounded by Liu Pang's forces. In the night, he heard the Han enemy forces all singing the songs of Ch'u as if they had already conquered Ch'u, his territory. The *Shih-chi* records his last moments. He had with him his beautiful Lady Yü and his horse Dapple. He composed this song, which appears in *Zen Sand* as verse 21^{+}.30:

My strength plucked up the hills,
My might shadowed the world,
But the times were against me,
And Dapple runs no more.
When Dapple runs no more,
What then can I do?
Ah, Yü, my Yü,
What will your fate be? (WATSON 1993A, *Han I*, 45)

He then mounted his horse and with 800 cavalry broke through the Han ranks and escaped into the night with several thousand Han forces in pursuit. The Han pursued him, but in battle after battle, Hsiang Yü cut through his enemy until he was finally backed up against the Yangtze River. When he had first set out to take the empire years earlier, he had led his forces across the Yangtze. At the end, he refused to cross back over and instead turned to face the Han forces who surrounded him, cut his own throat, and died. In phrase 20.4 his concubine Yü applauds his fighting spirit: "The soldiers of Han already hold the land. From all four sides come voices singing the songs of Ch'u. The great king has exhausted all his strength. But how can I, a lowly concubine, go on living ?"

For historical background, see LOEWE 1986, esp. 110–19 and WATSON 1993A, *Han I*, 17–48.

Hsiao Ho (Ch.) Shōka (J.) 蕭何

Hsiao Ho (?–193 BCE) was one of three advisors who assisted Liu Pang, later known as **Han Kao-tsu**, in establishing the Han Dynasty. Originally, Hsiao Ho had been prime minister of his local state, acquiring a reputation for thorough understanding of laws and letters. Subsequently he became the military advisor responsible for keeping Liu Pang's army well stocked with provisions.

When Liu Pang entered the Ch'in capital city of Hsien-yang, he did not allow his army the usual looting of the enemy's treasures. Only Hsaio Ho gathered up the maps and documents that had been used by the Ch'in ministers and officials (7.51).

According to legend, when Hsiao-ho fought against the Shan-yü, the chief of the Hsiang-nu nomads, he deceived and captured his enemy by saying that he had a silver city in his home country that he was willing to sell (7.216, ZGJI 351, IRIYA et al., 1992, II, 122). But biographies of Hsiao Ho make no mention of his ever taking part in such military action (Burton Watson personal communication, 4 November 1997). Hsaio Ho's biography is ch. 53 of the *Shih-chi.* See WATSON 1993A, *Han I*, 91–8.

Hsiao-hsiang (Ch.) Shōshō (J.) 瀟湘

Hsiao-hsiang is the name of the place where the Hsiao River empties into the Hsiang River, near Lake Tung-t'ing in modern Hunan Province, a location famed for its beauty. Phrase 5.383 is "Night rain passes through Hsiao-hsiang," describing one of the Eight Famous Views of Hsiao-hsiang 瀟湘八景.

Hsieh San-lang ➛ under **Shasanrō**

Hsü Yu ➛ **Shun**

Hua-liu (Ch.) Karyū (J.) 驊騮

In Chinese legend a fabulously swift horse, one of eight prize horses belonging to King Mu of the Chou Dynasty (HYDCD 12.867).

Huai-an (Ch.) Kaian (J.) 槐安

In the legend of Huai-an, which means "Acacia Peace," a man, whose custom was to drink beneath the large acacia tree by the side of his house, one day was escorted by mysterious envoys through an opening in the tree. Inside he discovered an entire empire, whose king invited him to marry his daughter. Subsequently he became an official in this kingdom and assumed the post of governor of one of its frontier states. After a twenty-year career, however, the king put him in a chariot and sent him back out of the acacia tree, whereupon he awoke from his drunken slumber. In some versions of the story, it is said that a pot of yellow millet that the man had put on to boil before he fell asleep was still only half-cooked. The story is told in Bauer and Franke 1964, 93–107. For some references to the development of this story in novels and drama, see Yao 1985, 149–50. Hakuin named one of his major works *Kaiankokugo* 槐安國語 (*Words from the Land of Acacia Peace*).

Huang-ti ➛ Yellow Emperor

Hui-yüan (Ch.) Eon (J.) 慧遠

Hui-yüan is an early Chinese Buddhist (334–417) cited as a precursor to the development of organized Pure Land Buddhism in China. He formed the White Lotus Society at the temple Tung-lin ssu 東林寺 on Mount Lü for studying the *Nirvana Sutra* and reciting the Buddha's name. The verse at 14.728 can be taken two ways. (1) Hui-yüan's head has turned white from his great efforts to save people by including them in the Lotus Society. (2) Hui-yüan, however, did not include everyone in the society. He excluded Hsieh Ling-yün (Sha Rei-un in J.) saying he was not pure of heart. The verse can then be taken to mean, as Hui-yüan is already white-haired with age, we must hurry if we are to do something for Hsieh Ling-yün's salvation.

Hun-tun (Ch.) Konton (J.) 混沌 | 渾沌

From *Chuang-tzu*, Inner chapter 7: The emperor of the South Sea was called Shu [Brief], the emperor of the North Sea was called Hu [Sudden], and the emperor of the central region was called Hun-tun [Chaos]. Shu and Hu came to meet from time to time in the territory of Hun-tun, and Hun-tun treated them very generously. Shu and Hu discussed how they could repay his kindness. "All men," they said, "have seven openings so they can see, hear, eat, and breathe. But Hun-tun alone doesn't have any. Let's try boring him some!" Every day they bored another hole, and on the seventh day Hun-tun died (translation adapted from Watson 1968, 97).

Imperial avenues *Gyogai* (J.) 御街

The imperial avenues were roads that originated at the imperial palace and were reserved for the exclusive use of the emperor and members of his immediate family when he went forth in procession on official functions. Needham (1971, 4–8) has described the extensive system of highways constructed by the First Emperor of Ch'in. In the vicinity of the capital, these highways were nine-chariot-lanes wide, with the inner lanes reserved for the emperor and his entourage. Although Morohashi 10157.33 says that the term 御街 refers to walkways within the grounds of the imperial palace, the way the term is used in Zen verses suggests there must have been grand impressive avenues that led away from the imperial palace into the distance (see, for example, 14.238, 14.685).

Inch and foot *Sun, shaku* (J.) 寸, 尺

A *sun* (J.) is a unit for measuring length, one-tenth of a *shaku* (J.). A *shaku* was about a foot long (23 cm during the Han period, 31 cm during the T'ang; see *Shinjigen* 1224–5). In *Zen Sand*, *shaku* and *sun* have been translated "foot" and "inch" (e.g., 4.262).

Suntetsu (J.) 寸鐵, "an inch of iron," is a dagger or other other small weapon. *Sanzun* (J.) 三寸 "three inches" is sometimes an abbreviation for 三寸舌 "three-inch tongue" (7.261). These two phrases are combined (三寸鐵 "three inches of iron") to refer to the Buddha's tongue, and by extension to the Buddha's teaching (7.261, 14.723).

Indra's net *Teimō, Taimō* (J.) 帝網

帝 refers to 帝釋天 (J. Taishakuten), the Buddhist name for the Indian god Indra. Indra had a net of jewels, each of which reflected the reflections in all the other jewels, creating infinite reflections within reflections. This image was used in Hua-yen philosophy to explain the mutual interrelatedness of all causes and conditions (8.296). ZGS 8.186 gives the reading *teimō* while Oda 1954, 1214, gives *taimō*.

Inexhaustible lamp *Mujintō* (J.) 無盡燈

This well-known image has two meanings. First, the lamp of the dharma is inexhaustible in the sense that it is always alight and never stops burning. And second, just as the flame of one lamp can light another lamp, and it in turn can light another, and so on and on, so also one person's awakening can trigger another person's, and that person can awaken another, and so on without end. Tōrei, the disciple of Hakuin, named his work *Mujintōron* with just this image in mind (ZGDJT 1209a).

Inferno at the gate *Ōmon no wazawai* (J.) 殃門累

"Inferno at the gate" is a Chinese proverbial saying that connotes a great misfortune with unseen consequences. When the city gate of the Sung capital was on fire, people used the water in the ponds to put out the conflagration, with the result that all the fish died. The fire at the gate led to the death of the fish (Yang Liyi 1987, 170–1).

Inka (J) Accreditation 印可

Inka is an abbreviation for *inka shōmei* 印可証明, or accreditation to teach. If the Zen teacher judges that the practitioner's own awakening has fully ripened and that the practitioner has the ability to teach others (two different things, 宗 and 説), then the teacher will confer an accreditation recognizing maturity of awakening and giving permission to teach. It is sometimes a paper document but not always so. Different lineages have different traditions for conferring *inka*.

Intercalary month ➛ **Repeated month**

Intimate, intimate friend *Chiin* (J.) 知音

The term *chiin* literally means "know sound" but is translated here as "intimate friend." The term refers to the story of Po Ya 伯牙 and his close friend Chung Tzu-ch'i 鍾子期. When Po Ya played his *ch'in* lute, Chung Tzu-ch'i knew without needing explanation what Po Ya felt. When Chung Tzu-ch'i died, Po Ya smashed his lute and never played again, for he felt no one could understand his music. This story can be traced to the *Lieh-tzu*, a Taoist work that is now thought to have been written about 300 CE, though composed in the style of the third century BCE. See *The Book of Lieh-tzu* (Graham 1990) for the story of Po Ya (109–10) and Graham's Introduction for discussion of the dating of the text. See also chapter 4 of the Introduction, pages 56–61 above.

Iron hammerhead without a socket *Muku no tettsui* (J.) 無孔鐵鎚

An "iron hammerhead without a socket" is a solid chunk of iron without any way to attach a handle. It is a metaphor for something that cannot be grasped and manipulated (ZGDJT 1202d, ZGJT 441).

Iron ring of mountains ➛ under **Sumeru**

Iron Ox of Shen-fu *Senbu | enpu) no tetsugyū* (J.) 陝府鐵牛

Shen-fu is an old name for an area on the Yellow River in modern Shenhsi. The Iron Ox was the local protector god. It was said to be huge in size—so huge that it supported the Yellow River on its back, with its head south of the river and its tail north. It was said that Yü the Great used the Ox at the time of the great flood (KZS #1130n).

Isle of Parrots Ōmushū (J.) 鸚鵡洲

The Isle of Parrots, paired together with the **Yellow Crane Pavilion**, is a famous landmark in Hubei Province on the Yangtze River. The picturesque Isle of Parrots lay in the waters right across from the Yellow Crane Pavilion (14.36).

Jade rabbit ➛ under **Moon**

***Jambū* tree** ➛ under **Sumeru**

Jewel in the clothing, jewel in the robe *Eju* (J.) 衣珠

The *Lotus Sutra*, ch. 8, contains the parable of the jewel sewn into the robe. A destitute man visiting a close friend gets drunk and falls asleep. Without waking him, the friend sews a jewel into the lining of his robe and then leaves. Years later when the man is in desperate poverty, they meet again. The friend then tells the other how he has been carrying around a jewel in his robe without knowing it. The *Lotus Sutra* goes on to explain that this jewel is a symbol for the wisdom that the Buddha planted in human beings ages ago.

Jōjūmotsu, jōjū no mono (J.) Permanent things 常住物

Literally "permanent things," this term can also refer to the fixed property or possessions of a monastery (ZGDJT 555d). The offices of a monastery are called *jōjū*, as opposed to the *dōnai*, meditation hall, which houses the monks who do not have office.

Jōmyō (J.) 浄名 Another name for **Vimalakīrti.**

Jujube *Natsume* (J.) 棗

The jujube was considered by Taoists to be a fruit of immortality.

Kalpa (Skt.) *fō, kō* (J.) 劫

A *kalpa* is an ancient Indian unit for measuring time. Immeasurably long, its length is explained metaphorically as the length of time it takes for the *kalpa* stone to wear away.

Doomsday fire *Gokka tōnen* (J.) 劫火洞然

The great fire in the *kalpa* of destruction is called *gokka tōnen*, here translated "doomsday fire." The image of a great conflagration that consumes the entire universe is so dramatic that, apart from any cyclical theory of universes, the term *gokka tōnen* came to be used as a symbol of total annihilation (see *Heki* 29).

Four *kalpa* *Shikō* (J.) 四劫

This describes the cycle of creation and destruction of universes. The first *kalpa* is that of creation or formation, *jōkō* (J.) 成劫, in which a universe is created; its six worlds come into existence and sentient beings populate them. The second is the *kalpa* of existence or continuation, *jūkō* (J.) 住劫, in which buddhas appear in the universe and the life span of human beings first decreases from 84,000 years to 10 years at the rate of 1 year every century and then increases again to 84,000 years. The third is the *kalpa* of destruction, *ekō* (J.) 壞劫, during which the universe is destroyed in a great fire. The fourth is the *kalpa* of annihilation, *kūkō* (J.) 空劫, in which there is nothing. Then the cycle starts all over again. Each such *kalpa* is actually a long *kalpa* composed of twenty smaller *kalpa* (ZGDJT 427a).

***Kalpa* stone** *Gosseki* (J.) 劫石

The characters 劫石, read *kōseki, kōshaku, gōseki*, or *gosseki,* are here translated *kalpa* stone. How long is a *kalpa*? Imagine a huge stone cube forty *yojana* in width, length, and height. A *yojana* is a measure of distance, estimated by different sources at anywhere from 7 kilometers (Nakamura et al., 1995, 814) to 160 kilometers (Daitō 1991, 370). Suppose a *yojana* is 100 kilometers; then the *kalpa* stone is a huge cube 4,000 kilometers on each side. Once a century, an *apsara* (angel) from heaven flies across its surface, dragging its gossamer sleeves across the stone's face. A *kalpa* will have passed when the friction from its sleeves has worn away the stone.

Kankosui ➛ *Kareta*

Kannon ➛ **Kuan-yin**

Kanzan ➛ **Han-shan**

Kao-tsu ➛ **Han Kao-tsu**

Kareta (J.) Withered 枯れた

Kareta, meaning "old, withered," is an extremely important concept in Zen practice. A mature monk of accomplishment strives to embody Zen totally, to radiate awakening, wisdom, and compassion in every word and deed. But because this awakening itself becomes an object of conceptualization and attachment, the truly serious practitioner must undergo a second awakening to rid himself of the first awakening, the "stink of Zen" (5.151, 5.152). Thus beyond the mature stage of Zen practice in which a person's awakening radiates through words and deeds, there is a further stage in which the practitioner exudes no trace of awakening. Once the practitioner rids himself of any whiff of Zen awakening, he is called *kareta*, "withered."

Many images express the complete ordinariness of the *kareta* master, such as the "**big bug**" 大蟲, the tiger who has lost its tail and teeth. Another image is that of an "old drillhead" (*kankōsui* 閑古錐 or *rōkosui* 老古錐), which suggests a wizened master who has lost the sharpness of youth. *Kan* 閑 implies that the master lives at leisure (ZGDJT 178d, ZGJT 68, 488). *Kareta* is the quality that, in the fine arts, Hisamatsu labeled "lofty dryness" 枯高 (1971, 31).

Karōtō (J.) Fireplace, keeper of the fires 火爐頭

"Fireplace" is a tentative translation for *karōtō* in 7.404. *Karōtō* also appears in ZGJI 287, 火爐頭無賓主 *Karōtō ni hinju nashi* "In the fireplace, there is no guest or host." The ZGJI commentary is that "all are host when everyone is gathered in a circle around a fire." The character 頭 may indicate a person as well as a place. Just as the monk in charge of vegetable gardening is the 園頭 and the monk in charge of the bathhouse is the 浴頭, so also 火爐頭 may be the monk in charge of the fireplaces and stoves. The original source seems to be *Jōshū-roku* 320, 師示衆云 老僧三十年前在南方火爐頭有箇無賓主話。 直至如今 無人擧著 (Suzuki and Akizuki 1964, 55). James Green translates this, "The master instructed the assembly saying, 'Thirty years ago when I was in the south, I was the monk in charge of the fires and I had a conversation without host and guest. To this very day no one has said anything'" (1998, 104).

Kāśyapa (Skt.) Kashō (J.) 迦葉

Kāśyapa, also known as Mahākāśyapa, "Great Kāśyapa," is considered one of the

Buddha's ten great disciples. Kāśyapa, reputed to be the most advanced in ascetic practice, is often paired and contrasted with Ānanda, reputed to be the most learned and to have had the best memory for all the Buddha's discourses (ZGJI 287). The strengths of the two disciples thus illustrate the two sides of Zen practice. Kāśyapa and Ānanda are listed as the second and third patriarchs following Śākyamuni Buddha.

Kāśyapa figures in the important kōan "Śākyamuni raises a flower" (MMK 6). In front of all his followers who had gathered to hear a discourse, the Buddha merely held up a flower in silence. Only Kāśyapa understood and smiled. The Buddha said, "I have the true Dharma eye, the marvelous mind of nirvana. This I now transmit to you, Mahākāśyapa" (ZD 152, also 255–6). This story, which cannot be traced to any Indian source, is used to illustrate the "mind-to-mind transmission" of Zen. See pages 56–8 above for a discussion of this story and its relation to the long Chinese tradition of silent communication.

In East Asian literature, Kāśyapa is sometimes called *Onkō* (J.), "drinker of light," a translation of the Sanskrit name (e. g., 7.66 "The 'drinker of light' raised his eyebrows at the flower"). It is said that Mahākāśyapa's body glowed so brightly, other people found it hard to look at him; it was as if he had drunk the light of the sky, sun, and moon (Jimbo 1974, 153).

Keeper of the fires ➛ ***Karōtō***

Kenkon ➛ **Heaven and earth**

Ki (J.) Dynamism, energy, impulse, action 機

In Zen texts, *ki* 機 and *zenki* 禪機 are extremely difficult to translate. The character 機 (J. *ki* or *hata*) originally meant a weaver's loom and in many phrases is used with this meaning (10.326, 10.449, 14.144, 14.572). It connotes a mechanism and is part of the modern Japanese compound *kikai* 機械 "machine." In other branches of Buddhism, *ki* denotes the potential of the practitioner or disciple (Inagaki 1984, 178) and by extension the practitioner or disciple himself (ZGDJT 191d). The Zen term *kien* 機緣, which means "disciple and master," shares this meaning (ZGJT 78).

In Zen, however, *ki* often refers to some movement of mind (ZGDJT 191cd) in contrast to stillness or solidity. For this reason, Japanese Zen texts sometimes put the *furigana* for *hataraki*, "working," "activity," "action" beside the character.

In the kōan curriculum described in the Preface, the first classes of kōan are *hosshin* 法身 "Dharma-body" and *kikan* 機關, translated "dynamic activity." Here the *ki* in *kikan* is *hataraki*, Zen activity, and to be contrasted with *hosshin* "Dharma-body," and stillness in Zen. This contrast thus resembles the relation between "body" and "function" (體用) in Chinese philosophy, or between *hajū* and *hōgyō* (**taking in and letting go**). See also page 21 above.

Sometimes *ki* indicates the method in contrast to the goal. Here *ki* refers to the teacher's skillful means rather than to the practitioner's potential. Thus the term *kikan* is interpreted as the mechanism or skillful means by which a teacher guides his students (ZGJT 78). The Zen teacher's skill is usually described as both totally disguised and deadly sharp (7.60, 7.382). In these contexts, *ki* has been translated "blade," taking a cue from compounds like *kihō* 機鋒 "*ki*-spear" (7.60, 7.111, 7.383).

Although *ki* usually indicates Zen activity or Zen energy—and therefore something that one would want to cultivate—in some verses the movement of mind labeled *ki* is considered negative, as in "Once forget all impulses (*ki*), then great emptiness is flawless" (8.18, see also 7.262).

Because of the great variety of meanings, *Zen Sand* has deliberately avoided trying to translate *ki* with a single word. Instead, *ki* has been translated "loom," "impulse," "blade," "dynamism," "energy," "act," "power," "potential," "spirit" depending on what seemed the best to fit the particular context (10.92). The compound *kizen* 機前 has similarly been translated by a variety of different expressions, depending on context: "in one fell swoop" (10.81).

Kin ➛ **Catty**

King Wen Wen Wang (Ch.) Bunnō (J.) 文王

King Wen is the legendary virtuous hero who started the rebellion against the tyrant Chou 紂, the last king of the Yin Dynasty. His son King Wu 武王 (J. Buō), completed the rebellion and assumed the throne as the first king of the Chou 周 Dynasty (see *Shih-chi*, ch. 4). King Wen was early eulogized in the *Book of Songs* (nos. 235, 240, 244); subsequent Chinese philosophical and poetic literature frequently alludes to these florid images (7.350, 8.217, 8.320, 8.350, 8.358, 9.23, 10.453, 10.454). His son, King Wu, is mentioned less frequently in *Zen Sand*, but there is a well-known passage taken from the Mencius in which he is mentioned (8.355).

Phrase 10.453 reads: "On the day that King Wen became emperor, he paid respect to King Chi three times." King Chi is King Wen's father. In Confucian ritual, a son visits his father twice daily to inquire about his well-being. King Wen, being extraordinarily filial in spite of his position, visited his father three times.

King Wu ➛ **King Wen**

Ko Hung (Ch.) Kakkō (J.) 葛洪

Ko Hung (283–343) is an important figure in Taoism because of his role in developing alchemical practices for the attainment of immortality. Born in Danyang, southeast of Nanking, he later took the name Pao-p'u-tzu 抱朴子, which is the title of his major book. Losing his father when he was 13, he thereafter sold firewood to buy writing materials and spent his time copying books to study. From early youth he started to learn the practices for becoming a *hsien*, Taoist immortal, but got caught up in the numerous rebellions and civil disturbances of the time. His life took him to many places, but important for *Zen Sand* is the fact that at one point he went south and secluded himself on the mountain **Lo-fu-shan** 羅浮山 (J. Rafuzan), where he practiced *lien-tan* 煉丹 (J. *rendan*), the alchemy of converting cinnabar to gold (NOGUCHI et al. 1994, 69–70).

Kōjō ➛ **Directed upwards**

Konron ➛ *K'un-lun*

Ku-su Terrace *Kosotai* (J.) 姑蘇台

The Ku-su Terrace was a pleasure pavilion built by King Fu-ch'ai for his beautiful concubine **Hsi-shih.** In Chinese poetry, it became a symbol for the inevitable fall of pomp and power (ZD #196n). Phrase 16.22 reads: "On the Ku-su Terrace, we do not discuss the *Spring and Autumn Annals*. In front of a patch-robed monk, would you theorize about the dark mystery?" To discuss the *Spring and Autumn Annals* means to discuss history (ZGJI 694). "Dark mystery" is associated with philosophical Taoism. See **Three mysteries** below.

Kuan-yin Kannon (J.) 觀音

The Bodhisattva of Compassion is known by several names: Kannon (J.) or Kuan-yin (Ch.) 觀音, the "observer of sounds"; Kanzeon (J.) or Kuan-shih-yin (Ch.) 觀世音, "the observer of the sounds of the world"; and Kanjizai (J.) or Kuan-tzu-tsai (Ch.) 觀自在, "free observing."

The Bodhisattva started off in India as the male Avalokiteśvara (Skt.), but in China came to be depicted in female form. Sometimes he/she was depicted as a young innocent maiden, sometimes as a sexually alluring mature woman, sometimes as a maternal figure. In iconographic study it is common to distinguish several varieties of Kuan-yin: the Thirteen-headed Kuan-yin, the Kuan-yin of a Thousand-Hands and Thousand Eyes, the White-robed Kuan-yin, the Horse-headed Kuan-yin, etc. Continuing research has shown the influence of Tibetan stories, Chinese local folk legends, and even Christian images of Mary in shaping the images of Kuan-yin (YÜ 1994, 2001).

More important to Zen kōan practice is the image of Kuan-yin as presented in the *Heart Sutra* (J. *Hannya Shingyō*) and the *Kuan-yin Sutra* (J. *Kannon-gyō*), the 25th chapter of the *Lotus Sutra*. The *Heart Sutra* presents the bodhisattva giving a discourse on *prajña* wisdom, the teaching on emptiness. The 25th chapter of the *Lotus Sutra* depicts the compassion and skillful means of the bodhisattva, who is capable of appearing in any one of thirty-three forms in order to save beings in peril (7.87). These two sutras thus present the two basic thrusts of Ch'an/Zen Buddhism: wisdom and compassion.

The Bodhisattva also appears in folk stories, some of which are relevant to the understanding of *Zen Sand* phrases (e.g., 14.166). On the Golden Sands River lived a beautiful girl whom many men hoped to wed. She said, "I will teach you how to chant sutras and will consider any man who learns the Universal Gateway Chapter of the *Lotus Sutra* in one evening." Next morning, twenty men had learned the Chapter. She refused them, saying, "I cannot marry you all but will consider any man who can learn the *Diamond Sutra* in one evening." By the next morning there were ten who could do this. Again she refused, saying, "I will consider anyone who can learn the *Lotus Sutra* within three days," and only a young man named Ma could do this. She and Ma were wed, but when she entered their house, she at once fell dead and her body rotted away. Then a monk appeared who together with Ma opened her coffin and discovered only a golden chain on the bones of a skeleton. The monk said, "This was Kuan-yin, who changed her physical appearance to help you." And with that he disappeared. Ever since, in the Shensi Gorge there are many people who can chant sutras (Yü 2001, 419–20).

Heki 89 is an important kōan: "How does the Bodhisattva of Great Compassion use her thousand hands and thousand eyes? Just like her hand reaching behind her for the pillow at night."

K'un-lun (Ch.) *Konron* (J.) Chaos 渾崙 | 崑崙 | 渾淪

The term *k'un-lun* has several meanings. K'un-lun-shan (J. Konronzan) refers to a mountain, or mountain range, that is said to be the home of the fabled immortal, the **Queen Mother of the West**. There is also a tribe of people called the K'un-lun.

In Taoist creation myth, *k'un-lun* is the formless chaos that preceded the division into *yin* and *yang*. The term can also simply mean "black" (7.56). In Zen texts, *k'un-lun* is used with all these meanings without clear discrimination, but since in *Zen Sand* it seems to refer to formless chaos quite frequently, it has either been translated "chaos" or left as *k'un-lun* (5.129, 5.130, 5.131, 5.132, 5.208). For a review of recent scholarship, see Birrell 1993, 183–5.

In 4.222 *konron* is used adverbially: 渾崙呑棗 *Konron ni natsume o nomu* "He gulps down the jujube whole." *Konron ni* is used adverbially to show the swallowing is done blindly, in one gulp, without discrimination. Since the jujube was thought to be a fruit of immortality, this verse puns on the meaning of *konron*.

Lake Tung-t'ing Dōteiko (J.) 洞庭湖

Lake Tung-t'ing in Hunan Province is the largest freshwater lake in China. Chinese poetry regularly referred to it and its "Eight Scenes" as symbols of scenic beauty.

Land within the passes ➤ **Han Kao-tsu**

Landscape

Several terms, such as 前山 "mountain in front"; 中山 "central mountain"; 主山, "host mountain"; 前川 "river in front"; and others make little sense unless understood as parts of an idealized landscape in which there is a central mountain in the north facing south, two flanks of lesser mountains curving out east and west and then turning south to form a rough horseshoe, and two streams flowing in from east and west to meet in a single stream flowing out south. According to Chinese *feng shui* 風水 concepts of siting, these roughly are the features of a properly sited grave, a house, a formal garden, and the imperial city plan. See, for example, 6.125: "The main mountain is high, the surrounding mountains are low." The term for the central mountain in the north, "host mountain," implies that the surrounding mountains are "guest mountains" (Iriya et al. 1992, II, 233; Hirata 1982, 244).

Layman P'ang (Ch.) Hō koji (J.) 龐居士

Hō koji, or Layman P'ang, is another interesting lay figure in the lore of Chinese Ch'an. Although a lay person, he was just as awakened to Zen as any monk. In fact, the impression given by his Recorded Sayings is that both his wife and his daughter were just as awakened as any monk. He is the main figure of the well-known kōan "Layman P'ang and Good Snowflakes" (*Heki* Case 42), which contains his oft-quoted verse at awakening (10.217-8). His recorded sayings have been translated into English (Sasaki et al. 1971).

Li (Ch.) Ri (J.) 李

"Fourth son Li." See under **Chang.**

Li Kuang ➛ **General Li**

Li Ling (Ch.) Riryō (J.) 李陵

Li Ling, a military man like his famous grandfather, the Han **General Li** Kuang, served Emperor Wu during the Former Han Dynasty, leading expeditions against the Hsiung-nu nomads on the far northwestern borders of the empire. In his last expedition, he led a small force of 5,000 footsoldiers into Hsiung-nu territory and encountered the Shan-yü, the leader of the Hsiung-nu, with a cavalry of 30,000. So able was Li Ling's leadership that his little force of 5,000 was able to inflict great damage upon the cavalry. Far outnumbered, Li Ling was eventually captured alive. The Hsiung-nu much admired his great military leadership (18.16) and kept him prisoner for twenty years (10.397).

Li Ling's biography forms part of the chapter on Li Kuang in Pan Ku's *History of the Former Han* and is translated into English in Watson 1974, 24–33.

Li Lou (Ch.) Rirō, Riru (J.) 離婁

In Chinese legend, in the age of the Yellow Emperor, Li Lou was a man famous for his extremely sharp eyesight. It was said that he could distinguish the hair tips of **autumn down**. He is often paired with **Shih K'uang**, famous for his extremely sharp hearing. See the story at **Hsiang-wang**.

Li Po (Ch.) Rihaku (J.) 李白

"Li Po (701–761)," according to NIENHAUSER, "generally shares or competes with **Tu Fu** for the honor of being the greatest of the T'ang poets" (1986, 549). He cultivated a reputation for eccentricity and love of wine, depicting himself in his poetry as constantly drunk and gazing at the moon (WALEY 1950). *Zen Sand* includes numerous verses taken from his poems (in the Fourteen-Character Verses alone, 14.7–8, 14.67–8, 14.144–5, 14.154, 14.181, 14.219–20, 14.223, 14.335, 14.421, 14.448, 14.585, 14.663–4, 14.696). Some of them are among the most memorable verses in T'ang poetry. There are numerous studies of his poetry and many translations (see NIENHAUSER 1986, 549–51).

Li Ssu (Ch.) Rishi (J.) 李斯

Li Ssu (280?–208 BCE) was Chancellor of the Ch'in Dynasty (221–207 BCE), the first dynasty to succeed in uniting all of China into one empire. Li Ssu is remembered as the official responsible for poisoning Han Fei-tzu, his competitor for office, and for the notorious Burning of the Books (BODDE 1938: 62–77, 80–4). After the death of the First Emperor, the powerful eunuch Chao Kao 趙高 (J. Chōkō) used forged documents to eliminate the crown prince and in his place install on the throne the youngest son, Hu-hai 胡亥 (J. Kogai), a youth of only twenty-one. Then Chao Kao assumed virtual control of the government and in the name of Hu-hai managed to have Li Ssu himself executed under imperial edict. This is the incident behind verse 16.15. Li Ssu and his son were sentenced to receive the "five punishments" (branding the forehead, cutting off the nose, cutting off the feet, death by flogging, exposure of the head and corpse in the marketplace). In the end, though, it seems he was actually executed by being cut in two at the waist. This was followed by extermination of his family to three degrees (BODDE 1938, 52). Li Ssu's biography constitutes ch. 87 of the *Shih-chi* (WATSON 1993A, 179–206). BODDE 1938 presents a detailed study of the man, with its own translation of *Shih-chi*, ch. 87.

Life-and-death illness *Kōgō* (J.) 膏盲

In ancient Chinese physiology, *kō* 膏 was the fatty tissue at the bottom of the heart, and *gō* 盲 was the diaphragm separating the chest cavity from the intestinal organs. The confined area between these two regions, *kōgō*, was considered very hard to treat medically. To say that "the illness has got into the *kōgō*" implied that there was no hope for the patient. Used as a metaphor for the life-and-death struggle of Zen practice (14.395, ZGDJT 310a).

Life-stealing magic charm *Datsumyō no shinpu* (J.) 奪命神符

Literally "a divine tally for stealing your life away," this is a "metaphor for the spiritual power attained after the experience of the Great Death" (ZD 279). The phrase *datsumyō no shinpu* is often paired together with the "dharma cave of talons and tusks" (J. *hokkutsu no sōge;* see **Talons and tusks**). Both refer to the strenuous and challenging practices of the Zen training hall.

Light and dark *Kōin* (J.) 光陰

The two characters literally mean "light and shadow" or "light and dark" but the compound together means "time," since the passing of the days is the constant alternation of daylight and darkness. In most Zen monasteries, at dawn and dusk—that is, when dark changes to light and back again—a monk marks the time by beating a mallet against a thick wooden slab. The slab bears the inscription 生死事大, 光陰可惜, 無常迅速, 時人不待: "Life and death are the great matter. Be watchful of your time. All is impermanent and passes swiftly away. Time waits for no one."

Ling-yün ➛ **Reiun**

Liu Hsia-hui ➛ **Hsia-hui**

Lo-fu-shan (Ch.) Rafuzan (J.) 羅浮山

The mountain Lo-fu-shan in Canton Province in south China is strongly associated with Taoism (8.2, 14.576). In addition to its scenic beauty and clean water, it is famous for herbal drugs, since its humid climate favors the growth of the kind of trees and herbs used in Taoist alchemy. The mountain began its association with Taoism when **Ko Hung** and his wife came in 326–334 to research methods for converting cinnabar to gold as a means of gaining immortality (Noguchi et al. 1994, 588).

Lo-yang Rakuyō (J.) 洛陽

Situated in the northeast region of present-day Honan Province, the city of Lo-yang was important in both the political and religious history of China. During the Sui and T'ang periods, the Chinese emperors maintained two capital cities, moving the imperial residence back and forth between **Ch'ang-an** in the west and Lo-yang on the east. Though Lo-yang was known as the Eastern capital, it was always the stronger economic power, benefiting from its geographical position as the center through which goods from the south intersected with the vast east-west river transportation system (14.682). When the emperor was in residence in Lo-yang, the city became the center for the civil service administration and for military command. Impressive monuments like the Tower of Five Phoenixes (14.238) were built. Its markets were filled with hustling sellers and wealthy buyers (14.441–2). Though it was outshone by the greater glory of Ch'ang-an, nevertheless the name of the city of Lo-yang also connoted beauty, urbanity, and sophistication (14.33, 14.708).

Lo-yang figures prominently in the history of Buddhism in China. The first

Buddhist monks and first Buddhist texts to reach China were housed in the White Horse Temple, built in Lo-yang (10.116). The first major translations of Buddhist texts were done in Lo-yang, and the first patriarch of Ch'an, **Bodhidharma**, was said to have visited Lo-yang and been so impressed by the beauty of the temple Yung-ning ssu (J. Einei-ji) that he put his hands together and uttered "Namu, Namu." Eka Daishi, the monk who became the Second Patriarch after cutting off his arm before Bodhidharma, was born in Lo-yang. The drama of the **Sixth Patriarch** was partly played out in Lo-yang: Ho-tse Shen-hui (J. Kataku Jinne), the monk who campaigned to have his master Hui-neng declared the Sixth Patriarch, came from the temple of Ho-tse ssu in Lo-yang, the temple that gave him his name.

Long, wide tongue *Kōchōzetsu* (J.) 廣長舌

Kōchōzetsu (J.), literally "long, wide tongue," is one of the thirty-two marks of the Buddha's body. It is often used as a metaphor for the Buddha's skillful eloquence: when he spoke, every listener heard in his own language. A related expression is *sanzun tetsu*, 三寸鐵, "three inches of iron," which also refers to the Buddha's tongue and his eloquence in explaining the Dharma.

Lord Five Ram-Skins Goko taifu (J.) 五羖大夫

Lord Five Ram-Skins is Po-li Hsi or Pai-li Hsi, 百里奚 (J. *Hyakuri Kei*), a statesman famed for his virtue, who served under Duke Mu of Ch'in (659–621 BCE). When the state of Ch'u took Po-li Hsi captive, Duke Mu offered five black ram skins for his return. He was thereafter known as Lord Five Ram-Skins (WATSON 1993A, *Qin*, 9). Duke Mu made him prime minister of Ch'in and within seven years Po-li Hsi had so strengthened the state that it had become the hegemon over the other states (YANG and YANG 1979, 67; WATSON 1993A, *Ch'in*, 96–7).

Lou-lan (Ch.) Rōran (J.) 樓蘭

The minor state of Lou-lan lay several hundred miles past the Jade Gate barrier on the far western border of the Han empire. It was one of many such minor states that the Han empire hoped to use in its continuing fight with the Hsiung-nu nomads. In the introduction to his novel titled *Rōran* (translated into English as *Lou-lan Stories* [INOUE 1979] and made into a movie, *Rōran*), the Japanese historical novelist Inoue Yasushi says that Lou-lan was first noticed by the Chinese about 120 or 130 BCE and disappeared about 77 BCE. To the average Han Chinese male subject to conscription into the army, "Lou-lan" probably suggested a faraway desolate outpost from which one would very likely never return.

Lu Pan (Ch.) Roban (J.) 魯般

Lu Pan is the name of a famous carpenter-mechanic who is said to have lived at the time of Confucius. He is now worshipped as the god of carpenters (GILES 1939, #1424).

Lu-neng ➛ NAME under **Sixth Patriarch**

Lung Men ➛ **Dragon Gate**

Mahāsthāmaprāpta (Skt.) Shih-chih (Ch.) Seishi (J.) 勢至

The Bodhisattva Mahāsthāmaprāpta is associated with Amitābha Buddha. He stands to the right of Amitābha Buddha as guardian of wisdom, while **Kuan-yin** stands to the left as guardian of compassion.

Maheśvara (Skt.) Makeishura (J.) 摩醯首羅

Maheśvara was originally the Indian god Śiva, creator god of the universe. In Buddhism Maheśvara is said to rule the universe in defense of the Dharma. He is extremely fierce in appearance, with three eyes and eight arms (NAKAMURA 1981, 1278; ZGDJT 976c). Phrase 14.105 contains a pun: "Maheśvara knows numbers but cannot distinguish colors, but when you enter willows, that's green, and when you enter flowers, that's red." The character for "color" 色 can also mean "form" (as opposed to emptiness), and in Buddhism Maheśvara is the god of the realm of form (色界).

Maitreya (Skt.) Mi-lo (Ch.) Miroku (J.) 彌勒

Just as Śākyamuni is the Buddha of the present age, Maitreya is the Buddha of the future. Even now, Maitreya sits in deep *samādhi* in the Tuṣita heaven awaiting final reincarnation into this world. In Chinese Buddhism the so-called laughing Buddha, Pu-tai 布袋 (J. Hotei), is said to be an incarnation of Maitreya.

Man from Tseng ➛ **Mo Yeh**

Mandarin ducks ➛ under **Matrimonial harmony**

Mañjuśrī (Skt.) Wen-shu (Ch.) Monju (J.) 文殊

The Bodhisattva Mañjuśrī is familiar to most Zen monks, since the principal image of the *zendō* (meditation hall) is that of Mañjuśrī. There he is called the *shosso-san* (in correct pronunciation, *shōsō* 聖僧 "holy monk"). He has an attendant called the *jisha* or ***shōji***. When a monk patrols the zendō with *keisaku* stick in hand, he is the embodiment of Mañjuśrī and the *keisaku* is Mañjuśrī's sword.

In iconography, Mañjuśrī is often paired with the Bodhisattva **Samantabhadra** (Fugen Bosatsu). Mañjuśrī, representing wisdom 智, stands to the left of Śākyamuni Buddha, while Samantabhadra, representing principle 理, stands to the right. Mañjuśrī is often shown riding a lion while Samantabhadra rides an elephant.

In Zen kōan practice, Mañjuśrī is the bodhisattva of highest attainment of wisdom, so much so that he is called the "teacher of the seven Buddhas." In this role he appears in the *Vimalakīrti sūtra* as the only one of the Buddha's disciples willing to make a sick call on the ailing Vimalakīrti (the other bodhisattvas having begged off, unwilling to let the shallowness of their wisdom be compared to the depth of Vimalakīrti's). In MMK 42, Mañjuśrī, who is so advanced in wisdom, is unable to bring a woman out of samadhi, while Mōmyō, a novice bodhisattva, is able to do so at once.

Matrimonial harmony, symbols of

Zen verses and phrases sometimes use symbols of matrimonial harmony, exploiting the fact that they connote a harmony of paired opposites, the necessity of two sides of a duality, ineffability, etc.

BIRDS WITH SHARED WINGS *Hiyoku no tori* (J.) 比翼鳥

Birds with shared wings were a Han symbol of matrimonial harmony. One bird had only one right eye and one right wing; the other had one left eye and one left wing. They could fly only when joined together (CAMMANN 1953, 210).

BRANCHES WITH A COMMON GRAIN *Renri no eda* (J.) 連理枝

The stem of one tree is grafted into the root of another tree. The branches of the resulting tree are said to display a common grain (*Shinjigen* 1003).

MANDARIN DUCKS *En'ō* (J.) 鴛鴦

Because of their beautiful plumage, which resembled the luxurious robes of imperial courtiers, mandarin ducks symbolized wealth and luxury (10.119). But they also symbolized love and matrimonial harmony. Male and female mandarin ducks were said to develop so strong an attachment that if one died, the other would pine away. The poet Wen T'ing-yün 溫庭筠 wrote, "With you, I would at once be your mandarin duck mate, and set to rest all my desire to traffic with the world" 與君便是鴛鴦侶, 休向人間覓往還 (KSMKJT §378). Images of pairs of ducks were often embroidered onto the covers of bedding that a bride presented at the time of marriage. Phrase 14.69 uses this imagery in a Zen context: "The mandarin ducks that I've embroidered I will let you see, but the golden needle that made them, do not give to another."

PAIRED FISH, FISH WITH PAIRED EYES *Himoku* (J.) 比目

Himoku literally means "paired eyes." The *himoku* is a fish with only one eye. Only when two fish align themselves side by side can they see to swim (*Shinjigen* 549). They are similar to the *hiyoku*, BIRDS WITH SHARED WINGS (CAMMANN 1953, 210; BODDE 1975, 155).

The parallelism in Chinese verse often required the poet to say the same thing in two ways. Phrase 14.597 is "If I could be paired fish with you, I would not begrudge even death. Let us become mandarin ducks and we will not envy even the immortals."

Mi-lo ➣ Maitreya

Min Tzu-ch'ien (Ch.) 閔子騫

Min Tzu-ch'ien, a disciple of Confucius, was famed for his filial piety (*Analects* XI, 4). His mother died when he was a child. His father married again and had two children by the second wife. She favored her children and neglected Min Tzu-ch'ien. The father noticed this neglect and in anger ordered the second wife to leave his home. But Min Tzu-ch'ien said, "If mother is here, then one child is cold; If mother is gone, won't three children be cold?" (WALEY 1938, 245–6; 10.423)

Mite *Shōmei* (J.) 蟭螟 | 蜼螟

In Chinese legend, the mite is an insect so tiny it can make its nest in the whiskers of a mosquito. It symbolizes the extremely small (Morohashi 19119.112; ZGDJT 236.b).

Mo-tzu (Ch.) Bokushi (J.) 墨子

Mo-tzu, one of the philosophers of the so-called Hundred Schools, is remembered for his theory of universal love and his studies in logic and in military science. 8.367 contains the phrase "Mo-tzu lamented the dyeing of thread." This refers to ch. 3 of the text *Mo-tzu*: "Watching a dyer of silk at work, Motse [Mo-tzu] sighed, saying: What is dyed in blue becomes blue, what is dyed in yellow becomes yellow.... Therefore dyeing should be done with great care. This is true not only with silk dyeing; even a country changes its color in response to its influences" (MEI 1977, 18).

Mo Yeh sword *Bakuya* (J.) 鏌鎁劍

In the ancient state of Wu, the swordsmith Kan Chiang 干將 (J. *Kanshō*) made a pair of fabulous swords. He named these swords, one male and one female, after himself and his wife Mo Yeh. One version of their story has been inserted into the Commentary of Case 100 of the *Hekigan-roku* (omitted in CLEARY and CLEARY 1977). The story is as follows:

> One summer the wife of the King of Wu, while enjoying the evening cool, embraced a metal pillar and felt herself pregnant. Subsequently she gave birth to a chunk of iron. The King of Wu had Kan Chiang make this chunk of iron into swords. Three years went by and two swords were finally made, one male and one female. Kan Chiang presented the female sword to the king but secretly kept the male sword. The king kept his in a case but he kept hearing the sound of a voice crying from inside. The king consulted his ministers, one of whom said, "There are male and female swords. The one that is crying is lonely for the male sword." The king was very angry and had Kan Chiang taken into custody with the intention of having him killed. Kan Chiang, who had already hidden his sword inside a roof post, managed to tell his wife Mo Yeh, "The sun rises from the north door; on the south mountain, there is a pine; the pine is born from a stone; the sword

is inside that." His wife afterwards gave birth to a son whom she named Mei-chien Ch'ih 眉間赤 (J. Mikenjaku). When the son turned fifteen, he asked his mother about his father. His mother then related the above incident. They split open the post and found the sword that had been so long in her thoughts. After that, night and day, the son was filled with the desire to avenge his father. Hearing of this, the King of Wu spread the word there would be a reward for the person who could capture Mei-chien Ch'ih. Immediately Mei-chien Ch'ih fled. Presently he met a traveler who said, "You must be Mei-chien Ch'ih." "That's right." The traveler said, "I am from Mount Tseng 甑 (J. Shō). I have been thinking for a long time about how you could avenge your father." Ch'ih said, "My father was innocent but he was forced to drink poison tea. What is your idea and what do you want?" The traveler said, "What I really need is your head and the sword." Ch'ih then promptly gave him the sword and his own head. The traveler took these to the King of Wu, who was very pleased. The traveler said, "Please heat up some oil and let's stew this." Right away the king threw Ch'ih's head into a cauldron. The traveler then lured the king, saying, "The head is not cooking." When the king went to take a look, the traveler from behind cut off the king's head with his sword and dropped it into the cauldron. There the two heads bit at each other. The traveler was afraid that Ch'ih would not win, so he decapitated himself to assist him. Then there were three heads all biting at each other. In a while, all three heads were cooked (IRIYA et al. 1992, III, 271–2; see also BIRRELL 1993, 221–7 for other versions of the legend).

The image of the sword is frequently used as a symbol of the ***zenki*** of the enlightened master (7.580, 14.77). But the image of the Mo Yeh sword is doubly interesting, since the man from Tseng uses it to cut off his own head (10.145). *Zen Sand* verses mention the Mo Yeh sword, the female sword, but in the above story the female Mo Yeh sword is given to the king and it is the male Kan Chiang sword that is used by the man from Tseng.

Monkey cry 猿啼 | 猿叫 | 猿聲

In Chinese literature, the call of the monkey was thought to resemble a human voice crying in sadness and grief. Phrases 14.248, 14.116, and 14.432 make this connection explicit, but the nuance is there in many other verses (10.250, 10.183, 14.152, 14.193, 14.201, 14.353, and others).

Moon

The moon is one of the most frequently used images in Chinese poetry, and in Zen is one of the standard images for Zen awakening. There were, however, complex legend and lore about the moon in Chinese literature, some of which is relevant to understanding the Zen use of this image. Since a toad was said to live in the moon, expressions like *kosen* "lone toad" refer to the moon, as in 14.224: "The lone toad shines brilliant, the thousand mountains are still, at the long, drawn-out roar, heaven and earth are startled." The "lone toad" implies the moon, and the moon is here used to refer to Zen awakening. The verse then can be read as an expression of the two sides of Zen awakening, stillness and startle, ***hajū*** and ***hōgyō*** (see also 10.279). The moon is also called "cassia circle" 桂輪 (J. *keirin*), because a great cassia tree is said to grow on the moon (7.122). The cassia is a type of cinnamon tree, whose bark is used for fragrances and spices. These images can be combined, as, for example, in "toad cassia" 蟾桂 (10.534).

A rabbit or hare was also said to live in the moon. Perhaps this is a Chinese remnant of the *Jātaka* tale about the hare in the moon. The moon was also called "jade rabbit" because a jade rabbit was said to pound the elixir of immortality underneath the cassia tree. 14.540 reads "Deep in the white clouds, the golden dragon dances. Within the blue waves, the jade rabbit is startled." Here golden dragon refers to sun and jade rabbit to moon. The moon in the waves is a standard image for the realization of awakening in the busyness of daily life.

Chinese folk legend said that a rabbit became pregnant if it gazed at the moon and that a pearl was conceived when moonlight entered the open mouth of an oyster shell. These are the associations behind *Heki* 90. To the Chinese, the pearl was associated with the moon; the *yin* of the moon congealed within an oyster to create a pearl. The pearl was also considered a wish-fulfilling gem, and by association, in some contexts, the pearl symbolizes enlightenment itself (see **Black dragon pearl**). Because pearls are round like an eyeball and luminous like the moon, they were ground up and made into a medicine for eye ailments (Schafer 1963, 242–4).

Morning clouds, evening rain ➛ Clouds and rain

Moth eyebrows *Gabi* (J.) 蛾眉

"Moth eyebrows" were considered a sign of great feminine beauty (14.4, 14.93, 14.122, 14.423). Reference books give the explanation that beautiful **eyebrows** were long and curved like the antennae of a moth (e.g., Morohashi 33082.10), but Birrell says that moth eyebrows were "thick dark eyebrows" made by applying kohl in a thick broad line over and beyond the natural line of the eyebrow (1986, 319). A beautiful woman's eyebrows were also said to resemble the shape of long narrow willow branches which rose upwards and whose ends curved gracefully down (14.407).

Mount of Five Elders Gorōhō (J.), Wu-lao-feng (Ch.) 五老峯

The Mount of Five Elders is Mount Wu-lao (Ch.), a famous mountain in Chiang-hsi Province, considered a great scenic site because of its five peaks. Li Po built a dwelling here (ZGDJT 362). It was said the first three peaks belonged to the human world, while the other two belonged to the gods (ZGJI 659; 14.227, 14.528, *Heki* 34).

Mount Wu-t'ai Wu-t'ai-shan (Ch.) Godaisan (J.) 五臺山

The great mountain Wu-t'ai-shan is located in north Shan-hsi Province. Wu-t'ai means "Five Peaks." The mountain has a center cone, the lowest of the five, and four other peaks in each of the four directions, the highest of which reaches 9,500 feet above sea level. The mountain, said to be the residing place of the Bodhisattva Mañjuśrī, is one of the four Buddhist mountains of China, the others being P'u-t'o-shan in the east (home of Kuan-yin), O-mei-shan in the west (home of P'u-hsien), and Chiu-hua-shan in the south (home of Ti-tsang). Wu-t'ai-shan, with more than a hundred temples on its slopes, is a popular pilgrimage site. Pilgrims on the mountain roads are careful to treat everyone they meet, whether beggar or peasant, with great reverence, since it is known that Mañjuśrī has appeared to pilgrims in such disguise (ZGDJT 350a).

Mountain monk *Sansō* (J.) 山僧

Sansō "mountain monk" is used as a first person pronoun, equivalent to "I," "me."

Mountain of blades ➛ Five hells without interval

Moxa *Gai* (J.) 艾

Moxibustion is a treatment in traditional Chinese medicine in which small lumps of dried moxa, or mugwort grass, are burned on the skin.

Musk deer ➛ Deer musk

Mustard seed *Ikke* 一芥

A mustard seed is tiny, but in these verses, it can cover the whole world (12.4).

Nata, Prince Nata Taishi (J.) 那吒

Nata (Skt. Nalakuvara) is another Indian deity adopted into Buddhism as one of its protectors (14.28, 14.454). A powerful demon-king, he is one of the five sons of Bishamonten (Skt. Vaiśravaṇa) and is traditionally represented as extremely fierce in appearance, with three faces and eight arms (7.361, 7.388, 7.429, 7.430). In every hand he wields an iron club, a symbol of his tremendous destructive power. His ferocity allows no approach (5.295; ZGJI 370 and 374, ZGJT 356).

Kattō-shū Case 261 is one of the first *hosshin* kōan: "Prince Nata cut his flesh and returned it to his mother, cut his bones and returned them to his father; then, revealing his true appearance and wielding his great spiritual power, he expounded the Dharma for his mother and father." This kōan is based on the following story. When he was born, Nata immediately started to cause havoc by overturning the palace and trying to pull the tendons from a dragon. Fearing that he might eventually cause great misfortune, his father tried to have him killed. At this Nata was enraged. With a knife, he cut off all his own flesh and gave it back to his mother; he cut up all his own bones and gave them back to his father. He thus repaid his debt to his parents and, free from their authority, he went to the realm of ultimate bliss in the West to serve the Buddha (MOCHIZUKI 1958, 3995; Anthony YU 1983, IV, 131).

Night-shining jewel *Yamyōju* (J.) 夜明珠

The night-shining jewel (7.396) was so called because it was so brilliant it glowed even at night. It is thus an apt symbol for the undimmed light of Buddha-nature (ZGJT 1239b). Several of the jewels could be strung together to make a jewel screen 夜明簾 (14.683). There is a possibility that the night-shining jewel was the phosphorescent eyeball of a whale (SCHAFER 1963, 237). Needham suggests that it was a stone cut from mineral fluorspar imported into China from Syria. Such a jewel would glow when heated or scratched in dim light (NEEDHAM and RONAN 1978, 71).

Nine heavens *Kyūten* (J.) 九天

There is more than one explanation possible for the term "nine heavens" (14.288, 14.383, etc.). Nine heavens would result if heaven were divided into the traditional Chinese 3 x 3 grid: one heaven would be assigned for each of the eight directions and the center. The term could also refer to heaven conceived as 9 vertical levels (Morohashi 167.472).

Nine mountains and eight seas ➛ Sumeru

Nine-tiered imperial palace *Kyūjūjō* (J.) 九重城

"Nine-tiered palace" (7.98) is a literary term to indicate the residence of the emperor (HYDCD 1–740).

Nine years facing the wall ➛ under **Bodhidharma**

North Star *Hokuto* (J.) 北斗

Hokuto, literally "north dipper," refers to the constellation known as the Big Dipper in the West. The full phrase is "Northern dipper, seven stars" 北斗七星 (5.363, 10.485, 14.37). In addition to indicating the direction north, the north dipper indicated time. Since in one cycle of night and day the handle of the dipper turned through one revolution, close observers could estimate the time from the angle of the handle (*Shinjigen* 133).

O-pang (Ah-fang, A-pang) Palace Abōkyū (J.) 阿房宮

The First Emperor of the Ch'in Dynasty built the O-pang Palace for his imperial capital in the Shang-lin Park near the city of Hsien-yang in 212 BCE. The palace is a symbol in Chinese literature for splendor and luxury on a vast scale (5.6, 8.258, 12.144). If it had actually been built according to the dimensions given in the *Shih-chi*, the palace would have been incredibly large: 675 meters by 112 meters (see TWITCHETT and LOEWE 1986, 102, for a discussion of these dimensions). It was said that the upper part of the palace could seat 10,000 persons, and on the lower part five great flagpoles 11.2 meters high were erected. The summit of the Southern Mountains was declared the gateway to the palace and covered walkways led from it to the palace itself. An elevated walkway led from the palace north across the Wei River to the city of Hsien-yang. The *Shih-chi* says that over 700,000 persons condemned to castration and convict laborers were assigned to building the palace and to the other great construction, the First Emperor's mausoleum (WATSON 1993A, *Ch'in*, 56).

"When the Six Kings were destroyed, the world became one. When the Szechwan mountains were laid bare, the O-pang Palace emerged" (12. 144) is a couplet taken from Tu Mu 杜牧, "O-pang-kung fu" 阿房宮賦. The "Six Kings" is a reference to the six states that united in 240 BCE to oppose the state of Ch'in. The O-pang Palace was of such a scale that the surrounding mountains were laid bare to provide lumber to build it.

When Hsiang Yü finally entered the city of Hsien-yang with his troops, he set fire to the O-pang and other Ch'in palaces. This is the event referred to in 8.258: "How sad—the man of Ch'u's single torch has scorched the earth." This too is a verse taken from Tu Mu's "O-pang-kung fu." It is said that the palaces burned for three months (WATSON 1993A, *Han I*, 33).

Old barbarian ➛ BARBARIAN under **Bodhidharma**

Old man on the frontier who lost his horse *Uma o shissuru saiō* (J.) 塞翁失馬

On the northern frontiers was an old man whose horse wandered off. Neighbors said, "What misfortune!" "Is that so?" said the old man. A day later, the horse came back bringing with it another horse, fine and strong. People said, "What great luck!" "Is that so?" said the old man. The next day, the old man's son tried to ride the new horse but was thrown and broke a leg. Neighbors said, "What misfortune!" "Is that so?" said the old man. A little while later, the barbarians attacked the border and all able-bodied young men were conscripted into the army. The son could not go because of his broken leg. In the army, nine out of ten died, but the old man and his son survived (*Huai-nan-tzu* 淮南子, 人間訓).

Old monk *Rōsō* 老僧

The characters literally mean "old monk" but they are often used as a first person indicator, equivalent to "I" or "me."

Original face ➛ under **Sixth Patriarch**

Oshō (J.) 和尚

The term *oshō* is a general term for priest or monk. In Japanese contexts, however, it can also be used in the second person, meaning "you" if the person to whom one is speaking is a priest or monk.

Paired fish ➛ under **Matrimonial harmony**

Pāpīyas (Skt.) *Hajun* (J.) 波旬

In early Buddhism, the *pāpīyas* was an evil spirit who interfered with the practice of the Buddha and bodhisattvas. The *pāpīyas* was not clearly distinguished from Māra, the god of evil. A related figure is ***yakṣa*** (ZGDJT 1019b).

Patch-robed monk *Nōsō, Nōsōge* (J.) 衲僧 | 衲僧家

The traditional Indian monk's robe was a large rectangular piece of cloth made of rags patched together and then dyed a dirty yellow color. It was wrapped around the body and then draped over the left shoulder, leaving the right shoulder bare. "Patch-robed monk" can mean Buddhist monk in general, but in Zen texts it means the Zen monk in particular (ZGDJT 1007B). When Buddhism came to China, the patched robe was combined with native Chinese clothing, so that by the T'ang a monk in formal dress wore two layers of clothing: an under layer of tailored Chinese robes similar to T'ang court dress, and a top layer of a rectangular patched cloth draped over the left shoulder. The Japanese Zen monk's *rakusu* 絡子, a small bib-like garment, is an abbreviation of the patched robe and still retains the patchwork pattern. Legend says that it was made during the T'ang Buddhist persecution of 845 so that Buddhist monks could wear the robe hidden beneath ordinary clothing. On Buddhist robes, see IZUTSU 1970, KYŪMA 1989.

Peach *Momo* (J.) 桃

Mention of the peach evokes a cluster of associations in Chinese literature. In the *Book of Songs*, the peach tree is used as a symbol for a beautiful young woman (16.60). The image of peach petals floating on water brings to mind T'ao **Yüan-ming**'s Peach Blossom Spring, the idyllic valley on the other side of a cave from which flowed a stream of water through a peach grove. The fruit of the peach is associated with the Taoist immortals' search for longevity. Legend says that in the garden of the **Queen Mother of the West** there grows a peach tree that blossoms once every three thousand years. Eating this fruit confers immortality (10.71). Taoist immortals are said to keep a diet that includes blue peaches (Morohashi 24334.124; see 14.486). In Zen, mention of peach flowers immediately brings to mind the story of **Reiun** Shigon Zenji, who experienced awakening at the sight of peach blossoms (10.379, 14.506).

Permanent things ➛ ***Jōjūmotsu***

Persian ➛ **BAREFOOT PERSIAN** under **Bodhidharma**

P'eng-lai (Ch.) Hōrai (J.) 蓬萊

In Chinese Taoist folk legend the terms P'eng-lai and P'eng-lai-shan 蓬萊山 (Mount P'eng-lai) were names for the residence of the immortals (14.154, 14.338, etc.). Usually it was said to be an island in the seas east of China, but it was also sometimes said to be a mountain in the interior continent. There the elixir of long life and immortality was made (*p'eng* and *lai* are the names of herbs). The P'eng-lai Palace, a building in the imperial capital, was built by the T'ang Emperor Kao-tsung.

Pi-lo Monument *Hekiraku no hi* (J.) 碧落碑

The Pi-lo Monument (4.555, 6.238) was a T'ang Dynasty monument in the Pi-lo Kuan Taoist temple. It was inscribed in ancient characters written in a style so unique that not even master calligraphers could make an exact copy (ZGJT 415).

Pick ➛ **Awl**

Pierced-eared traveler ➛ under **Bodhidharma**

Pine wind *Shōfū* (J.) 松風

The sound of wind sighing through the branches of mountain pine trees was thought to be a particularly natural and beautiful sound (7.300, 10.556, 14.168). To the Chinese poet's ear, the sound of water boiling in a tea kettle resembled the sound of wind in the pines (7.446, 14.271). In the modern tea ceremony there is still a great deal of attention paid to the quality of sound made by water boiling in an iron kettle over hot coals in the tea room, and to the stillness of mind required to appreciate the sound.

Po Ya ➛ **Intimate**

Po Yi and Shu Ch'i (Ch.) Hakui, Shukusei (J.) 伯夷｜叔齊

At the very end of the Yin Dynasty, Po Yi and his younger brother Shu Ch'i were heirs to a small kingdom. Their father named the younger brother Shu Ch'i as successor, but when the father died, Shu Ch'i offered the throne to the older brother, Po Yi. Po Yi insisted that Shu Ch'i take the throne as the father had wished. Being unable to decide, both fled the state. Thus did they acquire a reputation for being good men pure in virtue.

At this time, **King Wu** was engaged in a rebellion against the king of the Yin Dynasty. Though the Yin king was an evil ruler, nevertheless it was still an act of disloyalty to rebel against him. Po Yi and Shu Ch'i reprimanded King Wu for disloyalty. He refused to punish them, recognizing their upright motivation (14.635). When King Wu overthrew the Yin king and established the new Chou Dynasty, the two brothers refused to "eat the grain of Chou" and withdrew to Mount Shou-yang 首陽 (J. Shuyō), where they eventually starved to death (10.235). Their story is ch. 61 of the *Shih-chi* (Watson 1958, 11–15).

Poison bird wings ➛ **Poison blackbird**

Poison blackbird *Chinchō* (J.) 鴆鳥

The poison-winged blackbird has feathers that contain a virulent poison (20.10). Soaking a feather in wine makes poison wine 鴆酒 (J. *chinshu*, Morohashi

46727.3). Painting the poison on the head of a drum makes the poison-painted drum 塗毒鼓 (J. *zudokko, zudokku*); when the drum is beaten, all who hear it die (8.48, 8.385, 14.599). *Zudokko* is also the title of the Japanese Rinzai monks' handbook (Fujita 1922). One of the kōan collections contained in the *Zudokko* is the *Chin'u-shū* 鴆羽集, "The Collection of Wings of the Poison Blackbird."

Poison-painted drum ➛ **Poison blackbird**

Pole star *Hokushin* (J.) 北辰

The characters 北辰 literally mean "northern dragon." The Han Chinese thought that heaven turned around an axis that was marked by the pole star, the star that remained fixed in place while the other stars revolved around it. The star, it was said, ruled the heavens as the emperor ruled the earthly world. Thus the pole star was called the Celestial Emperor and nearby stars called Prince, Concubine, or some other name taken from the imperial court. The Confucian *Analects* depicts the *chün-tzu* 君子 (J. *kunshi*), the cultivated person, as a human still point in the midst of flux. "The Master said, He who rules by moral force (*te*) is like the pole-star, which remains in its place while all the lesser stars do homage to it" (Waley 1938, 1).

For a discussion of exactly what star the Chinese designated the pole star and the point around which the sky seems to turn, see Needham 1959, §20 "Astronomy," 171–461.

Princess(es) of the Hsiang *Shōkun* (J.) 湘君

In the singular, this refers to the goddess or consort of the Hsiang River 湘江 to whom ritual sacrifices were made in ancient China. In the plural, it refers to the daughters of the legendary Emperor Yao, who gave them to his successor Emperor **Shun**; when Shun died, they dutifully drowned themselves and became the princesses of the Hsiang. There are, however, several different accounts. See Waley 1955, 33; Birrell 1986, 308; Schafer 1980.

Queen Mother of the West Hsi Wang Mu (Ch.), Seiōbo (J.) 西王母

The Queen Mother of the West was said to dwell in the **K'un-lun** Mountains in the far west and to be surrounded by troops of spiritual beings (or sometimes it is said, by large numbers of youths, partners for Taoist sexual immortality practices). In her garden grew special peach trees that once in 3,000 years put forth fruit. Those who ate the peach would gain immortality (10.71; Birrell 1993, 171–5; Cahill 1995).

Rabbit horns and turtle hairs *Tokaku kimō* (J.) 兔角龜毛

Since rabbits do not have horns and turtles do not have hair, "rabbit horns and turtle hairs" symbolize things that are thought to be real but which do not exist (ZGJT 331; 5.58). The conventional or dualistic way of thinking both falsely imputes permanent existence to things and also classifies them into dualistic categories. Thus it is possible to say, "Turtle hairs are long, rabbit horns are short" (6.55, also 7.26).

Real and apparent ➛ **Five Ranks**

Red eyes *Sekigen, sekigan, shakugan* (J.) 赤眼

"Red eyes" has two connotations. First, it is a term for a turtle (Oda 1954, 800; ZGJT 248). Second, it signifies a person who has overcome the discriminative thinking of conventional consciousness (ZGDJT 652). It is unclear what association redness of the eyes has with either of these. The second of these two meanings applies to 14.332: "The flaming tile broke through the solid layers of ice. Red eyes collide with the burning brush." Here red eyes signify an awakened mind and the burning bush signifies the burning of the passions. This interpretation creates a nice parallel with the first verse; both become metaphors for Zen in action that cuts through the dross of intellectualization and the burning passions.

Red dust *Kōjin* (J.) 紅塵

Red dust is the dust that arises from carts and horses passing back and forth. It thus symbolizes the busyness and defilement of the everyday world.

Reiun (J.) Ling-yün (Ch.) 靈雲

Ch'an monk Ling-yün Chih-ch'in 靈雲志勤 (J. Reiun Shigon), a Dharma heir to Kuei-shan Ling-yu (J. Isan Reiyū), is most remembered for attaining awakening when he saw peach flowers in bloom. His verse is much quoted in Zen:

> Some thirty years I sought an expert swordsman.
> How many times leaves fell, how many times branches burst into bud!
> But from the instant I saw the peach flowers blooming,
> From that moment to this I have had no doubts.
> (*Keitoku dentō-roku* 11, T 51: 285a; translation from ZD 292)

In response to this, the Zen monk **Gensha** Shibi (14.506) wrote his own verse:

> For thirty years, it was always the same,
> How many times had the falling leaves emitted their gleams of light?
> Then he took one step out beyond the great sky,
> And his perfect voice and body matches that of the Dharma King.
> (*Gensha kōroku*, MZZ 126.357)

Relaxing the hands ➛ ***Suishu***

Repeated month, intercalary month *Jungetsu, Uruuzuki* (J.) 閏月

In the ancient Chinese lunar calendar, the six major months had thirty days and the six minor months had twenty-nine days, for a total of 354 days in a year. Since this is approximately 10–11 days short of the solar year, within a few years the human calendar and the solar seasons became unsynchronized. To adjust for this mismatch, from time to time an extra month was inserted into the calendar—once in every three years, twice in five years, and seven times in nineteen years. This extra month was inserted by repeating one of the regular months so that the same month occurred twice that year. The second such month was the "repeated month" or "intercalary month" (10.511; *Shinjigen* 1059).

Restored cinnabar *Kantan* (J.) 還丹

Ko Hung, an early authority in Taoist longevity practices, claimed that while breathing exercises, calisthenics, and herbal medicines could extend life, they could not prevent ultimate death. To attain the condition of not aging and not dying, one had to ingest restored cinnabar and potable gold. Restored cinnabar was so called because ordinary cinnabar, thought to be a mercury sulphate compound, could be refined to produce pure mercury. This in turn could be refined further to produce an even purer mercury product, which, because it was red and had the appearance of ordinary cinnabar, was called restored cinnabar (Noguchi et al. 1994, 79; Ware 1981, 68–96).

In Zen, the term "restored cinnabar" and other such Taoist terms are used figuratively in relation to practices of self-transformation.

Ring of iron mountains ➛ Sumeru

River and Lake *Gōko* (J.), *Chiang-hu* (Ch.) 江湖

This term in Zen texts is usually an abbreviation for Chiang-hsi 江西 (J. Kōsei) (14.446) and Hunan 湖南 (J. Konan), and although its two characters 江湖 literally mean "river" and "lake," it connotes the world of Zen practice. The Chiang-hsi area was the domain of Baso Dōitsu (709–788) 馬祖道一 (Ch. Ma-tsu Tao-i), while Hunan was the domain of Sekitō Kisen (700–790) 石頭希遷 (Ch. Shih-t'ou Hsi-ch'ien), the two greatest Chinese masters of the eighth century. A Ch'an monk serious about practice would find himself going back and forth between "the river and the lake," that is, going back and forth between Baso and Sekitō (ZGDJT 309b). The term *gōko* turns up also in text titles such as the *Gōko fūgetsushū* (J.) 江湖風月集 *(The River and Lake Wind Moon Collection)*, an anthology of poetry and commentary from several Zen monks and an important source of capping verses, and the *Gōko hosshiki bonbaishō* (J.), 江湖法式梵唄抄 *(The River and Lake Handbook of Protocol and Chant)*, an instruction book for performing Zen rituals.

Robber Chih (Ch.) Tōseki (J.) 盜跖

In Chinese legend, just as Po Yi and Shu Ch'i became symbols of virtuous conduct, so also Robber Chih, along with **Chieh and Chou**, epitomized viciousness and evil. *Chuang-tzu,* ch. 29, devoted entirely to stories of Robber Chih, records a fictitious conversation between Confucius and Robber Chih, in which Confucius comes upon Robber Chih as the latter snacks on minced human livers.

Confucius gives his usual sermon about virtue, but Robber Chih, speaking in the voice of a Taoist philosopher, denounces Confucius's Way and sends the great teacher scurrying (Watson 1968, 323–31).

Robe and bowl ➛ under **Bodhidharma**

Roc *Hō, taihō* (J.) 鵬 | 大鵬

The image of the great roc bird, taken from the first chapter of *Chuang-tzu*, is similar in some ways to the image of the *garuda* bird found in South and Southeast Asian literature. With one flap of its huge wings the roc flies 90,000 miles, sailing over the oceans and snapping up dragons for food.

Rod ➛ ***Shippei***

Sacred fetus *Shōtai, seitai* (J.) 聖胎

At the very end of formal kōan training comes a period called *shōtai chōyō* (J.) 聖胎長養 "long nurturing of the sacred fetus" (4.278, 14.47–8). See explanation in chapter 2 of the Introduction, pages 27–9.

Sahā (Skt.) This sorrowful world *Shaba* (J.) 娑婆

Shaba is the Japanese pronunciation of the Sanskrit *sahā*, the world in which we live. The term is used in contexts that stress the fact that it is impure and full of suffering.

Samantabhadra (Skt.) Fugen (J.) 普賢

Although the Bodhisattva Samantabhadra, "Universal Sagacity," is an important individual personality in East Asian Buddhism, in Zen verses he is almost always paired with **Mañjuśrī** (7.207, 14.305, 14.500, 14.602). They are the two attendants to Śākyamuni, Samantabhadra representing principle 理 and standing to the right of Śākyamuni, with Mañjuśrī representing wisdom 智 and standing to the left. In art and sculpture, Mañjuśrī is often shown riding a lion while Samantabhadra rides an elephant. Sometimes Mañjuśrī and Samantabhadra are paired with **Han-shan** and Shih-te (12.137). See also **Sudhana**.

Samatagezu (J.) Yes! 不妨

Samatagezu literally means "does not interfere," as in 14.419. But it is also a Chinese idiom implying approval and praise: "Yes!"

Sand-spitter *She-kung* (Ch.) *Shakō* (J.) 射工

According to legend, this nasty little turtle-like creature, about one or two inches in length, lived in mountain streams. The inside of its mouth was formed like a crossbow. It filled its mouth with sand, which it spat at passing shadows. If it struck the shadow of a person, that person sickened and died (7.208; HYDCD 2.1264; Mathews #7680). This image is said to describe a person who attacks another through malicious gossip and backstabbing.

Second Patriarch *Niso* (J.) 二祖

The Second Patriarch is Eka 慧可 (Ch. Hui-k'o), the disciple who cut off his arm and presented it to **Bodhidharma** to show his sincerity. This incident forms the basis for the kōan "Bodhidharma and Peace of Mind" (MMK 41, *Kattō-shū* 1).

Sessa takuma (J.) Cutting, grinding, filing, polishing 切磋琢磨

The *Book of Songs* 55 uses this phrase to describe a lord as polished as a jewel: "Delicately fashioned is my lord, as thing cut, as thing filed, as thing chiselled, as thing polished" (Waley 1937a, 46). The phrase is quoted in the Confucian *Analects* (1, 15) and is used in Confucianism to describe the training and self-discipline of a *chün-tzu* 君子 (J. *kunshi*), the morally and ritually cultivated person. By extension, it is used in Zen to describe Zen practice. In a monastery, the phrase takes on a social aspect: the monks are like stones rubbing against each other, mutually polishing each other.

Seven articles *Shichiji* (J.) 七事

There are several explanations of the seven articles. ZGJI 152 lists seven military articles: bow, arrow, knife, etc. ZGJT 184 lists possessions of a monk: three robes, one bowl, incense burner, whisk, prostration cloth, paper bedcloth, and bathing articles. Cleary and Cleary 1977, 103 and 163, lists the seven qualities of character of a great teacher.

Seven-hall complex *Shichidō garan* (J.) 七堂伽藍

Many Chinese Ch'an and Japanese Zen monasteries were built with seven main structures. The three largest buildings were, starting at the south, the Mountain Gate (*Sanmon* 山門), the Buddha Hall (*Butsuden* 佛殿), and the Lecture Hall (*Hattō* 法堂), aligned one above the other on the central north-south axis. On a parallel axis on the west side (again starting from the south) were the Latrine (*Tōsu* 東司) and the Monks' Hall (*Sōdō* 僧堂). On a parallel axis on the east side (again starting from the south) were the Bath House (*Yokushitsu* 浴室) and the Kitchen-Office (*Kuin* 庫院). The entire complex of a present-day Zen monastery is called a *sōdō*, but originally the *sōdō* was just one of the seven buildings of the *shichidō garan*. The original *sōdō* building was much larger than the present monastery *zendō*. It was divided into east and west halls, with each hall housing several zazen platforms capable of seating hundreds of monks (Collcutt 1981, 171–221, ZGDJT 別 10-38).

Shang Yang (Ch.) Shōō (J.) 商鞅

Shang Yang (12.53) was one of the original Legalists. An official in the Warring States period, his ideas about harsh punishment and strict enforcement of laws were implemented by the state of Ch'in, which went on to conquer all other states and form the first empire. In the end, he was driven from court by palace intrigue. He fled and sought lodging from an innkeeper, but the innkeeper refused him, saying, "According to the laws of Lord Shang, I shall be punished if I take in a man without a permit." Eventually he was captured. King Hui of Ch'in had his corpse torn limb from limb by chariots, and his family was wiped out. For Shang Yang's strict punishments, see Bodde 1938, 166–9. His biography is *Shih-chi* 68, translated in Yang and Yang 1979, 60-9. For a translation of his writings, see Duyvendak 1963.

Phrase 12.53 reads "Shang Yang put into law 'dragging by chariots,' Wu Ch'i's tyranny was 'dismembering the body.'" It is unclear what the original source of this verse is, but the *Huai-nan-tzu* 淮南子 contains the line 商鞅立法而支解, 吳起刻削而車裂, which reverses the attribution of the two punishments: "Shang Yang put into law 'dismembering the body', Wu Ch'i's tyranny was 'dragging by chariots.'"

Shao-lin ➛ under **Bodhidharma**

Shao-shih ➛ under **Bodhidharma**

Shasanrō (J.) Hsieh San-lang (Ch.) 謝三郎

The name Shasanrō has two uses in *Zen Sand*. First, it can be used generally to mean the third son (三郎) of the Sha 謝 (Ch. Hsieh) family. Son number three is regarded as uneducated and therefore unable to count or even read the four characters written on a Chinese coin (7.209, 8.186; ZGDJT 472).

Second, Shasanrō often refers to a particular individual, the Chinese Ch'an monk known also as Gensha Shibi 玄沙師備 (Ch. Hsüan-sha Shih-pei; 835–908), a monk in the lineage of Seppō Gison 雪峯義存 (Ch. Hsüeh-feng I-ts'un; 822–908). Before he came into Zen, he was a fisherman. He left the lay life at age thirty and eventually received Seppō's Dharma. Gensha is brother disciple to the famous Ummon Bun'en 雲門文偃 (Ch. Yun-men Wen-yen; 864–949), and the two are said to have established the reputation of their master Seppō. Gensha appears in kōan cases MMK 41, *Heki* 22, 56, 88. The image of the fisherman clings to him throughout his life (14.592). See also Cleary and Cleary 1977, 258–9.

Shih K'uang (Ch.) Shikō (J.) 師曠

In Chinese legend, during the Warring States period, Shih K'uang was famous for his extremely sharp hearing. It was said that he could hear the beating of the wings of a butterfly on the far side of a hill (ZGJI 590). He is often paired together with **Li Lou**, famous for his extremely sharp eyesight.

Shih-te ➛ **Han-shan**

Shikai ➛ **Four seas**

Shippei (J.) Rod 竹篦

A *shippei* is an S-shaped bamboo rod, sometimes carved and decorated with silk cord, used by a Zen master mainly for ritual purposes. It is sometimes employed to hit monks (8.203, 10.66, 10.215; ZGDJT 491).

Shōji (J.) Holy attendant (to the *shōsō*) 聖侍

Every Buddhist meditation hall has an image of a buddha or bodhisattva called the *shōsō* 聖僧, literally, "holy monk." In Zen monasteries the image is that of **Mañjuśrī**. The holy attendant to Mañjuśrī, also known as *jisha* 侍者 (**attendant**), is a higher ranking monk. He takes care of the ritual surrounding Mañjuśrī (placing flowers, incense, meals, etc. before the image). As the representative of Mañjuśrī, he sits on the seat nearest the door and monitors the exit and entrance of monks from the meditation hall. He looks after the welfare of the monks in general; this includes daily tasks such as serving tea and special tasks such as taking care of those who become ill.

Shōsō (J.) 聖僧 Holy monk

The holy monk is the Buddhist image that oversees the meditation hall of a monastery. In Mahayana, the image is that of Mañjuśrī; in Theravada, that of Kāśyapa or Subhūti. See also ***Shōji.***

Shōsoku (J.) Actuality, condition, the facts | News, information, report 消息

The term *shōsoku* is composed of two characters that individually imply breathing out and breathing in, and that more generally allude to the alternation of positive and negative, rising and falling, conventional and ultimate, etc. It thus can mean the actuality or condition of things. In a narrower and more modern usage, it means information or report.

Shou-yang ➛ Po Yi and Shu Ch'i

Shout ➛ Stick and shout

Shu Ch'i ➛ Po Yi and Shu Ch'i

Shun (Ch.) Shun (J.) 舜

In Chinese literature, the sage kings **Yao**, Shun, and **Yü** (J. Gyō, Shun, Yu) are exemplars of selfless virtue, and the age in which they are said to have lived is always nostalgically considered a golden age. Yao refused to pass the throne on to his own unworthy son and instead offered it to the worthy Hsü Yu 許由 (J. Kyoyu). Hsü Yu was so virtuous that legend says he not only refused Yao's offer (14.159, ZGJI 611) but hurried off to wash his ears in a stream to cleanse them of their defilement. His friend Ch'ao-fu 巣父 (J. Sōfu) was a person of equally spotless integrity; he led his ox upstream so that it would not be contaminated by the water in which Hsü Yu had washed his ears (8.252, 12.31; ZD #188). Eventually Yao passed on the throne to Shun, very poor in material wealth but of great unselfish virtue (10.255, 14.142).

When Shun was still a young child, his mother died and his father remarried.

A second son, named Hsiang, was born. The father liked Hsiang and began to despise his first son. The entire family hated Shun so much that over the years both the father and Hsiang made serious attempts to kill him. Shun miraculously escaped every time and always exhibited exemplary conduct toward the members of his family (10.342). This story is given in the *Shu ching* (The Book of History), *Yao tien* and *Shun tien* chapters (LEGGE 1985, vol. III, 15–27).

Silla Shinra (J.) 新羅

Silla began as a small ancient tribal state in Korean history, said to have been founded in 57 BCE and located in the southeast part of the Korean Peninsula. It grew in size and power, becoming one of the Three Kingdoms that dominated the Korean Peninsula from the fourth century on. In 668 Silla succeeded in unifying the entire Korean Peninsula. Although it imitated many Chinese institutions and imported much Chinese culture, Silla created the distinctive language, culture, and geographical boundaries of the modern country of Korea.

During the T'ang Dynasty, to the Chinese the name Silla connoted a very distant place, a "nowhere" place, somewhat as "Siberia" does in modern English. When a verse says an arrow flew off to Silla (4.628), it means the arrow has shot off to a faraway place beyond ordinary knowledge (5.392, 8.253).

Six directions *Rikugō* (J.) 六合

The six directions are the four primary directions plus heaven and earth (Morohashi 1453.84). 14.571 may be using the six directions as a metaphor for the consciousnesses.

Six realms *Rokudō* (J.) 六道

The six realms of rebirth are heaven, *asura,* human, animal, hungry ghost, and hell. The six realms are sometimes paired with the **four births** as a literary expression for *saṃsāra*, the cycle of birth and death.

Sixteen feet *Jōroku* (J.) 丈六

Jōroku 丈六 is an abbreviation for *ichijō rokushaku* 一丈六尺, "one *jō*, six *shaku*," here translated as "sixteen feet." The body of the Buddha was said to be sixteen feet long. *Jōroku no konjin* (J.) 丈六金身, "the sixteen-foot golden body," is a set phrase referring to the Buddha. Images of the Buddha were often made sixteen feet high, or some multiple of this height.

Jō and *shaku* (Ch. *chang* and *ch'ih*) are units of measurement in ancient China. 1 *jō* is 10 *shaku,* making *ichijō rokushaku* equal to 16 *shaku*. See **inch and foot**.

Sixth Patriarch *Rokuso* (J.) 六祖

Hui-neng 慧能 (638–713) is called the Sixth Patriarch because, of the legendary founders of the Ch'an school, he is the sixth-generation successor in Chinese Ch'an after **Bodhidharma**, the First Patriarch. The legend of Hui-neng is recounted in the *Platform Sutra of the Sixth Patriarch*, one of the most important texts outlining the Ch'an school's version of its own history. All current Ch'an/Zen lineages trace their roots back to him. Recently, however, scholars such as YANAGIDA (1967, 1977), YAMPOLSKY (1967), and others, using documents uncovered at Tun-huang, have challenged the Ch'an school's account of its own early history. They imply that the legend of Hui-neng was created by a later generation of Ch'an monks and then read as history. The same modern scholarship argues that the entire legend of an unbroken lineage of twenty-eight generations of patriarchs in India and six generations of patriarchs in China underwent numerous revisions until it attained its present form and was accepted as orthodoxy.

Within early Zen texts, two different accounts of Hui-neng's life circulated, one describing his early life and one describing his later life. Eventually these were combined together, but the different elements do not all fit neatly together. Dumoulin has attempted the reconstruction of a consistent biography (DUMOULIN 1990, I, 129–37).

Because Rinzai kōan training uses elements of the Sixth Patriarch legend to express points in its teaching, the historical factuality of the Sixth Patriarch legend is not of great concern. The following points of the Sixth Patriarch legend are important for the understanding of capping phrases.

NAME

The Sixth Patriarch's surname was Lu 廬 (12.98), his personal name Hui-neng 慧能 (J. Enō). He is also known as Lu-neng 盧能 (J. Ronō).

HEARING THE *DIAMOND SUTRA*

The early death of his father forced Hui-neng and his mother into extreme poverty. He collected brushwood to sell in the marketplace. One day he carried firewood to the home of a buyer and there happened to overhear someone chanting the *Diamond Sutra*. At this, he was awakened. Legend says the line was 應無所住而生其心 (J. *Ō mu sho jū ni shō go shin*) , "Arouse the mind that abides in no place" (8.47; T 48.348).

FIFTH PATRIARCH, HUNG JEN, AT HUANG-MEI

The man who chanted the *Diamond Sutra* told Hui-neng that he had been taught by Hung-jen 弘忍 (J. Gunin). At twenty-four Hui-neng left his home village to train with Hung-jen. Hung-jen's monastery was at Feng-mu-shan in the district of Huang-mei, and in the later legend of Hui-neng, the name Huang-mei-shan 黄梅山 (J. Ōbaizan, "Yellow Plum Mountain") is used to identify both the monastery of the Fifth Patriarch and also the place where it was located.

BARBARIAN FROM THE SOUTH

When Hui-neng said that he had come from Ling-nan 嶺南 in the south, Hung-jen asked, "If you are a southern barbarian, how can you become a buddha?"

Hui-neng replied, "There is no south or north in Buddha-nature." Impressed, Hung-jen put Hui-neng to work in the threshing room, where he hulled rice for eight months. He was "the visitor who was husked" of verse 6.284.

WALL POEMS

The aging Fifth Patriarch told his monks each to write a verse, saying that he would pass the robe of Dharma succession to anyone who could express his awakening. The head monk, Shen-hsiu, was considered by all to be the most advanced in Dharma and the obvious candidate. No one else wrote a verse. Late at night, Shen-hsiu wrote his poem on the wall of a corridor:

> The body is like the bodhi tree,
> The mind is like a clear mirror.
> At all times we must strive to polish it,
> And must not let the dust collect. (Yampolsky 1967, 130)

The illiterate Hui-neng had someone read it for him. At once, he knew that the writer had yet to awaken completely, and in response he composed a poem of his own. There are several versions of Hui-neng's poem, but the one most important for Zen kōan training is given in phrase 20.15:

> 菩提本無樹 *Bodai moto ju naku,*
> 明鏡亦非臺 *Meikyō mata dai ni arazu,*
> 本來無一物 *Honrai mu ichi motsu,*
> 何處惹塵埃 *Izure no tokoro ni ka jin'ai o hikan.*

> Bodhi originally has no tree,
> There is no mirror on a stand.
> Fundamentally there is not one thing,
> Where then can dust collect?

Heki 94 Verse Comm. also quotes the poem, but its version of the last line is 爭得染塵埃 *Ikade ka jin'ai ni somuru koto o en,* "How can it be defiled by dust?" Other versions are given in Yampolsky 1967, 132.

TRANSMISSION OF THE ROBE

Hung-jen recognized Hui-neng's awakening, but, fearing the jealousy of the monks against the illiterate and unordained "southern barbarian," he called Hui-neng to his room in secret at midnight, expounded the *Diamond Sutra,* and gave him the robe, making him the Sixth Patriarch. Then Hui-neng, on the Fifth Patriarch's instruction, fled south to hide.

ORIGINAL FACE

Monks from the monastery pursued him for months and finally caught up with him at the Ta-yü ling Peak 大庾嶺 (J. Taiyurei), where Hui-neng preached the Dharma: "Not thinking of good, not thinking of evil, at this very moment, what is your original face before the birth of your mother and father?" (MMK 23, *Kattō-shū* 1).

MIND IS MOVING

After going into seclusion in the south as an unordained lay person, Hui-neng came to hear a lecture by the famous monk and teacher Yin-tsung 印宗 (J. Injū) on the *Nirvana Sutra.* Two monks were arguing over the temple flag flapping in the wind, one saying the flag was moving, the other saying the wind was moving. Hui-neng said that it was neither flag nor wind but mind that was moving. See MMK 29, *Kattō-shū* 91.

ORDINATION

Yin-tsung recognized the quality of Hui-neng's mind and questioned him. Hui-neng for the first time revealed that he had received the robe from the Fifth Patriarch. After this, Yin-tsung gave him ordination and Hui-neng became a Buddhist monk.

PAO-LIN SSU 寶林寺 (J. Hōrin-ji) **at Ts'ao-ch'i** 曹溪 (J. Sōkei)

One version of his biography says that after getting ordained under Yin-tsung, Hui-neng went to the temple of Pao-lin ssu at Ts'ao-ch'i. Another version of his biography says that at age thirty, he met and impressed a Buddhist nun at Pao-lin ssu, after which he was ordained and lived there for three years (DUMOULIN 1990, I, 131). In any case, Hui-neng lived out the rest of his life at Pao-lin ssu preaching the Dharma. The second part of the *Sixth Patriarch Platform Sutra* is a record of Hui-neng's talks given on the teaching platform.

Since all other lineages died out, the Zen of Hui-neng became the mainstream tradition to which all schools of Zen in all countries now belong. Because he lived at Ts'ao-ch'i, the Sixth Patriarch's Dharma teaching is referred to as Ts'ao-yüan 曹源 (J. Sōgen), "the Ts'ao wellspring." "One drop of water from Ts'ao-yüan" (5.219) refers to the enlightenment of Hui-neng, and his teaching lineage is likened to a flow of water through history. 14.446 continues the metaphor: "One drop of water among the bamboos at Ts'ao-ch'i overflowed and gave rise to the eighteen rapids of Chiang-hsi," the Ch'an schools of the mid-T'ang. A verse not in *Zen Sand* reads 曹源一滴毒波浪濫, "A drop of water from Ts'ao-yüan is a poisonous tidal wave."

VERSE UPON TRANSMISSION

Just before he died, Hui-neng recited the verses composed by the previous five patriarchs at the time they transmitted the robe and Dharma. Bodhidharma's verse has been received into the body of *jakugo* verses (10.566–7).

Slash the boat *Ken satte funabata o kizamu* | *Funabata o kizande ken o motomu* (J.) 劍去刻舟 | 刻舟求劍

In a well-known Chinese folktale, a man on board a boat dropped his sword overboard while crossing a river. He immediately made a mark on the side of the boat to mark the spot where the sword had fallen (呂氏春秋 *Master Lü's Spring and Autumn Annals*, cited in YANG 1987, 48–9).

Snake in the wine cup is a reflection of a bow 盃弓蛇影

A certain official had a brother-in-law who suddenly took ill and stopped coming to visit. When the official questioned him, the brother-in-law explained that the last time he visited he saw a snake wriggling in his wine cup. He nevertheless drank the wine but afterwards became quite sick. The official, remembering that there was an archer's bow hanging on the wall, realized that his brother-in-law had seen the reflection of the bow in his cup of wine and mistaken it for a snake. When the brother-in-law heard the explanation, suddenly his sickness disappeared (7.73; from 晉書、樂廣傳 cited in YANG 1987, 188-9).

Snap the fingers *Danshi* (J.) 彈指

Snapping the fingers has many meanings. A snap of the fingers indicates an instant, an extremely short period of time (14.443). It is also a ritual way to awaken someone from sleep. In MMK 42, Mañjuśrī snapped his fingers three times in order to awaken a woman from *samādhi* but could not do so, while the novice bodhisattva Mōmyō succeeded after only one snap of his fingers (12.238). Snapping the fingers in front of a shrine is a ritual purification; in a memorial service, it chases away evil spirits. One snaps the fingers in front of a door to request permission to enter (ZGDJT 836c). Several of these meanings are combined in 12.128.

Sōten (J.) "Oh, God!" 蒼天

Although *sōten* literally means "blue heavens," this phrase is used in Zen texts to indicate a cry for pity, a plea for mercy, equivalent to "Oh, my God!" in English (4.351, 6.46; ZGJT 167).

Southern dragon *Nanshin* (J.) 南辰

A constellation, often paired with **North Star** (12.120).

Spiritual shoots ➛ **Auspicious grass and spiritual shoots**

Spring and autumn *Ch'un ch'iu* (Ch.), *Shunjū* (J.) 春秋

The compound "spring and autumn" indicates the passing of the seasons and thus means one year or many years (since the term does not distinguish singular and plural). The *Spring and Autumn Annals*, one of the traditional five Confucian classics, is an extremely brief chronicle of events for the state of Lu for the years 722–481 BCE. For this reason, this period of history is called the Spring and Autumn period. A subsequent historical work, the *Tso chuan* 左傳, filled out the brief description of events by dramatizing them and setting them into an explicitly didactic moral frame. There are English translations in WATSON 1989 and

LEGGE 1985, vol. V. To discuss the *Spring and Autumn Annals* means to discuss the moral lessons of history (16.22). Of importance to 14.450 is the legend that Confucius himself had written the *Spring and Autumn Annals*. Mencius was the first to make this claim (*Mencius* III, B, 9; IV, B, 21).

Steal a sheep *Yō o nusumu* (J.) 攘羊

In *Zen Sand* verses (4.393, 6.176), mention of stealing a sheep is usually a reference to the following passage from the Confucian *Analects* XIII, 18:

> The duke of Sheh informed Confucius, saying, "Among us here there are those who may be styled upright in their conduct. If their fathers have stolen a sheep, they will bear witness to the fact." Confucius said, "Among us, in our part of the country, those who are upright are different from this. The father conceals the misconduct of the son and the son conceals the misconduct of the father. Uprightness is to be found in this" (LEGGE 1985).

Steelyard *Kō* (J.) 鉤

The character 鉤 means a hook or curved piece of metal such as a belt hook, a crescent ornament, or steel hook (e.g., 4.434, 14.9, 14.363), but it can also mean the hook of a steelyard (10.156). A steelyard is a simple balance. A scaled arm is suspended off-center and the object being weighed is hung on a hook on the short end of the arm. On the long end, a counterweight can be moved back and forth across the scaled arm to determine the weight of the object. *Jōbanjō* 定盤星 are the graduations on the scale arm (SRZGK #1300) referred to, for example, in verse 10.156: "Know the meaning of the steelyard's hook. Do not fix your attention on the graduation marks." In other words: keep your eye on the ball, not on the scoreboard.

Stick and shout *Bōkatsu* (J.) 棒喝

The stick and the shout are the favorite teaching methods of **Tokusan** and Rinzai, respectively (8.90, 10.92, 10.234, 12.9, 12.149).

Stock, cangue *Ka* (J.) 枷 | 架

The stock or cangue was a large block of wood that was locked around a person's neck as punishment. Often the details of the prisoner's crime would be written on the block both to increase his public humiliation and to discourage others from committing the same crime. Larger stocks that could accommodate two or more people were sometimes fixed to the ground, usually in a public place. As added punishment, sometimes the wrists were locked into shackles or similar stocks.

Stone woman *Sekijo, umazume* (J.) 石女

"Stone woman" is used colloquially to mean a barren woman, unable to bear children (5.207). But in *Zen Sand*, the barrenness of the stone woman is also used occasionally as a metaphor for the no-self of Zen (10.363, 14.381, 14.630, 16.13). The stone woman is often paired together with the **wooden man**.

Straw dogs *Sūku* (J.) 芻狗

Straw dogs (5.196, 10.493) are small images of dogs made of straw placed on altars during early Chinese ritual sacrifice in the Chou Dynasty. During the ritual they were treated as sacred objects, but as soon as the ritual was over they were "trampled on, head and back, by passers-by; to be swept up by the grass-cutters and burned" (WATSON 1968, 158–9). The *Tao-te ching*, ch. 5, contains the line, "The Sage is not humane; He regards the common people as straw dogs" (HENRICKS 1989, 57).

Su Wu (Ch.) Sobu (J.) 蘇武

In the second century BCE, Su Wu was sent as envoy of the Han empire to the Hsiung-nu tribe. There he met former Han envoys and soldiers who had traded loyalties and gone over to the side of the Hsiung-nu. They tried to persuade him to do so as well. Su Wu utterly refused and was kept prisoner for nineteen years. The Han government asked for his return but the Hsiung-nu pretended that he was dead. Then Su Wu tied a letter to a goose, which flew all the way to the capital and was shot down by the emperor in his own courtyard. When confronted with the evidence that he was alive, the Hsiung-nu released him. 10.397 describes the moment when Su Wu and **Li Ling**, another longtime prisoner, parted. Su Wu's story can be found in WATSON 1974, 34–45.

Sudhana, the youth Sudhana-*śreṣṭhi-daraka* (Skt.) Zenzai Dōji (J.) 善財童子

Sudhana (12.128) is the pilgrim hero of the *Gaṇḍhavyūha*, the last section of the *Avataṃsaka sūtra*. In his quest for enlightenment Sudhana first meets the great Bodhisattva Mañjuśrī, who directs him to fifty-two other teachers, each of whom embodies an aspect of awakening. These teachers appear in many different guises—Buddhist, Brahmin, lay, monk, young girl, young boy, old mendicant, devout nun, prostitute, great warrior king, night goddess—thus exemplifying Buddhist *upāya*, or skill-in-means.

The fifty-first teacher is Maitreya, the Buddha of the Future, who opens the door to the many-storeyed tower of Vairocana by snapping his fingers, thus allowing Sudhana to enter. Sudhana sees that the interior of the tower is infinite and contains other towers that themselves also have interiors that are infinite. Sudhana also sees all the past, present, and future practices of Maitreya and of all the many thousands of buddhas under whom he practiced. This image illustrates the Hua-yen teaching of the Dharma world of the unhindered interpenetration of phenomena with phenomena. Maitreya then sends Sudhana onward to the fifty-second teacher, who is Mañjuśrī, the bodhisattva who was his first teacher. Finally, Sudhana meets the Bodhisattva Samantabhadra, his fifty-third teacher, who touches Sudhana on the head and brings about the inconceivable liberation.

The fifty-three stages of Sudhana's pilgrimage match the fifty-three stages of the career of the bodhisattva as outlined in the *Bodhisattva-bhūmi*, the first part of the same *Avataṃsaka sūtra*. The Sudhana story of the stages of enlightenment spread into popular conceptions of Buddhism because it was easier to understand than the philosophical explanation of the stages of the *Bodhisattva-bhūmi*. Illustrated versions of the story appeared. It is also sometimes said that the fifty-three checkpoints on the great Tōkaidō Highway between Tokyo and Kyoto reflected the fifty-three stages of the bodhisattva path. For translations of the *Avataṃsaka sūtra*, see Cleary 1984. For a synopsis of the story of Sudhana, see Cleary 1987.

Phrase 20.13 of *Zen Sand* reads "Tokuun, that old blunt **drillhead**, how many times has he come down from **Wonder Peak**? He hires another fool and together they haul snow to fill in the well." *Heki* 23 Main Case Comm. includes part of the story of Sudhana meeting Meghaśrī (J. Tokuun biku 德雲比丘), a master teacher who, it is said, had never come down from the top of Wonder Peak. Sudhana searched for him for seven days and failed to meet him. Then later Sudhana met him on another mountain, at which point he received Tokuun's teaching. Tokuun biku is referred to as a *kankosui* 閑古錐, an "old blunt drillhead," to indicate that he is a wizened master who has lost the sharpness of youth (see ***Kareta***).

Suishu (J.) Relaxing the hands 垂手

A monk in training always carries the hands in a ritual position, either in *gasshō* or in *shashu*. *Suishu*, literally "dangling hands," is neither of these positions. One relaxes the hands and lets them hang naturally. The phrase implies the putting aside of formality and ritual (ZGJT 236–7) and the extending of the hands of compassion to others (ZGDJT 630c). The title of the tenth Oxherding Picture is *Nitten (nyutten) suishu* 入鄽垂手, "Entering the Marketplace with Relaxed Hands" (8.331). The title implies that in the final stages of Zen practice, one returns from the mountain to the marketplace and lives a life without formality; the hands are relaxed and open to others, the position of natural compassion (e.g., *Heki* 7 Main Comm., *Heki* 96 Main Comm; see also 7.242, 10.144).

Sumeru, Mount Shumisen (J.) 須彌山

In the Indian Buddhist cosmology, at the center of the universe stands a huge mountain called Sumeru or Meru (Skt.), referred to by many *Zen Sand* phrases and verses. The name Sumeru is transliterated into Chinese as Hsü-mi 須彌 and into Japanese as Shumi. It is translated by a variety of terms: 妙高山 *Myōkōzan*, Wondrous High Mountain; 妙高峯頂 *Myōkōhōchō*, Wondrous High Peak; 妙光山 *Myōkōzan*, Wondrous Light Mountain; 妙峯 *Myōbu*, Wonder Mountain; 妙峯頂 *Myōbuchō*, Wonder Mountain Peak; 妙峯孤頂 *Myōbukochō*, Lone Wonder Mountain Peak (12.127, 14.164, 14.665). These terms in general connote a mountain peak above the turmoil of the world (14.655, 20.13). It is also sometimes referred to as the Diamond Mountain 金剛山 Kongōsen (J.) (10.369).

Legend says that Mount Sumeru has a height of 160,000 *yojana*, half of which is under water. The height above water is thus 80,000 *yojana*, or in Sadakata's estimate, 560,000 kilometers. (By comparison, the circumference of the earth at the equator is about 6,380 km and the distance from the earth to the moon is about 384,400 km.) A being on the top of Mount Sumeru looks far down upon the sun and moon, which revolve in a flat orbit above the horizon.

Sumeru stands on a square base and has four faces. The north face of Sumeru is yellow gold, the east face is white silver, the south face is emerald, and the west face is crystal glass. Seen from the side, Sumeru resembles a stepped hourglass with a narrow waist and a top half that widens into a vast plateau upon which rest the heavens. On the top plateau of Sumeru resides Indra (renamed in East Asia 帝釋天, J. Taishakuten), a god in the Indian pantheon who has been absorbed into Buddhism as the ruling guardian god. His lieutenants, the four guardian gods 四天王 (J. *shitennō*), each guard one of the four faces.

The geography of Mount Sumeru is sometimes described as "nine mountains and eight seas" 九山八海 (J. *kyūsen hakkai*). The first mountain is Sumeru itself at the center. Around Sumeru are seven concentric rings (actually squares) of mountain chains, each surrounded by a sea, and finally around the outermost sea is the circular Ring of Iron Mountains 鐵圍山 (J. Tetchisen) (5.272, 10.369).

In the vast sea between the last square of mountains and the circular Ring of Iron Mountains float the four great continents 四洲 (J. *shishū*), each with a distinctive shape. To the east of Sumeru is Pūrvavideha (J. Tōhotsubadai), shaped like a half-moon; to the north is Uttarakuru 欝單越 (J. Uttan'otsu), square in shape; to the west is Aparagodānīya 西瞿耶尼 (J. Saikuyani), circular in shape (12.91, 14.501); and to the south is the triangular-shaped Jambūdvīpa 南贍部 (J. Nansenbu, Nan'enbu), 南贍部洲 (J. Nansenbushū), or 南贍部提 (J. Nansenbutei). Its triangular shape resembles India and the position of Mount Sumeru to its north corresponds to the position of the Himalayas as seen by the people of India. The continent Jambūdvīpa is so called because of the *jambū* tree 閻浮樹 (J. *embuju*), a great towering tree that dominates the continent (7.50). Also called the *uḍumbara* (Skt.) tree, it is said to bloom only once in three thousand years (ZGJI 370). Its flower is the 曇華 (J. *donge*) or 優曇華 (J. *udonge*) (7.360).

In phrase 14.501, Tōhotsuutai 東弗于逮 is a variant of Tōhotsubadai 東弗于婆提, or Pūrvavideha (Skt.), the continent that lies to the east of Mount Sumeru; Saikuyani is the continent to the west. Jih-hsia (lit., "Under the Sun") and Yüeh-chih (lit., "Tribe of the Moon") here are probably ancient names for countries that lay outside the borders of China.

In Buddhist temples, the main altar in front of a Buddhist image and the platform upon which the Buddhist image itself rests are often shaped like Mount Sumeru and are called *shumidan* 須彌壇. The *shumidan* has a wide base upon which are placed narrower and narrower steps; at mid-height, the steps then increase in width (SADAKATA 1997).

Sun

Numerous Chinese literary expressions refer to the sun, including "golden dragon" 金龍 (J. *kinryū;* 14.169, 14.540) and "golden crow" 金烏 (J. *kin'u*), because a three-legged crow is said to reside in the sun (5.194, 6.63, 8.99, 12.120, 14.135). A three-legged frog 三脚蝦蟆 (J. *sankyaku no gama*) is also said to live in the sun (7.176).

Sword *Ken, tō* (J.) 劍、刀

The sword has many meanings in the phrases of *Zen Sand.* It is the symbol of intrinsic wisdom, and for this reason Mañjuśrī is often depicted as holding a sword (e.g., 14.675). The treasure sword of the Vajra king also symbolizes the sword of diamond wisdom (7.64, 8.144, 8.172). A Zen master's *zenki* 禪機 (see ***Ki***) is likened to a sword or a blade (7.111, 8.384). The sword of Zen insight cuts one thing into two (4.34) and two things into one (4.33), and is called the sword that deals out both life and death (6.147, 10.541, 12.145, 14.711).

In Chinese legend there have been many famous swords, some with proper names, such as the **Mo Yeh sword**, the **T'ai-a sword**, the **Dragon Spring sword** and the **Hair-cutter sword.**

Sword in the king's storehouse *Ōkō no katana* (J.) 王庫刀

In a story in the *Nirvana Sutra*, there was a prince who made friends with a poor man. The poor man coveted a jeweled sword that the prince possessed, and one night in his sleep he mumbled "Sword, sword." He was overheard and at once taken prisoner. Questioned by the king, the man said that he had not stolen the prince's sword. The king asked, "What kind of sword did you see in your dream?" The man answered, "It was shaped like the horn of a mountain goat." The king laughed and said, "In the king's storehouse, there is no such sword. You have never seen the sword of the prince" (ZGJT 51; 8.48, 8.437–8).

Symbols of matrimonial harmony ➛ Matrimonial harmony

Taking in and letting go *Hajū hōgyō* (J.) 把住放行

Zen activity is divided into two aspects, *hajū* and *hōgyō*, which, depending on context, can be understood as taking in and letting go, withdrawing and releasing, straightening up and relaxing, and so on. When the bell rings to start a period of meditation, this is *hajū*; when the bell rings to end a period of meditation, this is *hōgyō*. Daily cleanup and work periods are *hajū*, and are appropriately done in silence and with concentrated attention; tea break, however, is a time of *hōgyō*. In the middle of the afternoon, the wooden *han* is struck to signal *hōsan* 放參, release from practice. In the ancient schedule of the monastery, this signaled a short period of free time, *hōgyō*, for the monks. The account books of the monastery are not labeled "credit" and "debit" but *hajū* and *hōgyō*. The intense *hajū* of the *rohatsu ōzesshin* in the winter, the meditation retreat that commemorates the Buddha's enlightenment, is followed by the *hōgyō* of *tōji tōya* 冬至冬夜, the eve of the winter solstice. The evening is declared a period of *josaku* 除策 "removal of the *keisaku*," special food is served, the monks engage in entertainment, and the senior monks serve the junior monks. Although outside observers often think that a monastery's activities are all *hajū*, in fact the schedule is deliberately created to balance *hajū* and *hōgyō*. The entire universe exhibits *hajū* and *hōgyō* (12.119, 14.563).

Talons and tusks *Sōge* (J.) 爪牙

The characters for this term can be translated either "talons and tusks" or "claws and teeth." This term was originally a metaphor for the civilian officials and the military who assisted a ruler. In Zen, however, the talons and tusks (or claws and teeth) refer to the spiritual powers—such as determination, faith, understanding, etc.—that are required for, or that result from, Zen practice and the realization of awakening. The "Dharma cave of talons and tusks" (J. *hokkutsu no sōge* 法窟爪牙) refers to the Zen training hall. In some contexts, *sōge* has a slightly different nuance and refers to the sharpness and force of *zenki* (see ***ki***), the dynamic aspect of Zen (8.368; see also *Shinjigen* 630, ZD 278).

T'ai-a sword *Taiaken* (J.) 太阿劍

T'ai-a is the name of a famous sword in Chinese legend. In the ancient past, before the state of Wu was destroyed, there appeared in the sky a purple light that grew brighter and brighter. The poet and statesman Chang Hua enquired of the astrologer Lei Huan about the cause of the purple light. Lei Huan said it was the spirit of a magic sword reaching up to the heavens. Chang Hua traced the source of the light and finally came to a spot on the ground where he unearthed a stone casket. Inside were two swords, one inscribed with the name T'ai-a and the other with the name Lung-ch'üan 龍泉 (J. Ryōsen), "**Dragon Spring.**" Lei Huan and Chang Hua each took a sword, but Lei Huan commented that because the swords were magic, they would eventually come together again (Jimbo 1974, 829; Birrell 1986, 328). See also **Sword.**

T'ai-kung Wang (Ch.) Taikō Bō (J.) 太公望

The term "T'ai-kung" was once the title of a rank (Great Duke), but in the Chou Dynasty it was used as a respectful form of address for father, either one's own or another's, or for any elderly person. In *Zen Sand*, however, T'ai-kung often refers to a particular person, T'ai-kung Wang (J. Taikō Bō), otherwise known as Lü Shang 呂尚, the man who became advisor to **King Wen**, one of the founders of the Chou Dynasty (8.264). Because the last king of the previous Yin Dynasty, King Chou 紂, was particularly evil, Lü Shang had voluntarily gone into exile. When Wen set out to overthrow the last Yin king, he was given a prediction that he would meet a man of hidden talents who would render him great assistance. He encountered Lü Shang fishing by the Wei River and identified him as that man. He addressed him, saying, "You are the elder (太公 *tai kung*) that I have been looking for (望 *wang*)," and gave him the name T'ai-kung Wang. Subsequently Lü Shang helped him overthrow the last Yin tyrant and establish the Chou Dynasty.

Lü Shang is also known as "the fisherman of the Wei River" (Morohashi 5834.147; *Shinjigen* 239).

T'ang Yü (Ch.) Tōgu (J.) 唐虞

T'ang Yü is a conventional way of referring to **Yao** and **Shun**. Yao's reign title was T'ao-t'ang 陶唐 (J. Tōtō) and Shun's reign title was Yu-yü 有虞 (J. Yūgu). The second characters of the two reign titles have been combined.

T'ao Yüan-ming ➛ Yüan-ming

Ten directions *Jippō* (J.) 十方

The ten directions are the four cardinal directions, the four in-between directions, and up and down.

Ten isles *Jishū* (J.) 十洲

In Chinese legend, the Ten Isles refer to the ten islands where the Taoist immortals, *hsien,* are said to reside (14.300, 14.301, 14.414, *Daijigen* 237). See also **Three Islands, Three Mountains.**

Ten thousand phenomena *Banzō, banshō, manshō* (J.) 萬象

Ten thousand things *Banbutsu, banpō* (J.) 萬物, 萬法

"Ten thousand" is used here not as a precise number but to indicate the infinite differentiatedness of the phenomenal world.

Ten thousand years *Banzai* (J.) 萬歳

The shout " Ten thousand years!" is the common shout of celebration and congratulation. 5.385 is "The mountains ring with shouts of 'Ten thousand years!'" ZRKS 5.148n explains that when Emperor Wu of the Former Han Dynasty climbed a mountain to perform the Shan sacrifice, his attendant ministers heard the mountains echo three times with shouts of "Ten thousand years!" as if the mountains and all of nature were congratulating the emperor.

Thief, bandit *Zoku* (J.) 賊

The image of the thief or bandit is used in several ways in the verses of *Zen Sand.* In the Chinese tradition, the five thieves are joy 喜, anger 怒, pleasure 樂, grief 哀, and lust 欲. But in the Buddhist tradition, the thieves are the six senses. "The six evil spirit thieves" (惡鬼六賊 *akki rokuzoku*) refer to the six sense-objects (color, sound, odor, flavor, contact, thing 色聲香味觸法 *shiki, shō, kō, mi, soku, hō*) (ZGDJT 7c). Since the senses are part of mind itself, "It's hard to guard against thieves from within" (4.94) and easy to mistake a thief for a son of the house (4.354).

The term "thief" also is used to describe the activity of a Zen kōan (7.379) and the skillful means of a Zen master (4.209, 5.223). A skillful master uses the bandit's spear or horse and turns it against him (5.224, 5.226). And one Zen master facing another another Zen master is "One thief knows another thief" (4.217).

Thirty years *Sanjū nen* (J.) 三十年

Thirty years is often said to be the minimum necessary for Zen training (5.140; ZGJT 160).

Thirty-two marks *Sanjūni sō* (J.) 三十二相

When the Buddha was born, a seer examined his body and discerned the thirty-two bodily marks (4.239) of a *cakravartin*, a great wheel-king. These include long ear lobes, folds around the neck, webbing between the fingers, a curl between the eyebrows, a fleshy protuberance on the skull, wheel signs on the soles of the feet, a long wide tongue, saliva that improves the taste of food, and so on. The list varies with the text consulted.

Three bodies of the Buddha *Trikāya* (Skt.), *Sanshin* (J.) 三身

The three bodies of the Buddha are the:

Dharma-body (Skt. *dharmakāya*, 法身 Ch. *fa-shen*, J. *hosshin*),
Reward-body (Skt. *sambhogakāya,* 報身 Ch. *pao-shen*, J. *hōjin*),
Transformation-body (Skt. *nirmāṇakāya,* 化身 Ch. *hua-shen*, J. *keshin*, or 應身 Ch. *ying-shen*, J. *ōjin*).

The Dharma-body is the absolute aspect of the Buddha. It is not a body in the usual sense for it is not material and not particular. Though it is coextensive with the universe, it is not an object of sense or cognition since the Dharma-body also arises as the consciousness that senses and cognizes.

The Transformation-body is the Buddha in his material appearance as Śākyamuni, the human being who appeared in history, lived, practiced, attained awakening, and died.

The Reward-body is the body that a bodhisattva attains as a result of endless practice. The buddhas mentioned in the sutras, such Amitābha Buddha, are reward-body buddhas, neither buddha in absolute aspect nor buddha in historically concrete form.

Three borders *Sanben* (J.) 三邊

During the Han Dynasty, the term "three borders" referred to three areas on the frontier across the north, specifically Yu-chou 幽州 in the far northeast, Ping-chou 幷州 in the north center, and Liang-chou 凉州 in the northwest. The term gradually came to refer generally to the border of the country as a whole (ZGJT 163; 14.281, 14.286). In some *Zen Sand* verses, the three borders can be taken as a metaphor for the **three poisons** in Buddhism (ZGJI 626).

Three dark gates ➛ **Three mysteries**

Three Dynasties *Sandai* (J.) 三代

The Three Dynasties were the three ancient dynasties before the Ch'in Dynasty created a single empire: Hsia 夏 2205–1766 BCE; Shang 商 1766–1122 BCE (known also as the Yin 殷 Dynasty from 1401 BCE); and Chou 周 1122–1251 BCE. The three dynasties were idealized by the Confucians, who depicted them as a golden age of moral human conduct (8.184).

Three in the morning and four in the evening *Chōsan boshi* (J.) 朝三暮四

In the ancient state of Sung there was a man who kept a large number of monkeys, so many that he found it difficult to keep them fed and satisfied. When he reduced their food to three chestnuts in the morning and four in the afternoon, they got angry at him. Then he gave them four in the morning and three in the afternoon and they were satisfied. This story appears in several texts, among them *Lieh-tzu* and *Chuang-tzu.*

Three islands *Santō* (J.) 三島

The Three Islands are the same as the **three mountains**, the fabled islands of the immortals in the eastern sea (HYDCD 1.224). The phrase "Ten Isles and Three Islands" 十洲三島 is a set phrase connoting the realm of Taoist immortals.

Three learnings *Sangaku* (J.) 三學

The three learnings in Buddhism are precepts, meditation, and wisdom 戒定慧 (J. *kaijōe*). These are based on the early Buddhist threefold classification of the Eightfold Noble Path: precepts or *śīla* (Skt.), which include right speech, right action, right livelihood, and right effort; meditation or *samādhi* (Skt.), which includes right mindfulness and right concentration; wisdom or *prajñā* (Skt.), which includes right view and right intention. The three learnings, in turn, were later incorporated into the Six Perfections or *pāramitā* (Skt.), which were generosity *(dāna),* precepts *(śīla),* fortitude *(vīrya),* patience *(kṣanti),* meditation *(dhyāna),* and wisdom *(prajñā).*

Three-legged frog ➛ **Sun**

Three moments *Sansai* (J.) 三際

The three moments are past, present, and future (ZGJT 198).

Three mountains, three sacred mountains *Sanzan* (J.) 三山

In Taoist legend, the three mountains were the place where the immortals resided and where the elixir of immortality could be obtained. The three mountains (蓬萊, 方丈, 瀛州) were usually said to be islands in the ocean, sometimes thought to be mountains in the far west of China. Sea expeditions to find the Three Isles were sometimes sponsored by Chinese emperors, most notably Ch'in Shih Huang Ti, and some of these expeditions may have actually reached the shores of Japan. In the **K'un-lun** mountains to the far west of China, Hsi Wang Mu, the **Queen Mother of the West**, was said to have a kingdom where the peach tree of immortality grew. It blossomed only once every three thousand years and anyone who ate the fruit thereof attained immortality.

Three mysteries, three dark gates *Sangen* (J.) 三玄

Although the term appears to have entered Zen from Taoism (Morohashi 12.478 says it refers to the three texts: *Lao-tzu*, *Chuang-tzu*, and *I ching*), it is mainly associated with Rinzai. The introduction to the *Rinzai-roku* says of Rinzai, "With his three dark gates and three vital seals he pounded and shaped the monks" (Watson 1993b, 3). ZGDJT 392b explains the three mysteries as, first, the mystery within the body (體中玄), second, the mystery within words (句中玄), third, the mystery within the mystery (玄中玄) (see also *Heki* 15 Verse Comm). Rather than assign some individual meaning to the "three mysteries and three necessities 三玄三要, (J. *san'yō*), in the early stages of practice it is better to think of them as simply insight into Zen (14.273).

Three necessities *San'yō* (J.) 三要

In the *Rinzai-roku*, the three necessities are paired with the **three mysteries**. ZGDJT 392b explains the three necessities as, first, language that creates no differentiation, second, the absorption of the 1,000 sages directly into the mysteries and necessities, and third, the overcoming of all language. Rather than assign some individual meaning to the three mysteries and three necessities, in the early stages of practice it is better to think of *sangen san'yō* "the three mysteries and three necessities," as simply insight into Zen.

However, in Japanese Rinzai Zen since the time of Hakuin, the three necessities can also refer to the Great Root of Faith (*daishinkon* 大信根), the Great Ball of Doubt (*daigidan* 大疑團), and the Great Overpowering Will (*daifunshi* 大憤志). See also above, pages 6–7.

Three periods *Sango* (J.) 三期

"Three periods" is a literary expression for the monastic training term (12.18). The ninety days of the summer retreat were divided into three periods 三期 of thirty days each (Oda 1954, 45, 101). The early monks in India originally followed a rule of not sleeping under the same tree more than one night. Because of heavy rains during the summer months, however, they began the custom of taking a fixed residence for the three months of summer. Thus "rain period" 雨期 *uki* (J.), "summer" 夏 *ge* (J.), and "fixed residence" 安居 *ango* (J.) all came to refer to a monastery's training term (6.261). A Japanese Rinzai monastery now has a winter training term that is called *fuyu no ge* (J.) 冬の夏, literally, "winter summer."

Three poisons *Sandoku* (J.) 三毒

The three poisons of Buddhism are greed, anger, and ignorance (貪瞋癡 J. *tonjinchi*).

Three Sovereigns and Five Emperors *Sankō gotei* (J.) 三皇五帝

The set phrase "Three Sovereigns and Five Emperors" refers in Chinese legend to the very first beings to initiate human culture (14.274, *Heki* 3 Verse Comm.).

The Three Sovereigns are Fu Hsi 伏羲 (J. Fushi), Nü Wa 女媧 (J. Joga), and Shen Nung 神農 (J. Shinnō). These three are obviously deities since they do not have human bodies. Fu Hsi and Nü Wa are male and female divinities whose upper bodies are human in form but whose lower bodies are dragon tails. They are shown in iconography with tails intertwined and holding in their hands set squares and compasses to symbolize that they bring civil order to human culture. Fu Hsi was said to have devised the system of the **eight trigrams** of the *I ching*. The third sovereign, Shen Nung, in iconography is shown with the head of an ox and a plow in his hands, thus symbolizing his bringing agriculture to humankind. He is also said to be the creator of the sixty-four hexagrams of the *I ching*.

The Five Emperors are human. The first of the five is the **Yellow Emperor** and the fourth and fifth are **Yao** and **Shun**. The second and third emperors are descendants of the Yellow Emperor, but almost all details of their lives and personalities have been lost. **Yü, the Great**, is often thought to be one of the Five Emperors but is not; still, in Chinese legend he is closely associated with Yao and Shun.

Three steps *Santai* (J.) 三臺

The term "three steps" has more than one meaning, but often in *Zen Sand* it refers to the dance and music performed during banquets in the imperial palace during the T'ang period (e.g., 7.167, 7.268). One imagines that at each step, a new round of food and drink would be served, accompanied by a new style of music and dance performed by specialist entertainers. Apparently the music was quite fast, so dancing the three steps must also have been quite fast (Morohashi 12.1212; ZGJT 324; ZGDJT 403c).

Three stages ➛ **Dragon Gate**

Three thousand worlds *Sanzenkai* (J.) 三千界
Three-thousand-realm universe *Sanzen sekai* (J.) 三千世界
Sanzen sekkai (J.) 三千刹界
Great thousand-realm universe *Daisen sekai* (J.) 大千世界
Daisen shakai (J.) 大千沙界

Each of the ten realms of beings includes the other nine in itself. Thus there are one hundred realms altogether. These one hundred realms have each the ten factors of being 十如是 (J. *jūnyoze*), making one thousand realms. These one thousand realms can each be seen in the three realms of existence: the realms of sentient beings, nonsentient beings, and the ***five skandha*** that constitute all beings, both sentient and nonsentient (see DAITŌ 1991, 288).

The term *daisen shakai* 大千沙界 literally means "great thousand sands universe," the sense being that the universes are as numerous as grains of sand (14.409).

Three worlds *Sangai* (J.) 三界

The three worlds are the world of desire, the world of form, and the world of formlessness. Sometimes the term also means the three worlds of past, present, and future.

Toad ➛ Moon

Tokusan (J.) Te-shan (Ch.) 德山

Tokusan is Tokusan Senkan 德山宣鑑 (Ch. Te-shan Hsuan-ch'ien, 780/2–865), a well-known monk in the line of Seigen Gyōshi 青原行思 (Ch. Ch'ing-yüan Hsing-ssu) and himself the master of Seppō Gison 雪峯義存 (Ch. Hsüeh-feng I-ts'un) and Gantō Zenkatsu 巖頭全奯 (Ch. Yen-t'ou Ch'üan-huo), who appear with him in MMK 13. He appears in several other important kōan, including MMK 28, *Heki* 4, *Kattō-shū* 203.

Tokusan is often paired with Rinzai because of their teaching methods: Tokusan for his stick (*Kattō-shū* 203) and Rinzai for his shout (8.90, 12.9, 12.149). Once Tokusan said, "Tonight, no dialogue. I'll hit anyone who asks a question." A monk stepped forward and immediately Tokusan hit him. The monk said, "I haven't even asked my question yet. Why did you hit me?" Tokusan asked, "Where are you from?" The monk said "**Silla**." Tokusan said, "You should have been hit before you even boarded the boat" (*Kattō-shū* 203). See also CLEARY and CLEARY 1977, 230–2.

Tongs and hammer, forge *Kantsui*; *kentsui* (J.) 鉗鎚

The two characters literally mean "tongs and hammer," the tools of the blacksmith, but the phrase is used in Zen to refer to the Zen teacher's skillful training methods. To enter into Zen training is like entering a blacksmith's forge to be put upon the master's anvil. See also the similar expression **Fire pit and bellows.**

Tower of Five Phoenixes Gohōro (J.) 五鳳樓

When the founder of the Liang during the Five Dynasties period made Lo-yang his capital, he constructed the Tower of Five Phoenixes. Thus the tower is the symbol of the capital Lo-yang (14.238, ZGJI 618, Morohashi 257.1023).

Tree of Swords ➛ Five hells without interval

Trigram ➛ Eight trigrams

True listener ➛ **Intimate**

Ts'ao-ch'i ➛ PAO-LIN SSU under **Sixth Patriarch**

Tu Fu (Ch.) Toho (J.) 杜甫

Tu Fu (712–770) competes with **Li Po** for the title of greatest poet of the T'ang period. While Li Po cultivated an image of Taoist nonchalance and enjoyment of wine and nature, Tu Fu expressed in his poetry his strong sense of Confucian duty to his country and emperor. He twice failed at the imperial examinations and was thus unable to obtain an official position of any significance. All his life, his career was buffeted by political turbulence (such as the An Lu-shan rebellion of 755). His poems are noted for their realism and detail, their eloquent expression of human emotion, and their skillful use of language and rhythm. He is explicitly mentioned in *Zen Sand* verses (7.203, 14.117), and many other verses are drawn from his poetry (7.320, 10.6, 10.132–3, 10.159, 14.334, 14.355, 14.370, 14.475, 14.622, among others).

Turtle hairs ➛ **Rabbit horns and turtle hairs**

Twelve causal conditions *Jūni innen* (J.) 十二因緣

Innen 因緣 translates *pratītya-samutpāda* (Skt.), dependent origination or causation. The twelve causes are ignorance (*avidyā*), karmic volition (*saṃskāra*), consciousness (*vijñāna*), name and form (*nāma-rūpa*), the six sense-organs (*ṣaḍ-āyatana*), contact (*sparśa*), sensation (*vedanā*), desire (*tṛṣṇā*), grasping (*upādāna*), existing (*bhava*), birth (*jāti*), and old age and death (*jarā-maraṇa*). Although the doctrine of *pratītya-samutpāda* is the subject of much detailed philosophical analysis in Buddhism, in *Zen Sand* the term *Jūni innen* is used in a much looser way, and accordingly has been translated by a variety of terms: "interconnectedness," "causality," "karma," as well as "twelve causal conditions" (5.17, 12.114, 14.277, 14.620).

Two peaches *Nitō* (J.) 二桃

In the state of Ch'i, Duke Ching had three retainers who were fierce fighters able to vanquish any enemy, but they were also proud and unlikely to give their full allegiance to any lord. He presented two peaches to the three, saying "Let the two most virtuous eat." Two ate the peaches right away and then realized that the third had shown the greatest virtue by letting them eat the peaches. In shame they committed suicide. The third, in his loneliness, committed suicide as well (晏子春秋, 內篇諫下 cited in HYDCD 1.131; 14.30).

Uḍumbara ➛ under **Sumeru**

Ummon (J.) Yun-men (Ch.) 雲門

Ummon Bun'en 雲門文偃 (Ch. Yun-men Wen-yen; 864–949) was a disciple of Seppō Gison 雪峯義存 (Ch. Hsüeh-feng I-ts'un; 822–908) and himself the head of one of the Five Houses of Chinese Ch'an. Numerous difficult kōan are attributed to Yun-men, including *Heki* 14, 15, 27, 39, 47, 54, 60, 62, 77, 83, 86, 87 and MMK 21. The *Record of Yun-men* has been translated into English (App 1994).

Vairocana (Skt.) Biru (J.) 毘盧

Vairocana 毘盧遮那 (J. *Birushana*) is the principal Buddha in the Hua-yen (J. Kegon) school of Buddhism. Sculptures of Vairocana are often of huge gigantic size, such as the rock-cliff sculptures at Lung-men in China and the image at Tōdai-ji at Nara, Japan. This is most likely because, unlike Śākyamuni or Amitābha Buddha, Vairocana Buddha is not a savior figure but the expression of a philosophical concept, *dharmakāya*. The image of great size is often part of the nuance in the verses in which Vairocana is mentioned. Vairocana is described as seated on a lotus throne of a thousand petals, each one of which is itself a universe with its own Buddha, and each of these worlds in turn contains a hundred million further worlds (Sickman and Soper 1971).

Vajra *Kongō* (J.) 金剛

Vajra has several meanings. The *vajra* is a Buddhist ritual implement, a decorated shaft usually made of heavy metal that has at each end a head with three or five rounded prongs whose points flare out and then curve into the center. Sometimes called the thunderbolt or diamond club 金剛杵 of Indra, it was originally an Indian weapon of war but was taken up into Buddhism to symbolize the all-conquering power of Buddha.

Vajra can also refer to the *Vajra* gods 金剛力士 (J. *kongō rikishi*), the fierce guardian gods whose huge images stand outside temple gates.

Vajra as an abstract noun also refers to the ultimate strength and brilliance of Buddhist awakening. It is often translated "diamond" or "adamantine." The *Vajracchedikā sūtra* (J. *Kongō-kyō*) is translated as the *Diamond Sutra.*

Vimalakīrti (Skt.) Yuimakitsu (J.) 維摩詰

Vimalakīrti is the hero of the *Vimalakīrti nirdeśa sūtra*, a major representative work of East Asian Mahāyāna Buddhism. Vimalakīrti is a bodhisattva living as a layman engaged in the world of commerce in the cosmopolitan city of Vaiśalī. His understanding of the Dharma far surpasses that of the other bodhisattva disciples of Śākyamuni. In the history of Chinese Buddhism, Vimalakīrti legitimates the idea that ordained monks are not specially privileged and that lay people are just as capable of understanding and practicing the Dharma.

In the dialogue that appears in chapter 9 of the sutra, the Buddha sends the Bodhisattva Mañjuśrī with a host of lesser bodhisattvas to pay a sick call on Vimalakīrti. In the ensuing dialogue Mañjuśrī asks the bodhisattvas to expound nonduality. Many give their explanations, but in the end Mañjuśrī points out that nonduality is not expressible in language. He then turns to Vimalakīrti for his exposition of nonduality. Vimalakīrti remains silent, uttering not a word. This story of Vimalakīrti's "thunderous silence" has been taken up as an independent kōan (*Heki* 84).

Vimalakīrti's residence measured ten feet square (*hōjō* 方丈), and, because of this, Kamo no Chōmei entitled his work *Hōjōki* 方丈記, *Record of a Ten-foot-Square Hut*. Within a Rinzai monastery compound, the abbot's quarters are called the *hōjō*, and the abbot himself is sometimes called Hōjō-san.

There are several translations of the *Vimalakīrti nirdeśa sūtra* into English, including LUK 1972, THURMAN 1976, and WATSON 1997.

Vipaśyin (Skt.) Bibashibutsu (J.) 毘婆尸佛

In the theory of the Seven Buddhas of the Past, Vipaśyin Buddha, the first of the Seven Buddhas, appeared in the world many ***kalpa*** ago. Śākyamuni, who appears in our age, is the seventh. The name Vipaśyin connotes an incredibly ancient time, long past the human ability to count.

Vulture Peak Ryōzen (J.) 靈山

The Vulture Peak (Skt. Gṛdhrakūṭa, J. Ryōzen 靈山, an abbreviation for Ryōjusen 靈鷲山) is the the site where the Buddha preached the *Lotus Sutra*. In Zen, however, it is associated with the story in which Śākyamuni, instead of verbally preaching the Dharma to the assembled disciples, simply raised a flower in silence, at which **Kāśyapa** smiled (MMK 6; 12.146, 14.558).

Wait by the stump for a rabbit *Kuize o mamotte to o matsu* (J.) 守株待兎

A man in the ancient state of Sung was ploughing his field when he saw a rabbit run by chance headlong into a stump and die. He stopped working and thereafter waited by the stump for other rabbits to run into the stump (*Han Fei-tzu*, cited in YANG 1987, 32–3; 8.129, *Heki* 7 Verse *agyo*, 8 Intro., 20 Verse Comm., 95 Intro.).

Watch *Kō* (J.) 更

In early China the night was divided into five two-hour periods, here called "watches." The first watch 初更 (J. *shokō*) was the period about 7–9 PM. The third watch 三更 (J. *sankō*) was the period between 11 PM and 1 AM, and in *Zen Sand* has often been translated "midnight." The fifth watch 五更 (J. *gokō*), the period about 3 to 5 AM, is sometimes translated here as "dawn."

Wen Wang ➛ **King Wen**

Whisk *Hossu* (J.) 拂子

The *hossu* was used originally in India for keeping away insects, but in China and Japan it became a primarily ritual instrument used by the Zen master. It is basically a bundle of long horsetail or yaktail hairs to which a handle is attached.

Whisks for Buddhist ritual use are made from fine white hair, have lacquered handles, and are decorated with tassels of appropriate color.

White Glade talisman *Hakutaku no zu* (J.) 白澤圖

The White Glade talisman (10.17) was a drawing of a fantastic animal, with eyes on its sides and stomach, said to have arisen from the White Glade during the time of the Yellow Emperor in China. Despite its grotesque appearance, it spoke human language and scared away goblins and wild spirits. The Yellow Emperor had drawings made, and these were circulated widely as a charm for scaring away evil spirits. A reproduction was used on the cover of the journal *Zen Bunka* Fall 1997 (no. 163), and a drawing exists in the collection of the temple Dairyū-ji, in the city of Gifu, Japan (ZGJT 47; personal correspondence from Patricia Fister, 12 January 1998).

Wild fox *Yakozei* (J.) 野狐精

The fox in Chinese and Japanese folklore is a cunning and mischievous being, part animal and part demon-spirit, which assumes human shape to deceive people. The Zen term *yakozei,* "wild fox spirit," carries these connotations into the area of Zen practice, but has more than one meaning. A *yakozei*, for example, can be a person who has learned Zen through books and theory without personal experience. Such a person can deceive novices with his facile speech and learned explanation, just as foxes do humans. At another level, *satori* itself is called *yakozei*. ZRKS 10.425 is 吐出野狐涎再服平胃散 *Yakoen o hakidashi, futatabi heiisan o fuku su,* "He spits out that wild fox slobber, and once more drinks a potion to relieve his stomach." ZGJI 555 comments: "He spits out that mistaken fox-*satori* mind and once more takes up practice from scratch."

The opposite of the *yakozei* is *Zen tenma* 禪天魔, "Zen devil," one who has had only the experience of Zen and lacks the discipline of the study of texts, teaching, and skill-in-means.

The fact that the fox shifts shape, now in human shape, now in fox shape, is not necessarily a bad thing. In MMK Case 2, "Hyakujō and the Fox," Mumon uses the shiftiness of the fox as a metaphor for Buddhist impermanence and no-self.

Yakoen or *yakosen* 野狐涎, "fox slobber," is the saliva of the wild fox, said to be a poison (ZGDJT 329; 16.44, 20.10).

Withered ➛ *Kareta*

Wonder Peak, Wondrous High Mountain, Wondrous Light Mountain, Wonder Mountain Peak ➛ **Sumeru**

Wooden man *Bokujin, mokujin* (J.) 木人

A "wooden man" is a puppet pulled on strings, or a scarecrow dummy. But in

Zen, the lifelessness of the wooden man can connote the no-self of Zen (ZGDJT 194d, 1148d). See also **Stone woman**.

Wrestle in front of horses *Bazen sōboku* (J.) 馬前相撲

"To wrestle in front of horses" symbolizes the need to be decisive and fast (7.385; ZGJT 378, ZGJI 455, SRZGK 853).

Wu (Ch.) Go (J.) 吳

The state of Wu was one of several early Chinese states. It carried on a long hateful rivalry with the state of Yüeh 越 through generations of rulers. Finally in 493 BCE, King Fu-ch'ai of Wu (ruled 495–473 BCE) inflicted a crushing defeat on the state of Yüeh and humiliated its king, Kou Chien, by forcing him to be his personal servant doing degrading tasks. After three years, Kou Chien was released under promise that Yüeh would be a vassal state of Wu and would not train any soldiers or try to rearm. Kou Chien, however, harbored a deep desire for revenge. Legend says that to keep this desire constantly alive, he slept on a bed of brushwood. Outwardly he maintained no army but secretly he trained troops. He encouraged his people to have many children, looking forward to the day when his people would again be strong. He studied every aspect of state affairs, looking for a way to strike back at Wu. His prime minister Fan Li brought to him a plan.

As tribute to King Fu-ch'ai, Kou Chien sent the beautiful **Hsi-shih** to be the Wu king's concubine. Originally a rustic girl from the country, **Hsi-shih** was chosen because of her great beauty to come to the Yüeh court, where she was trained for three years in the arts of a courtesan—music, dancing, entertainment, and the arts of allure and seduction. King Fu-ch'ai of Wu was totally enamored of the beautiful Hsi-shih and built the sumptuous **Ku-su Terrace** as a pleasure pavilion for her. Advisors to King Fu-ch'ai, like **Wu Yuan**, tried to warn the king that Hsi-shih had been sent as part of a plot to overthrow Wu, but Fu-ch'ai was too infatuated to heed the warnings and neglected affairs of state.

Then King Kou Chien of Yüeh struck. In a disciplined march his army easily overran the Wu capital. Fu-ch'ai sent a court official to Kou Chien asking for his life to be spared, and Kou Chien, remembering that his own life had been spared twenty-three years earlier when he had been defeated by Fu-ch'ai, allowed the Wu king to live. When, however, the defeated King Fu-ch'ai realized that Hsi-shih had been part of the plot to destroy him, he took his own life in 473 BCE. Legend says that Hsi-shih, out of loyalty to the king she so long deceived and who was so in love with her, took her own life to join him in the **Yellow Springs**.

The chapters in *Shih-chi* dealing with Kou Chien and of Wu Yuan have been translated into English by YANG and YANG 1979, 35–46, 47–59.

Wu Ch'i (Ch.) Goki (J.) 呉起

Wu Ch'i (?–378? BCE) was a Warring-States general famous as a brilliant strategist and recognized as an authority equal to Sun Tzu in the art of war. He was well known for his extreme cruelty and ruthlessness. For example, when he was serving in the army of the state of Lu, the state of Ch'i attacked. Wu Ch'i's wife was from Ch'i; Wu Ch'i killed her to show his commander his loyalty. He was known as a soldier's soldier, living exactly the same tough life as his foot soldiers in order to cultivate their loyalty. But he enforced discipline with such cruelty and ruthlessness that in the end the noblemen of his own state rose up against him and killed him. His biography is included with Sun Tzu's in *Shih-chi* 65, translated in YANG and YANG 1979, 28–35.

Wu-t'ai ➛ Mount Wu-t'ai

Wu Wang ➛ King Wen

Wu Yuan (Ch.) Goun (J.) 伍員

See also **Wu.** Within King Fu-ch'ai's court was the elderly Wu Yuan 伍員 (also know as Wu Tzu-hsü 伍子胥), famous for his rectitude and one of the few persons to have influence with Fu-ch'ai. Old Wu Yuan had been counselor to King Fu-chai's father when the father had been battling to maintain the state of Wu. When the old king was unsure of whom to appoint heir apparent, Wu Yuan persuaded him to appoint Fu-ch'ai. Wu Yuan's story is ch. 66 of the *Shih-chi.*

Yakṣa (Skt) *Yasha* (J.) 夜叉

In early Buddhist legend, the *yakṣa* was an evil spirit of extremely frightening appearance, said to inhabit forests and places with water. The *yakṣa* was eventually adopted into Buddhism as one of the **eight beings** charged with protecting the Dharma. A related figure is ***pāpīyas.***

Yajñadatta (Skt) Ennyadatta (J.) 演若達多

The *Laṅkāvatāra sūtra* tells the story of Yajñadatta, who loved to look into the mirror every morning to see his face. One morning, he held up the wrong side of the mirror and could not see his face as usual. Thinking the devil had cut off his head, he ran around in a panic searching for it (ZGJT 446).

Yang Kuei-fei (Ch.) Yōkihi (J.) 楊貴妃

The dramatic and tragic life story of Yang Kuei-fei (719–756) has provided material for much Chinese poetry, drama, and literature. Though she was an actual historical figure, her persona in literature is far more legend than fact. Yang Kuei-fei was born to an official of the T'ang bureaucracy and raised by an ambitious uncle who early recognized her potential and gave her the best education possible at home. By age sixteen she was exceedingly beautiful, had mastered the Five Classics of Confucianism, and was skilled in music, dance, and the composition of poetry. Her beauty was described according to the classic Chinese conventions: a face like a lotus flower, eyebrows arched like willow branches, "bones of jade," and so on. She was also ambitious and understood how to use the arts of allurement.

In 735 Hsuan Tsung 玄宗, also known as Ming Huang 明皇, the "Brilliant Emperor" of the T'ang Dynasty, arranged a marriage between her and his eighteenth son. She so entranced Hsuan Tsung, however, that he took her as his own concubine and married his son off to another woman. Emperor Hsuan Tsung conferred upon her the title Kuei-fei, "imperial concubine." At the same time, her uncle, cousin, and three sisters also received positions of rank in the court. Because of this, it is said that parents at the time prayed for the birth, not of sons, but of pretty daughters.

The emperor took a liking to a nomadic tribesman named An Lu-shan, who presented himself as an uncultured simpleton. Yang Kuei-fei also took a liking to him but for different reasons. Under the very gaze of the aging emperor, Yang Kuei-fei and the young An Lu-shan carried on an illicit affair for years. Hsuan Tsung suspected nothing and even made An Lu-shan a general in his army. An Lu-shan, however, had enemies at court, including Kuei-fei's cousin, Yang Kuo-chung, a master at court intrigue. Yang Kuo-chung craftily arranged for An Lu-shan to be made military governor on the frontier to fight the barbarians. This attempt to get rid of An Lu-shan backfired.

In his latter years, Hsuan Tsung more and more dallied with Yang Kuei-fei and neglected affairs of state. Meanwhile his court seethed with intrigue and unrest broke out in the provinces. The T'ang empire had constantly to expend great military effort in confronting the barbarian tribes on its frontiers. An Lu-shan, who had made himself the powerful leader of one of the T'ang Dynasty's strongest armies, seized the opportunity to enter into a conspiracy with the barbarians against the T'ang court. The officials and generals of the court maneuvered desperately to save their own skins and forsook the defence of the country against the rebellion. As Hsuan Tsung dithered, An Lu-shan's forces marched toward the capital, storming through one city after another. When the rebel was almost at the gate, Hsuan Tsung finally gathered up Yang Kuei-fei, her relatives, attendants, and a military guard and fled for the area of Szechuan. It was the summer of 756.

On arrival at Ma-wei, the soldiers in the military guard rebelled and first killed Yang Kuo-chung, Kuei-fei's cousin. When Hsuan Tsung confonted them, they declared their loyalty to the emperor but only on condition that he hand over for execution Yang Kuei-fei, whom they held responsible for the calamity to the nation. It was her relatives who had filled the court with corruption and intrigue and it was her secret lover An Lu-shan who was spreading fire through the countryside. Unable to escape their demands, he had to hand over Yang Kuei-fei to the soldiers. Thus the brilliant life of the most beautiful and powerful woman of the T'ang Dynasty came to an ignoble end.

Hsuan Tsung's great fascination with Yang Kuei-fei's beauty and his prolonged mourning for her are the subject of much famous Chinese poetry, some of which has found its way into the Zen phrase books. Verses by Li Po on Yang Kuei-fei (14.181, 14.421, 14.663) and by Po Chü-i 白居易 from "The Everlasting Sorrow" 長恨哥 about Hsuan Tsung's longing for Yang Kuei-fei (14.297–9) are used as capping phrases to kōan. See SHU 1981A.

Yao (Ch.) Gyō (J.) 堯

Yao is always paired with Shun, the last two of the virtuous Five Emperors of antiquity. See the more detailed note at **Shun**.

Yellow Crane Pavilion Kōkakurō (J.) 黄鶴樓

The Yellow Crane Pavilion, overlooking the Yangtze River, is a famous landmark in Hubei Province. Right across from it in the river lay the picturesque Isle of Parrots. Long ago there used to be a drinking place here run by a man called Hsin. A strange old man used to come to Hsin's place to drink. Though he never had any money, Hsin never pressed him for payment. One day, after this had gone on for some time, the old man took the peel of an orange and with it drew a picture of a yellow crane on a blank wall. Later when customers would clap their hands and sing, the crane on the wall would flutter and dance. The bar became famous and Hsin became wealthy. Ten years went by and the strange old man appeared again. He blew a flute, a white cloud came down, the crane flew down from the wall. The old man climbed onto the back of the crane and then rode the white cloud off into the sky. Afterwards Hsin built a large pavilion that he named the Yellow Crane Pavilion after the drawing of the yellow crane (Morohashi 47926.138).

Yellow Emperor Huang-ti (Ch.) 黄帝

Huang-ti, the Yellow Emperor, is the first of the Five Emperors. His surname is Hsien-yüan 軒轅, a name possibly taken from the name of his birthplace. Several traditions have developed around him. First, he is a culture hero; as one of the Five Emperors, he is said to have taught humans the arts of culture and civilization. Second, he is revered as an ideal and powerful sovereign ruler, one who both heeds the advice of his counselors and succeeds in creating a civilized empire. In legend, he is often depicted as fighting in battle with other emperors, his own half-brother, and a fierce spirit-figure called Ch'ih Yu 蚩尤. Third, he is revered by the Huang-Lao 黄老 school of Taoists as one of their ancestors. The Taoists depicted him as practicing immortality techniques (alchemy, sexual techniques, medicine). Through later elaboration of the legends surrounding him, the Yellow Emperor has become a magnificent figure symbolizing all of Chinese culture and civilization (BIRRELL 1993, 130–7; *Shih-chi*, ch. 1).

Yellow-headed One Kōtō, Ōzu (J.) 黄頭

This term translates the Sanskrit *Kapila*, a region in ancient India associated with Śākyamuni. The Yellow-headed One is thus a literary expression for Śākyamuni (ZGDJT 121, ZGJT 137).

Yellow Plum Mountain ➣ FIFTH PATRIARCH, HUNG JEN under **Sixth Patriarch**

Yellow Springs *Kōsen* (J.) 黄泉

"Yellow Springs" is a Chinese expression for the land of the dead.

Yen Hui (Ch.) Gankai (J.) 顏回

Yen Hui is one of Confucius's two leading disciples, both known for their earnest attitude toward self-cultivation. Tragically for Confucius, Yen Hui died young. When he learned that Yen Hui had died, Confucius exclaimed, "Heaven is destroying me! Heaven is destroying me!" (*Analects* XI, 8).

Yü (the Great) U (J.) 禹

In the legendary history of China's early period, the sage kings Yao and Shun passed on their legacy of virtuous rule to Yü. Many legends describe Yü, but he is best known as the person who saved the world from the great flood. He is credited as the water engineer who caused all of China's Nine Rivers to flow to the east. In the process, he is also said to have created the famous three-step waterfall called the **Dragon Gate**. Because he expended so many years of long labor to save the people from the great flood, he is revered as one of the great sage kings along with Yao and Shun. In other myths, Yü is described as the demigod responsible for demarcating the Nine Provinces of China. For a survey of the legends of Yü, see BIRRELL 1993, 146–59.

On the peak called Kou-lou, the main peak of Mount Heng-shan in Hunan Province, there is a shrine to Yü. The monument there is said to contain seventy-seven characters and to be the oldest such inscribed stone monument in China (Morohashi 7962.1, 7962.2).

Yu-chou (Ch.) Yūshū (J.) 幽州

Yu-chou was a northwestern boundary state in ancient China; it had a reputation for being cold, barren, and desolate. It was often contrasted with **Chiang-nan**, a southern state reputed to be a paradise, famed for its beautiful landscape, women, food, and so forth.

Yü Jang (Ch.) Yoshō (J.) 豫譲

Yü Jang was a retainer who served several noble clans before coming to stay in the house of Chih Po, who recognized his abilities and treated him with respect. The house of Chih had long been in bitter struggle with other noble houses, and eventually Chih Po and all his heirs were killed in a battle with the house of Hsiang. Hsiang-tzu, head of the house of Hsiang, so hated Chih Po that he had Chih Po's skull lacquered and used it as a wine cup.

Yü Jang felt a fierce loyalty to his deceased master. The *Shih-chi* attributes to him the words that have become 12.50: "A warrior dies for one who knows him. A woman dresses for one who loves her." He swore to avenge his master's death. After one unsuccessful attempt to kill Hsiang-tzu, Yü Jang disguised himself by painting his body with lacquer to induce sores like those of a leper, and drinking lye to hoarsen his voice. He changed his appearance so much that when he begged in the marketplace, his own wife did not recognize him. He then hid under a bridge that Hsiang-tzu would soon cross, intending to jump out and kill him. When Hsiang-tzu reached the bridge, however, his horse shied. He sent men to investigate and they discovered Yü Jang.

As a last request, Yü Jang asked for Hsiang-tzu's coat. Hsiang-tzu respected Yü Jang's strong sense of loyalty to his past master and gave him the coat. Yü Jang slashed the coat three times, ritually fulfilling his vow to avenge his master. He then fell upon his own sword, killing himself (6.271, 9.13). Yü Jang's story is told in *Shih-chi*, ch. 86, "Assassin-Retainers" (史記刺客豫讓傳). A translation can be found in YANG and YANG 1979, 386–9, and in Burton WATSON's 1961 2-volume edition of *Records of the Grand Historian of China*. His 1993 3-volume translation, though longer overall, contains only an excerpt of "Assassin-Retainers," and the story of Yü Jang is not included.

Yüan-ming (Ch.) Enmei (J.) 淵明

Yüan-ming is T'ao Yüan-ming (Ch.) 陶淵明, born T'ao Ch'ien 陶潛 (365?–427). Though he lived before the rise of Ch'an in China, his poetry is regarded as expressing the spirit of Ch'an (ZGJT 155). Several verses in *Zen Sand* presuppose knowledge about Yüan-ming. In the early part of his life, he started a career as a scholar-official in the imperial bureaucracy and held a succession of government positions. Then in mid-career, he suddenly resigned from public life to take up a life of farming and living in nature. His poems deal with living in nature, drinking wine, contentment in poverty, and living according to the desires of one's own heart. Despite times of extreme poverty, political upheaval, and family misfortune, he displays in his poems an attitude of deep serenity.

His "Preface to the Poem on the Peach Blossom Spring" 桃花源詩 established a major image in Chinese poetry. A man was making his way up a mountain stream when he came upon a grove of peach trees whose whirling petals and fragrance filled the air. The water came from a spring in a small cave at the base of a hill. Entering the cave, he eventually came out onto a plain where there were people, houses, farms, animals, and children all living a happy and carefree life. They welcomed him warmly and told him that their ancestors several generations earlier had fled the constant warfare of their time and that over the years, they had lost all contact with the outside world. After several days of warm hospitality, the man passed through the cave and returned to his former life. He told the local governor of his discovery, but when they tried to find the peach grove and the spring again, they could not locate it (12.72; Watson 1984, 142–3).

His poem "Drinking Wine" 陶淵明飲酒 has become a model of the poetry of the recluse in Chinese culture. Five verses from it have been included in *Zen Sand* (10.550–4). Because of his poem "Homeward ho!" 歸去來 (read in J. *kaeri nan iza*), the phrase *kaeri nan iza* immediately brings to mind T'ao Yüan-ming.

Some images are associated with Yüan-ming, such as wine drinking, chrysanthemums, and the three paths of a recluse scholar's garden. The poem "Homeward ho!", which explains his reasons for resigning, contains the lines, "The three paths were overgrown with weeds, but the pines and chrysanthemums were still there." A formal Chinese garden had three paths planted with pine, chrysanthemum, and bamboo (Morohashi 12.404).

Yüeh ➛ Wu

Yüeh Yi (Ch.) Rakki (J.) 樂毅

During China's Warring States period, General Yüeh Yi was in the service of the state of Yen 燕. Intelligent and popular with his troops, he once led a five-state coalition of armies in a massive action against the state of Ch'i 齊, taking more than seventy of its cities. For this he was granted the title of duke by the king, and given a fief. When the king died, however, the next king did not like Yüeh Yi, and as a result Yüeh Yi left Yen to go to the state of Chao 趙. When he left the Yen soldiers trembled in fear, and with good reason. The general who succeeded Yüeh Yi suffered defeat in battle, causing the king to regret having driven Yüeh Yi away (*Shih chi,* ch. 80, Morohashi 15399.49).

Zenki* ➛ *Ki

Bibliography

Aitken, Robert
1984 *The Mind of Clover: Essays in Zen Buddhist Ethics.* San Francisco: North Point Press.
1990 *The Gateless Barrier: The Wu-men Kuan.* San Francisco: North Point Press.

Aizawa Ekai 相澤恵海
1907 禪學要鑑 [Essentials for Zen Study]. Tokyo: Kawase Shobō.

Akizuki Ryōmin 秋月龍珉
1972 臨済録 [Record of Rinzai]. Tokyo: Chikuma Shobō.
1979 禅問答 [Zen Dialogue]. Tokyo: San'ichi Shobō.
1981 禅のことば [Zen Words]. Tokyo: Toppan Insatsu.
1987 公案実践的禅入門 [Kōan: A Practical Introduction to Zen]. Tokyo: Chikuma Shobō.

Allan, Sarah
1991 *The Shape of the Turtle: Myth, Art and Cosmos in Early China.* Albany, NY: State University of New York Press.

Allan, Sarah, and Alvin P. Cohen, eds.
1979 *Legend, Lore and Religion in China: Essays in Honor of Wolfram Eberhard on His Seventieth Birthday.* San Francisco: Chinese Materials Center.

App, Urs T.
1994 *Master Yunmen.* New York: Kōdansha.

Asahina Sōgen 朝比奈宗源
1935 臨濟錄 [Record of Rinzai]. Tokyo: Iwanami Shoten.
1937 碧巖錄 [Blue Cliff Record]. 3 vols. Tokyo: Iwanami Shoten.
1941 禪の公案 [Zen Kōan]. Tokyo: Yūzankaku.

Bauer, Wolfgang, and Herbert Franke, eds.
1964 *The Golden Casket: Chinese Novellas of Two Millenia.* New York: Harcourt, Brace and World.

Berling, Judith A.
1987 "Bringing the Buddha Down to Earth: Notes on the Emergence of *Yü-lu* as a Buddhist Genre." *History of Religions* 27/1: 56–88.

Bielefeldt, Carl
1986 "Ch'ang-lu Tsung-tse's *Tso-ch'an* and the 'Secret' of Zen Meditation." In Gregory 1986, 129–62.
1997 "Kokan Shiren and the Sectarian Uses of History." In *The Origins of Japan's Medieval World*, ed. by Jeffrey P. Mass. Stanford: Stanford University Press. 295–317.

Birrell, Anne
1986 *New Songs from a Jade Terrace: An Anthology of Early Chinese Love Poetry.* Harmondsworth: Penguin.
1993 *Chinese Mythology.* Baltimore: Johns Hopkins Press.

BLYTH, R. H.
1949 *Haiku,* vol. I: *Eastern Culture.* Tokyo: Hokuseido Press.

BODDE, Derk
1938 *China's First Unifier: A Study of the Ch'in Dynasty as Seen in the Life of Li Ssu.* Leiden: E. J. Brill.
1975 *Festivals in Classical China: New Year and Other Observances during the Han Dynasty 206 BC–AD 220.* Princeton: Princeton University Press.

BRAVERMAN, Arthur
1989 *Mud and Water: A Collection of Talks by the Zen Master Bassui.* Berkeley: North Point Press.

BREWITT-TAYLOR, C. H., trans.
1959 *Romance of the Three Kingdoms.* Rutland and Tokyo: Charles E. Tuttle.

BUSSHO KANKŌKAI 仏書刊行会
1983 Gidō Shūshin 義堂周信, ed. 貞和類聚祖苑聯芳集, 新撰貞和集 [Jōwa Era Collection of Classified Verses Inherited from the Ancestors, New Selection of the Jōwa Era Collection]. 大日本仏教全書 143. Tokyo.

BUSWELL, Robert E.
1987 "The 'Short-cut' Approach of K'an-hua Meditation: The Evolution of a Practical Subitism in Chinese Ch'an Buddhism." In GREGORY 1987, 321–77.
1992 *The Zen Monastic Experience: Buddhist Practice in Contemporary Korea.* Princeton: Princeton University Press.

CAHILL, Suzanne
1995 *Transcendence & Divine Passion: The Queen Mother of the West in Medieval China.* Stanford: Stanford University Press.

CAMMANN, Schuyler
1953 "Types of Symbols in Chinese Art." In *Studies in Chinese Thought,* ed. by Arthur F. Wright. Chicago: University of Chicago Press.

CHANG Chung-yuan
1969 "Interfusion of Universality and Particularity." *Original Teachings of Ch'an Buddhism: Selected from The Transmission of the Lamp.* New York: Random House. 41–57.

CHIEN, Cheng
1992 *Sun-Face Buddha: The Teachings of Ma-tsu and the Hung-chou School of Ch'an.* Berkeley: Asian Humanities Press.

CLEARY, Thomas
1984 *The Flower Ornament Scripture: A Translation of the Avatamsaka Sutra.* 3 vols. Boulder: Shambhala.
1987 *Entry into the Realm of Reality. The Text: A Translation of the Gandavyuha.* Boston: Shambhala.
1990 *Book of Serenity.* Hudson, NY: Lindisfarne Press.
1993 *No Barrier: Unlocking the Zen Koan.* New York: Bantam Books.
1998 *The Blue Cliff Record.* Berkeley: Numata Center for Buddhist Translation and Research.

CLEARY, Thomas, and J. C. CLEARY
1977 *The Blue Cliff Record.* Boulder: Shambhala.

COLLCUTT, Martin
1981 *Five Mountains: The Rinzai Zen Monastic Institution in Medieval Japan.* Cambridge: Harvard University Press.

CONZE, Edward
1959 *Buddhist Scriptures.* Harmondsworth: Penguin.

COOPER, Arthur
1973 *Li Po and Tu Fu.* Harmondsworth: Penguin.

Daichū-ji 大中寺

1966 釋大眉禪師雲關窟廣錄 [Great Record of Shaku Taibi Zenji Unkankutsu]. Numazu, Shizuoka: Daichū-ji.

Daitō Shuppansha

1991 *Japanese-English Buddhist Dictionary* 日英佛教辭典. Revised edition. Tokyo: Daitō Publishing.

Davis, A. R.

1968 "The Double Ninth Festival in Chinese Poetry: A Study of Variations upon a Theme." In *Wen-lin: Studies in the Chinese Humanities,* ed. by Chow Tse-tsung. Madison: University of Wisconsin Press. 45–64.

De Bary, W. T., Wing-tsit Chan, and Burton Watson

1960 *Sources of Chinese Tradition.* 2 vols. New York: Columbia University Press.

DeWoskin, Kenneth

1982 *A Song for One or Two: Music and the Concept of Art in Early China.* Ann Arbor: University of Michigan Center for Chinese Studies.

Ding Wangdao 丁往道選譯

1988 *100 Chinese Myths and Fantasies.* 中国神 及志怪小説一百篇. Taipei: Taiwan Shang-wu Yinshukuan.

Dumoulin, Heinrich

1990 *Zen Buddhism: A History.* Vol. i: *India and China;* vol. ii: *Japan.* Trans. by James W. Heisig and Paul Knitter. New York: Macmillan (vol. i, 1988; vol. ii, 1990).

Dumoulin, Heinrich, and Ruth Fuller Sasaki

1953 *The Development of Chinese Zen after the Sixth Patriarch in the Light of Mumonkan.* New York: First Zen Institute of America.

Duyvendak, J. J. L.

1963 *The Book of Lord Shang.* Chicago: University of Chicago Press.

Ebersole, Gary L.

1983 "The Buddhist Ritual Use of Linked Poetry in Medieval Japan." *Eastern Buddhist* 16/2: 50–71.

First Zen Institute of America

1947 *Cat's Yawn.* New York: First Zen Institute of America. (13 numbers from 1940 to 1941)

Forman, Robert K. C.

1986 "Mysticism and Pure Consciousness Events." *Sophia* 25: 49–58.

1990 (ed.). *The Problem of Pure Consciousness: Mysticism and Philosophy.* New York: Oxford University Press.

1993 "Mystical Knowledge: Knowledge by Identity." *Journal of the American Academy of Religion* 51: 705–38.

Foulk, T. Griffiths

1993 "Myth, Ritual, and Monastic Practice in Sung Ch'an Buddhism." In *Religion and Society in T'ang and Sung China,* ed. by Patricia B. Ebrey and Peter N. Gregory. Honolulu: University of Hawai'i Press. 147–208.

2000 "The Form and Function of Kōan Literature: A Historical Overview." In Heine and Wright 2000, 15–45.

Fox, James J.

1988 "Introduction." In *To Speak in Pairs: Essays on the Ritual Languages of Eastern Indonesia,* ed. by James J. Fox. Cambridge: Cambridge University Press. 1–28.

Fujita Genro 藤田玄路, ed.

1922 塗毒鼓 [Poison-Painted Drum]. Kyoto: Kenninji Sōdō (vol. i, 1917; vol. ii, 1922). Contains 塗毒鼓句集 [Poison-Painted Drum Phrase Collection].

Fung Yu-lan

1952 *A History of Chinese Philosophy.* Princeton: Princeton University Press. 2 vols. Trans. by Derk Bodde.

Gallwey, W. Timothy

1974 *The Inner Game of Tennis.* New York: Random House.

Gardner, Daniel K.

1991 "Modes of Thinking and Modes of Discourse in the Sung: Some Thoughts on the *Yü-lu* ('Recorded Conversations') Texts." *The Journal of Asian Studies* 50/3: 574–603.

Gidō Shōshin 義堂周信

1939 空華日用工夫略集 [Summary Collection of Flowers of Emptiness from Daily Practice]. Ed. by Tsuji Zennosuke 辻善之助. Tokyo: Taiyōsha

Giles, Herbert. A.

1939 *A Chinese Biographical Dictionary* [Ku chin hsing shih tsu p'u]. Shanghai: Kelly & Walsh.

Graham, A. C.

1960 *The Book of Lieh-tzu.* New York: Columbia University Press.

1986 *Yin-Yang and the Nature of Correlative Thinking.* Singapore: Institute of East Asian Philosophies. Occasional Paper and Monograph Series No. 6.

1992 "Poetic and Mythic Varieties of Correlative Thinking." *Unreason Within Reason: Essays on the Outskirts of Rationality.* LaSalle, Illinois: Open Court. 207–23.

Green, James T.

1998 *The Recorded Sayings of Zen Master Joshu.* Walnut Creek, CA: Sage Publications.

Gregory, Peter N.

1986 *Traditions of Meditation in Chinese Buddhism.* Honolulu: University of Hawai'i Press.

1987 *Sudden and Gradual: Approaches to Enlightenment in Chinese Thought.* Honolulu: University of Hawai'i Press.

Haga Kōshirō 芳賀幸四郎

1973 一行物 [Scrolls]. Kyoto: Tankōsha.

1974 続一行物 [More Scrolls]. Kyoto: Tankōsha.

1977 続続一行物 [More and More Scrolls]. Kyoto: Tankōsha.

1984 又続一行物 [Still More Scrolls]. Kyoto: Tankōsha.

Haga Kōshirō, Ōsaka Kōryū, and Karaki Junzō

1977 "Japanese Zen: A Symposium." *The Eastern Buddhist* 10/2: 76–101.

Hakuin Ekaku 白隠慧鶴

1922 洞上五位偏正口訣 [Five Ranks of the Crooked and the Straight: The Oral Teachings of the (Monk) Who Lived on Mount Tō]. In Fujita 1922.

Harada Sogaku 原田祖岳

1977 参禅の階梯 [Stages in Zen Practice]. Tokyo: Kokusho Kankōkai.

Hawkes, David

1985 *The Songs of the South: An Ancient Chinese Anthology of Poems by Qu Yuan and Other Poets.* Harmondsworth: Penguin.

Heine, Steven

1990 "Does the Kōan Have Buddha-Nature?" *Journal of the American Academy of Religion* 58: 357–87.

1994 *Dōgen and the Kōan Tradition: A Tale of Two Shōbōgenzō Texts.* Albany: State University of New York Press.

1999 *Shifting Shape, Shaping Text: Philosophy and Folklore in the Fox Kōan.* Honolulu: University of Hawai'i Press.

Heine, Steven, and D. S. Wright, eds.

2000 *The Koan: Texts and Contexts in Zen Buddhism.* Oxford: Oxford University Press.

HEKIAN Shūdō 碧菴周道, compiler
1982 *Zenrin gokushō* 禅林語句鈔 [Zen Sangha Words and Phrases]. Tokyo: Nigensha.

HENDERSON, John B.
1984 *The Development and Decline of Chinese Cosmology*. New York: Columbia University Press.
1991 *Scripture, Canon, and Commentary: A Comparison of Confucian and Western Exegesis*. Princeton: Princeton University Press.

HENRICKS, Robert G.
1989 *Lao-Tzu: Te-Tao Ching*. New York: Ballantine Books.
1990 *The Poetry of Han-shan*. Albany: State University of New York Press.

HIGHTOWER, James Robert
1965 "Some Characteristics of Parallel Prose." In *Studies in Chinese Literature: Harvard-Yenching Institute Studies* XXI, ed. by John L. Bishop. Cambridge: Harvard University Press. 108–38.

HIRANO Sōjō 平野宗浄
1983 *Daitō Kokushi goroku* 大燈国師語録 [Record of Daitō Kokushi]. Tokyo: Kōdansha.
1988 "Den Daitō senkushū (Hōshun-in zō)" 伝大燈撰句集(芳春院蔵) [Collection of Selected Zen Phrases Attributed to Daitō (Hōshun-in Archives)]. *Zen Bunka Kenkyūjo Kiyō* 15: 561–600.

HIRATA Seikō 平田精耕
1988 禅語事典 [Zen Word Dictionary]. Kyoto: PHP.

HIRATA Takashi 平田高士
1969 無門関 [*Mumonkan*]. Tokyo: Chikuma Shobō.
1982 碧巌集 [*Hekiganshū*]. Tokyo: Daizō Shuppan.

HIRO Sachiya ひろさちや
1988 日本語になった仏教のことば [Buddhist Words That Have Become Japanese]. Tokyo: Kōdansha.

HISAMATSU Shin'ichi
1971 *Zen and the Fine Arts*. Trans. by Gishin Tokiwa. Tokyo: Kodansha International.

HOFFMAN, Yoel
1975 *The Sound of One Hand: 281 Zen Kōans with Answers*. New York: Basic Books.
1977 *Every End Exposed: The 100 Kōans of Master Kidō with the Answers of Hakuin Zen*. Brookline, MA: Autumn Press.
1978 *Radical Zen: The Sayings of Jōshū*. Brookline, MA: Autumn Press.

HOLZMAN, Donald
1956 "The Conversational Tradition in Chinese Philoosophy." *Philosophy East and West* 6: 223–30.

HORI, Victor Sōgen
1994 "Teaching and Learning in the Rinzai Zen Monastery." *Journal of Japanese Studies* 20/1: 5–35.
1999 "Translating the *Zen Phrase Book*." *Bulletin of the Nanzan Institute for Religion and Culture* 1999: 44–58.
2000 "Kōan and Kenshō in the Rinzai Kōan Curriculum." In HEINE and WRIGHT 2000, 280–315.

HSIEH Ding-Hwa Evelyn
1994 "Yuan-wu K'o-ch'in's (1063–1135) Teaching of Ch'an *Kung-an* Practice: A Transition from the Literary Study of Ch'an *Kung-an* to the Practical *K'an-hua* Ch'an." *Journal of the International Association of Buddhist Studies* 17/1: 66–95.

HUANG Yen-kai, ed.
1964 *A Dictionary of Chinese Idiomatic Phrases*. Hong Kong: Eton Press.

IIDA Rigyō 飯田利行, ed.
1975 禅林名句辞典 [Dictionary of Well-Known Zen Sangha Phrases]. Tokyo: Kokusho Kankōkai.

1994 禅林用語辞典 [Dictionary of Zen Sangha Language]. Tokyo: Kashiwa Bijutsu Shuppan.

IIDA Tōin 飯田窿隱, ed.

1955 槐安國語提唱錄 [Record of Lectures on the Kaiankokugo] Kyoto: Kichūdō.

IJŪSHI 已十子, ed.

1688 禪林句集 [Zen Sangha Phrase Collection]. Kyoto: Baiyō Shoin reprint.

IMAEDA Aishin 今枝愛眞, ed.

1971 五燈會元索引 [Index to a Compendium of the Five Lamps]. Tokyo: Rinrōkaku.

IMAI Fukuzan 今井福山 and Nakagawa Shūan 中川渋庵, eds.

1935 禅語字彙 [Zen Glossary]. Tokyo: Hakurinsha.

INAGAKI, Hisao

1984 *A Dictionary of Japanese Buddhist Terms*. Kyoto: Nagata Bunshodō.

1991 *A Glossary of Zen Terms*. Kyoto: Nagata Bunshodō.

INOUE, Y.

1979 *Lou-lan Stories*. Trans. by James T. Araki. Tokyo and New York: Kōdansha.

IRITANI Sensuke 入谷仙介 and Matsumura Takashi 松村昂, eds.

1970 寒山詩 [Cold Mountain Poems]. Tokyo: Chikuma Shobō.

IRIYA Yoshitaka 入矢義高

1991 臨済録 [Record of Rinzai]. Tokyo: Iwanami.

1996 「句双紙」解説 [An Explanation of Zen Phrase Books]. In YAMADA, IRIYA, and SANAE 1996, 564–80.

1997 (ed.) 景徳伝灯録三, 四 [Ching-te Era Record of the Transmission of the Lamp, vols. III and IV]. Kyoto: Zen Bunka Kenkyūjo.

IRIYA Yoshitaka 入矢義高, KAJITANI Sōnin 梶谷宗忍, and YANAGIDA Seizan

1981 雪竇頌古 [Setchō's Old Cases with Verses]. *Zen no goroku 15*. Tokyo: Chikuma Shobō.

IRIYA Yoshitaka 入矢義高 and KOGA Hidehiko 古賀英彦, eds.

1991 禅語辞典 [Zen Word Dictionary]. Kyoto: Shibunkaku.

IRIYA Yoshitaka 入矢義高, MIZOGUCHI Yūzō 溝口雄三, and SUEKI Fumihiko 末木文美士, trans.

1992 碧巖録 [*Hekigan-roku*]. 3 vols. Tokyo: Iwanami Shoten.

ISHIKAWA Umejirō 石川梅次郎 and HAMA Hisao 浜久雄, eds.

1962 詩韻含英異同辨 [Superior Poetic Rhymes]. Tokyo: Shōundō.

ITŌ Kokan 伊藤古鑑

1970 禪と公案 [Zen and the Kōan]. Tokyo: Shunjūsha.

IWAMOTO Yutaka 岩本 裕

1972 日常仏教語 [Everyday Buddhist Words]. Tokyo: Chūo Shinsho.

IZUTSU, Gafū 井筒雅風

1970 袈裟史 [History of the Kesa]. Tokyo: Yūzankaku.

JIMBO Nyoten 神保如天 and ANDŌ Bun'ei 安藤文英, eds.

1974 禪學辭典 [Dictionary of Zen Study]. Kyoto: Heirakuji Shoten.

KAJITANI Sōnin 梶谷宗忍, ed.

1977 宗門葛藤集 [Tangled Vine Collection]. Kyoto: Hōzōkan.

KAMATA Tadashi 鎌田 正 and YONEYAMA Toratarō 米山寅太郎

1980 漢詩名句辞典 [Dictionary of Well-Known Verses from Chinese Poetry]. Tokyo: Daishūkan.

KANAYA Osamu 金谷 治

1971 荘子 [Chuang-tzu]. 4 vols. Tokyo: Iwanami Shoten.

1997 老子 [Lao-tzu]. Tokyo: Kōdansha.

KAO, Yu-kung, and Tsu-lin MEI

1978 "Meaning, Metaphor, and Allusion in T'ang Poetry." *Harvard Journal of Asiatic Studies* 38/2: 281–356.

Katō Shōshun 加藤正俊

1998 "'A Lineage of Dullards': Zen Master Tōjū Reisō and His Associates." *Japanese Journal of Religious Studies* 25/1–2: 151–65.

Katz, Steven T.

1978 "Language, Epistemology and Mysticism." In *Mysticism and Philosophical Analysis*, ed. by Steven Katz. New York: Oxford University Press. 22–74.

1983 "The 'Conservative' Character of Mystical Experience." In *Mysticism and Religious Tradition*, ed. by Steven Katz. New York: Oxford University Press. 3–60.

1992 "Mystical Speech and Mystical Meaning." In *Mysticism and Language*, ed. by Steven Katz. New York: Oxford University Press. 3-41.

Kawase Kazuma 川瀬一馬

1942 句雙紙考 [Thoughts on *Kuzōshi*]. In 積翠先生華甲壽記念論纂 [Memorial Volume to Sekisui Sensei on His Sixtieth Birthday], ed. by Noguchi Shinji 野口信二. Tokyo: Ippan Insatsu. 119–44.

1979 句雙紙假名抄解説 [An Explanation of the Kana Annotated Phrase Book]. Tokyo: Kotenseki Fukusei Sōkan Kankōkai.

Keene, Donald

1977 "The Comic Tradition in Renga." In *Japan in the Muromachi Age*, ed. by J. W. Hall and Toyoda Takeshi. Berkeley and Los Angeles: University of California Press. 241–77.

Kim, Hee-jin

1985 "Introductory Essay: Language in Dogen's Zen." *Flowers of Emptiness: Selections from Dōgen's Shōbōgenzō*. Lewiston and Queenston: Edwin Mellen Press. 1–47.

1988 "The Reason of Words and Letters; Dogen and Kōan Language." In *Dogen Studies*, ed. by W. R. LaFleur. Honolulu: University of Hawai'i Press. 54–82.

Kimura Akira 木村 晟, ed.

1995 聚分韻略(無刊記本)の典拠資料(漢文注) [*Shūbun inryaku* (unpublished edition) with Exact References (Kambun Annotation)]. Tokyo: Daikūsha.

Kimura Akira 木村 晟 and Katayama Seiken 片山晴賢, eds.

1984 禪林句雙紙集 [Collected Versions of the *Zenrin kuzōshi*]. Tokyo: Kobayashi Insatsu.

Kino Kazuyoshi 紀野一義

1988 仏教のキイ・ワード [Buddhist Key Words]. Tokyo: Kōdansha.

Kita Takashi 来田隆, ed.

1991 句双紙抄総索引 [Comprehensive Index to the Annotated *Kuzōshi*]. Osaka: Seibundō.

Kokuyaku Zenshū Sōsho Kankōkai

1974 国訳虚堂和尚語録 [Record of Master Kidō, in Japanese Translation]. 国訳禅宗叢書第二輯第六–八巻 [*Kokuyaku zenshū sōsho*, Second Collection, vols. vi–viii. Tokyo: Daiichi Shoten.

Komazawa Daigaku Zengaku Daijiten Hensansho 駒澤大學禪學大辭典編纂所

1977 禪學大辭典 [Lexicon of Zen Studies]. Tokyo: Daishūkan.

Kraft, Kenneth

1988 (ed.) *Zen: Tradition and Transition.* New York: Grove Press.

1992 *Eloquent Zen: Daitō and Early Japanese Zen.* Honolulu: University of Hawai'i Press.

Kudō Sumiko

1975 "Shibayama Zenkei, 1904–1974." *Eastern Buddhist* 8/1: 149–54.

Kusumoto Bun'yū 久須本文雄

1982 禅語入門 [Introduction to Zen Language]. Tokyo: Daihōrinkaku.

Kuzōshi 句雙紙

n.d. 蓬左文庫 [Hōsa Collection] ざ Manuscript number 123-15 部門一二三 番号一五. Nagoya: Hōsa Bunko.

Kyūma Eichū 久馬慧忠
1989 袈裟のはなし: 仏のこころとかたち [Stories of the Buddhist Robe: The Heart and Form of Awakening]. Kyoto: Hōzōkan.

Lai, Whalen
1980 "Further Developments of the Two Truths Theory in China." *Philosophy East and West* 30: 139–62.
1983 "Sinitic Mandalas: The Wu-wei-t'u of Ts'ao-shan." In Lai and Lancaster 1983, 65–86.

Lai, Whalen, and Lewis R. Lancaster, eds.
1983 *Early Ch'an in China and Tibet.* Berkeley: Berkeley Buddhist Studies.

Lau, D. C., trans.
1970 *Mencius.* Harmondsworth: Penguin.
1979 *Confucius: The Analects.* Harmondsworth: Penguin.

Lattimore, David
1973 "Allusion and T'ang Poetry." In *Perspectives on the T'ang*, ed. by Arthur F. Wright and Denis Twitchett. New Haven and London: Yale University Press. 405–39.

Legge, James T.
1985 *The Chinese Classics:* vol. i, *Confucian Analects, The Great Learning, Doctrine of the Mean*; vol. ii, *The Works of Mencius*; vol. iii, *The Shoo King*; vol. iv, *The She King, or The Book of Ancient Poetry*; vol. v, *The Ch'un Ts'ew with the Tso Chuen.* London: Oxford University Press (reprint, Southern Materials Center).

Lewis, Zenrin Chidō Robert E.
1996 *The Book of the Zen Grove.* 2nd ed. Jacksonville: Zen Sangha Press.

Ling Yün 凌雲 and 白牧 Bai Mu, eds.
n.d. 禪林慧語 [Zen Sangha Words of Wisdom]. Taipei: Ch'ang-ch'un Shushufang.

Liu, James J. Y.
1988 *Language Paradox Poetics: A Chinese Perspective*, ed. by Richard John Lynn. Princeton: Princeton University Press.

Liu Wu-chi and Lo Yucheng, eds.
1975 *Sunflower Splendor: Three Thousand Years of Chinese Poetry.* New York: Anchor Books.

Lo Kuan-chung
1959 *Romance of the Three Kingdoms.* 2 vols. Trans. by C. H. Brewitt-Taylor. Rutland and Tokyo: Charles E. Tuttle.

Loewe, Michael
1986 "The Former Han Dynasty." In Twitchett and Loewe 1986, 103–222.

Loori, John Daido
1994 *Two Arrows Meeting in Mid-Air: The Zen Koan.* Boston: Charles E. Tuttle.
n.d. *108 Koans of the Way of Reality.* Mount Tremper, NY: Mountains and Rivers Order. (Unpublished)

Loy, David
1988 *Nonduality: A Study in Comparative Philosophy.* New Haven and London: Yale University Press.

Luk, Charles (Lu K'uan Yü)
1961 *Ch'an and Zen Teaching.* 3 vols. London: Rider.
1972 *The Vimalakīrti Nirdeśa Sūtra.* Berkeley: Shambhala.

Luo Zhu-feng 羅竹風, ed.
1990 漢語大詞典 [Great Dictionary of Chinese], 12 vols and index. n.p. Hanyu Dacidian Chubanshe.

Lynn, Richard John
1987 "The Sudden and Gradual in Chinese Poetry Criticism: An Examination of the Ch'an-Poetry Analogy." In Gregory 1987, 381–427.

1994 *The Classic of Changes: A New Translation of the I Ching.* New York: Columbia University Press.

MAENO Naoaki 前野直彬, ed.

1962 唐詩選 [Selected T'ang Poetry]. 3 vols. Tokyo: Iwanami Shoten.

MAIR, Victor, ed.

1994 *The Columbia Anthology of Traditional Chinese Literature.* New York: Columbia University Press.

MAJOR, John S.

1993 *Heaven and Earth in Early Han Thought.* Albany: State University of New York Press.

MARK, Lindy Li

1979 "Orthography Riddles, Divination, and Word Magic: An Exploration in Folklore and Culture." In ALLAN and COHEN 1979, 43–69.

MASUNAGA Reihō 増永靈鳳 and FURUTA Shōkin 古田紹欽, eds.

1967 現代禪講座別巻禪語小辭典 [Modern Zen Lectures, Special Issue: Shorter Zen Dictionary]. Tokyo: Kadokawa.

MATHER, Richard B.

1976 *Shih-shuo Hsin-yü: A New Account of Tales of the World* (by Liu I-ch'ing) 世說新語. Minneapolis: University of Minnesota Press.

MATSUBARA Taidō 松原泰道

1972 禅語百選 [One Hundred Selected Zen Phrases]. Tokyo: Shōgakkan.

MCRAE, John

1992 "Encounter Dialogue and the Tranformation of the Spiritual Path in Chinese Ch'an." In *Paths to Liberation: The Marga and Its Tranformations in Buddhist Thought*, ed. by Robert E. Buswell and Robert M. Gimello. Honolulu: University of Hawai'i Press. 339–69.

2000 "The Antecedents of Encounter Dialogue in Chinese Ch'an Buddhism." In HEINE and WRIGHT 2000.

MEI Yi-pao, trans.

1977 *The Works of Motze.* Taipei: Confucius Publishing Co.

MINER, Earl

1979 *Japanese Linked Poetry.* Princeton: Princeton University Press.

MIURA Isshū and Ruth Fuller SASAKI

1965 *The Zen Koan.* New York: Harcourt.

1966 *Zen Dust: The History of the Koan and Koan Study in Rinzai (Lin-chi) Zen.* Kyoto: The First Zen Institute of America.

MIYAZAKI Ichisada

1981 *China's Examination Hell.* New Haven: Yale University Press.

MOCHIZUKI Shinkō 望月信亨, ed.

1958 望月佛教大辭典增訂版 [Mochizuki Buddhist Lexicon, Revised Edition]. Tokyo: Sekai Seiten Kankō Kyōkai.

MOHR, Michel

1993 "Examining the Sources of Rinzai Zen." *Japanese Journal of Religious Studies* 20/4: 331–44.

1999 "Hakuin." In *Buddhist Spirituality II: Later China, Korea, Japan, and the Modern World.* Edited by Takeuchi Yoshinori with James W. Heisig, Paul L. Swanson, and Joseph S. O'Leary. New York: Crossroad Publishing. 307–28.

MOROHASHI Tetsuji 諸橋轍次, compiler

1960 大漢和辭典 [Great Chinese-Japanese Dictionary]. 13 vols. Tokyo: Daishūkan Shoten.

1979 *Chūgoku Koten Meigen Jiten* 中国古典名言事典 [Encyclopedia of Famous Sayings from the Chinese Classics]. Tokyo: Kōdansha.

MORRELL, Robert E.

1985 *Sand and Pebbles Shasekishū: The Tales of Mujū Ichien, A Voice for Pluralism in Kamakura Buddhism*. Albany: State University of New York Press.

MOTE, F. W.

1959 "Confucian Eremitism in the Yüan Period." In *Confucianism and Chinese Civilization*, ed. by Arthur F. Wright. Stanford: Stanford University Press, 252–90.

MUJAKU Dōchū 無著道忠 and HIRANO Sōjō 平野宗浄, eds.

1971 定本臨濟禪師語録 [Definitive Text of the Record of Rinzai Zenji]. Tokyo: Shunjūsha.

MUJAKU Dōchū 無著道忠 and Yanagida Seizan 柳田聖山, eds.

1979 Vol. I, 禪林象器箋 [Notes on Zen Images and Implements]; vol. II, 葛藤語箋, 禪林句集辨苗 [Tangled Vine Word Notes, *Zenrin kushū* Petals and Sprouts]. Kyoto: Chūbun Shuppansha.

MURAKAMI Tetsumi 村上哲見, ed.

1978 三体詩 [Collected Poems in Three Styles]. 4 vols. Tokyo: Asahi Shinbunsha.

NAKAMURA Hajime 中村 元

1977 仏教語源散策 [Browsing through Buddhist Word Origins]; 続仏教語源散策 [More Browsing through Buddhist Word Origins]. Tokyo: Tokyo Shoseki.

1981 仏教語大辞典 [Lexicon of Buddhist Terms]. Tokyo: Tokyo Shoseki.

NAKAMURA Hajime 中村 元, FUKUNAGA Mitsuji 福永光司, TAMURA Yoshirō 田村芳朗, and IMANO Tatsu 今野 達, eds.

1995 岩波仏教辞典 [Iwanami Buddhist Dictionary]. Tokyo: Iwanami Shoten.

NEEDHAM, Joseph

1959 *Science and Civilization in China*, vol. III: *Mathematics and the Sciences of the Heavens and the Earth*. Cambridge: Cambridge University Press.

NEEDHAM, Joseph, and Colin A. RONAN

1978 *The Shorter Science and Civilization in China*, vol. I: Cambridge: Cambridge University Press.

NEEDHAM, Joseph, and WANG Ling, eds.

1956 "Correlative Thinking and Its Significance." In *Science and Civilization in China*, vol. II: *History of Scientific Thought*. Cambridge: Cambridge University Press. 279–303.

NEEDHAM, Joseph, with WANG Ling and LU Gwei-Djen

1971 *Science and Civilization in China*, vol. IV, part 3*: Civil Engineering and Nautics*. Cambridge: Cambridge University Press.

NEEDHAM, Joseph, with WANG Ling and Kenneth Girdwood ROBINSON

1962 *Science and Civilization in China*, vol. IV, part 1: *Physics and Physical Technology*. Cambridge: Cambridge University Press.

NEEDHAM, Joseph, and Robin D. S. YATES

1994 *Science and Civilization in China*, vol. V, part 6*: Military Technology—Missiles and Sieges*. Cambridge: Cambridge University Press.

NIENHAUSER Jr., W. H., Charles HARTMAN, Y. W. MA, and Stephen H. WEST, eds.

1986 *The Indiana Companion to Traditional Chinese Literature*. Bloomington: Indiana University Press.

NISHIBE Bunjō 西部文浄

1985 禅語の味わい方 [How to Savor Zen Phrases]. Kyoto: Tankōsha.

NISHITANI Keiji

1982 *Religion and Nothingness*. Trans. by Jan Van Bragt. Berkeley: University of California Press.

Nitta Daisaku 新田大作
1967 禅と中国思想 [Zen and Chinese Thought]. In 講座禅第一巻禅の立場 [Lectures on Zen, vol. I, The Standpoint of Zen], ed. by Nishitani Keiji 西谷啓治. Tokyo: Chikuma Shobō. 85–111.

Noguchi Tetsurō 野口鐵郎, Sakaide Yoshinobu 坂出祥伸, Fukui Fumimasa 福井文雅, and Yamada Toshiaki 山田利明, compilers
1994 道教事典 [Encyclopedia of Taoism]. Tokyo: Hirakawa Shuppan.

Obata Buntei 小畠文鼎
1938 近世禪林僧傳 [Modern Zen Monk Biographies], vol. III. Kyoto: Shibunkaku.

Obata Shigeyoshi
1935 *The Works of Li Po, the Chinese Poet*. Tokyo: Hokuseido Press.

Oda Tokuno 織田得野
1954 佛教大辭典 [Dictionary of Buddhism]. Tokyo: Daizō Shuppan (revised ed.)

Odake Fumio 小竹文夫 and Odake Takeo 小竹武夫, trans.
1971 史記 [Shih Chi]. 2 vols. Tokyo: Chikuma Shobō.

Ogata Sohaku
1990 *The Transmission of the Lamp: Early Masters*. Wolfeboro, NH: Longwood Academic Press.

Ogawa Tamaki 小川環樹
1962 蘇軾 [Su Shih]. Tokyo: Iwanami Shoten.

Ogawa Tamaki 小川環樹 and Mori Mikisaburō 森三樹三郎, trans.
1978 老子荘子 [Lao-tzu and Chuang-tzu]. Tokyo: Chūō Kōron.

Ogawa Tamaki 小川環樹, Nishida Taiichirō 西田太一郎, and Akatsuka Makoto 赤塚 忠, eds.
1968 新字源. Tokyo: Kadokawa Shoten.

Ogura Yoshihiko 小倉芳彦, trans.
1988 春秋左氏伝 [Mr. Tso's Commentary on the Spring and Autumn Annals], 3 vols. Tokyo: Iwanami Shoten.

Ōmori Sōgen 大森曹玄
1967 公案の禅 [Kōan Zen]. In 講座禅, 第二巻: 禅の実践 [Lectures on Zen, vol. II: The Practical Application of Zen], ed. by Suzuki Daisetsu 鈴木大拙 and Nishitani Keiji 西谷啓治. Tokyo: Chikuma Shobō.
1994 碧巖録 [*Hekigan-roku*]. Tachibana Kyōyō Bunko, 2 vols.

Otobe Kaihō 乙部魁芳, ed.
1918 禪門公案大成 [Zen School Kōan Compilation] Tokyo: Kōmeisha.

Owen, Stephen
1975 *The Poetry of Meng Chiao and Han Yü*. New Haven and London: Yale University Press.
1977 *The Poetry of the Early T'ang*. New Haven and London: Yale University Press.
1985 *Traditional Chinese Poetry and Poetics*. Madison: University of Wisconsin Press.

Palmer, Martin, ed.
1986 *T'ung shu: The Ancient Chinese Almanac*. Boston: Shambhala.

Pas, Julian F.
1987 *The Recorded Sayings of Ma-tsu*. Lewiston and Queenston: Edwin Mellen Press.

Payne, Robert, ed.
1949 *The White Pony*. London: George Allen and Unwin.

Plaks, Andrew H.
1988 "Where the Lines Meet: Parallelism in Chinese and Western Literatures." *Chinese Literature Essays Articles Reviews* 10: 43–60.

Pollack, David
1976 Linked Verse Poetry in China: A Study of Associative Linking in "Lien-chu" Poetry with Emphasis on the Poems of Han Yü and His Circle. Ph.D. diss. University of California, Berkeley.

1979 "Literature as Game in the T'ang." In ALLAN and COHEN 1979, 205–24.
1986 *The Fracture of Meaning: Japan's Synthesis of China from the Eighth through Eighteenth Centuries.* Princeton: Princeton University Press.

POWELL, William F., trans.
1986 *The Record of Tung-shan.* Honolulu: University of Hawai'i Press.

PROUDFOOT, Wayne
1985 *Religious Experience.* Berkeley: University of California Press.

RED PINE, trans.
1989 *The Zen Teaching of Bodhidharma.* San Francisco: North Point Press.

REID, David
1990 *Japanese Emperors, Empresses and Eras Correlated with the Western Calendar.* Tokyo.

REPS, Paul
1934 *The Gateless Gate.* London: John Murray. Reprinted in REPS 1957.
1957 *Zen Flesh, Zen Bones.* Rutland, VT: Charles E. Tuttle Co.

ROBINSON, G. W.
1973 *Wang Wei: Poems.* Harmondsworth: Penguin.

ROGERS, Michael C.
1968 *The Chronicle of Fu Chien: A Case of Exemplar History.* Chinese Dynastic Histories Translations, No. 10. Berkeley: University of California Press.

ROHSENOW, John S., ed.
1991 *A Chinese-English Dictionary of Enigmatic Folk Similes.* Tucson: University of Arizona.

ROSEMONT, Henry, Jr.
1970 "The Meaning is the Use: Koan and Mondo as Linguistic Tools of the Zen Masters." *Philosophy East and West* 20: 109–19.

SADAKATA Akira
1997 *Buddhist Cosmology: Philosophy and Origins* [Eng. translation of *Shumisen to Gokuraku*]. Tokyo: Kosei Publishing.

SAHN, Seung
1993 *The Whole World Is a Single Flower: 365 Kong-Ans for Everyday Life.* Rutland and Tokyo: Charles E. Tuttle.

SANAE Kensei 早苗憲生
1996 句双紙の諸本と成立 [*Kuzōshi* Texts and their Development]. In YAMADA, IRIYA, and SANAE 1996, 581–606.

SASAKI, Ruth Fuller
1956 "Anthology of Zen Poems." *Zen Bunka* 禅文化 4: 22–6.
1975 *The Record of Lin-chi: The Recorded Sayings of Ch'an Master Lin-chi Hui-chao of Chen Prefecture.* Kyoto: The Institute for Zen Studies.

SASAKI, Ruth Fuller, IRIYA Yoshitaka, and Dana R. FRASER
1971 *The Recorded Sayings of Layman P'ang: A Ninth-Century Zen Classic.* New York and Tokyo: Weatherhill.

SATŌ Taketoshi 佐藤武敏
1974 長安: 古代中国と日本 [Ch'ang-an: Ancient China and Japan]. Tokyo: Hōyū Shoten.

SAUSSY, Haun
1993 *The Problem of a Chinese Aesthetic.* Stanford: Stanford University Press.

SAWYER, Ralph. D., trans.
1996 *The Complete Art of War: Sun Tzu, Sun Pin.* Boulder: Westview Press.

SCHAFER, Edward H.
1963 *The Golden Peaches of Samarkand.* Berkeley: University of California Press.
1967 *The Vermilion Bird: T'ang Images of the South.* Berkeley: University of California Press.

1980 *The Divine Woman: Dragon Ladies and Rain Maidens in T'ang Literature*. San Francisco: North Point Press.

SCHLOEGL, Irmgard

1975 *The Zen Teaching of Rinzai* [Record of Rinzai]. Berkeley: Shambhala.

SEKIDA Katsuki

1977 *Two Zen Classics: Mumonkan and Hekiganroku*. New York: Weatherhill.

SEKIGUCHI Shindai 関口眞大

1967 達磨の研究 [A Study of Bodhidharma]. Tokyo: Iwanami Shoten.

SELLMAN, James

1979 "The Kōan: A Language Game." *Philosophical Quarterly* 7. Supp.: 1–9.

SENZAKI Nyogen and Ruth S. MCCANDLESS

1964 *The Iron Flute: 100 Zen Kōans with Commentary by Genrō, Fugai and Nyogen*. Rutland and Tokyo: Charles E. Tuttle.

SHAKU Seitan 釋清潭 and Hayashi Kokei 林古溪, eds.

1924 作詩關門 [Gateway to Poetry Composition]. Tokyo: Heigo Shuppan.

SHARF, Robert H.

1995A "The Zen of Japanese Nationalism." *In Curators of the Buddha*, ed. by Donald S. Lopez. Chicago: University of Chicago Press. 107–60. Originally published in *History of Religions* 33: 1–43.

1995B "Buddhist Modernism and the Rhetoric of Meditative Experience." *Numen* 42: 228–83.

1995C "Zen and the Way of the New Religions." *Japanese Journal of Religious Studies* 22: 417–58.

SHENG-YEN

1987 *The Poetry of Enlightenment: Poems by Ancient Ch'an Masters*. New York: Dharma Drum.

1990 *The Infinite Mirror*. New York: Dharma Drum.

SHIBANO Kyōdō 柴野恭堂

1980 禅録慣用語俗語要典 [Basic Dictionary of Traditional Readings and Colloquial Language in Zen Texts]. Kyoto: Shibunkaku.

SHIBAYAMA Zenkei 柴山全慶, compiler

1972 訓註禪林句集 [Annotated Zen Sangha Verse Collection]. Kyoto: Kichūdō.

1974 *Zen Comments on the Mumonkan*. Trans. by Sumiko Kudo. New York: Mentor.

1980 毒語心經 [Poison Words Heart Sutra]. Kyoto: Kichūdō.

1984 無門關 [*Mumonkan*]. Kyoto: Kichūdō.

SHIBAYAMA Zenkei 柴山全慶 and JIKIHARA Gyokusei 直原玉青

1969 江湖風月集 [River and Lake, Wind and Moon Collection]. Osaka: Sōgensha.

1975 禅の牧牛図 [Zen Oxherding Pictures]. Osaka: Sōgensha.

SHIGEMATSU Sōiku

1981 *A Zen Forest*. New York and Tokyo: Weatherhill.

1988 *A Zen Harvest*. San Francisco: North Point Press.

SHIMANO Eido

1988 "Zen Kōans." In KRAFT 1988, 70–87.

SHINMURA Izuru 新村出

1960 広辞苑. Tokyo: Iwanami Shoten.

SHŌGAKU TOSHO 尚学図書

1982 ことわざ大辞典 [Lexicon of Proverbs]. Tokyo: Shōgakkan.

SHORE, Jeff

1996 "Kōan Zen from the Inside." *Hanazono Daigaku bungakubu kiyō* 花園大学文学部紀要 [Hanazono University Faculty of Arts Bulletin] 28: 1–52.

1997A "Translation: Selections from Akizuki Ryōmin's *Kōan: An Introduction to Zen Practice*." *Hanazono Daigaku bungakubu kiyō* 花園大学文学部紀要 [Hanazono University Faculty of Arts Bulletin] 29: 193–236.

1997B "The Fundamental Kōan of Humankind: Making It Our Own." *Hanazono Daigaku zengaku kenkyū* 花園大学禅学研究 [Hanazono University Research in Zen Studies] 75: 68–87.

SHU Chiung

1981A *Yang Kuei-fei.* Singapore: Graham Brash Pte. Ltd.

1981B *Hsi Shih.* Singapore: Graham Brash Pte. Ltd.

1981C *Chao Chün.* Singapore: Graham Brash Pte. Ltd.

SICKMAN, Laurence, and Alexander SOPER

1971 *The Art and Architecture of China.* Harmondsworth: Penguin.

SMITH, Richard J.

1991 *Fortune-tellers and Philosophers: Divination in Traditional Chinese Society.* Boulder: Westview Press.

SNYDER, Gary

1983 *Axe Handles.* San Francisco: North Point Press.

SOOTHILL, William Edward and Lewis HODOUS, eds.

1962 *A Dictionary of Chinese Buddhist Terms.* Kaohsiung and Taiwan: Buddhist Culture Service (revised ed.).

SPRUNG, Mervyn, ed.

1973 *The Problem of Two Truths in Buddhism and Vedanta.* Dordrecht: Reidel.

STEINHARDT, Nancy S.

1990 *Chinese Imperial City Planning.* Honolulu: University of Hawai'i Press.

SUDNOW, David

1978 *Ways of the Hand: The Organization of Improvised Conduct.* Cambridge: Harvard University Press.

SUDŌ Ryūsen 須藤隆仙

1982 仏教故事名言辞典 [Dictionary of Well-Known Historical Buddhist Expressions]. Tokyo: Shinjinbutsu-ōrai-sha.

SUN Yu 孫瑜, trans.

1982 *Li Po: A New Translation* 李白詩新譯. Hong Kong: Commercial Press.

SUZUKI, Daisetz T.

1953 *Essays in Zen Buddhism, Second Series.* London: Rider.

SUZUKI Daisetsu , UI Hakuju 宇井伯壽, and INOUE Tetsujirō 井上哲次郎, eds.

1952 禅の講座, 第三巻: 禅の公案と問答 [Lectures on Zen, vol. III: The Zen Kōan and Kōan Dialogue]. Tokyo: Shun'yōdō.

SUZUKI Daisetsu 鈴木大拙 and AKIZUKI Ryōmin 秋月龍珉

1964 趙州禪師語錄 [Recorded Sayings of Zen Master Jōshū]. Tokyo: Shunjūsha.

SUZUKI Shijun 鈴木子順

1935 新編, 江湖風月集鑿空抄講義 [Pointless Lectures on the *Fūgetsu-shū*, New Edition]. Tokyo: Reisen-in.

SWANSON, Paul L.

1989 *Foundations of T'ien-t'ai Philosophy: The Flowering of the Two Truths Theory in Chinese Buddhism.* Berkeley: Asian Humanities Press.

TAIWAN K'AIMING SHU-TIEN 臺湾開明書店

1955 十三經索引 [Index to the Thirteen Classics]. 2 vols. Taipei.

TAKAHASHI Hiroshi 高橋 浩

1988 禅の知恵ものしり辞典 [The Know-It-All's Dictionary on Zen Wisdom]. Tokyo: Daiwa Shuppan.

TAKASAKI Jikishō 高崎直承, ed.

1934 從容錄 [Book of Serenity]. Tokyo: Kōmeisha.

TAN Shilin

1992 *The Complete Works of Tao Yuanming.* Hong Kong: Joint Publishing Co.

THURMAN, Robert A., trans.
1976 *The Holy Teaching of Vimalakīrti: A Mahayana Scripture.* University Park: Pennsylvania State University Press.

TOKIWA Gishin
1991 "Hakuin Ekaku's Insight into 'The Deep Secret of Hen (Pian)-Sho (Zheng) Reciprocity' and His Koan 'The Sound of a Single Hand.'" *Journal of Indian and Buddhist Studies* 39/2: 989–93.

TŌREI Enji Zenji
1989 *Discourse on the Inexhaustible Lamp.* Comments by Daibi Zenji, trans. by Yoko Okuda. London: Zen Centre.

TSUCHIYA Etsudō 土屋悦堂, ed.
1957 禪林世語集 [Zen Sangha Vernacular Phrase Collection]. Kyoto: Kichūdō.
1973 新纂禪語集 [A New Compilation of the Zen Phrase Collection]. Compiled under the direction of Unkankutsu Shaku Taibi Rōshi 雲關窟釋大眉老師. Kyoto: Kichūdō.

TWITCHETT, Denis, ed.
1979 *The Cambridge History of China Volume 3: Sui and T'ang China, 589-906.* Cambridge: Cambridge University Press.

TWITCHETT, Denis, and Michael LOEWE, eds.
1986 *The Cambridge History of China,* vol. I: *The Ch'in and Han Empires, 221 BC–AD 220,* Cambridge: Cambridge University Press.

UEDA, Makoto
1982 *The Master Haiku Poet Matsuo Basho.* Tokyo and New York: Kodansha.

UEDA Shizuteru 上田閑照 and YANAGIDA Seizan 柳田聖山
1982 十牛図 [Ten Oxherding Pictures]. Tokyo: Chikuma Shobō.

UEKI Hisayuki 植木久行
1995 唐詩歳時記 [Glossary of Seasonal Words in T'ang Poetry]. Tokyo: Kōdansha.

UI Hakuju 宇井伯壽
1937 禪宗史研究 [Studies on the Zen School]. Tokyo: Iwanami Shoten. 第二禪宗史研究 [Vol. II: Studies on the Zen School]. Tokyo: Iwanami Shoten.
1938 コンサイス佛教辭典 [Concise Buddhist Dictionary]. Tokyo: Daitō Shuppan.
1943 第三禪宗史研究 [Vol. III: Studies on the Zen School]. Tokyo: Iwanami Shoten.

VERVOORN, A.
1990 *Men of the Cliffs and Caves: The Development of the Chinese Eremitic Tradition to the End of the Han Dynasty.* Hong Kong: The Chinese University Press.

WADDELL, Norman
1980 "Zen Master Hakuin's Poison Words for the Heart." *Eastern Buddhist* 13/2: 73–114.
1996 *Zen Words for the Heart: Hakuin's Commentary on the Heart Sutra.* Boston and London: Shambhala.

WALEY, Arthur, trans.
1937A *The Book of Songs.* London: George Allen and Unwin.
1937B "Appendix I: The Allegorical Interpretation." In WALEY 1937A. 335–7.
1938 *The Analects of Confucius.* London: George Allen and Unwin.
1949 *The Life and Times of Po Chü-i, 772-846 AD.* London: George Allen and Unwin.
1950 *The Poetry and Career of Li Po.* London: George Allen and Unwin.
1955 *The Nine Songs: A Study of Shamanism in Ancient China.* London: George Allen and Unwin.

WANG, Youru
1997 "An Inquiry into the Limnology of Language in the *Zhuangzi* and in Chan Buddhism." *International Philosophical Quarterly* 37/2: 161–78.

WARE, James R.
1981 *Alchemy, Medicine and Religion in the China of AD 320: The Nei Pien of Ko Hung*. London: Dover.
WATSON, Burton
1958 *Records of the Historian: Chapters from the Shih Chi of Ssu-ma Ch'ien*. New York: Columbia University Press.
1961 *Records of the Grand Historian of China, translated from the Shih Chi of Ssu-ma Ch'ien*. 2 vols. New York: Columbia University Press.
1964 *Basic Writings of Mo Tzu, Hsün Tzu, and Han Fei Tzu*. New York: Columbia University Press.
1968 *The Complete Works of Chuang Tzu*. New York: Columbia University Press.
1974 *Courtier and Commoner in Ancient China*. New York: Columbia University Press.
1986 *The Columbia Book of Chinese Poetry*. New York: Columbia University Press.
1988 "Buddhism in the Poetry of Po Chü-i." *Eastern Buddhist* 21/1: 1–22.
1989 *The Tso Chuan: Selections from China's Oldest Narrative History*. New York: Columbia University Press.
1992 "Buddhist Poet-Priests of the T'ang." *Eastern Buddhist*. New Series 25/2: 30–58.
1993A *Records of the Grand Historian by Sima Qian Revised*, 3 vols. Hong Kong and New York: Chinese University of Hong Kong and Columbia University Press.
1993B *The Zen Teachings of Master Lin-chi*. Boston: Shambhala.
1994 *Selected Poems of Su Tung-p'o*. Port Townsend, WA: Copper Canyon Press.
1997 *The Vimalakirti Sutra*. New York: Columbia University Press.
WATTS, Alan W.
1957 "Za-zen and the Kōan," *The Way of Zen*. New York: Random House. 154–73.
WELCH, Holmes
1967 *The Practice of Chinese Buddhism 1900-1950*. Cambridge: Harvard University Press.
WILHELM, Richard
1967 *The I Ching or Book of Changes*. Trans. by Cary F. Baynes. Princeton: Princeton University Press.
WILLIAMS, C. A. S.
1976 *Outlines of Chinese Symbolism and Art Motifs*. New York: Dover Publications.
WITTGENSTEIN, Ludwig
1958 *Philosophical Investigations*. Trans. by G. E. M. Anscombe. Oxford: Basil Blackwell.
WRIGHT, Dale S.
1992 "Rethinking Transcendence: The Role of Language in Zen Experience." *Philosophy East and West* 42: 113–38.
1998 *Philosophical Meditations on Zen Buddhism*. Cambridge: Cambridge University Press.
2000 "Kōan History: Transformative Language in Chinese Buddhist Thought." In HEINE and WRIGHT 2000, 200–12.
WU Juntao, trans.
1985 杜甫詩英訳一百五十首 [Tu Fu: One Hundred and Fifty Poems]. Shaanxi Renmin Chuban.
XIAO Tong
1996 *Wen Hsüan: Literary Selections*, 3 vols. Trans. by David R. Knechtges. Princeton: Princeton University Press.
XU Yuan-zhong, LOH Bei-yei, WU Juntao, trans.
1987 *300 Tang Poems: A New Translation*. Hong Kong: The Commercial Press.
YAMADA Toshio 山田俊雄, IRIYA Yoshitaka 入矢義高, and SANAE Kensei 早苗憲生, eds.
1996 庭訓往来句双紙 [Teikun Ōrai *Kuzōshi*]. Tokyo: Iwanami Shoten.
YAMAMOTO Shungaku 山本峻岳
1920 和訓略解禪林句集 [Zen Sangha Phrase Collection with Japanese Readings and Concise Explanations]. Tokyo: Kōyūkan.

YAMPOLSKY, Philip
1967 *The Platform Sutra of the Sixth Patriarch*. New York: Columbia University Press.
1971 *The Zen Master Hakuin: Selected Writings*. New York: Columbia University Press.
1988 "The Development of Japanese Zen." In KRAFT 1988, 140–56.

YANAGIDA Seiji 柳田征司
1975 「句雙紙抄」の諸本とその方法 [Varieties of "Annotated Phrase Books" and Their Methods]. *Kokugo kokubun* 国語国文 44: 1–22.

YANAGIDA Seizan 柳田聖山
1967 初期禅宗史書の研究 [Research into Historical Texts of the Early Zen School]. Tokyo: Hōzōkan.
1976 初期の禅史 [Early Zen History], 2 vols. Tokyo: Chikuma Shobō.
1972 臨済録 [Record of Rinzai]. Tokyo: Daizō Shuppan.
1983 "The 'Recorded Sayings' Texts of Chinese Ch'an Buddhism." In LAI and LANCASTER 1983, 185–205.
2000 解題 [Bibliographical Note]. In YANAGIDA and SHIINA 2000, 691–704.

YANAGIDA Seizan 柳田聖山 and SHIINA Hiro 椎名宏雄, eds.
2000 點鉄集 [Forging Iron Collection]. 禅学典籍叢刊第十巻下 [Zen Classical Text Collection, vol. x/2]. Tokyo: Rinsen Shoten.

YANG Hsien-yi and Gladys YANG
1979 *Selections from Records of the Historian, written by Szuma Chien*. Peking: Foreign Languages Press.

YANG Liyi 楊立義, compiler
1987 *100 Chinese Idioms and their Stories* 中國成語古事 一百篇. Hong Kong: Commercial Press.

YAO, Karl S. Y., ed.
1985 *Classical Chinese Tales of the Supernatural and the Fantastic*. Bloomington: Indiana University Press.

YOSHIDA Sumio 吉田澄夫
1938 天草版金句集の研究 [Studies on the Amakusa Golden Verse Collection]. Tokyo: Tōyō Bunko Kankō.
1941 句雙紙抄について [*Kuzōshi* Commentary Texts]. In 安藤教授還暦祝賀記念論文集 [A Collection of Commemorative Essays for Professor Andō on His Sixtieth Birthday], ed. by Uematsu Yasushi 植松 安. Tokyo: Sanseidō. 1171–91.

YOSHIKAWA Kōjirō 吉川幸次郎
1996 論語 [Analects]. Tokyo: Asahi Shinbunsha.

YOSHIZAWA Katsuhiro 吉澤勝弘, ed.
1999 諸録俗語解 [Explanation of Colloquial Language in Several Texts]. Kyoto: Zen Bunka Kenkyūjo.

YU, Anthony
1983 *Journey to the West*. 4 vols. Chicago: University of Chicago Press, 1977–1983.

YÜ Chün-fang
1979 "Ta-hui Tsung-kao and *Kung-an* Ch'an." *Journal of Chinese Philosophy* 6: 211–35.
1994 "Guanyin: The Chinese Transformation of Avalokiteshvara." In Marsha Weidner, ed., *Latter Days of the Law: Images of Chinese Buddhism 850–1850*. Kansas City: Spencer Museum of Art, copublished with University of Hawai'i Press. 151–81.
2001 *Kuan-yin: The Chinese Transformation of Avalokiteśvara*. New York: Columbia University Press.

YU, Pauline
1980 *The Poetry of Wang Wei*. Bloomington: Indiana University Press.

YU Sun, trans.
1982 *Li Po: A New Translation*. Hong Kong: Commercial Press.

Zen Bunka Kenkyūjo 禅文化研究所
n.d. 景徳傳燈録 [Ching-te Era Record of the Transmission of the Lamp]. Kyoto: Zen Bunka Kenkyūjo.
1991A 定本禅林句集索引 [Index to the Standard Text of the *Zenrin kushū*]. Kyoto: Zen Bunka Kenkyūjo. Based on a Meiji 19 (1886) reprint.
1991B 禪語辭書類聚 [Classified Zen Phrase Dictionary]. Kyoto: Zen Bunka Kenkyūjo.
1992A 禪語辭書類聚二 [Classified Zen Phrase Dictionary, vol. II], 無著道忠著葛藤語箋 [Mujaku Dōchū's *Tangled Vine Word Notes*]. Kyoto: Zen Bunka Kenkyūjo.
1992B 唐詩選三体詩総合索引 [Joint Index for the *Tōshisen* and *Santaishi*]. Kyoto: Zen Bunka Kenkyūjo.
1993 禪語辭書類聚三 [Classified Zen Phrase Dictionary, vol. III]: *Hekigan-roku funishō* 碧巖録不二抄 [Nondual Commentary on the *Hekigan-roku*]. Kyoto: Zen Bunka Kenkyūjo.

CLASSICAL SOURCES CITED BY NAME

Analects 論語. See Lau 1979, Legge 1985, and Waley 1938.
Book of Serenity 從容錄. T 48.226–96. See Cleary 1990 and Takasaki 1934.
Book of Songs (Book of Odes, Book of Poetry) 詩經. See Waley 1937A and Legge 1985, vol. IV.
Chuang-tzu 荘子. See Kanaya 1971, Ogawa 1978, and Watson 1968.
Great Learning 大學. See Legge 1985, vol. I.
Hekigan-roku 碧巖錄. T 47.713–811. See Cleary and Cleary 1977, Cleary 1998, Hirata 1989, Iriya et al. 1981, Iriya et al. 1992, Ōmori 1974, and Sekida 1977.
Jōshū-roku 趙州禪師語錄. See Suzuki and Akizuki 1964 and Green 1998.
Kattō-shū 葛藤集. See Fujita 1922 and Kajitani 1977.
Keitoku dentō-roku 景德傳燈錄. T 51.196–467. See Ogata 1990, Iriya 1993, 1997.
Mencius 孟子. See Lau 1970 and Legge 1985.
Mumonkan 無門關. T 48.292–9. See Aitken 1990, Cleary 1993, Hirata 1969, Sekida 1977, Reps 1934, and Shibayama 1974, 1984.
Platform Sutra of the Sixth Patriarch 六祖壇經. T 48.345–65. See Yampolski 1967.
Rinzai-roku 臨濟錄. T 47.495–507. See Akizuki 1972, Asahina 1935, Iriya 1991, Mujaku and Hirano 1971, Schloegl 1975, Yanagida 1972, and Watson 1993B.
Shih-chi 史記. See Odake and Odake 1971, Watson 1958, 1961, 1993A, and Yang and Yang 1979.
Song of Enlightenment by Yung Chia 永嘉證道歌. T 48.395–6. See Fujita 1922.
Songs of the South 楚歌. See Hawkes 1985 and Waley 1955.
Tao-te ching 道德經. See Henricks 1989 and Kanaya 1997.
Ten Oxherding Pictures 牧牛図. See Shibayama and Jikihara 1975, and Ueda and Yanagida 1982.
Tso chuan 左傳. See Legge 1985 and Watson 1989.
Ummon kōroku 雲門廣錄. T 47.544–76. See App 1994.
Vimalakīrti nirdeśa sūtra 維摩經. T 14.519–36. See Luk 1972, Thurman 1976, and Watson 1997.

Index